1 MONTH OF
FREE
READING

at

www.ForgottenBooks.com

By purchasing this book you are eligible for one month membership to ForgottenBooks.com, giving you unlimited access to our entire collection of over 1,000,000 titles via our web site and mobile apps.

To claim your free month visit:
www.forgottenbooks.com/free927662

ISBN 978-0-260-09606-7
PIBN 10927662

SESSIONAL PAPERS

VOLUME XXXIX.—PART IX.

Third Session of Eleventh Legislature

OF THE

PROVINCE OF ONTARIO

SESSION 1907

TORONTO:

Printed and Published by L. K. CAMERON, Printer to the King's Most Excellent Majesty

1907.

Printed by WARWICK BRO'S & RUTTER Limited, Printers,
TORONTO.

LIST OF SESSIONAL PAPERS.

TITLE.	No.	REMARKS.
Saint Joseph Island, kinds of Patents issued to locatees	57	*Not printed.*
Secretary and Registrar, Report	40	*Printed.*
Statutes, Distribution of	72	*Not printed.*
Succession Duties, Estates unsettled	58	"
Supplementary Revenue, amounts credited to cities, towns, etc.	59	"
Surrogate Courts, Orders-in-Council	56	"
Temiskaming and N. O. Railway, Report	8	*Printed.*
Temiskaming and N. O. Railway, cash expenditure on construction	60	"
Text-book Commission, Report	49	"
Titles, Fees received by Master of	55	*Not printed.*
Toronto Electric Light Company, date of incorporation, etc.	52	"
Toronto University, Auditor's Report	13	*Printed.*
Vegetable Growers' Association, Report	18	*Printed.*
Women's Institutes, Report	24	*Printed.*

LIST OF SESSIONAL PAPERS.

Arranged in Numerical Order with their Titles at full length ; the dates when Ordered and when presented to the Legislature ; the name of the Member who moved the same, and whether Ordered to be Printed or not.

CONTENTS OF VOL. III.

No. 10. . Report of the Inspector of Insurance for the year 1906. Presented to the Legislature, 30th March, 1907. *Printed.*

No. 11. . Loan Corporations, Statements by Building·Societies, Loan and other Companies, for the year 1906. Presented to the Legislature, 7th March, 1907. *Printed.*

. CONTENTS OF VOL. IV.

No. 12. . Report of the Minister of Education, for the year 1906, with the Statistics of 1905. Presented to the Legislature, 27th February, 1907. *Printed.*

No. 13. . Auditors' Report to the Board of Governors University of Toronto, on Capital and Income Accounts, for the year ending 30th June, 1906. Presented to the Legislature, 30th January, 1907. *Printed.*

No. 14. . Report of the Ontario Agricultural College and Experimental Farm, for the year 1906. Presented to the Legislature, 21st March, 1907. *Printed.*

CONTENTS OF VOL. V.

No, 15. . Report of the Ontario Agricultural and Experimental Union of the Province, for the year 1906. Presented to the Legislature, 21st March, 1907. *Printed.*

No. 16. . Report of the Fruit Growers' Associations of the Province, for the year 1906. Presented to the Legislature, 21st March, 1907. *Printed.*

No. 17. . Report of the Fruit Experimental Stations of the Province, for the year 1906. · Presented to the Legislature, 21st March, 1907. *Printed.*

No. 18. . Report of the Vegetable Growers' Association for the year 1906. Presented to the Legislature, 21st March, 1907. *Printed.*

No. 19. . Report of the Entomological Society. for the year 1906. Presented to the Legislature, 21st March, 1907. *Printed.*

No. 20. . Report of the Bee-Keepers' A-sociation of the Province, for the year 1906. Presented to the Legislature 21st March, 1907. *Printed.*

No. 21. . Report of the Dairymen's Associations of the Province, for the year 1906. Presented to the Legislature, 21st March, 1907. *Printed.*

No. 22. . Report of the Live Stock Associations of the Province, for the year 1906. Presented to the Legislature, 21st March, 1907. *Printed.*

CONTENTS OF VOL. VI.

No. 23. . Report of the Poultry Institute of the Province, for the year 1906. Presented to the Legislature, 21st March, 1907. *Printed.*

No. 24. . Report of Women's Institutes of the Province, for the year 1906. Presented to the Legislature, 19th February, 1907. *Printed.*

No. 25. . Report of the Farmers' Institutes of the Province, for the year 1906. Presented to the Legislature, 20th March, 1907. *Printed.*

No. 26. . Report of Agricultural Societies of the Province (Fairs and Exhibitions), for the year 1906. Presented to the Legislature, 19th February, 1907. *Printed.*

No. 27. . Reports of the Horticultural Societies of the Province, for the year 1906. Presented to the Legislature, 21st March, 1907. *Printed.*

No, 28. . Report of the Bureau of Industries of the Province, for the year 1906. Presented to the Legislature, 21st March, 1907. *Printed.*

No. 29. . Report of the Inspectors of Factories for the year 1906. Presented to the Legislature, 21st March, 1907. *Printed.*

No. 30. . Report of the Bureau of Labour for the year 1906. Presented to the Legislature, 11th March, 1907. *Printed.*

CONTENTS OF VOL. VII.

No. 31. . Report of the Commissioner of Highways, for the year 1907. Presented to the Legislature, 20th February, 1907. *Printed.*

No. 32. . Report of the Ontario Game Commission, for the year 1906. Presented to the Legislature, 19th March, 1907. *Printed.*

No. 33. . Report of the Department of Fisheries, for the year 1905. Presented to the Legislature, 8th March, 1907. *Printed.*

No. 34. . Report upon the Archives of the Province, for the year 1906. Presented to the Legislature, 20th March, 1907. *Printed.*

No. 35. . Report of Work relating to Neglected and Dependent Children of Ontario, for the year 1906. Presented to the Legislature, 20th March, 1907. *Printed.*

CONTENTS OF VOL. VIII.

No. 36. . Report of the Provincial Board of Health, for the year 1906. Presented to the Legislature, 30th January, 1906. *Printed*

No. 37. . Report of the Inspector of Division Courts, for the year 1906. Presented to the Legislature, 20th March, 1907. *Printed.*

No. 38. . Report of the Inspector of Legal Offices, for the year 1906. Presented to the Legislature, 22nd February, 1907. *Printed.*

No. 39.. | Report of the Inspector of Registry Offices, for the year 1906. Presented to the Legislature, 12th April, 1907. *Printed.*

No. 40.. | Report of the Secretary and Registrar of the Province, for the year 1906. Presented to the Legislature, 20th March, 1907. *Printed.*

No. 41.. | Report upon the Lunatic and Idiot Asylums of the Province, for the year ending 30th September, 1906. Presented to the Legislature, 20th March, 1907. *Printed.*

No. 42.. | Report upon the Prisons and Reformatories of the Province, for the year ending 30th September, 1906. Presented to the Legislature, 11th March, 1907. *Printed.*

No. 43.. | Report upon the Hospitals and Charities of the Province, for the year ending 30th September, 1906. Presented to the Legislature, 12th February, 1907. *Printed.*

No. 44.. | Report upon the Operation of Liquor License Acts, for the year 1906. Presented to the Legislature, 20th March, 1907. *Printed.*

CONTENTS OF VOL. IX.

No 45.. | Report of the Provincial Municipal Auditor, for the year 1906. Presented to the Legislature, 1st February, 1907. *Printed.*

No. 46.. | Supplementary Return from the Record of the several Elections in the Electoral Divisions of Cardwell, Hamilton East, West Middlesex and Carleton, since the General Elections on January 25th, 1905, shewing: (1) The number of Votes Polled for each Candidate in the Electoral District in which there was a contest; (2) The majority whereby each successful Candidate was returned; (3) The total number of votes polled in each District; (4) The number of votes remaining unpolled; (5) The number of names on the Voters' Lists in each District; (6) The population of each District as shewn by the last Census. Presented to the Legislature, 24th January and 12th April, 1907. *Printed.*

No. 47.. | Report upon the state of the Library. Presented to the Legislature, 2nd January, 1907. *Not printed.*

No. 48.. | Report of the Hydro-Electric Power Commission of the Province, for the year 1906. Presented to the Legislature, 12th April 1907. *Printed.*

No. 49.. | Report, with the evidence, of the Text-book Commission. Presented to the Legislature, 1st February, 1907. *Printed.*

No. 50.. | Copies of Orders-in-Council, under section 27, of the Act respecting the Department of Education. Presented to the Legislature, 11th February, 1907. *Not printed.*

No. 51. . Return to an Order of the House of the sixteenth day of March, 1906, for a Return shewing the names of all License Inspectors appointed since the first day of February, 1905, together with their addresses and the dates of their appointment ; the business or occupation of each Inspector prior to his appointment and the present occupation or business, other than their official business, of each such Inspector. Presented to the Legislature, 11th February, 1907. Mr. *McMillan. Not printed.*

No. 52. . Return to an Order of the House, of the thirtieth day of January 1907, for a Return giving the following information regarding the Toronto Electric Light Company, Limited. 1. Date of incorporation. 2. Applicants for Incorporation. 3. Objects of the Company. 4. Names of the Provisional Directors. 5. Amount of Capital. 6. Increase of Capital Stock. 7. Names of the Directors and Shareholders of the Company, according to the last Return to the Government. Presented to the Legislature, 11th February, 1907. Mr. *Hoyle. Not printed.*

No. 53. . Return to an Order of the House of the nineteenth day of February, 1907, for a Return of copies of all correspondence between the Government, or any member or official thereof, and any other person or persons, with reference to the dismissal of James Gillespie, of Picton, from the office of Sheriff of the County of Prince Edward. Presented to the Legislature, 26th February, 1907, Mr. *Currie. Not printed.*

No. 54. . Return to an Order of the House of the seventh day of February, 1907, for a Return shewing :—(1) List of names of Police Magistrates and Justices of the Peace in and for the County of Essex, on the 31st January, 1905. (2) List of names of Police Magistrates and Justices of the Peace in and for the County of Essex, appointed since February 1st, 1905. (3) Names of those who have qualified as Police Magistrates, or Justices of the Peace, in the County of Essex. Presented to the Legislature, 27th February, 1907. Mr. *Auld. Not printed.*

No. 55. . Return of all Fees received by the Master of Titles under Rule 77 of the Land Titles Act, for the year 1906. Presented to the Legislature, 5th March, 1907. *Not printed.*

No. 56. . Copies of Orders-in-Council commuting the Fees payable to His Honour Judge Finkle and increasing the commutations paid to His Honour Judge Benson, His Honour Judge McDonald, His Honour Judge Hardy and His Honour Judge Snider, under Section 187 of the Judicature Act and Subsection 2 of Section 84 of the Surrogate Courts Act. Presented to the Legislature, 5th March, 1907. *Not printed.*

No. 57. . Return to an Order of the House of the thirteenth day of February, 1907, for a Return shewing the various kinds of Patents issued to Locatees on St. Joseph Island. Presented to the Legislature, 5th March, 1907. Mr. *Smith (Sault Ste. Marie). Not printed.*

No. 58. . | Return to an Order of the House of the twenty-fifth day of February, 1907, for a Return shewing all Estates now unsettled upon which Succession Duty was claimed by the Treasury Department where the due date was on or before the first day of January, 1905, and the estimated amount of duty due and the reasons why unsettled. Presented to the Legislature, 7th March, 1907. Mr. *Kerr   Not printed.*

No. 59. . | Return to an Order of the House of the eighth day of March, 1907, for a Return shewing the amounts credited to the cities, towns, villages and organized townships in the Province of Ontario, from the sum received under Section 2, Subsection 5, of the Supplementary Revenue Act, 1899, as amended from time to time, and also the amount charged against each such city, town, village or organized township, respectively, for the maintenance of inmates of lunatic or other asylums in the Province under the provisions of Subsection 2, of Section 4, of Chapter 9 of the Statutes of 1906. Presented to the Legislature, 11th March, 1907. Mr. *Hislop.   Not printed.*

No. 60 . | Statement shewing cash expenditure on construction of the Temiskaming and Northern Ontario Railway, as of December 31st, 1906. Presented to the Legislature, 14th March, 1907. *Printed.*

No. 61. . | Return to an Order of the House of the sixth day of March, 1907, for a Return of:—1. Copies of all correspondence between the Government, or any Member or Official thereof and any person or persons, relating to the cancellation or granting of a liquor license to the Palace Hotel, at Fort Frances. 2. Copies of all correspondence between the Government, or any Member or Official thereof and any person or persons, relating to the cancellation or granting of a liquor license to one Thomas Wilson, at Fort Frances 3. Copies of all correspondence between the Government, or any Member or Official thereof and any person or persons, relating to the resignation or dismissal of the License Inspector or any member of the Board of License Commissioners at Fort Frances. Presented to the Legislature, 20th March, 1907. Mr *McDougal.   Not printed.*

No. 62. . | Report of the Ontario Railway and Municipal Board upon certain Bills amending the Municipal Act *in re* the Conmee clauses, referred to the Board by the Standing Committee on Municipal Law, in the Session of 1906   Presented to the Legislature, 19th March, 1907. *Not printed.*

No. 63. . | Report upon the Feeble-minded in Ontario. Presented to the Legislature, 15th April, 1907. *Printed.*

No. 64. . | Return to an Order of the House of the eighth day of March, 1907, for a Return of copies of all correspondence and papers relating to or in the matter of the protest of Mr. Chisholm Livingstone and the Davis Estate, against the purchase price awarded them by the arbitrators for their property for the Queen Victoria Niagara Falls Park. Presented to the Legislature, 20th March, 1907. Mr. *Fraser.   Not printed.*

No. 65.. | Report upon the Horse Industry of Ontario, for the year 1906. Presented to the Legislature, 21st March, 1907. *Printed.*

No. 66.. | Return to an Order of the House, of the first day of March, 1907, for a Return shewing the number of Mining Companies incorporated in the year 1906, also total amount paid into the Treasury Department from incorporation of Mining Companies in 1906, including licenses to companies previously incorporated. Presented to the Legislature, 21st March, 1907. Mr. *Pearce. Not printed.*

No. 67.. | Return to an Order of the House, of the twenty-seventh day of February, 1906, for a Return shewing, according to Counties:— 1. How many persons held Commissions and were qualified as Justices of the Peace, within the Province, on the 7th day of February, 1905. 2. How many persons held Commissions on the 7th day of February, 1906. 3. How many persons were included in the General Commission of the Peace, issued by the present Government. 4. How many of the persons named in such General Commission were continued in office from previous Commissions. Presented to the Legislature, 21st March, 1907. Mr. *Ross. Not printed.*

No. 68.. | Return to an Order of the House, of the seventh day of February, 1907, for a Return shewing :—₁. The names of Counties which have adopted the "Alternative Method" of selecting Jurors under the Amendment of 1902 to the Jurors' Act. 2. For a Comparative Statement shewing the expenses incurred under the old and new system in said Counties from the years 1902 to 1906, both inclusive. 3. The Counties (if any) in which the "Alternative Method" has been repealed and have returned to the old system of selecting Jurors. Presented to the Legislature, 22nd March, 1907. Mr. *Hoyle. Not printed.*

No. 69. | Return to an Order of the House, of the sixth day of March, 1907, for a Return of copies of all correspondence between the Government and the Northumberland-Durham Power Company, with respect to a lease of water power at Healey Falls. Presented to the Legislature, 3rd April, 1907. Mr. *Pense. Not printed.*

No. 70., | Return to an Order of the House, of the seventh day of February, 1907, for a Return, shewing the number and names of the settlers located in the Township of Gaudette and Hodgins in the District of Algoma, since the year 1906. Presented to the Legislature, 5th April, 1907. Mr. *Smith (Sault Ste. Marie). Not printed.*

No. 71.. | Documents and correspondence regarding Petawawa Camp. Presented to the Legislature, 15th April, 1907. *Printed.*

No. 72.. | Statement of distribution of Revised and Sessional Statutes. Presented to the Legislature, 17th April, 1907. *Not printed.*

No. 73. . Copy of a letter from His Honour A Constantineau, Judge of the Counties of Prescott and Russell, addressed to the Attorney-General of Ontario in the matter of the case Chatillon *vs.* Bertrand. Presented to the Legislature, 18th April, 1907. *Not printed.*

No. 74. . Return to an Order of the House of the twenty-second day of March, 1907, for a return of copies of all correspondence between the Nipissing Mines Company, or any Official thereof and the Government, or any Member thereof, relating to the property, or title thereto, of the said company, or any part or or parcel thereof situated in the Cobalt District; or to any application relating to the same; its title, or to the operation of the mines of the company, made by or on behalf of the company, or any of its Directors or Officers. Presented to the Legislature, 18th April, 1907. Mr. *McMillan, Not printed.*

Tenth Annual Report

OF

Provincial Municipal Auditor

1906

PRINTED BY ORDER OF THE
LEGISLATIVE ASSEMBLY OF ONTARIO

TORONTO:
Printed and Published by L. K. CAMERON, Printer to the King's Most Excellent Majesty
1907

WARWICK BRO'S & RUTTER, Limited. Printers,
TORONTO.

la M.A.

To His Honour the Honourable W. Mortimer Clark,
Lieutenant-Governor of Ontario.

May it Please Your Honour :

I have the honour to present to you the report of the Provincial Municipal Auditor for 1906.

J. J. FOY,
Attorney-General.

Parliament Buildings,
Toronto, 2 January, 1907.

PARLIAMENT BUILDINGS,
TORONTO, 2nd January, 1907.

To THE HONOURABLE J. J. FOY, K.C., M.P.P.,
Attorney-General.

SIR,—I have the honor to present to you my report for the year 1906.

J. B. LAING,
Provincial Municipal Auditor.

REPORT OF THE MUNICIPAL AUDITOR.

PARLIAMENT BUILDINGS,

TORONTO, 2 January, 1907.

To THE HONOURABLE J. J. FOY, K.C., M.P.P.,

Attorney-General for Ontario.

SIR,—I have the honour to submit to you the tenth annual report of the Department of the Provincial Municipal Auditor.

There were no unfinished audits of municipalities carried forward from 1905.

The following municipalities have presented petitions for audits during the year 1906, which have been granted and acted upon:

Township of Goderich, County of Huron.
      "   Finch, County of Stormont.
      "   Roxborough, County of Stormont.
      "   Sandwich West, County of Essex.
Town of Cobourg, County of Northumberland.
City of St. Thomas, County of Elgin.
Town of Stayner, County of Simcoe.
Township of Orford, County of Kent.
      "   Colchester North, County of Essex.
Village of Iroquois, County of Dundas.
Town of Napanee, County of Lennox.
      "   Wallaceburgh, County of Kent.
      "   Haileybury, District of Nipissing.

The following municipalities have presented petitions to the Government for audits, which so far have not been acted upon:

City of Windsor, County of Essex.
Township of Rochester, County of Essex.
Front of Yonge and Escott, County of Leeds.
Village of Morrisburgh, County of Dundas.

In the case of the last four municipalities mentioned, I made my usual preliminary inspection, but did not consider an audit necessary and so reported.

There have been some important drainage audits, as in the case of the Townships of Orford, Colchester North, Finch and Roxborough, which I have no doubt will do these municipalities much good. In these four townships the examination and proper arrangement of the drainage accounts have formed the principal feature in the audits, and were very much appreciated by the ratepayers. If it were possible to have similar examinations in other townships, it would be a good thing, as I am satisfied from what I know there are very few townships having drainage accounts, which are kept as they should be. This is a very weak spot in the municipal accounting, this same question of drainage accounts, and is sure to lead to trouble if not better attended to. I am alluding to the state of the drainage accounts, throughout the whole Province. In this connection it must also be noted that Treasurers and municipal office generally should be treated with more consideration as regards the remuneration they receive. There is little encouragement for an official to do his duty, when he receives the pittance often doled out to him. Say $30 to $50, and often less. I have made the remark before that no Treasurer should receive less than $100 per annum, where the annual income of the municipality exceeds $2,000. Of course there are a few townships in the new districts where the income will not pass $1,500, but they are getting fewer every year, and will soon cease to be in the gradual improvement of the country.

Township of Goderich, County of Huron.

The total receipts of this township for 1904, were $18,685.29, and the total payments, $16,523.30, leaving a cash balance in the Treasurer's hands of $2,161.99. The receipts for 1905 were $19,444.04, and the payments, $14,958.44, leaving in the Treasurer's hands, $4,985.60, which was mostly deposited in the Bank of Montreal, Goderich.

The assessment of the Township was for 1905, $2,004,228.00. Collector's roll for 1904 was $12,012.08, paid in full. For 1905, $14,411.46, also paid in full except about $30, returned to County Treasurer. Tax rate 7 6-10 mills on dollar, without school rates. There are no debentures except one small school debenture. Treasurer receives $75 per annum, and has been in office since 1895.

A strongly signed petition for a Government audit was presented to the Government, and granted by them. The audit disclosed no deficiency in the accounts, but the result was beneficial as bringing about an improvement in the Treasurer's books, which up to that date had not been well kept.

The audit by the Government appointee will be found at the end of this report, giving full particulars of the finances of the Township, which appear to be in a very healthy state.

At the end of this report will be found the principal portions of the Auditor's reports. I have eliminated some of the matter which is not of general interest.

The following is a list of the inspections and examinations made by myself during the year of 1906 : —

JANUARY, 1906.

Town of Trenton, County of Hastings.

Total receipts for 1904 .... $170,800 22
Total payments for 1904 .... 172,541 71

Balance overdrawn in Ontario Bank.................. $1,741 49

Total assessment of Municipality, $1,238,261.00. Collector's roll for 1904 $28,305.00, of which $1,000 was still due at the date of my visit. Tax rate, 24 mills. Government form of cash book fairly well kept. There is urgent need for better management in the affairs of this municipality. I can note some improvement since my last visit, but there is great room for more, especially in the collection of taxes, which are much behind. The Treasurer receives $300 per annum and has been in office three years. There is a sinking fund of $2,899.03 in Ontario Bank, Trenton.

31st December, 1904.

Assets.		Liabilities.	
Taxes in arrears	15,943 67	Debentures	....
Invested in debentures	4,966 80	Dam and flume	$51,267 34
Lands	5,149 24	Electric works	6,000 00
Buildings and furniture......	5,300 00	Bonus to manufacturers	10,000 00
Schools sinking fund	19,500 00	All other objects	88,767 95
Water works power	2,899 03	Current loans....................	9,145 00
Land and flume	75,000 00	Ontario Bank overdraft......	1,741 49
Fire hall appliances	10,000 00	Outstanding orders, liabili-	
Electric light, buildings and		ties	5,065 62
plant	9,000 00	Administration of Justice...	....
Booms and piers	6,000 00	Yearly payment to county...	1,500 00
Bridge across river	20,000 00		
Stone crusher, etc.	1,000 00		
Due by Gilmour & Co......	827 45		
Cash in collector's hands ...	700 55		
	$176,286 74		$173,487 40

Village of Morrisburg.

A numerously signed petition was presented to the Government from this municipality and in accordance therewith I went down to Morrisburg and made a careful examination of the books, so as to report on the advisability of the audit asked for by the petitioners. I did not consider there was sufficient to justify me in putting the ratepayers to the expense of an audit and so reported to the Government, who went no further in the matter. The following is the position as I found it:—

Total receipts for 1905 .... $51,371 68
Total payments for 1905 .... 50,185 23

Balance in Molsons Bank, Morrisburg............... $1,186 45

Total assessment of municipality, 1905, $564,750.00. Collector's roll, same year, $13,625.50. Paid in full except about $110 remitted by Council. Tax rate, 24 mills. I found a new Treasurer had been appointed for the new year at $65 per annum, which was $10 less than his predecessor received, who was a very competent man and resigned because he did not get the advance he thought he was entitled to.

31st December, 1905.

Assets.		Liabilities.	
Water works system	$31,000 00	Debentures	$49,715 80
Electric light system	31,000 00	Molson's Bank	15,853 62
Collegiate Institute	10,000 00	Miscellaneous	763 42
Public schools	9,000 00		
Fire department	1,000 00		
Granolithic walks	15,000 00		
Stone crusher	300 00		
Miscellaneous	4,105 74		
	$101,405 74		$66,332 84

APRIL.

Township of Colchester North, County of Essex.

A largely signed petition for a Government audit was presented from ratepayers of this Township, and after a preliminary investigation by myself an auditor was appointed and his report will be found attached hereto. . The following are the figures of my preliminary enquiry:—

Total receipts for 1904	$37,605 42
Total payments for 1904	37,505 50

Balance Imperial Bank of Canada, Essex.........	$99 92

Total receipts for 1905	$30,709 65
Total payments for 1905	29,917 01

Balance Imperial Bank of Canada, Essex.........	$792 64

Total assessment of municipality, $679,025.00. Collector's roll for 1904, $15,660.38. Paid in full. Tax rate, without school rates, County and Township 5 mills, including special, etc., and Drainage 7 mills. Treasurer's salary $125 per annum, in office eight years.

31st December, 1905.

Assets.		Liabilities.	
Cash in bank	$ 792 64	Consolidated debt	$ 1,362 75
Taxes, 1905	16,100 58	Tile drainage	1,258 56
Town hall	1,300 00	Debentures	35,436 90
Drainage dues	6,333 62		
	... $24,526 84		
Add. drains in township .... $			$38,058 21

Town of Walkerville, County of Essex.

Total receipts for 1904	$142,233 47
Total payments for 1904	143,091 60

Overdrawn balance Canadian Bank of Commerce, Walkerville	$858 13

Total receipts for 1905	$207,976 47
Total payments for 1905	207,866 20

Bal. Canadian Bank of Commerce, Walkerville	$110 27

Total assessment of municipality for 1905, $3,386,553. Collector's roll for 1905, $54,976.66. Paid on this to date, $50,038.31. Tax rate, including schools and library, 13 9-10 mills. Treasurer's salary, $200.00 per annum. In office since 1890.

31st December, 1905.

Assets.		Liabilities.	
Schools	$ 65,000 00	Debentures	$205,912 72
Police station	4,000 00	Interest unearned	84,827 57
Barn and stable	4,450 00	Sundries	2,852 00
Miscellaneous	3,371 23		
Frontage and local improvements	192,976 05		
Outstanding accounts	2,432 07		
Cash in bank	110 27		
	$272,339 62		$208,764 72

Township of Orford, County of Kent.

A numerously signed petition from ratepayers of this Township was presented to the Government, and after the usual preliminary inspection by myself, the prayer of the petition was granted. The Auditor's report, which is a very valuable one, particularly as regards the drainage system of the Township, will be found at the end of this report.

The following was the position of the Township at the end 1905 : —

Total receipts for 1904	$38,050 01
Total payments for 1904	33,397 67
Balance in Molsons Bank, Highgate.................	$4,652 34
Total receipts for 1905	$30,069 37
Total payments for 1905	22,515 22
Balance in Molsons Bank, Highgate.................	$7,581 15

Total assessment of Township for 1904, $1,329,275; for 1905, $1,733,175. Collector's roll for 1904, $19,451.20; paid in full. Collector's roll for 1905, $19,985.93; balance nearly paid at date. Tax rate, 6 mills for 1904, 5 mills for 1905, without school rates. Treasurer's salary, $115 per annum. In office five years.

31st December, 1905.

ASSETS.		LIABILITIES.	
Town hall and lock-up......	$1,300 00	County rate	$2,289 99
Interest in Moravian bridge.	2,000 00	Debentures	6,733 97
Safe	475 00	do	7,942 15
Cash in bank	7,554 15	Coupons	917 77
Back taxes	2,848 76	Tile drains	2,886 00
Gravel pits	600 00		
Sundries	41 18		
	$14,819 09		
*Drainage account	....		$20,769 88

Village of Iroquois, County of Dundas.

A largely signed petition for a Government audit from ratepayers of this municipality was presented to the Government, and after a preliminary inspection by myself an auditor was appointed, whose report will be found attached herewith. The following are the figures as found by me : —

Total receipts for 1904	$58,552 13
Total payments for 1904	59,620 66
Overdrawn balance due Molsons Bank, Iroquois...	$1,068 53
Total receipts for 1905	$45,201 77
Total payments for 1905	46,904 34
Overdrawn balance due Molsons Bank, Iroquois...	$1,702 57

Assessment of municipality, $339,994. Collector's roll for 1905, $10,091.02. Tax rate, 29.68 mills on dollar. Treasurer's salary, $25 per annum. Fifteen years in office, now resigned.

*See report attached herewith.

31st December, 1905.

Assets.		Liabilities.	
Stone crusher	$ 500 00	Current liabilities	$ 3,463 52
Fire department	575 00	Debentures in full	81,267 17
Town hall	5,000 00		
" scales	125 00		
" piano	150 00		
Water works and electric light	50,000 00		
Schools: High, 10,000; Public, 5,000	15,000 00		
Granolithic walks	15,372 86		
Shoe factory in liquidation..	3,000 00		
Balance old taxes	400 00		
	$90,122 86		$84,730 69

MAY, 1906.

County of Lincoln.

Total receipts for 1905	$62,523 33
Total payments for 1905	58,028 46
Balance Imperial Bank of Canada, St. Catharines	$4,494 87
Receipts to 1st May, 1906	$27,141 33
Payments to 1st May, 1906	25,615 29
Balance Imperial Bank of Canada, St. Catharines	$1,526 04

Total assessment of County, $9,734,500.00. County levy for year, $26,-530.86, which was paid in full at the date of my visit except one small amount of $522. There are no debentures owing by this County. The Treasurer has been in office since 1895 and receives a salary of $900, which is scarcely enough for the responsibility he shoulders, and might be increased to $1,000 without hurting any interest. His accounts are a credit to him and the County affairs are in good shape. Their total indebtedness on 31st December, 1905, was $16,351.85, and their assets, which included $87,000 for Court House and County Property Industrial Home recently erected, $26,000. Cash and sundries $6,107.08, amounted in all to $119,-107.08. The County rate is only 2 1-5 mills in the dollar. There is an additional charge of 7-10 mills in dollar for ratepayers benefited by the Queenston and Grimsby Road, which amounts to $5,114.96, or about one-fifth the total rate. A goodly record.

City of St. Catharines, County of Lincoln.

The assessment of this municipality for 1906 was $5,759,960, and the tax rate 22 1-10 mills in the dollar. Total receipts for 1905 were $379,597.53, total payments $379,125.16, leaving a balance on hand of $472.37. The receipts up to 1st April, 1906, were $40,898.99, and the payments $40,431.47, leaving a balance on hand of $467.52.

The assets of the City amount to $962,449.28, of which the Waterworks Department amounts to $400,189.69, sewers $75,698.25, sidewalks $62,-187.16, City land and buildings, $118,496.50, Public Library $33,000, schools $63,940.50.

The liabilities amount to $1,157,868.58, against which there is a sinking fund account in bank and bonds of $57,258.08. The liabilities are nearly all in the form of debentures. Treasurer's salary is $1,200 per annum, and as he also keeps the Library and the Schools' accounts he is a very busy man and should have an assistant. It would pay the municipality to give him a competent assistant.

The Collector's roll for 1905 amounted to $117,491.52, of which there was due at the date of my visit in 1906 the sum of $9,163.59.

Town of Niagara, County of Lincoln.

Total receipts for 1905	$27,021 95
Total payments for 1905	26,985 89
Balance	$36 06
Receipts to 21st May, 1906	$8,954 43
Payments to 21st May, 1906	8,382 21
Balance in Sovereign Bank, Niagara	$572 22

Total assessment of municipality, $551,995.00. Collector's roll for 1905, $13,177.68. Balance unpaid at date of visit, $2,138.51. Tax rate, 24 mills in dollar. Treasurer's cash book, well kept. Treasurer has been in office seven years and receives a salary of $600 per annum.

31st December, 1905.

ASSETS.		LIABILITIES.	
Real estate, including Court House	$25,000 00	Debentures	$38,637 81
Water works	34,000 00	Sovereign Bank	6,425 00
Electric light	17,500 00	County rate	836 00
Fire department	2,500 00	Sundry accounts	1,245 00
Taxes uncollected	5,282 94		
Miscellaneous	4,895 18		
	$89,178 12		$47,143 81

Village of Beamsville, County of Lincoln.

Total assessment of municipality, $238,529.00. The tax rate 20 mills in dollar.

Total receipts for 1905	$ 8,784 02
Total payments for 1905	10,144 83
Overdrawn balance Bank of Hamilton, Beamsville	$1,360 81
Receipts to 21st May, 1906	$4,259 28
Payments to 21st May, 1906	3,909 64
Balance Bank of Hamilton, Beamsville	$349 64

Collector's roll for 1905, $4,551.08; mostly paid. Books of Treasurer fairly well kept. Treasurer receives $50 per annum and pays out of that his premium to the Guarantee Company, which amounts to $15. The assets are $27,290.86, which includes Waterworks, $17,000, and Schools, $6,000. Liabilities, $18,313.41; mostly debentures.

Township of Gainsboro', County of Lincoln.

The equalized assessment of this Township for 1905 was $1,194,870.00. Tax rate, without schools, 5 mills in dollar. Total receipts for 1905 were $11,280.35 and payments $11,097.61, leaving a balance on hand of $182.74. There is no bank account kept by Treasurer. For some reason not apparent the accounts of 1906 had not been written up in the cash book at the date of my visit. The Treasurer has been in office 17 years and receives a salary of $50 per annum. I cannot commend his bookkeeping. The assets and liabilities will neither of them exceed $1,500.

Township of Clinton, County of Lincoln.

The total receipts of this Township for 1905 were $18,375.41, and the payments $18,452.97, leaving a balance on hand of $77.50 on the 1st January. Receipts to 21st May, 1906, were $2,475.86, and payments $2,640.53, being an overdraft of $164.67. The Treasurer produced no Auditor's report or Collector's roll for 1905, or Assessor's roll. The bank book shows an overdraft of $1,463.81. These books are the most unsatisfactory I have seen in the County. Treasurer has been in office three years and receives a salary of $70 per annum.

Township of Grantham, County of Lincoln.

Total receipts for 1905	$11,569 52
Total payments for 1905	10,030 79
Balance in Sovereign Bank, St. Catharines......	$1,538 73
Receipts to 1st May, 1906	$2,342 92
Payments to 1st May, 1906	1,009 47
Balance in Sovereign Bank, St. Catharines......	$1,333 45

Total assessment of municipality for 1905, $1,259,200.00. Tax rate, 3 8/10 mills without school rates. Collector's roll, $9,689.32; paid in full less about $16. Treasurer acts as Clerk also, and for dual office receives $300 per annum. The assets on the first of the year consisted of the cash in bank and there were practically no liabilities. A well-managed municipality. Treasurer keeps his books well and has done so for 23 years.

Village of Merritton, County of Lincoln.

Total receipts for 1905	$19,196 60
Total payments for 1905	18,638 97
Balance on hand and in bank	$557 63
Receipts to 21st May, 1906	$5,082 10
Payments to 21st May, 1906	4,863 83
Balance in Sovereign Bank, St. Catharines.........	$218 27

Total assessment of municipality, $699,746. Tax rate, 23 mills in dollar. Collector's roll, $16,077.30; settled in full. Treasurer appointed 1st

January, 1906. Salary, $100 per annum. Books accurately kept. The liabilities consist of $37,591.06, nearly altogether debentures; and the assets $93,588.03, of which the principaly item is $75,000 for Waterworks. A thriving community.

Village of Port Dalhousie, County of Lincoln.

The total assessment of this municipality for 1905 was $389,044.00. Tax rate, 25 mills in dollar. Collector's roll for 1905 was $6,025.06, which was paid in full, except about $35. Total receipts for 1905, $11,942.00. Total payments, $8,966.68. Balance on hand and in bank first of year, $2,975.32. Balance at date of my visit in May, $792,17. Treasurer keeps his books well and receives a salary of $50 per annum. He has been in office 13 years. Total assets, including water privilege valued at $6,500, amount to $15,630.53. Liabilities, chiefly debentures, amount to $16,607.09.

Township of South Grimsby, County of Lincoln.

The total receipts for 1905 were	$10,189 28
The total payments for 1905 were	8,021 94
Balance in Treasurer's hands	$2,167 34
Receipts to 23rd May, 1906	$2,336 13
Payments to 23rd May, 1906	462 62
Balance in Treasurer's hands	$1,873 51

Total assessment of Township, $696,787.00. Tax rate, 6 4/10 mills in dollar without school rates. Collector's roll for 1905, $8,281.36; paid in full less $20, remitted by Council. Treasurer's salary $50 per annum. In office 26 years. Treasurer keeps no bank account. The liabilities at close of year 1905 were $3,600. Assets, $2,600.

Township of Louth, County of Lincoln.

Total assessment of Township for 1905 was $797,046. Tax rate, 7 7/10 mills without school rates. Total receipts for 1905 were $15,823.37. Payments, $15,561.66. Balance in Treasurer's hands 1st January, 1906, was $261.71. On 24th May, 1906, there was a balance overdrawn of $570.72. Collector's roll, $12,012.60; mqstly paid. Treasurer receives a salary of $75 per annum and has been in office 11 years. Assets and liabilities aboht even at the end of year; $1,200 would cover each of them.

Township of North Grimsby, County of Lincoln.

Total receipts for 1905	$10,504 40
Total payments for 1905	9,172 41
Balance in Bank of Hamilton, Grimsby............	$1,331 99
Receipts to 21st May, 1906	$2,780 30
Payments to 21st May, 1906	4,122 93
Overdrawn balance Bank of Hamilton, Grimsby	$1,342 63

Total assessment of Township, $875,095.00. Collector's roll for 1905, $9,307.81; paid, $9,076.38; balance to County Treasurer and remitted, $231.43. Tax rate, 5 3/10 mills without school rates. Treasurer acts as Clerk also and for dual position receives $200 per annum. His books are well kept. The assets on 31st December., 1905, amount to $2,811.85, and the liabilities to $1,923.24.

Township of Niagara, County of Lincoln.

The assessment of this municipality for 1905 was $940,783.00. Tax rate, 9 mills in the dollar without school rates. Total receipts for 1905 $13,862.60. Payments, $13,530.17, leaving a balance of $332.43, which is in the Imperial Bank, Niagara Falls. The cash balance at the date of my visit in May was $542.07 in Sovereign Bank, Niagara-on-the-Lake. Collector's roll for 1905 was $10,891.10, which was paid in full less $24.13, remitted by Council. Treasurer keeps his books fairly well. He has been in office three years and receives $100 per annum. The liabilities at close of year were almost nil, and the assets were represented chiefly by cash in bank, as above, $332.43.

June, 1906.

Town of Lindsay, County of Victoria.

The total receipts of this Town for 1905 were.........	$159,153 48
The total payments of this Town for 1905 were.........	158,446 58
Balance on hand and in Ontario Bank...............	$706 90
Receipts to 1st June, 1906	$32,543 63
Payments to 1st June, 1906	32,174 51
Balance on hand and in Ontario Bank...............	$369 12

Total assessment of Town, $2,269,290.00. Collector's roll for 1905, $74,848.36, of which there was due on 1st June $12,703.73. Tax rate, 29 mills for public school supporters, 29¼ mills for separate school supporters. The Treasurer, who also acts as Clerk, receives $1,600 for holding the two positions, and keeps his books very well. The sinking fund amounts to $26,592.29, partly in mortgages but principally in cash in Ontario Bank. The total assets amount to $291,509.48, of which the school property, $80,-200, and local improvement fund, $72,369.93, constitute the largest items. The liabilities amount to $362,733.81, made up of debentures, $332,761.43; indebtedness to Ontario Bank, Lindsay, $21,701.90, and the balance sundry smaller amounts.

County of Victoria.

Total receipts for 1905	$92,641 22
Total payments for 1905	91,708 92
Balance, Bank of Montreal, $912.92; cash on hand, $19.38	$932 30
Receipts to 1st June, 1906	$22,693 39
Payments to 1st June, 1906	21,703 06
Balance, Bank of Montreal, $904.17; cash on hand, $86.16	$990 33

Total County levy for 1905, $25,603.00; paid in full by 1st June, 1906. Equalized assessment of County, $11,656,215.00. Tax rate, 2 1/5 mills in dollar. Treasurer has been in office many years and is a most efficient officer. He receives $1,700 per annum for the dual position of Clerk and Treasurer. Total assets, of which the largest item is County property valued at $81,558.64, amount to $131,494.18. Liabilities, $62,106.15, of which the largest item is debentures, $40,000.

Village of Fenelon Falls, County of Victoria.

Total receipts for 1905	$11,108 44
Total payments for 1905	9,618 08
Balance Bank B. N. America, Fenelon Falls......	$1,490 36
Receipts to June, 1906	$4,107 98
Payments to June, 1906	3,010 95
Balance Bank B. N. America, Fenelon Falls......	$1,097 03

Total assessment of municipality, $401,609.00. Collector's roll for 1905, $7,028.60; abatements, $420.22; balance paid. Tax rate, 17½ mills in dollar. Treasurer's salary, $60 per annum; ten years in office. Books fairly well kept. Total assets, $107,939.90. Liabilities, $85,125.30, which includes debentures for $15,000 for an industry that unfortunately collapsed.

Village of Omemee, County of Victoria.

Total assessment of Village, $188,841.00. Tax rate, 14 mills in dollar.

Total receipts for 1905	$11,316 46
Total payments for 1905	11,127 24
Balance in Treasurer's hands	$189 22

Collector's roll for 1905, $2,717.07; paid in full less about $15. Treasurer gets $30 per annum and has been in office 15 years. He is an excellent officer and should get double at least of his present salary. Liabilities consist of debentures, $7,000, for schools and local improvements. Assets, Fire Hall and small cash balance as above.

Township of Emily, County of Victoria.

Total receipts for 1905	$14,940 95
Total payments for 1905	14,060 80
Balance in Treasurer's hands	$880 15
Receipts to 1st June, 1906	$1,066 44
Payments to 1st June, 1906	300 07
Balance in Treasurer's hands	$766 37

Assessment of municipality, $1,370,316.00. Collector's roll for 1905, $12,428.18; paid in full less a small exemption of $27. Tax rate, 4 6/10 mills. Treasurer has been in office 18 years and receives a salary of $95 per annum. He is a careful and good official.

Township of Verulam, County of Victoria.

Total Receipts for 1905	$15,408 12
Total Payments for 1905	13,435 80
Balance on Hand and in Bank	$1,972 32
Receipts to 1st June, 1906	$2,158 71
Payments to 1st June, 1906	558 12
On hand and in Bank of British North America, Fenelon Falls	$1,600 59

Total assessment of Township, $514,076 00. Collector's Roll for 1905, $9,096.35. Paid in full less $15 to County Treasurer. Tax rate 8 2-10 mills without schools. Treasurer keeps books very well and receives a salary of $100 per annum. The liabilities consist of a School Debenture of $500, and a Railway Debenture of $10,000. Assets $3,320.71, which includes cash balance at close of year of $1,972.32. Treasurer has been in office 15 years.

Village of Bobcaygeon, County of Victoria.

Assessment of municipality, $180,000. Tax rate 23 mills on $.

Total receipts for 1905	$9,091 79
Total receipts for 1905	5,662 75
Balance in Treasurer's hands	$3,429 04
Receipts to 1st June, 1906	$28,739 84
Payments to 1st June, 1906..................................	11,959 19
	16,780 65
Cash on hand	1,057 26
Bank of British North America, Fenelon Falls	$15,723 39

Treasurer receives $35 salary per annum, which is not half what he earns this year, especially as the Village has installed an Electric Light System causing double work. He has been in office 15 years and is also Treasurer of the Township of Verulam. Collector's roll for 1905, $4,280.24. Paid in full less abatement of $50. There are railway debentures of $11,000 and assets of $9,266.04 (1905). The Electric Light debentures will be shown this year (1906).

Township of Fenelon, County of Victoria.

Total receipts for 1905	$10,898 34
Total payments for 1905	10,669 02
Balance in Treasurer's hands	$229 32
Receipts to 1st June	5,483 07
Payments to 1st June	4,799 52
Balance in Treasurer's hands	$683 55

Total assessment of Township, $781,800. Paid in full except abatement, $65.27. Tax rate 5 3-10 mills without school rates. Assets $5,459.39. Liabilities, $6,915.29. Treasurer's salary, $65 per annum. Books only fairly kept. In office 8 years.

Township of Eldon, County of Victoria.

Total receipts for 1905	$17,107 02
Total payments for 1905	16,079 43
Balance in Ontario Bank, Lindsay......................	$1,027 59
*Receipts to 1st June, 1906	2,586 97
Payments to 1st June, 1906	1,911 64
On hand and in bank	$675 28

Total assessment of Township, $1,779,789.00. Collector's roll for 1905, $12,209.03. Paid in full except $50 remitted. Treasurer receives $300 per annum for acting as Clerk and Treasurer also. He keeps his accounts fairly well. The assets at 31st December, 1905, were $2,065.71, and the liabilities $5,055.60. Tax rate, 3 1-3 mills without schools.

Village of Woodville, County of Victoria.

Total assessment of municipality, $121,041.00. Tax rate, 15c on the $.

Total receipts	$4,086 71
Total payments	3,769 99
Balance in Treasurer's hands ...., ...	$316 72
Receipts to 1st June, 1906	$564 87
Payments to 1st June, 1906	558 28
Balance in Treasurer's hands	$6 59

Collector's roll for 1905, $1,841.65. Paid in full less than $6.50 rebate. Treasurer receives $20 per annum, and has been in office since 1897. Total assets, $4,616.72, and liabilities, $3,360.00.

Township of Ops, County of Victoria.

Total receipts for 1905	$28,194 97
Total payments for 1905	27,294 79
Balance on hand and in bank of Montreal, Lindsay	$900 18
Receipts to 1st June, 1906	$1,213 16
Payments	1,121 76
Balance on hand...	$91 40

Assessment of Township, $1,820,465.00. Collector's roll for 1905, $16,-750.16. Paid in full less County Treasurer, 22.54; abatements, $94.59. Tax rate, 5¾ mills on $. Treasurer has been in office 2 years, succeeding his father, an old and trusted official. He gets a salary of $125 per annum and does his work well. Total assets, $8,395.70. Total liabilities, $18,031.31.

2 M A.

Township of Somerville, County of Victoria.

Total receipts for 1905	$8,118	43
Total payments for 1905	8,825	15

Overdrawn Bank of British North America, Fenelon Falls	$706	72

Receipts to 6th June, 1906	$2,928	96
Payments	1,624	41

Balance on hand, $370.57; in Bank of British North America, $933.98	$1,304	55

Assessment of Township, $204,340.00. Collector's roll for 1905, $7,-345.89. Balance due 7th June, $2,186.95. Tax rate about 12 mills without school rates. Treasurer is a new appointment. He gets $56 per annum salary. There is a sinking fund well invested of $9,286.15, which is included in assets, making a total of $16,575.31, and liabilities are $17,745.88.

Townships of Digby, Longford and Laxton, County of Victoria.

Total receipts for 1905	$3,232	74
Total payments for 1905	2,687	84

Balance in hands of Treasurer...........................	$544	90

Assessment of municipality, $148,561.00. Tax rate, 7 8-10 mills without school rates. Collector's roll, $2,896.53. Paid in full less $30 abatement. Treasurer in office 1 year. He receives $50 per annum. Total assets, $3,543.97. No liabilities.

Township of Bexley, County of Victoria.

Total receipts for 1905	$6,332	25
Total payments for 1905	6,299	20

Balance in Treasurer's hands	33	05

Total assessment of municipality, $230,018.00. Tax rate, 11½ mills without school rates. Collector's roll, $4,314.20, mostly paid. Treasurer receives $60 per annum. In office 8 years. Books fairly well kept. Assets $7,086.04; liabilities, $7,669.00.

Township of Mariposa, County of Victoria.

Total assessment of Township, $2,959,928.00. Tax rate, 4 6-10 mills without school rates.

Total receipts for 1905	$38,422	73
Total payments for 1905	37,251	12

On hand and in bank	$ 1,171	61

2a M.A.

Receipts to 6th June, 1906	$3,063 53
Payments to 6th June, 1906	2,242 37
On hand and in bank (Ontario, Lindsay)	821 16

Collector's roll for 1905, $25,441.02. All paid except $15 returned to County Treasurer. Treasurer has been in office 3 years and receives $150 per annum. Books not kept as well as they might be. Total assets, $7,822.70; liabilities, $11,255.68.

Township of Dalton, County of Victoria.

Total receipts for 1905	$2,222 00
Tôtal payments for 1905	1,990 40
Balance in hands of Treasurer	$231 60

Assessment of municipality, $51,665.00. Collector's roll, $1,468.27. All paid except $24.35 sent to County Treasurer. Tax rate 23 mills on dollar, including school rates. Treasurer receives a salary of $60 per annum and has been in office 20 years. Books not very well kept. Assets, $541.67; liabilities, $213.10.

Township of Carden, County of Victoria.

Total receipts for 1905	$4,436 32
Total payments for 1905	4,402 34
Balance in Treasurer's hands	$33 98
Receipts to 6th June, 1906	$639 77
Payments to 6th June, 1906	482 59
Balance in Treasurer's hands	$157 18

Assessment of Township, $242,964.00. Tax rate, 12 mills on dollar, without school rates. Collector's roll, $2,995.13. Paid to within $100 on 6th June, 1906. Treasurer in office 15 years. Salary $50 per annum. Books fairly well kept. Assets at close of 1905, $647.15; liabilities, $1,615.75.

Township of Tyendinaga, County of Hastings.

Total receipts for 1905	$19,515 44
Total payments for 1905	16,638 35
Balance in Treasurer's hands .....:......................	$2,876 69
Receipts to 1st June, 1906	$2,884 15
Payments to 1st June, 1906	925 84
Balance in Treasurer's hands	$1,958 31

Total assessment of Township, $1,386,597.00. Tax rate, 6 mills, without school rates. Collector's roll for 1905, $16,168.16. Paid in full less $253.38

cancelled by Council. Books fairly well kept. Treasurer in office since 1890, and receives $175 per annum. Assets, $32,911.03, mostly consisting of Schools and Township hall. Liabilities, $266.92. No debentures.

City of Belleville, County of Hastings.

Total receipts for 1905	$222,948 64
Total payments for 1905	218,519 58
Balance Bank of Montreal, Belleville	$4,429 06
Receipts to 1st June, 1906	$90,186 26
Payments to 1st June, 1906	81,840 39
Balance Bank of Montreal, Belleville	$8,345 87

Total assessment of municipality, 1905, $3,806,460; 1906, $3,936,770.00. Tax rate 23½ mills. Collector's roll for 1905, $91,660.32. Paid on, $73,-265.61. Treasurer keeps books very well and receives $1,000 per annum. He has been in office 4 years. Sinking funds: Bank of Montreal, $23,259.75. Local debentures, $48,994.78. Total assets, including the above sinking funds, $673,976.04. Total liabilities, $945,706.66, which amount includes an indebtedness to Bank of Montreal, Belleville, of $25,611.40.

County of Hastings.

The total assessment of the County for 1905 was $11,780,000. County rates for 1905 amounted to $43,586, of which amount there was paid in 1905 the sum of $42,237.83. The total receipts for 1905 were $131,005.21. Total payments, $130,990.25. Receipts to 1st June, 1906, $62,685.41. Payments, $62,526.28. Tax rate for County, 3 7-10 mills. Treasurer has been in office 2 years and keeps the County accounts well and accurately. He receives a salary of $1,250 per annum. Total assets at close of year, which include the amount of $75,000 for County buildings, amount to $130,139.07. Liabilities, which include a liability to the Merchants' Bank of Canada of $40,035 for an overdraft, amount to $60,925.09. This overdraft on the Bank was reduced at the date of my visit in June, 1906, to $19,602.24.

Town of Deseronto, County of Hastings.

Total receipts for 1905	$29,422 90
Total payments for 1905	26,612 24
Balance Bank of Montreal, Deseronto	$2,810 66
Receipts to 1st June, 1906	$3,453 82
Payments to 1st of June, 1906	7,758 90
Balance overdrawn due Bank of Montreal, Deseronto	$4,305 08

Total assessment of municipality, $1,093,906.00. Tax rate, 21 mills, for all purposes. Collector's roll, $22,994.08. Paid in full except struck off Roll, $63.53, and uncollectable, $25.73. Treasurer acts as Clerk also, and for the dual position gets $500 per annum. I found his books well kept and the Town finances in good shape. Total assets amount to $75,109.12. Total liabilities, all debentures, $58,040.00.

Village of Tweed, County of Hastings.

Total receipts for 1905	$13,312 97
Total payments for 1905	12,947 85
Balance in Sovereign Bank, Tweed	$365 12
Receipts to 1st June, 1906	$3,445 50
Payments to 1st June, 1906	3,369 88
Balance in Sovereign Bank, Tweed	$75 62

Total assessment of municipality, $583,089.00. Tax rate, 13 mills for public school supporters; 11 mills for separate school supporters. Collector's roll, $6,865.04. Paid to this date, $6,580.81. Treasurer has been in office 15 years and receives a salary of $50 per annum, which should be doubled. Total assets are $23,448.84. Liabilities, $12,598.88.

Township of Hungerford, County of Hastings.

Total receipts for 1905	$14,781 11
Total payments for 1905	14,848 54
Due Treasurer	$67 43

No entries made in cash book for 1906. No assessment roll or collector's roll provided. No auditor's report shown. The Treasurer receives $100 per annum and has been in office 14 years. On this occasion he appears to have utterly ignored the spirit of the Act, as I could get no information from him and he is old enough to know better.

Township of Sydney, County of Hastings.

Total assessment of municipality, $2,102,707. Tax rate 5 5-10 mills, without school rates.

Total receipts for 1905	$28,234 63
Total payments for 1905	28,412 65
Balance overdrawn due Bank of Commerce, Belleville	$178 02
Receipts to 20th June, 1906	$11,712 78
Payments to 20th June, 1906	11,130 92
Balance in Bank of Commerce, Belleville	$581 86

Collector's roll for 1905, $22,751.15. Paid in full less $6.76. Treasurer has been in office one year and is doing very well for a beginner. He receives $100 per annum. At date of my visit there were practically no liabilities, and the assets were represented by cash in bank.

Township of Thurlow, County of Hastings.

Total receipts for 1905 .... $21,529 97
Total payments for 1905 .... 19,293 41

Balance Bank of Commerce, Belleville $2,236 56

Receipts to 21st June, 1906 .... $9,872 96
Payments to 21st June, 1906 .... 9,629 14

Balance Bank of Commerce, Belleville $243 82

Total assessment of Township, $2,069,150.00. Tax rate, 5 3-10 mills without school rates. Collector's roll for 1905, mostly paid. Treasurer has been in office since 1877 and is a very capable officer. He receives $80 salary per annum. Assets and liabilities are about even, viz., $9,000.

Township of Huntingdon, County of Hastings.

Total receipts for 1905 .... $8,697 89
Total payments for 1905 .... 9,935 09

Balance due Dominion Bank, Madoc $1,237 20

Receipts to June 21, 1906 .... $5,116 60
Payments to 21st June, 1906 .... 5,031 29

Balance in Treasurer's hands $85 31

Total assessment of municipality, $548,870.00. Tax rate, 8.60 mills without school rates. Collector's roll 1905, $8,704.77. Due on this roll at date of inspection, $584.35. Treasurer in office 2 years. Receives salary of $80 per annum. Assets and liabilities nearly even, about $6,000.

Township of Elzevir and Grimsthorpe, County of Hastings.

Total assessment of municipality, $318,975.00. Tax rate, 5 mills, without school rates.

Total receipts for 1905 .... $4,312 78
Total payments for 1905 .... 5,661 20

Balance due J. C. Dale & Co., private bank, Madoc $1,348 42

Receipts 1st June, 1906 .... $2,098 00
Payments 1st June, 1906 .... 1,912 27

Balance due J. C. Dale & Co.'s Bank $185 73

Collector's roll for 1905, $4,384.13. Paid in full less about $100 for remission by Council. Treasurer acts as Clerk also, and for both offices receives $130 per annum. Books poorly kept. Assets at close of year, $5,734.06. Liabilities, $3,814.00.

Township of Limerick, County of Hastings.

Total receipts for 1905	$2,415 50
Total payments for 1905	2,351 96
Balance on hand	$63 54
Receipts to 20th June, 1906	$1,538 43
Payments to 20th June, 1906	804 17
Balance in Treasurer's hands	$734 26

Total assessment of municipality, $60,215.00. Tax rate, 12 mills on the dollar, without school rates. Collector's roll, $1,707.60. Paid in full less about $30. Treasurer acts as Clerk also and receives $135 for both offices. He has been in office 20 years and is a very worthy man, although not much of a book-keeper. He may improve, however. Total assets about $1,500. Liabilities, $600.

Township of Tudor and Cashel, County of Hastings.

Total assessment of municipality, $108,038.00. Tax rate, 8 7-10 mills, without school rates.

Total receipts for 1905	$3,733 08
Total payments for 1905	3,557 20
Balance in Treasurer's hands	
Receipts to June, 1906	$1,629 00
Payments to June, 1906	1,157 95
Balance in Treasurer's hands	$471 05

Collector's roll for 1905, $2,901.95. Paid to date of inspection, June, 1906, $1,419.48. Treasurer in office 3 years. Salary $35 per annum. Assets at close of 1905, $2,899.19. Liabilities, $1,766.29.

Township of Rawdon, County of Hastings.

Total receipts for 1905	$17,776 67
Total payments for 1905	16,742 19
Balance on hand, $375.44, and in bank, $659.04	$1,034 48
Receipts to 21st June, 1906	$6,610 29
Payments to 21st June, 1906	6,384 97
On hand, $43.48, and in Sovereign Bank, Stirling, $181.84	$225 32

Total assessment of Township, $1,171,035.00. Tax rate, 8 mills, without school rates. Treasurer has held office since 1900 and receives $80 per annum. Books fairly well kept. Total assets at close of 1905, $6,616.35. Liabilities, $5,171.70.

JULY.

Town of Sault Ste. Marie, District of Algoma.

Total receipts for 1905 .... $215,426 91
Total payments for 1905 .... 168,465 90

Balance on hand, $504.72; in Canadian Bank of
    Commerce, Sault Ste. Marie, $46,456.29 ... $46,961 01

Cash Book for 1906 not written up. Total assessment of Town, $3,-950,333.00. Tax rate, 20 mills on the dollar. Collector's roll for 1905, $79,006.66. Due 1st June, $22,403.92. Treasurer has been in office 3 years and receives a salary of $600 per annum. He should have an assistant as he has too much to do and is unable to keep up his work as well as he should. There is a sinking fund of $23,739.19. Altogether the assets of the Town amount to $456,376.43, and the liabilities, which are chiefly debentures, $642,673.22. The finances of the Town appear gradually to be getting into better shape.

Township of Plummer Additional, District of Algoma.

Total receipts for 1905 .... $5,278 63
Total payments for 1905 .... 4,764 76

Balance on hand, $46.10, and in Bank of Com-
    merce, Sault Ste. Marie, $467.77............... $513 87

Cash Book for 1905 not written up. Total assessment of municipality, $82,877.00. Collector's roll for 1905, $2,775.67. All paid but $137.56. Tax rate, 7 mills, without school rates. Clerk and Treasurer's salary, $60 per annum. Total assets, $4,313.98. Liabilities, $3,423.68.

Town of Steelton, District of Algoma.

Total receipts for 1905 .... $50,976 40
Total payments for 1905 .... 47,077 53

Balance on hand, $99.46, and in Imperial Bank,
    Sault Ste. Marie, $3,799.41 .... $3,898 87

Receipts to 5th July, 1906 .... $21,564 68
Payments to 5th July, 1906 .... 20,825 52

Balance on hand, $59.43, and in Bank (Imperial),
    $669.73 .... $729 16

Total assessment of municipality, $345,107.00. Tax rate, 14 mills on the dollar. Collector's roll for 1905, $16,867.19. Balance due 1st July, $6,291.42. Treasurer has been in office 2 years and keeps his books fairly well. He receives a salary of $400 per annum. Total assets at close of 1905, $36,410.23. Liabilities, $20,335.34.

JULY.

Township of St. Joseph, District of Algoma.

Total assessment of Township, $167,585.00. Tax rate, 14 mills without school rates.

Total receipts for 1905	$5,182 00
Total payments for 1905	5,009 40
Balance on hand	$172 60
Receipts to 1 July, 1906	$2,546 75
Payments to 1 July, 1906	1,917 30
Balance in hands of Treasurer	$629 45

Collector's roll for 1905, $3,933.46, paid in full. Treasurer receives $70 per annum. Has been in office 3 years. Books well kept. Total assets at close of year, $4,929.86. Liabilities, $4,990 60.

Township of Tarentorus, District of Algoma.

Total receipts for 1905	$9,041 31
Total payments for 1905	8,581 52
Balance on hand, $100.60. Imperial Bk., Sault St. Marie, $359.19	$459 79
Receipts to 5 July, 1906	$3,985 19
Payments to 5 July, 1906	1,995 24
Balance on hand, $172.91. Imperial Bk., Sault St. Marie, $1,817.04	$1,989 95

Total assessment of Township, $327,340.00. Tax rate, 12 mills without schools. Collector's roll for 1905, $5927.02. Non-resident, $173.90. paid within $400.00. Treasurer has been in office 2 years and receives a salary of $100 per annum. Total assets at close of 1905, $8,216.77. Liabilities about $200.

Township of Korah, District of Algoma.

Total receipts for 1905	$7,347 48
Total payments for 1905	7,308 55
Balance in Bk. of Commerce, Sault St. Marie	$38 93

1906 Cash book not written up. Total assessment of Township, $404,-567.00. Tax rate, 8 mills in dollar without schools. Collector's roll, $6,471.47. Paid on this $3,176.77. Treasurer receives $100 per annum. Been one year in office. Total assets at close of year, $9,760.79. Liabilities, $1,302.68.

Town of Bruce Mines, District of Algoma.

Total assessment of municipality, $166.060. Tax rate, 2c. in dollar.

Total receipts for 1905	$4,700 24
Total payments for 1905	3,736 51
Balance in Treasurer's hands	$963 73
Receipts to 1st July, 1906	$2,036 28
Payments to 1st July, 1906	1,971 35
Balance in Treasurer's hands	$64 93

Collector's roll for 1905, $3,458.96. Paid in full, less abatements and credits, $238.16. Treasurer acts as Clerk also, and for dual office receives $125 per annum. Books fairly well kept. Total assets at close of 1905, $3,112.14. Liabilities, $3,575.00.

Town of Thessalon, District of Algoma.

Total receipts for 1905 ....:	$24,499 45
Total payments for 1905 ....'	21,762 63
Balance on hand, $543.86. In Sovereign Bk., Thessalon, $2,192.96	$2,736 82
Receipts to 1 July, 1906	$13,099 95
Payments to 1 July, 1906	12,935 59
Balance on hand and in Sovereign Bk., Thessalon	$164 36

Total assessment of Town, $300,000.00. Tax rate, 24 mills in dollar. Treasurer has been in office 4 years, and receives salary of $70 per annum. Assets which comprise Water Works, and Electric Light at the close of year 1905, amount to $42,688.84, and Liabilities, $33,823.18.

Township of Thessalon, District of Algoma.

Total receipts for 1905	$3,350 68
Total payments for 1905	2,386 02
Balance on hand and in Sovereign Bk., Thessalon	$964 66
Receipts to 1st July, 1906	$2,494 15
Payments to 1st July, 1906	1,696 91
Balance on hand, $61.16, and in Sovereign Bk., Thessalon $736.08	$797 24

Total assessment of Township, $111,152. Tax rate, 9 mills in dollar without school rates. Collector's roll for 1905, $2,683.25. Paid in full, deducting $100 for rebates, &c., by council. Treasurer receives $30 per annum for salary, and has been in office 2 years. Total assets at close of 1905, $4,085.00. Total liabilities at close of 1905, $3,500.00.

Town of Port Arthur, District of Thunder Bay.

Total receipts for 1905	$1,367,433 05
Total payments for 1905	1,366,360 25
Balance in hands of Treasurer	$1,072 80
Receipts to 1st July, 1906	$881,640 91
Payments to 1st July, 1906	873,870 54
Balance on hand, $1,581.97, and in Ontario Bank, Port Arthur, $6,188.40	$7,770 37

Total assessment of municipality, $5,405,241.00. Collector's roll for 1905 and arrears, $67,379.09. Balance due 1 July, $12,803.63. Tax rate, 16 mills in dollar. Treasurer has been in office since 1893, and receives $2,000 per annum for acting in the dual capacity of Clerk and Treasurer. He is a very busy man, having to look after the Water Works and Electric Light Departments. Of late he has also had the Electric Railway between Fort William and Port Arthur to add to his numerous other duties. So it would appear that the Town should now pay for an assistant. He certainly needs help if it has not already been provided.

The total assets of this thriving Town to the close of 1905 were $753,-197.44. Of this amount Water Works stand for $247,204.98. Electric Light System, $36,525.84. Electric Railway System, $153,872.57. Further power developments, $90,023.02. Liabilities amount to $678,139.39, chiefly debentures. The many natural advantages coup'ed with the recent railway developments all promise to make this a highly prosperous community.

Township of Shuniah, District of Thunder Bay.

Total receipts for 1905	$9,217 10
Total payments for 1895	8,404 08
On hand and in bank	813 02
Receipts to 1 July, 1906	$3,328 49
Payments to 1 July, 1906	2,429 97
Balance on hand and in bank	$898 52

Total assessment of Township, $174,897.06. Tax rate, 1¾ cents in dollar. Collector's roll for 1905, $4,693.64. Balance due 1 July, $2,395.80. Clerk and Treasurer's salary, $225 per annum, in office 3 years. Total assets at close of 1905, $9,018.33. Total liabilities, $7,616.83.

Town of Fort William, District of Thunder Bay.

Total receipts for 1905	$58,391 75
Total payments for 1905	188,541 78
Balance overdrawn in Bank of Montreal, F. William	$130,150 03

Receipts to 1 June, 1906 .... $105,967 62
Payments to 1 June, 1906 .... 73,287 99

Balance deduct from above, leaving $97,4ı0.40.
Due bank, 1 June, 1906 .... $32,679 63

Total assessment of Town, $4.642,850.00. Tax rate, 23 mills, 1905; 18 mills, 1906. Assessment being raised. Collector's roll, 1905, $85,973.40. Balance due on 1 June, 1906, $12,927.28. Treasurer in office 1 year. Appears to be a competent official. Salary of $1,200 per annum. Sinking fund, part cash and part Town Debentures amount to $113,642.33. At the end of the year 1905, total assets amount to $771,001.25. In this amount are included Electric Light Plant, Water Works and Telephone, $226,500. Real estate, the new Town Hall, $124,267.73. School build'ngs, $88,530. Local Improvements, $167,000. Liabilities amount to $717,675.28, mostly debentures. There is, however, included in this amount due the Bank of Montreal of $165,830.94. This municipality appears to be enjoying the same degree of prosperity as the sister town of Port Arthur, the circumstances in both cases being very much the same.

Township of Neebing, District of Thunder Bay.

Total receipts for 1905 .... $8,670 86
Total payments for 1905 .... 7,764 14

Balance on hand and in Bank of Montreal, Fort
William $906 72

Cash book for 1906, not written up. Total assessment of Township, $207,120.00. Tax rate, 20 mills on dollar. No schools in Neebing. Collector's roll for 1905, $4,142.40, $1,939.30, arrears of taxes. Paid on $3,741.49. Treasurer receives $150 per annum. Has only been in office 3 months, and has scarcely had time to get the books fairly started. Total assets at close of 1905, $9,559.93. Liabilities, $14,157.94.

Township of Paipoonge, District of Thunder Bay.

Total receipts for 1905 .... $8,567 62
Total payments for 1905 .... 8,997 96

Balance overdrawn in Bk. of Montreal, Ft. William $430 34

Receipts to 1st July, 1906 .... $12,848 28
Payments to 1st July, 1906 .... 9,727 96

Balance in Bk. of Montreal, F. William............ $3,120 32

Total assessment of municipality, $180,949. Tax rate, 6 mills without school rates. Collector's roll, 1905, $6,973.83. About $4,000 due on 1st July, 1906. Treasurer acts as Clerk also, and receives for joint office, $150 per annum. In office about 2 years. Assets at close of year 1905, $13,681.87. Liabilities, $13,459.77, chiefly debentures.

Township of Oliver, District of Thunder Bay.

Total receipts for 1905	$4,900 42
Total payments for 1905	4,835 62
Balance in hands of Treasurer	$64 80
Receipts of 7th July, 1906	$654 40
Payments to 7th July, 1906	566 78
Balance on hand and in Ontario Bk., Pt. Arthur.	$87 62

Total assessment of municipality, $201,150.00. Tax rate, 6 mills without school rates. Collector's roll, $4,886.50. Due about $1,000 at close of year. Treasurer has only been one year in office, and the books are only fairly well kept at present. He is to get $60 per annum.

Total assets at close of 1905, $6,209.65. Total debentures, $3,400.00. The assets include an item of $945.10, deposited in the Bk. of Montreal, Ft. William, as a sinking fund.

Town of Kenora, District of Rainy River.

Total assessment of municipality, $1,770,869. Tax rate, 25 mills in the dollar.

Total receipts for 1905	$482,252 12
Total payments for 1905	474,810 54
Balance Imperial Bk of Canada, Kenora...........	$7,441 58
Receipts to 1st July, 1906	$216,612 83
Payments to 1st July, 1906	217,441 30
Balance overdraft in Imperial Bk. of Canada, Kenora	$828 47

Collector's roll for 1905, $54,924.11. Paid on 1905-6, $53,843.69. Balance due, $1,080.42. Sinking funds in bank, $4,176.83. Treasurer acts as clerk also, and for the dual position receives $1,500 per annum. He has been in office 4 years, and is accurate and industrious. Total assets at close of 1905, were $403,303.08. The principal items of this amount being Water Works, $163,439.81. Electric Light and Telephone systems, $65,307.83. School property, $47,865.62. Liabilities, $353,588.32 made up of bills payable, $55,000, and debentures, &c., $298,588,32.

Township of Keewatin, District of Rainy River.

Total receipts for 1905	$13,155 15
Total payments for 1905	13,213 00
Balance overdrawn in Bk of Ottawa, Keewatin...	$57 85
Receipts to 1st July, 1906	$534 49
Payments to 1st July, 1906	3,584 25
Overdrawn Bk of Ottawa, Keewatin	$3,049 76

On the occasion of my visit of inspection, the cash book did not appear to be written up, which was a surprise to me, as this Treasurer's books have always on former occasions been in perfect order. I have no doubt the omission was speedily rectified, the Treasurer being a good business man. His salary is $50 per annum, and he has been 8 years in office. Total assessment of municipality, $409,096.00. Tax rate, 16½ mills, without school rates. Collector's roll for 1905, $6,013.37. At date of my visit in July, 1906, there was still a balance unpaid of $672.63. The total assets at close of 1905, were $15,948.98, and the liabilities nearly all debentures, $18,-899.95.

Town of Fort Francis, District of Rainy River.

Total receipts for 1905	$46,263 36
Total payments for 1905	45,661 85
Balance in Bank of Commerce, Fort Francis......	$601 51
Receipts to 15th July, 1906	$17,298 22
Payments to 15th July, 1906	14,049 90
Balance in Bank of Commerce, Fort Francis............	$3,248 32

Total assessment of municipality, $800,000.00. Tax rate, 17 mills on dollar. Collector's roll for 1905, $12,023.18. Paid on 16th July, $7,161:48. Treasurer receives $150 per annum salary. Has only been in office 4 months. Total assets at close of 1905, $42,027.57. Liabilities consisting of bills payable, and debentures chiefly the latter, $33,868.66.

Township of McIrvine, District of Rainy River.

Total receipts for 1905	$1,103 91
Total payments for 1905	999 52
Balance Bk. of Commerce, F. Francis...............	$104 39
Receipts to 1st July, 1906	$645 91
Payments to 1st July, 1906	413 81
Balance Bk. of Commerce, F. Francis...............	$232 10

Total assessment of Township, $61,646.00. Tax rate, 12 mills, without school rates. Collector's roll for 1905, $1,234.34. About half paid. Treasurer acts as clerk also. For both offices, he only receives $25 per annum. Considering the salary he gets, his books are not badly kept. Total assets at close of 1905, $789. Liabilities, $300.

Township of Alberton, District of Rainy River.

Total receipts for 1905	$2,965 65
Total payments for 1905	2,573 34
Balance Bank of Commerce, F. Francis...............	392 31

Receipts to 1st July, 1906	$865 61
Payments to 1st July, 1906	574 10
Balance Bank of Commerce, F. Francis	$291 51

Total assessment of Township, $100,000. Tax rate, 9 mills without school rates. Collector's roll for 1905, $2,272.89. Still due, $600.00. Treasurer acts as clerk also, receiving for both offices, $50 per annum. The books are not well kept. Total assets about $1,000. Liabilities school debentures, $700.

Township of Morley, District of Rainy River.

Total receipts for 1905	$3,262 76
Total payments for 1905	3,066 48
Balance on hand and in Bk. of Commerce, Rainy River	$196 28

Cash book for 1906 not written up. Total assessment of Township, $119,212.00. Tax rate, 8 mills without school rates. Collector's roll for 1905, $2,806.07. Paid, $1,798.02. Treasurer acts as clerk also, and receives for the double duty, $125 per annum. Assets at close of 1905, $2,322.60. Liabilities, $1.057.50.

Municipality of Emo, District of Rainy River.

Including Townships Carpenter, Lash and Aylsworth.

Total receipts for 1905	$5,805 98
Total payments for 1905	5,460 54
Balance in Treasurer's hands	$345 44

Cash book, 1906, not written up. Total assessment of municipality, $246,072.00. Tax rate, 6 mills, without school rates. Collector's roll for 1905, $4,510.16. Paid on account, $3,673.07. Treasurer and clerk in one, $50 per annum. Books poorly kept. Total assets at close of 1905, $3,775. Liabilities, $3.892.

Municipality of LaValle, comprising Townships "Devlin, Burriss and Woodyat," District of Rainy River.

Total receipts for 1905	$3,488 67
Total payments for 1905	2,784 26
Balance on hand, $482.67, and in Bk. of Commerce, F. Francis, $221,74	$704 41

Cash book, 1906, not written up. Total assessment of municipality, $271,024.00. Tax rate, 4 mills without school rates. Collector's roll for 1905, $3,283.25. Paid on, 2,848.10. Treasurer has been in office 2 years, and receives a salary of $35 per annum. Total assets at close of 1905, $2,471.82. Liabilities, $859.

Municipality of Chapple, consisting of Townships Barwick, Roseberry, Dobier, Shenston, Mather and Tait, District of Rainy River.

Total receipts for 1905	$5,982	07
Total payments for 1905	5,981	48
Balance on hand		59
Receipts to 17th July, 1906	$1,563	40
Payments to 17th July, 1906	1,507	69
Balance on hand	$55	71

Total assessment of Township, $245,812.00. Tax rate, 8 mills without school rates. Collector's roll for 1905, $6,300.28. About $1,600, due 17th July, 1906. Treasurer has only been in office 4 months, but promises well. Salary, $45 per annum. Total assets at close of 1905, $7,296.88. Liabilities, $3,997.89.

SEPTEMBER.

Town of Georgetown, County of Halton.

Total receipts for 1905	$21,395	70
Total payments for 1905	21,395	70
Receipts to 27th Sept., 1906	$16,612	10
Payments to 27th Sept., 1906	15,353	66
Balance in Merchants' Bank of Canada, Georgetown	$1,258	44

Total assessment of Municipality, $408,073.06, for 1906. Collector's roll for 1905, about $80,000. About $500 unpaid Sept., 1907. Tax rate for 1905, 20 mills; for 1906, 23 mills. Clerk and Treasurer's salary combined, $250.00. Is a good, careful officer and has held the position 1 year. Assets, including Waterworks $40,000, and Schools $20,000. Total, $81,306.39. Liabilities, chiefly debentures, $61,916.50.

Township of Holland, County of Grey.

Total receipts for 1905	$9,875	01
Total payments for 1905	9,874	59
Balance		42
Receipts to 1 Sept. 1906	$4,774	50
Payments to 1 Sept., 1906	4,132	21
Balance on hand in Merchants' Bank, Chatsworth	$642	29

Total assessment of Municipality, $1,353,348.00. Collector's roll for 1905, $11,728.11; practically paid in full. Tax rate 4 mills on dollar, without School rates. Treasurer keeps Township books fairly well and receives

$100 per annum. He has been in office for 19 years. The County rate, $1,829, may be said to be the only liability, and there are assets of over $5,000, mostly taxes in arrears.

September.

Township of Sydenham, County of Grey.

Total assessment of Municipality, $1,902,562.00. Tax rate, 4 8-10 mills on the dollar.

Total receipts for 1905	$20,052 12
Total payments for 1905	19,010 69
Balance in Sovereign Bank, Owen Sound	$1,041 43
Receipts, 1 Sept. 1906	$9,930 50
Payments, 1 Sept., 1906	9,104 94
Balance in Sovereign Bank, Owen Sound	$825 56

Collector's roll for 1905, $17,186.03; paid in full except $32.25, defaulters. Tax rate, 4 8-10 mills on dollar less school rates. Treasurer has only been in office 2 years, but keeps the Township books very well; salary, $105 per annum. Liabilities are about $3,000, and cash assets about $1,500.

Township of Artemesia, County of Grey.

Total assessment of Municipality, $1,076,695.00. Tax rate 7 mills on dollar without school rates.

Total receipts for 1905	$24,949 32
Total payments for 1905	22,307 52
Balance on hand and in Standard Bk., Flesherton	$2,641 80

Cash Book for 1906 not produced.

Treasurer has been in office 11 years and receives a salary of $100 per annum. Total assets, $11,061.45. Liabilities, $12,510.95. Amongst' the assets there is an item of $6,349.87, Standard Bank deposit on account of sinking fund.

Township of Egremont, County of Grey.

Total receipts for 1905	$17,734 17
Total payments for 1905	16,898 52
On hand and in Ontario Bank	$835 65
Receipts to 1 August, 1906	$5,211 94
Payments to 1 August, 1906	1,986 48
On hand and in Bank	$3,225 46

3 M.A.

Total assessment of Municipality, $1,540,775. Tax rate 4 mills on dollar without school rates. Collector's roll for 1905, $14,257.70; paid in full less $32 (one defaulter). Treasurer only keeps his books fairly well. He has been in office two years and receives $100 per annum. School debentures form a liability of $8,191.55, and there was a balance of cash on hand at end of 1905 of $835.65.

Township of Derby, County of Grey.

Total receipts for 1905	$21,677 79
Total payments for 1905	19,456 24
Balance on hand and in Traders' Bank, Owen Sound	$2,221 55
Receipts to 1 Sept., 1906	$7,350 33
Payments to 1 Sept., 1906	6,872 14
Balance in Treasurer's hands	$478 19

Total assessment of Township, $976,397.00. Tax rate 6 mills on dollar without school rates. Collector's roll for 1905, $10,278.34; all paid except $12.65. Treasurer's books are fairly well kept. He has been in office 3 years and receives a salary of $75 per annum. Assets at close of 1905, $7,223.06. Liabilities, chiefly debentures, $6,378.20.

Township of Sarawak, County of Grey.

Total assessment of municipality, $350,198 for 1905. Tax rate 22 mills including school rates.

Total receipts for 1905	$12,696 94
Total payments for 1905	11,187 87
Balance on hand and in bank	$1,509 07
Receipts to 1 Sept., 1906	$3,234 99
Payments to 1 Sept., 1906	3,173 73
Balance in Molsons Bank, Owen Sound	$61 26

Collector's roll for 1905, $7,519.57; paid within $100. Treasurer in office since 1899; receives salary of $60 per annum. Total assets, $4,035.40. Liabilities, mostly R. W. debentures, $9,838.56.

Township of Glenelg, County of Grey.

Total assessment of municipality, $763,050.00. Tax rate about 7 mills without school rates.

Total receipts for 1905	$13,277 29
Total payments for 1905	11,035 91
Balance in Treasurer's hands	$2,241 38

3a M.A.

Receipts to 1st Aug., 1906 .... $2,554 82
Payments to 1st Aug., 1906 .... 1,999 92

Balance in Treasurer's hands $554 90

Collector's roll for 1905, $10,129.69; paid in full except about $16. Treasurer keeps the Township books well, and receives a salary of $100 per annum. He has been in office 3 years. Assets amount to $4,001.38, and consist of cash $2,241, and town hall. . There are no liabilities.

Township of Bentinck, County of Grey.

Total receipts for 1905 .... $15,020 75
Total payments for 1905 .... 14,539 88

Balance in Standard Bank, Durham $480 87

Receipts to 1st Sept., 1906 .... $4,454 89
Payments to 1st Sept., 1906 .... 2,675 74

Balance, in Standard Bank, Hanover, $151.93;
in Merchants Bank, Durham, $1,627.22...... $1,779 15

Total assessment of municipality, $1,802,845.00. Tax rate 4 mills on dollar without school rates. Collector's roll for 1905, $13,524.40; paid in full, less about $50, uncollectable. Treasurer has been 22 years in the service of the Township and receives $100 per annum. A good and faithful officer. The assets were $3,561.69 at the end of 1905, and there were no liabilities.

Township of Osprey, County of Grey.

Total receipts for 1905 .... $17,625 29
Total payments for 1905 .... 16,595 59

Balance in Treasurer's hands $1,029 70

Receipts to 1st Sept., 1906 .... $2,861 91
Payments to 1st Sept., 1906 .... 2,188 62

Balance in Treasurer's hands $673 29

Total assessment of municipality, $1,043,625.00. Tax rate 8 mills without school rates. Collector's roll for 1905, $13,483.79; all paid except about $20. Treasurer has been in office 2 years and receives a salary of $100 per annum. Assets at close of year 1905, $1,906.31. Liabilities $3,628, chiefly school debentures.

Township of Sullivan, County of Grey.

Total receipts for 1905 .... $16,896 95
Total payments for 1905 .... 14,962 72

Balance in treasurer's hands $1,934 23

Receipts to 1st Sept., 1906 .... $3,001 93
Payments to 1st Sept., 1906 .... 2,714 50

Balance in Treasurer's hands $287 43

Total assessment of municipality, $1,822,000. Tax rate about 10 mills including school rates. Collector's roll for 1905, $14,192.58; paid in full except about $150. Treasurer has been in office 17 years. He cannot, however, be said to keep the Township books in a satisfactory manner. In fact they are most unsatisfactory, although it must be stated that I found no evidence of dishonesty. The assets at close of 1905 were $4,108.50, and liabilities about $200. There are no debentures against the Township.

Township of Proton, County of Grey.

Total assessment of municipality, $1,372,450.00. Tax rate 5¼ mills on dollar.

Total receipts for 1905 .... $25,005 12
Total payments for 1905 .... 21,308 92

Balance in Bank of Hamilton, Dundalk............ $3,696 20

Receipts to 15th Sept., 1906 .... $8,499 17
Payments to 15th Sept., 1906 .... 7,559 80

Balance in Bank of Hamilton, Dundalk........... $939 37

Collector's roll for 1905, $15,964.33; paid in full less $400, defaulters' list. Treasurer has been in office about 4 years and keeps Township books very well. He receives $150 annually. Total assets at close of year 1905 were $8,199.60, and the debentures on drainage and school account amounted to $10,000.00

Town of Thornbury, County of Grey.

Total receipts for 1905 .... $9,158 39
Total payments for 1905 .... 8,918 40

Balance in Bank of Toronto, Thornbury............ $239 99

Receipts to 1st Sept., 1906 .... $4,664 64
Payments to 1st Sept., 1906 .... 4,097 60

Balance on hand and in Bank of Toronto, Tilsonburg $567 04

Total assessment of Town, $261,772.29. Tax rate, 19 mills on dollar. Collector's roll for 1905, $4,997.05; paid in full less $8.40. Treasurer is very good officer, although he only receives $50 per annum, which should be mended. Has been in the position since 1903. Total assets, $5,290.73. Liabilities, chiefly debentures, $7,040.87.

Township of Normanby, County of Grey.

Total receipts for 1905	$23,961 22
Total payments for 1905	23,734 55
Balance in Traders' Bank of Canada, Ayton......	$226 67
Receipts to 1st Sept., 1906	$4,034 60
Payments to 1st Sept., 1906	4,030 63
Balance on hand	$3 97

Total assessment for 1905, $2,164,505.00. Tax rate 4 mills, without school rates. Collector's roll for 1905, $18,156.35; paid in full. Treasurer has been in office since 1904, and receives a salary of $100 per annum. He is a good and trusty officer. Assets at close of 1905 were $2,318.32. No liabilities.

Town of Meaford, County of Grey.

Total assessment of municipality, $857,327.00, for 1905. Tax rate 27 3-10 mills.

Total receipts for 1905	$135,558 94
Total payments for 1905	119,165 35
Balance, Molsons Bank, Meaford, $6,863.34; Merchants Bank, Meaford, $9,530.25	$16,393 59
Receipts to 14th Sept., 1906	$56,431 71
Payments to 14th Sept., 1906	52,940 81
Balance, Molsons Bank, $1,544.56; Merchants Bank, $1,946.34	$3,490 90

Collector's roll for 1905, $20,224.57; about $200 still due on this roll. Treasurer keeps the Town books very well. He receives a salary of $200 per annum and has been in office 5 years. The assets of the Town amount to $162,839.71, which include at the end of 1905: Cash, $16,393.59; schools, $20,000; Waterworks, $30,000; local improvements, etc., $71,000. Liabilities, $172,500, nearly all debentures.

Village of Markdale, County of Grey.

Total assessment of municipality, $263,615 for 1905. Tax rate, 15 mills on dollar.

Total receipts for 1905	$12,040 62
Total payments for 1905	11,932 45
Balance in Lucas Bank, Markdale	$108 17
Receipts to 10th Sept., 1906	$2,009 30
Payments to 10th Sept., 1906	1,995 62
Balance in Lucas Bank, Markdale	$13 68

Collector's roll for 1905, $4,627.31; paid in full. Treasurer is a highly competent officer, but received only a salary of $35 for the last 15 years, which should be increased considerably. Total assets amount to $13,568.32, and liabilities, mostly debentures, to $5,761.08.

Village of Dundalk, County of Grey.

Total receipts for 1905	$18,978	46
Total payments for 1905	18,880	89
Balance in Lucas Bank, Markdale	$97·	57
Receipts to 1st Sept., 1906	$18,251	13
Payments to 1st Sept., 1906	18,541	29
Balance overdrawn in Lucas Bank, Dundalk......	$290	16

Total assessment of Village, $200,175.00. Tax rate, 18 mills on dollar. Collector's roll for 1905, $4,237.75; paid in full, only a deficit of $2. Treasurer has been in office nearly 20 years. Receives a salary of $50 annually. Accounts well and accurately kept. Assets over $25,000. Liabilities about the same, allowing for interest on debentures.

County of Grey.

Total receipts for 1905	$126,504	56
Total payments for 1905	86,184	69
In Molsons and Merchants Banks, Owen Sonud...	$40,309	87
Receipts to 1st Sept., 1906	$62,829	52
Payments to 1st Sept., 1906	43,120	63
In Molsons and Merchants Banks, Owen Sound...	$19,708	89

Equalized assessment of County, $29,343,476.00. County rates for year, $42,458.03. Tax rate, 1½ mills. Treasurer in office 33 years last June, salary $1,400 per annum. Is an excellent officer in every respect. At the close of year 1905 the total assets, including sinking funds, $11,467.61. Cash, $40,309.87; Court House, Gaol, House of Refuge, $118,338.60; and miscellaneous, $5,452.36, amounted to $175,568.44. The liabilities, including municipal debentures guaranteed by County, $105,897.00, amounted in all to $141,047.35. Altogether the County is in a first class financial position.

Town of Owen Sound, County of Grey.

Total receipts for 1905	$141,877	29
Total payments for 1905	130,012	00
Balance, on hand, $35.56; in Traders' Bank, Owen Sound, $11,829.73	$11,865	29
Receipts to 1st Sept., 1906	$188,190	15
Payments to 1st Sept., 1906	165,191	21
Balance, on hand, $31.15; in Traders' Bank, Owen Sound, $22,967.79	$22,998	94

Total assessment of municipality, $4,454,997.00. Collector's roll for 1905, $99,630.94; about $1,500 due 1st Sept., 1906. Tax rate, 21 mills for Public school supporters; 21 7-10 for Separate school supporters. Treasurer's salary, $1,500 per annum, out of which he paid $312 for clerical assistance. There is a new arrangement from 1st May, 1906, by which the Treasurer is paid $1,100 per annum, his assistant $800, and a lady assistant $312 per annum. Town pays for premium to Treasurer's Guarantee insurance. Sinking funds in cash in Traders' Bank, $50,520.27. In Town debentures, $92,-772.68. Total, $141,192.95. Waterworks amount to $155,243.00, and rates due. Gas plant, $67,623.11. Electric plant, $66,298.18. Altogether the assets at the end of 1905, including the above items, amounted to $823,960.33, and the liabilities, including debentures $703,376.08, to $823,597.23. The mayor and council appear to have made great improvements in their office arrangements the last year or two and also in their financial methods.

OCTOBER, 1906.

County of Ontario.

Total receipts for 1905	$158,774	79
Total payments for 1905	130,587	06
. In Western Bank of Canada, Whitby, $28,127.44; on hand, $60.29	$28,187	73
Receipts to 21st May, 1906	$54,272	20
Payments to 21st May, 1906	47,779	54
In Western Bank, Whitby, $6,303.12; on hand $189.54	$6,492	66

Total assessment of County, $21,099,219.00. County levies for 1905, $35,000, paid in full. Tax rate, 1 5-8 mills on dollar. Treasurer keeps the County books well, receiving $1,350 per annum. He has been in office 16 years last January. Total assets, including County property, $50,000. House of Refuge, $28,000. Miscellaneous, chiefly cash in bank, $29,666.56. Make in all, $107,666.56. Liabilities amount to $51,700.94.

Town of Whitby, County of Ontario.

Total receipts for 1905	$112,072	26
Total payments for 1905	111,807	40
Balance on hand and in bank	$264	86
Receipts to 1st Oct., 1906	$63,899	40
Payments to 1st Oct., 1906	63,900	85
Balance overdrawn	$1	45

Total assessment of Town, $927,174. Collector's roll for 1905, $22,-979,97, of which $3,119.70 remains unpaid. Tax rate for 1906, 26/10 mills on dollar. Clerk acts as Treasurer also, has been in office ten years and receives $550 per annum. Total assets, which include Waterworks, $51,724.76;

electric light, $22.476.74; schools, $25,000, amount altogether to $149,-
128.18. Liabilities amount to $156,885.50, principally debentures. The
Waterworks are said to be run at loss of $3,500 per annum and the Electric
Light shows a clear profit of $2,000 per annum.

OCTOBER.

Village of Port Perry, County of Ontario.

Total receipts for 1905	$15,093	11
Total payments for 1905	15,001	25
Balance in Bank of Commerce, Whitby	$91	86
Receipts to 30th Sept., 1906	$6,030	60
Payments to 30th Sept., 1906	6,078	18
Balance overdrawn, Bank of Commerce, Whitby...	$47	58

Total assessment of municipality, $451,857.00. Tax rate, 27 mills in
dollar. Treasurer has been in office 25 years and receives $100 per annum.
Total assets at close of 1905, $50,532.80. Total liabilities at close of 1905,
$54,255.74.

Town of Oshawa, County of Ontario.

Total receipts for 1905	$59,746	14
Total payments for 1905	59,676	70
Balance in Treasurer's hands	$69	44
Receipts to 27th Nov., 1906	$65,592	62
Payments to 27th Nov., 1906	65,998	15
Balance overdrawn	$405	53

Total assessment of municipality, $1,700,000 for 1906. Tax rate, 26
mills in dollar. Treasurer 11 years in office; salary $175 per annum. Total
assets, $238,216.67, which include water works. $111 000. School property,
$24,100. Mortgages on real estate, $50,035.51. Granolithic walks, $10,156.83;
sewers $19,000. Liabilities, $238,589.30; chiefly debentures.

Township of Scott, County of Ontario.

Total receipts for 1905	$14,692	94
Total payments for 1905	13,690	74
Balance on hand, $97.25; in Dominion Bank, Ux- bridge, $904.95	$1,002	20
Receipts to 1st Sept., 1906	$3,541	18
Payments to 1st Sept., 1906	3,059	17
Balance in Dominion Bank, Uxbridge	$482	01

Total assessment of Township, $1,024,745.00. Tax rate, 5.7-10 mills, without school rates. Collector's roll for 1905, $11,160.85, paid. Treasurer keeps Township books correctly and receives salary of $100 per annum; has been in office 8 years. Including a Clergy Reserve Fund of about $5,000, the total assets amount to $6,780.54. The only liability is Drainage Debenture, $384.67.

Township of Mara, County of Ontario.

Total receipts for 1905	$16,506	91
Total payments for 1905	16,165	59
Balance in Traders' Bank of Canada, Orillia	341	32
Receipts to 1st Oct., 1906	$3,894	48
Payments to 1st Oct., 1906	3,319	44
Balance on hand, $174.47; in Traders' Bank of Canada, Orillia, $400.57	$575	04

Total assessment of Township, $1,659,477.00. Collector's roll, $12,-103.33; paid in full less remissions by Council and non resident taxes, $600. Tax rate, 5 mills in dollar; without school rates. Treasurer keeps books fairly well; has been in office 34 years and receives $100 per annum. Total assets, including $1,000 for Town Hall, $3,308.66. Total liabilities, School and Drainage Debentures, $3,615.16.

Township of Brock, County of Ontario.

Total receipts for 1905	$23,591	33
Total payments for 1905	22,374	31
Balance on hand and in Western Bank, Sunderland	$1,217	02

Cash Book 1906 not written up.

Total assessment of municipality, $2,723,163.30. Collector's roll for 1905, $17,651.54; nearly all paid. Tax rate, 3½ mills, without school rates. Treasurer in office 6 years; receives salary of $100 per annum. There is no liability of the Township, and the assets amount to $3,196.96, which includes above cash balance of $1,217.02 and the Township Hall. This at close of 1905.

Township of Whitby West, County of Ontario.

Total receipts for 1905	$19,106	92
Total payments for 1905	19,055	04
Balance in Dominion Bank, Whitby	$51	88
Receipts to 30th Sept., 1906	$5,360	85
Payments to 30th Sept., 1906	5,155	19
Balance on hand and in Bank	$205	66

Total assessment of Township, $1,511,581.00. Collector's roll for 1905' $12,594.92; paid in full less deductions, $30. Tax rate, 4 1-10 mills, without school rates or special tax. Treasurer has been in office 10·years and receives salary of $90 per annum. The assets at close of 1905 amounted to $1,369.13, and the liabilities to $219.69.

Township of Whitby East, County of Ontario.

Total receipts for 1905	$18,000 25
Total payments for 1905	17,707 13
Balance in hands of Treasurer	$293 12

1906, not written up.

Total assessment of municipality, $1,651,160.00. Tax rate, 3 8-10 mills, without school rates. Collector's roll for 1905, $13,336.09; paid in full less $55 uncollectable. Treasurer has been in office 21 years; salary $75 per annum. Total assets at close of 1905, including Municipal Loan Fund item of $3,200, amount to $5,000.79. Liabilities amount to $1,030.70.

Township of Pickering, County of Ontario.

Total receipts for 1905	$41,490 35
Total payments for 1905	44,468 61
Balance, due Sovereign Bank, Claremont	$2,978 26
Receipts to 1st Oct., 1906	$14,168 31
Payments to 1st Oct., 1906	13,408 22
Balance, in Sovereign Bank, $497.23; in Western, $260.27; on hand, $2.59	$760 09

Total assessment of Township, $3,348,619.00. Tax rate, 3 8-10 mills, without school rates. Collector's roll, $30,363.51; paid in full. Treasurer in office 12 years; receives a salary of $150 per annum. At close of year 1905 the total assets were $5,593.17, and the liabilities $6,132.55.

Town of Uxbridge, County of Ontario.

Total receipts for 1905	$39,768 71
Total payments for 1905	39,685 22
Balance in Treasurer's hands	$83 49
Receipts to 3rd Oct., 1906	$16,440 41
Payments to 3rd Oct., 1906	16,039 76
Balance in Dominion Bank, Uxbridge	$400 65

Total assessment of municipality, $500,338. . Tax rate, 25 mills in dollar. Collector's roll for 1905, $12,866.60; paid in full except $90; defaulter's list. Treasurer is a very good officer and has been 8 years in the position. He receives $100 per annum, which should be increased fifty per cent. considering the work he does. The assets at the close of the year 1905 amounted to $65,336.35. This includes a sinking fund of $14,165.05; water works, $10,000, and schools, $13,000. Liabilities amounted to $35,279.12; principally debentures.

Township of Uxbridge, County of Ontario.

Total receipts for 1905	$17,201 45
Total payments for 1905	17,199 23
Balance in Treasurer's hands	$2 22
Receipts to Sept., 1906	$5,309 62
Payments to Sept., 1906	5,593 91
Balance overdrawn in Gould's Bank, Uxbridge ...	$284 29

Total assessment of Township, $998,435.00. Tax rate 6 5-10 mills, without school rates. Collector's roll for 1905, $12,157.54; paid in full except about $75, returned to County Treasurer. Treasurer keeps the Township books fairly well, and has been in office 16 years. He receives an annual salary of $100. The Township has a railway debenture debt of $19,000, against which there is a sinking fund of over $13,000, in cash and securities. The only other indebtedness is $2,000, to Gould's Bank, Uxbridge.

County of Dufferin.

The total assessment of this County for 1905 was $9,610,280.00. Tax rate, nearly 1½ mills.

Total receipts for 1905	$27,532 01
Total payments for 1905	25,398 81
Balance in Canadian Bank of Commerce, Orangeville	$2,133 20
Receipts to 16th October, 1906	$15,764 90
Payments to 16th October, 1906	15,068 91
Balance in Canadian Bank of Commerce, Orangeville	$695 91

County levies for 1905, $13,936.20; paid in full. Treasurer has been in office since January, 1893, and receives a salary of $1,000 per annum. He is an accurate and careful Treasurer. Total assets of the County at the close of 1905 were, including $40,000 for County property, $45,273.02. Liabilities, $3,061.56. A very carefully handled County in every respect.

Town of Orangeville, County of Dufferin.

Total receipts for 1905	$68,177 85
Total payments for 1905	67,928 45
Balance in Canadian Bank of Commerce, Orangeville	$249 40

Receipts to 16th October, 1906 .... $34,403 26
Payments to 16th October, 1906 .... 31,738 01

Balance in Canadian Bank of Commerce, Orange-
    ville $2,665 25

Total assessment of Town, $965,352.00. Tax rate, 24 mills in 1905; 22 mills in 1906. Collector's roll for 1905, $25,104.33; paid in full except for cash discounts, and $194 doubtful debts. Treasurer has been in office since 1879 and is a very good and faithful officer. He only gets $300 salary, which should be increased fifty per cent. at least, as the Town work takes up all his time. The assets of the Town at the close of 1905 were $91,815.66, which includes sinking fund, $17,782.05, water works system, $51,014.74. Liabilities, which were chiefly debentures, amounted to $140,568.69.

Village of Shelburne, County of Dufferin.

Total receipts for 1905 .... $13,650 48
Total payments for 1905 .... $12,132 07

Balance on hand and in Union Bank, Shelburne... $1,518 41

Receipts to 16th October, 1906 .... $3,620 26
Payments to 16th October, 1906 .... 3,017 95

Balance in Union Bank, Shelburne $602 31

Total assessment of municipality, $414,512.00. Collector's roll for 1905, $8,715.09; paid in full. Tax rate, 17½ mills in dollar. Treasurer in office since spring 1906; salary $70 per annum. Total assets, $398.50, including water works, $17,900.00. Liabilities, $27,791.27; debentures.

Township of Melancthon, County of Dufferin.

Total receipts for 1905 .... $17,502 13
Total payments for 1905 .... 17,132 56

Balance in Treasurer's hands $369 57

Receipts to 1st October, 1906 .... $4,786 06
Payments to 1st October, 1906 .... 4,595 33

Balance in Treasurer's hands $190 73

Total assessment of municipality, $1,965,647.00. Tax rate, 3¼ mills, without school rates. Collector's roll for 1905, $14,669.59; paid in full excepting $56, defaulters' list. Treasurer in office 13 years; salary per annum $100. Total assets at close of 1905, 854.16. Liabilities, $1,130.00.

Township of Mulmur, County of Dufferin.

Total receipts for 1905 .... $18,712 38
Total payments for 1905 .... 18,429 97

Balance in Treasurer's hands $282 41

Receipts to 12th October, 1906	$4,826 24
Payments to 12th October, 1906	4,778 62
Balance in Treasurer's hands	$47 62

Total assessment of municipality, $1,461,550.00. Tax rate, 4 4-10 mills, without school rates. Collector's roll, $13,771.97; paid in full less $1.74. Treasurer in office 12 years; salary $125 per annum. Total assets at close of 1905, $1,615.08. Liabilities, $1,198.36.

Township of Garafraxa East, County of Dufferin.

Total receipts for 1905	$12,798 83
Total payments for 1905	12,069 89
Balance in hand of Treasurer	$728 94

1906; not written up.

Total assessment of municipality, $1,139,662.00. Tax rate, 3 8-10 mills, without school rates. Collector's roll for 1905, $10,201.38; paid in full. Treasurer's books poorly kept; in office 9 years; salary $85 per annum. At close of 1905 assets were the above cash balance, $728.94, and liabilities the balance of a bridge debenture for $2,500.

Township of Amaranth, County of Dufferin.

Total receipts for 1905	$19,320 11
Total payments for 1905	18,591 86
Balance in hands of Treasurer	$728 25
Receipts to 13th October, 1906	$3,995 76
Payments to 13th October, 1906	3,961 25
Balance in hands of Treasurer	$34 51

Total assessment of municipality, $1,516,000. Tax rate, 2 8-10 mills, without school rates. Collector's roll for 1905, $12,821.19; paid in full except about $18.38. Treasurer has been in office 2 years; salary $65 per annum. Total assets at close of 1905, $2,579.93. Liabilities, $3,116.16.

Township of Mono, County of Dufferin.

Total receipts for 1905	$18,523 16
Total payments for 1905	16,158 54
Balance, Bank of Commerce, Orangeville	$2,364 62
Receipts to 5th October, 1906	$3,836 02
Payments to 5th October, 1906	3,592 04
Balance on hand and in bank	$243 98

Total assessment of municipality, $1,555,260.00. Tax rate, 4 3-10 mills, without school rates. Collector's roll for 1905, $14,387.77; paid in full. Treasurer keeps Township books well; in office 6 years; salary, $100 per annum. Assets at close of year 1905 consisted of cash, $2,364.52, in Bank of Commerce. There were no liabilities.

County of Renfrew.

Total receipts for 1905	$60,911 36
Total payments for 1905	60,340 67
Balance on hand and in Bank of Ottawa, Pembroke	$570 69
Receipts to 22nd October, 1906	$62,145 92
Payments to 22nd October, 1906	57,847 11
Balance, Bank of Ottawa, Pembroke	$4,298 81

Total assessment of County, equalized, $18,437,471.00. Tax rate, 1 33-100 mills in dollar. County levy for 1905, $25,045.17; balance unpaid in October, $775.26. Treasurer is an excellent officer and has been in office for 15 years; he receives a salary of $1,000 per annum. The total assets of the County at the close of 1905 were $86,623.28, which included sinking fund, $13,867.17, County buildings, 50,000.00, etc. The liabilities were $60,748.95, which consisted of debentures, $53,739.14; borrowed from Bank, $5,000.00, and the balance in miscellaneous.

Town of Pembroke, County of Renfrew.

Total receipts for 1905	$97,654 01
Total payments for 1905	99,799 82
Balance overdrawn, Bank of Ottawa, Pembroke ...	$2,145 81
Receipts to 16th October, 1906	$73,180 57
Payments to 16th October, 1906	73,199 75
Balance overdrawn, Bank of Ottawa	$19 18

Total assessment of municipality, $1,272,700.00. Tax rate, 17.30 mills, Public School supporters; 18.80, Separate School supporters. Collector's roll for 1905, $43,850.00; on which $2,000 is still due; 1904 roll paid in full. Treasurer has been in office 17 years and is a capable officer. He receives the modest salary of $375 per annum, which is scarcely enough for his many duties. The water works system is placed in the assets at $75,000.00. The assets of the Town, inclusive of the water works, amounted at the end of 1905 to $251,978.02, and the liabilities amounted to $200,203.07, of which the debenture debt made $150,506.00.

Town of Arnprior, County of Renfrew.

Total receipts for 1905	$92,299 66
Total payments for 1905	83,731 57
Balance on hand and in Bank of Ottawa, Arnprior	$8,568 09

Cash Book 1906 not written up.

Total assessment of Town, $1,071,446.00. Collector's roll for 1905, $29,705.30; about $15,000 due 1904-5. Tax rate, 22 mills, Public School supporters; 28 mills Separate School supporters. Treasurer has been in office 30 years and receives a salary of $300 per annum. His books are not up to date and the finances of the Town are decidedly in the same position, there being a poor system of collections. The assets of the Town, including the water works system, $102,909.53, amount to $248,281.67, and the liabilities to $207,971.55. This sum is made up of debentures mostly, but there is rather a depressing liability of $70,000 to two chartered Banks. Probably debentures are going to be issued to cover this rather unusual item.

Town of Renfrew, County of Renfrew.

Total receipts for 1905	$43,724	82
Total payments for 1905	69,697	30
Balance overdrawn in Banks	$25,972	48
Receipts to 22nd October, 1906	$32,130	16
Payments to 22nd October, 1906	42,909	63
Balance overdrawn in Banks	$10,779	47

Total assessment of municipality, $1,309,342.00. Collector's roll for 1905, $25,305.47; due on this roll, $2,927.61. Tax rate, 2 cents on Public School supporters; 3 3-10 on Separate School supporters. Treasurer in office 34 years; salary $375 per annum. Total assets, including $100,000 for water works and sewerage plant, amount to $233,312.86. Liabilities, including Bank overdrafts, $41,695.49, total $191,299.02. The books of this municipality are rather complicated in their entries and an audit would do good.

OCTOBER.

Village of Cobden, County of Renfrew.

Total assessment of municipality, $318,180. Tax rate, 9 2/10 mills in dollar.

Total receipts for 1905	$5,174	71
Total payments for 1905	5,465	55
Balance overdrawn on Bank of Ottawa, Cobden	$290	84
Receipts to 1st October, 1906	$1,196	64
Payments to 1st October, 1906	1,372	61
Balance overdrawn Bank of Ottawa, Cobden......	$175	97

Collector's roll for 1905, $3,142.62; paid. Treasurer has been in office for six years and receives $25 salary per annum. Assets at close of 1905 amounted to $1,906.46, and liabilities to $10,800, chiefly debentures for schools and local improvements.

Townships of Wilberforce and North Algona, County of Renfrew.

Total assessment of municipality, $802,367. Tax rate, 3 5/10 mills without school rates.

Total receipts for 1905	$7,601 55
Total payments for 1905	6,470 07
Balance in Treasurer's hands	$1,131 48
Receipts to 1st October, 1906	$3,160 98
Payments to 1st October, 1906	2,620 28
Balance in Treasurer's hands	$540 70

Collector's roll for 1905, $6,287.09; paid in full less remitted, $101.27. Treasurer's salary, $60 per annum; been in office 36 years. Total assets at end of 1905, $2,860.73. Liabilities, $2,182.07.

Township of Admaston, County of Renfrew.

Total assessment of municipality, $784.795.00. Tax rate, 4 mills in dollar without school rates.

Total receipts for 1905	$8,544 29
Total payments for 1905	7,627 68
Balance on hand, $403.56; in Bank of Ottawa, $513.05	$916 61
Receipts to 23rd October, 1906	$1,081 45
Payments to 23rd October, 1906	237 70
Balance on hand and in bank...........................	$843 75

Collector's roll for 1905, $7,194.50; balance due at date, $341.36. Treasurer has been in office 32 years; salary, $60 per annum. Total assets at end of 1905, $4,794.09. Liabilities, $1,738.14.

Village of Eganville, County of Renfrew.

Total receipts for 1905	$10,219 88
Total payments for 1905	9,445 79
Balance on hand and in Merchants' Bank, Eganville	$774 09
Receipts to 17th October, 1906	$10,759 40
Payments to 17th October, 1906	9,689 39
Balance on hand and in bank	$1,070 01

Total assessment of municipality, $319,798.00. Tax rate, 18¼ mills in dollar. Collector's roll for 1905, $6,018.32; paid in full less defaulters, $46.84. Treasurer has been in office five years and keeps the Village books very well. He receives $35 per annum, which might be increased without hurting any interest. The total assets of the Village are $8,477.50, and the liabilities $5,854.54.

Township of Grattan, County of Renfrew.

Total receipts for 1905	$2,919	82
Total payments for 1905	2,764	05
Balance in Merchants' Bank, Eganville.....:......	$155	77
Receipts to 4th September, 1906	$2,627	46
Payments to 4th September, 1906	2,476	99
Balance in Merchants' Bank, Eganville...............	$150	47

Total assessment of Township, $364,365. Collector's roll for 1905, $3,658.16; paid. Tax rate, 12 mills, including school rates. Treasurer in office three years. Keeps books very well. Salary $25 per annum. Total assets at close of 1905, $2,802.32. Liabilities, $1,147.65.

Townships of Bagot and Blythfield, County of Renfrew.

Total receipts for 1905	$5,981	55
Total payments for 1905	5,054	17
Balance in hands of Treasurer	$927	38
Receipts to 1st October, 1906	$1,534	85
Payments to 1st October, 1905	1,051	27
Balance in hands of Treasurer	$483	58

Total assessment of municipality, $153,296. Tax rate, 10 mills without school rates. Collector's roll, $3,891.08; settled in full except non-resident taxes, $118.13. Treasurer has been in office 25 years and receives a salary of $50 per annum. Total assets at close of 1905, $2,827.38. Total liability, $500.

Townships of Rolph, Buchanan and Wylie, County of Renfrew.

Total receipts for 1905	$3,463	29
Total payments for 1905	2,930	98
Balance in Treasurer's hands	$532	31
Receipts to 16th October, 1906	$3,131	08
Payments to 16th October, 1906	2,559	69
Balance in Treasurer's hands	$571	39

Total assessment of municipality, $184.117.00. Tax rate, 5¼ mills in dollar without schools. Treasurer has been in office since 1893. He receives $30 per annum for salary. Total assets at close of year, $3,807.04. Total liabilities, $3,014.00.

4 M.A

Townships of Head, Maria and Clara, County of Renfrew.

Total receipts	$920 30
Total payments	814 00
Balance in Treasurer's hands	$106 30
Receipts to 23rd October, 1906	$913 22
Payments to 23rd October, 1906	788 68
Balance in Treasurer's hands	$124 54

Total assessment of municiality, $67,314.00. Tax rate, 10 mills in the dollar for all rates. Treasurer's books poorly kept; salary $20 per annum since September, 1906. The assets at close of 1905 were about $200 and there were no liabilities.

Township of Horton, County of Renfrew.

Total assessment of municipality, $532,353.00. Tax rate, 3 2/10 mills without school rates.

Total receipts for 1905	$10,649 50
Total payments for 1905	4,493 10
Balance on hand, $286.34; and in Bank of Ottawa, $5,870.06	$6,156 40
Receipts to 19th October, 1906	$7,486 72
Payments to 19th October, 1906	1,367 06
Balance on hand and in bank	$6,119 66

Collector's roll for 1905, $4,153.32; balance due on this roll, $178.51. Treasurer keeps books fairly well and gets a salary of $40 per annum. Total assets at close of 1905, $13,540.40. Liabilities, $439.08.

Township of McNab, County of Renfrew.

Total assessment of municipality, $1,171,916.89. Tax rate, 4 9/10 mills without school rates.

Total receipts for 1905	$20,892 40
Total payments for 1905	12,689 29
Balance on hand, $3,540.06; and in Bank of Ottawa, Arnprior, $4,663.05	$8,203 11
Receipts to 1st October, 1906	$9,909 17
Payments to 1st October, 1906	5,110 68
Balance Bank of Ottawa, Arnprior	$4,798 49

Collector's roll for 1905, $13,257.72; paid in full less exemptions ($54.20), defaulters' list, $121.62. Treasurer has been in office 27 years and is a careful officer. He receives $75 per annum. There are no liabilities and the assets consist of cash on hand and in bank, as stated above, on 31st December, 1905.

4a M A.

Townships of Alice and Fraser, County of Renfrew.

Total assessment of municipality, $781,230 (equalized). Tax rate, 6 mills, including school rates.

Total receipts for 1905	$4,209 62
Total payments for 1905	4,085 71
Balance in Treasurer's hands	$123 91
Receipts to 18th October, 1906	$2,186 13
Payments to 18th October, 1906	2,124 81
Balance in Bank of Ottawa, Pembroke	$61 32

Collector's roll for 1905, $3,721.00; paid in full. Treasurer in office one year; salary, $35 per annum. Total assets at close of 1905, $1,446. Liabilities, $715.

Township of Bromley, County of Renfrew.

Total receipts for 1905	$32,427 86
Total . payments for 1905	31,796 77 ·
Balance in Treasurer's hands	$631 09
Receipts to 8th October, 1906	$3,450 99
Payments to 8th October, 1906	3,394 02
Balance in Treasurer's hands ....·.....:.	$56 97

Total assessment of municipality, $1,430,279.00. Tax rate, 4½ mills, including school rates. Collector's roll, $7,527.66; $7,451.04 paid; defaulters' list, $76.62. Treasurer's salary, $40 per annum; in office two years. Books poorly kept. Assets at close of 1905, $3,031.59. Liabilities, $9,382.96.

Townships of Hagarty, Sherwood, Jones, Burns and Richards, County of Renfrew.

Total receipts for 1905	$7,181 26
Total payments for 1905	6,645 82
Balance according to books	$535 44
Balance according to Auditors	547 79
Receipts to 26th October, 1906	$2,649 77
Payments to 26th October, 1906	2,149 31
Balance according to cash book	$500 46

Tax rate, 9 mills in the dollar, including school rates. Treasurer in office 19 years; salary, $85 per annum. Books poorly kept. Total assets $1,647.69. Liabilities, $3,100.00.

Township of Petawawa, County of Renfrew.

Total receipts for 1905	$1,626 55
Total payments for 1905	2,038 07
Balance due Treasurer	**$411 52**
Receipts to 1st October, 1906	$682 99
Payments to 1st October, 1906	985 15
Balance due Treasurer ..,...........................	**$302 16**

Total assessment of municipality, $150,646.00. Collector's roll for 1905, $1,591.94; none paid at date. Treasurer in office since 1900; salary, $25 per annum. Books well kept. Total assets at close of 1905, $2,791.94. Liabilities, $411.52 due Treasurer, as above.

Township of Pembroke, County of Renfrew.

Total receipts for 1905	$2,161 75
Total payments for 1905	2,584 05
Balance due Treasurer	**$423 30**
Receipts to 15th October, 1906	$1,697 56
Payments to 15th October, 1906	1,886 90
Balance due Treasurer	**$189 34**

Total assessment of municipality, $421,184 (equalized). Tax rate, 1.65 cents in the dollar, including all rates. Collector's roll for 1905, $2,544.37; nothing paid so far this year. No bank account. Treasurer in office ten years; salary $25 per annum. Books well kept. Total assets, $4,544.37. Liability, due to Treasurer as above, $189.34.

Township of Westmeath, County of Renfrew.

Total receipts for 1905	$15,109 17
Total payments for 1905	15,014 17
Balance in hands of Treasurer	**$95 00**
Receipts to 1st August, 1906	$13,398 19
Payments to 1st August, 1906	13,031 19
Balance in hands of Treasurer	**$367 00**

Total assessment of municipality $1,747,256.00. Collector's roll for 1904, $14,527.78; paid in full less $86, defaulters and refunds. Tax rate, 4½ mills, not including schools. Books fairly well kept, but no bank account. Treasurer has been in office 20 years, but is only receiving $50 per annum, which seems very poor remuneration for so much work. Total assets, including school property, $16,988.00. No liability. Taxes for 1905, $13,188.08; paid in 1906.

Township of Raglan, County of Renfrew.

Total receipts for 1905	$2,663	84
Total payments for 1905	2,110	17
Balance on hand and in bank	$553	67
Receipts to 1st October, 1906	$2,497	20
Payments to 1st October, 1906	2,074	29
Balance on hand, $270.21; and in Bank of Ottawa, Renfrew, $150.70	$422	91

Total assessment of Township, $59,225. Tax rate, nearly 4 mills in the dollar; all charges included. Books fairly well kept. Treasurer acts as Clerk also and only receives $15 per annum, which is surely not half enough for what he does. Assets and liabilities at close of 1905, nearly equal at $1,850.

NOVEMBER.

County of Huron.

Total receipts for 1905	$173,621	52
Total payments for 1905	168,982	27
Balance on hand and in banks	$4,639	25
Receipts to November, 1906	$90,795	70
Payments to November, 1906	90,504	78
Balance on hand and in banks	$290	92

Total assessment of County $42,501,400.00 (equalized). County rates for 1905, $51,372.45; paid with the exception of one Township about $1,600. Tax rate, 1 4-5 mills on dollar. Sinking fund, $43,009.03; invested in mortgages. Treasurer 23 years in office; salary, $1,350 per annum. Books well kept. Total assets at close of 1905, $161,967.68, which includes County property ($67,000), and House of Industry ($20,000). Liabilities, $119,320.13, which includes $93,000 in debentures.

Town of Clinton, County of Huron.

Total receipts for 1905	$35,761	91
Total payments for 1905	23,914	70
Balance in Molsons Bank, Clinton	$11,847	21
Receipts to 1st November, 1906	$22,654	70
Payments to 1st November, 1906	21,115	57
Balance in Molsons Bank, Clinton	$1,539	13

Total assessment, $724,400. Tax rate, 20 mills. Collector's roll for 1905, $16,243.77; paid in full less $77.47 remitted by Council. Treasurer has been in office two years; keeps Town books accurately and well. Salary, $100 per annum. Total assets at close of 1905, $97,402.44. Total liabilities at close of 1905, $61,937.09.

Town of Seaforth, County of Huron.

Total receipts for 1905	$42,508	84
Total payments for 1905	38,605	28

Balance on hand, $789.65; Dominion Bank, Seaforth, $3,113.91 ..... **$3,903 56**

Receipts to 1st November, 1906	$70,160	92
Payments to 1st November, 1906	65,347	77

Balance in Dominion Bank, Seaforth **$4,813 15**

Total assessment of Town 1905, $651,326.00; 1906, $670,463.00. Collector's roll for 1905, $16,289.00; due November, 1906, $226.01. Tax rate for 1905, 19 mills; for 1906, 20½ mills. Treasurer acts as Clerk also and for the dual position receives $450 per annum. Sinking fund amounts to $25,601.40. Total assets, inclusive of sinking fund, $108,392.80. Liabilities, chiefly debentures, $91,289.20.

Town of Goderich, County of Huron.

Total receipts for 1905	$136,690	93
Total payments for 1905	134,767	04

Balance on hand and in Bank of Montreal, Goderich **$1,923 89**

Receipts to 12th November, 1906	$97,765	51
Payments to 12th November, 1906	88,519	17

Balance on hand, $895.80; in Bank of Montreal, Goderich, $8,350.54 .... **$9,246 34**

Total assessment of Town, $1,604,092; Collector's roll for 1905, $35,-328.51. Paid in full less $100. Tax rate, 25 mills 1905, 22 mills 1906. Treasurer in office 20 years; salary, $540 per annum. Books well kept. Sinking funds, in cash, mortgages and debentures, $48,446.14. Total assets at close of 1905, including Water Works ($75,923.63), electric light plant ($35,692.37), amount in all to $301,360.58. Liabilities, chiefly debentures, to $270,554.85.

Township of Goderich, County of Huron.

Total receipts for 1905	$19,944	04
Total payments for 1905	14,964	79

Balance in Treasurer's hands **$4,979 25**

Receipts to 12th November, 1906	$10,550	25
Payments to 12th November, 1906	9,922	79

Balance in Sovereign Bank of Canada, Goderich **$627 46**

Total assessment of Township, $1,472,425.00. Collector's roll for 1905, $14,411.46; paid. Tax rate, 7 6/10 mills without school rates. Treasurer has been in office 11 years; keeps books fairly well. Salary, $75 per annum. Total assets consist of cash on hand $4,979.25, 31st December, 1905. Total liabilities amount to $4,138.30. An audit of this Township by a Government auditor is attached herewith.

Township of Ashfield, County of Huron.

Total receipts for 1905	$17,091 70
Total payments for 1905	16,311 15
' Balance in Treasurer's hands	$780 55
Receipts to 1st November, 1906	$11,343 26
Payments to 1st November, 1906	11,079 28
Balance in Treasurer's hands	$263 ,98

Total assessment of municipality, $1,697,218. Collector's roll for 1905, $15,698.46; paid in full. Tax rate, 5.03 mills without school rates. Treasurer has been in office six years at a salary of $95 per annum. Assets at close of 1905 amounted to $6,363.61. Liabilities, $3,957.55.

Village of Blyth, County of Huron.

Total receipts for 1905	$14,938 64
Total payments for 1905	12,756 64
Balance in Bank of Hamilton, Blyth..............	$2,182 00
Receipts to 14th November, 1906	$8,847 44
Payments to 14th November, 1906	8,466 77
Balance in Bank of Hamilton, Blyth	$380 67

Total assessment of municipality, $283,409.15. Collector's roll for 1905, paid in full. Tax rate, 18 mills 1905, 21 mills for 1906. Treasurer has been Clerk also for 11 years and for dual office receives $90 yearly. Sinking fund amounts to $2,332.50, deposited in Bank of Hamilton, Blyth. Total assets, including the above sinking fund, amount to $29,426.88. Liabilities, consisting chiefly of debentures, to $27,056.14.

Township of Usborne, County of Huron.

Total receipts for 1905	$26,405 03
Total payments for 1905	21,723 25
Balance	$4,681 78

1906 not written up.

Total assessment of municipality, $1,866,632.00. Collector's roll for 1905, $21,970.36; practically paid in full. Tax rate, 5.06 mills in the dollar without schools. Treasurer keeps books fairly well; has been in office 10 years and receives a salary of $80 per annum. Assets at close of 1905 amounted to $4,900.20, and liabilities to $145.00.

Township of Hay, County of Huron.

Total assessment of municipality, $2,296,260.00. Tax rate, 3 mills in dollar without school rates.

Total receipts for 1905 .... $21,499 88
Total payments for 1905 .... 20,818 15

Balance on hand and in bank $681 73

Receipts to 10th November, 1906 .... $6,411 29
Payments to 10th November, 1906 .... 5,114 18

Balance in Sovereign Bank of Canada, Zurich... $1,297 11

Collector's roll for 1905, $18,142.11; paid in full except returns to County Treasurer, $148.70. Tax rate, 3 mills in dollar without school rates. Treasurer's books well kept. He has been in office six years and receives $100 per annum. Total assets at close of 1905 amounted to $3,393.79, and liabilities, $2,862.03, drainage debentures.

Village of Hensall, County of Huron.

Total assessment of Village, $311,000.00. Tax rate, $13\frac{1}{2}$ mills in the dollar.

Total receipts for 1905 .... $8,856 97
Total payments for 1905 .... 8,607 08

Balance in Sovereign Bank, Hensall.................. $249 89

Receipts to November, 1906 .... $5,175 45
Payments to November, 1906 .... 4,443 81

Balance in Sovereign Bank, Hensall $731 64

Collector's roll for 1905, $4,025.39; paid in full less $25 remitted by Council. Treasurer has been in office seven years. He does not keep the Village books very well, but then he does not get much encouragement; $15 per annum is all the salary he gets. The assets at close of 1905 were $969.89, and the liabilities, chiefly debentures, amounted to $14,052.28.

Township of Colborne, County of Huron.

Total assessment of Township, $1,859,000. Tax rate, 4 6/10 mills without school rates.

Total receipts for 1905 .... $13,066 21
Total payments for 1905 .... ·10,775 21

Balance on hand and in Bank of Commerce,
    Goderich $2,291 00

Receipts to November, 1906 .... $4,257 66 ·
Payments to November, 1906 .... 3,877 33

Balance in Treasurer's hands $380 33

Collector's roll for 1905, $9,213.66; paid in full. Treasurer keeps the Township books fairly well. He has been in office five years and receives $70 per annum. Total assets at close of year 1905, $3,629.66. Total liabilities, $8,555.50.

Township of Hullett, County of Huron.

Total receipts for 1905	$25,102 63
Total payments for 1905	23,188 05
Balance on hand and in Bank of Hamilton, Blyth	$1,914 58
Receipts to 14th November, 1906	$9,716 17
Payments to 14th November, 1906	5,799 22
Balance Bank of Hamilton, Blyth	$3,916 95

Total assessment of Township, $1,913,335.00 (1905). Collector's roll for 1905, $19,239.23. Paid in full except about $8 uncollectable. Tax rate, 6 2-10 mills on dollar, without school rates. Treasurer officiates as Clerk also and is a very competent official. For the dual position he gets $275 per annum and has held it for 17 years. There is close on $4,000 in the Treasury to pay the bonus to the Guelph and Goderich Railway when it is running. Besides this the assets on the 31st December, 1905, amounted to $2,689.97, and the liabilities to $3,744.25. This appears to be a carefully managed Township.

Township of McKillop, County of Huron.

Total receipts for 1905	$26,434 41
Total payments for 1905	24,060 38
Balance in Treasurer Ross' hands	$2,374 03
Receipts to 1st November, 1906	$7,227 98
Payments to 1st November, 1906	5,443 59
Balance on hand, $151.95; in Dominion Bank, Seaforth, $1,632.44	$1,784 39

Collector's roll for 1905, $19,369.98. Paid in full less $107.60 uncollectable. Tax rate, 5 5-8 mills, without school rates. Treasurer has only been in office since June, 1906. He is to receive a salary of $80 per annum. The assets at the close of 1905 amounted to $29,741.68, and the liabilities to $26,910.51.

Township of Stanley, County of Huron.

Total assessment of municipality, $2,005,009.00. Tax rate, 3 8-10 mills, without school rates.

Total receipts for 1905	$22,220 85
Total payments for 1905	20,949 51
Balance in hands of Treasurer	$1,271 34

Receipts to November, 1906 .... $4,866 05
Payments to November, 1906 .... 4,855 83

Balance in hands of Treasurer $10 22

Collector's roll for 1905, $14,601.96. Paid. Treasurer has been in office 27 years and receives $75 per annum which is scarcely enough for so able and experienced an officer. The assets of the Township at the close of 1905 were $2,737.03, and the liabilities $3,380.00.

Township of Tuckersmith, County of Huron.

Total assessment of municipality, $2,007,654. Tax rate, 5½ mills, without school rates.

Total receipts for 1905 .... $25,593 33
Total payments for 1905 .... 25,445 62

Balance $147 71

Receipts to 9th November, 1906 .... $8,898 84
Payments to 9th November, 1906 .... 8,505 22

Balance on hand and in bank $393 62

Collector's roll for 1905, $15,935.64. Paid in full. Treasurer keeps Township books very well and has been in office 6 years. He receives a salary of $100 per annum. There is a School fund of nearly $18,000 invested in mortgages, and besides about $2,500 in other assets. The liabilities on same date, 31st December, 1905, were $5,000 in debentures. A carefully managed Township.

Township of East Wawanosh, County of Huron.

Total receipts for 1905 .... $12,969 35
Total payments for 1905 .... 9,564 63

Balance on hand, $265.79. In Dominion Bank,
    Wingham, $3,138.93 .... $3,404 72

Receipts to 1st October, 1906 .... $5,495 61
Payments to 1st October, 1906 .... 5,415 03

Balance in Treasurer's hands $80 58

Total assessment of municipality, $1,464,040.00. Tax rate, 3 1-10 mills on dollar, without school rates. Collector's roll, $9,589.16. Paid in full. Treasurer keeps the Township books very well. He has been in office 10 years and receives $85 per annum. Assets on 31st December, 1905, amounted to $3,613.63, mostly cash, and liabilities, $2,660.35.

Township of Morris, County of Huron.

Total receipts for 1905	$24,161 89
Total payments for 1905	16,376 34
Balance in Bank of Hamilton, Wingham	$7,785 55
Receipts to 15th November, 1906	$14,530 82
Payments to 15th November, 1906	8,469 43
Balance in Bank of Hamilton, Wingham	$6,061 39

Collector's roll for 1905, $14,350.00. Paid in full. Tax rate, 4½ mills on the dollar, without school rates. Treasurer has been in office 16 years and receives a salary of $100 per annum. Assets on 31st December, 1905, amounted to $9,615.55, principally cash, and the liabilities to $13,330.80.

Township of Turnberry, County of Huron.

Total assessment of municipality, $1,319,305. Tax rate, 3.60 mills without school rates.

Total receipts for 1905	$12,944 57
Total payments for 1905	11,322 47
Balance in Bank of Hamilton, Wingham	$1,622 10
Receipts to 1st November, 1906	$6,359 93
Payments to 1st November, 1906	4,977 59
Balance in Bank of Hamilton, Wingham	$1,382 34

Collector's roll for 1905, $9,513.48. Paid in full less $15.26 remitted by Council. Treasurer keeps books very well, in office 20 years, and receives $100 per annum. The assets at close of year amounted to $2,503.16, principally cash items, and the liabilities to $2,911.00, chiefly for County rate.

Township of Stephen, County of Huron.

Total assessment of Township, $2,750,779.00. Tax rate, 3 mills, without school rates.

Total receipts for 1905	$17,088 61
Total payment for 1905	14,620 84
Balance on hand and in bank	$2,467 77
Receipts to 15th November, 1906	$11,253 79
Payments to 15th November, 1906	9,044 76
Balance on hand, $1.63; in Sovereign Bank, Crediton, $2,207 40	$2,209 03

Collector's roll for 1905, $17,026.65. Paid in full less $86.62 written off but subsequently partly paid. Treasurer only one year in office. Receives salary of $90 per annum and gives promise of being a good officer. Total assets at close of 1905, $3,259.26, principally in cash. Liabilities, $4,420.53. Principally County Rate, $3,694.50.

DECEMBER.

Town of Haileybury, District of Nipissing.

A largely signed petition from Haileybury ratepayers having been received by the Government, I was instructed by the Attorney-General to proceed with a preliminary inspection of the books and finances of the Town, to ascertain the advisability of granting an audit by a Government Auditor. I found there was ample cause for an audit which was proceeded with at once, and I herewith attach the report of the auditor. I understand that the ratepayers of Haileybury were well satisfied with the result. The expense of the audit was $330.50.

The audit of Haileybury concludes my work for 1906.

I am, Sir,

Your obedient servant,

J. B. LAING,

Provincial Municipal Auditor.

Township of Goderich Report.

Oscar Hudson, Auditor, Toronto.

To the Reeve and Council of the Township of Goderich, County of Huron, Province of Ontario:

Acting by an Order-in-Council, dated the 12th day of January, 1906, and through instructions from the Provincial Municipal Auditor, Mr. J. B. Laing, I conducted at the Town of Goderich, an audit of the books, vouchers, moneys and accounts of the municipality of the Township of Goderich, County of Huron, for the eleven years ending with 1905.

Upon my arrival I interviewed the chief petitioners for the audit to ascertain their principal grounds for complaint and was informed in common by them as follows:—

That no specific charges were made but,—

1. That the printed statements and reports of the Treasurer and Auditors were not complete nor framed in a sufficiently explanatory manner.

That the explanations thereof when demanded were not freely nor clearly given so that the ratepayers could form opinions thereon.

3. That the sudden rise in the Township rate from 3 3-10 mills in 1904 to 5 mills in 1905 needed full explanation.

4. That the books, accounts and vouchers in use were not such as would readily furnish information even to the officials themselves, so that inquiries by members of the Council could not be satisfied by an easy reference to such records.

5. That information ought to be given said officials how entries should be made, what books were needed and how documents should be treated and taken care of.

It became my duty therefore not only to deal with the regular technical verification of the Treasurer's and Collector's accounts for the period under review, but also to meet the foregoing complaints and suggest methods for their avoidance in the future. Treating them in their order I found:

1. That the Auditors' statements, although giving in detail all items of expenditure and partly so of receipts, did not classify them so that the rate-payers might see at a glance the full receipts from each source of income, nor their full expenditure in any general direction with which they might be familiar.

(a) The taxes collected were stated in one amount, without specifying the purpose of each levy, the assessment sum levied on, the rate, or the yield, so that a ratepayer could not tell what sum the Township or the School Section had the disposal of.

(b) The expenditure upon roads and bridges in the several divisions in-cluded only the sums spent by the respective commissioners, although large amounts had been paid by the Council direct and placed under other head-ings. Expenditure other than those authorized to be made by Commissioners under by-law and which apply to respective divisions, were made by Council and charged under headings of "Gravel" or "Miscellaneous." These have been for 1904 and 1905 segregated as nearly as possible to the divisions bene-fiting therefrom, in the attempt to show the full cost of maintenance of each road division which the printed statements did not correctly exhibit. In the accompanying statements I have sought to represent all the results in more understandable form for the above two years, being the periods mostly called into question. With such modifications as the future may call for, this form of statement might be, with advantage to the general body of ratepayers, adopted by their Council when setting before them the annual account of their stewardship.

(c) *Treasurers' Statements.* Section 304 of the Municipal Act, 1903, Subsection 6, requires that "The Council of every Town, Township or Vil-"lage shall hold a meeting on the 15th day of December in each year, if that "day is a Sunday, then on the Monday following, and shall immediately "tnereafter publish a detailed statement of receipts and expenditure for the "portion of the year ending on the day of such meeting *together with a state-*"*ment of the assets and liabilities and uncollected taxes.* A similar state-"ment in detail respecting the *last 15 days of the preceding year* shall be "attached thereto." The purpose of this enactment being evidently to in-form the ratepayers upon the financial doings of the Council *before next nomination day* since the auditors' statement for the year would not be forth-coming until the following month. Such of these statements as have been shown me have a decidedly confused appearance—being only a mass of un-arranged details instead of a Cash Statement of Receipts and Expenditures showing a cash balance and followed by a Balance Sheet of the current Assets and Liabilities showing either a surplus or deficit; the two distinct classes of statements have been blended into one, whereof, the balance is incorrectly exhibited or omitted altogether. Moreover, any obligations by the Township remaining unpaid at the 15th of December and paid before the end of that month were in some cases not shown. Particularly was this the case of the 1904 statement which entirely omitted mention of the liability of $571.25 for the cement bridge in No. 2 Division although the obligation was incurred prior to that date. Moreover, the Cash statements for "the

15 days of the preceding year" was apparently never prepared. The intention of the Act is to give the ratepayers complete statements from the 15th of December in one year to the 15th of December in the next, each one commencing where the other left off. It is to be hoped that these statements will be properly rendered in future.

2. To expect a satisfactory explanation is to imply the ability on the part of someone to furnish it, and doubtless the books as they have been kept did not enable the officials to respond off hand to enquiries, otherwise it must have been with them an instance of *"lucus a non lucendo"* and dissatisfaction was the result. Certainly a simplification of the financial records would have permitted prompt and full explanation at any time it may have been demanded.

3. The jump in the Township rate for 1905 meant upon the assessment of $1,471,505 an additional income of over $2,500, and it was due the ratepayers to know why such an addition was needed, as also what became of it. In brief. it may be said that 1905 was entered upon with a cash deficit of $1,217.07, closing with a surplus of $940.04. This alone would have almost explained where the excess levy was; the balance of $324.89 being used in the year's expenses.

In round figures 1904 opened with a deficit of .... $ 177
And closed with one of   1,217

Showing expended for the year in excess of the Town
ship levy.. $1,040

due mainly to Maitland Hill and cement bridge expenditures, which, however, might have been provided for by debentures or by an increased rate for 1904, so that the above deficit had not occurred.

While 1905 started with a deficit from 1904 of............ $1,217
Closing with a surplus of   940
Or a gain over the year's expenses by $2,157

but 1905 has the advantage of an extra levy of 17c. on each
$100 assessed, or an income increased by $2,500
Of which the current expenses took only   343

The remainder being used to change a deficit into a surplus $2,157

The accompanying statements will more fully explain this.

4. Of the books and accounts, and especially of the vouchers, there is much to be said in criticism.

(a) The Ledger is needlessly diffuse in receiving all the details from the Government Cash Book. It was written up from the Treasurer's rough Cash Book, or Day Book as he called it, and from which he copied all items in full, under headings suited to those of the annual statement and arranged his vouchers in the order of the entries in the respective ledger accounts, so grouping them, but without much regard to dates. These Ledger totals when brought together constituted such a summary of his own Cash Book as the Government one would have automatically afforded had the summation of its columns been carried throughout the year.

This book should contain the entries which are generally needed but once a year, into the following accounts.

(1). *Collector.*

   (*a*) To be charged with the full amount of the Roll when certified to by the Clerk.

   (*b*) To be credited with the payments as he makes them to the Treasurer.

   (*c*) To be credited with the returned taxes when sworn to by him and given to the County Treasurer.

   His accounts will then balance.

(2) *Arrears of Taxes.*

   (*a*) To be charged with the balance in County Treasurer's hands 1st January, 1906.

   (*b*) To be charged with arrears of 1905.

   (*c*) To be charged with percentages on 1st May.

   (*d*) To be credited with any collections paid over by the County Treasurer.

   (*e*) To be credited with any abatements allowed by Council.

   This account will then agree with the County Statment and Land Register.

(3) *Township Revenue.*

   To be credited with the Township levy, Statute Labor, Dog Tax, etc., and with any revenue from casual sources, or any fractional levies in excess of county or debenture requirements.

   To be charged with Township expenditures for the year of the nature of Roads and Bridges, Salaries, Miscellaneous, School Grants, etc.

(4) *School Levies.*

   Credit with the general and special amounts to be levied on the sections, also those granted by the Township and the Legislature.

   Charge with the amounts handed over to the trustees on requisition or by Inspectors' orders.

   The account will then close itself.

(5) *Debenture Levies.*

   Credit with the sums to be raised each year and debit the payments of each debenture falling due as made—which will close the account.

(6) *County Treasurer.*

   Credit the amounts of the County rate. Debit payments to him—and the accounts will close.

(*b*) *Cash Book.* His rough Cash Book was again copied into the Government one, but as the columns were not used in proper relation to the Ledger accounts, nor the additions carried forward, and, moreover, as the book was not in consecutive use nor did it respond to a test of correctness for the past year, it had to be disregarded in favor of the Ledger itself. The Treasurer, however, under my instructions and explanation of its proper use, will recontinue the Government book from the first of the year as adequate if properly kept for all purposes as the Annual Statement, and for reference during the year. It would almost seem superfluous to endorse the admirable simplicity of this book and its adaptability to the preparation of statements were it not that some Treasurers appear to regard it only as a nuisance. Size is its only drawback, except perhaps that some purple down rulings to alternate with the red would relieve the landscape and guide the wearied eyes of the Treasurer across the stretches of red to the column for his figures to rest in.

(c) *Journal.* The use of this book as intended by Section 291 of the Municipal Act has not been made. Its purpose is to record all entries of transactions other than Cash by which the Township is or will be affected. The summary of the Collector's Roll as soon as ready should be journalized in the following manner for 1904, as an illustration:

```
21st Sept., 1904.   Collector 'of Taxes, Dr.... $12,016 20
    To County Treasurer ...........................    $2,796 75
    To Township Revenue ..........................     3,386 89
    To School Trustees for grant....................     1,491 00
        For general purposes ....................     2,660 01
        For Building Fund .......................     1,024 69
        For Debenture No. 3 ....................       620 62
        For Debenture of Hullett .................        36 24
                                                      _____
                                                      $12,016 20
```

and the uncollected taxes as returned by the Collector should have been charged to the proper account for same, thus:

```
15th Dec., 1904.   Arrears of Taxes, Dr. .........     4 12
    To  Collector  ......................................              4 12
```

The debenture issue for 1902 for the benefit of S. S. No. 6 could have been recorded as follows:

```
15th May, 1902.  S. S. No. 6 Debenture, Dr. ...  $753 92
    To Debenture No. 6, due 15th May, 1906...              376 46
    To Debenture No. 7, due 15th May, 1904...              376 46
```

The County percentage reported by that Treasurer would be journalized as follows:

```
1st May, 1904.  Arrears of Taxes, Dr. .........     1 24
    To Township Revenue ..........................              1 24
```

(d) *Assessor's Roll.* This as prepared for the past 7 years by the same official has been duly sworn to by him, but only latterly bears evidence of any careful preparation and correctness. Its original figures have, however, in some cases been altered to correspond with changes by the Court of Revision or through errors discovered. This is not permissible. Any amendments must only be noted against such assessments and reference made to the sanctioning power. Once sworn to, the original entries must stand, but it should only be certified when the completeness is assured. Its arrangement along haphazard lines of route is not to be commended as it does not split up the Township into such limited areas that an omitted assessment may be quickly detected by one conversant with any area. To assess as often as possible in even hundreds of dollars would shorten and simplify the assessor's and collector's work of calculation, also of copying and proving correctness. The acreage shown by assessor's roll varies every year. This is of course absurd as the Township boundaries are not elastic. The need of a map to give the entire and correct area is necessary to prove the full area upon the roll. It is important that the Assessor's Roll be kept in exact agreement with that of the Collector.

(d) Also that the ratepayers' names therein follow in the same order, and moreover be readily found.

Maps. A skeleton map of the Township may be easily prepared for each year with lot numbers and with locations numbered in correspondence with the rolls, and the acreage shown of each holding or section so that instant reference can be made for any ratepayer's name and place. These should be grouped according to school sections and numerically arranged so that the map may form an index to both books. Mr. J. A. Fowler, Civil Engineer, of Goderich, upon considering the foregoing requirements, has offered to prepare a map of about $4\frac{1}{2}$ feet by 2 feet for $15, and to make tracings therefrom for $1.50 each. Colored figures will clearly designate the meanings of the numbers thereon, while colored lines will exhibit the different boundaries of school sections, road divisions or polling divisions if needed. A small pocket map with a leaf to each school section could be carried by the assessor so that no area may escape him.

(e) *Collector's Roll.* The classification here is in accordance with school sections, but arrangement of the assessment therein does not follow any particular plan as to show the exhaustion of each lot area. Extra work is entailed upon the Township Clerk whose duty it is to prepare this roll, through having to pick out the numbers of each section from the Assessor's roll. These two should correspond page for page, thus the work of copying into the second would be easier and far more certain to avoid the mistakes which have been discovered in my agreements of the two rolls for the various years and a memorandum of which is submitted herewith. The different arrangement of the two rolls has occasioned an immense amount of detail checking in order to effect a reconcialiation, as this work was particularly requested by the petitioners. Upon the completeness and correctness of the Assessor's roll depends the income of the municipality and the copying of its values into the Collector's roll ought to be made self provable at every stage. Considering the difficulties attending this work and that of rate calculations, the Township Clerk performed it with surprising accuracy and thoroughness. The various school rates have been tested against each sectional assessment, and the Township and Country rates against the total. The full levies are clearly shown and certified to in each summary. The Collector in handling receipts has failed to mark the dates upon which he received the taxes, there is therefore no clue to the length of time such funds were in his hands; and his collection books omit all dates also, except those of his payments to the Treasurer.

The roll books are poorly made, the paper being inferior and the binding weak, while the down rulings are all in red instead of alternating colors, so as to classify the columns and guide the eye. The books are liable to fall to pieces and the ink runs into the soft paper. It would be well if some government printer could make up a large number of these rolls, after a proof has been carefully passed, and sell them direct to the municipalities so that they would not be dependent on local dealers.

(f) *Accounts.* Nearly all passed in minutes, although some very important items are not recorded. It was the duty of the Clerk who wrote the orders signed by the Reeve to have had such payments properly sanctioned, although these exceptions were apparently due to oversight in writing up the minutes by the Councilman acting as secretary of the meetings. Except those signed by the road commissioner, no orders should be issued until an invoice or memorandum of the account requiring payment shall have been laid before the Council by the Clerk, and such document ought to bear the date of passing by rubber stamp and the number of the order given therefor.

5 M.A.

These vouchers, moreover, should be carefully filed according to their number for future reference. There are but few documents to explain more fully than appears on the order the nature of the payment and the explanations such payments had to be received by me verbally as many papers which could have made entries clearly were mislaid. This has been a serious matter both in time spent getting information, and in its insufficiency when obtained.

A *Vault* or more safe accommodation is badly needed to guard the books and papers; and some town arrangement might be made for such protection; at present these are lodged in the residence of the Clerk or Treasurer. The former having only a small safe.

(*g*) *Orders on Treasurer.* The orders are to bearer and endorsed generally by the Reeve, Clerk or Councilman intending to make the payment and whom the money was given by the Township Treasurer for that purpose. There is a very limited number of acknowledgments of the money by the parties to whom the orders were made payable. As a rule the payments were made through the agency of some official and no direct receipts obtained therefor. This has been a long standing but most reprehensible practice and the weakness of it has been so strongly drawn to the attention of the officials that a new form of order should be adopted payable by a bank, to be chosen by the Council, upon proper endorsement by the payee. The form of order is suggested below:

(Counterfoil of Stub.)   (Endorsement on Back.)
Order No. ....   Received the within named sum
Payable to ....   in full payment to date of order.
Amount, $ ....
For ....
Date   ....   (Endorse here.)

Municipality of the Township of Goderich.

............day of............190...   Order No.......... Voucher No........
       (Date of passing.)
To the Bank of.................at Goderich, Ontario.
       Pay to the order of....................the sum of...........Dollars, $......
being for ....
.........day of.........190...   ....(Reeve.)
       (Date of issue.)   ....Road Commissioner.
....
       (Countersigned by Treasurer.)

These orders should be on strong paper, loosely bound in books of 100 each and numbered consecutively throughout the series. The counterfoils ought to be similarly numbered with plenty of room for particulars. The books should also be numbered thus: No. 1, for orders 1 to 100; No. 2, for orders 100 to 200, and so forth, and the Treasurer ought to call in the stubs when the book is finished before issuing another. Each Commissioner to have one as at present.

Road Commissioners have been each year authorized by by-law to issue their own orders to the Treasurer for divisional maintenance up to the amount of $250 each, which in almost every instance has been exceeded—with these orders also proper acknowledgment were absent. This laxity can be easily overcome when the orders are properly endorsed for the future.

5a M.A.

(*h*) *Bank Account.* No bank account for the Township has been kept. The Collector handing to the Treasurer all his collections, out of which the latter made payments of such orders as were presented to him at those times, generally the bulk of them for gravel, salaries, etc. The Township levy collections in November and December of each year were thus pretty well used up by the 15th, and the school levies by that time handed to the Trustees. Yet the levy for the County, not payable until the following February, and the levies for meeting school debentures in January or later, as also any unused Township funds were retained in the sole possession or personal custody of the Treasurer. Apart from the risk to Treasurer in retaining much cash unbanked, there is the question of interest to be obtained from the bank upon monies which it is possible to deposit for any stated time until actually needed. The private bank account of the Treasurer will not satisfactorily take the place of one for the Township. His own money and that of his trust as Treasurer must be kept apart as required by law, which has nothing to say as to the trustworthiness or otherwise of any official, but makes a general rule applicable to all. By section 291, par. 7, Municipal Act, 1903, a by-law may be passed authorizing an account with a chartered bank in the Town of Goderich in the name of the Township of Goderich, into which all receipts shall be paid as soon as possible and from which only payments are to be made upon the signature of the Reeve, the countersignature of the Treasurer and the endorsement of the payee.

The Treasurer or the Collector of Taxes should as soon as possible after the receipt of the same deposit in said account all monies received by him, to bear interest at the current rate. Whenever possible the payee of an order should endorse it before payment by the Treasurer; but to meet the convenience of those payees who wish their orders cashed beforehand the Treasurer might be authorized to advance out the receipts to the Reeve or Clerk or to any Councilman the sum necessary to prepay such order and shall take an interim receipt therefor to be exchanged for the original orders when same are returned to him duly endorsed by the payee thereof; and which orders shall be deposited in the said bank as part of the receipts out of which the amounts were advanced.

(*h*) It will thus still be possible for the commissioners or officials to make payments as heretofore and without requiring any one to cash orders at the bank, but it would be well to get as many orders paid by the bank as can be arranged, with a view to utilizing this course to a greater extent each year until finally the bank makes all payments except the most trifling ones.

(*i*) *Tax Bills.* It is fairly claimed that the present tax notices do not inform the ratepayers of their assessment against the rate levied for each purpose, so that they may check the correctness of the amount charged. The form in use might be substituted by the one hereunder as enabling the ratepayer to figure out his own taxes and prove the payment demanded from him. The Collector, moreover, would on the stub retained have a record of the exact date of any payments to him and with the name and amount previously filled in could check the amount received instantly. The payment dates could then be marked on his roll, while the undated stubs would prove arrears.

(*j*) *School Levies.* The school trustees are not advised beforehand of the amount to be collected to cover their requisition, nor do they give a proper order on the Treasurer for the amount. The make up of this amount, when paid them, has not been clearly stated as might have been done in the summary of the Collector's roll.

The sectional amount to be levied in response to their requisition might be reported by the Clerk to the trustees upon the following form so that when collected they may sign the order therein made for payment to their secretary-treasurer, who will acknowledge receipt thereon.

(*k*) *Township Grants to Union Schools.* Where any school section is shared with another Township the arbitrated portion of the grant should be set out in the minutes as a record of the sum payable to their section and as an authority to the Treasurer for making such payment to the nominee of the trustees of such school section and reference distinctly made to the certified document of the award in which the equalization is shown fixing the percentage. No such records appear though the awards were produced. The one of 1900 omits 6 per cent. of one of the section grants, hence only $1,491 has been paid to the schools since 1901 instead of $1,500 to the ten schools. As to how many schools there are in each year in the Township, and whether union or non-union, the rolls and maps should confirm.

(*l*) *Debentures.* The wording of the debentures is found somewhat incomplete and the inconsistencies were pointed out. They are written by hand and taken up in the neighborhood. Debentures when issued for school or other purposes in limited numbers should be suitably engrossed and passed upon by the solicitor. They should be numbered consecutively and each one recorded in the debenture register with particulars of its principal, interest, date of issue, date of payment, purpose for which given, where payable, and authority for its issue, and also bear an endorsed acknowledgment of its discharge from the last holder with the date of same. A receipt for them must be taken when the debentures are handed over to the school trustees. Only verbal testimony from the Ex-Reeve was tendered as to the 1902 debentures being handed to the trustees of School Section No. 2. It is necessary, of course, that such liability once created by Council, even if it be not for merely Township purposes or only to be liquidated by future levies, should be immediately recorded and the full amount placed to the credit of a debenture account, charging the particular school or construction account for which it was raised. Such entry should go through the journal as outlined, and as each debenture is lifted a reversal transfer of the amount made from one account to the other depressing both liability and asset.

(*n*) *Tax Arrears.* The County Treasurer's books were the only continuous record and a statement was kindly furnished from which a new start can be made to follow the defaulters in the Township books. This should have not been necessary as each amount in arrears should have been carefully followed until paid. A memorandum account with each defaulter might be kept, starting with the balance shown by the County Treasurer's statement at the close of 1905 and adding thereto the 1905 arrears. All payments hereafter by him to the Treasurer must be put to the credit of the separate delinquents, and each year's default charged to the proper parties, so that your books will show who is still in arrears and subject to percentage of tax sale. If he will go a step further than this, I cannot do better for the Township Treasurer than by endorsing the recommendation by F. H. Macpherson, F.C.A. (who is well qualified to give such an opinion), that he keep a land register similar to the one so well kept by the County Treasurer and follow his method of recording all arrears; starting it with the unpaid taxes as shown in the balance sheet for 1905, and on the 1st of May adding thereto the County percentages and the defaulters of each ensuing year and crediting any collections, so that the balance of the County Treasurer's annual statement may coincide with that of his own.

(n) *By-laws and Minutes.* These, although in crude form, generally conveyed the intention fairly well in view of the fact that the Clerk had to draft them without legal assistance. Two of these recurrent by-laws were quite disregarded, one to limit the expenditure of road commissioners, the other to limit the borrowing of money temporarily. The minutes have been noted by a Councilman as secretary and then copied, and were often more or less incomplete. The habit of crowding the writing and neglect to make side notations make a reference very difficult.

It must be borne in mind that by-laws are made to be regarded. If in borrowing money or in granting amounts for expenditure the sums are exceeded, personal liability may attach to the officials concerned with the payments. The agenda book will be found of great service in conducting meetings so as to ensure a full report of proceedings. All business known to come before the meeting should be entered before hand, the accounts to be passed listed, the motions to be laid drafted, those to be present and the order of business noted and what transpires written up as it comes along. In this manner proceedings can be correctly followed without chance of omissions in a busy session, and the minutes can be written up at any time therefrom. Plenty of space is needed in the minute book and separate paragraphs made for each of the matters dealt with. Marginal headings, and if possible an index to same, will facilitate reference to past proceedings. A suitable form and wording in which minutes should be written into the minute book has been given to the Clerk, so that proceedings can be recorded in regular order and with regard to the essential points common to all meetings such as:

1. Number of meeting.
2. How called.
3. Regular or special.
4. Place, date and hour.
5. Names of those present or absent.
6. Previous minutes and by-laws confirmed.
7. Business arising therefrom.
8. Discussions and resolutions.
9. Reports of officials or committees.
10. Discussions and resolutions.
11. New business.
12. Discussions and resolutions.
13. Passing of accounts.
14. Adjournment to date or call.
15. Signature of Clerk and Reeve confirming.

By-laws. There are generally set forms in use for the principal ones of these, which may be seen in the offices of the Town or County. It would be well to consult solicitor if any unused ones are prepared; and it is sufficient to state that the main features are:

1. The number for the year or preferably up to date.
2. The citation of the Act under which the power is exercised.
3. The purpose expressed in brief and general terms.
4. The occasion for the enactment or a statement of associated facts making it expedient.
5. The inferential legislation intended with the method of its accomplishment and the scope of its application.
6. The date of passing and of going into effect.

The Township Clerk could be well guided in the drafting of these, and the manner in which they are recorded, by consulting the by-law book of the Town of Goderich, which the acting Clerk kindly allowed me to scan and expressed his willingness to offer its form if desired. The annual by-laws for striking rates have not regularly mentioned the school rates. The Clerk's explanation for these omissions is that the school trustees fail to file their requisition to him in time. Such officers are bound to have these in by 1st of August, and it should be insisted upon that they comply.

(o) *Treasurer's Receipts.* A receipt book should be kept and on acknowledgment given therefrom for all monies received from whatever source entry being made to correspond on the counterfoil and receipts numbered consecutively. By section 294a, Municipal Act, 1903, it is incumbent on the Treasurer to produce statements each year from the Treasurer of the County or of any municipality from whom money *may* have been received, showing what his full receipts from such outside sources may have been during the year, also that all orders paid by him are sanctioned by minutes or higher authority. In such instances where no transactions have taken place during the year, it is expected that the Treasurer will obtain certificates from adjoining or adjacent municipalities to that effect . He should get similar assurance from License Inspectors, Pound Keepers, etc. A sincere effort to satisfy the auditors that all receipts are in will have their very marked appreciation.

Enquiries had to be made of the Treasurer of the County, and of the Townships of Hullett, Stanley, Baysville and Colborne, and of the Town of Clinton, also of the License Inspectors, Pound-Keepers, etc., as to monies paid into Goderich Township with the result of confirming entries in the Treasurer's books as including all receipts from such outlying sources for at least eight years back in some cases. This information ought to be always on file and laid before the auditors each year after being passed before Council by the Reeve. All such receipts should, of course, be found in the counterfoil of the Treasurer's receipt book. The Treasurer is also required to furnish other municipalities with similar statements of his payments to them. This has not been attended to.

5. In regard to this desideratum it has been my aim to enlighten the officials in the matter of their responsibilities, also in the manner of their financial work, and have discussed freely the most practicable methods of making it clear and comprehensible. The auditors have been advised upon the method of conducting their enquiries and of preparing the annual statements so that as little need as possible may arise for questioning its correctness. I must express satisfaction with the readiness with which information was furnished, although regretting it was not always sufficient nor in good form as evidence. The Township Treasurer has taken great responsibilities for limited pay and his work if not in required form has at least the merit of fair correctness and ample proof of payments. The Township clerk has apparently had an unnecessary amount of labor upon the rolls. His work bears evidence of most painstaking effort and is in the main very well done indeed; although his accounts and receipts have not been all carefully kept. His remuneration has been a very uncertain quantity, but on the average is rather less than over a fair return upon the work he has been called upon to do. The following of bad precedents, added to the oversight of many of the statutory requirements and the lack of proper instructions in the use of books and of forms, are the chief reasons why the verification of the work of these officials has not been adequately compassed by the auditors and which have prolonged the work of this commission. The result of which must be carefully studied by them so that the annual audits of the future may be sufficient assurance to your ratepayers.

Acknowledgment is due Mayor Tilt, of Goderich, for his courtesy in allowing the use of a room' in the Town Hall which was most suitable as a location and of convenient size for work and for the numerous interviews with the various petitioners and Township and other officials which occupied considerable time in the getting of requisite information upon the conduct of Township affairs during the period. From the books of the County treasurer and clerk there was no trouble in obtaining exact and explicit statements of their dealings with the Township, and I am much indebted to those officials for their aid and readiness in that respect.

A copy of the auditors' statement for 1895 shows a balance on hand of $3,659.11, while the one for 1896 brings it forward as $3,625.12, showing a difference as against the treasurer of $33.99 in the year broken by the change of treasurers. The error is a purely clerical one but it is difficult to understand how it escaped the attention of the auditors. Unfortunately the treasurer has to suffer for their oversight and to make good (unless it can be otherwise explained) the above amount (less subsequent small errors of 40 cents against him and 25 cents in his favor) as $34.14. There being no record in the past of any interest having accrued to the Township from its surplus funds, and the auditors having declared that any such had always been the perquisite of the various treasurers—none is considered in connection with the above account.

Balance in treasurer's hands at 6 April, 1906, $159.10, as shown in Government cash book at that date, has been deposited in an account with the Sovereign Bank at Goderich in the name of the treasurer until such time as the council pass a by-law changing it to that of the Township. In an interview with the accountant of that bank he stated his readiness to loan funds to the Township on demand notes at 6 per cent. per annum. also to allow interest on weekly balances at 3 per cent. per annum. He was likewise agreeable to the method of orders as laid down in this report and will carry out the plan of receiving them in lieu of cash and of treating them as checks. Any order paid at their Clinton branch to be at par. This agreement will considerably smooth the way of the treasurer, earn interest for the Township and give to all orders their fulness.

It is only fair to the officials who have aided the audit that expenses of attending be granted them. Their honesty and loyalty to the Township interests is undoubted and the ratepayers are to be congratulated upon having the services of such able and conscientious men as the present clerk and treasurer.

Assessment.

It will be seen upon attached statement how much the valuations have declined within the period. This can hardly be in accordance with the actual trend of values. It seems a matter of common knowledge that the good lands of the Township are under-assessed by 25 per cent. at least. There is no advantage in this. The credit of the Township suffers, while the rate is made to appear unduly high. The assessor is bound by the Act to cash values of all properties, and penalties are attached for non-adherence. Each ratepayer under-assessed imposes an extra burden on his fellows while the lower the assessment the less apparent are the differences between them. So long as the mischevious method of taxing improvement prevails the law requiring it must be conscientiously followed out. Upon the request of this Township the County caused a valuation to be made in 1905 of the properties in 26 municipalities with a view of better equalization basis, which if adopted will result in a reduction of several hundred dollars in favor of Goderich Township in the county rate. Even then the valuators after a test of 64 parcels found this Township assessment very considerably understated and forthwith added thereto 50.13 per cent. to bring it up to their standard. Your population seems to have decreased in the past 11 years by about 11 per cent.; the live stock by about 13 per cent., while the acreage cleared has increased 12 per cent. The factors which are making for progress within the borders of your municipality are the incoming railroads, the greater use of the lake port, increased banking facilities, the proximity of a growing town, and the stability and progressiveness of your ratepayers generally, as judged from those with whom I have had the pleasure of contact. The ease of tax collections and immunity from debenture debt of any consequence evidence an exceptional degree of prosperity. The subsidence of emigration to the west from your district must soon occur and your loss in number be recovered in time.

Statute Labor.

The pathmasters are advised by the clerk upon very suitable forms immediately after the Court of Revision of the names upon the roll of men from 21 to 60 years, their assessments and equivalent days. The pathmasters must add to this list any non-assessed person and return it before 1st of August marked for those whose work is not done. The clerk should bind these reports and summarize into the collector's roll to show the number of days, the rate and amount to be collected from those whose work is not done. The summary should be laid before the council and passed by them before the pathmasters are released from their duty.

School Taxes.

In 1896, 1897 and 1898 there are small school refunds to those over the three mile limit. Such as are made should not come out of the Township money but be reclaimed from the section receiving the amounts in the first instance. In these occurrences, however, the ratepayers were not strictly entitled to such refunds.

Gravel Payments.

These should be charged in the cash book in the columns for each road division. Any of these accounts unpaid at the close of the year ought, of course, to appear as liabilities. There is a payment in 1898 of an account for four years preceding, having been apparently lost sight of.

Maitland Hill.

It appears that the council of Colborne Township voted Goderich Township, in 1903, the sum of $100 towards the above work, but that through failure to pass the by-law necessary for such payment, the contribution could not legally be made. The suit for recovery entered against Colborne did not succeed in the Division Court and is being referred to the High Court. As the outcome is doubtful on legal ground the asset of the claim can only be taken on trust. Solicitor's opinion, however, advises that there is reasonable chance of settlement, so I have allowed it to stand. The costs of the case, however, which are quite heavy, were not shown as a liability on the printed statement.

Cement Bridge.

The minutes of council, for some unexplained reason, did not record the acceptance of a tender for its construction in No. 2 division some time in August, 1905. There appears to be no sanction of the council for payment of the account, although the acknowledgment for the money is exhibited. The payment, moreover, did not appear in the treasurer's statement referred to as for the last half of December, 1904.

Loans.

Sums have been borrowed from private sources on notes signed by reeve and treasurer and authorized by by-law, without the name of the lender being made known, nor the rate of interest. The bank ought to be able to discount the corporation paper as readily as others and at an even better rate. Loans made in this way would not be open to question on the grounds of favoritism. Some of these overran their due dates, interest being allowed the lender to the date of payment. This date, however, was merely in memorandum on the back of a note without the signature of the one to whom the repayment was made. It is difficult to say whether the note was lifted before or after its due date. The treasurer should have a care that all payments for interest are receipted for. These notes, moreover, were issued in some years in excess of the amount permitted by by-law.

Estimates.

Such are to be placed in writing by the clerk before the council early in each year so that the Township levy rate may be struck to cover the amount of contemplated expenditure and assented to by the council for the purpose. This estimate might be copied *in toto* into the minutes or attached thereto by reference to the document. The neglect to record such estimates in the past is to be regretted and the actual expenditures could not be compared with the expected ones.

Extra Remuneration.

The question raised as to what fees or perquisites the clerk is entitled to retain or receive may be best settled by his agreement with the council at their first meeting, since it is merely one of how much remuneration he shall altogether enjoy for all services of whatever character by which the Township generally is benefited, seeing that special attention has to be given by him to matters not in the regular course of his duties as clerk and of his pay therefor, yet essential to Township affairs.

Solicitor.

It seems that reference has been made to his opinion only upon litigated affairs involving the conduct of a suit, whereas, in the regular course of the council business his advice might have been frequently sought by the clerk when framing by-laws of importance, preparing debentures or justifying certain expenditures. It is not to be expected that a clerk can be so well acquainted with the Acts as to decide safely without occasionally needing such aid.

Arbitration Costs.

Payments have been made out of Township funds of $185 in 1902, $41.25 in 1900, and $54.50 in 1905 towards expenses of arbitration proceedings connected with School Section No. 4. These costs were fairly chargeable to that section to have been recovered in the usual levy from its ratepayers. The solicitor's opinion has been given upon that point and will serve as a future guide for matters of this kind.

Literature.

The expenditure for books, papers, periodicals, etc., for the guidance and instruction of the clerk or any member of the council might be taken exception to were it not for the fact that the clerk was playing a "lone hand" in advising the reeve and council as to the legislation which would affect their acts. The purchases were evidently made with the intention of safeguarding the council proceedings.

Legislative Grant.

Since the monies therefrom are receivable and distributed by the treasurer in his official capacity it would seem proper to pass the entries therefor through his cash book at the proper dates and furnish vouchers accordingly when the funds are handed to the school treasurers.

All of which is respectfully submitted.

Signed OSCAR HUDSON,

Chartered Accountant.

Toronto, 30th March, 1906.

———————

Township of Goderich Report.

Collector's Receipt Book.

Mr. ....

S. S. No..............Assessor's No...19......

Received of ....day of.............................19......

Receipt No. ....$..

Municipality of the Township of Goderich.

Mr. ....

S. S. No..............Assessment No..

Con. ....Lot ....

According to previous notice you were assessed for the year 19......on $...............
upon every $100 of which you are requested to pay as hereunder not later than 14th December.

County rate ....at ....cents. $...............
Township " ....at .... " $...............
School section rate ....at .... " $...............
Special school rate ....at .... " $...............
(For debenture No........)...........................at .... " $...............
Statute labor ....$...............
Dog tax ....$...............
Arrears of taxes ....$...............
Five per cent. thereon ....$...............

$...............

Demanded....................day of..19......
Received....................day of..19......
....Receipt No............

(Collector's signature.)

TOWNSHIP OF GODERICH REPORT.

School Trustee's Order for Funds.

To Mr...Treasurer
of the municipality of the Township of Goderich:

On demand pay to the order of the Secretary-Treasurer, Mr.................................
the sum of ....dollars $................. being
the amount of taxes levied by your municipal council for the school purposes of our
Section No.............as per council By-law No.................and in accordance with our
requisition dated...............day of..............................190......

Dated at ....}   ....Trustees of
this............day of ....190..... }   .... School Section
                                           .... No. ....

Memorandum explaining the above levy.

Assessment of Section No.........$...............cents on every $100.............. $...............
Township grant ....,.....per cent. of $150................................ $...............
Special levy ....at............cents........ $...............

N.B.—The Legislature grants will be paid only on order from Inspector. No other
order than above will be recognized by council.
Received the above amount in full payment
....Secretary-Treasurer.

.........................day of.........................190......

TOWNSHIP OF GODERICH REPORT.

No.....

Municipality of the Township of Goderich.

(Form for the use of School Trustees.)

............day of...................................190.........   Requisition for levy for 19.........

To the Township Clerk:

You are hereby desired to collect for us from the ratepayers of our
section of general school purposes... $...............
Also a special levy for .... $...............
These to be in addition to the Township grant due us of........................ $...............

....}
....}   Trustees of
....}   •   ....School No.........

N.B.—The Act demands that this notice shall be filed with the Township Clerk
not later than the first day of August in each year, you are therefore requested to
return this promptly.

Advice of levy made.

............day of.........................19......

To the above Trustees:—

You are advised that a levy is being made in response to the above
    requisition of..............mills on assessment of $............... to yield... $...............
The proportion of the Township grant is............... .... $...............
Special levy as above stated .... $...............

Making a total payable 15th December... $
    which sum will be paid only on presentation of an upon the form
    herewith enclosed.

MUNICIPALITY OF THE TOWNSHIP OF GODERICH, COUNTY OF HURON, ONT.

Balance Sheet..................... *At the close of the Year 1905.*

Assets.

By tax arrears with County Treasurer uncollected	$	8 87
" " " in " " hands		5 36
" " " for 1905		32 81
" cash in hands of Township Treasurer		4,979 25
" claim against Colborne Township *re* Holmesville Hill—settlement of which is pending		100 00
" Hullett Township for their proportion of Union School 4, debenture No. 4 ....—...		99 09
		$5,225 38

Liabilities.

To County Treasurer for levy of 1905	$3,808 00	
" Union school for debenture No. 4 with interest, due 28th January, 1906	330 30	
" solicitor's expenses *re* Maitland Hill.............................	65 68	
" balance, being surplus available for 1906 expenditure......	1,021 40	
		$5,225 38

*The last of Union School No. 4 debentures No. 5 for $330.30 falls due 28th January, 1907, and will be provided for by special levy in 1906 upon that section as to 70 per cent., and as to 30 per cent. upon Hullett Township, which should be collected by them in 1906.

*There are unrecorded assets the property of the municipality such as escaped taxes $16.43, the safe used by the clerks bought in 1897 for $32.50, and a grader bought in 1892 for $225, and also various scrapers bought for road commissioners in 1897, $43, and in previous years.

MUNICIPALITY OF THE TOWNSHIP OF GODERICH, COUNTY OF HURON, ONT.

Income and Expenditure for the year 1905.

(For Township purposes only.)

To deficit at 1st January, 1905, as per balance sheet then...	$1,105 76	
" expenses paid during 1905	3,718 77	
" school grant paid during 1905	1,491 00	
" short levied for debenture No. 4	4 59	
" solicitor's costs *re* Maitland Hill, etc.............................	65 68	
" surplus at 31st December, 1905	1,021 40	
By township levy for the year	....	$7,357 50
" county rate over levied	....	17 88
" statute labor levies	....	25 50
" increase in tax arrears	....	2 92
" sundry receipts	....	3 40
	$7,407 20	$7,407 20

The cost of this report to the municipality of the Township of Goderich as per Mr. Hudson's account was $395.25.

MUNICIPALITY OF THE TOWNSHIP OF GODERICH, COUNTY OF HURON, ONTARIO.

STATEMENT OF AGREEMENT OF ROLL FROM 1895 TO 1905, INCLUSIVE.

Year	Assessor's Rolls as found. $	Assessor's Roll (less revisions) corrected. $	Township Rate. c.	County Rate. c.	Collector's Roll as found. $	Collector Roll Shortrated. $		Escaped Taxes. $ c.
1895	1,520,477	1,521,877	.30	.25	1,521,877			
1896	1,515,177	1,515,117	.32	.17	1,515,117			
1897	1,505,222	1,503,122	.34	.20	1,502,722	400	Samuel Blair	2.36
1898	1,491,195	1,494,895	.34	.15	1,494,895			
1899	1,499,700	1,493,800	.34	.15	1,493,800			
1900	1,484,445	1,487,400	.32	.15	1,486,400	1000	Thos. C. Naftel	6.00
1901	1,482,070	1,483,825	.31	.15	1,483,325	500	Peter Steep	3.00
1902	1,482,520	1,481,925	.31	.15	1,481,875	50	John Gel	.30
1903	1,479,445	1,479,000	.33	.18	1,479,000			
1904	1, 34380	1, 24885	.33	.19	1,472,235	50 600	Chas. G. Middleton Edward Wise	.32 4.02
1905	1,472,425	1,471,580	.50	.26	1,471,505	75	William Isn	.73
	16,405,426				16,402,751	2675		*16.43

T. C. Naftel's assessment was omitted from assessment roll. Other errors arose from its faulty arrangement.

* This amount will be placed on collector's roll in 1906.

Correct,
Jos. E. Whiteley,
Nixon Sturdy,
March 24, 1906.

MUNICIPALITY OF THE TOWNSHIP OF GODERICH, COUNTY OF HURON, ONTARIO.

TREASURER'S CASH STATEMENT FOR THE FULL YEAR OF 1905.

To Balance in Treasurer's hands, 1st January, 1905 .... $2,161 99
   Held in Trust for County Rate, due 14th Feb, 1905 ... $2,672 30
   Held in Trust for Debenture No. 3, due 28th Jan, 1905 ... 330 30
   Held in Trust for Debenture No. 2, due 15th May, 1905 ... 376 46
      3,379 06
      1,217 07
Less deficiency in Township Revenue 2,161 99

" Receipts from Legislative Grant to Schools 270 00
" Receipts from Taxes (on each $100 assessed) 14,378 65
      2,975 96

School Levies ...
  Separate 8 49
  No. 1 .... $139,325 @ 17c 228 28
  No. 2 .... 150,374 @ 23c 345 84
  No. 3 .... 149,787 @ 15c 224 60
  Union 4 .... 125,900 @ 6c 75 54
  Union 2 .... 15,683 @ 17c 26 66
  Union 10 .... 15,600 @ 44c 68 64
  No. 5 .... 181,900 @ 17c 309 19
  No. 6 .... 126,456 @ 28c 354 07
  No. 8 .... 102,160 @ 25c 255 35
  No. 9 .... 158,650 @ 18c 285 57
  No. 10 .... 148,120 @ 27c 399 92
  No. 11 .... 157,550 @ 25c 393 81
      $1,471,505 $2,975 96

Township Levy—$1,471,505 @ 50c 7,357 50
Statute Labor 25 50
County Levy—$1,471,505 @ 26c 3,825 88
School Debentures, (Township proportion):
No. 4 Union—$125,000 @ 18c 226 62

Taxes collectable per Collector's roll 14,411 46

By County Treasurer, for 1904 Levy $2,672 30
" Debentures redeemed (with interest) 706 76
  Union No. 4 School Debenture No. 3 ... $330 30
  Section No. 6 " No. 2 ... 376 46
      706 76

" School Trustees 4,736 96
  For 1905 School Levy (per contra) ... 2,975 96
  " Township Grants ... 1,491 00
  " Legislative Grant (per contra) ... 270 00
      4,736 96

" Loans repaid (per contra) 3,400 00
" Township expenses (except School Grant) 3,718 77
  Roads and Bridges, No. 1 ... 463 72
  " " No. 2 ... 434 27
  " " No. 3 ... 547 63
  " " Nos 4 and 6 ... 717 18
  " " No. 5 ... 544 64
      2,707 44
  Salaries and Allowances ... 630 91
  Stationery, Printing, Postage and Literature ... 92 27
  Election Charges, Township and Provincial ... 85 00
  Law and Arbitration ... 56 50
  Rent ... 30 00
  Charities ... 8 00
  Interest on Temporary Loans ... 99 65
  Miscellaneous ... 9 00
      3,718 77

" Balance in Treasurer's hands, 31st December, 1905 .... 4,970 25
  Held in Trust for County Rate, due the 14th Feb, 1906 ... 3,808 00

Held in Trust for Debenture No. 4, due 28th Jan., 1906	231 21	
Cash available for Township expenses for 1906.	940 00	
		4,979 25
		$20,214 04

Less Arrears handed County Treasurer ..		32 81	
		14,378 65	
Receipts from Loans on Corporation Notes			3,400 00
Feb. 10th—Jos. Whitely, @ 5%	1,000 00		
May 6th—C. A. Whitely, @ 5%	500 00		
May 26th—Wm. Driver, @ 5%	700 00		
July 4th—C. B. Middleton, @ 5%	1,000 00		
Oct. 4th—Nixon Sturdy, at 6%	200 00		
		3,400 00	
Receipts from sales of Waste Timber, etc.			3 40
			$20,214 04

MUNICIPALITY OF THE TOWNSHIP OF GODERICH, COUNTY OF HURON, ONTARIO.

Treasurer's Cash Statement for the full Year of 1904.

To Balance in Treasurer's hands from 1903 .... 3,225 93

Held in Trust for County Rate, due 14th Feb, 1904 ... 2,672 30
Held in Trust for Debenture No. 2, due 28th Jan., 1904 ... 330 30
Held in Trust for Debenture No. 1, due 15th May, 1904 ... 376 46
Held in Trust for Dancey over-payment ... 24 40
    3,403 46
    177 53
Less Deficiency in Township Revenue 3,225 93

" Receipts from Legislative Grant 279 00
" Receipts from Taxes (on each $100 assessed) 12,012 08
    2,660 01

School Levies:

Separate		8 41
No. 1	$139,260 @ 17c.	228 26
No. 2	150,604 @ 15c.	225 73
No. 3	145,092 @ 20c.	290 18
No. 4 Union	126,125 @ 45c.	567 54
No. 2 Union	15,333 @ 20c.	30 66
No. 10 Ubn.	15,100 @ 15c.	22 64
No. 5	182,600 @ 12c.	219 12
No. 6	127,006 @ 15c.	190 47
No. 8	102,625 @ 28c.	287 34
No. 9	158,750 @ 15c.	238 06
No. 10	148,210 @ 15c.	222 30
No. 11	161,630 @ 8c.	129 30
$1,472,235		$2,660 01

School Building, Union:—
No. 4—$126,125 @ 81½c. 1,024 69
School Debentures (Township proportion):—
Union No. 14—$126,125 @ 19c. ... 239 61
Union No. 10—$15,100 @ 24c. ... 36 24
No. 6—$127,006 @ 30c. ... 381 01

By County Treasurer for 1903 Levy 2,672 30
" Debentures redeemed (with interest) 706 70
    Union No. 4 School Debenture No. 2 ... 330 30
    Section No. 6 " No. 1 ... 376 46
    706 76
    5,490 94

" School Trustees ...
    For 1904 School Levy (per contra) ... 2,660 01
    " Township Grant ... 1,491 00
    " Legislative Grant (per contra) ... 279 00
    " Union No. 4 Building (per contra) ... 1,024 69
    " Union No. 10, towards Hullett Debenture (per contra) ... 36 24
    5,490 94

" Loans repaid (per contra) 2,985 00
" Township Expenses (except School grant) 4,947 30

Roads and Bridges, No. 1	394 94	
" No. 2	365 42	
" No. 3	589 16	
" Nos. 4 and 6.	722 05	
" No. 5.	613 43	
Cement Bridge No. 2	607 70	
Maitland Hill Expenditure (grants contra)	677 59	
Salaries and Allowances		3,970 29
Stationery, Printing, Postage and Literature		684 38
Law and Arbitration		83 18
Rent		58 05
Charities		34 00
Interest on Temporary Loans		5 00
Miscellaneous		74 50
Statute Labor Taxes refunded		7 00
Dancey Taxes overpaid refunded		6 50
		24 40
		4,947 30

Statute Labor and Dog Tax (refund contra)....		20 00
Township Levy—$1,472,235 @ 33c............		4,857 89
County Levy—$1,472,235 @ 19c............		2,796 75
Total Taxes collectable per collector's roll..	12,016 20	
Less arrears handed to County Treasurer...	4 12	
Collections paid over to Township Treasurer	12,012 08	2,985 00
" Receipts from Loans on Corporation Notes........		
May 20th—C. A. Whitely, @ 6%........	900 00	
July 4th—Nixon Sturdy, @ 6%........	1,000 00	
Aug. 10th—Jos. Whitely, @ 6%........	800 00	
Sept. 15th—Nixon Sturdy, @ 6%........	285 00	
	2,985 00	
" Receipts from sundry sources....		462 28
Hullett Township, re Boundary line......	7 55	
County Treasurer, on account of Tax arrears..	55 64	
County Treasurer, balance of Co. grant—Maitland Hill...	250 00	
Clinton Town, balance grant—Maitland Hill...	50 00	
Hullett Township, 30% Union 4 School Debenture and Interest....	99 09	
	462 28	
		$18,964 29

" Balance in Treasurer's hands on 31st Dec, 1994..........		2,161 99
Held in Trust for County Rate, due 14th Feb, 1905....		2,672 30
Held in Trust for Debenture No. 3, due 28th Jan., 1905.		330 30
Held in Trust for Debenture No. 2, due 16th May, 1905 ...		376 46
	3,379 06	
	1,217 07	
Less Deficiency in Township Revenue........		2,161 99
		$18,964 29

6 M.A.

The Hon. J. J. Foy,
Attorney-General of the Province of Ontario.

Sir,—Pursuant to the instructions of J. B. Laing, Esq., Provincial Municipal Auditor, in accordance with the Order in Council of the 29th January last, I beg to report that I have made a careful inspection and audit of the books, accounts, vouchers and moneys of the Municipal Corporation of the Township of Finch, in the County of Stormont, and herewith submit the following reports:

(a) General report on the affairs of the Township.

(b) Assets and liabilities of the Township, showing the net debt as at 14th April, 1906, with the unpaid promissory notes and debentures at 31st December, and the surplus or deficit on each year's transactions, in 1898 and seven following years.

(c) The state of each drain account, giving such information as will enable the ratepayers to understand the present position of each drain, which reports will, I trust, have your approval.

All which is respectfully submitted.

J. R. Adamson,

Auditor.

To the Reeve and Council of the Township of Finch, Ont.:

Gentlemen,—The petition presented to Hon. J. J. Foy, Attorney-General for Ontario, set forth that your desire is to know the standing of the municipality's finances at the 31st December in each year since 1897, giving a statement of the

Assets and Liabilities,
Net Debt,
Unpaid Promissory Notes, and
Debentures,

at each 31st December.

In accordance therewith I have carefully examined the books and vouchers for 1905 and 1906, and all postings and entries since 31st December, 1897. The errors found have been few and unimportant, but I have made a large number of alterations in the classification of the entries which has had the effect, in many cases, of taking very considerable sums out of the general accounts and charging them to specific drains or bridges.

There are a few special matters to which I would beg to refer.

Moriarty Drain. Winchester paid lately its debt to Finch of $160.42, but interest is due to the amount of ———.

Foley Creek. Osnabruck Township owes $111.83 to the original construction account, and $61.48 under the amending by-law, upon which amounts the interest due this Township is $24.43 and $4.65 respectively.

Stephenson Drain. Winchester paid its debt to Finch of $425.20, but interest is due to the amount of $32.75.

Russell Township owes $30 and $2.50 interest to the same drain and it would be well to apply for payment of this account.

Whissel Creek. Cambridge Township owes $78.89 with $1.75 interest and there seems to be no good reason why the amount should not be paid.

Payne River and Beaver Creek. In 1902 a deputation went to Toronto and interviewed the Provincial Government with the object of obtaining assistance in this drainage scheme which affected a very large extent of

6a M A.

country. This was granted to the extent of $4,000, and the Townships interested, Osnabruck, Roxborough and Finch, agreed to divide the expense of the deputation in proportion to the amount each received. This was allotted, Roxborough $28.62 and Osnabruck $13.41. Unfortunately the clerk made a mistake in the notices, and Roxborough only paid $15.21, leaving $13.41 still due.

There appears also to be a claim of $21 against A. McKinnon for old bridge timber which may as well be collected without further delay.

Blue Creek Extension. The position of this matter has been fully set out in the report of the financial position of the drain and need not be repeated here, but deserves the serious consideration of the Council. I beg to hand herewith the letters of 12th March and 2nd April of this year from His Honor Judge Rankin regarding this matter.

Lalonde Drain. This Township has a claim against Roxborough of $265.14 which is directly the result of the then reeve, Dr. Crain, disregarding the rule that all amounts, without distinction, should be passed by Council before being paid. The amount due to Roxborough on this drain construction has been past due for some time and they placed it in the hands of Maclennan, Cline & Maclennan for collection. When the reeve instructed the treasurer to pay it, he forgot that the referee had allowed Finch expenses besides those regularly allowed, which expenses as above should have been deducted from the amount paid to Roxborough.

In this connection I would again refer to the large number of payments made last year before being submitted to Council. This practise cannot be too strongly condemned, as it does away with the proper control which Council ought to exercise over the affairs of the Township. I have been glad to learn that a stringent by-law has been passed this year affirming the principle that nothing is to be paid until the item has passed the Council.

1898.

There appears to be a book in which the then Treasurer, T. J. Hamilton, entered the details of many transactions which are only entered in the cash book in lump sums, but the most diligent search for this book has failed to discover it anywhere. I have been, therefore, unable to obtain as full details of the transactions of this and the following year, especially as regards drains, as I would have liked. There appears to have been a surplus of assets over liabilities in that year of $404.38.

1899.

The same remarks apply to the details for this year, in which there appears to have been a surplus of $160.20. It was in this year that a note for $665 was given to Anthony McGowan, which is running still.

1900.

This year marks the commencement of the effect of the drainage system upon the finances of the Township. In going over the accounts of the drains, there seems to have been several cases in which the engineer was far too low in his estimates. The result was, of course, a deficit, then an amending by-law, then, very often an appeal to the County Judge, and as no one is perfect in this world, the mistakes were pointed out, the individuals to be benefited by the drain were relieved and, as a last result, the Township had to pay the bill. If you will excuse my speaking plainly, it has seemed to me, in the course of this investigation, somewhat childish that men who have endeavored to do their very best, as I honestly believe every Reeve has done, should be blamed for increasing the debt of the Township when the truth has been that circumstances, facts and figures, have been too strong for each of them. There has been an increasing expenditure, very largely uncontrollable, and the revenue has not increased as rapidly. Anyone who considers the subject for a moment will acknowledge that expenditure, however wisely and skilfully made, must have time to develop results before these can be obtained. As it is impossible to obtain results from drainage in a year, or even a few years for that matter, the expenditure and consequent deficits have gone on piling up as a snowball gathers the farther it is rolled. It is evident that this is the result of the large drainage expenditure, and if those who have been doing the drainage will just consider how long it will require from the first digging of the drain, to their obtaining the full benefit to their lands, just so soon will the effect of the Township revenues be noticeable. I know that theoretically each drain should pay strictly for itself, but theories, however plausible, seldom work out practically, and, as I have mentioned there is so often, from one cause and another, a deficit in drainage accounts which the whole Township must bear and which increases the debt whether the Reeve will or no. It is a matter which is entirely beyond his control however good a financier he may be.

1901.

The notes current, which last year amounted to $3,471.31, crept up this year to $5,900.60, exemplifying the point that in many cases the Reeve may be as honestly desirous as it is possible for a man to be of keeping down expenditure, but the business of the Township must first be properly carriew on, and when there are increasing demands for proper expenditure the liabilities are bound to increase. And why should they not? Surely Finch does not wish to be distinguished as an unprogressive Township? And where there is progress there must be increased expense. There is, however, one point in connection with Township notes which should be carried out, unless under very exceptional circumstances. Sec. 435 of the Revised Statutes provides that the Reeve may borrow money on Township notes, until the taxes have been collected. Sometimes a Reeve provides the money wherewith to pay off the notes he has given for the Township and the money is applied to the payment of other urgent demands. This should be prevented as much as possible.

1902.

In going over the accounts of the various years I have been unable to avoid the reflection that the testing of a Reeve's reputation as a financier by his record in any particular year is a mistaken way of looking at things. Let us take time to see the results of this work before coming to a decision. What has become of our public spirit? Why should any man who has successfully aspired to take the first position in the Township be either praised or blamed merely on the issue of dollars and cents? Is it not much more important to spend money, if the spending in a wise way means greater benefit of any kind to the Township, than the saving of it is? The smaller the mental capacity of the man, the more apt he is to be penny wise and pound foolish, while the larger the mental calibre, and the better the business man, the more likelihood there is, not of lavish and foolish expenditure, but of there being a far-sighted looking ahead and the endeavor, at least, to make such a reasonable use of money as will ensure a considerable benefit to the community at large.

In this year the same thing happened as did last year, namely, that a drain expenditure of $773.80, for the Dunbar drain, came in late in the year. This amount has been entered also as an asset, since the ratepayers are perfectly good for it.

1903.

That three years should run along with no very large amount of difference in the deficit shows how small a margin there is in the expenditure over which the Reeve can exercise control. There is a large expenditure left unprovided for at the end of this year for which there is no evidence of any provision having been attempted to be made.

1904.

The annual deficit increased very much this year, the bills payable running up to the large sum, at the end of the year, of $14,749.01. The drainage schemes are evidently being a serious difficulty, the amounts spent on drains increasing to $10,656.40 at 31st December. This ought to be provided against by taking action to provide in time for expenditure which is known in advance.

Now that banking facilities are so universal it may be well for the Council to do as is done in some other Townships and keep the drainage moneys in a separate account. When money is required in advance a note for that special drain can be discounted and the interest charged to the drain to which it properly belongs. This will be an incentive to the Reeve to look ahead and obtain funds by the sale of debentures in the regular way, and so avoid paying bank interest.

I would take this opportunity to recommend that the funds of the Township be kept in an account in some chartered bank in the name of the Township and entirely distinct from the funds belonging to the Treasurer personally.

1905.

I enclose herewith a schedule showing the amount paid this year without first having been submitted to Council. It is only necessary to refer to this list to show to what a length the disregard for ordinary business methods have gone. The net debt is $9,926.70.

Finally let me protest, in the most energetic manner, against anything I have said above being taken, even as attempting, to whitewash anyone. such was very far from my intention, and I have nothing but condemnation for the loose and irregular manner in which the affairs of the Township were conducted in 1904 and particularly in 1905. The rules the present Council has laid down for their guidance, so far as payments are concerned, are the right ones and, if adhered to, will enable the Council to keep the control of the expenditure which they ought to have. Let me say that I consider the combination of the Clerk and Treasurership in some competent man's hands an important move in the right direction as soon as it can be arranged. The keeping of the accounts of the Township is a much more complicated matter now than it was a few years ago, and special knowledge is required to keep things straight.

There is a good opportunity for some leader in the Township to take the experience of the Townships in the westerly part of the Province and advocate tile subsoil drainage and the improvement of the roads. Anyone who considers the matter will see that the reason of the bad roads in spring is because they are water soaked, then frost heaves them up and the thawing does the rest. If the foundation of the road is dry the frost will have no effect in the way of heaving, and good roads all the year round will be the result, with proper gravelling, of course. A three-inch tile drain down the centre of the road will be a most efficient remedy. The benefit to be derived from drainage has been amply seen and quite as great benefit can be derived from subsoil drainage. Try it, and you will find that the increased value of the crop for two years will pay for the draining, while the land is increased fully twenty-five per cent. in value. All which is respectfully submitted.

J. R. ADAMSON,

Auditor.

REPORT ON THE FINANCIAL POSITION OF THE DRAINS IN THE TOWNSHIP OF FINCH.

Blue Creek Drain.

T. H. Wiggins, Engineer, report dated 16th February, 1898. Provisionally adopted 16th April, 1898.

The total cost of the work was estimated at...$1,581 63		
The contract was taken by J. H. Quinn at......	$1,126 11	
The Township costs have been	477 83	
Debentures were sold which provided		$1,665 00
Leaving at credit of the drain	61 06	
	$1,665 00	$1,665 00

Blue Creek Extension.

T. H. Wiggins, Engineer, report dated 12th August, 1898. Provisionally adopted 3rd October, 1898.

The total cost of the work was estimated at...$1,550 00		
The contract was taken by T. & J. Gagnon at	$2,656 86	
The debentures sold produced		$1,894 20
Leaving a deficit of		762 66
	$2,656 86	$2,656 86

In 1903 the Council endeavored to pass an amending by-law, which was provisionally adopted 29th June, 1903, and to which the Engineer added estimated costs of $322.02, making a total of $1,084.68 to be raised. This was appealed against by the interested parties to Judge Liddell who ordered as interpreted by the Council the sum of $611.50 to be deducted from the sum of $844.68 assessed against the interested parties, thereby leaving the whole $611.50, besides $240 already assessed against the roads of the Township, to stand against them.

The present position of the drain is as follows :—

Deficit as above			$ `.62 66
Costs as estimated by the Engineer			;ᴜᴜ ᴜᴜ
Total assessed against lands and roads			$1,084 68
Of which there was assessed against lands		$ 844 68	
Less struck off by Judge Liddell		611 50	
			$2,333 18
And against roads ....$ 240 00			
To which must be added the amount struck off			
by Judge Liddell	$611 50	$851 50	$1,084 68

F. D. McNaughton appealed to Judge Rankin, drainage referee, who gave judgment on 10th February, 1905, that the applicant could not succeed in having the by-law set aside, but that he was entitled to a declaration that the by-law should not be made a basis for future assessments or for damages, and he was given his costs of the application. This leaves the matter in a somewhat unsatisfactory position. Judge Rankin is evidently of opinion that the $611.50 should have been deducted from the whole amount of $1,084.68, and not from the $844.68, but states that this was done by the Council and that he has no authority to interfere. It remains, therefore, for the Council to decide whether they will continue the present assessment or whether it can be placed upon the basis favored by Judge Rankin, viz.: $473.18 against the lands, and $611.50 against the roads of the Township. Of the $233.18 the interested parties paid $172.26, leaving a balance of $60.92 which, with interest $3.41, makes the amount assessed against those who did not pay in advance. Of this, the first assessment of $14.44 has been paid.

Blair-McRae Drain.

This drain was completed in 1899, Roxborough being the initiating Township, and the amount claimed from Finch was $403.05. This amount was not paid, however, until 16th Sept., 1902, by which time interest to the amount of $58.63 had accrued, leaving a balance of $52.63 at the debit of the drain. It is unfortunate that the $403.05 was not paid when due and interest thereby saved, as the amount at the debit of this drain must result in loss to the Township as a whole since it evidently cannot be charged to the drain.

Butternut Creek Drain.

T. H. Wiggins, Engineer, report dated 20th July, 1898. Provisionally adopted 3rd Sept., 1898.

The total estimated cost was $3,914 36			
The contract was taken by T. & J. Gagnon at	$3,168 80		
And other costs were	833 23		
Debentures were sold which provided		$3,667 50	
There was received from Cambridge		57 25	
And from Roxborough		358 31	
J. A. Cockburn's fees in 1905 and 1906 were..	1 00		
Leaving a balance at the credit of the drain of	80 03		
	$4,083 06	$4,083 06	

Interest to the amount of $60.30 was paid by Roxborough and had been credited to the drain, but as Township funds were used, the drain has no right to it.

Campbell-Adams Drain.

T. H. Wiggins, Engineer, report dated 18th March, 1897. Provisionally adopted 15th May, 1897.

The estimated cost was $4,488 49		
The contract was taken by Holmes & Bruce at	$3,141 68	
The other costs were	961 72	
The debentures realized		$2,233 00
Advance assessments were paid amounting to		967 01
Amounts were charged in error and charged back		203 50
And the surplus distributed among the interested parties was	632 67	
	$4,736 05	$4,736 05
There stand at the debit of the drain, J. A. Cockburn's fees for 1905 and 1906.........	1 00	

Casselman Creek Drain.

T. H. Wiggins, Engineer, report dated 1st Sept., 1896. Provisionally adopted 28th Sept., 1896.

The total cost was estimated at..................$3,133 68		
The contract was taken by Clark & Connely, who threw it up before finishing it. They were paid	$2,247 40	
M. McMillan finished the work for.............	582 57	
Other costs were ....,	811 45	
Interest on advances on individual payments	61 35	
Other charges since have been	139 66	
Debentures sold realized		$2,382 00
Interested parties paid in advance of assessment		507 92
Osnabruck paid		482 99
Judge struck off interest		61 35
Leaving at the debit of the drain		408 17
	$3,842 43	$3,842 43

Judge Riddell ordered "the interest charged" to the amount of $79.35 to be deducted from the amount of the by-law, but the only interest charged in the books is the $61.35 mentioned above, while the by-law never reached its first reading, and there is no trace, either in the minutes or elsewhere, of what the amount was. I have therefore only allowed the amount of interest charged in the books, viz., $61.35. If interest on the balance, which was $329.66 at that time, was charged, it would have amounted to about $50 more.

J. A. Cockburn, fees, 1906, 50 cents.

Dunbar Drain.

T. H. Wiggins, Engineer, report dated 26th April, 1902. Provisionally adopted 9th Sept., 1902.

Osnabruck was the initiating Township.

The Engineer's estimate of 26th April, 1902, ratified by By-law 6, 1903, shows as follows : —

Estimated cost of construction in Finch \$1,232 40		
Less Engineer's allowance for McEwan award............	\$ 253 00	
Less Engineer's allowance for farm crossings...............	128 00	
Less Engineer's allowance for other expenses.............	200 00	
Balance at debit due to Osnabruck...........................	651 40	
	\$1,232 40	\$1,232 40

As the amount claimed by Osnabruck is \$665.30 it is clear that the amount standing at debit of the drain is not an asset, but has merely been entered as a matter of record.

The Engineer's report states the amount necessary to be raised by Finch as \$773 80		
Less, allowance for private drains	\$ 44 00	
Less, allowance for McEwan award	209 00	
Less, allowance for Campbell-Adams drain	88 56	
Less, allowance for farm crossings	128 00	
Less, allowance for expenses of drawing By-law, Courts Revision, etc.	100 00	
Leaving a balance due Osnabruck	204 24	
	\$773 80	\$773 80

Leaving the Township in debt to the above extent as the payments on debentures and advance payments have been used for other purposes.

Gregnon Drain.

The initiating Township was Russell. The drain was closed up in 1901, leaving \$2 at its credit.

Hebert Drain.

The initiating Township was Russell. This drain was closed up in 1901, leaving \$3.13 at its credit.

Foley Creek and Amending.

Geo. L. Brown, Engineer report dated 29th May, 1901. Provisionally adopted 22nd June, 1901. Amending report W. H. Magwood, Engineer, date 24th Feby., 1904. Provisionally adopted 12th May, 1904.

The total cost of the original drain was............ \$3,571 30		
Other costs were 128 94		
Debentures realized	\$2,227 26	
There is due from Osnabruck	111 83	
Advance assessments paid amounted to	165 80	

Debentures sold for amending, realized	1,122 57	
There is due from Osnabruck, on amending.....................	61 48	
The Engineer awarded Thos. Foley for farm crossing	12 50	
Leaving a balance at the debit of the drain of..............		. 23 80
	$3,712 74	$3,712 74

Johnstone Main Drain.

D. R. Brown, Engineer, report dated 20th May, 1895. Provisionally adopted 15th June, 1895. The total estimated cost was $3,496.96. The particulars of this drain are in a book used previous to 1896, and which cannot now be found. There is a balance at the debit of the drain of $24.61.

Johnstone Drain Improvement.

T. H. Wiggins, Engineer, there was a subsequent report made by W. H. Magwood, Engineer, dated 22nd August, 1904. Provisionally adopted 29th June, 1903, which was finally amended by Magwood's report of 24th July, 1905.

T. H. Wiggins estimated the cost at...........................	$947 60	
W. H. Magwood reports an estimated cost of...........	1,737 03	

The interested parties appealed to Judge Rankin, Drainage Referee, which appeal was heard on 10th Nov., 1904. The referee ordered that the assessments be reduced by $571.70 *pro rata*.

The cost of the work, including the cost of the Referee's court was	$2,051 07	
Advance assessments have been paid of		$333 60
One annual assessment has been paid, amounting to..............		167 65
Leaving the balance, for which debentures are being sold......		1,549 82
	$2,051 07	$2,051 07

It ought to be explained that the $571.70 struck off the individual rate-payers by the referee, and assessed upon the Township, was on account of the failure of the original engineer to make the contractors take out a quantity of hard pan from the bottom of the drain. The engineer was not present at the Referee's court to give any explanation of this which possibly he might have done, had he been called. As a result of the Referee's decision, the annual cost of the Township is $185.74.

Lagrove—McIntyre and Amending Drain.

Geo. L. Brown, Engineer, reported dated 16th July, 1900. Provisionally adopted 10th August, 1900.

The total estimated cost was $1,400 00		
The actual cost was $2,698 37		
Debentures sold under the original by-law		$700 77
Advance assessments paid		1,059 86
Interest		1 19
Debentures sold under amending by-law		725 30
Two assessments paid before debentures were sold		205 48
J. A. Cockburn, fees entering on roll 1 00		
Balance at debit		6 77
	$2,699 37	$2,699 37

Lalonde Drain.

The initiating Township was Roxborough. T. H. Wiggins, Engineer, report dated 2nd May, 1901. Amending report dated 10th March, 1902.

Amount assessed against Finch, which was paid 5th May 1902. $110 20

The Amending By-law was provisionally adopted 12th May, 1904.

The amount assessed against Finch, was against, which Finch appealed	$892 20
This appeal was heard on 19th Nov., 1903, and the assessment was reduced to	446 10
This amount was not paid to Roxborough until 19th July, 1903, by which time it amounted to	471 10
and Mclennan, Cline & Maclennan, in whose hands the claim had been placed for collection, insisted upon a further payment of interest of	12 22

It is evident this interest cannot be charged to the drain, so that it will probably be a loss to the Township. In remitting the amount to Roxborough, the expenses to which Finch had been put should have been deducted. The refere's decision placed Finch's costs at $161.33, and application should be made to Roxborough for it without delay. There stands at the debit of the drain, $265.14.

This payment of $471.10 was one of the many which were made without first having been submitted to Council, and the very loose manner in which the transaction was carried through emphasises the necessity of the rule, being strictly enforced, that all payments must be authorized by Council before being made.

McNaughton—Munro Drain.

T. H. Wiggins, Engineer, report dated 17th August, 1898. Provisionally adopted 3rd October, 1898.

The estimated cost was	$1,022 70		
The actual cost was		$1,127 12	
Debentures realized			$1,026 10
Advance payments were			54 00
Interest on money advanced before sale of debentures		12 48	
J. A. Cockburn's fees		50	
Balance at debit of drain			60 00
		$1,140 10	$1,140 10

Moriarty Amending.

W. H. Magwood, Engineer, report dated 19th April, 1904. Provisionally adopted 2nd June, 1904.

Estimated cost	$1,154 96	
Unpaid assessments under original by-law	545 48	
Debentures		$756 09
Advance assessments		707 92
Amount paid by Winchester		160 42
Costs underestimated by Engineer		27 76
Allowances made to Moriarty and McClusky		40 00
Balance at debit of drain		8 25
	$1,700 44	$1,700 44

Paquet—McMahon Amending.

W. H. Magwood, Engineer, report dated 6th May, 1904.   Provisionally adopted 8th July, 1904.

The total cost of the original drain was	$2,179 47	
Other costs were	808 50	
	$2,987 97	
Debentures sold, realized		$2,280 50
The Township of Russell, paid		430 00
Witness fees in Referee's Court, were		45 15
Interest refunded, amounted to		1 50
Debentures on amending by-law, realized		234 36
The costs re amending by-law	116 73	
There is due from the Township of Russell	....	56 03
Balance at debit of drain	....	56 08
	$3,104 70	$3,104 70

It seems to be the regular practise of engineers never to allow enough to provide for the full costs of a drain, and it would be well, especially in amending by-laws, to look closely into this in future in order that these constant debit balances may be avoided. In this case the engineer estimated the costs at $64.50, while the books show that the actual costs (as above) were $116.73.

Payne River and Beaver Creek Amending.

T. H. Wiggins, Engineer, report dated 8th July, 1901.   Provisionally adopted 24th Sept., 1901.

T. & J. Gagnon took the contract at	$10,011 65	
Other costs were	2,453 76	
	$12,465 41	
Debentures sold, realized	....	$2,534 00
Roxborough, paid	....	5,217 44
Osnabruck, paid	....	2,941 49
There was advanced to pay the Township's portion of the expenses of the deputation to Toronto, to obtain some assistance from the Ontario Govt	....	10 17
The portion of the grant was	493 30	
Refund re McNaughton, suit was	75 00	
While the drain owes this Township...$12,465.41	————	$1,762 31
Osnabruck paid on amending by-law	....	$492 84
Roxborough paid on amending by-law	....	895 42
Debentures sold, realized	....	385 00
J. A. Cockburn's fees	50	
Treasurer's fees	3 00	
Balance at credit	7 45	
Carried forward	1,762 31	
	$1,773.26	$1,773 26

On 5th May, 1902, $25.37 was received from Roxborough Township, and credited to the money, had been expended, the drain had no title to it. Making this correction, will leave $17.92 due to the Township.

Roxborough Payne River.

T. H. Wiggins, Engineer, report undated. Prvisionally adopted 9th June, 1898. Initiating Township Roxborough.

Total estimated cost to Finch $289 20		
Debentures sold, realized	....	276 00
Amount paid Roxborough	232 00	
Other expenses	44 00	
	$276 00	276 00

Stark Creek Amending.

W. H. Magwood, Engineer, report dated 9th May, 1904. Provisionally adopted 2nd June, 1904.

The total cost was	$1,996 58	
Debentures sold, realized ....:.....................	....	$1,304 33
Expenses re amending by-law	140 26	
Debentures sold under amending by-law	....	734 40
Balance at debit of drain	....	98 11
	$2,136 84	$2,136 84

Steele-McElpheran Drain.

Geo. L. Brown, Engineer, report dated 17th June, 1899. Provisionally adopted 16th August, 1899.

Total cost was estimated at $867 79		
J. M. Lazette, contractor received	$399 50	
Other expenses were	597 20	
Debentures sold, realized	....	$499 49
Roxborough paid, including fees and disbursements	....	466 50
Interest paid to Roxborough in above	51 19	
J. A. Cockburn's fees, 1905	50	
Balance at debit of the drain	....	101 40
	$1,048 39	$1,048 39

Stephenson Amending Drain.

W. H. Magwood, Engineer, report dated 11th Feb., 1904. Provisionally adopted 21st April, 1904.

J. H. Fetterley, contractor received	$2,644 70	
Other costs were	1,170 95	
Debentures sold for	....	$1,772 66
Winchester paid	....	726 38
Russell paid	....	35 43
Interested parties paid on amending by-law	....	323 97
Debentures sold under amending by-law for	....	596 15
Winchester paid under amending by-law	....	425 20

Russell owes, under amending by-law		30 00
Balance at debit of the drain		78 65
	$3,988 44	$3,988 44

The $30 from Russell might as well be collected, and the debit balance reduced to the amount mentioned above.

Smirl-McConnell Drain.

T. H. Wiggins, Engineer, report dated 19th January, 1903. Provision-ally adopted 1st August, 1903.

The Contractor was paid, as per Engineer's report	$2,486 05	
Other costs were	653 41	
Received from sale of Debentures		$3,322 74
Allowances as per Engineer's report, due under by-law of 21st August, 1905, not yet paid		49 00

Whissel, Improvement and Amending.

W. H. Magwood, Engineer, report dated 7th May, 1904. Provisionally adopted 11th July, 1904.

Original cost as per by-law 537/'96..................	$6,975 89	
Cambridge paid		$1,893 00
Debentures realized		5,039 85
Charged in error, and charged back		45 00
Balance to credit	1 96	
	$6,977 85	$6,977 85
Improvement as per by-law, 8/'00, balance to credit..............		1 96
Total cost	$3,396 00	
Debentures realized		2,032 42
Cambridge paid		128 00
Balance to debit		1,233 62
	$3,396 00	$3,396 00

Amending, Provisionally adopted, 11,7,'04.

At debit	$1,233 62	
Additional cost	274 15	
	$1,507 77	
Of which Cambridge share	$78 89	
Of which Finch share	1,301 73	
Finch's taxed costs re appeal	75 88	
Deficit	51 27	$1,507 77
Cash received from interested parties		146 99
Due from Cambridge		78 98
First assessment paid		149 27
Balance still to collect		$1,152 62
		$1,507 77

Wiseman Drain.

No final report has yet been made by the Engineer, so that no by-law has yet been passed.

The Treasurer's books show the amount at debit of the drain to be $2,670 19

Stoney Creek.

This drain was initiated by Winchester Township. Finch appealed, and nothing has since been done.

The amount at the debit of the drain is $36.52.

All which is respectfully submitted.

REPORT ON ASSETS AND LIABILITIES OF THE TOWNSHIP OF FINCH.

1898.

Liabilities.

County rate of 1898 unpaid at 31st December, 1898............	....	$1,001 07
Drains, balances to their credit—		
Blue creek	$163 61	
Campbell-Adams drain	488 65	
Payne River and Beaver Creek	356 41	
Roxborough and Payne River	352 00	
Whissel creek	3 46	
		1,244 13
Amounts unpaid on by-laws as per treasurer's report	....	148 49
Surplus for the year	....	404 38
		$2,798 07

Assets.

Cash in treasurer's hands at 31st December, 1898...............	$ 798 80	
Taxes due from collector at 31st December, 1898...............	1,034 59	
Drains, amounts due by them—		
Blue creek extension	$118 10	
Butternut creek	317 85	
Casselman creek	151 31	
Johnstone drain	8 11	
McNaughton-Munro drain	114 85	
Paquet-McMahon drain	145 72	
		855 94
D. & W., Fourney award		101 64
Russell Tp., Stevens & McConnell award		7 10
		$2,798 07

1899.

Liabilities.

County rate for 1899 unpaid at 31st December, 1899..........................		$1,255 93
Bills payable—		
Anthony McGowan, dated 1st March, '99, at 5 per cent.	$655 00	....
Interest from 1.3, '99, to 31.12, '99.......................	27 71	
Wm. Steele, dated 7th March, '99, at 5 per cent......	575 00	
Interest from 7.3, '99, to 31.12, '99...........................	22 44	
		1,290 15

Brought forward			2,546 08

Drains, balances to their credit—
Blair-McRae drain, Township Roxborough

owes	$409 05		
Less expenses	64 08		
	$344 97		
Interest from 16.5, '99, at 5 per cent.........	10 77		
		$355 74	
Blue creek	....	72 06	
do extension	....	304 70	
Butternut creek	....	512 14	
Campbell-Adams drain	....	138 21	
McNaughton-Munro drain	....	131 30	
Steel-McElheran drain, due from Rox-			
borough	$369 96		
Less amount at debit	368 33		
		1 63	
Whissel creek	....	1 96	
			1,517 74
Deposits on contracts, R. Fleming		$ 5 00	
Jas. Steele		10 00	
W. J. McElheran		20 00	
M. J. Lazette		50 00	
A. O. McMillan		100 00	
T. & J. Gagnon		450 00	
Interest on last from 10.4, '99, to 31.12, '99......................		14 50	
			$649 50
Amounts due contractors—			
T. & J. Gagnon on Butternut		$400 00	
Blue creek extension		100 00	
Payne River & B. C.		200 00	
		700 00	
S. S. No. 16 not paid until 24.3, '00..		33 50	
John Morrison, salary as collector for 1899		60 00	
Amounts unpaid on by-laws as per treasurer's report		65 25	
Payne River & B. C. not distributed			$493 30
			$6,065 37
Surplus for the year			160 11
			$6,225 48

Assets.

Cash in treasurer's hands at 31st December, 1899			$2,166 12
Balance of taxes due from collector 31.12, '99			2,060 36
Drains, amounts due by them—			
Casselman		$268 31	
Gagnon		31 50	
Johnstone		19 61	
McIntyre-Lagrove		140 50	
Pacquet-McMahon		147 22	
Payne River & B. C.	$1,036 66		
Less Govt. grant	493 30		
		543 36	
			1,150 50
McEwan award, as per resolution of council,			
25.11, '99	....	65 65	
Roxborough, due to Butternut creek	$358 31		
Less their costs	22 75		
Interest from 3.12, '99	1 49		
		337 05	

Cambridge Township, due to Butternut creek...	....	57 25
Roxborough Township due Steele-McElheran...	$396 31	
Less their costs	26 37	
	$369 94	
Interest	5 20	
		375 14
Roxborough Township, their share of expenses of deputation to Toronto *re* Govt. assistance to Payne R. & B. C....	13 41	
		$6,225 48

1900.

Liabilities.

County rate for 1900 unpaid		$1,154 78
Bills payable—		
Frank Charlebois, dated 19th Sept., 1900, at 6 per cent.	$300 00	
Interest from 19.9, '00, to 31.12, '00............................	5 20	
Sam. Cameron, dated 28th Sept., 1900, at 6 per cent...	700 00	
Interest from 28.9, '00, to 31.12, '00	10 50	
John A. Cockburn, dated 19th Sept., 1900, at 6 per cent.	200 00	
Interest from 19.9, '00, to 31.12, '00........................	3 50	
John A. Cockburn, dated 19th Sept., 1900 at 6 per cent.	1,000 00	
Interest from 19.9, '00, to 31.12, '00 ....'.	17 40	
Anthony McGowan, dated 1st March, 1899, at 5 per cent.	665 00	
Interest from 1.3, '99, to 31.12, '00	60 96	
John Currie, Sr., dated 15th Sept., 1900, at 6 per cent.	500 00	
Interest from 15.9, '00, to 31.12, '00	8 35	
		$3,471 31
Debentures due and unpaid—		
No. 1, Steele-McElheran	$ 50 24	
No. 1, McIntyre-Lagrove	102 74	
		152 98

This last should have been put on the collector's roll for 1900 to provide for the debentures falling due 1st January, 1901, but was omitted.

Drains, amounts to their credit—		
Blue Creek	$ 72 06	
Blue Creek extension	22 10	
Butternut	14 09	
Campbell-Adams	138 21	
		246 46
Public schools unpaid in 1900	....	144 63
Deposits on contracts, W. J. McElheran	$ 20 00	
T. & J. Gagnon on Butternut......	300 00	
do on Blue Cr. ex.	50 00	
		370 00
Roxborough Tp. due on Blair-McRae drain	$344 97	
Interest from 16.5, '99, to 31.12, '00, at 5 per cent............	28 02	
		372 99
Amounts paid on by-laws		811 77
Finch amount retained to meet garnishee		109 08
		$6,834 00

Assets.

Cash in treasurer's hands at 31st December, 1900	$ 102 53	
Amount due from collector at 31st December, 1900	1,771 45	
Drains, amounts due by them—		
Blue Creek extension	....	
Int. Casselman creek	$ 61 35	
Casselman	268 31	
Finch sewer	53 53	
Foley creek	45 58	
Herbert drain	28 23	
Johnstone	19 61	
McNaughton-Munro	45 02	
Paquet-McMahon	177 72	

7 M. A.

Payne River & B. C.	1,733 31	
Stark creek	1 25	
Steele-McElheran	407 26	
Stephenson	40 70	
Whissel	28 04	
		61 35
		2,858 06
Roxborough Tp. due on Steele-McElheran	$396 31	
Less their costs	26 37	
	$369 94	
Int. from 18.9, '99, to 31.12, '00	23 85	
		393 29
Roxborough Tp. due on Butternut..................	358 31	
Less their costs	22 75	
	335 56	
Int. from 3.12, '99, to 31.12, '00	18 29	
		353 85
Roxborough Tp., Payne River and B. C. share of		
expenses re Govt. grant	$13 41	
Int. from 5.11, '99, to 31.12, '00	74	
		14 15
Cambridge Tp., Butternut creek		57 25
		$5,551 08
Int. Casselman creek		61 35
Deficit for the year		1,221 57
		$6,834 00

$6,834 00

1901.

Liabilities.

County rate of 1901 unpaid at 31st December, 1901............................		$1,149 20
Bills payable—		
Frank Charlebois, dated 15th Oct., '01, at 6 per cent...	$600 00	
Int. from 15.10, '01, to 31.12, '01	7 50	
Frank Charlebois, dated 19th Sept., '00, at 6 per cent...	300 00	
Int. from 19.9, '00, to 31.12, '01	23 20	
John Currie, Sr., dated 15th Sept., '00, at 6 per cent...	500 00	
Int. from 15.8, '01,, to 31.12, '01	8 75	
John Currie, Sr., dated 15th Oct., '01, at 6 per cent...	200 00	
Int. from 15.10, '01, to 31.12, '01	2 50	
Sam. Cameron, 28th Sept, '00, at 6 per cent............	700 00	
Int. from 28.9, '00, to 31.12, '01	52 50	
J. A. Cockburn, dated 19th Sept., '00, at 6 per cent...	200 00	
Int. from 19.9, '00, to 31.12, '01	15 40	
Thos. Fleming, dated 25th March, '01, at 6 per cent...	400 00	
Int. from 25.3, '01, to 31.12, '01	1 80	
Thos. Fleming, dated 17th May, '01, at 6 per cent...	250 00	
Int. from 17.5, '01, to 31.12, '01	9 38	
Robt. Meldrum, dated 29th Oct.. '01, at 6 per cent...	700 00	
Int. from 20.10, '01, to 31.12, '01	7 00	
Anthony McGowan, dated 1st March, '99, at 5 per cent.	665 00	
Int. from 1.3, '00, to 31.12, '01	4 21	
Victor Beehler, dated 2nd March, '01, at 5 per cent...	800 00	
Int. from 2.3, '01, to 31.12, '01	33 6?	
Chas. Pratt. dated 25th March, '01, at 6 per cent......	300 00	
Int. from 25.3, '01, to 31.12, '01.............................	13 50	
		$5,900 60
Deposits on contracts, H. Bingham	$225 00	
J. H. Fetterley	250 00	
do	250 00	
Phil Empey	125 00	
	....	850 00

7a M. A.

Drains, balances to their crerit—

Blair-McRae drain due Roxborough	$409 05	
Less our costs	61 08	
	$344 97	
Int. from 15.4, '99, to 31.12, '01..............................	45 27	
	$390 24	
Blue creek	62 56	
Butternut balance due from Roxborough... $335 56		
Less at debit of drain 143 71		
	191 85	
Campbell-Adams	138 21	
Gregnon	2 00	
Herbert	3 13	
Whissel	268 74	
		$1,056 73

Debentures due but unpaid in 1901—

No. 1, Whissel	$245 58	
No. 1, Herbert	63 85	
No. 1, Gagnon ....:	57 15	
No. 2, Steele-McElheran	50 24	
No. 4, Roxborough Payne River	55 16	
No. 4, Blue creek	194 88	
No. 4, Payne River & B. C.	215 10	
No. 6, Johnstone	426 32	
		1,308 28
King Bridge Co., for Berwick iron bridge	....	1,193 00
Amounts unpaid on by-laws	....	1,111 84
Drainage and law costs *re* Ault and Empey suits		308 00
Roxborough Tp. *re* Lalonde drain, due 26th Oct., '01........	$1,102 00	
Int. from 16.10, '01, to 31.12, '01, at 5 per cent........	11 78	
	$1,113 78	
Less amount due Finch	45 58	
		1,068 20
D. P. Cameron, salary as collector for 1901		60 00
Empey costs		9 73
		$14,005 85

Assets.

Cash in treasurer's hands at 31st December, 1901		$ 251 45
Amount due collector for 1901		3,298 53
Drain amounts due by them—		
Blue creek extension	$617 50	
Casselman	{ 61 35	
	{ 268 31	
Finch sewer	234 23	

$53.53 of this amount was marked.paid in 1900, but the amount is not entered in the cash book. $180.70, the balance, was transferred to general account, but I can find no order of council for this.

Foley creek	157 20	
Johnstone	24 61	
Lagrove-McIntyre at cr............................ $1,298 38		
Less at dr.. 858 41		
Leaving at cr.................................... 439 97		
There stood at the contractor's dr........ 1,533 52		
Which would leave at dr..................... 1,098 55		
And two assessments were collected but		
not credited 205 48		
Leaving at debit of the drain	893 07	

McNaughton-Munro		47 02	
Paquet-McMahon		177 72	
Payne River & B. C.		859 76	
Stark		209 68	
Steele-McElheran at debit	$386 85		
Due from Roxborough	369 94		
		16 91	
Stephenson		1,407 24	
			4,913 25

The amount of $726.38 was paid by Winchester on 28th Nov., 1902, and Russell paid $35.43 on 20th April, 1904, but these amounts are not specified in the Engineer's estimate in the by-law. They appear to be included in the above amount of $1,407.24.

Roxborough Tp., Steel-McElheran		$369 94	
Int. from 18.9, '99, to 31.12, '01		43 85	
		$413 79	
do Butternut		$335 56	
do 3.12, '99, to 31.12, '01		34 95	
		370 51	
do Payne River & B. C.		$870 05	
do 24.9, '01, to 31.12, '01		11 78	
		881 83	
			1,666 13
			$10,129 36
Interest Casselman creek			61 35
Assessments under Lalonde drainage by-laws			1,102 00
			$11,262 71
Deficit			2,713 14
			$14,005 85

1902.

Liabilities.

County rate for 1902 unpaid at 31st December, 1902			$1,205 20
Bills payable—			
Anthony McGowan, dated 1st March, '99, at 5 per cent.	$665 00		
Int. from 1.3, '99, to 31.12, '92	127 46		
Frank Charlebois, dated 19th Sept., '00, at 6 per cent.	300 00		
Int. from 19.3 '02, to 31.12, '02	14 00		
Frank Charlebois, dated 16th Oct., '01, at 6 per cent.	600 00		
Int. from 15.3, '02, to 31.12, '02	28 50		
J. A. Cockburn, dated 19th Sept., '00, at 6 per cent.	200 00		
Int. from 19.12, '02, to 31.12, '02	35		
Sam. Cameron, dated 28th Sept., '00, at 6 per cent.	700 00		
Int. from 28.9, '02, to 31.12, '02	10 50		
Victor Beehler, dated 2nd March, '01, at 5 per cent...	800 00		
Int. from 2.3, '01, to 31.12, '02	73 33		
Chas. Pratt, dated 25th March, '01, at 6 per cent...	300 00		
Int. from 25.12, '01, to 31.12, '02	18 37		
John Currie, Sr., dated 15th Sept., '00, at 6 per cent.	500 00		
Int. from 15.9, '02, to 31.12, '02	8 75		
John Currie, Sr., dated 15th Oct., '01, at 6 per cent.	200 00		
Int. from 15.10, '02, to 31.12, '02	2 50		
Robt. Meldrum, dated 29th Oct., '01, at 6 per cent.	700 00		
Int. from 29.10, '02, to 31.12, '02	7 00		
			$5,255 76
Debentures due but unpaid in 1902—			
No. 1, Foley creek	$273 69		
No. 1, Lalonde	99 07		
No. 6, Paquet-McMahon	205 22		
No. 1, Stark	160 29		
No. 1, Stephenson	217 77		
No. — U. S. S., No. 17	19 91		
No. 6, Whissel	453 48		
			1,429 43

Drains, balance at their credit—

Blue creek	$ 61 56	
Butternut	149 83	
Gregnon	2 00	
Hebert	3 13	
Dunbar, due Osnabruck $665 30		
Less paid this year 42 00		
	623 30	
McIntyre-Lagrove, two assessments collected	205 48	
Payne River & B. C.	19 95	
		1,065 25
Deposits on contracts, Fetterley	$250 00	
do do	250 00	
do Phil. Empey	135 00	
do Wm. Johnstone	39 20	
		664 20
P. D. Cameron, salary as collector		60 00
Amounts on by-laws due and unpaid		831 97
		$10,511 81

Assets.

Cash in treasurer's hands at 31st December, 1902	$ 29 52	$ 29 52
Balance of taxes uncollected	2,477 40	2,477 40
Drains, amounts due by them—		
Blair-McRae	....	
Blue creek extension	761 16	
Casselman	{ 268 31	
	{ 61 35	

$61.35 of interest struck off by Judge Liddell in '05 not included in above amount of $268.31.

Foley creek	137 84	
Johnstone	38 61	
Lalonde	32 83	
McNaughton-Munro	47 02	
McIntyre-Lagrove	139 35	
Paquet-McMahon	230 82	
Dunbar, assessments under by-law	773 80	
Moriarty	280 25	
Steele-McElheran	49 71	
Stark	62 20	
Stephenson	527 72	
Whissel	1,311 95	
Finch sewer	258 83	

This is a very doubtful asset owing to the proceedings having been taken under The Municipal Drainage Act, and parties allowed to strike off their names afterwards, which required permission from the County Judge.

		4,920 40
Osnabruck, *re* Foley creek construction............................		111 83
Int. on Casselman creek		61 35
Deficit for the year		7,539 15
		2,911 81
		$10,511 81

This is the only year between 1898 and 1905 in which all the notes signed by the Reeve during the year were paid during that year.

1903.

Liabilities.

County rates for 1903 unpaid		$1,330 77
Bills payable—		
Wm. Armstrong, dated 5th Sept., '03, at 5 per cent...	$882 00	
Int. from 5.9, '03, to 31.12, '03	14 60	
Anthony McGowan, dated 1st March, 1899, at 5 per cent.	665 00	

Int. from 1.3, '00, to 31.12, '03 .... 160 70
Frank Charlebois, dated 19th Sept., '00, at 6 per cent. 300 00
Int. from 15.3, '03, to 15.6, '03, at 6 per cent., then
   5 per cent. 11 60
Frank Charlebois, dated 15th Oct., '01, at 6 per cent... 600 00
Int. from 15.3, '03, to 15.6, '03, at 6 per cent., then
   5 per cent. 23 75
John A. Cockburn, dated 19th Oct., '00, at 6 per cent. 200 00
Int. from 19.12, '02, to 15.6, '03, at 6 per cent., then
   5 per cent. 12 75
Sam. Cameron, dated 28th Sept., '00, at 6 per cent... 700 00
Int. from 28.9, '02, to 15.6, '03, at 6 per cent., then
   5 per cent. 47 50
J. R. Crysler, dated 16th April, '03, at 6 per cent... 800 00
Int. from 16.4, '03, to 15.6, '03, at 6 per cent., then
   5 per cent. 29 66
Thos. Fleming, dated 8th August, '03, at 5 per cent... 200 00
Int. from 8.8, to 31.12, '03 .... 7 90
Robt. Meldrum, dated 19th Oct., '03, at 5 per cent... 700 00
Int. from 28.10, '03, to 31.12, '03 .... 8 85
Robt. Meldrum, dated 27th May, '05, at 5 per cent... 200 00
Int. from 27.5, '03, to 31.12, '03 .... 5 80
Felix Behler, dated 20th April, '03, at 5 per cent... 1,400 00
Int. from 20.4, '03, to 31.12, '03 .... 49 60
John Wright, dated 23rd July, '03, at 5 per cent... 200 00
Int. from 23.7, '03, to 31.12, '03 .... 4 38
                                                               $7,224 09

Debentures due and unpaid in 1903—

Blue creek extension	No. 5	$162 65
Butternut	No. 5	314 74
Gagnon	No. 3	57 15
Hebert	No. 3	63 85
Johnstone	No. 7	426 32
Paquet-McMahon	No. 7	205 22
Payne River & B. C.	No. 2	89 86
Whissel	No. 7	453 48
Campbell-Adams	No. 7	155 63
Blue creek	No. 6	194 88
Casselman	No. 7	166 02
Foley	No. 2	273 69
Lagrove-McIntyre	No. 4	102 74
Lalonde	No. 2	99 07
McNaughton-Munro	No. 5	71 31
Roxborough, Payne River	No. 6	55 16
Payne River & B. C.	No. 6	215 10
Stark	No. 2	160 29
Steele-McElheran	No. 4	50 24
Whissel	No. 3	245 58

                                                                3,780 75

Public schools, S. S. No. 6 .... $399 60
              S. S. No. 11 .... 302 14
              Russel Separate No. 8 .... 6 00
                                                              707 74

Drains, for amounts due to them—

Blue creek .... $ 61 56
Casselman, Sutherland & Foley drain 55 00
Butternut creek 149 83
Gregnon drain 2 00
Hebert drain 3 13
Osnabruck, due to Dunbar drain 204 24
McIntyre-Lagrove, two assessments collected but not
   credited 205 48
Payne River & B. C. 19 95
                                                              701 19

Deposits on contracts, M. McMillan	107 50	
do do	107 50	
do J. H. Fetterley	250 00	
do Wm. Johnstone	39 20	
		504 20
Amounts due and unpaid on by-laws		627 86
		$14,876 60

Assets.

Cash on hand at 31st Dec., 1903		$ 54 35
Amount due from collector for 1902	$ 140 09	
do 1903	2,550 21	
		2,690 30
Drains, for amounts due to them—		
Blue creek extension, amending by-law...	$884 68	
Less Judge Liddell's decision	611 50	
		233 18
Blair-McRae drain	....	
Int. Casselman creek	61 35	
Casselman drain	268 31	
Dunbar drain	68 71	
Finch sewer	283 43	
Foley creek, including amount due from Osnabruck...	1,340 29	
Johnstone drain	285 42	
Lalonde drain	155 97	
McNaughton-Munro drain	47 02	
McIntyre-Lagrove drain	143 60	
Moriarty drain	1,529 44	
Paquet-McMahon drain	177 72	
Smirl-McConnell drain	203 56	
Stark creek	592 75	
Steele-McElheran drain	49 71	
Stephenson drain, including amounts due from Winchester and Russell	707 76	
Whissel creek	1,233 62	
Wiseman drain	15 23	
Johnstone, upper portion	$ 55 46	
		{ 61 35
		{ $10,135 83
Osnabruck, due on construction Foley creek	$111 83	
Interest from 13.8, '01, to 31.12, '03, 5 per cent....	14 55	
		126 38
Lumber in stock		211 50
		{ $10,473 71
		{ 61 35
Deficit for the year		4,341 54
		$14.876 60

1904.

Liabilities.

County rates for 1904 unpaid at 31st Dec., 1904		$1,766 76
Bills payable—		
Robert Meldrum, dated 5th Sept., '03, at 5 per cent.	$882 00	
Int. from 5.11, '04, to 31.12, '04	5 19	
Robt. Meldrum, dated 27th Jan., '04, at 5 per cent...	200 00	
Int. from 27.11, '04, to 31.12, '04	1 17	
Robt. Meldrum, dated 23rd July, '03, at 5 per cent...	200 00	
Int. from 23.11, '04, to 31.12, '04	1 17	
Robt. Meldrum, dated 29th Oct., '01, at 5 per cent...	700 00	
Int. from 29.10, '04, to 31.12, '04	6 04	
Robt. Meldrum, dated 27th May. '03, at 5 per cent...	200 00	
Int. from 27.11, '04, to 31.12, '04	93	
Robt. Meldrum, dated 26th May, '04, at 5 per cent...	800 00	

Int. from 26.12, '04, to 31.12, '04		54
Robt. Meldrum, dated 30th Jan., '04, at 5 per cent...		300 00
Int. from 30.11, '04, to 31.12, '04		1 27
Sam. Doran, dated 31st August, '04, at 5 per cent...		400 00
Int. from 31.8, '04, to 31.12, '04		6 33
D. N. McLean, dated 30th Jan., '04, at 5 per cent...		200 00
Int. from 30.1, '04, to 31.12, '04		9 17
John Doran, dated 22nd Feb., '04, at 5 per cent......		400 00
Int. from 22.2, '04, to 31.12, '04		17 09
John Doran, dated 22nd June, '04, at 5 per cent......		100 00
Int. from 31.8, '04, to 31.12, '04		2 63
John Doran, dated 30th Aug., '04, at 5 per cent......		250 00
Int. from 31.8, '04, to 31.12, '04		4 21
John Ruddy, dated 26th Jan., '04, at 5 per cent......		500 00
Int. from 26.11, '04, to 31.12, '04		2 38
Robt. Armstrong, dated 22nd June, '04, at 5 per cent.		300 00
Int. from 22.6, '04, to 31.12, '04		7 89
Anthony McGowan, dated 1st March, '99, at 5 per cent.		665 00
Int. from 1.3, '99, to 31.12, '04		194 02
John A. Cockburn, dated 19th Sept., '00, at 5 per cent.		200 00
Int. from 31.5, '04, to 31.12, '04		4 70
Sam. Cameron, dated 28th Sept., '00, at 5 per cent...		700 00
Int. from 28.9, '04, to 31.12, '04		9 05
Thos. Fleming, dated 8th Aug., '03, at 5 per cent...		200 00
Int. from 8.8, '03, to 31.12, '04		13 97
Thos. Fleming, dated 12th Feb., '04, at 5 per cent...:		1,200 00
Int. from 12.2, '04, to 31.12, '04		52 93
Thos. Fleming, dated 20th April, '04, at 5 per cent...		275 00
Int. from 20.4, '04, to 31.12, '04		9 60
Thos. Fleming, dated 23rd May, '04, at 5 per cent...		1,000 00
Int. from 23.5, '04· to 31.12, '04		29 31
Thos. Fleming, dated 29th July, '04, at 5 per cent...		100 00
Int. from 29.7, '04, to 31.12, '04		2 12
Thos. Fleming, dated 26th Aug., '04, at 5 per cent...:		500 00
Int. from 26.8, '04, to 31.12, '04		8 69
Thos. Fleming, dated 31st Aug., '04, at 5 per cent...		150 00
Int. from 31.8, '04, to 31.12, '04		2 50
J. C. Duhamd, dated 20th April, '04, at 5 per cent...		1,400 00
Int. from 20.6, '04, to 31.12, '04		37 24
John Smirl, dated 29th July, '04, at 5 per cent..........		200 00
Int. from 29.7, '04, to 31.12, '04		4 24
C. B. Pratt. dated 27th Jan., '04, at 5 per cent......		500 00
Int. from 27.1, '04, to 31.12, '04		23 15
John Wright, dated 20th April, '04, at 5 per cent...		425 00
Int. from 20.4, '04, to 31.12, '04		14 84
Victor Beehler, dated 11th July, '04, at 5 per cent....		200 00
Int. from 11.7, '04· to 31.12, '04		4 74
V. Beehler, dated 11th July, '04, at 5 per cent........		800 00
Int. from 11.7, '04, to 31.12, '04		18 95
V. Beehler, dated 8th Aug., '04, at 5 per cent........		300 00
Int. from 8.8, '04, to 31.12, '04		5 95
		——————— $14,749 01

Debentures on collector's roll 1904, paid 1905—

No. 6 Butternut	$314 74
No. 6 McNaughton-Munro	71 31
No. 8 Casselman	166 02
No. 8 Campbell-Adams	155 63
No. 7 Payne River & B. C.	215 10
No. 7 Blue creek	194 88
No. 4 Whissel improvement	245 58
No. 5 Steel-McElheran	50 24
No. 6 Blue creek extension	162 65
No. 9 Johnstone Main	426 32
No. 5 McIntyre-Lagrove	102 74
No. 3 Payne River & B. C., amending	89 86
No. 3 S. S. No. 3	130 00
do Coupons	26 00
No. 3 Stark creek	160 29

No. 3 Foley ..	273 69	
No. 3 Lalonde	99 07	
No. 3 Stephenson	217 77	
		3,101 89

Schools, due but unpaid in 1904—

Government grant S. S. No. 17	$ 35	
School debentures	66 60	
		66 95
D. P. Cameron, salary as assessor	....	60 00
Amounts under by-laws and orders not paid in 1904........	....	1,108 41

Drains, for amounts to their credit—

Blue creek	$ 61 56	
Butternut creek	81 03	
Casselman, Sutherland & Foley private drain	31 00	
Foley drain, T. Foley farm crossing	12 50	
Dunbar drain, due from Osnabruck under by-law No. 6, 1903	204 24	
Fournier drain, Wm. Johnston estate	39 20	
Gregnon drain	2 00	
Hebert drain	3 13	
Lalonde drain, for amount due Roxborough as per referee's decision ...... $446 10 Less amount of our costs to date 167 52	278 58	
McIntyre-Lagrove drain	205 48	
Payne River & B. C.	7 95	
Wiseman drain, M. McMillan for his deposit	135 00	
		1,061 67
Hamilton Bridge Co.		620 00
		$22,534 69

Assets.

Cash in treasurer's hands at 31st Dec., 1904	.	$2,202 03
D. P. Cameron, collector for 1903	$ 114 16	
do 1904	4,498 34	
		4,612 50

Drains, for amounts due by them—

Blue creek extension	$ 64 33	
Casselman	288 31	
Finch sewer	283 43	
Foley creek	1,037 43	
do due by Osnabruck	173 31	
Johnstone drain	1,151 50	
do upper portion	117 38	
McNaughton-Munro drain	59 50	
McIntyre-Lagrove drain	143 60	
Moriarty drain	707 05	
do due by Winchester	160 42	
Paquet-McMahon drain	271 32	
Smirl-McConnell drain	2,780 86	
Stark creek	726 25	
Steele-McElhern drain	100 90	
Stephenson drain	586 84	
do due by Winchester	425 20	
do Russell	30 00	
Whissel creek	1,191 73	
do do due by Cambridge	78 89	
Wiseman drain	278 15	
		10,665 40
Deficit for the year	.	5,063 76
		$22,534 69

1905.

Liabilities.

Balance due treasurer			$ 24 55
Drains, for amounts due by them—			
Blue creek	$ 61 06		
Blue creek extension, costs in appeal as per Judge			
Rankin's decision	43 40		
Butternut creek	141 33		
Dunbar drain due Osnabruck	204 24		
Gregnon drain	2 00		
Hebert drain	3 13		
Payne River & B. C.	7 95		
Smirl-McConnell drain	123 31		
Whissel creek, W. B. Lawson's costs in appeal as per			
Judge Rankin's decision	94 19		
		631 21	
D. D. Cameron, salary as collector		95 00	
County rate for 1905 unpaid		1,740 97	
M. McMillan, balance of deposit re Payne River bridges and balance			
of contract as per Engineer's report		111 16	
Public school moneys due but unpaid in 1905		1,960 80	
Separate school, Russell		6 00	
Hamilton Bridge Co.		2,768 00	
Gravel and hauling, Mannion bridge, 1905		70 65	
do Station Road, Crysler		118 00	
Debentures due but unpaid in 1905—			
Butternut drain No. 7.....................................	$314 74		
Casselman creek No. 9.....................................	166 01		
Foley creek No. 4.....................................	273 69		
Lalonde drain No. 4.....................................	99 07		
McNaughton-Munro No. 7.....................................	71 31		
Stark creek No. 4.....................................	160 29		
Steele-McElhern No. 6.....................................	50 24		
Stephenson No. 4.....................................	217 77		
Whissel improvement No. 5.....................................	245 58		
No. 4 S. S. No. 3	130 00		
Coupons	19 50		
		1,748 20	
Bills payable—			
John Doran, dated 22nd Feb., '04, at 5 per cent......	$400 00		
Int. from 22.8, '05, to 31.12, '05	7 20		
John Doran, dated 30th Aug., '04, at 5 per cent......	250 00		
Int. from 22.8, '05, to 31.12, '05	4 16		
D. E. Seese, dated 1st March, '05, at 5 per cent......	300 00		
Int. from 1.3, '05, to 31.12, '05, at 5 per cent........	12 50		
D. E. Seese, dated 27th June, '05, at 5 per cent......	435 00		
Int. from 27.6, '05, to 31.12, '05	11 16		
W. J. Dey, dated 14th March, '05, at 5 per cent......	430 00		
Int. from 8.11, '05, to 31.12, '05 .....↑................	3 15		
W. J. Deay, dated 8th June, '05, at 5 per cent......	683 89		
Int. from 8.11, '05, to 31.12, '05	5 00		
R. Meldrum, dated 29th Oct., '01, at 5 per cent......	700 00		
Int. from 29.4, '05, to 31.12, '05	23 33		
R. Meldrum, dated 27th May, '03, at 5 per cent......	200 00		
Int. from 27.5, '05, to 31.12, '05	5 95		
R. Meldrum, dated 5th Sept., '03, at 5 per cent......	882 00		
Int. from 5.5, '05, to 31.12, '05	28 80		
R. Meldrum, dated 27.1, '05, at 5 per cent...............	200 00		
Int. from 27.5, '05, to 31.12, '05	5 95		
R. Meldrum, dated 30th Jan., '04, at 5 per cent......	300 00		
Int. from 30.5, '05, to 31.12, '05	8 75		
S. Doran, dated 31st Aug., '04, at 5 per cent........	400 00		
Int. from 31.8, '04, to 31.12, '05	19 20		
John Ruddy, dated 26th Jan., '04, at 5 per cent......	500 00		
Int. from 26.11, '05, to 31.12, '05	2 38		

Anthony McGowan, dated 1st March, '99, at 5 per cent.	665 00
Int. from 31.12, '04, to 31.12, '05	33 25
J. A. Cockburn, dated 19th Sept., '00, at 5 per cent...	200 00
Int. from 31.5, '04, to 31.12, '05	15 83
Sam. Cameron, dated 28th Sept., '00, at 5 per cent...	700 00
Int. from 12.9, '05, to 31.12, '05	10 10
J. C. Duhame, dated 20th April, '03, at 5 per cent...	1,400 00
Int. from 20.6, '05, to 31.12, '05	27 24

                                                                     2,363 17

M. Breyare for land and damages at Swale br...........	....	138 95
Munro Trust	200 00	
Int. on same to 31.12, '05	7 06	

                                                                     207 06

Amounts outstanding under by-law 1.12, '04	18 45
do do 9.1, '05	9 75
do do 21.8, '05	57 00
do do 24.10, '05	61 28
do do 15.12, '05	766 74
do do 15.12, '05	290 80
Thos. Foley for farm crossing Foley creek	12 50
Amounts as per Road Superintendent's certificates, 1905	229 74

Township's portion of drains as per by-law ...	$5,892 02	
Amount of above payable in 1906	923 86	
Being liabilities not presently payable.		

                                                         $19,996 75

Assets.

Balance of taxes due from D. R. Cameron for 1904		$ 100 26	
do D. D. Cameron for 1905		1,638 09	
Drains, amounts due from them—			
Blue creek extension	$ 50 89		
Campbell-Adams	1 00		
Casselman	409 47		
Foley creek	7 55		
do due by Osnabruck	173 31		
Dunbar drain	89		
Johnstone main drain	1,549 82		
do upper portion.......	117 38		
Lalonde drain	265 14		
McNaughton-Munro drain	60 50		
McIntyre-Lagrove	6 77		
Moriarty drain due by Winchester	160 42		
do	10 14		
Paquet-McMahon	114 19		
Payne River & B. C.	17 92		
Stark creek	167 00		
Steele-McElhern drain	101 90		
Stephenson drain due by Winchester......	425 20		
do by Russell	30 00		
Stoney creek	36 52		
Whissel creek	1,242 67		
Wiseman creek	2,670 19		
		7,618 97	
Finch sewer		190 99	
A. McKinnon, offer for bridge timber		21 00	
Ontario Govt. grant for bridges		2,500 00	
Osnabruck share of exp. deputation to Toronto		15 21	
Roxborough do do		13 41	
United Counties lunatics expenses		42 00	
			$12,139 93
Deficit for the year			7,856 82
			$19,996 75

DEBT OF THE TOWNSHIP OF FINCH AS AT 14TH APRIL, 1906.

Liabilities.

Munro Trust	$200 00	
Int. from 1.1, '06, to date	2 74	
		$202 74
Bills payable—		
Sophia C. Dey	$5,000 00	
Int. from 17.1, '06, to date	59 59	
John Doran	400 00	
Int. from 17.1, '06, to date	5 48	
John Doran	250 00	
Int. from 1.1, '06, to date	3 42	
John Smirl	150 00	
Int. from 1.1, '06, to date	2 05	
D. E. Seese	300 00	
Int. from 1.1, '06, to date	4 11	
D. E. Seese	435 00	
Int. from 1.1, '06, to date	5 96	
W. J. Dey	683 89	
Int. from 1.1, '06, to date	9 37	
W. J. Dey	430 00	
Int. from 1.1, '06, to date	5 89	
S. Doran	400 00	
Int. from 1.1, '06, to date	5 48	
D. N. McLean	200 00	
Int. from 1.1, '06, to date	2 74	
John Ruddy	500 00	
Int. from 1.1, '06, to date	6 85	
John Ruddy	400 00	
Int. from 17.1, '06, to date	4 77	
Anthony McGowan	665 00	
Int. from 1.1, '06, to date	9 11	
Sam. Cameron	700 00	
Int. from 1.1, '06, to date	9 59	
J. C. Duhame	1,400 00	
Int. from 1.1, '06, to date	19 18	
H. L. McMillan	400 00	
Int. from 17.1, '06, to date	4 77	
Wm. Steele, Jr.	1,000 00	
Int. from 1.3, '06, to date	6 16	
Morris Servage	400 00	
Int. from 6.3, '06, to date	2 47	
Victor Beehler	2,000 00	
Int. from 17.1, '06, to date	32 84	
D. D. Cameron	300 00	
Int. from 9.3, '06, to date	1 48	
		16,206 20
Drains, for amounts to their credit—		
Blue creek	$ 60 06	
Butternut creek	80 03	
Dunbar drain due to Osnabruck	204 24	
Foley creek, due to T. Foley for farm crossing	12 50	
Gregnon drain	2 00	
Hebert drain	3 13	
Smirl-McConnell drain	183 28	
		645 24
Debentures due but unpaid—		
No. 4 Stephenson drain	$217 77	
No. 4 Foley creek	273 69	
No. 4 Stark creek	160 29	
No. 4 Lalonde drain	99 07	
		750 82

Separate school, Russell			6 00
Amounts due under orders and by-laws of 1905 not yet paid			66 68
Harkness & Milligan, law costs re Blue creek extension appeal as per Judge Rankin's decision			43 40
W. B. Lawson, law costs re Whissel appeal as per Judge Rankin's decision			94 19
			$18,015 27

Assets.

Cash in treasurer's hands		$ 373 78	
Due from D. P. Cameron, collector for 1904	$100 26		
Due from D. D. Cameron, collector for 1905	153 09		
		253 35	
Drains, for amounts due by them—			
Blue creek extension	$ 50 89		
Campbell-Adams drain	1 00		
Casselman drain	408 67		
Dunbar drain	89		
Foley Creek	7 55		
do due by Osnabruck	173 31		
Johnstone Main drain	1,549 82		
do upper portion	117 38		
Lalonde drain	265 14		
McNaughton-Munro drain	60 50		
McIntyre-Lagrove drain	6 77		
Moriarty drain	10 14		
Paquet-McMahon drain	114 19		
Payne River & B. C.	17 92		
Stark creek	167 00		
Steele-McElhern drain	101 90		
Stephenson drain	110 63		
Stoney creek	36 52		
Whissel creek	1,242 17		
Wiseman drain	2,670 19		
		7,112 58	
Finch sewer		190 00	
United Counties		106 25	
A. McKinnon for bridge timber		21 00	
Osnabruck Tp. re Payne River & B. C.		15 21	
Roxborough Tp. do		13 41	
			8,086 57
Net debt			$9,928 70

All of which is respectfully submitted.

The cost of this audit to the municipality of the Township of Finch as per Mr. Adamson's account, was $473.00.

REPORT ON THE POSITION OF THE ACCOUNTS OF THE TOWNSHIP OF ROXBOROUGH WITH THE SURPLUS OR DEFICIT AT THE END OF EACH YEAR, 1897 TO 1904 INCLUSIVE, AND FULL REPORT FOR THE YEAR 1905.

To the Reeve and Council of the Township of Roxborough:

GENTLEMEN,—In accordance with the instructions given me by J. B. Laing, Esq., Provincial Municipal Auditor, I have made a careful audit of the books and vouchers of the Township, from the last Government Audit of 8th Sept., 1897, to the 31st Dec., 1905, and have much pleasure in stating that

I found all the Treasurer's vouchers in perfect order, the only mistakes found being against himself, to correct which I have placed to his credit the sum of $63.97.

My principal work has been the writing up of a Drainage Record book from which the Clerk will in future make the entries on the Collectors' rolls, of the assessments payable under the various drainage by-laws in the Township, which with the number of names to be entered under each are as follows:

Drain.	Number of Interested Parties.
Aux Raisins River	66
Blair-McRae Drain	52
Blair-Shanks "	16
Boundary "	22
Butternut Creek	6
Deslile Drain	15
Dewar "	29
Duff-McMillan Drain	12
Fraser Creek	50
Hart "	86
Henry Drain	24
Monkland Drain	260
Morrison-Munroe	52
McElheran-Munroe	15
McGregor Creek	54
Maclennan Drain	32
McNeil-McDonell	29
McRae-McDonell	52
Macmillan Drain	15
North Branch and Mackintosh Drain	324
Payne River	430
Steele-Hough Drain	35
Steele-McElheran Drain	14
Stewart Creek	56
Tayside "	56
Thompson-Ferguson Drain	54
Upper Moose Creek	127

Total number of names 1,983

The Moose Creek was not entered because the debentures are practically paid off, the last being due this year.

The preparation of this drainage book will, I believe, result in a very considerable saving to the Township, as well as enable the Clerk to get the Collector's rolls prepared in proper time, and assist him to stop what have apparently been serious leaks in the Township finances. To enable him to effect this completely, however, it will be necessary for the Council to instruct the Engineer, or other competent person, to examine and report upon a good many of the assessments, principally in the south-western part of the Township, and particularly the Payne River and Hart Creek. There have been so many and intricate changes in the ownership of the lands, since these were assessed under the by-laws, that it is in many cases impossible to tell who should now be assessed and how much the assessment should be. Had the Drainage Record book been in use from the commencement of the several drains the changes in ownership would have been noted as they occurred, but now a proper report will be required, which can best be furnished by the Township Engineer. In giving the instructions for this it will be well to make them general, as the assessments on some of the other drains will probably require to be looked into.

I would again, respectfully, draw the attention of the Council to the imperative need of furnishing the Clerk and Assessor with plans of the Villages of Avonmore and Moose Creek, so as to enable these to be properly assessed and the taxes due collected. As matters now stand there is a constant annual loss to the Township from the vagueness of the descriptions given in these Villages, while, if the properties were mentioned by lot, this would not occur.

I have also prepared a Debenture book, giving the amounts received from the sale of the several issues of debentures, the date of maturity of the payments, and those already made.

In comparing this with the Drainage Record book, I found that, for the Payne River, five issues of debentures had been made, two of which were under By-law 12 of 1898, which authorized the issue of $13,883.14, $10,500 first being issued on account and $3,300 later. A subsequent By-law No. 26 of 1901, passed as an amending by-law to the Outlet, could not be found, there being no trace of it in either the books or minutes. I obtained a copy from Mr. J. G. Harkness, Barrister, who had drawn the by-law for fifteen annual payments of $83.25 each. Five of these debentures have been paid by the Township, and I beg to recommend that the first of these be placed upon the Collector's roll this year, and one each year in future until the issue is paid off. I have treated the debentures already paid as an asset as at 31st December, 1905.

I have also written up the Municipal Cash book for the years 1903, 1904 and 1905, so that the Treasurer can now continue it and will find it a very material assistance in enabling him and others to see clearly the exact position of Township affairs..

I beg to submit herewith a statement of the Net Debt of the Township as at 31st Dec., 1905, when it was $5,185.90, with approximate estimates of the amount at 31st Dec. in each year for 1897, 1898, 1899, 1900, 1901, 1902, 1903 and 1904. The amounts are sufficiently exact for all practical purposes, and the obtaining of exact data would have entailed a very considerable amount of work, which I did not consider myself warranted in spending the time to obtain.

If the Council will carry out the above suggestions as to the assessments on the drains and plans of the Villages, there is no reason why the small indebtedness of the Township cannot be paid off gradually without going to the expense of issuing debentures, but I would take this opportunity of drawing the attention of the Council to the unfortunate results which arise from striking the general rate of taxation too low, so that it will not produce the amount required to carry on the business of the Township, and consequently the indebtedness is increased instead of diminished.

All which is respectfully submitted.

J. R. ADAMSON,

Auditor.

Moose Creek, Ont., 24th July, 1906.

GENERAL.

Net Debt of the Township of Roxborough as at 31st December, 1905.

Liabilities.

Amount due the treasurer	$ 4,164 37
Bills payable, current	5,000 00
Interest thereon to 31st December, 1905	128 79
Balance of county rate for 1905 unpaid	2,759 51
Balance of school taxes unpaid	3,639 19
Assessments placed on roll of 1905 to provide for debentures maturing 1906	8,735 28
M. Maloney, salary as collector, 1905	30 00
Alex. Cummings, do	30 00
Unpaid under by-laws	714 17
C. C. Munro, salary as assessor and expenses	82 46
	$25,283 77

Assets.

Balance of taxes for 1905	$24,981 16	
Less collected in 1905	5,300 00	
		$19,681 16
Debentures paid by township, and to be charged to the interested parties—		
Payne No. 5, T debentures of $83.25 each............	416 25	
		20,097 41
		$5,185 36

Contingent Liability.

Drainage debentures not presently payable—

					Township portion.
Aux Raisins River	28 at	$113 26	each	$3,171 28	$ 16 18
Blair-McRae	9 at	298 31	"	2,684 79	30 74
" Amending	11 at	64 68	"	711 48	....
Blair-Shanks	10 at	124 53	"	1,245 30	1 91
Boundary	11 at	72 59	"	798 49	3 69
Delisle, last of three provided for............		....		....	....
Dewar, debentures not yet sold		....		....	16 65
Duff-McMillan, digging		....		....	3 26
Fraser Creek	6 at	585 10	"	3,513 60	116 03
Hart Creek	8 at	150 53	"	1,204 24	12 17
Henry	14 at	185 56	"	2,597 84	27 42
Lalonde	10 at	379 79	"	3,797 90	234 13
" Amending	13 at	323 14	"	4,200 82	....
McElheran	8 at	88 36	"	706 88	30 44
" Amending	7 at	96 79	"	677 53	....
McGregor Creek	2 at	188 23	"	376 46	1 52
North Branch & McIntosh.....................	15 at	611 89	"	9,178 35	41 26
Maclennan	7 at	107 54	",	752 78	10 51
Macmillan	8 at	89 49	"	719 92	20 77
" Amending. Last of five provided for.					
McNeil-McDonell	13 at	126 49	"	1,644 37	15 90
McRae	8 at	287 75	"	2,301 00	22 76
" Amending		....		1,100 00	....
Monkland	15 at	688 69	"	10,330 35	72 39
Morrison-Munroe	17 at	283 71	"	4,823 07	19 83
Moose Creek, Upper	1 at	538 95	"	538 95	21 31
Payne, Main	6 at	944 39	"	5,866 34	104 95
Outlet	8 at	441 08	"	3,528 64	....
No. 2 Main	9 at	296 68	"	2,670 12	....
Main Am.	3 at	74 90	"	224 70	....
Outlet Am.	9 at	83 25	"	749 25	....
Steele-Hough	13 at	202 51	"	2,632 63	6 51
Steele-McElheran	9 at	89 02	"	721 18	2 54

Stewart Creek .... 8 at	348 19	each	2,785 52	80 51
" Am. .... 9 at	202 05	"	1,818 45	....
Tayside Creek. Last of 10 provided for.				
Thompson-Ferguson .... 9 at	230 33	"	2,072 97	23 78
" Am. ....11 at	125 10	"	1,376 10	....
			$82,335 29	$937 16
S. S. No. 19, Monkland .... 4 at	61 65	"	246 60	
Total			$82,581 89	

STATEMENT OF RECEIPTS AND EXPENDITURES FOR THE YEAR 1905.

1905.

Jan.	19.—To H. M. Campbell on account taxes for 1904......		$ 470 00	
Jan.	30.— " "	......	430 00	
Feb.	26.— " "	......	718 00	
March	22.— ..	......	132 49	
April	26.— "	......	218 42	
May	1.— ::	......	200 00	
May	30.— ..	......	7,927 42	
July	24.— .. "	......	100 00	
Nov.	10.— " "	......	523 00	
Dec.	30.— " in full for 1904.			
	Less exemptions $310 44			
	Non-resident 27 40			
			567 57	
				$11,336 90
Jan.	9.—E. Maloney on account for taxes for 1904......		$ 100 00	
Jan.	17.— " "	......	147 00	
Jan.	20.— " "	......	575 00	
Feb.	6.— "	......	990 13	
Feb.	28.— " .	......	171 00	
Feb.	28.— "	......	1,754 24	
March	18.— ..	......	526 61	
April	12.— "	......	380 00	
April	26.— "	......	129 79	
May	10.— "	......	362 58	
June	15.— "	......	93 50	
July	24.— " ..	......	314 16	
July	24.— .. "	......	68 40	
Nov.	13.— " in full for 1904.			
	Less exemptions $203 74			
	Non-resident 83 82		69 31	
				5,681 72
Dec.	2.—To E. Maloney on account taxes for 1905......		$1,100 00	
Dec.	5.— " "	......	800 00	
Dec.	9.— " "	......	1,900 00	
			3,800 00	
Dec.	16.—To A. Cumming "	......	....	1,500 00
Dec.	30.—To county treasurer, non-resident taxes.............	......		140 03
June	25.—To R. H. Coleman, statute labor commuted......		$ 3 75	
June	25.—To C. P. R. "	......	3 50	
July	24.—To C. A. R. "	......	5 25	
				12 50
June	25.—To A. E. Fetterley, share of licenses.................		$274 17	
Dec.	16.— " "	....	151 67	
				425 84
Jan.	3.—To A. D. Cummings for fines		$ 32 00	
Nov.	10.— " "	....	15 00	
Dec.	9.—To J. K. McRae for fines		2 00	
				49 00
Subsidies and refunds— .				
Ontario Government for north branch drain...	$ 68 99			
" Hart Creek	6 75			
			$ 75 74	
Jas. McDonald, refund p. by-law			15 00	
				90 74

8 M. A.

Receipts from loans—
Miss Jessie Munroe on note	$ 50 00	
J. W. Crawford "	300 00	
Neil McLean "	1,200 00 .	
		1,550 00

Miscellaneous—
Dividend from liquidators of Ville Marie Bank	$ 73 53	73 53
Timber on road allowance—		
David Campbell	7 25	
A. Barrett	2 00	
D. McKercher	6 00	
		15 25
Gravel, John Campbell	$ 1 50	
John McPhail	48	
		1 98
		$24,677 49

Dec.   31.—Amount due the treasurer at this date 4,164 37

$28,841 86

Expenditure.

Roads and bridges	$ 2,275 98
Award ditches	659 14
Debentures retired	8,543 97
Refund of taxes	44 78
Charity	218 50
Printing	141 08
Law costs	244 97
County rates	1,718 69
Public schools	8,134 11
Loans and interest	1,683 52
Board of Health	61 50
Municipal Government	1,204 34
Miscellaneous	55 80
Avonmore Police Village	446 00
	$25,432 88

Jan.   1.—Amount due the treasurer 3,408 98

$28,841 86

Details of Expenditure.

Roads and Bridges.

D. G. Morrison, repairs to bridge lot 5, con. 1	$ 1 50
Alex. Robertson, travelling 9 mile road 18 and 19/4	50 00
Jas. McDonald, ditching 9 mile road C and D/1	14 25
Peter McLeod, ditching Finch boundary	15 00
Dan. McDonald, for gravel	80
Francis Richard, ditching	1 50
Alex. Robertson, gravelling	56 50
Dugald McGillivray, removing stones from Finch boundary	10 07
Luke Lalonde, filling washout on headline con. 6 and 7	18 00
John McDonald, for bridge on headline 23/4 and 5	5 00
Donald Grant, for gravel	6 60
Robert Wilson, for wire fence	8 00
Jas. D. McIntosh, damage from water on headline	15 00
Jos. Chartrand, ditching headline con. 7 and 8	8 00
Isidore Champagne, repairing culvert	8 00
Jas. Cumming, repairing road 1 and A/6	16 50
F. D. McLeod, ditching 12 and 13/6	25 00
John Johnston, culvert and gravelling con. 7	20 00
Alex. Aubin, wire fence on 6 and 7/7	32 85
Louis Lalonde, ditching cons. 6 and 7	4 00
Thos. Dewar, irons for bridge, Moose Creek	3 36
Jas. D. McDonell, gravelling C/1	9 09
Herman Fusee, for road to gravel pit	1 20

8a M. A.

Peter McLeod, ditching on Finch boundary	10 00
Nathaniel Ferguson, wire fence 6/2	4 68
Wm. Cameron, wire fence 6/2	11 08
Barney Bender, wire fence 7/2	6 66
Donald McLean, repairing road 12 and 13/6	2 00
Wm. Haley, work on Council road 17 and 18/2	6 00
John Legault, repairing culvert 16 and 17/9	3 00
Jacob Ruport, removing stones con. 1 and 2	5 00
Hugh McDiarmid, ditching 27/4	10 00
Jeremiah Collinson, ditching 35/2	7 00
Alex. Aubin, bridge on headline con. 6 and 7	16 75
Frank McLeod, ditching Finch boundary	20 00
D. A. Gibson, gravelling 30 and 31/4	20 00
Sinclair McRae, work on Finch boundary	3 50
Edgar McConnell, gravelling 30 and 31/2	15 00
S. Waldrof, gravelling Cornwall boundary	20 00
Finlay McRae, culvert Finch boundary	13 50
Jas. Shanks, for gravelling in 1904	42 05
Nathan Robertson, road making on 9 mile road 6 and 7/3...	7 00
Louis Bray, for gravelling Plantagenet boundary	10 00
A. G. Dewar, repairing culvert con. 2	2 50
Alex. Watts, for gravelling	15 00
Nap. Brabant, ditching 6 and 7/10	12 75
" gravelling 6 and 7/10	15 80
Herman Fusee, gravelling 13 and 14/2	10 00
Esdree Fabre, bitching between cons. 9 and 10	15 00
Jack Willard, repairing road 6 and 7/6	27 00
J. Crawford, repairing bridge con. 1 and 2	3 50
Alex. Aubin, grading 6 and 7/8	25 75
F. McLeod, removing stumps and repairing bridge Finch boundary	123 40
John Rombough, gravelling 26/3	25 00
" " Finch boundary	16 80
John Steele, wire fencing Osnabruck boundary	7 68
Alex. McPhail, gravelling 12 and 13/9	13 33
J. B. Runnions, gravelling Cornwall boundary	10 00
John Delaney, gravelling 18 and 19/3	20 00
Alex. Carther, part payment for gravel pit	34 00
Geo. Grant, for gravel	6 75
Don. Alguire, for ditching 20/4 and 5	50 00
Don. Grant, for gravel	2 70
Matt. Sproule, wire fencing	7 56
Peter McLeod, work on Finch boundary	26 00
Dav. Gibson, gravel on 9 mile road 31/1	20 00
" " 33/2	10 00
Nathan Robinson, ditching 3 and 4 con.	19 50
Sam. Robinson, ditching 2/3 and 4	21 00
A. A McEwen, gravelling and culvert con. 5	25 00
Norman McNeil, wire fencing	2 16
Larue, work on Cambridge road	12 50
John McLaughlin, wire fencing 30 and 31/3	3 78
Alph. Seguin, ditching 12/6	6 75
D. McPhail, ditching 12 and 13/9	5 00
W. R. Majerrison, gravelling 6 and 7/7	8 00
H. Lalonde, digging Township portion Ferguson Award	30 75
D. McRae, gravel 6 and 7/3	17 00
Hugh McMillan, gravel	4 70
Rod. McQuaig, ditching A/6	7 32
Alex. Cameron, A/6	13 25
Frank Bray, gravelling 8/10	5 00
D. Campbell, work on 9 mile road 30 and 31/3	5 00
Dan. Gibson, work on 30 and 31/4	3 50
Nap. Deguire, wire 12 and 13/3	6 66
Peter McLeod, ditching Finch boundary	15 00
W. Raney, work on headline 22/4 and 5	41 25
Jas. Hartibese, brushing 12 and 13/10	30 00
J. & T. Gagnon, for timber and lumber	23 60
J. Hartibese, brushing 12 and 13/10	30 00

Hugh Cameron, ditching 12 and 13/3	25	00
Finlay McPherson, for road to gravel pit	2	00
C. Montgomery, grading Kenyon boundary	10	00
Chas. Quail, repairing bridge between 9/2	37	00
Peter Ashlin, ditching 6 and 7 con.	5	00
D. McNeil, wire 18 and 19/2	2	52
Thos. A. Duff, for gravel	25	68
S. Waldruff, gravel 30 and 31/3	1	20
W. Tolmie, for culvert 18 and 19/6	25	00
W. A. McIntosh, ditching	5	00
Alex. Stewart, road job 22/4 and 5	8	75
F. D. McLeod, for work on 12 and 13/6	6	00
J. A. Brown, road job 18 and 19/3	28	00
Peter McLeod, for work on Finch boundary	13	00
John R. McDonald, culvert and ditching 12 and 13/6 and 7...	48	50
D. D. McLeod, 6 day's work and load of tile from Avonmore...	14	50
John Shannon, repairing bridge 9/2 and 3	17	50
" "	6	00
Dan. Leclair, for wire fencing	3	24
John McLennan, for bridge 18/6	50	00
Jas. Crawford, Jr., cleaning out ditch	4	00
Jas. Hartibese, brushing 12 and 13/10	10	00
Mich. Labroche, repairing bridge A/7		50
Peter McLeod, ditching Finch boundary	7	80
A. Aumelle, ditching Cornwall boundary	12	00
Ant. Laprierre, repairing bridge lot A	1	00
A. A. Fraser, for wire fencing	2	34
Ed. Delaney, ditching 9 mile road 18 and 19/3	10	00
Dav. McGregor, repairing bridge	24	00
Sandy McGregor, repairing road A/7	2	50
Jas. Grant, for apple trees injured in gravel pit	8	00
D. L. Campbell, gravelling 14/1	25	00
W. Bender, building bridge on J. F. Maloney's award, con. 1	14	00
John F. Maloney, gravel	15	00
Thos. Robinson, repairing road con. 5	3	50
Abram Lalonde, work on Cambridge road	104	65
J. Raney, brushing 9 mile road	3	75
J. Campbell, ditching 9 mile road 30 and 31/4	3	00
A. McMillan, gravel got from him	26	40
Don. Alguire, gravelling 22/4 and 5	3	25
Jas. McBain, repairing bridge at Monkland	2	25
W. H. Munroe, repairing bridge	1	00
W. Kinnear, for winter road per by-law	5	00
Alex. Lalonde, bridge 28/5	20	00
McEwen & Munroe, for gravel	25	00
John McDonald, 131 loads gravel at 6c.	7	86
John Crawford, for culvert on McEwen & Crawford's award...	20	00
Geo. McConnell, for cedar for bridge	1	00
F. McRae, for gravel	22	50
John Rombough, removing stones 30 and 31/5	8	00
W. M. Eamon, gravel	19	33
Jas. Miller, for crossing 2/2	3	25
John Hill, gravel	10	00
Alex. Scott, filling old crossing 4/1	9	90
Abram Lalonde, gravelling Cambridge road	14	00
Peter McLeod, work on Finch boundary	6	00
A. A. McDougall, trip to Cornwall re Highways	3	00
W. J. McCart, in full of account for tile	83	63

$2,275 98

Award Ditches.

C. H. Fullerton, fees Thompson's award	15	00
" Grant's award	15	00
" Dyer's award	3	00
" McRae's award	6	00
" Sabourin's award	3	00
D. F. Ferguson, for labor on Ferguson's award	6	00
J. S. McDonald, culvert "	19	00

John McDermid, assisting Engineer, McDermid's award......		1 75
Thos. Davidson, " "		75
E. Dorey, " Davidson's award		75
John McDermid, " "		1 15
John Shannon, work on Johnston's award		18 88
Alex. D. Kennedy, for work done on Ferguson's award......		9 00
C. H. Fullerton, fees on Maloney's award		21 00
" Duff's award		. 49 50
" Ferguson's award		30 00
D. A. McDermid, re McDermid's award		35
S. Brunett, re Ferguson's award ....'		3 15
E. J. McDonald, digging Watt's portion of D. F. Ferguson's award		9 00
Joe. Blondin, work on Ferguson's award		6 00
W. Raney, work on Alguire's award		2 07
" cleaning McNeil's award		8 50
Peter Ashlin, cleaning McEwen & Crawford's award		6 50
Don. McLean, re Davidson's award		55 00
Sam. Miller, re Alguire's award		7 30
W. Wert Thompson's portion Alguire's award		13 05
" McNeil's award		8 75
J. Meyers, work on Sabourin's award		10 00
Jas. McBain, building bridge on Ferguson's award		16 00
F. Finlayson, re Grant's award		4 00
F. Dyer, re McRae's award		4 00
S. Mills, work on Solomon's award		20 00
Joe. Sabourin, re Dyer's award		6 00
John St. John, re Leclair's award		7 25
C. H. Fullerton, fees re Saya's award		28 18
" Sabourin's award		31 76
" Dorey's award		36 50
Sabourin's award		44 70
" D. H. McDermid's award		21 15
W. Wert, work done on Solomon's award		4 50
S. Mills, " "		5 50
J. Grant, " Maloney's award		2 50
Don. McRae, " McRae's award		16 90
Fr. McLeod, " Dorey's award		2 50
Ed. Beauchamp, . " Sabourin's award		65
F. Brunett, 1 day at Sabourin's award		2 00
" 1 trip to Saya's award		2 00
A. A. McDougall, 1 day at McEwen & Crawford's award		2 00
J. Lalonde, work on Maloney's award		3 75
John Bender, "		1 25
Jas. Bender, "		2 50
D. D. McDonald, ...		35
Jas. Bender, "		1 80
John Crawford, re notices re Ferguson's award		2 00
" 1 day at court re Dyer's award		2 00
" 1 meeting, Sabourin		2 00
" 1 "		2 00
" 1 meeting McClafferty's		2 00
" 1 meeting re Aubin's		2 00
" 1 trip to Clark's re awards		1 50
" 1 meeting re Davidson's		2 00
" 1 day at court re Sabourin's		2 00
" 1 trip to Cornwall re Sabourin		2 00
" 1 trip with Engineer		2 00
" 1 meeting re Duff's		2 00
" 2 " re Ferguson's		4 00
" 1 " re Sabourin's		2 00
" 1 " re Dorey's		2 00
" 1 " re H. H. Campbell's		2 00
" 1 trip to Daniel's, north branch		1 50
" 1 trip to Cornwall re awards		2 50
" 1 meeting at Johnston's		2 00
" 1 · " Maloney's		2 00
" 1 trip to P. McCafferty's		1 50

John Crawford,	1 day at court	2 00	
	" 1 " Maloney's	2 50	
	" 1 trip with Engineer to Maloney's	2 00	
	" 1 meeting, D. D. McIntyre's	2 00	
	" 1 D. McDermid's	2 00	
Victor Begg, refund taxes *re* Sabourin's award		3 75	
John Bovineau, *re* Dorey's award		3 75	
Duncan McRae, assisting Engineer *re* McDermin's		95	
			659 14

Debentures Retired.

Lalonde No. 4	$379 79	
Thompson-Ferguson No. 4	230 33	
Blair-Shanks No. 4	124 53	
Fraser No. 4	585 10	
McMillan No. 4	62 61	
Tayside No. 8	510 17	
Payne No. 5	74 90	
McLennan No. 1	107 54	
Morrison-Munroe No. 1	283 71	
Payne No. 7	944 39	
Steele-McElheran No. 4	89 02	
Payne No. 4	83 25	
Upper Moose Creek No. 7	538 95	
North Branch No. 3	611 89	
Monkland No. 3	688 69	
Boundary No. 3	72 59	
Stewart No. 4	202 05	
Blair-McRae No. 4	64 68	
Thompson-Ferguson No. 2	125 10	
McElheran No. 1	96 79	
Payne No. 5	296 68	
Lalonde No. 1	323 14	
McMillan No. 6	89 49	
Blair-McRae No. 6	298 31	
McRae No. 6	287 75	
Stewart No. 6	348 19	
Monkland School No. 6	61 65	
Hart No. 7	150 53	
Payne No. 7	441 08	
Delisle No. 2	94 48	
McElheran No. 2	88 36	
McGregor No. 8	188 23	
		$8,543 97

Refund of Taxes.

Ed. Blair	$11 01	
John Johnston	12 42	
D. Blair	37	
J. Mackenzie	1 21	
Peter Munroe	13 20	
W. Montgomery	2 20	
Victor Begg	4 37	
		$ 44 78

Charity

Geo. Shaver, for coffin to bury child	$ 10 00
Thos. Dey, coffin for Paul Lapierre	8 00
" for Swguin	8 00
Sick Children's Hospital, Toronto	2 00
Janet McQuaig	15 00
D. J. Norman	5 00
Noah Disho	4 00
Mrs. McGillivray	20 00
Mrs. Quesnelle	3 00
Lacelle	16 50
Wm. Raney, for coffin for Widow Aumelle	5 00
Dr. Stewart, account in full to date	20 00

Mrs. Stephenson	5	00
Mrs. Braya	5	00
St. Paul's Home, Cornwall	80	00
Xavier Braya	10	00
J. Lemon	2	00

$218 50

Printing.

Gleaner	$ 12	00
Maxville Advertiser	3	00
Gleaner, printing Auditor's Report	23	00
" voters lists	38	00
" 100 municipal bills	3	00
Treasurer, by-law 40/'05	22	00
Municipal World in full of account	40	58

$141 58

Law Costs.

Maclennan, Cline & Maclennan re Ville Marie Bank	$100	00
P. McLafferty, costs of suit against the Township	16	75
D. McDermid, witness fees re Ville Marie Bank	7	50
" 2 day's in Cornwall	6	00
Maclennan, Cline & Maclennan, in full re Ville Marie Bank ...	70	00
" in full of account rendered 4th July, 1904	11	02
Gogo & Styles re McLafferty's case	10	70
W. R. Majerrison, one day at court re Watts case	2	00
F. Burnett, " "	2	00
Treasurer, " "	2	00
A. A. McDougall, " "	2	00
J. Crawford, 3 days at Cornwall re Ville Marie Bank	7	50
Treasurer, " "	7	50

$244 97

County Rates.

County Treasurer on account county rates	$1,000	00
" in full for 1904	218	69
" on account 1905	500	00

$1,718 69

Public Schools

Balance of school rates for 1904	$3,734	11
On account for 1905	4,400	00

$3,134 11

Loans and Interest

Neil McLean	$1,200	00
School sec. No. 5	325	00
Interest on above	23	52
Neil McLean's note	60	00
" J. A. Cumming's note	55	00
" J. A. Crawford's note	20	00

$1,683 52

Board of Health

Dr. Whitaker. fees as Medical Health Officer for 1904	$ 34	00
A. H. McMillan, for P. McLafferty	10	00
John Crawford, Reeve, 1 meeting	2	00

$ 61 50

Municipal Government.

Chas. Kahalie, Sanitary Policeman during diphtheria	$14	00
J. K. McRae. Polling Booth No. 7	4	00
Dan. Montgomery, Polling Booth	4	00
Chas. Quail. do	4	00
R. C. McGregor, do	18	00

J. K. McRae, D. R. O.		6 00
do for auditing, 1904, and filing report		12 00
R. C. McGregor, fees as Township Clerk and by-laws		199 34
Peter Munros, D. R. O.		6 00
A. H. McMillan, one trip to Cornwall		2 50
R. C. McGregor, placing drainaige assessment on Collector's roll		32 00
J. Crawford, salary as Reeve for 1904		75 00
D. D. Cameron, for Polling Booth, Provincial Election		4 00
Joel Myers, do do		4 00
John Crawford, Reeve, on account of expenses for 1905		50 00
Jas. Shanks, for Road Commissioner for 1904		25 00
Jas. Quail, additional for Polling Booth		1 00
H. M. Campbell, salary as Assessor for 1905		125 00
Ed. Maloney, salary as Collector for 1904, $40, and postage ...		43 50
R. C. McGregor, as per By-law 29, 1905		10 40
do forwarding Collector's roll to Reeve		1 00
D. D. McLeod, Road Commissioner for 1905 and extras		26 00
Dav. Campbell, do do		30 00
W. H. Munroe, do do		33 00
H. M. Campbell, Collector for 1904		40 00
F. Brunett, trip to Cornwall *re* road		3 00
John Crawford, Reeve, trip to Moose Creek		2 00
do 3 trips to Cornwall		7 50
do 1 trip *re* Ville Marie Bank		2 50
do 1 trip to Clerk		2 00
do notifying Council of 2 special meetings.		4 00
do 1 trip to Bank, Twp. account		2 00
do 1 day selecting jurors		2 00
do salary as Reeve		26 00
F. Brunett, do as Councillor		26 00
A. H. McMillan, do do		26 00
W. R. Majerrison, do do		26 00
J. H. Wert, fees as Auditor for 1904		10 00
A. A. McDougall, salary as Councillor for 1904		26 00
R. C. McGregor, salary as Clerk		200 00
Alex. Stewart, as Caretaker of Hall and repairs		7 60
Treasurer's salary for 1905		50 00
J. K. McRae, auditing accounts for 1904 and filing report ...		12 00

$1,204 34

Miscellaneous.

Fire insurance premium on Township Hall		$7 75
Exchange on Tayside Debenture		1 00
do Payne do		20
do do do		1 25
do Steele-McElheran		37
Alex. Stewart, repairs to Township Hall		3 25
Exchange on several debentures		38
R. C. McGregor, copies of drain account, sent Department of of Public Works		3 00
Exchange on Lalonde Debenture		50
Dr. McIntosh, examining a lunatic		5 00
Emerson Warner, sending lunatic to Cornwall		3 50
Exchange on a number of debentures		2 75
Township portion of D. Ferguson's award		3 00
F. Brunett, three meetings of Division Court in Hall		15 00
P. McLeod, on Township account *re* McElheran Drain		2 50
J. Crawford, trip to Cornwall *re* Aux Raisins Drain		2 00
do telephone account		25
do meeting with Clerk *re* Finch boundary.............		1 50
Alex. Stewart, repair and banking of Hall		1 60
do repair of stables		1 00

55 80

Avonmore Police Village.

Amount of special assessment		$339 54
do License Fees		106 46

$446 00

Aux Raisins River.

1904.		
Dec. 31.—By amount due Treasurer..................................		$501 00
1905.		
Jan. 12.— " Michael Maloney, 2 meetings...... $...........		$4 00
" S. Hough, 2 "		4 00
" A. H. McMillan, 2 "		4 00
" F. J. McRae, 2 "		4 00
" R. C. McGregor, Clerk, by-law 23/'04		4 00
" *Gleaner*, notices for by-law.........		1 00
" Maclennan, Cline & Maclennan...		1 08
To proceeds of debentures sold.........	1,849 18	....
By exchange in remitting proceeds...		1 85
" D. H. McDermid, trip to Toronto re Government grant...........		24 00
" J. J. McLaughlin, trip to Toronto re Government grant...		24 00
" Extra to Treasurer, by-law 40/'05		3 00
" W. R. Marjerrison, Councillor, 3 meetings		6 00
" F. Brunett, Councillor, 3 meetings		6 00
" J. Crawford, trip to Toronto re Government grant...............		24 00
" J. Crawford, 2 meetings of Council		4 00
" Exchange on cheque for debentures		1 00
" A. A. McDougall, Councillor, 3 meetings		6 00
Roxborough expenses to date.............................		$677 05
which are finally to be deducted from the proceeds of debentures and the balance at present paid to Osnabruck		1,172 13
	$1,849 18	$1,849 18

Blair-McRae Drain.

1904.		
Dec. 31.—To balance on hand	$169 87	
1905.		
Dec. 15.—By extra to Treasurer, by-law 40/'05.................	....	3 00
" balance carried forward	....	166 87
	$169 87	$169 87

Blair-Shanks Drain.

1904.		
Dec. 31.—By amount due Treasurer	$195 35	
1905.		
October.— " Maclennan, Cline & Maclennan	3 00	
" Elias McDermid	8 09	
" Joe Sauve, refund of taxes	1 35	
" Extra to Treasurer, bylaw 40/'05	3 00	
Dec. 31.—Amount due Treasurer		$210 79

Boundary Drain.

1904.		
Dec. 31.—By balance due Treasurer	$191 05	
1905.		
Dec. 16.— " H. D. McKinnon, inspecting	6 75	
" extra to Treasurer, by-law 40/'05	3 00	
Dec. .— " amount due Treasurer		$200 82

Butternut Creek.

1904.
Dec. 31.—By balance due Treasurer $260 21
1905.
Dec. 15 —To amount collected from interested parties........ $ 34 08
      31.— " balance due Treasurer 226 13

                                    $260 21 $260 21

Deslile Drain.

1904.
Dec. 31.—To balance on hand $95 22
1905.
Dec. 15.—By extra to Treasurer, by-law 40/'05 .... $ 3 00
      31.— " balance on hand 92 22

                                    $95 22 $95 22

Dewar Drain.

1905.
            To A. R. McLennan for deposit $100 00
July 10.—To D. Dewar & Sons, assessment................ 32 50
           "   Archie McDonald,   "   10 75
Oct. 6.— "   W. H. Williamson,   " 21 75
           "   Duncan Campbell,   "   29 75
           "   Malcolm Campbell,   " 40 00
Nov. 18.— "   Thos. McEwen,   "   E. 1/4, 5/5   2 00
           "   Alex. Forbes,   "   25 10
           "   Alex. Perrier, ... 8 00
           "   Hiram Robinson. 18 65
           "   A. Dewar, ... 30 00
           "   Peter McEwen,   " 16 10
Dec. 31.— "   Balance due Treasurer 813 80
           By C. W. Fullerton, fees as Engineer............... .... $ 40 00
           "   *Gleaner,* printing by-laws 10 00
           "   *Gleaner,* printing tenders 2 00
           "   A. R. McLennan, on account of contract........ .... 350 00
           "   A. R. McLennan, on account of contract...... .... 150 00
           "   *Gleaner,* posters for bridges........................... .... 1 00
           "   C. H. Fullerton, as per by-law 23/'05........ .... 25 00
           "   A. R. McLennan, on account of contract...... .... 450 00
           "   A. Dewar, distributing by-laws 2 00
           "   A. Dewar, bridge, 4th and 5th Con. Station O. 27 00
           "   *News,* printing notices 3 58
           "   Extra to Treasurer, by-law 40/'05............... .... 3 00
           "   W. R. Marjerrison, 2 Council meetings......... .... 4 00
           "   W. R. Marjerrison, 1 day at drain, by-law
                40/'05 .... 2 00
           "   F. Brunett, Councillor, 2 meetings............... .... 4 00
           "   John Crawford, Reeve, trip to drain, by-law
                40/'05 .... 1 75
           "   John Crawford, trip to Clerk 1 50
           "   A. A. McDougall, Councillor, 2 meetings...... .... 4 00
           "   C. H. Fullerton, Engineer, on account of fees 50 00
           "   Harkness & Milligan, drawing by-law............ .... 15 00
           "   Harkness & Milligan, making copy 2 66

                                    $1,148 49 $1,148 49

Fraser Creek.

1904.
Dec 31.—By balance due Treasurer $351 36
1905.
Jan. 25.— "   C. H. Fullerton, fees on survey..................... 25 00
           "   Alex. McPherson, assistance on survey 3 75
Dec. 15.— "   Extra to Treasurer per by-law 40/'05........ 3 00
           "   John Crawford. Reeve, trip to drain per
                by-law 38/'04 .... 2 00

Dec. 31 — "   balance due Treasurer $385 11

Hart Creek.

1904.			
Dec. 31.—To balance on hand		$101 03	
1905.			
By W. M. Rainey, for work		....	$ 6 60
" paid by-law pay sheet		....	109 11
" Treasurer, trip to pay Government grant, by-law 40/'05		....	5 00
" Extra to Treasurer, by-law 40/'05		....	3 00
" Estel Hough, inspecting drain		....	2 00
Dec. 31.—To amount due Treasurer		24 68	....
		$125 71	$125 71

Henry Drain.

1904.			
Dec. 31.—To balance on hand		$1,560 55	
1905.			
Jan. 12.—By M. Maloney, 3 meetings...............................		....	$ 6 00
" S. Hough, 3 "		....	6 00
" A. H. McMillan, 3 meetings.......................		....	6 00
" F. J. McRae, 3 "		....	6 00
" C. H. Fullerton, Engineer, on account of fees		....	20 00
" Sam Henry, per Engineer's report.................		....	120 00
" R. C. McGregor, Clerk, by-law 23/'04.........		....	2 00
" R. C. McGregor, Clerk, 3 meetings..............		....	6 00
" R. C. McGregor, as p. Engineer's report, by-law 23/'04		....	25 00
" Denis St. Denis, crossing and allowance.........		....	44 00
" Dechar St. Denis & Son, assistance on survey		....	15 75
" M. A. Stewart, on account of contract.........		....	200 00
Aug. 28.— " M. A. Stewart, on account of contract.........		....	300 00
" C. H. Fullerton, per McEwen		....	25 00
" M. A. Stewart, on account of contract.........		....	500 00
" News, printing second tenders		....	5 85
Dec. 14.— " M. A. Stewart, on account of contract.........		....	400 00
" Dacher St. Denis, for trees cut as per by-law		....	2 00
" Gogo & Stiles, their account of 21 Nov., 1904		....	75 00
" Extra to Treasurer, by-law 40/'05		....	3 00
" John Crawford, trip to bank, by-law 38/'04...		....	1 00
" John Crawford, 3 meetings of Council		....	6 00
" C. H. Fullerton, on account of fees............		....	50 00
Dec. 31.—To balance due Treasurer		264 05	....
		$1,824 60	$1,824 60

Lalonde Drain.

1904.			
Dec. 31.—To balance in hand		$252 30	
Jan. 12.—By M. Maloney, 3 meetings..		....	$ 6 00
" S. Hough, 3 "		....	6 00
" A. H. McMillan, 3 "		....	6 00
" F. J. McRae, 3 "		....	6 00
" Peter McLeod, cleaning out drain...............		....	43 11
" MacLennan, Cline & MacLennan....................		....	47 09
" Peter McLeod, inspecting		....	4 00
" John H. Merkley, overpaid on debentures......		....	16 00
" R. C. McGregor, Clerk, by-law 23/'04.........		....	5 00
" R. C. McGregor, 3 meetings, by-law 23/'04...		....	6 00
July 24.— " R. C. McGregor, re debenture and certificate by-law 23/'04		....	1 25
" Exchange on cheque to Tp. Finch		....	1 00
" MacLennan, Cline & MacLennan		....	3 87
Dec. 14.— " Peter McLeod, inspecting and cleaning drain		....	19 50
" Extra to Treasurer, by-law 40/'05................		....	3 00
" F. Brunet, trip to drain, by-law 40/'05.........		....	2 00
" John Crawford, Reeve, to Ottawa re Government grant		....	2 50
" John Crawford, trip to Cornwall, by-law 38/'04		....	2 50
" trip to drain		....	1 50

Dec.	14.—By trip to bank		....	2 00
	" trip to Cornwall		....	2 50
	" trip to Finch on drain account.................		....	2 50
	" 3 trips to bank *re* drain		....	6 00
	" trip to Avonmore *re* drain		....	2 00
	" trip to Treasurer		....	2 00
	" 3 meetings for drain		....	6 00
	" witness fee Finch *re* drain		....	2 50
	" 2 trips to Cornwall		....	4 50
	" balance on hand		....	523 30
	To cheque from Finch per MacLennan, Cline & MacLennan		471 10	
	5.— " interest on same		12 22	
			$735 62	$735 62

McElheran Drain.

1904.				
Dec.	31.—By amount due Treasurer		$............	$70 11
1905.				
Jan.	12.— " M. Maloney, 1 meeting...................		....	2 00
	" S. Hough, 1 "		....	2 00
	" A. H. McMillan, 1 "		....	2 00
	" F. J. McRae, 1 "		....	2 00
	" Maclennan, Cline & Maclennan		....	47 83
	" R. C. McGregor, Clerk, by-law 23/'04........		....	2 00
	" R. C. McGregor, debentures and certificate by-law 23/'04......................................		....	1 25
	" Maclennan, Cline & Maclennan		....	1 04
	" Extra to Treasurer, by-law 40/'05.............		....	3 00
	" John Crawford, Reeve, by-law 38/'04—			
	2 trips to Cornwall		....	5 00
	2 days at Cornwall		....	4 00
	1 meeting of Council		....	2 00
June	1.—To received from Finch per order of the Referee, through Maclennan, Cline & Maclennan		80 00	
	" balance due Treasurer		64 23	
			$144 23	$144 23

McGregor Creek.

1904.				
Dec.	31.—To balance on hand		$50 94	
1905.				
Dec.	16.—By extra to Treasurer, by-law 40/'05.........		....	$ 3 00
	" balance on hand		....	47 94
			$50 94	$50 94

North Branch and McIntosh Drain.

1904.			
Dec.	31.—By balance due Treasurer		$387 49
1905.			
Jan.	3.—To grant from Ontario Government.................	$2,000 00	
June	18 — " John Ferguson, on three months' note........	1,553 00	
July	13.— " Ed. Alguire, on six months' note................	1,340 00	
July	15.— " Ottawa Bank note....................................	500 00	
Aug.	16.— " " "	600 00	
Aug.	28.— " " "	1,000 00	
Sept.	1.— " " "	1,300 00	
Sept.	18.— " " "	2,500 00	
Nov.	13.— " Wm. McIntosh, on one year's note..............	1,500 00	
	" Alex. McIntosh, " "	275 00	
Oct.	4.— " Alex. Dewar, note	1,680 00	
Oct.	23.— " Ottawa Bank, on note	2,000 00	
Nov.	26.— " F. Richard, on note	2,000 00	
Dec.	15.— " John Ferguson, on note	1,361 90	
	" Geo. T. Ferguson, on note.......................	404 17	
Jan.	18.—By Cornwall Township for their share of Government grant	....	655 46
	" C. H. Fullerton, on account fees	....	50 00

Jan.	18.—By pay list to interested parties	....	1,293 35
	" Kenyon Township, for their share of Government grant	....	14 44
	" J. K. McRae, for preparing and paying pay lists	....	36 75
Feb.	13.— " J. & T. Gagnon, contractors, per resolution of Council	....	500 00
March	20.— " J. & T. Gagnon, contractors, Estimate B	....	800 00
	" Exchange of cheque for above	....	1 50
	" J. & T. Gagnon, contractors, estimate on note	....	175 00
June	14.— " J. & T. Gagnon, on account contract	....	500 00
	19.— " John Ferguson, for note given him	....	1,300 00
	" interest on above	....	52 56
July	13.— " Ed. Alguire, for note given him	....	1,100 00
	" Interest on above	....	53 90
	" Ed. Alguire,, for note given him	....	49 50
	" interest on above	....	2 43
	15.— " J. & T. Gagnon, on account contract	....	500 00
Aug.	28.— " J. & T. Gagnon, on account contract as per Engineer's certificate	....	1,500 00
	" M. Maloney, for culvert	....	23 00
	" Jas. Quail, for work	....	3 75
	" Jas. Harrison, for work	....	2 25
	" Bernard Campbell, for work	....	3 75
	" C. H. Fullerton, on account of fees	....	50 00
	" Cory Alguire, 2½ days with Engineer	....	3 00
Sept.	23.— " J. & T. Gagnon, on account of contract	....	1,800 00
Oct.	3.— " J. & T. Gagnon, on account of contract	....	750 00
Oct.	4.— " Alex. Dewar, for note given him	....	1,600 00
	" interest on above	....	80 00
	" Wm. McIntosh, for note given him at one year	....	1,350 00
	" interest on above	....	67 50
Nov.	13.— " Alex. McIntosh, for note at one year	....	200 00
	" interest on above	....	10 00
Nov.	23.— " J. & T. Gagnon, on account contract	....	2,000 00
	" J. & T. Gagnon, on account contract, 10% on McIntosh Branch by-law 31/'05	....	300 00
Dec.	15.— " John Ferguson, for note given him	....	1,553 00
	" interest on above	....	37 07
	" J. & T. Gagnon, interest on deposit, by-law 33/'05	....	60 00
	" J. & T. Gagnon, discount on notes given on Estimate B, by-law 33/'05	....	95 00
	" M. Maloney, inspecting as per by-law	....	64 00
	" D. J. Norman, clearing timber out of drain	....	2 00
	" Treasurer, 10 trips to bank, by-law 40/'05	....	16 00
	" trip to Ottawa re contract, by-law 40/'05	....	6 00
	" Treasurer, extra for 1905, by-law 40/'05	....	3 00
	" W. M. Majerrison, Councillor, 4 meetings	....	8 00
	" F. Brunet, " 4 "	....	8 00
	" A. A. McDougall, " 4 "	....	8 00
	" John Crawford, Reeve, 2 trips to bank	....	4 00
	" John Crawford, trip to D. W. McIntosh re note, 39/'04	....	2 00
	" John Crawford, trip with Eng. to drain	....	2 00
	" John Crawford, trip to Cornwall	....	2 50
	" C. H. Fullerton, on account fees	....	175 00
	" J. & T. Gagnon, for assistance by-law 40/'05	....	24 00
Dec.	31.— " balance in hand	....	723 87
	Total	$20,014 07	$20,014 07

McLennan Drain.

1904.		
Dec.	31.—To balance in hand	$49 44
1905.		
Dec.	31.— " balance due Treasurer	89 65

Jan.	12.—By	M. Maloney, Councillor, 3 meetings............	....	6	00
	"	S. Hough, " 3 "	....	6	00
	"	A. H. McMillan, " 3 "	....	6	00
	"	F. J. McRae, " 3 "	....	6	00
	"	C. H. Fullerton, Engineer, on account fees...	....	20	00
Feb.	27.— "	D. H. McMillan, for labour on drain............	....	2	19
	"	D. Campbell, " "	....		94
	"	R. C. McGregor, Clerk, by-law 23/'04...........	....	6	00
	"	R. C. McGregor, as per Engineer's report......	....	15	00
	"	R. C. McGregor, " " "	....	1	25
	"	John McLennan, " " "	....	11	15
	"	Gogo & Stiles, for their acount for 1904......	....	10	00
Dec.	15.— "	Extra to Treasurer, by-law 40/'05............	....	3	00
	"	John Crawford, Reeve, by-law 38/'04...........	....	22	00
	"	John Crawford, trip to Clerk............	....	1	50
	"	John Crawford, 3 meetings of Council........	....	6	00
	"	Harkness & Milligan, preparing by-law........	....	15	56
	"	John Crawford, for telephone message............	....		50
			$139 09	$139	09

McMillan Drain.

1904.					
Dec.	31.—By	balance due Treasurer	$29 60		
	"	Mrs. Nelson Campbell, for crossing...............	5 00		
Dec.	15.— "	Extra to Treasurer, by-law 40/'05...............	33 00		
Dec.	31.—To	balance due Treasurer...................................		$37	60

Neil-McDonell Drain.

1905.					
		To deposit from McNeil	$ 70 00		
July	14.— "	R. McLennan, assessment	59 30		
	"	Uriah Shaver, "	50 00		
Sept.	15.— "	McNeil, "	120 00		
	"	Donald McKinnon, "	3 00		
Dec.	12.— "	proceeds of debentures	1,358 34		
April	13.—By	M. Eamor, for labour	....	$ 14	48
	"	C. H. Fullerton, Engineer, on account fees...	....	35	00
	"	*Gleaner*, printing by-laws	....	10	00
	"	W. Raney, distributing by-laws	....	2	00
	"	*Gleaner*, printing tenders	....	2	00
July	24.— "	R. McLennan, labour allowed	....	36	90
	"	Uriah Shaver, per Engineer's report............	....	17	45
	"	McNeil-Eamor, contractors	....	300	00
	"	Norman McNeil, work per Engineer's report	....	38	40
	"	A. H. McMillan, per Engineer's report.........	....	1	75
	"	McNeil-Eamon, contractors	....	392	50
	"	News Printing Co., for notices	....	3	57
	"	McNeil-Eamon, deposit returned	....	70	00
	"	John Delaney, per Engineer's report............	....	93	90
	"	Wm. Tait, "	....	47	10
	"	Wm. Raney, "	....	25	90
	"	Harkness & Milligan, drawing debentures......	....	16	29
	"	D. McDonald, farm crossing, per Engineer's report	....	94	85
Dec.	19.— "	D. McDonald, per Engineer's report............	....	19	55
	"	Alex. Johnson, "	....	16	05
	"	John Johnston, "	....	67	00
	"	Mrs. McEwen, "	....	22	40
	"	Sandy McDonald, "	....	22	85
	"	Treasurer, trip to bank, by-law 40/'05........	....	1	50
	"	Treasurer, extra per by-law 40/'05...............	....	3	00
	"	W. R. Marjerrison, 2 Council meetings........	....	4	00
	"	F. Brunett, 2 "	....	4	00
	"	A. A. McDougall, 2 "	....	4	00

Dec.	19.—By Harkness & Milligan, drawing by-law	....	15 00
"	" Harkness & Milligan, drawing copies............	....	2 67
"	" John Johnston, farming crossing, allowed......	....	7 50
Dec.	31.— " balance in hand	....	274 03
		$1,6656 64	$1,665 64

McRae Drain.

1904.

Dec.	31.—By balance due Treasurer		$1,025 90
1905.			
Dec.	19.—To proceeds of debentures sold	$1,100 00	
"	" Bank of Ottawa, on demand note.................	1,000 00	
Dec.	31.—By Bank of Ottawa, for demand note..............	....	1,000 00
"	" interest on above	....	48 37
"	" extra to Treasurer, by-law 40/'05................	....	3 00
	To Quinn & Co., deposit forfeited	240 00	
	By balance in hand ....,	....	262 73
		$2,340 00	$2,340 00

Monkland Drain.

1904.

Dec.	31.—To balance in hand	$1,367 39	
1905.			
Dec.	22.— " J. T. Ferguson, on 6 months' note..............	410 00	
"	" Silas McDermid, on note	1,000 00	
Jan.	12.—By M. Maloney, 1 meeting of Council...............	....	2 00
"	" S. Hough, 1 " "	....	2 00
"	" A. H. McDougall, 1 meeting of Council........	....	2 00
"	" F. J. McRae, 1 " "	....	2 00
"	" C. H. Fullerton, Engineer, on account fees...	....	25 00
"	" R. C. McGregor, dividing Government grant	....	12 00
"	" R. C. McGregor, 1 meeting of Council........	....	2 00
"	" Jas. Quail, for work	....	1 50
"	" Angus Harrison, for work	....	1 50
"	" Cory Alguire, for work	....	1 50
Nov.	15.— " Philip St. John, return of overcharge, p.		
	by-law	....	1 00
"	" J. & T. Gagnon, 10 per cent. on contract, by-		
	law 31/'05	....	817 90
"	" J. & T. Gagnon, p. Engineer's report, 33/'05	....	883 20
"	" J. & T. Gagnon, extras as p. by-law 33/'05...	....	1,600 00
"	" interest on deposit, by-law 33/'05	....	60 00
"	" M. Maloney, inspecting, by-law 33/'05.........	....	34 00
"	" Treasurer, paying Govt. grant, by-law 40/'05	....	3 00
"	" Treasurer, 6 trips to bank, by-law 40/'05......	....	11 00
"	" Treasurer, extra, by-law 40/'05	....	3 00
"	" W. R. Marjerrison, 2 meetings of Council......	....	4 00
"	" F. Brunett, 2 " "	....	4 00
"	" John Crawford, trip to Ottawa *re* Govern-		
	ment grant	....	2 50
"	" John Crawford, 1 meeting of Council...........	....	2 00
"	" A. A. McDougall, 2 meetings of Council......	....	4 00
"	" C. H. Fullerton, Engineer, on account fees...	....	75 00
"	" J. & T. Gagnon, for assistance by-law 40/'05	....	25 50
"	" Jas. Daniels for bridge	....	25 00
Dec.	31.—To balance due Treasurer	827 21	
		$3,604 60	$3,604 60

Morrison-Munroe Drain.

1904.

Dec.	31.—To balance on hand	$1,234 54	
1905.			
Jan.	12.—By M. Maloney, Councillor, 1 meeting............	....	$ 2 00
"	" S. Hough. " 1 "	....	2 00
"	" A. H. McMillan, " 1 "	....	2 00
"	" F. J. McRae, " 1 "	....	2 00
"	" Chris. & John McDonald, for work done......	....	25 00
"	" Alex. Cummings, crossing and private ditch	....	58 43

Jan.	12.—By	R. C. McGregor, Clerk, by-law 23/'04..........	....	2 00
	"	R. C. McGregor, re debentures, by-law 23/'04	....	4 25
July	10.— "	Jos. Britton, contractor, on account...........	....	375 00
	"	A. H. McMillan, interest on $1,000 note......	....	25 00
Aug.	9.— "	Joe. Britton, contractor, on account...........	....	100 00
Sept.	15.— "	Joe Britton, contractor, on account...........	....	200 00
	"	C. H. Fullerton, Engineer, on account fees	....	25 00
	"	Oddfellows, interest on note, 6 months.........	....	25 00
	"	A. S. McIntosh, refund taxes, by-law 36/'05...	....	7 13
Dec.	5.— "	Joe Britton, contractor, on account...........	·...........	300 00
	"	Joe Britton, contractor, for bridge..............	....	90 00
	"	interest on deposit as p. by-law....................	....	40 00
	"	Gogo & Styles, account of 1904....................	....	75 00
	"	A. S. McIntosh, bridge, $44 and $21, as per Engineer's report	....	65 00
	"	Extra to Treasurer, by-law 40/'05...............	....	3 00
	"	A. H. McMillan, 6 months' int. on note......	....	25 00
	"	John Crawford, Reeve, by-law 38/'04..........	....	2 50
	" " "	trip to bank	....	1 00
	" " "	trip to Cornwall	....	2 50
	" " "	2 trips to Clerk	....	4 50
	" " "	trip to Reeve Kenyon	....	2 50
	" " "	trip to Cornwall	....	2 50
	" " "	1 meeting of Council	....	2 00
	"	C. H. Fullerton, Engineer, on account fees...	....	50 00
	"	Wm. McIntosh, bridge	....	16 00
December.—To		balance due Treasurer	298 82	
			$1,533 36	$1,533 36

Moose Creek, Moose Creek Extension and Upper Moose Creek.

1904. Dec.	31.—To	balance in hand	$1,162 47	
1905. Nov.	1.—By	Debenture No. 9, paid	....	$822 93
	"	Exchange on cheque	....	1 00
Dec.	15.— "	Extra to Treasurer, By-law 40, 1905	....	3 00
	"	Transferred to Moose Creek Extension per instructions of Reeve Crawford	....	240 72
	"	balance in hand	....	94 22
			$1,162 47	$1,162 47
1904. Dec.	31.—By	balance due Treasurer		904 35
1905. Jan.	25.— "	J. K. McRae, inspecting, 1904		5 00
	"	C. H. Fullerton, Engineer, on account, fees		10 00
	"	Ottawa Bank, for note paid		1,000 00
	"	Interest on above		48 37
	"	Extra to Treasurer, By-law 40, 1905		3 00
Jan.	3.—To	proceeds of Demand note to Bank of Ottawa ...	$1,000 00	
	"	Transferred from Moose Creek per instructions of Reeve Crawford	240 72	
	"	Transferred from Upper Moose Creek	70 00	
	"	Part levy of taxes for 1905	400 00	
	"	To be levied on the interested parties	300 00	
	By	balance in hand	....	40 00
			$2,010 72	$2,010 72
1904. Dec.	31.—To	balance in hand	$100 59	
1905. Dec.	15.—By	extra to Treasurer, By-law 40, 1905	....	3 00
Dec.	31.— "	Transferred to Moose Creek extension as per instructions of Reeve Crawford	....	70 00
	"	Balance in hand	....	27 59
			$100 59	$100 59

Payne River.

1904. Dec.	31.—By balance due Treasurer		$131 09
	" D. McKinnon, refund taxes, By-law 23, 1904		6 61
	" Extra to Treasurer, By-law 40, 1905		3 00
	To balance due Treasurer		$140 70

Steel-Hough Drain.

1905. Aug.	8.—To A. R. McLennan, deposit	$168 35	
Dec.	12.— " Proceeds of debentures	2,175 00	
	By C. H. Fullerton, Engineer, By-law 17, 1905 ...	....	50 00
	" Exchange on deposit cheque	....	25
Sept.	12.— " Paid to different parties for work as per by-law	....	29 69
	" A. R. McLennan, Contractor, on account	....	850 00
	" Gleaner, printing	....	6 75
Oct.	10.— " A. R. McLennan, Contractor, on account	....	800 00
Nov.	28.— " " " in full	....	33 57
	" " " deposit	....	168 00
	" Harkness & Milligan, drawing debentures	....	16 29
	" A. H. McMillan, work	....	2 50
	" H. Hough, farm crossing, $6, and $7.50 as per Engineer's report	....	13 50
	" H. Hough, work	....	1 25
	" J. Raney, assistance on drain	....	8 00
	" Joe Raney, report and farm crossing	....	36 00
	" W. Majerrison, Councillor, two meetings	....	4 00
	" F. Brunet, " two "	....	4 00
	" W. C. Hough, farm crossing per Eng. report...	....	14 00
	" A. A. McDougall, Councillor, two meetings	....	4 00
	" Harkness & Milligan, drawing by-laws	....	15 00
	" " " for copies	....	2 67
April	12.— " Silas Cook, per Engineer's report	....	16 00
Dec.	31.— " balance in hand	....	267 88
		$2,343 35	$2,343 35

Steele-McElheran Drain.

1904. Dec.	31.—By balance due Treasurer		101 54
1905. Dec.	16.—By extra to Treasurer, By-law 40, 1905		3 00
	31.—To balance due Treasurer	$104 54	
		$104 54	$104 54

Stewart Creek.

Dec.	31.—To balance on hand	$672 90	
1905. Jan.	12.—By M. Maloney, Councillor, 1 meeting	....	2 00
	" S. Hough, " 1 "	....	2 00
	" A. H. McMillan, " 1 "	....	2 00
	" F. J. McRae, " 1 "	....	2 00
	" C. H. Fullerton, Engineer, on account	....	10 00
	" R. C. McGregor, Clerk, By-law 23, 1905	....	2 00
	" Ed. Sauve, assessment on East Branch	....	2 70
	" Gleaner, printing tenders	....	50
	" " printing tenders for sand	....	1 00
Sept.	20.— " Ed. Sauve, cleaning drain	....	25 00
	" " "	....	125 00
	" Nelson Sauve, "	....	144 00
	" Extra to Treasurer, By-law 40, 1905	....	3 00

9 M. A.

Dec.	15.—By B. Brunet, 1 trip to drain, By-law 40, 1905...	....	2 00
	" John Crawford, Reeve, By-law 38, 1904—		
	1 trip, letting contract	....	2 00
	1 meeting of Council	....	2 00
	1 day at the drain	....	2 00
	" balance in hand	....	243 70
		$672 90	$672 90

Tayside Creek.

Dec.	31.—By balance due Treasurer	$35 47	
	" Alex. McPhail, cleaning and inspecting	14 00	
	" Jas. McPhail, "	4 00	
	" Alex. McPhail, "	8 00	
	" Extra to Treasurer, By-law 40, 1905	3 00	
	" Balance due Treasurer		$64 47

Thompson-Ferguson Drain.

1904.			
Dec.	31.—By balance due Treasurer		$446 11
1905.			
Dec.	16.— " Extra to Treasurer, By-law 40, 1905		3 00
Dec.	31.—To balance due Treasurer	$449 11	
		$449 11	$449 11

Position of the Drainage Accounts in the Township of Roxborough.

Aux Raisins River.

Osnabruck is the initiating Township. The sale by Roxborough of their share of the thirty year debentures produced $1,849.18, from which the expenses incurred by this Township have to be deducted. At the 31st Dec., 1905, these amounted to $677.05.

Blair-McRae Drain

This drain has been completed and there is a balance of $166.87 at its credit.

Blair-Shanks Drain.

This drain is completed and there is a balance due the Treasurer as at 31st Dec., 1905, of $210.79.

Boundary Drain.

This drain is completed and owes the Treasurer, as at 31st Dec., 1905, $200.82.

Butternut Creek.

The balance due the Treasurer is $226.13, with four more assessments of $34.08 each to collect. There will then be a small deficit which can be levied *pro rata*.

Deslile Drain.

This drain is completed, leaving a balance of $95.22 on hand.

9a M. A.

Dewar Drain.

The contractor has not yet received his deposit, there being some work still to be completed to the satisfaction of the engineer. The debentures not yet having been sold, there is a balance due the Treasurer of $813.99.

Duff-McMillan Drain.

The contract for the digging of this drain was let this year and is at present unfinished.

Fraser Creek.

Owing to quicksand running in this drain has had to be cleaned out at a cost of $652.58, for which the Ontario Government made a grant of $300. After applying this amount, there remains the sum of $385.11 due the Treasurer for which some provision will have to be made.

Thompson-Ferguson Drain.

The contractor for this drain is claiming a considerable sum of money, the liability for the payment of which would have to be settled in court. The drain has a note for $500 standing against it, the proceeds of which to the extent of $449.11 has been used up to 31st Dec., 1905.

Hart Creek.

There was a small surplus of $101.03 on hand for this drain as at 1st Jan., 1905, which was divided *pro rata* among the interested parties, the consequence being that by the 31st Dec. in the same year there was $24.68 at its debit. There are small expenses that come in against each drain for some years after it is dug, and it is usually prudent to retain on hand any small surplus, such as the above, to provide for these.

Henry Drain.

This drain owes the Treasurer $264.05 besides which there will probably be $80 to $100 to be paid to the contractor out of his deposit, after he has done some work required by the engineer.

Lalonde Drain.

A note for $2,000 was given on account of this drain which, with interest to 31st Dec., 1905, amounted to $2,357.52, of which, as at that date, there remained a balance on hand of $523.30, leaving a deficit of $1,834.22 to be provided for.

McElheran Drain.

This drain is completed. During 1905 Finch paid the $80 due by them on account, leaving $64.23 due the Treasurer as at 31st of last December.

McGregor Creek.

There remains a balance in the Treasurer's hands of $47.94, which will provide for any small charges which may come in.

North Branch McIntosh Drain

This drain appears to have cost, up to 31st Dec. last, $34,910.40, and is not yet finished. The large amount of rock encountered, for which the engineer, T. H. Wiggins, did not make a sufficient allowance, has enormously increased the cost of the drain over the original estimates.

McLennan Drain.

This drain is completed, there being, as at 31st Dec. last, $89.65 due the Treasurer.

McMillan Drain.

This drain is also completed and there stands an amount of $37.60 at its debit.

Neil-McDonell Drain.

This drain was commenced and completed in 1905. There is a balance at its credit of $274.03.

McRae Drain.

This contract was let to Quinn & Co., who made default and did not complete the work. The Council then went on with it by day labor, with the following result:

Quinn & Co., while at work, were paid.........................$2,760 00
The Township costs and amount paid for labor was......... 1,598 83

Making a total of $4,358 83

Against which there is held Quinn & Co.'s deposit of $240. There is $22.73 at the credit of the drain.

Monkland Drain.

This drain has been completed and there are now current notes amounting to $1,410 and interest, besides $827.21 due the Treasurer, making $2,-237.21 in all, at the debit of the drain.

Morrison-Munroe Drain.

This drain is not yet completed. There is an amount of $298.82 due the Treasurer, besides a note current for $1,000, making $1,298.82 and interest at its debit.

Moose Creek, Moose Creek Extension, and Upper Moose Creek.

In 1901 the Ontario Government made a grant to assist in building the outlet for these drains.

The last debenture payable on the Moose Creek falls due 1st Nov. 1906, to provide for which the necessary assessments were put on the collector's roll for 1905, while the one falling due 1st Nov., 1905, amounting to $822.93, was charged to the drain, $417.45 only being collected.

There is at the debit of the extension $970.72, for which no assessment has been levied.

At the credit of the Upper Moose Creek there is $87.59.

The most reasonable way of settling these accounts appears to be to charge the united account with the deficit $967 72

And credit what has been collected 667 72

Leaving to be levied on the interested parties to the extension $300 00 And I beg to recommend that this be done.

Payne River.

Five by-laws have been passed by this drainage scheme, four only of which have as yet been placed on the collector's roll. The last should have been placed on the roll for 1902, but as the original by-law had not been received from the former clerk, and there was no trace of it in the minutes, nothing was known of it until the discrepancy between the number of issues of debentures and the annual assessments was found by the Government Auditor. A copy of the by-law was obtained from J. G. Harkness, Esq., who had prepared it.

I beg to recommend that the first annual assessment for this debenture, which calls for an annual payment of $83.25 only, be placed on the roll for 1906 and fourteen following years. The assessments are small and in some cases are limited to levies for one to seven years only.

There remains a balance due the Treasurer as at 31st Dec. last of $140.70.

Steele-Hough Drain.

This drain was commenced, and finished in 1905. There is a balance on hand of $267.88.

Steele-McElheran Drain.

This drain is completed, leaving $104.51 due the Treasurer.

Stewart Creek.

This drain has been completed and, owing to an inflow of quicksand, has been cleaned out. The amount to the credit as at 31st Dec. last is $243.70.

Tayside Creek.

The last debenture on this drain falls due on 1st January, 1907. There is an amount due the Treasurer of $64.47.

Drains.

Balances as at 31st Dec., 1905.

Blair-Shanks, for amount due Treasurer		$210 79		
Boundary,	"	200 82		
Butternut,	"	226 13		
Dewar,		813 99		
Fraser,		385 11		
Hart Creek,		24 68		
Henry,		264 05		
McElheran,		64 23		
McMillan,		37 60		
McLennan,		89 65		
Monkland,		827 21		
Morrison-Munroe,		298 82		
Payne River,	"	140 70		
Steele-McElheran,		104 54		
Tayside,		64 47		
Thompson-Ferguson,	"	449 11		
			4,201 90	
Aux Raisins River, for balance in hand		$1,172 13		
Blair-McRae drain,	"	166 87		
Deslile,	"	95 22		
Lalonde,	"	523 20		
McGregor,		47 94		
North Branch,		728 87		
McNeil-McDonell,		274 03		
McRae Creek,		22 73		
Moose Creek,		67 82		
Moose Creek Extension,	"	40 00		
Upper Moose Creek,	"	27 59		
Steele-Hough,		267 88		
Stewart Creek,		243 70	3,677 98	

Balance due Treasurer as at 31st Dec., 1905 .... $523 92

APPROXIMATE STATEMENT OF SURPLUS OR DEFICIT AT 31ST DEC., IN EACH YEAR.

1897.

H. M. Campbell, Reeve.

Assets.

Balance of cash in Treasurer's hands as at 31st Dec.	$235 30		
" taxes uncollected	3,577 37		
	$3,812 67		
Less assessments placed on roll to provide for debentures (drainage) maturing in 1898	822 93		
		$2,989 74	

Liabilities.

Balance due for County rates	$1,912 66		
" school taxes	449 35		
Amount unpaid under by-laws	2,001 62		
Excess of liabilities over assets	....	1,373 89	
	$4,363 63	$4,363 63	

     I have had no means of checking the amount unpaid under by-laws, which was placed by the Auditors for the year at $2,001.62. Looking at the amounts in other years it seems more reasonable to expect that it should have been $1,001.62, in which case the deficit would have been $373.89. As I mentioned to Council this is a very unsatisfactory way of estimating assets and liabilities.

1898.

H. M. Campbell, Reeve.

Assets.

Cash in Treasurer's hands	$450 75	
Balance of taxes uncollected	6,108 62	
	$6.559 37	
Less assessments placed on roll to provide for debentures maturing 1899	2,773 35	
		$3,786 02

Liabilities.

Balance due for County rates	$1,642 16	
" school rates	1,000 79	
Unpaid under by-laws	751 43	
Excess of assets over liabilities	391 64	
	$3,786 02	$3,786 02

1900.

Assets.

Balance of cash in Treasurer's hands	$535 98	
" taxes uncollected	7,403 47	
		7,939 45

Liabilities.

Balance of school taxes	$1,317 03	
" County rate	2,726 66	
Unpaid under by-laws	300 00	
Excess of liabilities over assets	....	1,457 49
	$9,396 94	$9,396 94

1901.

Assets.

Balance of cash in Treasurer's hands	$549 04	
" taxes uncollected	8,601 35	
Bills payable	700 00	
		$9,850 39

Liabilities.

Balance of school taxes	$2,000 00	
" County rates	2,700 90	
Unpaid under by-laws	600 00	
Debentures maturing 1902	6,874 61	
Excess of liabilities over assets	....	2,325 12
	$12,175 51	$12,175 51

1902.

Assets.

Balance of taxes	$8,676 07	
Bills payable	1,780 00	
		$10,456 07

Liabilities.

Balance due Treasurer	$1,065 22	
" school rates	1,514 97	
" County rates	959 34	
Unpaid under by-laws	500 00	
Debentures maturing 1903	8,247 78	
Excess of liabilities over assets	....	1,831 24
	$12,287 31	$12,287 31

1902.

John Crawford, Reeve.

Assets.

Balance of taxes	$8,676 07	
Bills payable	1,780 00	
	$10,456 07	
Less assessments placed on roll to provide for debentures maturing in 1903	7,962 48	
		2,473 59

Liabilities.

Balance due Treasurer	$1,065 22	
" for County rates	959 34	
" for school taxes	1,514 97	
Unpaid under by-laws	500 00	
Excess of liabilities over assets	....	1,565 94
	$4,039 53	$4,039 53

1903.

James Norman, Reeve.

Assets.

Balance of taxes uncollected	$12,392 37	
Bills payable	1,400 00	
	$13,762 37	
Less assessments placed on roll to provide for debentures maturing 1904	8,270 42	
		5,491 95

Liabilities.

Balance due Treasurer	$859 11	
" for County rates	1,684 21	
" for school taxes	1,978 43	
Unpaid under by-laws	1,514 92	
Excess of liabilities over assets	....	544 52
	$6,036 67	$6,036 67

1904.

John Crawford, Reeve.

Assets.

Balance of taxes uncollected	$17,436 17	
Bills payable	3,325 00	
	$20,761 17	
Less assessments placed on roll to provide for debentures maturing in 1905	8,481 60	
		12,279 57

Liabilities.

Balance due Treasurer	$3,408 98	
" County rates	2,001 25	
" school rates	3,734 11	
Unpaid under by-laws	703 40	
Avonmore Police Village	119 24	
Excess of assets over liabilities	2,311 86	
	$12,279 57	$12,279 57

1905.

John Crawford, Reeve.

Assets.

Balance of taxes uncollected	$19,681 16	
Bills payable	1,550 00	
	$21,231 16	
Less assessments placed on roll to provide for debentures maturing in 1906	8,780 42	
		$12,450 42

Liabilities.

Balance due Treasurer	$4,164 37	
" for County rates	2,759 51	
" school taxes	3,639 19	
Unpaid under by-laws	517 14	
Excess of assets over liabilities	1,370 33	
	$12,450 74	$12,450 74

Auditor.

REPORT ON THE POSITION OF THE ACCOUNTS OF THE TOWNSHIP OF ROXBOROUGH WITH SURPLUS OR DEFICIT AT THE END OF EACH OF THE YEARS 1897 TO 1904 INCLUSIVE, WITH FULL REPORT FOR THE YEAR 1905.

To the Reeve and Council for the Township of Roxborough:

GENTLEMEN,—In accordance with the instructions given me by J. B. Laing, Esq., Provincial Municipal Auditor, I have made a careful audit of the books and vouchers of the Township, from the last Government Audit of 8th Sept., 1897, to 31st Dec., 1905, and have much pleasure in stating that I found all the Treasurer's vouchers in perfect order, the only mistakes found being against himself, to correct which I have placed to his credit as at 31st Dec., 1905, the sum of $63.97.

My principal work has been the writing up of a Drainage Record book, from which the Clerk will in future make the entries on the Collector's rolls, of the assessments payable under the various drainage by-laws of the Township, which with the number of names under each are as follows:—

Drain.	Number of Interested Parties.
Aux Raisins River	66
Blair-McRae Drain	52
Blair-Shanks "	16
Boundary "	22
Butternut Creek	6
Deslile River	15
Dewar Drain	29
Duff-McMillan Drain	12
Fraser Creek	50
Hart "	86
Henry Drain	24
Monkland Drain	260
Morrison-Monroe Drain	52

McElheran Drain	15
McGregor Creek	54
Maclennan Drain	32
McNeil-McDonell Drain	29
McRae "	52
Macmillan "	15
North Branch and Mackintosh Drain	324
Payne River	430
Steele-Hough Drain	36
Steele-McElheran Drain	14
Stewart Creek	56
Tayside "	56
Thompson-Ferguson Drain	54
Upper Moose Creek	127

Total number of names 1,983

The Moose Creek was not entered because the debentures are practically paid off, .ne last falling due in 1906.

The preparation of this drainage book will, I believe, result in a very considerable saving to the Township, as well as enable the Clerk to get the Collector's rolls prepared in proper time, and assist him to stop what have apparently been serious leaks in the Township finances. To enable him to effect this completely, however, it will be necessary for the Council to instruct the Engineer, or other competent person, to examine and report upon a good many of the assessments, principally in the south-western part of the Township, and particularly the Payne River and Hart Creek. There have been so many and intricate changes in the ownership of the lands, since these were first assessed under the by-laws, that it is in many cases impossible to tell who should now be assessed and how much the assessment should be. Had the Drainage Record book been in use from the commencement of the several drains the changes in ownership would have been noted as they occurred, but now a proper report will be required, which can best be furnished by the Township Engineer. In giving the instructions for this it will be well to make them general, as the assessments on some of the other drains will probably require to be looked into.

I would again, respectfully, call the attention of the Council to the imperative need of furnishing the Clerk and Assessor with plans of the Villages of Avonmore and Moose Creek, so as to enable these to be properly assessed and the taxes due collected. As matters now stand there is a constant annual loss to the Township from the vagueness of the descriptions given in these villages, while, if the properties were assessed by lot number, this would not occur.

I have also prepared a Debenture book, giving the amounts received from the sale of the several issues of debentures, the date of maturity of the payments, and those already made.

In comparing this with the Record book, I found that, for the Payne River, five issues of debentures had been made, two of which were under By-law 12 of 1898, which authorized the issue of $13,883.14, $10,500 first being issued on account and $3,300 later. A subsequent By-law, 26 of 1901, passed as an amending by-law to the Outlet, could not be found, there being no trace of it either in the books or minutes. I obtained a copy from Mr. J. G. Harkness, Barrister, who had drawn the by-law, for fifteen annual payments of $83.25 each. Five of these debentures have been paid by the Township, and

I beg to recommend that the first of them be placed on the Collector's roll for 1906 and one in each year afterwards until the issue is paid off. I have treated the debentures already paid as an asset as at 31st Dec., 1905.

I have written up the Municipal Cash book for the years 1903-4 and 1905, so that the Treasurer can now continue it, and will find it of very material assistance in enabling him and others to see clearly the exact position of Township affairs.

I beg to submit herewith a statement of the net debt of the Township as at 31st Dec., 1905, when it was $5,185.90, with approximate statements of the amount at 31st Dec. in each of the years 1897-8-9 1900-1-2-3 and 1904. The amounts are sufficiently exact for all practical purposes, and the obtaining of exact data would have entailed a very considerable amount of work, so that I did not consider myself warranted in spending the time necessary to obtain it.

If the Council will carry out the above suggestions as to assessments on the drains and plans of the Villages, there is no reason why the small indebtedness of the Township cannot be paid off without going to the expense of issuing debentures, and the saving in taxes now lost will, I believe, pay the whole cost of this audit within two years. I would take this opportunity of drawing the attention of the Council to the unfortunate results which arise from striking the general rate of taxation too low, so that it will not produce the amount required to carry on the business of the Township, and consequently the indebtedness is increased instead of diminished.

All of which is respectfully submitted.

J. R. ADAMSON,
Auditor.

Moose Creek, Ont., 24th July, 1906.

The cost of this audit to the Township of Roxborough as per Mr. Adamson's account was $816.50.

TORONTO, ONT., April 20th, 1906.

To His Honour the Lieutenant-Governor of Ontario in Council:

SIR,—By authority of an Order-in-Council approved by your Honour on the 6th day of March last, and under instructions from the Provincial Municipal Auditor, I proceeded on the 11th of same month to Windsor for the purpose of making an inspection, examination and audit of the books, accounts, vouchers and moneys of the Municipal Corporation of the Township of Sandwich West, in the County of Essex.

2. This audit had been petitioned for by certain ratepayers of the said Township, who requested that it cover the period of the last ten years.

Treasurer.

3. During the first four years covered by this audit Mr. J. D. Lajennesse was Treasurer, and during the time before he started the Municipal Cash book now in use, the entries made by hi mare difficult to follow, I have, however, satisfied myself as to the correctness of his accounts, with the exception of the balance shown on 4th Con. Drain repairs By-law No. 250, reference will be found to this balance under statement of drains, and whilst it may have been properly distributed, I was unable to find entries therefor.

Mr. Ferdinand Pare has been Treasurer for the past six years, and his
keeping of the cash book shows painstaking work and method.   His additions
were correct, and the vouchers were fastened together to correspond with the
pages of the cash book, in proper rotation, and up to the last audit, bore the
"audit" stamp, the auditors initialling the back of each package only.   The
vouchers lack in one essential, in that in many cases, no endorsement by the
party to whom the warrant is payable appears, the word "paid" generally
being used.

This arises to some extent from the fact that many warrants are held
until turned over to the Collector on account of taxes, and this official, when
accepting same, has not secured a proper receipting of the warrant.   The Collector is in fact an important medium of exchange between warrant holders
and the Treasurer, with the result that the latter's transactions in cash are
materially lessened, a desirable result where banking facilities are not locally
available.

Cash Book.

4. I recommend as follows : —

(a) That all warrants held by the Treasurer as vouchers be properly endorsed by the party to whom same are payable, or if received by some one
else on behalf of said party the endorsement to state the fact.

(b) That the Auditors appointed for the year complete their audit up to
the 31st day of December of the year for which they are appointed, and not
carry their work beyond that date.   An interim audit can be made at any
time during the year, but the result of each audit should be shown upon or
attached to the Cash Book page containing the termination of the period over
which audit extends.

(c) That the balance of cash on hand on 31st December of each year alone
be carried forward to the 1st of January following, and that additions of both
debits and credits be carried from page to page up to the 15th of December
when to the totals then shown be added the totals for period 16th to 31st of
December previous, thus giving the totals for the municipal year.   There is
no advantage in making a summary of each page should it be thought desirable to make a summary by months, then the totals at the end of each month
should be added to the summation of the succeeding one; that is January
additions will be carried to the end of February, and these to the end of March
and so on through the year.

(d) That the Treasurer enter in a separate column under " Drain Awards,
etc.," all payments made by him which are to be placed by the Clerk upon
the roll for collection.   This will enable the former, by comparing the total
additions to the roll, to ascertain that for all such disbursements proper
charge has been made.

(e) That it be the duty of the Clerk to notify the Treasurer in writing
of any sums due to or payable by adjoining Townships on account of drains
or other matters, together with any subsequent adjustment, and that the
Treasurer enter at the top of each drain account the information, thus enabling him to see that a proper settlement is finally made.

Arrears of Taxes Book.

5. Since the "Arrears of Taxes" book was opened by Mr. Pare, such
arrears have been well looked after.   I find, however, on comparing the book
with the records of the County Treasurer that some unimportant differences

exist, and I recommend that the Treasurer make the necessary corrections in his book in accordance with Schedule "I" attached hereto, and which list agrees with the County Treasurer's book. I find that the County Treasurer returned to the Clerk for the purpose of having placed upon the roll 1902, taxes on part of Lot 32 and on 2nd Con., amounting to $4.83 (four dollars and eighty-three cents. This was not placed on the roll, and if not now collectable and subject to there being no reason for this omission, I consider the Clerk to be responsible therefor, and I have carried it as an asset of the Township.

Assessors.

The assessment rolls are added by pages only, and usually in pencil, no summary of the totals is given, the grand total only being shown. The additions of the several pages should in future be properly completed, and following the last of the roll, a recapitulation by pages of the totals thereon shown, which added would give the grand total. The rolls bear the certificate of the Assessor, showing them to have been handed to the Clerk not later than the 30th of April in any year.

Clerk.

7. Mr. Ernest Bondy has been Clerk of the Township for the full period of this audit, and I consider him well qualified by knowledge and experience to carry out in a proper manner the work devolving upon him. In some particulars (to which reference is made under the separate heading), the work has not been done in as systematic a manner as its importance requires. To the lack of information which should be readily obtainable, thereby occasioned, as also that several of the Collector's rolls were not to be found, was due a considerable expenditure of time on my part, which under proper conditions would not have been required.

Collector's Rolls.

8. It has been the practice of the Clerk to enter the names of the ratepayers in alphabetical order, in this departing from the order in which the names appear on the assessment roll. The additions of the sub-divisions of assessed value have not been made, nor even the total assessed value in all cases. No summary of the pages is shown.

I recommend as follows:—

(a) That the Collector's roll follow page for page, the names as shown on the assessment roll.

(b) That the columns showing the sub-divisions of assessed value to be added, thereby providing a check on the addition of the column showing total assessment.

(c) That the rate of levy for County, Township and schools, both general and special, be shown.

(d) That special drain debenture levies be kept as much as possible in separate columns, and that a special column be used for "Drain Awards, etc.," and for this purpose the next supply of Collector's rolls purchased should be of a pattern giving more columns for use.

(e) That the following recapitulations be entered at the end of the roll:—

1st. Recapitulation, showing number of page and amount thereon divided under the different drain debenture levies, also one column for drain award charges and totalled.

2nd. Recapitulation, showing number of page and amount thereon of total assessed value for the purposes named and levies under separate headings of the County, Township, commutation, dogs, arrears, etc., and totalled.

3rd. Recapitulation, showing number of page and amount thereon of total assessed value for school purposes, also under separate columns the amounts levied in each school section for general, also for special rates, and totalled.

The above to be then tabulated, thus showing total on roll. The following gives settlement with the Treasurer for the last ten years.

Roll 1896.

Total as per return made to Bureau of Industries	$10,021 02
Receipts from Collector as per cash book	9,947 34
Shortage	$73 68

I have not carried this shortage to the debit of Mr. F. St. Louis, the Collector, as I have received from Mr. Benetean, then Reeve, and Mr. Bondy the Clerk, certificates that deductions for errors equal to the shortage were made on the roll after returns were sent to the Government. The roll books for this year were not to be found.

Roll 1897.

Total as per returns made to Bureau of Industries	$10,706 92
Add arrears returned from the County Treasurer	96 11
	$10,802 03
Receipts from Collector as per cash book	$10,816 58

This surplus is probably due to additions to the roll on accountant of statute labor. The roll book for this year was not to be found.

Roll 1898.

Total as per returns made to Bureau of Industries	$11,862 75
Add arrears returned from County Treasurer	13 16
	$11,875 91
Receipts from Collector as per cash book	$11,875 91

The roll book for this year was not to be found.

Roll 1899.

Total as per returns to Bureau of Industries	$12,270 62
Add arrears returned from County Treasurer	72 29
	$12,342 91
Receipts from Collector as per cash book	$12,310 62
Shortage	$32 29

This shortage I have carried as a charge against Mr. F. St. Louis, the Collector, as I have had no explanation as to how it occurred.

The roll book for this year was not to be found.

Roll 1900.

Total as per returns made to Bureau of Industries	$13,439	63
Add arrears returned from County Treasurer	39	17
	$13,478	80
Receipts from Collector as per cash book	13,477	32
Shortage	$1	48

This shortage is small and probably arose through some correction of the roll, and I have not thought it necessary to carry it as a charge against the Collector.

The roll book for this year was not to be found.

I have carried as a charge against Mr. F. St. Louis the sum of $12.46, being taxes on the roll 1900 on W. part Lot 11 of 1st Con. I understand that these taxes were returned from the County Treasurer to be again put upon the roll, it was found they had been paid when due, either to Mr. St. Louis or to an agent appointed by him, and the Council in April, 1905, issued a warrant to the then Collector to settle the matter. I cannot find that the Council had the power to make this allowance, but in view of their action I have not added interest to the original amount, which is due from and which should be paid by Mr. St. Louis. · ·

Rolls 1901, 1902, 1903 and 1904.

The rolls for these years were furnished me and agree with the returns as shown by the cash book.

Roll 1905.

No returns are shown on account of this roll up to the 31st December last, but during January and February receipts total $2,576.93, and the Collector is at present working on the collections. I have noted on the book two undercharges and one overcharge, in all a short charge of $6.25 and due to error in computation of school taxes. If too late to correct on this roll they should be carried forward to that of next year.

I was greatly hampered in my work owing to so many of the Collectors' rolls being missing.' In order to determine the Drain Debenture levies due to be placed upon the rolls for the years 1896 to 1900, I called for the rolls from 1886, with the result that the books for the years 1887, 1889 and 1895 to 1900, inclusive, were not to be found. The most important were the books covering the period 1895 to 1900, and Mr. St. Louis, then Collector, acknowledged to having received back at least some of these for the purpose of adjusting between himself and certain ratepayers taxes returned by him to the Treasurer as paid, but he claims to have duly returned the books when this was done. However this may be, the result evidences a lack of care in the safekeeping of these records which should not be permitted in the future.

By-law Book.

9. The By-law Book is not indexed, which should be done at once. I recommend that in future drain by-laws be entered in a separate book, and that in this connection the assessment table showing levies on individuals as also "Roads," be the assessment as confirmed by the Court of Revsion, and also that in the event of allowances for farm bridges, etc., such allowances be settled by warrant on the Treasurer, and not by making correction in the assessment table as then determined. In some cases it was difficult, if not impossible, owing to the numerous alterations of figures in the assessment table, to determine the amount properly chargeable to "Roads."

Further that in the event of a by-law being amended, a supplementary by-law be passed to cover such changes.

I attach (Schedule 2) a form of by-law, with figures based upon last year, which form I recommend for the annual levies.

In all cases the by-laws should show the date when finally passed.

Court of Revision.

10. The minutes of meetings of the Court of Revision seldom show the signature to same of the Chairman, although always signed by the Clerk. This omission should not occur.

Drain and Watercourse Book.

11. The entries in this book are not complete. The Clerk informs me that his practice is to enter all such charges on the Collector's roll from the certificate furnished by the Engineer, and by reference to copies contained in the books of Mr. Newman, Engineer, I satisfied myself as to the correctness of this statement so far as the roll books were available.

I recommend that for every payment made by the Township, which is to be settled for by being placed on the roll for collection, an entry be made in this book. Such entry should show the date and to whom paid, also warrant number, also the names of contributors with amount due from each.

The Clerk, after having duly entered on the Collector's roll, should mark against the charge "Entered on Collector's Roll of 190—."

Drain Accounts.

12. I attach statement Schedule No. 3 showing the position of the several drain accounts, so far as the books were available, to determine the same. When the work is sufficiently advanced to permit of it being done, the Council should, without delay, arrive at an adjustment with the neighboring Townships contributing to such works, the Clerk to advise the Treasurer of the result.

Schools, Special Rates.

13. By reference to Schedule No. 2 it will be seen by Schedule (B.) that the amounts collected from the several school sections on roll 1905 varies from the amounts asked for and paid as follows:—

S.S.	Amount levied.	Amount paid.	Over-payment.	Under-payment.
	$ c.	$ c.	$ c.	$ c.
No. 2..........	555 33	500 00	....	55 33
" 3..........	400 70	400 00	....	70
" 5..........	311 33	300 00	....	11 33
" 6..........	403 58	400 00	....	3 58
' 7..........	254 67	250 00	....	4 67
" 8..........	239 69	237 00	....	2 69
" 9..........	256 70	275 00	18 30	....
" 10...........	20 22	19 25	....	97
Separate No. 1	1,044 91	1,050 00	5 09	....
" " 2 & 5	269 00	269 72	72	....
" " 4	456 47	450 00	....	6 47
Sandwich.......	28 76	28 73	....	3
	$4,241 36	$4,179 70	$24 11	$85 77

The net amount underpaid of $61.66 I have carried as a liability, and although it may not be considered necessary to make an adjustment in the majority of cases the amount over-collected in S. S. No. 2 should be paid to the Trustees or taken into consideration when making the next levy. I recommend that in future the actual amount produced by the levy be paid to the school sections contributing.

Assets and Liability Statement.

14. I attach Schedule No. 4, a statement of the standing of the Township as on the 31st of December last.

Amongst the available assets I have included the amount of $23.50, being a payment on account of Engineer's charges on Pajot drain, which amount had already been paid. On reference to Mr. Newman's books I am satisfied that the amount was received in his office through an oversight, and the matter was at once put right by re-payment to the Treasurer.

I also attach Schedule No. 5, a statement of the drain balances on hand; also Schedule No. 6, statement of the drain indebtedness to be provided for by annual levies.

The property of the Township in Town Hall or road repairing machines has not been taken into account.

The Town Hall and contents are insured in the London Mutual Fire Insurance Company.

15. I inspected the bond of Mr. Albert Dufour, Collector, which is for $8,000, signed by Thomas Dufour and Arsane Dufour, and dated the 2nd of December, 1905.

The bond of Mr. Ferdinand Pare, Treasurer, for a similar amount and signed by R. C. Benetean and Nazaire Pare, bears the date of 22nd April, 1905. Mr. Pare will furnish a bond ·for the current year so soon as the Council take action upon this report.

16. I communicated with the Treasurers of the adjoining municipalities asking for a statement of their cash transactions with the Township of Sandwich West, and I was favoured with the information excepting in the case of the Township of Sandwich East; two letters which I addressed to Mr. W. A. St. Louis, Treasurer of that Township, remaining unanswered.

17. The deposit accounts of the Collector and the Treasurer have been kept as such in the banking house of Messrs. John Curry & Co., Windsor,

10 M.A.

whose handling of the Township's banking business has, I believe, been in every way satisfactory to the Council. I would, however, respectfully draw the attention of the Council to the desirability of, in the handling of public funds, taking advantage of the facilities of the generally acknowledged stronger position of a chartered bank.

18. The recommendations which I have made in this report are based upon the continuance of the present system of books, and without bringing into use journal and ledger. Should the Council desire to do so, they could no doubt make satisfactory arrangements with some one in Windsor (where such expert assistance is available) to carry the several accounts into the ledger from the books of account as now kept by the Clerk and Treasurer and who would continue their work as in the past.

19. I shall be pleased to furnish further explanation and to advise with the Council on any matter or recommendation arising out of this report.

I have the honour to be, Sir,

Your obedient servant,

J. George,

Chartered Accountant.

Schedule No. 1.

Arrears of Taxes as of 31st December, 1905, as given by County Treasurer.

1st.	E. P. 54	$31 26
	R. P. 54 and 55	10 64
B.A.	149 and 150	1 65
"	257 and 258	5 89
"	½ of 250, lot 251	1 59
'	126	2 29
"	151 N. ¼ 152	77
"	132, 133, 134	1 67
"	½ of 250 (1903 and 1904 taxes)	· 69
"	139 and 140	1 25
"	225	1 96
'	163	39
'	143, 144	77
"	76, 77, 78, 79	2 68
"	131	56
"	136, 137, 138	3 97
'	203	72
'	227	3 08
'	145, 146	61
"	293, 294, 305, 306, 325, 326	5 36
"	40, 41, 57, 58	3 51
"	2	6 63
'	297, 298	1 54
'	24, 25	3 12
"	93, 94, 97, 98	9 06
	Campbell Ave., 69	7 71
"	208, 209	2 56
"	55, 56, 128, 129, 130, 197	7 33
"	295, 296, 303, 304	3 91
"	26, 27	3 25
'	61	3 42
'	Lot 1	3 12
'	38, 39	3 12
"	67, 68, 69	3 34
'	100, 101	5 68
"	117, 120, 121	4 75
"	187, 188, 189, 190, 191	3 12
"	265, 266, 260, 261, 262	5 14

10a M. A.

A.B.	320, 321, 322, 323, 324	10 28
"	318, 319, 194, 195, 196	9 06
"	122, 123	1 11
"	80, 81, 82, 83	2 68
"	147, 148, 156, 153	4 74
	2nd, N. ½ 79	3 84
	West London, lots 4, 5, 6	3 58
"	7, 8, 9	5 61
	Wellington Ave., 84, 85, 86	7 08
"	243, 244, 245, 246, 17, 18, 19, 20, 21, 222, 223, 224	5 42
W.N.	90, 91, 234, 235, 236	4 42
	2nd pt. lot 87	4 25
B.A.	54	2 45
"	267	1 51
"	213, 214, 215	5 42
"	135	1 17
	Wellington Ave., 127, 128	3 51
"	119, 210	1 98
"	25	3 51
"	10, 11, 12, 13	2 07
	5 E. pt. 4	5 04
"	240, 241	2 73
	West London, 17, 18	4 17
"	299	1 17
	247, 248	1 59
"	283 N. 7-101	93
"	313	77
"	300	77
"	207, 217, 57	2 64
"	1 N. E. pt. 27	10 83
"	228	71
"	229	79
"	50 and 51	1 03
"	105	95
		$283 92

NOTE.—That taxes amounting to $2.77 on Bridge Ave., lot No. 277, were written off by County Treasurer in accordance with minutes of Council of April 19, '04.

SCHEDULE No. 2.

By-Law No.

Being a by-la v to fix the rates for the levy and collection of taxes for the Township of Sandwich West, for the year 1905.

Finally Passed, 1905.

Whereas the Municipal Council of Sandwich West, deem it necessary and expedient to pass a by-law for said purpose.

And whereas the total assessment of the Township of Sandwich West, liable for Township rate, county rate, and special on roads for drainage is the sum of $785,645, and the total assessment liable for general school rate is the sum of $605,491.

Therefore the Municipal Council of the Township of Sandwich West, enacts as follows:—

1. That for raising the sum of $1,472, for county purposes, a rate of mills on the dollar, of the assessed value of the whole rateable property of the Township of Sandwich West, be levied and collected.

2. That for raising the sum of $3,136, for Township purposes, a rate of mills on the dollar, of the assessed value of the whole rateable property of the Township of Sandwich West, be levied and collected.

3. That for raising the sum of $130.78, as recited in column No. 6, Schedule "A" for special rates on roads for drainage purposes, a rate of mills on the dollar, of the assessed value of the whole rateable property of the township of Sandwich West, be levied and collected.

SCHEDULE "A".

No. of By-law.	Name of drain.	No. of levy.	Total No. of levies.	Annual on lands.	Annual on roads.
				$ c.	$ c.
337	Chappus D. O.....	5	5	73 41	5 12
349	Chappus....	2	5	300 04	49 65
351	Bisetts	3	5	67 76	21 24
: 52	Cahill	2	5	87 66	15 12
359	4 Con	1	5	135 87	39 65
				$674 87	$130 78

4. That the amounts specified in column 5, Schedule "A", shall be levied in accordance with the several by-laws pertaining thereto.

5. That for public and separate school purposes, a rate on the dollar, of the assessed value of the whole rateable property in each school section be levied and collected for the maintenance of the said schools for the year 1905, in accordance with the Statutes of Ontario, 1 Edward, Chap. 39, Section 71, and that the rates in each section be the rates set opposite the number of the section in column 6, Schedule B.

SCHEDULE "B".

No. of Section.	Assessment.	Amount levied.	Township portion.	Rate.	Total rates.	Trustees' requisitions.
	$	$ c.	$ c.		$ c.	$ c.
1	25,435	....	150 00	......	705 33	....
2	122,342	555 33	150 00	4.55	705 33	500 00
3	133,564	400 70	250 00	3.	650 70	400 00
5	166,238	311 33	150 00	4.7	461 33	300 00
6	73,766	403 58	250 00	5.5	653 58	400 00
7	74,041	254 67	150 00	3.4	404 67	250 00
8	31,953	239 69	150 00	7.5	389 69	237 00
9	69,367	256 70	150 00	3.7	406 70	275 00
10	8,785	20 22	15 00	2.3	35 22	19 25
County......			69 85		69 85	....
	605,491	2,442 22	1,334 85	. ...	3,777 07	2,381 25
Separate.						
No. 1........	75,139	1,044 91	....	14.	....	1,050 00
" 2 & 5.....	37,362	269 00	....	7.2	....	269 72
" 4	70,217	456 47	....	6.5	....	450 00
Sandwich....	3,285	28 76	....	8.¾	....	28 73
	791,494	1,799 14	....	....	....	1,798 45

6. That for raising the sum of $1,334.85, as recited in column 4, Schedule "B" for general school rate, a rate of mills on the dollar, shall be levied and collected upon all the rateable property liable therefor.

7. That the Clerk shall also enter in the collector's roll for the year 1905.

DITCHES AND WATERCOURSES' AWARDS.

Enter here the different awards with the amount to be collected on each (against the names entered in Drain Award Book, enter the No. on roll and year charged).

Dogs. Enter number and total charges.

STATUTE LABOR.

Pathmaster.	*Person Charged.*	*No. on Roll.*	*Amount.*

ARREARS OF TAXES.

Name of Owner.	*Description of Property.*	*No. on Roll.*	*Amount.*

DRAIN ACCOUNTS.

SCHEDULE No. 3.

1886. Cahill Drain By-law No. 157 (10 years at 6 per cent.)

By sale of debt, C. B. 614	....	$3,462 20
To cost of work, C. B. 615	$3,382 90	
To refund on same including Township C. B. 360	79 30	
	$3,462 30	$3,462 30

1906.
Sept. 3.—Paid deb. 346, 22· coupons, $20.78...................................   367 00

Levies on Lands.

1886, $409.87.	1891, $376.09.
1887, roll missing.	1892, $376.09.
1888, $376.09.	1893, $327.95.
1889, roll missing.	1894, $327.95.
1890, $376.09.	1895, roll missing.

1886. Marais Drain By-law No. 159 (10 years at 6 per cent.)

By sale of deb.	C. B. 619	....	$1,457 00
To work and expenses	" 619	$1,362 30	
To refunds including township share	" 368	94 70	
		$1,457 00	$1,457 00

(No vouchers produced.)

1896.
Sept. 3.—Paid deb 145 70   8 75   336 $154 45
1895.
Sept. 15.—Paid deb 145 70   17 50   332   163 20

Levies on Lands.

(1886 not on this.)	1892, $141.98.
1887, roll missing.	1893, $154.41.
1888, $136.00.	1894, $154.41.
1889, roll missing.	1895, roll missing.
1890, $141.98.	1896, roll missing.
1891, $141.98.	

1886. 4th Con. Drain, By-law No. 162 (10 years at 6 per cent.)

By sale of deb.	C. B. 622	....	....	$1,331 00
By Sandwich East	622	....	....	288 00
To work and expenses	622	....	$1,608 20	
To refunds including township portion	366	....	10 80	
			$1,619 90	$1,619 90

(No vouchers produced.)

Levies on Lands.

1886, not on roll.	1892, $137.77.
1887, roll missing.	1893, $136.48.
1888, $137.77.	1894, $136.48.
1889, roll missing.	1895, roll missing.
1890, $137.77.	1896, roll missing.
1891, $137.77.	

1890. 3rd Concession Drain, By-law No. 214 (5 years at 5 per cent.)

By sale of deb.	C. B. 621	....	....	$1,826 87
By Township of Sandwich E.	621	....	....	293 70
To work		....	$2,033 50	
To refunds including township share C.B. 364		....	87 07	
			$2,120 57	$2,120 57

1896.
Sept.   3.—Paid deb. 407.00, coupons 20.35, C. B. 336 .... $427 35

Levies on Lands.

1890, roll missing.	1893, $277.71.
1891, $278.44.	1894, $277.71.
1892, $278.44.	1895, roll missing.

Assessment, lands	$278 37	
roads	135 93	
		$414 30

1890. Basin Drain, By-law No. 215 (5 years at 5 per cent.)

By sale of deb.	C. B. 620......		....	$565 85
To work and expenses	C. B.	......	542 30	
To refund including township portion C. B. 369......			23 55	
			$565 85	$565 85

1896.
Sept.   3.—By reduction of deb. C. B. 336 .... $132 35

Levies on Lands.

1891, $100.74.	1894, $100.72.
1892, $100.74.	1895, roll missing.
1893, $100.72.	

Assessment lands	$100 74	
roads	31 05	
		$131 79

1892. Cahill Drain, Outlet By-law No. 230.

By sale of deb.	C. B. 617......		....	$2,833 00
By Sandwich East	617......		....	383 00
By transfer from Marais	231......		....	258 74
To work			$2,956 16	
To portion of debenture			361 93	
To refunds including township portion 363........			156 65	
			$3,474 74	$3,474 74

1897.
July   20.—Paid deb. and coupons $626 34
1898.
Aug.   29.—   "   " 597 87
        By portion of deb. charged to cost 361 93

Levies on Lands.

1892, not on this roll.   1895, roll missing.
1893, $239.98.   1896, roll missing.
1894, $479.96.   1897, roll missing.

Marais Drain Repair, By-law No. 236.

By sale of deb.   C. B. 618......   .... $1,689 00
To work $1,430 26
Transfer to Cahill Dr'n Outlet, By-law No. 230, 618   258 74
                                         $1,689 00 $1,689 00

(No vouchers produced.)
1896.
Jan.   11.—Paid deb.   333..   390 33
Oct.   6.—   "   340..   389 27
1897.
Oct.   11.—   "   352..   390 21
1898.
Sept.   10.—   "   8..   390 01

Levies on Lands.

1893, $212.39.   1896, roll missing.
1894, $212.39.   1897, roll missing.
1895, roll missing.

Assessment of lands $212 98
                roads 175 49
                                              $388 47

Janisse Drain By-law No. 249.

By sale of deb. C. B. 623................................   .... $670 59
To work   622................................   634 46
Refunds   367................................   36 13
                                    $670 59 $670 59

(No vouchers produced.)
1896.
Sept.   21.—Paid deb. C. B. 340.. $154 97
1897.
Oct.   20.—   "   356..   154 97
1898.
Sept.   10.—   "   8..   154 86
1900.
June   20.—   "   34..   154 82
1899
Oct.   7.—   "   29..   154 79

Levies on Lands.

1895, roll missing.   1898, roll missing.
1896, roll missing.   1899, roll missing.
1897, roll missing.   1900, roll missing.

1894. 4th Con. Drain Repairs, By-law No. 250 (3 years.)

By sale of deb. C. B. 613	....	$655 77
Sandwich South	....	124 59
To work	$741 15	
To balance	39 21	
	$780 36	$780 36

(No vouchers produced.)

1896.
Oct.   5.—Deb. C. B. 340.. $240 52
1897.
Oct.   11.— "   352..   240 64
1898.
Aug.   29.— "   8..   241 25

Levies on Lands.

1894, not in this roll.   1897, roll missing.
1895, roll missing.   1898, roll missing.
1896, roll missing.   1899, roll missing.

I cannot find entries to show that above balance of $39.21 was distributed.
The levy according to by-law shows on lands $179.56 and on roads $97.96, in all
$277.52. I cannot ascertain if the levy was reduced to agree with the reduced cost
of work (estimated $755.77 debentures sold for $655.77 as roll books are missing.)

1896. Chappus Drain Improvement, By-law No. 261.

Debentures, C. B. 148......................................	....	$964 00
Interest, 148......................................	....	21 10
To work	$945 12	
To balance transfers to Chappus drain outlet......	39 98	
	$985 10	$985 10

1897.
Oct.   11.—Paid deb. C. B. 352.. $222 78
1898.
Oct.   29.—   "   8..   223 01
1899.
Oct.   7.—   "   29..   223 00
1900.
June   20.—   "   34..   222 69
1901.
July   24.—   "   50..   222 68

Levies on Lands.

1896, roll missing.   1899, roll missing.
1897, roll missing.   1900, roll missing.
1898, roll missing.   1901, not in this roll.

Cahill Drain Improvement, By-law No. 273.

1897.
Aug.   30.—By sale of deb., C. B. 143...............................   .... $1,408 00
            To work and expense $1,410 40
                                                                       $1,410 40 $1,408 00

1898.
Oct.   15.—Deb. and coupons, C. B. 14.. $325 21
1899.
Oct.   7.— "   "   C. B. 29..   325 21
1901.
July   3.— "   ..   C. B. 50..   325 21
1901.
Nov.   27.— "   60..   325 21
1902.
Oct.   8.— "   "   73..   325 21

Levies on Lands.

1897, roll missing,	1900, roll missing.
1898, roll missing.	1901, $271.10.
1899, roll missing.	1902, not in this roll.

Assessment, lands $271 10
            roads 50 89
                                             $322 09

Cahill Drain Outlet Improvement, By-law No. 274 (5 years at 5 per cent.)

1897.
Oct.   30.—By sale of deb., C. B. 144............................ .... $1,085 00
Oct.   23.—By cash Sandwich South 144......................... .... 175 00
          To work and expenses $1,271 07
          By general funds 11 07
                                          $1,271 07 $1,271 07

1898.
1899.
Oct.   7.—   "   ..   29.................................   250 61
1900.
Nov.   9.—   " .   44.................................   250 61
1901.
Oct.   14.—   "   56.................................   250 61
1902.
Oct.   8.—   "   73.................................   250 61

Levies on Lands.

1897, roll missing.	1900, roll missing.
1898, roll missing.	1901, $197.20.
1899, roll missing.	1902, not in this roll.

Assessment, lands $197 20
            roads 53 31
                                               $250 51

Domouchelle Drain, By-law No. 284 (5 years at 5 per cent.)

1897.
Aug.   9.—By sale of deb., C. B. 142 .... $528 92
1899.
Nov.   14.—By interest 3 50
          To work and expenses $528 92
1900.
Jan.   9.—To township funds 3 50
                                           $532 42 $532 42

1898.
Oct.   15.—Deb. and comp., C. B. 14................................ $122 17
1899.
Oct.   7.—   "   29.....................   122 17
1900.
Oct.   19.—   "   42.....................   122 17
1901.
Oct.   14.—   "   56.....................   122 17
1902.
Oct.   22.—   "   54.....................   122 17

Levies on Lands.

1897, no rolls.	1900, no rolls.
1898, no rolls.	1901, $105.55.
1899, no rolls.	1902, not in this roll.

Assesment, lands $105 55
            roads 16 46
                                             $122 01

Basin Drain Repairs, By-law No 288.

1893.			
	By sale of deb., C. B. 145.................................	....	$580 36
1899.			
Nov.	14.—By interest	....	10 35
	To work	$441 36	
	To transfer to Marais Drain, see minutes of council		
	Oct. 7/99	108 00	
1900.			
Jan.	9.—Transfer of township funds, see minutes of council		
	Jan. 5/00	41 37	
		$590 71	$590 71

1899.			
Sept.	19.—Deb. and coupons C. B. 21...		$134 05
1900.			
Aug.	9.— " 39...		134 05
1901.			
Sept.	4.— 55,..		134 05
1902.			
June	14.— 70...		134 05
1903.			
Aug.	18.— 85...		134 05

Levies on Lands.

1898, roll missing.	1901, $102.39.
1899, roll missing.	1902, $102.39.
1900, roll missing.	1903, not in this roll.

Assessment, lands	$102 39	
roads	31 62	
		$134 01

Marais Drain Repairs, By-law No. 289 (5 years at 5 per cent.)

	By sale of deb., C. B. 145	....	$504 50
	" Sandwich, East	....	367 30
	" transfer Bassin drain No. 288	....	108 00
	" interest	....	4 60
	To work and expenses	$949 98	
	" balance in bank	34 42	
		$984 40	$984 40

1899.			
Sept.	19.—Deb. and Comp., C. B. 21...		$116 53
1900.			
Aug.	9.— " 39...		116 53
1901.			
Sept.	4.— " 55...		116 53
1902.			
Jan.	14.— " 70...		116 53
1903.			
Sept.	18.— " 85...		116 53

Levies on Lands.

1898, roll missing.	1901, $97.65.
1899, roll missing.	1902, $97.65.
1900, roll missing.	1903, not in this roll.

Assessment, lands	$97 65	
roads	19 03	
		$116 68

4th Con. Drain, By-law No. 299 (5 years at 5 per cent.)

	By sale of deb., C. B. 146	....	$1,080 00
1899.	" Sandwich South	....	236 00
Nov.	14.— " interest	....	7 55
	" township funds	....	5 00
	To work and expenses	$1,121 00	
	" transfer to 3rd con., minute of council Dec. 20/98	200 00	
	" township funds, minutes of council Jan. 8, 1900	7 55	
		$1,328 55	$1,328 55
1899.			
Sept.	8.—Deb. and Coupons, 20..		$249 45
1899.			
Aug.	9.— " 39...,..............		249 45
1901.			
Sept.	4.— " 55..		249 45
1902.			
June	14.— " 70..		249 45
1903.			
Sept.	18.— " 85..		249 46

Levies on Lands.

1898, roll missing.	1901, $171.29.
1899, roll missing.	1902, $171.29.
1900, roll missing.	1903, not in this roll.

Assessment, lands	$171 29	
roads	75 86	
		$247 15

3rd Con. Drain, By-law No. 300.

1898.			
	By sale of deb., C. B. 146	....	$1,102 00
1899.			
Dec.	17.—Sandwich South	....	221 00
	" transfer from 4th con.	....	200 00
	" interest	....	10 65
	To work and expenses	$1,512 25	
1900.			
Jan.	6.— " transfer to township funds	6 00	
	" transfer to 3rd con. No. 379	5 40	
		$1,523 65	$1,523 65
1899.			
Sept.	8.—Deb. and coupons, C. B. 20............................		$254 53
1900.			
July.	4.— " " 39...............................		254 53
1901.			
Sept.	4.— " " 55...............................		254 53
1902.			
June	14.— " " 70...............................		254 53
1903.			
Aug.	18.— " " 85...............................		254 53

Levies on Lands.

1898, roll missing.	1901, $182.34.
1899, roll missing.	1902, $182.34.
1900, roll missing.	1903, not in this roll.

Assessment, lands	$182 34	
roads	79 58	
		$261 92

Dougal Road Drain Repair, By-law No. 301 (5 years at 5 per cent.)

By deb., C. B. 147	....	$472 00

1899.
Nov. 14.—To interest 4 50
 " work $469 41
1900.
Jan. 9.— " township funds 7 09

| | $476 50 | $476 50 |

1899.
Sept. 25.—Deb. and · coupons, 27.. $109 02
1900.
Oct. 9.— " 40.. 109 02
1901.
Oct. 14.— " 56.. 109 02
1902.
Aug. 29.— " 73... 109 02
1903.
Sept. 18.— " 85... 109 02

Levies on Lands.

1898, roll missing.　　　　　　　1901, $72.23.
1899, roll missing.　　　　　　　1902, $72.23.
1900, roll missing.　　　　　　　1903, not in this roll.

Assessment, lands $72 23
　　　　　 roads 37 12

| | | $109 35 |

6th Con. Outlet, By-law No. 302 (5 years at 5 per cent.)

By sale of deb., C. B. 147................................... .... $779 00

1899.
Nov. 14.— " interest " 147.................................. .... 4 60
 To work and expenses $777 50
 " balance in bank 6 10

| | $783 60 | $783 60 |

1899.
Sept. 10.—Deb. and coupons, C. B. 21.. $179 93
1900.
Oct. 9.— " " 40... 179 93
1901.
Oct. 14.— " 56... 179 93
1902.
Aug. 29.— " 73... 179 93
1904.
Nov. 31.— " 92... 179 93

Levies on Lands.

1898, roll missing.　　　　　　　1901, $118.74.
1899, roll missing.　　　　　　　1902, $118.74.
1900, roll missing.　　　　　　　1903, not in this roll.

Assessment, lands $118 74
　　　　　 roads 61 25

| | | $179 99 |

\

2nd Marais Drain Repairs, No. 306 (5 years at 5 per cent.)

	By sale of deb., C. B. 148............................	....	$254 00
1899.			
Nov.	14.— " interest	....	4 30
	To work and expenses	$ 71 00	
	" amount paid Sandwich East	179 00	
1900.			
Jan.	9.— " transfer township funds (minutes of council Jan. 8th, 1900)	2 00	
	" balance in bank	6 30	
		$258 30	$258 30
1899.			
Nov.	14.—Deb. and coupons, C. B. 30........................		$58 67
1900.			
Oct.	25.— " " 44..............................		58 67
1901.			
Nov.	27.— " 66..............................		58 67
1902.			
Oct.	8.— " 73..............................		58 67
1904.			
April.	7.— " 93..............................		58 67

Levies on Lands.

1898, roll missing.   1901, $38.63.
1899, roll missing.   1902, $38.63.
1900, roll missing.   1903, not in this roll.

Assessment, lands	$38 63	
roads	19 72	
		$58 35

Taylor-Gunn, By-law No. 313.

March	3.—By sale of deb., C. B. 149.....................	....	$461 00
	" Sandwich South, 149...................	....	115 87
June	30.— " interest	....	4 44
	To work	$505 25	
	" refunds ....—.............................	76 06	
		$581 31	$581 31
1900.			
Aug.	9.—Deb. and coupons, C. B. 39....................		$106 48
1901.			
Oct.	14.— " " 56..........................		106 48
1902.			
Aug.	14.— " 72..........................		106 48
1903.			
Sept.	18.— " 85..........................		106 48
1904.			
Aug.	12.— " 97..........................		106 48

Levies on Lands.

1899, roll missing.   1902, $56.74.
1900, roll missing.   1903, $56.74.
1901, $56.74.   1904, not in this roll.

Assessment, lands	$56 74	
roads	50 21	
		$106 95

Bank pass-book shows a credit of 1 60
Being warrant No. 360, 4th Aug, 1900, Henry
    Petrimoulx $1 40
    Balance 20
                                                                    $1 60

Recommended that the balance of $1.60 as shown by bank pass-book be transferred to township account and that a warrant be issued to Mr. Henry Petrimoulx to replace warrant No. 360.

Langlois Drain, By-law No. 315.

1889.				
Oct.	20.—By sale of deb., C. B. 149....................................	....		$849 00
	" interest to June 30/00	....		5 46
	To work and expenses	$781 00		
	" surplus distributed	73 46		
		$854 46		$854 46
1901.				
Oct.	14.—Paid deb. 56..			$196 03
Nov.	1.— " 59..			196 03
1902.				
Oct.	8.— " 73..			196 03
1904.				
March	31.— " 92..			196 03
1905.				
Jan.	9.— " 101..			196 03

Levies on Lands.

1899, roll missing.   1902, $165.97.
1900, roll missing.   1903, $165.97.
1901, $165.97.   1904, not in this roll.

Bank pass-book shows a balance of 41 cents., being warrant No. 344, Aug. 4, 1900, Randolph Hantais, 41 cents.

Recommended that the balance of 41 cents. as shown by bank pass-book be trans. ferred to township account and that a warrant be issued to Mr. R. Hantais to replace warrant No. 344.

Lennon Drain, By-law No. 316 (5 years at 5 per cent.)

1899.				
Oct.	20.—By sale of deb.	....		$947 00
1900.				
March	3.—Sandwich, South	....		374 00
1899.				
Dec.	18.— " loan	....		200 00
1900.				
June	30.— " interest			3 30
	To work and expense	$1,215 35		
	" payment of loan	200 00		
	" refunds	108 95		
		$1,524 30		$1,524 30
1900.				
Nov.	9.—Deb. and coupons, C. B. 44...			$218 66
1901.				
Nov.	27.— " " 60..			218 66
1902.				
Oct.	8.— " " 73..			218 66
1904.				
April	7.— " 93..			218 86
Dec.	22.— " 99..			218 66

Levies on Lands.

1900.
1899, roll missing.   1902, $208.17.
1900, roll missing.   1903, $208.17.
1901, $208.17.   1904, not in this roll.

Assessment, lands	$208 17
roads	29 58
	$237 75
Bank pass-book shows a credit of	$0 37
Being voucher No. 318, Aug. 4/00, Allen Drouillard	25
" No. 321, Aug. 4/00, Jos. Marchesean............	12
	$0 37

Recommended that the balance of 37 cents. as shown in bank pass-book be transferred to township and that warrants be issued to replace Nos. 318 and 321.

Tecumseh Drain, By-law No. 331.

1900.				
Nov.	30.—By sale of debentures, C. B. 150........................		....	$488 00
1901.				
Sept.	30.—By City of Windsor		....	218 38
	To work and expenses ....:		$541 50	
	Balance in bank		164 88	
			$706 38	$706 38
1901.				
Nov.	27.—Deb. and coupons, C. B. 60................................			$112 71
1902.				
Dec.	22.— "	74...		112 71
1904.				
April	7.—	93...		112 71
March	21.—	99...		112 71
1905.				
Nov.	14.—	111...		112 71

Levies on Lands.

1900, roll missing.   1903, $96.75.
1901, $96.75.   1904, $96.75.
1902, $96.75.   1905, not in this roll.

Assessment, lands	$96 75
roads	16 55
	$113 30

Chappus Drain Outlet, By-law No. 337.

1901.				
Sept.	6.—By transfer from Chappus drain improvement,			
	By-law No. 261		....	$ 39 98
	Sale of deb.		....	341 02
	To cost of work		$381 00	
			$381 00	$381 00
1902.				
Aug.	29.—Paid deb. 73..			$78 77
1903.				
Sept.	18.— "	85...		78 77
1904.				
Sept.	3.— "	97..		78 77
1905.				
Aug.	26.— "	109..		78 77

Levies on Lands.

1901, $73.74.   1904, $73.41.
1902, $73.74.   1905, $73.41.
1903, $74.80.

  J. Curry & Co., deb. due Sept. 6th, 1906 .... $78 77
  Assessment, lands $73 41
      roads 5 12
                            $78 53

Chappus Drain, By-law No. 349.

1902.
Oct. 27.—By loan on note 141......................... $........... $140 50
1903.
Oct. 20.— " ." " 141.........................   ....   397 47
1904.
Aug. 13.— " sale of debentures 141.....................   ....   1,712 00
Nov. 2.— " " " 141.....................   ....   1,512 79
1905.
Nov. 20.— " interest 28 75
    " loan on note 35 24
1903.
Oct. 20.—To note with interest paid....................   147 47
1904.
Aug. 12.— " " " 413 57
Nov. 2.— " debs., sold in error and paid with interest...   1,731 21
    " cost of work 1,531 50
    " balance in bank 3 00

                   $3,826 75 $3,826 75
1905.
Aug. 12.—Paid deb. 109 .... $345 54

Levies on Lands.

Taxes, 1904, $309.04.   1905, $309.04.

J. Curry & Co., deb. due 12th Aug., 1906.......................... $345 54
    " " 1907..........................   345 54
    " " 1908..........................   345 54
    " " 1909..........................   345 54
    Note with int. due 23rd May, 1906..............   36 12

(This entry is noted.)
 "This amount is a charge against the benefited parties and should be levied in 1906 roll."
  Assessment, Lands $309 04
      Roads 49 65
                       $353 69

 If this assessment table has not been altered, it would appear that levies as made on "lands" for 1904 and 1905, if continued, will produce more than sufficient to meet note in addition to debentures to mature, and levies on "lands" should be amended accordingly.

East Branch of Cahill Drain, By-law 351.

1902.
Dec. 9.—By loan on note 140......................... $........... $ 91 00
1904.
Jan. 27.— " " " 140.........................   ....   136 25
1905.
Nov. 14.— " " " 140.........................   ....   400 00
1906.
Nov. 20.— " " " 140.........................   ....   276 73

1904.
Jan. 27.—To paid note with interest................................. 96 25
1905.
Nov. 14.— "   "   " 148 73
      "   cost of work 649 00

                                         $903 98 $903 93

No debentures have been issued nor levies made.
J. Curry & Co., note with interest due 17th May, 1906......................... $410 00
            "   "   23rd May, 1906........................... 283 73

Bissette Drain, By-law No. 351.

1902.
Dec. 9.—By loan on note C. B. 138................................... .... $144 00
1903.
Sept. 2.—Sale of deb. 138.. .... 387 32
Sept. 5.—To paid note with interest............................... 149 32
      "   cost of work 382 00

                                         $531 32 $531 32

1904.
Sept. 2.—To paid deb. 97 .... $89 46
1905.
Aug. 26.— "   "   109 .... 89 46

Levies on Lands.

1903, $67.76.   1905, $67.76.
1904, $67.76.

J. Curry & Co., deb. due 2nd Sept., 1906... $89 46
       "   "   1907.................................. 89 46
       "   "   1908.................................. 89 46
         Assessment, lands $67 76
                roads 21 24
                                             $89 00

Cahill Drain of 1902, By-law No. 352.

1902.
Dec. 9.—By loan on note C. B. 139................................. $............ $159 00
1903.
Oct. 20.— "   "   "   139............................... .... 245 90
1904.
Aug. 12.—Sale of deb. 139.. .... 443 00
Sept. 17.—Received from Sandwich South 333 00
1903.
Oct. 20.—To paid note with interest................................. 165 90
1904.
Aug. 12.— "   "   " 255 78
         Cost of work 664 95
         Balance in bank 94 27

                                      $1,180 90 $1,180 90

1905.
Aug. 12.—To paid deb. $102 29

Levies on Lands.

1905, $87.66.   1904, $87.66.

J. Curry & Co., deb. due 12th Aug. 1906.. $102 29
       "   "   1907.................................. 102 29
       "   "   1908.................................. 102 29
       "   "   1909.................................. 102 29

         Assessment, lands $87 66
                roads 15 12
                                           $102 78

11 M.A.

Fourth Con. Drain, By-law 359.

1903.				
Oct.	20.—By loan on note C. B. 136	$...........		$275 50
1904.				
Aug.	12.—Sale of deb. 136		....	1,015 80
Dec.	15.—Received from Sandwich South		....	200 00
Aug.	12.—To paid note with interest		236 75	
	" cost of work		961 65	
	" balance in bank		242 90	
			$1,491 30	$1,491 30
1905.				
Jan.	9.—To paid deb. C. B. 114			$234 62

Levies on Lands.

1905, $136.87.

J. Curry & Co., deb. due 12th Aug.,	1906			$234 62
" "	1907			234 62
" "	1908			234 62
" "	1909			234 62
	Assessment, lands		$136 87	
	roads		39 65	
				$176 52

As the debentures are for $234.62 each this assessment shows an annual shortage of $58.10, which, providing the assessment on ''lands'' has not been altered (and of this I can find no record), should be yearly transferred from above balance to Township funds.

Ferrari Drain, By-law No. 361.

1903.				
Dec.	7.—By loan on note C. B. 135	$...........		$173 00
1905.				
Nov.	14.— " " 135		....	189 26
	To paid note and interest		189 26	
	" cost of work		173 00	
			$362 26	$362 26

No debentures have been issued nor levies made.

J. Curry & Co., note due 17th May, 1906, with interest $193 51

Third Con. Drain, By-law No. 379.

1903.				
Oct.	20.—By loan on note C. B. 137	$...........		$316 00
Oct.	31.—Transfer from 3rd Con. Drain, By-law No. 300		....	5 40
1904.				
Sept.	20.—Loan on note		....	850 00
Dec.	15.—Received from Sandwich South		....	300 00
1905.				
Nov.	14.—Interest to June, 1905		....	10 68
	Loan on note		....	700 00
1904.				
Sept.	20.—To paid note with interest		330 65	
1905.				
Nov.	14.— " " "		899 50	
	Cost of work		934 65	
	Balance in bank		17 19	
			$2,182 08	$2,182 08

No debentures have been issued nor levies made.

J. Curry & Co., note with interest, due July, 17, 1906 .... $723 50

11a M. A.

Dobson Drain, By-law No. 381.

1905.
Nov. 20.—By Loan on note C. B. 134............................	$.............	$59 00
To cost of work	59 00	
	$59 00	$59 00

No debentures have been issued nor levies made.

J. Curry & Co., note with interest due 23rd May, 1906............................ $60 50

Grand Coulee Drain, By-law No. 382.

1905.
Nov. 20.—By loan on note C. B. 133...............................	$.............	$49 00
To cost of work	49 00	
	$49 00	$49 00

No debentures have been issued nor levies made.

J. Curry & Co., note with interest due, 23rd May, 1906............................ $50 25

Schedule No. 4

The Township of Sandwich West, as of 31st December, 1905.

Available Assets.

Due from F. St. Louis, Collector, on roll 1899........................	$ 32 29	
Due from F. St. Louis, Collector, being taxes on W. pt. lot 11 of 1st Con. on roll 1900..	12 46	
Amount of Warrant No. 1,072 re Pajot drain........................	23 50	
Arrears of taxes returned by County Treasurer but omitted from roll 1902	4 83	
Arrears of taxes with County Treasurer..............................	283 92	
Collector's roll for 1905 .... $11,639 98		
Add net for errors 6 25		
	11,646 23	
Cash on hand	16	
To be transferred from balance on 4th Con. Drain, By-law No. 359, for first debenture paid	58 10	
(See under statement of Drains.)		
Balances in Bank on,—		
Taylor-Gunn Drain, By-law No. 313..................................	1 60	
Langlois Drain, By-law No. 315....................	41	
Lennon Drain, By-law No. 316..................................	37	
		$12,063 87

Township of Sandwich West, as of 31st December, 1905.

Current Liabilities.

Outstanding warrants	$7,789 78	
County rate	1,472 00	
House of Refuge	78 21	
Collector's salary	100 00	
Debentures to be paid from taxes collected,—		
Cahi'l Drain, By-law No. 352...................... $102 29		
Bisette " " 351...................... 39 46		
Chappus " " 349...................... 345 54		
Chappus Drain Outlet, By-law No. 337........ 78 77		
	616 06	
Adjustment of school section special rate levy, 1905 roll.........	61 66	
Due Henry Petrimoulx, Warrant No. 360 of Aug. 4, 1900......	1 40	
" Rudolph Hantais, " 344 " "	41	
" Alex. Drouil'ard, " 318 " "	25	
" Jos. Marchesseau, " 321 " " ...	12	
Surplus	1,943 98	
		$12,063 87

SCHEDULE No. 5.

The Township of Sandwich West, as of the 31st December, 1905, Contingent, Asset and Liability Statement.

DRAIN BALANCES.

Assets.

Balances standing to the credit of the several drain accounts as given below $569 06 $569 06

⸱   These balances are represented by deposit accounts in the bank of Messrs. J. Curry & Co., and bear interest at the rate of 4 per cent. per annum. Interest has not been computed.

Liabilities.

Marais Drain repairs, By-law	No.	289............................	$ 34 42
6th Con. Drain Outlet,	"	302............................	6 10
2nd Marais Drain repairs,	"	306............................	6 30
Tecumseh Drain,	"	331............................	164 88
Chappus "	..	349............................	3 00
2nd Con. "	..	359............................	242 90
3rd Con. "		379............................	17 19
Cahill Drain of 1902,	..	352............................	94 27

                                                             $569 06

The cost of this audit to the Municipality of the Township of Sandwich West, as per Mr. George's account, was $354.07.

SCHEDULE No. 6.

Township of Sandwich West, as of December 31st, 1905.

STATEMENT OF DRAIN INDEBTEDNESS TO BE PROVIDED FOR BY ANNUAL LEVIES.

Debentures.

Chappus Drain, By-law No. 349, due Aug. 12,	1907..............	$345 54	
"	"	"	1908..............	345 54	
"	"	"	1909..............	345 54	
				$1,036 62
Bisette Drain, By-law No. 351, due Sept. 2,	1907..............	$89 46	
"	"	"	1908..............	89 46	
				178 92
Cahill Drain, By-law No. 352, due Aug. 12,	1907..............	$102 29	
"	"	"	1908..............	102 29	
"	"	"	1909..............	102 29	
				306 87
4th Con. Drain, By-law No. 359, due 12th Aug.	1906..............	$234 62	
"	"	"	1907..............	234 62	
"	"	⸜ "	1903..............	234 62	
			1909..............	234 62	
				933 48

Being face value (principal and interest) of debentures issued. $2,460 89

Notes. (Adding interest to due date.)

Chappus Drain, By-law No. 249, due 23rd May, 1906............	$ 36 12
East Branch Cahill Drain, By-law No. 350, 17th May, 1906...	410 00
" " " 23rd May, 1906...	283 73
Ferrari Drain, By-law No. 361. due 17th May, 1906..............	193 51
3rd Con. Drain, By-law No. 379, due 17th July, 1906............	723 50
Dobson Drain, By-law No. 381. due 23rd May, 1906............	60 50
Grand Coulee Drain, By-law No. 382. 23rd May, 1906............	50 25

                                             $1,757 61

                                             $4,218 50

Cobourg Town Council.

We have made a careful and exhaustive audit of the financial transactions of the above Council for the year 1905, and submit the following report:—

The receipts from all sources during the year amounted to $74,223.72, which, with the balance of $2,511.45 on the 1st day of January, 1905, gives $76,735.17 to be accounted for by the Town Treasurer.

The accompanying statement shows the various sources of receipts and the details of expenditure.

With regard to the receipts from taxes ($39,421.78) it will be noticed that $787.78 has reference to the 1903 account, $8,821 to the 1904, and $29,813.00 to the 1905 account. On the 31st December, 1905, the following balances were owing on the respective tax rolls:—

1903	$ 103 00
1904	1,341 47
1905	12,670 95
	$14,115 42

In connection with these arrears we beg to draw attention to the general condition of the collection work. The assessment roll for 1905, which should have been handed to the Town Clerk on the 30th day of April, was not completed until the 25th day of May. The Court of Revision dealt with abatements and exemptions on the 28th June and the roll was finally certified to by the Judge on the 26th day of July.

A by-law of the Council on the 30th of October authorized the collection of taxes and the tax roll did not reach the Collector's hands until early in November. We understand from your Collector that in addition to the usual difficulties attendant on collection of taxes, he has from time to time been hampered in the performance of his duties by interference on the part of members of the Council. We consider this a great detriment to the best interests of the Council's finances and we would suggest that the Council instruct the Collector to return his tax roll on a certain date and let it be definitely understood that the Council's order is final. We are further of opinion that it would be advisable to collect the taxes in two instalments.

This method would, we think, not only meet the convenience of a large section of the taxpayers, and thereby facilitate the Collector's duties, but also save the Council a large proportion of the interest paid on moneys borrowed to carry on the work of the Town until the taxes are collected. The Councils of 1904 and 1905 instructed the Collector to collect fines of five per cent, on all taxes not paid by a certain date, but we regret to report that these orders were not rigidly enforced. In certain instances members of the Council have asked the Collector not to press for the fines, and in consequence we have no means of verifying the amount received in this way.

We are glad to be able to state that our endeavours to clear up the 1903-04 tax rolls have been fairly successful and, thanks to the prompt action taken by your present Council at our instigation, the balances of taxes due for 1903-04 have been materially reduced.

We have carefully examined all abatements and exemptions and report that generally they are in fair order. We consider the by-law passed by the Council exempting the Golf Club from general rates on an assessment of

$1,500 to be illegal, and the exemption by-law in the case of the Cobourg Matting Co. expired on the 1st day of June, 1904. In the latter instance we have included the proportion due from 1st June to 31st December in the balance owing on the 1904 tax roll as shewn above. In the case of the Golf Club, however, we would suggest that the Council take solicitor's opinion as to the advisability of endeavouring to collect.

We regret to note that in one or two instances accounts owing by the Council have been adjusted by an abatement on the tax roll. The Assessment Act does not permit of abatements of this nature and we need not point out the sinister motives that might be attributed to a Council that authorizes or countenances such a pernicious system of account keeping. Not only are the published accounts misleading and inaccurate but the system is objectionable from every point of view. We would suggest that in every case accounts owing by the Council should be paid by cheque and we cannot imagine a reason that would warrant a variation from this method.

A sworn statement of arrears of taxes chargeable against lands should be handed to the Treasurer by the Collector at the time of returning the roll, and we find these returns duly entered in a book of account kept by the Treasurer for the purpose.

With regard to the compilation of the tax roll, we would suggest that the Town Clerk take steps to see that the roll is arithmetically correct in every particular before handing it over to the Collector, and we are strongly of opinion that the Collector should be supplied with a fire-proof safe to guard the roll and other valuables.

Poll tax realized $29 and was collected late in the year. We are of opinion that if greater efforts were put forth this tax should produce a larger revenue.

Dog tax is included in the Collector's roll and shows under the head of taxes, but we desire to draw attention to a considerable drop in the receipts from this source since the collection has been taken out of the hands of the Chief of Police. We are of opinion that dog tax can be more efficiently collected by the Chief of Police, and would suggest that the duty be again handed over to him supposing your Solicitor sees no legal objection, and we would further advise the use of a proper receipt book and the issue of a tag in every instance.

The revenue from Town licenses was $393.25, which, we think, should have been collected earlier in the year.

Temporary loans from the bank amounted to $27,500. During the year $16,500 was repaid so that on the 31st December, 1905, there was a balance of $11,000 owing the bank on the Council's note. Of this balance $2,000 is chargeable against sidewalks, for which debentures will be issued on the completion of the work, leaving a difference of $9,000, which may be considered as a current liability of the Town.

The sum of $554.50 was paid to the bank for interest during the year, of which $345.65 was owing on the 31st December, 1904. The difference, viz., $208.85, together with $270 interest accrued to 31st December, 1905, gives $478.85 as the total interest charge for the period under review.

We should mention that the Council pays 6 per cent. for its accommodation and would suggest that an endeavour be made to secure a lower rate.

With regard to the expenditure, your Treasurer has produced properly endorsed cheques and vouchers for all payments, and, with one or two minor exceptions, we find them in good order. With regard to the grant of $350 to the Benevolent Fund we consider your Council should be either represented in the Committee or that the financial statement of the fund be audited by your Treasurer, and we are also of opinion that the payment of $103.04 to the Old Boys' Fund is illegal.

We find the Council's property is duly insured, but we consider that $17,000 on the Town Hall does not cover the risk.

The debenture debt on the 31st December, 1905, was $233,580.00, to which should be added the $2,000 expenditure on sidewalks referred to above.

Of this total ($235,580) the sum of $22,800 is in respect of local improvements and school debentures. The difference, viz., $212,780, is the net debenture debt against general rate and is a charge of over $42.00 per head, calculated on a population of 5,000. We understand your Council contemplates a further issue of debentures in the near future.

We regret to report that there has been no investment of moneys for Sinking Fund purposes, though we find that year by year the requisite amount has been included in the estimates and assessed for. Unfortunately, however, the Councils of 1902 and 1903 were working under large deficits and the mony raised to meet Sinking Fund charges was diverted to other uses. The Council of 1904 took upon itself to wipe out the accumulated deficit and partially successful.

On the 31st December, 1905, $2,481.82 should have stood at the credit of the Sinking Fund.

In the statement of assets and liabilities, which follows, this amount appears as a liability and with an estimated surplus of $700 when the assets are realized, the Council should take immediate steps to see that the Statutory requirements in relation to the Sinking Fund are carried out. We desire to call the Council's particular attention to this section of our report and would emphasize the necessity for immediate action. During such time as the Council have failed in their duty to invest the Sinking Fund the general rates have borne a charge of $147.36 for interest.

In a general review of the finances of the Council during the year we desire again to call attention to the collection of taxes. We believe your Collector to be quite capable of performing his duties in an adequate manner but would urge the necessity of the Council stipulating for the return of the roll on a definite date.

Further, we would advise he be untrammelled in the carrying out of this work by orders form individual members of the Council, definite or implied.

We consider the appliances available for filing office records, etc., are totally unsatisfactory, and it is a pressing necessity that this matter be attended to without delay.

In conclusion we desire to place on record our high appreciation of the efficient manner your Treasurer has prepared his accounts for audit and the valuable assistance he has rendered us in the performance of our duties.

Cobourg Town Council.

1. Report should be read in conjunction with financial statement and statement of assets and liabilities.

2. Since drafting the report I have thought of one or two matters that might be referred to, but they are of minor importance though I think they should be noted.

3. So far as the 1905 accounts are concerned, there is nothing to warrant an investigation.

4. There is no doubt what has taken place in the past was sufficient reason for discontent amongst the taxpayers, but the more serious matters occurred years ago.

5. One matter, the payment of a bonus of $5,000 to Dick Ridout was, of course, illegal and unwarranted but the payment was afterwards legalized by a special Act of Parliament.

In connection with this matter a Judge living in the Town used it as a lever to secure a reduction of his assessment. He intimated to the Council that unless his assessment was reduced to a certain amount he would bring on a claim against the Council for making an illegal payment.

6. Another bone of contention is the disposition of the monies in the hands of the Town Trust Commissioners. The Commissioners were appointed to stand between the Town and the bondholders at a time when the Town's credit was questionable. A fortunate deal with the Dominion Government helped to re-establish the Town's finances and removed the *raison d'etre* of the Commissioners.

At the time of relinquishing their duties there was a balance of something like $10,000 in their hands, and I do not know whether it was handed over to the Town or spent by the Commissioners in improvements to the opera house.

No one seems to know very definitely what was done with it, and, of course, it did not come within the province of my work to look carefully into the matter. This, however, is a matter of the past.

7. I think the fact that no Sinking Fund has been provided for is a very serious matter.

The Consolidated Municipal Act is very clear and definite on this point and neglect to provide for it is considered a misdemeanour inasmuch as there is a penalty imposed.

The money has been assessed for but it has been diverted to other uses.

8. There are evidences that the Councillors have treated their duties in a very careless way.

They have failed to take their Solicitor's advice and any suggestion made by the Treasurer as to the advisability or legality of any action has been considered as interference.

The Council should be made to understand that as a body corporate they can only do what the law provides what they may so do and in a manner as set out in the statute.

9. I consider the books in use quite inadequate to the Town's requirements, but I understand the cash book is the stereotyped pattern required to be used by the Provincial Government.

10. There are no records of assets in any shape or form. The bookkeeping system provides for nothing of the sort.

H. VIGEON, F.C.A.

Mr. Vigeon's charges for this audit amounted to $200.

Report of the Investigation of the Account of the Municipal Corporation and
Board of Education of the City of St. Thomas.

Acting under the authority of an Order-in-Council dated the 19th day of March, 1906, I, Harry Vigeon, of the City of Toronto, Chartered Accountant, was instructed to make an inspection, examination and audit of the books, accounts, vouchers and moneys of the Municipal Corporation of the City of St. Thomas.

In pursuance of the said authority such investigation has been made, and I beg to report as follows:—

1. The Auditors who were appointed in the year 1900 to make a special investigation suggested certain improvements in the method of keeping the accounts and also made sundry suggestions as to the office routine. These recommendations have not all been adopted. Had they been carried out they would have tended towards the more efficient conduct of the City's business transactions and have provided material from which could be obtained a more intelligible statement of the City's financial position.

2. *Assessment Rolls.* The assessment rolls have been carelessly compiled. There has been no system of check whatever in the details nor has any attempt been made to reconcile the total of the Collectors with the assessment roll.

The rolls of 1901-2-3-4 provide striking instances in support of this statement.

In 1901 the amount collected was $1,410.57 less than estimated in the assessment roll, and this after full provision being made for commuted taxes, etc.

The roll of 1902 shews a deficiency of $5,148.18. On Folio 5 of the assessment roll the total is taken as $240,950.00, whereas it should be $24,-950.00. At the rate of 19.5 mills on the dollar $4,212 of the above difference is accounted for.

The assessment roll of 1903 totals up to $5,154,988, and at 21 mills on the dollar should have produced $108,254.00. The correct total of the Collector's roll was, however, only $98,547.

On Folio 92 of the assessment roll the total is, by an error in footing, shown as $411,110
whereas it should be 41,110
a difference of 370,000
which at the above tax rate accounts for $7,770 of the difference.

These discrepancies have seriously affected the estimates and I desire to lay particular stress on this section of my report as if even the footing only of the roll had been checked the errors would have been discovered and subsequent deficiencies avoided.

In connection therewith the duties of the City officials are not clearly defined. It is difficult, therefore, to say who is to blame in the matter. It would be well for the Council to give this subject of defining the duties of the officials careful consideration and determine on whom should rest the responsibliity of seeing that the assessment and Collector's rolls are correctly compiled.

A code of standing orders assigning the duties, responsibilities and office hours of the several officials is urgently needed to obtain such efficiency of work as their position warrants.

The recapitulation of the assessment roll should shew separately the total assessable value of property where taxes have been commuted. A reconciliation could then be readily made between the assessment and Collector's rolls.

In some instances property has been entirely omitted and consequently the taxes lost to the Council. There have been many cases of this kind,— the present arrangements for taking the assessment will minimize chances of similar omissions in future.

No connection is shewn between the total assessment and the annual estimates, whereas in point of fact they are closely allied. Unfortunately the practice has been to prepare the estimates in the months of June or July, and even sometimes later, treating as a total, the expenditure up to that date irrespective of the year in which such expenditure was incurred.

The estimates should and could be prepared earlier in the year—the previous year's assessment forming a guide to the finance committee when considering the same.

Whether the estimates have not been prepared with due care, or whether the Council has not considered the estimated revenue, the fact remains that in every year within the scope of this investigation the estimates have been exceeded. They should be prepared in greater detail, and the appropriation carefully watched against the expenditure, and reported to the council periodically.

(3) *Collector's Rolls.* By-laws provide that the assessment roll should be in the hands of the City Clerk on the 15th April. Councils have very un-wisely allowed this time to be considerably extended so that the time in which the roll could be prepared for the collector was so short that proper care and attention could not be given to its correctness.

No check was made before handing the same to the collector, and this together with a lack of time is advanced as the cause of numerous errors in the correct compilation of the roll. Under the present arrangements the auditor verifies the correctness of the roll before the collector takes same in charge, and the assessor is now required to return the roll to the clerk before the 15th of February in each year.

It is to be hoped that the council will not again so unwisely extend the time, and thus cause the financial affairs of the municipality to be dis-arranged.

Owing to the short time at disposal, and the absence of suitable check, school taxes have not been shewn separately as required, nor has the roll been footed before delivery to the collector. Had this simple precaution been taken the discrepancies noted above would have been discovered.

The collector deposits all moneys direct to the credit of the municipal-ity, and has properly accounted for his total collections. The collector's cash books do not shew clearly how and when the taxes were collected, but the collector states that such moneys are kept separate and deposited periodi-cally.

The tax roll of 1900 was underfooted by $100, and this error being dis-covered by the auditors of the 1901 account, your collector deposited $100 to the credit of the municipality in February, 1902, after the 1900 roll was apparently closed.

The new form of cash book which it is proposed to use in the collector's department, is in my opinion suitable for the requirements.

As a whole, the taxes have been carefully collected—the uncollectable amount being trifling.

The collector deposits from time to time large sums to the credit of the general account irrespective of whether such sums are general or frontage.

The moneys should be kept quite separate, and deposits made to the account (General or Frontage), on which they are collected.

Taxes chargeable against lands have been duly recorded in a register kept by the Treasurer, and interest added yearly. Amounts written off, have in the majority of cases, been sanctioned by resolution of council. It is necessary that council's authority should be obtained in every case.

I would draw council's attention to the practice of refunding taxes after they have been paid to the collector. In my opinion in almost every in-stance the payment was illegal.

The Assessment Act clearly provides for the finality of the assessment roll after its revision by the court, and where a tax-payer has failed to appeal to the Court of Revision, on the ground of an over-assessment, the council has no option but to demand payment in full.

I have discussed this matter with the City Solicitor, and on general grounds he is of the same opinion.

(4) *General Account.* Having carefully examined the records of the various sources of revenue, I herewith report that your Treasurer has duly accounted for the moneys belonging to the city which he has received.

There have been from time to time certain small omissions which, however, your city auditors have drawn attention to, and which have been properly credited to the municipality.

Taxes.

It would be greatly to the interest of the council's finances if arrangements were made for a more prompt collection of taxes.

The tax rolls have, as a rule, been prepared late in the year, and consequently the Council has had to borrow money to meet current expenses.

I have no doubt whatever that the present method could be greatly improved upon, but any improvement would depend on the early compilation of the assessment roll, and the preparation of the estimates in February, or not later than March in each year.

Licenses.

The receipts from this source shew considerable variation year by year. The following are the amounts received since 1899:

1900	$3,930 00
1901	2,499 00
1902	4,099 00
1903	3,638 00
1904	5,097 00
1905	2,429 00

Licenses due on year are in many cases not paid over to the Treasurer until the following year. All licenses should be paid and credited to the municipality in the year they are due.

No milk licenses were collected in 1905.

The License Inspector's Department has been fully criticized by your present city auditor.

Mr. Shaw states that his multifarious duties have prevented him keeping such account of his collections as the extent and importance of this branch of the city's ravenue demands.

The records of this department are imperfect—no proper system of registering "Licenses" being kept, and therefore the proper checking of the work is practically impossible.

Appended to this report is a suggested rearrangement of the license collection.

Dog Taxes.

Here again I notice considerable differences year by year, and proper records and registers are lacking.

1900	....	$312	00
1901	....	588	00
1902	....	295	00
1903	....	181	00
1904	....	311	00
1905	....	572	00

The above figures suggested criticism, and your inspector accounted for the falling off in ravenue in 1902-3-4 by the reduction in the dog tax.

Poll Tax.

I note your council has ceased to collect this tax.

Police Court Fines.

These have been properly recorded in a register kept by the chief of police, and the sums paid over to the Treasurer have baen accounted for.

Fines paid to the gaoler are now handed over to the Police Department, and through it to the Treasurer. This course permits the chief of police to have a record of every case in his own register, which was not possible when the gaoler paid to the Treasurer direct.

Miscellaneous Receipts.

Premiums and accrued interest on the various debentures issued have been accounted for as have also amounts realized from sale of land in 1902, market rents and sundry items.

(5) *Disbursements*. The disbursements are vouched, and are all in order with the exception of refunded taxes, which I have called attention to under paragraph 3 of this report.

(6) *Board of Education*. Receipts have been accounted for, and payments properly vouched.

Thesé accounts have been well and creditably kept, although the records are not in accordance with the requirements of the department.

(7) *Frontage*. This account seems to be in a very unsatisfactory condition.

The special auditors who were appointed in 1900, reported against the system which obtained at that time of keeping frontage separate from general account. Acting on this recommendation, frontage and general taxes were combined in the tax roll of 1900.

The first result of this seems to have been that the amount ultimately transferred from the combined to frontage account was $6,000 less than the sum collected for frontage purposes, nor can I discover that this amount has since been transferred.

Frontage account was supplemented by loans from the bank, and general account benefited to the extent of this $6,000.

In the following year the formar method of separating frontage and general taxes was reverted to, and this is by far the more satisfactory way of dealing with these accounts, and I know of no legal objection to the course.

Payments on frontage account are charged to the individual improvements by the City Treasurer, and a record of the cost of the work is further kept by the city engineer.

The amount for which debentures have been issued to meet the cost of such works has been determined by the city engineer from the records of cost kept in his department.

In the past no attempt has been made to reconcile the "Costs" as between the Treasurer's account and the engineer's. Each account in the Treasurer's books has been charged with interest for an amount qual to the difference between the cost of the works as shewn by his books, and the assessable value as certified to by the engineer.

The amount provided yearly on the tax roll is the exact amount necessary to meet the payment of debentures, and interest on those works for which debentures have already been issued.

Money for current capital expenditure is raised by loans from the bank, and repaid from the debenture issue made in the year following the completion of the work. As the taxes are not collected in the year in which they are due, further loans have to be obtained to meet the debenture payments, and consequently there must ever be a small deficiency on account of interest for which no provision is made in frontage account, or in general account.

On the other hand there is occasionally a small surplus arising from the issue of debentures at a premium, and I would suggest that an equitable and possible way of dealing with such surplus would be to credit it to a special fund against which could be charged any shortages consequent on issuing debentures at a discount, and also the deficiency on interest account referred to above.

As local improvement debentures are sold on the credit of the municipality at large, and general account has to meet shortages from issues at a discount—it would seem fair that general account should receive the benefit of any premium obtained. As the municipality, however, has commuted itself to the frontage plan, it is desirable that the two accounts should be kept separate and the special fund as outlined would appear to be satisfactory.

A statement showing the condition of frontage account as on the 31st December, 1905, is herewith submitted. In it the $6,008.00, owing by general account in respect of the 1900, tax roll, and an advance of $4,000.00 in 1904 have been included.

The statement No. 2 discloses a difference in the neighborhood of $7,-000.00, which has been occasioned by insufficient levies, and the shortage in sinking fund to retire debentures falling due for repayment on the 25th of November, 1905.

The general frontage account is charged with such items as cannot be immediately appropriated to any particular work. It has been charged with the cost of a steam-roller, and I would suggest that this be taken over by the City's General Account, and frontage works charged with the use of it, and general account credited. It is certainly important that general frontage account should be written off yearly by distributing the amount over the various capital works in proportion to their cost at the end of the year.

In this way all expenditure under local improvements would be provided for in the debenture issue.

The City Treasurer prepares no estimates of the amount required annually to meet debenture and interest payments on frontage account, and I would recommend that such an estimate be prepared from the debenture, register and agreed with the amount placed on the frontage tax roll.

The method of accounting, which obtains with regard to local improvements is not clear, and is, in my opinion, inadequate.

The matter has been discussed with your City Treasurer and auditor, and certain suggestions have been made which they approve of, and which I have reason to believe will be put into practice without delay.

It is imperative that the council give this matter early consideration as a deficincy to be dealt with at once. In conjunction with it of course will be the deficiency shewn under general account referred to later in the report.

(8) *Accounting.* Speaking generally, a thorough reorganization of the method of keeping the municipal accounts is necessary.

A list of suggestions which I consider suitable for the city's requirements has been handed to your Treasurer, the adoption of which would tend to efficiency in the accounting system.

The rolls as I have before pointed out are not prepared in conformity with the requirements of the Assessment Act, nor is their accuracy determined before handing over to the collector.

No proper record is kept of the amount of school taxes raised yearly.

The heat, light and power plant, and street railways should be assessed and charged with their proper proportion of school and other taxes.

The waterworks are exempted under the Waterworks Act, but in the case of the other utilities a correct accounting system would certainly suggest that taxes should be charged annually.

The amounts raised yearly on the requisition of the Board of Education have not in any year, excepting 1905, been paid over in full to that body.

The balance has been appropriated for general purposes. This is not satisfactory, as it does not disclose the correct rate for school taxes. The total levies should be handed over to the Board, and any surplus at the end of the financial year should be taken into account by them when preparing their estimates for the current period.

The council's attention must be drawn to the capital liability of $50,000 for street railways, and for which no provision is being made for repayment.

The interest charge of $2,000 is paid yearly out of the general account. The street railways being permanently in the possession of the council, steps should be taken to liquidate this debt at maturity. The bonds mature in 1928, or 22 years from this date.

A sinking fund should be created, and such an amount paid into it yearly as will provide the necessary sum at their maturity. This matter should be dealt with immediately as there is every probability that in the near future large sums will be required for the renewing of roadbed, equipment, etc.

The annual accounts should be prepared on the income and expenditure basis, and any deficiency on street railways, after charging it with interest on debenture issue of $15,000 should be made good out of general funds, and the amount provided for in the estimates for the ensuing year.

Before closing my report on the municipal portion of the city's account, I would draw the Council's attention to the report of your present city auditor on the 1905 accounts. He remarks "No provision has ever been made for depreciation in any of the permanent assets of the city," and urges the council to give the matter their careful consideration.

The City Hall, school buildings, etc., are kept in a good state of repair out of revenue, and the yearly payments for debentures and interest are also a charge to this account.

Year by year as the debentures mature and are paid off, the various properties are becoming of more value to the city, relatively to the debenture debt, and in the case of the City Hall, school and other buildings, in addition to their relative value, there is also an actual appreciation consequent on the appreciation in land values.

In order to depreciate the city's permanent assets as suggested a reserve or sinking fund would be created, and would be a further charge on revenue, and consequently tend to increase taxation. When the debenture debt was liquidated, the council would possess in addition to the capital asset an invested amount equal to the original debenture issue so that the tax-payers would in reality have paid twice the value of the property in question.

In the case of the street railways, waterworks and light, heat and power plants, it might be advisable when the capital debt has been paid to create a reserve fund for providing for capital replacements.

I trust the foregoing remarks will make my views on the subject clear to the council.

Statement No. 1 appended news a deficiency of $30,002.28 on general account. Against this deficiency must be put an amount of $21,845.52 for which debentures have recently been issued under a special act passed on the 10th of April, 1906.

The net deficiency, viz., $8,156.75, is the amount which the Council has to consider in connection with the deficit on frontage account of $6,630.61, being a total deficit of $14,787.37.

(9) *Water Works.* The records kept in this Department are not such as will admit of a satisfactory check. The water rates roll is compiled as a rule from the previous one as regards the number of houses and name of street, but the quarterly charge to the account is not made in any of the records, therefore there is no means of determining whether the cash paid is the proper or even the full amount of the water taker's indebtedness.

The roll is not footed and no attempt is made to arrive at the exact amount of revenue due in any one quarter, half-year or year. The system of accounting, subject to one or two variations, if properly carried out should give good results.

I have drafted and submit a new form of register which your Treasurer and Auditor have agreed to adopt, and which will tend to greater efficiency in the future.

(10) *Street Railways.* The statement submitted, No. 3, shews the condition of the street railway's accounts as on the 31st December, 1905.

In it is included the $50,000 guaranteed debt referred to earlier in my report, and to liquidate which no provision has yet been made. It will be observed that the deficit has already amounted to the sum of $10,225.15.

I would draw the Council's attention to the value of the undertaking as per your Engineer's report. His valuation of $8,600 shews an appreciation of $16,000 over the book value. I have reason to think that the street railway should soon become a revenue producing concern.

Your City Auditor has drawn attention to the number of free passes issued, and I would further remark on the practice of giving rebates to picnic parties and baseball players.

Having looked carefully into several instances where grants of $5.00 per game have been made to the latter, I found little or no advantage has accrued therefrom.

Complaints have been made that the cash and tickets in conductors' boxes do not agree with the reports. As the latter are made up by the conductors from memory, it is not strange that they do not agree. Suitable registers would provide some check, but I understand there are only two in use.

The annual accounts of this undertaking should be compiled strictly on the income and expenditure basis, and the books balanced periodically. The invoices for all purchases are in order, but no distinction is made between capital and revenue. It is essential that this division should be made and

the annual financial statement prepared so as to shew clearly the actual surplus or deficit. The books of account are well adapted for giving this information and it should be insisted upon.

Payments have been vouched and I report the same correct.

(11) *Heat, Light and Power Plant.* These accounts are creditably kept
and the statement submitted by your City Auditor discloses clearly the condition of the undertaking as on the 31st December, 1905.

(12) *Amasa Wood Hospital.* The accounts in connection with the above
are in order, but here again I must advise that the annual statement be prepared on the income and expenditure basis.

On the 31st December, 1905, there were accounts owing amounting to
$740.96, which does not appear in your Auditor's report. On the other hand,
patients' fees received in December ($187.85) and fees due by patients on the
31st December, 1905, are not brought into account.

(13) *Recommendations.* The following recommendations should be put
into force and strictly adhered to:—

1. All cheques be signed by the Treasurer and countersigned by the chairman or other member of the finance committee.

2. Orders to the Treasurer for payments under contracts to be signed by
chairman of spending committee.

3. The Treasurer to see that all orders to him for payments are properly
certified.

4. Orders for stores should be given on suitably printed order forms and
duplicates kept on file. This recommendation will apply to all the Council's
departments, and would be of considerable help when preparing the annual
accounts.

5. Assessment roll to be prepared by a certain fixed rate and the Council
to permit of no extension. The roll to be footed by the Assessor and checked
by a responsible official prior to its being handed to the Clerk, and the recapitulation to shew separately the total assessable value of property where
taxes have been commuted, and also where only a portion of the taxes is
charged.

6. Collector's roll to be prepared by a certain fixed rate, checked by a
responsible official, and reconciled with the assessment roll.

7. Collector be instructed to return roll by a certain fixed date and no
extension of time permitted.

I would point out that the 1905 roll is not yet returned, although the
Council, by resolution, instructed the Collector to return same on 15th May,
1906.

8. When roll is handed to Collector, Treasurer to prepare journal entry
charging the Collector and crediting the various services with such sums as
the estimates provide.

Further, he will debit such accounts as licenses, dog taxes, rents receivable, etc., with the estimated revenue in each case.

9. The Treasurer will open an account for bills payable and interest.

10. The Treasurer to balance his ledgers monthly.

11. Treasurer to charge sundry taxpayers with exact amount owing on
account of local improvements as on 31st December, 1905.

Sundry taxpayers' account will also be debited annually with the further
assessments for local improvements and debentures account credited with the
corresponding issue.

Sundry taxpayers' account will be credited annually with the total of
the frontage Collector's roll and Collector's account charged.

The balance of sundry taxpayers' account, together with expenditure on new work, should equal the balances of debentures account, bills payable, cash and Collector's account.

12. Treasurer to agree his ledger cost of new work with Engineer's account of same.

13. Treasurer to reconcile amount of annual debenture issue for frontage expenditure with his ledger accounts of same.

14. Register of licenses to be prepared and revised as occasion requires. This register to be the basis on which the licenses are collected.

15. New registers to be obtained by the Water Commissioners as accompanying form of ruling, and from it consumer's account in general ledger to be charged with the quarterly amount due and revenue account credited. Explanation in detail of this working has been made to your Treasurer and Auditor.

16. In his annual inspection of the various properties, the Assessor to inspect and record the particulars of the water service, and from his records water register to be checked and revised.

17. That Council define by by-law the duties and responsibilities of the various civic officials.

18. That the Collector obtain a guarantee bond from a guarantee company instead of being bonded by private individuals as at present.

The above recommendations will tend towards greater efficiency in the accounting of the municipality, and I would urge the Council to take the necessary steps to put them into operation without delay.

In conclusion I desire to place on record my appreciation of the courtesy which your officials have extended to me in the course of my work.

HARRY VIGEON,
Chartered Accountant.

Toronto, 23rd June, 1906.

STATEMENT SHOWING POSITION OF GENERAL ACCOUNT ON 31ST OF DECEMBER, 1905.

Liabilities.

Debentures maturing Jan. 1st, 1906	$1,118 30	
Coupons　　　" "	3,116 06	
Imperial Bank on bills payable	54,000 00	
County of Elgin, Administration of Justice	2,675 00	
Accounts owing	2,934 27	
Frontage account, balance of 1900 roll	6,008 89	
Frontage account, temporary loan	4,000 00	
		$73,852 52

Assets.

Cash on hand and in Bank	$6,145 56	
Balance of taxes due on 1905 roll	21,978 27	
Taxes returned against lands, Frontage account	137 61	
Street Sprinkling assessments, 1904 and 1905	3,369 10	
Dog taxes uncollected	18 40	
Licenses due and not paid	1,582 00	
Police fines paid over in 1906	95 25	
Bell Telephone Co., rent, Dec., 1905	125 00	
Golf Club, rent, 1905	123 75	
Board of Water Commissioners, balance of surplus revenue, 1905	10,230 72	
Sundries	44 58	
Deficiency, 31st Dec., 1905	30,002 28	
		73,852 52

12 M.A.

STATEMENT SHOWING POSITION OF FRONTAGE ACCOUNT AS ON DECEMBER 31ST, 1905.

Liabilities.

Debentures and coupons due in 1906 provided for in 1905 tax roll	$30,573 32	
Bills payable	25,000 00	
General account—		
Street Sprinkling, for amounts raised in Frontage Tax Rolls 1904-1905	3,369 10	
		58,942 42

Assets.

Roll, 1900, due from General account	$6,008 89	
" 1904, "	12,993 42	
" 1905, "	8,864 30	
Expenditure on works unfinished at 31st Dec., 1905	18,906 19	
General account—		
Temporary loan	4,000 00	
Cash on hand	1,539 01	
Balance, being deficiency	6,630 61	
		58,942 42

ST. THOMAS STREET RAILWAY.

Liabilities.

Debentures, original issue		$50,000 00	
" No. 2		13,972 40	
City of St. Thomas—			
Amount received from City	$5,861 90		
Amount paid by General account on account of Street Railway—			
Jan. 1902, coupons	$1,000 00		
" 1903, "	2,000 00		
" 1904, "	2,000 00		
" 1905, "	2,000 00		
Oct. 1904, deb. and coupons	1,103 72		
" 1905, "	1,103 73		
		9,207 45	
		15,069 35	
Car tickets sold and outstanding		Unrecorded	
Unpaid accounts		1,021 28	
			80,063 03

Assets.

Value placed on works when taken over	50,000 00	
Plant, rolling stock and equipment charged to capital account since that date	14,729 92	
	$69,729 92	
Undertaking valued by Engineer at 31st Dec., 1905 at $86,000.00		
Cash on hand and in Bank	50 96	
Unexpired insurance premiums	57 00	
Revenue account—		
*Amount at debit, including sundry capital items charged against this account	10,225 15	
		80,063 03

*This is the amount which the Street Railway has cost the City to date, but it should not be included in the City Balance Sheet as an asset.

Mr. Vigeon's charges for the services of himself and his staff in the matter of this audit (inclusive of expenses for travelling) were $1,000.00.

12a M. A.

STAYNER, Ont., May 4th, 1906.

AUDITOR'S REPORT OF THE TOWN OF STAYNER, IN THE COUNTY OF SIMCOE, AND
PROVINCE OF ONTARIO.

To His Honor the Lieutenant-Governor-in-Council :

SIR,—In accordance with a petition of certain ratepayers of the Town
of Stayner, I received an order from the Provincial Municipal Auditor,
dated 6th March, 1906, to proceed to the Town of Stayner to make an inspection, examination, and audit of the monies, books, accounts, vouchers of
the above-named municipal corporation.

I have the honor to submit herewith report of my audit and inspection.
The deceased treasurer, having been also collector and clerk, the audit has
been an extremely difficult one, all sources of personal information having
been cut off.

The heir of said late treasurer being desirous to do what was right in
covering up the deficiency of his late father, made an offer to the Council
of the said Town of Stayner, in which he was willing to pay into the Town
treasury what would be considered more than could be obtained out of the
late treasurer's estate or bond. The following resolution was passed by the
Council of the Town of Stayner, reading as follows:

Stayner, May 4th, 1906. As requested, I beg to submit the following
true copy of a resolution passed at an adjourned special meeting of the Council of the Town of Stayner, held in the Council Chamber this morning.
Moved by Councillor Livingstone, seconded by Councillor Perkins, that the
communication from H. W. Jakeway, Esq., making an offer of Three thous-
and five hundred dollars (₃,500.00) in full of all claims for shortage in his
late father's accounts with the Town of Stayner as treasurer, be received
and accepted, and that the clerk be instructed to notify Mr. Jakeway by
registered letter this afternoon.

My audit extended from March 10th, 1906, to Dec. 31st, 1906. I discovered the following shortage:

School Board, Cash .... $ 189 67
Town Cash 4,485 64
                                                                       ―――――――――
    Total shortage $4,675 31

The whole respectfully submitted.

    I have the honor to be, Sir,

                        Your obedient servant,

                                J. D. ANDERSON,

                        Chartered Accountant, Dominion Association.

FINAL RECAP., TOWN CASH, DEC. 31ST, 1901, TO MARCH 10TH, 1906.

Dec. 31, 1901.—Cash on hand, per cash book	$154 94	
Overdraft in Bank	....	$2,188 06
Dec. 31, 1902.—Receipts as marked paid on roll, 1902, found		
in blotter, etc., water books	10,016 57	
Arrears collected, $58.44, corroborated	1,636 29	
Disbursements, per cash book	....	9,221 81
	$11,807 80	$11,403 87
		$403 93

	Balance down from 1902	$403 93	
Dec. 31, 1903.—Total receipts on roll, etc., 1903	10,337 92	
	Total disbursements in cash book, 1903	....	7,452 05
		$10,741 85	$7,452 05
			3,289 80
	Balance from 1903	$3,289 80	
Dec. 31, 1904.—Total receipts on roll, etc., 1904	35,223 76	
	Disbursements per cash book	....	34,722 60
		$38,513 56	$34,722 60
			3,790 96
	Balance from 1904	$3,790 96	
Dec. 31, 1905.—Total receipts on roll, etc., 1905	40,904 37	
	Disbursements	....	39,820 43
Mar. 1906.—Cash in Bank	....	395 62
	Cash in safe	....	4 05
	Overdrawn salary	10 41	
		$44,705 74	$40,220 10
	Balance		4,485 64
	Net shortage in Town cash		$4,485 64

Gross Receipts and Disbursements, Town Cash.

	Cr.	Dr.
Dec. 31, 1901.—Overdraft ,..	....	$2,182 06
Cash on hand	$154 94	
Dec. 31, 1902.—Receipts and disbursements	11,652 86	9,221 81
Dec. 31, 1903.—Receipts and disbursements	11,905 06	7,452 05
Dec. 31, 1904.—Receipts and disbursements	36,095 08	34,722 60
Dec. 31, '05-6.—Receipts and disbursements	41,310 39	39,820 43
Balance in Bank, March, 1906	....	395 62
Balance in safe	....	4 05
Overdrawn salary, 1905	10 41	
	$101,128 74	$93,798 62
		7,330 12
	$101,128 74	$101,128 74

Apparent shortage as per individual yearly Town cash sheets,	1902.........	$403 93
not considering balances	1903.........	4,453 01
	1904.........	1,372 48
	1905-6......	1,100 70
		$7,330 12
Less yearly arrears not considered in them	1903.................	$1,567 14
until ascertained, arrears	1904.................	871 32
	1905-6...............	406 02
		2,844 48
		$4,485 64

The above is a true extract of the books, vouchers and papers of the Town of Stayner, as discovered by me.

Dated at Stayner, Ont., this March 10th, 1906.

J. D. ANDERSON,
Chartered Accountant.

Report of Town Cash Book, 1905.

1. There was such a wide difference between the Town cash book and Bank pass book as to the balance on hand 31st December, 1904, that the accompanying statement of receipts and disbursements for 1905 is compiled without taking into consideration any balance on hand, December 31st, 1904, and which is yet to be ascertained.

2. Though a statement of receipts and disbursements for 1905 had been rendered, I found the cash book not added up for the latter part of the year.

3. I found omissions to enter resident taxes amounting to $2,716.50 over and beyond taking for granted a pencil entry of $1,000.00 on folio 106 (presumably to be inked over afterwards), likewise ommissions to enter $132.90 water rates, also small amounts received for fines, arrears, and interest.

I also find omissions to enter monies paid out amounting to a large sum. These payments I have corroborated by cheques, vouchers, and letters found in a miscellaneous lot of papers and memoranda dating back over ten years, also by answers to inquiries made by me.

4. School grants were deposited in the town account, and school cheques used to pay town accounts.

5. To put down a date was the exception, not the rule.

6. The monies borrowed, and received for sale of debentures are mixed together, likewise repayment of loans, debentures, coupons, and interest.

7. In several places acid had been used to erase.

8. There are entries of arrears of taxes amounting to $195.00, the details of which I can find no clue, the arrears book not having been kept up for many years past.

9. The cemetery being an asset of the town, it was necessary to go through the receipts.

10. Practically speaking, no ledger entries have been made for 1905.

11. No journal was kept.

12. Only one lot of debenture entries in debenture register, being issue of 1899, though four lots are current and being paid.

13. No entries in by-laws for past year, though some have been past.

14. Minutes not written up.

15. No entries for non-resident taxes in non-resident tax book.

16. Only one entry in the arrears of taxes book under date of 1905.

17. As the town owns the cemetery, I checked over the receipts for lots sold and find them correct.

18. The books clearly show a lack of knowledge of bookkeeping.

19. The complete absence of dates upon payment of taxes received makes it impossible to determine whether interest also was due.

20. It was necessary to compile the arrears from the tax rolls of different years, after discovering what was unpaid, as the arrears book has not been posted for four or five years.

No attempt was made to separate school grants and improvements, payment of different debentures.

There are omissions to enter in cash book, cash received amounting to $1,426.50, and interest amounting to $9.36. Said items being marked paid on the roll, and corroboration being discovered in a memoranda book.

The absence of dates in the cash book, and the fact of not having the bank pass book balanced for months at a time, coupled with the disregard as to order of papers, vouchers, etc., and the lack of knowledge of the first principle of bookkeeping, makes it impossible to balance the books except annually.

TOWN CASH.

Town Cash, 1902.

With and without considering balance on hand from 1901.

Receipts.

Resident taxes marked paid on roll and entered in cash book and blotter	$3,691 96	
Resident taxes marked paid on roll, not in blotter	123 71	
Resident taxes marked paid on roll and blotter, not entered in cash book	1,651 64	
		$5,467 31
Arrears of taxes entered in cash book		1,636 29
Dog tax		1 00
Water rates		618 61
Licenses		368 00
School grants		147 00
Loans		3,332 45
Fines		15 50
Miscellaneous		49 70
Cemetery		17 00
		$11,652 86

Disbursements.

Salaries and allowances	$477 59	
Printing, advertising and stationery	174 95	
Fire and water	149 89	
Roads and bridges	535 33	
Charity	24 35	
Debentures	1,387 92	
Bills payable	3,500 00	
Interest	9 25	
County rate	368 53	
School account	1,900 00	
Light	355 20	
Miscellaneous	318 80	
Rent, Council Chamber	20 00	
		9,221 81
Apparent balance, not taking into consideration balance from 1901		$2,431 05
Balance as above	$2,431 05	
Cash on hand per cash book, Dec. 31, 1901	154 94	
	$2,585 99	
Less overdraft, Bank, Dec. 31, 1901	2,182 06	
Actual balance, Dec. 31, 1902	$403 93	

Taking 1901 audit as a basis, the cash book and bank pass books agreeing.

Town Cash, 1903.

Considering no balance on hand Dec. 31st, 1902, yet to be ascertained.

Receipts.

Resident taxes marked paid on roll, and entered in cash book and blotter	$4,064 70	
Resident taxes marked paid on roll, not entered in cash book or blotter, per schedule	290 51	
Resident taxes marked paid on roll, and entered in cash book, but omitted from blotter	998 57	
	5,353 78	
Arrears of taxes entered in cash book (only details of $168.35 corroborated).	1,567 14	
Water rates ($2.78 omitted in cash book)	856 86	
Licenses	372 75	

Government school grants	289 00
Loans	3,324 75
Fines	20 00
Poll tax	12 00
Interest	·26 78
Cemetery	82 00
	$11,905 06

Disbursements.

Salaries and allowances	$466 20
Printing and stationery	85 00
Fire and water	283 57
Law costs	15 00
Roads and bridges	341 97
Charity	29 05
Bills payable (including interest)	3,486 98
Interest	4 95
County rate	359 43
School account.	1,689 00
Electric light	384 80
Board of Health	24 75
Miscellaneous	261 35
Rent, Council Chamber	20 00
	7,452 05

Apparent balance short, not taking into account balance from 1902 .... $4,453 01

The cash book and bank account agree on an overdraft Dec. 31st, 1902, of $1,431.50. Whereas on Dec. 31st, 1903, the cash book shows $4,212.08 on hand, and the bank book same date $1,019.57 overdraft.

Town Cash, 1904.

Considering no balance on hand from 1903, yet to be ascertained.

Receipts.

Resident taxes marked paid on roll and entered in cash book and blotter	$4,150 63
Resident taxes marked paid on roll, not entered in cash book or blotter, per schedule	110 69
Resident taxes marked paid on roll and entered in blotter, but omitted from cash book	1,315 81
	$5,577 13
Arrears of taxes entered in cash book only (details of $111.85 corroborated).	871 32
Water rates	853 72
Licenses	384 95
Government school grants	139 00
Loans	28,078 90
Fines	29 00
Interest	9 36
Miscellaneous (old sidewalk)	115 30
Cemetery ($4.00 omitted in cash book)	22 00
Poll tax	14 40
Total receipts	**$36,095 08**

Disbursements.

Salaries and allowances	$478 24
Printing, stationery	115 59
Insurance	15 50
Fire and water	207 02
Roads and bridges	266 83
Charity	41 20
Debentures, repayments	2,775 84
Bills payable (loans)	18,378 90

Interest	133 25	
County rates	452 61	
Schools and improvements	3,819 50	
Electric light	362 20	
Board of Health	22 82	
Miscellaneous	263 08	
Rent, Council Chamber	10 00	
Granolithic sidewalks	7,380 02	
		34,722 60
Balance		$1,372 48

Balance $1,372.48 should be on hand without taking into consideration the balance from 1903, yet to be ascertained.

Whereas the Treasurer's cash book shows Dec. 31st, 1903, $1,495.88 on hand, the bank pass book shows an overdraft of $1,019.57 on same date.

On page 93 of the Town cash book there is an error in entering twice $500.00 paid into the school account, corroborative proof having been ascertained through the kindness of the manager of the Bank of Toronto.

The water rates check up correctly.

An omission to enter $4.00 occurs in the cemetery receipts.

The arrears of taxes are entered in lump sums amongst the current year. I fail to discover any memo or book giving details amongst the papers, except the corroboration of one entry of $111.85 in the receipt stubs.

TOWN CASH, JAN. 1ST, 1905, TO MAR. 10TH, 1906.

Considering no balance on hand from 1904.

Receipts.

Resident taxes, 1905	$6,259 30	
Arrears (corroboration of $211.02 discovered)	406 02	
Water rates	886 76	
Licenses	332 35	
School grant	138 00	
Debenture sales	12,480 54	
Loans	20,578 52	
Fines	27 00	
Miscellaneous	88 90	
Cemetery	113 00	
		$41,310 39

Disbursements.

Salaries and allowances	$652 38	
Printing, stationery	158 19	
Insurance	14 60	
Fire and water	173 80	
Law costs	25 00	
Roads and bridges	511 51	
Charity	44 68	
Debentures	2,481 89	
Interest	38 78	
County rates	532 49	
Schools (including refund of moneys used)	2,940 00	
Electric light	430 07	
Board of Health	28 08	
Miscellaneous	288 70	
Granolithic sidewalks	2,818 69	
Rent, Council Chamber	18 00	
Administration of justice	1 45	
Bills payable	28,662 15	
		39,820 43
		$1,489 96

Cash in Bank	$395 62	
" sate	4 05	
		399 67
		$1,090 29
Overdrawn salary, say 15 days		10 41
Town Treasurer's shortage 1905 and 1906		$1,100 70

Not taking into consideration balance from 1904 yet to be ascertained. December 31st, 1904, cash book calls for a balance on hand of $931.00, whereas the bank pass book shows an overdraft of $1,320.40, not including shortage as School Treasurer.

REPORT OF WATER BOARD BOOKS OF THE TOWN OF STAYNER, ONT.

.Compiled by J. Donald Anderson, Chartered Accountant, Windsor, Ont., by order of the Provincial Municipal Auditor, acting under instructions from the Lieutenant-Governor in Council, at the request of a petition from the ratepayers of Stayner, Ont.

Report of Water Rates, 1905.

Total Water Rates $946 96	
Collections per blotter and stubs and entered direct in cash book...... 886 76	
Uncollected as below	$60 20

Waterworks Ledger.

Folio	4. Stewart, F. J. (Mrs.)	$6 00
"	15. Honsberger, Dr.	3 50
"	19. Perkin, S. L.	2 00
"	60. Glenn, Hugh	3 30
"	76. Perry, S. G.	4 00
"	77. Cain, Mrs. P.	4 00
"	96. Cheeseman, B.	8 00
"	101. McSherry, P.	2 00
"	116. Briggs, J. T.	9 00
"	118. Emes, T.	4 00
"	122. Peattie, Jas.	4 40
"	137. Walton, M.	4 00
"	148. Weatherup, W. J.	4 00
"	158. Watson, A.	2 00
		$60 20 $60 20

Remarks re Waterworks.

The water rates are payable semi-annually in advance. There was fully one-third of the users not charged up with their rates, likewise their payments would not be placed to their credit. I obtained the list of said payments from a memoranda book, and the receipt stubs discovered in the Treasurer's surgery. No book or water register was extant showing a complete list of water users, consequently considerable difficulty was encountered. But with the assistance of the newly appointed Treasurer and ex-civic officials, what is considered a complete list has been prepared. I would suggest having a proper register of water users.

Re Water Board, 1902-3-4.

As it was the custom of the late town Treasurer to merely enter the water board receipts as thy came in, direct to the ledger, with the exception of a few small omissions which I have made memo. in the town cash book, they check up correctly. I might here remark that so-called water ledger is merely a journal, the debit being used for the credit side, from lack of knowledge of bookkeeping.

Town Cash Report, 1902, 903, 1904, 1905, of the Town of Stayner, Ont.

Basing balance on Dec. 31st, 1901, to March 10th, 1906.

Compiled by J. Donald Anderson, Chartered Accountant, Windsor, Ont., by order of the Provincial Municipal Auditor, acting under instructions from the Lieutenant-Governor in Council, at the request of a petition from the ratepayers of Stayner, Ont.

RECAPITULATION OF SCHOOL BOARD CASH OF THE TOWN OF STAYNER, ONT.

	Dr.	Cr.
Dec. 31/'01.—Balance on hand taken as a basis	$ 222 70	
Dec. 31/'02.—Receipts, per schedule No .B1	3,120 76	
Disbursements, per schedule No. B1	....	$2,994 49
Balance down	....	348 97
	$3,343 46	$3,343 46
Balance from 1902	$ 348 97	
Dec. 31/'03.—Receipts per schedule No. B2	2,674 15	
Disbursements per schedule No. B2	....	$2,825 94
Balance down	....	170 18
	$3,023 12	$3,023 12
Balance from 1903	$ 170·18	
Dec. 31/'04.—Receipts per schedule No. B3	4,432 75	
Disbursements per schedule No. B3	....	$4,474 14
Balance down	....	128 79
	$4,602 93	$4,602 93
Balance· from 1904	$1,128 79	
Dec. 31/'05.—Receipts per schedule No. B4	4,035 27	
Disbursements per schedule No. B4	....	$3,973 88
Cash in bank	....	51
Balance down	....	189 67
	$4,164 06	$4,164 06
School Treasurer's shortage		·$189 67

Corroboration.

	Dr.	Cr.
Dec. 31/'01.—Balance on hand as a basis	$222 70	
" '02·—Balance per schedule No. B1	126 27	
" '03·—Balance per schedule No. B2	....	$178 79
" '04·—Balance per schedule No. B3	....	41 39
" '05·—Balance per schedule No. B4	61 39	
Cash in bank	....	51
Shortage as above	....	189 67
	$410 36	$410 36

The above is a true extract of the books, vouchers and papers of the School Board of the Town of Stayner as discovered by me.

J. D. ANDERSON,
Chartered Accountant, Dominion Association.

STAYNER, Ont., March 10th, 1906.

Report re School Board, 1905.

Owing to the fact that the late Town Treasurer was also Treasurer of the School Board, and having seen evidences in the town books that Government grants belonging to the School Board had been used for town purposes, also that there were discounted notes entered in the bank book of said board notwithstanding money was due the School Board from the town; also I could not make the School Board cash book balance in any way or agree with the bank pass book, necessitating a strict examination of the cash book from January 1st, 1905, to date of taking charge, March, 1906.

1st. That after September, 1905, the late Treasurer quit attempting to show his balances of cash on hand.

2nd. That cheques were issued out of the school check book for town purposes.

3rd. That he had omitted to enter as cash paid out cheques to the amount of $194.55.

4th. That he drew without authorization on January 26th, 1906, his salary of $20.00 for year 1906, usually payable the following December.

5th. That he, as Treasurer, has sole right to sign cheques on the school account, cheques not being countersigned.

6th. That on September 12th, 1905, he drew a cheque payable to himself, without authorization, for $30.00.

7th. That all payments authorized by the School Board have been checked into a cash book and found to agree.

8th. His cash book shows a balance on hand January, 1905, of $618.34; whereas the bank pass book shows only $9.22.

9th. Therefore, eliminating the 1904 balance all together, I find the total receipts for government, town and county grants, including notes, discounts, fees, etc., for 1905, amount to.................................... $4,035 27

Disbursements corroborated by cheque or voucher 3,973 88

Balance	$ 61 39
Overdrawn salary	20 00
Unauthorized personal drawings	30 00
	$111 39
Less balance in bank	51
	$110 88

10th. This leaves an apparent shortage in school for year 1905, not taking into consideration the balance carried from 1904 yet to be ascertained of $110.88 as above.

11th. The total receipts were	$4,035 27
The total deposits in bank were	3,949 00

The difference not deposited is		$86 27
evidently composed of the only currency handed him, viz.:		
School fees	$21 50	
Sale of old woodshed, stoves, etc., corroborated by stubs of receipts given	64 77	
	$86 27	$86 27

General Remarks.

The proceeds of notes discounted for school purposes in the school bank account amount to $609.00, whereas when repaid with interest came to $625.00, thereby causing a loss of $16.00 to the School Board instead of the Town.

I advise: That the cheques issued should be countersigned by some officer of the School Board to prevent personal use of funds, as has been done by the late Treasurer. That the Government grant sent by the Treasury Department July 4th, 1905, was not entered in the cash book until January, 1906.

SCHOOL BOARD, 1902.

With and without taking into consideration balance on hand December 31st, 1901.

Receipts.

Fees	$ 20 00	
Government grant	200 00	
County grant	300 00	
Local municipal grant	1,900 00	
Loans	700 76	
		$3,120 76

Disbursements.

Teachers' salaries	$2,020 80	
Other salaries	103 00	
Fuel and supplies	110 92	
Repairs	29 05	
Printing and stationery	5 46	
Equipment, maps, etc.	6 30	
Sundries	8 90	
Loans and interest	710 06	
		$2,994 49
Balance on hand not considering 1901		$126 27
Balance on hand	$126 27	
Balance on hand Dec. 31st, 1901, taken as a basis	222 70	
Total balance on hand Dec. 31, 1902		$348 97

I find the books of the School Board, for the year 1902, correct to a cent, and consider it safe in taking as a basis the balance on hand December 31st, 1901, of $222.70.

SCHOOL BOARD, 1903.

Balance from 1902 not considered until ascertained.

Receipts.

Fees	$ 27 50	
Government grants	489 00	
County grants	200 00	
Local grants	1,400 00	
Loans	557 65	
Total receipts		$2,674 15

Disbursements.

Teachers' salaries	$1,975 28	
Other salaries	119 00	
Fuel and supplies	81 35	
Repairs	90 15	
Printing, stationery	13 52	
Sundries	8 64	
Loans, interest	565 00	
		$2,852 94
Excess of disbursements		$178 79
Less cheque No. 6,528, drawn by Treasurer to himself		25 00
		$153 79

There was supposed to be on hand, according to the cash book, December 31st, 1902, $348.97; and bank book, $208.43.

No corroboration of the school fees for 1903 are extant beyond the sum of $15.50, the papers having been destroyed or lost.

The Treasurer, having power to sign cheques and there being no countersigning required, I cannot find any explanations for a cheque Number 6,528, drawn payable to himself for $25.00, all other vouchers being present.

SCHOOL BOARD, 1904.

Balance from 1903 not considered until ascertained.

Receipts.

Fees (omitted in cash book)	$ 34 85	
Government grants	339 00	
County grants	200 00	
Local municipal grant	2,060 00	
Debentures	1,600 00	
Loan	198 90	
Total receipts		$4,432 75

Disbursements.

Teachers' salaries	$2,169 32	
Other salaries	165 00	
Fuel and supplies	94 97	
Repairs	47 68	
Stationery	20 32	
Equipment, maps, etc.	10 83	
Insurance	65 40	
School improvements	1,678 52	
Sundries	22 10	
Repayment of loans	200 00	
		$4,474 14
Excess of disbursements		$41 39
Total receipts		$4,432 75
Total deposits		4,399 90
		$32 85
Evidently school fees		$34 85
Less the only currency deposited to cover an overdraft		2 00
		$32 85

The balance on hand, according to the school cash book, December 31st, 1903, was $195.18; and according to the bank pass book, $31.22. That there was a balance on hand is established by the fact that the disbursements exceed the receipts. I discovered an error in entering amongst his receipts, a $500.00 entry twice, which accounts for the extremely large discrepancy between the bank account and the school cash book balance carried to January, 1905.

Not a single cent of the school fees received for this year (1904), was entered in his cash book.

School Board, 1905-6.

Balance from 1904 not considered until ascertained.

. Receipts.

Fees	$21 50	
Sundries (sale of seeves, etc.)	64 77	
Government grant, received August, 1905, entered in cash 1906	338 00	
County grant	200 00	
Local municipal grant	2,802 00	
Loans	609 00	
Total receipts 1905		$4,035 27

Disbursements.

Teachers' salaries	$2,183 70	
Other salaries (including overdraft Treasurer $50.00)	222 50	
Fuel and supplies	340 61	
Repairs	34 94	
Examinations	10 00	
Printing and stationery	5 75	
Equipment, maps, etc.	8 00	
Improvements, buildings, etc.	533 25	
Sundries	10 13	
Repayment on loan	625 00	
Total disbursements '		$3,973 88
Add unauthorized overdraft		61 39
Add unauthorized salary for 1906		30 00
		20 00 .
		$111 39
Less cash on hand, in bank		51
Apparent shortage for 1905 to March, 1906		$110 88

Considering there was no balance on hand January 1, 1905, of which the school cash books call for $618.34, though bank pass book only shows $9.22, necessitating going back through 1904 to ascertain balance on hand at end of 1904.

Memo.

Receipts, 1905 to March, 1906		$4,035 27
Deposited in bank		3,949 00
Difference		$86 27
Evidently the only currency handled being,—		
School fees	$21 50	
Sale of old materials	64 77	
		$86 27

All of the above are corroborated by vouchers, cheques, minutes of School Board.

Uncollected Taxes, 1902, 1903, 1904, of the Town of Stayner, Ont.

Compiled by J. Donald Anderson, Chartered Accountant, Windsor, Ont., by order of the Provincial Municipial Auditor, acting under instructions from the Lieutenant-Governor-in-Council, at the request of a petition from the ratepayers of Stayner, Ont.

UNCOLLECTED TAXES.

DETAILS ROLL, 1902.

Folio No.	Name.	Uncollected Taxes.	Interest Collected.	Taxes paid on Roll not in Blotter.
1	John A. Cameron	....	....	$23 40
4	Joseph Purdy	$1 95		
5	Donald McNab	....	$0 98	
6	Margaret Jones	17 00		
6	Sam'l Coborn	18 85	.	
7	Donald McLean	2 34		
7	John Bettas	....	52	.
8	Duncan Paul	5 20		
13	Willard Sage	....	....	13 00
15	Andrew Robertson	7 80		
15	John S. Garrod	5 20		
17	Andrew Robertson	7 80		
18	John McKee	....	39	
19	Duncan McDonald	....	35	
19	Matilda Watson	....	....	9 10
19	John Honsberger	....	....	50 40
20	John A. Garrod, jr.	....	....	5 20
20	Angus L. Woodard	....	....	10 10
24	W. J. Craven	2 43		
26	P. McSherry	....	5 45	
26	E. C. Oliver	....	1 74	
29	M. McColeman	7 50		
31	P. McSherry	11 67		
31	Andrew Heron	14 65		
31	Finley Campbell	....	60	
31	Sumerfeldt Estate	....	06	
31	P. McSherry	....	....	81
32	Alex. Nicol	15 60		
32	A. J. F. Sullivan	....	83	
33	John Robertson Estate	10 10		
33	Peter Driver	4 55		
33	Confederation Life Co.	....	85	
34	Jas. Fleming	....	....	10 40
36	C. Robinson	5 20		
37	P. McSherry	1 04		
37	A. Madden	78		
37	E. Weston	....	53	
40	John Bettas	....	52	
40	John Hisey	....	....	1 30
41	Mary Farqueson	2 08		
41	John Lang	1 30		
41	Robt. Lee	1 95		
41	Henry Allen	65		
42	Angus I. Woodard	78		
42	Sarah Woodard	....	03	
43	Jas. Coulter	1 95		
44	Jas. C. Dunlop	13 00		
45	George Gibb	....	57	
		$161 28	$13 42	$123 71

UNCOLLECTED TAXES.

DETAILS ROLL, 1903.

Folio No.	Name.	Uncollected Taxes.	Interest Collected.	Taxes paid on Roll not in Blotter.
4	A. T. Johnston	....	$0 18	
4	John Ayers	....	....	$1 88
5	Donald McNabb	$11 88		
6	S. Coborn	18 13		
6	Margaret Jones	12 50		
8	D. Paul	....	25	
8	Neil McEachern	....	....	3 00
8	Margaret McLaughlin	....	....	5 63
9	Nesbitt Estate	7 50		
12	F. J. Stewart	....	1 43	28 50
12	C. E. Jakeway	....	....	45 00
14	G. T. Railway	....	....	86 25
14	G. T. Railway	....	....	17 25
14	H. W. Jakeway	....	....	6 25
15	A. Robertson	7 50		
17	Wm. Robertson	7 50		...
17	Alex. McTaggert	....	22	
18	John Goodwin	8 75		
18	John McKee	7 50		
18	John McDonald	6 88		
18	Alfred Schell	....	2 75	
18	John Honsberger	....	4 85	48 50
20	Angus Bell	5 63		
20	John Laphan	....	50	
21	Pat. McSherry	12 50		
21	Robt. Fleming	6 00		
24	W. J. Craven	2 25		
24	John McEachern	50		
26	H. W. Jakeway	....	37	
26	Pat. McSherry	....	10 50	
26	Alex. Hadden	11 25		
28	Annie Hargrave	....	30	
28	Eliz. Cruickshank	....	25	
29	John Coborn	....	....	10 00
29	Mary Adair	7 25		
31	Pat. McSherry	....	1 20	12 00
31	Jonathan Baker	12 50		
31	Somerfeldt Estate	....	....	1 25
32	A. J. F. Sullivan	....	1 60	
32	Alex. Nicol	1 25		
33	E. C. Cross	....	....	20 00
33	Peter Driver	4 38		
33	Chas. O'Brien	10 63		
35	Trustees R. C. Church	46 25		
35	Neil McEachern	....	....	5 00
37	Anthony Madden	76		
37	Edmund Weston	10 38		
38	Robt. Howie	....	1 13	
39	Wm. McBeth	....	75	
41	Robt. Lee	2 88		
41	Henry Allen	63		
41	J. T. Lang	1 25		
41	Mary Farquarson	2 00		
42	J. L. McCarthy	2 50		
43	Jas. Coulter	1 88		
44	Wm. McBeth	....	75	
45	Thos. Higgs	....	30	
		$230 81	$26 83	$290 51
	Less error in interest	....	05	...
	Memo.	$230 81	$26 78	$290 51

34 Robt. Grainger, marked paid on blotter, not marked paid on roll, $5.00.

UNCOLLECTED TAXES.

DETAILS ROLL, 1904.

Roll No. Page.	Name.	Uncollected Taxes.	Overpaid.	Paid Interest	Paid on Roll not in Blotter.
1	....	....	$0 03		
3	Mary Stuart	$10 42			
4	Levi. Ayers	1 95			
4	Jas. Weatherup	7 80			
5	W. B. Henderson	2 60			
5	Donald McNabb	....	....	65	
9	Wm. McGill	....	....	65	
9	Nesbitt Estate	7 80			
12	J. Lamont	....	....	10	
12	Chas. E. Jakeway	....	....	....	$46 80
14	Finlay Campbell	6 50			
14	H. W. Jakeway	....	....	....	6 50
15	A. Robertson	7 80			
15	M. Burkholder	....	....	70	
16	Mowat Estate	1 95			
17	Wm. Robertson	7 80		......	
17	Jos. Johnston	....	....	26	
17	John Little	....	....	20	
17	Alex. McTaggert	....	....	23	4 78
18	F. J. Hill	....	....	71	7 86
18	Alfred Schell	28 60			
18	John Martin	7 80			
18	John Goodwin	....	....	35	
20	Angus M. Woodard	....	....	1 01	11 11
20	Angus Bell	5 85			
20	D. Nobes	....	....	20	
20	John Laphan	....	....	52	
21	Pat. McSherry	13 00			
22	Margaret Jones	13 00			
23	Wm. O'Helia	4 00			
24	W. J. Craven	2 60			
24	John McEachern	65			
26	Pat. McSherry	113 10			
28	Mrs. Gillespie	....	03		
29	Simon Spiker	5 85			
29	Mary Coffee	....	....	70	14 70
31	Pat. McSherry	....	....	62	13 10
32	D. Somerville	....	....	61	
35	N. McEachern	....	....	26	
36	John Ball	....	....	65	
37	John Beardon	7 80			
37	Anthony Madden	78			
37	Alex. Nicol	1 56			
37	Edmund Weston	11 75			
38	Robert Howie	....	....	58	
38	Thos. Reazin	.	....	02	
40	John Bettas	13 00			
41	Robt. Lee	2 85			
41	Henry Allen	65			
41	J. T. Long	1 30			
41	Mary Farquarson	2 08			
42	J. L. McCarthy	2 60			
42	Sarah Woodard	....	....	06	71
42	A. M. Woodard	....	....	06	08
42	Bridget Walsh	....	....	....	4 55
43	Thos. Mike	....	....	29	
43	Jas. Coulter	1 95			
44	Wm. McBeth	5 20			
45	Angus Hayman	11 40			
		$312 09	$0 06	$9 30	$110 69

13 M A

Recapitulation Collector's Rolls, 1902, 1903, 1904, of the Town of Stayner, Ont.

Compiled by J. Donald Anderson, Chartered Accountant, Windsor, Ont., by order of the Provincial Municipial Auditor, acting under instructions from the Lieutenant-Governor-in-Council, at the request of a petition from the ratepayers of Stayner, Ont.

RECAPITULATION COLLECTOR'S ROLL, 1892.

Page No.	County rate.	Town rate.	Debenture rate.	Dogs.	P. School rate.	Totals.
	$ c.	$ c.	$ c.	$ c.	$ c.	$ c.
1	22 89	113 15	86 90	5 00	124 10	352 10
2	11 46	56 55	43 50	1 00	62 04	174 55
3	44 77	221 75	170 26	2 00	243 12	681 90
4	21 64	107 30	82 35	1 00	117 61	329 90
5	9 33	45 82	35 31	1 00	50 33	141 79
6	2 47	12 26	9 41	....	13 43	37 57
7	10 30	50 43	38 97	1 00	55 39	156 09
8	3 30	16 26	12 52	1 00	17 84	50 92
9	6 91	34 10	26 23	1 00	37 41	105 65
10	5 30	25 96	20 04	4 00	28 52	83 82
11	6 38	31 64	24 27	3 00	34 69	99 98
12	12 56	61 80	47 59	1 00	67 85	190 80
13	8 84	43 35	33 42	2 00	47 64	135 25
14	11 10	54 60	42 05	....	59 95	167 70
15	6 79	33 45	25 75	3 00	36 71	105 70
16	85	4 25	3 25	....	4 65	13 00
17	4 31	21 15	16 31	2 00	23 23	67 00
18	12 04	59 04	45 52	6 00	64 88	187 48
19	6 74	33 25	25 58	1 00	36 48	103 05
20	6 54	52 11	24 75	1 00	35 27	99 67
21	8 04	39 64	30 51	4 00	43 49	125 68
22	1 78	8 65	6 70	1 00	9 52	27 65
23	3 36	11 25	8 61	3 00	12 33	37 45
24	1 70	8 04	6 34	1 00	8 88	25 96
26	28 90	142 97	109 85	3 00	156 77	441 19
27	20 41	100 85	77 52	....	110 62	309 40
28	6 62	32 43	25 04	....	35 62	99 71
29	8 49	41 95	32 25	2 00	46 01	130 70
30	3 48	16 98	13 12	....	18 68	52 26
31	5 99	29 06	22 50	1 00	32 02	90 57
32	7 44	36 90	28 32	5 00	40 44	118 10
33	7 27	35 88	27 60	3 00	39 36	113 11
34	3 41	16 70	12 88	2 00	18 36	53 35
35	6 62	32 60	25 08	2 00	35 80	100 10
36	4 48	22 00	16 94	....	24 18	67 60
37	3 77	18 31	14 20	3 00	20 14	59 42
38	3 14	15 28	11 82	....	16 82	47 06
39	7 08	34 95	26 88	....	38 34	107 25
40	4 88	24 11	18 54	....	26 44	73 97
41	97	4 39	3 51	....	4 91	13 78
42	1 11	5 29	4 14	....	5 84	16 38
43	2 48	11 55	9 02	2 00	12 76	37 75
44	7 53	37 26	28 60	....	40 88	114 27
45	4 98	24 68	18 95	4 00	27 05	79 66
	367 29	1,809 92	1,392 97	72 00	1,986 41	5,628 59

13a M. A.

Total tax roll as above $5,628 59
Interest collected per schedule 13 42
                                                             $5,642 01

Collected per roll and blotter part in cash book $5,343 60
Marked paid on roll not in blotter part in cash book as per
    detail roll schedule 123 71
Interest per schedule 13 42
                                                               $5,480 73

Uncollected taxes, 1902, per schedule No. A1.. $161 28

RECAPITULATION COLLECTOR'S ROLL, 1903.

Page No.	County rate.	Town rate.	Debenture rate.	Dogs.	P. School rate.	Totals.
	$ c.	$ c.	$ c.	$ c.	$ c.	$ c.
1	27 50	108 10	86 40	5 00	123 76	348 76
2	16 95	65 40	53 25	4 00	76 28	215 88
3	52 30	301 70	164 40	2 00	235 35	655 75
4	26 25	101 31	82 44	4 00	118 14	332 14
5	10 87	41 95	34 14	1 00	48 94	136 90
6	2 65	10 21	8 34	....	11 93	33 13
7	11 86	45 82	37 20	1 00	53 39	149 27
8	3 84	14 82	12 06	....	17 30	48 02
9	8 54	32 96	26 82	3 00	38 45	109 77
10	5 85	22 59	18 36	2 00	26 33	75 13
11	7 50	28 92	23 58	2 00	33 75	95 75
12	15 60	60 24	48 96	1 00	70 22	196 02
13	10 52	40 53	32 97	2 00	47 26	133 26
14	12 50	48 26	39 24	1 00	62 56	163 56
15	7 95	30 66	24 99	2 00	35 78	101 38
16	1 20	4 62	3 78	1 00	5 40	16 00
17	5 00	19 31	15 69	2 00	22 51	64 51
18	15 11	58 43	47 34	4 00	68 00	192 88
19	6 75	26 07	21 18	1 00	30 39	85 39
20	7 45	28 75	23 40	2 00	33 54	95 14
21	9 20	35 48	28 92	3 00	41 40	118 00
22	2 10	8 10	6 60	2 00	9 45	28 25
23	2 65	10 21	8 34	3 00	11 93	36 13
24	1 92	7 44	6 00	1 00	8 65	25 01
26	29 45	113 78	92 38	1 00	132 33	369 13
27	24 20	93 20	76 20	....	108 90	302 50
28	17 24	66 59	54 09	1 00	77 60	216 52
29	10 10	38 96	31 74	3 00	45 46	129 26
30	4 02	15 51	12 63	....	18 09	50 25
31	6 89	26 63	21 60	....	31 02	86 14
32	8 94	34 47	28 11	3 00	40 24	114 76
33	8 72	33 65	27 37	1 00	39 28	110 02
34	4 00	15 45	12 57	....	18 01	50 01
35	7 70	29 78	24 12	1 00	34 67	97 27
36	5 25	20 28	16 47	....	23 64	65 64
37	4 17	16 14	13 05	3 00	18 80	55 16
38	2 95	11 41	9 24	....	13 28	36 88
39	8 95	34 51	28 09	1 00	40 28	112 83
40	5 84	22 58	18 30	....	26 29	73 01
41	1 06	4 13	3 29	1 00	4 78	14 26
42	1 26	4 89	3 93	....	5 69	15 77
43	2 85	11 04	8 91	1 00	12 84	36 64
44	8 54	32 96	26 82	1 00	38 44	107 76
45	6 62	25 52	20 82	2 00	29 79	84 75
	440 81	1,701 34	1,384 18	68 00	1,990 26	5,584 59

FINAL RECAPITULATION ROLL, 1903.

Total tax roll as above $5,584 59
Total net interest collected per schedule............................. 26 78
                                                                                        $5,611 37
Collected per blotter and roll $2,984 70
Collected per roll not in blotter and part omitted in cash book   290 51
Omitted in cash book, marked paid in blotter and on roll,
    including error under collected (5)............................... 2,078 57
Interest collected 26 78
                                                                                        $5,380 56

Uncollected taxes, 1903, per Schedule No. A2...................................... $230 81

RECAPITULATION COLLECTOR'S ROLL, 1904.

Roll page.	County rate.	Town rate.	Water debenture rate.	Dogs.	Public School rate.	Total.
	$ c.	$ c.	$ c.	$ c.	$ c.	$ c.
1	27 03	99 90	72 93	6 00	105 74	311 60
2	22 29	82 20	60 06	3 00	87 00	254 55
3	59 49	219 44	180 30	1 00	232 24	672 47
4	31 22	115 12	84 08	....	131 88	352 30
5	11 24	41 41	30 28	4 00	43 82	130 75
6	1 90	7 01	5 12	....	7 42	21 45
7	13 61	50 11	36 63	1 00	53 05	154 40
8	4 15	15 24	11 15	....	16 13	46 67
9	10 15	37 49	27 37	1 00	39 65	115 66
10	6 81	25 05	18 33	-2 00	26 51	78 70
11	8 63	31 87	23 26	....	33 74	97 50
12	18 48	68 19	49 79	4 00	72 19	212 65
13	10 66	39 29	28 71	2 00	41 59	122 25
14	14 37	52 86	38 67	....	62 25	168 15
15	9 28	34 25	25 02	3 00	36 23	107 78
16	2 02	7 43	5 43	....	7 87	22 75
17	5 77	21 23	15 52	....	22 48	65 00
18	14 66	53 97	39 47	3 00	57 13	168 23
19	7 95	29 31	21 41	1 00	31 03	90 70
20	8 30	30 58	22 36	1 00	32 36	94 60
21	12 10	44 60	32 59	2 00	47 21	138 50
22	3 51	12 96	9 46	1 00	13 72	40 65
23	3 14	11 55	8 44	6 00	12 23	41 36
24	2 26	8 27	6 08	1 00	8 74	26 35
26	41 32	152 54	111 36	3 00	161 48	469 70
27	22 74	84 08	61 32	....	89 00	257 14
28	25 65	94 81	69 22	4 00	100 32	294 00
29	11 82	43 53	31 83	3 00	46 07	136 25
30	4 63	17 09	12 47	1 00	18 07	53 26
31	6 53	23 93	17 53	....	25 33	73 32
32	10 87	40 05	29 26	4 00	42 41	126 59
33	11 45	42 28	30 86	1 00	44 76	130 35
34	5 88	21 66	15 84	2 00	22 92	68 30
35	9 09	33 58	24 51	1 00	35 52	103 70
36	6 47	23 77	17 40	2 00	25 16	74 80
37	5 04	18 63	13 61	3 00	19 66	59 94
38	3 35	12 37	9 04	....	13 07	37 83
39	9 86	36 31	26 52	2 00	38 46	113 15
40	6 74	24 91	18 17	....	26 36	76 18
41	1 24	. 4 48	3 30	1 00	4 76	14 78
42	1 66	6 12	4 47	....	6 47	18 72
43	3 30	12 09	8 87	1 00	12 79	38 05
44	9 84	36 37	26 50	....	38 41	111 02
45	7 50	27 71	20 21	3 00	29 34	87 76
	514 00	1,895 54	1,384 75	73 00	2,012 57	5,879 86

FINAL RECAPITULATION ROLL, 1904.

Total tax roll above	$5,879 86	
Total interest collected per schedule	9 30	
Over collected	06	
		$5,889 22
Collected per blotter and roll	$5,466 44	
Marked paid on roll not in blotter	110 69	
		$5,577 13
Uncollected taxes on roll 1904, as per Schedule No. A3..........................		$312 09

No recapitulation, and none of the additions except the total column on each page of this roll, were made, resulting in the discovery of a few small errors.

Recapitulation Collector's Roll and Uncollected Taxes, 1905, of the Town of Stayner, Ont.

Compiled by J. Donald Anderson, Chartered Accountant, Windsor, Ont., by order of the Provincial Municipial Auditor, acting under instructions from the Lieutenant-Governor-in-Council, at the request of a petition from the ratepayers of Stayner, Ont.

The cost to the Municipality of Stayner of this audit was $730, which included Mr. Anderson's travelling expenses, etc.

Report of Collector's Roll, 1905.

My first observation was there seemed to be an excessively small amount collected on the roll 1905, and that there was not a single date where marked paid.

All evidence had to be produced from a heterogeneous mass of papers for, let it be remembered, that for sixteen years the late Town Treasurer also occupied the positions of Collector and Clerk of the Town, Treasurer of the School Board and cemetery, editor and owner of a newspaper and printing office, medical practitioner and insurance examiner, etc., and had only lately moved everything under the one roof. Even the Town safe contained a mixture of papers from 1898 to 1906, many of no value. Most important vouchers and books were scattered all over the printing department and the surgery. However, from this mass of papers I extracted positive evidence of collections amounting to $6,259.30 on roll 1905, whereas only $1,510.87 was marked paid. A memoranda in the back of a book proved to be the tax collections of 1905, corroborated subsequently by discovery of receipt stubs.

Other payments were marked paid directly on the roll, no other evidence until receipts were produced at my request.

The addition of only half a dozen columns of the tax roll was made, which when completed resulted in the discovery of many errors in cross addition. The balance being $3.27 in favour of the Town, no recapitulation of rolls was ever attempted.

By some oversight no poll tax was collected in 1905. (It generally runs about $14.00.)

Accompanying herewith please find a complete recapitulation of 1905 tax roll, vide exhibits attached, accompanies this report, also list of unpaid taxes, 1905, vide exhibit attached.

RECAPITULATION ROLL, 1905, to March, 1906.

1	10	11	12	14	15	16	17	18
No. of Roll page.	Total value of real property.	Value of personal property other income.	Amount of tax income.	Total value and amount of real and personal property and tax income.	County rate 2 M. on the $.	Town rate 4 $\frac{3}{10}$ M. on the $.	Special debenture pavement 1 $\frac{4}{10}$ M. on the $.	Special debenture reservoir 4 M. on the $.
	$ c.	$ c.	$ c.	$ c.	$ c.	$ c.	$ c.	$ c.
1	15,025 00	2,540 00	834 00	18,399 00	36 80	79 08	25 79	7 37
2	12,250 00	....	492 00	12,742 00	25 48	54 79	17 82	5 10
3	5,200 00	....	....	5,200 00	10 40	22 36	7 28	2 08
4	25,780 00	7,260 00	....	33,040 00	66 08	141 95	46 20	13 25
5	16,100 00	4,975 00	....	21,075 00	42 15	90 61	29 45	8 55
6	6,120 00	250 00	40 00	6,410 00	12 82	27 51	8 97	2 58
7	2,050 00	....	40 00	2,090 00	4 18	8 98	2 93	84
8	4,535 00	75 00	365 00	4,975 00	9 95	21 38	6 98	3 00
9	2,865 00	....	....	2,865 00	5 73	12 27	4 02	1 16
10	2,395 00	....	....	2,395 00	4 79	10 30	3 32	96
11	5,375 00	250 00	....	5,625 00	11 25	24 79	7 84	2 26
12	9,275 00	700 00	258 00	10,233 00	20 46	43 92	14 35	4 12
13	11,325 00	....	85	11,410 00	22 82	49 01	15 98	4 59
14	8,650 00	....	158 00	8,808 00	17 62	37 87	12 32	3 53
15	8,085 00	1,581 00	....	9,666 00	19 33	41 54	13 48	3 88
16	6,650 00	....	100 00	6,750 00	13 50	28 97	9 45	2 72
17	7,775 00	....	....	7,775 00	15 55	33 41	10 89	3 12
18	9,435 00	....	250 00	9,685 00	19 37	41 64	13 53	3 88
19	1,700 00	....	....	4,700 00	9 40	20 18	6 56	1 90
20	6,475 00	500 00	....	6,975 00	13 95	29 97	9 74	2 26
21	5,600 00	250 00	....	5,850 00	11 70	25 16	8 16	2 34
22	19,935 00	5,457 00	1,763 00	27,155 00	54 30	116 61	38 02	10 92
23	11,900 00	4,425 00	100 00	16,425 00	32 85	10 65	22 89	6 58
24	14,960 00	1,250 00	260 00	16,470 00	32 94	70 71	23 05	6 60
25	6,325 00	510 00	....	6,835 00	13 67	29 38	9 57	2 74
26	3,480 00	....	....	3,480 00	6 96	14 98	4 85	1 40
27	3,590 00	500 00	....	4,090 00	8 18	17 53	5 72	1 66
28	5,810 00	250 00	....	6,060 00	12 12	26 04	8 49	2 42
29	6,920 00	....	65 00	6,985 00	13 97	30 02	9 78	2 80
30	3,080 00	....	100 00	3,180 00	6 36	13 65	4 45	1 28
31	7,525 00	....	....	7,525 00	15 05	32 35	10 51	3 02
32	3,170 00	....	....	3,170 00	6 34	13 58	4 43	1 29
33	5,770 00	760 00	....	6,530 00	13 06	27 97	9 14	2 64
34	4,550 00	....	340 00	4,890 00	9 78	20 98	6 86	1 98
35	775 00	....	....	775 00	1 55	3 24	1 10	32
36	2,385 00	250 00	....	2,635 00	5 27	11 28	3 69	1 08
37	4,860 00	....	....	4,860 00	9 72	20 82	6 83	1 98
38	2,900 00	....	....	2,900 00	5 80	12 48	4 04	1 16
	285,600 00	31,783 00	5,250 00	320,633 00	641 25	1,377 91	448 48	128 36

RECAPITULATION.

Real property....................$283,600 00
Personal property..... .... 31,783 00
Income....................... 5,250 00

Total......................$320,633 00

County rate, 2 mills or $641.25.

RATES.

County.....................: .... 2 mills
Town.............................. 4$\frac{3}{10}$ "
Pavement....................... 1$\frac{4}{10}$ "
Reservoir........................ $\frac{4}{10}$ "
Waterworks....................... 4$\frac{4}{10}$ "
School .... 6$\frac{7}{10}$ "
Debentures..................... 1$\frac{4}{10}$ "

                      20 mills

RECAPITULATION ROLL, 1905, to MARCH, 1906.

1	19	21		23		26	27
No. of Roll page.	Special debenture waterworks 4⁴⁄₁₀ M. in the $.	Special frontage.	No. of dogs.	No. of bitches.	Rate on each.	Public. General 6⁴⁄₁₀ in the $.	Public. Debentures ⁸⁄₁₀ in the $.
	$ c.	$ c.				$ c.	$ c.
1	79 10	13 37	1	1	3	125 10	14 74
2	54 81	14 11	5	....	5	86 64	10 20
3	22 36	4 58	1	....	1	35 36	4 16
4	141 98	1 47	1	....	1	224 84	26 50
5	90 66	11 12	1	....	1	143 31	16 88
6	27 54	13 47	1	....	1	43 63	5 15
7	8 98	8 75	....	....	....	14 21	1 68
8	21 38	4 35	....	....	...	33 82	3 99
9	12 28	....	1	....	1	19 53	2 31
10	10 32	....	2	....	2	16 29	1 92
11	24 20	2 51	1	....	1	38 27	4 31
12	43 92	11 38	3	....	3	69 67	8 22
13	49 03	14 06	2	....	2	77 62	9 15
14	37 89	2 10	3	....	3	59 88	7 05
15	41 57	4 97	1	....	1	70 62	8 34
16	29 00	7 28	1	....	1	45 94	5 42
17	33 41	9 28	....	....	....	52 89	6 23
18	41 68	....	5	....	5	65 85	7 75
19	20 18	....	2	....	2	32 00	3 78
20	30 00	10 86	3	....	3	47 57	5 59
21	25 18	....	2	....	2	39 78	4 68
22	116 70	93	1	....	1	184 76	21 80
23	70 67	25 22	....	....	....	111 71	13 15
24	70 84	21 95	4	....	4	112 00	13 13
25	29 40	7 61	2	....	2	46 47	5 47
26	14 94	....	1	....	1	23 72	2 80
27	17 45	9 90	1	....	1	27 86	3 30
28	26 08	10 96	4	....	4	41 20	4 85
29	30 04	6 34	2	....	2	47 49	5 60
30	13 65	11 11	....	....	....	20 65	2 56
31	32 35	7 49	1	1	3	51 19	6 03
32	13 60	2 71	2	1	4	21 60	2 56
33	27 99	4 24	1	....	1	44 47	5 27
34	20 97	1 03	....	....	....	33 29	3 94
35	3 32	....	1	....	1	5 32	65
36	11 29	....	....	....	....	17 95	2 14
37	20 83	....	2	....	2	33 10	3 92
38	12 48	....	2	....	2	19 72	2 32
	1,378 07	243 15	60	3	66	2,185 22	257 79

RECAPITULATION.

County	$ 641 25	20 mills on $320,633 00	$6,412 66
Town	1,377 91	Special	243 15
Pavement	448 48	Dog	66 00
Reservoir	128 36	Excess levy	4 42
Waterworks	1,378 07		
School	2,185 22		
Debenture	257 79		
Dogs	66 00		
Special frontage	243 15		
	$6,726 23		$6,726 23

RECAPITULATION ROLL, 1905, TO MARCH, 1906.

1	30	32	33	34	35	36	39
No. of Roll page.	Total taxes, 20 amount	Marked paid on roll by Treasurer.	Received by Treasurer not marked paid on roll.	Collected since interest date.	Interest.	Errors in favor of town.	Uncollected March 10th.
1	384 35	104 38	278 61				1 36
2	273 95	74 32	199 63				....
3	109 58	33 00	76 48				10
4	663 27	140 60	517 67				5 00
5	433 73	44 61	373 51	5 00	25		15 61
6	142 67	48 97	88 70				
7	50 55	....	50 55				
8	103 85	17 50	77 62				8 73
9	58 30	16 80	41 50				
10	49 90	8 70	41 20				
11	116 63	6 00	62 00			1	48 64
12	219 04	113 14	105 90				
13	244 26	48 12	80 37	17 82	87		98 45
14	181 26	23 16	145 10				13 00
15	204 73	88 74	98 59				17 40
16	143 28	17 00	100 18	8 00	40		18 10
17	164 78	8 72	119 31	14 75	74		22 00
18	198 70	52 00	130 70				16 00
19	96 00	12 50	77 50				6 00
20	152 84	26 98	126 12			54	28
21	119 00	33 00	40 50				45 50
22	545 04	146 26	366 27				32 51
23	353 72	99 25	219 47	10 00	50		25 00
24	355 27	96 22	260 38			1 33	
25	146 31	37 80	108 51		45		
26	70 60	....	65 60	5 00	25		
27	92 60	11 94	59 20			10	21 74
28	136 16	23 74	103 64				8 78
29	146 04	10 00	125 04	3 00	15		10 00
30	73 71	20 98	53 73			1 00	
31	160 99	59 81	101 18				
32	70 11	11 63	37 58	7 00	35		13 90
33	135 78	80	130 27			29	5 00
34	98 83	34 80	52 03				12 00
35	16 50	....	8 40				8 10
36	52 70	90	34 80				17 00
37	99 20	10 50	88 70				
38	60 00	38 00	32 00				
	6,726 23	* 1,510 87	† 4,678 36	‡ 70 07	** 3 96	3 27	†† 470 20

```
Total levy ......................................................    $6,726 23
Over collected ..................................................         3 27
Interest ........................................................         3 66
* Collected previous to interest date ...........................    $1,510 87
† Collected not marked paid on roll ..............................     4,678 36
                                                                     $6,189 23
‡ Collected since November 30th, per list ........................        70 07
** Interest ......................................................         3 96
                                                                     $6,263 26
†† Uncollected to date, per list .................................       470 20
                                                                     $6,733 46    6,733 46
```

ROLL, 1905.

DETAILS OF ROLL BY ROLL OF OUTSTANDING TAXES.

Folio.	Uncollected Taxes, 1905.	Roll No.	
1	Reynolds, F............	4	$1 36
3	Dixon, Jno................................	40	10
4	Hood, Jno................................	49	5 00
5	Bannerman, H............?.	60	10 50
	Clark, Jno.	64	2
	Maynard, Geo. et. al.................	69–70	5 09
8	Bettes, J. W.............................	90	8 73
11	Bell, Morg...............................	113	63
	Johnston, Geo.........	115	5 00
	Briggs, A.	122	8 50
	Briggs, J. T..............	123	12 51
	Briggs, J. T. & A. T.....................	124	13 00
	Nesbitt, Jas.............................	130	9 00
13	Peattie, Jas.	148	15 12
	Jakeway, C. E	151	51 67
	Stewart, Mrs. M. E., et. al............	153	31 66
14	Atkinson, T. H..........................	62	13 00
15	Jakeway, H. W........................	185	7 00
	Campbell, E. (G.T.R.)	190	5 40
	Campbell, F.............................	190	5 00
16	Shirk, T. B..............................	157	12 10
	Robertson, Andrew.....................	208	4 00
	Mowat, O. Est..........................	211	2 00
17	Robertson, Wm.........................	212	6 00
	Bradbury, Jno., et. al	221–6	16 00
18	Goodwin, Jno	236	8 00
	Martin, E. J., et. al....................	237–8	8 00
19	Bell, Angus..............................	258	6 00
20	Lockup	272	26
	Fleming, R.	281	2
21	McBeth, A	285	14 00
	Jones, M.................................	144	13 00
	Church, E. C., Trustees..................	286	16 00
	Craven, John	292	2 00
	McEachern, John, et. al.................	293	50
22	Jakeway, C. E...........................	151	10 50
	Pearson, H. C.	306	17 00
	Devlin, S. L.	14	1
	Perry, S. G..............................	311	5 00
23	Jakeway. H. W..........................	185	15 00
	Cook, Jos	317	5 00
	Brown, Fred.............................	106	5 00
27	McSherry, P.............................	276	3 56
	Summerfeldt, Est........................	355	2 16
	Buist, D.................................	357	1 22
	Baker, Jonathan........................	361	2 80
	Herron, Andrew, et. al..................	362	12 00
28	Perry, Geo	311	8 78
29	O'Brien, Chas	370	10 00
32	Madden, Anthony	324	70
	Nicol, Alex.	419	1 20
	Richmond, R I., et. al...................	318	12 00
33	Beckett, S. G............................	378	5 00
34	Bettes, John and J.W....................	90	12 00
35	Lee, R...................................	446	5 00
	Allen, Hy................................	447	50
	Long, Thos..............................	448	1 00
	Farquison, Mary........................	449	1 60
36	McCarthy, L............................ ..	450	2 00
	Struthers, Josephine et al..............	452	7 00
	Walsh, B................................	454	4 00
	Mike, Tony	460	4 00
			$470 20

STAYNER, Ont., May 2nd, 1906.

MUNICIPAL CORPORATION OF THE TOWN OF STAYNER, ONT.

Dr. To J. Donald Anderson, Chartered Accountant, Auditor, etc.

March 9.—To railroad fare, Windsor to Stayner and return...		$ 16 10
March 10.— " hotel and expenses Toronto, interview with Provincial Municipal Auditor to receive instructions		3 00
April 23.— " railroad fare, Toronto and return; at resolution of Council		4 35
" hotel and expenses in Toronto		3 00
" assistant's account, Richmond		35 00
" " " Doner		20 00
" Globe Hotel bill		81 00
" Telegram, stationery and supplies		2 50
" typewriting, Miss O'Brien		15 00
" hotel, Toronto, returning to Windsor, rendering report to Provincial Municipal Auditor		3 00
" personal service, including instruction to Clerk and Treasurer, anticipated to be finished Thursday evening		578 00
		$760 95
May 4.—By cash		300 00
		$460 95
Deduction by special request of Mr. J. B. Laing, Provincial Municipal Auditor		30 95
		$430 00

Certified correct,   Approved,
    J. B. LAING,   J. J. FOY,
    Prov. Municipal Auditor.   Attorney-General.
6th May, 1906.

Memorandum to the Honourable the Attorney-General re Town of Stayner.

Mr. Anderson of Windsor has completed his report in this matter, having ascertained the indebtedness of the late Treasurer to the Corporation to be $4,485.64, which was compromised by the payment of $3,500 by his son, H. W. Jakeway. I consider the settlement a good one under the circumstances. Mr. Anderson made a very effective audit, which I have certified to, and, to make it as light as possible to the Corporation, have deducted $30.95 by special request of the Mayor.

                              J. B. LAING,
                    Provincial Municipal Auditor.

                          Stayner, May 4th, 1906.

J. D. ANDERSON, ESQ., Auditor.

Dear Sir,—As requested, I beg to submit the following true copy of a resolution passed at an adjourned special meeting of the Council of the Town of Stayner, held in the Council Chamber this morning:

"Moved by Councillor Livingstone, seconded by Councillor Perkin,—

"That the communication from H. W. Jakeway, Esq., making an offer of $3,500.00 (three thousand five hundred dollars) in full of all claims for shortage in his late father's accounts with the Town of Stayner as Treasurer be received and accepted, and that the Clerk be instructed to notify Mr. Jakeway by registered letter this afternoon."

                              Yours truly,
                          ALEX. HISLOP,
                                    T. Clerk.

REPORT OF SPECIAL INSPECTION, AUDIT AND EXAMINATON OF THE BOOKS, ACCOUNTS, VOUCHERS AND MONEYS OF THE MUNICIPAL CORPORATION OF THE TOWNSHIP OF ORFORD IN THE COUNTY OF KENT.

By A. F. Falls, Chartered Accountant.

Chatham, Ont., Octo. 24, 1906.

Upon authority of an Order-in-Council approved by His Honor, the Lieutenant-Governor of the Province of Ontario, the twenty-fourth day of April, 1906, Alexander Frederick Falls, Chartered Accountant, of the City of Chatham, was commissioned to make an inspection, examination and audit of the books, accounts, vouchers and moneys of the Municipal Corporation of the Township of Orford, in the County of Kent, under the Provisions of Chapter 228, R.S.O. 1897.

In pursuance of said authority, the said Alexander Frederick Falls, hereby reports that he has made an inspection, examination and audit of the books, accounts, vouchers and moneys of the said Corporation.

The audit is made on the petition of certain ratepayers addressed to the Provincial Municipal Auditor.

The petition requests that the examination shall extend over the period from the year 1887, and shall embrace an inspection, examination and audit of the books, accounts, vouchers and moneys in the hands of the Treasurer and Collector, and all matters and things in connection with the drainage by-laws of the municipality, or affecting the same, whether in the hands of the Clerk, Treasurer, Collector or anyone else on behalf of the said municipality, and also any bonus by-laws.

On Thursday, August 23, 1906, the petitioners, councillors and other ratepayers were invited to meet at Byfield Hall, Highgate, to make any charge or complaint respecting the manner the affairs of the Township were being conducted. The reasons leading up to the circulation of the petition for a special audit appear to have been :—

1. The drainage work accounts were not carried on in such a manner as to show the standing of the accounts of the different drains.

2. The impression that the Council had failed to collect deficiencies on certain drains, for which sums had been charged to the general funds, and to make rebates when the cost of the work was less than the estimates.

3. The report of a special audit in 1901 was not published.

4. The Tile Drainage money in the hands of the Provincial Treasurer has not been dealt with.

5. The manner in which Angus Smith, C. E., delayed the construction, inspection and completion of drains.

6. A desire for positive information as to the financial standing of the Corporation.

7. That drainage and other papers could not be procured from the Clerk when repairs were required, necessitating new surveys.

Scope of the Audit.

The inspection, audit and examination under the Order-in-Council covers the accounts of the municipality from 1887.

Besides the other accounts, the following were investigated in particular :—

ASSESSMENT AND COLLECTOR'S ROLLS.
DEBENTURES.
ACCOUNTS WITH HOWARD AND ALDBOROUGH TOWNSHIPS.
DRAINAGE ACCOUNTS.
SCHOOL SECTION ACCOUNTS.
ACCOUNTS OF TREASURERS.
TILE DRAINAGE ACCOUNTS.
DITCHES AND WATERCOURSE AWARDS.

Officers.

Henry Watson, the present Clerk, has held office during the entire period covered by this audit.

Thomas H. Ridley was Treasurer from 1888 to 1894 inclusive.

John S. Foster, Treasurer from 1895 to March, 1903, inclusive.

John D. Gillis was Treasurer for the year 1887, also since March, 1903, and is the present Treasurer.

Assessment Rolls.

The assessment rolls are in the proper form. The description of land owned by railways is not given in detail. No record appears of property exempt from taxation.

The minutes of the Court of Revision on the assessment roll are too brief, in many instances where changes are made, the owner's name only is mentioned, without any description of the property, the amount originally assessed, or after passed passed upon by the court, are omitted.

Many of the changes in the assessments made by the Court of Revision were done by erasing the original amount in the assessment roll, and inserting another, instead of ruling a line through the original, and inserting the altered amount with red ink. The minutes frequently only state the amount of increase or reduction, which makes it impossible to tell if amount altered to is correct. The minutes of the Court of Revision on the assessment roll for 1905 are fully recorded.

In a few instances items appear in the tax rolls, that are not on the assessment roll, or recorded in the minutes of the Court of Revision.

May 26th, 1896, Court of Revision minutes state J. H. Jones assessed Part 56 S. T. R. $300.00 income, this item appears on the assessment roll of 1896 in pencil, but is omitted from the tax roll. This is the only instance of an item on the assessment roll not appearing on the tax roll.

Collector's Rolls.

The collector's rolls of each year have been examined. Alterations have been made after the rolls were placed in the collector's hands. There are no records in the minutes of the council authorizing some of the changes.

The rolls are all properly certified by the Clerk, but have never been delivered on or before Oct. 1st, as required by Sec. 131, Asst. Act, R. S. O. The summary or schedule does not state the amount levied for each school section separately, but gives the total of the school levies in one amount; the rates as shown in the summary differ in some instances for the sum of the details as shown on the pages of the roll, but have generally been found correct. The roll of 1901 contained an error of $94.55. This is referred to in anther paragraph.

The collector's declaration has frequently been omitted to be signed. The 1905 collector's roll was not returned by Alp. 8th, 1906, in accordance with the act, causing a loss of interest to the Township of $3.15. Ten per cent. interest is added when the roll is in the County Treasurer's hands on May 1st, Sec. 169, Asst. Act. The roll was returned by Collector on May 3, 1906.

The collector's rolls since 1892 as a rule have the date entered on which taxes were paid, the roll of 1905, however, has a number of items against which the date of payment does not appear.

The collector's settlement with the Treasurer should be entered at the back of the roll with full particulars, stating number on the roll, name and amount of items uncollected referred to, with the date on which any allowances were made by resolution of Council.

Duplicate required under section 147 have not been made. The Clerk has neglected to notify those in arrears as required by section 147, Asst. Act R.S.O. The Treasurer overlooked sending a return to the County Treasurer of the unpaid taxes on 1905 roll, $31.58, when roll was returned to him May 3, 1906.

No record has been kept by the treasurer of any arrears of taxes returned to the County Treasurer. An account should be kept and the amount, if any, included in the assets.

The roll of 1901, as recapitulated by the Clerk, showed the total taxes, $94.55 less than the actual items on the roll. The error was in the school taxes. The collector made no declaration in the roll, but reported it fully collected on March 22, 1902, to the Council. Settlement was made with the Treasurer on the recapitulation of the Clerk, instead of the actual additions of the tax roll. This should have been discovered by the auditors of 1902 if they had properly audited the roll. This error was communicated to the executors of the estate of John A. McArthur, who was collector for that year. The difference was gone into with them in the presence of the Clerk. A cheque was promptly issued to the Township by the executors for $94.55, and appears among the assets in the attached statements.

The Township on Dec. 31, 1905, had no arrears of taxes against lands in the municipality in the County Treasurer's office.

The Municipality owes a debt of gratitude to the late John A. McArthur, who collected the taxes of the Township for many years, and to whose zeal and energy in the work the unique position of not having any arrears of taxes in the County Treasurer's Office can be attributed.

Debentures.

In some instances one debenture only has been issued for principal covering a period of years, with coupons attached for the annual payments of principal and interest. These coupons, covering the annual payment of both principal and interest for each year instead of the interest only, are not in accordance with the by-laws, and are altogether irregular. There should be one debenture for principal maturing each year, with coupons for interest only.

One series of debentures issued in 1902 in this manner, the lake Erie and Detroit River Railway Bonus of $2,000.00 under by-law No. 253, three coupons covering interest and principal, $247.08 each, have been paid. There are outstanding seven coupons of $247.08 each, attached to a debenture for the original principal sum of $2,000.00. The last of these coupons will mature Jan. 1, 1912. Till then the debenture for $2,000.00 will be held, although principal is paid annually.

.. This manner of issuing debentures might cause the municipality. loss. The principal is in the debenture and also included in the coupons, thus showing double liability.

The record of particulars of the outstanding debentures was not properly kept, and had been altered and transferred from one book to another several times. A proper debenture record book, which was much needed, was procured and written up; it contains particulars of all the debentures and coupons issued and unpaid on Dec. 31, 1905.

The Treasurer should keep this record written up in the future.

The debentures in connection with the drainage works are rarely issued in accordance with the by-laws. It has not been the custom to include in the amount, for which debentures were issued, the Township's portion for roads, even when provided in the by-law.

Frequently the issue was delayed till after one levy was placed on the roll.

The system of paying the Township's portion out of the general funds on all drains in the year the work was performed, instead of issuing debentures as provided by the by-laws under which they were constructed, the same as for the ratepayers' portion for which the money should be provided by the sale of debentures; together with the fact that what debentures were sold, were for even amounts instead of the estimate by the engineer as set forth in the by-law, has simply meant, that all the drainage work has been carried on by the general funds of the Township.

Debentures were issued on Cornwall Drain By-law 316, Dec. 3, 1904, for $525.00. Engineer's report was $524.95 on lands and roads, which was reduced at Court of Revision, Oct. 1, 1904, by. $52.00. The over issue of debentures on this drain was $52.05. No levy was made for the drain in 1905, although first debentures matures on Jan. 1, 1906.

The Treasurer, in his sworn evidence, stated that the debentures were issued for amounts to suit the borrowers. He was advised from time to time by the Reeve to issue debentures for a certain sum to ratepayers named, the rate of interest was sometimes mentioned. In January, 1904, $825.00 of debentures were issued to J. McWilliams at 5 per cent. on Eastlake, Drain, by-law 307. On Sept., 1904, were issued to John A. McArthur at 4 per cent. on McKerracher Drain, by-law 308. On Oct., 1904, $600.00 were issued to Mrs. Maud H. Logan, at 4 per cent. on King Drain, by-law 291. On Nov., 1904, $500.00 were issued to John A. McArthur at 4½ per cent. on Gosnell Drain, by-law 294. On Dec., 1904, $525.00 were issued to Charles Slade at 4½ per cent. on Cornwall Drain, by-law 316.

The method of issuing debentures for sums not in accordance with the by-laws is in keeping with the manner in which the finances of the Township have been handled. It has been less work for the Treasurer to borrow from the bank to provide funds to conduct the Township affairs, than to be issuing debentures for all the drains. Since March, 1903, when the present Treasurer assumed office for the second time, debentures have only been issued for one-third of the drains constructed under the Municipal Act.

The debentures were sold by private arrangement and almost entirely to the ratepayers; the question of rate was not fixed in the by-law, but limited (not exceeding five per cent.) Had they been sold by tender, better rates of interest would have been procured in many instances, and the legality of the issue in accordance with the by-law insisted on by the purchaser.

Townships of Howard and Aldborough.

There is no record of any account with either Township, except such memo. as the Clerk made of amounts due when asking for a settlement.

The adjustment of the accounts was usually made by committees appointed for the purpose. There is record of some of the written reports as to how settlements were arrived at. From inquiry it was learned that verbal reports were frequently made. Orders were issued for lump sums, "settlement of drainage matters" is the information as to what the payment was for. In only one instance the details appeared on the back of the order, the minutes record the motion that an order be drawn for a stated amount in settlement of drainage matters.

Settlements were made at intervals, sometimes not for two or three years. Allowances or deductions from items to affect a settlement or in lieu of interest accrued were made, without proper records being retained.

The Treasurer when asked for information in connection with these accounts, had no records at all of any of the transactions except as appeared in his cash book. He kept no continuous ledger, never used a journal, and had no account with either Township.

It was necessary to examine the audit reports of both Townships after receiving statements from the Treasurers. The statements were incomplete.

The accounts of the treasurers of Howard and Aldborough Townships were examined. They had no records of items under the ditches and watercourses Act, except such as was furnished them by the Clerk. From their records information was secured which was not in the records produced in Orford Township.

Drainage Accounts.

No ledger accounts whatever were kept showing the cost of construction of the different drains. They were never credited with proceeds of debentures and money commuted. The disbursements only were recorded year by year under the drain indicated on the warrant of the Council, or order of the commissioner. These were shown in the annual audit in detail under the head of the drain named or under the miscellaneous drains, but no-credits at all were mentioned, nor was any balance brought forward from the previous year.

Owing to the absence of a properly kept ledger, much information was required that could not be found in minutes of Council, on orders issued for payments, among the accounts on file, or in any of the records produced. It was necessary to take evidence from the Clerk, Treasurer, and members of the present and former councils.

The present Treasurer, who was auditor of the Township for some years previous to his appointment in 1903, stated under oath, that he had not included the drainage accounts in the annual audit report among the assets and liabilities, because he could not tell whether they were an asset or a liability, owing to the way records were kept.

In 1904 an attempt was made by the Treasurer to open up drainage accounts in the ledger, of such as had been recently constructed. This, however, was not satisfactory, owing to the fact that many of the drains taken into account were repairs on old drains, on which the previous balance was unknown, and not included. The collection of levies to meet debenture issues have also been included with cost of construction.

The absence of a proper record of the accounts of the drains, whereby the financial condition of drain could be ascertained promptly, has been a great source of inconvenience to the ratepayers and loss to the Township.

The fact that practically all the drainage construction and costs of the drainage suits have come out of the general funds of the Township, will no doubt be a surprise to the ratepayers in general, as well as to some of those who have occupied the positions of Reeve and members of the Council. This is very clear, however, when it is known that for all the drainage work constructed since Jan. 1, 1900, debentures have only been issued to provide money for the construction of five drains; and only in one instance, that of the Cornwall Drain, by-law 316, has the amount levied against Township roads been included in the debentures sold.

All the drains constructed, against which there are collections to be made, are indebted to the general funds as well as those for which the engineer's estimates have been exceeded.

The practice of the Council has been to provisionally adopt the by-law, hold the Court of Revision, and finally pass the by-law. In some of the by-laws provision was made for borrowing the entire amount, as estimated by the engineer, and in others the amount assessed against lands only was to be provided by sale of debentures. The amount against roads would then have to be provided out of the general funds. This was practically commuting the Township's portion of the work. Debentures were only issued when the Treasurer was so instructed by the Reeve. Nearly all drainage debentures were issued for even amounts, and in not one single instance in the last ten years have they been issued strictly as set forth in the by-law.

Under the above conditions it is not to be wondered at, that the drainage accounts of the Township could not be satisfactorily explained. The financial standing of the affairs of the Township could not be shown, without taking into account the condition of the account of each drain. This has never been done.

The usual method of providing funds for drainage work, and the only legal way (in my opinion) is by the issue of debentures under the by-law authorizing the construction. If any ratepayers commute the amount they are to pay, the debentures to be issued are reduced by the amount paid in. Against funds so provided the commissioner or engineer, appointed under the same by-law which provides for the funds, can draw orders for the work set forth in the by-law. Unless the funds are provided as set forth in the by-law authorizing the expenditure, no other funds are available for use, and the Treasurer should refuse payment and report to the Council. There is no provision in the act whereby the general funds of the Township can be used as they have been by the officials of the Township of Orford for years.

It is astonishing that this practice should have been so long permitted, of constructing drains out of general funds when the by-laws provided for the sale of debentures to furnish the money. The general funds providing the money and remaining a creditor of the drain till such time as all the annual levies had been collected.

Owing to irregularities in the by-laws, and the manner of conducting the affairs in the construction of drains, it is not possible to arrive at the standing of the drainage accounts by the ordinary methods, namely:— Crediting the drain with proceeds of debentures and commuted taxes, and charging up all disbursements.

The manner in which Engineer Angus Smith has neglected his work of attending to the construction and inspection of drains has put the township to considerable annoyance, and caused the ratepayers to make complaints, and in some instances suits have been entered. Frequently his absence from the Township for long periods at a time, has caused the construction of drains to remain unfinished from year to year, and in many instances sub-commissioners have had to be appointed to continue the work. Contractors have been held back in their payments, with great annoyance to the rate-payers. This has a tendency to increase the cost of other drainage work in the township. From the evidence of members of the present and former councils, it is evident that there has not been proper inspection of drainage work after the completion of the work. In some instances work has not been inspected for a year after it was performed, at which time, owing to the light nature of the soil, it would not be possible to tell if earth in the drain had been washed in since, or had not been fully removed when constructed.

It would be a wise precaution, before drains were finally taken over as finished from the contractor, that a written report to the Council from the Reeve should be required; the commissioner not to receive an order for his commission until the Reeve became responsible to the ratepayers that the work had been performed in accordance with the profile. If the contractor was paid before the work was properly executed, the commission would be a guarantee for any unfinished work.

On all the drainage accounts no interest has been added to any of the balances.

Drains have not been charged with many small items expended owing to the lack of information. The Council meetings, as Court of Revision, were not charged to any drain, nor a number of orders passed for committee work on drains, the names of the drains, the names of the drains not being designated in the minutes, in which they were recorded, nor on the order for the amount.

All drainage levies authorized by by-laws have been traced, and those which have not been collected are mentioned in this report.

The drain by-laws passed during the years 1904 and 1905, when Clerk was under salary, had not been charged with Clerk's fees. The charges have now been included against the proper drains.

An analysis of all the drain accounts has been made since 1887 to Dec. 31st, 1905, charging up all disbursements and crediting the amount as contained in the engineer's report embodied in the by-laws. Reference is made only to those as is thought necessary.

Ashton Drain.

The disbursements for this drain in 1892 do not appear in the printed audit report at all.

By law 329, finally passed Dec. 15, 1905. The schedule was changed by Court of Revision, but was not altered by the Clerk in the by-law book, or on the copy of by-law handed the Treasurer. The amounts on the original against J. H. Ashton and Chas. Ashton have been commuted. There is yet due from J. H. Ashton $2.00, and Chas. Ashton $1.40, which was added on their lots by the Court of Revision.

After placing the total amount of engineer's report contained in by-law 320 to the credit of the drain, there is on Dec. 31, 1905, a credit balance of $1,327.40 to meet the cost of the work under construction.

Aldborough No. 2 Drain.

This drain originated in Aldborough Township, with levies against two Orford ratepayers on lands, and the Township on roads. In 1901 the clerk drew $16.00, $6.00 for fees and $10.00 for publishing by-law number 279,

14 M.A.

although a few typewritten copies only were struck off. In 1903 for by-law number 303, the clerk received $15.00, $5.00 for fees and $10.00 for publishing. This charge of $15.00 should have been deducted from $72.00 paid Aldborough Township on March 10th, 1906. The $15.00 must be recovered from Aldborough Township.

In 1901 this drain was improved on report of Angus Smith, engineer. Ten and twelve inch tile were used, covered over with an open drain above the tile for flood water. This did not provide sufficient outlet. In 1903 on report of Alex. Baird, engineer, the tile was removed from the lower portion, and an open drain made instead. All lands assessed in 1901 were again assessed in 1903. The Aldborough audit report of 1905 shows tile sold in 1903, $160.90, in 1904, $236.84. And on Dec. 31, 1905, a surplus of $350.07 standing to the credit of the drain. This is an asset of the drain constructed in 1901, and must be distributed to the two townships in proportion to their respective aggregate assessments on lands and roads. Orford, $107.50; Aldborough, $1,726.80. Orford should apply for rebate.

Cornwall Drain.

Under By-laws number 187 in 1892, and number 316 which was finally passed Oct. 1, 1904, debentures were sold for $525.00 on Dec. 3, 1904, a sum greater than the by-law called for. Construction was completed in 1905. No levy was placed on the roll of 1905, nor could a copy of the by-law be found transcribed in the by-law book. The clerk gave no explanation why he omitted to copy by-law or make a levy in 1905. There is a credit balance on Dec. 31, 1905, of $7.05.

Cranberry Marsh Drain, West Branch.

This drain was in litigation with the Township of Howard. The total paid out by Orford Township was $561.11 of this $263.25 the cost of arbitration was levied under an amending By-law No. 278, of 1901, against lands and roads, and was collected in 1901, 1902 and 1903.. The balance $297.86, the cost of the appeal remains as an overdrawn account.

The minutes of the Township Council of Sept. 17, 1896, read:—"In the matter of the Cranberry Marsh Drain, the parties assessed all signed a request to appeal to the referee, which was done."

"Moved by Sifton and Gosnell and resolved that the clerk be instructed to go to Chatham and receive proper plans of service through the advice of a solicitor in connection with the appeal to the referee on west branch of Cranberry Marsh Drain."

There is a reference in the minutes when the amending By-law No. 278 was passed, that the amount inserted was in accordance with an agreement. No document of this nature could be found, nor any particulars in regard to it, further than what is stated above.

Cruickshank's Drain.

Under By-law 123 of 1886, 186 of 1892, and 300 of 1903. In the year 1898 the drain was repaired, and a pro rata levy made, covering the costs of cleaning, and expenses, $297.50. This did not cover all the charges, as $25.00 was paid C. Bergy as commission on the drain, making the total, $322.30. This whole transaction was put through without any by-law. Some

14a M.A

of the ratepayers complained of the heavy taxes, and by resolution had half of their portion carried over with 6 per cent. added till 1899.

The work done under by-law 300 of 1903 was very much delayed. There is a suit against the Township by some of the ratepayers which has not yet been disposed of.

After placing to the credit of this drain the amount due from Aldborough as on Dec. 31, 1905, and which was paid in March, 1906, there is a credit balance of $45.41. There have been some law costs incurred in 1906, which have not been taken into consideration, as the amount is not known till the suit is concluded.

This drain was carefully gone into, and, owing to the fact that it is in litigation, it is not deemed wise to comment on it further than to say, for the purpose of arriving at a settlement, the engineer has relinquished his claim for commission.

Dube's Drain.

Under by-law 288 of 1902, the Court of Revision made some changes when they first met and then adjourned. When they again met, and finally passed the by-law, more changes were made. The changes on the schedule, from which the amounts are placed on the tax rolls, does not agree with those recorded in the minutes of the Court of Revision, and the Clerk's explanation sworn to is as follows:—

"Frequently at the Court of Revision the changes were marked on copy of by-law being perused, and usually confirmed before Court of Revision ended, and from that be embodied in the by-law book. There seems to be $4.00 more added to land than deducted from lands. I am sure the schedule from which the collections have been made are correct with the exception of the extra addition of $4.00 I cannot account for."

The incomplete records of the changes by the Court of Revision make it impossible to know what they really were.

On the roll 1905, John Schuller was charged 43c., which should have been $1.43. The correction will be made on the roll of 1906, with the last levy under the by-law. On Dec. 31, 1905, this drain shows a debit balance of $16.85.

Duffus Drain.

This drain has been constructed, improved and repaired under by-laws 160 of 1890, 173 of 1891, 200 of 1893, 261 of 1900, and 304 of 1903. Some of the repairs have been under pro rata levies, and the records are not as clear as they might and should be. There is a surplus standing to the credit of the Duffus Drain, on Dec. 31, 1905, of $112.91, as the result of by-law 160 of 1890 levying a greater amount than was expended. This sum should be rebated the ratepayers or applied to repair the drain if it now requires it.

Eastlake Drain.

One of the ratepayers on this drain complained that when petition was asked for repairs to this drain prior to passing by-law 307 of 1903, the original papers could not be found by the Clerk. This necessitated the outlay of $40.00 for new plans and profile.

There is a credit balance on Dec. 31, 1905, of $35.27.

Foster Drain.

Constructed under By-law 257, of 1899, by Angus Smith, Engineer, as commissioner. Some orders were issued by S. H. Foster as Commissioner. One of these dated June 6th, 1900, $19.80, was issued by S. H. Foster, Commissioner, payable to himself for work, a most irregular and improper procedure. While a member of Council in 1901, S. H. Foster also sold gravel to the municipality. Owing to his absence in the North West, the matters were not taken up with him personally, or examined further.

On Dec. 31, 1905, the drain account was overdrawn, $11.43.

Desner Drain.

Constructed under By-laws 169, of 1891, and 246 of 1898. There is a surplus standing to the credit of this drain on Dec. 31, 1905, of $80.16, which should either be refunded or used to reduce the levies, when the drain is again repaired.

Gosnell Drain.

Under By-laws 180, of 1892, 240 of 1897, and 294 of 1903. The schedule of by-law 294 was changed at the Court of Revision, no mention is made of striking off $2.00 assessment of A. J. Stone, in the body of the minutes. A pencil memo was the only authority on which this was done.

The Clerk's evidence in this drain is as follows:—"The change in Stone assessment, $2.00, was made by some authority of Council which I cannot recall. The assessment against the Michigan Central Railway, 70c., and Lake Erie & D. R. R., 70c., omitted from 1905, seems to be an error."

These items will be corrected on the roll of 1906.

There is a balance on Dec. 31, 1905, standing to the credit of this drain of $43.81.

Haycroft Drain.

Under By-laws 213 of 1894, and 317 of 1905. Work was started in 1905, and is being completed in 1906. No debentures have been issued to furnish funds for this work as provided in by-law. It is being constructed out of the general funds, to the credit of which the levies as made will go. This irregular method is referred to elsewhere in this report.

After crediting the drain with the full amount, $350.65, as contained in the engineer's report, there is a credit balance of $267.66, against which the balance of work done in 1906 is to be charged.

Highgate Drain.

This is the most complicated of all the drains constructed in the Township. By-laws and their levies have been changed by agreements and resolutions of Council, and ratepayers were permitted to perform work in lieu of assessment.

By-law 241 in 1899; the following levies were omitted from 1899 roll:—

D. McMackon,	Part Lot 6, Con. 5,	37c.
Rev. D. Pomeroy,	Part Lot 6, Con. 6,	37c.
Mrs. S. E Johnston,	Part Lot 7, Con. 6,	35c.

The following were added at the Court of Revision, but were never embodied in the by-law when finally passed. These have never been collected, and are an asset of the Township.

W. R. Attridge $5 00
J. Beattie 1 85
F. Phoenix 7 00
James Attridge 4 00

$19 14

In reference to these the evidence of the Clerk is:—"I cannot find where the items which amount to $19.14 have been collected on the rolls; the items $5.00, $1.85, $7.00 and $4.00, total $17.85, are not embodied in the by-law."

By-law 277 of 1901, for $224.00 was attacked, and proceedings to have it quashed instituted. A settlement was arrived at without an amending by-law, which placed $90.96 against lands on roll of 1901; the amount against roads was $10.23, and ratepayers performed work to the value of $24.80. This left the drain on Dec. 31, 1901, overdrawn $55.85 which, owing to the illegal methods adopted, cannot now be collected and is a loss to the Township.

By-law 295 of 1903, to improve the upper portion of this drain. The levies have all been collected on the rolls of 1903, 1904 and 1905. Complaints, that the work has never been completed, were made by some of the ratepayers. The old tile was sold, and has been credited to the drain. A rebate of $20.00 was passed in 1905 by the Council for the tile sold, but orders were not issued till 1906. On Dec. 31, 1905, there is standing to the credit of the upper portion of the drain $84.94 which, after the rebate of $20.00 is charged, will leave $64.94 remaining to the credit. This can be used to complete the unfinished work complained about.

Ingram Drain.

Constructed under by-law 293 of 1902. No debentures were sold to provide funds for the work. There are two levies not yet collected, those of 1906 and 1907.

The engineer's estimate was exceeded by $144.15, the amount the drain is overdrawn on Dec. 31, 1905.

An amending by-law must be passed to cover that amount.

King Drain.

Constructed under by-law 125 of 1886, 202 of 1893, and 291 of 1902. After crediting up the amount due from the Township of Aldborough, which was paid on March 10, 1906, the drain shows a credit balance of $4.36 on Dec. 31, 1905.

The amount expended in 1906 has yet to be charged.

During the present year the Council has had under consideration the complaint of one of the ratepayers which may lead to litigation.

Massey Drain.

There are the Leitch, Hornal and Wylie branches, as well as the main drain, care has not always been exercised to keep them separate. The last by-law covering Wylie branch only, is shown by itself.

The following items under By-law 212 of 1894, were omitted from the roll of 1897 : —

Jas. R. McDonald, Lot 15, Con. 8	....	$0 29
Robert Hornal, Lot 17, Con. 8	....	5 32
John McKay, Lot 18, Con. 8	....	5 32
Alex. McWilliams, w ½ Lot 19, Con. 8	....	2 62
		$13 55

The Clerk in his evidence stated :—"I think that my attention was called to this by some ratepayer on the drain. It was never placed on the roll however."

The engineer's allowance for advertising by-law 212 was $20.00, and Clerk's fees $18.60. The Clerk drew in 1894, voucher 223, payable to his printer, $15.00, vouchers 333, 409 and 481, payable to himself for $15.00, $15.00 and $18.60, a total of $63.60, or $25.00 more than allowed by the by-law. This amount has been charged to the Clerk in schedule 5.

In connection with by-law 174, there was considerable extra work, owing to change on account of ratepayers having the privilege to tile, instead of having open drains. For the services of investigating, changing levies and reporting to Council on this, and the McCallum drains, the Clerk was allowed on Massey drain, $20.50 extra, and on McCallum, $5.50; these payments are over and above the $25.00 charged back to the Clerk. In his evidence he states : "The $25.00 appears by the vouchers that I received that amount more than the engineer's allowance. Two sets of by-laws were gotten up."

The Massey drain shows, after crediting it back with $25.00, (drawn by the Clerk more than contained in the engineer's estimates referred to above), a credit balance of $42.79 on Dec. 31, 1905, against which there is a liability of $19.42 due to Wm. Desmond for over collection against Lot 16, Con. 7, on the roll of 1897. The amount had previously been commuted, and should not have been placed on the roll.

The By-law No. 327, passed in 1906 for the Massey drain, is not included in above statement: the sale of debentures as provided should furnish the funds to be placed to the credit of the drain and used for meeting expenditures mentioned in the by-law.

McCallum Drain.

On July 31, 1901, D. Reavie requested the Council to deepen the outlet of this drain, the Clerk was instructed to notify the engineer. On Sept. 11, 1901, the Council minutes show on motion of Long and Webster, "engineer's report was accepted and that the work be proceeded with in accordance with the same, and assessments placed on the roll in pro rata to original. Also that Joel Wootten be appointed commissioner, to see that the work be properly done." The work was proceeded with the same year and paid for.

No by-law has been passed for it nor has it been placed on the roll. James Rendall, a ratepayer on the drain, in giving evidence, swore:—"I went into the Clerk's office, Oct. 18, 1903, and asked for copy of engineer's report of Aug. 29, 1901. That I wanted to pay my asesssment on it. He said there was no such report or no such drain to pay on."

The Clerk could give no explanation for not having a by-law passed, and the amount collected on the roll.

In 1903, D. Graham was charged $5.93, on the roll which should have been $3.96. There is due him $1.97, amount overcharged. This amount must be charged to the drain when paid.

On Dec. 31, 1905, this drain account was overdrawn, $131.39, which will be recovered when a proper by-law is passed to collect the amount on the engineer's report of Aug. 29, 1901.

McCaughrin Drain.

This was constructed under by-law No. 250 of 1898. In the year 1898, J. S. Foster took credit for paying voucher No. 477, T. Garlick, $25.00, and in 1899 again took credit under voucher 31, for paying the same order. In 1899 the drain was completed, and showed with the above item charged twice, an overdraft of $38.50. On April 19, 1901, nearly two years after the drain was completed, J. S. Foster got an order from the Council for $26.00, which read, "amount paid on McCaughrin." One of the vouchers in 1899 on this drain for $20.00 is missing. No authority has been shown for the $26.00 of April 19, 1901. The items of $25.00 and $26.00 with interest have been charged to Mr. Foster. The engineer's report after the drain was completed does not include these two items as expenditures.

On Dec. 31, 1905, there is a debit balance of $13.50 after crediting the drain with $51.00, due from Mr. Foster.

McKerracher Drain.

In the audit report of 1888 this drain was reported with others as overdrawn. A dispute arose, between the Clerk and the auditors, which was referred to the County Judge, by the Council under section 477 of the Municipal Act. Between the time the resolution was passed, and Judge Bell made his report, by-law No. 151 was passed June 18, 1889, amending by-law number 122 of 1886, covering the amount, this drain was overdrawn. Under this by-law 151 of 1889, two sets of debentures were issued and sold, the first on Oct. 8, 1889, for $314.00, the second on April 24, 1891, for $320.00. The proceeds of both went to the credit of the general funds, and the debentures as they matured were paid out of the same fund.

Collections against the ratepayers were only made once, and went into the general funds.

This goes to show how utterly careless the finances of the Township were handled.

The Court of Revision made changes on the schedule of by-law 308 in 1903 before it was finally passed. The Clerk made some of the changes on the copy of the by-law he had embodied in the book for that purpose; but omitted to change the following, although he had typewritten copies struck off, including them:—

OMISSIONS.

Raised.		Lowered.	
Jas. R. Gosnell ....$ 3 00			
Lake Erie R. R.......... 10 00		F. S. Scott $5 00	
Mich. C. R. R............. 5 00		John H. Knapp 5 00	
W. J. Raycraft 2 00		Angus D. Gillis 5 00	
D. M. Gillis 1 00		Angus D. G'llis 5 00	
Pro rata on Culvert.... 18 00		Robert McLaren 3 00	
Mrs. Kemp McKellar			
Lot 13, Con. 5......... 2 00		$23 00	
Albert Blue 3 00			
$44 00			

The collections under this by-law, on the rolls of 1904 and 1905, have been made without taking the above mentioned changes in schedule, into account at all. Some ratepayers have paid more than they should have, and others less. The levy against the L. E. & D. R. R., was omitted from the rolls of 1904 and 1905, in error by the Clerk. The levy against the Mich. Central R. R., for 1905, was also omitted from the roll, up to and including 1904, all the taxes of this railway were commuted by by-law. All these errors have been corrected and properly entered in the drainage levy book, which was procured and written up, and can be seen at the Clerk's office. The proper amounts will be placed on the roll of 1906. The Clerk's explanation of the errors is:—

"I had no idea there were any errors of that nature, and cannot account for the changes not being made in the by-law."

The Court of Revision minutes read, "On reduction of 40 per cent. Culvert pro rata." On inquiry it was learned, that the Township was to pay at least 40 per cent. of the cost of this culvert; which including excavation and temporary bridge cost $507.94. The drain, when complete and paid for, will be overdrawn, $268.18. The Council must authorize the crediting of the drain and charging general funds with the Township's portion of the Culvert.

After crediting the drain with the full amount of the engineer's estimate in by-law 308, and the amount added by the Judge to cover court costs, and charging all disbursements to Dec. 31, 1905, there is a credit balance of $89.62.

The work of construction was not then completed. The above amount is all that has been provided by existing by-laws, for expenditure on the drain.

Morrison Drain.

By-law 315 was abandoned. Costs incurred were to be placed on the roll of 1904.

The Clerk did not include the amounts for publishing $10.00, and Clerk's fees, $12.00, as he did not receive the fees at that time, but was under salary. He was of the opinion, as he did not receive the fees personally, they should not be charged. The Township sustains this loss through the Clerk's proper interpretation.

North Marsh or Arnold Creek Drain.

There was a refund from the Township of Howard of $145.05, for which orders were issued, rebating to all the ratepayers, except the Township's portion for roads, on Dec. 8, 1894. On Dec. 17, 1894, an order was issued for $6.00 to H. Watson, "special work rebating North Marsh Drain." Again a year later, on Dec. 16, 1895, another order was issued to H. Watson for $8.00, "allowance on drain, North Marsh." No transaction whatever took place between Dec. 17, 1894, and Dec. 16, 1895. He had previously drawn in 1890, when by-law 164 was put through, $20.00 on by-law, and for 2 days with reeve, $4.00, besides $6.00 was paid Jas. Rendall for serving by-laws. In 1891, Nov. 17, the Clerk drew for By-law 171, $15.00 and $10.00; again on Dec. 16 for services $5.00. My opinion is that he had been fully compensated prior to 1894 for all services in connection with the drain. The Clerk's evidence is as follows:—"I claim work was done for these two orders, or I would not have put in account for them." To the question how do you account for the $8.00 in 1895, as there was no rebating in that year, he replied, "There must have been some reason for the issue of the order."

The fact that these orders were passed by the Council does not make it legal for a Clerk to draw practically 10 per cent. of the amount to be rebated on a drain. He has already been paid in excess of the engineer's report for Clerk's fees, and the full amount allowed for publishing the by-law in his own printing office, in direct violation of his declaration of office.

The two items, $6.00 and $8.00, have been charged to H. Watson, as shown in schedule 5.

Potter Drain.

Constructed under by-law 201 of 1893, shows on Dec. 31, 1905, a credit balance of $83.97. This amount should be rebated to the ratepayers pro rata unless the drain is shortly to be repaired. In such case this amount may be applied to reduce the levies for the new work.

Stover Drain.

This drain was constructed under by-law No. 80 of 1884, which was duly registered. Litigation took place. The auditors in 1888 reported the account overdrawn. A dispute arose between the Clerk and the auditors, which under section 477 of the Municipal Act, on motion of Jonas Gosnell and Peter Spence was referred to the County Judge. The original report of Judge Bell and evidence taken could not be produced by the Clerk. On pages 33 and 34 of the audit report of 1888 his report is published. In reference to the Stover Drain, it states the following:—"With respect to the Stover Drain I find that, owing to heavy incidental expenses, caused by litigation and otherwise, there is a large amount due to the township as shown by the auditor's report."

"This is properly an asset of the township, and can be realized by a proper by-law in that behalf."

The same Clerk that was in office then is Clerk now. The mover of the resolution was in council for 1888 and 1889, and Reeve from 1892 to 1896 inclusive; the seconder was in the council 1888, 1889 and 1890. Yet there never has been a by-law passed, or motion recorded in the minutes from that day till the present, bearing on the subject, or any effort made to collect the sum of $1,504.14, which is the amount the account was overdrawn in 1888, after all disbursements and credits are included. No interest has been included in the above amount.

The loss to the Township alone on this amount at 5 per cent. since Jan. 1, 1889, to Jan. 1st, 1906, is $1,534.08. Had the same action been taken on this drain as the McKerracher, loss would have been averted, besides reimbursing the general fund the amount due it.

Stover Drain (News).

This drain, under by-law 311 of 1903, shows an overdraft of $18.00, amount of allowance to H. Watson, Clerk, for preparing by-law. The amount should have been deducted from the Township of Howard, when payment was made on Dec. 15, 1905, of $138.40. The $18.00 must be collected from Howard in the next settlement.

South Marsh Drain.

Constructed under by-laws 144 of 1886, 152 of 1889, 229 of 1896, and 259 of 1899. On Dec. 31, 1905, after crediting up the full amount of engineer's reports in every instance, there is a credit balance of $19.06.

In 1890 there was placed in error against the property of Jas. Congo, on the roll for this drain, $6.80. The amount was remitted by Council, and an order passed refunding the money. This should have been levied against N. ½, Lot 2, Con. 2, A. McLaughlin, but has never been placed on the roll or collected; it must now be collected. In the same year $7.15 was placed against the property of Sam Bentley in error, and refunded, which should have been on roll against S. ½, Lot 2, Con. 2, Samuel McAllister. This must also be collected, as it has not been put on the roll, or paid to the Treasurer. The Clerk's explanation is:—"I thought this had been paid to the Treasurer. I do not known if they were paid or not. They were not put on the roll."

Tinline and Hogg Drain.

By-law 319 of 1905, was abandoned on Oct. 18, 1905. The costs incurred, $45, must be collected from ratepayers on the drain. Engineers' fees not yet paid.

Wylie Branch of Massey Drain.

Constructed under By-law 310 of 1903, shows on Dec. 31, 1905, a credit balance of $53.14.

The by-law distinctly states the first collection to be made in the year 1904. Nothing appears on the tax roll till the year 1905. The Clerk placed the amounts on the roll according to the Engineer's original report, not taking into account at all the changes by the Court of Revision, in the assessment on the drain. Two of the ratepayers, N. Littlejohn and W. Goodbrand, detected the error in the amount they were charged, and had the amounts over collected rebated. The others will be rectified on the roll of 1906 as shown by Schedule XI. attached.

The Clerk's evidence on this is:—"Changes by Court of Revision were not made in the By-law book and levy of 1905, as reported by the Engineer without changes. This was entirely overlooked."

The neglect to levy taxes against a drain, as called for in the by-law, and to make changes as ordered by the Court of Revision on a by-law, is of too serious a nature to be passed over without special reference.

Wilson Drain.

In 1897, By-law 245 was passed and afterwards abandoned. It was later constructed under By-law 305 of 1903, and shows a debit balance on Dec. 31, 1905, of $0.75.

When By-law 245 was abandoned, a levy was made for the costs; this relieved the Clerk of the work of placing the levies on the roll for the three years mentioned in by-law, for which he was paid in the receipt of the amount allowed for by 'the Engineer. Instead of placing the levy against each parcel of land for three years, he calculated and placed on the roll one year only, an amount pro rata to cover the costs incurred. In placing the costs on the roll no charge at all was made against some descriptions of property.

The Engineer's allowance for publishing by-law was $15.00 and Clerk's fees $12.00; the Clerk drew $16.00 and $12.00 also as proprietor of Monitor office $11.00 more, which does not appear to have been passed by the Council. The clerk's evidence is:—"It is evident I got the money and recall tha' it was for putting the costs on the drain pro rata to the ratepayers. Cannot explain why some levies were omitted from' roll, but must have been 'some reason for it."

The item of $12.00, drawn in excess of what the by-law calls for, is an illegal payment, and has been charged to the clerk in Schedule 5.

McGregor Creek and Buller Drains.

These drains originated in the Township of Howard. Lands and roads in Orford Township were assessed to contribute to the cost of construction. At the request of the ratepayers, Orford resisted the levies as being excessive. The matter was arbitrated, and finally referred to the Referee. The litigation covered a long period, during which time all costs incurred were paid out of the general funds of the Township.

Angus Gillanders, Reeve of Orford in 1904, gave the following evidence under oath:

"Referee's report was made in 1904, while I was Reeve; it contained no direction as to costs. I am a ratepayer on the drain, and believe the drain should pay all costs the Township was not able to recover from Howard. Howard never made a demand for the money till 1905. I talked the matter of costs over with George Raycraft, Reeve of 1905. He asked my opinion about it. I told him that, owing to the nature of the case, the long time it had been pending, and the sum we had recovered from Howard had gone to the credit of General Funds, it would be as well to pay the balance of costs out of General Funds as a great deal of the costs paid out were unnecessary to the real case at issue. It would be hard to define what were really the costs. A number of witnesses were taken to Chatham and kept there for days and not heard at all. I was speaking then as a ratepayer.'

Geo. Raycraft, Reeve in 1905, swears as follows:

"McGregor Creek and Buller Drin By-law was not passed because we were busy with other matters, and the by-law was not p$_r$epa$_r$e$_d$. I am of the opinion that all the costs were chargeable to the drain, and to be collected from the ratepayers. The Clerk furnished some figures which I cannot remember, but they were less than the amount saved by the suit." .

Jonas Gosnell, ex-Reeve of Orford Township, swore:

McGregor Creek and Buller Drain By-laws were passed in 1906. I have discussed the question of costs incurred on suits, but do not know that I said anything to the Councillors or Clerk. I am of the opinion that the General Funds should stand all the costs, as it was a test case, the uplands being assessed for benefit of the low. I am a ratepayer on the drain in both Orford and Howard. I am of the opinion that legally the drain should bear all the costs, and believe that the ratepayers signed a petition to the Council that they would stand all costs of the suit."

R. A. Spence, Reeve for 1906, swore as follows:

"The Clerk, H. Watson, urged that no law costs be added to the by-laws for McGregor Creek and Buller when filling in the amounts, and he filled simply the amount awarded by Referee to be paid over to Howard by Orford, adding $24.00 to one, and $35.00 to the other for cost of getting up the by-laws. My opinion was that the ratepayers should pay the costs on these and all other drains. In 1905, I discussed the matter with the then Reeve, Geo. Raycraft, and he thought the drains should pay the costs."

Henry Watson, Clerk, sworn, stated:

"I furnished the figures myself from the award, adding $24.00 to one, and $35.00 on the other. These charges were to cover cost of preparing and passing by-laws. Council did not instruct me to collect only amount of Referee's award. There is no doubt that the Council was aware of the costs that had been incurred when passing the by-law in 1906. There were discussions over it, and they thought that the Referee would have instructed otherwise if he had thought they were justified in collecting costs from parties interested on the drain. The question of costs was not discussed in 1904 that I know of. I do not think the question of by-laws was discussed nor figures to be inserted in 1905. My reason that law and other costs should not be collected from ratepayers on the drain, is because the Referee did not specially state that costs were to be charged to the ratepayers. I had memorandum of some of the expenditures, and know there was a large sum paid out on them. The orders charged to McGregor Creek and Buller drains were all passed in Council at the time the orders were issued, and were properly chargeable to the McGregor Creek and Buller Drains, Account, for services performed or expenditures mentioned."

The minutes of the Council show that the litigation was at the instance of the ratepayers on the drain, who guaranteed to become responsible pro-rata for costs incurred.

On Dec. 31, 1905, the McGregor Creek and Buller Drains' account was overdrawn $2,390.68, after crediting it with $435.75 recovered from Howard. This does not include any interest whatever.

The Referee's decision relieved the ratepayers by reducing the original Engineer's report by $2,507.50. Yet to date they have not been levied with one dollar of the money paid out by the Township from its general funds to obtain that result. The by-laws passed this year are merely to provide the amount due the Township of Howard.

Under Section 77, Chapter 226, R.S.O., there must be amending by-laws passed to re-imburse the General Funds the amount paid out for the benefit of these drains.

McMillan Drain.

After crediting the full amount of the Engineer's report, authorized under By-law 316, of 1903, no debentures were sold to provide funds, there is on Dec. 31, 1905, a credit balance of $266.60, the work was not finished in 1905.

SCHOOL ACCOUNTS.

Section One.

A Bank account has only been kept since Jan. 1st, 1906. There has not been any interest credited on funds in hands of Treasurer.

Secretary-Treasurer is remunerated $10.00 per annum.

Section Two.

A Bank account has been kept for years and interest credited.

Some pages had been removed from Cash Book. These were later produced, and had been torn out because of an error in entering the accounts. In 1903 there was borrowed on a note $175.00 and the amount properly entered. On payment of the note it was entered as $170.00 and $4.25 interest. There is $5.00 due to the late Treasurer, whose son is now Treasurer.

The Section leased the land on which the school stands, for 100 years, from A. Crawford and Hon. David Mills. Since the death of the latter, the property has come into possession of his son, E. B. Mills, who is one of the trustees of the section, and is in receipt of $1.00 per year for rent from the Section of which he is trustee. He must either cease to be landlord or trustee. It is not legal to be both.

Section Three and Four.

When the present Secretary, Robert McLaren, was appointed in 1895. no funds were turned over from his predecessor. The balance of funds at that time, as shown by the Cash Book, was $241.80, deposited with T. H. Ridley, banker, who was then also Township Treasurer. This amount has been lost to the section by the failure of Ridley. The fact that this amount was not carried forward in the Cash Book was not mentioned by the Auditors, A. R. McDonald and W. B. Tait, when certifying to the correctness of the statement, which omitted the balance of $241.80. There is no record in the minutes to show that the ratepayers were informed of this loss to the Section.

For 1897 the Secretary-Treasurer was remunerated $10.00, since then nothing has been paid. The use of the money of the Section is in lieu of compensation for services.

The non-resident taxes of 1887, amounting to $6.40 were paid to J. C. McDonald, by Township order dated Jan. 12, 1889, but it is not in Cash Book of the Section. This fact was communicated to Mr. McDonald, and an opportunity given of examining the books and records of the Township and Section, but was not taken advantage of.

The amount of $6.40 and interest is an asset of the Section, and should be collected from J. C. McDonald, of Ridgetown, Ont.

Section Five.

No interest has been credited since 1896, for funds in hands of Arch. McLaren, who has been Secretary-Treasurer since ɯat date. $5.00 annually is paid the Secretary-Treasurer for his services. No bank account is kept in the name of the section.

Section Six.

A Bank account is kept; there is no interest credited as the section borrows early in each year.

Geo. E. Lee, Secretary-Treasurer, in 1900, entered the Legislative Grant in the Cash Book as $92.00, the amount which he received was $94.00. On his attention being called to the fact, he promptly paid the $2.00 to rectify the error.

The Secretary-Treasurer, Dr. D. P. McPhail, receives $10.00 per annum for his services.

Accounts are paid by cheque on the bank, signed by the Secretary-Treasurer, with seal of Section attached. They are not recorded in the minutes of the Board.

Section Seven.

James Goodbrand, one of the Trustees, is Secretary. D. T. Gillis, the Treasurer, is not a Trustee. The Secretary received no remuneration for services. The Treasurer, by resolution of the Trustees, has the use of the funds of the Section as compensation for services. He is under bond signed by himself only.

No Bank account is kept in the name of the Section; orders are signed by Trustees, but seal is not attached. There was on Jan. 1, 1906, $722.68 on hand and due from the Township. The Treasurer's books showed $419.38, and did not include $303.30, order on Township, which he collected on Jan. 3, 1900. This was sufficient to meet the expenses of the Section for about eighteen months, based on the previous six years' expenditures. The remuneration of Treasurer by allowing him the use of funds, on motion of the Trustees, is illegal. The question is one that should be dealt with by the annual meeting and a sum fixed.

It is only fair to the Treasurer of this Section, who is remunerated by the use of the funds, to state that he had nothing to do with fixing the rate, further than informing the Trustees of the balance.

J. C. McDonald received on Jan. 12, 1889, order from the Township for $4.00 in payment of non-resident taxes for 1887 for S. S. No. 7. This item, (like that of $6.40 on the same date, of Section 3 and 4,) has not been entered in the Cash Book of this Section. The amount, $4.00, and interest is an asset of the Section, and should be collected from J. C. McDonald, of Ridgetown, Ont.

Some small supplies have been furnished the Section by Trustees Jas. Goodbrand and W. J. Raycraft, while they were Trustees. This is contrary to the Act.

Section Nine.

C. Bergy, Secretary-Treasurer, is remunerated $5.00 per annum. Trustee J. B. McDonald has furnished the Section with material and services as follows:

Sept. 17, 1901, Painting School House .... $ 4 75
April 28, 1902, Pump 2 35
Dec. 30, 1902, New Pump and putting down 12 40
Aug., 1903, Tile.. 1 00
Oct. 10, 1904, Fixing Pump 3 85

Joseph Hornal, Trustee, was paid for work performed painting School House, Dec. 24, 1901, $4.12.

This is contrary to the Act.

Section Ten.

R. Heatherington, Secretary-Treasurer, is paid $5.00 per annum; there is no resolution since 1901 at the annual meeting covering the same.

No Bank account is kept in the name of the Section.

In this Section, Wm. Richardson, Peter Clark, M. T. Dickson, R. F. Dickson and S. McArthur have furnished material while Trustees, for which they have been paid, contrary to the Act.

Section Eleven.

John Lather, Secretary-Treasurer, is remunerated $5.00 yearly. Trustees requisition the Township for such a small levy that they are compelled to borrow three times yearly to meet their expenditures. The money borrowed on note is not entered in the Cash Book at all; the only entry made is for amount of interest when the note is paid. This is improper as the Cash Book should show all the cash transactions.

General Remarks on School Accounts.

Sections one, two, six and twelve keep bank accounts. All the others, the funds are in the hands of the Treasurer of the Section.

Bonds have only been found in the Clerk's office for Robert McLaren, of Section 3 and 4, and D. T. Gillis, of Section 7.

Interest is seldom credited on funds held by Treasurers. An account should be kept in chartered banks, in the name of the Section, and any interest derived go to the Section. The services of the Treasurer can only be legally fixed at the annual meeting, and should in no instance be by the use of the funds on hand, but by a specified sum.

In not one Section are orders drawn on the Treasurer, signed by the Trustees, with the seal of the Section attached, authorizing the payment of money. Section 7 is the only one that issues orders at all, and they omit the use of the seal. The minutes do not contain authority to the Treasurer for payments, except for occasional large expenditures. The impression, that as long as the accounts passed the annual audit and general meeting, was all that was required, has influenced the action of every Section in not recording in the minutes the authorization of payments, or amounts of accounts.

The books of some Sections have been audited by persons who had transactions with the Section during the period audited. This is irregular and should not be permitted.

The supply of wood is frequently sold at the annual meeting to the lowest bidder. In some instances Trustees have secured the contract.

The absence of any device accompanying the Government and other grants, when received by the Treasurer of the Section, has prevented his producing any documents to enable the auditors annually to verify his receipts. The result has been that the correctness of the annual receipts has been assumed.

Frequently the cash balance at the end of the year, as shown in the books, does not present the true standing of the finances of the Section. The amount levied by the Township on the roll is seldom paid over by the Township Treasurer on Dec. 15th, as required by the Act. Some Sections included the amount among their receipts, holding the order issued by the Township and unpaid, in lieu of cash; others make no entry until the actual cash is paid over.

While the affairs of some Sections are well conducted, there is room for improvement in the way in which the business of others is carried on.

The courtesy extended by the officers of all the Sections in the course of this audit was very much appreciated.

Accounts of Treasurers.

Thomas H. Ridley.

The accounts of Thomas H. Ridley, Treasurer for the years 1888 to 1894 inclusive were carefully examined. The items and interest in Schedule VI., amounting to $493.64, are due the Township and have not been accounted for. This is in addition to the amount of $241.80 loss of School Sections 3 and 4.

John S. Foster.

The accounts of John S. Foster, Treasurer for the years 1895 to March, 1903, have been examined as closely as the records would permit. The vouchers for the year 1897 were missing, and have not yet been located. No vouchers were turned over to J. D. Gillis by Mr. Foster, who thinks the missing vouchers must have been destroyed when he moved about a year ago. Some time was occupied in verifying transactions of 1897 that could be checked from other sources.

No journal was ever kept. The ledger opened in 1901, when a special examination was made of the accounts of the Township, soon fell into disuse, except as a memoranda of the disbursements under the different heads. There never was an account with the Collector, charging him with the amount of the tax roll, and crediting the various accounts with the appropriations. It was absolutely impossible for the Treasurer to tell the standing of any of the accounts of the divisions or drains, in the manner in which his books were kept. The reason given why a proper ledger and journal was not kept, is that the remuneration was not sufficient.

In 1899, $40.00 was charged as premium on Treasurer's bond. This was a duplicate of a charge already entered in 1898. Mr. Foster's evidence on this is as follows:

"In reference to the premium on my bond as Treasurer, I remitted each of the three last years that the bond was in force by the Employers' Liability Assurance Corporation, Limited, $40.00 each year. The $40.00 entered in the cash book by me as voucher No. 44 in 1899 is an error, and is chargeable to me, as the amount had already been charged in 1898, as voucher 571. The first year's premium was paid by voucher number 433, April 19, 1895, and was remitted to the Company by H. Watson, Voucher 711 Dec. 16, 1895, for $23.50 balance on Treasurer's bond, marked pay to T. H. Hammond or bearer, and endorsed H. Watson; I do not know what it is for, as Voucher 433 paid the premium in full for that year."

The $40.00 has been charged to J. S. Foster, and in included in Schedule VII.

On Oct. 10, 1902, John Bloom paid J. S. Foster $162.00, commuting his taxes on the Ingram Drain. After corresponding without avail, a subpoena was sent to Mr. Bloom to produce the original receipt. It was produced and shown to Mr. Foster, who, under oath, stated:

"Receipt for $162.00, J. Bloom, dated Oct. 10, 1902, was not entered in the books till Dec. 14, 1904. I had a few loose receipts at the store, and issued it from them, and overlooked entering it in the Township book. It was not entered till I gave up the position as Treasurer. I only balanced the Township cash at intervals. I did not detect that the cash was over at the close of the year 1902, although I had received $162.00, which was not entered."

Interest has been charged Mr. Foster on this money from the time received till paid over to the Township. See Schedule VII.

The Township of Alborough, on March 17, 1900, issued an order for $55.54, payable to Orford Township, for Cruickshank's Drain, $30.76, and Ditches and Watercourses, $24.78. The only entry in Orford books is on May 21, 1900, $40.18, from Alborough on Drains. I examined the original order at West Lorne. It was endorsed by J. S. Foster, Treasurer of Orford.

The difference between amounts received and entered in the books, $15.36, is charged Mr. Foster in Schedule VII.

A proper municipal cash book has not been kept since 1898. It has been regularly audited and certified. An error in the additions of $100.00 in 1901 was not detected by John D. Gillis and A. R. McDonald, the Auditors of that year. A corresponding mistake was made in their report in the recapitulation of the total disbursements of roads and bridges. of $100.00; this made their statement agree with the Treasurer's books. This amount is charged J. S. Foster, as he took credit for paying out $100.00 more than he should have.

The funds of the Township were not all deposited in the Bank, and although the Treasurer states he balanced the cash at intervals, the omissions and errors mentioned, as shown in Schedule VII., indicate that there was, was, to put it in the mildest term, gross carelessness in the handling of of trust funds. There is no other excuse for a business man charging up the same item in the accounts of two years as Mr. Foster admits under oath to have done, in the case of the charge to the McCaughrin Drain, of $25.00, and $40.00 premium on his bond.

The items charged to Mr. J. S. Foster are detailed in Schedule VII, amounting to $303.56, statement of which has been furnished him, with the request to have the Treasurer advise when the amount was paid into the Township account.

John D. Gillis.

The accounts have been examined of John D. Gillis, Treasurer during the year 1887, who was again appointed in 1903, and is still Treasurer.

15 M.A

No entries appeared in the cash book for the year 1906 when this audit was started in May. The records of the Treasurer, outside of the cash book, were more in the nature of a memoranda than a ledger.

All items that pass through the cash book do not appear in the bank account. The balance in the bank is greater than that shown in the cash book, caused by the Treasurer paying some orders with his own funds and not passing them through the bank at all.

In 1903, orders payable by the County Treasurer in favor of School Sections to the amount of $420.00 were charged to the Township account by the Treasurer in error. The Auditors did not detect this mistake. In Dec., 1904, the amount was recovered from the County. The interest on this amount at 5 per cent. from the dates indicated on the orders has been charged the Treasurer, as it was clearly his error. The Township account should not have been charged these amounts.

The neglectful manner in which the issue of debentures was treated is deserving of severe criticism. The Treasurer was aware that drains were being constructed. He was paying orders drawn by the Commissioners, chargeable to drains which he knew he had not provided the funds for, by the issue of debentures.

The excuse that he was not sufficiently paid, or that he was not furnished with a copy of the by-law, is no valid excuse.

He knew what the remuneration was when he accepted the office. It is not to be wondered at that the affairs of the Township were muddled, when it is known that the present Treasurer, who has been Treasurer for years before 1888, had audited the Township accounts frequently since 1888 to 1903, and is now holding the office of Treasurer again since 1903, stated under oath :

"I audited the books of the Township for years. I never brought forward the balances in drain accounts from year to year. The drain accounts were not included as assets or liabilities in audits. There was nothing to go by; could not tell if they were an asset or a liability. Did not mention the fact in any of our written reports."

"Outside of the Taxes, we did not check the sources of revenue, to see if any were not accounted for by the Treasurer."

"When I became Treasurer in 1903, and tried to start drain accounts, then found I could not get a starting point, but showed partial statements of the drains that were alive."

"I kept no accounts with Howard or Aldborough (Townships), nor carried forward any balance of any accounts from year to year. The appropriations were not entered in the ledger at all. I never kept a journal. I do not know that I ever read the duties of a Treasurer in the Municipal Act."

"I have added the cash book of 1901 through to-day and find there is $100.00 too much in the additions, as shown in the audit report; the total disbursements should be $31,825.16, which leaves the amount of $100. due the Township from J. S. Foster to straighten the error."

The evidence above mentioned shows the manner in which the finances and books of the Township have been conducted.

The cash book, which is practically the only book kept by the Treasurer, is neatly and carefully written up.

The amounts charged to John D. Gillis and due the Township are shown on Schedule VIII.

15a M.A.

Clerk's Office and Records.

Henry Watson has been Clerk of the Municipality for over thirty years. The office used by him as Clerk is in connection with his residence. It is not supplied with facilities for properly filing documents. He keeps his personal papers mixed with those of the municipality.

Considerable delay in this audit was occasioned by the manner in which books, documents, reports, and other papers were filed. After asking for different papers required during the commencement of the audit, and delayed by the Clerk not finding them readily, it was found necessary to take all the papers, books, documents and reports procurable from the Clerk's office to the parlors of the hotel, where the audit was being conducted, sort them, so those of each drain would be together, and any papers could be readily referred to when required. Many of the papers, reports and documents were missing, and have not yet been produced. They include engineer's reports on municipal drains, awards under the Ditches and Watercourses Act, judgments and papers in connection with some of the suits.

The Clerk produced some books, which he claimed as his personal property, in which were copies of statements furnished various departments of the Government and County Clerk, records of the amounts required to be raised for the different school sections, notation as to notices and awards under the Ditches and Watercourses Act, figures on some of the accounts rendered Howard and Aldborough Townships, certified copies of by-laws about the year 1875. These books contained the only record of filing of awards under the Ditches and Watercourses Act, till the year 1902, when a proper book was secured for that purpose. The date of filing is not endorsed on the awards, nor are they recorded in the registry office.

A complete list of all the books used by the Clerk for the Township purposes was made. Had he claimed the minute books of the Council as personal property, it would not be more absurd.

Over twenty years ago a copy of the Schedule of each by-law was put in a separate book from that in which the by-law was embodied, showing each description of land, the total amount against it, as well as the amount to be placed on the roll each year during the life of the by-law. A most proper method to safeguard the placing on the roll of all the amounts required to be collectd under drainage by-laws.

For the past ten years that method was abandoned as entailing too much work. All the levies since are figured out in the pook in which the certified copy of the by-law is embodied. This has caused many of the errors and omissions referred to elsewhere under the head of the different drains.

In a few instances the minutes of the Council are not signed by both the Reeve and Clerk.

Pages 298 to 309 of the minute book in use in 1890 were cut out, between the parts of the book used for recording the minutes and the by-laws. These pages appear to have been blank. No reason was given except that they were used sometime when paper was required and none was at hand. There is nothing to indicate that they were removed from any improper motive.

In 1895, a bond No. 120, for $4,000.00, on J. S. Foster, Treasurer, was issued by the Employers' Liability Assurance Corporation, Limited. In reply to a letter of Aug. 1, 1906, the Head Office of the Company write, "Bond was first issued in 1895, the yearly premium being $40.00, which was paid for four successive years, the bond expired 1899." The following charges appear in the Township Cash Book:

1895
April 19. Voucher 433, Guarantee Co. or bearer, endorsed, pay
    J. S. Foster, signed H. Watson .... $ 40 00
1895
Dec. 16.   Voucher 711, pay T. H. Hammond or bearer, balance
    Treas. bond, endorsed H. Watson 23 50
1896.
Dec. 4.   Voucher 443, Receipt G. H. Merritt, Prem. Treas.
    Bond 40 00
1898.
Jan. 17. Voucher 20, Receipt Guarantee Co., Prem. Treas. Bond   40 00
Dec. 28. Voucher 571, Guarantee Co., Prem. Treas. Bond...   40 00
1899.
Jan.   Voucher 44, Employers' Liability Co., ... 40 00

                                                     $223 50
Company received as premium as per their letter $160 00

Overcharged the Township 63 50
Of this amount Voucher 44 has been charged to J. S. Foster   40 00

Leaving an amount as shown on Voucher 711 .... $ 23 50

The Clerk produced letters showing that of this money he paid $16.50, the amount of premium on bond in London Guarantee Company which was cancelled. The balance of this item, $7.00, is included in charges to Henry Watson, Clerk, in Schedule V.

The accounts passed by the Council, and orders issued, were frequently based on verbal reports. Those on file showed that in 1887 the Commissioners reported in detail the orders they issued, with a statement of their commission for the same. As time went on the methods have become more lax, till at present a verbal report of members of the Council, for the commissions due them, or a memo on a slip of paper, which is not retained, has become the custom, and all that is now required.

One Councillor, under oath, stated that a lease for a gravel pit was reported to Council verbally by him, in August, 1906, as of no further value to the municipality. It was considered cancelled by verbal discussion at the board. No resolution was considered necessary by the Clerk, who stated that all that was necessary was to endorse the fact on the lease. Attention was called to this by the lessor of the pit enquiring from me if the lease was among the papers in use in the audit. He desired the lease returned as he had been informed that it was cancelled.

Many transactions of a similar nature were not recorded in minutes or records, but based o verbal reports or statements. A great deal of time was unnecessarily occupied to ascertain the authority for transactions which would have been avoided had proper records been kept.

It was not till the year 1903 that the orders drawn by the Township were made payable to order. Prior to that time many orders passed by the Council, drawn payable to different persons or bearer, were edorsed by the Clerk, and for which no receipt or account from the party in whose favor the order was drawn were on file. Many of these, owing to lapse of time since the transaction took place, could not now be verified. Those of recent date that could be reached have been communicated with. In the case of the account with the *Municipal World*, of St. Thomas, orders have been passed for their bills, which were endorsed by the Clerk, and remittances not made for the amount at the time. The statements received showed that a running account was kept, and payments made as it suited the convenience of the Clerk. The last few years the orders, as passed by the Council, have been sent direct, and bear proper endorsement.

The items in the Engineer's reports on municipal drains for Clerk's fees have in some cases been exceeded by orders passed by the Council; these are referred to under the drains to which they are charged. The item for publication of by-law, which is the Engineer's limit of the cost of publication and service of the by-law has been handled by the Clerk in a most unusual and improper manner. For many years the Clerk, an officer of the municipality, conducted a newspaper, published the by-laws, and received in every instance the full amount of the estimate of the Engineer for the publication. The printing of voters' lists, audit reports, and all other work that he was capable of turning out, was furnished the municipality by the Clerk. Such transactions are in direct violation of his declaration of office, which is as follows:

"That I have not received, and will not receive, any payment or reward, or promises of such, for the exercise of any partiality, or malversation, or other undue execution of the said office, and that I have not by myself, or partner, either directly or indirectly, any interest in any contract, with or on behalf of the said Corporation, except arising out of my office as clerk."

The printing of by-laws, voters' lists, or audit reports is just as much a contract under the above declaration as building a bridge or digging a drain.

Tile drainage debenture No. 64, Duncan Ross, issued Jan. 1, 1893, under by-law 68, was marked in the Clerk's record book, "paid Nov. 17, 1903." On examining the paid debenture it was found that thirteen coupons, $7.36 each, were paid to the Government. The last coupon paid matured Jan. 1, 1905. Only twelve levies were placed on the tax rolls. The Township paid out $7.36 more than they have received. This amount and interest is charged to the Clerk. The following is the sworn evidence of Henry Watson, Clerk, in explanation of the transaction:

"Debenture No. 64, Duncan Ross, was paid to the Government some time after Nov. 17, 1903, the date it is marked paid in the tile drainage levy book by me. I had correspondence for Mr. Ross with the Government, and found out what they required. I do not know just how much I remitted, but the $49.47 marked in book was paid in the first place to me by Ross, and I held the money in my safe till it was settled with the Government. I cannot tell anything more about it, nor do I know why the thirteenth coupon was collected by the Government on the debenture."

The Government records show that they did not receive the money in settlement of this debenture till Jan. 3, 1905. Further comment on this is unnecessary.

A by-law was submitted to the ratepayers in 1898 for a bonus to the Lake Erie and Detroit River Railway of $2,000.00, the Railway to pay $75.00 for cost of submitting the by-law and to deposit that amount in the Traders Bank, Ridgetown. The money was transferred to the Clerk on the authority of a letter, copy of which is as follows:

To the Manager Traders Bank, Ridgetown:

Nov. 11, 1898.

DEAR SIR,—The L. E. & D. R. R. Co. deposited $75.00 in your bank to defray expenses for submitting a by-law in their interests, in the Township of Orford.

You will please place same at Clerk's disposal, so as to pay Dep. Returning Officers and accounts on his cheque and oblige.

. Truly yours,

JOS. HORNAL,

Reeve of Orford.

The Clerk was very active in procuring the passage of the by-law. The way the $75.00 was handled by the Clerk personally, instead of through the hands of the Township Treasurer, and the Council passing the accounts in the usual way, is so improper and irregular that the matter called for special investigation. The Clerk's sworn evidence on the subject is as follows:

"The Lake Erie by-law in Nov., 1898, was submitted to the ratepayers, the Railway to pay expenses. I know they paid me for submitting the by-law, and expense in conection with it. There was money deposited in Traders Bank, Ridgetown, $75.00, to meet the expenses of by-law, and by letter of Reeve was placed to my credit to pay costs of election expenses. I paid all the expenses of the by-law, none of the money belonged to the Township, nor was paid into it. I do not know how much I got personally. I cannot say I got much over $75.00, and anything I got was compensation for services in endeavoring to have the by-law passed."

How is it possible to harmonize the above sworn evidence with the declaration of office of a Clerk of a Municipality? The paid officer of one corporation accepting remuneration from another whose interests cannot possibly work in unison, cannot be more properly described by any other than the vulgar word "Graft."

In April, 1903, a remittance was made to the Sawyer Massey Co., Limited, Hamilton, Ont., of $8.50 for goods supplied in March, 1903. On April 23, 1903, they returned 85c. to the Clerk, being 10 per cent. discount on invoice paid within thirty days. There is no trace of this in the books of the Township. The Clerk could give no explanation. The amount is charged to him in Schedule V.

The Tile drainage book in use is one designed by the Clerk; the way it is kept written up, and the records it contains, reflect credit on that officer.

My criticism of the Clerk may appear to be harsh, but the facts are, that the affairs of the Township were fairly well conducted by him twenty years ago, and the careless and neglected manner in which he has performed his work in recent years cannot be attributed to his ignorance or inability to properly perform the duties of the office of Clerk.

Tile Drainage.

Under By-law 68, many of the ratepayers took adavntage of the provisions of The Tile, Stone and Timber Drainage Act.

Debentures of $100.00 each were issued for twenty years for all amounts borrowed. Those issued prior to Jan. 1st, 1887, were at five per cent., and the annual payment of $8.00 for twenty years, which in that time paid the interest and principal.

All amounts borrowed after Jan. 1st, 1887, were at four per cent. with annual payment of $7.36 instead of $8.00.

The reduction from five to four per cent. applied to all amounts borrowed prior to Jan. 1st, 1887, and for which debentures were outstanding with coupons attached for $8.00 payable yearly.

On Oct. 18, 1888, the Treasury Department of the Ontario Government, holders of the debentures, wrote Hy. Watson, Clerk, in reply to his letter of the 15th, enclosing a statement showing the number of payments yet to be made on debentures of each year's issue at five per cent., showing what payments and parts of payments (the last to mature in every instance) would be cancelled by the reduction of interest.

This statement could not have been understood by the Clerk. Instead of continuing to collect $8.00 from the ratepayers on every $100.00 borrowed at five per cent., he placed $7.36 on the roll for all, regardless of the rate at which the debentures are issued. The Township has paid the $8.00 coupons yearly out of the general funds for the debentures issued at five per cent., against which the Clerk placed on the roll only $7.36 each. The amount paid by the Government in excess of that collected from the ratepayers is $471.68. This sum is standing to the credit of the Township of Orford in the hands of the Treasury Department of the Ontario Government.

The Council should pass a resolution applying to the Government for a refund of this $471.68, the surplus of Tile Drainage debentures. This amount when received is to be placed to the credit of the General Funds.

Reference to Tile Drainage Debenture 64, Duncan Ross, has already been made under the heading of Clerk's Office and Records.

Under By-law 211 the amount charged Geo. Raycraft on Lot 13, Con. 4, was $4.52; the proper amount is $5.52. The difference, $1.00, will be placed on the roll of 1906.

In 1889, D. D. McTavish, w ½ Lot 68, N. T. Road, was charged on the roll $14.70, in error for $7.36. This amount was all refunded on Dec. 26, 1889, Voucher 352, $7.35, and on Feb. 21, 1890, Voucher 505, $7.35. Only half should have been refunded. By refunding the two amounts of $7.35, leaves it that no collection for 1889 was made on account of this property at all. There must be an extra $7.36 placed on the roll of 1906 to cover this omission.

All the tile drain levies of 1889 were placed on the roll as $7.35 in error for $7.36.

Under By-law 226, S. McDonald borrowed $200.00 on April 27, 1896. No collection was made in 1896 (a memo mentioned that this was requested by Mr. McDonald). The Township paid coupons on Jan. 1, 1897, $7.36 on each $100.00, or $14.72, which has not yet been collected. The collection in 1897 met the Coupon due Jan. 1, 1898. The collections on this by-law are one year behind. There must be placed on the 1906 roll against this property an extra $14.72 to cover the amount the Township has advanced. The terms of a by-law cannot be changed to suit the convenience of a ratepayer.

In checking over $474.56 of Tlie Drainage Coupons paid by the Treasurer on Jan. 25, 1906, it was found that Coupon No. 18, Debenture No. 56 $7.36, due Jan. 1, 1908, was paid instead of that of 1906 in error, two years in advance of its maturity. The coupons of debentures 51, 52 and 53, due Jan. 1, 1906, have not been presented for payment.

The debenture book, which I have procured and written up, includes all the Tile drainage debentures in detail. Each coupon should be marked off by entering the Cash Book folio on which the charge appears. If this is followed out, coupons outstanding or paid in advance will be promptly seen.

On Sept. 21, 1905, the Treasurer paid an order in favor of Thos. J. Johnston, $198.00; this with order to A. J. Stone, $2.00, for inspection, amounted to $200.00, a Tile Drainage loan under By-law 320. The debentures were not issued for this till July 14, 1906. It is included in my statement of assets. The Township was out the use of this amount till July 14, 1906, owing to the Reeve and Clerk drawing an order on the Treasurer before the money was received from sale of debentures. The Treasurer should have seen that the debentures were issued when he entered the order in his Cash Book.

Ditches and Watercourses.

Drains constructed under the Ditches and Watercourses Act have been handled in a very indifferent manner. There is no record of the filing, or passing of these, in the minutes of the Council. The awards or agreements are not endorsed showing the date they were filed with the Clerk. On Nov. 24, 1902, an Award book was started in which is recorded particulars of drains constructed under this Act. Prior to that date the only record is found in books which are claimed by the Clerk as personal property.

There were over ninety drains constructed under Awards or Agreements, and on these the Township has sustained considerable loss by the neglect of the Clerk in omitting to add seven per cent. interest on all items placed on the roll, as required by Sec. 27 and 30. The Engineer, when reporting the completion of work he had sold to others than those awarded to do the work, mentioned the description of property to which the amount was to be charged on the roll, stating 7 per cent. to be added. The printed By-laws revised by the Clerk in 1903, the adding of seven per cent. is also mentioned

Considerable time was spent in securing information owing to many of the original awards, Judge's reports and documents not being on file in the Clerk's office; none of these are on record in the Registry Office of the County.

No separate account was kept at all of any of the awards or other drains as should be done.

The General Fund has not received credit for any fees that should be included in the awards of the Engineer for Clerk's services since Jan. 1, 1904, from which time the Clerk was paid a salary. He advised the Engineer he could include fees if he wished, but that he did not get them as he was paid by salary.

Reference only is made to such awards as is deemed necessary.

Attridge Award.

Dec. 1, 1890.—Report of Thos. Scane, Engineer.

Wm. Pierson	$2 60
Peter Allison	2 60
Municipality	2 60
James Attridge	2 60
John Steele	2 60

There is no trace of these costs being placed on the roll.

Downie Award.

Of Jan. 24, 1903, assessment against C. Bergy, Lot 25, Con. 11, $3.00, does not appear to have been collected on the roll.

Gladstone Award.

There is to be collected from lands in Orford Township... $4 75
Township portion 50
                                                                  ———
                                                                  $5 25

These will be placed on the roll of 1906.

Hepburn Drain Award.

There is considerable expense incurred by litigation on this drain. The Judge's award and all other papers in connection with this suit were not produced by the Clerk. The Township paid $635.41 more than was collected. The evidence taken on this subject indicated that the Township sustained this loss, which they could not recover.

McTavish Drain Agreement.

On Dec. 1, 1902, an agreement was drawn by the Clerk, and later executed, under which the Township was to construct a drain, and the parties to the agreement were to contribute the amounts stated. Two of the parties paid the Treasurer the amount agreed. Neil Ford paid $3.00 to Dan. Ferguson, the Commissioner, who handed this amount to the Contractor on on account. This amount was deducted from the contractor when the work was finally paid for.

There was no note of what rate or amount the contract was let for, nor could it be ascertained from any of the parties interested. The evidence taken showed that the $3.00 was deducted. No record of this agreement appeared in the Clerk's office except the original document itself. The amounts not paid have never been placed on the roll. The Clerk could not make any explanation why they had been omitted from the roll. The amount uncollected is as follows:

Angus Thompson (since paid) $14 00
Ford Bros. 10 00
T. H. Ford 2 00
                                                                  ———
                                                                  $26 00

These will be placed on the roll of 1906.

Mobey Award.

There was an appeal against this award before Judge Bell, in 1906, and the amount of $16.95 and interest at 7 per cent. will be collected on 1906 roll.

Nicholls Award.

An appeal was made against this award in 1900. The amounts paid in as guarantee of costs were held by the Clerk instead of handing amounts to the Treasurer. This manner of handling the funds gave rise to the impression that the Clerk got the amount in compensation for services. The Judge allowed costs, $27.50; there was paid out $31.10. Of this amount Angus Smith, Engineer, was overpaid $2.50, which is charged to him in Schedule XII.

Webster Award.

This award of 1896, allows Angus Smith, Engineer, $12.00, and Henry Watson, Clerk, $4.00 making a total of $16.00. During the same year this drain was charged the following:

Oct. 31, 1896, Angus Smith, Webster drain Voucher 379.........$12 00
Dec. 15, 1896, H. Watson   do   460......... 4 00
Dec. 15, 1896, Angus Smith,   do   467......... 16 00

The last item paying the amount of the first two a second time. All these vouchers were payable to bearer, and endorsed by Henry Watson. The Clerk in his evidence stated :

"I do not remember anything about it."

The amount, $16.00, improperly issued to Angus Smith has been charged to him in Schedule XII.

Scott and Ward Award.

Award dated Nov. 7, 1901, of Angus Smith, Engineer, was appealed against, and Judge Bell gave his award Feb. 7, 1902. There was paid out to witness $3.46 in excess of the Judge's award.

All expenditures of Township's portion of awards and agreements should only be made on written report of the Commissioner, stating price at which work was let, filed with the Clerk, and passed by the Council. The absence of such reports has made it absolutely impossible to properly check many of the expenditures.

The expenditures must be all charged up in separate accounts for each award drain. Proper entries will be made by the Treasurer at the end of the year charging General Funds with the Township's portion of each and crediting the drain account. All amounts collected on the tax roll will be charged the Collector through the journal and credited to the proper accounts. In this way all omissions from the tax rolls will be detected by the drain showing an overdrawn account.

By-laws.

The principle underlying all imposition of taxes and expenditure of money by a municipality is, that it must be authorized by by-law, properly drawn, and regularly carried through its different stages.

The originals were seldom found; copies of most by-laws appear in a book for that purpose; those appointing officers for recent years are kept in separate book.

Records of the by-laws imposing the rate for some years could not be found. The minutes do not always show that they had been passed. The details of estimates on which the rates were based are not in the minutes. There is no record in the minutes or other records of the Township of a by-law, resolution or statement showing that appropriations were made for the years 1904 and 1905.

The Clerk states, "There were no years that by-laws were not passed levying rates. There may be years that the by-laws were not embodied." He, however, has not been able to produce any figures of 1904 and 1905 appropriations.

A by-law setting forth in detail the different amounts required to be raised and the rates necessary to provide them, must be passed annually, and a proper record in detail kept by the Clerk.

The drainage by-laws do not state the rate of interest at which the debentures are to be issued. They limit the rate not to exceed five per cent. This has caused a higher rate to be inserted in some instances than the money could have been produced for, had there been any competition.

Some provide that the Township's portion of the cost of construction of a drain is to be paid out of the General Funds instead of by sale of debentures. This has a tendency to disorganize the finances. The amount chargeable against roads yearly on all drains should be included in the estimates and provided for the general Township rate. The money to pay for the Township portion of the work should be provided by sale of debentures, the same as that of lands, and not taken out of General Funds in one year, as has been the method in the past.

Frequently appropriations by by-laws, have been amended by resolution of the Council. A by-law is necessary to be passed always to amend a by-law, unless there is a clause inserted making provision for supplementary appropriations, by resolution of Council, in the original by-law.

The drainage by-laws have not been registered for many years.

The omission by the Clerk, to properly draw up and record by-laws, setting forth the annual appropriations for the years 1904 and 1905, and other omissions are attributed by him to ill-health.

The remuneration paid to members of the Council is by resolution, which is illegal. A by-law must be passed covering this, when this is done, it might be well to fix the remuneration of the Councillors, at a lump sum, covering all services as Councillors and Commissioners, and mileage for the year, making the only exception, witness fees in cases heard outside the Township.

Divisions.

Commissioners are appointed, usually from the Council to look after the six road divisions, into which the Township is divided.

Appropriations were made each year with the exception of 1904 and 1905, the amounts were never credited the divisions by the Treasurer. No record was kept to ascertain whether the amount appropriated was exceeded.

From 1890 to the end of 1903, the appropriations recorded have been exceeded in all but Number Six Division. The Commissioners were paid on the amount expended by them. The more they expended, the greater their compensation. For years no detailed statement has been handed the Council, of the orders issued. The only means the Council or ratepayers had of ascertaining the expenditures in the different divisions was from the printed audit report annually.

The Commissioners never turned their stubs in annually for the use of the Auditors. These were all asked for, but comparatively few were produced, except those of recent years.

The amounts expended by the divisions is not a special levy to the division, but a part of the general Township rate. The amount the divisions exceeded the appropriations cannot be ascertained owing to there being no record of the 1904 and 1905 appropriations.

In opening the ledger on Dec. 31, 1905, the accounts of the Division have no balances brought forward. Each division is now credited with the amount of the appropriation for 1906, and it is the duty of the Treasurer to refuse payment of any orders issued by the Commissioners which will overdraw the account, until funds are provided in a legal manner by an amending by-law.

Police Village of Highgate.

In 1902 an agreement was made with the Township. The Trustees were to receive credit for all County and Township rates raised on the Tax Roll, on property within the boundaries of the Police Village, less a lump sum of $190.00. This agreement continued in 1903, since which the amount deducted has been raised to $200.00 by resolution. A new agreement should be drawn.

The minutes of the Police Trustees show that one of the Trustees, on motion, has been appointed a Commissioner. He has assumed control of the Police Village. The minutes do not show that any expenditures, except for water tanks, received the sanction of the other Trustees. The Commissioner received the Pathmaster's list and noted thereon in some instances what action was taken in each case. On some of the lists only a tick in pencil was made when the item referred to was disposed of by cash payment, work performed, or was uncollectable.

J. G. Crosby was Secretary of the Trustees for the years 1902 to 1905, inclusive. All cash collected on the Pathmaster's List was supposed to go through his hands.

In checking the Pathmaster's List against the entries in the cash book it was found there were a number of items each year marked paid, or ticked to indicate that they had been disposed of, which did not appear in the cash book.

In August, 1906, the Cash Book for 1904 had not been balanced, although there was a published statement issued for the year 1905. In his evidence on this Mr. Crosby swore:—

"The balance shown Jan., 1905, represented the balance as between the Township and the Police Village, taken from the Township Treasurer's statement."

"The amount the Township raised for the Police Village did not pass through the hands of the Secretary. Orders were drawn direct on the Township Treasurer, signed only by the Commissioner.

The evidence of Mr. Crosby explains the manner the affairs were carried on, which is as follows:—

"I never paid my road work, but considered it as performed in lieu of services. I got no other remuneration. I supplied no goods directly, but other Commissioners purchased small supplies from me. paying cash."

"The money on the (pathmaster's) roll was handled in cash by me, or offset against labor. Those marked on the roll as paid, and not appearing in the cash book, are either parties who were unable to pay. or twice assessed as man and wife, or the services have been performed for the amount."

The roadwork unpaid has been charged to Mr. Crosby in Schedule IX.

Among the orders for which Mr. Crosby took credit as paying in 1904, thirty-six in all, seventeen are not signed by Geo. Gosnell, the Commissioner, or any of the Trustees. One of these unsigned orders for $45.00 is in favor of Geo. Gosnell for services. This order was never written out till 1906, after the books were asked for in connection with this audit, it was dated back Dec. 20, 1904. The evidence on this showed that only $8.00 cash had been paid to G. Gosnell, and entered in the cash book, the $37.00 was held by Mr. Crosby, on account of money owing him in his store by Mr. Gosnell, without being entered in the books of the Police Village.

One item, $3.61 to C. Crichton, dated Dec. 15, 1903, was entered as paid twice, in 1903 and 1904, this is charged to Mr. Crosby in Schedule IX. The vouchers for the year 1903 are missing, the stubs only could be furnished to check the entries against.

There are no by-laws passed by the Trustees. Neither by-law nor resolution is recorded in the minutes regarding granolithic walks, regulating the amount chargeable to the property benefited. A. J. Stone, Commissioner for 1905 and 1906, stated in his evidence:—

"The custom has been for the Commissioners to perform services, and be remunerated for them."

"I was not aware that the Police Village was owing Geo. Gosnell anything. I understood that Jan. 1, 1905, there were no liabilities, with only a small balance on hand."

"We charge at the rate of two and one-half cents per square foot frontage tax for all granolithic walks. This is by resolution of board. No charge is made for gravel walks, the crossings are at the general cost of the village."

Mr. Stone in 1905 drew $45.00 for services as Commissioner and work on roads of the Police Village, issuing orders to himself for the same. No statement setting forth the details of the services performed, no resolution of the board, appears for this payment.

The following payments have been made to Police Trustees during their term of office:—

1902	C. Crichton	$ 6 37
"	W. Reycraft, Commissioner	44 27
1903	C. Crichton	3 61
"	W. Reycraft, Commissioner	53 80
1904	John Hardy	26 87
"	Geo. Gosnell, Commissioner	45 00
1905	A. J. Stone, Commissioner	45 00

From the above it will be seen that the Commissioner who has signed all orders on the funds received from the Township, as well as that collected on the Pathmaster's list, has been in receipt of over ten per cent. of the net amount received from the Township, exclusive of statute labor.

The Commissioner, or Inspecting Trustee, has never been legally appointed as required by Sec. 735 of Consolidated Municipal Act of 1903.

The minutes of Police Trustees do not contain a proper record of the business transacted. By-laws should be passed regulating the price charged for granolithic walks, and other regulations as set forth in sections 736 to 750 of Consolidated Municipal Act of 1903.

A statement of the standing of the accounts of the Township, and J. G. Crosby, with the Police Trustees, is shown in Schedules IX. and X.

General Remarks.

A considerable amount of laxity has prevailed with regard to the granting of orders by the Council. No order should be passed or issued without
first procuring an original detailed account in writing, setting forth the
goods furnished or services performed. This should be kept on file by the
Clerk, and his authority for issuing the order.

The Auditors appointed have in a number of instances had transactions
with the municipality during the year they audited. The most glaring is
that of H. G. Gilmore, in 1903, who received no less than fourteen orders, for
different services and material supplied the various divisions and drains,
amounting to $111.40.

The Auditor's declaration of office contains the following, "That I had
not directly or indirectly any share or interest whatever in any contract or
employment with, by or on behalf of such municipal corporation during the
year preceding my appointment, and I have not any such contract or employment except that of Auditor for the present year."

The bonds of John D. Gillis, Treasurer, private sureties, have been examined and are in order, those of the collector were not examined, as the
tax roll had been returned prior to the commencement of this audit. Guarantee bonds are recommended to be procured in the future.

The renting of the Town Hall, Highgate, was deputed to Thos. Mickle,
caretaker. He kept no proper record of the moneys that passed through his
hands, but reported verbally to the Council yearly, paying the amount as
reported, to the Treasurer. No regulations governing prices to be charged
were fixed. The matter should be properly regulated by by-law. Written
statements should be made regularly to the Council of receipts in detail. All
the expenditures must be passed by the Council. There is no insurance on
any of the assets of the Township.

James S. Swanton, Pathmaster for 1905 for Muirkirk division, collected
money and retained it after he ceased to hold office. He also cashed a Township order for special grant for sidewalk after he ceased to be pathmaster.
He admitted under oath having $31.75 on hand which he had not then turn-
ed over to the Township Treasurer. This has since been paid to the Treasurer as required by Sec. 13 of By-law 4 of Consolidated By-laws of Township.

Frequently orders have been passed for gravel and other material supplied, covering a period of more than a year, on a verbal report. This, like
many other transactions, could not be verified. Accounts should only be
passed on written statement certified by the Commissioner or Councillor.

All the leases of gravel pits were not found, none of those produced were
recorded in the Registry office. It would be in the Township's interest if all
leases and drainage by-laws were registered.

The Treasurer never kept account of when appropriations were exceeded
or knew how the accounts stood.

Orders were issued by Commissioners who are not under bond and whose
actions do not come to the knowledge of the Council or public till the audit
report is published yearly, and not then if any of the orders are outstanding.
Such loose methods only open the door for irregularities and fraud and should
be stopped.

During the period covered by this audit, some of the members of the
Council could have been disqualified for transactions they had with the municipality.

The salary of $100.00 for the services of Treasurer of the Township is good compensation for the way the work has been done, but is small remuneration for the office if the services are properly performed and accounts kept as they should be. The salary paid the Clerk, $500.00, compared more favorably with that of officials of other municipalities. It might be added that I have yet to find a Municipal Clerk or Treasurer who is overpaid for properly performing the duties of his office.

General Accounts of the Township.

The accounts of the municipality have had a thorough examination. The printed audit reports have in most instances contained all the details of receipts and expenditures as entered in the cash book. It is not deemed necessary to furnish them in this report.

The manner in which the drainage expenditure was provided out of the

In the statement of assets, presented herewith, is included the amounts against lands on the drains, among the assets not immediately available, showing the amount each year, and the placing outstanding drainage debentures as liabilities not immediately payable, of the general fund. Had the drains been constructed according to by-laws, the amount uncollected on drains would equal the amount of unpaid drainage debentures outstanding.

In the statement of assets presented herewith, is included the amounts the general fund has advanced by paying in one year, when the drains were constructed, the whole of the Township's assessment against roads instead of providing by sale of debentures and charging only the portion due each year, the same as the ratepayers. The general fund has paid in advance in this way for 1906, $463.55; for 1907, $393.47; for 1908, $103.72, a total of $960.74 up to Dec. 31, 1905, which should not be charged till due, as above stated, if the finances were properly managed.

The general fund should receive credit for all Clerk's fees chargeable to drains and awards, the Clerk is paid his salary out of the general fund. Hereafter an order shall be drawn chargeable to the drain for these amounts in favor of the general funds and handed to the Treasurer as authority for the transfer. This would be passed through his cash book as a receipt to general funds and debited to the drain it is properly chargeable to.

I have charged all municipal drains with amount of Clerk's fees omitted. No allowance was inserted in awards for Clerk's fees. The Township has sustained a loss of the amount the engineer should have allowed.

The accompaniyng Schedule I. shows on Dec. 31, 1905 : —

Available assets	$13,154 48
Current liabilities	12,702 87

Leaving a surplus of available assets over current liabilities of...$ 451 61
  To this must be added;
Assets not immediately available, drainage levies against lands,

To be collected, 1906	$2,587 48	
To be collected, 1907	2,181 48	
To be collected, 1908	752 10	
		$5,521 06

Township's portion for roads advanced,
Not payable till 1906 ....$ 463 55
Not payable till 1907 .... 393 47
Not payable till 1908 .... 103 72
$960 74
Drainage accounts overdrawn 4,567 03

$11,500 44
Less drainage debentures not immediately payable,
Due Jan. 1, 1907 ....$1,494 60
Due Jan. 1, 1908 .... 893 45
Due Jan. 1, 1909 .... 190 55
$2,578 60

Surplus of assets available and not immediately available, over liabilities current and not immediate-
ly payable $8,921 84

The surplus of $8,921.84 includes the amounts due from officials of the Township as well as the overdrawn accounts on drains.

Not a dollar of the $4,567.03 overdrawn drain accounts is available till such time as proper by-laws are passed and debentures sold. Already too much interest has been lost by the Township on these items.

The affairs of the Township, as far as the financial position is concerned may be said to be in a satisfactory condition. All known assets and liabilities are included with the exception of items referred to in this report. The account of Angus Smith, engineer, contains claim for extra services, which is disputed on the ground that the work was not properly attended to. There is $1850 overpayment on the Webster drain and Nichols award, which is to be deducted.

The direct financial benefit of this audit to the Township is given in Schedule XV., showing the items, which amount to the large sum of $6,-493.38, none of which was previously included in the assets of the Township in the Auditor's report to Dec. 31, 1905.

The bonds of ex-officials held by the Clerk have not been commented on. These had better be referred to the Township Solicitor.

Recommendations.

(1) That a by-law striking the rate be passed yearly and recorded, showing in detail the amounts to be levied for each purpose, including the rates for different school sections, as required by the Assessment and Public School Acts.

(2) That in recapitulation of the tax roll, the rate as well as the amount it represents on the roll for each school section be recorded in detail, not in a lump sum as has been done.

(3) That the Assessor include in this roll detailed statement of all railway property, valuing separately that in each school section so the Clerk can place the proper amounts for each section on the roll. At present the value is divided by estimate.

(4) That the exempted property in the Township be detailed at the back of the roll with valuation for reference.

(5) That the lands owned by one person in two school sections be separately assessed, not together in one amount, as has been frequently done. A map showing the school sections should be furnished the Assessor. One was paid for by the Treasurer.

(6) That the Collector mark in his roll the date he received each payment. That he return the roll before April 8th, with statement of uncollected taxes, and settlement with ᴜᴀe Treasurer recorded in the back of the roll, with duplicate for the Clerk.

(7) That no change be permitted to be made in the collector's roll after placed in his hands, without resolution of Council, a copy of which shall be attached to the roll.

(8) That the Collector deposit all monies direct to the credit of the Township bank account, Sec. 19, chapter 228 R.S.O.

(9) That records of all Courts of Revision on the assessment roll or drainage assessments be kept in a book specially provided for that purpose, in which full descriptions and value shall be given of all property on which any changes are made.

(10) That all by-laws be written in the by-law book in consecutive numerical order with a proper index at the front.

(11) That proper means be provided for filing the records of the Township by furnishing a tin box for each year in which the accounts, vouchers and records arranged in order can be deposited. The vouchers to Dec. 31, 1905, are at present in the vault of Molsons Bank, Highgate, for safe keeping.

(12) That notices be sent to all persons who have taxes in arrears, Sec. 147 Asst. Act, and return made to the County Treasurer.

(13) That all schedules against lands and roads for drainage purposes be kept written up in the book provided, and the Clerk enter therein the number on the collector's roll against which the annual levies are entered.

(14) That all reports of committees be in writing and incorporated in the minutes of Council.

(15) That an office with vault be provided by the Council for the Clerk with provision for the proper filing and safely protecting the documents and vouchers. The insecurity from fire of the records at present should be remedied. The loss would entail expense many times the cost of a vault and office.

(16) The accounts in writing should be submitted to Council, certified by a member thereof before payment, and filed in such manner that they can be readily referred to.

(17) That reports be in writing and properly filed with the Clerk.

(18) That the Commissioners of the divisions or drains report monthly to the Treasurer all orders issued by them, on a form which will be provided for the purpose as follows:—

To the Treasurer of Orford Township.

Statement of Orders issued by...
Commissioner for ....
For month ending ...., 190...

No.	Date.	In favor of	Services performed.	Amount.	To be charged to.

16 M.A.

The Treasurer will file these statements for the use of himself and Auditors.

(19) That the Treasurer report monthly to the Council the Commissioners' orders paid since previous report as follows :—

Highgate, Ont.

....190...

To the Reeve and Council of Orford Township.

I beg to report that I have cashed the following Commissioners' orders and submit the same for your approval and confirmation :

Statement No..............for month of.................., 190..

No.	Date.	Issued by	Charged to	In Favor of	Service Performed.	Amount.

On motion of.............................., seconded by..............................., the action of the Treasurer be confirmed and his statement recorded in minutes and filed with the Clerk. The above motion was passed at meeting of Council..........................., 190......

(20) That no order signed by the Reeve and Clerk, or Commissioners become chargeable to the funds of the Township till countersigned by Treasurer. A rubber stamp for all but the Treasurer's signature can be procured.

(21) That the cash book be kept written up regularly and balanced not less frequently than monthly, after the vouchers are returned from the bank.

(22) That the funds of the Township be kept separate from those of the Treasurer so that the balance in the bank will equal that in the cash book.

(23) That the Treasurer enter up all arrears of taxes returned to the County Treasurer in his ledger, and make his return to the County Treasurer promptly on receipt of the roll from the collector.

(24) That the Treasurer deposit all moneys, when received, in the bank account, and make no payments except by countersigning orders passed by Council or issued by Commissioners, except fixed charges such as debentures and coupons and any other items fixed by by-law or statute payable without reference to the Council.

(25) That a bill book be provided to contain a proper record of all notes issued by the municipality.

(26) That the Treasurer only issue acknowledgments of money in his receipt book, which I have had numbered by machine, every receipt form must be accounted for.

(27) That the ledger be properly kept and regularly balanced. In it shall be kept an account of each drain or award, and the different divisions. That no miscellaneous drain account be opened, but the ledger as opened by me and written up to Oct. 20, 1906, be continued, so that at all times it will show the correct standing of the Township affairs.

(28) That the debenture redemption account, through which all payments of drainage and other debentures, and levies to meet them, only shall pass, for all debentures issued properly under the by-laws which authorize them.

16a M A.

(29) That the journal provided be used, through which any transfers will be entered and the appropriations be placed on the tax roll charged to the collector and placed to the credit of the proper accounts. The amount at debit of the collector's account in the ledger will indicate the amount of unpaid taxes.

(30) That early payments of taxes be encouraged so the County rate and school sections will all be paid before end of the year. This can be done by amending the by-law imposing a percentage on taxes unpaid on Dec. 15th in each year.

(31) That orders issued by the School Trustees on the Township Treasurer to pay the Treasurer of the school section for the "amount levied" without stating the amount, be discontinued, and a stated amount inserted with the seal of the section attached in every instance.

(32) That the drainage account opened for each individual drain or award drain in the Treasurer's ledger, shall remain until closed out by cash payment, sale of debenture, or written off by resolution of Council if found impossible to collect from the interested parties. In these accounts nothing should appear but the cost of construction.

(33) That all funds for constructing drains be provided by sale of debentures. The Township's portion of cost of construction to be included in the debenture issue. The proceeds of the sale of debentures and cash commuted to go to the credit of the drain. That if there is a surplus it be deducted from the next annual levy against the drain, or rebated pro rata by orders issued in favor of the ratepayers. That if there is an overdraft, a proper amending by-law be promptly passed, and the deficiency collected from the ratepayers on the drain.

(34) That on all drainage expenditures the Reeve be authorized to make inspection and a written report to the Council when advised by Engineer or Commissioner that the work is completed. The commission on the work to be withheld till such report is made. This will prevent the passing incompleted work or overpaying the contractor. The commission held will be a guarantee to cover any deficiencies found by the Reeve.

Conclusion.

The absence of a proper system of filing records, accounts and documents in the Clerk's office, with no ledger accounts or journal kept by the Treasurers covering the nineteen years over which the audit extended, has caused twice the time to be occupied and expense incurred in the investigation than would have otherwise been necessary. Accounts have had to be made up in detail for each one of the awards, school sections, divisions, drain and other accounts for the nineteen years covered; necessitating the writing of over one hundred and fifty letters, and the examination of Howard and Aldborough books pertaining to Orford accounts, an enormous amount of work in separating the items chargeable to the different accounts to which they properly belonged; this all had to be done before a conclusion could be reached. There were many irregularities, but only those of the greatest importance are referred to in this report. It is not deemed necessary to give further details than contained in the schedules attached.

I desire to call the attention of the Council to the fact that the affairs of the Township during the year 1906 have been conducted in a similar manner to that of past years, and that owing to the irregularities in the methods of carrying on the business and financing the drainage and other expenditures, that unless the books are annually audited by some competent person they will again become muddled and a great deal of benefits derived from the expense of this audit will be lost to the Township.

Accompanying this report are :—

(*a*) A debenture register up to date.

(*b*) A drainage levy book in which are written up the schedules of all drainage by-laws in detail, of drains against which collections are yet to be made.

(*c*) A ledger for the Treasurer, opened up on Dec. 31, 1905, according to this report, and into which I have entered all transactions for the year 1906 to Oct. 20th, including the charging the collector of 1906 with the tax roll, and crediting the divisions and other accounts with the appropriations.

(*d*) A journal for the use of Treasurer in which are the entries for 1906 tax roll.

It is a source of regret that I cannot compliment the officials of the Township on the manner in which the business of the municipality has been conducted.

I desire to thank the officers and members of the Council for the willing manner in which they have rendered substantial assistance from time to time during the continuance of the audit.

The attention of the Council is called to section 14, chapter 228, R.S.O. 1897, which requires that the recommendations made in this report shall be carried into effect.

I shall be pleased to furnish any further explanations or advise with the Council in reference to any of the matters mentioned and recommendations contained in this report.

All of which is respectfully submitted.

A. F. FALLS,
Chartered Accountant.

CHATHAM, ONT., Oct. 24th, 1906.

SCHEDULES OF REPORT OF SPECIAL INSPECTION, EXAMINATION AND AUDIT OF THE BOOKS AND ACCOUNTS OF THE MUNICIPAL CORPORATION OF THE TOWNSHIP OF ORFORD.

BY A. F. FALLIS, CHARTERED ACCOUNTANT.

LIST OF SCHEDULES.

The schedules referred to in this Report are :—

Schedule XII.—Claim of Angus Smith, C.E., also list of payments by the Township
    to him since 1901.
Schedule XIII.—Municipal Drain Balances Dec. 31, 1905.
Schedule XIV.—Treasurer's Ledger Balance on October 20, 1906.
Schedule XV.—Statement of Assets included as result of this Audit.

TOWNSHIP OF ORFORD.

FINANCIAL POSITION AS ON DEC. 31, 1905.

Assets.   Schedule I.

Available Assets—

Cash on hand Dec. 31, 1905		$7,554 15	
Tax roll, 1905, total	$19,991 15		
Collected	17,145 00		
		2,846 15	
Tile drain advance to T. J. Johnson, Sept. 21st, 1905—			
Debentures not issued till July 14, 1906	....	200 00	
Tile drainage surplus, due from Ontario Government when applied for	....	471 68	
Police Village of Highgate, overdraft	....	61 58	
Township of Aldborough—			
Clerk's fees, Aldborough No. 2 drain	$15 00	●	
Part Patterson bridge, townline	93 75		
		108 75	
Township of Howard—			
Clerk's fees on Stover drain	....	18 00	
John A. McArthur Estate—			
Error by clerk recapitulating 1901 roll paid since	....	94 55	
McGregor Creek and Buller drains—			
By-laws 323 and 324, passed to pay Howard, debentures not yet issued	....	670 00	
Crandell drain—			
Amount due Aldborough, for which by-law not yet passed or debentures sold	....	95 50	
Drainage levies omitted—			
Atridge award	10 40		
Downie award	3 00		
McTavish agreement	28 00		
Highgate drain	19 14		
Massey drain	13 55		
South Marsh drain	13 95		
G. Raycraft, drain	1 00		
D. D. McTavish tile drain	7 36		
S. McDonald, tile drain	14 72		
		111 12	
T. H. Ridley, ex-Treasurer—			
Schedule VI		493 64	
J. S. Foster, ex-Treasurer—			
Schedule VII		303 56	
J. D. Gillies, Treasurer—			
Schedule VIII		27 82	
Henry Watson, Clerk—			
Schedule V		97 98	
			$13,154 48

Assets not immediately available.
Drainage accounts not available till amending
by-laws are passed and debentures sold—

Butler drain	$ 1 65
Cranberry Marsh, west branch	297 86
Dube's	16 85
Foster	11 43
Ingram	141 15
McCaughrin	13 50
McCallum	133 36
McGregor Creek and Buller	2,390 68
McPhail extension	6 79

Morden	39	
North Marsh	48	
Stover	1,504 14	
Tinline and Hogg	45 00	
Wilson	75	
		$4,567 03

General fund assets—

Drainage levies against lands, to be collected on Roll 1906	$2,587 48	
Drainage levies against lands, to be collected on Roll 1907	2,181 48	
Drainage levies against lands, to be collected on Roll 1908	752 10	
		5,521 06

Township portion of drain advanced—

Due in 1906	$ 463 55	
Due in 1907	393 47	
Due in 1908	103 72	
		960 74

Total assets not immediately available.................................	$11,048 83

Passive assets.
    Debentures—

Tile drain	$2,259 52	
Moravian bridge	1,006 98	
Lake Erie and Detroit River bonus......	1,292 60	
School section 3 and 4	1,092 00	
		$ 5,651 10

Fixed assets.

Town hall, lot and lock-up, Highgate		$ 300 00
Safe in clerk's office		200 00
Road machines	$ 150 00	
Howard gravel pit	300 00	
McLaren gravel pit	150 00	
Calhoun gravel pit	100 00	
Blue gravel pit	100 00	
L. Gosnell gravel pit	200 00	
		1,000 00
Interest in Moravian bridge ....:................		2,000 00
		$ 3,500 00

Recapitulation of assets.

Available assets	$13,154 48	
Assets not immediately available	11,048 83	
Passive assets	5,651 10	
Fixed assets	3,500 00	
		$33,354 41

TOWNSHIP OF ORFORD.

Liabilities.

Current liabilities. Debentures and coupons—   Dec. 31, 1905.

Moravian bridge	due Dec. 31, 05...	$277 50	
Tile drainage	Jan. 1, '06...	489 28	
Lake Erie & Detroit R. Ry.	Jan. 1, '06...	247 08	
School section No. 3 and 4	Jan. 1, 06...	401 10	
Cornwall drain	Jan. 1, '06...	200 35	
Gosnell drain	Jan. 1, '06...	276 20	
King drain	Jan. 1, '06...	328 70	
McKerricher drain	Jan. 1, '06...	560 00	
Eastlake drain	Jan. 1, '06...	190 55	
			$2,970 76

Township of Howard—

Orford portion, McGregor creek and Buller drains	....	670 00

Township of Aldborough—
Amount due on drains paid Mch. 10, 1906... $ 120 55
Crandell drain 95 50
                                                   216 05

Schools—
W. J. Ferguson, sec. No. 1 .... $ 507 00
Robt. McLaren, sec. 3 and 4 ....   645 20
D. P. McPhail, sec. 6 ....   1,220 10
Jas. Goodbrand, sec. 7 ....   303 30
R. Heatherington, sec. 10 ....   304 30
John Lather, sec. 11 ....   304 30
                                                   3,284 20

County rate—
J. C. Fleming Co., Treasurer, 1905 rate 2,289 99

Charity—
Jonas Gosnell, Co. Clerk, House of Refuge, 1905 ....   222 32

Attridge award—
Geo. Moody, tile 27 00

Dubs drain—
Judge Woods, order Nov. 15, 1901 ....   5 00

Drain accounts balances—
Ashton drain $1,327 40
Cruickshanks 45 41
Cornwall 17 05
Crouch 2 00
Duffus 112 19
Eastlake 35 27
Gesner 80 16
Gosnell 43 81
Haycroft 267 66
Highgate tile portion 84 94
King 4 36
Massey 23 37
McKerricher 89 62
McMillan 266 60
Potter drain 83 97
Saw Mill Creek 1 00
South Marsh 19 06
Wylie branch of Massey 52 14
                                                   2,556 73

McCallum drain—
Amount due D. Graham, overcollected 1903 ....   1 97

Massey drain—
Amount due W. Desmond, overcollected 1897 ....   19 42

General fund—
Div. 1, Geo. Moody, tile   1905... $ 8 10
"   2, Harry Lewis, work   1905...   6 00
"   3, Wm. McDonald, grading   1905...   4 50
"   4, D. McMackon   1904...   7 84
"   5, Geo. Moody, tile   1905...   5 00
         A. J. Stone, grading   1905...   5 00
"   6, W. Bishop, putting in tile   1905...   4 25
         Geo. Moody, tile   1905...   1 27
         Geo. Moody, tile   1905...   45
E. Townline, J. McFarlane   1905...   10 00
A. McDiarmid, fees on McDonald award......   9 00
               Gillis   " 7 00
               Mobey   " 8 00
               Miller   :: 8 00
               Summers 8 00
               Allison   " 6 00
McDonald award, W. McDonald, work 2 00
J. B. Peets, meetings and commissions 1905...   21 50
J. D. Gillis, treasurer, salary   1905......   103 00
L. Tape, collector, salary   1905......   78 00
E. Patrick, gravel   1905......   18 50
Jos. Swanton, grant   1905......   15 00
Jas. McLaren, gravel   1904 and 1905......   48 00

Municipal world	15 92	
Canadian Sewer Pipe Co., balance	11 35	
Commutation, Highgate Police Village	27 75	
		$439 43

Total current liabilities		$12,702 87
Available assets over current liabilities		451 61
		$13,154 48

Liabilities not immediately payable.
  Drainage debentures—
  Payable out of general fund,

Due Jan. 1, 1907	$1,494 60	
Due Jan. 1, 1908	893 45	
Due Jan. 1, 1909	190 55	

Total liabilities not immediately payable		$2,578 60
Assets not immediately available over liabilities not immediately payable		$ 8,470 23
		$11,048 83

Deferred liabilities.
  Debentures—

Tile drainage	$2,259 52	
Moravian bridge	1,006 98	
Lake Erie & D. R. Ry., bonus	1,292 60	
School section 3 and 4	1,092 00	
		$5,651 10

Recapitulation of liabilities—

Current liabilities	$12,702 87	
Liabilities not immediately payable	2,578 60	
Deferred liabilities	5,651 10	
Surplus, total assets over liabilities	12,421 84	
		$33,354 41

STATEMENT OF ASSETS AND LIABILITIES GENERAL AS ON DECEMBER 31ST, 1905.

Assets—

		Schedule II.
Available assets as per statement		$13,154 48
Assets not immediately available as per statement		11,048 83

Fixed assets—

Town hall, lot, Highgate	$ 300 00	
Gravel pits, road machines, etc	1,200 00	
Interest on Moravian bridge	2,000 00	
		3,500 00

Passive assets—

Tile drain assessment to mature	$2,259 52	
Moravian bridge assessment to mature	1,006 98	
Lake Erie & D. R. R. bonus assessments to mature	1,292 60	
School assesements to mature	1,092 00	
		5,651 10
		$33,354 41

Liabilities—

Current as per statement		$12,702 87
Liabilities not immediately payable as per statement		2,578 60

Deferred liabilities—

Tile drainage debentures	$2,259 52	
Moravian bridge debentures	1,006 98	
Lake Erie & D. R. R. debentures	1,292 60	
School debentures	1,092 00	
		5,651 10
		$20,932 57
Balance		$12,421 84
		$33,354 41
Surplus	$12,421 84	

Made up as follows : —
Available assets over current liabilities .... $ 451 61
Assets not immediately available over liabilities not immediately pay-
able 8,470 23
Fixed assets 3,500 00

$12,421 84

DEBENTURE LIABILITY.   Schedule III.

By-law 149, School Section No. 3 and 4, $5,000.00.

Number.	Principal.	Due.	Coupons.	1906.	1907.	1908.	1909.
17	$333 00	Jan. 1, '06		$16 50			
18	347 00	Jan. 1, '07		17 35	$17 35		
19	364 00	Jan. 1, '08		18 20	18 20	$18 20	
20	381 00	Jan. 1, '09		19 05	19 05	19 05	$19 05
	$1,422 00			$71 10	$54 60	$37 25	$19 05

By-law 253, Lake Erie and Detroit River Bonus, $2,000.00.

4	$187 38	Jan. 1, 1906	
5	194 87	Jan. 1, 1907	These are the proper amounts of principal due
6	202 67	Jan. 1, 1908	yearly.
7	210 78	Jan. 1, 1909	Equal annual payment of interest and princi-
8	219 20	Jan. 1, 1910	pal is $247.08.
9	227 98	Jan. 1, 1911	
10	237 10	Jan. 1, 1912	
	$1,479 98	Principal liability.	

Only one debenture was issued for $2,000.00, with ten coupons of $247.08 each attached to cover principal and interest due annually. There remains outstanding the debenture of $2,000.00, and seven coupons of $247.08 each.

This improper method of issuing debentures makes the township liable for the original principal sum in the hands of the holder of the debenture till all annual payments of interest and principal have been made, and the debenture itself surrendered.

By-law 291, King Drain, $600.00.

Number.	Principal.	Due.	Coupons 1906.	1907.	1908.
1	$300 00	Jan. 1, 1906	$14 35		
2	300 00	Jan. 1, 1907	14 35	$12 00	
	$600 00		$28 70	$12 00	

By-law 294, Gosnell Drain, $500.00.

1	$250 00	Jan. 1, 1906	$13 10		
2	250 00	Jan. 1, 1907	13 10	$11 25	
	$500 00		$16 20	$11 25	

By-law 307, Eastlake Drain, $825.00.

2	$156 75	Jan. 1, 1906	$33 80	One coupon	
3	164 00	Jan. 1, 1907	25 95	"	
4	172 85	Jan. 1, 1908	17 70	"	
5	181 50	Jan. 1, 1909	9 05		
	$675 70				

By-law 308, McKerricher Drain, $1,500.00.

1	$500 00	Jan. 1, 1906	$20 00		
2	500 00	Jan. 1, 1907	20 00	$20 00	
3	500 00	Jan. 1, 1908	20 00	20 00	$20 00
	$1,500 00		$60 00	$40 00	$20 00

By-law 316, Cornwall Drain, $525.00.

1	$175 00	Jan. 1, 1906	$ 8 45		
2	175 00	Jan. 1, 1907	8 45	$ 7 90	
3	175 00	Jan. 1, 1908	8 45	7 90	$ 7 90
	$525 00		$25 35	$15 80	$ 7 90

By-law 260, Moravian Bridge, $2,250.00.

6	$228 00	Dec. 31, 1905	$49 50	One coupon
7	·237 12	Dec. 31, 1906	40 38	"
8	246 61	Dec. 31, 1907	30 89	"
9	256 47	Dec. 31, 1908	21 03	
10	266 78	Dec. 31, 1909	10 72	
	$1,234 98			

By-law 68, Tile Drainage.

Principal and interest—

$489 28..Jan. 1, 1906
353 28..Jan. 1, 1907
323 84..Jan. 1, 1908
294 40..Jan. 1, 1909
287 04..Jan. 1, 1910
272 32..Jan. 1, 1911
242 88..Jan. 1, 1912
213 44..Jan. 1, 1913
147 20..Jan. 1, 1914
73 60..Jan. 1, 1915
29 44..Jan. 1, 1916
14 72..Jan. 1, 1917
7 36..Jan. 1, 1918
$2,748 80

Recapitulation of debentures unpaid on Dec. 31, 1905—

School section No. 3 and 4	$1,422 00	
Moravian bridge	1,234 98	
Lake Erie & D. R. R. bonus	1,479 98	
King drain	600 00	
Gosnell drain	500 00	
Eastlake drain	675 70	
McKerracher drain	1,500 00	
Cornwall drain	525 00	
Tile drainage	2,748 80	
		$10,686 46

COLLECTOR'S TAX ROLLS. Schedule IV.

Year.	Clerk's warrant to Collector.	Collector's Declaration.	Date returned to Treasurer.	Arrears.
1887	Nov. 14, 1887	Feb. 18, 1888	Feb. 18, 1888	$125.88
1888	Oct. 1888	Mar. 19, 1889	Mar. 19, 1889	169.28
1889	Nov. 1889	June 3, 1890	June 3, 1890	210.46
1890	Oct. 27, 1890	Not signed	Sept. 2, 1891	70.62
1891	Oct. 31, 1891	May 3, 1892	May 3, 1892	134.75
1892	Oct. 25, 1892	Mar. 30, 1893	Mar. 30, 1893	29.51
1893	Nov. 6, 1893	All collected	Mar. 31, 1894	None
1894	Nov. 19, 1894	Apl. 25, 1895	Apl. 25, 1895	22.60
1895	Nov. 9, 1895	Not signed	Apl. 11, 1896	12.52
1896	Nov. 10, 1896	None	None	None
1897	Nov. 15, 1897	Apl. 5, 1898	Apl. 5, 1898	3.60
1898	Nov. 7, 1898	Not signed	Mar. 1, 1899	7.21
1899	Nov. 2, 1899	Not signed	Mar. 30, 1900	5.28
1900	Oct. 27, 1900	None	None	None
1901	Oct. 26, 1901	None	None	None
1902	Oct. 13, 1902	None	Mar. 28, 1903	None
1903	Oct. 27, 1903	Mar. 25, 1904	Mar. 25, 1904	3.02
1904	Oct. 24, 1904	Mar. 10, 1905	Mar. 10, 1905	None
1905	Oct. 31, 1905	May 3, 1906	May 3, 1906	31.58

The Collector's Rolls have not been delivered for collection any year as required by the Act. Section 131, Assessment Act, R.S.O., requires roll to be in collector's hands on or before first of October.

Account with Henry Watson, Clerk.

To Sept. 1, 1906.
SCHEDULE V.

Date.		Principal.	Interest.
1894.			
Dec. 17.—Voucher 487, rebating North Marsh Drain, 11 years 257 days		$ 6 00	$ 3 51
1895.			
Dec. 8.—Voucher 487, rebating and postage North Marsh Drain, 10 years 266 days		8 00	4 29
The above were charges for rebating $145.05 refund from Howard Township.			
1898.			
Sept. 17.—Voucher 331, overpayment on Wilson Drain, 7 years 347 days		12 00	4 77
1894.			
Nov. 26.—To overpayment of Engineer's allowance for Clerk's fees and publication on Massey Drain, Vouchers 223, 333, 409, 481, 11 years 278 days		25 00	14 70
1895.			
Dec. 16.—Voucher 711, F. H. Hammond, or bearer, balance on Treasurer bond premium, order endorsed by H. Watson, $23.50; amount of earned prem. on London Guarantee bond cancelled, $16.50; 10 years 258 days		7 00	3 75
1903.			
April 23.—Amount remitted by Sawyer-Massey Co., Ltd., as discount of 10 per cent. on $8.50 order, 3 years 130 days		85	15
1905.			
Jan. 1.—Thirteenth coupon on tile drainage deb, 64 Duncan Ross; marked paid in record book on Nov. 17, 1903, money not received by Government, till Jan. 3, 1905, 1 year 242 days		7 36	60
		$66 21	$31 77
Interest		31 77	
Total		$97 98	

Account with Thomas H. Ridley, Ex-Treasurer.

SCHEDULE VI.

Date.		Principal.	Interest.
1890.			
Nov. 26.—McPhail Extension Drain, J. Randall; costs commuted, marked paid in Clerk's books, not entered in Treasurer's books, 15 years 278 days		$ 2 30	$ 1 82
1895.			
Jan. 21.—Draft on Clerk by J. W. Shackleton, Minutes, page 171, state ex-Treasurer's default charge ex-Treasurer, page 20, Audit Report, 1895, 11 years 222 days		20 50	11 90
1889.			
Feb. 28.—From Township of Howard account of ditches and watercourses; marked in H. Watson's book turned over to Treasurer, 17 years 185 days		4 65	4 07
1890.			
July 30.—From County Treasurer for non-resident taxes, 16 years 30 days		248 50	199 90
Principal		$275 95	$217 69
Interest		217 69	
Total		$493 64	

Account with J. S. Foster, Ex-Treasurer.

Date.	Principal.	Interest.
1899.		
Jan. 15.—To Voucher 31, McCaughrin Drain; previously charged in 1898 as Voucher 477; interest on above to Sept. 1, 1906, at 5 per cent., 7 years 228 days	$25 00	$ 9 53
1899.		
Jan. 1.—To Voucher 44, premium on Treasurer bond previously charged in 1898 as Voucher 571; interest on above from Jan. 1, 1899, at 5 per cent.	40 00	15 32
1900.		
May 21.—To Aldborough Order No. 158, March 17, 1900, endorsed by J. S. Foster, Treasurer, and passed through Traders' Bank, Ridgetown, April 6, 1900, for Cruickshanks Drain $30.76, and Ditches and Watercourses $24.78; total $55.54. Entered in Treasurer's cash book as $40.18. 5 years 102 days	15 36	4 05
Dec. 17.—To rebate on note due Jan. 7, 1901, at Molson's Bank, Ridgetown, not entered in cash book; 5 years 257 days	1 30	33
1901.		
April 19.—To Voucher 867 to J. S. Foster for amount paid on McCaughrin Drain. No particulars of what this is made up could be obtained from the minutes or officers. The order was issued two years after the work was reported completed by the Engineer; interest from April 19, 1901, at 5 per cent.	26 00	6 97
Dec. 31.—To error in additions of cash book. The Auditors made an error of same amount in addition of totals of road and bridges disbursements; interest from Dec. 31, 1901, at 5 per cent., 4 years 243 days	100 00	23 32
1903.		
March 10.—To cash from M. Driver, for settlement on Irvine roadway, not entered in cash book; interest March 10, 1903, at 5 per cent., 4 years 243 days	20 00	3 47
1904.		
Dec. 14.—To interest on money paid by J. Blum on Ingram Drain on Oct. 10, 1902, $162.00, not entered in cash book of the Township till Dec. 14, 1904. From Oct. 10, 1902, to Dec. 14, 1904, at 5 per cent.	....	17 63
	$227 66	$80 62
Principal	227 66	
To interest	80 62	
	$308 28	
Dec. 14.—By interest on order issued June 13, 1903, to J. S. Foster in full for account and services as Treasurer, $62.75, not used till settlement in Dec. 14, 1904, of the J. Blum item above; interest June 13, 1903, to Dec. 14, 1904......	4 72	
Total	$303 56	

Account with John D. Gillis, Treasurer.

Date.	Principal.	Interest.
1904.		
Dec. 15.—To cash from Gabriel Clark for gravel deposited in bank to Township account but not entered in cash book; interest on above to Sept. 1, 1906	$ 1 60	$ 14

Dec.   14.—To interest on 7 orders on County Treasurer to
School Sections, charged to Township account
by J. D. Gillis, from dates as shown on the
original orders in County Treasurer's office,
Chatham, to date money recovered from
County, Dec. 14, 1904.

1903.

Oct.	3.—D. P. McPhail, Sec.	6 County grant	$100 00	....	$ 5 99
	" "	6 Leg. "	100 00	....	5 99
	" "	6 County "	160 00	....	10 58
Oct.	13.—Peter Clark,	10 County "	15 00	....	88
	" "	10 County "	15 00	....	88
Oct.	14.—Robt. McLaren, "	3 & 4 Leg. "	15 00	....	88
	" "	County "	15 00	....	88

	$ 1 60	$26 22
To interest	26 22	
Total	$27 82	

J. G. Crosby, Secretary of Police Trustees of Police Village of Highgate.

Date.	SCHEDULE IX.	
	Disbursements.	Receipts.
1902—By statute labour	$.........	$128 50
To sundry labour supplies, etc.	110 39	
1903—By statute labour	....	228 60
To sundry labour supplies, etc.	182 63	
1904—By statute, frontage and fines	....	184 35
To sundry labour, supplies, etc.	285 57	
1905—By statute labour, drain, etc.	....	175 50
To sundry labour, supplies, etc.	181 48	
Balance	....	43 12

	$760 07	$760 07
Disbursements over receipts	....	$43 12
To order C. Crichton entered 1903 and 1904	$3 61	

To G. Gosnell, Sr., statute labour not entered...........	$ 1 50	
" W. Smale, " "	1 50	
" Mrs. E. Eastlake, " "	1 50	
" J. Scott, " "	75	
" J. G. Crosby, 4 years' statute labour, 1904 and 1905 marked performed by services as Secretary; 1902 and 1903 credited, but later offset by not crediting other cash payments	9 00	

1906.

Jan.	26.—To order from Township statute.		
	Labour 1904 roll	27 75	
	Balance due police village	....	2 49

	$45 61	$45 61

Amount due Police Village of Highgate from J. G. Crosby....................	$2 49

Township Account with Police Village of Highgate.

	SCHEDULE X.	
1902—By levy on roll 1902	$.........	$535 50
To deductions as per agreement	190 00	
To orders paid	252 16	
1903—By levy on roll 1903	....	541 35
By statute labour on roll 1903	....	17 25
To deduction as per agreement	190 00	
To orders paid	480 83	
1904—By levy on roll 1904	....	541 35
To deduction as per agreement	200 00	
To orders paid	350 70	

1905—By levy on roll 1905	....	513 37
By statute labour roll 1905	....	12 00
To deduction as per agreement	200 00	
To orders paid	358 71	
Balance overdrawn	....	61 58
	$2,222 40	$2,222 40

1905.
Dec.   31.—To amount overdrawn $61 58
        (This does not inclue order outstanding.)   •
        D. McMackon paid in 1906...............................   6 50

The statute labour placed on the roll in the year 1904 $27.75; was paid to J. G. Crosby in 1906, but is charged to him in account as shown in Schedule IX.

TOWNSHIP OF ORFORD.

WYLIE BRANCH OF MASSEY DRAIN, BY-LAW 310.   Schedule XI

Statement of Assessments against Lands.

Con.	Lot.	Name.	Amount as per Engineer's Report.	Amount as revised by Court of Revision.	Annual levy.	Amount on roll 1905.	To collect, 1906.	To collect, 1907.
			$ c.	$ c.	$ c.	$ c.	$ c.	$ c.
8	15	J. B. McDonald..........	2 50	1 25	47	97	44	Nil.
8	16	Thomas Lee......	4 00	2 00	75	1 50	75	Nil.
8	17	R. Hornal	9 00	4 50	1 65	3 33	1 62	Nil.
8	18	John McKay.............	4 00	2 00	75	1 50	75	Nil.
8	W. ½ 19	Mrs. McWilliams........	2 00	1 00	37	75	36	Nil.
7	12	L. J. Gosnell............	6 00	6 00	2 20	2 25	2 15	2 20
7	W. ½ 13	George Swanton..........	4 50	8 00	2 94	1 70	4 18	2 94
7	E. ½ 13	N. Littlejohn(rebated 1905, $10.37)	14 50	14 50	5 33	16 10	4 93	5 33
7	14	J. S. Foster	60 50	50 50	18 55	22 25	14 85	18 55
7	15	Thomas Routledge	34 50	34 50	12 67	12 74	12 60	12 67
7	16	William Desmond.......	65 00	60 00	22 03	23 95	20 11	22 03
7	17	J. W. Reycraft..........	38 00	38 00	13 95	14 00	13 90	13 95
7	18	Norman Adrain	40 50	40 50	14 87	14 62	15 12	14 87
7	19	W. Goodbrand (rebated, 1905, $3.64)...........	24 00	10 00	3 67	8 85	2 13	3 67
6	10	L. Gosnell	10 50	35 75	13 10	3 55	22 65	13 10
6	W. pt. 11	L. Gosnell	7 50	24 50	9 00	2 76	15 24	9 00
6	E. pt. 11	R. Swanton.............	52 00	52 00	19 10	19 10	19 10	19 10
6	12	B. Brosnahan	23 00	18 00	6 61	8 50	4 34	6 61
6	14	B. Brosnahan	1 00	Nil.	Nil.	38	Nil.	Nil.
5	W. ½ 11	W. Fenton....·..........	50	50	18	19	17	18
			403 50	403 50	148 19	158 99	155 39	144 20

SCHEDULE XII.

Statement of A. Smith's Claim Against Orford, Stratford, April 5, 1906.

Letting King Drain .... $38 00•
  "   Ingram Drain ....   24 00•
  "   McKerricher Drain 45 00
  "   Gosnell, Upper Portion 10 00
  "   Gosnell, Lower Portion 20 00
  "   Highgate Drain 12 00

Survey plans, Tinline Hogg Drain .,	58 50	
Amending same	10 00	
Attending meeting on drain	5 00*	
Survey and Irwin Drain	28 50	
		$251 00
Less *re* Tinline and Hogg Drain		15 00

Amount of Claim April 5, 1906		$236 00
Paid June 7, 1906, as shown above	$67 00	
Paid Sept. 15, 1906, order of A. Smith in favour of Solomon Gosnell	6 00	
		73 00

Amount claimed	$163 00

Deductions for Overpayments.

1896.

Dec. 15.—To overpayment on Webster Drain Award, Voucher 467	$16 00	
(Previously paid by Vouchers 379 and 460.)		
To overpayment on Nichols' Award Drain, awarded by Judge $7.50; amount paid $10.00	2 50	
		18 50

Amount still claimed by A. Smith, C.E.	$144 50

The Following Payments Have Been Made to Angus Smith, C.E., Since Jan. 1, 1901.

1901.

Sept.	28.—Ashton Drain	$30 00
Oct.	11.—Butler Drain, survey	23 75
Jan.	14.—Foster Drain, commission	26 00
May	21.—Bateman Drain, survey	16 50
Sept.	14.—Rowland Drain	7 50
Oct.	11.—McCallum Drain, plans	10 50
	Dubs Drain	16 00
	Schindler Drain	16 50
Nov.	15.—Dubs Drain	5 00
Dec.	16.—Ward Drain Award	12 00
	Duffus Drain Award	18 00
Jan.	14.—McGregor Creek Drain, services	40 00
1902.		
Feb.	28.—Ward Award, amending	5 00
May	23.—Dubs Drain, plans	46 50
July	2.—Dubs Drain, report	6 50
	King Drain	2 75
Sept.	9.—King Drain	53 25
	Ingram Drain	28 50
1903.		
Nov.	14.—Clearville Bridge, Engineer	28 75
Dec.	15.—Rowland Drain	7 50
	Gosnell Drain	38 50
Nov.	14.—McCallum Drain	36 00
	Cruickshanks Drain, survey	38 50
Nov.	13.—Duffus Drain	37 50
March	21.—Downie Drain	22 00
	McDonald Drain	16 50
Nov.	14.—Highgate Drain, survey	16 50
	Eastlake Drain, survey	40 00
	Dubs Drain. superintending	30 00
	Wilson Drain	41 50
1904.		
Jan.	11.—Wylie Drain, survey	42 00
Jan.	27.—Abray Award, allowance	16 50
	Shankie Drain, allowance	10 00

*Paid June 7, 1906.

Oct.	1.—Gosnell Drain, Court of Revision		4 00
	Gosnell Drain, Upper Portion		10 00
	Ingram Drain, Court of Revision		2 00
	King Drain, Court of Revision		2 00
June	4.—McKerricher Drain, witness		9 00
June	17.—McKerricher Drain, plans and survey		110 00
1905.			
Oct.	28.—McCallum Drain, commission		18 00
Feb.	10.—Morrison Drain, survey		28 50
Feb.	3.—Cornwall Drain, plans		28 00
1906.			
Sept.	15.—Order (A. Smith) paid Solomon Gosnell		6 00
June	7.—Letting King Drain		38 00
	Ingram Drain		24 00
	Attending meeting on drain		5 00

Statement of Balances of Municipal Drain Accounts as on December 31, 1905.

Ledger Folio.		SCHEDULE XIII.	
250	Ashton	$........	$1,327 40
252	Butler	1 65	
254	Cruickshanks	....	45 41
266	Cornwall	....	17 05
255	Cranberry Marsh, West Branch	297 86	
256	Crouch	....	2 00
272	Dubes	16 85	
257	Duffus	....	112 91
258	Eastlake	....	35 27
259	Foster	11 43	
260	Gesner	....	80 16
286	Gosnell	....	43 81
490	Haycroft	....	267 66
294	Highgate, Tile Portion	....	84 94
298	Ingram	144 15	
300	King	....	4 36
302	Massey	....	23 37
261	McCaughrin	13 50	
262	McCallum	133 36	
263	McGregor Creek and Buller	2,390 68	
310	McKerracher	....	89 62
254	McMillan	....	266 60
265	McPhail Extension	6 79	
267	Morden'	39	
268	North Marsh Drain	48	
269	Potter	....	83 97
270	Saw Mill Creek	....	1 00
271	South Marsh Drain	....	19 06
273	Stover	1,504 14	
304	Tinline and Hogg	45 00	
274	Wylie Branch of Massey	....	52 14
275	Wilson	75	
		$4,567 03	$2,556 73

Treasurer's Ledger Balance as on October 20th, 1906, after Crediting up Appropriations and Making Entries for 1906 Tax Roll.

Folio.	Title.	SCHEDULE XIV.	
		Debit.	Credit.
1	Division 1	$............	$ 177 20
10	" 2	....	131 32
20	" 3	....	266 25
30	" 4	....	140 77
40	" 5	....	226 25
50	" 6	....	162 50
60	East Town Line	....	92 00
70	West Town Line	....	37 50
80	Roads and Bridges	....	1,165 38
90	Charity	....	241 46

94	Noxious Weeds (no appropriations)	14 00	
98	Law Costs (no appropriation)	7 00	
100	County Rate	....	1,815 93
101	Stationery and printing (no appropriation)	177 12	
108	School Section 1	....	600 49
109	" 2	....	952 86
111	" 3 and 4	....	912 72
112	" 5	....	430 70
113	" 6	....	2,128 14
114	" 7	....	511 05
115	" 9	....	550 88
116	" 10	....	613 26
117	" 11	....	610 75
112	" 12	....	405 30
119	Union School Section 5	....	27 72
110	Schools	....	25 60
120	Sheep and Dog	....	204 85
130	Election Expenses (no appropriation)	84 25	
140	Commutation	....	40 75
150	Donations and Grants (no appropriation)	35 00	
160	Miscellaneous	....	43 72
170	Debenture Redemption Account	....	3,119 81
181	Police Village of Highgate, overdraft after crediting all 1906 levies	71 55	
193	Salaries (no appropriation)	773 60	
200	Interest (no appropriation)	46 45	
201	Bills payable	....	4,000 00
202	Thos. H. Ridley, ex-Treasurer	493 64	
202	J. S. Foster, ex-Treasurer	303 56	
202	J. D. Gillis, Treasurer	27 82	
202	H. Watson, Clerk	97 98	
203	Ontario Government	471 68	
203	Muirkirk Road Division	....	35 75
203	Road Division No. 58	....	1 15
208	Arrears of Taxes, from roll of 1905	31 58	
211	Lawrence Tape, Collector, 1906	21,598 70	
218	Fixed Assets	4,100 00	
220	General Funds	....	12,510 31
230	Tile Drain Advances	....	1 00
231	Cash, overdrawn	....	252 72
250	Asher Drain	....	470 94
252	Butler Drain	1 65	
253	Crandell Drain	79 07	
254	Cruickshanks Drain	....	45 41
255	Cranberry Marsh Drain, West Branch	297 86	
256	Crouch Drain	....	2 00
257	Duffus Drain	....	112 91
258	Eastlake Drain	....	35 27
259	Foster Drain	11 43	
260	Gesner Drain	....	80 16
261	McCaughrin Drain	13 50	
262	McCallum Drain	2 87	
263	McGregor Creek and Buller Drains (old)	2,390 68	
263	McGregor Creek and Buller Drains (new)	670 00	
264	McMillan Drain	....	236 60
265	McPhail Extension Drain	6 79	
266	Cornwall Drain	88 95	
267	Morden Drain	39	
268	North Marsh or Arnold Creek Drain	48	
269	Potter Drain	....	83 97
270	Saw Mill Creek Drain	....	1 00
271	South Marsh Drain	....	19 06
272	Dubs Drain	16 85	
273	Stover Drain (old)	1,504 14	
274	Wylie Branch of Massey Drain	....	52 14
275	Wilson Drain	75	
286	Gosnell Drain	271 98	
290	Havcroft Drain	43 34	
294	Highgate Tile Drain	....	66 42

17 M.A.

298	Ingram Drain	168 15	
300	King Drain	113 02	
302	Massey Drain	52 21	
304	Tinline and Hogg Drain	45 00	
305	Tinline Johnston Drain	12 75	
310	McKerricher Drain	199 38	
326	Aldborough Township	13 25	
328	Howard Township	....	652 00
330	Mobey Award	16 80	
331	Clark Award	1 50	
331	Gladstone Award	3 25	
332	Brooks Award	....	56 00
332	Leverton Award	....	8 00
334	Fence Views Award	....	2 00
		$33,359 97	$33,359 97

The by-law for 1906 did not provide for all the accounts as indicated above, by the words no appropriaton.

The Police Village of Highgate has exceeded the levy of 1906 and the commuted taxes on 1906 roll. The account shows that they had drawn $71.55 on account of 1907 taxes.

SCHEDULE XV.

As a Result of this Audit the Following Amounts are Found to be Due the Township, which were not Previously Included as Assets.

Provincial Government, Tile Drain surplus	$471 68	
Township of Howard, Stover Drain fees	15 00	
Township of Aldborough, No. 2, drain fees	18 00	
Angus Smith, Engineer, overpayment	18 50	
Henry Watson, Clerk	97 98	
John D. Gillis, Treasurer	27 82	
John S. Foster, ex-Treasurer	303 56	
T. H. Ridley, ex-Treasurer	493 64	
John A. McArthur, Estate (since paid)	94 55	
		$1,540 73
Drainage accounts overdrawn, detailed in Schedule XIII	....	4,567 03

Drainage Collections Omitted from Rolls.

Attridge Award	$10 40	
Downie Award	3 00	
McTavish Agreement	28 00	
Highgate Drain	19 14	
Massey Drain	13 55	
South Marsh Drain	13 95	
Dubes Drain	1 00	
Gosnell Drain	1 40	
McKerricher Drain	72 10	
Geo. Raycraft, Tile Drain	1 00	
D. McTavish, Tile Drain	7 36	
S. McDonald, Tile Drain	14 72	
		$185 62
Tile Drain advance on Sept. 21, 1905, to T. J. Johnston, Debentures not issued till July 14, 1906		200 00
		$6,493 38

Cost of this audit to the Township of Orford, including services of staff and travelling expenses as per Mr. Falls' account, was $1,506.63.

17a M.A.

TORONTO, 15th July, 1906.

*To the Reeve and Council of the Township of Colchester North, County of
Essex.*

GENTLEMEN,—Under authority of an Order-in-Council approved by His
Honour the Lieutenant-Governor the 4th day of May last, and in accordance
with instructions from the Provincial Municipal Auditor, I proceeded on
the 9th inst. to the Town of Essex for the purpose of making an inspection,
examination and audit of the books, accounts, vouchers and moneys of your
said Township.

This audit is made upon the petition of certain ratepayers, addressed to
His Honour the Lieutenant-Governor of Ontario, who desire it to extend for
sixteen years from 1st January, 1890; no specific charges being made, the
audit being simply asked for upon general grounds, reference being merely
made to the imperfect system of bookkeeping and an improper state of affairs
in connection with the finances of said Township.

The offices of Clerk and Treasurer during the period under inspection
were occupied as follows :

Mr. I. A. Coulter, Clerk, held office until May, 1897, when he was succeeded by Mr. A. C. Atkinson, still holding office.

C. E. Weldon, Treasurer, 1885 to 1898, succeeded by the present Treasurer, Mr. Henry Baker.

Municipal Cash Book.

Prior to the introduction of the new Government municipal cash book
in 1898, I regret to say the system adopted was of a very inferior and incomplete nature, numerous errors occurring, fortunately not of a serious nature,
and which were rectified under my examination.

In order to take full advantage of the present method and reap the full
benefit of its good points, is to carry the addition of each column forward to
the end of each month, a summary being made annually to enable the auditors to verify the grand totals. If this system is properly carried out you
have practically in each column a ledger and cash book combined.

Following out the above suggestions, there will be no absolute necessity
of entries into the ledger being made more than once a month, except perhaps "sundry items" which necessarily will require to be arranged into their
separate accounts.

Ex-Treasurer Weldon's Accounts.

I have carefully scrutinized these accounts, this having been made the
subject of a searching investigation and audit in 1898, and a settlement
arrived at based upon the audit mentioned.

I append corrected statement which differs considerably with the one
upon which the settlement was made :

Statement re Weldon.

1898.		$ c.	1898.			$ c.
April 11..	To Balance C.B.......	3,625 07	June 27.	By Cash..............		1,000 00
" 11..	" Stat. Labor, 1896...	165 00	Aug. 2.	" Notes.............		1,100 00
			" 2.	" Sundries..........		124 00
			" 2.	" Cash..............		267 00
				" Cash in Bank......		131 00
				" Balance..........		1,165 07
		$3,787 07				$3,787 07

As shown above, the loss to the Township is $1,165.07 instead of $989.23, as reported by the Auditors.

This loss to the Township never would have occurred had the necessary precautions been taken at the time with the view of ascertaining the financial standing of the Treasurer's bondsmen who are personally liable for this discrepancy. Evidently no great effort was ever made to see that the loss was made good by the responsible parties.

Assessment Rolls.

These rolls I have carefully gone over, checking with the Collector's rolls as far as the material at hand would permit, for the years 1890 to 1905, inclusive.

I am pleased to report that I found them in mostly every instance fairly well kept, although there is still room for improvement. The separate pages are added, and the grand totals are shown, but no summary of the various pages to enable the auditors to verify the same.

There being no more important and responsible position than that of the Assessor, the assessment constituting the foundation upon which the taxes are levied, and the taxes practically the entire income of the municipality.

This being the case, I trust that the above suggestions will not be lost sight of, but carefully noted and carried out, as it is most essential that in work of this kind the very best methods should be employed to avoid the possibility of errors.

Collector's Rolls.

The Collector's rolls for the several years have also been examined and found fairly accurate, with the exception of a few instances hereinafter related.

The Collector's roll should contain full particulars prescribed by law (R.S.O. Chap. 224, Sec. 129 to 132). If this had been fully carried out in every case, and the totals from each page had been properly tabulated at the end of the roll, the totals of the separate pages could have been made to prove the correctness of the grand totals.

As the Collector's roll is one of the most important financial documents of the municipality, I would strongly urge that it be thoroughly checked and revised before being handed over to the Collector. Should any alterations be required in the assessment roll by the Court of Revision after the Collector's roll has been prepared, which is found very often necessary, it is the duty of the Clerk to alter and initial same, after which no alterations whatever of any kind should be made.

F. Sweet, Collector's Roll 1897.

Correct amount	$15,571	96
Roll shows	15,472	16
Shortage	$99	80

F. L. Sweet, Collector's Roll 1901.

Correct amount	$15,270	72
Roll shows	15,260	72
Shortage .....:..	$10	00

D. A. Brush, Collector's Roll, 1903.

Correct amount page	$513	79
Roll shows	512	79
Shortage	$1	00

Ledger Folio 52.

F. Sweet is charged in 1897 with roll	$15,472	16
Accounted for only	15,422	16
Shortage	$50	00
Total shortage	$160	80

And chargeable as follows:

F. Sweet, Collector	$99	80
F. L. Sweet, "	10	00
D. A. Brush, "	1	00
Henry Baker, Treasurer	50	00
	$160	80

Debenture Account.

These accounts, as a rule, are carefully kept.

Checking with the register cash book and also with the by-law book, when a question of moneys raised on debentures were involved, I found that in every respect the funds were properly accounted for.

If the Treasurer, when entering in his cash book in detail the amount realized from the sale of debentures, that is the principal premium and accrued interest, received an account of each issue of debentures; and if raised for drainage purposes, he will be able to credit each drain with its proper proportion of the sale of debentures, at the same time setting forth the exact standing of each.

In every instance only the principal and premium should be placed at the credit of the drain, the interest being placed at the credit of interest account or general fund.

This in my opinion is only proper, as during the construction of the drain the Township has paid interest on funds borrowed for that purpose, unless, of course, the debentures have been sold in advance, which is not often the case.

In order to place this account properly upon the ledger, the following journal entry is necessary:—

Collector's Account, *Dr.* $............
                    To Debenture Account $............

    To amount levied and placed on Collector's
    roll to meet debentures at maturity by-laws.

As the debentures mature and are paid they are debited to this account, the balance at credit showing exactly what the Treasurer should have on hand for the purpose of meeting debentures when due, and also showing debenture liability of Townships.

Sinking Fund.

There is no Sinking Fund debentures in every instance being issued upon the annuity or instalment plan.

Vouchers.

To have examined every item over a period of sixteen years might have possibly occupied months instead of weeks. It was, therefore, desirable to discriminate as to what was necessary and what was unnecessary. After giving the matter due consideration, I decided that my special attention should be given more to the general vouchers, the assessment and Collector's rolls, debenture coupons, drainage accounts, etc.

Bank Account.

Although an account with the Sovereign Bank of Canada is kept, I cannot by any means commend the system at present in use and adopted by the Treasurer, it leaving the Township open and entirely at the mercy of the bank, a small pass book being his only record.

It is usually more convenient to keep the bank account in the check book instead of opening an account in the ledger, a book for this purpose being furnished by the bank. As deposits are made the amounts should be entered on the left-hand, or debit, side of the check book. As checks are drawn the amounts of the checks should be entered on the right-hand, or credit, side of the check book, and the stubs filled out, showing to whom the checks were given, the amount of each and date. By adding each side and carrying forward the amounts a balance may when necessary be struck, and at the end of the month the check book balanced, so that if anything is wrong it can be made known and remedied. All checks should be numbered, making it an easy matter at the end of each month to ascertain how many checks are still outstanding, in which case the balance shown in the bank pass book will exceed that in the check book by just the amount of check or checks that have not been received and paid at the bank. Deface or destroy the signatures of all cancelled checks, arrange them according to their numbers so that they can be referred to at any time.

In making the above suggestions it is not by any means my intention to attempt to do away with or discredit the splendid system adopted and set forth in the Government municipal cash book, but would insert that as instructed all bank transactions be fully recorded therein, using this merely as a safeguard and further check upon the accuracy of the most important branch of the Township's financial affairs.

Bills Payable.

No systematic record of promissory notes issued has been kept, which seems almost incredible, as it is evidently a very popular method used by the Township towards raising funds for various purposes, judging by the large sums borrowed by this means from time to time.

A bill book is exceedingly useful, full particulars of each bill being entered as to date when payable, where payable, etc. The total of these notes given during the month or year is then shown by an addition, and is posted to the credit of "Bills Payable Account," which I opened in the Treasurer's new ledger; when notes mature and are paid these amounts are debited "Bills Payable Account," the balance of this account, therefor, will always show what bills the Township has to meet, the total amount of the outstanding notes, as shown in the "bill book," agreeing, if correct, with the balance in the ledger.

It is not necessary to enter the renewals of notes in the cash book, as is at present the case, the interest paid being sufficient, full particulars of renewals being found in the bill book. If the amount of the note is reduced the Treasurer should charge the amount by which it is reduced, and also the interest paid. By this method it does not give the impression that more money is being borrowed than is actually the case.

Commissions.

In the matter of payments on account of commissions on drainage work, etc., it would appear that a considerable amount of laxity has prevailed; in very few instances any stated rate nor amount being mentioned in the by-laws, as a basis to work on, consequently warrants seem to have been granted at will regardless of the fact, or evidently without the knowledge, that in a great many instances these commissions had already been overpaid. This is not as it should be. The ratepayers' moneys are handled by the Council, who are in a position of trust, and they cannot be too careful in disbursing these moneys, especially when making payments to themselves.

I annex a statement citing a few instances of over-payments made, as above referred to, taking as a basis 3 per cent. on the actual expenditure on each drain or local improvement scheme

				Correct Amt.	Paid.
Edgar drain, By-law No. 341				$30 00	$63 00
East Town line drain, By-law No. 376				19 38	42 00
Walls	"	"	377	23 34	47 91
12th Con.	"	"	378	40 20	56 75
10th	"		386	24 30	42 00
8th	"		388	99 10	145 50
				$236 32	$397 16
Over-paid commissions				160 84	
				$397 16	

The by-law should distinctly state the rate or amount of the appropriation to be used for the purpose of payments to Commissioners; and the Treasurer should be instructed to refuse to honor Commissioners' warrants when such appropriation has been exhausted, unless otherwise ordered by resolution of the Council.

Drainage Accounts.

These accounts during the period under review have been very numerous and have been keenly scrutinized, taking up a very considerable time, especially when I found the manner in which these various accounts had been dealt with during the past number of years, double entry being simply ignored.

In treating with those local improvements, an account should be opened in the ledger for each work undertaken by the Township, whether it be for drainage or any other local improvement work, and all expenditure in connection with the cost of construction should be charged, and levies made, debentures sold, moneys received from other interested Townships, or otherwise credited. By this means the exact standing of any of these accounts can be ascertained at any time, and when the construction of the work has been completed, should a surplus or deficit exist, it can be dealt with in the usual way.

I attach separate statements to this report giving the standing of a number of the more important drainage schemes as at 31st December, 1905.

13th Concession Drain. By-law 242. The balance standing at the debit of this drain, as shown by the Treasurer's books, is $25.00. The Engineer estimates the cost at $1,741.20. There was raised by the issue of debentures the sum of $1,741.20, and I find the actual expenditure to be $1,766.20, leaving a balance due the Township as above.

Lapain Drain. By-law 246. A balance of $86.76 stands at the credit of this drain; the estimated cost per Engineer's report being $1,118.00, debentures for this amount being issued. I find the actual expenditure to be $1,031.24, leaving a surplus to this drainage scheme, as stated above, of $86.76.

Canaan Drain. By-law 404. The Engineer's report on this drainage work estimates the cost at $799.70 for completing same. I find the expenditure to be $821.20, and there was realized by the sale of debentures the sum of $799.70, leaving a deficit of $21.50.

10th Concession Drain. By-law 279. The Engineer's estimate of cost for the completion of this drain is $369.00, Garfield North paying as her share, being benefited to that extent, the sum of $211.00. The levy on the interested ratepayers amounted to $158.00, showing a balance due by the drain of $21.14 after allowing for the expenditure amounting to $390.14.

Snyder Drain. By-law 301. The estimated cost of this drain per Engineer's report is $644.50, apportioned as follows: Township of Colchester North $182.68, Gosfield North $382.70, and Gosfield South $79.12, and I find the expenditure to be $679.75. A yearly levy for five years was made upon the interested ratepayers of the Township; giving effect to the above charges and credits, the drain shows a debit balance of $35.25.

Foster Drain. By-law 307. The Engineer's report on this work of completion estimates the cost at $1,326.75. The expenditure I find to be $1,049.22. The sale of debentures realized $1,326.75, and to this has to be added the sum of $18.00 premium realized on the sale of same, leaving a surplus to this drain of $295.53.

Essex Improvement Drain. By-law 353. The Engineer's report on this improvement work estimates the cost at $2,322.75, apportioned as follows: Town of Essex $524.19; Township of Colchester North, $1,798.56. I find the expenditure to be, per Treasurer's books, $2,386.43, the sale of debentures realizing $1,798.56. Allowing for the above charges and credits, the standing of this drain is a debit balance of $63.68.

Walker Drain. By-law 355. The report by the Engineer on this work gives an estimate of the cost at $6,316.68. I find the expenditure to be $6,317.49, apportioned as follows: Township of Colchester North, $6,205.68; Anderdon, $77.00, and Railways, 34.00; Colchester North's share being raised by the sale of debentures for that amount. Giving effect to the above expenditures and credits, this drainage scheme shows a small shortage of 81 cents.

10th and 11th Side Road Drain. By-law 362. The cost of this improvement scheme, as shown by the Treasurer's books, is $1,296.58, and the Engineer's estimate $1,416.20. The sale of debentures realized $1,416.20, leaving at credit of this drain $119.62.

Sweet Drain. By-law 364. A balance of $43.42 stands at the credit of this drain. The Engineer estimated the cost at $513.42, and I find the expenditure to be $470.00, debentures being issued for the amount of the estimated cost, realizing par.

Walls Drain. By-law 377. This drain shows a credit of $28.65, the Engineer showing an estimated cost of $778.70, and according to the Treasurer's books an expenditure of $750.05; the amount of the estimated cost being raised by the sale of debentures for that amount.

12th Concession Drain. By-law 378. The balance standing at the credit of this drain, according to the Treasurer's books, is $26.20. I find the expenditure to be $1,313.80, and the Engineer's estimated cost $1,340.00; debentures being issued to meet this cost, leaving a balance as above.

9th Concession S. R. Drain. By-law 422. This drain shows a small debit of $24.67 according to the Treasurer's books. The Engineer's report on the work estimates the cost at $1,443.60 and I find the expenditure to be $1,468.27. There was realized by the sale of debentures $1,443.60, which, deducted from the amount expended, shows balance mentioned.

8th Concession Drain West. By-law 388. The Engineer's report on this improvement scheme estimates the cost at $3,302.90, and I find the expenditure to be $3,311.40. There was realized by the sale of debentures the sum of $3,302.90, which, deducted from cost of construction, shows a shortage of $8.50.

7th Concession and C. S. R. Drain. By-law 400. According to the Treasurer's books there is standing at the credit of this drain the sum of $98.23. The Engineer's report on this work estimates the cost at $764.00, and I find the actual cost as per expenditure to be $665.77, and there was realized by the sale of debentures, including a small premium, the sum of $535.75. To this has to be added the sum of $228.25 received from the Township of Colchester South, being benefited to that extent. Giving effect to the above charges and credits, this drain shows a surplus as above.

Boyd Drain (Repairs). By-law 401. There is a balance of $36.10 to the credit of this repairing work, as shown by the Treasurer's books. I find the actual expenditure to be $589.35 and the Engineer's estimated cost $625.45, the issue of debentures realizing this amount.

McLean Drain. By-law 406. The estimated cost of this repairing work is $5,676.50, and I find the expenditure to be $5,449.90, the Townships of Colchester South, Malden and Anderdon being assessed for $1,667.82, $219.80

and $438.40, respectively. There was raised by debentures the sum of $3,350.48, and a premium of $52.75 on the sale of same. Giving effect to the several charges and credits, there remains at the credit of this drainage scheme $279.35.

8th Concession Drain East. By-law 407. As shown by the Treasurer's books, there is a balance of $105.10 standing at the credit of this drain. The Engineer's report on this work estimates the cost at $3,805.80, apportioned as follows : Township of Colchester South, $1,165.85 ; Township of Colchester North, $2,639.95. I find the actual expenditure to be $3,736.20. The issue of debentures realized the sum of $2,639.95, and a premium of $35.50. Giving effect to the above credits and charges, there remains a surplus to this drain as above mentioned.

Boyle Drain (Improvement). By-law 413. This drainage improvement scheme shows a credit balance of $32.75, the Engineer's estimated cost being 749.60. There was raised by the issue of debentures the sum of $749.60, realizing a premium of $5.25 on their sale. I find the expenditure to be, according to the Treasurer's books, $722.10, thus showing a surplus to this drain as aforesaid.

14th Concession West Drain. By-law 416. A balance of $26.73 stands at the debit of this drain. The estimated cost is $374.45, and I find the expenditure to be $403.93. The sale of debentures realized $374.45 and a small premium of $2.75. Giving effect to the different charges and credits, I find a debit balance as shown above.

Caya Drain (Improvement). By-law 417. The Engineer's estimated cost on this work is $547.85, and I find the expenditure to be $551.68, and there was raised by the issue of debentures $347.35 and a small premium of $2.25. The Township of Colchester South paid to the Township of Colchester North $200.50, being interested to that extent. Giving effect to the above, there remains a small debit balance of $2.08.

McKersic Drain (Improvement). By-law 421. A balance of $11.95 remains at the credit of this drain. The report on this work estimates the cost at $666.00, and I find the expenditure to be $654.05. The sale of debentures realized $666.00, leaving a small surplus as above.

14th Concession and Wilton Drain. By-law 430. The cost of improvement on this drainage work was estimated per Engineer's report at $5,938.00, the Town of Essex contributing as her share the sum of $271.25. I find the expenditure to be $6,108.59, debentures issued realizing $5,666.75 and also a premium of $62.85; allowing for the above charges and credits, this drain shows a shortage of $107.74.

McKee and Shuell Creek Drain. By-law 436. The estimated cost of this drain per Engineer's report is $3,400.00, and the expenditure I find to be $3,289.20. The issue of debentures realized $1,734.51, to which has to be added a premium realized on their sale of $36.00. The Township of Anderdon contributed as her share $1,665.49, being benefited to that extent. After crediting and charging the above items, I find this drainage scheme shows a surplus of $146.80.

Bowler Drain. By-law 437. There is a small shortage of $7.25 on this work. The Engineer estimates the cost at $893.00 and the expenditure I find to be $907.25. The issue of debentures realized $893.00 and also a premium on their sale of $7.00. Giving effect to the above expenditures and credits, there is a small debit balance to this drain as shown above.

Statement showing the surpluses and deficits of the several drainage schemes above referred to as at 31st December, 1905 : —

				Surplus.	Deficit.
13th Concession Drain,	By-law	242		$.........	$ 25 00
Lapain	"	"	246	86 76	....
Canaan	"	"	404	....	21 50
Snyder	"	"	301	....	35 25
Foster	"	"	307	295 53	....
Essex Improvement	"	"	353	....	63 68
Walker	"	"	355	....	81
10th & 11th S. Road	"	"	362	119 62	....
Sweet	"	"	364	43 42	
Walls	"	"	377	28 65	....
12th Concession	"	"	378	26 20	....
9th "	"	"	422	....	24 67
8th "	"	"	388	....	8 50
7th "	"	"	400	98 23	....
Boyd (repairs)	"	"	401	36 10	
McLean	"	"	406	279 35	
8th Concession	"	"	407	105 10	....
Boyle	"	"	413	32 75	....
14th Con. West	"	"	416	....	26 73
Caya	"	"	417	....	2 08
McKersic	"	"	421	11 95	....
14th Con. & Wilton	"	"	430	....	107 74
McKee and Shuell	"	"	436	146 80	....
Bowler	"	"	437	....	7 25
10th Concession	"	"	279	....	21 14
				$1,310 46	$344 35

Canard River Scheme. This river scheme seems to have been the source of a good deal of comment among a number of the ratepayers, principally on account of the large expenditure, and partly owing to the failure in carrying out the proposed scheme, an appeal being made to Referee Rankin, which was quashed on account of not having a majority on the petition.

During the years 1900, 1901 and 1902 charges amounting to $2,565.31 are made against this scheme, and, as will be seen by the annexed statemnt, composed principally of engineers' and lawyers' fees, with the view of ascertaining the advisability of carrying out the proposed project. In the absence of any by-law being passed, which would have authorized the charging of these various items to this special work, the charges were made against the general funds, and which is now being carried as an asset of the Township, evidently with the hope that perhaps some day in the near future the proposition will be looked upon with more favour and carried through, and in this case the amount chargeable against the several ratepayers. I do not see, however, that I would be justified in including this very doubtful debt in my statement of assets.

STATEMENT OF EXPENDITURE re CANARD RIVER SCHEME.

1900.		No. Ck.	
Oct.	13.—J. S. Laird, work	151	$100 00
	" to pay assistants	135	127 50
No.	10.—J. S. Laird, work	178	100 00
	J. Bottom, assistant engineer	176	17 25
Dec.	8.—J. S. Laird, work	211	100 00
	A. C. Atkinson, trip to Amherstburg	190	2 50
1901.	D. R. Davis, Jr., assistant engineer	202	24 00
Jan.	14.—J. S. Laird	11	100 00

Feb.	9.—D. R. Davis, Jr. 22		20 80
	A. C. Atkinson, copy roll 24		6 00
	J. S. Laird, copies 23		11 35
	" 30		100 00
March	9.— " 37		101 50
	D. R. Davis, Jr. 38		25 00
April	13.—A. C. Atkinson, expenses of meeting 54		30 00
	J. S. Laird 51		300 00
May	11.—J. R. McEwan 78		14 00
	D. R. Davis, Jr. ....: 79		156 00
June	8.—J. S. Laird 97		23 25
	D. Kennedy 85		5 50
	25.—J. S. Laird 108		20 00
July	13.—A. C. Atkinson 123		28 00
Aug.	10.—Brett & Auld 165		3 00
Oct.	12.—D. R. Davis, Jr. 202		50 00
	" 203		2 40
	30.—J. S. Laird 206		5 00
Nov.	11.—Brett & Auld 239		127 16
	27.—J. S. Laird 246		8 00
Dec.	14.—A. C. Atkinson, Court of Revision 244		18 00
1902.	" extra work 316		100 00
April	12.—I. A. Coulter, two trips to Chatham 75		10 00
	J. S. Laird 70		200 00
June	14.—J. H. Rodd, law costs 113		356 14
Aug.	23.—Wilson & Co. 165		10 75
Sept.	16.—I. A. Coulter, services on D. R. Davis' acct. ...198		3 00
Nov.	8.—D. R. Davis, law costs 237		208 55
	J. H. Rodd, " 238		33 66
	A. C. Atkinson, to pay witnesses 239		17 00
			2,565 31

Consolidated Debt.

In response to a number of enquiries with reference to the present standing of this debt, I append for the information of those interested a detailed statement giving the number of payments made and also the amount due, which will be seen has been reduced to one installment of $680.40, due 1st June, 1907.

Statement of Consolidated Debt.

Date of Debentures.	Time to Run.	Amount of each Debenture.	Amount of each Debenture and Coupon.	When Payable.
1887.		$ c.	$ c.	
June 1	1 year	257 00	682 00	June 1, 1888, paid.
	2 "	270 00	682 15	" 1889 "
	3 "	283 00	681 65	" 1890 "
	4 "	298 00	682 50	" 1891 "
	5 "	312 00	681 60	" 1892 "
	6 "	329 00	683 00	" 1893 "
	7 "	344 00	681 55	" 1894 "
	8 "	362 00	682 35	" 1895 "
	9 " ，	379 00	681 25	" 1896 "
	10 "	399 00	682 30	" 1897 "
	11 "	419 00	682 35	" 1898 "
	12 "	439 00	681 40	" 1899 "
	13 "	462 00	682 45	" 1900 "
	14 "	485 00	682 35	" 1901 "
	15 "	509 00	682 10	" 1902 "
	16 "	535 00	682 65	" 1903 "
	17 "	562 00	682 90	" 1904 "
	18 "	589 00	681 80	" 1905 "
	19 "	619 00	682 35	" 1906 "
	20 "	648 00	680 40	" 1907
		8,500 00	13,643 10	

Non-Resident Rolls. I found on examination of these rolls since 1890, to be practically correct, and that same had been returned to the County Treasurer in almost every case within the statute time.

Township Books. If the council is desirous of receiving the full benefit as a result of the present audit; the new Township books supplemented by me, and the methods suggested, should be taken full advantage of and the accounts kept properly written up.

Refunds and Supplementary Levies. It is strongly advisable that the Council should go carefully over the several drainage schemes, and when surpluses or deficits appear make the necessary refunds or levies so that those open accounts can be closed and the balances not carried along from year to year.

School Accounts. These accounts were found in a satisfactory condition. Although large amounts of the municipal funds have been expended during the sixteen years under review, I found on examination, as far as time and material at hand would permit, that all monies received to be fully accounted for.

Salaries. The officials' salaries, especially of the Treasurer' are altogether inadequate for the amount of work performed, and it is better that their salaries should be increased than that any of their work should be done incompletely. Any reasonable increase would never be felt by the Township, and at the same time imbue in the minds of the ratepayers more confidence, by the increased accuracy of the accounts.

Warrants. In every case when issuing warrants where a by-law governs same, mention number of by-law. This will prove most beneficial in diminishing numerous errors in charging wrong accounts, so often done, and at the same time will be of great assistance to the Treasurer in making his entries. Some of the warrants I found not properly endorsed, but if a check was issued in payment, the endorsation was found upon the check.

Conclusion. In concluding this report, I must express my thanks to the Reeve, the Clerk, the Treasurer and others for the valuable assistance rendered me, all of whom evinced the utmost willingness in explaining and giving all necessary information in the course of my examination and audit. The Township is to be congratulated, and extremely fortunate in having such a capable and painstaking official as the present Reeve, Mr. J. A. Coulter, under whose careful methods the Township has greatly benefited.

I shall be pleased to furnish further information or to advise with the Reeve or Council in regard to any of the matters contained in this report. All of which is respectfully submitted.

A. P. Scott,

Auditor.

Toronto, 15th July, 1906.

Statement of Receipts and Expenditures to 31st December, 1905.

Receipts.

Balance from 1904	$99 92
Cash checks and warrants from Collector	14,457 76
Township of Anderson	1,587 49
County Treasurer	784 71
"	147 68

I. Miller, rent of hall	2	00
Check, Hutchinson	12	13
Return to County Treasurer, Collector's	677	26
County Treasurer, non-resident refund	257	28
" half share County grants, bridge over South Branch of Canard	270	45
County Treasurer, school grant	225	00
Sale, debentures, By-law 442 for S. S. No. 9	1,000	00
Premium on above	57	00
Accrued interest	21	04
Sale, debentures, By-law 443, Coulter S. R. Drain	1,958	25
Premium	32	75
Accrued interest	30	05
Gosfield North, part payment for work E. T. L.	51	85
Municipal loan	2,500	00
"	500	00
Sale, debentures, By-law 445, Sucker Creek Drain	1,968	30
Premium	42	70
Accrued interest	21	03
Municipal loan	1,000	00
"	500	00
"	2,000	00
Colchester South or Caya Drain	215	00
" 7th Con., Olsen Suit	290	00

30,709 65

Expenditure.

General	$348	37
Roads and bridges	3,054	53
Salaries	752	00
Legislative grant	232	90
Refund	239	13
Debentures	5,493	90
Coupons	1,972	31
Charity	180	50
Half share, work Gosfield N. E. T. L.	54	96
Deneau award	1	00
Maloche "	16	75
Schools	5,401	19
Election expenses	44	35
County Treasurer	1,990	71
Imperial Bank	1,001	94
Steers' award	13	00
Hutchinson award	11	75
Barlow "	9	00
Postage	14	98
Sheep killed	37	30
Printing	24	00
Commission	85	00
Olsen Case	129	14
Drainage	8,806	30
Balance, excess receipts over expenditure	792	64

30,709 65

ASSETS AND LIABILITIES.

Assets.

Balance on hand	$792	64
Uncollected roll of 1905	16,100	58
Drainage accounts	3,795	04
Town Hall, road machine and gravel pits	1,300	00

21,988 26

Linbilities.

Consolidated debt	$682	35
Debentures	5,243	80
Imperial Bank	5,500	00
Tile drains	191	36
Due County	1,161	84
Unpaid Township school warrants	4,288	94
Sundry unpaid warrants	612	00
Drainage accounts	1,743	66
Balance, showing amount of assets over liabilities	2,564	31
	21,988	26

The cost of this audit to the Township of Colchester North as per Mr. Scott's account was $395.90.

To His Honor the Honorable W. Mortimer Clark, Lieutenant-Governor of Ontario:

MAY IT PLEASE YOUR HONOR,—In accordance with instructions from the Provincial Government Auditor, I have made an examination of the books and accounts of the Village of Iroquois, from January 1st, 1896, to December 31st, 1905, and herewith submit the following statements:

(1) Abstract statements of receipts and disbursements for the years 1896 to 1904, inclusive.

(2) Abstract and detailed statements of every branch of the receipts and disbursements of the municipality for 1905.

(3) Abstract and detailed statements of the receipts and disbursements of the Treasurer for the two months ending February 28th, 1906, when the former Treasurer gave up office. This statement shows a balance of $89.68 due the late Treasurer, which shoud be repaid to him.

(4) Statement in detail of the debenture debt of the Village.

(5) Statement of the amount required each year to retire maturing debentures and pay interest on debentures.

(6) Approximate statement of amount expended on capital account on the waterworks, electric light plant and power house, from 1899 to 1905.

The books of the Treasurers of the High and Public School Boards were examined as well as those of the Light and Water Commission and found well and correctly kept. The municipal cash book was fairly well kept, but no ledger was kept by the Treasurer. This omission will not occur again, as the present Treasurer has promised to keep one.

There was no bank account until 1904, when one was opened with the local branch of the Molsons Bank.

I find that it has been the custom to purchase supplies from merchants who were, at the time of the purchase, members of the Village Council. While this may be necessary at times in a small village where sources of suppy are limited, it has been done to a much larger extent than there was any necessity for and should be carefully avoided in future.

No proper facilities are afforded for the safe-keeping of the Village documents and records. I would recommend that steps be taken to provide such at once.

It was desired by a number of the ratepayers that a statement be given of the cost of the Waterworks and Electric Light System under the different departments. This has been done, as far as was possible where no special attention was given, at the time, to keeping the accounts separate and where much of the work and plant were common to both departments.

I desire to thank the Clerk for his valuable assistance in the way of explanations and looking up documents, and all the officials with whom I came in contact for their uniform courtesy.

From the Village Solicitor, who was associated with me, I received assistance of the most useful kind. His care and attention to searching out and arranging vouchers and documents very materially shortened my work.

In conclusion I would suggest that no municipality can expect to gain anything by an economy in the matter of officials' salaries. To pay a treasurer ten dollars a year is certainly not an adequate remuneration.

All of which is respectfully submitted.

THOS. D. MINNES,
Special Auditor.

KINGSTON, Oct. 11th, 1906.

STATEMENT OF AMOUNT REQUIRED EACH YEAR TO MEET DEBENTURE AND INTEREST PAYMENTS.

Year	Amount	Year	Amount
1906	$6,996 68	1920	4,729 85
1907	6,508 43	1921	4,729 85
1908	6,621 44	1922	4,729 85
1909	6,597 44	1923	4,729 85
1910	6,573 44	1924	3,846 86
1911	6,549 44	1925	2,255 37
1912	6,525 44	1926	2,255 37
1913	6,501 44	1927	2,255 37
1914	5,769 76	1928	2,255 37
1915	5,745 76	1929	2,255 37
1916	5,721 76	1930	2,255 37
1917	5,097 76	1931	1,098 77
1918	5,097 76	1932	1,098 77
1919	5,097 76		

DEBENTURE DEBT OF THE VILLAGE OF IROQUOIS ON DECEMBER 31ST, 1905.

High School Building, By-law 194.

Matures 1906	375 00

High School Equipment, By-law 205.

Matures 1906	$166 66	
" 1907	166 66	
		332 32

Fire Appliances, etc., By-law 253.

Matures 1906	308 36

Intake Pipe, By-law 289.

Matures 1906....	$212 46	Matures 1914....	290 76	
" 1907....	220 96	" 1915....	302 39	
" 1808....	229 79	" 1916....	314 49	
" 1909....	238 99	" 1917....	327 07	
" 1910 ...	248 55	" 1918....	340 15	
" 1911...		" 1919....	353 76	
" 1912...	268 83			3,886 27
" 1913....	279 58			

Granolithic Walks, By-law 320.

Matures 1906....	$537 79	Matures 1910....	$629 13	
" 1907....	559 30	" 1911....	654 32	
" 1908....	581 66	" 1912....	680 48	
" 1909....	604 94			4,247 62

Waterworks Extension, By-law 306.

Matures	1906....	$433 86		Matures	1919....	$722 41
"	1907:....	451 21		"	1920....	751 31
"	1908....	469 26		"	1921....	781 36
"	1909....	488 03		"	1922....	812 63
"	1910....	507 55		"	1923....	845 12
	1911....	527 85		"	1924....	878 93
"	1912....	548 97		"	1925....	914 08
"	1913....	570 93		"	1926....	950 65
"	1914....	593 76		"	1927....	988 67
"	1915....	617 52		"	1928....	1,028 22
"	1916....	642 22		"	1929....	1,069 35
"	1917....	667 90		"	1930....	1,112 13
"	1918....	694 62				18,068 54

Electric Light, $6,000 Issue, By-law 310.

Matures	1906....	$60 00		Matures	1912....	$600 00
"	1907....	300 00		"	1913....	600 00
"	1908....	600 00		"	1914....	600 00
"	1909....	600 00		"	1915....	600 00
"	1910....	600 00		"	1916....	600 00
	1911....	600 00				5,760 00

Electric Light, By-law 326.

Matures	1906....	$381 08		Matures	1920....	$659 90
"	1907....	396 32		"	1921....	686 29
"	1908....	412 17		"	1922....	713 74
"	1909....	428 66		"	1923....	742 29
"	1910....	445 80		"	1924....	771 98
	1911....	463 63		"	1925....	802 86
"	1912....	482 18		"	1926....	834 98
"	1913....	501 46		"	1927....	868 37
	1914....	521 52		"	1928....	903 11
"	1915....	542 39		"	1929....	934 24
"	1916....	564 08		"	1930....	976 80
"	1917....	586 64		"	1931....	1,015 87
"	1918....	610 11		"	1932....	1,056 51
"	1919....	634 51				17,942 49

Shoe Factory, By-law 330.

Matures	1906....	$435 37		Matures	1916....	$645 20
"	1907....	453 31		"	1917....	671 00
"	1908....	471 44		"	1918....	697 80
"	1909....	490 30		"	1919....	725 70
	1910....	509 91		"	1920....	754 74
"	1911....	530 31			1921....	784 99
"	1912....	551 52		"	1922....	816 35
	1913....	573 58		"	1923....	849 04
"	1914....	596 52				11,177 90
"	1915....	620 32				

Consolidation of Debt, By-law 316.

Matures	1906....	$366 42		Matures	1916....	$569 04
"	1907....	382 91		"	1917....	594 64
"	1908....	400 14		"	1918....	621 39
"	1909....	418 14		"	1919....	649 36
"	1910....	436 96		"	1920....	678 58
	1911....	456 62			1921....	706 12
"	1912....	477 17		"	1922....	741 03
"	1913....	498 64		"	1923....	774 38
"	1914....	521 08		"	1924....	809 22
"	1915....	544 53				10,649 37

18 M.A.

Granolithic Walks, By-law 348.

Matures 1906....	$323 18	Matures 1916....	$501 89	
" 1907....	337 73	" 1917....	524 48	
" 1908....	352 93	" 1918....	548 08	
" 1909....	368 81	" 1919....	572 75	
" 1910....	385 40	" 1920....	598 52	
" 1911....	402 75	" 1921....	625 46	
" 1912....	420 87	" 1922....	653 60	
" 1913....	439 81	" 1923....	683 01	
" 1914....	459 60	" 1924....	713 75	
" 1915....	480 28			9,392 90

$82,141 77

Expenditure on Water and Light Plant.

Arbitration	$3,234 70
Waterworks	22,824 14
Power house and plant	9,041 03
Electric plant	9,099 92
	44,199 79

Abstract Statement of the Receipts and Disbursements of the Village of Iroquois for the Years from 1896 to 1904 Inclusive.

1896.

Receipts.

Balance, December 31st, 1895	$1,642 95	
Taxes, 1895	617 92	
Taxes, 1896	4,691 60	
Non-resident taxes	4 35	
Rents	282 00	
Fines	7 00	
Streets	26 10	
License fund	324 59	
Government school grant	138 59	
Sale of old hose	2 50	
Loan from High School Board	512 50	
		8,249 51

Disbursements.

High school	$1,620 00	
Public school	1,560 22	
Roads, sewers, etc.	1,175 88	
Public Library	150 00	
Note and interest	525 00	
County rate	135 83	
Salaries	203 76	
Fire protection	192 55	
Printing, postage, etc.	74 16	
Town hall	103 85	
Charity	108 30	
Legal expenses	13 53	
Water power rent	70 00	
Miscellaneous	14 50	
Balance	2,301 93	
		8,249 51

18a M. A.

1897.

Receipts.

Balance, December 31st, 1896	$2,301 93	
Taxes	5,038 26	
Streets	6 55	
Rents	262 00	
Fines	3 00	
Government school grant	132 00	
License fund	320 11	
		8,063 85

Disbursements.

Debentures	$1,235 41	
Fire protection	231 05	
County rate	492 00	
Salaries	202 64	
Miscellaneous	77 09	
Streets	1,175 38	
Charity	101 00	
Town hall	180 11	
Printing, etc.	101 64	
Public Library	150 00	
Public school	1,477 46	
High school	614 00	
Legal expenses	53 71	
Water power rent	35 00	
Balance	1,937 36	
		8,063 85

1898.

Receipts.

Balance, December 31st, 1897	$1,937 36	
Taxes	6,489 72	
Fines	76 00	
Rents	173 00	
License fund	332 84	
Government school grant	133 00	
Streets	13 24	
Loan	700 00	
		9,855 16

Disbursements.

Streets	$1,553 82	
Charity	71 25	
Town hall	48 78	
Public Library	150 00	
Debentures	1,144 58	
County rate	403 27	
Water power rent	35 00	
Fire protection	89 20	
Legal expenses	142 20	
Miscellaneous	33 09	
Salaries	296 80	
Printing, etc.	50 53	
Public School	1,633 00	
High School	1,452 00	
Loan and interest	708 10	
Balance	2,043 54	
		9,855 16

1899.

Receipts.

Balance, December 31st, 1898	$2,043 54	
Taxes	6,459 82	
School grant	144 00	
License fund	285 89	
Fines	1 00	
Rents	197 50	
Bills payable	3,000 00	
Debentures	5,000 00	
		17,131 75

Disbursements.

Salaries	$532 74	
Printing	94 92	
Interest	433 68	
Law costs and damages	1,082 45	
Streets	1,123 77	
Charity	99 40	
Schools	3,026 50	
Debentures	750 36	
Fire protection	108 10	
County rate	554 90	
Town Hall	21 10	
Intake pipe	3,087 94	
Bills payable	3,000 00	
Public Library	150 00	
Water works	698 42	
Vaccine points	76 60	
Miscellaneous	147 52	
Balance	2,143 35	
		17,131 75

1900.

Receipts.

Balance, December 31st, 1899	$2,143 40	
Taxes	4,848 45	
School grant	157 00	
License fund	314 20	
Fines	12 00	
Rents	98 00	
Bills payable	3,000 00	
		10,573 05

Disbursements.

Charity	$105 00	
Schools	3,180 60	
Miscellaneous	281 46	
Salaries	130 35	
Damages	70 52	
Law costs	2,654 70	
Waterworks Arbitration	170 94	
County rate	201 96	
Suction pipe	199 72	
Streets and sewers	1,490 17	
Town Hall	37 10	
Printing, etc.	68 10	
Interest	529 63	
Debentures	928 70	
Fire protection	200 75	
Balance	323 35	
		10,573 05

1901.

Receipts.

Balance, December 31st, 1900	$323 35	
Taxes and water rates	5,711 80	
License fund .:..	311 80	
Sale of tile	9 80	
Rents	134 75	
Bills payable .:..	6,000 00	
Gilbert Bros.	50 00	
School grant	148 00	
Witness' fees, A. McInnes	6 00	
Debentures sold	19,865 20	
		32,560 70
Balance due Treasurer		922 42
		$33,483 12

Disbursements.

Salaries	$234 00	
County rate	330 12	
Debentures	1,302 97	
Printing, etc.	234 26	
Interest	1,219 61	
Fire protection	172 23	
Streets and sewers	1,316 19	
Waterworks and Arbitration	19,373 88	
Waterworks	1,447 40	
Power house	2,425 76	
Charity	109 25	
Town Hall	51 35	
Schools	2,939 80	
Bills payable	2,000 00	
Miscellaneous	326 30	
		33,483 12

1902.

Receipts.

Taxes and water rates	$9,314 54	
Rents	210 00	
License fund	297 34	
School grant	138 00	
Sale of plank	8 00	
Bills payable	29,203 65	
Debentures sold	6,006 66	
		45,178 19

Disbursements.

Balance due Treasurer, 1901	$922 42	
Streets and sewers	798 52	
Printing, etc.	121 88	
Salaries	270 60	
Schools	1,978 90	
Charity	116 00	
Bills payable	17,101 60	
Debentures	1,455 72	
Waterworks	174 38	
Interest	2,157 09	
Law costs	484 45	
Fire protection	64 35	
Power House	12,101 65	
Town Hall	204 26	
Granolithic walks	5,302 43	
Miscellaneous '...	417 70	
County rate	144 65	
Balance	1,360 59	
		45,178 19

1903

Receipts.

Balance, December 31st, 1902	$1,360 59	
Taxes and water rates	8,389 96	
School grant	128 00	
License fund	314 67	
Rents	138 00	
Debentures sold	24,490 00	
Bills payable	42,555 05	
Dr. Stephenson, for walk	82 19	
J. M. Cook, for building	75 00	
C. G. Electric Co., deposit	1,000 00	
Lumber sold	4 00	
		78,537 46

Disbursements.

Salaries	$261 45	
Printing, etc.	279 91	
Interest	3,292 98	
Law costs	6 45	
Streets and sewers	1,674 52	
Charity	111 61	
Schools	3,195 12	
Debentures	2,246 75	
Fire protection	447 91	
County rate	707 42	
Bills payable	54,409 70	
Town Hall	49 21	
Miscellaneous	1,752 53	
Water, heat and light	7,824 40	
Stones	117 75	
Balance	2,659 75	
		78,537 46

1904.

Receipts.

Balance, December 31st, 1903	$2,659 75	
Taxes	7,530 31	
School grant	119 00	
Licenses	280 00	
Rents	220 00	
Debentures sold	11,642 30	
Bills payable	34,614 00	
Water and Light Commission	1,472 67	
Tile sold	4 10	
Refund	10 00	
Balance due Treasurer	1,068 53	
		59,620 66

Disbursements.

Salaries	$234 66	
Printing, etc.	224 03	
Interest	3,324 79	
Law costs	20 50	
Streets and sewers	1,628 72	
Charity	160 33	
Schools	3,483 64	
Debentures	3,539 43	
Bills payable	24,450 00	
Town Hall	55 95	
Miscellaneous	619 33	
Water and Light Commission	1,392 57	
Excelsior Shoe Co.	12,000 00	
Granolithic walks	8,486 71	
		59,620 66

Received from Collector, arrears of taxes		$1,004 10
" licenses		140 00
" rents		161 50
" debentures:		
Consolidating debt	$11,000 00	
Interest on same	61 00	
		11,061 00
Granolithic sidewalks	$9,702 17	
Premium on same	237 43	
		9,939 60
Received from loans:		
Molsons Bank	$5,800 00	
Dis. on same	59 90	
		5,749 10
Molsons Bank	$5,800 00	
Dis. on same	50 90	
		5,749 10
Molsons Bank	$500 00	
Dis. on same	6 50	
		493 50
Molsons Bank	$800 00	
Dis. on same	3 65	
		796 35
Received from Collector, taxes		8,748 85
" H. A. Brouse, fines		2 00
" for school purposes		122 00
" from miscellaneous:		
Stone and wood	$82 00	
Rebate on $800.00 loan	30	
" $500.00 "	11 90	
		94 20
Received from water and light		1,127 47
" Collector, dog taxes		13 00
		45,201 77

ABSTRACT STATEMENT OF EXPENDITURE OF THE VILLAGE OF IROQUOIS FOR THE YEAR 1905.

Balance due treasurer from audit of 1904	$1,068 53	
Paid cash for salaries and allowances	365 41	
" printing, postage and advertising	256 24	
" interest	4,421 17	
" law costs	10 00	
" roads and bridges	1,095 95	
" charity	76 90	
" school purposes	3,420 80	
" debentures and coupons	3,479 31	
" fire protection	38 50	
" county rates	1,096 15	
" loans current	30,985 15	
" town hall	59 94	
" miscellaneous	218 65	
" sewers	77 15	
" water and light	237 85	
		$46,907 70
Total receipts	$45,201 77	
Balance due treasurer	1,705 93	
		$46,907 70
Total expenditures		$46,907 70

DETAILED STATEMENT OF EXPENDITURES.

Salaries and allowances.

W. J. Forward, salary as collector for 1904	$25 00
Alton Locke, salary as constable	8 00
G. H. Dany, salary as poll clerk	2 00
Alton Locke, opening and cleaning hall	4 68
A. J. Ross, salary as auditor	6 00
G. H. Parlow, salary as auditor	6 00
G. S. Hanes, Dep. R O., Dom. R. S. Co. by-law	4 00
T. Coulter, poll clerk " "	2 00
P. S. Johnston, " "	2 00
Jas. Flanagan, Dep. R. O.	6 00
S. Moore, constable "	1 00
C. E. Cameron, Court of Revision	8 00
Jas. Flanagan, Court of Revision, selecting jurors	10 88
W. A. Coons, Court of Revision, and salary as assessor	42 50
Alton Locke, constable......:	1 50
Jas. McDonald, "	1 50
E. Lewis, " ....:..	1 50
I. Hilliard, legal services	133 85
Jas. Flanagan, salary as clerk	60 00
C. E. Cameron, selecting jurors	4 00
Alton Locke, salary	10 00
W. J. Forward, salary as collector for 1905	25 00

$365 41

Printing, Postage and Advertising.

R. S. Pelton, printing	$49 59
Municipal World, supplies	7 55
W. J. Forward, Collector's Guide	50
Municipal World	5 00
R. S. Pelton, printing	22 46
" "	126 34
" "	24 88
Jas. Flanagan, *Municipal World*, stationery	8 33
R. S. Pelton, printing	4 13
Jas. Flanagan, clerk's postage	7 00

$256 24

Interest.

Mrs. McGinn, interest on note.............................			$50 00
Guy Brouse,	"	....	71 01
Miss E. Stirling,	"	....	53 81
Est. H. J. McGinn,	"	....	91 28
John Larmour,	"	....	50 00
C. E. Cameron,	"	....	189 30
W. J. Marsh,	"	....	84 15
Mary Robertson,	"	deb. No. 6....................	163 62
Molson's Bank,	"	note..........................	50 90
"	"		50 90
"			50 90
			3 65
	"	overdraft	11 35
	"	"	4 50
		"	6 35
	"	note	6 50
	"	deb. No. 5	739 43
"	"	deb. No. 2	463 88
Mrs. Guy Brouse,	"	deb. No. 4	77 60
Archie Stirling,	"	note..........................	99 72
Molson's Bank,	"	deb. No. 3	190 58
"	"	" 11	30 10
"	"	" 1	436 59
"	"	" 3	732 35
	"	" . 19	37 50
	"	" 18	25 00
	"	" 1	495 00
	"	" 4 (Est. A. Patton)........	155 20

$4,421 17

Law Costs.

John Harkness, attg. Court of Appeal	$8 00
G. H. Dany, legal advice Bouck case	2 00
	$10 00

Roads and Bridges.

M. McNally, sewer tile	$15 23
L. Cameron, lumber	15 75
Frank Rolland, work at crusher	12 30
Chas. Hawley, labor and teaming	5 98
Wm. Wallace, labor	1 13
Alva Serviss, labor and teaming	1 50
Geo. Serviss, labor at snow	63
Thos. Serviss, "	63
Ira McGee, "	63
Ed. Lewis, labor	14 62
Wm. Wallace, labor	1 25
Ed. McRobie, labor	4 51
W. A. Coons, ploughing snow	10 00
L. N. Tanney, work at crusher	19 45
Hare & McInnis, account	67 39
W. A. Coons, ploughing snow	17 50
Ed. McRobie, "	6 50
Elgin Serviss, labor at snow	1 25
Frank Rolland, "	1 25
Ed. Lewis, roadwork	21 25
Chas. Hawley, "	5 88
Geo. Raney, "	1 25
W. A. Munroe, taking levels	55 00
Ed. Lewis, labor	13 25
Chas. Hawley, "	3 87
Wm. Wallace, "	2 13
Jesse Lewis, "	1 25
Fred. Stone, "	1 50
Tim. Coloren, "	1 25
Ed. Lewis, "	18 75
Wm. Wallace, "	3 13
Jno. McRobie, "	3 00
Jesse Lewis, "	2 38
Wm. Anderson, labor	2 38
Chas. Hawley, labor and teaming	16 33
Robt. Wright, use of field winter road 1904-1905	6 00
Harvey Lackerbie, blacksmith account	4 05
Ed. Lewis, labor	12 50
Chas. Hawley, "	7 13
Wm. Wallace, "	3 75
Ed. Lewis, "	27 13
Chas. Hawley, "	23 38
Ed. Lewis, "	18 13
Chas. Hawley, "	15 88
H. Serviss, "	5 63
H. Coons, "	75
Jas. Stamp, "	63
E. Rolland, "	75
John English, "	75
John Armstrong, "	13
Frank Rolland, "	1 80
Sam. Rolland, "	1 88
Est. A. Patton, "	28 09
Jas. Stamp, "	1 25
Hiram Serviss, "	1 25
Wm. McGee, "	1 25
Chas. Hawley, "	1 88
Archie Currie, blacksmith account	2 65
Ed. Lewis, labor	14 38
Chas. Hawley, "	5 38
Ed. Lewis, "	6 88

T. A. Thompson, "	13 17	
Ross Bros., supplies	4 27	
Hare & McInnis, supplies	54 63	
S. Landon, supplies	1 70	
Ed. Lewis, labor	7 50	
Chas. Hawley, labor	2 88	
L. Cameron, lumber	45 41	
Walter Weston, stone	3 00	
W. J. Forward, stone	2 00	
W. A. Coons, work at snow	3 00	
Dolan & Son	414 71	
		$1,095 95

Charity.

Hotel Dieu, Mrs. J. Shaver	$10 00	
Mrs. J. Hess, for M. Briggs	6 00	
C. E. Cameron, expenses to Cornwall *re* Briggs	2 75	
Alton, Locke, tramps	4 40	
Mrs. Elgin McKnight, for N. Tanguay	6 00	
Alton Locke, tramps	50	
" "	75	
" "	25	
Harkness & Milligan *re* Briggs	25 00	
St. Joseph's Home	15 00	
Mrs. Elgin Knight, for charity	2 25	
Alton Locke, tramps	50	
Mrs. J. Shaver, charity	3 50	
		$76 90

Debentures and Coupons.

Mary Robertson, deb. No. 6................................	$204 29	
Molson's Bank, " 5................................	417 17	
Molson's Bank, " 2................................	419 11	
Mrs. Guy Brouse, " 4................................	20 00	
Molson's Bank, " 3................................	517 10	
" " 11................................	293 66	
" 1................................	309 27	
3................................	366 42	
" 19................................	375 00	
18................................	166 66	
1................................	350 63	
" 4 (Est. of A. Patton)................	40 00	
		$3,479 31

School Purposes.

E. McNulty, High School, balance of 1903 account...............	$312 44	
" " account of 1904	600 00	
T. Coulter, Public School, account of 1904	450 00	
" " "	84 00	
" " "	252 36	
" " Government grant	122 00	
E. McNulty, High School	400 00	
" "	300 00	
T. Coulter, Public School	750 00	
" "	150 00	
		$3,420 80

Fire Protection.

W. J. Fisher, A. B. Carman fire	$11 00	
" Geo. Raney fire	20 75	
" inspecting underwriters	6 00	
Jas. McNairn, hydrants	75	
		$38 50

County Rates.

Geo. Stacey, Co. Treasurer	$200 00	
" " for 1903 and 1904	896 15	
		$1,096 15

Loans, Current.

Guy Brouse, note...	$1,400 00	
Miss E. Stirling, "	1,000 00	
Est. H. J. McGinn, " ....:.................	2,688 00	
John Larmour, "	1,000 00	
C. E. Cameron, "	2,000 00	
Mrs. Wm. Bannon, "	860 00	
W. J. Marsh, "	2,000 00	
Molsons Bank, "	5,749 10	
" "	5,749 10	
" "	5,749 10	
" "	796 35	
Archie Stirling, "	200 00	
Molsons Bank, "	493 50	
Archie Stirling, "	1,300 00	
		$30,985 15

Town Hall.

Alton Locke, opening and cleaning hall	$7 50	
Geo. Raney, cleaning hall	1 50	
Alton Locke, opening hall	3 25	
" "	2 00	
" "	2 00	
" "	3 50	
" "	1 00	
" "	1 00	
" "	4 00	
A. J. Osborne, repairing hall	2 00	
Alton Locke, opening hall	2 00	
" "	4 00	
J. W. Brouse, wood	4 00	
T. A. Thompson, coal	16 69	
Alton Locke, opening hall	4 50	
" "	1 00	
		$59 94

Miscellaneous.

A. J. Osborne, carpenter work	$ 2 65	
Jas. Shannon, polling booth	4 00	
Rev. J. M. McAllister, public library	150 00	
Mrs. C. E. Harkness, supplies	95	
T. E. A. Stanley, type writing	3 00	
Canadian Rubber Co., supplies	2 00	
Jas. W. Tindale, telephone	6 10	
Wm. Henderson, polling booth	3 00	
Ira W. Beckstead, polling booth	4 00	
Jas. W. Tindale, telephone	1 15	
Bank exchange on debentures	1 25	
Express	2 40	
Canadian Express	55	
J. Williams, water power	35 00	
J. Flanagan, registering by-law	2 60	
		$218 65

Sewer Account.

Ed. Lewis,	labor	....	$22 00
Chas. Hawley,	"	....	17 63
E. Rolland,	"	....	8 63
Elijah Serviss,	"	....	7 63
T. Caloren,	"	....	9 25
E. McRobie,	"	....	4 38
L. Mattice,	"	....	5 63
M. Redmond,	"	....	2 00

$77 15

Water and Light.

Water and Light Commissioners $228 85
" " " 9 00

$237 85

$46,907 70

Current Assets.

Arrears of taxes 1900	....	$ 6 30
" 1901	....	5 40
" 1902	....	21 66
1903	....	21 56
.. 1904	....	161 97
" 1905	....	1,944 84
Arrears of dog taxes 1905	....	39 00
Judgment Iroquois vs. P. Keefe	....	278 40

$2,479 13

Balance 3,573 77

$6,052 90

Current Liabilities.

Balance due Village Treasurer	....	$1,705 93
County rate for 1905	....	508 41
Due Public School Treasurer	....	790 90
Due High School Treasurer	....	1,647 54
Molsons Bank, overdraft	....	1,400 12

$6,052 90

ASSETS AND LIABILITIES OF THE VILLAGE OF IROQUOIS ON DECEMBER 31ST, 1905.

Assets.

Boiler, engine and crusher	....	$500 00
Hose reel and wagon	....	75 00
Fire hose and Babcock	....	500 00
Town hall and site	....	5,000 00
Town scales	....	125 00
Waterworks and electric light system	....	50,000 00
Public school and site	....	5,000 00
High school and site	....	10,000 00
Special rate on granolithic walks	....	5,998 39
Shoe factory and site	....	3,000 00
Town piano	....	150 00

$80,348 39

Balance 5,376 15

$85,715 54

Liabilities.

Balance of current liabilities	....	$3,573 77
Debentures—		
High school building	....	375 00
High school equipment	....	333 32
Fire appliances, etc.	....	308 36
Intake pipe	....	3,886 27

Waterworks	18,068 54
Electric light	5,760 00
Granolithic walks	4,247 62
Water and light	17,942 49
Shoe factory	11,177 90
Consolidation of debt	10,649 37
Granolithic walks	9,392 90

$85,715 54

ABSTRACT STATEMENT OF RECEIPTS OF THE VILLAGE OF IROQUOIS FROM 1ST JANY., 1906.
TO 28TH FEBY., 1906.

Received from arrears of taxes	$1,207 28
" dog taxes	19 00
" licenses	163 34
" rents	31 00
" loans, A. Stirling note	1,000 00

$2,420 62

ABSTRACT STATEMENT OF EXPENDITURES FOR THE VILLAGE OF IROQUOIS FROM 1ST JANY.,
1906, TO 28TH FEBY., 1906.

Balance due Treasurer from audit of 1905	$1,705 93
Paid cash for printing, postage and allowances	27 97
" roads and bridges	10 20
" charity	15 00
" town hall	9 00
" Miscellaneous	222 65

$1,990 75

Balance due corporation	$429 87
Balance in bank	519 55

Balance due Treasurer	$89 68

DETAILED STATEMENT OF EXPENDITURES.

Printing, Postage and Allowances.

Municipal World, supplies	$ 5 32
W. J. Forward, postage and exchange	90
R. S. Pelton, printing account	20 85
Jas. Flanagan, express account	90

$27 97

Roads and Bridges.

P. A. Wallace, blacksmithing account	$ 5 20
Edmund Lewis, labor	5 00

$10 20

Charity.

St. Joseph's Home	$15 00

School Purposes.

I. Coulter, public school	$150 00

Town Hall

Alton Locke, opening hall nine times	$ 9 00

Miscellaneous.

Eugene Serviss, rebate on dog tax	$ 1 00
T. J. Johnston, inspecting scales	1 65
J. D. Williams, water rent	70 00
J. M. McAllister, public library	150 00

$222 65

High School.
Receipts.

Balance as per audit from 1904	$1,100 42	
From municipality of Iroquois, 1903	312 44	
" " " 1904	600 00	
Government maintenance cheque	735 18	
Leeds and Grenville for year ending 30th June, 1905	281 26	
Breakages in laboratory	2 24	
Cheque, Arthur Brown, Deptl. Exam's	31 90	
From municipality of Iroquois, 1904	300 00	
" " " 1904	400 00	
From county grant	2,239 00	
		$6,002 44

Expenditures.

T. E. A. Stanley, salary	$1,060 00	
Jas. McGuire, "	810 00	
Nellie Rose, "	645 00	
W. G. Anderson, . "	900 00	
Ed. McNulty, " secretary	20 00	
A. W. Jackson, " caretaker	200 00	
Ed. McNulty, express account	2 80	
E. Mills, repairs to furnace	55 40	
Hiram ·Serviss, labor	6 86	
Wm. Briggs Co., supplies	18 45	
C. W. Robson, labor	17 25	
Hare & McInnis, supplies	8 65	
Ed. McNulty, cash account	4 09	
Morang & Co., books	3 00	
H. A. Brouse, coal	18 00	
T. Coulter, supplies	6 45	
B. F. Smith, supplies	42 00	
A. H. Dixon, gravel	4 00	
U. McAllister, salary	50 00	
Arthur Brown, I. P. S.	34 50	
T. E. A. Stanley, ent. exams	37 05	
Water and light	66 67	
Wm. Crobar, labor	15 00	
Education Pub. Co., supplies	7 20	
A. F. Sherman, postage	5 00	
Ross Bros., supplies	39 15	
" coal account	80 30	
" coal and supplies	40 60	
R. S. Pelton, printing	50 00	
A. W. Jackson, wood	16 00	
W. A. Bowen, Ent. and Deptl. Exams.	43 90	
J. W. Armstrong, painting	349 75	
T. A. Thompson, coal, lumber and supplies	186 98	
J. W. Tindale, supplies	15 70	
A. J. Osborne, labor	1 60	
Steinburger, Hendry & Co., supplies	68 56	
To balance	1,073 00	
		$6,002 44

Total receipts	$6,002 44	
Total expenditures	....	$4,929 44
Balance in Treasurer's hands	....	1,073 00
	$6,002 44	$6,002 44

Public School.
Receipts.

Balance as per audit of 1904	$140 02	
From municipality of Iroquois	450 00	
" "	336 66	
From Legislative grant	122 00	
From assessment No. 3, 1905	173 53	
From assessment, Iroquois	750 00	
		$1,972 21

Expenditures.

W. A. Bowen, salary	$525 00	
Nancy Thompson, "	181 18	
Sophia Donaldson, "	285 00	
Jennie Thompson, "	160 05	
Ethel Armstrong, "	160 05	
A. M. Harkness, "	110 89	
J. L. Harkness, "	118 81	
Maggie Munroe, "	108 81	
Sam. Moore, salary, caretaker	85 00	
Ross Bros., accounts	55 43	
T. A. Thompson, account for coal	69 34	
Can. Pub. Co., account	2 88	
Harry Tisdale, labor	75	
A. J. Osborne, account	21 85	
Wm. Crobar, account	4 12	
Geo. Stewart, labor	1 75	
Jas. Tindale, account	1 80	
C. E. Keeler, account	13 33	
J. W. Armstrong, painting	55 50	
Steinburger, Hendry & Co., account for blackboards	12 24	
H. A. Brouse, account for coal	33 70	
Globe Pub. Co., account	1 25	
Thos. Coulter, account, supplies	16 82	
Hare & McInnis, account, supplies	25 66	
Water rent	10 00	
		$2,061 21
Total receipts	$1,972 21	
Total expenditures	....	$2,061 21
Balance due Treasurer	89 00	
	$2,061 21	$2,061 21

PUBLIC LIBRARY.

Receipts.

Balance on hand as per audit of 1904	$ 14 95	
Proceeds oyster supper	32 10	
Municipal grant	150 00	
Department of Education	23 63	
Citizens' subscriptions	39 60	
Further subscriptions	13 00	
		$273 28

Expenditures.

law.

Paid note Molsons Bank	$ 25 00	
" I. B. Beckstead, rent	132 50	
" Jas. Flanagan, insurance	8 75	
" *Gazette* Pub. Co. to 31st Dec., 1915	3 38	
" *Success*	1 00	
" *Daily Globe*, 3 mos.	1 00	
" R. S. Pelton, printing bills	1 50	
" Secretary for postage	1 03	
" note Molsons Bank	45 00	
" interest on note	1 30	
To balance	52 82	
		$273 28
Total receipts	$273 28	
Total expenditures	....	220 46
Balance in Treasurer's hands	....	52 82
	$273 28	$273 28

General Statement of Water, Light and Power Commissioners.

Receipts for Water and Light.

Water rent	$1,130 05	
Electric light	1,682 77	
Lamp sold	35	
Barrel sold	60	
Tape sold	40	
		$2,814 17

Payments for Running Expenses and Repairs.

Rufus Barton, salary	$491 67
Geo. McInnis, "	360 00
Allan McInnis, salary for 1904	40 00
Allan McInnis, postage for 1904	3 06
Canadian General Electric Co., account	269 96
Alva Serviss, express and freight	13 31
J. W. Tindale, telephone account	24 95
Inland Revenue, Deptl. Registration	10 00
P. A. Wallace, blacksmith account	7 65
Frank Rolland, labor	1 00
E. Lewis, "	24 76
Chas. Hawley, "	21 15
Geo. W. Serviss, "	6 40
A. T. McLatchie, repairs	55 25
T. A. Thompson, account	215 67
M. E. Barkley, labor	3 00
R. Barton, sale leather	55
T. J. Johnston, horse hire	3 25
R. S. Pelton, printing account	8 50
G. A. Bouck, blacksmith account	3 85
C. Robson, account	25 00
C. E. Cameron, expenses to Ottawa	11 20
" postage and telegrams	3 65
W. A. Coulter, expenses to Ottawa	8 00
Hamilton Engine Packing Co., account	20 10
Canada Rubber Co., packing	2 70
Queen City Oil Co., account	31 36
Wm. McGee, labor	1 25
S. Frayne, account	18 40

	$1,686 70	
Paid to Village Treasurer	1,127 47	
	$2,814 17	$2,814 17

Receipts and Expenditures for Capital Account.

Receipts.

Received from Village Treasurer	$237 85

Payments.

L. N. Tanney, account	$40 00
C. Robson, account	25 00
W. G. Anderson, for wire	15 00
Canadian Gen. Electric Co., account	8 44
" " "	9 60
Canada Foundry Co., account	4 50
R. H. Buchanan Co., account	25 95
E. Lewis, labor	21 25
C. Hawley, labor	16 00
C. E. Keeler, account	4 88
S. Landon, account	58 23
Canadian Gen. Electric Co., account	9 00

	$237 85	$237 85

DETAILED ACCOUNT OF WATER RENT COLLECTED DURING THE YEAR 1905.

W. N. Abbott	$16 50
Mrs. W. Bannon	4 50
M. E. Barkley	9 50
Mrs. A. Beach	6 75
M. F. Beach	9 00
Jas. Collison	7 69
W. A. Bowen	11 00
Bowen Bros.	8 33
R. V. Moore	16 67
Wm. Bolke	4 50
W. E. Bowen	9 00
Guy C. Brouse	12 00
Donald Brouse	15 00
Mrs. Geo. P. Brouse	12 00
Jas. Ballis	8 00
W. A. Munroe	6 42
Rev. Geo. Rogers	6 00
A. B. Carman	34 00
Mrs. D. A. Cameron	9 00
Jesse Barkley	4 50
Alex. Barkley	1 00
C. E. Cameron	9 00
Thos. Coulter	24 00
Wm. A. Coons	6 00
Guy C. Ault	6 00
John H. Currie	11 00
Rev. A. H. Whalley	9 00
E. M. Dakin	16 12
John Parlow	11 00
John G. Doran	9 00
John F. Armstrong	9 00
Mrs. S. Doran	9 00
Mrs. N. M. Dany	9 00
T. S. Edwards	11 00
W. A. Fisher	9 00
W. J. Forward	10 00
Chas. Hawley	9 00
Wm. Hartle	9 00
Chas. Holmes	9 00
Mrs. C. E. Harkness	11 00
C. E. Keeler	11 00
T. W. Hare	10 50
Mrs. H. McGinn	3 00
Dr. Parlow	9 00
Jas. McDonald	6 00
Rev. J. M. McAllister	11 00
Mrs. McQuaig	4 50
Thos. Johnston	10 00
Wm. J. Marsh	9 00
Mason Mills	11 00
Johiel Wert	6 00
John W. Armstrong	6 00
John McKercher	9 00
Allan McInnis	8 75
Arthur Patton	9 17
H. Montgomery	25 00
H. H. Ross	17 00
M. Redmond	12 00
M. Y. Edwards	7 25
J. Myers	3 50
H. A. Brouse	9 00
Gordon Serviss	6 00
High School	30 00
M. B. Fluidall	6 00
G. R. Sipes	7 00
N. G. Sherman	2 50
J. F. McGuire	3 25

I. W. Beekstead	6 50
G. D. Van Arnam	6 75
T. A. Thompson	15 00
Rev. R. Corrigan	9 00
W. D. Rutherford	5 66
Mrs. J. E. Tuttle	6 00
L. N. Tanney	4 50
Mrs. Jas. Johnston	6 00
W. J. Fisher	6 00
Jas. W. Tindale	11 00
Jas. Powell	11 00
L. Cameron	9 00
Public School	10 00
Chas. Burnside	3 00
Dr. Johnston	7 50
Jesse Lewis	6 00
S. Larne	6 00
E. McNulty	8 00
S. Landon	15 00
B. F. Smith	8 00
Chinese Laundry	1 50
Mrs. A. Serviss	6 00
Dr. Stephenson	11 00
J. W. Brouse	9 00
D. Fink	4 50
J. H. McNairn	4 50
S. Frayne	8 00
Richard Candor	1 00
John Goudie	6 00
W. G. Anderson	9 00
Chas. Rose	6 00
Mrs. E. Morrison	6 00
Skating Rink	15 00
English Church	12 00
The Molsons Bank	4 00
J. L. Cook	10 00
Z. Seeley	6 00
Geo. Van Camp	6 00
E. Lewis	1 50
Silas Redmond	6 00
Mrs. J. Donnelly	1 87
Fred. Coulter	1 88
Chas. Robson	6 00
Philip A. Wallace	3 50
Herb. Serviss	9 00
Wm. Clarke	5 50
Wm. Nicholson	8 00
John Watkins	6 00
Mrs. D. Savor	1 50
Alva Serviss	1 50
Miss E. Bailey	1 66
W. I. Shaver	9 00
Geo. Donaldson	2 00
M. S. Cassan	9 00
Jas. McGowan	3 00
Wm. McGee	9 00
Jas. A. Rose	2 25
Stephen Liezert	75
Wm. E. Fisher	6 00
W. A. Feader	5 75
Geo. E. Caldren	7 17
John McInnis	8 68
R. S. Pelton	42 75
Mrs. Simon Barkley	2 00
W. L. Redmond	2 48
Edward Roberts	6 00
W. A. Shaver	75
P. S. Johnston	75
W. J. Sharra	1 00

19a M.A.

Wm. Munroe	4 00
Gordon Strader	1 00
D. O. Bowen	2 50
Richard Neal	5 00
Total	$1,130 05

Detailed Account of Electric Light Rents Collected During the Year 1905.

High School	$36 67
Peter Ouimet	50
Jas. Shannon	63
C. W. J. Haworth	52
G. D. Van Arnam	5 06
Mrs. N. M. Dany	13 97
Miss B. Baldwin	5 96
T. W. Hare	19 25
John Parlow	12 15
Geo. Thompson	9 40
R. S. Pelton	22 35
Miss A. Piche	8 30
A. J. Osborne	3 19
Mrs. Neil Wright	4 13
M. S. Cassan	9 14
G. H. Dany	4 60
Mason Mills	14 19
Calvin Burnside	7 33
Rev. R. Corrigan	15 18
J. Alford	176 00
Mrs. J. E. Tuttle	6 80
Rev. J. M. McAllister	16 42
M. F. Beach	13 75
W. D. Rutherford	8 72
J. Harper	9 85
J. Alford	13 02
W. D. McCormack	42
Archie Currie	5 04
W. E. Bowen	5 23
Herb. Serviss	6 38
W. N. Abbott	12 38
W. G. Anderson	9 63
J. L. Cook	8 03
John L. Adams	9 13
W. A. Feader	9 13
Chas. Rose	6 38
Geo. Donaldson	10 60
Dr. Johnston	9 20
Mrs. D. Bowen	6 82
C. W. Holmes	1 25
Chas. Burnside	3 25
Stirling Wood	2 76
Mrs. D. A. Cameron	1 45
Frank R. Bullis	31
Stephen Liezert	2 16
J. B. Speirs	39
P. S. Johnston	1 41
W. J. Sharra	38
W. A. Munroe	1 45
W. J. Fisher	5 28
B. F. Smith	23 51
E. McNulty	40 81
Allan F. Sherman	5 00
C. & M. Mills	42 13
Gordon Serviss	9 63
T. A. Thompson	21 56
Thos. Johnston	8 88
Dr. Parlow	11 66
W. J. Marsh	24 97

N. Guay	4 29
W. E. Bowen	18 37
T. A. Doran	13 75
Z. Seeley	11 00
J. W. Tindale	36 72
G. R. Sipes	27 50
Ross Bros. & Co.	19 69
Edmond Lewis	1 37
Mrs. C. E. Harkness	22 70
Hare & McInnis	34 38
Allan McInnis	14 86
H. Montgomery	75 63
A. O. U. W.	14 67
Thos. Coulter	27 46
H. H. Ross	16 72
Jas. A. Rose	12 13
C. E. Cameron	13 97
Presbyterian Church	10 78
Angus McInnis	6 42
Mrs. J. Powell	14 19
The Bowen House	95 70
Arthur Patton	24 00
Odd Fellows	11 00
John McInnis	8 56
Mrs. J. Donelly	75
Thos. Coulter	1 13
A. B. Carman	28 16
The Molsons Bank	18 81
Jas. McNulty	20 63
C. E. Keeler	20 52
Mrs. Amos Serviss	12 55
J. N. Forward	14 19
Free Masons	9 46
W. A. Short	15 45
Chinese Laundry	84
Methodist Church	45 87
Geo. A. Bouck	1 75
Currie Bros.	1 50
John H. Currie	15 99
Robert Wright	6 88
Mrs. A. Beach	3 87
M. B. Flindall	8 69
Wm. N. Wilson	4 68
Wm. A. Fisher	26 40
Donald Brouse	16 06
Mrs. H. McGinn	2 50
S. Larne	8 35
S. Landon	11 43
Geo. W. Serviss	4 13
John G. Doran	5 50
E. M. Dakin	14 72
Nancy Roberts	3 63
J. D. Bullis	8 47
M. Redmond	5 22
J. W. Brouse	10 31
L. Cameron	11 02
St. John's Church	20 13
Wm. McGee	4 62
John F. Armstrong	6 38
Mrs. Geo. P. Brouse	11 00
Holiness Movement	3 63

Total	$1,682 77

The cost of this audit to the Municipality of the Village of Iroquois, as per Mr. Minnis' account, was $145.

WATER RENTS DUE AND UNPAID 31ST DECEMBER, 1905.

Allan F. Sherman	$16 80
C. W. J. Haworth	1 50
Nancy Roberts	11 12
G. D. Van Arnam	2 25
L. N. Tanney	1 50
N. Guay	10 00
W. A. Wallace	5 37
G. T. Railway	15 00
J. H. McNairn	1 50
Fred Coulter	3 75
Philip Wallace	2 50
J. B. Speirs	1 00
L. Maltice	1 50

Total	$73 79

ELECTRIC LIGHT RENTS DUE AND UNPAID 31ST DECEMBER, 1905.

G. T. Railway	$45 83
C. W. J. Haworth	42
Allan F. Sherman	24 58
Excelsior Shoe Co., for 1904	47 50
Mrs. J. E. Tuttle	66
J. Alford	1 21
Chas. Holmes	1 08
Frank R. Bullis	40
John Keeler	50
N. Guay	7 55
Thos. Coulter	25 88
Fred. Coulter	2 25
W. A. Short	3 25
M. Redmond	1 16

Total			$162 27
Total water rents due		$73 79	
Mrs. A. Beach, credited	$1 12		
John McKercher, credited	2 25		
		3 37	
Balance water rents due			70 42
Total electric light rents due			162 27
Total water and light rents due			$232 69

TOWN OF NAPANEE REPORT.

OSCAR HUDSON, Auditor.

Toronto.

*To the Mayor and Council of the Town of Napanee, County of Lennox and
Addington, Province Ontario :*

The petition of your ratepayers last July for an audit of the books and
accounts of their corporation, was acted upon with the sanction of the Provincial Government, given to Mr. J. B. Laing, Provincial Municipal Auditor, through whom my instructions to conduct it were received.

A circular letter was directed to each of the petitioners, as per schedule
——— with list of the signers attached, inviting their attendance, and any
communication affecting the purpose of the enquiry.

From the interviews held nothing was gleaned giving the character of a
special charge to any complaint made.

Enquiries from many quarters also failed to disclose the ground work
for the enquiry, to be more than as set forth in the following paragraphs.

The enquiry appears to have been instituted for the following reasons:—
1. The Treasurer's cash book was thrown into confusion through the introduction of an additional bank account.
2. The Collector for 1905 had received monies in excess of the roll amount, and had offered to hand over such surplus, with information as to its origin if recompensed for so doing. ·
3. The impression prevailed that the Collectors of 1903 and 1904 had made settlements upon incorrect bases.
4. The times within which duties were dischargeable by Assessors and Collectors were not regarded.
5. The books and papers of the corporation were improperly cared for.
6. The accounts of the Treasurer were lacking completeness and clearness.
7. Appropriations could not be compared with expenditure.
8. Assessments were unreliable, and the Assessor's and Collector's rolls were contradictory.
9. The auditing was too perfunctory. .
10. The school accounts should be looked into.
11. Definitions of duties of officials were needed.

The procedure of the investigation, therefore, was to discover and rectify the errors in the cash account, to ascertain how the Collector's roll permitted escaped taxes; the basis on which their settlements were made; the method of preparing the rolls; and generally to inspect the work of the officials, the care of records, systems of accounts and finance, and such other matters as might arise in connection therewith.

The Town Hall was placed at the disposal of the Commission and every courtesy and attention was shown by the various officers of the year in aid of the audit.

Numerous letters, however, had to be written to summon attendance, and to obtain the requisite statements and information.

The lack of adequate knowledge of the facts was apparent in the case of some officials, likewise the loose keeping of documents essential to the enquiry, the result of which is as follows.

Report 2.　Enquiry and Procedure.

Assessor's Roll, 1905.

This book, prepared by W. L. Bennett, has not been sworn to by him. It appears to have been incompleted when handed in, and additions made subsequent to the preparation of the Collector's roll therefrom which would sufficiently explain why the latter roll did not include all the taxes to be levied.

The summary certified to by the Clerk, after revision, showed an assessment of $1,091,750, whereas a present summary of its figures gives the total of $1,115,870 of which errors in addition amount to $4,970, and changes to the amount of $19,150, forming part of the assessments omitted by the Collector's roll.

The estimates for 1905 and the tax rates therefor, rested upon an erroneous assessment, which, from its insufficiency, imposed an extra burden on the ratepayers.

On page 5, the assessments of the Bay of Quinte Rly., and of H. R. Sherwood, have the appearance of having duplicated page 2 to the amount of $3,089.

If changes were made by him, the Assessor showed ignorance of the law and serious negligence in letting so many properties escape his notice or in the copying of his blotter into his roll, which he informs me was done for him by juniors.

With the preceding rolls to guide his work for 1905, and previous experience ,this roll might have been better done.

As to whether the Assessor's roll for 1905, with its alterations, now covers all assessable properties cannot be definitely ascertained without the aid of a proper map and the assistance of a committee, chosen for their acquaintance therewith, and with the business standing of merchants, etc.

The Act makes remissness of duty on the part of an assessor a very grave offence, it should therefore be the duty of the Council to see that he is competent, well paid, and has every facility, legal and otherwise, for performing his work.

The roll must be handed in by the 30th of April, final and complete in every particular, sworn to, and so placed before the Court of Revision to sanction all changes.

Report 3. Collector's Roll, 1905.

Collector's roll, 1905, prepared by W. A. Grange, Clerk, from the Assessor's roll, and delivered to T. F. Ruttan, Collector, 14th Nov., instead of 1st Oct., 1905, not added nor certified.

Errors have been found in its additions and extensions, as per schedule B, amounting to $58.72, of which $54.00 was recovered.

Omissions of assessments also occur in the sum of $22,939, also as per schedule C, showing escaped taxes of $618.68, of which now remains $178.93 to be reviewed for collection.

Settlement of Collector with the Treasurer, 2nd June, 1906, shown on schedule A, was made on the basis of the roll as handed him, and agrees therewith, but is without certificate.

Credits taken therein are for:—

(1) Taxes remitted by Court of Revision, documents signed by Clerk, but minutes of the Court proceedings not obtainable.

(2) Tax arrears, $218.47, listed but not sworn to.

(3) Balance of $3.35 written off by Council.

(4) Cash payments per cash book, which prove that the bank pass book of the trust account kept by the Collector, into which all his monies were deposited, except the extra collections made.

Among the taxes remitted is an amount for $540 to the Napanee Waterworks, from their assessment of $20,000. The remission is to offset their water bill for 1905 for the same amount, and which should have appeared among the expenses for that year instead of being covered up as taxes lost. Of the escaped taxes, the Collector recovered the sum of $572.60, per list given the Treasurer, being monies tendered by those ratepayers to the Collector, who thereby discovered the omissions from his roll, and that certain assessments were omitted from the Assessor's roll for 1905, these being traced through the Assessor's blotters for 1903 and 1904. His work in doing this must have been very considerable, and the Council, desirous of recompensing him, passed on the 18th June the following resolutions:—"That the Collector be paid 10 per cent. on all money that he has collected and paid over to the Town, for which he is to give a full explanation to the satisfaction of the Council," and further "That the Council accept Mr. Ruttan's explanation as satisfactory." The breadth of this is at once apparent. The sum re-

ceived by the Collector in this connection was $114.81, being ten per cent.
upon the extra collections of $572.60 and upon an amount of $575.56, shown
in a statement prepared by the Treasurer as having been overpaid him by
the Collector. This statement was not correct, but according to the latter
official the Treasurer was prepared to make a settlement upon that basis,
whereupon the Collector offered, if compensated, to make a correct settlement, which he did on 2nd June.

A motion to rescind the foregoing resolution was followed by one to
legally recover the commission paid.

Report 4. Collector's Roll, 1905.

The position of the Collector in this matter appears to be that he did
work in rectifying the figures of the Assessor and of the Treasurer outside
of his duties as Collector, and for which he sought payment.

It would have been better if the Collector, when the first intimations of
the incorrectness in the rolls appeared, had brought the matter immediately
and officially before the Council, through the Clerk, and had sanction before the extra expense was incurred. No additions or summary of the Collector's roll having been made, the Treasurer was unable to tell the amount
due by the Collector, hence his incorrect statement. The Collector, of
course, should not have accepted the roll from the Clerk until such certified
summary had been shown, and the Treasurer ought to have been notified by
the Clerk of the amount before the roll left his hands.

The Council acted apparently without a solicitor's advice, unwittingly
overriding the by-law fixing the pay of the Collector. It was undoubtedly
their intention to recompense Mr. Ruttan for his extra services, not as a collector but as a corrector of errors.

As the matter is in suit and the issue rests upon legal grounds, the ver-
dict of the court will solve the situation.

Other statements are presented as follows:—

Schedule B.—Collector's own summary after correction of errors in additions and extensions.

Schedule C.—Corrected summary supplemented by taxes on omitted assessments showing agreement of Collector's and Assessor's rolls.

Schedule D.—Further corrections of summary by addition of taxes discovered from parties not on the Assessor's roll, and showing how Collector's
settlement should have appeared.

The work of bringing the two rolls into harmony and focusing the result
has occupied a very long time owing to the confusion and errors thereon.

With the final balance of $179.93 the Court of Revision has now to deal.
Also with tax arrears per schedule E from 1904, amounting to $56.17, ap-
parently unpaid since, and not forwarded into the 1905 roll for the reason
given by the Clerk that they could not be identified with lands in the Assessor's roll of 1905, although such lands did appear in the rolls of 1904.

The Assesor's and Collector's rolls are intended to correspond page for
page, and no such difficulty as occurred could have arisen if they had been
properly prepared.

The Collector's roll should show against each assessment the separate
rates levied for County, school, and general purposes.

Report 5. Collector's Roll, 1905.

Collector's roll, 1904, handed to F. C. Bogart by J. E. Herring, Clerk,
without certificate, as required by section 95, and not having the proper summary according to section 94 of the Assessment Act. The amount called

for by this roll has been accounted for per schedule F with the exception of $27.74, being a difference in interest items.

Credits taken in this settlement include as in 1905 the Napanee Water-works bill of $540, really an expense on 1904.

Vouchers for these credits are most unsatisfactory and should not have been accepted by the Treasurer until put in proper form.

The uncollectable taxes reported as $60.86 bear no approval by the Court of Revision.

The tax arrears were sworn to in accordance with section 115 of the Act, but schedule H therein relating to tax demands is apparently disregarded.

The Collector deducted his salary from his settlement, although the Council only could authorize the payment. The Treasurer should have charged himself with $1.50 as received on account of taxes and then taken credit for the salary payment, which is therefor omitted from the 1904 Treasurer's statement.

Section 109, par. 4, Assessment Act, obliges a Collector to pay the Treasurer all his monies weekly. This has not been done in 1904 and 1905. The Collectors in these cases kept trust accounts with the Merchants' Bank and paid therein all monies, with the exception of a few hundred dollars, disbursing therefrom to the Treasurer in even sums at irregular times. No interest is allowed in his pass book on the balances, meanwhile the Town overdraft was suffering interest.

Section 109, subsection 1, Assessment Act, orders return of Collector's roll before 14 December, clearly for the purpose of the Treasurer's statement to the 15th of that month; Council may, however, extend that time to 1st of February next, not later. Such resolutions were passed, yet the Collector for 1904 settled 23rd August, 1905, and the Collector for 1905, 2nd June, 1906. A by-law fixed 1st November as the date of final payment, afterwards extended to 1st December, after which interest of 1 per cent. per month is imposed. Owing to the difficulty of verifying the dates upon which the Collector receives the several taxes, the imposition of interest charges is largely in his hands, and considering that over one-third of the taxes each year are unpaid at the end of it and the remainder extended from four to six months longer, the question of interest charges is a very important one.

Report 6. Collector's Roll.

The Collector's roll being returnable (by resolution) not later than 1st Feb., and a clear statement of arrears then rendered by him at the time his service ends, and it devolves upon the Treasurer to impose the additional percentages up to 10 per cent. and to receive all arrears.

There has been so far no distinction made in the Treasurer's books between current tax receipts and arrears.

The final arrears for Collector's settlements run often largely over $200, but the citizens, generally, cannot be aware of this, as the annual statements are ready before more than two-thirds of the taxes are paid.

Collector's roll, 1903, was handed W. Rankin about 15th October and settlement made by him August 25th, 1904 per schedule G. His payments were made as monies were received and his roll presents a very clear finish.

Collector's rolls, 1902 and 1901, by W. A. Empey and R. A. Shorey, respectively show settlements complete as to cash payments, but with vouchers more or less inefficient. The latter Collector settled 9th Dec., 1901, for the 1900 roll.

Assessor's Roll, 1904.

Assessments to the sum of $2,880.00 per schedule F were omitted from Collector's roll of that year, showing escaped taxes for $77.75 to be dealt with by the Court of Revision and placeable on this year's roll. Lack of adequate comparison of one roll with the other is responsible for errors of this kind.

Assessor's rolls, 1903, 1902, 1901, have been compared with those of the Collectors for those years, and although lacking in completeness of summaries, etc., as with the others, have been accounted for throughout.

Alphabetical arrangement is to be deprecated, if completeness is aimed at.

Assessments are not of names, but of objects, persons only be the subjects of taxation.

The lines to follow are those of location, street, block, and lot numbers.

A map will aid this very materially, permitting exact descriptions, now erratic.

A card system may be compiled therefrom to furnish the alphabetical arrangement essential to the preparation of voters' lists.

Were the assessments confined in all reason to the location values, the valuations would attain absolute precision. As the law now stands, however, buildings and businesses, with their indefinite and changing values, have to be regarded.

Report 7. Assessor's Rolls, 1904, 1903, 1902, 1901.

A map of the Town is badly needed as the latest one dates back to 1878. No Assessor can properly perform his duties without some such guide. After a thorough survey is made, a large map can be produced to be hung in the Town Hall. From this sectional ones can be prepared for the wards, then reduced ones in pocket edition for the Assessors and other officials. Tracings in skeleton form will permit changes being marked from one year to another as discovered by the Assessor. Colored lines will show school, municipal and legislative divisions.

The description of properties by the Assessor cannot be at present depended upon, as much trouble is given the Clerk in preparing his rolls and voters' lists in sequence. Exactness in this respect must be shown by the assessor.

A map, moreover, would be practical guide to any citizen in search of the assessment roll, which is open to such inquiry, for the location of certain lands, their size, improvements and values, with the names and businesses of the occupants.

Plans of the various buildings might be kept on file with a recital of the uses to which they are put and the materials of which composed, etc., etc., with a direct reference to the Assessor's roll.

An index book or card system by which the names of the ratepayers could be arranged alphabetically with the years in which they were assessed and the number of assessment, would also aid the Assessor and the Clerk.

Report 8. Map.

Assessor's Roll, 1906.

The Town's full tax income depending entirely upon the correctness of the Assessor's roll, and the same Assessor acting in 1906 as in the two preceding years, in which no certainty exists that all properties were covered by him, the responsibility now rests upon the Council to cause the present year's assessment roll to be gone over by a committee, with the assistance of the map herein recommended, so that a firm basis may be had of the rolls of succeeding years.

It appears to have been too much the practice to copy names from one Assessor's roll into another and assess therefrom in lieu of using the names on the preceding year's roll to guard against possible omissions from the current one.

The roll for this year was summarized by me for the purpose of the estimates recently made, and which pressed for attention.

The rolls have been verified with one another and with the settlements made thereon as far back as 1900. Age, illness, death or absence of officials connected therewith earlier than that, made it inadvisable to prosecute enquiry farther in view of the substantial correctness of the rolls, other than the most recent ones.

The re-summarizing work entailed during examinations, together with the corrections of additions, has occasioned an immense amount of work.

In hardly any instance has the list of arrears carried from one year to another been clearly accounted for by giving dates of interim payments to Treasurer, authority for remissions thereof, or location of amounts when carried into succeeding roll. The task of discovering their disposal, therefor, has been a difficult one. The Treasurer should have furnished the Clerk with such amendment to the list given him at the time of the Collector's return, as was the result of subsequent payments thereon to him direct, which list the Clerk ought to have introduced into the roll intact.

The special book kept by the Treasurer for delinquents is suited for that purpose, and should be carefully continued. The defaulter's list sworn to by the Collector upon his return of his roll posted thereto, interest added and each subsequent payment credited. The balances may then be given the Clerk for the next roll. Only in this way will the arrears be watched.

Collector's Rolls.

Settlements made with Treasurers by the Collectors will best appear at the end of each roll, and be assented to in writing by both. Sworn declarations of tax arrears must also be so made.

The Clerk must prepare and certify to the correctness of the Summary of the roll before handing it over.

Report 9.   The Rolls, Assessor's and Collector's.

He must enumerate the various purposes of the levy in his summary, as for:— Ordinary expenditure, Debentures and interest, School monies, County rate.

The Treasurer will thereupon charge the Collector with the amount in his ledger, and by journal entry give credit to the accounts for which levies are made.

A perfect comparison with the Assessor's roll is also essential.

Observance of these rules will give permanency and clearness to final results and be in conformance to the Act designed to protect ratepayers.

Government cash book has been kept neatly and systematically, and, previous to the present year, with apparent exactness. The only bank account up to 8th May last was with the Merchants' Bank.

On that date the proceeds of a series of debentures were deposited in the Crown Bank, the funds to be used for electric light installation.

The requisite entries for the subsequent transactions with the bank were not sufficiently made. This matter was attended to and the two bank accounts straightened out to 31st July of this year, and again to 31st August.

A balance of the cash book itself was then struck with the result of finding an amount, $308.40, due by the Treasurer, certified to by him as produced from the totals of his figures as they stood at 1st August.

All his entries and additions were gone over for this year, but only $80.00 was discovered in reduction of the above, the balance being unexplainable.

His August entries, made during my visit, also fell into disorder and more work was entailed in adjusting them. This unsatisfactory condition of the cash book and other books in his care made it imperative that the Treasurer should be superseded, and my letter to the Council, per schedule O, indicated this.

His present incapacity may be traced to an accident 18th Dec. last, which to a man over 80 years old was serious, since when, from all accounts, he has been unable to discharge his duties properly. His faithful diligence being so noticeable in prior years in his work, the cause for his retirement is, the more regrettable after his 15 years of service.

The annoyance and delay arising from his inability to explain entries prolonged unduly the investigation and increased its difficulties.

The voucher book contains all payments by date and consecutive number, name of payee, name of account chargeable and amount, also spaces for signature of recipient and witness.

This book is thoroughly well kept but the signatures are very often not those of the payees, thus proof of payment to the proper parties is not assured.

Were all payments made by the proper Council warrants on the bank through the Treasurer, sufficient acknowledgments would be had by endorsement and the keeping of this book would be unnecessary as it is copied verbatim into the cash book.

Paylists emanating from Council meetings often follow the actual payments by the Treasurer instead of preceding them, thus confirming instead of authorizing them. This, if continued, gives too much freedom to the Treasurer and leads to laxity. He should be permitted by law only to prepay necessary salaries, wages, and perhaps freight items.

Accounts dealt with by the Council requires to be first certified by some member of the board or qualified official, then marked with date of passing and consecutive number of payment, also with the name of the account affected. A suitable rubber stamp may be used for this.

Pay lists and accounts ought to be immediately filed in order of number and kept for reference and audit.

Very much time was lost in seeking information in this form.

Pay lists are ill-arranged, and some were missing.

Receipt Book.

Receipts have counterfoil signed by whom the monies were paid, and the corresponding receipt bearing Treasurer's signature as recipient thereof are numbered in rotation and so entered in the cash book. The cash book has been excellently kept and is thoroughly adapted to its purpose as a voucher for the cash receipts.

Report 10.   Voucher Book and Receipt Book.

Ledger.

Into it are posted in detail all items from the cash book under the headings corresponding to its column. This work is superfluous and exceedingly heavy. Except as to items in the miscellaneous column it is only necessary to carry yearly totals into the ledger accounts, so that at the end of the financial year the ledger may prove the cash statement, which can be wholly prepared from the cash book columns.

The ledger has no appearance of having been balanced, one year being run into the next, without a line or total to break the period.

The book as kept is antiquated, cumbersome and of little convenience. Its main purpose is to furnish figures for the auditor's statement from cash book totals, and to carry such accounts in detail that cash book columns cannot be spared for, or that arise from the journal entries. Accounts with the Collector, tenants, delinquents, debentures, County Treasurer, School Trustee, licensees, Legislature, adjacent municipalities, sundry debtors, etc., are herein to be kept, as also the permanent asset accounts.

It should be properly balanced and closed annually, re-opening with the figures of the balance sheet.

Treasurer's statement of 15th December, 1905, was hastily completed for him by the Clerk and Chairman of Finance, as an accident prevented his personal attention to it. The figures of its cash portion were prepared with general exactness from the cash book, but the balance sheet was evidently drawn up from disconnected memoranda, since mislaid.

The cash statement for the balance of the year, as prepared by the Treasurer himself and certified by the Auditors, closes with a stated bank overdraft of $3,246.48, whereas the true amount is $3,355.42, showing that at that date the cash on his hands was $108.94, although the fact was not recognized by the auditors.

The balance sheet, similarly prepared and audited, contains assets and liabilities dependent upon lists all trace of which appears to have been lost. This lamentable carelessness made the verification of such accounts as tax arrears and sundry creditors impossible within a reasonable time, and the proof of debentures ascertainable only by tedious extraction from the debenture book.

Balance Sheet, 1905.

Schedules H and I exhibit the financial position of the corporation at the close of last year.

It differs from that of the auditor's statement then in respect to the following items:

1. Cash in hands of Treasurer, $108.94, was by them treated as reducing bank overdraft.

Report 11.   Ledger, Treasurer's Statement, Balance Sheet, 1905.

2. Bank overdraft (allowing for unpaid checks) was greater by the above sum.

3. Tax monies unpaid failed then to include rates for watering, dogs, 1904 arrears, and to deduct discount already allowed, with provisions for remissions.

4. Cement walks unpaid for were figured too high.

5. Sundry creditors for current Town account unpaid, were shown by the Auditors at $4,653.52. The most diligent enquiry of them and of the other officials failed to produce explanation in any form whatever of the composition of this debt. It is, therefore, a matter of conjecture that some amounts of the electric light contracts had been included. As against the asset of cash expenditure only, this was unreasonable. Moreover, the contracts were not signed until 3rd May, nor does it appear that any important work performed to the close of the year was then unpaid in terms of agreement.

It was a matter of considerable time and uncertainty to search out the items paid this year that affected last one, and which compose the sum under this heading.

6. A distinction is now made between passive and active assets, in order to show the funds available towards expenditure for the ensuing year, separated from the general surplus, which may be regarded as highly satisfactory.

7. It is obvious that 1906 was entitled to a much larger working surplus than $2,059.09 from 1905, considering debentures and interest maturing immediately and the slowness of tax collections. This year ought to deal more liberally with its successor in this respect.

8. Rents unpaid were entirely omitted from the Auditor's statement.

Schools.

The school rate for 1905 was 7½ mills, while the requisitions from the Board of Education made in 1905 called for $8,300, of which $400 was paid before the end of 1905.

The liability of $7,900.00 has gradually been reduced to $2,900.00 at 31st July, 1906, without interest being charged for the Town's use of such school money meanwhile. It would seem proper for the Town to treat all school monies, not immediately paid over, as a loan from the Board of Education, or if held in trust, to deposit same to the credit of a trust bank account, and confine their borrowing to banks and debentures. The balance of $2,900.00 due the Board of Education, if not needed by them for expenses of the year to which the sum belongs, should be applied towards their levy of this year, and the school tax be lessened thereby.

Report 12. Balance Sheet 1905, and Schools.

The Court of Revision proceedings have not been formed into minutes. The conduct of the meetings must have been quite informal, as its dealings were not generally on petition, but upon presentation of facts by the Collector or Clerk. Remissions were made then the only record of which appears in vouchers issued to the Collector by the Clerk. Exception was taken in the minutes of 6th March, 1905, to the Council dealing with rebated taxes, Council should constitute the court, three of whom are a quorum. The Town Clerk is the Clerk of such court. Its proceedings and decisions are required to be certified by the Chairman, and to be of clear record. The first sitting may be the 25th May, and ought to dispose of all claims at once. Its business is to deal with all complaints arising from the preparation of the assessment roll, or from the settlement of the Collector's roll, and to authorize and sanction all changes therein. The Assessor being bound to the figures of his roll by affidavit, and the Collector by the summary of his roll certified by the

Clerk, it is obvious that any relief must proceed from the powers that gave them office, the agent of which is the Court of Revision. The considerable remissions made each year were worthy of more careful attention, and of being granted only when circumstances to justify them were not only discussed thoroughly, but so placed upon record that the Treasurer or Collector might be justified in reducing the roll amount by them, and that future reference would find such explanations as are at this date almost entirely absent. The court having power until the 1st of July following to remit taxes of the preceding year, and the Collector having to return his roll before the 1st February following, it would seem that the Treasurer, having arrears to collect, is the official to whom such vouchers should issue.

Street Watering.

Petitioners have applied to Council, and reference made to Streets Committee. The watering was done upon the requisition of two-thirds of either owners or occupiers, who were taxed accordingly. Objections to payment were apparently passed upon by Court of Revision, as the Clerk issued vouchers thereon. A motion in Council, 16th July, 1906, endeavoured to throw the cost upon the general funds upon the grounds of general benefit to all citizens of having main thoroughfares so treated. This is the reasonable view until the residents of a particular street can be bound without exception to the specal charge for watering it, in which case the driver should report daily his time and route, when engaged on that work, so that the accounts may be prepared against residents for the Clerk to enter upon the roll.

Snow Shovelling.

Citizens have been expected to do their own, but where it has been neglected the Streets Committee are expected to get it done and report the cost. Whatever information may have reached the Clerk for the charges upon the roll is not now available.

Report 13. Court of Revision, Street Watering and Snow Shovelling.

The collectors of 1904 and previous years, had the collection of such charges for the preceding winters, but the winter of 1904-5 has not been represented on the rolls. Its severity must have rendered corporation work needful.

Cement Walks.

These have been constructed upon petition to Council of all land owners affected, and reference to Streets Committee, who, in terms of petition, may charge such parties one-half of the cost, payable over three years, any private walks being payable in full immediately. This would have been clear enough if the Streets Committee had made proper reports to the Treasurer of the amounts collectable in connection therewith, and if the Treasurer had either kept proper accounts with each debtor or caused the Clerk to add the sums to the Collector's roll of each year. None of those courses were followed except in 1904, when the Chairman of that year exhibited a proper list of charges, with full explanations, but which theyTreasurer recorded only in an intricate memorandum form in his ledger. From the absence of proper information the acceptance was forced of a rough memoranda from the Treasurer, verified as far as possible, and showing unpaid, 31st July, 1906, for

cement walks, constructed to the end of 1904, $227.21. As to those under-
taken in 1905 no information is obtainable. The works of 1906, as completed,
should be reported as above suggested by the Chairman, and the Treasurer
must charge them to the petitioners immediately and open accounts against
the debtors for 1904, mentioned above.

Richard Street Sewer.

The debts shown in the following list, appearing in the balance sheet
of 1905, are explained by the Treasurer as payable when the street carrying
the sewer has been gravelled. No record can be found of such a contract,
and the cost of the work must be considered against such asset, if it remains.
It is imperative meanwhile that accounts be opened with these parties in the
ledger, awaiting the action of the Streets Committee, who should deal finally
therewith.

Fraser	$ 4 43
Mill	4 43
Kimmerly	4 43
Light	18 56
Vrooman	16 11
Wright	11 69
Lane	6 88
Waitman	6 88
Total	$73 41

Report 14. Snow Shovelling, Cement Walks, Richard Street Sewer.

Electric Light Debenture Money, $35,000.

On May 8, 1906, the Finance Committee, from previous powers conferred, deposited proceeds of $34,657.05 in Crown Bank, and reported accord-
ingly to the Council; also electric light expenditure to date as $8,400.75,
which sum was then withdrawn from the Crown Bank and deposited in the
Merchants' Bank, to the credit of the Town current account, to recoup it for
such expenditure advanced therefrom.

Electric Light Expenditure.

Payments to 31st August, 1906, date from 1st September, 1905, by-law
being passed 24th July, 1906.

Such payments amount to $20,259.39, excluding the costs of confirma-
tory legislation as not entering into original estimates, for which the loan was
intended.

It is found that labour and supplies have been used in house-wiring and
equipment.

A careful account of these must be kept and used against the property
owners.

I am informed that Town labour used by contractors was paid for by
them.

A careful analysis of the whole expenditure when completed should be
presented to Council at an early date and bear relation to the headings of the
original estimate.

The liabilities are estimated at $12,600 to contractors and engineer. The remaining accounts are not in evidence.

More carefulness is needed in the care of and arrangement of these important papers.

Commissioners are now needed to take charge of the power plant and its operation.

Separate books and bank account will be necessary in connection therewith.

Extension work must be separate from that for the benefit of house owners or of the Town property.

Electric Light Debenture.

Thirty-five thousand dollars produced $34,657.05, being sold to City and District Savings Bank, Montreal, at a discount of $1,275.00, or over $3\frac{1}{2}$ per cent., and with accrued interest of $932.05 added to 2nd May, 1906, at the time of purchase by remittance. This sum was held over from 3rd to 8th, pending arrangements with the proper depositary.

Report 15. Electric Light Debenture Money, Expenditure and Debenture.

No entries were made for these in the cash book, nor did the debenture register contain the proper record of these debentures. The immediate registration of this information is necessary; 1906 Statutes contain the special legislation this year that legitimized the issue, and gives printed information concerning them.

Bank Accounts.

The trust accounts kept by the Collectors for 1902, 1904 and 1905 for the reception of tax monies, were lacking some important features.

1. No monies ought to have been removable therefrom except upon the signatures of Mayor and Treasurer.

2. All of the taxes collected should have gone therein on the day after collection.

3. Such deposits could have been, by duplicate . slip, reported to the Treasurer.

4. Interest upon the running balance might have been arranged.

The Treasurer is thereby saved the handling of money.

The Collector would be released after deposit.

The Town's funds would be safeguarded and under its control.

The settlement with the Collector would have been much clearer and easier.

School and debenture monies could have been drawn out and passed into special trusts accounts for these until their payment over.

The current account of the Treasurer would, of course, be added to therefrom, only as needed.

Tax Monies.

The handing over of tax monies to the Treasurer by the Collector may be obviated by taking advantage of Sec. 40, Chap. 7, R.S.O., which states:—

"The Council of any municipality may, by by-law, direct that monies payable to the municipality for taxes or rates, and upon such other accounts

20 M. A.

as may be mentioned in the by-law, shall be by the Collector of Taxes, or by the person charged with the payment thereof, paid into such chartered bank as the Council may by such by-law direct, to the credit of the Treasurer of the municipality, and in such case the person making payment shall obtain a receipt from the bank thereof and produce the same to the Municipal Treasurer, who shall make the proper entries therefor in the books of the municipality." Your municipality, in adopting a by-law with the foregoing intent, would free its Treasurer from very great responsibility, and avoid all questions as to dates and amounts of the Collector's payments, and ensure the safekeeping of its funds. The Treasurer's work would then be one of mere bookkeeping, and the vouchers for his receipts would emanate from a strong source.

Report 16. Electric Light Debentures, Bank Accounts and Tax Monies.

Town Vault.

It is astonishing that no Town vault or safe accommodation exists for the protection of books and papers, and it is incumbent upon the Council to have this security afforded without delay. The Town Hall premises admit of a vault being easily built, with access from the Treasurer's office. It should be capacious enough for inspection of records inside, fitted with an electric hand lamp and having good ventilation. Shelving all round may be spaced to fit the variously sized books, and pigeon holes labelled for all documents, books, papers and records of all kinds ought to be placed in the vault after the day's business, and no one allowed access thereto except the proper officials. Charter, original by-laws, deeds of property, leases and contracts, insurance policies and receipts, bonds of officials, plans and specifications, are some of the most important papers to be protected in the Town premises, as the safe in the Clerk's business office cannot be the proper receptacle; nor is his office the place in which to transact Town business.

Town papers in the custody of the Treasurer are scattered all over his office, no attention is shown to have been paid to their arrangement, endorsement or filing. Several days were spent in assisting him in the search for the most ordinary documents. Confusion in this respect is reported to have existed for many years in the offices of both the Clerk and Treasurer. Immediate steps ought to be taken by the Council to have all books, documents and memoranda having reference of any character whatever to the civic affairs, carefully collected, scanned by a competent person, and placed in suitable divisions for each year in the vault herein suggested as a necessary container thereof. The expensive filing cabinet now standing in the Council Chamber appears to have been given up, as no papers later than early in 1905 appear therein. Its proper use ought to be recontinued at once. The Assessor's rolls for 1903 and 1904 were not obtainable for two weeks owing to the Assessor's absence, the Clerk in whose custody they should have been not knowing their whereabouts.

Council minutes are in good form and fully signed. Marginal notations of the substance of each minute would, if properly indexed, serve as a useful reference to matters having come before the Council. It must be an exceedingly troublesome affair at present for the Clerk to find the meeting before which any particular matter came. Some of the resolutions are resolvable into by-laws, and should have been so treated. And your Solicitor's scrutiny of minutes is desirable before their confirmation at the next meeting. A little more space and more time given to writing up the minutes would make them more readable than many at present are.

20a M.A.

An agenda book will also be found to be of much service in recording matters to come before the Council. Committee reports ought to appear in full in the minutes, and more insistence used in requiring such reports.

Report 17. Town Vault, Town Papers and Council Minutes.

Tax Payment Dates.

No dates appearing in the Collector's roll for 1905 against the sums collected, it is not apparent how long the Collector had such sums in his possession. A by-law passed in 1893 fixed the date of tax payments as 1st November, subsequently extended to 1st December, by resolutions of the Council in lieu of an amending by-law. Whatever final date is fixed by this year's Council must be embodied in the by-law. An earlier date than hitherto observed is highly desirable and after the first year's change had removed the unpleasantness of havin~ the tax demands of one year ride too close on that of the next, would be acceptable for several reasons : —

1. Town funds from this source would practically be all in before the annual statement, leaving thereon only genuine tax arrears and exhibiting same to the ratepayers.

2. School and County monies could be paid over or carried into trusts account before the close of the year and cease as liabilities.

3. The vexatious list of sundries unpaid would disappear, and all current liabilities be cleared off.

4. The Treasurer's cash statement would thus be a complete income and expenditure statement for the whole year by excluding items carried over from the preceding year, and including all payments now carried as liabilities to the next year, and it would thus set forth to the ratepayers what they really wish to know, *i. e.*, what has been their income and what their expense.

5. The ratepayers can probably find the money more easily in the fall than in the spring, and, given a liberal discount for prepayment, would favour it more than in the past.

6. The unsightly feature of a chronic bank overdraft on the annual balance sheet would be replaced by that of a substantial balance wherewith to meet the maturing obligations of the early part of the succeeding year, after the use of which, resort could be had to the bank until tax collections were resumed.

7. The Collector's duties would occur within the year of his appointment, less of his time would be occupied, and his remuneration be made more acceptable.

8. The advantage to the Town of a good clear balance sheet lies in the higher credit that awaits its debentures.

9. The saving of bank interest occurring now from protracted overdrafts is worth regarding.

10. A by-law fixing 1st September for final payment, coupled with discount offerings in preceding months, might well be passed by your Council, interest rates of 1 per cent. per month thereafter would then have more significance.

11. The expense of discount and gain of interest would then affect the year of levy. With the roll in his hands 1st July, the Collector could start his collections with any prepayments tendered that month. The completion of the Assessor's roll 1st of May, and its revision by 1st June, would give one month in which the Clerk could prepare his roll.

Report 18.   Tax Payment Dates.

Solicitor.

Any irregularities of officials alluded to in this report have obviously
arisen from a light view taken of their responsibility. Their ignorance of the
requirements of the Act is explainable by the frequent changes of such
officials, and to the consequent difficulty of new ones becoming well acquainted with their duties in the time of their first term. Neglected attention to
the dates upon which the rolls ought to be handed over and returned, coupled
with incomplete affidavits, certificates, vouchers, summaries and statements,
and careless preparation of the rolls, dragged along the period of collection,
confused the roll with alterations and gave rise to remissions that might have
been forestalled, made the settlement with the Collector crude memoranda.
The recurrence of such conditions may be best avoided by causing the officials
to be quite conversant with every phase of their duties. To accomplish this
the aid of the Town Solicitor is of prime importance. No one is better situated to advise the officials as to their work so far as the law requires it to be
done, so that no excuse remains for digressions. His remunerations should
allow of consultations to this end. In respect to the justification of payments, the validity of by-laws, the form of resolutions and their distinction
from by-laws, and the various dates that the act fixes for certain purposes,
his opinion may be called for with much advantage to the Council. Much
stress is laid upon the importance of the assistance this official can render to
the Council, the members of which cannot be held in fairness to be acquainted with the significance of all municipal legislation.

By-laws.

These are in three books. The first runs from 19th January, 1855, to
5th April, 1880. The second runs from 5th April, 1882 to 9th January, 1905.
The third runs from 9th January, 1905, to present date. The sequence of
numbers is frequently broken. The book of by-laws between 5th April, 1880,
and 3rd April, 1882 (if any), cannot be found. The first two books are
crudely indexed. The third one has no index attached. All officials complain of the difficulty of finding by-laws and amended interpretation.

The by-laws number over one thousand, and as no consolidation has been
made for many years it is highly important that they be condensed and
clarified at an early date, printed with proper index, and published to the
ratepayers in well-bound form, so that all may be conversant with the Town
ordinances.

There is no present way of finding a by-law except by hunting through
the 200 folios that contain them, or by referring to a very ineffectual index.
The Clerk, Magistrate and Chief admit their inability to find within a reasonable time, or with any certainty, the by-laws and amendments applicable to
cases as they arise, and these alone are reasons for having them consolidated.

The signature of the Clerk must be put to every by-law copied into the
by-law book to attest its accuracy.

Report 19.   Solicitor and By-laws.

Estimates.

Were a more vigorous effort made towards collecting taxes within the
year of levy, the delay in estimates would cease. These could be entered
upon in June, when the revised assessment was known, and cover expenditure
from the first of the year to its close.

The method of overlapping estimates on to the next year is most distracting to those of the ratepayers who desire to know whether certain expenditures are kept within bounds, and seemingly it is no less confusing to a finance committee who have so far been more dependent upon the piecing of the two years' portional figures by the Treasurer than upon the exact showing of the whole year's cash statement, which should be their most reliable guide.

To shift the unexpended appropriations upon the shoulders of an incoming Council leads only to a similar action on their part when their term ends.

It would be better financial policy to have each year's Council make estimates for its own year, expend only the income of that year with an obligation to favour its successor in office with such a reasonable bank balance as will at least take care of yearly expenditure. Failing this, temporary resort can be had to the bank until tax time comes around again.

Town Rentals.

Buildings on the west side of Centre Street were acquired by the Town from the Gibbard Company in lieu of bonus to them. Rentals, according to Treasurer's ledger memoranda, are $175 p.a. from C. Anderson, who is two years in arrears to July last, and Chas. Stevens at $86.00 p. a. paid to 4th January, 1906. Leases should be signed and held by Clerk and proper ledger accounts kept by the Treasurer for these or any other tenants. Certified admissions of their debts have been obtained.

Licenses.

It is requisite that a register for these be prepared at an early date. In this would appear licensees' names, locations, businesses, dates of their payments and years so covered. Billiard rooms, playhouse, butchers, dogs, etc., with Town portion of hotel licenses are entitled to be clearly and amply set forth in a register for the purpose.

Debentures.

A schedule of those maturing this and subsequent years has been prepared as per schedule for the guidance of estimates. A cancelled debenture file is requisite to properly account for these and coupons. A more suitable debenture register is likewise needed and a form will be offered if desired.

Report 20. Estimates, Town Finances, Licenses, Debentures.

Estimates made last year in by-law 722 on 4 Oct., 1905, following the custom of previous years, sought to forestall expenditure between the periods of 1st Aug., 1905, and 1st Aug., 1906, although it is mentioned as "current expenditure for the said year" as the Act requires. If the latter review be assumed, the position is resolved as follows: —

Estimated expenditure to close of 1905..................		$38,797 88
Actual expenditure for the year............	$37,589 99	
Liabilities at its close	15,750 46	
		53,340 45
Over expended during 1905		$14,542 57

Of which electric light debenture money anticipated.   5,539 17

Showing a shortage of 9,003 40
If the intention of the estimates was to cover as well, expenditure for
the first seven months of the succeeding year, as for the last five of the cur-
rent one, then the comparison stands:
Estimated expenditure $38,797 88
Actual expenditure, exclusive of electric light const.,
    1 Aug., 1905, to 1 Aug., 1906 ...... $30,055 22
Liabilities at 1 Aug., 1906, approximately   8,000 00
Liabilities at 1 Aug., 1906, approximately   8,000 00

                                                            38,055 22
                                          —————— $38,055 22

Showing an amount to be recovered from ratepayers
    by levy or debenture $742 66
A retrenchment is herein illustrated of the first seven months of 1906,
as compared with those of 1905.

Report 21.   *Balance Sheet, 1905, Schedule.*

Trunk Sewers.

By-law 698 passed by Council in October, 1904, to take effect 7 of
November, provided for the raising of debentures of $5,000.00 for the con-
struction of sewers.
Expenditure in this direction was begun the preceding August, and
totalled, $5,098.26 for the year.
The Council for that year were under the impression that this expendi-
ture could be made, and debentures be sold without the submission of a
by-law to the people.
The non-disposal of such debentures was explained by this neglect.
The estimates for that year were thus exceeded, yet the Council be-
queathed to 1905, a current surplus of over $2,000.00.
To legalize the issue, and effects its sales would place the present Council in funds.
Until this is done, the ratepayers are borrowing the sum of, from the
bank on an overdraft at 5 per cent.
The loan in this form will be repayable by the present ratepayers,
whereas debentures will extend it also to those of succeeding years.
Expenditure in 1905, of $2,247.75 under this heading, indicates further
work in contemplation.
This must be anticipated by sufficient debenture issues, so that permanent cost may be shared by posterity.
Part of the prime cost, and all of the maintenance of public works are
charges enough against one year's income.

Board of Education.

The school books and accounts were gone into and found to have been
kept carefully and systematically by the Secretary Treasurer for the past
twelve years, M. W. F. Hall.

The passing of accounts for payments might have been accomplished more clearly with the aid of a rubber stamp, and the signature of Chairman of Board or Committee to every one. Orders on Treasurer should emanate from trustees.

The receipt book must be used for all monies received, without exception, the counterfoil thus constituting vouchers for all income.

The balance on hand is certified to by the Merchants Bank, that portion for the High School being sufficient for the remainder of the year, and that of the public school probably coming somewhat short.

The estimates date forward from 1 August, instead of covering the calendar year only.

This method imposes appropriation upon the succeeding board for them to disregard at will.

Earlier appropriations are therefor required which a good balance during the year in the bank, or in the town's custody, would take care of.

The year's levy would thus restore the balance for use by the next year's board.

School supporters understand their tax to be for the current year's expenses.

The annual statement enables comparison of appropriations with expenditure when both cover the same period.

The Council may demand the estimate at any time, and it must be in before the 2nd of August.

Solicitor's guidance in the accomplishment of a change, would naturally be needed.

That section 16 of the High School Act requires estimates twelve months in advance, does not fix the date for such, and signifies only that borrowing shall be unnecessary by having funds at call of next year's board.

Section 65 Public School Act requires estimates for the current year.

Report 23.　　　　　Board of Education.

Payments to councilmen have been customary for many years, and the resolution for such, mention the remuneration at for committee work during the whole year. It has doubtless been well earned in the majority of cases, and the citizens were aware of such payment by the Treasurer's statement. Sec. 280, Municipal Act allows the Council to remunerate the Mayor, but the members are not so legislated for. Here again Counsel's advice has not been taken, and it would be well for him to now prescribe the proper course to pursue.

Town Properties.

A proper register of these is not in the possession of the Clerk. Such should contain a thorough description of the land, buildings, giving dates of acquirement or construction, location, size, original cost and subsequent additions thereto, with any further facts that will convey to future councilmen the origin, composition and value of such recurring assets of the balance sheet as are represented by the sum of $16,000. An official valuation of this aggregation of real estate would furnish its full description, and support the exhibited surplus for debenture holders.

Auditors.

The detail of their work has been well done within the compass of their view of it. It is however necessary for their criticism to extend further than the more clerical correctness. This report will doubtless indicate the further lines that may be reasonably followed by them.

Salaries.

The duties of Auditors, Clerk, Treasurer, Collector and Assessor in a town of such size call for men of experience, and ability to a larger extent than heretofore, since the standard of ability among citizens generally, is steadily rising, and demands fuller and quicker response from its government.

Permanence of officials is also much to be desired, as long acquaintance-ship, with civic affairs leads to better knowledge of the Town's requirements, and raises no new questions of reliability or capacity of officials. The duties of such officials must be performed morethoroughly in future, even though more work is entailed. It seems certain that capable men will not offer themselves permanently for the pay now afforded.

Your Council would act well therefore, in advancing some of the salaries.

Assistance to the audit was particularly rendered by the Chairman of Finance, Dr. T. W. Simpson, to whose courtesy and acquaintance with Town affairs, I am much indebted.

Report 24. Payments to Councilmen, Town Properties, Auditors, Salaries, Assistance to Audit.

Town of Napanee.

T. F. Ruttan, Collector, in account with Robert Mill, Treasurer.

Settlement of 1905 Roll as made by Collector, 2nd June, 1906.

To taxes collectable for 1905, as per collector's own summary	$30,079 42	
To interest charges as per collector's own summary	227 07	
By discount allowed as per collector's own summary	....	$ 127 10
By payments to treasurer, as entered in cash book	....	28,489 73
C. B. 48, Oct. 17, '05....... .... $	151 27	
55, Nov. 25, '05	2,500 00	
56, Nov. 27, '05	1,500 00	
57, Dec. 1, '05	4,000 00	
57, Dec. 1, '05 ....:	2,500 00	
57, Dec. 2, '05	2,500 00	
60, Dec. 13, '05	1,000 00	
61, Dec. 21, '05	1,000 00	
63, Dec. 30, '05	3,000 00	
65, Jan. 9, '06	2,000 00	
67, Feb. 6, '06 ....:..................	1,000 00	
68, Mar. 2, '06	1,000 00	
69, Mar. 13, '06 ......,...................	1,000 00	
70, Apr. 2, '06	1,000 00	
74, Apr. 24, '06	1,000 00	
Apr. 27, '06	1,000 00	
75, May 2, '06	1,000 00	
.., May 14, '06	1,000 00	
79, June 2, '06	322 26	
June 2, '06	16 20	

$28,498 73

By voucher for rebates (less duplicates 42.67—28.52)............	....	1,425 12
" " Madole	....	14 58
" " watering	....	28 14
" " arrears	....	218 47
By balance for rebates underpaid	.........:	3 35

$30,306 49 $30,306 49

Schedule A.

TOWN OF NAPANEE.

Correction of Collector's Summary, 1905.

Total taxes per collector's summary	$30,079 42
Add. interest per collector's summary	227 07

$30,306 49

Less discount per collector's summary	127 10

Amount accounted for by the collector	$30,179 39
Add. errors in drawing off tax totals p. 41, $4.10, East Ward, $5.00......	9 10

$30,188 49

Less errors in additions ot tax total, p. 41, $2.36, p. 42, $8.25	8 61

$30,179 88

Plus errors in extensions of taxes 54 82

p. 13	$ 1 00
15	1 00
41	1 94
42	2 10
43	46
47	1 62
59	54 00

$62 12

Less p. 69 ....:......	7 30

$54 82

$30,234 70   13 18

Plus errors in interest additions	
Recap. addition	$10 00
p. 52	3 20

$13 20

Less p. 6	2

$13 18

$30,247 88   9 77

Less errors in discount additions		
Recap. addition		$10 00
Less p. 44 ....:........	$0 21	
p. 37	2	
		23

. $9 77

Collector's summary after correction of errors ....,...................	$30,238 11

Schedule B.

TOWN OF NAPANEE.

Agreement of Collector's Roll with Assessor's Roll for 1905.

1,093,006	Assessments entered at 27 mills	$29,510 30
	Watering	396 70
	Dog tax	114 00

			113 73
Arrears			113 73
Interest			240 25

	$30,374 98
Less discount	136 87

	$30,238 11

22,039 Assessments omitted at 27 mills			$618 68
p. 5	Bay of Quinte Ry.	$850 00	$22 96
	Sherwood, H. B.	644 00	17 39
	" "	600 00	16 20
	" "	775 00	20 92
	.. ..	220 00	5 94 .
	" "	700 00	18 90
9	Mrs. A. J. Empey	750 00	20 25
11	Jones Mauley	1,350 00	36 45
17	McGee, Jas.	400 00	10 80
19	Mulligan, Jno.	900 00	10 80
	McCullough, J.	150 00	4 01
	McNeil	4,200 00	112 27
21	Peterson, F.	225 00	6 32
27	Whitemarsh, F.	100 00	4 05
29	Wales, Robert	150 00	4 10
36	Chambers, H.	300 00	8 10
	Jones, M.	175 00	4 75
46	Hawley, Jno.	450 00	12 03
	Hawley, M. S.	375 00	10 02
49	Laughlin, F.	450 00	12 03 .
	McBain. J.	550 00	14 85
50	Miller, S.	1,300 00	34 75
55	Harshaw, P.	2,700 00	72 42
61	Wilson	500 00	13 50
	Coates, J.	1,000 00	27 00
65	Craig, J.	2,000 00	54 00
68	Gleason, G.	350 00	9 45
70	Kinkley, G. E.	75 00	2 02'
73	McCabe & Earl	600 00	16 20
74	Pringle, E.	100 00	2 70

	$22,939 00	$618 68

$1,115,945 00
        75 00 less error in copying.

$1,115,870 00 per assessor's roll.
        Corrected total of collector's roll $30,856 79

Schedule C.

Town of Napanee.

Collector's Statement for 1095 as it appears after adjustment of the Rolls.

To corrected total of collector's roll	$30,856 79		
" tax collection extra thereto, apparently derived from assessor's omissions			75 13
By collections of taxes omitted from collector's roll handed in 19 June, 1906	....		$572 60
" collections of taxes entered in collector's rolls handed in from 17 Oct., 1905, to 2 June, 1906	....		28,469 73
" rebates allowed by council	....		1,471 19
" arrears of taxes	....		218 47
" balance of omitted taxes, etc., as follows...................	....		179 93

Errors in extensions of roll	$ 4 72	
Asst. 291 Mauley Jones, short paid............	12 15	
" 109 Bay of Quinte Ry.	22 96	
" 110/6 Sherwood, H. B.	17 39	
" 117 " "	16 20	$83 41
" 124 " "	20 92	
" 125 " "	5 94	

Asst. 218	Empey, Mrs. A. Z.	20 25
" 126	Sherwood, H. B.	18 90
" 901	Chambers, H.	8 10
" 1538	Wilson	13 50
" 1327	McCabe & Earl	16 20
" 1544	Pringle, E.	2 70
		$179 93

N.B.—The above balance $83.41 marked, has reference to possible duplicate assessments as mentioned in report.

$30,931 92 $30,931 92

Schedule D.

TOWN OF NAPANEE.

Amended memo. of settlement with Treasurer, R. Mills, 23 August, 1905.

F. C. Bogart, collector for 1905.

To amount of roll			$28,504 14
1,017,504 at 27 mills	$27,472 61		
Watering	388 54		
Snow shovelling	30 50		
Dog tax	103 00		
Arrears	309 46		
Interest	321 00		
	$28,625 11		
Less discount	120 97		
	$28,504 14		
By remissions, etc.		....	$1,023 62
" uncollectables		....	60 86
" tax arrears		....	237 38
" salary		....	150 00
" cash payments		....	27,004 54
			$28,476 40
Short paid		....	27 74
		$28,504 14	$28,504 14

Assessor's Roll for 1904.

Revised amount	$1,020,384 00
Collector's roll above	1,017,504 00
Shortage	$ 2,880 00

Collector's Roll, Omissions for 1904, at 27 mills.

A. R. 28	Monetan	300	$ 8 10
" 38	Cook	150	4 05
" 51	Boyes	900	24 30
" 64	Vacant	1,530	41 30
		2,880	
Escaped taxes of 1904			$77 75

N.B.—Arrears of taxes from 1903 not in 1904 roll, are on Clarksville lots, Nos. 31 and 32 and amount to $17.01, in addition to above.

Schedule F.

TOWN OF NAPANEE.

W. Rankin, Collector, 1903, in account with R. Mills, Treasurer.

Final settlement of 1903, Collector's Roll, 25 August, 1904.

To amount of roll		$28,426 19	
1,014,806 at 27 mills	$27,399 76		
Watering	345 18		
Snow shovelling	21 45		
Dog tax	95 00		
Arrears from 1902	348 75		
Interest	316 02		
	$28,526 16		
Less discount	99 97		
	$28,426 19		
To difference in figures		52	
By cash payments		....	$27,153 79
" remissions and exemptions		....	233 42
" errors rectified		....	153 11
" uncollectable taxes		....	346 39
" Napanee waterworks		....	540 00
		$28,426 71	$28,426 71

N.B.—Assessor's roll contained an error in addition of $2,000 arrears of 1902, not paid or remitted, have appeared in 1905 roll.

Schedule G.

BALANCE SHEET 31ST DECEMBER, 1905.

Current Assets.

By cash in Treasurer's hands		$ 108 94	
" tax monies not paid		11,540 40	
Collector's roll for 1905	$30,828 54		
Less cash payments $18,151 27			
Less discount allowed 136 87			
	18,288 14		
	$12,540 00		
Less rebates estimated	1,000 00		
Including $362.01 in his hands................	$11,540 00		
By electric light debenture monies divertible to current account in refund of advances	$............	5,539 17	
" supplies on hand	....	126 94	
" cement walks, property owners' proportion	....	387 78	
" Richard Street sewer	....	73 39	
" Dundas Street sewer	....	33 00	
" rentals unpaid	....	386 50	

Current Liabilities.

To school monies, 1905, unpaid	7,900 00	
" County rate, 1905, unpaid	2,600 00	
" sundry Town accounts per list	1,895 04	
" Merchants' Bank, overdraft	3,355 42	
" surplus available for 1906, current expenditure, debentures and interest	2,445 57	
	$18,196 03	$18,196 03

Fixed Assets.

By Town buildings and real estate, estimated.....................	$............	$16,000 00
" Land used by Board of Health, "	....	....	100 00
" Public Library, "	....	....	3,250 00
" Isolation Hospital, ::	....	....	325 00
" Harvey Warner Park,	....	....	1,300 00
" Public Schools,	....	....	15,000 00
" Collegiate Institutes, ..	....	....	26,500 00
" Fire appliances,	....	....	5,000 00
" Water sprinklers,	....	....	475 00
" Fire alarms,	....	....	1,100 00
" Weigh scales, ..	....	....	300 00
" Electric light construction,	....	....	5,539 17
" Office furniture,	....	....	100 00
" Surplus from current account, . "	....	....	2,445 57

Deferred Liabilities.

To Debenture portion of electric light expenditure	5,539 17	
" Debentures maturing annually	38,548 70	
" Surplus over bonded indebtedness	33,346 87	
	$77,434 74	$77,434 74

List of Debtors on Account of Cement Walks, 30th June, 1906.

Perry, J. J.	$ 2 95
Casey, Mrs.	6 60
Harshaw, A. T.	63 00
Perry Estate, Jas.	28 75
York, David	4 00
Mills, Geo.	6 60
Meagher, W. H.	29 95
Frizzell, Wm.	9 98
McCabe Estate, P. N.	4 64
Riddell, J. T.	2 60
Ward, Dr.	1 00
Chinneck, F. ....:	12 60
Cliff, G. A.	8 24
Herring, J. E.	12 72
Wilson, W. G.	11 14
Waller, T. H. & W. T.	22 44
	$227 21

Accounts Paid in 1906, Contracted in 1905.

Herrington, W. S.	$ 75 00
Kelly, H. W.	12 98
Doller, N.	20 45
Rankin, Wm.	20 00
Grange, W. A.	25 00
Graham, J. J.	25 00
Mill, R.	25 00
Potter & Blanchard	12 50
Madole & Wilson	34 99
Mair & Bro., G. L.	50 00
Pollard, E. J.	39 00
Perry, E. B.	7 50
Websdale, A. E.	10 00
Templeton, Wm.	37 50
Cowan, G. W.	75 00
Wilson, Jno.	20 80
Light, R.	38 32
Pringle, C.	25 15
Vanluven, F. C.	30 00
Canadian Locomotive Co.	64 00
Lapum, E. S.	10 00
Stevens, Chas.	28 55

McLaughlin, E.	4 90
Sine, A. D.	3 60
Bruce, Alexander	170 00
Board of Trade	25 00
Grange, J. T.	15 00
Alexander, A.	15 00
Vanluven, F. C.	76 30
Wilson Bros.	28 00
Madden Bros.	60 50
Gutta Percha & Rubber Co.	270 00
Town of Napanee, extra water service	540 00

Total	$1,895 04

Town of Napanee, October 20, 1902.

R. A. Shorey in Account with Corporation of Napanee.

To amount of taxes for 1901..............................	$............	$26,446 55
" Interest	407 15	
By discount	93 81	
		313 34

		$26,759 89
By cash October 2 per list.................................	$25,598 53	
" Dogs uncollectable	16 00	
" Remitted by Council	78 71	
" Exemptions	299 00	
" Uncollectable	569 53	
" Vouchers from Council	198 12	
		$26,759 89

Thomas G. Empey in Account with the Corporation of Napanee.

To amount of taxes for 1902..............................	$............	$28,467 85
" Interest	274 72	
" Discount	124 77	
		149 95

		$28,617 80
By cash paid	$............	$27,306 48
" Dogs uncollectable	32 00	
" Watering and snow shovelling	4 72	
" Taxes remitted	260 85	
" Taxes uncollectable	420 93	
" Taxes exempted	592 82	
		1,311 32
		$28,617 80

List of 1904 Arrears (Exclusive of Percentage) Introducible Into Collector's Roll for 1905 but Not Discoverable Therein.

Assessment	85	Cartwright,	P. & J. R............................		$13 59
"	86	"	"		4 86
"	87	"	"		9 72
"	87	"	::		2 03
"	88	"	"		2 02
"	1664	Hamilton,	J. A.		6 75
"	1745	Cartwright,	R. J.		2 70
"	1777	Pringle,	E.		14 59
					$56 17

1905 Tax Collections Apparently Derived from Assessor's Omissions.

McPharland	$ 8 10
McFarland	8 18
McCabe & Douglas	5 40
McCoy, Mrs. Jas.	12 15
Briggs, Jno.	2 79
Cunningham	17 38
Kellar, J. M.	9 73
Close, Lucy	9 45
Symington (error)	1 95
	$75 13

Letter to Dr. T. W. Simpson.

Dr. T. W. Simpson, Napanee, Ont.

MY DEAR DOCTOR,—Enclosed letter *re* Treasurer seems proper at this time. Will you present it. If you have any particular reason of policy against doing so, please communicate with me at once.

Yours truly,

(Sgd.) OSCAR HUDSON,

Chartered Accountant.

Letter to Mayor and Council.

To the Mayor and Council of the Town of Napanee, Ont.:

GENTLEMEN,—As a preliminary to the conclusion of my report upon the Audit of your Town Accounts;

It has been forced upon me to bring to your notice the inability of your Treasurer to continue his present duties.

His age and infirmity render him incapable of properly conducting the work, or of caring for the books, papers and monies of the town.

It is with exceeding regret that this view of his competency must be taken, but the responsibility of his position renders his continued performance of its duties inimical to the interests of the ratepayers.

His length of service and faithful discharge of duty entitle him to your utmost consideration.

The painstaking care shown in the books brought under my notice satisfy me of his honesty, and that until recently he must have been a highly capable official.

His willing and courteous attention to all enquiries have been gratifying, although the much needed information has, through his loss of memory, been utterly unobtainable, much to the detriment of this enquiry.

The Cash Book has been adjusted for him for this year, but unfortunately shows a balance that he is not able to explain, $220 at 1st August.

In justice to him, therefore, it is wiser that he be immediately relieved of further responsibility.

Yours truly,

(Sgd.) OSCAR HUDSON,

Chartered Accountant.

Report 25. Letter to T. W. Simpson and to Mayor and Council.

Letter to Petitioners, Sept. 5, 1906

As the Government is desirous of fully satisfying the purposes of the Commission of Enquiry, instituted in response to the petition which omits any specific charges, you are invited, as one of the petitioners, to present individually, or through a committee, during my attendance at the Town Hall next week, any facts bearing upon the investigation, and your reasons for requiring it, in order that the lines of enquiry may not be unnecessarily extended.

List of Petitioners.

T. W. Simpson.	V. Kouber.
Dudley L. Hill.	M. J. Nomile.
D. N. Parks.	Robert Boyes.
Albert D. Root.	H. Ming.
T. B. Wallace.	J. McGee.
H. N. Smith.	G. H. VanAlstine.
W. C. Smith.	F. Markle.
M. Taylor.	G. W. Gibbard.
A. E. Websdale.	A. C. Baker.
M. S. S. Madole.	W. E. Vine.
J. A. Hambly.	H. E. Fralick.
W. K. Pringle.	R. J. Wale.
F. H. Carson.	W. A. Frizzell.
A. F. Chinneck.	C. Frizzell.
Thos. Symington	J. J. Minchinton.
Ed. Boyle.	H. Babcock.
Will. H. Boyle.	H. E. Smith.
John Lowry.	

SCHEDULE E.—MUNICIPALITY OF THE TOWN OF NAPANEE.

Debenture Principal and Interest maturing in 1906 and following years.

	1906		1907		1908		1909		1910 and later.		Outstanding.	
	Principal.	Interest.	Principal.	Interest.	Principal.	Interest.	Principal.	Interest.	Principal.	Interest.	Principal.	Interest.
	$ c.	$ c.	$ c.	$ c.	$ c.	$ c.	$ c.	$ c.	$ c.	$ c.	$ c.	$ c.
...ed By-law No. 332, ...ssed 28th ...une, 19.., $4,500.00 @ 6 %, ... 62, ...hal l evy $2,438, ...ties July 1	2,300 00	69 00	......								2,300 00	69 00
High School By-law No. 438, ...ssed July 1, 19.., $6,000.00 @ 5 %, Nos. 36-40, Annual levy $481, ...ties July 1..	377 00	104 13	396 50	85 32	416 00	65 50	436 50	44 70	457 50	22 87	2,083 50	322 57
High School By-law No. 454, ...ssed July 2, 19.., $3,800.00 @ 5%, Nos. 55-60, ...ual l evy $305, ...ties July 1	227 50	77 46	239 00	66 02	251 00	54 07	263 50	41 52	567 00	28 34	1,548 00	267 41
Swing Bridge By-law No. 465, issued Dec. 15, 19.., for 30 years, $20,000.00 @ 4 %, Nos. 7-30, Annual levy, $1, 156.00, ...ties December 15 ...	270 29	114 12	282 45	101 91	295 16	89 21	308 44	75 93	1,378 96	62 05	2,535 30	443 22
N. T. & Q. Railway B-law No. 98, ...ied Dec. 15, 1899, for 30 ...ars, $20,000.00 @ 4 %, Nos. 29, Annual levy 1 $56, ...ties Dec. 15 ...	451 20	705 20	469 20	687 20	488 00	668 40	507 60	649 20	1,5718 60	7,412 80	17,634 60	10,122 80
N. T. & Q. Railway By-law No. 616, ...ssed Aug. 2, 19.., for 30 ...ars, $10,- 000.00 at 4 %, Nos. 39, Anal levy $578, maturities August 2 ...	217 00	361 38	225 60	352 60	234 60	343 60	244 00	334 20	8,113 10	4,031 00	9,034 30	5,422 78
High School By-law No. 412, issued July 3, 19.. for 20 ...ars, $12,000.00 @ 5 %, Nos. 17-20, Annual levy 19, 1...ties July 1	793 00	170 68	832 00	131 00	873 00	89 40	915 00	44 75	......	......	3,413 00	436 83
Electric light By-law No. 718, ...ssed July 24, 19.. for 30 ...ars, $35,000.00 @ 4 %, Nos. 7-30, Anal levy $2,024, maturities September 1	624 05	1,400 00	649 01	1,375 04	674 97	1,349 08	701 96	1,322 09	32,350 01	20,275 29	35,000 00	27,721 50
	5,260 04	3,002 02	3,093 76	2,799 09	3,232 73	2,659 26	3,377 00	2,513 39	58,585 17	31,832 35	73,548 70	42,806 11

21 M. A.

ABSTRACT STATEMENT.

INCOME AND EXPENDITURE NAPANEE PUBLIC SCHOOLS FROM JANUARY 1ST TO SEPTEMBER 12TH. 1906.

Income.

1906.	Cash balance			$267 49	
					$267 49
Jan.	1.—Municipal grant, balance 1905-6	259	$5,000 00		
	Legislative grant	259	402 00		
				5,402 00	
	Fees	258	8 00		
	Interest	258	50 78		
	Miscellaneous	258	7 00		
				65 78	
				$5,735 27	

Expenditure.

Salaries—

C. H. Edwards	250	$602 00		
Miss E. Harrison	250	211 75		
" J. F. Walsh	251	211 75		
" M. E. Fraser	251	211 75		
" F. G. Hall	252	211 75		
" Mata Wales	252	211 75		
" Mabel Caton	253	211 75		
" J. E. Mair	254	211 75		
" E. N. Parks	254	211 75		
" E. R. Baker	254	211 75		
Supply teacher	253	14 00		
E. Walker	254	216 50		
Wm. Burley	253	80 00		
Secretary-Treasurer	255	75 00		
			$2,893 25	
Supplies	257	$211 66		
Repairs	257	69 03		
Expense	257	60 22		
Printing	257	4 75		
Fuel	257	49 80		
			395 46	
Balance on hand			2,446 56	
			$5,735 27	

ABSTRACT STATEMENT INCOME AND EXPENDITURE NAPANEE COLLEGIATE INSTITUTE FROM JANUARY 1ST TO SEPTEMBER 12TH, 1906.

1906.

Income.

Jan.	1.—Cash balance			$1,639 83	
					$1,639 83
	Legislative grant	215	$1,091 84		
	County grant	214	2,700 00		
	Fees	214	84 00		
	Interest	214	27 90		
				3,903 74	
				$5,543 57	

Expenditure.

Salaries—

U. J. Flach	209	$844 20	
M. R. Reid	209	665 50	
R. A. Croskery	210	605 00	
Miss E. Henry	210	484 00	
" M. Smith	211	363 00	
" M. A. Nicholl	211	363 00	
Samuel Wilson	212	216 00	
Secretary-Treasurer	212	25 00	
			$3,566 20

21a M. A.

Repairs	212	$ 8 60	
Supplies	213	170 13	
Fuel	212	74 80	
Expense	213	20 62	
Printing	213	12 00	
Library	213	22 05	
Insurance	214	11 50	
Examinations	215	183 54	
			503 24
Balance on hand			1,474 13
			$5,543 57

Cost of this audit to the Municipality of Napanee, as per Mr. Hudson's account, was $492.45.

To the Mayor and Council of the Town of Wallaceburg:

GENTLEMEN,—Under the authority of an Order-in-Council approved by His Honour the Lieutenant-Governor on the 24th of March, 1906, I have made an inspection, examination and audit of the books, accounts, vouchers and moneys of the Town of Wallaceburg, in the County of Kent, and beg to report as follows:

According to my instructions, my audit has been confined to the period from 1st January, 1901, to 1st January, 1906.

The Town Treasurer has been in office nearly twenty years; his bond is dated 8th January, 1887; one of the sureties died some years ago, and the bond may now be considered of little value.

I have compared the vouchers and the sources of revenue carefully with the entries in the Cash Book and have balanced the latter. On the face of it, the balance $710.64 found in the cash book is correct. I find, however, that there are changes to be made in the items of cash receipts, etc. The following should be debited to the Treasurer:

Difference between balance of 1900 as shown by Auditor's statement and Treasurer's cash book	$ 5 00	
Short debit on June 1st, 1901, $272.50 for Licenses should be $292.50	20 00	
Purchase of one-half interest in Town Hall piano	100 00	
Moneys in Treasurer's hands on account of Cemetery as per statement herewith	58 00	
	$133 00	
Against which the Treasurer should receive credit for error in balance, 10c., over debit in taxes, $1.59	1 69	
	$181 31	

The total added to the cash balance would be $181.31 and the correct balance on 31st December, 1905, will be $991.95. The amount to credit of the municipality in Bank of Montreal on that date was $890.08.

I submit herewith a statement showing the cash balance at the close of each year. From this it will be seen that there were balances at credit of the Treasurer at close of 1901, $414.79; 1902, $639.79; 1903, $1,603.99. This credit balance was paid in 1904 and converted into a debit balance of $149.24.

The orders and vouchers for the years 1901, 1902 and 1903 are very irregular. A large number of orders are signed by the Town Clerk alone, some do not appear to have been passed by the Council and many of the vouchers are without the signature of the payee. It appears to have been considered that the possession of the voucher was sufficient evidence of payment. This, of course, is quite erroneous. No voucher is complete unless it bears the signature of the proper payee. In the years 1904 and 1905 there is a great improvement, the form of order and voucher is an excellent one and care has been taken that all necessary signatures have been attached.

In some cases I find that the Council had directed payments to be made upon the certificate or under the direction of a committee or individual member of the Council, but I do not find that any certificate from the committee or member of the Council was obtained before making the payment. In all cases where I considered that the orders or vouchers were defective, I made enquiries, the result of which satisfied me that the payments were proper ones.

In the year 1901 orders number 282 and 312 were for the same debt, and the payee, George Woods, received payment twice of his claim, $4.37.

At the end of the year 1903 the Town Clerk was overpaid on salary account $5.00 and the Engineer was overpaid $6.66.

In September, 1901, a settlement was made with Mr. C. Macgregor upon his contract for construction of granolithic walks. In this settlement Mr. Macgregor was allowed $137.80 for 53 barrels of cement. There does not appear in the minutes of the Council any authority for this purchase nor for the subsequent sale of the cement. In the following year $50.55 appears to have been realized from the sale of the cement.

In the year 1901 a contract was made with S. Thibedeau for the purchase of 150 thousand bricks for fire hall at $5 per thousand. On March 7th, 1901, $730 was paid Mr. Thibedeau and $25 on April 6th, 1901, making all $755. Of this sum $730.00 was charged to Blight & Fielder, the contractors for the Fire Hall. I find in Mr. Thidedeau's book an entry of the delivery of 146 thousand brick at Fire Hall. Mr. Thibedeau explains that the balance of the brick, 5 thousand, was delivered elsewhere for other purposes of the municipality.

In the same year, 1901, vault doors were purchased by the municipality and $55 paid therefor. $50 only appears to have been charged by Blight & Fielder.

On the 5th December, 1904, there appears upon the minutes of the Council a resolution "that an order for Seventy-two dollars and fifty cents be granted to D. C. MacDonald for taxes paid in error on post office." Upon reference to list of persons in arrear of taxes it will be found that during the period of my audit the taxes on Post Office were not paid. Mr. MacDonald explains that the taxes referred to and refunded were paid previous to 1901. As my audit does not extend back earlier than 1901, and as this matter came before the Council, who no doubt took proper care to investigate before passing the resolution, I accept Mr. MacDonald's statement.

On December 2nd, 1902, the basement of Town Hall was rented to Mr. Gollogly at $3 per month. I do not find that any part of the rent has yet been paid.

The by-laws which have been passed in each year to raise money for current expenses of the municipality are erroneously based upon the amount of taxes in arrear and unpaid, presumably under the authority of section 189 of Assessment Act, Chapter 23, of 1904, which permits the issue of debentures not exceeding in amount one-half of the arrears.

I find by minutes of Council that the Council has on several occasions by resolution remitted taxes on account of losses by fire and also grants have been made for decoration purposes. I am unable to find any legal authority for either of these cases. Taxes may be remitted under section 112 of the Assessment Act, but only for the reasons there set out. Under section 591 of the Municipal Act, grants for certain purposes therein specified may be made by by-law but the grants above mentioned are not included and in any case the grant must be made by by-law and not by resoultion.

Re Shepherd Moses.

On the 8th September, 1904, a child eleven years old, named Shepherd Moses, was convicted by the Police Magistrate of larceny and committed to the Victoria Industrial School for a period not extending beyond the time when he shall have attained the age of twenty-one years. The Police Magistrate further certified that the Town of Wallaceburg was liable to pay to the Industrial School for the maintenance of the child $1.25 a week. On Deecmber 19th, 1904, the Treasurer was instructed by resolution of Council to accept a draft at the rate of $1.25 per week. The expenses of conveying the child to the School have also been paid. This conviction and order were made under the authority of Chapter 304 of R.S.O., amended by Chapter 39, 1903, Ont. These acts refer only to Counties, Cities and Separated Towns, and as the Town of Wallaceburg does not come under any of these three heads, the Police Magistrate had no jurisdiction to take an order against the municipality; the order should have been made against the County of Kent. This is an important matter as the charge amounts to $65 per year and may continue for a period of ten years. Proceedings should be taken to have the order varied under the provisions of section 36, Chapter 259, R.S.O. This section (36) provides that unless the municipality moves to set aside the order in respect of maintenance within one month after receiving copy of the order, the municipality shall be deemed to have consented to the order and shall be stopped from denying liability thereunder. When considering the effect of this clause it must not be forgotten that the word "municipality" when used in this Act, and of course in this section 36, means a "County, City or Town separated from the County" (see Interpretation Clause). This section therefore does not affect the Town of Wallaceburg and no delay in moving against the order can make this municipality liable.

Floating Debt.

As there appears to have been some misunderstanding and some doubt in the minds of the ratepayers as to this debt, I give a short statement of its growth taken from the Town Cash Book, which is submitted herewith. The balance on 31st December, 1900, is given in my statement as $16,140.71, in the Auditor's statement of 1900 as $15,940.71, a difference of $200. This occurs by reason of a payment of $200 in 1900 which was improperly applied in reduction of principal instead of payment of interest. A by-law dated June 14, 1904, was passed for the purpose of consolidating the floating debt, and from the debentures issued thereunder the sum of $23,795.90 was realized on September 24th, 1904. At the commencement of the year 1904 the floating debt amounted to $25,340.34, this on the 24th September, when proceeds were realized, amounted to $29,554.85. Of the proceeds of debentures $15 was paid to the bank for expenses, 270.41 for accrued interest on the debt, leaving the balance of debt on September 30th, $6,044.36. This balance had increased on 31st December, 1904, to $9,353.15. In the year 1905, the debt still further increased, and on the 31st December of that year was $15,200, all held by the Bank of Montreal. Besides this amount it is claimed that a considerable sum has been collected for Public School purposes but retained and used for the general purposes of the municipality. I refer to the School balance hereafter. It is true that the bills, of which the floating debt is almost entirely composed, were from time to time discounted for the direct purpose of meeting debentures falling due and other liabilities of the municipality, but the fact remains that in each year a rate had been imposed upon the taxpayers for. the payment of these debentures, and if the monies thus raised had not been diverted to other purposes, the debentures would have been met from that source. The real deficit will be found else-where. The true cause no doubt is that the receipts from year to year for Town purposes fell far short of the amounts expended for these purposes, the total deficit on this account for the five years being upwards of $27,000. The increase of the debt in 1904 appears excessive in comparison with the two previous years; this is partly due to the fact that the Treasurer was advancing moneys which at the end of 1903 amounted to $1,603.99 and which were paid back to him in 1904. The taxes received in 1902 were likewise nearly $2,000 more than the levy for that year. There have been several over charges of interest on Bills Payable, particulars. of which have been handed to the Treasurer for correction.

The Debenture Debt.

The balance at this account on December 31st, 1900, was $70,237.75, being $1,015.96 in excess of the amount stated in Auditor's Report for that year. I submit a brief statement showing the yearly payment and the balance at the close of each year. The balance at close of 1905 being $101,-670.53. Two large amounts have been added to this debt during the last five years, viz.: $30,000 bonus to Sugar Company in 1901 and $24,000 consolidation of floating debt in 1904. The increase in the debt in five years is $31,432.78.

Asessment and Taxes.

I have checked the Collector's Rolls with the Assessment Rolls in each year of the period of my audit.

In the year 1903, I find an assessment of L. H. Side, $1,200, which was not carried into Collector's roll. As this assessment was properly made and the Collector's roll has not yet been returned, I am of the opinion that the latter can still be amended. The assessment is the basis of the debt, the Collector's roll is merely the means used for the collection of the debt, and the omission of any proper assessment from it does not cancel the debt. I would suggest an amendment of the Collector's roll by resolution of Council; the Collector should then give Mr. Side the necessary legal notices and if he refuses to pay an action can be brought in the Division Court. Mr. Side, however, should not be prejudiced; he should have the same advantages in the way of discount as if the proper entry had been made upon the roll.

I have compared the Collector's cash receipts with the Treasurer's Cash Book and find all correct, and all cash accounted for except a few small items amounting in all to $16.11 made up as follows:

1904.

July 23, Charles Reed ...., ...	$5 46
September 5th, Alexander Grant	4 00
Thomas Simpson...	2 00
December 31, Mrs. Brabeau	4 00
March 2nd, L. Lacroix, balance	65

$16 11

These items do not appear to have been paid over by the Collector to the Treasurer.

It is worthy of note that in the five years poll tax has been returned in one year only and also that dog tax returned in 1901 and 1903 amounted only to the small sums of $25 and $12 respectively.

The Collector has not made separate entries of taxes and interest received by him (in all cases), it has therefore been found impossible to balance the Collector's rolls with any degree of accuracy. I have, however, made an estimate of the amount of taxes paid upon each roll, and have arrived at an estimated balance for each year. This estimate varies considerably from the amount of taxes actually remaining unpaid on the rolls of 1901 and 1903. I have checked the items of taxes received in 1905 with the Collector's rolls of the different years and find them correct. It would be advisable to have the moneys received in the years 1901-2-3-4 compared with the different rolls. This could be done by your Collector with the assistance of the Clerk or Treasurer without any expense to the municipality.

The question of discount on taxes is one, of course, entirely within the discretion of the Council, but it might be well to consider if the advantages are not over-balanced by the loss to the municipality. The total amount of discounts allowed in the municipality for the last five years amount to

1901 ....$ 341 61
1902 .... 486 33
1903 .... 537 12
1904 .... 559 19
1905 .... 593 29

Total in five years $2,517 54

This large amount has been allowed to ratepayers who are best able to pay their taxes, and a large part of it has been allowed upon taxes which were paid the day before or within a few days of the time when they could with no difficulty have been collected at par. Five per cent. for a day, a week or a month appears to be a very high rate of interest.

Free Library.

The vouchers of the years previous to 1905 have not been preserved. I was therefore unable to audit the books except for the year 1905, which I found correct. The books appear to have been regularly audited and have been properly balanced. I submit statement showing receipts and expenditure for the five years, the balance on hand on 31st December, 1905, being $411.21. It is the duty of the Library Board to submit estimates to the Council before 15th February yearly of sums required by the Board, and it is the duty of the Council to levy and assess a sum sufficient (not more) but not requiring in any case a rate exceeding ½ mill (upon certain conditions ⅔ of a mill) on the dollar. It is not intended by the Act that the Library Board should create a surplus or that so large a sum as $411.21 should remain on hand at the close of the year.

Cemetery.

I have examined the books kept by the Caretaker, the Town Clerk and the Treasurer. I find certain moneys in the Treasurer's hands of which I submit a statement. In the Clerk's register there appear the names of certain person who have apparently received deeds for Cemetery lots but who do not (in Treasurer's books) appear to have paid the purchase money. A list of these names has been placed in the hands of the Treasurer for investigation. The system of accounts in connection with the Cemetery is fairly good, except in one or two particulars. The greatest defect appears to be that the Town Clerk issues the deeds whilst the Treasurer is supposed to receive the purchase money; in consequence deeds appear to have been issued without payment of purchase money. In the early years of the cemetery's existence no registry of lots sold or occupied was kept; it is now therefore impossible to ascertain from the books what lots remain unsold.

Non-resident Lands.

The non-resident branch of the tax department appears to have been somewhat overlooked. The lots assessed as non-resident are few, and from the books it is impossible to say with certainty what tax is against any particular lot. I have made all possible searches in the rolls, etc., and have prepared and delivered to the Treasurer a brief statement of the result. From this and from further investigation which the Treasurer has undertaken the accounts can be written up to date.

Police Accounts.

I find the accounts of the Police Court in a very unsatisfactory condition and have not been able to make an audit as no proper books have been kept. The Police Magistrate does not keep a cash book and the Town Clerk has not acted as Police Clerk as required by the Municipal Act. I have obtained from the Police Magistrate a statement of the fines paid in to the Town Treasurer, the total for five years being $431.80. The Town Treasurer's cash book shows the receipt of a much larger amount, namely $754.37.

Wallaceburg Electric Light Co.

I submit a statement of the accounts with the Electric Light Company for five year, showing orders issued and cash paid to the Company. From this statement it would appear that the Company is indebted to the town $305.35, but it will be noticed that accounts have been passed and orders issued for 19 quarters only in the five years for street lighting, the quarter overlooked is apparently the first quarter of the year 1903. If the omitted quarter (322.50) be added to the account the balance would be $17.15 in favor of the Company.

Balance Sheet.

I submit a statement of assets and liabilities as they stood on the 31st December, 1905. This statement is chiefly of value for the purpose of comparison with a similar statement made by the Auditors at the close of 1900. During the 5 years assets have decreased from $57,178.99 to $51,763.74 chiefly owing to the decrease of cash on hand. Liabilities have increased from $85,162.50 to $117,614.53, an increase of $32,452.03. Excess of liabilities over assets in 1900 was $27,983.51; at close of 1905 it was $65,850.79, an increase of $37,867.28.

Permit me briefly to direct your attention to the Auditor's balance sheets of the years 1900, 1901, 1902 and 1903, (1904 is not before me), and the different results arrived at by the respective auditors. For the purpose of comparison I give here the totals in each year as given by the balance sheets:

Year.	Assets.	Liabilities.	Deficit.
1900	$57,178 99	$85,162 50	$27,983 51
1901	47,272 72	85,452 67	38;179 95
1902	112,548 38	114,045 35	1,496 97
1903	114,150 97	109,497 37	*4,653 60

*Surplus.

It would appear from these figures that, notwithstanding $30,000 had in the meantime been given away, the municipality in its financial affairs had improved in a miraculous manner and in an exceedingly short time. A very cursory examination of the Town's accounts during that period will disclose quite a contrary condition of affairs. These statements are chiefly for the information of the ratepayers, but have been (unintentionally no doubt) misleading. The discrepancies are the result of inaccuracy, and of the different methods of treating the assets adopted by the different auditors. The Auditors of 1901, 1902 and 1903, appear to have overlooked the balances in the cash book for these years, which in each case happened to be a liability. In the statement of 1903, the floating debt is placed at an amount very much less than the correct one. Sewers in 1902 are valued as an asset at $10,000, and in 1903, (in the published statement) at $1,000, the addition would indicate that this is an error in the published statement, but in any case it is misleading to the public. In the case of municipality, the question often arises, "what are properly classed as assets?" It appears to me that only those assets which might (in case of insolvency) be used in payment of liabilities should be set off against liabilities, and then only at their cash value. If this rule were applied to your municipality your total of assets would be very much reduced.

Re Sugar Company.

I desired to make some investigation into the relations of the sugar company with the Town, but have been unable to do so as no copy of the agreement between these two parties can be found in any of the Town offices.

Public Schools.

I have carefully examined the books, accounts and vouchers in connection with the public school.

The Treasurer's books of account and vouchers are in good order, and have been very well kept, and with a few not important exceptions are correct. Three vouchers in 1902, one in 1903, one in 1904, are not properly signed by the payee, and voucher number 75 in 1903 is missing. The payments in each of these cases appear to have been proper.

The minutes of school board meetings do not disclose a very precise method of doing business.

No security has been taken from the Treasurer as required by section 18, chapter 89, Ontario, 1901.

Section 81 of chapter 89, Ont., 1901, which provides that all agreements between trustees and teachers shall be in writing signed by the parties thereto, and sealed with the seal of the corporation has been altogether ignored. I have been informed that no agreement in writing has been made with any teacher during the last five years. In at least one case a teacher was engaged without even the passing of a resolution.

In several cases no mention is made of the amount of salary to be paid.

On the 5th May, 1903, R. L. Soper, offered to purchase lots 91, 92, 133, 134, for the sum of $400, with five per cent. payable monthly, the offer was approved of by the committee appointed to make the sale, the purchaser was let into possession, placed a house on the lands, and has since paid the taxes on the lots, yet no action appears to have been taken by the school board, either to accept or reject the offer, or to collect the purchase money, and no part of the purchase money appears to have been paid. The agreement would now be held to be binding, and the purchase money should be collected.

Requisition has not always been properly made to the Council for moneys required in each year. This should not be neglected as the requisition is the basis for the rate to be levied by the Council.

I submit herewith statements showing receipts and expenditure of the school for five years, and also the levies made by your Council, and the payments made to school board, showing a balance due the school of $744.00. The Town Treasurer informs me that there is a further amount due the school on account of collections made to equal Legislative grants in the years prior to the period of my audit.

It is claimed that a considerable amount is owing by the Council to the school board, the board has a cash balance on 31st December, 1905, of $139.83, and have also a debt due to the school of $400 for sale of lots, in all about $2,000. I need scarcely say that the school board is supposed to receive yearly an amount sufficient to meet their annual expenditure, a surplus is not contemplated by the Public School Acts.

Fire Hall.

I submit an account in connection with the building of the fire hall, in which there is balance due the Treasurer of $4.33.

To facilitate reference, and for other various reasons all moneys received or paid on behalf of the corporation should be entered in the cash book. this rule has not been observed in connection with this account.

In my audit I have been greatly assisted by the Treasurer, the Town Clerk and the collector. Each one of these gentlemen has promptly and cheerfully given every explanation asked for, and has facilitated a thorough investigation. The system of book keeping is a good one. The books of the Treasurer and Town Clerk are particularly neat, and whilst the collector's are not so neat, it must be said that his task has been a very difficult one, his errors have been unimportant, and under the circumstances very few.

Recommendations.

1. A new bond should be taken from the Treasurer, preferably that of a surety company.

2. Care should be taken that all orders be properly marked for their respective accounts, and all receipts and payments entered in each book under proper heads.

3. No orders should be issued by the Clerk without the authority of the Council, in cases where the Council has delegated its authority to a committee, the order of the chairman should be produced to the Clerk, and filed away for the use of the auditors. There are of course cases of emergency where orders must be issued before consulting the Council. In all such cases the order should be submitted to the Council for approval at its next meeting.

4. A ledger account should be opened with the collector, a separate account for each year's roll. He should be charged with the whole of taxes on the roll, and credited with payments as he makes them, of taxes collected. A balance can then be struck at any time, and the amount remaining unpaid on the roll be readily ascertained. In order that this may be done, the collector must keep separate in his books, and returns the amount paid for taxes, and interest and care must also be taken by the collector and Treasurer to keep separate the amounts paid on the different rolls.

5. By-laws for raising money for current expenditure should be under the authority of section 435 of the Municipal Act, amended by Act of 1904, section 15, and should recite amount of estimates, and necessity for providing for current expenditure.

6. Deeds for cementry lots should be issued, and purchase money be received by the same official, either the Treasurer or the Clerk who would this become responsible for the receipt of the purchase money before delivery of the deed. A short form of deed should be prepared with a stub attached, deed and stub to be numbered consecutively. The caretaker of the cemetry should also report to the Treasurer when any plot is first taken up or occupied.

8. The Town Clerk should be required to act as Police Clerk as provided by section 480 of the Municipal Act, and should keep a record of all informations taken, all fines imposed, and all moneys received.

9. To facilitate checking similar items in collector's roll, and assessment roll should have similar numbers. Each page in the collector's roll should terminate with the same serial number as the corresponding page in assessment roll.

10. Reports of committees of Council sould always be in writing, and preserved for reference.

11. All agreements between public school teachers, and the school trustees should be in writing. Section 81, chapter 39, 1901, Ontario, is imperative.

12. A special effort should be made to get in arrears of taxes, and have collector's rolls returned. I found five rolls in the collector's hands. A state of affairs which needs no words from me to condemn it.

13. Auditors should be required to make clear and impartial statements such as will make known to the ratepayers the true financial standing of the corporation.

All of which is respectfully submitted.

J. W. SHARPE,

Auditor.

27th July, 1906.

The following statements accompany this report, viz.:
1. Town balance sheet.
2. Statement of Wallaceburg, E. Light Company.
3. Yearly cash balances.
4. Statement of taxes collected.
5. Public School in account with corporation.
6. Statement of debenture debt.
7. Statement of floating debt.
8. Treasurer in account with Cemetry.
9. Public library receipts and expenditure.
10. Corporation receipts and expenditure.
11. Fire hall building account.
12. Public school receipts and expenditure.

Fire Hall Building Account.

Amount of deposit in Bank	$5,000 00	
Interest on same	44 79	
Balance due Treasurer	4 33	
		5,049 12

1901.
March	7.—Paid S. Thibideau for bricks	$730 00	
Aug.	7.—Paid M. Martin for plans	102 00	
Aug.	17.—Paid Blight & Fielder on contract	500 00	
Ang.	30.—Paid Blight & Fielder	500 00	
Sept.	16.—Paid Blight & Fielder	500 00	
Sept.	28.—Paid Blight & Fielder	300 00	
Sept.	29.—Paid J. & J. Taylor, vault doors	55 00	
Oct.	12.—Paid Blight & Fielder	400 00	
Nov.	4.—Paid Blight & Fielder	500 00	
Dec.	24.—Paid Firemen's grant	195 00	
Dec.	28.—Paid Blight & Fielder in full	1,267 12	
			5,049 12

Account of Blight and Fielder.

Cash as above	$2,700 00	
146 thousand of brick	720 00	
Vault doors	50 00	
Freight on	2 31	
55½ barrels cement at $2.40	133 20	
Cartage	1 37	
Cheque to balance	1,267 12	
Total contract price		4,884 00

RECEIPTS AND EXPENDITURE OF THE PUBLIC SCHOOL OF THE TOWN OF WALLACEBURG FOR THE YEARS 1901, 2, 3, 4 AND 5.

Expenditure.

Salaries to teachers	$19,604 29	
Salaries to others	2,407 93	
Fuel, etc.	2,183 66	
Repairs	1,223 72	
Examinations	214 20	
Printing	449 63	
Equipment	423 16	
Insurance	140 83	
Sundries	464 13	
Balance on hand	139 83	
		27,251 38

Receipts.

Balance from 1900	$174 00	
Grants from Government	2,104 00	
Municipal taxes	22,222 88	
County grant	1,674 50	
Sundries	170 00	
Fees received	906 00	
		27,251 38

Balance Sheet.

Total receipts for the years 1901, 1902, 1903, 1904 and 1905.

Resident taxes	$93,815 38	
Dog tax	394 00	
Rents	989 31	
Licenses	4,130 98	
Legislative grants for schools	1,504 00	
Loans	55,024 94	
Fines	574 37	
Cemetery	1,187 75	
Miscellaneous	2,347 68	
Non-resident tax	178 23	
Debentures	54,000 00	
Coupons	674 27	
Interest	241 27	
Balance from Auditor's report of 1900	5,761 62	
		220,823 80

Expenditure.

Salaries and allowances	$11,563 34	
Printing, etc.	1,112 69	
Insurance	593 26	
Fire, water and gas	13,119 93	
Roads and bridges	12,000 05	
Charity	835 77	
Debentures	22,567 22	
Coupons	16,443 57	
Bills payable	55,965 65	
Interest	7,463 03	
Public Library	1,500 15	
Granolithic walks	4,978 85	
County rate	3,655 06	
Schools, Public	1,504 00	
" taxes	22,222 88	
Schools, Separate	7,103 71	
Board of Health	1,089 31	
Town Hall	917 76	
Miscellaneous	3,282 08	
Bonus to Sugar Company	30,000 00	
Cemetery	1,586 14	
Law costs	427 38	
Balance in Treasurer's hands	891 95	
		220,665 80

THE WALLACEBURG PUBLIC LIBRARY.

Receipts for Years 1901-'05.

Balance from 1900	$147 46	
Receipts in 1901	422 80	
Receipts in 1902	533 12	
Receipts in 1903	406 48	
Receipts in 1904	614 28	
Receipts in 1905	505 59	
Total receipts for 5 years		2,649 73

Expenditure for 5 Years.

Light and School (1901)	$7 77	
Salaries	765 20	
Newspapers and magazines	272 70	
Books	919 52	
Lectures	1 00	
Miscellaneous	272 33	
Balance on hand, 31st December, 1905	411 21	
		2,649 73

THE TREASURER.

In Account with Wallaceburg Cemetery.

1901.—To receipts as per register	$188 50	
By debit in Town cash book	....	156 00
" allowed off. not paid in	....	6 00
1902.—To receipts as per register	272 00	
By debit in Town cash book	....	228 00
" allowed off, not paid in	....	25 50
1903.—To receipts as per register	225 25	
By debit in Town cash book	....	233 75
" allowed off, not paid in	....	3 50
1904.—To receipts as per register	204 00	
By debit in Town cash book	....	215 50
1905.—To receipts as per register	227 00	
By debit in Town cash book	....	230 00
To cash, Mrs. Schaaf	10 00	
" Pangburn	3 50	
" McCrary	1 00	
" Fullmer	10 00	
" Arnold	15 00	
By balance in Treasurer's hands	....	58 00
	$1,156 25	$1,156 25

STATEMENT SHOWING YEARLY INCREASE OF FLOATING DEBT OF THE TOWN OF WALLACEBURG.

Debt, 1st January, 1901	$16,140 71	
Increase in 1901	3,675 91	
Debt, 1st January, 1902	$19,816 62	
Increase in 1902	2,083 38	
Debt, 1st January, 1903	$21,900 00	
Increase in 1903	3,440 34	
Debt, 1st January, 1904	$25,340 34	
Increase in 1904	7,523 30	
	$32,863 64	
Consolidated in 1904	23,510 49	
Debt, 1st January, 1905	$9.353 15	
Increase in 1905	5,846 85	
Debt, 1st January, 1906		15,200 00

Wallaceburg, July, 1906.

Statement Showing Growth of Debenture Debt of the Town of Wallaceburg.

Total December 31, 1900	$70,237 75	
Paid in the year 1901	4,509 12	
Total December 31, 1901	$65,728 63	
Bonus to sugar company	30,000 00	
	$95,728 63	
Paid in 1903	3,583 23	

Total December 31, 1902	$92,145 40
Paid in 1903	4,488 14
Total December 31, 1903	$87,657 26
Paid in 1904	5,019 14
	$82,638 12
Consolidated debentures in 1904	24,000 00
Total December 31, 1904	$106,638 12
Paid in 1905	4,967 59
Total December 31, 1905	$101,670 53

(The payments above mentioned do not include the amounts paid for interest coupons.)

The balance is made up as follows:

By-law for granolithic walks	$3,673 81	
By-law 55, Fire Hall	3,886 27	
Consolidation of 1895	13,166 99	
Bonus to sugar company	26,855 11	
North Wallaceburg School	1,925 82	
Sydenham Glass Co., stock	9,124 49	
By-law 57, floating debt and granolithic walks	19,431 34	
By-law 93, consolidation	23,606 70	
		$101,670 33

The Corporation of Wallaceburg in Account with Wallaceburg Public School.

Balance due schools as shown by Town Treasurer's ledger account	$ 990 64	
Levy public schools in 1901	3,713 24	
To equal Government grant	291 00	
Levy for Public Schools, 1902	3,959 00	
To equal legislative grant, 1902	291 00	
Levy for Public Schools, 1903	3,800 00	
To equal legislative grant for 1903	304 00	
Levy for Public Schools, 1904	4,500 00	
To equal legislative grant, 1904	309 00	
Levy for Public Schools for 1905	4,500 00	
To equal legislative grant for 1905	309 00	
Legislative grant for five years	1,504 00	
		$24,460 88

Payments to School Treasurer as Shown by Town Treasurer's Cash Book.

Paid in 1901 on 1901 account...	$4,054 00	
" 1901, legislative grant...	291 00	
" 1902 on 1902 account..	3,866 00	
" 1903 " 1902 "	675 00	
" 1903 " 1903 "	3,909 49	
" 1904 " 1904 "	5,189 00	
" 1905 " 1904 "	933 39	
" 1905 " 1905 "	4,809 00	
		$23,726 88
Balance unpaid		$744 00

WALLACEBURG, July, 1906.

Statement of Taxes Collected.

Total in year 1901..	$15,440 67	
" 1902..	19,573 22	
" 1903..	18,008 25	
.. 1904..	19,983 03	
" 1905..	20,810 19	
Total collected in five years............................		$93,815 36

TOTALS ON EACH ROLL.

Roll of 1897.

Collected	in	1901	$ 53 87
"		1902	69 56
"		1903	54 28
"		1904	4 15
			$181 86

Roll of 1898.

Collected	in	1901	$569 28
"		1902	334 52
"		1903	59 21
..		1904	2 24
			965 25

Roll of 1899.

Collected	in	1901	$1,307 18
"		1902	1,223 56
"		1903	116 17
::		1904	24 34
			2,671 25

Roll of 1900.

Collected	in	1901	$3,822 05
"		1902	2,258 31
"		1903	465 88
..		1904	170 62
..		1905	1 31
			6,718 17

Roll of 1901.

Collected	in	1901	$9,688 29
"		1902	3,385 83
"		1903	1,079 61
..		1904	669 64
		1905	3 16
			14,826 53

Roll of 1902.

Collected	in	1902	$12,247 44
"		1903	2,664 00
"		1904	1,977 06
::		1905	378 85
			17,267 35

Roll of 1903.

Collected	in	1903	$13,569 10	
"		1904	3,371 60	
"		1905	1,888 93	
				17,829 63

Roll of 1904.

Collected	in	1904	$13,763 38	
"		1905	3,901 61	
				17,664 99

Roll of 1905.

Collected	in	1905	$14,602 43	
				14,602 43

Total on all rolls		$93,727 46
Non-resident tax		33 90
Poll tax		54 00
Total for five years		$93,815 36

Statement Showing Cash Balances at End of Each Year Commencing with Balance at End of 1900, $5,761.62, Taken from Auditor's Statement of 1900.

Year.	Debits.	Credits.		Balance.
1900	$ 5,761 62	$	Dr.	$5,761 62
1901	21,824 58	28,000 99	Cr.	414 79
1902	68,830 40	70,324 52		
1902	8,050 03	6,780 91	Cr.	639 79
1903	22,030 73	23,000 26		
1903	6,580 14	6,574 81	Cr.	1,603 99
1904	65,348 95	61,674 61		
1904	....	1,921 11	Dr.	149 24
1905	26,024 19	28,337 05		
1905	6,154 28	3,255 12		
1905	156 41	....	Dr.	891 95
	$230,761 33	$229,869 38		
	229,869 38			

Balance 1905	$891 95	

The Town of Wallaceburg in Account with the W. E. Light Company.

1901.   *Payments as Per Cash Book.*

April	10.—138	Quarter ending March	$............	$305 00
June	31.—220	....	....	305 00
Sept.	31.—234	....	....	305 00
Dec.	31.—	....	....	305 00
1902.				
May	15.—	For wiring and fixtures	133 69	
		March quarter and lamp	11 60	305 00
June	30.—	....	....	322 50
Sept.	30.—	Street lighting and supplies	2 75	322 50
Dec.	11.—261	Coal	6 00	
	261	Cinders	9 00	
Dec.	31.—	....	....	322 50
1903.				
Feb.	6.—	Supplies (1902 account)	3 00	
May	21.— 62	Lighting (Municipal buildings)	....	93 96
March	28.—	....	....	322 50
July	23.—	June quarter	....	322 50
Oct.	3.—	September quarter	....	322 50
Dec.	26.—	Bal. of September quarter	12 50	
Dec.	31.—345	December quarter	....	322 50
		For municipal buildings, etc.	2 70	94 12

22 M.A.

1904.				
April	6.— 68	To April 1 and supplies less $6.40 reduction	75	316 10
May	16.—141	Account June quarter	....	100 00
June	14.—184	Account	....	150 00
July	27.—250	Account June quarter	....	-40 00
Aug.	5.—274	September quarter	....	100 00
Oct.	15.—351	Bal. of Sept. quarter less $31.96 reduction...	50	213 36
Dec.	23.—449	Street lighting, etc. (including municipal buildings)	11 80	416 62
1905.				
April	5.— 80	Supplies	7 75	
May	3.—125	Account April quarter	....	94 09
	126	Account April quarter	2 13	228 41
July	5.—205		....	334 71
Aug.	22.—261	Account	6 75	
Oct.	5.—321	$340 less $9.52	2 25	330 48
Nov.	16.—325	Balance	....	9 52
1906.				
Feb.	8.— 28	Street lighting, supplies, etc., to December 31, 1905	30 58	434 12

	$243 75	$737 45
Supplies, etc., carried down		243 75
Total cash paid		$6,981 20
Orders as per statement herewith		6,675 67
Balance		$305 53
Less Dr. in cash book		18
		$305 35

Orders Issued.

March	8.—137	Balance ($200 having been paid November 8, and $105 on December 28, 1900)	$ 15 00	
Aug.	12.—272		307 50	
Dec.	31.—413		610 00	
1902.				
April	2.—483		316 60	
	484		133 69	
Sept.	3.—147		325 25	
Oct.	9.—188		3 00	
Nov.	3.—213		322 50	
Nov.	7.—228	To December 31, 1901	305 00	
Dec.	5.—260		9 00	
	261		6 00	
1903.				
April	8.— 31	To December 31, 1902	322 50	
May	6.— 69		93 96	
July	8.—116		322 50	
Dec.	2.—239		334 65	
Dec.	26.— 43		419 32	
1904.				
April	4.—103		316 85	
Oct.	10.— 66		313 96	
July	5.—258		289 72	
Dec.	20.—282		428 42	
1905.				
March	7.—239		6 75	
April	5.—266		7 75	
May	2.—319		94 09	
May	3.—326		228 41	
May	2.—320		2 13	
July	5.—387		334 17	
Oct.	3.—473		332 73	
Nov.	11.—498		9 52	
1906.				
Feb.	.— 60		464 70	
				$6,675 67

STATEMENT OF ASSETS AND LIABILITIES OF WALLACEBURG ON 31ST DECEMBER, 1905.

Assets.

Available—

Cash on hand	$891 95	
Taxes on roll of 1901	504 65	
" " 1902	446 16	
" " 1903	523 04	
" " 1904	2,492 54	
" " 1905	5,886 40	
Balance on Thomas property	119 00	
Balance due from Agricultural Society	800 00	
		$11,663 74

Permanent—

Fire Hall and contents	$9,500 00	
Town Hall	7,000 00	
Public Schools	20,000 00	
Cemetery	3,000 00	
Town dock	200 00	
Street scraper	200 00	
Sprinkler	200 00	
		40,100 00

Total assets	$51,763 74

Cost of this audit to the Municipality of Wallaceburg, as per Mr. Sharpe's account, was $528.00.

Liabilities.

Due Bank of Montreal	$ 15,200 00
Debentures unpaid (not including coupons)	101,670 53
Due School Board, say	744 00
Total liabilities	$117,614 53
Assets	51,763 74
Excess of liabilities over assets	$65,850 79

TOWN OF HAILEYBURY.

TORONTO, ONTARIO, January 21st, 1907, ·

TO THE MAYOR AND COUNCIL OF THE TOWN OF HAILEYBURY:—

Gentlemen,—Under authority of an, Order-in-Council approved by His Honor the Lieutenant-Governor of Ontario, the 12st ultimo, and in accordance with instructions from The Provincial Municipal Auditor, I proceeded to the Town of Haileybury, for the purpose of making an inspection, examination and audit of the books accounts, vouchers and moneys of the Municipal Corporation of the said Town of Haileybury, in the District of Nipissing.

The audit is made upon the petition of certain ratepayers, addressed to His Honor the Lieutenant-Governor of Ontario. Nothing specific is charged; the audit being simply asked for, upon general grounds, reference being made to the reported muddled condition of the books, owing to the inexperience and incapacity of the officials and Council that have had charge of affairs since incorporation over two years ago.

The incorporation of Haileybury was proclaimed as a town in August, 1904. The first Mayor and Council elected were—

Mayor—P. T. Lawlor.

Councillors—R. Little, S. Norfolk, G. A. Adair, J. McLellan, E. R. Summers, W. S. Heron.

H. D. Graham, Clerk; Jos. Bell, Treasurer.

1906.

Mayor—C. C. Farr.

Councillors—S. Briden, T. H. Thompson, F. B. Warner, Robert Little, A. J. Murphy, S. Norfolk.

H. D. Graham, was succeeded by J. D. McMurrich, as clerk, and later by Paul A. Cobbold, the present clerk, on the 13th of November, 1906; John T. Kelly succeeding Joseph Bell on the 5th September, 1905, as Treasurer.

1907.

The newly elected Mayor and Council are as follows:—

Mayor—P. T. Lawlor.

Councillors—Geo. T. Hamilton, Arthur ⅃erland, Cyril Young, W. H. Wilson, S. Briden, A. E. Whitley.

BY-LAWS PASSED BY THE COUNCIL OF HAILEYBURY.

1904.

No. 1, Sept. 26.—Appointing Auditor, Clerk, Treasurer, Medical Health Officer, Board of Health, Constable and Sanitary Inspector.

No. 2, Sept. 26.—Against Indecent Posters, Gambling, Houses, Horse Racing or Furious Driving, Beggars, Indecently Clothed Persons, and use of Fire Arms.

No. 3, Sept. 26.—To Borrow $500.00 from Union Bank on promissory note.

No. 4, Oct. 10.—Regarding Pool Tables, etc.

No. 5, Oct. 10.—Regarding Disorderly Houses.

No. 6, Nov. 8.—Regarding Appointment of Assessor.

No. 7, Nov. 8.—Regarding Assessment Roll.

1905.

No. 8, Feb. 6.—Appointment of Assessor.

No. 9, April, 3.—Regarding Taverns and Shop Licenses.

No. 10, April 3.—Regarding Pedlars.

No. 11, April 3.—Appointment of Sanitary Inspector.

No. 12, May 1.—Regarding Vehicles on Sidewalks.

No. 13, May 1.—Dog Tax.

No. 14, May 1.—Regarding Carters or Draymen.

No. 15, June 5.—Appointing D. Myles, Member Board of Health.

No. 16, June 5.—J. Coats appointed Constable.

No. 17, June 5.—Borrowed $650.00 Union Bank.

No. 18, July 10.—Regarding Pounds, and running at large of Animals, etc.

No. 19, Sept, 1.—Loan of 559.52 from Union Bank.

No. 20, Sept. 5.—J. T. Kelly, appointed Treasurer.

No. 21, Sept. 19.—Borrowed $500.00 from Union Bank.

No. 22, Oct. 3.—Regarding Beach Bros. Contract, ratifying Contract between Town and Beach Bros.

No. 23, Nov. 18.—E. C. Wright, appointed Collector.

No. 24, Nov. 18.—E. Provost appointed Sanitary Inspector.

No. 25, Dec. 15.—Chas. Warner appointed Collector.

No. 26, Dec. 15.—Borrowed $500.00 from C. A. Foster.

No. 27, Dec. 15.—D. Myles and R. J. Hancock appointed Members of Local Board of Health.

1906.

No. 28, Feb. 8.—A. E. Whitley appointed Assessor and Collector for year 1906.

No. 29, Feb. 7.—By-law No. 1 Amended re Hotel Licenses.

No. 30, Feb. 27.—Regarding lease of Fire Engine.

No. 31, March—Borrowed $1,500.00 from Union Bank.

No. 32, March—Dr. Jackson appointed Medical Health Officer.

No. 33, March—Borrowed $1,000.00 from Union Bank. Stables.

No. 34, April—To license and regulate owners of Livery Stables.

No. 35, April—To authorize and provide for licensing of Pool Rooms, etc.

No. 36, April—Appointing Inspector of Buildings and regarding Buildings, Chimneys.

No. 37, July 31.—Borrowed $5,000.00 from Union Bank.

No. 38, Nov. 13.—Appointing P. A. Cobbold, Clerk of Town.

No. 39, Dec. 13.—To authorize purchase of Steam Fire Engine.

No. 40, Dec. 13.—h. A. Day appointed Poll Clerk.

No. 41, Dec. 13.—Regarding hour for holding nominations.

No. 42, Dec. 15.—H. A. Day appointed Collector.

No. 43, Dec. 18.—For authorizing the levying and collecting of Annual Rates.

No. 44, Dec. 18.—Authorizing rebate to Fire Sufferers.

No. 45, Dec. 18.—Appointing F. A. Day, Solicitor for Town.

No. 46, Dec. 18.—Authorizing issue of Debentures for the sum of $10,-000.00.

No. 47, Dec. 18.—Authorizing issue of Debentures for the sum of $10,000.00.

RATES STRUCK FOR 1906.

No rate having been struck for the current year, owing to the fact, that the Mayor and Council were entirely in the dark regarding the present financial standing of the Town, being evidently unable to obtain any definite idea from the Treasurer, owing to the condition of his books, I was accordingly requested on my arrival to prepare at the earliest possible momnt, from the material at hand, a financial statement setting forth as nearly as possible the present position of the Town. After its completion and at my request a meeting of the Council was called, and held in the office of F. A. Day, Solicitor for the Town, when I presented my statement to the meeting, which finally passed the by-law fixing the rate as follows:—

General rate 16 mills on the dollar.

School rate 3½ mills on the dollar.

School Debenture rate ½ mill on the dollar.

Total 20 mills on the dollar, being 7 mills less than 1905.

Total Assessment per Collector's Roll,	$444,457	at 16 mills,
	7,111 31	at 16 mills,
School, General, $444,457 at 3½ mills,	1,555 45	at 16 mills,
School Debentures, $444,457 at ½ mill,	222 38	at 16 mills,
		at 16 mills,
Total taxes per Collector's Roll, 1906,	$8,889 14	at 16 mills,

Municipal Cash Book.

I regret to say on examination, I found this very important book in a most deplorable condition, receipts, in many 'nstances, as well as payments, not being entered until the end of the year, and in some cases not at all, although various sums had been received and paid during the year. The same system prevailed 'n regard to other important items.

This is totally foreign to all accepted ideas of the correct method of keeping a cash book. Payments and receipts ought to be entered as they are paid or received. Each individual payment or receipt should be at once entered, with date and all needful particulars. The entries of taxes in the cash book, also should agree with the receipts given by the Treasurer to the Collector.

The present Municipal Cash Book, is a most valuable book in every detail. If it is properly kept and full advantage taken of its excellent system, the Treasurer should have no trouble whatever in balancing his cash in a few minutes.

The proper and only way to keep a cash book is to enter every transaction as it occurs, and show how it occurs, excepting perhaps in the renewal of notes. The same note might eas'ly appear more than once in the same year, which gives an impression that more money has been borrowed than is actually the case. If the amount of the note is reduced, the Treasurer should charge the amount by which it is reduced, and also the interest paid. Full particulars of renewals of notes will appear in the bill book.

The cash book should be balanced every year, and transactions of each year, as far as possible should be kept separate and distinct.

By authority of the Provincial Municipal Auditor I have written up and balanced the cash book from 1904, to date 31st December, 1906, so that the future Treasurer will have no difficulty in following the entries, in writing up the items for the year 1907.

Cash Book balance as shown on the 31st December, 1906......... $2,587 47
Cash in bank and on hand 2,560 65

                                                                        $26 82
T. & N. O. Ry., cheque received by Treasurer in error, and deposited in Union Bank 45 00

Cash deficit, and due by Treasurer $71 82

This discrepancy will be considerably reduced by a credit of arrears of Treasurer's salary, not yet fixed, and also one or two miscellaneous items, particulars of which at present cannot be ascertained, owing to the loss of the documents in the late fire.

The Treasurer, I may say, has shown every inclination to have the matter straightened up.

Bank Account.

This most important branch of the Treasurer's work, has been, I found, sadly neglected, and needless to say has been the means of giving me a good so that if anything is wrong it can be made known and remedied. All though an account is, kept with the Union Bank, and large sums passing yearly through their hands, no attempt was evidently ever made to ascertain if the bank's books agreed with the Town's, it leaving the Town open and entirely at the mercy of the bank. My thanks are due to the able assistance given me by your genial bank manager, Mr. Bagshaw, in assisting in adjusting this rather complicated affair.

It is a most convenient way to keep the bank account in the cheque book, a book for this purpose being furnished by the bank. As deposits are made, the amounts should be entered on the left hand or debt side of the cheque book. As cheques are drawn, the amounts of the cheques should be entered on the right hand, or credit side of the cheque book, and the stubs filled out showing to whom the cheques were given, the amount of each, and date. By adding each side and carrying forward the amounts a balance may, when necessary, be struck, and at the end of the month, the cheque book balanced, so that if anything is wrong it can be made known and remedied. All cheques should be numbered, making it an easy matter at the end of each month to ascertain how many cheques are still outstanding in which case the balance shown in the pass book, will exceed that in the cheque book by just the amount of cheque or cheques that have not been received and paid by the bank. Arrange the cheques according to their numbers, so that they can be referred to at any time; also deface or destroy the signatures of all cancelled cheques. All bank transactions should also be fully recorded in the Municipal Cash Book as instructed.

Debentures.

The Treasurer when entering in his cash book the amount realized by the sale of debentures, that is the principal, premium and accrued interest, received on account of each issue of debentures, should in every instance credit debenture account with only the principal and premium (if any) the interest being placed at the credit of general fund or interest account, the town having paid interest on funds borrowed for the purpose for which the debentures were issued, unless, of course, the debentures have been sold in advance, which is not often the case.

Warrants.

When a by-law governs same in every instance mention the number of the by-law on the warrant. This will prove most beneficial in diminishing numerous errors in charging wrong accounts, so often done, and at the same time will be of great assistance to the Treasurer in making his entries. The warrants I found in a great many instances wrongly numbered—the same number appearing several times—and in some cases not properly signed, taking up a considerable amount of my time in tracing the amounts relative to the warrants, and also in checking with the cheque book. Everything possible should be done to make the auditor's work more simple, and it would be well that in every instance on the return of the cheque or cheques, for which warrants have been issued, to attach the warrant to the cheque, and file in its proper place for future reference.

Assessment Rolls.

The assessment rolls have been compared with the collecor's rolls for 1905 and 1906 and found correct.

Collector's Rolls.

The collector's rolls for each of the years 1905 and 1906, have been carefully gone over and found correct; 1906 roll having been thoroughly examined and checked by me before being handed over to the collector.

The assessment rolls and collector's rolls are of similar size, and have generally the same number of lines on each page, with the apparent object that each page of the one shall correspond with the corresponding page of the other. There is a decided advantage in this. When the clerk adds up the assessment as entered on each page of the collector's roll, and finds that the totals correspond with the same pages of the assessment roll, he might be practically sure his figures so far are correct, and he can proceed with confidence to his calculations of the various rates, and to the completion of the roll.

The Assessment Act, section 130 (2) requires that the clerk shall append a table setting forth:

1. The total amount of taxes levied in the roll.

2. The name, amount and aggregate proceeds of each separate rate levied.

This abstract settlement is required by the auditors in order to enable them to make a complete and satisfactory audit.

Electric Lighting.

Electric lighting of the town as at present, under agreement with Beach Bros. & Company. The agreement is dated the 3rd day of October, 1905, and has to run ten years from said date, with privilege of renewal if so desired. For the benefit of those interested, I annex an abstract from said agreement which may throw a little light on the matter, and at the same time give the ratepayers a clearer conception of the present position of the town with Beach Bros. & Company:

"That the said Company (Beach Bros. & Co.) during ten years next after the date hereof, and during any renewal of this contract furnish and provide a system of electric lighting for the streets of the said municipality by as many arc lights of 1200 candle power each, and as many incandescent lights of 32 or 50 candle power each as the said corporation (town) may require, the same to be paid for at the respective rates hereinafter provided, the number of which lights may be increased from time to time as the said corporation shall require at the same rate respectively, provided that the said corporation will during each and every year of ten years, and the term of renewal thereof pay the minimum sum of $500.00 per annum for such street lighting. The said Company shall provide, furnish, supply and maintain all the necessary plant of modern construction and sufficient capacity, and all poles, wires and supports and connections, and all other things that may be required for the purpose of giving efficient service, and will whenever necessary, promptly make all repairs and renewals of all and every of the same."

Town rates street lighting $65.00 per annum 1200 candle power
"   "   "   23.00 "   "   50   "   "
"   "   "   15.00 "   "   32   "   "

Resident Rates 16c. per Kilewatt, according to meter of 25 light capacity, and one cent per light per month, for each meter of over 25 light capacity.

Minute Book.

Is fairly well kept. It would save the Clerk a lot of valuable time and trouble if he would make up as far as possible a complete list of all the bills to be submitted to Council, and have those that are approved passed by one motion.

By-law Book.

The examination of the by-laws in the municipality's by-law book revealed a good deal of carelessness, numerous instances occuring where the signature of both Mayor and Clerk were missing.

Roads and Sidewalks (Improvements).

This most important and necessary work has already cost the town nearly $9,000.00, which sum has been drawn from the general funds of the town, in order to meet the daily expenditures. In order to repay the said sum a by-law has been passed authorizing the raising by way of debentures, the sum of $10,000.00, payable in ten yearly instalments of $1,000.00 each, with interest at the rate of 5 per cent. per annum. To meet the following annual payments, a special annual levy will be made upon all rateable property, for the purpose of defraying the aforesaid debt with interest, as follows:—

YEAR	No.	INTEREST	PRINCIPAL	TOTAL ANNUAL AMT.
1907	1	$500 00	$1,000 00	$1,500 00
1908	2	450 00	1,000 00	1,450 00
1909	5	400 00	1,000 00	1,400 00
1910	4	350 00	1,000 00	1,350 00
1911	5	300 00	1,000 00	1,300 00
1912	6	259 00	1,000 00	1,250 00
1913	7	200 00	1,000 00	1,200 00
1914	8	150 00	1,000 00	1,150 00
1915	9	100 00	1,000 00	1,100 00
1916	10	50 00	1,000 00	1,050 00

$10000 00 Principal

Memo of Moneys paid F. B. Warner, on Account of Wages re Street and Sidewalk Improvements.

June 26	Warrant $35	Account Wages		80	59
" 27	" 39	"		343	73
	" 40	"		403	86
July 13	52			797	90
	53			11	69
" 14	57			577	25
' 21	61			637	60
' 24	" 62	"		650	90
' 26	65			73	80
				$3,577	32
Pay List		$616 00			
"		637 59			
"		787 90			
		779 86			
				2,821	35

Balance due, for which there are no vouchers...... $ 755 97

I do not see, however, that I would be justified at present in including this amount in my Statement of Assets until further search is made for the missing documents.

Payments to Councillors.

In the matter of payments to Councillors, no doubt a great deal of laxity has prevailed, which seems to have been the source of a good deal of comment among a number of the ratepayers. This is not as it should be. The Council is in a position of trust handling the ratepayers' moneys, and they cannot be too careful in disbursing these moneys, more especially when making necessary payments to themselves.

The cash book reveals various payments to Councillors, for work undertaken by them for the town, which is an infringement of the Consolidated Municipal Act, Section 80; which reads: "No person having by himself or his partner any interest in any contract, with or on behalf of the corporation or having a contract for the supply of goods or materials to a contractor for work for which the corporation pays, or is liable directly or indirectly to pay or which is subject to the contract or supervision of the Council, or of any officer thereof on behalf of the Council, shall be qualified to be a member of the Council of any Municipal Corporation."

School Account.

The school accounts were carefully gone into, with the following results: that I found the town to be at present indebted to the Township Trustees to the extent of over $6,000.00. I append a statement showing as nearly as possible their present position.

Grounds	$150 00
Due on contract, new school	3,600 00
Borrowed on promissory note to meet current expenses............	2,524 45
	$6,274 45

Before the incorporation of Haileybury as a town, there was raised by debentures, for school purposes, $2,500.00, payable in twenty equal yearly instalments of $217.96 each. So far the township has been paying the instalments when due, and drawing on the town for her percentage, viz.: 75 and 90 per cent., equal to $163.97 and $196.16 in the years 1905 and 1906, being according to the equalization awarded by the assessor. The township, I understand, is very desirous of obtaining a dissolution and disposing of their interest to the town, but the price asked, I understand, is not according to their views, and matters will probably be settled by arbitration. I annex schedule showing the present standing of the school debenture debt:—

TOWNSHIP OF BUCK.

Schedule of By-law No. 25.

No.	Year Due.	Interest.	Principal.	Total.	
1	1904	$150 00	$ 67 96	$217 96	Paid
2	1905	145 92	72 04	217 96	"
3	1906	141 60	76 36	217 96	"
4	1907	137 01	80 95	217 96	
5	1908	132 16	85 80	217 96	
6	1909	127 01	90 95	217 96	
7	1910	121 55	96 41	217 96	
8	1911	115 76	105 20	217 96	
9	1912	109 64	108 32	217 96	
10	1913	103 14	114 82	217 96	
11	1914	96 25	121 71	217 96	
12	1915	88 95	129 01	217 96	
13	1916	81 21	136 75	217 96	
14	1917	73 01	144 95	217 96	
15	1918	64 31	153 65	217 96	
16	1919	55 09	162 87	217 96	
17	1920	45 31	172 55	217 96	
18	1921	34 96	183 00	217 96	
19	1922	23 98	193 98	217 96	
20	1923	12 34	205 62	217 95	

$2,500 00

Principal Paid, ... 216 36

$2283 64   Total Principal Debenture Debt.

Town's share 75%, $1,712.73, less 15% overcharged, $32.70,
   1906 . . . . $1,680 03
Township's share 25%, $570.91, add $32.70 overcharged, 1906. 603 61

$2,283 64

According to the School Act, the equalization of the assessments of the two municipalities for union school purposes, is made every three years and not every year, as has been done. Therefore the 75 per cent. being the equalization of the assessment awarded in 1905, should stand for three years from that date, and not be assessed again the following year at 90 per cent. I have therefor charged the difference 15 per cent., equal to 32.70, back to the Township as shown above.

Fire Protection.

The disastrous fire that devastated your town last August, though an unwelcome visitor, was no doubt the means of proving to a great extent the total inadequacy of your present fire fighting appliances; and also fortunately perhaps, the cause of stirring up the town to the fact, that better fire protection was absolutely necessary, in order to cope against the possibility of a recurrence of a similar nature. Accordingly, I am pleased to say that a by-law has been passed by the Municipal Council, dated the 18th day of December last, authorizing the purchase of a steam fire-engine and all the necessary fire appliances, including hose, ladders, etc., etc.; and also giving the Council power to purchase land suitable as a site for an engine-house and fire hall. For this purpose, the sum of $10,000.00 will be raised, by the issue of municipal debentures for this amount, in sums not less than $1,000.00 each, payable yearly, and bearing 5 per cent. interest, coupons to be attached to said debentures for payment of said interest.

In order to meet the ten yearly instalments of $1,295.05 as per annexed schedule, a special rate shall be levied on all the rateable property, in the said municipality of the town, for the purpose of paying the amount due each year, viz.:

YEAR	No.	INTEREST	PRINCIPAL	TOTAL ANNUAL AMT.
1907	1	$500 00	$ 795 05	$1295 05
1908	2	460 25	834 80	1295 05
1909	3	418 51	876 54	1295 05
1910	4	374 69	920 36	1295 05
1911	5	328 67	966 38	1295 05
1912	6	280 35	1014 70	1295 05
1913	7	229 61	1065 44	1295 05
1914	8	176 34	1118 71	1295 05
1915	9	120 41	1174 64	1295 05
1916	10	61 67	1233 38	1295 05

$10,000.00 Principal

Sanitary Conditions.

I regret that I am unable to compliment the town officials upon the manner in which the town's sanitary arrangements are conducted, there being undoubtedly great room for improvement, especially in so important and, I might say, serious a matter as this. However, I am pleased to know that the new Council, one and all, strongly advocate the installation of water works and sewage, and I hope before another year, you will see great strides made in this direction.

Of course it must be remembered that your town, though growing, is still in its infancy, and a great deal of discretion and caution is necessary in handling a project such as this. Large sums of money to disburse the heavy expenditures would be required, which would naturally fall on the heads of the ratepayers. I feel satisfied, however, from what I saw and heard of the new Council, that they have the town's interests at heart, and would do nothing rashly, that would perhaps be the means of placing your pushing and progressive town in financial difficulties.

Hound Chute.

This rather interesting, and at the same time important matter, has been thoroughly threshed out, and requires no further comments from me.

Salaries

I feel it my duty to point out that the salaries, especially of the Treasurer, are altogether inadequate for the amount of work performed; the transactions in a young and growing town naturally being more intricate than in an older and more settled municipality, yet I find that the salaries paid are less than in other places.

Conclusion

The town has to be congratulated upon the efficient services rendered by its late Mayor, Mr. C. C. Farr, and also its present Clerk, Mr. Paul A. Cobbald; but regret exceedingly I cannot say so much for the Treasurer, although during my examination and audit, all evinced the utmost willingness to assist, for which I desire to express my thanks.

I shall be·pleased to furnish further explanations to the Council or officials in connection with any matters contained in this report.

All of which is respectfully submitted,

A. P. SCOTT,

Accountant.

TORONTO, 21st January, 1907.

DETAILED STATEMENT.

1904, Receipts.

Loans from Bank		$500 00	
Fines		9 00	
Miscellaneous		1 50	
Expenditure over receipts		19 10	
			529 60

Expenditures.

Salaries and allowances		$4 50	
Printing, advertising and stationery		2 50	
Law costs, C. R. Biggar, Toronto		5 00	
Roads and bridges		433 00	
Election expenses		27 00	
Miscellaneous		57 60	
			529 60

1905, Receipts.

Cash from Collector		$1,442 07	
Dog taxes		34 00	
Licenses		286 84	
School grant		60 00	
Loans from Bank		3,079 55	
Fines		50 25	
Roads and bridges		2 17	
Miscellaneous		03	
			4,954 91

Expenditures.

Balance from 1904		$19 10	
Salaries and allowances		394 69	
Printing and stationery		101 67	
Fire assistance from New Liskeard		112 00	
Roads and bridges		1,704 49	
Repayments on loans		1,841 15	
Interest *re* Bank		59 95	
School grant (Government)		60 00	
Board of Health		18 25	
Miscellaneous, expenses, rents, hall for meetings, expenses, trips to Toronto, etc.		166 27	
Balance, receipts over expenditures		477 34	
			4,954 91

1906, Receipts.

Jan.	7.—Balance from 1905			$477 34
March	24.—Union Bank, note discounted			1,500 00
June	29.—	"	"	1,522 50
July	7.—	"	"	4,946 55
Aug.	15.—	"	"	2,000 00
Sept.	15.—	"	"	4,947 40
Sept.	15.—	"	"	989 40
Nov.	15.—	"	"	9,448 50
	28.—	"	"	4,368 95
	28.—			2,031 60

Dec.	19.—Licenses	62 00	
	19.—Licenses from Mr. Porter	45 00	
July	20.—School grant for February, 1906	55 00	
	20.—Cheque from Ferguson, North Bay	42 00	
Sept.	15.—From F. B. Warner	4 00	
July	21.—Pelkiers Dept. Account	10 00	
Sept.	27.—Fines ....,.....	5 00	
Oct.	25.—Fines	25 00	
Nov.	Non-resident taxes from E. O. Taylor	2 70	
	7.—Licenses	44 50	
Dec.	1.—Fines	30 50	
	1.—Cash from Collector, 1905 taxes	1,087 63	
June	7.—Union Bank, note discounted	1,000 00	
	Interest on loans	585 82	
Dec.	31.—John Coats, paid twice, returned	11 95	
	31.—J. H. Bell & Co., acct. charged but not paid	32 58	
	31.—The Haileyburian, acct. "	13 80	
	31.—W. Paul, cash returned, taking prisoner to North Bay	11 10	
	31.—S. Blackwell, cheque, acct. licenses	166 00	
			35,466 82

1906, *Expenditures.*

Roads and Bridges.

		Order No.		
May	8.—Chas. Nicholls, work on roads	11	$2 00	
	8.—Jas. Williams, work on roads......................	12	3 00	
	8.—A. W. Mitchell, cedar for sidewalks	14	6 72	
	12.—W. J. Wallace, work on streets	16	6 00	
	12.—D. Cook, work on streets	17	9 00	
	12.—Jas. Moore, plow destroyed by Town	18	15 00	
June	5.—F. B. Warner, lumber station shack	19	62 10	
	5.—A. Dickson, repairing sidewalk	20	6 60	
	5.—B. Drackley, lumber and teaming	21	8 10	
	5.—A. Dickson, repairing sidewalk	22	40	
	5.—R. H. Lemon, lumber acct., streets	24	7 30	
	5.—D. Laffiner, 4½ hrs. work on streets	26	7 87	
	5.—J. A. McKinnon, drawing sawdust	31	2 00	
Oct.	10.—Jas. Bullifant, teaming, etc.	82	33 75	
	10.—Wm. Hongo, "	84	14 06	
	10.—Pat. Hanley, "	85	16 30	
	12.—Wm. Robb.	...	24 75	
	15.—Thomas Cain, "	83	7 30	
	19.—Thomas Cain, work on roads	...	7 87	
	27.—Liskard Lumber Co., account	...	24 00	
	27.—Thomas Cain, work on roads	...	12 37	
				276 49

1906, *Hound Chute.*

July	27.—F. H. Thompson, trip to Toronto	44	$28 00	
	31.—Montgomery & Ferguson, supplies	46	23 73	
Sept.	14.—Hudson Bay Co., account	73	14 47	
June	29.—R. R. Hurd, work on Hound Chute	...	12 00	
				78 20

1906, *School Account.*

		Order No.		
Jan.	22.—Part payment to trustees	115	$500 00	
March	20.—Balance in full	116	100 00	
				600 00

1906, *Board of Health.*

April	2.—Arthur Geeting, work, Board of Health	3	$31 00	
	2.—H. D. Graham, account, Board of Health	4	28 50	
	2.—H. D. Graham, "	5	28 50	
	12.—A. G. Berry, work, Board of Health	6	2 81	
	17.—Jas. Brady, Board of Health	7	30 35	
June	5.—Dr. Jackson, Board of Health	28	15 00	
	5.—Wm. Reamebottom, Board of Health	29	1 00	

July	4.—McIntosh and Hamilton, Board of Health	35	21 73
	17.—Henry Dewitt, Board of Health	39	33 00
	24.—E. Philips, Board of Health	42	8 00
	31.—E. & S. Atkinson, Board of Health	45	19 50
	31.—Jas. Brady Board of Health	54	4 50
	31.—Montgomery & Worrell, Board of Health	55	27 00
	31.—Hudson Bay Co., Board of Health	56	38 53
	31.—T. F. Harty & Co., Board of Health	57	13 00
	31.—E. Prevost, Board of Health	58	1 00
	31.—C. C. Farr, fumigator, Board of Health	60	50
	31.—Hudson Bay Co., Smith's services	62	28 73
	31.—E. Phelps, cleaning Lake Shore	66	2 50
Aug.	15.—E. Phelps, cleaning Lake Shore	99	6 50
Sept.	27.—Wm. McCracken	106	79
Oct.	19.—F. Elliott, Board of Health	...	10 00
Dec.	8.—A. W. Mitchell, Board of Health	102	30 00
			382 44

1906, Printing, Advertising and Stationery.

		Order No.	
June	5.—*The Haileyburian*, printing	30	$13 80
Sept.	17.—H. Walsh, account	75	4 40
Nov.	5.—Rolph, Clark & Co., account ....:...............	...	25 50
Dec.	20.—Newsome & Gilbert	110	12 50
			56 20

1906, School Debentures.

Jan.	16.—Instalment, School Debenture		$163 97
Nov.	30.— " "		196 16
			360 13

1906, Bills Payable.

June	16.—Paid note due Union Bank		$569 55
	16.— " "		671 85
March	24.—. .. i		506 00
June	28.— "		1,522 50
Sept.	15.— "		6,000 00
Nov.	.. ..		5,000 00
	28.—		1,837 35
	28.—		2,031 60
	28.—		1,000 00
			19,138 85

1906, Improvement Fund.

		Order No.	
June	7.—D. Norando, work on streets	1	$16 27
	D. M. McCrader, "	2	16 27
	F. Dane, "	3	15 22
	F. Ainto, ...	4	13 12
	W. Pelecano, "	5	10 50
	C. Pacione, "	6	9 09
	D. Pacione, ...	7	8 75
	A. Dearno, ...	8	9 10
	A. Ulriaco, ...	9	6 12
	P. Esila, ...	10	6 12
	P. Wapascio, ...	11	6 12
	A. Martello, "	12	7 87
	A. Belle, ...	13	7 87
	G. Demont, ...	14	7 87
	B. Aikins, "	15	7 87
	F. Cambore, ...	16	7 35
	T. Faguno, ...	17	7 87
	A. Seibo, ...	18	9 10
	T. Seibo, ...	19	9 10
	T. Greer, ...	20	3 00

June	7—D. Brackley, work on streets			21	14 62
	D. Cook,	"		22	17 50
	A. G. Berry,	"		23	31 25
	A. G. Berry,	"		24	45 00
	A. Branche,	"		25	9 00
	P. Macator,	..		26	5 25
	Jas. Gabb,			26	2 25
	Walter Boy,	"	carrying water...	27	3 50
	P. Deanor,	"		28	9 10
	G. Dermot,	"		29	6 12
	Martin Beaupre,	"		30	18 00
	W. Troke,	::		31	26 25
	T. Menard,			32	9 22
	P. Gariski,	"		33	21 60
	Jno. Kirwin,	..		34	3 75
	26.—F. B. Warner,	"	for wages.........	35	80 59
	27.—W. Lewis, lumber for culverts, etc.			36	236 35
	A. G. Berry, work on streets			37	146 00
	H. Fiss,	"		38	13 95
	F. B. Warner, wages			39	343 77
	F. B. Warner			40	403 86
	28.—James Brown, work on streets			42	75 00
July	4.—S. Norfolk,	"		43	137 29
	18.—A. Dickson, grading sidewalks			44	40 75
	T. Green, street improvements			45	20 00
	10.—I. McClain,	"		46	21 25
	14.—G. Cruickshanks, "			47	5 00
	12.—McIntosh & Hamilton, re John Hogson			48	10 12
	Geo. Minika, street improvements			49	9 00
	Elliott & Beaupre, sidewalks			50	194 25
	13.—Myles & Co., street improvements			51	43 75
	F. Warner, wages			52	797 90
	F. Warner, wages			53	11 69
	Wilson Heron, two wheel scrapers			54	70 00
	14.—D. Lemaren, street improvements			55	8 00
	J. Lemaren,	"		56	8 00
	F. B. Warner, account, wages			57	577 25
	16.—Jno. McLellan, street improvements			58	38 75
	18.—C. C. Farr, for Geo. Eastwood per order			59	23 62
	20.—J. J. Montgomery, street improvement			60	29 00
	21.—F. B. Warner,	"	wages.	61	637 60
	24.—F. B. Warner,	"	" .	62	650 90
	25.—Jas. Brown,	"	salary	63	75 00
	G. Corbett, street improvements			64	7 00
	26.—F. B. Warner, wages			65	73 80
	28.—John Duggan, street improvements			67	23 61
	31.—J. E. Williams,	"	lumber..	68	409 85
Aug.	3.—M. G. Hunt,	"	wages.......	69	292 30
	4.—C. Johnson,	"	"	70	33 18
	G. Corbett,		"	71	22 50
	Harry Jewitt,	..	"	72	4 50
	J. Bulliwants,	"	"	73	15 00
	R. Creighton,		"	73	56 25
	H. Drackley,	. ..	"	74	24 18
	J. McIntyre,		"	77	21 93
	6.—J. McLean,		"	78	24 37
	D. Moriarty,		"	79	19 40
	R. J. Spence,		"	80	13 50
	T. Pictor,		"	81	18 00
	J. McLellan,	"	"	82	81 25
	A. G. Berry, team, wages			83	95 00
	S. Austin,	"		84	4 50
	W. Kidder,	"		85	18 00
	P. Moriarty,	"		86	24 75
	P. Moriarty,	"		87	31 25
	7.—J. McLean,	"		88	5 00
	10.—Thos. Cain,	"		91	13 50
	A. J. Murphy,	"		92	188 75

Aug.	19.—John Kirwin, wages, improvements	93	16 30
	13.—Elliott & Beaupre, sidewalks, repairs	94	227 30
	9.—J. Berry, wages, improvements	96	29 25
	H. Warner, "	97	22 50
	15.—H. C. Dunbar, lumber account	98	385 01
	16.—Peter Davey, drawing lumber	64	2 00
Sept.	14.—S. Norfolk, street improvements	70	164 91
	McLellan & Co., planking, etc.	100	237 38
	Charlton & Wilson, drains, etc.	101	268 91
	Montgomery & Ferguson, account	103	27 02
	17.—Little Bros., lumber, etc.	104	16 01
Oct.	11.—J. E. Williams, lumber for sidewalks	85½	683 25
Nov.	23.—Little Bros. & Co., street improvements	100	10 96
Dec.	18.—Thomas Cain, work on streets	104	1 12
			8,728 92

1906, Salaries and Allowances.

		Order No.	
May	8.—Chas. Warner	13	$31 75
July	16.—Walter Paul, salary	37	75 00
Aug.	24.—W. Woodhus, fees	43	18 00
	15.—W. Woodhus, police duty	63	9 00
	28.—Walter Paul, salary	65	75 00
	31.—J. D. McMurrich, expenses Toronto and salary	66	112 83
Sept.	10.—W. Woodhus, 19 days police duty	68	42 75
	14.—J. D. McMurrich, salary, etc.	71	190 52
	15.—A. Whitley, assessment	76	75 00
	14.—F. G. Garbutt, auditing, etc.	72	75 00
	22.—Walter Paul, salary	78	75 00
Oct.	6.—Chas. Riddler, police duty	79	73 00
	8.—William Stimson, "	80	2 25
	14.—Walter Paul, "	97	75 00
	17.—Walter Paul, "	88	75 00
Nov.	8.—Jas. McIntyre, night watchman	98	2 25
	Chas. Riddler, 32 days, watchman	93	72 00
Dec.	15.—Chas. Riddler, police duty	103	79 60
	20.—John Coats, police duty	109	15 45
	31.—Walter Paul, salary for June, not charged	...	75 00
			1,249 40

1906, Fire Department.

		Order No.	
May	9.—A. W. Mitchell, work on three ladders	15	$28 25
June	11.—J. D. McLeod, work on fire hall	27	3 25
July	4.—G. Pappleton, repairs to fire engine	33	7 75
	Hugh Cameron & Co., acct., gasoline engine	34	400 00
	12.—W. D. Woodhus, fire watching	36	5 00
	31.—Repairs to engine	48	72 39
	J. H. Shibley, expenses on engine	49	19 55
Sept.	13.—Angus McKelvie, New Liskeard	69	50 00
	19.—P. Sherwin, gasoline	77	6 00
Oct.	15.—W. T. Richardson, fire account	86	11 85
Nov.	8.—T. N. O. Railway, freight on pipe	96	1 35
	17.—Gutta Percha Rubber Co., fire hose	99	348 33
Dec.	31.—Walter Paul, watching fire, not charged	...	10 00
			963 72

Law Costs.

Nov.	5.—Judge Valin, assessment roll	94	$15 40
Dec.	1.—Express, taking prisoner to North Bay	101	11 10
			26 50

1906, Miscellaneous.

April	2.—Ed. Prevost, wood for jail	2	$2 00
	18.—A. W. Mitchell, "	8	1 00
May	1.—C. C. Farr, Austin's account, arrests	9	8 00
	C. C. Farr, Woodhus' account, arrests	10	6 00

23 M.A.

July	17.—W. J. Coats, w.c., jail	38	11	95
	19.—C. C. Farr, two trips to Toronto	40	56	00
	J. D. McLeod, "	25	9	00
June	5.—Thomas Cain, cleaning lockup	23	4	00
Aug.	4.—S. D. Briden, trip to Toronto	41	28	00
	24.—Morton & Hyams, account	...	19	50
July	31.—W. Berry, damage to Graham House	52	1	25
	F. Woodhus, suit for constable	53	33	00
Sept.	17.—J. J. Taylor, for safe	74	80	00
Oct.	15.—W. T. Richardson, repairs to jail	87	116	03

375 73

1906, Interest Account.

Nov.	30.—Union Bank, interest on loans	$585	82
	Union Bank, discount on $1,000 note	15	25
	Interest on overdrafts, current account	41	70

·642 77

1906, Recapitulation.

Roads and bridges	$276	49
Hound Chute	78	20
School Account	600	00
Board of Health	382	44
Printing and Stationery	56	20
School Debentures	360	13
Bills Payable	19,138	85
Improvement Fund	8,728	92
Salaries and Allowances	· 1,249	40
Fire Department	963	72
Law Costs	26	50
Miscellaneous	375	73
Interest Account	642	77

Total expenditures	32,879	35
Total receipts	35,466	82

Excess, receipts over expenditures $2,587 47

STATEMENT OF THE ASSETS AND LIABILITIES OF THE TOWN OF HAILEYBURY FOR THE YEAR ENDING 31ST DECEMBER, 1906.

Assets.

Balance per cash book	$2,587	47
Taxes in arrears, 1905	439	90
Collector's roll, 1906 (uncollected)	8,889	14
School House (Town's share)	5,500	00
Road machinery, scrapers, etc.	200	00
Gasoline fire engine	500	00
Union Bank drain	292	50
4,000 feet plank	64	00
Lumber in Italian's shack ....:	48	00
Cost of improvements to streets and sidewalks	8,728	92

27,249 93

Liabilities.

Loans from Bank to cover current expenses and street improvements	$16,135	55
Accrued interest on above to date	200	00
School grant (due by Town)	6,274	45
Arrears of salaries	280	00
Outstanding accounts and warrants	1,305	42
Excess of assets over liabilities	3,054	51

27,249 93

Cost of this audit to the Town of Haileybury, as per Mr. Scott's account, was $333.80.

Recommendations.

1. That the Treasurer and Collector be required to give guarantee bonds as security.

2. That a debenture register be kept.

3. That a bill book containing a proper record of all loans on promissory notes be kept.

4. That a proper record of all arrears of taxes be kept.

5. That the Collector's roll be thoroughly checked and certified by the Clerk before being handed to the Collector.

6. That no change be made in the Collector's roll by the Clerk after it has been handed to the Collector unless authorized by resolution of Council.

7. That the Treasurer pay all accounts by bank cheque.

8. That the by-laws of the Town when passed be properly signed by the Mayor and Clerk, and be sealed with the seal of the Corporation.

9. That the Collector's roll be placed in the hands of the Collector by October 1st, as required by Statute.

10. That the Treasurer shall furnish the Council with a monthly statement of receipts and expenditures, cash in the office and in the bank, and also a memo of all outstanding cheques.

11. That the bank account be balanced regularly at the end of each month.

AMOUNT PAID BY ONTARIO MUNICIPALITIES FOR GOVERNMENT AUDITS FOR THE YEAR 1906.

Township of Goderich, County of Huron, O. M. Hudson, Auditor	$395 25
Township of Finch, County of Stormont, R. J. Adamson, Auditor	473 00
Township of Roxborough, County of Stormont, R. J. Adamson, Auditor ...	816 50
Township of Sandwich West, County of Essex, James George, Auditor	354 07
Town of Cobourg, County of Northumberland, H. Vigeon, Auditor	200 00
City of St. Thomas, County of Elgin, H. Vigeon, Auditor	1,000 00
Town of Stayner, County of Simcoe, J. D. Anderson, Auditor	730 00
Township of Orford, County of Kent, A. S. Falls, Auditor	1,506 63
Township of Colchester North, County of Essex, A. P. Scott, Auditor	395 90
Village of Iroquois, County of Dundas, T. D. Minnes, Auditor	145 00
Town of Napanee, County of Lennox, O. M. Hudson, Auditor	492 45
Town of Wallaceburg, County of Kent, J. W. Sharpe, Auditor	528 00
Town of Haileybury, District of Nipissing, A. P. Scott, Auditor ... .'	333 80

$7,370 60

INDEX.

SUPPLEMENTARY RETURN

FROM THE RECORD OF THE

SEVERAL ELECTIONS

IN THE ELECTORAL DIVISIONS OF

CARDWELL AND EAST HAMILTON

Since the General Elections of January 25th, 1905, shewing:

(1) The number of Votes Polled for each Candidate in the Electoral District in which there was a contest;

(2) The majority whereby each successful Candidate was returned;

(3) The total number of votes polled in each District;

(4) The number of votes remaining unpolled;

(5) The number of names on the Voters' Lists in each District;

PRINTED BY ORDER OF
THE LEGISLATIVE ASSEMBLY OF ONTARIO

TORONTO:
Printed and Published by L. K. CAMERON, Printer to the King's Most Excellent Majesty
1907

Recapitulation of Votes Polled for each Candidate at the several Polling Sub-Divisions of the Electoral District of the Riding of East Hamilton in the County of Wentworth at an Election held on the Fourth day of December, 1906, and in Cardwell on the 21st September, 1906.

Electoral District	Sub-Div. No.	Scott	Studholme	Total No. of Votes Polled	No. of Votes remaining Unpolled	No. of Names on the Voters' Lists	No. of Ballot Papers sent out to each Sub-Division	Used Ballot Papers	Unused Ballot Papers	Rejected Ballot Papers	Spoiled Ballot Papers	Ballot Papers given to Voters who afterwards declined to Vote	Ballot Papers taken from Polling Places	Tendered sent out to each Sub-Division	Tendered Used	Tendered Unused	Population of each Constituency
East Hamilton.	1	51	49	100	98	198	250	100	150		1			30		30	
	2	54	63	117	109	226	250	117	132		1			30		30	
	3	38	22	60	56	116	150	60	89	1	1			20		20	
	4	46	49	95	113	208	250	95	253					25		25	
	5	36	45	81	66	147	200	81	119					20		20	
	6	29	58	87	92	179	200	87	113	1				20		20	
	7	35	79	114	83	197	250	114	136	1				25	1	25	
	8	47	91	138	119	257	300	138	161	1	2			30		30	
	9	43	108	151	139	290	350	151	198					35		35	
	10	55	49	104	127	231	250	104	143					25		25	
	11	49	29	78	93	171	200	78	122					20		20	
	44	25	13	38	59	97	150	38	112					19		19	
	45	28	81	109	124	235	250	109	141	1				25		25	
	46	48	74	122	141	263	300	119	177	2				30		30	
	47	39	80	119	136	255	300	135	179					30		30	
	48	51	84	135	154	289	350	148	163					40		40	
	49	49	99	148	152	300	350	94	199		2			25		25	
	50	28	66	94	113	207	250	83	154	1	2			20		20	
	51	33	50	83	107	190	200	106	116	1	1			30		30	
	52	44	82	126	126	252	300	116	171					25		25	
	53	34	72	106	87	193	250	143	142	1	1			30	2	30	
	54	42	74	116	101	217	250	108	133	1	1			25		25	
	55	32	70	111	129	240	300	111	138	1				30		30	
	56	66	77	143	130	273	250	143	155					30		30	
	57	46	62	108	112	220	250	108	141	2				25		25	
	58	43	82	125	114	239	250	125	125	1				30		30	

59	50	94	144	150	214	350	144	205					30		30
60	41	73	114	135	249	300	114	186					30		30
61	52	61	121	114	235	250	121	128					25		25
62	42	54	96	45	191	200	96	103	1				20		20
63	47	56	103	53	156	200	103	97					20		20
64	26	72	98	91	189	200	98	101					30		30
65	47	68	115	132	247	300	115	185	1	1			20		20
66	23	44	67	116	183	200	67	132					20		20
67	33	44	77	77	144	200	77	122	1	1			20		20
68	17	26	43	117	160	200	43	157					20		20
69	34	41	75	115	190	200	75	125					20		20
Totals	1,503	2,356	3859	4085	7164	9200	3859	5308	19	14			950	3	947
		1,503													
Majority for Studholme		853													

11—By Acclamation : Alexander Ferguson.

SUPPLEMENTARY RETURN

FROM THE RECORD OF THE

SEVERAL ELECTIONS

IN THE ELECTORAL DIVISIONS OF

WEST MIDDLESEX AND CARLETON

Since the General Elections of January 25th, 1905, shewing:

(1) The number of Votes Polled for each Candidate in the Electoral District in which there was a contest;

(2) The majority whereby each successful Candidate was returned;

(3) The total number of votes polled in each District;

(4) The number of votes remaining unpolled;

(5) The number of names on the Voters' Lists in each District.

PRINTED BY ORDER OF

THE LEGISLATIVE ASSEMBLY OF ONTARIO

TORONTO:
Printed and Published by L. K. CAMERON, Printer to the King's Most Excellent Majesty
1907

RECAPITULATION of Votes Polled for each Candidate at the several Polling Sub-divisions of the Electoral District of the West Riding of the County of Middlesex, at the Election held on the 13th and 20th days of February, 1907.

Electoral District.	Names and Numbers of Polling Sub-divisions.	Duncan Campbell Ross, Barrister, Town of Strathroy. (Ross.)	George Alexander Stewart, of the Town of Strathroy, Miller. (Stewart.)	Total number of votes polled.	Number of votes remaining un-polled.	Number of names on the Voters' Lists.	Rejected ballot papers.	Remarks.
West Middlesex. Stephen Blackburn, Returning Officer.	Township of Caradoc: Division 1	64	108	172	20	192	1	
	" " 2	46	67	113	27	140		
	" " 3	82	94	176	93	269		
	" " 4	109	43	152	58	210		
	" " 5	77	27	106	26	132		
	" " 6	77	57	134	24	158		
	" " 7	67	41	108	18	126		
	Township of Delaware: Division 1	73	35	108	12	120		
	" " 2	50	69	119	24	143		
	" " 3	45	51	96	17	113		
	" " 4	29	38	67	9	76		
	Township of Ekfrid: Division 1	51	39	90	8	98		
	" " 2	47	36	83	3	86		
	" " 3	49	52	101	16	117		
	" " 4	42	42	84	8	92		
	" " 5	46	43	89	10	99		
	" " 6	60	60	120	16	136		
	" " 7	39	36	75	9	84		
	Township of Metcalfe: Division 1	37	39	76	19	95		
	" " 2	12	49	61	12	73		
	" " 3	37	43	80	11	91	1	

The ballots now being unnumbered there appears to be no necessity for these statistics.

STEPHEN BLACKBURN, Registrar, West Middlesex.

Division						
" 4	33	59	92	18	110	
" 5	57	29	86	49	135	
Township of Mosa:						
Division 1	52	42	94	21	115	1
" 2	89	56	145	29	174	1
" 3	55	73	128	27	155	
" 4	48	28	76	10	86	
" 5	44	20	64	22	86	
Town of Strathroy:						
Division 1	60	52	112	24	136	1
" 2	50	22	72	23	95	
" 3	75	70	145	75	220	1
" 4	77	57	134	44	178	3
" 5	44	45	89	27	116	
" 6	60	53	118	33	146	
Village of Glencoe:						
Division 1	44	67	111	23	134	1
" 2	37	60	97	20	117	1
Village of Newbury:						
Division 1	35	46	81	24	105	
Village of Wardsville:						
Division f	23	36	59	26	85	
Totals	2,024 / 1,884	1,884				11
Majority for Ross	140					

Dated at Glencoe, the 25th day of February, 1907.

RECAPITULATION of Votes Polled for each Candidate at the several Polling Sub-divisions of the Electoral District of the County of Carleton, at an Election held on the 11th and 18th days of March, 1907.

Electoral District	Names and Number of Polling Sub-divisions	Wm. H. Bartin	Robert H. McElroy	Total number of votes polled	Number of votes remaining un-polled	Number of names on the Voters' Lists	Number of Ballot Papers sent out to each sub-division	Used ballot papers	Unused ballot papers	Rejected ballot papers	Spoiled ballot papers	Ballot Papers given to voters who afterwards declined to vote	Ballot Papers taken from pollingplaces	Number of tendered ballots sent out to each sub-division	Used	Unused	Population in each Constituency as shown by census	Remarks
Carleton	No. 1 Township of March	33	65	98	77	175	200	98	102					20		20		
	No. 2 "	26	35	61	78	139	200	61	139					20		20		
	No. 1 Nepean	47	31	78	34	112	200	78	122					20	1	19		
	No. 2 "	15	9	24	18	42	100	24	76					20		20		
	No. 3 "	27	40	67	39	106	200	67	133					20		20		
	No. 4 "	54	26	80	28	108	200	81	119					20		20		
	No. 5 "	36	14	51	30	81	100	51	49	1				20		20		
	No. 6 "	63	23	87	25	112	200	87	25	1				20		20		
	No. 7 "	29	62	91	90	181	300	91	112					20		20		
	No. 8 "	9	71	81	94	175	300	81	219	1				21		21		
	No. 10 "	10	38	48	34	82	101	48	52					20		20		
	No. 11 "	20	19	39	37	76	300	39	62					20		20		
	No. 1 North Gower	33	67	100	94	194	204	100	200					20		20		
	No. 2 "	14	37	51	76	127	200	51	163					20		20		
	No. 3 "	8	62	71	61	132	200	71	129					20		20		
	No. 4 "	10	29	39	43	82	200	39	161	1				20		20		
	No. 5 "	1	26	27	28	55	200	27	173					20		20		
	No. 1 Marlborough	13	20	33	89	122	193	33	167					20		20		
	No. 2 "	12	32	44	58	102	185	44	149					20		20		
	No. 3 "	9	32	41	70	111	200	41	144					20		20		
	No. 1 Village of Richmond	13	17	30	36	66	200	30	170					20	1	19		
	No. 1 Tp. of Goulbourn	24	44	71	57	128	200	71	129					20	1	19		
	No. 2 "	3	37	47	47	94	101	47	54					20	4	16		
	No. 3 "	4	37	41	64	105	174	41	133					20		20		
	"	25	24	49	85	134	202	49	163					20		20		

James M. Argue, Returning Officer.

Having no Census Returns, I cannot furnish population.

" 4	39	41	80	36	116	200	80	120					20		
" 5	54	56	111	56	167	300	111	189					20		
" 6	19	29	48	26	74	100	48	52					20		
No. 1 ... Huntley	51	42	94	32	126	200	94	106					20		
" 2 "	26	205	233	48	281	299	233	68					20		
" 3 "	34	5	40	50	90	102	40	62			1		20		
" 4 "	29	20	49	49	98	100	49	51			2		20		
No. 1 ... Fitzroy	37	31	68	89	157	200	68	132			1		20		
" 2 "	32	63	95	117	212	225	95	130					20		
" 3 "	23	61	84	102	186	201	84	117					20		
" 4 "	31	59	90	34	124	200	90	110					20		
No. 1 Tp. of Torbolton	13	48	62	81	143	200	62	138					19		1
" 2 "	34	58	92	104	196	199	92	107					20		
Totals	960	1,625	2,589	2,216	4,805	7,190	2,593	4,597		4	4		760		8752
Majority for R. H. McElroy		950													
		665													

HYDRO-ELECTRIC POWER COMMISSION

of the

Province of Ontario

FOURTH REPORT

OTTAWA VALLEY AND ST. LAWRENCE RIVER DISTRICT

Printed by Order of the Legislative Assembly of Ontario.

March 15th, 1907

COMMISSION

HON. ADAM BECK, London, Chairman.

GEO. PATTINSON, M.P.P., Preston.

JOHN MILNE, Hamilton.

STAFF—

CECIL B. SMITH... ... .*Chief Engineer.*

W. G. CHACE.................*Asst. Engineer.*

S. B. CLEMENT...............*Asst. Engineer.*

E. RICHARDS..............*Electrical Engineer.*

H. G. ACRES.............*Hydraulic Engineer.*

E. C. SETTELL....................*Secretary.*

FOURTH REPORT.

OTTAWA VALLEY AND ST. LAWRENCE RIVER DISTRICT.

To his Honour,

The Lieutenant-Governor of Ontario:—

The undersigned Commissioners appointed by your Honour by Commission bearing date the 26th day of January, 1906, beg leave to submit the following report, as their fourth report upon the matters authorized and directed to be enquired into.

Your Commissioners made enquiries and obtained information from various sources, but did not find it necessary to hold formal sittings in this district, as the information which they have obtained has been given freely to members of their engineering staff, who have thoroughly canvassed this district both as to its hydraulic possibilities and its present industrial demands.

Your Commissioners have foreborne to give in detail the names of their informants or the particulars of the information acquired from them, but have used the knowledge and facts so acquired for the purposes of computation, comparison, etc., and for the production of the results which they have now the honour to report.

The detailed scientific and technical information obtained has been tabulated and arranged by the Engineer employed by your Commissioners and is contained in his report which is submitted as an appendix hereto.

The following are the matters on which your Commissioners were authorized and directed to report, with the report upon each subjoined:—

DEMAND FOR ELECTRIC POWER.

(1) *"The present and probable demand for hydraulic and electrical power in the various districts capable of being supplied from the different water-powers within the jurisdiction of the Province of Ontario."*

In this fourth report your Commissioners deal with that portion of the Province of Ontario which lies east and north of the territory already similarly dealt with in the second and third reports already issued, and which, for the purposes of this report, may be called the Ottawa Valley and St. Lawrence River District. (See map accompanying this report.)

For convenience, the towns in this district have been assembled into three groups, but the grouping has no special significance, being geographical only.

The demand for electrical power will, in almost all cases, depend upon the relative cost of electricity as compared with that of steam, gas or other local source of power. The cost of electricity is dependent upon the distance over which it is transmitted and upon the quantity transmitted. As it is only feasible to transmit the power in large quantities, trunk transmission lines capable of carrying large quantities must be constructed at the outset; therefore the cost increases with the distance, and a point is eventually reached at such a distance from the generating station that electrical can no longer compete with steam or other local power.

Again the exhaust steam and heat from the steam plant of some factories is used in the process of manufacture, and it could not be expected that electricity would be adopted by manufacturers of this class for power only, as their production of steam and heat for manufacturing purposes apart from power would increase rather than diminish their expenses; and in many instances waste material is used in the production of steam; such industries have been excluded from the consideration of the extent of the market at present in sight. The capital cost of abandoning steam plants would also, in many cases, be considerable, and the ability of small users of power to bear this loss must always be a factor in the finding of a market.

Experience shows that where the distribution is controlled by private corporations, the distribution area remains restricted, and from the information obtained by your Commissioners they are able to say that the trend of affairs with private corporations has been, not to compete for business and thus keep down prices for consumers, but to amalgamate or otherwise destroy competition, and then to fix the prices according to the slight saving which they may be able to induce particular customers to make. The natural result of this has been to force individual consumers, where the circumstances justified it, to instal generating plants of their own, or to adhere to existing methods, rather than place themselves at the mercy of large combinations formed for the purpose of preventing competition and keeping up the price of electrical power.

An examination of the Engineer's appendix Tables I., II. and III. will show that over the greater part of this district, hydraulic power is in an advanced state of development, there being 13,000 H.P. used direct in mills, etc., and 14,000 H.P. devoted to the production of electricity, in addition to which there are several power stations having permanent works of somewhat greater capacity, ready for the installation of additional machinery.

On the other hand, it is significant that, in several localities, the adjacent water powers are fully developed and further progress is temporarily checked by the necessity of developing more distant water powers to meet further demands, and evidently, unless these demands are of considerable immediate extent, there is a hesitancy on the part of private companies to enter a field already partially or almost entirely supplied from a source of power which has reached its limit. Considerable transmission systems may be expected in this district in the near future, particularly in the new mining field adjacent to Lake Temiskaming.

As a result, however, of your Commissioners' enquiries in the various manufacturing centres of this district as to the present and probable market for electrical power, it appears that under favorable conditions a total demand of 6,400 H.P. is at present existent, but that, of this total, a considerable proportion can be supplied locally or by transmission systems, already under construction or constructed: and again in some small towns at a distance from other towns requiring power and distant also from water powers, there does not appear to be any opportunity to meet the small probable demands, until such are augmented by some special requirement of considerable extent.

To meet the demands at present existing in certain towns, however, the Commissioners' Engineer has studied the grouping of these towns in relation to certain water powers at present undeveloped. In the Commissioners' second report it was suggested that Kingston should obtain electrical power from the water powers of the Trent river, but as an alternative and, as a means of enabling Gananoque to receive similar benefits, a source of power at Waddington, N.Y., (opposite Morrisburg) could be drawn upon, to meet the requirements of Kingston, Gananoque, Prescott, Brockville and Cornwall. This development is capable of generating 15,000 H.P., but owing to the fact that the source of power is in United States territory, no estimate thereon included in this report. Assuming that Kingston and Cornwall could be otherwise provided for, a limited development has been estimated upon, for the supply of electrical power to Prescott and Brockville.

Similarly, High Falls on the Mississippi river may be developed either for the requirements of Perth, Smith's Falls and Carleton Place only, or by careful storage, the capacity may be increased so as to meet the present needs of Brockville and Prescott also, and studies have been made for such developments. Any of the investments indicated would be in stable communities in which the demands for power are certain to increase from year to year.

In the mining district adjacent to Cobalt, there is a present large market for electrical power for use in mines, and doubtless this market will tend to increase for some years, but while there are ample undeveloped water powers on the Montreal river to meet the requirements of such a market, your Commissioners do not suggest a large development at present, until it has been more fully demonstrated that the market mentioned is sufficiently stable to warrant large investments.

Should the Iroquois, High Falls and Fountain Falls developments be undertaken, there would, in the opinion of your Commissioners, be an immediate market for some 4,000 H.P., provided the power is offered at reasonable and attractive rates, but considering the insecurity of the future, it would appear that a somewhat higher rate for power in the Cobalt mining district should be considered justifiable, than would be the case in firmly established communities with diversified industries and resources.

UNDEVELOPED LOCATIONS.

(2) *"The location, capacity and capital cost of development of the various water powers within the legislative jurisdiction of the Province of Ontario at present undeveloped, but whose development is required to supply the present and probable needs of the surrounding districts, and to ascertain the cost of the attendant transmission plant necessary to the utilization of electrical and hydraulic powers to be provided from the aforesaid water powers within the respective surrounding districts."*

A systematic tabulation of the water powers of the various rivers in this district based upon gaugings and meterings, supplemented by information derived from other sources, has been carried out during the past eighteen months, and although more minute information, particularly with reference to dry weather flow, could be obtained by continuing the work, it is felt that a fairly accurate hydraulic knowledge of the district has been obtained.

Along the St. Lawrence river, which has no laterals in this part of Ontario, except a small stream at Gananoque, a peculiar situation has been created by the construction of the various ship canals.

These canals can be used to a limited extent as head races for power developments, but evidently extensive use is objectionable to the navigation interests, due to the creation of currents, and therefore no very extensive constructions of this type need be expected. The St. Lawrence has enormous potential water powers, and the future outlook in this locality would seem to be in the nature of very extensive developments, possible only by placing dams in the main river, or else, as at Hoople Creek, near Cornwall, by means of an expensive head canal, circumventing and not interfering with the ship canals themselves.

The Ottawa river and its tributaries is a magnificent source of water power, and whilst the construction of the Georgian Bay and Ottawa ship canal would create conditions more favorable than at present to such water powers, both as to first cost of construction and freedom from ice trouble of operation, still, even under present conditions, the possibilities are very great.

The Ottawa river itself abounds in opportunities, which will be taken advantage of as soon as the mineral and timber resources of its watershed are more fully exploited, but the attendant first investments will be heavy, owing to the large volumes of water to be handled, and nothing short of permanent constructions on a large scale should be encouraged.

The tributaries of the Ottawa in Ontario are less valuable as sources of water power than those in Quebec Province, but being in some cases, as on the Rideau and Mississippi rivers, easily developed, have made considerable progress. On the other hand, the Madawaska, Petawawa, Bonnechere and Montreal rivers abound in undeveloped water powers of considerable magnitude, and as the sources of these rivers are in forest areas abounding in lakes, the regulation is very good and dry weather flow higher than normal.

Water powers developed in the Ottawa districts may be looked upon as good permanent investments from an hydraulic standpoint.

Table IV. of the Engineer's report gives the dry-weather continuous capacity of the various water powers of the district. An examination of this table will show the widespread and valuable latent sources of energy waiting for investment and use.

Your Commissioners in studying in detail the cost of developing and distributing electrical power have indicated the possibilities only as regards immediate requirements, in their consideration of Iroquois, (St. Lawrence), High Falls (Mississippi) and Fountain Falls (Montreal), and an examination of Table VI. will show that these are by no means large constructions.

The Mississippi river has other valuable water powers adjacent to High Falls and the Montreal river has 12,000 H.P. adjacent to the Cobalt mines.

In general, it may be said that, with the exception of a small area, lying between the St. Lawrence and Ottawa rivers and east of Smith's Falls, the whole district covered by this report is bountifully supplied with water powers capable of being developed for reasonable costs per horse power.

RATES AND PRICES.

(3) *"To ascertain the rates or prices that would require to be charged the various classes of consumers of hydraulic or electrical power within the respective districts in order to meet all expenditure of maintenence and operation."*

The ascertainment of the rates that would require to be charged for electrical power in order to meet expenditure of maintenance and operation is based upon the cost of necessary plant, for future calls upon it, original cost of construction, cost of maintenance and operation, and the probable market for electrical power, ascertained from local enquiries.

In order to ascertain the cost of delivering electrical energy in large quantities at particular distances, where now required, your Commissioners have made computations with respect to certain available markets, which may be conveniently and economically supplied from four generating plants through transmission systems and sub-stations, estimated upon in Part V. of the Engineer's report attached. It should be particularly noted that the basis of estimate is not the total present steam power used by the various industries, but that portion which the Commissioners' engineers, after consideration, denote as being probably available for conversion to electrical power, if such power were offered at reasonable rates.

Your Commissioners call attention to the fact, however, that when electricity is delivered at a municipal sub-station, as above, the cost of distribution among the consumers within such municipality must be added to this price in order to determine the cost to the individual municipal consumer.

In order to illustrate the cost of distributing power delivered at a sub-station, your Commissioners have caused estimate to be made for a distribution system for the town of Brockville, as this town already owns its own lighting station, etc., and in Part VI. of the Engineer's report will be found the results obtained, but it must be understood that local conditions, the proportionate amounts of lighting and power used, the variety of industries, hours of operation, etc., all point to the necessity of special local studies being made for each municipality and particular attention is directed to the fact that these estimates are based on all the power generated being used, and until

such is the case, a correspondingly higher (rg   must be made to
meet higher charges on investment, etc., etc.

Table XXII., Part V., also gives data   re   rd to the cost of
supplying a particular customer with powe at   considerable distance from a sub-station, the total cost to s h   nsumer being the
sub-station cost added to the secondary cost .ve' in the table.

SAVINGS.

(4) *"To enquire into and ascertain the nn   ' savings accruing
to the consumers in the various districts afo aia   y the substitution
of the rates or prices in the next preceding arc   aph for the rates
paid at present in the said district so far a: he   mmissioners may
be able to ascertain or estimate them."*

The saving which any customer may ol in   the introduction
of electrical energy on the basis of the Eng eer   cstimates depends
on the conditions under which he is at pres o .ating.

The customer may now be operating by ite   in which case he
must consider his present total fixed charges is l as cost of operation and then decide that he will allow s   sent plant to be
scrapped, or keep it as a standby or reserve to   of which must be
added the cost of a motor installation, as p Ta   XIII., Part VII.

If, on the other hand, a customer is alre y u   r electrical power
or light, the prospective saving may consist o   aging from a private company source with rates based on wh tl   'isiness will stand
to a municipal source based on the cost of rv   or if the municipality is already distributing electricity ge cat   from coal (as for
instance Brockville), then the prospective s in   ll be the lessened
cost of power to the municipality based on a lea   source of supply.

An intelligent study of tables XV., X I.   XVII. will give
a proper basis of comparison when taken a ng   h previous information contained in Engineer's report.

As to the actual rates which a municip ty   ld afford to make
when distributing power delivered in acc da   with Engineer's
estimates on a 4 per cent. cost basis, this wilde l upon such items
as the following:—Amount of 24 hour pow so   umber of limited
hour contracts during winter season, towr pu   ng with reservoir
capacity to carry over peak load, distance f   f customers from

distributing station, tc., etc. The introduction of hydro-electric power available throu hout the whole day and night makes marked changes in the indust al conditions of a town or city.

CAPITL COST OF UNDERTAKINGS.

(5) *"To enquire nto and ascertain the cash capital cost of the hydraulic and electri l power undertakings of existing companies located within the P vince of Ontario, the capacity and state of development thereof.'*

Your Commission s, following the policy outlined in their earlier reports, have not thou ht it necessary to consider any but the more important undertakin , where electrical energy is being generated for power, as well as lhting purposes and transmitted some distance.

A partial list of puts in the district coming under this head are Andrewsville, Mattaw Pembroke, Perth, Renfrew and Morrisburg. The St. Lawrence Pow· Co. and the Hawkesbury Electric Light and Power Co. have not furnished the necessary information asked for by your Commissioners.

The plant of the :emptville Milling Co. is located at Andrewsville on the Rideau rir and supplies the town of Kemptville with light and power over fifteen mile transmission line at 10,000 volts, three-phase. This pla has a generator capacity of 400 H.P., and the capital investment or generation, transmission, step-down transformation and local distribution is in the neighborhood of $65,000.

The Mattawa Electic Light and Power Co. have a plant on the Mattawa river, which pplies the town of Mattawa over a 3½ mile transmission line. The lant is a small one, having a present capacity of 150 H.P. The capal cost to date has been $, , including transmission and step-wn transformation.

The town of Pembke is to be supplied from a plant under construction on the Black iver in the Province of Quebec. When this installation is complete, it will have a capacity of about 1,500 H.P., with a 14 mile transmsion line. The estimated capital cost of the undertaking, exclusive f sub-station equipment, is about $125,000.

The town of Pert is supplied by the Canadian Electric and Water Power Co. from vo generat ox stations on the Tay river, three and four miles, respectvely, from e town. The rated capacity of such is the case, a correspondingly higher charge must be made to meet higher charges on investment, etc., etc.

Table XXII., Part V., also gives data in regard to the cost of supplying a particular customer with power at a considerable distance from a sub-station, the total cost to such consumer being the sub-station cost added to the secondary cost given in the table.

SAVINGS.

(4) "*To enquire into and ascertain the annual savings accruing to the consumers in the various districts aforesaid by the substitution of the rates or prices in the next preceding paragraph for the rates paid at present in the said district so far as the Commissioners may be able to ascertain or estimate them.*"

The saving which any customer may obtain by the introduction of electrical energy on the basis of the Engineer's estimates depends on the conditions under which he is at present operating.

The customer may now be operating by steam, in which case he must consider his present total fixed charges, as well as cost of operation and then decide that he will allow his present plant to be scrapped, or keep it as a standby or reserve, to all of which must be added the cost of a motor installation, as per Table XIII., Part VII.

If, on the other hand, a customer is already using electrical power or light, the prospective saving may consist in changing from a private company source with rates based on what the business will stand to a municipal source based on the cost of service, or if the municipality is already distributing electricity generated from coal (as for instance Brockville), then the prospective saving will be the lessened cost of power to the municipality based on a cheaper source of supply.

An intelligent study of tables XV., XVI. and XVII. will give a proper basis of comparison when taken along with previous information contained in Engineer's report.

As to the actual rates which a municipality could afford to make when distributing power delivered in accordance with Engineer's estimates on a 4 per cent. cost basis, this will depend upon such items as the following:—Amount of 24 hour power sold, number of limited hour contracts during winter season, town pumping with reservoir capacity to carry over peak load, distance of chief customers from distributing station, etc., etc. The introduction of hydro-electric power ·available throughout the whole day and night makes marked changes in the industrial conditions of a town or city.

CAPITAL COST OF UNDERTAKINGS.

(5) *"To enquire into and ascertain the cash capital cost of the hydraulic and electrical power undertakings of existing companies located within the Province of Ontario, the capacity and state of development thereof."*

Your Commissioners, following the policy outlined in their earlier reports, have not thought it necessary to consider any but the more important undertakings, where electrical energy is being generated for power, as well as lighting purposes and transmitted some distance.

A partial list of plants in the district coming under this head are Andrewsville, Mattawa, Pembroke, Perth, Renfrew and Morrisburg. The St. Lawrence Power Co. and the Hawkesbury Electric Light and Power Co. have not furnished the necessary information asked for by your Commissioners.

The plant of the Kemptville Milling Co. is located at Andrewsville on the Rideau river and supplies the town of Kemptville with light and power over a fifteen mile transmission line at 10,000 volts, three-phase. This plant has a generator capacity of 400 H.P., and the capital investment for generation, transmission, step-down transformation and local distribution is in the neighborhood of $65,000.

The Mattawa Electric Light and Power Co. have a plant on the Mattawa river, which supplies the town of Mattawa over a 3½ mile transmission line. The plant is a small one, having a present capacity of 150 H.P. ·The capital cost to date has been $,   , including transmission and step-down transformation.

The town of Pembroke is to be supplied from a plant under construction on the Black river in the Province of Quebec. When this installation is completed, it will have a capacity of about 1,500 H.P., with a 14 mile transmission line. The estimated capital cost of the undertaking, exclusive of sub-station equipment, is about $125,000.

The town of Perth is supplied by the Canadian Electric and Water Power Co. from two generating stations on the Tay river, three and four miles, respectively, from the town. The rated capacity of the two plants is 400 H.P. The total capital cost to date is $128,000, including development, transmission and distribution.

The town of Renfrew is supplied by the Renfrew Power Co.'s plant on the Bonnechere river. The present capacity of this plant is 400 H.P., and the capital cost to date $81,000. A 500 H.P. unit, which is now being installed, will cost about $30,000 additional, making a total capital investment of $110,000 for development and distribution.

The Rapide Plat Canal is utilized by the town of Morrisburg, which, at present, has a 250 H.P. plant in operation for lighting purposes only. The capital investment in connection with this plant is $35,000. A new plant of 1,100 H.P. capacity is now in course of construction, the cost of which is estimated at $75,000.

By comparison, it will be noted that the capital costs per H.P. in this district are, as a rule, higher than those in the district covered by the Third Report. This is due in a great measure to the lower heads under which the plants mentioned in this report operate, and the greater power-house capacity necessary to accommodate low-head machinery, also probably partly due to the fact that the developments above described are of small capacity.

POWER SUPPLIED AND UNDER CONTRACT BY THE EXISTING COMPANIES.

(a) *"The quantities supplied and contracted for and the rates charged and to be charged under such contracts by these companies for hydraulic and electrical power."*

In Part III. of the Engineer's Report, Table IV. will be found listed the amount of machinery installed at various points. It will be noted that in most cases the installations are for mills, and that very important industries in all the manufacturing centres of Eastern Ontario are operated by water powers. As regards water powers developing electricity, the most important are those at Ottawa, devoted to general power, street railway and lighting, and the St. Lawrence Power Co., near Cornwall, which lights the canal and supplies power to the Stormont Electric Light & Power Co. and to mills.

The prices or rates charged for power and light in various municipalities are set forth in Part IX., Table XIV. It may be noted that the only power distributed is that derived from water power, and that the charges for light at Cornwall, although the source of power is a very economical canal water power development, are practically the high:st rates given.

APPRAISEMENT OF UNDERTAKINGS.

(b) *The actual present value of the said undertakings, or such of them as may be required, after making such fair and reasonable allowances for existing conditions as in the judgment of the Commissioners seems necessary or expedient.*"

See Part V. of the Commissioners' report.

(c) *"To estimate the capital outlay, if any, necessary to complete these undertakings."*

At the present time the Renfrew Power Co. is increasing its machinery equipment some 500 H.P. and at cost of probably $20,000 to $30,000, and will soon be able to meet any immediate demands.

At Morrisburg, the municipality is constructing an 1100 H.P. hydro-electric station to supply the tin plate works with some 800 H.P. and will probably expend $75,000; the head canal being the ship canal itself and very inexpensive head works being all that is necessary therefor.

At Cornwall, the St. Lawrence Power Co., whose electric power station is on the Cornwall canal, some 5 miles west at Mille Roches, will, it is stated, soon install additional units of machinery beyond the two 1000 K.W. machines already installed. Such machinery equipment up to 4000 K.W. total can be installed in the present building at a cost of $25 to $30 per H.P.

The Pembroke Power Co. is constructing a system for transmitting from a power station being built on Black River in the Province of Quebec. Its estimated cost is shown in Part V. of the Commissioners' report.

On the Montreal river two incipient undertakings are becoming active, one at the "Notch," the second at Fountain Falls,—both proposing to meet the requirements of the Cobalt mining field and the municipal needs of Cobalt and Haileybury.

Near New Liskeard a small electric station is being built for supplying light and power. It is located on the Wabi river.

CONCLUDING REMARKS.

Your Commissioners respectfully submit that in the Central and Southern portions of the district the future needs of the various industrial centres will fully tax the capacity of the available smaller water powers, and the St. Lawrence river will need to be developed in a large way to fully meet requirements.

All over the northern portion, including the upper Ottawa valley and tributaries, there is ample water power available for generations to come, which will have a marked influence on the development of mineral and timber resources of this part of the Province.

All of which is respectfully submitted.

(Sgd.)   ADAM BECK,
                    Chairman.

(Sgd.)   GEORGE PATTINSON,

(Sgd.)   JOHN MILNE.

Toronto, March 15th, 1907.

APPENDIX

TO

FOURTH REPORT

Ottawa Valley and St. Lawrence Valley District

ENGINEER'S REPORT

ON

THE GENERATION, TRANSMISSION AND DISTRIBUTION OF ELECTRIC POWER

HONORABLE ADAM BECK,
      CHAIRMAN OF THE HYDRO-ELECTRIC POWER COMMISSION:

DEAR SIR:—
      Herewith find my report on the Ottawa Valley and St. Lawrence River District, extending as far north as the height of land.

The report deals with the present consumption of and demand for power, the sources of power developed or undeveloped and discusses in detail certain developments within economical transmission distance of various markets and indicates the cost of generating and transmitting the electrical energy required to meet present needs, based upon 4 per cent. return on investment.

                 Yours respectfully,

                    CECIL B. SMITH,
                          Chief Engineer.

TORONTO, CANADA,
      JANUARY 5TH, 1907.

INDEX.

INDEX TO TABLES.

Hydro- Electric Power Commission
of The
Province of Ontario

OTTAWA DISTRICT

N SHOWING TRANSMISSION LINES FROM
er Powers on the Ottawa River and
its Tributaries

Hydro-Electric Power Commission
of the
Province of Ontario
OTTAWA DISTRICT
PLAN SHOWING TRANSMISSION LINES FROM
Water Powers on the Ottawa River and
its Tributaries.
Scale: 15 Miles – 1 Inch

Nov. 1906

——— Transmission Lines now in Operation
- - - - Proposed Transmission Lines

PROVINCE OF QUEBEC

Ottawa River

L. Kippawa

Montreal R.

HEIGHT OF LAND

PROVINCE

ONTARIO

HEIGHT OF LAND

STATE

River

PART I.

GEOGRAPHICAL SUBDIVISIONS.

The District included in this Report is that bounded on the West by the Districts treated in Reports 2 and 3 already issued, on the South by the St. Lawrence River, on the East and North by the Ottawa River, the interprovincial boundary and the height of land south of Lake Abitibi. It has been sub-divided for convenience into three portions, viz., the St. Lawrence margin, the Central Ottawa valley and the Upper Ottawa valley.

The St. Lawrence River margin, which includes that district drained to the St. Lawrence, is the site of a number of towns of considerable commercial importance. This section is very narrow and no large tributary rivers exist here. The potential water powers on the St. Lawrence itself, are, as a rule, very large and have not been developed to any great extent, excepting in such cases as were made easy by reason of canal construction carried out by the Dominion Government for purposes of navigation. The only tributary river is the Gananoque, which, at the town of that name, has been successfully developed to yield its maximum output for the needs of the Water Power Association which carried out the work.

By far the greater portion of the peninsula lying between the St. Lawrence and Ottawa Rivers is drained by tributaries of the Ottawa. The elevation of the land surface above that of the Ottawa River is not very great and there are no lakes or marshes which would serve as storage basins to supplement the dry weather flow. As a consequence, the rivers, chief of which is the Nation, are subject to very great Spring floods and to periods of very low water.

Westward of and including the Rideau river, all the tributaries of the Ottawa flow from basins containing a large proportion of lakes and marshes and thus are better suited for the development of power. The relative elevation of the hinterland, too, becomes greater towards

the West, the total fall of the Madawaska for instance being over one
thousand feet, as is also that of the Petawawa.

The Mattawa river, however, lies in a valley extending from the
Ottawa only as far westward as Lake Nipissing, rising in this distance
less than two hundred feet. North of this valley, the country, while
retaining the character of that above described, has much less relative
elevation and there are fewer water-powers of importance.

PART II.

DEMAND FOR POWER.

As a basis for estimates, a full canvass was made by expert
assistants in each town of this District. In this canvass care was taken
to enquire and if possible ascertain whether or not the manufacturer
would be likely to adopt electrical power if it were available at reasonable rates. The canvass included also the present users of hydraulic
and of electric power. In the tables following (Nos. I. II. and III.)
there are given estimates of the amounts of power now available for
substitution of electric installation and of the amounts of Hydraulic
and Electric power already in service.

The map accompanying this report indicates the location of the
various cities and towns in the District, as well as a few of the chief
water-powers and also the specific transmission schemes which have
been adopted as appearing to best serve the requirements of markets
at present available.

It will be noted that but few towns have been included in the
transmission schemes which follow. This is due in some instances to
the fact that the local sources of hydraulic power have not been completely or economically developed and that careful use of these resources would satisfy the town's present requirements and probably
those of the immediate future. In other instances it is due to the fact
that the small amounts of power required would not warrant the expenditure necessary to supply the available market.

It will be further noted that in certain portions of this District,
there are very large powers, for which there is no apparent available
market existing. Such are many of those on the Ottawa, Madawaska
and Petawawa rivers.

TABLE I.

POWER CONDITIONS.

ST. LAWRENCE RIVER DISTRICT.

Municipality.	Population.	Average Total Power Used. H.P.	Average Hydraulic Power Used Direct. H.P.	Maximum Hydro-Electric Power Developed. H.P.	Steam Power Available for Electric Installation. H.P.	Remarks.
Brockville.....	9,000	900	..	..	900	
Cornwall.......	7,600	4,485	3,300	925	40	From St. Lawrence River Power Co., Mille Roches.
Iroquois.......	1,200	85	45	100		
Gananoque.....	4,000	900	800	180	35	Gananoque Water Power Association control and distribute water available at various seasons on 10-hour basis
Morrisburg...	1,700	200	135	267	..	Town building 1,100-h.p. plant for tin-plate works.
Prescott.......	3,035	215	..	..	150	

TABLE II.

POWER CONDITIONS.

CENTRAL OTTAWA VALLEY.

Municipality.	Population.	Average Total Power Used. H.P.	Average Hydraulic Power Used Direct. H.P.	Maximum Hydro-Electric Power Developed. H.P.	Steam Power Available for Electric Installation. H.P.	Remarks.
Hawkesbury...	4,500	2,900	1,400	800	..	Transmitted 10 miles by Hawkesbury E. L. & P. Co.
Vankleek Hill..	2,500	175	..	..	100	Light is now supplied by Hawkesbury E. L. & P. Co.
Alexandria.....	2,200	275	75	..	200	
Chesterville....	850	115	..	..	50	
Winchester.....	1,200	230	..	..	140	
Kemptville.....	1,400	90(a)	..	300	..	Lighting not included in (a.) Power transmitted 14 miles from Andrewsville
Merrickville....	1,100	350	350	40	.	
Smith's Falls...	5,700	815	..	1,500	500	
Perth..........	4,000	240	..	200	150	Transmitted for commercial lighting 3 and 4 miles.
Carleton Place .	4,000	505	205	185	300	
Almonte.......	3,000	865	750	225	80	Municipal plant to be enlarged.
Arnprior.......	4,300	520	380	160	170	
Ottawa........	67,600	16,075	5,250	8,650	400	Maximum.

TABLE III.

POWER CONDITIONS.

UPPER OTTAWA VALLEY.

Municipality.	Population.	Average Total Power Used. H.P.	Average Hydraulic Power Used Direct. H.P.	Maximum Hydro-Electric Power Developed. H.P.	Steam Power Available for Electric Installation. H.P.	Remarks
Renfrew........	3,500	585	170	530	150	Renfrew E. L. & P. Co. will soon enlarge plant.
Eganville......	1,100	300	300	100	..	..
Pembroke......	5,150	521	100	..	250	1,300-h.p. will soon be available from Waltham, P.Q., 13 miles.
Mattawa	1,700	75	50	90	..	3½ mile transmission.
Cobalt Mines...	..	2,800	..	..	2,200	Demand uncertain and rapidly growing.
Haileybury.....	1,215	200	..	..	200	Lighting only
New Liskeard..	2,700	200	..	..	200	Lighting chiefly.
Cobalt.........	..	200	..	..	200	Lighting only.

PART III.

SOURCES OF HYDRO-ELECTRIC POWER.

Of the water-powers in this District, those of the St. Lawrence and of the Ottawa rivers are the largest, and for the entire development of a water power on either a complete damming of a great river bed is necessary.

The St. Lawrence being a navigable stream throughout, and, at points of possible development by the Province of Ontario, an international stream, it is not at present necessary to consider here the question of making use of these water powers in this manner. Canals paralleling each of the rapids of the St. Lawrence have been built by the Dominion of Canada, thereby concentrating at one or more points the existing heads and providing to a limited extent water supply, which has been in whole or in part, utilized in nearly every case by private interests. In the table following is given a summary of the powers along this river, (1) involving the entire estimated low water flow, and, (2) derivable from the canal waters, either by diversion to the river or by utilizing the head at the various locks. The amount of power derivable from the canal waters depends upon the dimensions of the canal section and of the various inlets and passages at the locks, and upon the allowable velocity of the canal waters, which velocity is limited by the requirements of navigation.

The Ottawa river over a considerable portion of its course is a navigable stream and its waters are, moreover, interprovincial. This latter fact need not stand in the way of the intelligent and economical development of the water powers, although it has led to difficulties in the past. In the report following, estimates of power are based on the entire low water flow of the stream at each important fall or rapid. The construction of a 23 foot Georgian Bay Ship Canal, as is proposed, would altogether alter the profile of the Mattawa and Ottawa Rivers and would concentrate the entire fall of these rivers at the various necessary dams. A further result would be the reduction of the variation in the discharge of these rivers, an end desirable for canal operations as reducing the seriousness of the annual floods. Essential to such control of floods would be the damming of Lake Temiskaming and other lakes in the Upper Ottawa valley. An example of the effect of canalization and storage of flood waters may be noticed in the case of the Rideau river, the existence of whose dams and retaining works causes the discharge of the stream to be more than ordinarily regular.

In Part I., while discussing the geographical subdivisions of this district, reference was made to the fact that by far its greater portion contains many lakes and marshes. It was, moreover, thickly wooded, in time past, and in some portions even yet, with white pine and now with a dense second growth of birch, poplar, maple, spruce, etc. These conditions are likely to remain permanent, and thus the discharges of the rivers will probably retain their present character and dimensions.

Of the important Ontario rivers tributary to the Ottawa, the Nation river is peculiar in that it drains a comparatively low lying country well cleared of large timber, fairly well drained and without any lakes. Its low water flow is therefore very small and as a source of power the river has little value. The other principal tributaries have in their drainage areas numerous lakes and swamps; a few of these lakes are now under control by lumbermen, though many of the dams erected for this purpose are reaching an advanced stage of decay. For power purposes, the low water flow of the streams can be considerably increased and besides this in many cases, pondage sufficient to accommodate a peak load considerably greater than that indicated in the tables can be created in the immedate vicinity of the individual falls.

The discharge of most of these streams has been measured during the late summer and a unit rate of low water discharge per square mile of drainage area has been chosen. For the Quebec and upper Ontario tributaries, a larger unit has been selected as probably near to the truth, on account of this district being more heavily timbered, and thus the flow of the Ottawa at different points has been estimated. This is considered a fairly safe method, as the characteristics of the entire watershed, with the exception of the Nation river basin, are practically uniform.

The heads given are, in many cases, the results of approximate measurements by the commission's engineers; in others, they are derived from surveys made by other engineers, and in some cases they are taken from White's "Altitudes in Canada." The amount of fall shown in the tables as existing at any one point is a matter of arbitrary decision, as, should any given development be made, the working head chosen and the extent of existing rapids to be included should be arrived at only after a very careful estimate of the economics involved. Many lesser rapids have been entirely omitted from the lists below.

In many of those developments which have been made hitherto, the entire available head has not been made use of, for confirmation of which fact see Table IV. wherein it will be noted, as is the case at other places, that all but one of the developments at the Chaudiere Falls, Ottawa, operate under heads much less than the maximum available, thus generating a smaller amount of power than could have been obtained otherwise.

TABLE IV.

WATER-POWERS IN ST. LAWRENCE AND OTTAWA DISTRICT.

Water Power	Lowest Head, Feet	Estimated Minimum Low Water Flow c.f.s.	Minimum 24 Hour Power H.P.	Present Turbine Installation H.P.	Remarks
St. Lawrence Canals:					
Galops,					
*†Cardinal..............	8	......	......	200	Edwardsburg Starch Works.
*Iroquois..............	14	......	......	40	M. F. Beach.
				20	Town of Iroquois pumping and electric plants.
Rapide Plat,					
Morrisburg	11	1,410	1,410	......	Gibson lease, 60 H.P.
				250	Town of Morrisburg pumping and electric plants.
				1,100	New municipal lease for electric power.
Cornwall,					
*†Mille Roches..........	20	......	......	2,700	St. Lawrence Power Co. Normal head 28 feet.
Lock 20.............. .	8	1,400	1,000		
Lock 19..............	6	1,400	760		
Lock 18	7.5	1,400	950	800	Toronto Paper Mfg. Co.
				50	Municipal pumping.
*Lock 17.....	20	1,400	2,540	1,500 }	Canada Colored Cotton Company.
				1,200 }	
				200 }	
				80	Cornwall Street Ry. and Wm. Hodge flour mill.
' **St. Lawrence River:**...					
Galops, Cardinal and Iroquois Rapids..........	15	170,000	232,000		
Rapide Plat..............	11.5	170,000	178,000		
Long Sault..............	40	170,000	618,000	.....	St. Lawrence River Power Co., Massena, N.Y.
a Gananoque River	21	190	365	50	Cowan & Britton.
				50	O. D. Cowan.
				100	The Skinner Co
				150	Spring & Axle Co.
	14	......	......	250	Electric Light Plant.
				65	Rolling Mill.
				80	Ontario Wheel Works
				50	Parmenter & Bullock.
				90	Toronto Bolt & Forge Co.
				60	Canada Cabinet Co.
				40	St. Lawrence Steel and Wire Co.
	ʹ	......	......	95	Grist mill.
				20	Mitchell & Wilson.
				150	G. F. Jones.
				10	W. G. Gibson.
Ottawa River					
Carillon Dam............	16	17,400	25,300	.....	Present dam and rapids below.
Long Sault Rapids.......	43	17,400	65,300	1,200	Hawkesbury Lbr Co., head developed 8 feet.
Chaudiere Falls..........	35	11,500	36,300	3,600	J. R. Booth, 25 ft. head.
				1,850	Ottawa Electric Co, 22 ft. head.
				2,800	Ottawa Electric Co., 25 ft. head.
				1,600	Ottawa Electric Ry. Co. 20 ft. head.
				4,000	Ottawa Power Co , 25 ft. head.
				4,000	Municipal pumping, 27 ft. head
				7,000‡	E. B. Eddy Co , heads 16-21 ft.
				6,000‡	Ottawa & Hull Power Co, head 27-35 ft.
Little Chaudiere Rapid...	7	11,500	7,300	......	
Remous Rapid	3	11,500	3,140		
Deschenes Rapid........	9	11,500	9,400	2,100‡	Capital Power Co.
				1,200‡	Hull Electric Co.

TABLE IV.—Water-powers in St. Lawrence and Ottawa District.—*Continued.*

Water Power	Lowest Head Feet	Estimated Low Water Flow c.f.s.	Minimum 24 Hour Power H.P.	Present Turbine Installation H.P.	Remarks
Chats Falls	38	11,100	38,400		
Chats Rapids	12	11,100	12,100		
Portage du Fort	12	9,800	10,700		
*b*Calumet Island	..	9,800			
Roche Fendu	86	4,900	38,300	.....	Interprovincial Channel, 13 miles of rapids.
Calumet Falls	55	4,900	24,500	..... }	In Prov. of Quebec.
Mountain Chute	15	4,900	6,680	..... }	
*b*Allumette Island	..	8,600	......	......	
Les Allumettes	13	6,600	7,800	.....	Interprovincial Channel.
Paquet's	9	6,600	5,400	..... }	
Culbute	21	2,000	3,800	..... }	In Prov. of Quebec.
Des Joachims	27	7,830	19,200	..... J	
Rocher Capataine	41	7,130	26,600		
Deux Rivieres	13	7,080	8,360		
Trou	7	7,020	4,460		
L'Evieilles	8	7,020	5,100		
Rocky Farm, Johnson and Mattawa	17	6,950	10,700		
Les Erables Mountain	16	6,450	9,400		
Long Sault	49	6,440	28,700	.....	Six miles of rapids.
Nation River:					
Cripler	12	15	16	200	Bishop & Son flour mill and electric light plant.
High Falls	40	25	90		
Plantagenet	8	30	20	.....	Grist mill and wooler mill.
Rideau River:					
*c*From Perth, 3 miles	15	55	75	250 }	Electric light and power for Perth.
Tay River, 4 miles	10	55	50	250 }	
Smiths Falls	6	140	78	280	Electric light plant.
				90	Plough works.
	{ 18	140	230	{ 100	Woolen mills.
	17			300	Stove Works.
	17			500	Flour and planing mills.
	15			800	Flour mill.
	13			400	Municipal pumping
1 mile below Smiths Falls	18	140	230	500	Smith's Falls Electric Company.
Merrickville	26	215	505	.....	Possible development.
	12	215	235	120	Electric light plant.
				100	Sawmill.
				70	Malleable iron works.
				170	Flour mill.
				50	Woolen manufacture.
				50	Ploughs and stoves.
				120	Grist and saw mills.
				80	Furniture.
Andrewsville	11	220	220	250	Kemptville elec. supply.
Manotick	10	363	330	750	Grist mills.
Black Rapids	10	370	330		
Hog's Back	50	400	1,820	....	Saw and planing mills.
Ottawa	40	400	1,450	100	Foundry.
Mississippi River:					
King	24	140	305		
Otter	15	140	190		
Island	38	140	485		
Ragged	38	140	485		
High Falls	72	140	915		
Geddes Bros	15	140	130	.....	Grist mill.
Playfairville	15	150	200	.....	Saw mill.
Innisville	13	232	275		
Carleton Place	{ 12	250	272	.....	Possible development.
	8	......	......	200	Elec. light stations.
				250	Four mill.
	{ 8	250	182	.....	Possible development.
	{ 7	......	......	70	Engines.
	7	......	......	200	Woolen mills.
Appleton	16		360	...	Woolen mills.
Almonte	10	300	270	100	Flour mill.
				40	Flannel mill.
				30	Machine shop.
	{ 51	300	1,390	500	Woolen mills.
	26	......	......	250	Municipal elec. plant.
	22	......	......	190	Dress goods, etc.
	18	......	......	75	Woolen goods.
	14	......	......	150	Shoddy mill.
	7	......	......	100	Knitting mill.

TABLE IV.—Water-powers in St. Lawrence and Ottawa District.—*Continued.*

WATER POWER	Lowest Head, Feet	Estimated Low Water Flow c.f.s.	Minimum 24 Hour Power H.P.	Present Turbine Installation H.P.	REMARKS
Rosebank.................	23	320	670	.....	Woolen mill.
					Grist mill.
Packenham..............	18	330	540	.....	Flour mill.
Galetta..................	25	345	780	35	Woolen mill.
				80	Grist mill privilege.
Madawaska River:					
Palmer Rapids..........	17	635	980		
Omo Rapids............	7	650	410		
Snake Rapids...........	30	670	1,820		
Slate Falls.............	23	725	1,510		
Highland Chute.........	12	725	790		
Camel Chute and Rapids.	19	740	1,280	.....	Sawmill, 8 ft. head.
Colton Chute...........	18	750	1,230	.....	
Rapids.................	13	750	885	.....	
Deschenes Rapids and Rapids above..........	29	770	2,030	.....	
Rapids.................	7	770	490	.....	
Cedar Rapids...........	31	775	2,180	.....	
Mountain Chutes........	40	790	2,860	550	Electric plant for graphite mine, 20 feet head.
Norway Chute...........	8	790	575	.....	
Chain Rapids...........	15	810	1,100		
The Ducks.............	16	830	1,220		
Ragged Chute...........	16	830	1,220		
High Falls.............	78	830	5,960		
Barret's Chute..........	17	830	1,300		
Calabogie Rapids........	20	860	1,560		
Sixteen miles of Rapids, Arnprior..............	20	885	1,610	.....	Present dam dilapidated
	18	......	......	200	Grist mill.
	9	......	......	75	Machine shop
	9	......	......	75	Electric light plant.
	10	......	......	300	Sawmill
Bonnechere River.					
Rabitahl Cascades.......	405	20	730		
High Falls.............	30	20	55		
Eganville	14	105	135	300	Sawmill
				120	Flour mill and elec. plant
				40	Sash factory.
	12	105	115	300	Flour mill and elec. plant.
	12	105	115	.....	In process of developm't.
	46	110	460	.....	Possible development.
Fourth Chute....	15	......	......	700	Sawmill.
Third Chute............	21	110	210		
Renfrew................	37	140	470	500	Renfrew Power Co. (capacity being increased)
	20	140	255	100	Woolen mills.
				110	Sawmill and elec. plant.
				300	Renfrew Milling Co.
				50	Thos. Lowe.
	11	140	140	.....	Unused.
(Smith's Creek Branch)...	44	15	60	190	Sash factory.
First Chute.............	32	145	420		
Petewawa River:					
1st series rapids below Catfish Lake.........	119	120	1,290		
2nd do.	41	120	445		
3rd do.	80	120	875		
1st series rapids below Cedar Lake..........	29	145	380		
2nd do.	33	145	435		
3rd do.	36	145	475		
1st series rapids below Little Trout Lake......	18	190	310		
2nd do.	13	190	225		
On LaVieille Cr..........	31	60	170		
2nd series rapids below La Vieille Creek........	25	250	570		
3rd do.	16	255	370		
4th do.	27	255	630		
5th do.	24	255	560		
6th do.	44	255	1,000		
1st series rapids below Lake Travers.........	16	280	410		
3rd do.	41	280	1,050		
(Crooked Chute)					

TABLE IV.—Water-powers in St. Lawrence and Ottawa District.—*Continued.*

WATER POWER	Lowest Head, Feet	Estimated Low Water Flow c.f.s.	Minimum 24 Hour Power H P.	Present Turbine Installation H.P.	REMARKS
1st rapid above S. Branch.	13	280	330		
1st rapid below S. Branch..	13	375	445		
2nd do.	18	375	615		
At C.P.R. Bridge........	21	380	725		
2nd above mouth........	24	380	830		
1st above mouth........	21	380	725		
Indian River:					
Pembroke..............	9	30	25	......	Foster's mill.
Muskrat River.					
Pembroke..............	12	60	65	75	Grist mill.
				30	Woolen mill.
Mattawa River:					
Plein Chant........ .	17	160	250	.....	Electric light plant.
Paresseux..............	33	120	360		
Little Paresseux	8	120	95		
Talon............	42	60	230		
Montreal River.					
The Notch	100	750	6,500		
Fountain Falls.........	21	720	1,350		
Ragged Chute...	36	720	2,360		
Ragged Chute and Rapids below and above.......	54	720	3,500		
Hound Chute............	18	720	1,180		
Latchford	8	720	510		
Mattawapika...........	30	100	270		
Blanche River:					
Lot 12, Con. 3. Evanturel..	54	130	640		
Lot 1, Con. 3. Dack	26	130	310		
Lot 2, Con. 4. Dack......	34	130	400		
Lot 7, Con. 4, Dack......	22	130	260		
L. Wendigo Br..........	36	100	330		
1 mile below Lake Wendigo	36	100	330		
Wabi River:					
High Falls..............	81	30	220		
New Liskeard...........	100	30	270	200	New Liskeard Light and Power Co., under construction.

*Head least in periods of high water in the river.
†These plants take water from an upper reach of the canal and discharge it into the river.
‡Developments in Quebec Province.
*a*All consumption on 10 hour basis.
b The distribution of the discharge is uncertain and varies at different stages of the water. Certain existing dams at La Passe, Ont., and at Culbute and Bryson, Que., now control the water levels above.
*c*Upper Tay controlled for use on Rideau Canal.

PART IV.

GENERATION OF POWER.

As will be seen in the preceding tables, nearly every town in the district has electric light and power supplied from a hydraulic source. The most important developments are those of Ottawa, Cornwall, Hawkesbury, Morrisburg, Smith's Falls, Gananoque and Almonte. It may be said of most towns in this district that the local hydraulic power has been a large factor in fixing the location of the town. Several of the towns have, in their demand for electrical supply of light and power, outgrown the capacity of the early hydraulic developments and are now, or were until recently, in need of a supply from more extensive and more economical local developments, or from hydraulic sources external to themselves. In the former class are Almonte, Arnprior, Morrisburg and Renfrew; in the latter, are Carleton Place, Gananoque, Kemptville, Pembroke, Perth and Smith's Falls. Of the latter group, Kemptville is now supplied from a development at Andrewsville of a capacity of 400 H.P. by a transmission of 14 miles at 10,000 volts, and Pembroke will shortly receive a supply up to 1,300 horse power at 22,500 volts from a development at Waltham on the Black River in the Province of Quebec. Gananoque is isolated and cannot expect to receive a supply of hydro-electric power other than it now possesses unless Kingston should at some time be supplied from a hydraulic source along the St. Lawrence river. Of the former group, Morrisburg is constructing a second municipal plant and at Renfrew the privately owned Company is engaged in more than doubling its equipment of generating machinery. The Hawkesbury Lumber Company develop power under an eight foot head on the upper portion of the Long Sault Rapids on the Ottawa River, but the town itself is not supplied from a local source. The Hawkesbury Electric Light and Power Co. have a development at Calumet on the Little Nation River in Quebec, whence they supply, by means of a 10,000 volt transmission, Grenville in Quebec and Hawkesbury and Vankleek Hill in Ontario. It is understood that as relating to Cornwall, an agreement between the St. Lawrence Power Co. located at Mille Roches, 5 miles west of the town, and the Stormont Electric Light & Power Co., of Cornwall, stands in the way of a supply of municipal power to the people of this town, whose natural source of supply is at Mille Roches. The City of Ottawa is supplied from Chaudiere Falls by two systems of distribution, owned one privately and one municipality, the latter obtaining its power from a privately owned generating equipment in Hull, Que., the former generating its own power in Ontario.

A considerable market for electric power and light has developed recently in the Temiskaming district, where are the three towns of New Liskeard, Haileybury and Cobalt and where there is a rapidly growing demand for electric power for the numerous services connected with mining operations.

The following Table V. is a summary showing the variety of frequencies now in use in places in this district:

TABLE V.

Frequency.	Capacity K.W.	Used in.
60	17,745	Eleven towns and cities.
66	100	One town.
100	60	One town.
125	810	Five towns.
133	740	Three towns.

A frequency of 60 cycles per second has been chosen for purposes of the estimates following, as this frequently is in use already in serving a large majority of the urban population of the district and, as it harmonizes with the great bulk of the practice on this continent. This frequency is also satisfactory for all services and well within proper limits for transmission of the relatively small quantities of current to be transmitted, considering the greatest distance estimated upon is only 86 miles. The distances however, are great enough to prohibit the use of any frequency much in excess of 60. This fact must be borne in mind in estimating the cost of distribution for Prescott, Smith's Falls, Carleton Place and Perth, where, 125 and 133 cycle machinery is in use, and where it will be necessary, therefore, to install frequency changers, in addition to the ordinary sub-station equipment.

A proper estimate of the probable immediate future demands for electric power, which demands may be conveniently supplied from available water power developments, is peculiarly difficult on account of the number and character of the many hydro-electric plants now in service, but for the towns in the Southern portion of the district, some optional schemes have been developed. These include proposals to develop, (1) a twelve foot head at Iroquois, Ont., on the Galops canal for the supply of Brockville and Prescott; (2) a seventy-eight foot head at High Falls on the Mississippi River for (a) the supply of Prescott, Brockville, Carleton Place, Smith's Falls and Perth; (b) the supply of Carleton Place, Smith's Falls and Perth only; (c) a twenty-seven foot head at Fountain Falls on the Montreal River for the supply of the Cobalt Mines and Haileybury.

(1) IROQUOIS, ONT., DEVELOPMENT: This scheme involves the use of a power site already partially prepared by the Dominion Government when rebuilding the Galops canal. Water would be taken from just above the lock at the foot of the canal. Twelve feet at periods of high water in the St. Lawrence would be the probable minimum head. The capacity of such a plant would be limited by the maximum discharge of water permitted by the canal authorities and by the continuous flow of water already in service for power and canal purposes. There would be only a small peak load capacity in such a development.

As it is the practice of the management to close the canal periodically, it would be necessary to instal for power purposes an auxiliary steam plant of capacity equal to that of the hydraulic plant here estimated upon, but as it would be desirable that such steam plant or plants should be located in the cities where power is to be delivered, the costs and charges thereon are not estimated. Such reserve plants are those already in service at Brockville and Prescott. The water power conditions at this point will not admit of any considerable addition to the installation herein estimated upon, which is 1,200 H.P.

(2) HIGH FALLS DEVELOPMENT: The developments at this point here estimated upon are for (a) 2,400 horse power and (b) 1,100 horse power, respectively. The natural head at this point is seventy-two feet, which can be augmented, at least six feet, by drowning out small rapids above the falls. It will be noted that in Table IV. above the minimum capacity is given as 900 H.P. under present natural conditions. This capacity can be considerably increased by developing the unusually good storage facilities in the sources of the river, thus permitting an output, as suggested in Scheme A.

Should the market for power grow beyond the capacity of this water power, it would be feasible to develop Ragged and Island Chutes immediately up stream, which would, as one plant, be capable of like output.

(3) FOUNTAIN FALLS DEVELOPMENT: By use of a dam, whose crest would rise nine feet above present head water level, a twenty-seven foot head would be available, giving a minimum output of 1,750 horse power. Survey of the market has shown that there is installed or about to be installed in the mining district, 3,000 boiler horse power. Hydraulic development of 2,400 horse power capacity has been here estimated upon, and such a plant can, in view of the irregular nature of the load, carry the present probable demand.

In estimating the annual charges on this development and transmission, it has been kept in mind that the market being that of a mining camp, is of fluctuating character. On this account, the sinking fund charges have been calculated on a ten year basis, instead of thirty years, as is the case in towns in other portions of the Province, where the prospects of a future market are more assured. Also it is important to note that in the case of the Fountain Falls development, the sinking fund charges have been incorporated in the development and transmission cost per horse power and are consequently included in the final cost per horse power as given in the Summation Sheet.

TABLE VI.

ESTIMATED CAPITAL COST OF POWER DEVELOPMENTS.

Location of Water Power.	Head.	Net Amount of High Tension Power Generated H.P.	Total Capital Cost.	Cost Per H.P.
St. Lawrence River, Iroquois, Ont............	12	1,200	$179,000	$149 16
Mississippi River, High Falls, Ont., A.........	78	2,400	195,000	81.25
Mississippi River, High Falls, Ont., B.........	78	1,100	123,000	111.82
Montreal River, Fountain Falls, Ont..........	27	2,400	214,000	89.16

The capital cost in each case includes step-up transformer stations, one reserve generating unit in excess of each of the above mentioned capacities, and a spare transformer in each station.

TABLE VII.

ESTIMATED ANNUAL CHARGES ON FULLY DEVELOPED GENERATING PLANTS.

ITEMS	St. Lawrence River Iroquois	Mississippi River		Montreal River Fountain Falls
		High Falls Scheme A	High Falls Scheme B	
Operating Expenses including Step-up Transformation Losses...............	$6,864	$9,391	$6,390	$9,850
Maintenance and Repairs...............	5,119	3,840	2,491	3,903
*Replacement Fund....................	5,118	3,841	2,491	21,622
Interest at 4%.......................	7,151	7,777	4,908	8,539
Total Annual Charges.................	24,252	24,849	16,280	43,914
MUNICIPALITY	Distribution of Charges			
Brockville............................	$19,681			
Prescott.............................	4,571			
Brockville............................	.....	$10,629		
Prescott.............................	.....	2,532		
Smith's Falls........................	.....	5,818		
Carleton Place.......................	.....	3,507		
Perth................................	.....	2,363		
Carleton Place.......................	.....	.....	$4,927	
Smith's Falls	.....	.....	8,083	
Perth	.....	.....	3,270	
Haileybury...........................	.....	.....	.....	$ 3,704
Cobalt	.....	.....	.....	25,634
Kerr Lake............................	.....	.....	.....	14,576

*In the case of Fountain Falls, the figure under this head includes a 10 year sinking fund, of which mention has been made elsewhere in the report.

PART V.

TRANSMISSION OF POWER.

In connection with the hydraulic developments in the Ottawa Valley and that portion of the Province bordering on the St. Lawrence river, four transmission schemes have been considered; viz., one, 20,000 volts, three-phase, from Iroquois through Prescott to Brockville; one, 30,000 volts, three-phase, (Scheme A.) from High Falls through Perth and Smith's Falls to Brockville, Prescott and Carleton Place; one, 20,000 volts, three-phase, (Scheme B.) from High Falls through Perth and Smith's Falls, terminating at Carleton Place; one, 20,000 volts, three-phase, from Fountain Falls through the Cobalt Mining district, terminating at Haileybury.

In the following estimates, the use of high class wooden poles with concrete bases is assumed, the telephone line being mounted on the same poles.

The transmission table shows the capital cost and annual charges on the transmission lines from the step-up transformer station at the various points of development to the step-down stations at points of local distribution. The annual charges include depreciation and repairs, interest and cost of patrol.

The table of transformation details gives particulars concerning the proposed transformer stations. In all cases the step-up station is assumed as being built for full capacity at the outset, with equipment to be installed as required. The transformation charges provide for municipal taxes on building, insurance, depreciation, engineering and contingencies and interest during construction.

The summation sheet contains the charges for transmission, transformation and administration chargeable to each municipality, in addition to which is added in each case, the cost of power at the generating station. The final column is for 24 hour power at low-tension bus-bars of the various municipal sub-stations.

In connection with the transformation and summation sheets, it has not been considered advisable to discuss the question of three-quarter and half loads, as in former reports. If information in this connection should be required, the cost per horse power may be arrived at approximately by dividing total annual charges for any town by the amount of power delivered there.

	SMITH'S FALLS.		PERTH.		HAILEYBURY.		COBALT.		KERR LAKE.	
	Loss of Power.	Annual Charges.	Loss of Power.	Annual Charges.	Loss of Power.	Annual Charges.	Loss of Power.	Annual Charges.	Loss of Power.	Annual Charges.
	H.P.		H.P.		H.P.		H.P.		H.P.	
0										
4	11.8	$ 571								
9	23.1	912	9.2	$371						
3	34.9	$1,483	9 2	$371						
0										
0	14.4	1,298								
7	27.61	1,931	11.2	782						
7	42.0	$3,229	11.2	$782						
	...	.....	...	...	1.0	$ 739				
	...	.....	...	...	1.5	79	9.7	$ 537		
	...	.....	...	...	5.7	256	39 1	1,744	22.2	$991
					8.2	$1,074	48 8	$2,281	22 2	$991

TABLE VIII.

TRANSMISSION DETAILS.

IROQUOIS TO BROCKVILLE, 20,000 VOLTS.

Section.	Miles.	Size of Conductors. M.C.M.	Capital Cost per Mile. Equipment.	Right of Way, etc.	Engineering and Contingencies.	Total.	Capital Charges per Mile. Equipment.	Right of Way, Fencing, etc.	Engineering and Contingencies.	Total.	Total Capital Cost.	Total Capital Charges.	Patrol. Per Mile.	Total.	Total Annual Charges.	Full Load Loss of Power H.P.	Brockville. Loss of Power	Annual Charges.	Prescott. Loss of Power H.P.	Annual Charges.	Carleton Place. Loss of Power H.P.	Annual Charges.	Smith's Falls. Loss of Power H.P.	Annual Charges.	Perth. Loss of Power H.P.	Hailebury. Loss of Power H.P.	Annual Charges.	Cobalt. Loss of Power H.P.	Annual Charges.	Kerr Lake. Loss of Power H.P.	Annual Charges.
Brockville–Prescott	12	47.1	$1,560	$200	$372	$2,232	$1,248	$370	$376	1,910	$26,794	$1,703	30	$360	$2,113	25.5	25.5	$2,113	7.5												
Prescott–Iroquois	15	38.1	1,474	620	399	2,394	1,745			1,910	35,910	2,402	30	450	2,552	39.6	33.1	2,317	7.5	$535											
Total.	27										$62,694	$4,155		$810	$4,965	65.1	57.6	$4,430	7.5	$535											

HIGH FALLS TO CARLETON PLACE, 20,000 VOLTS.

Carleton Place–Smith's Falls	12	41.6	1,097	370	291	1,748	1,097			1,910	13,212	2,495	35	475	2,980	4.0			1.0	1,819	4.0	$2,680									
Prescott–Brockville	12	41.6	1,097	370	291	1,745	1,097				20,976	2,918	35	500	2,818		46.8	3,633	11.2	872			11.6	$571							
Brockville–Smith's Falls	21	66.0	1,376	370	349	2,055					49,944	3,545	35	589	4,535	58.0	21.6	1,643	10.1	269	7.2	344	23.1	912							
Smith's Falls–Perth	23	72.8	1,452	140	318	1,910	1,452				43,930	1,787	40	480	3,207	45.8	4.2	1,063	10.1	397	13.9	549	34.9	$1,463	9.2	$371						
Perth–High Falls												2,072	40	920	3,663	98.5			27.5	3,337	25.1	$3,771			9.2	$371						
Total.											$172,303	$12,168		$3,155	$15,322	207.3	110.6	$6,359													

HIGH FALLS TO CARLETON PLACE, 20,000 VOLTS.

Carleton Place–Smith's Falls	19	41.6	1,089	370	292	1,751					33,269	2,415	35	665	3,080	7.0	4.0		7.0		7.0	3,080	14.4	1,268	11.2	782						
Smith's Falls–Perth	12	35.4	1,069	370	295	1,505					28,600	1,804	35	320	2,080	55.3			23.3		16.8	780	37.61	1,531								
Perth–High Falls	23	69.1	1,444	140	317	1,901					43,723	2,970	40	920	3,900						32.5	1,177	42.0	$3,229	11.2	782						
Total.	54										$100,592	$7,039		$2,005	$9,058	85.4						$5,047										

FOUNTAIN FALLS TO HAILEYBURY, 20,000 VOLTS.

Haileybury–Cobalt	3	41.6	1,089	240	140	1,469					7,345	539	40	500	739	1.0			1.0							1.0	720	0.7			
Cobalt–Kerr Lake	13	17.2	1,027	438	162	1,627					7,861	495	40	446	896	17.0			17.0							1.5	79	39.1	1,744	22.2	399
Kerr Lake–Fountain Falls			2,779	140	384	3,303					42,086	2,811	40	480	2,911											5.2	358	48.8	$2,581	22.2	601
Total.	39										$57,292	$3,846		$880	$4,346	79.2										8.2	$1,074				

TABLE IX.

TRANSFORMATION DETAILS.

MUNICIPALITY.	Capacity H.P.	Capital Cost.					Annual Charges.				Source of Power.
		Building and Lot.	Equipment.	Engineering and Contingencies 10 per cent.	Interest during Construction 2 per cent.	TOTAL.	Maintenance and Depreciation.	Interest 4 per cent.	Operating.	TOTAL.	
Brockville.........	875	$2,100	$12,620	$1,472	$124	$16,516	$782	$661	Operating cost covered by line patrol and administration.	$1,443	} Iroquois, Ont., 20,000 Volts.
Prescott.........	308	1,100	8,340	944	208	10,592	550	424		974	
Brockville.........	875	2,100	18,600	2,070	155	23,225	1,110	929		2,039	High Falls, Mississippi River, Scheme A, 30,000 Volts.
Prescott.........	208	1,100	8,270	987	206	10,513	496	420		916	
*Smith's Falls....	304	1,600	17,042	1,864	410	20,916	1,122	836		1,958	
Carleton Place ...	300	1,100	10,023	1,112	244	12,479	631	499		1,130	
Perth...........	210	1,100	11,145	1,224	269	13,738	659	550		1,209	
In Place	300	1,100	9,470	1,057	233	11,860	583	475		1,057	High Falls, Mississippi River, Scheme B, 20,000 Volts.
*Smith's Falls....	504	1,600	14,160	1,576	347	17,683	852	707		1,559	
Perth	210	1,100	9,970	1,107	243	12,420	570	497		1,067	
Haileybury.......	200	1,100	9,520	1,062	234	11,916	566	477		1,043	} Fountain Falls, Montreal River, 20,000 Volts.
Cobalt..........	1,400	2,100	22,675	2,477	545	27,797	1,307	1,112		2,419	
Kerr Lake........	800	2,100	17,020	1,912	420	21,452	1,022	858		1,880	

*Switching Station.

TABLE X.
SUMMATION SHEET

Municipality	Population	Present Power Used. Total	Present Power Used. Portion admitting Electrical Installation.	Estimated Future Load.	Annual Charges. Generation including Step-up Transformation	Annual Charges. Transmission	Annual Charges. Step-down Transformation.	Annual Charges. Administration and Interswitching	Annual Charges. Total.	Total Annual Cost of 24 Hour Power at Low Tension Bus-bars, Step-down Transformer Station.	Source of Power.
Brockville	9,000	700	700	875	$19,681	$4,430	$1,443	$2,935	$28,489	$32.55	Ironquois, Ont. 20,000 Volts.
Prescott	3,035	215	150	208	4,571	545	974	665	6,745	32.42	
Brockville	9,000			875	10,629	6,359	2,039	3,498	22,525	25.68	High Falls, Mississippi River, Scheme A, 30,000 Volts.
Prescott	3,035			208	2,522	3,357	916	828	7,613	36.58	
Smith's Falls	5,700	815	300	504	15,818	1,483	1,958	1,351	11,190	22.20	
Glen Place	4,000	545	175	300	3,507	3,773	1,130	1,157	9,567	31.89	
Perth	4,000	210	150	210	2,363	371	1,209	785	4,728	22.51	
Carleton Place	4,000			300	4,927	5,047	1,057	1,515	12,546	41.82	High Falls, Mississippi River, Scheme B, 20,000 Volts.
Smith's Falls	5,700			504	8,083	3,229	1,559	2,480	15,351	30.45	
Perth	400			210	3,270	782	1,067	1,005	6,124	29.16	
Hanleybury	1215, 1 milef.	200	200	400	3,704	1,074	1,043	507	6,338	31.64	Fountain Falls, Montreal River, 20,000 Volts.
Cobalt	1 milef.	1,800	1,400	2,800	25,634	2,281	2,419	3,503	33,857	24.17	
Kerr Lake	1 milef.	1,000	800	1,600	14,576	991	1,880	1,950	19,437	24.29	

In the following table (XI.) is shown in condensed form the investment and annual charges for transmission and step-down transformation, also the cost per annum per horse power ready for distribution from the low-tension bus-bars in the various towns.

TABLE XI.

ITEMS	St. Lawrence River Iroquois	Mississippi River		Montreal River Fountain Falls
		High Falls Scheme A	High Falls Scheme B	
Total H.P. Distributed..	1,200	2,366	1.100	2,400
Total Investment including Step-down Transformer Stations.......	$89,802.00	$252,683 00	$142,555.00	$118,427.00
Investment per H.P. delivered...	74 86	110 90	129.60	49 34
Total Annual Repairs, depreciation, operation and administration ..	3,790 00	13,299.00	8,039 00	4,951.00
Interest 4%	3,592 00	10,107 00	5,702.00	4,737.00
Total.	7,382.00	23,406.00	13,741.00	9,688.00
MUNICIPALITY	Cost of 24 hour power per H.P. per Annum including line and step-down transformer losses.			
Brockville......	$32.55			
Prescott............................	32.42			
Brockville............................	.....	$25 68		
Prescott	.....	36.58		
Smith's Falls	.....	22.26		
Carleton Place.. . ...:	.....	31.89		
Perth	.....	22 51		
Carleton Place	.....	.....	$41.82	
Smith's Falls..	.....	.....	30.45	
Perth..........	.....	.....	29.16	
Haileybury........ ...	.....	.....	.....	$31.64
Cobalt. ....:	.....	.....	.....	24.17
Kerr Lake	.....	.....	....	24.29

INDIVIDUAL TRANSMISSION.

The various sub-stations have been estimated on the basis of transformation down to 2,200 volts, but the cost of distribution of power at this voltage will be dealt with in Part VI. Many instances arise. however, in which it is desired to supply a single large consumer or a small municipality at some distance from a sub-station. When this is the case the following table may be made use of. The total cost of power to such a consumer is ascertained by adding the rate per H.P. from this table to the cost of power at the nearest municipal sub-station. The charges for such a branch transmission do not include any allowance for right of way or telephone, it being assumed that the highways would be available for such low voltage lines.

TABLE XII.

SHOWING COST OF DISTRIBUTION FROM MUNICIPAL SUB-STATION TO
AN INDIVIDUAL CONSUMER, NOT COVERED BY LOCAL DISTRIBUTION.

Distance in Miles from Municipal Sub-station	Cost per Horse-Power per Annum for the Delivery of Various Amounts of Power.							
	50 H.P.	75 H P.	100 H.P.	150 H.P.	200 H.P.	250 H.P.	300 H P.	
2	$5.58	$4 20	$3 53	$2.92	$2.74	$2 60	$2.51	
3	6.89	5.20	4 41	3.60	3 25	3.10	3.03	2,300 Volts
4	7.92	6.18	5.20	4.27	3.93	3.72	3.86	
	8.87	7.18	5.98	4.96	4.55	4.32	4.17	
6	10 20	8 24	6.77	5.38	5.13	4.60	4 43	
8	14 10	10 14	8.40	6.97	6.24	5.79	5.58	11,000 Volts
10	16 12	12.13	9.54	8.31	7.68	6.96	6.17	
12	18.76	14.03	11.12	10.12	8.42	7.96	7.22	16,500 Volts
15	22.74	17.08	13.48	10.89	9.35	8.84	8.32	

PART VI.
DISTRIBUTION OF POWER.

The cost of distribution from the municipal sub-stations to the consumers' premises varies widely with different conditions and depends upon the distances involved, the magnitude of the demands of individual consumers, and the grouping of these consumers.

This cost of distribution will not necessarily, however, give the increase of cost to the consumer above that paid for the power by the municipality unless a method of charging be chosen which will take into account the difference between the sum of the consumers' maximum demands and the maximum demand on the station. If the charging rate for power were one composed of a flat rate based on maximum demand plus a rate per k.w.-hour or h.p.-hour actually registered by meter, then it would be approximately correct to say that the combined rate per horse power to the consumer should be the same as the cost of power at the sub-station plus the cost per horse power of the distribution service. Besides this the ordinary municipality has such various means of modifying the rates for power, such as limited-hour contracts with motor users, contracts with summer users of electric power, etc., that fair rates could only

be established after a careful study of the actual conditions after operations were begun. Under average conditions in a town demanding
1,000 H.P. or over, it could reasonably be expected that 10-hour power
could be sold at the same or even a lower rate, if based on maximum
demand than that charged the municipality for 24-hour power at the
sub-stations. In other words, the municipality might expect to profit
sufficiently from non-coincident peaks, 24-hour power for lighting,
pumping, general motor users, etc., to pay the cost of its distribution.

The cost of a distribution system for the town of Brockville has
been estimated on, the same being entirely independent of the one in
use at the present time. This includes completely equipped pole and
distribution lines and sufficient 2,200 volt 60 cycle power service transformers to carry the present motor load. Two banks of 2,200 volt
transformers have been assumed in this estimate as centrally located
in the town from which the lighting load would be taken, but it is
important to note that this estimate does not include the cost of lighting, distribution and lighting transformers. On this basis, it is found
that the total capital cost will be about $21,000 and the annual in-
terest, depreciation and operation charges attendant upon this investment would be $4,100.00. This charge on 950 H.P. gives a yearly rate
of $4.30 per H.P., which, added to the cost of low-tension power at the
sub-station, as given in Table X., gives an average yearly rate for 24
hour power, without any allowance for over-lapping. It is probable
that if suitable portions of the present distribution system were utilized, the capital cost would be materially reduced.

In connection with the smaller towns, it may be said that the
actual selling price of 10 hour power to the consumer would not be
appreciably greater than the cost of 24 hour power to the municipality
at the main sub-station, as given in the Report, if the facilities for the
double use of power be at all favorable.

PART VII.

MOTOR INSTALLATIONS.

To complete the information regarding the cost of electric power
to the consumer, the following table is given, showing the cost of induction motor service per H.P. per year.

TABLE XIII.

CAPITAL COST AND ANNUAL CHARGES ON MOTOR INSTALLATIONS,
POLYPHASE, 60-CYCLE INDUCTION MOTORS.

Capacity. H.P.	Capital Cost per H.P. Installed.	ANNUAL CHARGES.			
		Interest 5%	Depreciation and Repairs, 6%	Oil, Care and Operation.	Total per H.P. per Annum.
5	$39.00	$1.95	$2.34	$4.00	$8.29
10	36.00	1.80	2.16	3.00	6.96
15	30.00	1.50	1.80	2.50	5.80
25	25.00	1.25	1.50	2.00	4.75
35	22.00	1.10	1.32	1.75	4.17
50	20.00	1.00	1.20	1.50	3.70
75	19.00	.95	1.14	1.25	3.34
100	17.00	.85	1.02	1.00	2.87
150	15.00	.75	.90	.80	2.45
200	14.00	.70	.84	.70	2.24

By combining the costs given in this table with the cost of distributed power, as indicated in Part VI, the final or total charge per H.P. per year will be obtained.

PART VIII.

SINKING FUND.

In the above estimates for transmission and transformation, depreciation and replacement charges have been provided for which would replace the different classes of plant in periods ranging from 15 to 30 years. These charges would, therefore, amply serve the purpose of any sinking fund which might be considered needful. In the case of the generating plant estimates, however, these charges would not be sufficient for such a purpose in the so-called permanent portions of the development, comprising the dam, headworks, powerhouse, etc.

A forty year sinking fund to cover these portions of the development, amounting on the average to about $35.00 expenditure per H.P.

MUNICIPALITY.	Street Lighting per Year.
Alexandria........	32 c.p. $16.66
Arnprior..........	50 c.p. $6.50
Almonte..........	arc $65.00
	2,000
	50 c.p. $5.00
Brockville........	arc $62.25
	2,000
	32 c.p. $22.00
Carleton Place.....	32 c.p. $7.00
Cornwall..........	2,000 arc $82.
	25 c.p. $16.00
Eganville.........	50 c.p. $16.40
Gananoque........	5 amp. arc $42.
	115 v. moonlig
Hawkesbury......	50 c.p. $12.00
Iroquois..........	1,000 arc
	50 c.p. moonlig
Kemptville........	32 c.p. $15.0
Mattawa..........	1,200 arc $42.
	16 c.p. $2.00
Merrickville..... .	50 c.p.
	32 c.p.
Morrisburg........	52 c.p.
	rate not fixed
Ottawa...........	arc $52.00
Pembroke.........	arc $55.00
	1 a.m. moonlig

TABLE XIV.

RATES FOR LIGHT AND POWER.

Municipality.	Street Lighting per Year.	Commercial Incandescent Lighting. Meter Rate per K.W. Hr.	Commercial Incandescent Lighting. Flat Rate per 16 c.p. lamp per Year.	Residential Incandescent Lighting. Meter Rate per K.W. Hr.	Residential Incandescent Lighting. Flat Rate per 16 c.p. per Year.	Power. Flat Rate per H.P. per Year.	Source of Power.	Remarks.
Alexandria	32 c.p. $16.66 50 c.p. $6.50 arc $65.00 50 c.p. $-$5.00 2,000	8c.	$4.80 & down	8c.	$4.80 & down	...	Steam	Municipal.
Arnprior		15c.	$5.40; $3.00	9.6c.		...	W. & S.	Private.
Almonte			$3.90		$1.80	...	Water	Municipal.
Brockville	2,000 32 c.p. $62.25 arc 2,000	10c. & 14c	$9.00 & down	10c. & 14c.		...	Steam	Municipal.
Carleton Place	32 c.p. $22.00 32 c.p. $7.00	10c.		9c.		...	Water	Private.
Cornwall	2,000 arc $88.12 25 c.p. $16.00	13.5	arc $105.00 $5.30 down	13.5	$5.40	$30.00 25.00 20.00	Water	Private, transmitted 5 miles.
Eganville	50 c.p. $16.40	9c.—6c.	arc $73.00 $5.40		$1.55—$2.00		Water	Private.
Gananoque	5 amp. arc $43.00 115 v. moonlight		$3.00	8c.		6c. & 4c. per K.W. hr.	W. & S.	Private.
Hawkesbury	50 c.p. $12.00	8c.	$3.60 & down	8c.	$3.60—$2.40	$30.00 & down	Water	Private, 10 miles transmitted.
Iroquois	1,000 arc 50 c.p. moonlight		$2.50		$1.50	$15.00	Water	Municipal.
Kemptville	32 c.p. $15.00		$5.50— $4.55		$3.00 & down	$30.00	Water	Private, transmitted 14 miles.
Mattawa	1,200 arc $42.00 16 c.p. $2.00		$6.00 to $2.00		$4.00 to $2.00		Water	Private, transmitted 3½ miles.
Merrickville	50 c.p. 32 c.p. 52 c.p. rate not fixed		$7.30 to $3.65 $2.00		$7.30 to $3.65 $1.00		Water	Private.
Morrisburg							Water	Municipal.
Ottawa	arc $52.00	7.2c.	$2.52	7.2c.		$25.00 30.00	Water	Municipal and Private. (Limited contract $17.50.)
Pembroke	arc $55.00 1 a.m. moonlight		$6.00 to $3.60	12c. to 8c.			Water	Private, 13 miles, transmission being prepared.
Perth	2,000 arc $65.00 midnight		$6.00 & $3.00		$2.00		Water	Private and municipal.
Prescott	16 & 32 c.p. 7c. per K.W. hr. 1,000 c.p.	10c.		10c.			Steam	Municipal, rate for 1904 given.
Renfrew	1,100 c.p. $33.00 arc	10c.	$5.00 to $2.00 $3.65		$2.50	$20.00 25.00	Water	Private (two companies).
Smith's Falls	2,000 c.p. $57.50 ($66.25) arc	8c.			$1.85	20.00	Water	Private (two companies).
Vankleek Hill	32 c.p. $10.00 16 c.p. $6.00	10.5	$4.20 to $2.62		$4.20 to $2.52 $7.30		Water	Private, Hawkesbury E. L. & P. Co.
Winchester	32 c.p. $14.60 midnight			10c.			Steam	Private.

of capacity, would require a charge of 37 cents per H.P. to repay this expenditure in 40 years, interest being calculated at 4 per cent.

The special conditions governing the case of the Fountain Falls development have been set forth elsewhere in the Report.

PART IX.

EXISTING RATES.

In Table XIV. following will be found a statement of the lighting and power rates in a number of municipalities throughout the District.

PART X.

STEAM POWER.

In order to institute a comparison between the cost of electric power as has just been set forth and the cost of power generated by steam or producer-gas, the following tables have been compiled after a careful study of data available in technical journals and also from data collected by the Commission's engineers in various towns within the district under consideration. The capital costs have been compiled from information supplied by various makers of engines and other machinery. The tables represent average working conditions and assume a high class installation.

TABLE XV.

STEAM POWER PLANTS.

SHOWING CAPITAL COSTS OF PLANTS INSTALLED AND ANNUAL COSTS OF POWER PER BRAKE HORSE-POWER.

Size of Plant, H.P.	Capital Cost of Plant per H.P. installed.			Annual Cost of 10-hour Power per B.H.P.	Annual Cost of 24-hour Power per B.H.P.
	Engines, Boilers, etc., installed.	Buildings.	Total.		
CLASS I —Engines: Simple, slide valve, non-condensing. Boilers: Return tubular.					
10	$66.00	$40.00	$106.00	$91.16	$180.76
20	56.00	37.00	93.00	76.31	151.48
30	48.70	35.00	83.70	66.46	131.68
40	44.75	33.50	78.25	59.49	117.74
50	43.00	31.00	74.00	53.95	106.46
CLASS II.—Engines. Simple, Corliss, non-condensing. Boilers: Return tubular.					
30	70.70	35.00	105.70	61.14	117.70
40	62.85	33.50	96.35	55.50	107.10
50	59.00	31.00	90.00	50.70	97.73
60	56.00	30.00	86.70	47.42	91.34
80	50.00	27.50	77.50	43.86	85.41
100	44.60	25.00	69.60	40.55	79.19
CLASS III.—Engines: Compound, Corliss, condensing. Boilers: Return tubular with reserve capacity.					
100	63.40	28.00	91.40	33.18	60.05
150	53.70	24.00	77.70	29.83	54.63
200	50.10	20.00	70.10	28.14	51.72
300	45.90	18.00	63.90	26.27	48.83
400	43.55	16.00	59.55	24.84	46.12
500	41.25	14.00	55.25	23.73	44.21
750	40.50	13.00	53.50	23.56	44.02
1000	39.00	12.00	51.00	23.26	43.71
CLASS IV.—Engines: Compound, Corliss, condensing. Boilers: Water-tube, with reserve capacity.					
300	55.20	18.00	73.20	25.77	46.32
400	51.50	16.00	67.50	24.18	43.61
500	49.40	14.00	63.40	23.19	42.03
750	46.80	13.00	59.70	22.88	41.56
1000	44.80	12.00	56.80	22.47	41.11

NOTE:—Annual costs include interest at 5 per cent., depreciation and repairs on plant, oil and waste, labor and fuel (coal at $4.00 per ton). Brake horse-power is the mechanical power at engine shaft.

It will be noted that for a consumer requiring a large installation, operating for ten hours only, there appears to be little advantage to be derived from the use of transmitted electric power, provided the power is not to be distributed throughout a consumer's buildings by a complicated system of shafting, belts, etc. But in the majority of cases this condition obtains, and herein lies one of the specific advantages of electric power. Motors can be installed on each floor of the factory, or even on each machine, with but little loss in efficiency, and only such motors as are required to drive the machinery in use from time to time need be operated. In many cases due to this fact the total electric power consumption of a large factory would be reduced from 25 per cent. to 50 per cent. below that which is required under steam operation, working from a central station.

Again, where electric power is available throughout the 24 hours many industries will work night and day, thereby effecting a great economy, as is evidenced by a comparison of the cost of 24-hour steam or producer-gas power with 24-hour electric power.

Perhaps the most striking advantage to be derived from the use of electric power as compared with other power, is that the small consumer can obtain power at a rate which should not be appreciably greater than that made to the large consumer, although the present practice in selling electric power is to discriminate against the small consumer for the reason that electric power prices made by private companies are not based on cost of service, but are merely made with a view to displacing steam.

PART XI.

PRODUCER GAS POWER.

TABLE XVI.

SHOWING CAPITAL COSTS OF PRODUCER GAS PLANTS INSTALLED, AND
ANNUAL COSTS OF POWER PER BRAKE HORSE-POWER.

Size of Plant, H P.	Capital Cost of Plant per H.P. Installed.			Annual Cost of 10-hour Power per B.H.P.	Annual Cost of 24-hour Power per B.H.P.
	Machinery, etc.	Buildings.	Total		
10	$137.00	$40.00	$177.00	$53.48	$90.02
20	110.00	36.00	146.00	44.47	75.22
30	93.00	33.00	126.00	38.73	65.99
40	84.50	29.00	113.50	35.05	59.85
50	80.00	26.00	106.00	32.27	55.22
60	79.00	24.00	103.00	30.49	52.03
80	78.20	22.00	100.20	28.70	48.95
100	77.50	20.00	97.50	27.05	45.40
150	76.00	19.00	95.00	25.87	43.17
200	74.00	17.00	91.00	24.95	41.78
300	73.00	16.00	89.00	24.24	40.40
400	71.50	14.00	85.50	23.41	39.03
500	70.00	12.00	82.00	22.54	37.54
750	67.50	10.00	77.50	21.55	35.99
1000	65.00	8.00	73.00	20.46	34.66

NOTE.—Annual costs include: Interest at 5 per cent., depreciation and repairs on plant, oil and waste, labor and fuel (bituminous coal at $4.00 and anthracite coal at $5.00 per ton).

A reference to Table XV. will show that the cost of power developed by producer-gas plants and gas engines is less than that produced by steam plants of the same capacity. It may be said, however, that up to the present no very large installations of suction producers have been made, 250 to 300 horse-power being about the maximum. But this has been provided for in the table by assuming that the larger plants will be made up of several units, each unit being not greater than 350 H.P. capacity. While operation of producer-gas plants has not been going on many years, and complete knowledge on the subject is not available, with the information at hand it is believed that in many situations this form of power producer will be found more economical than a steam plant, and, therefore, a closer competitor of hydro-electric power. It must be remembered that the same objections hold against the producer-gas plant as those which have been mentioned in reference to steam plants, namely, that 24-hour power costs proportionately more than 10-hour power; that the small consumer does not have the great advantage obtainable by the use of electric power; and also that a central installation in a factory is all that is possible if electric motors are required in various parts of the factory, and the only prime mover available is steam or gas. This will make the cost of electric factory operation very expensive, and considerably higher than the power costs shown in Table XI. Speaking generally, however, it may be said that producer-gas plants have a bright future, and as the design and construction is perfected undoubtedly the capital cost will be reduced and the cost of power lessened.

TABLE XVII.

SHOWING THE EFFECT ON THE COST OF POWER OF A VARIATION IN THE PRICE OF COAL OF ONE-HALF DOLLAR PER TON.

Size of Plant. H.P.	Suction Producer Gas.		Steam.		
	10-Hour.	24-Hour.	10-Hour.		24-Hour.
10	$1.15	$2.53	Simple	$6.14	$13.47
20	1.13	2.46	Slide Valve	5.25	11.56
30	1.10	2.40	Engine.	4.71	10.35
40	1.07	2.33		3.56	7.84
50	1.04	2.29	Simple Automatic	3.37	7.41
60	1.01	2.24	Non-	3.26	7.16
80	.98	2.18	condensing.	3.15	6.97
100	.96	2.12		3.12	6.87
150	.94	2.07		1.75	3.85
200	.92	2.02	Compound	1.69	3.71
300	.90	1.98	Condensing.	1.62	3.60
400	.88	1.94		1.56	3.44
500	.86	1.89	Compound Con-	1.39	3.05
750	.82	1.81	densing; Water-	1.39	3.05
1,000	.76	1.72	tube Boilers.	1.39	3.05

HYDRO-ELECTRIC POWER COMMISSION

of the

Province of Ontario

FIFTH REPORT

ALGOMA, THUNDER BAY AND RAINY
RIVER DISTRICTS

Printed by Order of the Legislative Assembly of Ontario.
March 15th, 1907

COMMISSION

HON. ADAM BECK, London, Chairman.

GEO. PATTINSON, M.P.P., Preston.

JOHN MILNE, Hamilton.

STAFF—

Cecil B. Smith...	*Chief Engineer.*
H. G. Acres	*Asst. Engineer.*
W. G. Chace.................	*Asst. Engineer.*
S. B. Clement................	*Asst. Engineer.*
E. Richards..............	*Electrical Engineer.*
A. D. Griffin	*Field Engineer.*
F. W. Wilkins	*Field Engineer.*
G. T. Jennings	*Field Engineer.*
E. C. Settell...................	*Secretary.*

FIFTH REPORT.

ALGOMA, THUNDER BAY AND RAINY RIVER DISTRICTS.

To His Honour,
The Lieutenant-Governor of Ontario:—

The undersigned Commissioners appointed by Your Honour by Commission bearing date the 26th day of January, 1906, beg leave to submit the following as their fifth report upon the matters authorized and directed to be enquired into.

Your Commissioners caused enquiries to be made and information to be obtained from various sources, but did not hold formal sittings in those districts, as the information which was desired for the purposes of this report has been given freely to members of their engineering staff, who have thoroughly canvassed those districts both as to their hydraulic possibilities and present industrial demands.

During the summer of 1906, the members of the Commission, at that time, visited Port Arthur, Fort William and Kenora and examined the water powers and enquired into the conditions at these places.

The Engineers' reports indicate the great hydraulic potentialities of this portion of the Province, and your Commissioners desire to emphasize the value which these water powers have, owing to the wide district traversed by them, in relation to the future development of the timber and mineral resources of those districts. The detailed scientific and technical information has been obtained at considerable expense and under great difficulties, owing to the rugged natural conditions and unsettled parts through which most of the rivers of those districts flow; it has been tabulated and arranged by the Engineer employed by your Commissioners and is contained in his fifth report, which is submitted as an appendix hereto.

The following are the matters on which your Commissioners were authorized and directed to enquire, with the report upon each subjoined:—

DEMAND FOR ELECTRIC POWER.

(1) *"The present and probable demand for hydraulic and electrical power in the various districts capable of being supplied from the different water powers within the jurisdiction of the Province of Ontario.*

In this fifth report your Commissioners deal in general with that portion of Ontario comprising the judicial districts of Algoma, Thunder Bay and Rainy River, but have omitted that area north of the height of land owing to the sparseness of population and lack of demand for power in this region. Within the near future with the construction of the Transcontinental, Temiskaming and other railways, it may become advisable to make a fuller investigation of this area.

Many towns have been located at the conjunction of railway and water powers. Of these, we may mention Kenora, Fort Frances and Sault Ste. Marie. The prosperity these places have attained is largely due to the development of hydraulic power.

The demand for electrical power will, in almost all cases, depend upon the relative cost of electricity as compared with that of steam, gas or other power. The cost of electricity is dependant upon the distance over which it is transmitted and upon the quantity transmitted. As it is only feasible to transmit the power in large quantities, trunk transmission lines capable of carrying large quantities must be constructed at the outset; therefore, the cost increases with the distance, and a point is eventually reached at such a distance from the generating station that electrical can no longer compete with steam or other power.

It is an interesting fact, however, that at Port Arthur and Fort William, where coal is laid down at a very moderate rate, waterpowers have been developed somewhat commensurate with the present requirements, and to such an advantage that a strong feeling exists for increasing the supply of electrical energy by further developments.

The exhaust steam and heat from the steam plants of some factories is used in the process of manufacture and for heating purposes, which will prevent the adoption of electrical power in some cases, as the cost of steam and heat for manufacturing purposes, apart from power, would increase rather than diminish the expense.

Also in many instances waste material is used in the production of steam; such industries have not been included in the consideration of the extent of the market at present in sight. The capital cost of abandoning steam plants would also, in many cases, be considerable, and the ability of small users of power to bear this loss must always be a factor in the finding of a market.

As a result of your Commissioners' enquiries in the various towns and villages of these districts as to the present market for electrical power, it would appear that outside of the Victoria Mines, in the vicinity of which there is a completed development which is not at present utilized, there are only two markets at present open for supply, though these may be augmented by future demands of mines, mills, pulp-factories, etc. These are Thessalon and Bruce Mines, which can be supplied from the Mississauga River to at least the present demand of 150 H.P. and 500 H.P. respectively, and Port Arthur, which can supplement its present supply of 1,000 H.P., derived from its municipal water power, by the transmission of any quantity of power from the Nepigon or Kaministiquia Rivers.

In the opinion of your Commissioners, the outlook for a plentiful supply of electrical power at moderate rates will be of very great value in the establishment of industries at Port Arthur and Fort William, and as the Kaministiquia Power Co. has already a development delivering power to the latter city, it has been considered sufficient to indicate, by two estimates, the manner in which power may be most economically supplied to Port Arthur in any quantity likely to be required in the near future with the development of the mineral resources of Northern Ontario. It may be confidently anticipated, however, that the water powers adjacent to these mines will be utilized to supply the power required.

UNDEVELOPED LOCATIONS.

(2) *"The location, capacity and capital cost of development of the various water powers within the legislative jurisdiction of the Province of Ontario at present undeveloped, but whose development is required to supply the present and probable needs of the surrounding districts, and to ascertain the cost of the attendant transmission plant necessary to the utilization of electrical and hydraulic powers to be provided from the aforesaid water powers within the respective surrounding districts."*

A systematic tabulation of the water powers of the various rivers in this district based upon gaugings and meterings, supplemented by information derived from other sources, has been carried out during the past eighteen months, and although more minute information, particularly with reference to dry-weather flow, could be obtained by continuing the work, it is felt that a fairly accurate hydraulic knowledge of these districts has been obtained.

The natural storage of many of the rivers of these districts is very good, but in nearly all instances still better conditions can be obtained. by placing dams at the various lake outlets and holding water back for use during the dry season.

The Spanish, Vermilion, Ouaping, Mississauga, Serpent, Michipicoten, White, Black Sturgeon, Kaministiquia, Seine and Rainy Rivers are all capable of excellent storage regulation and the waste land, which would be flooded by such action; would be of a rocky character, having little present value. The Nepigon River is so extensive and the lake storage so enormous that it is not probable that any scheme of increasing its storage would be advisable.

The Dog Lake development, estimated at 14,000 H.P., can at a comparatively small expense, be doubled in capacity by a dam at the mouth of the lake and proper control of storage secured for a depth of 10 feet.

Your Commissioners having considered Port Arthur's present and probable future requirements, have made two estimates for supplying the same, and in Part IV. of the first appendix will be found estimates of the cost of alternative developments for supplying these requirements, and also to supply those of Bruce Mines and Thessalon from a source on the Mississauga River. Tables IV. and V. give estimates of capital cost and yearly charges on generating plant.

RATES AND PRICES.

(3) *"To ascertain the rates or prices that would require to be charged the various classes of consumers of hydraulic or electrical power within the respective districts in order to meet all expenditure of maintenance and operation.''*

The ascertainment of the rates that would require to be charged for electrical power in order to meet expenditure of maintenance and operation is based upon the cost of necessary plant for future calls upon it, original cost of construction, cost of maintenance and operation, and the probable market for electrical power, ascertained from local enquiries.

In order to ascertain the cost of delivering power to Port Arthur, Bruce Mines and Thessalon, your Commissioners have caused computations to be made for transmission systems and sub-stations for supplying and delivering the power generated at power stations on the Kaministiquia, Nepigon and Mississauga rivers, and in Part V. of the first appendix will be found the necessary calculations, based on delivering 6,000 to 14,000 H.P. at Port Arthur either from the Kaministiquia or Nepigon rivers, and to deliver 150 H.P. at Thessalon and 1,650 H.P. or 3,300 H.P. at Bruce Mines. This should meet future requirements for some time to come.

Your Commissioners call attention to the fact that when electricity is delivered at municipal sub-stations the cost of distribution to consumers within such municipality must be added to this price in order to determine the cost to the individual municipal consumer.

Table X., Part V., also gives data in regard to the cost of supplying a particular customer with power at a considerable distance from a sub-station, the total cost to such a consumer being the sub-station cost added to the secondary cost given in this table.

POWER SUPPLIED AND UNDER CONTRACT BY THE EXISTING COMPANIES.

(a) *"The quantities supplied and contracted for and the rates charged and to be charged under such contracts by these companies for hydraulic and electrical power."*

In Part III. of the first appendix, Table III., and Part IV. of the second appendix will be found listed the amount of machinery installed at various points. It will be noted that pulp grinding, flour grinding and mining operations constitute the present power market.

The prices or rates charged for power and light in various municipalities are given in Table XII of the first appendix, and the Kenora rates are given in Part IV. of the second appendix.

The difference in prices charged for power and light at Sault Ste. Marie and Kenora is very great, though the conditions are similar, in that both are free from long-distance transmission.

Your Commissioners believe that this and preceding reports cover the whole of the Province with the exception of the James Bay watershed. In making investigations, they have endeavored to get a survey of all important waters, so that the department might have on file particulars of the immense hydraulic resources available.

Your Commissioners desire to express their appreciation of the services rendered by the Chief Engineer and the Assistants associated with him in carrying out their portion of the work. The surveying and measuring of the streams, especially in the northern part of the Province, has called for much arduous work, which necessarily had to be performed under the most difficult conditions.

APPENDIX

TO

FIFTH REPORT

Algoma and Thunder Bay Districts.

ENGINEER'S REPORT

ON

THE WATER POWERS AND ON THE GENERA-
TION AND TRANSMISSION OF ELECTRIC
POWER GENERATED THEREFROM.

HONOURABLE ADAM BECK,

CHAIRMAN OF THE HYDRO-ELECTRIC POWER COMMISSION:

DEAR SIR,—

Herewith find my report on Algoma and Thunder Bay Districts, extending northward to the height of land and westward so as to include all of the watershed in the Province of Ontario draining into Lake Superior and Lake Huron.

The report deals with the present consumption of and demand for power, the sources of power developed or undeveloped and discusses in detail certain developments within economical transmission distance of various present markets and indicates the cost of generating and transmitting electrical energy necessary to meet the present requirements, based on 4 per cent. return on investment.

Yours Respectfully,

CECIL B. SMITH,

Chief Engineer.

TORONTO, CANADA,

MARCH 15TH, 1907.

INDEX

the future industrial development of the district. Lumber-

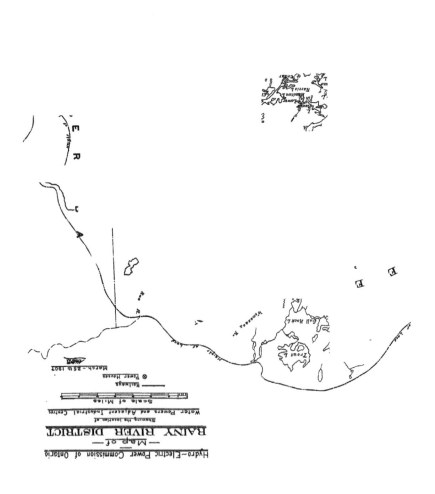

PART I.

GEOGRAPHICAL SUBDIVISIONS.

This report will deal with the hydro-electric conditions and present requirements of the extreme western portion of the Province, embracing practically the district of Rainy River. This district is probably the most copiously watered of any in the Province, water powers being abundant, and in many cases of considerable magnitude.

As in the case of Algoma and Thunder Bay districts, only the important water powers in the neighborhood of existing or prospective industrial centres have been examined in detail, the more remote power sources being discussed in a general way.

The whole of the district under discussion is embraced by one drainage area, being part of an immense system, the run-off of which reaches tide-water in Hudson's Bay by way of the Winnipeg River, Lake Winnipeg and the Nelson River.

The rivers in this district, as a general rule, are large and full flowing, with comparatively low heads, which disadvantage is in a measure offset by the splendid natural storage facilities offered by Rainy Lake, Lake of the Woods, Lac Seul and numerous other lakes of lesser magnitude plentifully distributed throughout the district.

The map accompanying this report indicates the location of the chief water falls or powers, such as those on the Rainy, Winnipeg, Seine, Wabigoon and English rivers.

PART II.

DEMANDS FOR POWER.

The power market in this district at the present time is confined almost wholly to the town of Kenora, where the population is sufficiently large to create a profitable municipal market, besides which there are several manufacturing establishments, chiefly flour mills, using a considerable quantity of power. Fort Frances, owing to its geographical situation as a border town, and to the hydraulic possibilities of the Koochiching Falls, will doubtless play an important part in the future industrial development of the district. Lumbering is now, and will be for some time to come, an important industry, and as the waste material from the mills furnishes abundant fuel for the generation of steam, none of the smaller towns need be considered as possible users of hydro-electric power.

The mineral areas in this district, though not actively developed at present, may at some future time attain sufficient importance to warrant development of such of the abundant existing water powers as may be convenient.

PART III.

SOURCES OF HYDRO-ELECTRIC POWER.

The most important rivers in this district are the Winnipeg, Rainy, Seine and English rivers.

Seine River:—This river takes its rise in Lac des Milles Lacs, and flows in a generally southwesterly direction to Rainy Lake. Though not possessing any tributaries of importance, its considerable length and good natural storage facilities combine to give it the uniform flow which is common to all the more important rivers in this district, and distinguishes them from most of the rivers of Algoma and Thunder Bay, tributary to the Great Lakes.

The mineral belt through which this river flows may possibly reach a stage of development sufficient to warrant the utilization of several favorable power sites, where economical development is feasible.

Rainy River:—This river rises in Rainy Lake, forms the international boundary between Ontario and Minnesota and discharges into the Lake of the Woods. This is one of the large rivers of Ontario, and permits of steamboat navigation to the foot of Koochiching Falls at the source of the river. This fall is now in process of development.

Winnipeg River:—This river, which is one of the largest in Canada, rises in the Lake of the Woods, and flows in a northwesterly direction to Lake Winnipeg, draining in its course the whole of Rainy River District, large portions of Southern Keewatin, Northern Minnesota and the western extremity of Thunder Bay District, in all about 55,000 square miles. Although the natural heads on this river are not great, the heavy minimum flow makes possible the development of very large blocks of power. Several developments in various stages of construction exist at the present time, and so far it has been found necessary to use only a fraction of the total discharge of the river.

English River:—This river is also a tributary of the Winnipeg River, the confluence being about fifty miles northwest of Kenora. This river rises in Scotch Lake, south of the main line of the C. P. R., and flows northwesterly for nearly 100 miles to Lac Seul, a lake in the same class as Lake of the Woods and Lake Nepigon, as regards size. After leaving Lac Seul, the river flows in a southwesterly direction for 250 miles to the junction with the Winnipeg River, forming a portion of the boundary between Ontario and the district of Keewatin. Apart from its great length, this river is remarkable, in that it consists mainly of a series of large lakes connected by short rapids and falls. For this reason, its natural storage facilities are unequalled elsewhere in the Province, with the possible exception of the Winnipeg River. The natural resources of the country through which the river flows are comparatively meagre, as the rock formation is not mineralized to any extent, being nearly all Laurentian granite. The timber, as a rule, is sparsely distributed, consisting principally of poplar and small spruce and jack pine, with a small percentage suitable for tie-timber.

In the following table is given a list of water powers in the territory covered by the report. Unless otherwise stated only those powers possessing fairly good natural heads have been included in this list, but it should be understood that in many localities rapids, or series of rapids, could be drowned out and an artificial head created by means of a dam. In most cases the question of back water damage would not be a serious one, so that the heads obtainable would be limited only by the capital investment in connection with the dam estimates thereon will be found worked out elsewhere in this report. construction.

The figures in the second column of this table indicate uniform low water flow, and it is important to note that in this district, in almost every case, the dam construction necessary in connection with any power installation would provide storage sufficient, not only for daily peak load demands, but also to appreciably augment the present low water flow during the dry-weather period. The system of artificial regulation could be extended as required, by constructing dams at the various lake outlets, such as those now constructed at

Kenora, and by so doing the minimum 24-hour flow can be very much increased, in fact, the power capacity of the district can be augmented until probably 40 per cent. of the annual rainfall could be utilized for power purposes.

Water Power.	Head	Estimated Low Water Flow C.F.S.	Min. 24 Hour Power. H.P.	Present Installation.	Remarks
SEINE RIVER:					
Seine Falls.................	11	800	800	....	
Island Falls...............	20	882	1,510	....	Minto Mine adjacent.
Lynx-head Chute.........	11	850	880	....	
Steep-rock Falls	40	960	2,900	....	
Sturgeon Falls............	13	1,120	1,320	....	
RAINY RIVER:					
Koochiching Falls	23	6,700	14,000	....	In process of development.
					½ of this available to Ontario.
WINNIPEG RIVER:					
E. Branch Kenora.	18	2.500	4,100	....	
W. " "	18	11,000	18,000	....	
Island Falls...............	45	14,500	59,300	....	Combined artificial head.
WABIGOON RIVER:					
Upper Fall, Dryden......	26	240	568	....	
Lower Rapids, "	22	240	480	....	
ENGLISH RIVER:					
Pelican Chute............	12	3,200	3,490	....	
Ear Rapids................	29	6,100	16,100	....	Combined artificial head.
Manitou Chute	28	7,000	17,800	....	
Fall.....	15	7,100	9,670	....	
Rapids..........	6	7,300	3,980	....	
Fall......	10	7,500	6,820	....	
Rapids	6	8,000	4,360	....	
Rapids ,....	6	9,000	4,910	....	
Kettle Falls	19	9,000	15,550	....	
Rapids	15	9,000	12,250	....	
Caribou Rapids	6	9,250	5,050	....	

PART IV.

GENERATION OF POWER.

At the present speaking, the only power developments operating in this district are located at Kenora, where the extensive hydraulic facilities of the Winnipeg River have for some time been partially utilized for power and lighting purposes.

The power being developed at the present time is as follows:—

Kenora Municipal Plant:—This plant, now in process of construction, is located at the eastern outlet of the Lake of the Woods, and is designed for an ultimate capacity of 4,000 H.P., half of which is to be installed immediately.   Of this portion, 1,000 H.P. is already contracted for, in addition to the municipal load of approximately 300 H.P. The conditions of the contract call for the construction of permanent works for full capacity of 4,000 H.P. and for the immediate installation of three units of 500 k.w. each. The power house and dam have already been completed and one unit put into service.

Lake of the Woods Milling Co.:—This company develops in the neighborhood of 2,000 H.P., water being taken from the Lake of the Woods by means of a flume.

Keewatin Flour Milling Co.:—This company has a 3,000 bbl. mill in process of erection, and will use about 1,500 H.P. of hydraulic power, for which a flume has been excavated and machinery installed.

As yet no active development has taken place on the main or western branch of the river, but some years ago, the Keewatin Power Co. constructed what is known locally as the Norman dam, across the western branch about 3-4 mile from the Lake of the Woods outlet.

The dam is constructed of rock fill, with heavy masonry sluiceway piers. Apart from a certain amount of leakage through the rock fill, the dam is in serviceable condition at the present time, and would admit the development of 20,000 minimum horse-power under present conditions.

At the present time the total average amount of power developed in the town of Kenora is in the neighborhood of 4,250 H.P., of which about 1,400 H.P. is the average amount of hydraulic power used direct, and 1,900 H.P. hydro-electric, the remainder, 950 H.P., being steam generated. Of this latter amount about 100 H.P. is available for electric installation.

As regards rates for power and light, the municipality charges 10 cents per kilowatt-hour for incandescent lighting and from $10.00 to $50.00 per horse power per year for power, this price being regulated according to the quantity contracted for.

At Fort Frances on Rainy River, the important international power of Koochiching Falls is being developed for the joint use of Fort Frances and the town of International Falls on the American side of the river. The natural head is about 23 feet. This will be increased to 27 feet when the power installation is completed. The estimated low-water capacity is about 16,500 H.P., and permanent works for full capacity are being constructed at the present time. At the present speaking, there is no market for power in either town, but the prospect of much improved railway facilities in the near future is expected to supply, in conjunction with cheap power, sufficient inducement for the establishment of manufacturing industries. A large proportion of the power it is expected will also be used for grinding the pulp output of the district. The development provides for the construction of two power houses, one on the Canadian and one on the American side of the river. Each power house will ultimately contain nine 1,000 k.w. units, which will be installed as the occasion demands.

Investigation as to present and probable and future demands for power would seem to indicate that the requirements of this district will be amply met for some time to come by the above-mentioned installations, until such time as mining or milling operations warrant special developments.

FIFTH REPORT.

INDEX.

INDEX TO TABLES AND MAPS.

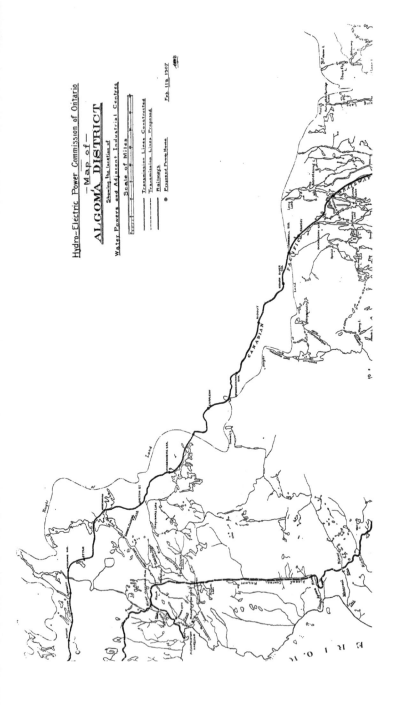

Hydro—Electric Power Commission of Ontario

— Map of —

ALGOMA DISTRICT

Showing the location of
Water Powers and Adjacent Industrial Centres

Scale of Miles

———— Transmission Lines Constructed
———— Transmission Lines Proposed
———— Railways
⊙ Proposed Power House

Feb. 11th, 1907

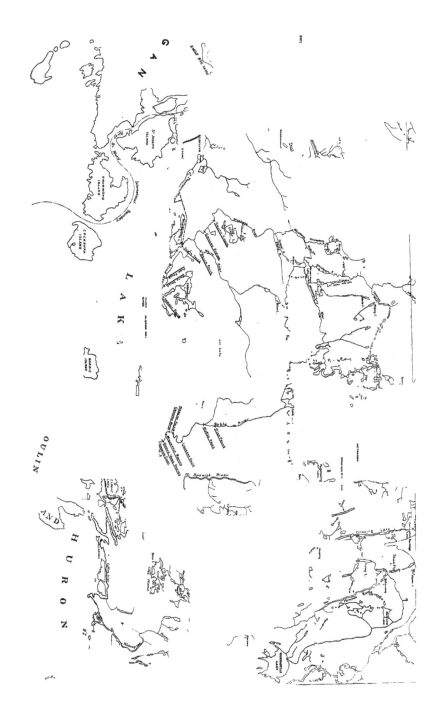

INSERT

OR MAP
HERE!

Hydro-Electric Power Commission of Ontario

— Map of —

THUNDER BAY DISTRICT

Showing the location of

Water Powers and Adjacent Industrial Centres

Scale of Miles

——————— Transmission Lines Constructed
– – – – – – – Transmission Lines Proposed
——————— Railways
⊕ Proposed Power House

Jan. 21ˢᵗ 1907

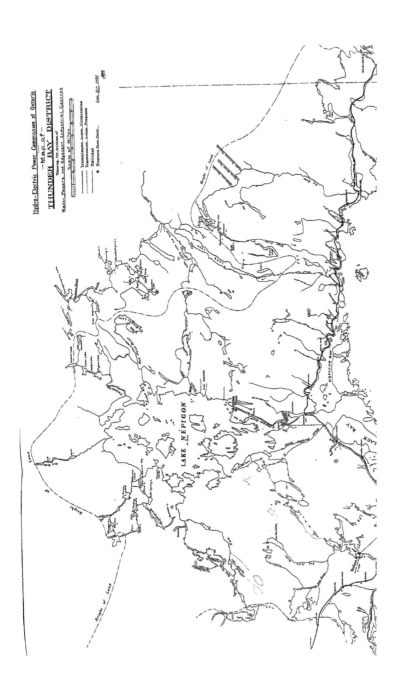

Hydro-Electric Power Commission of Ontario
— Map of —
THUNDER BAY DISTRICT
Showing the location of
Water Powers and Adjacent Industrial Centres
Scale of Miles

Transmission Lines Constructed
Transmission Lines Proposed
Railways
Proposed Power Plant

Jan. 31st 1927

PART I.

GEOGRAPHICAL SUBDIVISIONS.

This report deals with the Hydro-Electric conditions and present power requirements of that portion of the Province lying along the north shores of Lake Huron and Lake Superior, south of the height of land. This extensive territory is, to a large extent, unsettled and in many localities practically unexplored, but it has been determined that water powers capable of economical development, having an output far in excess of all present requirements, are distributed over its whole area.

Speaking generally, all the important water powers lying within the zone of influence of the Canadian Pacific, Algoma Central and Canadian Northern Railways, have been carefully examined in detail, but somewhat more general information concerning the more remote power sources of this territory has been considered sufficient, as surveys would have entailed an amount of investigation not warranted by present need.

The territory covered by this report includes two distinct drainage areas, of which the more easterly is that drained by Lake Huron. The portion of this to be considered extends west from Sudbury and the Wahnapitae River (already covered by the third report) to Sault Ste Marie and northward about 90 miles. It contains several rivers of considerable size, with the high heads which usually characterize the Laurentian rivers; consequently, many valuable powers exist, and as this is the more thickly settled of the two districts, there is a probability that many of the more promising water powers not already utilized will be taken up in the near future.

The second drainage area is that which extends north and westerly from the north shore of Lake Superior and from Sault Ste Marie westward to the International Boundary. Owing to the comparative proximity of the crest of the height of land to the north shore of Lake Superior throughout the greater part of its length, many of the rivers draining this watershed are short and turbulent, with high heads uniformly characteristic; falls of from fifty to one hundred and twenty-five feet being common.

The two exceptions to this are the Nepigon and Kaministiquia rivers, both of which have large drainage areas, and which possess splendid central lake storages into which the upper tributaries flow.

The maps accompanying this report indicate the location of the chief water falls or powers, such as those on the Spanish, Vermilion, Mississauga, St. Mary's, Montreal, Algoma, Michipicoten, Nepigon, Current and Kaministiquia rivers.

PART II.

DEMANDS FOR POWER.

Previous to the preparation of the following estimates, the various towns in the territory were visited by representatives of the Commission, whose canvass included information in connection with power at present used, power likely to be used in the immediate future, and the probable amount of electric power which could be disposed of to the consumer, if supplied at reasonable rates; this information is set forth in Tables I. and II.

There are at present comparatively few towns in the territory in which any extensive present or probable immediate future demand for power exists, but where any considerable demand was found which could not be supplied locally, it was considered advisable to indicate specific water power developments and transmission schemes by which these available markets could be most reasonably served, and detailed estimates thereon will be found worked out elsewhere in this report.

It must be borne in mind, however, that this whole district is mineralized particularly with iron ores, and that enormous tracts of pulp timber are yet untouched. It can therefore be confidently predicted that with improvements in the methods of electric treatment of ore and with advance in value of pulp, these water powers will form a more than ordinarily important factor in the development of this district. ·

TABLE I.

POWER CONDITIONS.

NORTH SHORE OF LAKE HURON.

Town.	Population.	Average Total Power Used H.P.	Average Hydraulic Power Used Direct. H.P.	Maximum Hydro-Electric Power Developed. H.P.	Steam Power Available for Electric Installation. H.P.	Remarks.
Copper Cliff...	2,000	3,000	....	3,000	....	Power controlled by Canada Copper Co. Plant at Turbine on the Spanish River.
Espanola......	....	10,000	8,000	2,000	....	Power on Spanish River, Spanish River Pulp and Paper Co.
Victoria Mines	300	550	....	....	500	Available power on Spanish and Vermilion Rivers.
Massey........	750	120	....	....	100	Available power on Sable River.
Blind River ...	1,200	820	200	100	100	Available power on Blind River.
Thessalon.....	1,350	800	....	....	150	Available power on Mississauga River.
Bruce Mines ..	860	600	....	...	500	Available power on Mississauga River.
S. S. Marie....	8,763	8,000	1,800	3,500	....	Power developed at St. Mary's Rapids.
Steelton.......	....	....	....	....	....	Available power at St. Mary's Rapids.

TABLE II.

POWER CONDITIONS.

NORTH SHORE OF LAKE SUPERIOR.

Town.	Population.	Average Total Power Used. H.P.	Average Hydraulic Power Used Direct. H.P.	Maximum Hydro-Electric Power Developed H.P.	Steam Power Available for Electric Installation. H.P.	Remarks.
Port Arthur...	10,206	4,000	....	950	2,400	Available power in Current, Nepigon and Kaministiquia Rivers. Current River at present developed by municipality.
Fort William..	10,426	6,000	....	1,500	900	Available power on Nepigon and Kaministiquia Rivers.

PART III.

SOURCES OF HYDRO-ELECTRIC POWER.

Of the rivers flowing into Lake Huron along the north shore, the Spanish, Vermilion and Mississauga are the most important as regards size and hydro-electric possibilities, numerous water powers admitting of more or less economical development existing on these rivers. Two plants are at present in operation on the Spanish River, furnishing power for pulp mills and mines.

This district contains valuable timber and mineral areas, factors which will in the near future have an important bearing in determining the economic value of the available water powers.

Rivers of lesser importance in the same district are the Blind, Sable, Serpent, Onaping and Whitefish.

At the head of Lake Huron is the important international power of the Sault Rapids on the St. Mary's River, which takes the total run-off of the Lake Superior basin. This power is partially developed on both sides of the river and forms the basis of operation for the industries established and controlled by the Lake Superior Corporation at Sault Ste Marie.

Along the north shore of Lake Superior, many fine water powers exist, which, in many cases have but little present economic value; exceptions being the Nepigon, Kaministiquia and Current Rivers, the importance of which is due to the fact that they are within transmission distance of the rapidly increasing power markets of Fort William and Port Arthur, and, especially in the case of the Nepigon, are of sufficient extent to use for grinding the pulp output of the Nepigon watershed.

In the following table is given a list of water powers in the territory covered by the report. As a rule, only those powers possessing fairly good natural head have been included in this list, but it should be understood that in many localities, rapids, or series of rapids, could be drowned out, and an artificial head created by means of a dam. In most cases, the question of back-water damage would not be a serious one, so that the heads obtainable would be limited only by the capital investment in connection with the dam construction.

The figures in the second column of this table indicate uniform low-water flow only, and it must be understood that in practically all cases enough local pondage can be obtained above the headworks to provide for a considerably increased peak capacity. It is not generally feasible, however, to obtain in this way storage sufficient to materially augment the natural dry-weather flow over a greater period than that required to take care of the daily variation of load demands, without a large relative expenditure for impounding storage reservoirs.

To this general observation, there are two notable exceptions, namely, Lake Nepigon, with 1,500 square miles of area, and Dog and Shebandowan Lakes, with 100 square miles of area, serving to create natural storages, which, in the case of Dog Lake, can be enormously increased in value by the expenditure of a small sum for construction of a dam at the outlet of the lake, which will raise the lake level ten to fifteen feet during high-water and hold the same for use when required at low-water periods.

TABLE III.

Water powers in the districts of Algoma and Thunder Bay on rivers tributary to Lake Huron and Lake Superior.

Water-power.	Head Feet.	Estimated Low Water Flow C.F.S.	Minimum 24 hr Power. H.P.	Present Installation. H P.	Remarks.
SPANISH RIVER:					
Espanola	62	1,800	10,145	10,000	Spanish River Pulp and Paper Co.
Nairn Falls.................	28	1,027	2,630		
High Falls............... ...	85	1,027	7,936	5,400	Canada Copper Co.
Norway Falls and Rapids...	40	935	3,400	....	Lot 9, Con. 1, Hyman.
Township, No. 108...	14	935	1,190	....	Above Agnes River.
Township, No. 108.........	32	855	2,429	....	Below " "
Metagama (rapids)..........	27	400	980		
" "	16	400	580		
Biscotasing "	26	266	630		
VERMILION RIVER:					
Wabageshik Rapid..........	15	720	980		
" Chute	42	720	2,750		
Soo Line Crossing....... ..	15	700	955		
Island Rapids...............	11	667	667		
Cascade	19	667	1,150		
Big Stoby Falls.............	35	640	2,040	1,350	Ver. River Power Co.
C.P.R. Crossing.............	11	500	500		
Larchwood.................	9	500	410		
Onwatin Lake.............	18	193	313		

TABLE III.—Water-powers in the districts of Algoma and Thunder Bay on rivers tributary to Lake Huron and Lake Superior.—Continued.

Water-power.	Head Feet.	Estimated Low Water Flow C.F.S.	Minimum 24 hr. Power. H.P.	Present Installation. H.P.	Remarks
ONAPING RIVER:					
High Falls	127	300	3,460		
Fall	15	300	410		
Fall and Rapids	22	240	480		
Rapids	17	180	278		
Onaping Chute (outlet)	11	147	147		
WHITE-FISH RIVER:					
White-fish Falls	47	117	500	....	At mouth of River.
Charleton "	58	85	450		
Long Lake	16	80	116	....	Combined with 9 ft. fall.
SABLE RIVER:					
Bridge Rapids	8	230	167		
Spanish Chute	38.5	230	805	....	½ mile from Massey.
Graveyard Chute	54	230	1,130		
Island Rapids	16	230	334		
Crooked "	19	230	397		
Meareau "	36	230	755		
Cameron Falls	45	230	940		
Long Rapids	16	230	334		
Ragged Rapids	24	200	435		
McKee Falls	39	160	567		
High Falls	51	130	603		
SERPENT RIVER:					
McCarthy's Chute	61	154	855		
1st Log-slide	63	140	800		
2nd "	36	140	460		
3rd "	26	140	380		
4th "	19	140	242		
Fall and Rapids below Whiskey Lake	35	40	128		
Rapids at Big Bear Lake	32	40	116		
BLIND RIVER:					
Blind River	12	96	105	80	Canada Saw Mill Co.
Cataract Falls	23	87	182		
White Falls	55	87	435	....	7¼ miles from Blind River.
High Falls	31	87	245		
Chiblow Lake (outlet)	45	87	356		
MISSISSAUGA RIVUR:					
1st Fall	20	1,050	1,910		
2nd Fall	21	1,050	2,000		
Slate Falls	32	1,050	3,045	....	Lot No. 12, Con. 6, Gladstone.
4th Fall	18	850	1,890		
5th Fall	31	850	2,400		
Squaw Chute	17.5	850	1,350		
Aubrey Falls and Rapids	117	750	7,980		
Fall	24	420	915		
Head of Lake Minneesagua	13	360	425		
" Fall	21	180	342		
" "	38	160	555		
WHITE RIVER: (E. Branch Mississauga).					
Bells Falls	17	210	327		
White Falls	16	100	145		
ST. MARY RIVER:					
Soo Rapids	18	60,000	98,200	6,500	Lake Superior Power Company.

TABLE III.---Water-powers in the districts of Algoma and Thunder Bay on rivers tributary to Lake Huron and Lake Superior.---Continued.

Water-power.	Head Feet.	Estimated Low Water Flow C.F.S.	Minimum 24 hr. Power. H.P.	Present Installa- tion. H.P.	Remarks.
GOULAIS RIVER :					
Lower Fall	61	200	1,109		
Upper Fall	52	125	591		
CHIPPEWA RIVER :					
Fall at mouth	61	85	470		
BATCHEWANA RIVER :					
Fall at mouth	34	110	340		
2nd Falls	35	110	850		Artificial head.
MONTREAL RIVER : (Algoma)					
Fall at mouth	165	340	5,100		
Upper Fall	170	340	5,250	....	Algoma Central cross ing.
AGAWA RIVER :					
Fall at mouth	90	175	1,430	....	Including backing up on rapids 10 ft.
MICHIPICOTEN RIVER :					
Michipicoten Falls	128	650	7,564	2,100	Algoma Power Co.
Cat Portage Falls	33	356	1,068		
Pigeon Falls	18	356	585		
Stony Portage Falls	91	234	1,940		
SHEQUAMKA RIVER :					
First Fall	27	292	715		First and second Fall would be combined by means of a dam at first fall.
Second Fall	22	292	585		
Third Fall	32	240	697		
MAGPIE RIVER :					
1st Fall, 2nd Fall, 3rd Fall..	113	256	2,630	....	At mouth of river.
4th Fall	77	256	1,790		
5th Fall	63	256	1,470	....	4 miles from Helen Mine.
DOG RIVER :					
Denison Falls	140	125	1,590		
WHITE RIVER :					
1st Fall	50	500	2,280	...	6 miles from L. Su- perior.
2nd "	40	500	1,820	....	6¼ miles from L. Su- perior.
3rd "	20	500	910	....	6¾ miles from L. Su- perior.
4th "	35	500	1,590	....	11¼ miles from L. Su- perior.
5th "	20	450	820	....	11¾ miles from L. Su- perior.
6th "	145	450	5 950	....	12¼ miles from L. Su- perior.
7th "	50	450	2,046	....	13¼ miles from L. Su- perior.
8th "	50	300	1,860	....	32 miles from L Su- perior.
9th "	20	300	545	....	27 miles below Monti- zambert.
10th "	33	250	750	....	25 miles below Monti- zambert
11th "	20	225	410	....	15 miles below Monti- zambert.
PIC RIVER :					
Lake Superior Portage	51	140	650	....	60 miles above Lake Su- perior.
White Otter Falls	42	130	495		
Sand Hill Portage	115	130	1,300		

TABLE III.---Water-powers in the districts of Algoma and Thunder Bay on rivers tributary to Lake Huron and Lake Superior.—Concluded.

Water-power.	Head	Estimated Low Water Flow C.F S.	Minimum 24 hr. Power. H.H.	Present Installation. H P.	Remarks.
STEEL RIVER :					
Simpson's Stretch.........	71	150	970	....	7 miles from Jackfish.
BLACK RIVER :					
Falls at mouth	106	75	725	....	7 miles east of Schreiber.
NEPIGON RIVER :					
‡Cameron Rapids....,......	39	5,500	19,500	....	14 miles from Nepigon Station.
Split Rock..................	15	5,500	7,500		
Island Portage..............	9.5	5,500	4,750		
Pine Portage Rapids........					
White Chute................	12	5,500	6,000		
Victoria Rapids.............	10	5,500	5,000		
Camp Miner Rapids........	7	5,500	8,500		
Virgin Falls.................	25	5,500	12,500	....	30 miles from Nepigon Station.
Flat Rock..................	38	5,500	19,000		
NEPIGON TRIBUTARIES :					
STURGEON RIVER					
No-ga-mi-non..............	42	250	955	....	Adjacent to iron deposits
Beaver Falls................	28	250	635	....	
RED PAINT RIVER ·	..	125	,...	....	No valuable water power.
OMBABIKA RIVER :	..	120	....	....	Good storage but no valuable power.
MUD RIVER : WABINOSH : GULL RIVER : }	..	....	....	....	Not explored.
BLACK STURGEON RIVER :	..	150	....	....	No valuable water power.
WOLF RIVER :					
First Fall..................	30	100	270	....	
Second Fall................	42	100	380	....	
CURRENT RIVER :					
Falls at mouth.............	86	*130	1,020	1,100	Port Arthur Municipal Plant.
Cascades	100	*100	910		
KAMINISTIQUIA RIVER :					
‡Mt. McKay and Kakabeka Falls Ry.................	25	830	1,887	....	Lot 2, Block A. Paipoonge.
Kakabeka Falls and Ecarte Rapids...........	180	800	13,100	10,000	Kaministiquia Power Co.
Rapids	10	800	728		
Rapids....................	33	450	1,350		
‡Dog Falls.................	347	450	14,200	....	25 miles from Port Arthur.
PIGEON RIVER :					
High Falls	110	125	1,250	....	At mouth of River.
Cascades	100	60	545		
ARROW RIVER :					
High Falls.................	37	60	202	....	At mouth of River.
KAWA-KASHKAGAMA RIVER :					
Upper Falls	14	100	127	....	North of height of land, (tributary to Kenogami.)
Howard Falls..............	21	100	190	....	

‡Proposed development.
* Estimated flow dependent upon adequate storage facilities (Fannings' report.)

PART IV.

GENERATION OF POWER.

In the district covered by this Report, there are comparatively few power developments in existence at the present time. Several of these, however, are of considerable magnitude. In the field of local distribution are included the Spanish River Pulp and Paper Co., Canada Saw Mill Co., Lake Superior Power Co. and the Port Arthur Municipal Plant.

The plant of the Spanish River Pulp & Paper Co. is located at Espanola on the Spanish River. The total development is for 15,-000 H.P., of which about 10,000 H. P. is being used at the present time, 8,000 H.P. being taken by direct connected pulp grinders and the remainder on lighting, motor and other loads.

The Canada Saw Mill Co. utilizes a small power at the mouth of the Blind River. The total output is required for the lighting load of the Company's mills and the Town of Blind River.

At Sault Ste Marie, the plant of the Lake Superior Power Co. has a turbine capacity of about 6,500 H.P. Of this 3,800 H.P. is electrical and the remainder is consumed by direct-connected pulp grinders and other pulp-mill machinery.

The Port Arthur Municipal Plant takes its water supply from the Current River. The maximum load on the plant is in the neighborhood of 800 H.P., which under present conditions is excessive. Steps are being taken to improve the storage facilities of the upper river in order to provide for 1,000 H.P. additional maximum capacity.

Of the Companies transmitting at high potential, the Canada Copper Co. and the Kaministiquia Power Co. are the only ones in operation at present. The power station of the Canada Copper Co. is located at Turbine on the Spanish River, and energy is transmitted twenty-two miles to the Company's plant at Copper Cliff over a duplicate transmission line, at 34,000 volts, three-phase 25-cycles. The present capacity of the plant is 5,400 H.P. and two additional units of 2,700 H.P. each are to be installed this year, making 10,800 H.P. in all.

The Kaministiquia Power Co. has an extensive plant at Kakabeka Falls on the Kaministiquia River, with a partial installation of 10,000 H.P., which, it is stated, is shortly to be doubled.   The plant is in operation at present and transmits power over a 25-mile double transmission line to Fort William at 25,000 volts, 3-phase, 60-cycles.

At Big Stoby Falls on the Vermilion River is the plant of the Vermilion River Power Co., which has an installation of 1,350 H.P. capacity.   This plant is within transmission distance of Victoria Mines, Copper Cliff and Sudbury, but is not in operation at present.

.   The Algoma Power Co. has a plant under construction at Michipicoten Falls, on the Michipicoten River.   This plant is to have an initial capacity of 2,100 H.P., the prospective market being the neighboring mines, of which there are a considerable number, the estimated demand being about 1,500 H.P.

The Mount McKay & Kakabeka Falls Power Co. propose to develop a 25-foot head on the Kaministiquia River in the Township of Paipoonge, about seven miles from Fort William, where it is the intention to drown out a series of rapids by means of a dam.   Under dry weather conditions, the flow would be sufficient to generate 1,500 H.P., but with storage and regulation, such as will be necessary in connection with plants on the upper river, this output could be doubled.   The capital investment necessary in this case will be very heavy, owing to the extensive dam construction.   It is understood that this power is required chiefly for the operation of a suburban electric railway.

A considerable number of towns in this district have sufficient water power latent in their immediate neighborhood to supply their probable needs when the demand arises.   Of these the following may be mentioned: Schreiber, 725 H.P. on the Black River, 7-mile transmission; Jackfish, 970 H.P. on the Steel River, 7-mile transmission; White River, 200 H.P. on the White River, adjacent to town; Blind River, 435 H.P. on the Blind River, 7 1-4-mile transmission; Massey, 805 H.P. on the Sable River, 1-2-mile transmission.

As a result of investigation as to present and probable immediate future demands for power in this district, three tentative schemes of development have been considered, by which these demands could be most reasonably met.   They are, (1) Dog Lake, at the head waters of the Kaministiquia, 347 feet natural head; (2) Cameron Rapids on the Nepigon, 39 feet natural head; (3) Slate Falls on the Mississauga 31 feet natural head.

(1) Dog Lake Development: This power is situated about 25 miles northwest of the towns of Port Arthur and Fort William. An effective head of 310 feet can be obtained by utilizing the difference in level between Big Dog and Little Dog Lake. The distinguishing feature of the development would be the construction of about 3,500 feet of head-water tunnel. The value of this power is due to the high head and the exceptionally good storage facilities of Dog Lake, which has an area of 53 square miles.

(2) Cameron Rapids Development: This power is situated on the Nepigon River, about 14 miles north of Nepigon Station. The very considerable economic importance of this power is due to the fact, already mentioned, that it is within transmission distance of Port Arthur and Fort William, and that it is available for the development of the extensive pulpwood areas of the Nepigon watershed. In addition to this, the remarkably favorable topographical conditions in the neighborhood of the power-site, and the magnificent storage facilities offered by Lake Nepigon, with its 1,500 square miles of area, which would obviate all necessity for artificial regulation for some time to come, combine to make this a most attractive proposition from an engineering standpoint.

(3) Slate Falls Development: This power is situated on the Mississauga River about 25 miles from the town of Bruce Mines. A head of 40 feet can be obtained here, and in view of the natural conditions, the scheme of development is simple. No natural storage basins are available in the vicinity, but the dam necessary for the development will provide storage sufficient for any daily peak load within the limit of the temporary overload capacity.

Details as to horse power to be developed, capital costs and annual charges will be found in table IV. and V. following. These estimates are based on information collected by the Commission's engineers and on such other information as was available and known to be authentic. In the half-load estimates, it is assumed that permanent works for full capacity will be constructed at the outset. This includes dam, forebay, foundations, buildings, etc.

TABLE IV.

ESTIMATED CAPITAL COST OF DEVELOPMENTS.

Location of water-power.	Net amount of power to be developed. H.P.		Total capital cost.		Cost per H.P.	
	Full Capacity.	Half Capacity.	Full Capacity.	Half Capacity.	Full Capacity.	Half Capacity.
Dog Lake	13,675	6,840	$832,000	$619,700	$61 00	$91 00
Cameron Rapids..........	16,350	8,250	815,000	600,000	50 00	73 00
Slate Falls................	3,686	1.843	357,600	260,000	97 00	141 00

The capital cost in each case includes step-up transformer stations, one reserve unit in excess of each of the above mentioned capacities and a spare transformer in each station.

TABLE V.

ESTIMATED ANNUAL CHARGES ON
GENERATING PLANTS.

Items.	Dog Lake.		Cameron Rapids.		Slate Falls.	
	Full Capacity.	Half Capacity.	Full Capacity.	Half Capacity.	Full Capacity.	Half Capacity.
Wages administration, step-up transformer losses....	$13,760	$11,296	$16,375	$14,390	$6,000	$6,000
Maintenance and repairs	16,427	10,632	17,827	11,478	6,634	3,868
Replacement fund........	15,927	10,132	16,727	10,978	6,334	3,669
Interest at 4 per cent......	33,278	24,787	32,561	24,008	14,308	10,400
Total annual charges.	$79,392	$56,847	$82,990	$60,854	$33,271	23,937

PART V.

TRANSMISSION OF POWER.

In connection with the hydraulic developments dealt with in the previous section, three specific transmission schemes have been assumed as best meeting present and probable future power requirements. They are as follows: (1) A line from Dog Lake to Port Arthur, Fort William and vicinity; (2) a line from Cameron Rapids on the Nepigon to Port Arthur, Fort William and vicinity; (3) a line from Slate Falls on the Mississauga, to Thessalon and Bruce Mines.

Detailed estimates on these schemes will be found in table VI. In all cases, the use of a high-class wood pole has been assumed, with telephone wires on the same poles. The transmission table (VI.) shows the capital cost and annual charges on the transmission lines from the step-up transformer station at the various points of development to the step-down stations at points of local distribution. The annual charges include depreciation and repairs, interest and cost of patrol.

The table of transformation details gives particulars concerning the proposed transformer stations. In all cases, the stations are assumed as being built for full capacity at the outset, with equipment to be installed as required. The transformation charges provide for municipal taxes on building, insurance, depreciation, engineering and contingencies, and interest during construction.

The summation sheet contains the charges for transmission, transformation and administration chargeable to each municipality, to which is added in each case the cost of power at the generating station. The final column is for 24-hour power at low-tension bus-bars of the various municipal substations.

In Table IX. is shown in condensed form the total investment and the annual charges for transmission and stepdown transformation: also the cost per annum per horse-power ready for distribution from the low-tension bus-bars in the various towns.

TABLE VI.

TRANSMISSION DETAILS.

SHOWING CAPITAL COST AND ANNUAL CHARGES.

Item.	Dog Lake to Port Arthur 33,000 V. 60 Cycles.		Cameron Rapids to Port Arthur 60,000 V. 60 Cycles.		Slate Falls to Bruce Mines 40,000 V. 60 Cycles.		Slate Falls to Thessalon 40,000 V. 60 Cycles.	
	Full Capacity.	Half Capacity.	Full Capacity.	Half Capacity.	Full Capacity.	Half Capacity.	Full Capacity.	Half Capacity.
Miles	25	25	75	75	26	26	16	16
Area of Conductors—M.c.m	300	150	150	95	83	83	83	83
Capital Cost per Mile :—								
Equipment	5,603.00	2,831.00	4,524.00	2,292.00	4,003.00	3,919.70	91.00	174.30
Right of way protection	100.00	100.00	100.00	100.00	195.70	191.70	4.30	8.30
Engineering and contingencies	1,140.00	596.00	925.00	478.00	839.00	821.50	19.00	36.50
Total	6,843.00	3,527.00	5,549.00	2,870.00	5,037.70	4,932.90	114.30	219.10
Total capital cost	$171,075.00	$87,925.00	$416,175.00	$215,250.00	$65,503.20	$63,823.70	$1,828.80	$3,509.30
Capital Charges per Mile :—								
Equipment	337.75	171.25	305.40	155.10	276.76	271.08	6.30	11.98
Right of way protection	5.50	5.50	6.50	6.50	10.75	10.50	.25	.50
Engineering and contingencies	68.65	35.35	62.20	32.10	57.48	56.30	1.31	2.49
Total	411.90	212.10	373.10	192.70	344.99	337.88	7.86	14.97
Total capital charges	$10,297.00	$5,303.00	$27,981.00	$14,452.00	$4,477.21	$4,363.48	125.76	239.52
Patrol	900.00	900.00	2,250.00	2,250.00	1,012.00	986.70	28.00	53.30
Total annual charges	$11,197.00	$6,203.00	$30,231.00	$16,702.00	$5,489.00	$5,350.00	$154.00	$293.00
Loss of power, H.P.	915.00	460.00	1,900.00	945.00	167.00	38.00	4.00	2.00

TABLE VII.

TRANSFORMATION DETAILS.

SHOWING CAPITAL COSTS AND ANNUAL CHARGES.

Item.	Port Arthur (Dog Lake Scheme.)		Port Arthur (Cameron Rapids)		Bruce Mines (Slate Falls.)		Thessalon (Slate Falls.)	
	Full Capacity.	Half Capacity.	Full Capacity.	Half Capacity.	Full Capacity.	Half Capacity.	Full Capacity.	Half Capacity.
Capacity, H.P.	12,382	6,187	14,025	7,010	3,300	1,650	150	150
Capital Cost:—								
Building and lot	16,000.00	16,000.00	21,000.00	21,000.00	7,000.00	7,000.00	3,000.00	Same station used as for full generation capacity.
Equipment	90,789.00	58,385.00	95,055.00	62,000.00	43,365.00	25,015.00	11,435.00	
Engineering and contingencies	10,528.00	6,839.00	11,995.00	8,300.00	5,196.00	3,602.00	1,444.00	
Interest during construction	2,327.00	1,501.00	2,558.00	1,826.00	1,143.00	770.00	318.00	
Total	$118,695.00	$76,725.00	$130,213.00	$93,126.00	$58,294.00	$39,287.00	$16,197.00	
Annual Charges:—								
Maintenance and depreciation	6,236.00	3,012.00	6,483.00	4,254.00	3,080.73	1,544.09	749.88	
Interest, 4 per cent	4,747.00	3,071.00	5,209.00	3,725.00	2,331.76	1,571.48	647.88	
Operation	4,000.00	4,000.00	5,000.00	4,500.00	4,400.00	4,000.00	1,000.00	
Total	$14,983.00	$10,083.00	$16,692.00	$12,479.00	$9,882.00	$7,476.00	$2,398.00	$2,398.00

TABLE VIII.

SUMMATION SHEET.

SHOWING ANNUAL COST OF POWER ON 24 HOUR BASIS AT SUB-STATION LOW TENSION BUS-BARS.

Item.	Port Arthur (Dog Lake.)		Port Arthur (Cameron Rapids.)		Bruce Mines. (Slate Falls.)		Thessalon (Slate Falls.)	
	Full Capacity.	Half Capacity.	Full Capacity.	Half Capacity.	Full Capacity.	Half Capacity.	Full Capacity.	Half Capacity.
Population :—	10,206	....	10,206	....	860	....	1,380	....
Annual Charges :—								
Generation, including step-up transformation....	79,382	56,817	82,990	60,854	31,825	22,109	1,446	1,48
Transmission..........	11,197	6,203	30,251	16,702	5,489	5,350	154	93
Step-down transformation.........	14,983	10,083	16,092	12,479	9,823	7,476	2,398	2,98
Administration	6,850	4,820	6,656	6,097	1,434	1,375	66	25
Total.......	$112,422	$77,953	$136,569	$96,132	$48,571	$36,310	$4,064	$4,644
Total H.P. developed.........	14,100	7,050	16,850	8,500	3,620	1,287	165	63
Net H.P. delivered, all losses deducted.......	12,382	6,187	14,025	7,010	3,300	1,650	150	80
Total annual cost of 24-hour power at low tension bus-bars, step-down transformer station........	$9.10	$12.60	$9.75	$13.70	$14.72	$22.00	$27.10	$30.92

TABLE IX.

TRANSMISSION INVESTMENTS.

Item.	Port Arthur (Dog Lake.)		Port Arthur (Cameron Rapids.)		Bruce Mines (Slate Falls.)		Thessalon (Slate Falls,)	
	Full Capacity.	Half Capacity.	Full Capacity.	Half Capacity.	Full Capacity.	Half Capacity.	Full Capacity.	Half Capacity.
Total H.P. distributed	12,382	6,187	14,025	7,010	3,300	1,650	150	150
Total investment, including step-down transformer stations	289,760	164,653	451,568	308,376	123,977	103,111	18,026	19,706
Investment per H.P. delivered	$23 40	$26.60	$32.20	$44 00	$37.55	$62.50	$121.00	$131.20
Total annual repairs, depreciation, operation and administration	14,600	9,700	28,861	16,846	10,353	8,702	1,831	1,908
Interest, 4 per cent	11,590	6,586	18,062	12,335	4,959	4,124	721	788
Total	$26,190	$16,286	$46,923	$29,181	$15,312	$12,826	$2,552	$2,691
Cost of 24-hour power per annum, including line and transformer losses	$9.10	$12.60	$9.75	$13.70	$14.72	$22.00	$27.10	$30.92

INDIVIDUAL TRANSMISSION.

The various sub-stations have been estimated on the basis of transformation down to 2,200 volts, but the cost of distribution of power at this voltage will be dealt with in Part VI. Many instances arise, however, in which it is desired to supply a single large consumer or a small municipality at some distance from a sub-station. When this is the case the following table may be made use of. The total cost of power to such a consumer is ascertained by adding the rate per H.P. from this table to the cost of power at the nearest municipal sub-station. The charges for such a branch transmission do not include any allowance of right of way or telephone, it being assumed that the highways would be available for such low voltage lines.

TABLE X.

SHOWING COST OF DISTRIBUTION FROM MUNICIPAL SUB-STATION TO AN INDIVIDUAL CONSUMER, NOT COVERED BY LOCAL DISTRIBUTION.

Distance in Miles from Municipal Sub-station.	Cost per Horse-Power per Annum for the Delivery of Various Amounts of Power.							
	50 H.P.	75 H.P.	100 H.P.	150 H.P.	200 H.P.	250 H.P.	300 H.P.	
2	$5.58	$4.20	$3.53	$2.92	$2.74	$2.60	$2.51	2,200 Volts
3	6.89	5 20	4 41	3.60	3.25	3.10	3.03	
4	7.92	6.18	5.20	4.27	3.93	3.72	3.86	
5	8.87	7.18	5.98	4 96	4.55	4.32	4.17	
6	10.20	8.24	6.77	5.38	5.13	4.60	4.43	
8	14.10	10.14	8.40	6.97	6 24	5 79	5.58	11,000 Volts
10	16.12	12.13	9.54	8.31	7.68	6.96	6.17	
12	18.76	14.03	11.12	10.12	8.42	7.96	7.22	16,500 Volts
15	22.74	17.08	13.48	10.89	9.35	8.84	8.32	

PART VI.

DISTRIBUTION OF POWER.

The cost of distribution from the municipal sub-stations to the consumers' premises varies widely with different conditions and depends upon the distances involved, the magnitude of the demands of individual consumers and the grouping of these consumers.

This cost of distribution will not necessarily, however, give the increase of cost to the consumer above that paid for the power by the municipality unless a method of charging be chosen which will take into account the difference between the sum of the consumers' maximum demands and the maximum demand on the station. If the charging rate for power were one composed of a flat rate based on maximum demand plus a rate per k.w.-hour or H.P.-hour actually registered by meter, then it would be approximately correct to say that the combined rate per H.P. to the consumer should be the same as the cost of power at the sub-station plus the cost per H.P. of the distribution service. Besides this the ordinary municipality has such various means of modifying the rates for power, such as limited-hour contracts with motor users, contract with summer users of electric power, etc., that fair rates could only be established after a careful study of the actual conditions after operations were begun. Under average conditions in a town demanding 1,000 H.P. or over, it could reasonably be expected that 10-hour power could be sold at the same or even a lower rate, if based on maximum demand, than that charged the municipality for 24-hour power at the sub-stations. In other words, the municipality might expect to profit sufficiently from over-lapping peaks, 24-hour power for lighting, pumping, general motor users, etc, etc., to pay the cost of its distribution.

PART VII.

MOTOR INSTALLATIONS.

To complete the information regarding the cost of electric power to the consumer, the following table is given, showing the cost of induction motor service per H.P. per year.

TABLE XI.

CAPITAL COST AND ANNUAL CHARGES ON MOTOR INSTALLATIONS,
POLYPHASE, 60-CYCLE INDUCTION MOTORS.

Capacity. H P.	Capital Cost per H.P. Installed.	ANNUAL CHARGES.			
		Interest 5%	Depreciation and Repairs, 6%	Oil, Care and Operation.	Total per H.P. per Annum.
5	$39.00	$1.95	$2.34	$4.00	$8.29
10	36.00	1.80	2.16	3.00	6.96
15	30.00	1.50	1.80	2.50	5.80
25	25.00	1.25	1.50	2.00	4.75
35	22.00	1.10	1.32	1.75	4.17
50	20.00	1.00	1.20	1.50	3.70
75	19.00	.95	1.14	1.25	3.34
100	17.00	.85	1.02	1.00	2.87
150	15.00	.75	.90	.80	2.45
200	14.00	.70	.84	.70	2.24

By combining the costs given in this table with the cost of distributed power, as indicated in Part VI., the final or total charge per H.P. per year will be obtained.

PART VIII.

SINKING FUND.

In the above estimates for transmission and transformation, depreciation and replacement have been provided for which would replace the different classes of plant in periods ranging from 15 to 30 years.

The charges would, therefore, amply serve the purpose of any sinking fund which might be considered needful. In the case of the generating plant estimates, however, these charges would not be sufficient for such a purpose in the so-called permanent portions of the development, comprising the dam, head-works, power house, etc.

A forty-year sinking fund to cover these portions of the development amounting, on the average, to about $50 expenditure per H.P. of capacity would require a charge of $0.55 per H.P. to repay this expenditure in 40 years, interest being calculated at 4 per cent.

PART IX.

EXISTING RATES.

In Table XII., following, will be found a statement of the lighting and power rates in a number of municipalities throughout the district:—

TABLE XII.

EXISTING RATES.

Municipality.	Street Lighting per Year.	Incandescent Lighting.				Power.	Source of Power.	Control
		Commercial.		Residential.		Flat rate per H.P. per Year.		
		Meter-rate per K.W. Hour in cents.	Flat rate per 16 C.P. Lamp per Year.	M-rate per K.W. Hour in cents.	Flat rate per 16 C.P. Lamp per Year.			
Fort William	$40 all night.	7.5	$6.40	7.5	$6.75	$25.00	Water and Steam.	Private and Municipal.
Fort Arthur	indefinite. all night.	6—10 15% off.	$4.80—$9.00 15% off.	7—10 10% off.	$2.40—$6.60 10% off.	....	Water.	Municipal.
Copper Cliff	2,000 c.p. indefinite,	....	$2.40—$4.80	....	$2.40—$4.80	....	Water.	Private.
Blind River	32 c.p.—$12 all and every night	....	$3.00—$4.80	....	$3.00—$6.00	....	Water and Steam.	Private.
Thessalon	1,200 c.p. Arc $76 all night.	....	$3.00	....	$3.00	....	Steam.	Municipal.
Bruce Mines	32 c.p.- $12	....	$3.00—$6.00	....	$3.00—$6.00	....	Steam.	Private.
Sault Ste. Marie	1,200 c.p. Arc $70 all night.	5—10	$6.00	5—10	$3.00—$6.00	$50.00	Water.	Private.

PART X.

STEAM POWER.

In order to institute a comparison between the cost of electric power as has just been set forth and the cost of power generated by steam or producer gas, the following tables have been compiled after a careful study of data available in technical journals and also from data collected by the Commission's engineers in various towns within the district under consideration. The capital costs have been compiled from information supplied by various makers of engines and other machinery. The tables represent average working conditions and assume a high-class installation.

TABLE XIII.

STEAM POWER PLANTS.

SHOWING CAPITAL COSTS OF PLANTS INSTALLED AND ANNUAL COSTS OF POWER PER BRAKE HORSE-POWER.

Size of Plant, H.P.	Capital Cost of Plant per H.P. installed.			Annual Cost of 10-hour Power per B.H.P.	Annual Cost of 24-hour Power per B.H.P.
	Engines, Boilers, etc., installed.	Buildings.	Total.		
CLASS I.—Engines Simple, slide valve, non-condensing. Boilers: Return tubular.					
10	$66.00	$40.00	$106.00	$91.16	$180.76
20	56.00	37.00	93.00	76.31	151.48
30	48.70	35.00	83.70	66.46	131.68
40	44.75	33.50	78.25	59.49	117.74
50	43.00	31.00	74.00	53.95	106.46
CLASS II.—Engines Simple, Corliss, non-condensing. Boilers: Return tubular.					
30	70.70	35.00	105.70	61.14	117.70
40	62.85	33.50	96.35	55.50	107.10
50	59.00	31.00	90.00	50.70	97.73
60	56.00	30.00	86.70	47.42	91.34
80	50.00	27.50	77.50	43.86	85.41
100	44.60	25.00	69.60	40.55	79.19
CLASS III.—Engines: Compound, Corliss, condensing. Boilers: Return tubular with reserve capacity.					
100	63.40	28.00	91.40	33.18	60.05
150	53.70	24.00	77.70	29.83	54.63
200	50.10	20.00	70.10	28.14	51.72
300	45.90	18.00	63.90	26.27	48.83
400	43.55	16.00	59.55	24.84	46.12
500	41.25	14.00	55.25	23.73	44.21
750	40.50	13.00	53.50	23.56	44.02
1000	39.00	12.00	51.00	23.26	43.71
CLASS IV.—Engines: Compound, Corliss, condensing. Boilers: Water-tube, with reserve capacity.					
300	55.20	18.00	73.20	25.77	46.32
400	51.50	16.00	67.50	24.18	43.61
500	49.40	14.00	63.40	23.19	42.08
750	46.80	13.00	59.70	22.88	41.56
1000	44.80	12.00	56.80	22.47	41.11

NOTE.—Annual costs include interest at 5 per cent., depreciation and repairs on plant, oil and waste, labor and fuel (coal at $4.00 per ton). Brake horse-power is the mechanical power at engine shaft.

It will be noted that for a consumer requiring a large installation operating for ten hours only, there appears to be little advantage to be derived from the use of transmitted electric power, provided the power is not to be distributed throughout a consumer's buildings by a complicated system of shafting, belts, etc. But in the majority of cases this condition obtains, and herein lies one of the specific advantages of electric power. Motors can be installed on each floor of the factory, or even on each machine, with but little loss in efficiency, and only such motors as are required to drive the machinery in use from time to time need be operated. In many cases due to this fact the total electric power consumption of a large factory would be reduced from 25 per cent. to 50 per cent. below that which is required under steam operation, working from a central station.

Again, where electric power is available throughout the 24 hours many industries will work night and day, thereby effecting a great economy, as is evidenced by a comparison of the cost of 24-hour steam or producer gas power with 24-hour electric power.

Perhaps the most striking advantage to be derived from the use of electric power as compared with other power, is that the small consumer can obtain power at a rate which should not be appreciably greater than that made to the large consumer, although the present practice in selling electric power is to discriminate against the small consumer for the reason that electric power prices made by private companies are not based on cost of service, but are merely made with a view to displacing steam.

PART XI.

PRODUCER GAS POWER.

TABLE XIV.

SHOWING CAPITAL COSTS OF PRODUCER GAS PLANTS INSTALLED, AND

ANNUAL COSTS OF POWER PER BRAKE HORSE-POWER.

Size of Plant, H.P.	Capital Cost of Plant per H.P. Installed.			Annual Cost of 10-hour Power per B.H.P.	Annual Cost of 24-hour Power per B.H.P.
	Machinery, etc.	Buildings.	Total		
10	$137.00	$40.00	$177.00	$53.48	$90.02
20	110.00	36.00	146.00	44.47	75.22
30	93.00	33.00	126.00	38.73	65.99
40	84.50	29.00	113.50	35.05	59.85
50	80.00	26.00	106.00	32.27	55.22
60	79.00	24.00	103.00	30.49	52.03
80	78.20	22.00	100.20	28.70	48.95
100	77.50	20.00	97.50	27.05	45.40
150	76.00	19.00	95.00	25.87	43.17
200	74.00	17.00	91.00	24.95	41.78
300	73.00	16.00	89.00	24.24	40.40
400	71.50	14.00	85.50	23.41	39.03
500	70.00	12.00	82.00	22.54	37.54
750	67.50	10.00	77.50	21.55	35.99
1000	65.00	8.00	73.00	20.46	34.66

NOTE.—Annual costs include: interest at 5 per cent., depreciation and repairs on plant, oil and waste, labor and fuel (Bituminous coal at $4.00 and Anthracite coal at $5.00 per ton).

A reference to Table XIII. will show that the cost of power developed by producer-gas plants and gas engines is less than that produced by steam plants of the same capacity. It may be said, however, that up to the present no very large installations of suction producers have been made, 250 to 300 horse-power being about the maximum. But this has been provided for in the table by assuming that the larger plants will be made up of several units, each unit being not greater than 350 H.P. capacity. While operation of producer-gas plants has not been going on many years, and complete knowledge on the subject is not available, with the information at hand it is believed that in many situations this form of power producer will be found more economical than a steam plant, and therefore a closer competitor of hydro-electric power. It must be remembered that the same objections hold against the producer-gas plant as those which have been mentioned in reference to steam plants, namely, that 24-hour power costs proportionately more than 10-hour power; that the small consumer does not have the great advantage obtainable by the use of electric power; and also that a central installation in a factory is all that is possible if electric motors are required in various parts of the factory, and the only prime mover available is steam or gas. This will make the cost of electric factory operation very expensive, and considerably higher than the power costs shown in Table VIII. Speaking generally, however, it may be said that producer-gas plants have a bright future and as the design and construction is perfected undoubtedly the capital cost will be reduced and the cost of power lessened.

TABLE XV.

SHOWING THE EFFECT ON THE COST OF POWER OF A VARIATION IN
THE PRICE OF COAL OF ONE-HALF DOLLAR PER TON.

Size of Plant. H.P.	Suction Producer Gas.		Steam.		
	10-Hour.	24-Hour.	10-Hour.		24-Hour.
10	$1.15	$2.53	Simple	$6.14	$13.47
20	1.13	2.46	Slide Valve	5.23	11.56
30	1.10	2.40	Engine.	4.71	10.35
40	1.07	2.33		3.56	7.84
50	1.04	2.29	Simple Automatic	3.37	7.41
60	1.01	2.24	Non-	3.26	7.16
80	.98	2.18	condensing.	3.15	6.97
100	.96	2.12		3.12	6.87
150	.94	2.07		1.75	3.85
200	.92	2.02	Compound	1.69	3.71
300	.90	1.98	Condensing.	1.62	3.60
400	.88	1.94		1.56	3.44
500	.86	1.89	Compound Con-	1.39	3.05
750	.82	1.81	densing; Water-	1.39	3.05
1,000	.76	1.72	tube Boilers.	1.39	3.05

APPENDIX

TO

FIFTH REPORT

Rainy River District.

ENGINEER'S REPORT

ON

THE WATER POWERS AND ON THE
GENERATION OF ELECTRIC POWER
THEREFROM.

HONOURABLE ADAM BECK,

CHAIRMAN OF THE HYDRO-ELECTRIC POWER COMMISSION.

DEAR SIR:—

Herewith find my report on the Rainy River District, being that portion of Ontario identical with the judicial district of Rainy River.

The report deals with the present consumption of and demand for power, and the sources of power developed and undeveloped. There are no long distance transmission systems in this district, and there does not appear at the present time to be any demand for such, unless the operating of certain mines might in the future require the transmission of power.

Yours respectfully,

CECIL B. SMITH,

Chief Engineer.

TORONTO, CANADA,
APRIL 15TH, 1907.

REPORT OF

Text Book Commission

1907

PRINTED BY ORDER OF

THE LEGISLATIVE ASSEMBLY OF ONTARIO

TORONTO
Printed by L. K. CAMERON, Printer to the King's Most Excellent Majesty
1907

Printed by WARWICK BRO'S & RUTTER, Limited, Printers,
TORONTO.

COPY OF AN ORDER-IN-COUNCIL APPROVED BY HIS HONOR THE LIEUTENANT-
GOVERNOR, THE 30TH DAY OF JUNE, A.D. 1906.

Upon the recommendation of the Honorable the Minister of Education,
the Committee of Council advise that under "The Act Respecting Enquiries
Concerning Public Matters," being chapter 19 of The Revised Statutes of
Ontario, 1897, the following persons be appointed Commissioners to enquire
into and report upon the reasonableness of the present prices of School Text
Books now on the authorized list, and to enquire also into the prices of such
publication elsewhere:

T. W. Crothers, Esquire, Barrister-at-Law, St. Thomas.

John A. Cooper, Esquire, Journalist, Toronto.

The Committee further advise that the Commission confer on the said
Commissioners the powers authorized by the above mentioned Act.

Certified,

J. LONSDALE CAPREOL,
Clerk, Executive Council.

COPY OF AN ORDER-IN-COUNCIL APPROVED BY HIS HONOR THE ADMINISTRATOR
OF THE GOVERNMENT OF THE PROVINCE OF ONTARIO, THE 16TH DAY OF
JULY, A.D. 1906.

Upon the recommendation of the Honorable the Minister of Education, the Committee of Council advise that Alexander Clark Casselman be
appointed Secretary to the Commission lately appointed to inquire into and
report regarding the prices of text books.

Certified,

J. LONSDALE CAPREOL,
Clerk, Executive Council.

COPY OF AN ORDER-IN-COUNCIL APPROVED BY HIS HONOR THE ADMINISTRATOR
OF THE GOVERNMENT OF THE PROVINCE OF ONTARIO, THE 16TH DAY OF
JULY, A.D. 1906.

Upon the recommendation of the Honorable the Minister of Education, the Committee of Council advise that George Lynch Staunton, K.C.,
Hamilton, be appointed Legal Counsel to the Commission lately appointed
to inquire into and report regarding the prices of text books.

Certified,

J. LONSDALE CAPREOL,
Clerk, Executive Council.

[3]

PROVINCE OF ONTARIO.

EDWARD THE SEVENTH, by the Grace of God, of the United Kingdom of Great Britain and Ireland, and of the British Dominions beyond the Seas, King, Defender of the Faith, Emperor of India.

To THOMAS WILSON CROTHERS, of the City of Saint Thomas, in the County of Elgin, Esquire, Barrister-at-Law, and JOHN ALEXANDER COOPER, of the City of Toronto, in the County of York, Esquire, Journalist, OUR COMMISSIONERS in this behalf.

GREETING :—

J. J. FOY, } WHEREAS in and by Chapter Nineteen of the Re-
Attorney-General. } vised Statutes of our Province of Ontario, en-
titled "An Act Respecting Inquiries concerning Public Matters," it is enacted that whenever the Lieutenant-Governor of Our said Province-in-Council deems it expedient to cause inquiry to be made into and concerning any matter connected with the good government of Our said Province, or the conduct of any part of the public business thereof, or the administration of justice therein, and such enquiry is not regulated by any special law, the Lieutenant-Governor may, by the Commission in the case, confer upon the Commissioners or persons by whom such inquiry is to be conducted, the power of summoning before them any party or witnesses and of requiring them to give evidence on oath, orally or in writing (or on solemn affirmation if they be parties entitled to affirm in civil matters), and to produce such documents and things as such Commissioners deem requisite to the full investigation of the matters into which they are appointed to examine, and that the Commissioners shall then have the same power to enforce the attendance of such witnesses, and to compel them to give evidence and produce documents and things, as is vested in any Court in Civil Cases.

AND WHEREAS it has been made to appear to the Executive Government of Our said Province that enquiries should be made upon the reasonableness of the present prices of the School Text Books now on the authorized list and to enquire also into the prices of such publications elsewhere.

NOW KNOW YE that WE, having and reposing full trust and confidence in you the said Thomas Wilson Crothers and John Alexander Cooper.

DO HEREBY, by and with the advice of Our Executive Council of Our said Province APPOINT you the said THOMAS WILSON CROTHERS and JOHN ALEXANDER COOPER to be OUR COMMISSIONERS in this behalf to INQUIRE INTO AND TO REPORT to Our said Lieutenant-Governor upon the reasonableness of the present prices of the School Text Books now on the authorized list and to enquire also into the prices of such publications elsewhere.

GIVING to you Our said Commissioners full power and authority to summon before you any party or witnesses, and to require him, or them, to give evidence on oath, orally or in writing (or on solemn affirmation if such party or witnesses is, or are, entitled to affirm in civil matters), and to produce to you Our said Commissioners such documents and things as you may deem requisite to the full investigation of the premises, TOGETHER with all and every other power and authority in the said Act mentioned and authorized to be by Us conferred on any Commissioners appointed by authority or in pursuance thereof.

AND WE DO REQUIRE you Our said Commissioners forthwith after the conclusion of such inquiry to make full report to Our said Lieutenant-Governor touching the said investigation together with all or any evidence taken by you concerning the same.

To HAVE, HOLD AND ENJOY the said office and authority of Commissioners for and during the pleasure of Our said Lieutenant-Governor.

IN TESTIMONY WHEREOF We have caused these OUR LETTERS to be made PATENT and the GREAT SEAL OF OUR PROVINCE OF ONTARIO to be hereunto affixed.

WITNESS: THE HORORABLE SIR WILLIAM MULOCK, K.C.M.G., Chief Justice of the Exchequer Division of Our High Court of Justice of Ontario, &c., &c., &c., Administrator of the Government of Our Province of Ontario.

AT OUR GOVERNMENT HOUSE, in Our City of Toronto, in Our said Province, this twelfth day of July, in the year of Our Lord one thousand nine hundred and six and in the Sixth year of Our Reign.

BY COMMAND,

THOMAS MULVEY,
Assistant Provincial Secretary.

REPORT OF

TEXT BOOK COMMISSION,

1907.

To His Honor the Honorable
WILLIAM MORTIMER CLARK, K.C.,
Lieutenant-Governor of the Province of Ontario.

MAY IT PLEASE YOUR HONOR:

The undersigned, having been appointed by Commission under the Great Seal of the Province, bearing date the 12th day of July, in the year of our Lord 1906, a Board of Commissioners—

"To inquire into and report to our said Lieutenant-Governor upon the "reasonableness of the present prices of the School Text Books now on the "authorized list and to inquire also into the prices of such publications else-"where," beg leave to report as follows:—

After notice thereof through the press your Commissioners held meetings for the taking of evidence, all of which were open to representatives of the press, as well as to the general public. The evidence was taken under oath and everyone who expressed a desire to make any statement before us was given an opportunity to do so.

Representative teachers, inspectors, educationists, experts in every department of book-making (including two from the United States) and all persons publishing school text books for Ontario, were summoned and testified before us. The paper used in the various books was chemically analyzed, and the expert report thereon forms part of the evidence returned herewith. Access was had to the correspondence on file in the Education Department respecting text books and agreements concerning the same.

We had expected to obtain assistance from a perusal of the evidence taken by the former Text Book Commission, but in this we were disappointed as it was not filed with their report, and the shorthand notes thereof had been destroyed.

Your Commissioners visited the largest publishing establishments in the United States, where many courteous and instructive interviews were accorded them. In Boston and Norwood two days were spent in go through the largest printing, binding, and publishing establishments. Every step and process in text book making, type-setting, plate making, printing and binding was thus studied where the most modern methods are to be found. Similar establishments in New York were visited where also the various steps in text book making were studied. Prices and methods of distribution were discussed with the leading publishers in Boston and New

York (where is published a large proportion of the school books used throughout the Union), and your Commissioners desire to acknowledge the great assistance, the adequate information and the generous treatment there received. We also had the advantage of examining many school books published and used in Great Britain and Ireland.

It is clear that text book publishing in Ontario has fallen behind the times. Most of the books produced to-day are no better than those produced twenty years ago, whereas in the United States and Great Britain great progress has been made. The paper used in the Ontario books is not equal to that used in the United States, and is much inferior to that used in Great Britain. As the demand for this kind of paper increases doubtless some of this inferiority will disappear. Concerning type-setting, some of the work done here is decidedly inferior, while plate making and press work are more nearly up-to-date. In binding the United States factories have special machinery and produce better work at lower prices.

Part of this general inferiority has been due to the absence of any insistent demand from the educational authorities, inspectors, or teachers for better work. The Department allowed slovenly work, and apparently the inspectors and teachers either hesitated to criticize or were unfamiliar with conditions elsewhere. We believe that just as good books may be produced in Canada as elsewhere if the authorities insist upon an equally high standard.

DEPARTMENT METHODS.

There are three general methods of producing text books which may here be considered. The Department may select an author to prepare a text book, then engage a publisher and fix the price at which the text shall be sold to the public. This is the method which, speaking generally, was adopted under the two previous Ministers of Education. The author selected was not necessarily the one who could produce the best text; the publisher had the price fixed for him and he immediately set to work to make the most money he could out of his contract. Consequently the present text books are unsatisfactory.

A second method may be considered. The Department might have all its texts prepared under its authority, make its own plates, own all the rights in the texts and then have them printed by tender. If the Department represented the whole of Canada instead of one Province this system might be expedient. For a single province to adopt such a plan would be expensive and cumbersome.

A third method would be to throw open to competition both writing and publishing. A text book may thus be produced for nine provinces instead of for one. Educationists would be stimulated to produce the very best both in literary and educational quality. Competition among publishers would result in the highest standard of book-making. This plan would be the best of the three if the Department will maintain uniformity in the text books used in all schools, especially in all public schools, and will authorize text books for only a limited period.

PUBLIC SCHOOL READERS.

The most important of the text books are the public school readers, and respecting those at present in use we think the Education Department took a wise course in the circumstances of the time in having them prepared by a board of educationists. But we are of opinion that there were several grave errors in the methods adopted by the Department to secure their mechanical make-up and publication—methods not calculated to give satisfactory results either as to quality or price—methods which in fact resulted in books inferior in material and workmanship and exorbitant in price, as admitted directly or substantially before us by the publishers themselves.

Mr. Gage, one of the three publishers of the readers, testified before us in part as follows:—"In conclusion, reverting to the publication of the "Ontario Readers, I would say they were fairly good books when issued "twenty years ago, but not as good as they should have been—not books "that a publisher would be proud of. They were prepared under the super- "vision of the Government and by men who had no experience in work of "this kind, and were therefore mechanically at least not up to the highest "standard. An examination not only of the reading books, but of many "other text books used in Ontario, when compared with those of other "Provinces, will force the conclusion that this Province is very much behind "other Provinces both in point of educational value and the mechanical "make-up of the book."

Mr. S. G. Beatty, of the Canada Publishing Company, another of the publishers, testified as follows:—

Q.—Are you aware that your Readers are not bound in the way that the Readers in England and the American Readers are bound?

A.—Yes.

Q.—And you never tried to make any improvement in them?

A.—Of course there are better methods.

Q.—Do you think the method in which you have bound these Readers is good enough for the purpose for which they are designed?

A.—No, I do not think it is.

Q.—You do not think the binding is good enough?

A.—No, I do not.

Q.—How would you suggest improving it?

A.—I would suggest thread stitching.

In 1884 the Government entered into an agreement with three publishing companies (W. J. Gage & Company, The Canada Publishing Company and Thomas Nelson and Sons) to publish the said readers according to certain specifications for a period of ten years from the 1st day of January, 1885, the maximum retail prices and the minimum discounts to be allowed being fixed thereby. This agreement was made without asking for tenders or in any way securing competition. It would have been better, we think, had the contract been made with one firm rather than with three, and for a period not exceeding five years; the specifications were loosely drawn, thus permitting the production of an inferior book without violating the letter of the agreement; the copyrights of the selections should all have been secured by the Department; wire stitching should not have been allowed at all.

When this contract was secured by the three publishers they apparently did not intend or anticipate that in carrying it out there should be any competition among them, and in fact there was none. The Government supplied each of the three publishers with a complete set of plates for the whole series of readers, and these firms had nothing to do but to print the books.

Shortly after the making of the contract, Thomas Nelson and Sons assigned their interest therein to the Copp, Clark Company, for $30,000, payable in ten yearly payments of $3,000 each.

From the first of January, 1885, till the first of July, 1896, these readers retailed as fixed by the said contract at the following prices:—

First Reader, Part I	10	cents.
First Reader, Part II	15	"
Second Reader	25	"
Third Reader	35	
Fourth Reader	45	

Five experts (for fuller report of experts' figures see appendix I) were examined before us as to the cost of producing these readers, including the printers' and binders' profits, the plates being supplied by the Department. One of these experts speaking for the Canada Publishing Company, gave the cost as follows, which differed but little from that given by the other four:—

	Cents.
First Reader, Part I	4.10
First Reader, Part II	5.75
Second Reader	7.75
Third Reader	10.50
Fourth Reader	12.00

It will be seen that the set of readers costing about 40 cents, was sold to the trade at about 95 cents, and retailed at $1.30. At an advance of six cents per set superior and satisfactory books could have been produced.

Comparisons are sometimes made of the retail prices of these readers with those used in the various states of the Union, but the conditions obtaining in Ontario differ so widely from those existing there that there is no fair basis for such a comparison. Here, the plates having been supplied by the Government, and a monopoly for ten years established, all elements of risk and uncertainty were eliminated. There, open competition prevails, resulting in better books and (having with it all the elements of risk, uncertainty and expense), higher prices.

COPYRIGHT ON SELECTIONS.

The copyright on the selections in the readers is worthy of special consideration, as it has played a leading role in connection with the existing contracts. When the Department prepared the readers, and made a contract for their publication for ten years from Jan'y 1st, 1885, the copyrights on the selections were not secured. Apparently both the Minister and the publisher were ignorant of the situation, or thought it a matter of small importance. The publishers issued the books containing copyright selections, and sold them without any fear that action might be brought against them by the British owners. In this they were justified by the general customs of British publishers and British writers. It has always been usual to allow quotations and selections from literary productions to be used in school books without charge, or on payment of a nominal fee. The publishers and the Government felt so secure that they did not trouble to pay the British copyright holders the courtesy of asking permission to reprint copyright selections. It is possible that the publishers regarded themselves as printers merely and not the real publishers.

Just before the ten year term expired, and when there was a prospect of a new contract being entered into by the Government, the three firms then printing the readers, (the Copp, Clark Co., the W. J. Gage Co., and the Canada Publishing Co.), seemed to have suddenly realised that the copyright matter was worth looking into. The contract was to expire at the end of December, 1894, and in 1893, Mr. H. L. Thompson, of the Copp, Clark Co., representing the three firms interested, went to England and took up the copyright matter with some of the holders. He went to Macmillans, showed them the readers, and gave them the first information on the subject. He arranged to pay Macmillans £50 a year for the right to publish thereafter the selections in which they held copyright. He also got the Macmillans to agree that they would allow no other firm in Canada to publish these while they, the three firms, published the readers. Both Mr. Thompson and Mr. Gage admit in their evidence that the object was to secure the copyrights so as to force a renewal of the contract from the Minister of Education, and to so arrange matters that no other firm could get in on the contract. It was arranged among the three firms before Mr. Thompson went to England, that the cost of securing the copyrights was to be borne in equal shares.

Not content with what Mr. Thompson secured, Mr. Gage also visited England and obtained some copyrights. He also induced one firm to bring an action against the Minister of Education, so as to convince him of the importance of the copyrights. . The action was only a "bluff" action, but it apparently had its effect.

Though the contract ran out at the end of December, 1894, it was not until March, 1896, that a new contract was made. Under this, the three firms secured what they had worked for, although some slight reductions were made in prices. The Second Reader was reduced from 25c. to 20c., the Third from 35c. to 30c., and the Fourth from 45c. to 40c. After the renewal of the contract, the Copp, Clark Co., paid Thomas Nelson & Sons from 2½ to 5% on their share of the business, the consideration for which was not made clearly to appear.

Perhaps the action of the publishers in thus forcing a renewal from the Government cannot be condemned from a business point of view, but the Government showed weakness in allowing its hand to be forced. The copyright selections might have been taken out and others substituted: or the Government might have questioned the publishers' rights in the courts. The British copyright holders would, in all probability, have refused to allow their names to be used in such a questionable way, had they fully understood the situation.

While the new contract seems to have contemplated that other publishers might come in and share the publication of the readers, it was found that the three publishers were practically masters of the situation, and had in substance secured for an additional period of ten years, the exclusive right to publish the said readers. For twenty-two years the Public School readers have been so published, and during that period the Public School children of Ontario have been required to use inferior readers, and to pay about $200,000 therefor more than what, in the circumstances, was a fair price. We arrive at this result after allowing the publishers 25% for selling and distributing.

We would recommend that if a satisfactory and modern set of readers cannot be secured one should be prepared by the Department, the copyright of all selections secured, the plates made, and that the printing be given out by tender, under proper specifications to one firm. In the new set greater attention should be paid to the size of type, quantity of matter on a page, quality of the illustrations, and color of the paper. Too great care cannot be taken in this regard so that the pupils will be able to read the books without straining eyes, even in poorly lighted school rooms.

We would also recommend that if the Department finds it necessary to continue the old readers for a short period, until a new set can be secured, that tenders be invited for the printing, and that the contract be given to not more than two firms, one preferably.

With regard to Primers, we would recommend that only one be authorized. Others might be recommended for supplementary reading, but in that case they should be bought by the school board, and kept in the school room. Where more than one Primer is authorized, children moving from one school section to another are put to extra expense if the same Primer is not in use.

Other Public School Books.

Other Public School Books.	Their cost.	Retail price.
	cts.	cts.
Public School Arithmetic	11	25
Public School Geography	21¼	75
Morang's Modern Geography	23¾	75
Our Home and its Surrounding (Morang)	10½	40
Rose's Public School Geography	21½	75
Public School Grammar	9⅔	25
Morang's Modern English Grammar	9⅔	25
Public School History of England and Canada	11 9/10	30
History of Dominion of Canada	16⅜	50
Duncan's Story of the Canadian People	21	50
Weaver's Canadian History	13 3/10	50
Public School Physiology and Temperance	9⅓	25
Public School Bookkeeping	9	25
Public School Algebra and Euclid	9	25
Public School Agriculture	11	30
Public School Domestic Science	9½	50
Ahn's First German Book	7 5/10	25
Ahn's Second German Book	14½	45

These cost prices include neither royalties nor cost of plates—the former being generally 10% on the retail price, and the latter varying according to the quantity manufactured.

It will be observed that in this list there are four geographies, four histories, and two grammars. There can be no economy with such a multiplicity of authorized books. The sales are spread over two or four books instead of being confined to one, consequently the prices charged for each must be higher, or the quality must be inferior. If but one grammar, one geography and one history were authorized, the sales would be sufficiently large to enable a publisher to issue a better book at a lower price.

A survey of the books mentioned above, shows that they are just as poor in workmanship as the readers. In fact, some of them are worse. The P. S. Arithmetic, the P. S. Grammar, Rose's P. S. Geography, and some of the histories are very bad typographically. The type is too small, the paper poor, and the press work of a low grade. Most of them are wire stitched, which is uniformly condemned both by teachers and experts. In mechanical execution, exception must be made of Duncan's Story of the Canadian People (Morang), Morang's Modern Geography, and Morang's Modern English Grammar. These three books have a modern appearance, and met with the approval of the experts who examined them.

The paper used in all text books should have no mechanical pulp in its composition.

Writing and Drawing Books.

The evidence of the publisher of the drawing and writing books shows that the prices are too high. The writing book schedule of prices is as follows:—

	Cost.	Wholesale.	Retail.
Nos. 1-6	1.35	5.25	7 cents.
No. 7	3.00	7.50	10 cents.

The drawing books run thus—

	Cost.	Wholesale.	Retail.
Nos. 1-5	1.55	3.75	5 cents.

As these books have been authorized for over six years, and the sales have been large, there has been plenty of profit to wipe out the original cost of plates and compilation. If they are to be continued, the price might reasonably be reduced at once to 3 cents for all except writing book No. 7, which should sell at 5 cents. The discount to the retailer may be left at 25% and still give the wholesaler an adequate profit.

The cost of scribbling and exercise books is a burden to parents, and some system should be devised to relieve them. In Toronto the pupils get all their supplies at a cost of 14c. per year, while in towns where the parents buy individually the cost will be nearly one dollar for each pupil.

High School Books.

The list of books authorized for High Schools and Collegiate Institutes is unnecessarily large, owing chiefly to there being more than one book authorized in a subject. In the authorized list there are two reading books, three books on Composition, two on Geography, two on British History, two on Canadian History, two on Arithmetic, two on Algebra, three on Geometry, three on Latin, and two on Bookkeeping. The method and matter to be taught has, surely long before 'this, become pretty well defined, and could be contained in one book of moderate size. Cheapness of production is almost out of the question when two or three books are authorized in a subject and produced by different publishers. Again, it often occurs that a pupil moves from one High School to another, and is compelled to buy new books to enable him to take up with the work with the class. In an extreme case, if a pupil had to purchase a new book in every subject where more than one is authorized it would cost him $8.45. If a pupil wishes to consult another authority on any subject, he may do so by making use of the School Library, now grown to respectable dimensions in every secondary school in the Province. In many cases where more than one book is authorized in a subject, one of them has been in use more than 10 years. While change for the sake of change is not always good, yet it is believed that a consultation should be held over every book that has been in use five years. If with slight revision it could be brought up to the standard of the best books published on that subject it should be authorized for another term of say 3 years. Should it be found unsuitable, a dying period should be granted it of not more than one year and another authorized. This change should be announced to the publisher and the public at the same time.

The price of nearly all the High School Books is too high, and could be materially reduced and still allow a fair profit to the publisher.

There is a heavy expenditure by pupils of High Schools and Continuation Classes for annotated texts in English Literature, Latin, Greek, French and German. The texts prescribed are usually padded by notes, and other matter causing the pupils to pay from 50 cents to $1.25 for selections that should cost less than one-third of those sums.

Enterprising publishers manufacture blank books with specially ruled lines to suit certain subjects at too great an advance on the price of ordinary foolscap paper.

Some means should be devised by the Education Department to prohibit the use of these blank forms. The pupil might do his own ruling on foolscap paper for all school exercises necessitating the use of blank forms.

High School Books.

High School Books.	Their cost.	Retail price.
	cts.	$ c.
High School Reader	19 7/10	50
The Principles and Practice, Oral Reading	11½	50
High School English Grammar	17 6/10	75
High School English Composition	13½	50
Elementary English Composition	12 7/10	40
High School Composition from Models	21¼	75
High School Geography	21 1/10	1 00
Morang's Modern Geography	23¾	75
High School History of England and Canada	18 6/10	65
Wrong's The British Nation	26 9/10	1 00
Myer's Ancient History, Greece and Rome (Canadian Edition)	21 6/10	75
Botsford's Ancient History for Beginners	28 1/10	1 00
History of the Dominion of Canada (Clement)	16¾	50
High School Arithmetic	16¾	60
Arithmetic for High Schools (De Lury)	13½	60
High School Algebra	16¼	75
Elements of Algebra (McLellan)	15¾	75
Elementary Plane Geometry (Baker)	9	50
Geometry for Schools, Theoretical (Baker)	12½	75
High School Euclid (J. S. McKay) and Thompson	10 7/10	50
First Latin Book and Reader	18 6/10	1 00
Primary Latin Book and Reader	20½	1 00
Hagarty's Latin Grammar	19 8/10	1 00
White's First Greek Book	20¼	1 25
High School Beginner's Greek Book	22 1/10	1 50
High School French Grammar and Reader	19¼	1 00
High School German Grammar and Reader	20½	1 00
High School Physical Science, Part I	10 4/10	50
High School Physical Science, Part II	17 7/10	75
High School Chemistry	10 6/10	50
High School Botany, Part II	13 4/10	60
High School Bookkeeping	16	60
Commercial Course in Practical Bookkeeping	15½	40
High School Cadet Drill Manual	9	40
High School Euclid (J. S. McKay)	10 4/10	75

These cost prices include neither the cost of plates nor royalties.

INSPECTION.

The system of inspection of text books on behalf of the Department has been entirely inadequate. The officers of the Government who have performed this duty have not had sufficient knowledge of the technical questions involved, have not been encouraged to make a special study of modern improvements in book-making and have not been specially remunerated for the extra duties imposed upon them. Your Commissioners would recommend that a special officer be appointed for this work at a special salary. Only thus can the Department protect itself and the public keep the standard of its books equal to the best elsewhere. Such an officer should have a library of his own to which should be added as they appear all the leading text books published in the United States or Great Britain. It should be part of his duty to keep in touch with the Department and also with the teachers and inspectors. He will thus discover early any defects in the books which are being sent out to the schools.

Free Text Books.

Everyone now favors a system of free education. A free school should include free equipment for the school—maps, globes, etc., etc., are now supplied free. And there seems no valid reason why text books and other school supplies should not be so provided. Indeed, there are many cogent reasons, which suggest themselves on a moment's reflection, why they should be so supplied. Objections here, as in other quarters, readily disappear before the basic principle that education is maintained in the general interests of the whole Province rather than for the individual or for any particular locality.

The evidence concerning free book systems now in vogue in many States and in the leading cities in the United States, in the City of Toronto and in the Province of Manitoba indicates that this is a subject to which the Department of Education should direct its serious attention. The success of a free text book system depends almost entirely on those who administer it. The teachers must exercise a watchful care over books to see that they are kept clean and in good condition. In Toronto and Kingston, cleanliness is aided by supplying a new manilla cover for each book twice a year. The evidence from these two cities as regards durability under the system is in strong contrast with that from Hamilton and Brantford. This emphasises the point mentioned above, that much depends upon those administering the system.

The advantages of a system of free text books will be found admirably set forth in the evidence given by Inspector Odell, Inspector Hughes and Mr. Macdonald of Kingston.

There is a marked tendency in all progressive communities on this continent towards this system. No place that has ever adopted it has gone back to the old system. It would be of special advantage in the newer and more sparsely settled districts in Ontario.

In Ontario, a beginning might be made by supplying readers and other public school books to all school boards at cost. Later on readers might be supplied to rural schools free of charge. The rural school boards purchase their books and supplies in such small quantities that they are not in a position to secure as close prices as the school board in a city the size of Toronto. All the evidence brought before your Commissioners indicates that on public school books alone, the Government might purchase for the school boards at a very large saving annually. In the State of Delaware, the books are supplied directly from the publishers to the school boards, but all bills are sent to the State treasurer, paid by him and the amount deducted from the annual grant. This system, with slight modifications, might be found admirably suited to this Province.

We append herewith a digest of the experts' report on the cost of the readers; the Secretary's report of the procedure and meetings; a short history of the Ontario text books prepared by him; a list of the selections in the readers which are believed to be still in copyright; a communication from Mr. Fletcher, Deputy Minister of Education for Manitoba, explaining their system of free text books; a schedule of the cost of text books and supplies in the City of Toronto.

All of which is respectfully submitted.

THOS. W. CROTHERS,
JOHN A. COOPER.

TORONTO, January 31st, 1907.

APPENDIX I.

CostT OF READERS AS ESTIMATED BY THE VARIOUS EXPERTS, PLATES BEING
SUPPLIED FREE BY THE DEPARTMENT.

	(1) Grantham.	(2) Southam.	(3) Fleming.	(4) Can. Pub. Co.	(5) Brainard.
	cts.	cts.	cts.	cts.	cts.
Part I	4.50	5.00	6.10	4.10	5.50
Part II	6.00	6.00	6.90	5.75	6.50
Second..........	11.25	10.50	9.50	7.75	10.00
Third...........	12.33	13.00	11.33	10.50	11.00
Fourth..........	12.50	15.00	13.75	12.00	11.00
	46.58	49.50	47.58	40.00	44.00

NOTE.—Numbers 1, 3 and 5 are for thread-sewing; 2 and 4 are for wire-
sewing, all estimates include printers' and binders' profits.

	Average of expert's estimates.	Present wholesale price.	Present retail price.
	cents per copy.	cts.	cts.
Part I	5.04	7.50	10
Part II	6.23	11.25	15
Second	9.80	15.00	20
Third................................	11.63	22.50	30
Fourth	12.85	30.00	40

	Estimated annual sales.	Cost to print.	Cost to consumer.
		$	$
Part I	90,000	4,536	9,000
Part II............................ ...	70,000	4,361	10,500
Second	37,000	3,626	7,400
Third................................	33,000	3,838	9,900
Fourth	17,000	2,185	6,800
		18,546	43,600

APPENDIX II.

SECRETARY'S REPORT.

TORONTO, Jan. 29th, 1907.

T. W. CROTHERS, Esq., K.C.,
  Chairman, Text Book Commission.

SIR,—I have the honor to submit herewith a report of the proceedings of the Text Book Commission.

The Text Book Commission met for organization in the office of the Honourable Dr. Pyne, Minister of Education, at 10 o'clock on July 20th, 1906.

Those present were:—
Mr. T. W. Crothers, K.C., Chairman.
Mr. John A. Cooper.
A. C. Casselman, Secretary.
G. Lynch-Staunton, K.C., Counsel.

The Commission was addressed by Dr. A. H. U. Colquhoun, Deputy Minister of Education, and Dr. John Seath, Superintendent of Education.

The Commission discussed methods of procedure and gave instructions to the Secretary to procure a room at the Education Department in which to hold the sessions of the Commission.

It was decided to prepare a list of questions on text books to be sent to the Inspectors of Public Schools and to the Head Masters of High Schools.

On July 31st, 1906, the Commission met at the office of the Secretary and discussed the questions prepared.

According to instructions a circular letter was ordered to be printed embodying these questions. A copy was sent to each Inspector of Public Schools on August 22nd, 1906, and the next day one was sent to each Head Master of a High School and Collegiate Institute.

A circular letter was also sent to the Secretary of the Public School Board in the cities of Hamilton, Toronto, Kingston and Brantford.

Another circular was sent to the Principals of twenty-two leading Public Schools in the Province.

Replies were received from thirty-nine (39) of the ninety-five (95) Inspectors and from twenty-seven (27) of the one hundred and forty Principals of High Schools and Collegiate Institutes.

The Secretaries of the Board of Education in the four cities replied, and those from Brantford and Kingston gave evidence before the Commission. The cities of Hamilton and Toronto were represented before the Commission by their Inspectors, Mr. Ballard and Mr. Hughes respectively. Mr. Hughes sent me a copy of each printed form used by the Board of Education in supplying free text books to the pupils.

Replies were received from but five of the twenty-two Principals of Public Schools.

Although the number of replies in some cases were not as large as anticipated, yet those who took the trouble to answer the questions asked, did so in a manner that convinced the Commission that there was abundant evidence to proceed with the investigation along the lines first determined upon.

The thanks of the Commission are tendered to those school officials who replied to the circular sent out.

2a T. B.

Many of the Inspectors and Teachers were dissatisfied with the binding and paper in the books, as indicated by their answers.

The Commission met again on the 5th of September and studied carefully the answers received to the circulars. It was decided to get Dr. F. B. Allan, of the University of Toronto, to make a chemical analysis of the paper of several of the authorized books and also of the paper in some American and British text books.

Mr. Geo. R. Byford, a binder, was engaged to report upon the binding of the authorized books.

The Commission adjourned to meet on the 19th of September for the hearing of evidence. The witnesses to be called were A. E. Coombs, Head Master of Newmarket High School, Albert O'Dell, Inspector of Public Schools for the County of Northumberland, Thomas Carscadden, Head Master of Galt Collegiate Institute, Dr. Fred. B. Allan, Lecturer in Chemistry, University of Toronto, Geo. Byford, bookbinder, Toronto, Richard Southam, President of the Mail Job Printing Co.

Before the public meeting on the 19th of September, I had typewritten a digest of the laws regarding text books in the States of the United States.

Mr. James Macdonald, the Junior Counsel, examined the agreements and correspondence in the Education Department and enlarged upon data contained in the return presented to the Legislature last session. His work aided the Commission very materially.

The first public meeting took place at 10 o'clock in the forenoon of the 19th of September, at the Education Department. Mr. Clarkson W. James took the official stenographic report of the evidence given by the above witnesses. His excellent transcription of the evidence taken before the Commission speaks for itself.

The next meeting of the Commission took place on Sept. 25th, 1906, when the following persons gave evidence: —

Frank N. Nudel, Assistant Registrar of the Education Dept.

Arthur C. Paull, Clerk of Records of the Education Dept.

John Macdonald, Secretary Board of Education, Kingston.

A. K. Bunnell, Secretary Public School Board, Brantford.

The Commission met again on Sept. 26th, 1906, when William C. Flint, S. C. Woodland and C. R. Hurst, delegates from Chapter No. 28 of the Bookbinder's Union appeared and gave evidence. The following were called and examined: —

J. F. Ellis, paper dealer, Toronto.

W. H. Ballard, Inspector Public Schools, Hamilton.

James L. Hughes, Chief Inspector of Schools, Toronto.

On the 24th of October the following gave evidence: —

H. M. Grantham, Toronto.

G. N. Morang, Publisher, Toronto.

John C. Saul, Mgr. of the Education Department, Morang & Co.

Frank Wise, President of the Macmillan Co. of Canada, Toronto.

On October 25th, the following gave evidence: —

A. W. Thomas, of the Copp, Clark Co., Publishers, Toronto.

E. M. Trowern, Secretary of the Retail Merchants' Association, Toronto.

Albert Britnell, Bookseller, Toronto.

Frederick Carman, Bookseller, Toronto.

E. S. Caswell, of the Methodist Book and Publishing House, Toronto.

Geo. M. Rose, of the Hunter, Rose Co., Publisher, Toronto.

The Commission met again to take evidence on November 5th, 1906, and the following gave evidence: —

Charles B. Fleming, of the Norwood Press, School Book Manufacturers of Norwood, Mass.

On the 6th the following were examined:—

G. N. Morang, H. M. Grantham and John C. Saul.

H. M. Wilkinson, Chief Clerk of the Education Dept., Toronto.

Arthur C. Paull.

On November 7th:—

H. L. Thompson, President of the Copp, Clark Co., Publishers, and W. J. Gage, President of the W. J. Gage Co., Publishers, gave evidence.

On November 8th:—

Dan. A. Rose, Publisher, Toronto, and Wilson F. Brainard, Publishing Expert, New York, gave evidence.

On December 19th, 1906:—

Charles Builder, Secretary, and S. G. Beatty, President of the Canada Publishing Co., gave evidence.

Wallace Nesbitt, K.C., read a statement of W. J. Gage before the Commission. A. F. Rutter, of Warwick Bros. & Rutter, gave evidence, and the Commission adjourned, having taken sufficient evidence upon which to make a report.

I have prepared a short history of text books in the Province of Ontario, and also collected the clauses relating to text books from the various Acts passed by the Legislature of the old Province of Canada and the Legislature of Ontario.

I have corresponded with the Departments of Education of the Provinces of the Dominion regarding text books. In the Province of Manitoba the Provincial Government supplies certain text books free to the pupils. I append an instructive letter from Mr. R. Fletcher, Deputy Minister of Education for Manitoba on the working of the system in that Province that is worthy of perusal. My thanks are due to the various officials in the other Provinces and in the United States that kindly replied to enquiries.

The officials of the Education Department of Ontario gave every aid to the Commission on the intricate text book question.

All of which is respectfully submitted.

                              A. C. CASSELMAN,
                              Secretary to the Commission.

APPENDIX III.

HISTORY OF SCHOOL TEXT BOOKS.

The settlement of Ontario dates from 1784, when the United Empire Loyalists came in large numbers to the Province. These people taught the rudiments of education in the home, the most common book, and in many cases the only one, being the family Bible. In 1789, the inhabitants petitioned Lord Dorchester to establish a seminary at Kingston so that the youth might have the advantage of higher education. He answered the petition by directing the Surveyor-General to set apart eligible portions of lands for the support of schools in all the new settlements.

When the Province of Upper Canada was set apart from Quebec in 1791, one of the first acts of Lieut.-Governor Simcoe was to propose to the home government that schools be established at Kingston and at Niagara, and a University at the Capital. Lower education might be provided by the parents aided by school lands. Higher education must be supplied by the British Government as the cheapness of education in the United States might induce some to send their children there, which would tend to pervert their British principles.

Simcoe, in his eagerness for a large population, admitted many emigrants from the United States with strong republican principles. These generally settled in groups, brought teachers from their old homes and insisted on their children using United States books.

The early missionaries of the Church of England opened schools in their districts, but the great trouble was to get books.

When Dr. John Strachan came to Upper Canada he was much inconvenienced by the want of books. To rectify this defect he compiled several treatises for the use of his pupils at Cornwall and York. His arithmetic published in Montreal in 1809 was the first school book specially prepared for schools in Upper Canada.

Although school books were scarce, many of the wealthier people and many of the larger private schools had libraries. The Ernesttown Academy announces in 1811 that scholars may have the use of the library for 15s. ($3.00). In 1812, Attorney-General Firth's large library of history, politics, law, science, poetry, classics and general literature was sold at York and this furnished an opportunity for many to buy books.

After the campaign of 1812 closed, a school was opened for the militiamen in garrison at Fort Henry at Kingston. All books, pens, paper and ink were provided free.

In 1813 the Rev. John Langhorn, of Ernesttown, presented his collection of books to the social library established at Bath. In 1814, a circulating library was established at Kingston. They offered a large number of children's books in exchange for rags or cash. A library was established at Niagara at an early date. The importance of these libraries to the people will be understood when it is known that they were about the only importers of books for sale to the people.

The first Common Schools Act was passed by the Government of the Province on April 1st, 1816. An annual grant of £6,000 was voted for maintenance. Teachers were to be British subjects, either by birth or naturalization. The trustees were required to report every three months to the District Board of Education the books used and the rules and regulations in force. If the books were not approved by the District Boards, others were to be provided by the subscribers. The Boards were empowered to expend not more than £100 yearly for the purchase of proper books for the use of the common schools of the District and to distribute them in any manner that may seem meet.

Dr. Strachan recommended for boys from 7 to 9 the following books in English:—Mavor's Spelling Book, Enfield's Lessons, Walker's Lessons, Murray's Lessons and Blair's Class Book.

This is the first attempt by government to regulate the kind of books to be used in the schools and also the first instance we have of supplying books free to the schools.

However, Gourlay reports that in scarcely one case in ten are the rules regarding proper school books adhered to, chiefly through neglect of the Trustees and the District Boards. Frequently he observed one pupil with Noah Webster's Spelling Book, while the one next to him was using Lindley Murray's. As the teaching in these days was individual, not in classes, it did not make very much difference if all the pupils had different books. In those early days there were no primers. The letters were printed by the teacher on a piece of smooth board, and after they were learned Mavor's spelling book was used. The Bible was used as a reading book, and in addition Cobb's and Carpenter's spelling books. Later, the English reader was used. Arithmetic was taught from Walkingame's and Daboll's books, both American works. The grammars in use were Lindley Murray's, Kirkham's and later Lennie's. For the first few decades of the 19th century geography was but little taught. The ones used later were Peter Parley's, Morse's and Olney's.

·   Many of these books were American in sentiment and described the American population as the most enlightened and free on the face of the earth, and their laws and institutions superior to any other in the world. This itself was objectionable, but worse still, the same books contained passages particularly hostile to everything British. Olney's geography, perhaps, offended most. Often the teacher was an American who never wearied of instilling into the pupils' minds false ideas regarding the parent state. Dr. Thos. Rolph in his statistical account of Upper Canada published in 1836, speaks strongly on this matter. Dr. Strachan in a statement submitted to Sir Peregrine Maitland, recommending the proposed University, pointed out that loyal youths may seek higher education in the United States and return, not so strongly attached to their native land, because of the calumnies contained in American books and taught in their schools. Dr. Ryerson, during the first few years of his superintendence, made strenuous efforts to place proper books in the hands of the pupils. Indeed one of the causes of the war of 1812 has been attributed to the use of American school books. The rebellion of 1837 was made possible by the sentiments derogatory to British institutions so common in the school books of Upper Canada just before that time. Even as late as June 5th, 1849, a letter from Mr. A. W. B. McDougall, of Pelham, was laid before the Upper Canada Board of Education stating that objectionable American school books were being used in the schools, that "The American Rebel Declaration on Independence of the 4th of July, 1886, is suspended in some Canadian schools, with Lexington and Bunker Hill pictures."

One of the charges of William Lyon Mackenzie against Sir John Colborne was—"causing his District Boards of Education to dictate to the teachers and school trustees what books they may or may not use."

By the School Act of 1824 a general Board of Education for Upper Canada was appointed by Lieut.-Gov. Maitland, with the Rev. Dr. Strachan as President, and as such was practically Superintendent of Education till the Board ceased to exist in 1832. This Board was empowered to spend £150 each year for books to be distributed to the District Boards. Mavor's Spelling Books were sent in quantities to the Boards and 2,000 copies, printed on cards, were contracted for, for the use of township schools.

·   The Select Committee on Education appointed by the House of Assembly in 1829 reported that the difficulties of procuring proper school books operated against the advancement of education in the Province; the encouragement not being sufficient to induce men of capital to embark in the printing and publishing of elementary books on reasonable terms. They advised that encouragement be given to the printing and publishing of elementary books in the Province and in all branches of their manufacture.

·   A Commission of Education in 1839 reported that great care should be taken in the selection of text books. They regretted to find that editions published in the United States are much used throughout the Province, tinctured as they are by principles which cannot be inculcated here without evil results. This Commission recommended that some means should be taken whereby the schools may be provided with text books at a cheap rate from Great Britain, or that a series of compilation or re-publications should be prepared and printed here as the school books appointed to be used in all the schools of the Province.

At the first session of the Parliament of United Canada in 1841, an Educational Bill was passed which authorized the appointment of a Superintendent of Education for the Province. The Act also provided for Township or Parish Commissioners. One of their duties was to prescribe a course of study and the books to be used in the schools within their jurisdiction. The Act also provided that the District Council should be the Board of Education for the District. This Board had power to apportion to each Township or Parish a sum not to exceed £10 in any one year for the purchase of books required.

Under the prerogative of the Crown, Rev. Robert Murray was appointed Assistant Superintendent for Canada West. In his report to the Governor-General he says that the Township Commissioners, except in a few cases, had not attended to their duty in regard to course of study and books to be used. Many of the books were old and antiquated and teachers from the multiplicity of texts cannot teach in classes. Parents in some cases objected to buy books because they contended that the School Bill provided for the supply of books by assessment on the township.

The Bill of 1841 was found to be utterly impracticable and was repealed by the Act of 1843. Rev. R. Murray was appointed Professor of Mathematics in the University of King's College on 25th September, 1844, and Rev. Dr. Ryerson was appointed Assistant Superintendent for Canada West. In the letter of the Provincial Secretary, selecting Dr. Ryerson for this office the first duty mentioned is "to provide proper school books." Having been granted leave of absence, Dr. Ryerson left Canada on Oct. 31st, 1844, about one month after his appointment to study the educational systems prevailing in Great Britain and Ireland and on the Continent, and also in the more advanced States of the American Union. The result of this trip was a "Report on the system of Public Elementary Instruction for Upper Canada," dated 27th March, 1846.

This report was lengthy and fully discussed every phase of the educational question. The proper kind of school books were discussed along with the best methods of teaching the various subjects. This valuable report formed the basis of all school legislation for some years and the school law of 1846 was founded directly upon it.

This law of 1846 provided for a Superintendent of Schools for Upper Canada and defined his duties. It provided for a Board of Education to advise the Superintendent upon all measures he may submit to them. They were to examine and recommend or disapprove of all books submitted to them for use in schools. The District Superintendents were to see that only such books as recommended by the Board of Education were used. The trustees of each section had the power to choose from the list furnished by the Board. This Act also provided for the formation of school libraries.

Dr. Ryerson found that the best series of school books was that known as the Irish National series, and at the first meeting of the Board of Education on July 21st, 1846, it was ordered that Dr. Ryerson should enquire at what prices the Commissioners of National Education in Ireland would engage to furnish the Board with their National Series of books, and also if they would grant permission to the Board to reprint editions of the books, if required. The Commissioners replied that they would supply the books at prices fixed for poor schools in Ireland, and permission was granted for reprinting the books in Canada.

The Board of Education recommended the Irish National Series for use in schools in Upper Canada on Oct. 27th, 1846. They then advertised for tenders for reprinting or the importing the Irish editions, fixing the maximum price for each publication. The Board after receiving several tenders granted permission to any publisher to import or publish the series upon conditions imposed by the Board.

To secure the uniform use of these books took some years, but Dr. Ryerson was equal to the task. By circular he explained to the District Superintendents the value of uniformity in text books and used every means to get the Irish series to gradually replace the others as they were used up. The Superintendents of the Niagara and Brock Districts were somewhat persistent in their application to use American books, but Dr. Ryerson was firm and took occasion to point out the superiority of the Irish National series.

No part of the Act of 1846 was assailed as much as the clause forbidding the use of foreign books. Dr. Ryerson and the Provincial Board were made the targets of abuse, yet no one dared to publicly advocate their use. The books were excluded because they were anti-British. They were unlike the books of any other nation. The books of Germany, France and Great Britain contain nothing hostile to the institutions of any other nation. Dr. Ryerson said further that in precisely those parts of Upper Canada where United States school books had been used most extensively, there the spirit of the insurrection of 1837 and 1838 was most prevalent.

Before introducing the School Bill of 1850, Hon. Francis Hincks decided to test public opinion with regard to the Acts of 1846 and 1847 by sending a circular letter to District Superintendents, teachers and others, asking their opinion. The replies to these must have been particularly gratifying to Dr. Ryerson as far as school books were concerned, because with hardly an exception everyone expressed himself in favor of the Provincial Board selecting the books for the sake of uniformity and spoke highly of the educational value of the Irish National Series. In the Act of 1850, these provisions were retained, but the Provincial Board of Education was changed to a Council of Public Instruction of nine members, which in 1874 was increased to eighteen, nine of which were elective.

In 1854 Dr. Ryerson was able to report that the Irish National Readers and the National Arithmetic were used in nearly all the schools of the Province. They acquired this degree of popularity under the sanction of the Council by their own intrinsic excellence, by their cheapness, and by their suitability for the purpose of daily instruction. It was exceedingly gratifying to have produced this result without compulsion or proscription.

One of the greatest aids to general education in Upper Canada was the system of Public Libraries authorized by the Act of 1850. Libraries might be established in townships or school sections. The Superintendent issued a catalogue of books from which selections might be made. Any section or township to share in the grant had to raise locally an amount equal to the grant from the Legislature. In 1855 the amount voted for Library purposes was £2,500. In addition to this, Dr. Ryerson advised that a grant be given for aiding Public and Grammar Schools to buy maps, globes and apparatus on the same terms as the establishment of Libraries. The Legislature concurred in this proposal and granted £2,500.

Provision for the purchase and distribution of books, maps, globes and apparatus was made by the Council of Public Instruction, and the Superintendent through the Depository. These articles were purchased in large quantities at the lowest rate, and sold at a much cheaper rate than through

the ordinary trade channels. At the time of the organization of the Depository, it was absolutely a necessary institution to aid the people to get
cheaply and easily whatever they required for Library or School. It
created a love for good books, and a market that the provincial booksellers
subsequently reaped a large benefit from when there was no longer any
reason for its continuance.

As stated before, Dr. Ryerson's aim was to secure uniformity in text
books, and if possible not more than one authorized book in a subject.
These two principles ensured the lowest price for books.

Another aim he had, was to make the books Canadian in sentiment,
to secure Canadian authors, and to have the books manufactured in Canada. In doing this he wished to protect the public, the publisher and the
author. The public was secured by government approval of matter, paper,
typography, binding and price. The publisher was secured by giving him
the exclusive privilege of publication for one year. The author was secured and encouraged by the publisher agreeing to pay the author a fair
royalty for the first edition, and for each subsequent revision.

In April, 1869, a regulation was issued containing this clause "All
new or revised editions, after January last, 1870, shall be printed in Canada, on paper made in the Dominion, and shall be bound therein."

In 1860, the Irish National Arithmetics were changed to the Decimal
system, lately adopted in Canada. In 1869 and 1870, Barnard Smith's
arithmetic was adapted to Canadian schools.

The Irish National Series of Readers, authorized in 1846, had been
useful and instructive books. Although not prepared for Canadian schools
they were the best set of readers published anywhere. On their introduction they were assailed because certain localities wished to use American
. Books.

During the last few years of their use the Canadian National sentiment had grown, and now an agitation arose for a Canadian National series. It can never probably be ascertained how much of this is due to Dr.
Ryerson and his school book policy. This much is known. He took charge
of the education of the youth of Upper Canada at a critical period in its
history. When he put off his mantle, the Dominion was an accomplished
reality beyond the shadow of a doubt.

The new readers "The Red Series" were prepared under the direction
of the Council of Public Instruction, by Dr. J. H. Sangster, Dr. McCaul,
Dr. Barclay and Dr. Ormiston. They were authorized as the Canadian
Series of Readers on January 4th, 1868, the copyright being vested in the
Chief Superintendent. They consisted of the First Book, parts I and II,
Second Reader, Third Reader, Fourth Reader and Fifth Reader. In 1870,
"The Advanced Reader" and a Spelling book called a "Companion to the
Readers," were published. James Campbell and Son, published this ser-
ies exclusively for three years. Mr. Warwick then shared in the publi-
cation, and in 1878, Adam Miller & Company, now the W. J. Gage Co.,
were allowed the same privilege, later another firm secured the right.
These readers continued in use until 1883.

In 1864, Lovell's Geography and "A History of Canada and the other
British Provinces," were authorized for schools. These books, with few
exceptions, mark the beginning of Canadian authorship in school books,
being written by Dr. J. George Hodgins, at that time Deputy Superintendent of Education.

These and revised editions of them continued in use for a number of
years, and to-day it would not be difficult to find many teachers and edu-

cationists to say that no better books on these subjects have been published since, in Canada.

When Mr. Crooks was Minister of Education, the Education Department made it known that the Canadian Series of Readers would be replaced by a new series. Three series were prepared and submitted to the Department for approval and authorization. These were—

(1) The Canadian Series, published by W. J. Gage & Co., being a publication of a publishing house in Scotland, adapted for Canadian schools.

(2) The Royal Readers, also published in Scotland, by Thos. Nelson & Sons, of Edinburgh, adapted for Canadian Schools, and published by James Campbell & Son.

(3) The Royal Canadian series wholly prepared in Ontario, and published by the Canada Publishing Co.

The first two series were recommended by the Central Committee, and were authorized on June 30th, 1863. For about a year before this the three firms had agents at every Teachers' Convention, seeking resolutions in favor of their series. The whole country was in a turmoil over the reader question. When Mr. Ross became Minister of Education he wished to have but one series. A composite series was proposed as a remedy, but the composition of the series agreed upon was not acceptable to the publishing houses interested. Mr. Ross then gave notice to the publishers, that the two series would be deauthorized as soon as a new series could be prepared, under the direction of the Education Department. The editorial work was placed in charge of John E. Bryant, William Little and L. E. Embree.

The series was authorized on the 26th day of November, 1884, and publication given to Thomas Nelson & Son, of Edinburgh, W. J. Gage & Co., and the Canada Publishing Co. These firms had the sole right of publication for ten years. Thomas Nelson and Son disposed of their right to the Copp, Clark Co., for an annual payment of $3,000. The agreements with these firms expired on the 26th of November, 1894, but another agreement was not made until March 26, 1896, giving a further exclusive right to these three firms for ten years from July 1st, 1896. The cause of delay in renewing the agreement was occasioned by the publishers of the Ontario Readers buying the exclusive right to use certain selections contained in the readers, for which neither the editors nor the Minister of Education, Mr. Ross, made arrangements to secure from the authors and publishers of these in Great Britain. Mr. Ross was in a measure compelled to renew the former agreement, or prepare a new set of readers. This agreement was renewed on July 1st, 1906, for a term of six months, by Dr. Pyne, the present Minister of Education.

It is of some interest to read the parts of the bills passed by the Legislature of Upper Canada relating to text books.

Session of 1841.

The District Council was to be the Board of Education for the District. One of their duties was "To apportion *to each Township and Parish*, a sum not exceeding *ten pounds*, in any one year, to be expended in the purchase of such books as may be *required*. One of the duties of the seven School Commissioners of each township was—"To regulate for each school respectively the course of study to be followed in such school, and the books to be used therein."

By the School Act of 1846, a Chief Superintendent of Education was provided for. One of his duties was—"To discourage the use of unsuitable and improper books in the Schools, or School Libraries, and to use all lawful means to provide for and recommend the use of uniform and approved text books in all the schools."

The General Board of Education were "To examine and recommend, or disapprove of all Books, Plans, or Forms which may be submitted to them, with a view to their use in schools; and no portion of the Government Grant shall be given in aid of any school in which any book is used, and which has been disapproved by the Board, and of which disapproval public notice has been given."

By this act, Common School Trustees were empowered "To select from a list of text books made out by the Board of Education for Upper Canada, under the sanction of the Governor in Council, as hereinbefore provided, the text books which shall be used in the school."

By the School Act of 1850, the Trustees of each School Section were empowered "To do whatever they may judge expedient for procuring Apparatus and Text Books for their school." And also, "To see that no unauthorized books are used in the school, but that the pupils are duly supplied with a uniform series of text books, sanctioned and recommended according to law."

The Board of School Trustees of each city and town had similar powers to Trustees of rural sections.

This act provided that the Local Superintendents and the Board of Trustees of the County Grammar School had power "To select from a list of text books recommended, or authorized by the Council of Public Instruction, such books as they shall think best adapted for the use of the Common Schools of such County or Circuit; and to ascertain and recommend the best facilities for procuring such books."

It will be seen that by this Act the Trustees as representatives of the people had power to procure text books in any way they may deem expedient, but manner in which such expenses were to be raised was to be left to a public meeting of the tax payers, called for the purpose, and if all the expenses is not provided for, the Trustees may raise the amount by voluntary subscription, or by rates on the parents sending children to school, or by rates on all taxable property of the school section.

By the Act of 1853, to amend the law relating to Grammar Schools, the Board of Trustees of such Grammar School were empowered to levy rates to supply apparatus, maps, text books, registers, and for any other necessary expenses of the schools.

School Law Regarding Text Books in Compendium of School Law of 1878.

Inspectors are "To prevent the use of unauthorized, and to recommend the use of authorized books in each school, and to acquire and give information as to the manner in which such authorized books can be obtained, and the economy and advantage of using them."

Trustees' duties are "To see that no unauthorized books are used in the school, and that the pupils are duly supplied with a uniform series of authorized text books, sanctioned and recommended by the Education Department," and also "To do whatever they may deem expedient in regard to procuring apparatus, maps, prizes, library and text books for their school."

By this Act (37 Victoria) School Boards of cities, towns and villages were given power "to procure suitable maps, apparatus, text and prize books," and to lay before the Municipal Council of the city, town or village, an estimate of the sums which they think requisite "for procuring suitable apparatus, and text, prize and library books for such schools."

The Education Department was empowered "To examine, and at its discretion, recommend or disapprove of text books for the use of schools or books for school libraries and prizes."

By the *Public Schools' Act*, of 1885, the duties of Trustees of Public Schools are "To see that no unauthorized books are used in the school, and that the pupils are duly supplied with a uniform series of authorized text books, sanctioned by the Education Department,—and to do whatever they may deem expedient in regard to procuring apparatus, maps, prize and library books for their school."

It will be observed that under this Act, the power that Trustees formerly held in regard to the purchase of text books is taken away. That is Trustees no longer had the power to supply books free to pupils, meeting the expense by a general tax on the ratepayers. This retrograde portion of act was not repealed until 1891.

By the *"Public Schools' Act*, of 1891,"* the Board of Trustees of cities, towns and incorporated villages shall have power:—"To collect at their discretion, from the parents or guardians of the pupils attending any Public School under their charge, a sum not exceeding twenty cents per month, per pupil, to defray the cost of text books, stationery and other school supplies, or at their discretion, to purchase for the use of pupils attending such schools, text books, stationery and other supplies at the expense of the corporation."

This privilege was not granted to rural public schools until the Act of 1896, which says, "It shall be the duty of the Trustees of all public schools, and they shall have the power to collect at their discretion from the parents or guardians of the pupils attending school, a sum not exceeding twenty cents per month per pupil, to defray the cost of text books, and other school supplies; or to purchase for the use of pupils, text books and other school supplies at the expense of the corporation."

The Education Department Act of 1901, was amended in 1904, by adding the following: "It shall be the duty of the Minister of Education, and he shall have power: "Also to apportion under the provisions of such regulations as may be made by Order in Council all sums of money voted by the Legislative Assembly for aiding public and separate school boards in rural districts to furnish certain text books free of cost."

The regulations of the Education Department, under which aid is granted for Free Text Books, are as follows:—

Free Text Books.

108. Any Public or Separate School Board in rural districts may by a resolution, decide to have certain text books purchased for the pupils free of cost to the parents or guardians.

109. The text books that may be provided in this way shall include only such readers as may be authorized for use in the Public or Separate Schools.

110. Any rural School Board which provides such text book free for the scholars shall be entitled to a grant, equivalent to one-half of the amount expended, from whatever money may be appropriated for the purpose by the Legislature.

111. Trustees shall have the right to purchase from either wholesale or retail dealers, and on such conditions as they may consider most desirable.

112. The Trustees are required to make proper arrangements for the care of the text books which become the property of the Boards; and the principal or a Teacher of the school shall be Librarian, and act under such instructions as may be given by the Minister of Education, the Inspector or the Trustees of the school concerned.

113. All applications for Legislative aid must be made, through the Public (or Separate) School Inspector, to the Minister of Education by the Trustees, who shall give all necessary information regarding the books purchased together with such vouchers from the booksellers as may be required. The Inspector will make application to the Education Department on a form to be provided.

114. All applications by trustees for Legislative aid must be made before the first day of October in each year, and after the books have been received. Any purchases made after that date, and before the same date of the succeeding year may be included in applications made the following year.

In 1904, the High Schools' Act was amended by adding to the duties of Trustees of High Schools or Collegiate Institutes the following:—"To collect at their discretion, from the parents or guardians of the pupils attending school, a sum not exceeding twenty-five cents per month per pupil, to defray the cost of text books and other school supplies," or to purchase for the use of pupils, text books and other school supplies at the expense of the corporation."

In 1906, the duties of Trustees regarding text books was repealed, and the following substituted therefor—

"To purchase, in case they deem it expedient, for the use of pupils attending school, text books and other school supplies; and, at their discretion, either to furnish the same to the pupils free of charge, or to collect for the use thereof from the respective parents or guardians of the pupils, a sum not exceeding twenty cents per month per pupil to defray the cost thereof."

APPENDIX IV.

REPORT AS TO COPYRIGHT OF SELECTIONS IN ONTARIO READERS COMPILED FROM EVIDENCE GIVEN BEFORE THE COMMISSION AND CORRESPONDENCE IN THE EDUCATION DEPARTMENT.

First Reader, Part I. No selections copyrighted.

First Reader, Part II. In 1900 The Copp Clark Co. secured permission for the three publishers of the Readers to use "My Doll," p. 29, and "What Birdie Says," p. 43. Mr. Saul says there is nothing in Part II now in copyright.

Second Reader. "The Baby," p. 16. On Dec. 11th, 1893, Mr. Gage secured copyright of this article from Chatto and Windus for *himself* solely for £1. On June 12th, 1893, Chatto and Windus extended the right to the other two firms *for 4 years* from June 1st, 1895, for payment of one guinea per annum. "Any further responsibility to be at our discretion." Chatto and Windus. "Grandpapa," p. 100, secured by Copp, Clark & Co. from the McMillan Co. "Good Night and Good Morning," p. 103, by Lord Houghton; bought by Mr. Gage *for himself* for one guinea from John Murray, on Dec. 19, 1893. "Two Sides to a Story," p. 102; bought from The Religious

Tract Society, *for himself* for one guinea on Dec. 20, 1893. "The Lazy Frog," for p. 120, called in the authority "The Gifted Frog," bought by Mr. Gage *for himself* for one guinea from George T. Browne, publisher of London Illustrated Reader. "The Squirrel," p. 83, by Norman McLeod; bought by Mr. Gage for the three firms for one guinea per annum for each firm. "Authorized to forbid on my behalf publication by any other firm for *three years* from date." Wm. Isbister (Charles Burnet & Co.), Jan. 1, 1895.

Second Reader. "The Squirrel," bought from T. D. M. Burnside, London, who probably represents heirs of Norman McLeod. Mr. Saul says "Tea," p. 43, and "Coffee," p. 68, from Blackwood's II Reader is probably in copyright. "The Lion," p. 72, from Blackie's III Reader; bought by Mr. Morang. "The Ostrich," p. 110, from Blackie's Third Reader; bought by Mr. Morang. The chances are that "A True Hero," p. 135, by Thomas Carlyle, was in copyright in 1885.

Third Reader. "The Hippopotamus," p. 55. "The Black Douglas," p. 83, from Battersea III Reader, purchased by Mr. Gage *for himself* for two guineas, which includes the price paid for the history of "A Piece of Coal," bought from Edward Stanford on Dec. 6, 1893. "The Farmer and the Fox," p. 71, by Froude. Mr. Gage applied but could not get exclusive right; at least no charge made—free. "Ho! Breakers on the Weather Bow," by Swain; in copyright yet (Saul); no record of any purchase. "A Narrow Escape," p. 111; probably copyrighted (Saul), from III English Fourth Reader. Original probably not copyrighted. "The Monster of the Nile," p. 173, by Baker; bought by Copp, Clark Co. from Macmillans; "Expires next year" (Saul). "The Thermometer," p. 179. "Heat," p. 194. Both from III English Reader; (Probably copyrighted) (Saul); original probably not copyrighted.

Third Reader. "Zlobane," p. 149, by Mrs. Gustafson; in copyright (Saul). No record of holder. "Trust in God and Do the Right," by Norman McLeod, p. 155; bought by Mr. Gage for three firms, Jan. 1st, 1895. "The Burial of Moses," Mrs. Alexander, p. 240. "The Road to the Trenches," Lushington, p. 221; bought by The Copp, Clark Co. from Macmillans, 12th July, 1900.

Fourth Reader. "Tom Brown," p. 17, Hughes. "Loss of the Birkenhead," p. 23, Doyle. "Discovery of Albert Nyanza," p. 77, Baker. "The Two Breaths," p. 214, Kingsley. "Song of the River," p. 295, Bright; were bought by The Copp, Clark Co. from Macmillans, 12th July, 1900. for the three firms. Probably some of these are out of copyright now. "Riding Together," p. 231, Wm. Morris; bought by Mr. Gage for one guinea; exclusive right, Dec. 14th, 1893. Other two firms not given rights. James Bain got consent of Mr. Morris for the Education Department to use any of the poems of Mr. Morris. "The Ride from Ghent to Aix," by Browning, p. 285, and "A Forced Recruit at Solferino," by Mrs. Browning, p. 287; bought by Mr. Gage *for himself*, the privilege to reprint from Smith, Elder & Co., but not exclusive right, November 28th, 1893. Mr. Bain reported that this firm refused Mr. Gage, but a letter to Mr. Gage shows as above. Smith, Elder & Co. granted to the Education Department privilege to use any of the extracts from Mr. and Mrs. Browning's Poems for a payment of £10 10s.

Fourth Reader. "Lament of the Irish Emigrant," by Lady Dufferin, p. 52; bought by Mr. Gage, December 19th, 1893, for 2 guineas; sole right for *himself* from John Murray. "The Black Prince at Cressy," p. 107, by Dean Stanley; bought by Mr. Gage for *himself* for £2 2s., Dec. 19th, 1893. "Shakespeare," p. 303, by Max Muller; bought by Mr. Gage for £5; exclusive copyright Dec. 19th, 1893. F. McMillan, of No. 7 Norham Garden, Oxford, gave the privilege. "The Fixed Stars," p. 93, by Proctor; bought by Dr. Bain for Education Department. "History of a Piece of Coal," p. 171 and 179; bought by Gage from E. Stanford, December 6, 1893, *for himself* only. 'Clouds, Rains and Rivers," p. 54, by Tyndall; purchased by Dr. Bain for Education Department. "Before Sedan," p. 199, by Dobson. Dr. Bain says Kegan, Paul & Co. sold this to Mr. Gage for one guinea, although it does not appear in the Gage correspondence put in to the Commission. "To Florence Nightingale," p. 230, by Edwin Arnold. Dr. Bain reports this sold to Mr. Gage, but no record in the Gage correspondence handed in. Mr. Saul says the following are in copyright: "The Little Midshipman," p. 25, by Jean Ingelow. "Among the Thousand Islands," p. 200, by Miss Machar, Kingston. "After Death in Arabia," p. 272, by Edwin Arnold. No record of purchase although Mr. Gage is reported as purchasing Arnold's other poem on p. 230, "The Founders of Upper Canada," by Ryerson, p. 282, in copyright. Held probably by Methodist Book Room.

The articles from Tennyson in these readers are all out of copyright now.

The word (Saul) after the statements in this report refers to the evidence given by John C. Saul who was examined on this matter.

It will be observed that Mr. Gage, in several cases, purchased the right to use certain selections for himself only. It appears then that The Copp, Clark Co. and The Canada Publishing Co. were publishing these selections without authority from the authors or the British publishers. Further, the privilege of using some selections was granted only for a stated term which has expired several years ago. Smith, Elder & Co. granted the privilege to Mr. Gage to reprint selections from the poems of Mr. and Mrs. Browning but not to the Copp, Clark Co. or The Canada Publishing Co. The same firm, Smith, Elder & Co., granted the same privilege to the Education Department.

APPENDIX V.

FREE TEXT BOOKS IN MANITOBA.

WINNIPEG, December 12th, 1906.

A. C. CASSELMAN, ESQ.,
    Secretary Text Book Commission,
        Education Department, Toronto, Ont. ·

SIR,—Your favor of the 4th received. The law for supplying free text books to our schools was passed at the 1903 session of the Legislature. I enclose herewith a copy of the Bill.

I understand that the legislation emanated from the Department of Education, but it had the approval of our Advisory Board and leading educationists.

I enclose herewith a list of the books which we are at present supplying. You will observe that we have begun at the bottom and are supplying the books for the junior grades. In our rural schools, in particular, the majority of the pupils are in the lower grades, many of them never getting beyond grade V or VI before quitting school.

By purchasing the books in quantities we are able to make arrangements whereby we can get the books at a lower rate, I believe, than the retail dealers.

In the case of "Morang's" Arithmetic, Book I, for instance, our contract price is considerably below the price at which the retail dealer can purchase the book.

The "requisition" for free texts is made out by the teacher and signed by both the teacher and the secretary-treasurer of the district, and at present we fill these requisitions whenever the same are received, provided as above, that the request is made on the form supplied by us. We send the books by express prepaid to the nearest railway point, and in some cases where the district is far back from the railway, we send the books by mail, postage paid; the requisition comes direct to the Department of Education and the books are furnished absolutely free.

The teacher is the custodian of the books and the ownership is vested in the district, the trustees having a certain responsibility, as you will see by the text of the Bill.

A pupil, on the promotion to a higher class, is sometimes given a book which has already been used. If a child loses or destroys a book before it has had the ordinary wear and tear which represents its life, then the parents of the child are supposed to replace the book.

I do not know that any complaints were made by the retail dealers at the time the free text system was inaugurated. We began with the readers and arrangements were made whereby each retail dealer could turn in his stock of these readers and receive value therefor.

So far, we find, speaking generally, the free texts are carefully used, and as the books are loaned to the pupils the children learn a lesson in the careful handling of the same, which aparently they were not learning when supplying their own books.

The Department favors the principle, and I believe the public generally favors it also. Any parent who wishes may buy books for his child, the use of the free text books not being compulsory. The advantage to the school lies in the fact that many children were not supplied with books previous to the inauguration of free texts, and it was not unusual for a teacher to have a class of six or eight with only two or three readers among the class. I cannot say, at the present time, just how far the Department may extend the system.

I believe some few districts are purchasing pencils, paper, ink, etc., for the school and paying for the same out of the general fund.

If I have not made any point as clear as you may wish, kindly advise me, and I will try again.

I have the honour to be,

Sir,

Your obedient servant,

(Sgd.) R. FLETCHER,

Chief Clerk.

DEPARTMENT OF EDUCATION, MANITOBA.

2. Section 48 of the 'Public Schools Act" is hereby amended by adding the following paragraph thereto:

(c) To see that suitable accommodation is provided for all free text books furnished by the Department of Education, and furthermore to see that the teacher or teachers keep an accurate statement of the receipts and distribution of such books in the records furnished by the Department, and that they fulfil all their duties in regard to such books.

3. Section 125 of the said Act is hereby amended by adding thereto the following paragraph:

(*k*) To see that suitable accommodation is provided for all free text books furnished by the Department of Education, and furthermore to see that the teacher or teachers keep an accurate statement of the receipt and distribution of such books in the records furnished by the Department, and that they fulfil all their duties in regard to such books.

4. Section 194 of the said Act is hereby amended by adding thereto the following paragraph:

(1) To keep an accurate record of the receipt and distribution of all free text books furnished by the Department of Education. To see that pupils take proper care of such books and also to see that every regulation with regard to such books is properly enforced.

S. B. Folio......................   Shipped via........................

                           Date................................

Department of Education, Manitoba.

Requisition.

The following books are required for the use of the pupils of the School District of......................Number.............................

Name of Book.	Number Required.

Certified correct

                       ....
                             Teacher or Principal.

                       ....
                              Secretary-Treasurer.

                             ....Post Office.

Books will be sent to the Secretary-Treasurer. Give nearest Railway Station below.

                       ....

                       ....

3 т. в.

Department of Education, Manitoba.

FORM OF AGREEMENT.

We, the Trustees of the School District of.....................................
Number........................do hereby agree to provide suitable accommodation for all Free Text Books furnished by the Department of Education.

We do further agree to see that the Teacher or Teachers fulfil all duties with regard to Free Texts, and that they keep a proper account of all books in the records furnished by the Department.

....
....
....
                                                     Trustees.

Dated this............day of...............190

Department of Education, Manitoba.

NOTICE.

The Department of Education will furnish free to the Trustees, on receipt of a properly certified requisition, the following books:—
Teacher's Record Book of Free Texts.
Principal's Record Book of Free Texts.
Victorian Readers:
    Primer, Grade I. ·
    First Reader, Grade II.
    Second Reader, Grade III.
Bi-Lingual Reader, French-English.
    (For Bi-Lingual Schools only).
Morang's Modern Arithmetic, Book I, Grades IV and V.
Geography: "Our Home and its Surroundings," Grades IV and V.
Royal Atlas for Manitoba Schools, Grades VI, VII and VIII.
                              COLIN H. CAMPBELL,
                         For the Department of Education.

Department of Education, Manitoba.

RECEIPT.

The School District of................................Number.....................
Received from the Department of Education the following books:

Name of Book.	Number of Books.

....
                              Secretary Treasurer
Dated this........................of...............190...
3a T. B.

APPENDIX VI.

Board of Education, Chief Inspector's Office.

COST OF FREE TEXT BOOKS AND SUPPLIES SINCE THEIR FIRST INTRODUCTION
IN TORONTO.

—	Pupils supplied.	Cost of Free Text Books.	Cost of Supplies.
1892	28,345	$4,380*	
1893	28,306	6,927	$10,334
1894	28,938	2,464	6,630
1895	28,877	4,917	6,209
1896	28,983	5,225	4,144
1897	29,390	1,568	3,822
1898	29,771	910	2,586
1899	29,885	1,043	2,101
1900	29,801	2,305	2,666
1901	30,075	2,109	4,119
1902	30,003	2,474	3,570
1903	29,746	2,710	2,853
1904	30,011	2,660	3,529
1905	30,334	4,563	3,740
Totals	412,465	$44,255	$56,303

*Inaugural Expense

Average cost per annum for text books $3,161
Average cost per annum for supplies 4,331
Cost per pupil for text books in 14 years .... 10¾c.
Cost per pupil for supplies in 13 years .... 13½c.

JAMES L. HUGHES,
Chief Inspector.

OFFICIAL REPORT OF THE EVIDENCE TAKEN BEFORE THE TEXT
BOOK COMMISSION AT ITS FIRST SITTING ON WEDNESDAY,
19TH SEPTEMBER, 1906.

MR. T. W. CROTHERS, CHAIRMAN; MR. JOHN A. COOPER, MR. GEORGE LYNCH-
STAUNTON, K.C., OFFICIAL EXAMINER AND COUNSEL; MR. JAMES A. MAC-
DONALD, COUNSEL FOR THE GOVERNMENT, AND MR. A. C. CASSELMAN,
SECRETARY.

Mr. Ernest A. Coombs, Principal Newmarket High School, being duly
sworn by Mr. T. W. Crothers, the Chairman of the Commission, was sub-
jected to the following examination by Mr. Staunton :—
By Mr. G. L. STAUNTON, K.C.
Q.—What is your name in full, Mr. Coombs?
A.—Ernest A. Coombs.
Q.—What is your profession?
A.—I am a High School Teacher and at present, Principal of the New-
market High School.
Q.—Are you a graduate of a University?
A.—Yes. I am a graduate of the University of Toronto.
Q.—You have been in your present position how many years?

A.—I am in my eighth year. I was four years Principal of the Richmond Hill School prior to that.

Q.—In your position have you had any opportunity of observing the durability of the school text books in the High Schools?

A.—Yes, I have.

Q.—As a result of your observations, have you any of those books with you?

A.—I have. (Witness here submits a number of books as exhibits.)

Q.—Have you any complaint to make as to the durability of those books?

A.—Well, there are some of them that are not satisfactory.

Q.—Are you speaking of them as a class?

A.—In a few cases, certain books, the English Grammar, for instance, has not been satisfactory. There are a few others; but the English Grammar is the most notable example that I have.

Q.—Have you a copy of the book here?

A.—I have. (Witness produces copy of Grammar in question.)

Q.—This book was purchased when?

A.—September 4th, 1905; it belonged to one of the girls in the school and cost 75c.; it is a High School Grammar.

Q.—Did you know the pupil that had it?

A.—I did.

Q.—Is that pupil careful with books?

A.—She is.

Q.—This book has been used for how long?

A.—About one year; that is, when I say one year, I mean, of course, that ten months is the actual school term.

Q.—It is pretty well out of business now, is it not?

A.—Yes, I suppose it is judging from its appearance.

Q.—Would you expect that book to last longer than one year?

A.—Yes, it should last three years at the very least. .

Q.—What is the matter with the book, you say it is not sufficiently durable?

A.—The binding and make-up of the book generally, is very unsatisfactory; I could get you an armful of books similar to this sample; and I may say with respect to the Grammar, that I have seen a copy taken from the teacher's room to the class room, and very seldom used, have to be repaired to hold it together in order that it might last out the year.

Q.—What do you say is defective about this book?

A.—There is something wrong with this, I suppose you would call it "mull," that goes across the back; I think that these sections being bound with wire are not as good as if they were sewn in.

Q.—Why do you object to wire being used in the fastening of these books?

A.—Well, for one reason, it rusts; and for another reason, there does not seem to be anything to assist in thoroughly fastening on the cover; there are no tapes, and if tapes were used it would materially strengthen the backs and prevent the books from becoming loose leaved.

Q.—You think, then, Mr. Coombs, that the use of "mull" is of no benefit at all?

A.—No sir, not as far as I can see. I am of the opinion that "mull" is no good whatever. In fact, I have thought that the glue, or whatever is used, seems to rot the "mull" and render it practically useless.

Q.—The substance of your evidence then, would seem to be, that these books should last at least from two to three years, or even longer, with ordinary careful handling, and that they really do not last but one year with ordinary careful handling? Is that what you mean to convey?

A.—Yes, you frequently find that to be the case; but I would not like to put it that strong; it is only the binding that is useless at the end of the year.

Q.—Have you any other objections to find with this book?

A.—No, I have not, except that the cover is not as it should be.

Q.—Do you find that when wire is used in the binding that it scratches the desk?

A.—Yes, there is an objection to the wire scratching the desk; but I have not noticed it myself, particularly with the Grammar.

Mr. Staunton here handed the witness a copy of the High School French book, published by Messrs. Hunter, Rose Co.

Q.—What do you think of that book, Mr. Coombs?

A.—The criticism on this book is very similar to that which has just been given with respect to the Grammar, but, the effect is not quite as glaring.

Q.—How old is the book that you hold in your hand?

A.—It was purchased in January, this year, by one of the girl pupils of the school.

Q.—Is she a very careful girl?

A.—Yes, I consider her a careful girl.

Q.—Is it your experience, Mr. Coombs, that this book is not reasonably durable even though it has had proper care in the hands of a careful pupil?

A.—Yes, this book should last during the whole of the High School course,—at least three years.

Q.—Is it intended to be used by one pupil only?

A.—It is.

Q.—How often do they have to renew these books?

A.—As a matter of fact, I do not know that the pupils are in the habit of buying new books before they complete their school course; but before they are through, the books are in shreds.

Q.—How do they make them last out?

A.—Oh, they manage as best they can by means of temporary binding.

Q.—Are all of these books as bad as that?

A.—No, I think the High School Grammar is the worst.

Q.—What is the relative cost of those books?

A.—The last book (the French book) costs one dollar, while the other book (the Grammar) costs seventy-five cents.

Q.—Now, Mr. Coombs, what is the next book that you wish to speak of?

A.—The High School Physical Science Book.

Q.—Well, how long has this book—(handing witness copy of book in question) been in use?

A.—This book has been in use about nine months.

Q.—Am I to understand that its present condition is the result of nine months' usage?

A.—Yes sir.

Q.—What kind of pupil used this book?

A.—The book was used by one of the girl pupils of the school.

Q.—Do you consider her a careful pupil, Mr. Coombs?

A.—I do.

Q.—Is this book then in the condition that you find them generally?

A.—Yes, but some are worse, and again some are in better condition.

Q.—How long should this book be used by a High School pupil?

A.—I would say about three years; sometimes it varies, but it should last at least for three years.

Q.—Is your criticism quite as strong against this book as it was against the other?

A.—Hardly. I have not seen as many of the Physical Science books as I have of the English Grammar, but that book, as well as others like it, is in very bad condition.

Q.—Which of the two books would be most used?

A.—The Grammar would be used more than the Physical Science.

Q.—Is the Physical Science book used much? Say how many times per week?

A.—We have two double lessons which would be equivalent to four lessons if given separately.

Q.—It is not used then every day?

A.—No. It would be equivalent to four lessons per week.

Q.—Is it a book that you give home lessons out of?

A.—Yes. All these books are to be taken home.

Q.—Now, here is a copy of the High School Chemistry. How long has this book been in use?

A.—I should say about six months.

Q.—And by a careful pupil?

A.—Yes, a girl.

Q.—It is in pretty bad condition, is it not?

A.—Yes. There are some places about the edges where acid has been dropped.

Q.—Well, never mind about that, tell me how often this book is used in the week?

A.—Three days per week.

Q.—Is it used as much as the Grammar?

A.—No.

Q.—Should it then be in a better or worse condition?

A.—It should be in a better condition.

Q.—When was it purchased?

A.—About six months ago.

Q.—So it has not been long enough in use to have had a hard life then?

A.—No, it has not.

Q.—What do you think of it as a sample of its class?

A.—It is about as good as those of its kind.

Q.—You consider it then a fair sample?

A.—Yes, I think it is a fair sample.

Q.—Have you any criticism to offer on the printing of any of the books you have produced here; any defects of type, etc.?

A.—No, I have nothing to say in that line; I am satisfied with the printing and the paper.

Q.—I am to understand then, that you have told me now all of the faults you have to find with the books produced?

A.—Yes, I think I have. I may say, however, that my own eyes are good, which may be the reason why I do not object to the type being small.

Q.—The next book that we will speak of, Mr. Coombs, is the Geography, entitled "Our Earth as a Whole." Where is this book published and by whom?

A.—It is published by Messrs. Morang Company, Toronto.

Q.—In what classes or forms is that book used?

A.—It is used in the First Form in the High School and the Senior Fourth in the Public School.

Q.—When was that book published?

A.—This book was in use, I should say, nearly nine months.

Q.—What does it cost?

A.—I am not able to give the price, but I think about sixty cents.

Q.—Was it in the custody of a careful pupil?

A.—Yes. It was purchased and used by a careful boy.

Q.—The book is in what condition now?

A.—I do not object to it on the same ground as the others; the maps came loose and certain leaves came loose; but the style of binding seems to be different, and to my mind, better.

Q.—You mean that here are tapes overlapping and sewn in a better manner so as to ease the back?

A.—Yes, that is my opinion.

Q.—Do you think that it is durable?

A.—Yes, the weakness complained of, is due to the fact that the leaves projected a little.

Q.—What do you think of the cover?

A.—I think the back is all right; it is better than most of them.

Q.—How long is that book supposed to last?

A.—In our school it would last about one year.

Q.—What is your opinion regarding its use in other schools?

A.—I would not care to say; I think some other witness may be able to answer that better than I can.

Q.—Now, Mr. Coombs, here is a copy of Hagarty's Latin Grammar used in the High Schools. Tell me how long that book has been in use?

A.—This book has been in use one year.

Q.—What is the cost of the book?

A.—It cost one dollar.

Q.—It is to be used for how long?

A.—Three years at least.

Q.—How many times during the week?

A.—Four times, and in some years, every day.

Q.—What is your criticism on this book?

A.—Well, in nearly every case, the cover pulls away from the cloth; the "mull" seems to be good; but for some reason or other, it seems to pull away.

Q.—Are there many instances of this kind?

A.—I could easily find an armful of these books that act just like this one; there seems to be some mis-fit.

Q.—Is there any other objection to it?

A.—No, except that the binding goes to pieces.

Q.—Who publishes this book, Mr. Coombs?

A.—It is published by the Morang Company.

By Mr. JOHN A. COOPER:

Q.—Do you not think, Mr. Coombs, that the weakness complained of, is due to the paper?

A.—Yes, it may be that; it is printed on extraordinary heavy paper.

By Mr. G. L. STAUNTON, K.C.:

Q.—The next book we have here is "The Commercial Course in Bookkeeping." Who publishes this book?

A.—It is published by the Copp, Clark Co., and costs forty cents per copy.

Q.—What is your criticism on this book?

A.—It has not a proper binding; this, you will observe, is a new book and has never been used; I was very careful not to pull on it, and you can see how it has gone. Here is one that has been in use about two months, with leaves out and whole sections loose. Here is another book that has been in use a little longer, and is all loose.

Q.—How long should these books last?

A.—We expect these books to last two years.

Q.—How long do they last?

A.—The pupils keep them two years, but they have to be repaired and sewed, in order to last out that period.

Q.—Now, here is a copy of the Public School Geography, published, I see, by The Canada Publishing Co., at a cost of seventy-five cents. What form is this book used in?

A.—We use it in the First Form.

Q.—What have you to say about this book?

A.—There is a similar criticism, but, in this case, it might be due to the weight of the contents.

Mr. STAUNTON: Never mind the cause, just tell us whether it goes to pieces or not.

WITNESS: Yes, it goes to pieces, the back comes off.

By Mr. STAUNTON, K.C.:

Q.—How long do you say that book has been in use?

A.—Six months; it was bought in January, 1905, but has been in use about six months; the boy was out of school.

Q.—Is that a fair sample of the durability of these books.

A.—Yes.

Q.—Have any of the books that you have brought here, been used by careless or negligent pupils?

A.—No, they have all had their usage.

Q.—What is next, Mr. Coombs, have you any other books to submit?

A.—No, I have no other books of the High School series, but I have brought an old book of my own.

Q.—What book is it?

A.—It is a Latin book, Harkness' First Latin book.

Q.—How long have you used it?

A.—Three years.

Q.—How much did it cost?

A.—I think about one dollar and twenty-five cents, but I am not positive; I used this book a great deal, I taught Classics, and it is as good as ever.

Q.—What other book have you got?

A.—I have a Todhunter's Algebra here that cost forty cents.

Q.—How many years have you used it?

A.—Four years, and it is still in a good state of preservation.

Q.—It is possible then, to produce a book that will not go to pieces in six months?

A.—Yes, I think so.

Q.—Will you please tell me, Mr. Coombs, if you can, what is the cost of an outfit of books for a High School pupil?

WITNESS: If I give you the approximate cost of a pupil starting, will that do?

Mr. STAUNTON: Yes, I mean the probable cost of a complete set of books for a pupil entering your school.

WITNESS: Well then, I would estimate the cost of a complete set of books, at nine dollars and seventy cents.

By Mr. STAUNTON, K.C.:

Q.—What books would be required to make up that amount?

A.—There would be, say,—

One P.S. Arithmetic	...at a cost of	$0	25
" " Grammar	" "		25
" " Geography	" "		75
" Story of Canadian People	" "		50
" British Nation	" "	1	00
" English Composition	" "		40
" H. S. Algebra	" "		75
" Elementary Geometry	" "		50
" Hagarty's Latin Grammar	" "	1	00
" High School French Grammar	" "	1	00
" " " Botany, Part II	" "		60
" Commercial Course in Bookkeeping	" "		40
" Drawing Book	" "		10
' Literature	" "		30
" Writing Book	" "		25
" Stenography Book	" "	1	25
and Note Books	" "		40

Making a total of $9 70

Q.—There are, I see, three books in this list that are used in the public schools' courses, which cost $1.25; so that if they have these books fit for use when they enter High School, it would only cost $8.45?

A.—Yes, that is correct.

Q.—Is there any reduction on these books?

A.—Yes. We got 20% off in order to compete with the T. Eaton Co.

Mr. STAUNTON: Then, as I figure it, if the pupil had three High School books with him on entering, it would cost him $8.45, unless Eaton comes to his rescue.

Mr. STAUNTON: Well now, suppose a pupil is going through for a teacher, that pupil would not require to take stenography?

A.—No, not in that case.

Q.—Or, in the case of others who do not desire to take languages, they would not require these books.

A.—No sir, but I am giving you approximately, the cost of a complete outfit.

Q.—Are there no other books required in the High Schools?

A.—There are, in some cases.

Q.—Name some of them?

A.—There are the Primary Latin Grammar, First Latin Book, and Hagarty's Latin Grammar.

Q.—Are there any other subjects?

A.—There are, in Geography, History, Geometry, and others.

Q.—Is that a good system to authorize more than one book? Is it necessary in your judgment?

A.—I think it is not a good system.

Q.—Do you approve of it?

A.—No, I do not. We teachers frequently have pupils come from other places who used a different book, and we say, this Latin book that you have, will not do here. (and it may be that this book is nearly new). The pupil's parents immediately want to know why it will not do and enter a strong objection to buying a new one, which, they ultimately have to do.

Q.—How are these books? Suppose in Newmarket they use one book, while in other places they use others, how is it arranged?

A.—The choice of books is left to the staff.

Q.—Is there any uniformity in the staffs of the Province?

A.—No, there is not.

Q.—Then, you simply pick out what you like, and the other man chooses what he likes, and you may be placed within two or three miles of each other, and yet you each have a different set of books?

A.—Yes, that is quite right.

Q.—Does this not affect the students in their studies?

A.—Yes, in some cases the books are arranged differently, and it is quite a difficult matter to take a child from one book and start him on another.

Q.—You think then, from an educational point of view, that it is not to be approved of?

A.—Yes, that is the idea; it is unsatisfactory from both points of view.

Q.—Have you any other points that you have thought about that you could assist the Commission on, Mr. Coombs?

Witness hesitates.

Mr. STAUNTON resumes: Were you going to speak on the advisability of having free text books? I would like to ask you whether, in your opinion, it would affect the cost of the books. Have you given the matter any thought?

A.—Well, my opinion is that a pupil should own his own books. I have formed a plan in the school, of trying to arrange so that each pupil might accumulate a little library of his own during his course, so that he will have something tangible when he leaves.

Q.—How do you manage it?

A.—Well, in the first year, we have him use certain books, and we get them in a style of binding that would be suitable, and the next year we get certain others, and so on, so that when he is through, he is the possessor of a little library of English literature, and we encourage him in that way to buy the very books that would be a pleasure for him to have in after years.

Q.—Have you ever ascertained, or endeavoured to ascertain what the cost per pupil is to the school or state where the books are furnished free?

A.—Well, the only information that I have had on that point, I have obtained from the reports of the Superintendent of Education in the United States, and from some reports that I have seen printed in Ontario where it has been tried.

Q.—You have had no wide experience of it?

A.—No, I have not.

Q.—Are these the only arguments you can advance as to the student owning the books?

A.—Well, the pupil would not use the book as carefully if he did not have to pay for it.

Q.—You do not think then, that a pupil has a greater reverence for books that are not his own?

A.—No. I do not; but I have had no experience in this matter.

The witness was here interrogated by Mr. J. A. Cooper.

By Mr. COOPER:

Q.—Mr. Coombs, in your evidence you spoke about books falling to pieces; apparently that is a matter of binding. You are probably aware that in most of the cities where free text books are used, they re-bind their books. Have you ever had any books re-bound for your pupils?

A.—No, but I have had some of my own re-bound.

Q.—Do you not think, if the books were owned by the High School Board, that they could be re-bound and still be good books?

A.—Yes, I think that is possible.

Q.—You say you tried to inculcate in your pupils the idea of having a library. How do you reconcile that statement with the one you made in your evidence that the books do not last?

A.—Well, I have not brought any of those books here; I do not encourage my pupils to keep books like that in their libraries.

Q.—Well, then, your answer is, that you are not in favor of the general idea of free text books.

A.—I do not favor it; but my idea of a library for pupils is not based on the ordinary text books. Most pupils would not take a delight in reading out of an Algebra after leaving school; but would take a delight in reading Tennyson and other standard works.

Q.—Then your idea of a library is only for standard English books used in the High School course?

A.—Yes, in a general sense it is.

Mr. STAUNTON: That will do, Mr. Coombs. Thank you, you may step down.

EVIDENCE OF MR. RICHARD SOUTHAM, PRESIDENT OF THE MAIL JOB PRINT-ING COMPANY, TORONTO.

By Mr. G. L. STAUNTON, K.C.:

Q.—What is your business Mr. Southam?

A.—Printing and Publishing, and to a certain extent we make books and give them to the publishers at a certain price.

Q.—What is the name of your Company?

A.—The Mail Job Printing Company.

Q.—Have you the capacity to turn out books such as the School Readers, and are you able to produce them?

A.—Yes.

Q.—Have you estimated upon these books?

A.—I have, on the Readers.

Q.—What have you estimated on, the Public or High School, the First Reader, Part one or two, or the Second, Third, Fourth and Fifth?

A.—On the First Reader, Part one.

Q.—How many of these Readers do you estimate are used each year in this Province?

A.—I understand that there are approximately, about 90,000 used in this Province each year.

Q.—What do you figure that you could produce them for?

A.—For five cents per book; that is to say, I am making these figures on the understanding that the plates would be supplied to us, and that all we would have to do, is set them up and print them.

Q.—What would it cost if you had to do all of the work; that is, produce the plates yourself?

A.—I could give you a price per book; but the plates are always furnished.

Q.—Well, then, I will assume that the plates are furnished to you, and that you are supplying the books in quantities, and will ask you then, knowing the number of books that are used in the Province in a year,— what would you take for a contract to produce these books, say for a term of ten years?

A.—I would produce Part I of the First Reader for five cents per copy; that would cost $4,500.00 for the first year.

Q.—How much do they cost at present?

A.—I believe they cost about $9,000.00 per year; that is the retail price; the wholesale price is about $6,300.00, taking them in this order at Printers' wholesale price, and retail price on an average of 70,000 books.

Part II.

Printer's Price.	Wholesale Price.	Retail Price.
6c per book.		
$4,200.00	$7,700.00	$10,500.00

This covers Parts I and II of the First Reader.

Second Reader, quantity 37,000 at 10½c. per book, making a total of $3,835.00, Printer's price. Wholesale price, $5,180.00. Retail price, $7,400.00.

Third Book, quantity 33,000, at 13c. per book. Printer's price, $4,-290.00. Wholesale price, $6,930.00. Retail price, $9,900.00.

Fourth Book, quantity 17,000 books, at 15c. per book. Printer's price, $2,550.00. Wholesale price, $4,760.00. Retail price, $6,800.00.

Fifth Book, quantity, 4,000 books at 20c. per book. Printer's price, $800.00. Wholesale price, $1,720.00. Retail price, $2,400.00.

Q.—Your figures, as I understand them, Mr. Southam, show that these books can be produced for less than the present Manufacturers' cost, which is about thirty-three per cent. higher than what might be considered a fair price?

A.—The comparisons are, that our price is about one-third lower than their prices.

Q.—If these books were printed by you, would you supply them ready for shipment in Toronto, to any part of the Province?

A.—Yes. Free on board the cars, or in Toronto warehouses.

Q.—Do you know anything about the binding of these Readers?

A.—Not particularly; I have had samples and I based my figures really on those books.

Q.—Would you bind them properly?

A.—Well, I think there is one objection to the binding, that is the wire sewing; some people seem to think a great deal of wire sewing, but wire sewing machines are, I think, out of date; there are better machines used now. The wire stitching is liable to rust a little, and certain sections of the books would pull away easily; there are other machines which sew with thread that I consider better than the wire machines. There should also be a tape running across the back of the book, and extending to the other side of the cover; that makes a flexible sling, and is not so liable to pull off as the other. The "mull' is now placed in like the tape would be, and I think the binding could be made quite a bit stronger. This is only my theory, I am not an expert binder.

Q.—You have simply estimated on these books as they are?

A.—Yes, I am taking them just as they are.

Q.—Now Mr. Southam, you have estimated on these books, understanding that the Government would supply you with the necessary plates. Now how much do you think you would add to the cost if you were to furnish the plates yourself?

A.—Well to make the plates for the set of six books would cost, I think, about $2,200.00.

Q.—That is, then, for the whole lot?

A.—Yes, for setting up and making plates for all these readers.

Q.—Have you figured on this?

A.—Yes. You can get electrotypes for two cents per square inch, and an electrotype for one of those pages is only worth fifty cents.

Q.—Is there any difference in the page when it is a picture, or when it is a type?

A.—No.

Q.—Do I understand you to say, that you would publish the book with the whole of the pictures or types, for the same money?

A.—If we have to furnish it, we would require to have the cuts of the pictures supplied to us, and that would be an extra. That is, an extra for making an illustration.

Q.—Can you tell me what that would be?

A.—No, I can not; one could figure it up, but it would take a long time,—It is so much per inch.

Q.—What would you expect to be supplied to you?

A.—Well, at the prices I have given you, we would expect to be supplied with complete electrotypes. If we get type-written copy, we would set it up. I am now speaking of an engraving; we would have to get photographs.

Q.—Have you included these plates and engravings in your figures?

A.—No, we have not touched them at all.

Q.—In both of your estimates then, these cuts, plates, or engravings, are supplied to you.

A.—Yes.

By Mr. JOHN A. COOPER:

Q.—Mr. Southam, how long have these sewing machines, that are used now to sew books, been in use among printers?

A.—Do you mean the wire machines?

Mr. COOPER: No, I mean thread machines.

A.—They have been in use about twelve years, but I do not know exactly when they were introduced.

Q.—The sewing with a thread machine is, you think, the better way?

A.—Yes, I think so.

Q.—Can the work be done as cheaply with a thread machine?

A.—It can. Approximately the difference in cost is very slight; hardly worth considering.

By Mr. G. L. STAUNTON, K.C.:

Q.—On your estimate, would you take a short contract, say, for five years?

A.—Yes. I based my estimate on a from five to ten years contract. Very well, that will do Mr. Southam. Thank you.

EVIDENCE OF DR. F. B. ALLAN, LECTURER ON CHEMISTRY IN THE UNIVERSITY
OF TORONTO.

By Mr. G. L. STAUNTON, K.C.:

Q.—What is your profession?

A.—I am a lecturer on Chemistry in the University of Toronto.

Q.—How long have you been on the University staff?

A.—I have been on the staff for thirteen years.

Q.—Dr. Allan, you were requested by the Secretary of this Commission
to prepare a chemical analysis of the paper in certain of the school text
books?

A.—Yes, I was supplied with eleven specimens of paper taken from the
following books:

1. Longman's Ship Historical Readers, 1903, English.
2. Macmillan's New Globe Readers, Book II, 1905, English.
3. New Education Readers, American Book Co., 1900.
4. Second Year Language Reader, American Macmillan & Co., 1906.
5. Public School History of England and Canada, 1906.
6. Practical Speller, 1906.
7. Public School Arithmetic, 1906.
8. High School Algebra, 1906.
9. Second Reader, 1906.
10. Second Reader, 1897.
11. Second Reader, 1885.

Q.—Did you make a chemical analysis of the paper?

A.—Yes, sir.

Q.—What did you find?

A.—I found from 30 per cent. to 35 per cent. of rag pulp and from 65
per cent. to 70 per cent. of wood pulp and some esparto grass.

Q.—You say you prepared a report of your finding?

A.—Yes, sir.

Q.—Is this the report furnished by you? (Hands witness a document).

A.—Yes, that is my report.

Q.—Well, Dr. Allan, I will read this report for the benefit of the Commission. (Reads copy of the following report).

COPY OF REPORT.

Chemical Laboratory, University of Toronto.

TORONTO, September 15th, 1906.

To the Secretary of the Text Book Commission:

SIR,—We beg to report that we have examined the eleven specimens
of paper submitted and find that they have the following composition:

1. Longman's Ship Historical Readers, 1903, English: 30-35 per cent.
rag pulp, linen; 65-70 per cent. chemical wood pulp, spruce; some esparto
grass.

2. Macmillan's New Globe Readers, Book II, 1905, English: 40-50
per cent. rag pulp, linen; 50-60 per cent. chemical wood pulp, spruce; some
esparto grass.

3. New Education Readers, American Book Co., 1900: 10-15 per cent. rag pulp, cotton; 85-90 per cent. chemical wood pulp, mostly poplar; considerable broken and crushed fibre.

4. Second Year Language Reader, American Macmillan & Co., 1906: Chemical wood pulp, poplar and spruce; considerable broken and short fibre, a small amount of rag.

5. Public School History of England and Canada, 1906: 90 per cent. chemical wood pulp, spruce; 10 per cent. mechanical wood pulp, spruce; much crushed and broken fibre.

6. Practical Speller, 1906: 5-10 per cent. rag pulp, cotton; 90-95 per cent. chemical wood pulp, largely spruce, some poplar; trace mechanical wood pulp.

7. Public School Arithmetic, 1906: 5-10 per cent. rag pulp, cotton; 80-85 per cent. chemical wood pulp, spruce; 10 per cent. mechanical wood pulp, spruce.

8. High School Algebra, 1906: 15 per cent. rag pulp, cotton; 75 per cent. chemical wood pulp, mostly spruce, some poplar; 10 per cent. mechanical wood pulp; much crushed and broken fibre.

9. Second Reader, 1906: 10-12 per cent, rag pulp, cotton; 30 per cent. chemical wood pulp, mostly spruce, some poplar; 8-10 per cent. mechanical wood pulp; much crushed and broken fibre.

10. Second Reader, 1897: 10-15 per cent. rag pulp, cotton; 85-90 per cent. chemical wood pulp, spruce.

11. Second Reader, 1885: 10 per cent. rag pulp*, cotton; 90 per cent. chemical wood pulp, poplar.

All of the papers submitted had rosin sizing.

Mechanical wood pulp, because of the process of manufacture, has a very short fibre. It is also affected by exposure to light and air. For these reasons it is only used in inferior papers. Examination of chemical wood pulp which has not been thoroughly bleached will indicate traces of mechanical wood pulp.

The fibre of spruce wood is longer and more slender than that of poplar and consequently felts better.

The fibre of rag pulp is longer and makes a better paper than chemical wood pulp.

Table Showing the Composition of Paper.

No.	Rag Pulp.	Chem. W. Pulp.	Mech. W. Pulp.	Remarks.
1.	30-35% linen....	65-70% spruce........	....	Some esparto grass.
2.	40-50% linen....	50-60% spruce........	....	Some esparto grass.
3.	10-15% cotton...	85-90% mostly poplar..	....	Considerable broken and crushed fibre.
4.	Cotton.........	100% poplar and spruce	....	Considerable broken and crushed fibre.
5.	....	90% spruce...........	10% spruce...........	Much crushed and broken fibre.
6.	5-10% cotton ...	90-95% largely spruce.	trace	
7.	5-10% cotton....	80-85% spruce........	10% spruce...........	
8.	15% cotton......	75% mostly spruce....	10%.................	Much crushed and broken fibre.
9.	10-12% cotton...	80% mostly spruce....	10% spruce...........	Much crushed and broken fibre.
10.	10-15% cotton...	85-90% spruce	....	
11.	10% cotton.. ...	90% poplar..	....	

*Includes all coniferous woods.

Q.—I see you have covered the ground pretty thoroughly in your analysis, Dr. Allan, but I would like to ask you whether, if the Department desires it, all the paper contained in those books could be submitted to a gentleman of your profession, from time to time, and ascertain definitely just what kind of paper it was getting?

A.—Yes, sir.

Q.—The Department need not take any publisher's word for it?

A.—Certainly not.

Q.—We could know what paper was being used in all of the books in the country?

A.—Yes, you could.

Q.—I suppose, Doctor, that publishers and manufacturers know quite well which is the proper paper to use for each kind of book?

A.—I do not know anything outside of what I have said.

By Mr. CROTHERS:

Q.—Dr. Allan, would you undertake to say what kind of paper should be used in school books; what percentage of these different kinds of pulp should be used?

A.—I would certainly think that mechanical wood pulp should not be used.

Q.—Then what quantity of chemical wood pulp should these papers contain?

A.—I do not think I would care to express an opinion on that.

Q.—But you do not think that mechanical wood pulp should be used?

A.—I would think not.

By Mr. G. L. STAUNTON, K.C.:

Q.—What is the difference between rag pulp and wood fibre?

A.—Well, what is known as rag pulp is manufactured from cotton and linen rags; the cotton consists of nearly pure cellulose fibre, while the linen is made up of fibres which have already undergone a treatment of maceration to remove the intercellular matter and leave the fibres quite clean. The wood fibre, commonly known as chemical fibre, can be produced by two processes, namely, the alkali and the acid process.

Q.—Well, Doctor, it will not be necessary for you to go into the process again, as the information is set forth very thoroughly in your report; but tell me please, which is the best pulp or fibre in your opinion, that produced by the chemical process or that produced by the mechanical process?

A.—If you mean chemical wood pulp as against mechanical wood pulp, I would say the chemical pulp, as it contains the best fibre; the mechanical pulp is a cheaper and inferior process.

Mr. STAUNTON: That will do, Doctor; thank you.

EVIENCE OF MR. ALBERT O'DELL, PUBLIC SCHOOL INSPECTOR.

By Mr. G. L. STAUNTON, K.C.:

Q.—What is your name?

A.—Albert O'Dell.

Q.—And your profession?

A.—Public School Inspector for the County of Northumberland.

Q.—How long have you been a Public School Inspector?

A.—For ten years.

Q.—Have you had any experience as to the durability of the books used in the Public Schools?

A.—Only as to what I have seen.

Q.—What have you seen?

A.—I have seen some very bad Geography books.

Q.—Have you any of them here?

A.—Yes.

Q.—What have you got?

A.—I have what you see here. (Witness produces a number of text books).

Q.—Well, then, we will speak first of the Geographies, are these Geographies used in the Public Schools?

A.—Yes.

Q.—Who publishes them?

A.—The Canada Publishing Company.

Q.—And the price is?

A.—The price is 75 cents each.

Q.—Do you know the age of these three?

A.—This one seems to have been purchased in 1905.

Q.—Do you know personally how long they have been in use?

A.—I do not; but I would say one is one year old, and the others two or three years old.

Q.—Do you know who owned these books? What sort of people were they? They look as if they had more than careful usage.

A.—They are owned by pupils in the various schools of my district.

Q.—This Ontario Reader; do you know the person who owns it?

A.—No, I do not; but the boy who owns it has had it since 1904. Here is one that is owned by a careless boy; this reader was bought in January, 1905; here is another one bought in 1905; this book is also in pieces; here is a book owned by a teacher bought in 1897.

Q.—Is the teacher careful?

A.—Yes, I think so; she uses this book daily.

Q.—Here is one bought in 1905; what do you say about that?

A.—That book belongs to a child in the country; I do not know her and cannot say whether she is careful or not.

Q.—Have you any more books there?

A.—Yes. (The witness produced eight readers, stating that some had been in use for one year and some for three or four years; but all of them in pieces.)

Q.—Here you have two Public School Arithmetics; one, I see, bought in 1902 and one in 1904, both of them all in pieces. Then you have a Public School Grammar; two of them I see were published by the Canada Publishing Company at 25 cents per copy; the first one being in 1904 and the second in 1900, both badly dilapidated. Then we have a copy of Gage and Company's Practical Speller and a copy of Gage and Company's Practical Grammar, bought in 1902; a copy of Public School History of England and Canada, Robertson's, bought in 1905. Now, are these books a fair sample of the books in your district that have been in use for any length of time?

A.—I would not like to say; there are some of them a great deal better. I would say that the Geographies are not well bound, and the Practical Speller is not well bound; but the others are an average; my chief objection is to the Geographies and the Speller.

Q.—The Geography and Speller are the ones you think require improvement?

A.—Yes.

Q.—Tell me, Mr. O'Dell, have you any information as to how the books might be cheapened?

4. T. B.

A.—Ninety-seven out of one hundred and sixty families have complained as to the cost of text books.

Q.—Where do they reside?

A.—In Cobourg.

Q.—What sort of people were they generally? What class were they?

A.—Well, they are artisans in the Town of Cobourg.

Q.—What other complaints did you have?

A.—I have complaints as to the number of text books; I find that one hundred and seventeen families out of one hundred and sixty find fault with the number of books they have to buy.·

Q.—In what way did they find fault?

A.—Well, that they had to buy too many books.

Q.—What other complaint did you have?

A.—There were very few found any fault with the binding or the quality of the paper.

Q.—Did you ever find more Geographies or more books in a family than you thought were necessary?

A.—Well, the experience of a principal of one of the schools was this way: he said sometimes there were two or three members of one family with only one Geography which passed from one room to the other, and when one pupil wanted it he had to get the text book from a brother or sister, which always led to confusion.

Q.—Did you find any books lying idle in families?

A.—Yes, and I am quite satisfied it will be an increasing ratio. Take, for instance, the Fourth Readers; I found out that in this one hundred and sixty families there were one hundred and fifteen Fourth Readers and but sixty of them were in use.

Q.—You say that there were only sixty of them in use and fifty-five lying idle?

A.—Yes, and the same might be said of other text books.

Q.—I am to understand then that the result of your enquiries satisfies you that nearly one-half of the text books purchased by the parents are lying unused in the houses?

A.—Yes.

Q.—Now, Mr. O'Dell, have you any suggestions to advance to decrease the cost of text books?

A.—I think that our girls and boys, since they are compelled to attend school, should be provided with free books.

Q.—What benefit would that be in your judgment?

A.—There are a great many advantages. I took occasion to find out from my teachers and I could not put it in better form myself. Here are a few quotations:

I. There is scarcely a class in which every pupil has all the books required. If the text books were free, all pupils would have an equal chance in so far as books are concerned.

II. Books are now bought, used for a year or two, and then thrown aside. The waste of books in this way alone must amount to an immense sum every year. With free books there would be no loss.

III. Children often remain at home when they cannot get books, and parents keep their children from school because they are unable to buy school books.

IV. Immigrants are coming into Canada by thousands; they are generally poor and have large families. It is often an impossibility for them to

4a T. B.

buy a full·supply of books at once and they are compelled to send their children to school.

V. Attendance between the ages of seven and fourteen is compulsory, therefore education should be free; otherwise the burden on the poor is greater than that on the rich. This is really class legislation.

VI. As a general rule, the family of the poor man is larger than that of the rich; this makes the burden of school books still greater.

VII. If the pupils and parents were responsible for the books, greater care would be taken of them. All would have good books and carefulness would be encouraged.

Q.—You appear to be an advocate of free text books, Mr. O'Dell, you believe it is the proper system?

A.—I do.

Q.—You think the parents would be more interested if text books were free?

A.—Yes, I think so. When parents would have to give an account for these books, they would see that better care was taken of them.

Q.—How would this affect the text books?

A.—Well, there would be fewer changes in the text books if the Government had to bear the expense.

Q.—Do you think there should be a variety of text books used?

A.—I think there should be but one set for the Province.

Q.—Then you would not allow different books on the same subject?

A.—No, I would not. I was talking to a dealer the other day and he said he had got tired and would not keep any more text books because there were too many kinds.

Q.—Would there be any advantage to the pupils if but one set of books were used?

A.—Why, yes; take pupils moving from one part of the Province to another; they would not have to buy different setts of books.

Q.—Have you any other reason?

A.—I think there would be better books.

Q.—Why do you think so?

A.—My reason for thinking so is that they would be under better supervision; there would be also a general saving in the expenditure.

Q.—Anything else?

A.—Yes, I think they could be produced cheaper with a free book.

Q.—Why do you think so?

A.—Because they would be produced in larger quantities, and the Government would produce them as near cost as possible.

Q.—You think, then, Mr. O'Dell, that there would be a large saving in the cost of the books?

A.—Yes, but of course we are not supposed to know very much about this as we are not in the business.

Q.—Have you any other reasons to advance in support of free text books?

A.—Yes. Confusion in caused in a school when only one book is furnished to a family, as, for instance, a Geography. So many parents object to paying seventy-five cents for a Geography for a child in the third book class when they have two or three children in the home attending school; it means at least three Geographies at seventy-five cents each, and parents strongly object to that sort of thing.

By Mr. Cooper:

Q.—Could that difficulty not be overcome by a division of the book?

A.—Yes, I think it could; the book is unnecessarily large for a child to handle.

Q.—You think that it would be advisable to have the Geography divided into two parts and have one part for the third class and one for the fourth class?

A.—I think so. I know a little girl in the third book this term and the actual cost to provide that little girl with books was $2.20.

By Mr. G. L. STAUNTON, K.C.:

Q.—Have you included scribbling books in that amount?

A.—I have included one.

Q.—How many more pencils and scribblers than you have included would she require during the term?

A.—About thirty cents more, or two dollars and fifty cents in all, would cover it.

Q.—Would the books be of any use to her at the end of the year?

A.—Yes, the Grammar and Reader.

Q.—I mean, if she goes into the next class?

A.—All but the Reader.

Q.—How many years would they be of use to her?

A.—For a child, it would be two years for the third, and two years for the fourth; these books should last for four years if average care is taken of them; if the books are properly bound.

Q.—How about the Arithmetic?

A.—The Arithmetic should last for two years in the third book and two years in the fourth book.

Q.—Do you think that those books you have produced here would last that time?

A.—I do not think some of them would; but the Grammar and the Arithmetic would.

Q.—Are there any other reasons?

A.—I think I have given you the principal reasons.

Q.—Have you any other points you could mention of interest to the Commission, Mr. O'Dell?

A.—I might say that I have one school in the county that is provided by the trustees with pens, pencils, paper, ink, etc. The secretary-treasurer of that school writes me to this effect:—He says, "The trustees think it the best way to furnish the school with these things," and it is a very great convenience, I must say; for very often a child comes to school without a pencil and the excuse is, that his father did not go to town, or else he forgot to buy one.

Q.—How much did this cost the trustees?

A.—The amount for last year was nine dollars and thirty-five cents.

Q.—How many pupils were there in attendance at the school?

A.—They averaged about twenty-one pupils.

Q.—What does the teacher think of this plan?

A.—The teacher approves, for she has always a supply in her possession and can, at any time, furnish a necessary article to those who are in need; so that no child is ever without the means to work with. However, she finds that, while some pupils are benefited, others are led to become careless and neglect their duty, depending on their teacher.

Q.—Do you think such would be the case if the supply were properly managed?

A.—No, of course I do not think it is properly managed; this teacher has only been there for about two months; otherwise, it would not be so expensive.

By Mr. Cooper:

Q.—Do you think it would be a good idea if a proper system was adopted?

A.—Yes, I think it would.

By Mr. G. L. Staunton, K.C.:

Q.—You think the trustees should supply everything?

A.—I think so, and another good reason is, that the children would have them at the beginning of the term; there would be no delay.

Q.—Do you know what it costs in Toronto for free text books, etc.?

A.—It costs a very reasonable amount. I spent one year in Toronto under the free text book system and am satisfied with it.

By Mr. Crothers:

Q.—Mr. O'Dell, you have been inspecting schools for ten years?

A.—Yes, and I taught for fifteen years.

Q.—Were the old text books in use then?

A.—No. I used them when a boy.

Q.—Has there been any deterioration in the binding since those days; those old Readers used to be handed down from father to son, did they not?

A.—I would say, that the same principle might be applied to almost everything, namely, that there has been a deterioration.

Mr. Staunton: That will do for the present, Mr. O'Dell.

Evidence of Thomas Carscadden, M.A., Principal Galt Collegiate Institute.

Mr. G. L. Staunton, K.C.:

Q.—What is your name in full, Mr. Carscadden?

A.—Thomas Carscadden.

Q.—How many years have you been a teacher, Mr. Carscadden?

A.—For thirty years.

Q.—How long have you been a Principal?

A.—Since 1884.

Q.—Have you any criticism to make, Mr. Carscadden, as to the binding of the High School books?

A.—I think it very imperfect and far from what it should be.

Q.—What imperfections have you found in the binding?

A.—Well, it breaks easily.

Q.—You have a number of books here?

A.—Yes, I have some eighteen or nineteen books with me. (Witness produces bag containing a number of books in very bad condition.)

Q.—Will you tell us, Mr. Carscadden, how long these books have been in use?

A.—Here is a Grammar, in use for three years.

Q.—Has it been carefully handled?

A.—Yes, somewhat carefully handled.

Witness: Here is a second High School Grammar in use for two years, and this is Delury's High School Arithmetic in use for two years, and here is one of the same books in use one year; all, you see, in very bad condition.

Q.—Who publishes Delury's books?

A.—The Canada Publishing Company.

Q.—What is the price of them?

A.—Sixty cents each.

Q.—Here is a High School Chemistry in use two years. Has it been used by a careful person?

A.—Yes, a careful boy.

Q.—Here are two High School Physics in use one year. How often is this book used?

A.—About three times per week.

Q.—Here is Baker's Geometry in use one year. Was this book used by a careful student?

A.—Yes.

Q.—The next one is a High School Algebra in use one year, published by Briggs, price 75c. How often is this book used?

A.—Four times per week.

Q.—Next we have a History of England and Canada, price 65c., published by Copp, Clark Co., in use for two years and in bad condition. Also a French Grammar and Reader, price $1.00, published by Copp, Clark Co. and used three years. What have you to say about them?

A.—I would say that this present condition is due to the bad binding; but the books that I complain of most are the French and German Grammars.

Q.—What German book do you mean?

A.—The German Grammar and Reader, price $1.00, published by Copp, Clark Co. Then there is "The Elements of Algebra," price 25c., published by The Canada Publishing Company. This book fell to pieces in two months, while this book, "Vergil's Æneid," fell to pieces in one year.

Q.—Here is a book called "Ancient History for Beginners." What do you think about that?

A.—In my opinion, it is fairly bound; but the Latin books by Hagarty I think, are very badly bound. Also the Principles and Practice of Reading by the Canada Publishing Company, I consider a poor type.

By Mr. CROTHERS:

Q.—Mr. Carscadden, have you noticed any deterioration in the binding in the last twenty years?

A.—Yes, I have noticed it.

Mr. G. L. STAUNTON, K.C.:

Q.—Are there any other books that you think are too large?

A.—Yes. I think Botsford's English History for Beginners is too heavy and would be better to divide it into two parts; that is, into the History of Greece and the History of Rome.

Q.—Are the specimens you have submitted about the average?

A.—Yes.

Q.—Have you any ideas as to how the cost of these text books might be reduced?

A.—No, I have not; I have not thought about it, but I think if the books were better bound, there might be some reduction in the cost to families where a number of books have to be purchased.

Q.—How long should these books last?

A.—I think they should be made to last, with care, from five to eight or nine years.

Q.—Then you think they should last through a family of three or four children?

A.—Yes, I think so.

Q.—What do you say about the average life of a book being eight years?

A.—I should say, that the books would require better care than the average care given them by pupils.

Q.—Is there anything you would like to tell the Commission?

A.—No, I have not thought of anything. The only thing is, the poor wearing quality of the text books, especially the binding.

By Mr. COOPER:

Q.—Mr. Carscadden, how do these books compare with the American books?

A.—The American books are very much better bound.

Q.—Do you think a binding like that used in Ahn's German Reader, a good one?

A.—Yes, I think the Class Book binding is the best.

Q.—For all classes of books?

A.—Yes. I think it would be a good binding for all classes of books.

By Mr. CROTHERS:

Q.—I understand you, Mr. Carscadden, that your chief objection is to the binding, not to the price of the books?

A.—Yes, the binding is so poor that in a month or so the book comes apart.

Mr. STAUNTON: That will do just now, Mr. Carscadden.

EVIDENCE OF MR. G. R. BYFORD, BOOK-BINDER, TORONTO.

By Mr. G. L. STAUNTON, K.C.:

Q.—What is your name in full, Mr. Byford?

A.—George Robert Byford.

Q.—You are a book-binder, I believe, Mr. Byford?

A.—Yes.

Q.—Of long experience?

A.—Yes, for fifty years.

Q.—Do you bind the books for the Toronto Public Schools?

A.—Yes. I have done so for several years.

Q.—I suppose you find that a good many books require re-binding?

A.—Yes; I have had over four thousand one summer.

Q.—The books that pass through your hands, Mr. Byford, in the matter of workmanship and binding, what would you say about them?

A.—I would say that they were very badly bound.

Q.—Has that been your experience in handling the Public School books?

A.—Yes.

Q.—Have you examined the books known as "The Ontario Reader" at the request of the Secretary of the Commission and made a report on them?

A.—Yes.

Q.—Is that report, that you now produce, is it a true and fair report?

A.—Yes, sir, it is.

Mr. STAUNTON: Give me your report and I will read it for the benefit of the Commission. (Witness hands examiner his report, which reads as follows:—

REPORT OF GEORGE BYFORD AS TO BINDING OF CERTAIN TEXT BOOKS.

First Book, Part I.

Binding of present edition is superior to that of 1885 in having the cover turned in at the sides and ends. This is according to contract, I understand. The sewing is done with an ordinary sewing machine and threads are loose at ends, which must be unsatisfactory. The sides covers are too light.

First Book, Part II.

This book is wire-stitched and has a heavier cover than Part I. The cover should be heavier still. In order to make the binding of First Book, Parts I and II as strong and durable as the other books, they should have end papers, heavier board covers, and should be properly sewn by hand or by special machine.

Second Reader.

Samples of Copp, Clark Co. edition, dated 25th March, 1885, and April 2nd, 1885, are well bound, thread sewn to tape with mull over the back.

Samples of the Canada Publishing Co., dated April, 1885, and December, 17th, 1885, are wire stitched and are not nearly so good as the Copp, Clark editions.

The thread sewn book would, in my estimation, wear ten times as long as the wire stitched.

The Copp, Clark Co. edition of 1890, which is thread sewn, but without tapes, is not quite so good as the 1885 edition, lacking the tapes, but is nearly as durable. I have examined the Canada Publishing Co. edition of 1889 and the present edition of the Copp, Clark Co. These are wire stitched and have no tapes and, therefore, have very little wearing quality.

The quality of cloth in all these editions is about equal, the last edition being a trifle better.

The board used in the Canada Publishing Co. edition of 1885 is mill board, that in the Copp, Clark Co. edition of 1885 is straw board; the Copp, Clark Co. edition of 1890 is straw board. The present editions are straw board. The Canada Publishing Co. edition of 1897 is straw board.

Mill board is 25 per. cent. more expensive than straw board and is much more durable and should be used.

Third Reader.

Examined four samples of the Copp, Clark Co. editions of 1885. All are thread sewn to cords, mull covered, with end papers.

The Canada Publishing Co. edition of 1885 is the same as Copp, Clark Co.

The Canada Publishing Co. edition of 1897 is wire stitched through a poor quality of mull, and each section may be pulled out of the book very easily.

The present edition is similar.

The wearing quality of these books must be very unsatisfactory.

Straw board is used in all the samples.

Cloth is satisfactory in all editions.

Fourth Reader.

Two samples of the Canada Publishing Co. editions of 1885 are thread sewn to cord, with mull over the back.

Two samples of the Copp, Clark Co., 1885, are wire stitched on mull, without tapes.

One sample of Canada Publishing Co. of 1885 is wire stitched on tapes.

Those thread sewn are the best; the wire stitched on tapes are second in quality; and wire stitched on mull are the poorest in wearing quality.

The edition of 1897 and the present editions are all wire stitched on mull and must prove very unsatisfactory.

The two Copp, Clark Co. editions of 1885 are straw board.

The Canada Publishing Co. editions of 1885 are mill board.

The Copp, Clark Co. edition of 1897 is straw board.

The Canada Publishing Co. present editions are mill board.

The cloth is fair and all have end papers.

High School Reader.

Machine stitched with thread, without cord or tapes. Poor mull glued over back.

This binding while not very durable is much better than wire stitching, for reasons stated. It would be much improved if tapes were added.

Practical Speller. Gage & Co.

Wire stitched to mull and open back. Must prove as unsatisfactory as readers.

Public School Geography.

Wire stitched to mull. Only three stitches used, which is too few for such a large book. The 1887 Canada Publishing Co. sample is thread sewn, but none of the later samples at all compare with this.

German Readers. E. Steiger & Co., New York.

The German Readers are hand sewn to cords with mull over the back and the cords frayed out and glued to the cover boards. They also have tight backs.

These must be the most durable of all the authorized books.

General Remarks.

Wire sewn books are very unsatisfactory, because the wire rusts and breaks through the sections, entirely destroying the books, even for re-binding. Moreover, the wire wears through the cloth at the back. Only a bit of thin mull and a piece of paper holds cover to the book. This should be strengthened by cord or tapes. Better still, the backs might be made tight. A sample of a well bound cheap book is Macmillan's Globe Reader, Book II, which is sewn on tapes in addition to mull.

By Mr. STAUNTON:

Q.—Mr. Byford, are you in favor of the binding?

A.—No, I do not approve of the wiring, if the book gets the least bit damp it turns rusty and leaves a hole right through the section.

Q.—How much longer would a book last if sewed with thread, than one with wire?

A.—I would say, a book sewed with thread, would last ten times as long, as one sewed with wire.

Q.—Now, Mr. Byford, you cannot mean ten times as long, surely?

A.—My reason for saying that a book sewed with thread would last ten times longer than one sewed with wire, is because directly the book gets damp the wire rusts and breaks through; then there are single sections that are not connected.

Q.—Is "mull" of any strength to the book?

A.—Yes, it helps to hold the cover on the book.

Q.—I thought there was no strength in the "mull"?

A.—The "mull" is no good to sew to wire, simply to hold the cover on.

Q.—I would like to ask which is the cheaper, mull board or straw board?

A.—Straw board is the cheaper.

Mr. STAUNTON: That will do, Mr. Byford, thank you.

MR. STAUNTON HERE RE-CALLED MR. THOMAS CARSCADDEN FOR FURTHER EXAMINATION.

Q.—Mr. Carscadden, do you find that this wire stitching scratches the desks?

A.—Yes, sir, and I find pupils complain that the books fastened with wire, scratch their hands at times very severely.

Mr BYFORD, re-examined by Mr. CROTHERS:

Q.—Mr. Byford, when you came to repair these books that are bound with wire, how did you repair them?

A.—Well, the wire has to be taken out and the books sewed with thread.

Q.—Then they are worth very much more when you get through with them than they were before?

A.—Yes, sir, the wire binding should only be used on small pamphlets.

Q.—Have you had this repairing for the schools for a number of years without a break?

A.—No, there was one year, about five years ago, that it was given to another tenderer.

Q.—And the binding was not as satisfactorily done during that year?

A.—No, it was not. There was a lot of trouble; the binding was done with wire and tin-tacking, and was not satisfactory, and after that, the repairing came back to me at my own price without a tender.

EVIDENCE OF MR. CLARKSON W. JAMES, SECRETARY EDUCATION DEPART-MENT AND PRIVATE SECRETARY TO THE MINISTER.

By Mr. G. L. STAUNTON, K.C.:

Q.—What is your name in full, Mr. James?

A.—Clarkson W. James.

Q.—Mr. James, you are Private Secretary to the Minister of Education.

A.—Yes, sir.

Q.—When did you assume your present position?

A.—On the first of December, 1905.

Q.—You are also the Secretary of the Education Department?

A.—Yes, sir.

Q.—Now, Mr. James, when you took over the duties of your office did you examine any of the documents that had accumulated there during the time of your predecessor?

A.—I did. It was necessary that I should do so in order that I might be seized of all the information possible pertaining to the office under my control.

Q.—Did you find any documents relating to text books among your files?

A.—Yes.

Q.—What documents did you find?

A.—I question my right to discuss any documents placed in my charge without the consent of my Minister.

Mr. STAUNTON: This Commission has the authority of the Minister of Education to obtain any documents from the files of the Department, that will throw any light on, or assist in this investigation, so that you may answer fully.

WITNESS: I discovered a number of letters and documents with reference to text books generally.

Q.—What were those letters about?

A.—They were copies of letters sent out to publishers and others with a view to obtain information regarding text books, prices, quality, style, etc., and the replies thereto.

Q.—What did you do with those documents and letters?

A.—I re-arranged them under their proper heads and filed them carefully away.

Q.—Will you produce them at the next sitting of the Commission?

A.—I will.

Q.—Tell me, Mr. James, do you know of a previous Commission having been appointed by the late Government to investigate text books?

A.—I do. I have a report of such a Commission, dated 12th November, 1897.

Q.—Who composed this Commission?

A.—(Judge) Edward Morgan, James Bain, Jr., and C. Blackett Robinson.

Q.—Have you a copy of the evidence then taken?

A.—No. There is no copy of any such evidence on my fyle.

Q.—Do you know who was the Secretary of that Commission?

A.—I believe Mr. Frank Nudel was the Secretary.

Mr. STAUNTON: That will do for the present, thank you.

The Commission then adjourned.

EVIDENCE TAKEN AT THE SECOND SITTING OF THE TEXT BOOK COMMISSION, 25TH SEPTEMBER, 1906.

Mr. J. A. MACDONALD, Examiner.

EVIDENCE OF MR. FRANK NASSAU NUDEL, TORONTO.

Q.—What is your name in full Mr. Nudel?

A.—Frank Nassau Nudel.

Q.—What is your official position in the Education Department?

A.—I am Acting Registrar at present.

Q.—Did you act in that position in November, 1897?

A.—I think I was Registrar in 1897.

Q.—Did you act in the capacity of Secretary to the Commission appointed in that year?

A.—I did.

Q.—Were notes of the evidence taken at the time?

A.—There were.

Q.—By you?

A.—Yes.

Q.—In shorthand?

A.—Yes, sir.

Q.—What did you do with the notes?

A.—Well, I made a transcription of the notes, a copy of which went to Mr. Nesbitt, and a copy to His Honour, Judge Morgan.

Q.—What did you do with your shorthand notes?

A.—I retained the note books for some two or three years after the report was printed and presented to the Legislature, and then destroyed the notes, after speaking to His Honour, who said there was no necessity to retain them any longer.

Q.—Did you go to Judge Morgan to ask him whether you should destroy them?

A.—I did not go exactly for that purpose, but I met him and asked him what I should do, if I might destroy them, and he said, as the report had been printed, that I might do so.

D.—Did you keep a copy besides the ones you made?

A.—I did not.

Q.—How many copies did you make altogether?

A.—I made three copies, one of which went to the Judge, and one to Mr. Nesbitt.

Q.—Mr. Nudel, is it usual for you to destroy your shorthand notes in a case like that?

A.—Well, I might say, that it was somewhat exceptional experience for me; I believe it is the custom of Secretaries to Ministers, that after a certain period has elapsed, copies of letters are made and put on fyle, that the notes are destroyed.

Q.—That is where there are copies on fyle?

A.—Yes.

Q.—But where no copies are on fyle?

A.—I might mention, that of course it was not directly an official report, that is, in connection with the Department.

Q.—But it was exceptional in this, that the notes were destroyed?

A.—Well, I was not instructed to have a copy of the evidence placed on fyle in the Department; I was instructed by the Commissioner that he would like copies of the evidence, and Mr. Wallace Nesbitt also asked that he be furnished with a copy of the evidence.

Q.—Then you handed over the notes extended to the Judge and Mr. Nesbitt, and there is no fyle of them in the Education Department?

A.—Yes, sir.

By Mr. COOPER:

Q.—Have you asked Judge Morgan to return those notes that you gave him?

A.—I did not. They were not returned to me, if returned at all.

Q.—To whom would they most likely be returned?

A.—I would only assume, that after the Commissioners made their report, that all documents would be returned to the late Minister, The Honourable Mr. Ross.

Q.—What clerk in the Department would have control or charge of these papers?

A.—In all probability, the first official who would handle them would be Mr. H. R. Alley, and then, if placed on fyle, they would go to Mr. Paull, the Clerk of Records.

By Mr. CROTHERS:

Q.—Is it not usual, that when a report· is made of such a Commission, to keep the evidence on which the report is founded?

A.—Well, Mr. Crothers, I cannot speak on that; the experience to me was somewhat a little exceptional, and I asked for instructions from Judge Morgan.

Q.—Well, did you ever know the evidence not to be fyled?

A.—Well, on similar occasions, any evidence that has been taken, such evidence is on fyle, that is, in regard to irregularities of teachers, etc., I believe they are on fyle.

By Mr. MACDONALD:

Q.—You say your superior officer was Dr. Ross; did you destroy the notes before consulting your superior officer?

A.—I did. I got any instructions I had from Judge Morgan.

That will do Mr. Nudel, thank you.

EVIDENCE OF MR. A. C. PAULL, EDUCATION DEPARTMENT, TORONTO.

By Mr. J. A. MACDONALD:

Q.—What is your name in full Mr. Paull?

A.—Arthur Charles Paull.

Q.—What is your official capacity in the Department of Education?

A.—Clerk of Records.

Q.—What position did you occupy in November, 1897?

A.—Well, practically the same position.

Q.—What are the duties of your office?

A.—Well, I may say, my duties are variable; in regard to the records, I keep charge of them and see that they are properly fyled away.

Q.—Then, if a record is required, you are the proper officer to ask for it?

A.—Yes.

Q.—You recollect the Commission of 1897, with regard to the cost of text books.

A.—Yes.

Q.—You have heard Mr. Nudel's evidence; he acted as Secretary of that Commission, extended the evidence and handed two copies to Judge Morgan, and one to Mr. Wallace Nesbitt, who represented the publishers on that occasion?

A.—Yes.

Q.—Did the report of the Commission come to your office?

A.—No; the report, as Mr. Nudel says, went to the Minister and then from him. I understand it was printed.

Q.—Where is the original report?

A.—I am not sure that such a report was ever fyled in the office.

Q.—Is it not usual to fyle a report of this kind in your office?

A.—Well, it should be fyled.

Q.—Can you say whether this report was fyled?

A.—I would not like to say for certain.

Q.—Where is the evidence upon which the report was based?

A.—Well, I have no recollection of seeing that; as far as I know, it was never received in the Department except it went to the Minister; I have no knowledge of it at all.

Q.—Are these notes now in the Department on fyle?

A.—No.

Q.—You have no knowledge of where they are?

A.—No, none whatever.

Q.—They could not have become mixed up in politics?

A.—I do not know as to that.

Q.—Have you any knowledge of the custom that prevailed in a Commission such as this was, in reference to the report, the fyling of it and the evidence upon which it was based?

A.—I think most of the Commissions that have been held, made their report and sent their evidence in complete.

Q.—Then this must have been an exception, and the report cannot be based on the evidence then taken?

A.—I do not know as to that.

Q.—Who was the Minister of Education at that time?

A.—The Honourable Mr. Ross.

By Mr. Cooper:

Q.—Have you made a special search through the records to find these notes, Mr. Paull?

A.—Yes, but have been unable to find them.

Mr. Macdonald: That will do Mr. Paull, thank you.

Evidence of Mr. John Macdonald, Kingston.

By Mr. J. A. Macdonald:

Q.—What is your name in full?

A.—John Macdonald.

Q.—Mr. Macdonald, you are the Secretary-Treasurer of the Board of Education for the City of Kingston, are you not?

A.—Yes, sir.

Q.—How long have you occupied that position?

A.—For fourteen years.

Q.—How is the Board of Education in Kingston situated; has it jurisdiction over public and high schools?

A.—They have jurisdiction over both; it is similar to the situation at Toronto.

Q.—Now what system prevails in Kingston as to the furnishing of text books to the pupils in the schools?

A.—We have a Fee System.

Q.—When was that system adopted?

A.—In 1902, and it was instituted in 1903.

Q.—How did it come to be adopted?

A.—Well, we experienced great difficulty in getting children to come to school, and also experienced great difficulty in having each child properly equipped to begin work.

Q.—Was there any agitation in the matter?

A.—Yes, there was some.

Q.—How did the agitation arise?

A.—It arose among the teachers first, and then the Trustees took it up: the teachers complained to the principals who consulted the inspector who communicated with myself.

Q.—There was an agitation then in the City of Kingston?

A.—Yes, in educational matters.

Q.—What shape did it take?

A.—Oh, it was confined to the teachers, trustees and officials.

Q.—Was any by-law necessary to introduce this system?

A.—No; it was wholly within the jurisdiction of the Board of Education; it is in the School Law, and we have that right under the Act.

Q.—Was there any opposition to the introduction of your system?

A.—No.

Q.—What method did you adopt in the purchasing of the books?

A.—By tender; I have the tender slips here. (Witness here hands tender slip to the examiner.)

Q.—How do you call for tenders?

A.—By advertising in the two daily papers in Kingston, it is purely local.

Q.—You did not go outside of the city to ask for tenders?

A.—No.

Q.—Then on what basis do you accept a tender?

A.—We accept the lowest tender.

Q.—Are you aware, Mr. Macdonald, of the nature of the contract existing between the Government, and the publishers to publish these school books?

A.—No sir.

Q.—Are you aware of the rate of discount that is provided under these contracts?

A.—No; I have heard of them, but I cannot say exactly.

Q.—What discount have you been able to secure from these local dealers?

WITNESS: Do you mean the difference between our purchase money, and the price of the goods?

Mr. MACDONALD: Yes, that is what I mean.

WITNESS: Yes, I should say 20 per cent.

Q.—The difference, then, between what you pay, and the retail price, would amount to 20 per cent. off the retail price; in other words, you save the pupil 20 per cent.?

A.—Yes.

Q.—Are you aware that you could save from 30 per cent. to 35 per cent. in buying from a wholesaler?

A.—Yes.

Q.—Under the terms of the contract existing between the Government and the publishers there is a rate of discount varying from 20 to 25 per cent. and 5 additional and another 5 additional, and you have been buying these books not knowing of the existence of such a condition?

A.—We would have to buy a certain quantity before we could get this discount which would be more than we require, and we find it a convenience in dealing with local dealers in that respect.

Q.—Then you denominate your system as the Fee System?

A.—Yes.

Q.—Who owns the property in the books?

A.—The Board; the pupil simply gets the use of the books.

Q.—Do they pay a rental?

A.—Yes, but the property remains in the Board. I have a slip here showing the rules on which a book is given to a pupil by the Board. (Witness here hands slip to examiner.)

The examiner here reads the following rules:—

Class..............................   .   Book No.....................
....School.

This book belongs to the Kingston Board of Education.

Conditions of Loaning.

1. Marking or defacing this book will be regarded as a serious offence.
2. In case of loss, destruction or material injury, this book must be at once replaced by the pupil.
3. This book may be replaced at cost through the Principal.
4. This book must not be taken from the school room without permission from the teacher.
5. This book must be returned to the teacher at the close of the term, or in case of removal of the pupil to another school.
6. In case of contagious disease, this book, if taken home, should be given to the Medical Health Officer, and a receipt taken from him therefor.

JOHN MACDONALD,
Secretary-Treasurer.
Board of Education.

Q.—How do the children or the pupils pay for their books?
A.—They pay at the beginning of each term, on the opening day, or the day after the opening.
Q.—What fees do they pay?
A.—I figure up the price of the books in each grade, and collect a fee to cover the cost.
Q.—Can you give me some idea as to what your total cost is for supplies, we will say for 1905?
A.—You mean books and supplies.
Examiner: Yes.
WITNESS: Well, the cost is $1,359.28.
Q.—That includes the cost of text books and various supplies, does it?
A.—Yes, everything.
Q.—What do the supplies consist of?
A.—Readers, Part I.
              Part II.
              Second.
              Third.
              Fourth.
    Writing Books.
    Ruled Work Books.
    Unruled Work Books.
    Exercise Books.
    Geographies, Public School.
    Grammars, Public School.
    Histories, Public School.
    Spellers, Public School.
    Physiologies, Public School
    Lead pencils.
    Slates.
    Slate pencils.
    Book Covers.
    Drawing Paper.
    Rulers.
    Foolscap Paper.

Pen Handles.
Pen Nibs.
Rubber Erasers.

Q.—Are there any other supplies?

A.—There are, of course, extras.

Q.—What extra supplies are there?

A.—Compasses.
Cardboard.
Raffia.
Folding Paper.
Carving Wood.
Carving Tools.
Wool.
Cotton.
Thread.
Needles.
Thimbles.
Scissors.
Darners.
Paint Boxes.
Paint Brushes.

Q.—So that for $1,359.28, you provide those necessary supplies for that year?

A.—Yes sir.

Q.—What revenue did you derive from this system of education for the year 1905?

A.—I did not bring that with me, but it just covers the cost; there was possibly about $30.00 over and above the fees, I might say about $1,365.00 taken in.

Q.—Then the Board is making no profit out of that system?

A.—None whatever, the Board merely buys the books and gives them to the pupils at the regular cost; we are always prepared to recommend a decrease in the fee.

Q.—How do you collect the fee?

A.—The teacher collects the fee from each class, and hands it over to the Principal of the school and he hands it over to me.

Q.—Do the teachers experience any difficulty in collecting fees?

A.—Well no, with the exception of two or three cases where the pupils are too poor to pay, in which cases, we remit the fee.

Q.—What is the relative proportion of the books and supplies?

A.—I was going to ask permission to explain this; all we paid for text books in that year was $73.00; that was the third year, in 1903 we paid $1,164.41, and in the second $100.30, and in the third year $73.65.

Q.—What was the cost this year?

A.—I think it will be less than $73.00, say $70.00 at the outside.

Mr. MACDONALD: Now this is a very marvelous sample of economy.

Q.—What is your total enrollment?

A.—2,575.

Q.—What average does that produce in the cost to the pupil?

A.—I did not figure it up, but would think about 14c.

Q.—Does that include supplies?

A.—No, simply text books alone.

Q.—What amount have you for supplies for 1905?

A.—$1,359.28.

Q.—Start with 1903?

5 T. B.

A.—$2,021.65.
Q.—For 1904?
A.—$1,274.13.
Q.—For 1905?
A.—$1,359.28.
Q.—Can you give me the amoun fo   06?
A.—No I cannot.
Q.—Do you think it will be as m h   last year?
A.—I should say it would be al ut   same, $1,350.00.
Q.—The total then, will show the v   for text books and supplies?
A.—Yes, I should say it would ve   about $1,500.00 per year.
Q.—What is the average to the p
A.—I would think, about 60c. p y   per pupil?
Q.—You think about 60c. is the v
A.—Yes, about that.   us some idea as to the value a
Q.—I would like you to be able g   unt, that is, what "quid pro
pupil in the Junior Third gets for is   it costs a pupil 70c. per year.
quo," you say that in the Junior Th t   n to a pupil in the Junior
What supplies and what text books e
Third for that fee?   ven unruled work books, one
A.—They get six ruled work l k   three pen holders, three
writing book, three exercise books, e
drawing books and one rubber erase
Q.—What is the value of these y   or 3c. a piece.
A.—The whole supply cost about 30
Q.—You sell them at the same te
A.—Yes.
Q.—That would amount to 18c. or   ix books?
A.—Yes
Q.—How many unruled work books   ou say?
A.—We give them seven in the Ju   Third.
Q.—At what cost?
A.—Those would be worth about 2c
Q.—Then there are the writing o   what is the value of them?
A.—Four cents (we make our o l   books).
Q.—What other supplies?
A.—We give them three exerci l   at 4c. a piece, then we give
them a 1.   ruler: this is worth a very ltle
Q.—W.   hat would that be worth
A.—Oh, riting Boabout 1c. anyway.
Q.—What d Work next?
A.—Then wed Work give them two or hr   n holders, as they use them;
these are worth ab Books.   out 2c. for the thee
Q.—Anything fees, Publ rther?   cils.
A.—Yes; we give Public them two drwr
Q.—How much a ublic Sci they worth   hen we give them a rubber
A.—They are wort lic School 3c. for th t   he use of a reader,—they get
eraser, worth about 1c.; Public S we also giv tl
the reader practically.   .?
Q.—What is the pri   e of the rad
A.—Yes.   supply them with different
Q.—Then in the diff   rent class.
books?   e give them just a reader,—we
    —Oh yes, but in ou   r Junior ir   than the Senior Third.
do   t Spellers and G   graphic lev

Q.—In the different class coming up from the Junior Third, I understand you supply a reade speller and geography; and to the Senior Fourth you supply a reader, a seller and physiology?

A.—Yes, that is right.

Q.—What about an arithmtic, do you supply that?

A.—No, we make the teaier teach all the arithmetic on the blackboard.

Q.—Do you not use an arhmetic in the schools?

A.—No, not in the hands of the pupils. I understand from the Inspector, that he can get better results from the teacher by putting everything on the board.

Q.—How high do you carr the sewing classes?

A.—Right up to the top.

Mr. MACDONALD: So that hen a boy leaves school he should be able to sew a button on his trouser

A.—Yes, that is about it.

Q.—Then the total value nounts to about 79c. per pupil?

A.—Yes.

Q.—What is the relative sving to the pupil?

A.—Well, there would be saving in quantity, for if he bought them he would use twice as many probably; the mere fact of having supervision by the teacher would make them last much longer.

Q.—Who did you say superises these matters?

A.—The teacher; and whe they get good results they speak of it indly.

Q.—What are the findings as far as the books are concerned, by the adoption of your system?

A.—Well, in the first plac it gives uniformity of equipment; every child in the school is equippedalike for the same work, and you can see the advantage of that when a cild is expected to move along at the same rate with others in his class. f you have one child half equipped, and another fully equipped, they cannot succeed the same, and we find it a very essential thing to have them equipped alike.

Q.—What effect has that sstem upon the attendance, does it help to keep the pupil at school any loner?

A.—Oh yes, we find that he children of immigrants from the Old Country, who come to our city get an earlier opportunity of attending school, otherwise, they would be in the city for three months or more before they would be able to sid their children to school,—not for lack of money but rather for lack of ime to get them properly equipped.

Q.—The foreign element ten would, therefore, have a ready access to your schools?

A.—Oh, yes.

Q.--Even if they have not the fee they need not lose one hour after they arrive in the city?

A.—Yes, they can come rigt along.

Q.—Do you think, Mr. Madonald, it is a financial advantage to the parent?

A.—I do, I think it is fully 50 per cent. in some cases.

Q.—What do you mean by 50 per cent.?

A.—It would lengthen the life of a book; the longer a book lives in a school under this system, the le fee would be charged.

By Mr. COOPER:

Q.—You mean to say then, hat the pupil will take better care of the book under the supervision of the teacher?

A.—$2,021.65.

Q.—For 1904?

A.—$1,274.13.

Q.—For 1905?

A.—$1,359.28.

Q.—Can you give me the amount for 1906?

A.—No I cannot.

Q.—Do you think it will be as much as last year?

A.—I should say it would be about the same, $1,350.00.

Q.—The total then, will show the average for text books and supplies?

A.—Yes, I should say it would average about $1,500.00 per year.

Q.—What is the average to the pupil?

A.—I would think, about 60c. per year.

Q.—You think about 60c. is the average per pupil?

A.—Yes, about that.

Q.—I would like you to be able to give us some idea as to the value a pupil in the Junior Third gets for this amount, that is, what "quid pro quo," you say that in the Junior Third class it costs a pupil 70c. per year. What supplies and what text books are given to a pupil in the Junior Third for that fee?

A.—They get six ruled work books, seven unruled work books, one writing book, three exercise books, one ruler, three pen holders, three drawing books and one rubber eraser.

Q.—What is the value of these books?

A.—The whole supply cost about $30.00, or 3c. a piece.

Q.—You sell them at the same rate?

A.—Yes.

Q.—That would amount to 18c. for the six books?

A.—Yes.

Q.—How many unruled work books did you say?

A.—We give them seven in the Junior Third.

Q.—At what cost?

A.—Those would be worth about 2c.

Q.—Then there are the writing books, what is the value of them?

A.—Four cents (we make our own writing books).

Q.—What other supplies?

A.—We give them three exercise books at 4c. a piece, then we give them a ruler; this is worth a very little.

Q.—What would that be worth?

A.—Oh, about 1c. anyway.

Q.—What next?

A.—Then we give them two or three pen holders, as they use them; these are worth about 2c. for the three.

Q.—Anything further?

A.—Yes; we give them two drawing pencils.

Q.—How much are they worth?

A.—They are worth 3c. for the two; then we give them a rubber eraser, worth about 1c.; we also give them the use of a reader,—they get the reader practically.

Q.—What is the price of the reader, 20c.?

A.—Yes.

Q.—Then in the different classes, you supply them with different books?

A.—Oh yes, but in our Junior Third we give them just a reader,—we do not put Spellers and Geographies lower than the Senior Third.

5a T. B.

Q.—In the different classes coming up from the Junior Third, I understand you supply a reader, speller and geography; and to the Senior Fourth you supply a reader, a speller and physiology?

A.—Yes, that is right.

Q.—What about an arithmetic, do you supply that?

A.—No, we make the teacher teach all the arithmetic on the black-board.

Q.—Do you not use an arithmetic in the schools?

A.—No, not in the hands of the pupils. I understand from the In-spector, that he can get better results from the teacher by putting every-thing on the board.

Q.—How high do you carry the sewing classes?

A.—Right up to the top.

Mr. MACDONALD: So that when a boy leaves school he should be able to sew a button on his trousers?

A.—Yes, that is about it.

Q.—Then the total value amounts to about 79c. per pupil?

A.—Yes.

Q.—What is the relative saving to the pupil?

A.—Well, there would be a saving in quantity, for if he bought them he would use twice as many probably; the mere fact of having supervision by the teacher would make them last much longer.

Q.—Who did you say supervises these matters?

A.—The teacher; and when they get good results they speak of it kindly.

Q.—What are the findings, as far as the books are concerned, by the adoption of your system?

A.—Well, in the first place, it gives uniformity of equipment; every child in the school is equipped alike for the same work, and you can see the advantage of that when a child is expected to move along at the same rate with others in his class. If you have one child half equipped, and another fully equipped, they cannot succeed the same, and we find it a very essential thing to have them equipped alike.

Q.—What effect has that system upon the attendance, does it help to keep the pupil at school any longer?

A.—Oh yes, we find that the children of immigrants from the Old Country, who come to our city, get an earlier opportunity of attending school, otherwise, they would be in the city for three months or more before they would be able to send their children to school,—not for lack of money but rather for lack of time to get them properly equipped.

Q.—The foreign element then would, therefore, have a ready access to your schools?

A.—Oh, yes.

Q.--Even if they have not the fee they need not lose one hour after they arrive in the city?

A.—Yes, they can come right along.

Q.—Do you think, Mr. Macdonald, it is a financial advantage to the parent?

A.—I do, I think it is fully 50 per cent. in some cases.

Q.—What do you mean by 50 per cent.?

A.—It would lengthen the life of a book; the longer a book lives in a school under this system, the less fee would be charged.

By Mr. COOPER:

Q.—You mean to say then, that the pupil will take better care of the book under the supervision of the teacher?

A.—Yes.

Q.—And you say that there would be a saving of 50 per cent. to the pupil?

A.—Yes, all round.

By Mr. MACDONALD:

Q.—What would it cost the parents if this system were not in force?

A.—About double that amount.

Q.—On the average then, you think, the fees are about 50 per cent. of what an ordinary parent would pay?

A. -Yes.

Q.—Have you any other advantages?

A.—No, I cannot think of any others at present.

Q.—I want to find out a little further regarding the life of the book being prolonged by reason of this system, in so far as the property in the book is concerned. Does a child take greater care of a book because it belongs to someone else than if it belonged to himself.

A.—Yes, we find that it does. This is why we state on our label "This book belongs to the Board of Education."

Q.—You mean then, that the book will last about twice as long?

A.—Yes, I find that we can make it last twice as long; it doubles the life of the book.

Q.—According to your evidence, Mr. Macdonald, if we had someone come here and say the books did not last very long, you would say that was the result of their system and not the books?

A.—Yes.

Q.—What influence does your system exert on the pupil as far as his remaining at school when they get up in a higher form?

A.— I have never thought of it in that light.

Q.—How does it strike you now; is there any inducement for a pupil to remain on after coming up to a higher class for the reason that the books are supplied cheaper?

A.—It never occurred to me to think of it in that light.

Q.—Now what do you do with the books, supposing there is thirty pupils in a class, and only twenty-five books in that same class; who would get the five new books, and who the twenty-five old ones?

A.—Now, there is just the trouble in the transfer of books, that is the only objection in our system.

Q.—Does that create jealousy among the pupils?

A.—It does create talk among the pupils, but the teachers are really very discreet in making these transfers, so that a clean child will not get a dirty book.

Q.—You mean to tell me then, that she gives dirty books to dirty children, and the clean books to the clean children?

A.—No, I would not like to say that.

Q.—Have you cases where pupils agree to purchase their own books?

A.—Yes.

Q.—What do you say to lost books, or books seriously damaged?

A.—We fine the pupil, that is, if they lose or damage the book through neglect; the fine is based upon the value of the book.

Q.—What tendency has your system towards cleanliness; in other words, are the pupils under your system likely to have the books any cleaner than if they owned them themselves?

A.—Decidedly so; the books are inspected regularly by the teachers.

Q.—Then the teacher supervises the books and the pupil with regard to their cleanliness?

A.—Yes; we have some pupils who keep their books perfect for years, but that is not of actual credit to the pupil as it would indicate that he did not use them much.

Q.—What advantage is accrued to the teacher from the adoption of this system? Will the supervision of the books entail extra duty on her part?

A.—She has her class to equip always, every day from the very beginning of the term to the end, so that she can get on with her work much better and do much better work.

Q.—Now, Mr. Macdonald, has the subject of infectious diseases ever been mentioned in connection with your system?

A.—Oh, yes.

Q.—Have any cases been reported during the time your system has been in force for the three years?

A.—Not that I have heard of; of course doctors blame the reason that pupils get sick on the schools, but I have not heard of it being attributed to our books.

Q.—In case an infectious disease is found to be in the home of a pupil what course do you adopt with the books?

A.—We immediately destroy everything in use by that pupil in the school.

Q.—Supposing these books were owned by the pupil, would you have the same ready access to destroy them in your capacity as Secretary of the Board?

A.—No, I would not consider that I had; but in the case of disease breaking out, we destroy the books immediately; that is one of the benefits of our system.

Q.—In the event of the books being owned by the pupil, then the only tendency would be to retain those books until the disease had disappeared?

A.—Yes, very likely.

Q.—Would not that be a means of conveying infectious germs?

A.—Yes.

Q.—So there is an advantage in the property being in the Board as against it being vested in the pupil, if for this reason only?

A.—Yes, decidedly so.

Q.—Was there any other objection raised in addition to that of the infectious disease being carried by the books?

A.—No, I do not think so; the transfer of the books was the main objection.

Q.—Mr. Macdonald, did you ever hear of any objection being made to the transfer of paper money for this reason?

A.—No, I never heard of money being refused on that ground.

Q.—Have you brought with you any samples of the books that are used in Kingston?

A.—Yes.

Q.—Just produce them, please. (Witness produces a number of text books and hands them to examiner).

Q.—Here is a book that has been in use for two years; do you know in whose hands that book has been?

A.—Yes, the name is there.

Q.—What class of pupil has this Third Reader belonged to?

A.—An average pupil.

Q.—Look at this book, please; what condition is it in?

A.—It is in good condition; there is not a loose leaf in it.

Q.—How do you account for it, Mr. Macdonald?

A.—I should say the daily supervision of the teacher and the control and possession of the book by the Board.

Q.—If it were the property of the pupil you would not expect it to be in as good condition?

A.—No.

By Mr. COOPER:

Q.—Was this book in use every day for two years?

A.—Yes.

Q.—Was it taken home every night?

A.—Yes.

Q.—Is that the only book you allow them to take home?

A.—No, they can take home every book if they get the permission of the teacher.

Q.—What is the difference then in giving the books and the pupils buying them?

A.—The only difference is that they have to exercise greater care when the books belong to the Board.

WITNESS: (Selecting a book from the pile) Here is a Fourth Book in use three years in excellent condition.

Q.—Have any observations or complaints been made to you by the teachers in regard to the binding of the books? If so, what books were complained of?

A.—Yes, objections have been made to the wire binding.

Q.—What is the objection to the wire binding?

A.—The wire bursts through the sections of the book and it has to be re-bound.

Q.—Have you found it necessary to repair the books?

A.—Yes.

Q.—What is your system of repairing?

A.—We have them re-bound; we have now a great many so far; all our books are now going into the fourth year.

Q.—How are they re-bound?

A.—They are stitched where the wire was and the back taken off and re-glued.

Q.—Do you find that quite as durable?

A.—They are quite as durable.

Q.—Then by this system you say you retain the life of the book two fold?

A.—Yes.

Q.—Is it customary to have a tight back?

A.—Yes.

Q.—Well, I think it is more readily bound that way.

Q.—Here is another Second Reader, in use two years, in bad condition; how do you account for the difference in the two books?

A.—Well, I think it is the fault of the pupils; they bend them back.

Q.—Do you consider if this wire bound book had been stitched with thread that it would have been better?

A.—Yes.

Q.—Does the wire scratch?

A.—Not in many, but I have noticed it before.

WITNESS (selecting book): Here is a good sample of the way a book goes to pieces when bound with wire.

Q.—I see that the back is fastened with mull and that it breaks away readily.

A.—Yes.

Q.—Now, here is a "History of England and Canada," published by Copp, Clark & Co., price 30c.; how long has this book been in use?

A.—Three years.

Q.—In whose possession has it been in that time?

A.—It has been in the possession of different pupils; the teachers tell me that this is the poorest bound book of the lot.

Q.—You say that the teachers find more fault with this History than any of the other books?

A.—Yes.

Q.—How long, in your opinion, should this book last?

A.—Under our supervision that book should last five years if it had been properly bound.

Q.—Are your books covered by the pupils?

A.—Yes.

Q.—I should imagine it had a tendency towards cleanliness?

A.—Yes, we give them two covers per year.

Q.—Do you do so wholly on sanitary grounds?

A.—Yes, and to preserve the cover.

Q.—Do you mean that you have no confidence in the covers of the books and you put on others?

A.—No, I would not say that.

Q.—Why does not the publisher put on a manilla cover?

A.—I do not know about that; it is covered by the pupil simply to keep it clean.

Q.—What does the re-binding cost you?

A.—Five and ten cents per book are the repairing prices.

Q.—Do you think it would be a good idea if all the publishers turned out their books with protecting covers on them?

A.—Well, they would have to keep on supplying them as they only last from two to three months.

Q.—What does these manilla covers cost?

A.—Twenty-four cents per hundred, or $2.40 per thousand.

Q.—Do you think the rapid wearing out of the covers on the books is the fault of the poor quality of cloth?

A.—No, I think it is rather from the use of the book.

Q.—In the matter of repairs, which books cost five cents and which books cost ten cents for repairing?

A.—It depends altogether on the damage done to the book; the smaller and less expensive ones are, of course, the cheapest to repair.

Q.—Those prices include stitching the books?

A.—Yes.

By Mr. COOPER:

Q.—If you were advising a man, Mr. Macdonald, would you advise him to see if the books were better sewn or better bound?

A.—Well, with regard to Readers I have an idea of my own.

Q.—What is your idea?

A.—My idea is from a hygienic standpoint; you get up a cheap reader that would stand one year only; and in the other grades separate the books into two parts so that each part would last only one year. In this way you

would have new books each class year and at a less expenditure, besides
doing away with the complaints as to danger from germs of disease..

By Mr. MACDONALD:

Q.—What Primer do you use in Kingston, Mr. Macdonald?

A.—Morang's.

Q.—How many are there authorized?

A.—I cannot say; I know there are two or three.

Q.—Have you a sample of that Primer with you?

A.—No, we just use these books one year and then destroy them.

Q.—Are you an advocate of free text books, Mr. Macdonald?

A.—Yes, very strong.

Q.—Ou what basis?

A.—On these three points, namely,—uniformity of equipment, individual equipment and a reduction of truancy.

Q.—These are the principal reasons, which you put forward for your plan in the system of Free Text Books?

A.—Yes.

Well, that is about all I shall ask you this morning, Mr. Macdonald, thank you. Call the next witness.

EVIDENCE OF MR. ARTHUR K. BUNNELL, BRANTFORD.

By Mr. MACDONALD:

Q.—What is your name in full?

A.—Arthur K. Bunnell.

Q.—What is your position?

A.—Secretary-Treasurer Public School Board.

Q.—Board of Education?

·A.—We have no Board of Education.

Q.—What is the jurisdiction of your Board?

A.—It is supreme in its own forms.

Q.—Are there then only Public Schools?

A.—Well, I should have added Technical School and School of Domestic Science.

Q.—How long have you occupied the position of Secretary-Treasurer to the Board?

A.—About thirteen years.

Q.—What system prevails in Brantford, Mr. Bunnell, as to text books?

A.—Practically the same system as that in Kingston, the "Fee System."

Q.—How is the fee levied?

A.—It is levied according to the classes; we have not changed our system for many years; we have the same fee every year.

Q.—What is that fee?

A.—The first book pupils pay 10c. three times per year; the second book pupils pay 10c. per month, and the fourth and fifth book pupils pay 20c. per month.

Q.—What was the total revenue in 1905?

A.—About $2,000.00.

Q.—How many pupils did you have that year?

A.—In 1905 we had 2,682 pupils.

Q.—What is the average cost per pupil?

A.—The average cost would be about 80c. per pupil; possibly a little less than that.

Q.—Per annum?

A.—Yes.

Q.—What do you give the pupils for that money?

A.—We give them their books and all supplies required for the conduct of their education; in the higher forms we give them the advantage of going to the Technical School; and to the girls, the privilege of attending the School of Domestic Science.

Q.—Do the supplies include those schools?

A.—Well, it is this way, we contribute a stated sum towards those schools; the Domestic Science is conducted by the Young Women's Christian Association and we pay a bulk sum per annum for the services received by the pupils.

Q.—There is then no tax levied upon the pupils to support these schools?

A.—No.

Q.—You pay all the fees of the pupils from your schools attending both the Technical School and School of Practical Science?

A.—Yes, we pay the total cost in connection with it.

Q.—Upon what basis do you levy those charges?

A.—From what I know it is based on the price the books cost the Board.

Q.—How do you buy your books?

A.—We buy by tender.

Q.—To whom do you extend the privilege of tendering?

A.—Latterly we have asked only the local dealers because we found it impossible to get outside tenders.

Q.—Why did you not go to the wholesalers?

A.—Because I found that invitations to tender sent by me were, by the wholesalers returned to our local dealers.

Q.—What publisher or wholesaler did that?

A.—I cannot remember at this moment.

Q.—Did you ask all publishers to tender?

A.—I cannot say; I got a list of firms and sent a notice to each.

Q.—What bulk or quantity did you offer to buy?

A.—Well, I can tell you about what we are using now; but I cannot remember in what year that happened or what the quantity was in that year.

Q.—Can you give me roughly the amount of supplies you required? I mean, of course, text books.

A.—Well, we would ask for supplies of everything?

Q.—Tell me, if you can, what the amount would be for text books?

A.—About $600.00 annually in text books.

Q:—Do you make application to the publishers for text books?

A.—No, we did not make any separate application; we simply called for tenders on books and supplies for the Brantford Public School Board from first of July to first of July.

Q.—You would not expect publishers to handle supplies would you?

A.—I do not know and therefore cannot state definitely as to that.

Q.—Well, your invitation to tender was sent to them then?

A.—No, it was sent to wholesalers in Toronto.

Q.—And they were returned?

A.—Yes, our local man told me that our request simply came back to him.

Q.—To whom did you send the notices?

A.—I do not know the names; I fancy the Principal of the school supplied me with the names.

Q.—What books do you supply to your pupils?

A.—Everything that they require.

Q.—Have you anything with you to show what books you supply to them?

A.—Yes, I have our tenders here for 1903 and 1904-5-6 and 7; that is, for text books and supplies.

Q.—Well, then, Mr. Bunnell, take those for 1906 and 1907.

A.—Here is Mr. Sutherland's tender for books and supplies for 1906 and 1907 :—

Arithmetics, P. S.	per doz.	$2 05
Bookkeeping Text, H. S.	per doz.	5 40
Bookkeeping C. C., No. 14	per doz.	2 00
Blotting paper as sample	per M.	75
Copy Books, Blanks as sample	per doz.	20
Composition Books, as sample	per doz.	25
Drawing Books Blank, as sample	per doz.	35
Drawing Paper, as sample	per M.	50
Erasers, Andrews' Dustless Cotton, Felt	per doz	35
Geography, P. S.	per doz.	6 25
Grammar, Morang, Buchler, 25c. edition	per doz.	2 25
History, P. S.	per doz.	2 43
Hygiene and Phys., Knight's	per doz.	5 50
Ink, Duckett's dry, half gallon cans	1 gal.	25
Ink, red, 2-oz. bottles	per doz.	36
Mammoth Ex. Books	per doz.	75
Mucilage, Staff, 2-oz.	per doz.	36
Numeral Frames, 144 Balls	each	25
Pencils, red or blue marking	per gross	2 20
Penholders, E. F. 2491-3178	per gross	1 50
Pens, Est. Falcon 048	per gross	45
Pencil Books, 200 pages	per doz.	23
Pencil Books, 100 pages	per doz.	15
Pen and Pencil Books, as sample	per doz.	35
Pitman Manual, 20th Cent. Phon.	per doz.	3 30
Reporters' Note Books, as sample	per doz.	45
Rulers, Foot, submit sample with in. and half in. mk. per 100	per 100	65
Readers, Part I, Can. Pub Co.	per doz.	90
Readers, Part II, Can. Pub. Co., new ed.	per doz.	1 34
Readers, Bk. III, Old kind	per doz.	2 57
Readers, Part 2, Morang	per doz.	1 32
Readers, Bk. IV, Old kind	per doz.	3 42
Spellers, P. S.	per doz.	2 00
Britannia History Readers, Introd.	per doz.	2 25
Britannia History Readers, Book I	per doz.	2 70
Britannia History Readers, Book II	per doz.	3 60
Britannia History Readers, Book III	per doz.	3 60
Britannia History Readers, Book IV	per doz.	3 60
Britain and Empire, Putnam	per doz.	5 00
Copy Book (Medial Slant), 1-6	per doz.	55
Crayons, White Waltham	per doz.	08
Crayons, Colored, best mixed	per doz.	60
Carbon Paper, for manifold	per 100	1 25
Canadian People, Duncan	per doz.	4 50
Century Cyclopædia of Names		
Dictionary, Funk and Wagnall Standard, 2 vols.		
Dictionary, Funk and Wagnall Standard, 1 vol.		9 50
Dictionary Student, Comp.		85
Envelopes, Commercial No. 7	per 1,000	60
Foolscap, ruled, cut, 10 lb.	per 1,000	73
Foolscap, ruled, cut, 12 lb.	per 1,000	84
Foolscap, ruled, cut, 14 lb.	per 1,000	1 00
Grammar, P. S.	per doz.	1 95

History of England, Symes & Wrong ....per doz.		$4 50
Maps ....35% off regular retail price.		
Physiology, P. S. ....per doz.		1 95
Pencils, slate, sharpened ....per box		9
Pencils, Bavaria 4487 Lead ....per gross		75
Pencils, Kangaroo ....per gross		1 70
Pencils, Faber's Sphinx H. B. ....per gross		1 75
Pencils, Faber's Polygrade, 1204 H. B. ....per gross		3 00
Paper Fasteners, R. or S 0 ....per 100		03
Paper Fasteners, R. or S 1 ....per 100		04
Paper Fasteners, R. or S 2 ....per 100		04
Paper Fasteners, R. or S 3 ....per 100		05
Paper Fasteners, R. or S 4 ....per 100		06
Rubber Bands, assorted sizes ....per box		15
Readers, Part I, Morang ....per doz.		90
Readers, Part II, Can. Pub. Co. ....per doz.		2 25
Readers, Bk. II, Morang ....per doz.		2 25
Readers, Bk. II, Old kind ....per doz.		1 72
Slates, Am. Best, 6 in. x 9 in. ....per doz.		52
Slates, Am. Best, 7 in. x 11 in. ....per doz.		58
Slates, Cloth Bound, 6 in. x 9 in. ....per doz.		80
Slates, Cloth Bound, 7 in. x 11 in. ....per doz.		1 00
Typewriter Paper ....per 1.000		45
Riverside Series Literature, paper ....each		12
Riverside Series Literature, cloth ....each		20
Morang Series Literature, paper ....each		12

Q.—Has that tender been filled?

A.—Yes, it is now in force.

Q.—On what basis did you purchase?

A.—We bought them on those prices.

Q.—Have you been able to figure out what the difference is?

A.—No, I am not familiar with it; you would have to take the retail price and figure it up.

Q.—That is then the cheapest you can buy?

A. Yes; we had two tenders on these lines.

Q.—Then your fee is based upon that system?

A.—Yes, it is supposed to be based upon that system.

Q.—Who has charge of the supervision of the text books and supplies?

A.—The Principal of each school primarily and the teachers under the Principal.

Q.—Are the children allowed to take the books home?

A.—They are.

Q.—How does your system work out in so far as prolonging the life of the books is concerned?

A.—Well as to that, I may say that latterly we have adopted the system of getting each of the pupils when they come into a class a new set of books, and when they leave we permit them to take their books with them; we found that the Medical Health Officer objected to the books being in use by so many pupils and last year we discarded the system and let the pupils take the books away.

Q.—Does that practice not increase the expenses?

A.—Yes.

Q.—To what proportion?

A.—It would increase the average by about 10 cents per head.

Q.—In whom then is the property of the book vested?

A.—It now rests with the pupil.

Q.—Is there any advantage in the vesting of the property in the pupil as against the Board?

A.—Well, the parents seem to be pleased that the children are allowed to take the books away from the school.

Q.—You let them have the books as a memento of their school days, I suppose?

A.—Yes, I guess that is the reason the parents are so pleased.

Q.—Now Mr. Bunnell, before we pass on to the question of Medical Inspection, I want you to take a pupil in the Junior Third and tell me what fee you collect from him?

A.—15 cents per month or $1.50 per year—of ten months.

Q.—Can you give me a comparative estimate of the value that you give in return for that amount?

A.—I cannot; that is under the supervision of the teacher, it is not in my knowledge.

Q.—You cannot give me an estimate?

A.—I cannot.

Q.—Now, Mr. Bunnell, referring back for a moment, you said something about the Medical Health Officer interfering and suggesting that the books should not be transferred from one pupil to another?

A.—Yes, sir.

Q.—Tell me then, how long the system of transferring the books was in force?

A.—Probably forty years.

Q.—In the City of Brantford?

A.—Yes, we have had free text books ever since I can remember.

Q.—Would you call yours a system of free text books?

A.—Yes, we call it free text books; it is not really free, but we call it so; it is really a "Fee Text Book System."

By Mr. CROTHERS:

Q.—When did you adopt the new system?

A.—I recommended the Board to adopt this system in 1905.

Q.—What were the characteristics of the free text books that prevailed prior to 1905?

A.—There was no difference in the books or in the fees; but we kept the books as long as we were able to pass them along to the pupils from one to another.

Q.—Now you give them new books each year and let them take them away.

A.—Yes, new books when required.

Q.—On what grounds did you make the change: because of the suggestions of the Health Officer? Had there been other complaints?

A.—Yes, great complaints, and the books got the benefit of the blame; they said they were the cause of the illness at all events.

Q.—Of course, that cry has had the effect of increasing the number of books bought?

A.—Yes.

Q.—And incidentally this helps the publisher?

A.—Well, if he was making any profit on it at all it would certainly help him.

By Mr. COOPER:

Q.—Did you ever hear of any other city on the continent that had adopted free text books and gone back on it?

A.—We have not gone back on it, and I do not know anything outside our own city.

Mr. Cooper remarks. (Yes, you have gone back on it, as far as I can see. Brantford stands unique in having discarded that system.)

Mr. J. A. MACDONALD: Now, Mr. Bunnell, I would like some more information concerning the advantages derived from your system. (Witness interrupting: I have a letter here from our Mr. J. P. Hoag, Brantford, which might be interesting to you.)

Mr. MACDONALD: Well, let us hear it.

(Witness here reads letter as follows):—

BRANTFORD, September 24th, 1906.

DEAR MR. BUNNELL,—Miss Purves informs me that our present system of supplying text books, etc., has been in operation for at least forty years.

Our fees are as follows:—

1st Bk. Pupils (Pt. I, Pt. II), 10 cents three times a year, Sept., Jan. and April.

2nd Bk. Pupils, 10 cents a month.

3rd Bk. Pupils, 15 cents a month.

4th Bk. Pupils, 20 cents a month.

5th Bk. Pupils, 20 cents a month.

These fees now just about pay for the books, previously a slight profit was made.

As you will notice, the cost for 1905-6 was very much higher than for any previous year. This is due to the fact that the Board has decided that the text books shall belong to the pupil on his completion of his course, *i.e.*, a boy finishing his third book work will take home as his own, his third reader, instead of having it serve for one or more other pupils.

I enclose a copy of the old rules for guidance of teachers in giving out supplies. Our supplies to-day cost more because we give better "lead pencils," slates (cloth bound instead of wood frame), "pens," etc., to the pupils. Besides we give geographies and histories to third book classes, whereas the former plan was to give only to fourth book classes and have teachers of third book give elaborate notes to the pupils.

The system is excellent as every pupil has his book, slate, pencil, etc., when it is needed, and if he is poor, he does not even have to pay fees. Supplies are got promptly and all books are alike; there is no trouble about changing text books as we can use up old stock before we change. Teachers experience little difficulty in collecting the fees, and the parents, I believe, like the system very well, since new books are given in each subject when it is begun. There are a great many details, which I cannot describe, however.

I have at the Central a list of books used for one year, for two years and in a few cases for three years. If you wish to take them with you to Toronto, please send a note by bearer to Mr. Aberhart and Mr. Jackson will pack them up and send to your address in Toronto, by express. The package will be somewhat large.

Yours truly,

(Signed) J. P. HOAG.

By Mr. MACDONALD:

Q.—Yes, I see Mr. Hoag gives practically the same information in his letter to you that you have given us here yourself?

Q.—Well now, Mr. Bunnell, coming back to the sanitary side of the question, are we to understand that the reason for adopting the system of allowing the pupils to retain the books and issuing new ones, was solely on sanitary grounds?

A.—No, I cannot say that, but it is one of the reasons.

Q.—What other reasons would there be?

A.—Oh, except that the children liked to have their own books to take home; and I have heard people remark that they pay fees for the books and they should be theirs.

Q.—Did you think your fees were so high that the parents were not getting value for their money?

A.—I never heard it that way.

Q.—Did the fees cover the cost before 1905?

A.—It covered the cost before we adopted the Technical School and Domestic Science.

Q.—Did it cover any more than the cost?

A.—Probably about $200.00 over and above.

Q.—Mr. Bunnell, in the system prevailing prior to 1905, were the pupils allowed to take their books home with them?

A.—Yes.

Q.—And you say they are still allowed the same privilege?

A.—Yes; they take them home to acquire their lessons at night.

Q.—What do you do in case disease breaks out in a home, that is, as far as the books are concerned?

A.—Well, the Medical Health Officer looks after that matter, as he is the proper person to deal with it.

Q.—I mean, what would the Board of Education do?

A.—We simply forbid the pupil coming to the school until he gets an order from the Medical Health Officer that he can come back.

Q.—How about the books?

A.—Well, they are not permitted to be returned to the school until we are satisfied by the Medical Health Officer that they are free from contagion.

By Mr. Cooper:

Q.—Do you think then, that you are dependent on the Medical Health Officer in such cases?

A.—Perhaps so, Mr. Cooper.

Q.—The point I wish to get at is, that by private ownership of the books, the pupils can bring them back whether there is any disease or not?

A.—No, I think we could object to anything that would affect the sanitary condition of the schools or the health of the pupils.

Q.—While you have a strictly legal right to object if you desire to, yet it remains practically with the Medical Health Officer to enforce conditions?

A.—Well, I have not charge of the actual running of the schools myself, but, subject to correction, I think you are right.

Q.—Suppose that the system of free text books prevailed, the Board would have control of the books and could order them destroyed; whereas it would not have the right or power in cases where the books were owned by the pupils; that is, I want to bring out the means by which infectious diseases could be prevented, that is, would there be less chance of a disease becoming contagious if the books were owned by the pupil or by the Board?

A.—That is too difficult for me and might better be answered by a medical man.

Q.—Well, put it this way; ownership by the pupil means that where disease exists in a home, the books are retained there while the disease is running its course and brought back to school after the disease is supposed to be gone?

A.—It is still too abstruse for me, I think it would be better to have a medical man give you an opinion on that; but I do not think that there would be a bit of difference, there would be no communication of disease in any case as the Medical Health Officer would not allow a child to return to school until the disease had been properly stamped out.

Q.—Well then, Mr. Bunnell, we will pass on to the subject of binding. Have any complaints reached you about the binding of the books?

A.—There were complaints some years ago, but that was when we were trying to make the books last a long time; under the present system that does not obtain.

Q.—You are satisfied under your system if they hold out one year?

A.—Yes; but in some cases I have known books last two and three years.

Q.—Now, Mr. Bunnell, you have heard the evidence of Mr. Macdonald, and you understand the nature of the Commission; is there any suggestion you can offer in connection with reducing the cost of text books, apart from the system prevailing in your city?

A.—No, I cannot say that I have, beyond the fact that we always try to buy our books as cheap as we can get them.

Q.—You are not sure then, that you are not paying more for your books under your system than if you bought them direct from the publisher?

A.—I don't know; but I think we buy them very close; I believe that our tenderers cut the prices down very low.

Q.—Are you aware of the contract that exists between the Government and the publishers which provides for a discount of 25 per cent. and an additional 5 per cent.

A.—I am not.

Q.—Have you had any complaints from parents as to your fees?

A.—No, not to my knowledge. If a child is not able to pay we admit him free; we do not keep any child from school because they cannot pay.

Q.—In what respect do you find your Fee System an advantage?

A.—We believe that the parents get better value for the money than if they were compelled to buy the books at retail price, or, in other words, the advantage comes by buying in bulk.

Q.—In your argument for free text books and a free system of education, would you not naturally desire to see the tax distributed among the rate-payers generally than among the pupils of the schools?

A.—Well, I do not know about that; the person who gets the direct benefit is not over charged as it is.

By Mr. Cooper:

Q.—Under your present system, I understand, that when pupils are promoted from one form to another you give them new books?

A.—Yes.

Q.—And when the books are worn out you give new ones to replace them without extra charge?

A.—Yes, that is our system.

Q.—Is there a public library in Brantford?

A.—There is.

Q.—Then, as I understand it, your present system has been in force for two years?

A.—Yes,

Q.—Have you increased the fee under this new system?

A.—No, not at all.

Q.—Yet it costs your Board a great deal more?

A.—Yes.

Q.—How is it that you have not increased your fee?

A.—We had a surplus and thought that we were entitled to use it in buying books.

By Mr. MACDONALD:

Q.—You have about the same number of pupils in Brantford as in Kingston, yet they get text books for $100.00 as against the $600.00 you expend. That is a very remarkable difference, is it not?

A.—It looks like it?

Q.—Do you not think the system is very expensive?

A.—No, I think it is in the handling of the books.

Q.—Were you careful to keep the books repaired?

A.—Under the previous system the teacher would have the books repaired.

Q.—So there was no sorting out of books to see if they required binding regularly?

A.—Well, I cannot say as to that.

Q.—You do no re-binding at all under your present system?

A.—I would not say that; a teacher may fix up a book for a child to enable him to use it; but that is not included in our system.

Q.—You see then, the difference between your system and the one in vogue in Kingston?

A.—I do, but they do not supply as many books as we do.

Q.—Did you bring down some of your books, Mr. Bunnell?

A.—Yes, sir.

Q.—You might produce them if you please?

(Witness produces package of books for inspection.)

Mr. Macdonald, selecting one, hands it to witness and asks: What book is that?

A.—A Second Book.

Q.—How long has it been in use?

A.—One year.

Q.—What is the next book?

Q.—A Public School History of England and Canada.

Q.—Who publishes it?

A.—Copp, Clark & Co.

Q.—How long has it been in use?

A.—Two years.

Q.—How many pupils have had possession of it?

A.—I cannot say; I do not know of more than one.

Q.—What is the next book?

A.—A Public School Grammar by H. T. Strang.

Q.—How long in use?

A.—Two years.

Q.—What condition do you consider that book is in?

A.—A used up condition.

Q.—How does the binding of that strike you? Do you think that the dilapidated condition is due to the binding?

A.—I would think it was the usage received.

Q.—Take the next book, what is that?

A.—A practical Speller, published by W. J. Gage.

Q.—How long in use?

A.—Two years.

Q.—The next one?

A.—Primer, by Morang; in use one year.

Q.—What condition is it in?

A.—Fair.

Q.—What next?

A.—A Public School Second Reader, by the Canada Publishing Company in use one year.

Q.—Very bad condition?

A.—Yes.

Q.—Your next one, please?

A.—Practical Speller, by W. J. Gage.

Q.—How long in use?

A.—One year.

Q.—In good condition?

A.—Yes.

Q.—How often has this book been used, daily?

A.—I cannot say.

Q.—Well, give me the next one?

A.—A Public School History of England and Canada, by Copp, Clark Co.; in use two years.

Q.—What condition?

A.—Fair condition.

Q.—The next one?

A.—Public School Grammar, in use three years and in very good shape.

Q.—What is the next?

A.—A Phonic Primer; in use one year.

Q.—Who is the Publisher?

A.—Morang.

Q.—What condition is that in?

A.—Fair condition.

Q.—What others have you there?

A.—Third Reader; Canada Publishing Company; in use one year and in bad condition. A Third Reader; in use two years; in better condition than the others.

Q.—Who is the publisher?

A.—Copp, Clark Co.

Q.—Next one?

A.—Fourth Reader, by Ayers; in use one year; in very bad condition—all broken.

Q.—How many more have you there?

A.—Three; Public School Geographies; the first one in use three years; the second in use two years, and the third in use one year.

Q.—These are all the books you have to produce?

A.—Yes sir.

Mr. MACDONALD: Thank you, Mr. Bunnell; that will do.

----

6 T. B.

EVIDENCE TAKEN AT THE THIRD SITTING OF THE TEXT BOOK
COMMISSION, SEPTEMBER 26TH, 1906.

G. L. Staunton, K.C., Examiner:

Evidence of Mr. W. C. Flint, Toronto.

By Mr. Staunton:
Q.—What is your name?
A.—W. C. Flint.
Q.—Are you a book-binder?
A.—Yes, for thirty years in Toronto.
Q.—Where are you employed?
A.—Carswell Company.
Q.—Are you in a union?
A.—Yes, International Book-binders' Union.
Q.—Have you been engaged in binding any of the books used in schools?
A.—Yes, four and a half years in W. G. Gage Company.
Q.—When were you there?
A.—About eight years ago.
Q.—What books were you in the habit of binding?
A.—I was foreman.
Q.—As a book-binder, do you consider wire as a proper binding?
A.—No sir.
Q.—If a book is contracted to be bound in a workmanlike manner, is that contract fulfilled in your opinion as a book-binder, by wire?
A.—I think not.
Q.—Why not?
A.—Wire holds sections separate by themselves to a piece of crash or mull on back of the book. Thread sewing is a kettle stitch connecting each section of the book together.
Q.—And what advantage is that?
A.—Because then one section cannot get away from another.
Q.—You say the whole binding must be destroyed before a section can escape where they are done with the thread stitch.
A.—If sewn by hand.
Q.—This book is supposed to be sewn with wire?
A.—What book are you looking at?

Mr. Staunton: Fourth Reader.
Witness: By whom?
Mr. Staunton: Canada Publishing Company.

Q.—Is it a good binding?
A.—A child getting hold of that book straight from the publishers, and opening it suddenly in centre, would break it through. The wire is just held by crash on the back of the book. Therefore, if one section gives, every other section will follow.
Q.—Why is wire used?
A.—Cheapness.
Q.—What is the difference in the cost between wire and thread stitch?
A.—Materially, very little difference in the single book. Going into the thousands it would make quite a difference. About one-third more if hand-sewn.

6a T. B.

Q.—So that it does not make a durable binding, and it has been in your judgment on account of the cheapness.

A.—Yes, on account of the cheapness.

Q.—Is it an up-to-date method of binding books?

A.—It is being discarded.

Q.—Who is discarding it?

A.—All American firms.

Q.—Now then, they tell us that Inspectors and teachers complain strongly that the books are not durable and give way. Do you blame it entirely on the wire, or is it some other defect in the binding of the books?

A.—A book sewn on the Smythe Sewing Machine is stronger than sewn by wire.

Q.—Then a hand-sewn book is best?

A.—The hand-sewn book is preferable.

Q.—Are the public school readers machine-sewn, or sewn by wire?

A.—They are machine-sewn.

Q.—What is the difference in the cost of machine and hand-sewn?

A.—About one-third of a cent; according to the thickness of the book.

Q.—Let me understand you.

A.—If a book has twenty sections it would cost about one-third of a cent more than by machine or wire stitching. Hand-sewn makes the kettle stitch, and wire machine only makes sections.

Q.—Are there sixteen or thirty-two sections?

A.—We fold them in sixteen and thirty-two.

Q.—Suppose twenty sections of thirty-two, is that more expensive than if twenty sections of sixteen?

A.—The size of the section makes the book bigger.

Q.—Are there any other defects in this binding?

A.—For school books, I claim all joints should be cloth.

Q.—You do not think straps sufficient?

A.—No, I do not.

Q.—Can you tell by examining that book (Arnold's First Latin Book) is that mull or cloth?

A.—I think that book has been pasted open. It is a good book.

Q.—Now to bind a school book, what difference does it make if it is pasted open?

A.—It is stronger.

Q.—What difference would it make in the cost of the binding of the school book, if it was bound in the same manner as Arnold's First Latin Book, that I show you?

A.—About one-half cent each.

Q.—Then this book would last for much longer than other books would?

A.—Yes.

Q.—It would not easily come apart?

A.—No sir.

Q.—What made that book go to bits like that?

A.—Wire stitching.

Q.—Do you blame it on the wire stitching exclusively?

A.—Yes, and the poor paper. The stronger the paper, the better the book.

Q.—Do you say that is poor paper and poor binding?

A.—I think it is.

Q.—The High School Arithmetic, published by the Hunter, Rose Company, at sixty cents, and I produce it now, and ask what do you think of the binding of the book?

A.—That book is very good.

Q.—You consider it fair binding?

A.—Yes.

Q.—You say it is well enough done; would you prescribe that system of binding for every book to be used in public schools?

A.—I would not.

Q.—Now, you say you would substitute cloth for mull.

A.—No, I would add cloth.

Q.—This book has no straps on it?

A.—No.

Q.—Would you turn out a book without straps?

A.—No, I would not.

Q.—How should it be sewn?

A.—Hand sewn.

Q.—You think that would be stronger than using tapes.

A.—That is the same as tapes.

Q.—Why would it not be stronger?

A.—Because it holds in three separate parts.

Q.—You admit, however, that if the tapes were put in it would make it stronger?

A.—Yes.

Q.—When you speak of cloth-bound you refer to that in this book?

A.—Yes.

Q.—Did you ever condemn these books before?

A.—No, not personally.

Q.—Did you ever say anything about it to the publishers.

A.—No, I did not know what agreement the publishers had with the Government. I did not know of the contract.

Q.—You say a tight binding is better than open binding?

A.—Yes.

Q.—Is it considered better to have tight binding?

A.—Yes.

Q.—Is it more or less expensive?

A.—More expensive.

Q.—Why?

A.—Extra work.

Q.—How much more expensive?

A.—Half a cent a book.

Q.—You would have cloth bound and hand-sewn, and close bound books?

A.—Not necessarily tight bound.

Q.—In either case it would cost one cent or one and a half cents more for the binding.

A.—About that.

Q.—It should not materially effect the profits on the school book.

A.—Not the profits the paper says they have at the present time.

Q.—What does it cost to bind these readers?

A.—Nine cents a piece.

Q.—How is the price made up?

A.—Folding, sewing, cloth boards and forwarding.

Q.—And includes then?

A.—Everything.

Q.—This book is furnished to the binder in sheets, and he supplies all material to bind it in its present shape for nine cents, now what profit does he make?

A.—The book literally would cost him six and one-half to seven cents.

Q.—Now you put in the highest cost at nine cents, you are sure it would not cost any more?

A.—Yes.

Q.—There is a book which has never been used at all, one of the High School Readers, that is broken. The outside paper is of no use, is it?

A.—No.

Q.—Now here is a Fourth Reader; that book is machine-sewn, is it not?

A.—Yes.

Q.—Now take that book, that ought to cost the binder four and a half cents or five cents?

A.—In what quantities?

Q.—In thousands?

A.—Yes.

Q.—Your way of binding it, what would it cost?

A.—Five and one-half cents.

Q.—To hand sew it?

A.—Yes, to hand sew it, and put cloth joints.

Q.—Tell me what kind of board is that?

A.—Mill board.

Q.—How can you tell it is mill board?

A.—It is a dark color.

Q.—Straw board is light in color?

A.—Yes.

Q.—What is mill board made of?

A.—All kinds of board, rubber. Anything.

Q.—By stamping, I understand, you to mean all that is on the outside of the cover, that includes the border?

A.—Yes.

Q.—Why did you come here this morning?

A.—We had a meeting, and we thought by the papers that the binders were getting blamed for the binding. We were appointed as a Committee to come, and if necessary, to ask any questions, we would be pleased to answer them.

Q.—What is your position in the Union?

A.—Vice-President.

Q.—What Union?

A.—Local Union No. 28.

Q.—You came here to give us any assistance you could?

A.—Yes, as citizens.

Q.—There is a book called First National Reader, is that a well bound book?

A.—Yes.

Q.—Does it recommend itself to you?

A.—Yes, sir.

Q.—Take that book and if you were asked to bind our Readers in the same way as that is bound, what would it cost?

A.—One to one and a half cents.

Q.—Would that book cost more than the book you recommend?

A.—No.

Q.—Then we can adopt either one or the other systems, what do you think of the Globe Reader, published by McMillan and Company?

A.—Very good.

Q.—Is that machine sewn with tape?

A.—No.

Q.—Is that good enough?

A.—Whoever is handling it. That book would go to pieces as well as any other.

Q.—It is better than ours, and not as good as the American, and not good enough in your opinion.

A.—No.

Q.—High School Algebra, published by Wm. Briggs. What do you think of the binding of this book?

A.—Good book.

Q.—Is that wire stitched?

A.—No, it is machine sewn.

Q.—Longmen's Historical Reader. What do you think of this book?

A.—That will last forever.

Q.—You think that is all right, do you?

A.—Yes, it is stitched right through.

Q.—Would that cost more than our books?

A.—Yes.

Q.—You think it an ideal book, do you?

A.—Yes, for cheap readers, tight back, and stitched through.

Q.—What do you say of these books?

A.—Not as good as the other.

Q.—Is it stitched through?

A.—Yes, sewn right through the book.

Q.—For books intended to be used by school children, is there anything can take the place of the hand-sewn?

A.—No, nothing.

Q.—Will machine sewn show through through all sections of the book?

A.—In backwards and forwards.

Q.—Will not the sewing that you speak of, be done in sections?

A.—Yes.

Q.—Then what holds the sections together?

A.—Kettle stitch.

Q.—Now you speak of the profits in the binding, that it can be bound for six and one-half or seven cents, would that include the wages of the binder?

A.—Yes.

Q.—How many of these books would a man bind in ten hours, say?

A.—Two hundred and fifty, taking them from the cutter.

Q.—Can some of them bind as many as one thousand a day?

A.—No, that is casing in.

Q.—I understand, Mr. Flint, that you were here lest there might be some reflection on the binders.

A.—Yes.

Q.—When at W. J. Gage's knowing that these books were being very poorly bound, why did you not point it out to them?

A.—I was not asked.

Q.—It did not strike you as your duty to point out to your employer that they were poorly bound?

A.—No, I did not have control over the school books.

Mr. STAUNTON: That will do Mr. Flint, thank you.

EVIDENCE OF MR. J. F. ELLIS, TORONTO.

By Mr. G. L. STAUNTON, K. C. :

Q.—What is your name?

A.—J. F. Ellis.

Q.—Your business?

A.—Paper dealer and member of the firm of Barber and Ellis.

Q.—Do you supply paper to the publishers for the school books?

A.—No.

Q.—Did you ever do so?

A.—Not directly.

Q.—You made an occasional jag?

A.—Yes in a small way; Mr. Barber was interested in mills that did supply paper.

Q.—Did you give evidence before any of the prior commissions?

A.—No, this is the first time.

Q.—Have you any idea of the use or abuse to which a Reader might be put in the Public Schools?

A.—Well, I taught for four or five years and saw a good deal of it; but we did not use these readers when I taught school, we had the old red ones. It is forty-five years since I promenaded these corridors.

Q.—Are you a practical paper-maker, Mr. Ellis?

A.—No I am not, I do not know how to make paper; no more than handling it.

Q.—Do you know what kind of paper should be in these books?

A.—I have a very good idea; I know what rates were given the publishers and I know pretty well what was paid for them.

Q.—Well then, if you were going to make a contract, what paper would you prescribe for the book? Say that you are the Minister of Education, and you want to buy school books, and you are going to prescribe a kind of paper to use in them, what kind would you prescribe?

A.—A rag and sulphur paper, a paper made partially of rags and partially of sulphur, called chemical pulp, about 25 per cent sulphate and 75 per cent rag.

Q.—You think it is the only common sense paper to prescribe?

A.—Yes. It is very easy for the Minister when he examines a book to ascertain what kind of paper it is.

Q.—He could send some of the paper to a chemical analyst?

A.—Yes, Mr. Coldthrite of the Printing Bureau, Ottawa, can tell you all about it. Any ordinary man can make a test and tell what nature of wood is in that paper. He cannot tell the proportion, but he can tell whether there is any ground wood in it.

Q.—What kind of paper is in these books?

A.—This is called Super Calendar.

Q.—What is that high finished paper made from, is there any rag pulp in it?

A.—That is made from sulphate and wood; I do not think there is any rag in it at all; I cannot tell you by looking at it without testing it.

Q.—What affect has the high finish on the paper?

A.—It is a litle more expensive; just shows off the goods, and is simply fancy.

Q.—What is that paper worth?

A.—I should say four and a quarter or four and a half cents per pound.

Q.—That is a pretty good price is it not?

A.—It is cheap for Super Calendar book.

Q.—Four and a half cents is cheap for that class of paper; is there any difference in the paper in that book and any of the others you know?

(Hands witness a High School Book)

A.—This may not be any better paper but that may be on account of it not being illustrated.

Q.—Is it as durable?

A.—Yes.

Q.—But you think it may be a cheaper paper?

A.—Yes, I think there would be a difference in the price.

Q.—What difference, Mr. Ellis?

A.—Oh, about one quarter of a cent a pound difference.

Q.—Do you think there is any rag in that paper?

A.—No, I think it is all wood.

EXAMINER: Here submitted a number of other books to the witness with the question:—

Q.—Examine these books, Mr. Ellis, and tell, please, whether in your opinion, the quality of the paper is the same all through.

By Mr. COOPER:

Q.—Mr. Ellis, in the paper used in these school books, should there be any mechanical wood pulp used?

A.—Well, Mr. Cooper, in my opinion, I think it is a mistake to use any mechanical wood pulp at all.

Mr. STAUNTON: That will do, Mr. Ellis, thank you.

EVIDENCE OF MR. W. H. BALLARD, PUBLIC SCHOOL INSPECTOR, CITY OF HAMILTON.

By Mr. G. L. STAUNTON, K.C.:

Q.—Mr. Ballard, your first name is?

A.—William H. Ballard.

Q.—Your occupation is?

A.—Inspector of Schools for the City of Hamilton since 1885—twenty-one years.

Q.—What method is adopted for supplying books to the school children in the Public Schools in Hamilton?

A.—We make out a list of books and supplies once a year and invite public competition.

Q.—Is it a Free System?

A.—No, I would not call it a Free System; the Board supplies all the books, but we collect a fee.

Q.—How much of a fee do you collect?

A.—In the lower classes ten cents, and the higher classes twenty cents per month.

Q.—To what classes do you charge the ten cents?

A.—Well, up to the second book.

Q.—Yes, but what classes are they?

A.—The Kindergarten, Junior First, Senior First are ten cents per month; for the rest it is twenty cents.

Q.—Do you make any profit on the amount expended for books and supplies by collecting those fees?

A.—Yes, we do.

Q.—How much?

A.—From three to four thousand dollars a year.

Q.—What do you do with the surplus? Divide it?

A.—No, it all goes into a general account.

Q.—How much do you collect per annum from the children in the Public Schools?

A.—About $11,000.00.

Q.—Can you give me the average for the last five years? The Commission wants to be able to form an opinion.

A.—There has been a very small addition in the last five years; I think it would average $11,000.00; it may be a little more or a little less.

Q.—Give me the average amount that you have expended on books and supplies for the children in the Public Schools in the last five years?

A.—I have the sums down as nearly as I could get them in the time allowed; the average would be about $6,000.00.

Q.—What was the average attendance, Mr. Ballard, at the Public Schools during that time?

A.—I have the attendance from the city hall Registers, as 8,114; that was the gross attendance.

Q.—Will you tell me what the total enrollment was during the five years, that is for each year, commencing with 1901?

A.—For 1901, 8,348; 1902, 8,144; 1903, 8,114; 1904, 8,166; 1905, 8,214.

Q.—What would the average be for the five years?

A.—I would say 8,157.

Q.—In the total number of pupils in attendance do you include the Kindergarten?

A.—I cannot tell you.

Q.—Have you the number of pupils attending the Kindergarten?

A.—No, I have not the number.

Q.—Well then, that 8,114, does that include or exclude the Kindergarten pupils?

A.—Exclude, I think.

Q.—What do you figure the average it would cost per pupil for the last five years?

A.—The average cost I have for the items is, $5,894.00 per year.

By Mr. COOPER:

Q.—I want to know this: I may tell Mr. Ballard it has not been proved to my mind yet, that in the City of Toronto it costs ten cents per year for books and fifteen cents for supplies, and it is stated here, that it costs about sixty cents for books and supplies in the City of Kingston; now Kingston is a much smaller place—can you account for it?

A.—Well, the only way in which I could account for it is that in Hamilton we never take the books back; when a pupil begins a new subject he gets a new book, while in Toronto they take the books back and re-bind them.

By Mr. STAUNTON:

Q.—Just tell us your system as it is in Hamilton, Mr. Ballard?

A.—The books are tendered for once per year by the local trade and the lowest tender gets the contract.

Q.—That is for the books and supplies?

A.—Yes, we supply everything; we make a schedule of what we require and in addition each school principal on the 30th June or shortly after makes out a statement in detail of the supplies he will need for his school and these are sent in to the tenderer and are on hand on the first of September, so that everything works out without any hitch.

Q.—Do you think the method you have in Hamilton a good one?

A.—I think so; we have had it for a very long time.

Q.—Do you understand the system of distribution in Toronto?

A.—Not fully.

Q.—Do you understand the system of any other place?

A.—No, excepting that the system in Brantford seems to be the same.

Q.—What do you think of the Free Book System yourself?

A.—I do not think I would favor it; I do not think it is good for a pupil to give him the idea that he is using something that is given to him or loaned to him.

Q.—Do you not think that if a person borrowed something he would take better care of it than if he owned it?

A.—I cannot say.

Q.—Would you not take better care of it yourself under those circumstances?

A.—I cannot answer that definitely, I am sure.

Q.—I suppose that if a pupil were given a book on the understanding that he had to give an account of its keeping while he had it, that better care would be taken of it than if it were his own property, and if the parents would have to make good any damage done to it, why that would be another incentive to take care of the book, would it not?

Witness hesitates.

Q.—Have you given the question thought, Mr. Ballard?

A.—Not in that particular aspect; but it struck me that the giving out of an old book would be always objectionable.

Q.—Why, Mr. Ballard?

A.—Well, if you pick out pupil "A" and give him or her an old book, while all the others have new ones, you create bad feelings.

Q. If others have old books, what is the difference?

A.—Well, I suppose books wear out from time to time; but we have to give them new ones.

Q.—Have you had any conversation or correspondence with those who have the free book system?

A.—No.

Q.—Did you ever know a free system to be abandoned after it has been once instituted?

A.—No, I am not aware of that side of it.

Q.—Have you heard of them having any trouble in Toronto in connection with their method?

A.—No, I have no definite information about that.

Q.—Your objections then, are that you think children would be mortified if they had old books given to them and that they would not take as good care of them as if they owned the books?

A.—Yes, that is my thought.

Q.—Is there any other objection?

A.—There might be sanitary objections.

Q —Don't you think there is a great amount of humbug in this matter of the insanitary state of books?

A.—Yes.

Q.—Don't you think there would be the same objections to the books in public libraries?

A.—Yes.

Q.—Well, taking a given number of children in a class, say forty children, it is alleged that there are objections on sanitary grounds to the use of the books. These children are all huddled together in that room and if they gather disease, would it not be taken from each other as well as from the books?

A.—Yes.

EXAMINER: I can understand a man who takes a book into his home being afraid that it might germinate disease in his family, but where children come together day after day, don't you think there would be greater danger?

WITNESS: Well, if there are any elements of danger in an old book, then a new book would be the best.

EXAMINER: No, I mean if the children bring disease in their clothes and persons, you know that it is alleged by medical men that the crowding of so many pupils in a room is in itself a menace to health?

WITNESS: Well, if any of the pupils were infected, there would, of course, be danger.

Q.—Well, Mr. Ballard, you say that you do not take back the books; now if there are two or three children in a family, and one is promoted out of the Third into the Fourth, and one from the Second into the Third, would you insist upon that child using his brother's book, or would you give him a new one?

A.—We would give him a new one.

Q.—Every child then secures a new book?

A.—Yes.

Q.—You include everything then, all books?

A.—We give everything the student needs but the strap, he carries them with all the school requirements.

By Mr. COOPER:

Q.—Have you any Manual Training?

A.—Not in the Public Schools.

By Mr. STAUNTON:

Q.—Have you a memo of the books and supplies with prices for the current year, Mr. Ballard?

A.—No, not for the current school year, but I have a list prepared by the secretary of the Board, that is a price list for books and stationery for our public schools showing the prices paid the contractor.

Q.—Will you produce it, please?

The witness here submitted the following statement:—

PRICE LIST FOR BOOKS AND STATIONERY—PUBLIC SCHOOLS, 1905-1906—CLOKE & SON, CONTRACTORS.

Article.		Price.
Arithmetics, P. S.	each	$0 17½
Arithmetics, H. S.	each	42
Arithmetics, Practical Problems, sample	each	03½
Algebra and Euclid, P. S.	each	17½
Blackboard Erasers, as per sample	each	03½
Blank Books, as per sample, 12 lbs.	each	01¾
Bookkeeping, H. S.	each	45½
Bookkeeping Blanks, P. S. L. No. 14, Copp, Clark	each	17½
Sets Bookkeeping Blanks, 3 in a set. as sample	per set	55
Blotting Paper, white, 80 lbs., cut as required	per ream	7 50
City Directories, 1906	each	2 50
Lang's Composition	each	07½
Copy Books, Blank, as sample, 16 lbs.	each	02
Copy Books, Gage's Business and Social Forms	each	07
Copy Books, Casselman	each	05
Boxes Crayons, White	per box	10
Crayons, White, Hard Dustless, American Crayon Co.	per box	25

Article.		Price.
Crayons, Pink, hexagonal	per box	$0 50
Crayons, Scarlet, hexagonal	per box	1 50
Crayons, Yellow	per box	65
Crayons, Green	per box	70
Crayons, Red	per box	40
Crayons, Blue	per box	65
Crayons, Orange	per box	65
Crayons, Purple	per box	65
Crayons, Umber	per box	60
Crayola, 41 B, Binney & Smith	per box	02½
Crayola, 54, Binney & Smith	per box	06
Dictionaries, Chambers' Etymological	each	76
Drawing Books, Blank, 16 pages, as sample	each	01¼
Drawing Books, No. 5	each	03½
Drawing Books, No. 6	each	01¼
Drawing Books, H. S., No. 1	each	07¼
Drawing Books, H. S., No. 2	each	07½
Drawing Books, Casselman	each	04
Drawing Paper, Prang's, 100 sheets in package	per package	05
Text Book of Art Education, 1 to 8, Prang	each	2 10
Teachers' Manual of Art Education, 1 to 8, Prang	each	25
Envelopes, large	per M.	2 00
Envelopes, No. 6	per M.	90
Envelopes, No. 7	per M.	90
Erasers, No. 60, Faber's	per box	82
Foolscap, unruled and cut, 12 lbs	per ream	90
Foolscap, 12 lbs., ruled both ends alike and cut	per ream	93
Foolscap, 12 lbs., ruled both ends alike and cut ¼ sheets	per ream	93
Foolscap, 14 lbs., ruled ¼ and ⅜ in. spaces and cut	per ream	1 22
Foolscap, 14 lbs., ruled ⅜ and ⅛ in. spaces and cut	per ream	1 22
Foolscap, 14 lbs., ruled 2-15 and 4-15 in. spaces and cut	per ream	1 22
Geography, P. S., New edition	each	52
Geometry, Baker's Elementary Plans, W. J. Gage	each	38
Grammars, P. S.	each	17½
Grammars, Buehler, 25c. edition	each	19
Histories, P. S.	each	21
Histories, H. S.	each	47
Ink, Black	per gallon	50
Ink, Red	per gallon	75
Ink, Stafford's, in quarts, Red	per quart	1 00
Ink, Stafford's, in quarts, Black	per quart	50
Maps, Canada, Copp, Clark Co.	each	3 30
Maps, Canada, W. & A. K. Johnstone	each	3 80
Maps, Ontario, W. & A. K. Johnstone	each	3 80
Maps, North America, Johnstone's Imperial Series	each	3 80
Maps, British Empire, Howard Vincent	each	4 25
Maps, Johnstone's Imperial Series, 72 x 63 ins.	each	3 80
Maps, Hamilton, Scarborough Co.	each	4 00
Note Books, Cloth	each	3½
Note Books, Paper	each	01
Note Books, Reporters', 224 pages	each	5½
Pencils, Lead, Scholastic H., Eagle Pencil Co.	per gross	1 40
Pencils, Lead, Scholastic H. B., Eagle Pencil Co.	per gross	1 40
Pencils, Lead, Eagle Pencil Co., Colored 700-750	per gross	4 40
Pencils, Slate	per box	07½
Penholders, Eagle Pencil Co., No. 320	per gross	31
Pens, 292 or 293, Gillett's	per gross	30
Pens, No. 1, Vertical, Eagle	per gross	36
Pens, No. 170, Eagle Public Pens	per gross	30
Pens, Esterbrook's School Pens	per gross	37
Physiology, P. S.	each	17½
Practical Speller	each	17½
Readers, H. S.	each	41½
Readers, 4th	each	30
Readers, 3rd	each	22½
Readers, 2nd	each	15
Readers, 2nd, Morang	each	19½

Article.		Price.
Readers, 2nd, Canada Publishing Co.	each	$0 19¼
Readers, 1st, Part 2, Morang	each	11½
Readers, 1st, Part 2, Phonic Primer, Can. Pub.	each	11¼
Readers, 1st, Part 1, Morang	each	07¼
Readers, 1st, Part 1 Phonic Primer, Can. Pub.	each	07¼
Munro's Primer	each	15
Rubber Bands, No. 60, assorted sizes	per box	95
Rulers, Hardwood, as samples, with round edge	each	01¼
Rulers, marked in half and quarter inches	each	01¼
Scribbling Books	each	02
Scribbling Paper, cut as required	per ream	1 20
Slates, wirebound	per gross	7 20
Slates, not wirebound	per gross	5 90
Manual of Phonography	each	30
Phonographic Reporters	each	36
Our Home and Its Surroundings, Morang, Pt. 1	each	30
Guide to Nature Study, Crawford	each	72
Nature Study, Morang	each	60
Flashlights on Nature, Grant Allen	each	88
Nature Study and Life, Hodge	each	1 25
Britannia History Readers, Introductory, Arnold	each	20
Britannia History Readers, Book 1	each	24
Britannia History Readers, Book 2	each	31
Britannia History Readers, Book 3	each	31
Britannia History Readers, Book 4	each	31
Miller's Brief Biographies, Copp, Clark	each	29
Putman's Britain and the Empire, Morang	each	50
Robert's History of Canada	each	85
Story of the Maple Land, Young	each	21
Morang's Modern Geography, Part II	each	46
The Story of the Canadian People, Duncan, Morang	each	38

T. BEASLEY,
Secretary of Board of Education.

Q.—What is the average life of each book that you buy, Mr. Ballard?

A.—We do not fully test them, but I find on enquiry that with ordinary care, the books answer the time we need them; it may be two years, sometimes three years, and sometimes one year.

Q.—Do you ever have to duplicate a book?

A.—We do not do that; if a pupil loses a book he has to replace it.

Q.—The teachers say that you have one uniform set of books throughout the schools?

A.—Yes, that is right; I think that costs less per head.

By Mr. CROTHERS:

Q.—What is the object, Mr. Ballard, in collecting from the pupils nearly twice the sum necessary to supply the books and supplies?

A.—Well, I don't know.

Q.—It would appear that you compel the poor man to help pay the rich man's taxes?

A.—Well, I suppose he pays for his education.

Q.—You collect about $11,000.00 and you pay out about $7,000.00, leaving a profit of $4,000.00?

A.—Yes, it runs from $4,000.00 to $5,000.00.

By Mr. J. A. COOPER:

Q.—Don't you think you are robbing the poor men of Hamilton?

A.—No, if a man is poor we exempt him altogether.

Q.—Don't you think yourself, it would be unwise to extend such a practice over the whole Province, that is, to have the various school boards collect the same fee from the parents, instead of asking from the parents the average cost of the books and supplies? Don't you think the purpose of your system of education is to afford every man an education for his children at the lowest possible cost, and to give every child, whether he is poor or rich, an equal opportunity; that is the spirit of the Act, I think?

By Mr. Staunton:

Q.—Do you think it discourages attendance at the schools?

A.—I do not think so; we have always had a very high average.

Q.—Do you think, with Mr. Cooper, that it contravenes the spirit of the Act?

A.—I do not think it contravenes it; the spirit of the Act is for free education; the attendance has been good and has always been good.

Q.—You do not find the children stay away from school on account of the price of books and supplies?

A.—No.

Q.—You do not find that the parents offer any objection to it?

A.—No, and in a case of indigence the truancy officer looks after it.

Q.—Any indigent pupils are supplied books free?

A.—Yes, we have no charge for these persons.

By Mr. Cooper: '

Q.—Have you ever investigated a system in any particular state or city as to the handling of text books in the public schools?

A.—No, not outside of the Province of Ontario.

Q.—Don't you think that every inspector should know something of modern methods?

'A.—Well, Mr. Cooper, we have to use the text books that the Province prescribes.

By Mr. Staunton:

Q.—What is the amount of taxation for school purposes in Hamilton?

A.—I do not remember that.

Examiner: The assessed value of the city is twenty-eight millions.

Witness: This year it is over that amount, I think.

Mr. Staunton: That will do, Mr. Ballard, thank you.

Evidence of Mr. Alexander Buntin, Toronto.

By Mr. G. L. Staunton, K. C.:

Q.—What is your name?

A.—Alexander Buntin.

Q.—Your business?

A.—Wholesale paper.

Q.—Your firm?

A.—Buntin, Reid.

Q.—Place?

A.—Toronto.

Q.—You are a practical papermaker?

A.—Yes.

Q.—How many years experience have you had?

A.—Seventeen years.

Q.—Did you give evidence before the last Commission?

A.—Yes.

Q.—When was that?

A.—In 1897.

Q.—Where was it held?

A.—Here.

Q.—Was it public or private?

A.—It was held at night time.

Q.—After dark you would call it?

A.—Well, it was 10 or 11 o'clock at night when I gave my evidence.

Q.—What did you give evidence on?

A.—As to the quality of the paper as to whether it was free from ground wood.

Q.—What books were shown to you? Do you recollect?

A.—I think samples of the different books, registers, etc.

Q.—What were you asked about it?

A.—They wanted to find out whether the party that had the contract for supplying paper was keeping up his contract and furnishing paper free from ground wood and I was there to test whether there was any ground wood in it.

Q.—What did you discover?

A.—That there was ground wood in it.

Q.—Your evidence then, went to show, that the contract was not lived up to.

A.—Yes.

Q.—What was your opinion?

A.—That it was simply a ground wood paper and should have been a rag paper.

Q.—What was the difference in the value of the two papers at that time?

A.—From three to four cents per pound, according to what the Government called for, and that which they were supplied.

Q.—You gave evidence to that effect?

A.—Yes, I submitted the paper to a chemical test before Judge Morgan and showed him,—why you could nearly make 'the wood grow.

Q.—Did any other people give evidence similar to you?

A.—They did not until after Judge Morgan saw the nitric acid test, and then they did.

Q.—Why do you prescribe rag paper for books of this kind?

A.—They call for a rag paper because they have an idea that it is a better paper, whereas it is not.

Q.—What is the best paper, Mr. Buntin?

A.—Sulphate and rag; or a soda and rag.

Q.—How could an ordinary person know there was rag pulp used?

A.—Well, in the mill they sometimes take up a piece and chew it into pulp, when the rag is easily distinguished.

Mr. J. A. MACDONALD: That would be what is commonly called "Chewing the Rag", would it not?

A.—It might be. (A voice: That is no doubt where the phrase originated).

Q.—Well, Mr. Buntin, how many processes are there used in the manufacture of chemical and mechanical wood pulp, can you explain them?

A.—Yes, it is this way, the preparation of wood used in the manufacture of paper is divided into two classes, namely, chemical and mechanical wood. In the first named there are two processes,— the sulphate and the soda process. In the preparation of the wood for the soda process, the bark is stripped from the wood and cut into chips, which pass through a mechanical duster to eliminate as much as possible all the dust and foreign matter that might otherwise go into the digestors. From the dusters the wood passes through into the digestors or boilers. These digestors are of several kinds: Horizontal, cylindrical, spherical, rotary or upright stationary. After the digestors have been charged there is a solution of

caustic soda introduced, after which the boiler or digestor is sealed and
steam turned on from 90 to 120 lbs. pressure.　In the soda process the time
consumed for thoroughly cooking the wood is from twelve to fifteen hours.
By giving it this extra time, it absolutely insures the thorough cooking of
the wood and remedies, to a large extent the tendency for a paper to shrink
on the presses.　An improperly cooked wood paper would shrink, whereas if
thoroughly cooked, this tendency is avoided. · After cooking the allotted
time, the steam is blown off, the digestors emptied and the cooked pulp
washed through several washings.　It is then fed into beating engines with
whatever per cent. of other stock is required and from there into the machines.

The sulphate or sulphuric acid process goes through a similar form
with the exception that the wood has to be more carefully overhauled.　The
bark is first removed, then all knots, blemishes, dark parts of the wood, etc.,
are removed previous to cooking.　The wood is then ground, crushed or
chipped, in order to insure the removal of imperfections in the heart of the
wood and to give the sulphuric acid an opportunity to get into all parts of
the fibre.　The digestors are of a similar style to those used in the soda
pulp, but instead of using the caustic soda, a solution is made up of bisul-
phate of soda and the wood is cooked from eighteen to twenty-four hours at
from 80 to 120 lbs pressure.　After cooking, the usual washing and the
same process takes place as in the soda pulp, etc.

By Mr. Staunton :

Q.—Then in either process great care has to be taken in order to get
good results.

A.—Yes.

Q.—And you consider sulphite and rag paper to be the better of the two?

A.—Yes, I consider it the best paper.

Q.—Did you examine the paper in each of the publishers' books?

A.—I examined probably six or seven of them.

Q.—Did you stumble on any of them that were living up to the contract?

A.—No.

Q.—How much paper is there in one of those Readers?

A.—About 60 lb. double royal.

Q.—How much does it weigh?

A.—I have no idea, but supposing that the paper mill supplies it to the
Publishers in the large sheets, 66 lbs. to 500 sheets, 27 by 41, that would
probably print thirty-two pages.

Q.—Look at these Readers, what do you say? Is it the same paper or an
improved paper?　Dr.Allan in his report says here at No. 9, that this paper
contains 10-12 per cent. cotton in the rag pulp, 80 per cent. mostly spruce
chemical wood pulp and that it is much crushed and broken in fibre.　What
do you remark, Mr. Buntin?

A.—Well, it is cheaper to-day and better to put in a little rag filler than
to use an all chemical pulp, besides, it would make it perhaps one cent or
one and three-quarter cents cheaper than rag pulp.　If you had it all rag
there would be no body in it and would be quite limp.

Q.—Well, what do you say to the analysis of Dr. Allan in No. 9; what
do you think of the quality of the paper?

A.—I should say, it would be a very good paper.

Q.—Then that paper described there is fairly good paper?

A.—Yes, for that purpose.

Q.—Do you say all the papers there (shows witness copy of Dr. Allan's
evidence containing his report on the different papers) are fairly good?

A.—Yes. They cannot make that American or Canadian papers, it is only to be found in British paper.

Q.—Well now, look at No. 3 Mr. Buntin, what do you say to that paper?

A.—It is supposed to be the best stock you can put in, very few mills can get it.

Q.—Are there any of the papers described in that schedule objectionable for text book purposes, Mr. Buntin?

A.—Well, I would not like to say without submitting them to a test myself.

Q.—Could you test them for us here?

A.—Certainly if I had the materials.

Q.—What do you require for such a test?

A.—Some pure nitric acid would answer the purpose.

Mr. Crothers, the Chairman of the Commission, here instructed the Secretary to obtain some pure nitric acid and Mr. Buntin proceeded to make his test to find ground wood.

Mr. STAUNTON — handing witness a book— look at this Public School History of Canada, published by Copp, Clark & Co., what do you find?

A.—There is about 25 per cent. ground wood in it.

Q.—Look at this book, it is "Longman's Ship Historical Reader", what do you find?

A.—This is free from ground wood.

Q.—In your tests there, Mr. Buntin, will you please explain how you know when a paper shows ground wood?

A.—Well, when I test the paper and find sulphate, the paper shows perfectly transparent like wax, it is then a pure sulphate paper, when it shows a yellow color or orange it is soda pulp paper, and when it turns brown it is ground wood.

Q.—But it does not necessarily follow that because a paper turns brown that it is made from ground wood?

A.—No, not always.

Q.—Well, referring again to the schedule prepared by Dr. Allan, sample four, is this list all alike?

A.—Yes.

Q.—Here is Macmillan's Second Year New Reader, what do you say about that?

A.— This book is altogether sulphate, soda and ground wood.

Q.—What proportion of ground wood is in that?

A.—Fifteen per cent. I should say, but this might lead you astray by the use of pulp insufficiently cooked.

Q.—Now, we will take this book, Morang's Modern Geography; just try that, will you?

A.—This is pure chemical paper; there may be a small percentage of rag, but there is no ground wood in it; it shows clear.

Q.—This next book is the "Ontario Latin Grammar", price one dollar, manufactured also by Morang?

A.—It is free from ground wood also.

Q.—How about this High School Algebra, by Briggs?

A.—It is also free from wood pulp.

Q.—Here is a Public School Physiology by Briggs, how is it?

A.—This paper shows a distinct trace of ground wood.

Q.—About what proportion would you say?

A.—About from 25 to 30 per cent. of ground wood in this book.

Q.—You think then, that there is a high percentage of ground wood in this book?

7 T. B.

A.—Yes.

Q.—Take this High School Bookkeeping book by Copp, Clark Co., what does it show?

A.—This book shows ground wood too.

Q.—Would you say a large quantity?

A.—No, not more than 10 per cent., which is a "filler."

Q.—You would not condemn a paper on that account?

A.—No I would not condemn any paper that did not contain more than twenty per cent. of the ground wood.

Q.—Well, take this book, a "Physical Science" Part 2, by Copp, Clark Co., what do you say?

A.—This paper is about the same as the other, there is a percentage. but not too high. If you do not soften down sulphate and soda pulp, the book would be all broken, the paper would stretch out and when handled much, cut or break.

Q.—Well what do you say the limit should be?

A.—Oh, any good paper would stand 25 per cent. without hurting it a bit.

Q.—Do you think then, that these papers are good if they have that filler in them?

A.—I say they are very good papers; they are good sulphate with a little amount of filler.

Q.—You would be satisfied with them?

A.—I may say, that they are good papers from what I know the market value of them to be; the paper is well enough made.

Q.—Here is a Public School Euclid and Algebra by Hunter, Rose & Company; has it too much ground wood pulp in it?

A.—No, not any of these books have any more than they can stand except the "Physiology."

Q.—Here is a Public School Euclid and Algebra by the Hunter, Rose Company, what do you say in this case?

A.—The paper is poor, it is not good enough paper.

Q.—How about the ground wood?

It is not carrying any more ground wood than it should carry for that quality of paper.

Q.—Take this Public School Arithmetic by the Canada Publishing Co.?

A.—There is a small percentage of soda pulp.

Q.—What do you say to this Public School Grammar, published by Canada Publishing Company.

A.—This is a sulphate paper.

Q.—The next will be this Public School Geography also by the Canada Publishing Co.; what kind of paper do you call that?

A.—I call it a pure sulphate paper.

Q.—Do you think it would be a stronger paper if there was a little filler in it.

A.—Well, it would be cheaper.

Q.—I understand that a little filler makes it more flexible?

A.—Yes: but on the other hand take "map" paper, you cannot use any ground wood in a paper prepared for maps, if there is any ground wood in it there would be a certain amount of expansion and the leaf containing the map would not be even with the others but project beyond the covers.

Q.—You should not put ground wood in map paper, then?

A.—No, we have a special paper made for maps that we guarantee.

Q.—Well, try this High School Botany, please; let me see, it is published by Gage & Company, what is it?

7a T. B.

A.—It is a pure sulphate paper.

Q.—Would you put in a little filler in that paper, Mr. Buntin?

A.—Well, when I was in the mill I always put in a little filler; I would have no way of telling whether my mechanical wood is properly cooked for the reason that my engineer might go asleep and the machine might run at perhaps 60 lbs. for two hours or more instead of running at 120 lbs., so that it would be impossible for me to tell whether it was properly cooked or not.

Q.—So then, it is hard to arrive at, or find the percentage of ground wood contained in a paper?

A.—Well, I might say, that in testing papers to ascertain the quantity of ground wood which they may contain, it is almost impossible, outside of a chemical analysis, to give the actual percentage of ground wood that may show in the nitric acid test such as I am using now. The difficulty arises from the fact, that the greatest bulk of wood used in the chemical process is spruce, the same as used in ground wood, but on application of nitric acid to the sheet of paper being tested, in the case of the wood being imperfectly cooked, the orange or yellow tint is strengthened materially, thus in many cases confusing the expert as to the difference between the uncooked chemical wood and the ground wood.

Q.—Well then, Mr. Buntin, what do you mean when you say it is a pure sulphate paper?

A.—I would say, in the case of a paper being made from pure sulphate wood which has been cooked the full length of time, that the nitric acid test would show, like in the case of some of these papers, a clear transparent stain, whereas the same paper in a batch of wood that had been improperly cooked, would show a distinct orange tint and would be liable to lead an expert to state that there was at least a small percentage of ground or mechanical wood in the composition of the paper.

Q.—How do you guard against it?

A.—The only way to guard against this mistake in the test, would be to watch closely with the glass, and the small fibres of the mechanical wood will come out more prominently than the rest; but the only absolute test would be to reduce the paper to pulp and allow the pulp to stand in contact for twenty-four hours with a solution of iodine in potassium iodide. The amount of free iodine is found by titration with sodium thiosulphate, and by deducting the amount of free iodine from the amount originally used, this will be found to correspond with the same percentage of wood used in the pulp under test. I would say, however, that a test like this is usually only made by a chemical analyst.

Q.—Well, we will continue by asking you to test this book, the Practical Speller, published by Gage & Company, what kind of paper do you call that?

A.—This is a well made paper; pure sulphate.

Q.—Here is a First Latin Book or Reader by Copp, Clark; how is it?

A.—I would say the same of this book.

Q.—Try this book, it is an American book, a Second German Book, by E. Steiger & Co., New York?

A.—This is a pure sulphate paper.

Q.—Now, Mr. Buntin, you gave your opinion on this paper before the Commission, and, as I understand, you condemned the paper as having too much ground wood in it?

A.—I did not exactly condemn it; there was an American gentleman who stated that there was no ground wood in it and I was brought up to give evidence, and I gave it as my opinion that there was a great percentage in it and I showed Judge Morgan that there was.

Q.—Was the American present at the time?

A.—Yes.

Q.—How did he take his medicine?

A.—He fell in with my view, stating that he had made only a casual examination.

Q.—Now, Mr. Buntin, I read in the report of that Commission on page 5 "A careful enquiry into the cost of 'publication' of these Readers and an examination of the make up of each book and the testimony of witnesses qualified to judge as to the material and workmanship employed in the publication has satisfied us that the Readers are of excellent and durable quality as to paper, typography, illustrations and binding, and in addition, have a very attractive appearance, which is not to be overlooked in the get-up of school books, and that the retail price now charged for each book is not excessive and should not be reduced to any lower prices than that to which the Minister of Education has, by recent agreement, reduced them, as the publishers and the trade generally will not at present prices realize more than a fair business profit from the sale of these books in connection with the other school books published by them." Now, was there any evidence given in your presence to justify that?

A.—No, I did not go into that question at all with them, Judge Morgan simply asked me if there was any ground wood in the paper and I said that there was.

Q.—The paper you saw then, on that occasion, was not good paper?

A.—I would not say that. They wanted to know whether the paper was being supplied according to contract and I said it was not.

Q.—It would not be up to the specifications of the contract, you think?

A.—No, when the contract called for it to be absolutely free from ground wood; besides, some of the paper was all ground wood.

Q.—You would not say that it was excellent paper would you, Mr. Buntin?

A.—No.

Q.—If you had been asked your opinion, would you have condemned it?

A.—Yes.

Q.—Did you hear anyone say that is was either excellent or desirable?

A.—No, I did not.

Q.—It was not in your opinion?

A.—No, it was not, it was an extra quality of "news."

Q.—You say it was an extra quality of "news," I suppose you mean that it should only be put in newspapers?

A.—Yes, that is it.

Q.—What is the value of the paper, that is, what would be the cost of the paper you have been examining, to the publisher, what would he pay for it at the mill?

A.—Well, for super calendar paper he ought to pay 4½ cents. per pound.

Q.—Is that 4½ cents. per pound net cost?

A.—That gives him one-third off.

Q.—Does it matter what large quantities?

A.—No, that is quality price.

Q.—Was there any evidence given as to the binding of these books?

A.—No, not while I was there, I was only up one night.

By Mr. COOPER:

Q.—Mr. Buntin, do you think the quality of the paper used in the school books superior or inferior to what you examined when here nine years ago?

A.—I think it is a better paper.

Q.—What would you say about the binding?

A.—All books should be properly sewn and bound, you seldom see a book that has been sewn go to pieces at the covers, besides, the cover has got to be put on good.

Q.—You agree with the evidence given by Mr. Flint, that we should bind them strongly?

A.—Yes, get your cover on firm so that it will not go to pieces.

That will do, Mr. Buntin, thank you.

MR. STAUNTON HERE RE-CALLED MR. W. C. FLINT, TORONTO, FOR FURTHER EXAMINATION.

By Mr. G. L. STAUNTON, K.C.:

Q.—(Handing witness a copy of Morang's Introductory Latin Grammar.) What kind of a book is that, Mr. Flint, is it hand sewn or machine sewn?

A.—It is machine sewn.

Q.—Are there tapes on this book?

A.—Yes.

Q.—How about book No. 2, you do not approve of it?

A.—No, the sewing is not as good as in No. 1.

Q.—There are no tapes in this book, are there?

A.—No, not in this book.

Q.—Now, take Morang's Modern Geography, that has no tape in it, has it?

A.—No.

Q.—What do you say of the binding of that book?

A.—It is not as strong as the first one.

Q.—The sewing, you think, is not good?

A.—No, of course, tape sewing is the strength of the book.

EVIDENCE OF MR. S. C. WOODLAND, BOOK-BINDER, TORONTO.

By Mr. J. A. MACDONALD:

Q.—What is your name?

A.—S. C. Woodland.

Q.—What is your occupation?

A.—Book-binder.

Q.—Where are you engaged?

A.—Brown Bros., Toronto.

Q.—How long have you been engaged in the business of book-binding?

A.—About eighteen years.

Q.—Why do you come to give evidence here?

A.—It was represented to Local Union No. 28, that there was a special Commission to enquire into the books and the Union decided to send a committee to sit and listen to see whether the blame for the bad binding was placed on the workmen or the publishers and to be of any assistance, so far as expert knowledge is concerned, to the Commission.

Q.—Were you reading the evidence as to the binding in the newspapers.

A.—I was.

Q.—And what did you decide?

A.—I decided that there were faults to lay all through; both in the manufacturing and the handling of the books afterwards.

Q.—What position does your Union take in regard to the binding in a large publishing house? Do you exercise a control over the work that the workmen put through?

A.—We exercise no control; only the manner of work.

Q.—And to the men?

A.—Only to the men individually as regards hours and wages.

Q.—How about their being union or non-union men, do you interest yourself in that question? You like union men to work in those places as largely as possible?

A.—Yes, that is our object, to have as many union men employed as possible and to encourage others to join the union.

Q.—Have you seen some of the books that are up here for investigation?

A.—I have only seen one book up to the present.

Q.—Cast you eye over that one. Do you notice any difference in that?

A.—In the first place, it is stiff in the joints, which, in a short time, will cause it to break away.

Q.—What caused that stiffness?

A.—On that they have a mull lining over the back, on account of the thinness of the board it will break open even; take another book, it will break free at the joint because the board is heavier; it breaks at the softest spot; the whole strain is upon these two hinges here.

Q.—Well, would a cloth joint make any difference?

A.—A cloth joint would solve the problem of the books coming out of the covers, take a strip of cloth 1½ inches wide and paste it on the back and sew it there in the ordinary way so that the strain of the book would be on the sewing.

Q.—Then your solution of the difficulty would be cloth joints to make the book more durable?

A.—Yes.

Q.—What do you say as to the wire binding?

A.—Wire binding has always been a failure for two reasons, one being that where the wire is clinched over these two pieces of wire (witness here shows the fastening to examiner) coming up here, it bursts the middle and will get short and cut through the paper before there is any strain on it at all.

Q.—You heard the evidence given by Mr. Flint as to the improvements which he suggested in the binding?

A.—Yes.

Q.—Do you agree with him in the main?

A.—Yes, his idea is good, but I am opposed to the joint mentioned by him.

Q.—How it that; why do you differ with him?

A.—Well, the only way I differ with him, is that the cloth should be put around the back further and instead of putting it on one leaf to put it on both leaves of the section.

Well, I will not ask you anything further now, Mr. Woodland.

EVIDENCE OF J. L. HUGHES, TORONTO.

By Mr. G. L. STAUNTON, K.C.:
Q.—What is your name?
A.—James L. Hughes.
Q.—You are?
A.—Chief Inspector of Public Schools in Toronto.
Q.—And have been for?
A.—Nearly thirty-three years.
Q.—You have in the City of Toronto free text books?
A.—Yes sir, and supplies.
Q.—Do you make any tax on the pupils?
A.—No direct tax; it comes out of the general taxation.
Q.—How long have you had that system?
A.—It was adopted in 1891 and put into operation in 1892.
Q.—Have you made a statement showing the cost of books and supplies from 1892 to 1905?
A.—Yes, sir.
Hands statement to examiner who reads it to Commission as follows:—

BOARD OF EDUCATION.

Chief Inspector's Office.

Cost of Free Text Books and Supplies since their first introduction in Toronto.

	Pupils Supplied.	Cost of Free Text Books.	Cost of Supplies.
1892	28,345	$4,380	
1893	28,306	6,927	*10,334
1894	28,938	2,446	6,630
1895	28,877	4,917	6,209
1896	28.983	5,225	4,144
1897	29,390	1,568	3,822
1898	29,771	910	2,586
1899	29,885	1,043	2,101
1900	29,801	2,305	2,666
1901	30,075	2,109	4,119
1902	30,003	2,474	3,570
1903	29,746	2,710	2,853
1904	30,011	2,660	3,529
1905	30,334	4,563	3,740
	412,465	$44,255	56,303

*Inaugural expense.

Average cost per annum for Text Books $3,161
Average cost per annum for supplies 4,331
Cost per pupil for Text Books in 14 years .... 10¾c.
Cost per pupil for Text Books in 13 years .... 13½c.

JAMES L. HUGHES,
Chief Inspector.

Q.—This statement is true, Mr. Hughes?

A.—Yes, sir, this statement is accurate, the accounts are audited by the official auditors, and you can rely upon it as sufficiently accurate.

Q.—You say that the average cost per annum for text books is $3,161.00.

A.—Yes.

Q.—And the average cost for supplies is $4,331.00?

A.—Yes.

Q.—You say the average attendance of pupils runs from 28,000 to 30,000 per year?

A.—Yes, sir.

Q.—The average cost per pupil for text books during the period of fourteen years is 10¾c., and the average cost for supplies covering the same period is 13½c. Do you mean to say that you supply all the pupils in the Public Schools with all their requirements of books and supplies for 24¼c.?

A.—Yes, sir.

Q.—Have you any doubt as to the advisability of adopting the Free Book System?

A.—We have found it very satisfactory.

Q.—What are its principal recommendations?

A.—Well, the pupils always have their books and supplies ready to begin on the opening day and are never without books which, of course, is a saving to the pupil.

Q.—The saving is very marked, is it not?

A.—Yes, sir.

Q.—Have you any idea what it would cost if the pupils had to buy these books?

A.—No, I never prepared an estimate.

Q.—Does the statement, submitted here, show the cost for all departments or classes in the schools?

A.—All but the Kindergartens, they are not included in this.

Q.—Do you furnish them with supplies?

A.—We do.

Q.—Have you an estimate showing the cost?

A.—I have not with me; but it costs say about $1,200.00 on the average for all our schools, and we have between five and six thousand children.

Q.—So it is a very small cost?

A.—Yes.

Q.—It does not cost any more than for the other children?

A.—No, about the same.

Q.—You supply the children with books, and when the books become dilapidated, I believe you bind them?

A.—Yes, we bind the books above the second Reader; we do not bind the smaller books.

Q.—You have a contract with Mr. Byford?

A.—Yes. He charges 10½c. to bind.

Q.—Do you find that re-bound books last as long as the first binding, or longer?

A.—Well, we find that they last quite as long.

Q.—Have you a tabulated statement showing the life of these books?

A.—Yes. Here is a statement showing the average life or usefulness in years.

(Hands Examiner following statement.)

Statement.

Text Books.	Average length of Usefulness in years.
High School Reader	8
Third Reader	6
Fourth Reader	6
P. S. Geography	6
P. S. History of England & Canada	6
History of Dominion of Canada, (Fifth Form)	6
P. S. Agriculture	6
Second Reader	5
Public School Arithmetic	5
Public School Algebra & Euclid	5
Public School Grammar	5
First Reader, Part II	3
P. S. Phonic Primer, Part II	3
Modern Phonic Primer, Part II	3
P. S. Phonic Primer, Part I	2
First Reader, Part I	$1\frac{1}{2}$
Modern Phonic Primer, Part I	$1\frac{1}{2}$
P. S. Copy Book	$\frac{1}{4}$

Q.—Does this statement include the re-bound books?

A.—No, it is before they are re-bound.

Q.—The average runs from six to eight years?

A.—Yes. The First Readers do not last so long.

Q.—These books pass through a great many hands, do they not?

A.—Yes, a book lasting from seven to eight years, passes through a great many hands.

Q.—Do you think the books are treated better under the Free Book System by the pupils?

A.—I do, that is one of the advantages that we claim for it; the pupils exercise greater care of the books.

Q.—Do they respect a Government book more than they do their own?

A.—Yes; we train them to believe it is theirs. Their fathers pay taxes and they know if they injure the book they have to pay for it.

Q.—If a child loses a book, what then?

A.—His father has to pay for it.

Q.—He has to be careful for two reasons then?

A.—Yes.

Q.—How do you carry out this plan of yours?

A.—In the first place, we have a Department that we call our Supply Department, with a gentlman in charge of that,—a clerk of supplies, who is employed by the city, and it is his business to supervise and look after them.

Q.—What does he do?

A.—He could tell you to-day, if you called him, how many books of each kind were in any school, and how many had been destroyed in the last fourteen years, and all the facts about them.

Q.—He keeps a history then?

A.—Yes; he has a record and account for every school which is made up every year.

Q.—What salary is he paid?

A.—$1,500.00 per year.

Q.—He is the custodian of all books?

A.—Yes. He receives all books from the publishers after the Board of Education advertises for tenders and awards contracts.

Q.—He receives tenders, does he?

A.—No, the Secretary of the Board receives the tenders, and the Board awards them; the clerk of supplies, under my direction, orders the books as they are required, you will understand that we order books twice a year.

Q.—Now, say that I am a teacher and I want to supply books for my class, what do I do?

A.—You have a form supplied to you from which you get a supply from the Principal.

Q.—What does the Principal do?

A.—He supervises all the requisitions and sends one large form similar to this to the clerk of supplies.

(Hands following form of Requisition to Examiner.)

(No. 27.)

THE BOARD OF EDUCATION, TORONTO.

Toronto,.................. 190

Mr. WM. KERR,
    Clerk of Supplies.

Dear Sir,—The following is a list of supplies in.............................
School for the month of ....

........Work Books (A).

........Work Books (B).

........Note Books.

........Exercise Books.

........Dictation Books.

........Business Forms, Senior.

........Business Forms, Junior.

........Book-keeping Blanks.

........Book-keeping Blanks, Senior 5.

    Book-keeping Blanks, Junior 5.

........Practice Drawing Paper.

........Junior (A) Drawing Paper.

........Senior (B) Drawing Paper.

........Special (C) Drawing Paper.

........Writing Books, ruled.

........Writing Books, unruled,

........Rulers, Senior Class.

........Rulers, Junior Class.

........Boxes Slate Pencils.

........Boxes Gillett's Pens, 292.

........Boxes of Eagle Pens, 190.

........Gross of Penholders.

........Gross of Lead Pencils, Work.

........Gross of Lead Pencils, Drawing.

........Boxes of Crayons, White.

........Boxes of Crayons, Assorted.

.........Blackboard Brushes.

.........Pointers.

.........Note Pads.

.........Memo Pads.

.........Sheets Exercise Paper, cap size.

.........Sheets Exercise Paper, note size.

.........Package Stamped Envelopes.

.........Package Note Envelopes.

.........Package Foolscap Envelopes.

.........Book Covers, small.

.........Book Covers, large.

.........Modulator.

.........Boxes Charcoal.

.........00 Notice of Absence, No. 1.

.........00 Notice of Punctuality, No. 2.

.........00 Notice of Susp's. to Parents, No. 3.

.........00 Notice of Susp's. to Inspector, No. 4.

.........00 Notice of Conduct, No. 5.

.........00 Transfer Pads, No. 6.

.........00 Notice of Inf. Dis. to Parents, No. 7.

.........00 Notice of Inf. Dis. M. H. Officers, No. 8.

.........00 Measles Forms, No. 9.

.........00 Vaccination Forms, No. 10.

.........00 Notice of Suspension to Inspector, No. 11.

.........00 Notice of Yard Duties, No. 12.

.........00 Notice of Teacher's Absence, No. 13.

.........00 Monthly Reports, Night Schools, No. 14.

.........00 Transfers, No. 15.

.........00 Monthly Reports to Inspector, No. 16.

.........00 Annual Reports to Principal, No. 17.

.........00 Examination Record Sheets, No. 18.

.........00 Marking Sheets, No. 19.

.........00 Labels for Text Books, No. 20.

.........00 Medical Certificates, Teachers, No. 21.

.........00 Medical Certificates, Pupils, No. 22.

.........00 Requisition Forms for Night School Supplies, No. 23.

.........00 Receipt Forms for Night School Supplies, No. 24.

.........00 Receipt Forms given for Text Books, Night Schools, No. 25.

.........00 Receipt Forms for Text Books, Day Schools, No. 26.

.........00 Requisition Forms for Supplies, No. 27.

.........00 Receipt Forms for Supplies, No. 28.

.........00 Requisition Forms for Kindergarten Supplies, No. 29.

.........00 Receipt Forms for Kindergarten Supplies, No. 30.

.........00 Monthly Reports of Inf. Disease, No. 31.

Extras ....

Extras ....

Extras ....

Extras ....

Extras ....

....

Principal.

Q.—And on receipt of this requisition, what does the Clerk of Supplies do?

A.—The Clerk of Supplies goes carefully over it to see whether it is a reasonable order, and passes it if he considers it is; if he has any doubt upon it, he consults me.

Q.—You are then, the Official Judge?

A.—Yes, the supplies are in my Department.

Q.—If you approve of the order, what happens then?

A.—It is passed on to the Store-keeper.

Q.—The man who puts up the supplies in packages?

A.—Yes.

Q.—Then you keep a supply of books in stock?

A.—No, we do not keep a supply in stock because we can obtain them easily. He first checks over each school, and any parcels that are being made up are put in that box and twice a month we have a delivery to the schools.—Do you hire a carter to deliver them?

A.—Yes, then these books are sent out with the invoices and the Principal, after comparing, signs a receipt and returns it.

Q.—Is this the form of receipt?

(Reads receipt form as follows.)

(No. 28.)

THE BOARD OF EDUCATION, TORONTO.

Toronto,....................... 190.......

Received from the Clerk of Supplies, Toronto Public School Board, the following Supplies for..........................School.

.........Work Books (A).

.........Work Books (B).

..........Note Books.

.........Exercise Books.

.........Dictation Books.

.........Business Forms, Senior.

....Business Forms, Junior.

.........Book-keeping Blanks, Senior 5.

.........Book-keeping Blanks, Junior 5.

.........Practice Drawing Paper.

.........Junior (A) Drawing Paper.

.........S nior (B) Drawing Paper.

.........Special (C) Drawing Paper.

.........Writing Books, ruled.

.........Writing Books, unruled.

.........Rulers, Senior Class.

.........Rulers, Junior Class.

.........Boxes Slate Pencils.

.........Boxes Gillett's Pens, 292.

.........Boxes of Eagle Pens, 190.

.........Gross of Penholders.

.........Gross of Lead Pencils, Work.

.........Gross of Lead Pencils, Drawing.

.........Boxes of Crayons, White.

.........Boxes of Crayons, Assorted.

.........Blackboard Brushes.

..........Pointers.
.........Note Pads.
.........Memo Pads.
.........Sheets Exercise Paper cap size.
.........Sheets Exercise Paper, note size.
.........Package Stamped Envelopes.
.........Package Note Envelopes.
.........Package Foolscap Envelopes.
.........Book Covers, small.
.........Book Covers, large.
.........Modulator.
.........Boxes Charcoal.
.........00 Notice of Absence, No. 1.
.........00 Notice of Punctuality, No. 2.
.........00 Notice to Susp's. to Parents, No. 3.
.........00 Notice to Susp's. to Inspector, No. 4.
.........00 Notice of Conduct, No. 5.
.........00 Transfer Pads, No. 6.
.........00 Notice of Inf. Dis. to Parents, No. 7.
.........00 Notice of Inf. Dis. M. H. Officers, No. 8.
.........00 Measles Forms, No. 9.
.........00 Vaccination Form, No. 10.
.........00 Notice of Suspension to Inspector, No. 11.
.........00 Notice of Yard Duties, No. 12.
.........00 Notice of Teacher's Absence, No. 13.
.........00 Monthly Reports, Night Schools, No. 14.
.........00 Transfers, No. 15.
.........00 Monthly Reports, to Inspectors, No. 16.
.........00 Annual Reports to Principal, No. 17.
.........00 Examination Record Sheets, No. 18.
.........00 Marking Sheets, No. 19.
.........00 Labels for Text Books, No. 20.
.........00 Medical Certificates, Teachers, No. 21.
.........00 Medical Certificates, Pupils, No. 22.
.........00 Requisition Forms for Night School Supplies, No. 23.
.........00 Receipt Forms for Night School Supplies, No. 24.
.........00 Receipt Forms given for Text Books, Night Schools, No. 25.
.........00 Receipt Forms for Text Books, Day Schools, No. 26.
.........00 Requisition Forms for Supplies, No. 27.
.........00 Receipt Forms for Supplies, No. 28.
.........00 Requisition Forms for Kindergarten Supplies, No. 29.
.........00 Receipt Forms for Kindergarten Supplies, No. 30.
.........00 Monthly Reports of Inf. Dis., No. 31.
Extras   ....
Extras   ....
Extras   ....
Extras   ....

....
                                                    Principal.

A.—Yes; the Principal is in charge of these books for his school, and
if he gives a wrong receipt he will have to pay for it. He takes a receipt
from his teachers, and they take receipts from their pupils, at the close of

the term the pupils receipts are taken out, and if a pupil does not return the books in harmony with those receipts his father has to make up the difference,—this is the form of receipt signed by the pupils on receipt of their books, and which is returned to them when their books are given back. (Hands examiner following form).

(No. 26.)
(Form F.)

TORONTO PUBLIC SCHOOLS.

Receipt to be Given for Books Received.

Toronto,................... 190.......

Received the Following Books ....
Teacher in Class No. ....
School.

........Arithmetics, High School.
........Arithmetics, Public School.
........Algebras, High School.
........Geographies, High School.
........Geographies, Public Schools.
........Grammars, High Schools.
........Grammars, Public School.
........Euclid, McKay's (Book 1 to 3).
........Euclid and Algebra, Public School.
........Histories, England and Canada, H. S.
........Histories, England and Canada, P. S.
........Readers, 1st.
........Readers, 2nd.
........Readers, 3rd.
........Readers, 4th.
........Readers, 5th.
........Readers, Supplementary.
........Singing Books.
........Practical Speller.
....
....
....
....

....

This form should be signed by pupils on receipt of their books, and returned to them when their books are given back.

Q.—Are the books kept during the holidays?

A.—No. We collect them all in before promotions are made; at the end of the mid-summer they are all collected and stored during the holidays.

Q.—So that I understand, that when the pupil gets a book he gives a receipt for it, and when he returns the book he receives his receipt back, and if he does not, he has to pay the value of the book?

A.—Yes.

Q.—So there is no opportunity for stealing or dishonesty if your system is carried out?

A.—No, the only possibility we have of losing a book, is by the parents moving away from the city without giving warning of it.

Q.—How many officers does this work require,—as I understand it, you have a clerk of supplies and a store-keeper; then you have to have a room?

A.—Yes, we have a room at the City Hall.

Q.—These are all the officers you require?

A.—Yes, except a carter.

Q.—These officers are an additional cost are they? What does the store-keeper cost?

A.—$650 per annum, I think is his salary.

Q.—Do you compel the children to take books from you, or can they bring their own books?

A.—They may bring their own books if they like.

Mr. STAUNTON: Just a minute, Mr. Hughes, I want to re-call Mr. Ballard to ask him a question.

Mr. BALLARD re-called was asked by Mr. Staunton:

Q.—Have you any paid officers in Hamilton in connection with your books and supplies, Mr. Ballard?

A.—No.

Examination of Mr. Hughes continued:

Q.—It is fair then, to add the salaries of these two officials,—$2,100.00 to the cost of the text books supplied to the children because it is an expense that otherwise would not be incurred?

A.—Yes.

Q.—Could you dispense with the services of any of your clerks if you did not have the free system?

A.—Yes, we could dispense with some of the clerks in my office.

Q.—You say that there is charged up here all the cost of the books for night schools, but you have not put in the night school pupils?

A.—Yes.

Q.—Do you think that the night school pupils would absorb some of the clerical assistants?

A.—Yes.

Q.—About how much?

A.—It would be fair probably to put it at one-third.

Q.—How many pupils are there in the night schools?

A.—We have fifteen classes in our night schools.

Q.—What is the total attendance?

A.—I would say about eight hundred.

Q.—They say this free school book system is objectionable on sanitary grounds, do you think there is anything in that?

A.—I do not think there is the slightest foundation for it whatever. The Medical Health Officer destroys the books belonging to the boys or girls who have disease, and he gives us a form stating that he has destroyed them; our label, which is in every text book, has a special clause to this effect.

Q.—Have you a copy of this label with you Mr. Hughes?

A.—Yes. (Hands label to examiner.)

(No. 20).

FORM G.

Class No................   Book No................

....School.

THIS BOOK BELONGS TO
THE BOARD OF EDUCATION, FOR THE
CITY OF TORONTO.

———

Conditions of Loaning.

1. Marking or defacing this book will be regarded as a serious offence.
2. In case of loss, destruction or material injury, this book must be at once replaced by the pupil.
3. This book may be replaced at cost through the Principal.
4. This book must not be taken from the school room without permission from the teacher.
5. This book must be returned to the teacher at the close of the term, or in case of removal of the pupil to another school.
6. In case of contagious disease, this book, if taken home, should be given to the Medical Health Officer, and a receipt taken from him therefor.

By Order,
THE BOARD OF EDUCATION
FOR THE CITY OF TORONTO.

Q.—You do not believe there is any danger then, from contagion, Mr. Hughes?

A.—No, I remember asking the Secretary of the State Board of Massachusetts, when I was there, whether he thought there was any danger from germs of disease in the books and he said:—"Do you use dollar bills in Canada?" and I said yes, and he said, "well, do you think there is any contagion in dollar bills?" I answered no, I do not think there is, and he stated, "then there is none in text books, you would get disease just as easy from the newspapers."

Q.—Have you all the forms used in connection with your system?

A.—Yes, I shall make a complete set for you.

Q.—You think then, this system is the best?

A.—Yes. I studied all the systems in the United States and I think we have adopted all the good ones.

Q.—Do you think it is imminently satisfactory?

A.—Yes.

Q.—Have you any samples of books with you?

A.—Yes. (Produces a large package of books). After six years' use in the schools we ask the teachers to condemn the books that they cannot approve of and send them into our office and we credit them with the books so sent in.

Q.—Do you ever send any of them back to them?

A.—Yes, if the books are in fairly good condition we send them back, and if we can bind the books over again we have them rebound.

Q.—You allow them to condemn a book because it is dirty, do you not?

A.—Oh, yes.

Q.—Mr. Hughes, are these books selected as a fair average lot?

A.—Yes.

Q.—You never saw these books before you received them?

A.—No, the messenger brought them to me at the door here.

Q.—What would say about this High School Reader?

A.—The High School Reader lasts with care about six years, we often find when the covers come off the books that we can rebind them ourselves by using cotton strips and book binders' paste, which holds the covers on as long as the books last.

Q.—In your opinion then, these strips should be used in binding "Readers?"

A.—I think so.

Q.—Have you received any compliments generally as to the quality of the binding?

A.—About eight years ago complaint was made that the High School Arithmetic covers came off too easily.

Mr. Cooper examined the books, singling out copies of Public School History of England and Canada, one in use since 1892 and one since 1896 and some for a longer term, all in fairly good condition.

By Mr. COOPER:

Q.—Is it customary for you to supply manilla covers on all your books, Mr. Hughes?

A.—Oh yes, all our books are covered like that.

Q.—How often are the covers changed?

A.—Twice a year.

Q.—Why do you put on these covers?

A.—To protect the books and to train the pupils in habits of cleanliness; we train the pupils to put on these covers as a matter of cleanliness.

(Mr. Hughes here demonstrated to Mr. Cooper how the pupils put the manilla covers on their books).

Mr. STAUNTON: Would you call this book well printed?

A.—Yes.

Mr. Staunton examined several copies of the Practical Speller produced by Mr. Hughes, some in use since 1892 and 1894, and found them to be all in fairly good condition.

Mr. COOPER: Did you ever have the pupils supplement the binding by the way of fixing books?

A.—We did until we adopted the plan of having them bound by a professional binder; but that was only when the cover came off. There is one feature that I might call your attention to in the making of good books out of old books. We have two grades in our schools and the first grade uses the first half of the book and the senior grade uses the second half and when we get the books in we can tear the first half out of one and the second half out of the other and thus have a new book by bringing the two good parts together.

Q.—Would it, in your opinion, be advisable to print separate Readers for the Junior Second, Senior Second, Junior Third and Senior Third?

A.—I think for cities that would be an advantage. We have in Toronto two sections of the Second Book, two of the Third and two of the Fourth, and I think separate Readers would be an advantage.

Mr. COOPER: There was a suggestion made that these small readers be bound cheaply so that they would not be expected to last a great length of time and then they could be thrown away and let every pupil as he came along get a new reader.

8 T. B.

A.—Well, in a sense, it would be an advantage but it would be much more expensive.

Q.—It does not greatly appeal to you then?

A.—Not from the citizens' standpoint.

Q.—Do you ever have complaints that the books are not in good condition?

A.—In the fourteen years I have not had fourteen complaints, with over 30,000 children using them, that the books were not in good condition.

Q.—What do you do in case of a pupil objecting to take a second hand book?

A.—I do not think we ever had such an objection.

Q.—You have no trouble then on that score?

A.—No.

Mr. STAUNTON: Do you know of any case where the parents buy their own books?

A.—I do not know of any case now; these were a few when we first started the system but I do not find it now.

Q.—Do you think the free text book system has a civilizing effect on our foreign population; do they come to school more freely on account of free text books?

A.—Oh yes, I think there is no doubt about that; it is a great feature in the poorer districts and all classes of people take advantage of it.

Q.—What effect has it on the attendance.

A.—Not any material effect.

Q.—In certain districts do you think the attendance would be much lower if they did not have free text books?

A.—Not much.

Q.—Does the free text book system tend to prolong the attendance where a boy gets up to the fourth class?

A.—Yes, I think it does. If a boy had to buy an expensive set of books it would induce some parents to take a boy from school.

Q.—Do you not think that free text books in the cities is one of the principal attractions to draw men with large families to the cities?

A.—If they thought about it, I suppose that would be an attraction; but I do not believe they would think about it; they come to the city because they think they can get their children to work. Other classes come because they have retired and wish their children to be educated in the Universities.

Mr. MACDONALD: Mr. Hughes, you point out that the condition of these books is attributed to the perfection of your system?

A.—Yes, I think so.

Q.—Both as to the cleanliness and economy?

A.—Yes.

Mr. STAUNTON: Will you tell the Commissioners, please, Mr. Hughes, some of the advantages arising out of the free text book system as you conduct it in Toronto?

A.—I believe that the free text book system as we have conducted it in Toronto during the last fifteen years is an excellent system. If I knew any better system I would suggest it to the Board of Education. It has the following advantages among others: —

(1) It is very much cheaper than any other system with which I am acquainted of supplying text books. I submit the following statement, which shows the cost of text books since 1892, and of school supplies since 1893. Pupils are not required to purchase any of the material which they use in school.

8a T. B.

(2) The plan of supplying text books free is in harmony with the general principle of free education. The same fundamental principle which has been accepted as a basis for free school buildings and free teachers provided by general taxation logically leads to the providing of free text books in the same way. The patriotic as well as the economic reasons for free national schools apply to free text books as well as to free buildings and free teachers.

(3) Free text books are of value in securing a better classification of pupils.

(4) Their use leads to more regular attendance, especially in the poorer districts of cities. Many poor people would shorten the years of attendance of their children at both ends of the school course if they had to purchase the text books required for their children. This would be especially true in the case of children who were about to be promoted to a higher class when they had reached the age of fourteen. The poor man who had to purchase a new set of expensive books for his child under such conditions would in many cases allow his child to leave school, rather than buy the books which were to be used for only a short time.

(5) It was always necessary to purchase text books for the children of some very poor people. The fact that their books were purchased for them and loaned to them, made an invidious distinction and placed the unfortunate children at a disadvantage compared with their fellow pupils. Free text books overcome this disadvantage entirely and place all children on an equal footing.

(6) The work of the school is not interfered with because all children have not the necessary text books.

(7) Experience in our schools has proved that the use of free text books is one of the best possible methods for training children to take good care of public property. This is a most important moral lesson.

(8) So far as I am aware the system of free text books has not been discontinued in any place where it has been adopted.

That will do, Mr. Hughes, thank you.

EVIDENCE OF MR. C. R. HURST, TORONTO.

Examiner, Mr. James A. Macdonald.

Q.—What is your name?

A.—C. R. Hurst.

Q.—What is your occupation, Mr. Hurst?

A.—Book-binder.

Q.—How long have you been a book-binder?

A.—About fifteen years.

Q.—Where are you employed now?

A.—In the Methodist Book Room.

Q.—Were you subpœnaed to give evidence here?

A.—No, sir.

Q.—How did you come to give evidence?

A.—For the same reason as Mr. Flint and Mr. Woodland; I am a member of the Committee.

Q.—You are then, a member of Local Union No. 28?

A.—Yes, sir.

Q.—And you decided to come and give evidence as to the binding?

A.—Yes, the papers said the binding was bad and we decided to come and give evidence if we were asked.

Q.—Is it the fault of the binder or the binding, this bad method?

A.—Well, it is not the fault of the book-binder, the workman, for he only carries out the instructions of his employers.

Q.—Look at this Second Reader, Mr. Hurst; is there any fault in this book?

A.—Yes, serious fault; I do not approve of the wire sewing.

Q.—Why do you not approve of that?

A.—Because it is not as good as thread sewing.

Q.—What do you think could be done to make this a stronger book?

A.—To have it sewn with thread.

Q.—Is the condition you find this book in the fault of the book-binder or the fault of the firm?

A.—It could not be the fault of the binder because he is working under instructions.

Q.—You have heard the evidence of the preceding witnesses, Mr. Flint and Mr. Woodland, as to how these books may be made with a cloth joint and thread sewn; do you concur with them in that respect?

A.—Yes, sir.

Q.—And in its present condition you think the book would go to pieces very readily?

A.—Yes.

Well, Mr. Hurst, I will not ask you anything more just now, but may later on.

The Commission then adjourned.

OFFICIAL REPORT OF THE EVIDENCE TAKEN BEFORE THE TEXT BOOK COMMISSION AT ITS FOURTH SITTING ON WEDNESDAY, 24TH OCTOBER, 1906. G. L. STAUNTON, K.C., EXAMINER.

EVIDENCE OF MR. H. M. GRANTHAM, TORONTO.

By G. L. STAUNTON, K.C.:

Q.—Your name is?

A.—H. M. Grantham.

Q.—And your occupation?

A.—Manufacturing books for Morang & Company.

Q.—How long have you been in the book business?

A.—Three years, and in the paper business four years.

Q.—Prior to that?

A.—Yes.

Q.—Were you in New York and obtained experience of the paper manufacturing down there?

A.—Yes. I was for some time down there.

Q.—In selling paper, of course you would come in touch with the publishers and what they publish; you know the value of school book papers and magazine papers well?

A.—Yes.

Q.—Since you have been with Morang & Company what has been your occupation?

A.—Looking after the manufacturing entirely.

Q.—Morang & Company are publishers in Toronto and publish a large number of books, do they not?

A.—Yes. School books, subscription books and novels for a time.

Q.—In producing these publications they are constantly making contracts with printing, binding and paper supplies, do they not?

A.—Yes. I look after that.

Q.—You make contracts with the different paper companies, printers and book-binders, do you?

A.—Yes.

Q.—You have done that for how long?

A.—Three years.

Q.—Your business requires that you should be in touch with and know what the current cost of school books is?

A.—Yes.

Q.—Do you profess to have a knowledge of the current cost of school books?

A.—Yes, certainly I have.

Q.—You have had an experience which would warrant you in saying that?

A.—Yes.

Q.—Be kind enough to look at these readers. (Witness is given copies of "Readers": First Part of First Reader, Second Part of Second Reader and Third and Fourth Readers.)

I would ask you, Mr. Grantham, to be kind enough to make me an estimate on the Ontario Readers of their cost to the publishers?

WITNESS: Of the manufacturer's cost, you mean?

EXAMINER: Yes, that is it; have you done so?

A.—Yes. I have an estimate here that shows it.

EXAMINER: Let us have it, please.

MANUFACTURING COST OF ONTARIO READERS.

Part I.—Ontario Reader.

Containing 64 pages, 2 32 page forms in black, no color work.

Manufacturing Cost on 100,000 Copies.

210 rms., 30 x 41, 70.5000 at 4¼ cents	$624 75
Printing, 2 32 page forms	262 00
Binding at 3 cents per copy	3,000 00
Total	$3,886 75

Cost per copy (3 9-10 cents) (4 1-2).

Part II—Ontario Reader.

Containing 96 pages, 3 32 page forms in black; no color work.

Manufacturing Cost of 100,000 Copies.

315 rms., 31 x 40, 70.500 at 4¼ cents	$937 10
Printing, 3 32 page forms	390 00
Binding at 3 7-8 cents	3,875 00
Total	$5,202 10

Cost per copy (5 1-5 cents) (6).

Ontario Reader—Second Book.

Containing 184 pages, 5 32 page forms and 1 16 page and 1 8 page.

Manufacturing Cost of 50,000 Copies.

298 rms., 31 x 40, 70.500 at 4¼ cents	$886 55
Printing, 5½ cents	400 00
Binding at 5½ cents per copy	2,750 00
Total	$4,036 55

Cost per copy (8 cents) (11¼).

Ontario Reader—Third Book.

Containing 280 pages, 8 32 page forms, 1 16 and 1 8 page.

Manufacturing Cost on 25,000 Copies.

225 rms., 31 x 40, 70.500 at 4¼ cents	$669 40
Printing, 10 forms	370 00
Binding at 6 cents per copy	1,500 00
Total	$2,539 40

Cost per copy (10 1-8 cents) (12 1-3).

Ontario Reader, Fourth Book.

Containing 344 pages, 10 32 page forms, 1 16 and 1 8 page.

Manufacturing Cost on 25,000 Copies.

278 rms., 31 x 40, 70.500 at 4¼ cents	$828 00
Printing, 12 forms	460 00
Binding at 7 cents per copy	1,750 00
Total	$3,038 00

Cost per copy (12 1-8 cents).

PLATE COST AND MANUFACTURING COST OF VARIOUS BOOKS PUBLISHED BY MORANG & CO.

Phonic Primer—Part I.

Containing 64 pages, 4 32 forms in black and 6 forms of color work.

Manufacturing Cost on 50,000 Copies.

105 rms.; 31 x 42½, 85.500 at 4½ cents pound	$401 65
Printing, 2 32's and 3 forms of color	559 50
Binding at 2¼ cents per copy	1,062 50
Total	$2,023 65

Cost per copy, 4 cents; plus royalty, ½ cent, 4½ cents.
Original cost of plates, $2,450.00.

Phonic Primer—Part II.

Containing 112 pages, 3 32 page and 1 16 page form in black and 3 forms of color.

Manufacturing Cost on 40,000 Copies.

147 rms., 31 x 46, 100.500 at 4½ cents pound	$661 50
Printing, 4 forms black and 3 color	420 00
Binding at 3¼ cents per copy	1,300 00
Total	$2,381 50

Cost per copy, 6 cents.
Original cost of plates, $2,466.31.

Modern Reader—Book I.

Containing 128 pages and 8 full page illustrations in two colors, 4 32 page 16-144 forms and 2 forms of color work.

Manufacturing Cost on 25,000 Copies.

183 rms., 31 x 46, 100.500 at 4½ cents	$823 50
Printing, 7 forms	224 00
26 rms., 23½ x 31½, 50.500 at 7½ cents	97 50
Printing, 2 color cuts	60 00
Binding at 7½ cents per copy	1,875 00
Total	$3,080 00

Cost per copy, 12 1-3 cents.
Original cost of plates, $1,051.50.

British Nation.

Containing 20 32 page forms and 1 8 page and 6 colored maps.

Manufacturing cost on 5,400 Copies.

111 1-20 rms., 31 x 42½, 80.500 at 4½ cents	$399 78
Printing forms, 20 32's and 1 8	280 55
Maps in 5 colors ....;.................	145 17
Binding at 14 cents per copy	756 00
Total	$1,581 50

Cost per copy, 29½ cents; royalty, 10 per cent., 10 cents, 39½ cents.
Total cost of plates, $1,359.07.

Story of the Canadian People.

Containing 15 32 page forms and one colored map.

Manufacturing Cost on 4,700 Copies.

72 rms., 31 x 42½, 85.500 at 4½ cents	$275 04
Printing forms, 15 32's	194 20

5,000 five color maps 42 65
Binding at 11½ cents 540 50

      Total $1,052 39
      Cost per copy, 10¼ cents; royalty, 1¼ cents, 11½ cents.
Total cost of plates, $1,180.00.

Modern English Grammar, 25 Cent Edition.

Containing 6 32 page forms.

Manufacturing Cost on 5,000 Copies.

34 14-20 rms., 30½ x 41, 75.500 .... **$97 06**
Printing forms, 6 32's 54 00
Binding at 7¼ cents 362 50

      Total $513 56
Cost per copy, 10¼ cents; royalty, 1¼ cents, 11½ cents.

Q.—What do you think of this book? (Hands witness one of the Canada Publishing Company's books.) Give me a fair criticism?

A.—Well, in the first place, there are no color cuts in it whatever; the printing is very, very poor; the illustrations are very poor and much behind the times; the paper might be a little better and the binding is, to say the least, very badly done. The mechanical work is not very good either.

Q.—Now then, take Part II of the Ontario Reader; you have estimated on that?

A.—Yes; for manufacturing 100,000 copies the cost would be 5 1-5 cents.

Q.—Give me your criticism on that book?

A.—It would be just about the same as I gave on Part I, except that I notice that there is wire stitching; where this kind of stitching is used, the wire rusts and leaves pull out; the illustrations in this book also seem to be very poor indeed. There is no reason now-a-days why we should not have color work in school books.

Q.—Take the Second Reader, published by Copp, Clark & Company; you have estimated on that, have you not?

A.—Yes; it would cost to manufacture that book in 50,000 copy lots, 8 cents per copy.

Q.—What do you say as to that book so far as its mechanical merits are concerned?

A.—Well, the type used is too small and the illustrations poor again; it is also bound with wire stitches and is about twenty years behind the times.

Q.—What about the paper?

A.—Well, as I said before, the paper is all the same; you could get better?

Mr. Cooper: In what way?

A.—Well, you might pay a little bit more for it. If you notice you will see that the sheet is what you might call flanked and notyperfectly smooth; it brings the cuts out very well, but there is a dirty murky color all through the sheet.

Mr. Crothers: Would that be caused by the presence of ground wood in the paper?

A.—No, not necessarily.

Mr. COOPER: Do you think the weight is heavy enough?

A.—No, I do not; there should be a clear surface and a little heavier weight, say 5 or 10 pounds to the ream.

Mr. STAUNTON: The next book that I was about to direct your attention to was the Third Reader. What is your estimate on that book?

A.—In 25,000 lots, the cost per copy would be 10 1-8 cents.

Q.—There are 280 pages in that book, are there not?

A.—Yes, but there is no color work.

Q.—Is that book as good as this one?

A.—Well, it all depends as to what you mean.

Q.—Well, have you any additional remarks to make on that book?

A.—No, I do not think it is any worse than the others.

Q.—Who is it published by?

A.—Copp, Clark & Company.

Q.—It is a wire stitched book too, is it not?

A.—Yes.

Q.—Then there is the Fourth Reader; this book contains 344 pages and you estimate I see on 25,000 lots?

A.—Yes, they can be made for 12½c. each.

Q.—What are the retail prices of those books?

A.—The retail price of First Reader, Part I, is 10c.; Part II, 15c., Second Reader, 20c., Third Reader, 30c. and Fourth Reader, 40c.

Q.—The Canada Publishing Company issue the Fourth Reader, while the Third Reader is published by Copp, Clark Company.

Q.—What you have to say about the Third Reader and the other books, does that apply to this Fourth Reader?

A.—Yes, and another point about the Fourth Reader is, in my opinion, that the type is smaller than need be; much smaller, and the binding is very, very poor.

Q.—I want to come back with you to the First Part of the First Reader, does Morang & Co. publish a book similar to that?

A.—Yes, we have our Primer, Part I.

Q.—Have you a copy with you?

A.—Yes, our book contains the same number of pages as the other book.

Q.—Does it sell for the same price?

A.—Yes, it sells for the same price; it contains the same number of pages with three color work all through the book.

Q.—What is three color work?

A.—I mean that the pictures are printed in blue, red and yellow.

Q.—Is that more expensive than mere black and white work?

A.—Yes, it means running the book through the presses three times more.

Q.—Well, does it increase the expense?

A.—Yes, certainly, it doubles the printing I should think.

Q.—What would you produce that book for?

A.—I have my own cost cards down at the office and have taken a memo from then and that Primer, Part I costs, say 4½c.

Q.—So that you have there what you call a modern book?

A.—Yes, it is so strongly made that you cannot possibly pull the cover off.

Q.—It is in three colors and a superior book to the others?

A.—Yes, it is in three colors, the type is better, the paper is clear and the binding is strong.

Q.—What do you say about the cover of that book?

A.—I think it will stand probably more than the cover you have there.

Q.—This is not as expensive a cover as it?

A.—No, possibly the other cover costs a little wee bit more, but as far as wear is concerned it will out-last it.

Q.—Are these books authorized in any other place than in this Province?

A.—No, they are just authorized here.

Q.—This books retails at the same price does it not?

A.—Yes, but from a mechanical point of view, our book is very much better.

Q.—Is your paper equal to or better than theirs in your opinion?

A.—In my opinion, I think ours is a better paper.

Q.—Now, I have another book here, namely, Part II, Morang's Modern Phonic Primer, this is the second part of the First Reader. Now, the engravings in this book, in my judgment, are very much finer than those in the other book. How much does it cost?

A.—That book costs us to manufacture 6c. There is three color work in that book; it contains 112 pages, three 32 and 16 forms in black and 3 forms in color. Have you noticed that there are some very good half-tones in it and nice large clear type and margins, the same as in part one, and bound in the same manner.

Q.—That on page 52 is very nice; do you consider that very good?

A.—Yes, that is a pretty little cut; there is also a cute little cut on page 61 which is very pretty and suggestive; and a full page cut opposite page 68 which livens up the book and makes it interesting.

Q.—This book costs you how much?

A.—Six cents per copy.

Q.—And sells for 15c. the same as the other?

A.—Yes.

Q.—You sell to the trade the same way as other books are sold, do you not?

A.—Yes, the same price; then you must remember the book costs far more to manufacture than the Ontario books on account of that color work.

Mr. CROTHERS: You say, Mr. Grantham, that this book costs six cents. Does that cover the literary part of the work?

A.—No, merely the paper, press work and binding; the plates are outside of that price entirely.

Q.—Were these plates prepared in Canada?

A.—Yes, most of them; there may be two or three that have not, but the majority of them were.

Q.—You mean the cuts were made in Canada?

A.—Yes.

Q.—How did you get the original of that cut?

A.—That was drawn by the Toronto Engraving Company as a matter of fact.

Q.—Then you employ original artists in that sense?

A.—Yes, as far as possible we do all this in Canada.

Q.—Did you buy the copyright of that picture?

A.—Probably there is no copyright on it; and if there is, we probably got permission to use it, or paid for it as the case may be.

Mr. CROTHERS: These books published by Morang & Company, Parts I and II First Book, seem to be very much superior in every way to the others in paper, printing and illustrations, do they not?

A.—Yes, according to our system, this Part I, Morang's Primer, only costs 3-5 of a cent more than Part I of the other; although the difference in cost is so small, yet it means a great deal when the total cost is so small.

Mr Staunton : It is like adding half an inch to the end of a man's nose, I should think?

Witness : Exactly so.

Mr. Staunton : I notice that your Part II contains 102 pages and the other contains 94 pages?

A.—Yes, I have noticed that, but then in our book there are some blank pages at the back that are numbered in; for instance, opposite page 74, and I have added these all in.

Q.—Then you do not profess. to say that there is more in this book than in the other?

A.—Possibly three or four, I have not counted them over carefully.

Mr. Crothers : How much more would it cost to put covers like these on other books?

A.—It would cost about half a cent more to do that.

Mr. Staunton : Come to the Ontario Readers now, I want to ask you about the paper; Part I and II of the Ontario Readers are referred to in the contract to be 66 lbs. to the ream of 512 sheets, now the contract that you have requires that there should be 85 lbs., how about that?

A.—Well, we are using 85 lb. paper to make them more substantial.

Q.— Do you know why you where given the worst of it?

A.—I do not, it certainly costs more money. We are putting very nearly 20 lbs. more to the ream at about 4½c. per lb. The paper on the Morang Primer, Part I, I think, is 80 lbs. to the ream and we have made it 5 lbs. better.

Q.—Perhaps you could not get 80 lb. paper?

A.—Oh yes, quite easily.

Q.—You mean to say then, that it sells in Ontario just on its merits?

A.—Yes. This book has in all 144 pages counting eight full page illustrations and costs us 11¼c.

Q.—Does this book correspond with the Ontario Second Reader, or does it compete with any other book? Do you sell it in competition?

A.—I cannot tell you that at all; Mr. Saul can tell you that.

Q.—The first book then, that you mark in your statement to me, is the Modern Reader, book one. This is the book is it? (Hands witness copy of Morang's Modern Reader, Part I).

A.—Yes, that is the one.

Q.—What does that book cost?

A.—11¼c. each copy.

Q.—Now, I am asking you exactly what it costs to publish the book per copy?

A.—That is the exact cost taken from my cost cards in the office.

Q.—Would there be any additional cost for plates, etc.?

A.—The additional cost for plates, etc., in that book would be about $600 or $700.

Q.—And you are estimating on an output of 25,000 copies?

A.—Yes, you put the cost at 11¼c. which includes a royalty of one cent which is charged against every book.

Q.—That book is then, in your mind, superior to any of those others in its mechanical construction, etc.?

A.—Very much so, on account of its color plates, etc., it is a better book altogether.

Q.—Tell me the cost of the plates used in Parts I and II of your Primer?

A.—The original cost of the plates in Part I was $2,450, Part II cost, say, $2,465. Our Modern Reader, First Book, was about $700.

Q.—Now then, take Modern Reader, Book II, that contains 284 pages, 8 full page illustrations, two colors, etc., that is right is it not?

A.—Yes.

Q.—You estimate that it would cost 12½c. and the plates $1,051?

A.—Yes.

Q.—Are all these books Canadian made?

A.—Yes, as much as possible; but we have had a little bit of artistic work done in the United States.

Q.—Now, take this copy of "The British Nation"—that book is a History of England, is it not?

A.—Yes.

Q.—Have you the present edition of "Wrong's" book here with you?

A.—No, but there is one here I think.

Q.—How is that book you have there put together? (Hands witness one of "Wrong's" books.)

A.—This book is sewn on tapes and is much better bound than the others.

Q.—Have you any difficulty in getting books sewn on tapes?

A.—Yes. I have had some difficulty; but sewing on tapes certainly makes a book much stronger, for if a book gets loose and the cover springs out, if it has a tape holding it on it makes it much better and renders the book stronger in every way.

Q.—You prefer books to be sewn on tapes then?

A.—Yes, I certainly do.

Q.—Now, that book of "Wrong's" is a large book, is it not?

A.—Yes.

Q.—It contains how many pages?

A.—About 650 pages.

Q.—And retails for how much?

A.—For one dollar a copy.

Q.—You estimate on 5,400 copies; has it a much smaller circulation?

A.—Yes, that is about the number we would like to estimate on.

Q.—The total cost I see, including royalty, is 39½c. and the cost of the plates $1,359. That is half the cost, the Americans carried the other half, did they not?

A.—Yes.

Q.—Is that book well constructed mechanically?

A.—Yes, except that it is not sewn on tapes; the printing is good and the illustrations as good as can be had; the paper is good and will print easily.

Q.—Is this book "The British Nation," an authorized book?

A.—Yes, authorized in the High Schools.

Q.—Take this book (hands witness copy of book entitled "Story of Canadian people.) Is it an authorized book?

A.—Yes, in Ontario.

Q.—How many pages does it contain?

A.—468 pages.

Q.—In your opinion, these books should be on tapes?

A. Yes.

Q.—This book is written by Mr. Duncan and sells at 50c.?

A.—Yes.

Q.—And costs you to produce it 27½c., including 5c. royalty to Mr. Duncan?

A.—Yes, that is right.

Q.—There are maps in this book, are there not?

A.—Yes, five colored maps.

Q.—You estimate on 4,700 copies for that book?

A.—Yes.

Q.—That is the actual cost you are stating, and not mere speculation, is it?

A.—No, I have a system in the office where I keep a copy of these costs and there can be no error; the cost is $1,180.

Mr Cooper: Are the maps in the "Story of Canadian People" by Duncan, lithographed or half-tone maps?

A.—Half-tone maps.

Mr. Cooper: Are you using half-tone maps all through?

A.—Yes, altogether.

Mr. Staunton: Do you say that these books are up-to-date?

A.—Absolutely up-to-date, look at the book, the paper is good, the types stand right out and the cuts are pretty.

Q.—Take this Modern English Grammar, price 25c., Public School edition, is it authorized?

A.—Yes, that contains 192 pages, and in 5,000 lots cost 11½c. each.

Q.—With a royalty of what?

A.—A royalty of 1¼c. each book.

Q.—You have no tapes on this book?

A.—No, that was bound last year and unfortunately we did not have the tapes.

Q.—If they had been done on tapes, would they have cost more money?

A.—No, practically no difference.

Q.—Here is a Reader by Baker and Carpenter, published by Mac-Millan Co. in 1906, what do you think of that book?

A.—That is a very well executed book, although I do not like the sewing idea, for the simple reason that you cannot open your book at the flap.

Q.—Where does it differ from yours in the opening?

A.—It differs in this way, that it is sewn through the whole book, and with new ones you cannot open them at the flap.

Q.—I am told, that it is really a better book when made that way?

A.—No, not unless sewn properly.

Q.—You think it will last as long?

A.—Yes.

Q.—Would these books cost more to have them bound in this way?

A.—No, I think the binding would be as cheap; it is very well printed, with good illustrations and good three color work.

Q.—Could it be produced as cheaply as yours?

A.—Oh yes, the cost is practically the same; but I think the binding is cheaper.

Mr. Cooper: Do you think the cloth hinge is superior to your hinge?

A.—No, I do not; the hinge is certainly preferable, but it is not better than our book.

Q.—Do you think the cloth hinge is better than that piece of "mull"?

A.—Yes. I have had some of our books bound that way by having a piece of heavy cotton pasted on the cover of the book as a means of strengthening the book.

Q.—Have you a sample of that book?

A.—No, I have not one with me, but can let you have one.

Q.—One publishing house in the States puts two pieces of cloth in addition to the "mull," instead of using the tapes to form a hinge, what do you think of that; would it be as strong as tapes?

A.—No, I would rather use the tapes as against double "mull." Instead of using the "mull' I have used heavy cotton without tapes up to the present.

Mr. STAUNTON: Where a book is sewn, you say it is better than where it is wire stitched?

A.—Yes, I cannot see why anyone uses wire stitching instead of sewing,—it is a little cheaper perhaps.

Q.—Is it cheaper?

A.—Yes, a little bit.

Q.—Can you say how much cheaper?

A.—No, I cannot tell you for I have never used wire machines.

Q.—You would give wire stitching no show on any terms?

A.—None, absolutely none.

Q.—Do you know of any firms in the United States using wire stitching?

A.—No, I do not.

Mr. CROTHERS: What did you say you figure the cost of composition and plates for these books at outside of the "cuts" altogether, Mr. Grantham?

A.—That is rather a hard question to answer: but I will say about $1.50 a page; there are, of course, all sorts of sundry costs, etc., but the cost would be about $1.50.

Q.—These prices you have given us here include the profit, printing, binding and paper, do they not?

A.—Yes.

Q.—Have you figured it out without any profits?

A.—No, I have not.

Q.—This is what these various books cost you, and you have them printed and bound by various printers and institutions in Toronto?

A.—Yes.

Q.—That is what you pay them?

A.—Yes.

Q.—It is done on competition?

A.—Yes. I go to the best houses I can, and they compete for the work.

Mr. STAUNTON: That will do thank you, Mr. Grantham.

EVIDENCE OF MR. G. N. MORANG, TORONTO.

Mr. STAUNTON: Mr. Morang, you are the head of the Company known as the Morang Publishing Co., are you not?

A.—Yes.

Q.—I believe some years ago,—in 1901, you had a decided wish to break into the publication of the "Ontario Readers"?

A.—Yes, I did.

Q.—Did you succeed in getting a piece of it?

A.—No, I did not.

Q.—What did you do; did you apply to the Department of Education?

A.—Yes, I applied in person, and I was told I could not have them.

Q.—You were told you could not have the Readers in 1901?

A.—Yes.

Q.—Do you know that there is an agreement with the publishers, made on the 24th March 1896, made with Gage & Co., The Canada Publishing Co., Copp, Clark Co., and Her Majesty the Queen, that they might with impunity allow any other person or firm to publish these books without fear or breach of contract,—did you know that?

A.—Yes, I have read it; but I could not get any reason from the Government why they did not want me to have them.

Q.—What good would it be to the Government to allow you to publish them?

A.—I offered them money, and it would be saving thousands of dollars in the pockets of the people if I was allowed to publish them.

Q.—At that time the Readers were being published by these three firms were they not?

A.—Yes. The Government had supplied a set of plates for these Readers, and the publishers were to pay $4,300 for the plates.

Q.—And did you expect, if you were allowed to participate in the publication of these books, to pay the same amount to the Government for the contract as they did?

A.—Having reference to a portion of the contract, I did. There was so much money to come into the Government's hands from every additional publisher that was allowed to print these books.

Q.—I notice that these books are all exactly the same color, covering inferior and superior, pictures and type, they do not look as if there was any competition at all; was there any?

A.—No, they combined and did it together.

Q.—How is it that each one turns out exactly the same book as the other?

A.—Well, I may say, they have that understanding.

Q.—Do you know as a matter of fact that these different firms print only part of the different books?

A.—I have heard that they check one another up and print a certain part so that they would not go ahead of one another; I do not say whether it is true or not,—of course I am not in the ring.

Q.—You are sorry no doubt?

A.—No, I do not think I would go in.

Q.—What was the reason you could not publish them?

A.—Well, they would not give me any satisfaction, and would not guarantee that I would be free from action by the holders of the copyrights, and I would not be misled.

Q.—But this agreement guarantees the Government against any suit for copyright. How could they mislead you?

A.—The British Publishers are the people to decide.

Q.—Well, is not the spirit of the Agreement with the Government, that those gentlemen who profess to own every Canadian Copyright of the various selections for these Readers, to the effect that they will give the Government control as far as other contracts are concerned as to copyright?

A.—Yes, it states that plainly in the agreement that they would not directly or indirectly interfere with the Government.

Q.—Did you try to know that you would run any risk if you published these Readers?

A.—I tried through the Government, but they would give me neither list of copyright, nor any guarantee that I would be free from suit.

Q.—Did they appear to want to help you in this thing ?

A.—No, they did not.

Q.—Did they obstruct you in any way?

A.—Yes, they obstructed me for years.

Q.—If you had received permission to publish these books, would it have been in your interest to have made better mechanical work than what is now in them?

A.—That was my intention; to make them of better paper and put in some color work in the First Book.

Q.—Then, if you had them, you would go by the rule, that the better the books the more of them you would sell,—is that it?

A.—Yes. I offered to give them immeasurably better value.

Q.—I see, Mr. Morang, that you say you would not put your "imprint" on these books,—did you mean that?

A.—Yes, I meant just what I said; I considered them very inferior from every point of view,—I am, of course, referring to the "Readers."

Q.—What is the matter with them, Mr. Morang?

A.—Well, in the first place, for what they get for them they should have better illustrations; the paper should be much better; I do not have to be an expert to tell you that these books are inferior, that is self-evident.

Q.—Well, tell me, Mr. Morang, did any person else try come in with you. Did Mr. Warwick endeavour to get into this business with you?

A.—No.

Q.—Were you ever in company with him discussing the question?

A.—No, I never talked with him a minute on it.

Q.—Well, did he make application to go into it?

A.—I understand that he did; but I could not find out definitely; I heard that Warwick had permission to print the books, and I corresponded with the Government, but could not get it out of them.

Q.—You could not find out whether it was true or not?

A.—No.

Q.—Who did you correspond with?

A.—Mr. Harcourt; he was Minister of Education at that time.

Q.—Did you correspond with the Hon. Mr. Ross?

A.—He sent for me one day and I went up to see him.

Q.—So that the Minister of Education, and the Premier were both conversant with the facts?

A.—Yes.

Q.—How long did your correspondence extend over?

A.—Oh, they sent me Private and Confidential letters that I could not show at the time, and I complained about it, but they persisted in sending them marked "Private" and "Confidential" notwithstanding that I desired business letters; but I got them to write letters that were not private and confidential extending over a period of two years. I protested strongly against having letters coming to me marked "Private," because I was dealing with a public question.

Q.—Have you a copy of any letters there, showing any of the points you mention?

A.—Yes, I have, here is a letter dated 21st January, 1902, explaining the situation.

(Witness reads following letter.)

January 21st, 1902.

JOHN MILLAR, ESQ.,
    Deputy Minister of Education,
        Toronto.

DEAR SIR,—We have the honour to acknowledge the receipt of your letter of the 15th inst., written by direction of the Minister.

We greatly regret that you do not treat our application to be allowed to publish the Readers in a reasonably businesslike way. You appear to be imbued with the idea that we really do not wnat to publish, but are only indulging in a literary correspondence with some other ulterior obiect. Now let us at once and finally disabuse your mind on this point. A house of our standing does not run its business on any such lines. We intend to get into the field if we are permitted to do so, and we maintain that we are entitled to have encouragement from the Department, and not have obstacles thrown in the way to deter us.

You decline to let us see the instruments under which the copyrights owned by the Department are controlled. It seems a very arbitrary and extraordinary proceeding that the Department should be unwilling to produce the documents of title to copyright property for which you wish us to pay for the permission to print. However, as the Department assures us that it owns the copyright of seven selections, we will act upon that assumption. If we are not to act upon such an assumption, we will thank you to say so in plain and unmistakeable language.

You then proceed to say that your Department cannot undertake to assist either party in the suit now pending in the courts. Such a remark cannot be made with the sanction of the Minister, and is entirely gratuitous on your part. We asked for this information *bona fide*, and *we resent the insinuation* that we are asking for it for the purpose of assisting us in the litigation we have brought against the three houses. We are at a loss to understand why, when you say you cannot give us the information we asked, you should without any reason for doing so add such a reflection upon our integrity. We do not believe you yourself think that in applying for this information we were seeking assistance in our litigation, and look therefore for some explanation for the unnecessary interjection of such a remark.

We have been trying honestly to find out whether the three houses concerned in publishing the Readers, so directly or indirectly control a number of copyrighted selections which appear in the Readers that our house cannot, nor can any other publishing house engage in the publication of the Readers without being subject to the penalties for copyright infringement from which the three combined houses are freed. We have asked for any information on this point which is within the knowledge of the Minister or the Department. The writer is aware that the Minister has stated, not officially of course, that the three houses do control the position in some such way as this, and any information you have on this point should in all frankness be given to us, in order that we may form an opinion as to whether these three houses really are the masters of the situation, or are merely making an empty threat which they cannot carry into effect. We are aware that these three houses combined, have, in point of fact, within the last few months frightened out of the field another publisher who had duly obtained authority to publish the Readers. However, as the Minister officially assures us that the Department has already provided that the present publishers shall not directly or indirectly be the means of causing

9 T. B.

any such interference on the part of English firms, we are content to abide
upon that assurance.

We asked further that some consideration might be allowed us by the
Education Department for the encroachment upon our rights in using extracts in respect of which our company *is prepared to satisfy the Department that it owns the copyrights.* Your only answer to this is that this
request will not be entertained because in any case no action can lie against
the Department for using such copyright selections. If you refer the
question to the legal advisers of the Department, you will learn that the
Minister of Education who compiled and copyrighted these Readers, made
the plates, and sold them to publishers, is just as much liable to the penalties for infringement of copyright in selections owned by outside parties
as the publishers who printed from the purchased plates. You say, however, that if any monetary allowance were made for these copyrights it
would be giving value without consideration in return. We do not understand this, and we think you will have some difficulty in explaining it
yourself, but we ask you to take legal advice upon the point and then recon-
sider our request.

You ask for evidence that if we enter into the field we will· produce
books of superior quality to those now being published. We refer you to
any of the educational works published by our house. If we publish the
Readers, they will be of the same class, any one of which is superior in
style and workmanship to the present Readers. The fact is, that we would
not put our imprint upon Readers such as are at present issued. If the
Minister is anxious that the public should receive the best text books for
their money he should take no objection to our assurance that we will
produce Readers unmistakably superior to those now in use, and at the
same cost to the purchaser and to our carrying out the assurance.

You conclude by saying that the Department is interested in guarding
the public interests, and not in assisting either party in the matter before
the courts. Again we say that such a remark cannot be made with the
sanction of the Minister, and again we resent in the strongest terms such
an unfounded insinuation against us and our advisers. We may retort
with justice that the Department appears to be interested in guarding not
the public interests, but the private interests of the three houses which are
generally thought to have a monopoly of the publication of the Readers.

Now permit us to recapitulate the position. We have from the outset
sought to put this transaction upon an honourable business basis, and we
cannot help thinking after reading over the whole correspondence again
that our efforts have not been met by the Department in the same way.

We have never· received straight answers to the questions we have
asked. The Department has never in definite language assumed a single
responsibility which it has been fairly asked to assume. The Department
has no knowledge of what copyrighted selections the three houses own; it
does not know whether they in fact own any. We hazard the statement
that up to the present time they have never received a legitimately registered transfer of a single extract in the Readers. We are refused any
consideration for the use of any extracts the copyright of which is undoubtedly our property and which was appropriated in the preparation of
the Readers, yet we are requested as a condition precedent to entering the
field, that we shall pay this considerable money to be handed over to these
three publishers for the use of certain unknown selections in which they
may have no property whatever, and the particulars of which they refuse
to disclose even to the Minister.

9a T. B.

We intend of course to retain all our rights and assume we will not be asked by the Department to waive them in any respect.

We have held ourselves ready to put the Department in possession of our entire position, to produce our titles to the copyrighted extracts we own and give any other information that may be desired. We have had little encouragement to proceed; it has been assumed and we have been told that we are not acting in good faith. Being now satisfied that we can get nothing further from the Minister or the Department and that that we must rest satisfied with the limited assurances contained in the correspondence and must submit to this demand for payment. and get voluntarily nothing from the Department for the use and continued use of our own property, we evidence our good faith by enclosing our cheque for $4,100, being the full amount required by the terms of the Order-in-Council as out-lined in your letter of Nov. 22nd, 1901, for the privilege of printing and publishing the Ontario Readers. We require the plates immediately for business reasons, and trust there will be no delay in supplying them to us.

Yours truly,

GEORGE N. MORANG & COMPANY, LIMITED,

(Signed) GEORGE N. MORANG.

Q.—You stated in your corespondence Mr. Morang, that you desired to put this transaction on an honourable business basis and that the Department have not been acting frankly with you?

A.—Yes, I got private interviews but got no satisfaction at all; they would write letters asking for all kinds of information which was entirely unnecessary and kept continually putting me off from month to month and year to year, and never onċe received straight answers to the questions we have asked.

Q.—That is a serious accusation to make against a Government Department, can you give me some justification for that?

A.—Well, it is just this, I asked Mr. Ross when he was Minister of Education, before he was Premier, if I could print the Ontario Readers, and he told me "No."

Mr. STAUNTON:

Q.—Did he refuse to give you any reason?

A.—Yes, he refused to give me any reason although I tried in every way to get it as I mentioned in my letter to his Deputy, the late Mr. Millar. and I could not get the Deparment to assume a single responsibility which they were fairly asked to assume.

Q.—What responsibility did you ask them to assume?

A.—Well I wanted to get a list of the copyright selections and to be protected against action by the owners of the copyrights in England.

Q.—And they would not meet your views in this respect, would they?

A.—No, they wanted me to give so much money.

Q.—Oh, did they; how much money did they ask you to put up?

A.—$4,100.

Q.—Then the Government had these plates made and sold them to the publishers and controlled the situation?

A.—Yes, and I knew full well that the minute I got those plates I would be jumped on by the copyright holders and could not publish them. and I asked the Government to show that they were the masters of the situation and hold me harmless in the matter.

Mr. STAUNTON: But they apparently should have been able to do that according to their contract with the publishers, in fact it is as plain as English can make it.

WITNESS: Apparently, but they would not guarantee to protect me.

Q.—You say the Government originally procured this set of plates and then sold them to those other publishers.

A.—Yes, and I may tell you that when we prepare a set of plates for Readers we have our own copyrights and other documents and are in a position to deliver the goods.

Q.—You guarantee your customers against action by copyright owners?

A.—Yes, they would be fools to buy the goods otherwise.

Q.—But the Government refused to do that with you and would not give you a list of the copyrights that they were selling and told you that you would have to take your chance, is that it?

A.—Yes.

Q.—And you think then that before the Government disposed of the right to publish these readers they should have made themselves secure as to copyright?

A.—Yes, I do.

Q.—And did they not do that?

A.—No, they did not, but I am told that a publisher who got a certain contract slipped over to England and got these copyrights behind the back of the Government.

Q.—Did you not go over to England too and try for some of those copyrights, the same as the representative of the other concerns did?

A.—Well, when I found that they did not act up to the basis of the agreement, I went over to England and I got some.

Q.—Why did you do that Mr. Morang?

A.—I said to myself, these fellows are holding the Government up and I will now hold them up.

Q.—So the Government really paid for the composition and the plates and did not control their own property?

A.—Yes.

Q.—I am told they renewed the contract with the publishers because the publishers controlled these copyrights,—is that right?

A.—I understand that it is.

Q.—Was there any necessity to renew the contract for any such reason?

A.—No there was not, it is mere humbug. In my opinion the copyright material in the books could have been taken out, and replaced by other matter, and, furthermore, the whole thing was only worth a few hundred dollars.

Q.—How do you know that?

A.—Well, we have done the same thing.

Q.—When you are talking of copyrights you mean the contents of the book, not the book itself?

A.—Yes,—I mean selections by English authors like George Eliot, Shakespeare and other English authors.

Q.—Did the others have the right in Canada to the sole publication of these books?

A.—Yes.

Q.—Then, in your various publications which are numerous, have you used articles which are copyrighted?

A.—No, only where we have obtained permission.

Q.—Have you got permission from anybody?

A.—Yes, here is permission from the Longmans, England, for the use of two selections,—they asked us ten shillings to print the poems of "James Lowe."

Here is permission from Blackie—Edinburgh, for one of George Mc-Donald's works, —for nothing.

And one from Mr. George Allen, publisher, London, for two selections from "The King of the Golden River", —for two guineas.

One from Robert Louis Stevenson (through Lloyd Osborne his executor) for the use of seven selections for which we paid five dollars each.

Q.—So that infringing your right on the use of those works is infringing on a mere nominal right?

A.—Yes I simply got permission to use them in these books. Then there is Mr. Kipling's works, I am his publisher and he allows me to use his works for nothing.

Q.—So that the cost of copyrights in so far as your experience goes, is merely nominal?

A.—Yes, if the Government had gone at it in anything like a business way they could have got all the copyrights they wanted for a mere nominal sum,—about $250.

Q.—And they could not have been held up by any publishers?

A.—No,—they could have made provision for that, and by giving six months' notice, they could have got over the difficulty,— that is, if they wanted to let any other people in.

Q.—As you evidently did not get in they lost that $4,100.

A.—Yes.

Q.—Did they send your check back to you?

A.—Yes.

Mr. COOPER:

Q.—You say that your $4,100 cheque was sent back to you,—was it at your own request?

A.—I do not remember whether I wrote to send it back or not,—I will look up the letter; but I never got the plates. I did write demanding the plates and my letter had not been in the Department ten hours before Mr. Ross sent for me and had my letter before him when I arrived at his office. I told him I wanted the plates and that he had not given me any guarantee that I would not be held up by the English owners of copyright; and he said he was sorry, but he could not let me have the plates. I was angry and told him that I had given my cheque and should have the plates. I told him that he had been fooling me for years. Mr. Ross then told me he would fix it up for me by authorizing two little Primers, and that is all I got out of it. He would not give me my cheque until he got ready to.

Q.—Do you mean to say, that you made no arrangement with him that you should have others authorized?

A.—I could not get any satisfaction out of him; he said the readers only had four more years to run and that I would have the other books at that time; he said he would authorize the other two books and he did so after going for him a lot.

Q.—We are to understand then that the cheque was returned to you on your own request on the understanding that you were to have the other books authorized instead of the Ontario Readers,—is that right?

A.—Yes, I merely said to him,—all I want you to do, Mr. Ross, is to carry out what you promised. I wanted my books authorized,—but I want to print the Readers and if I take the plates and print these Readers I will be at a loss for doing so and be held up.

Q.—You were a party then with Mr. Ross in coming to an agreement whereby you undertook to print other books?

A.—I was not a party to him under any circumstances,—I made no agreement with him whatever.

Q.—It would be wrong to let the impression go out that he sent you back your cheque and did not give you the plates.

A.—He would not have given me the plates.

Mr. Crothers:

Q.—You say Mr. Morang, that Mr. Ross told you, he could not prevent your being prosecuted?

A.—No,—he could not give me any assurance that I would not be.

Q.—Then did you say that you would not go on with it?

A.—I wanted an assurance that I would be protected and asked him if he really could give me the plates, and he said in plain English, he could not.

Q.—Then you arranged that your cheque would come back and he would authorize the other books?

A.—Yes.

Q.—So that you were not a party to any agreement?

A.—No, I was not; I was glad to get anything.

By Mr. Staunton:

Q.—You say that the Department has no knowledge of what copyright selections the three houses own?

A.—The Department never had a list of these copyright articles. I might say that in order to get copyright so that you can commence action you have to have it registered in "Stationers Hall," England. These men may have had permission to use these things in the Readers, but in order to commence action they would have to get the real owners of the copyright to do that. For instance, there is some of "Tennyson" in the Readers, and I know perfectly well those people would not come over here; but the people in England would.

Q.—Would the local publishers set them up to go for you?

A.—Yes, I firmly believe that was their desire.

Q.—So that the agreement made by a publisher with the Government then did not secure against any attack by the owners?

A.—Yes, that is it.

Q.—So that you might print one of those books and then for some insignificant article that appeared in the middle of it, an injunction would be got against you and you would be prevented from selling them?

A.—Yes and also heavily fined.

Mr. Cooper:

Q.—You say that in order to proceed against you, they would have to do so in England. How is it that you instituted a suit?

A.—Well, I registered my copyrights in "Stationer's Hall," England.

Q.—You were sueing then on the original contract which was bought outright?

A.—Yes.

Q.—Are you aware as to whether or not these publishers did the same thing as you did?

A.—I do not think they did,—I think they did not know enough about copyright to do so.

Mr. Staunton: Supposing that you have got permission to use these selections, and you have not gone to "Stationer's Hall" and registered them, would there be anything to prevent you from agreeing with me to allow me to use the extracts and then write to the people in England and say "Go after that fellow."

A.—No, there is not, and that is what I was afraid of,—I was well aware that the penalty was very great, and I knew full well that I would get into trouble.

Q.—So that you were not quibbling with the Government,—it was really a serious matter?

A.—Yes. Every offense would cost at least £10, and would be a very serious thing in printing a large edition of the book. It would simply ruin a firm to do that.

Q.—Then, you must know before your book is published or printed, that you are safe in printing and publishing that book, or it might mean ruin to you?

A.—Yes, absolute ruin.

Q.—You think then that the Government should have secured the copyright under lock and key before they used an extract?

A.—Most assuredly.

Q.—And the Government did not do so?

A.—No,—they could have taken out pieces if they wanted to, but they did not do so.

Q.—Now then, Mr. Morang, you say you were refused any consideration or privilege in the preparation of the "Readers?"

A.—Yes.

Q.—And I understand you to say, then, that after the Government had compiled these "Readers," you, as a matter of fact, went over to England and got possession of some of the articles that the Government had in their books?

A.—Yes,—they wanted me to give a consideration for some of those things and then bluffed me off.

Q.—You mean to tell me that you have to pay to the Government $4,100, and you have to also pay to the publisher a consideration for the use of the articles that are copyrighted in these "Readers?"

A.—Yes,—and further more to the publishing firm that secured the right.

Q.—You just said, Mr. Morang, that the Government wanted you to give a consideration for some of those articles; what articles were they; and what did they want you to give?

A.—They wanted me to give them $1,000 for the right to publish certain articles, and I made the statement that they had no right to charge for them, and I said I was prepared to show that I had a legal right to obtain them. Besides, they could give me neither guarantee nor assurance that I would be protected if I used them. Why, they even did not know what selections were copyrighted.

Mr. Cooper: I am told you brought suit against the other publishers. How did that suit turn out.

A.—Well, it was this way,—I got Blackie to assign me certain rights, and when I commenced suit one of the other firms went over to England and told Blackie what I was doing, and he went back on me and got out of it, and said he would not go with me in the suit,—I have all the correspondence with regard to it in the office if you want it.

Q.—The result then showed that your suit was of no use.

A.—Yes.

Q.—You said you registered your articles at "Stationer's Hall,"—why did you not sue on the registrations you had at the "Hall?"

A.—Because Mr. Blackie backed out.

Q.—Why did you not go on with your original registrations at the "Hall" which you claim to be so good?

A.—Well, there was no reason for going on because I would have had to commence the suit all over again, and there was no satisfaction in it unless Blackie helped me at that time. I could have commenced a law suit against Blackie to make him do what he said; but that would mean another law suit over in Scotland, and I was here in Toronto, so I threw the whole thing up in disgust. The fact of the matter is, that the fight I had with the Government cost so much money that I could not go on with it, and simply had to stop it.

Mr. STAUNTON: I see, Mr. Morang, that in a memo prepared for the Deputy Minister, dated 23rd October, 1901, this note:—"The agreement *re* Ontario Readers provides that any other publisher coming in afterwards shall pay for the plates $2,500,—$1,000 towards the present publishers' rights as to control of certain copyrights, and $3,000 to the Department for the right to publish. A total of $6,500 if for ten years. If a part of the time has expired, a proportional amount only of the $1,000 and $3,000 has to be paid.

If two applicants gain permission to print at the same time the $1,000 payment has to be borne equally between them.

If either Morang or Warwick is given permission now to print, the party would have to pay as follows for term January or July, 1902, to June 30th, 1906,—

For 4½ years' term, plates	$2,500 00
For Publishers' rights, 9-20ths of $1,000	450 00
For Government rights to publish 9-20ths of $3,000...	1,350 00
Total for a single applicant	$4,300 00

For term July, 1902, to June 30th, 1906, or four years as follows:—

For 4 years' term, plates	$2,500 00
For Publishers' rights, 4-10ths of $1,000	400 00
For Government right to publish 4-10ths of $3,000......	1,200 00
Total for a single applicant for four years' term...	$4,100 00

If under clause 6 of agreement, Morang and Warwick are considered to be applying at the same time, the $1,000 for publishers' rights in copyrights will be divided between them, and each would have to pay as follows:—

For term Jan., 1902, to June 30th, 1906, or a 4½ years' term, plates	$2,500 00
Nine-tenths of $500	225 00
Nine-twentieths of $3,000	1,350 00
Total	$4,075 00

For term July, 1902, to June 30th, 1906, or a four years'
    term, plates $2,500 00
Four-tenths of $500 .... 200 00
Four-tenths of $3,000 .... 1,200 00
                                                                   ——————
        Total $3,900 00

Note:—The agreement does not appear to allow anything off the price
of plates for shorter term. The price of plates include part of the original
cost of authorship, setting up, engravings, etc. Hon. Mr. Ross, years ago,
in debate contended that the original cost would in time be recouped from
sale of plates. Besides, the plates may be of value after the expiration of
present contract, as it always takes time before a new series can be got
ready, and time must be given for the old edition to die out.

There is but one set of plates on hand, and two more sets would have
to be got ready for Morang and Warwick. It will take some time, so a
decision should be arrived at soon if they want to begin January, 1902.

Q.—So it was just the sale of these plates to such people as you and
Warwick that was desired,—and you say that the Government did not encourage any other person to come in?

A.—No,—besides, I never got the plates.

Q.—Mr. Morang, do you mean to say, that you were asked to pay that
$1,000 for the use of selections which were not disclosed to you: were you
asked to pay money for something they had no property right in whatever,
and the principals of which they refused to disclose even to the Minister.
Do you mean to say that the Minister did not know whether or not it was
a *bona fide* claim?

A.—No, I assumed he did not.

Q.—Did you ask him to give you the names of the selections?

A.—Yes, and he could give me the names of only six; but I could not
get them to say what the other fellows had.

Q.—Right here I will ask you this, Mr. Morang, do you not know, as
a matter of fact, that the correspondence in the Department shows that
the "Ontario Government" did ask the publishers of Ontario Readers to
furnish them a list of copyright selections of the English authors, and that
request was made in November, 1901?

A.—I can not say that I do.

Q.—Well, here is a copy of a letter from the Minister to Gage and Co.,
Canada Publishing Co., and Copp, Clark & Co.:—

"Dear Sirs,—I am directed by the Minister of Education to state that
there does not appear to be on fyle in this Department any list of the copyrighted extracts in the Ontario Readers controlled by your firm, for the
use of which any subsequent publisher, if permitted to publish, would be
asked to pay to the present publisher $1,000.00, or a proper proportion of
that sum, as compensation for the use of such extracts. Will you kindly
furnish this Department, at your earliest convenience, with a statement of
the extracts referred to above, controlled by your firm.

                    Your obedient servant,
                        DEPUTY MINISTER."

    Now, here is the answer

                      "Toronto, December 3rd, 1901.

    Sir,—The W. J. Gage Company (Limited), has handed us your letter
of the 30th ult.

On perusal of the contract between the publishers and the Department, we do not find that the publishers have undertaken to supply any list of the copyrighted extracts, and as there is litigation now pending in the courts over the question of some of these extracts, we cannot advise the W. J. Gage Company (Limited), to supply such list at present.

　　　　We are, sir,　　　　　　　　　.
　　　　　　　　Your obedient servants,
　　　　　　　　　　(Signed) THOMPSON, HENDERSON &. BELL.

JNO. MILLAR, ESQ.,
　　Deputy Minister of Education,
　　　　Toronto.''

These are also two similar letters from Messrs. Thompson, Henderson & Bell, to the Deputy Minister under same date, representing The Copp, Clark Company (Limited), and the Canada Publishing Company.

Q.—Can you conceive of any motives that would warrant the action taken by these gentlemen?

A.—No, I cannot,—they simply wanted $1,000 from me.

Q.—Well, you see the reason given by their solicitors?

A.—Yes, I know that.

Q.—Now, here is an extract from a letter sent to you by the Department, December 5th, 1901. "Any publisher seeking permission to publish must assume any responsibility or risk not provided for by the present agreement between the Department and the present publishers." What have you to say to that?

A.—Well, they say that they would not assume any risk,—so that I would be simply at the mercy of the copyrighters.　　　　　　.

Q.—So far as you know then, Mr. Morang, did the Government endeavor to insist upon the publishers giving you the information you wanted?

A.—No,—after the suits were over we never got the list.

Q.—Did you ask for it?

A.—Yes.

Q.—You did not get it then, and you never got the list since?

A.—No.

Q.— That was the reason you did not publish these Readers, was it?

A.—Yes, that was the reason.

Q.—In the letter from the Department to you, dated December 27th, 1901, they give a list of seven selections which they say the Department control,—and they also say they are unable to get any others,—is that right?

A.—Yes.

Q.—Mr. Morang, in a letter from the Deputy Minister to you, under date of January 15th, 1902, he says as follows:—"You again ask in your third question.—'Can the Department give our company any satisfactory assurance that our publishing the Readers will not be interfered with by the owners of British Copyright extracts other than those above referred to?' and in reply the Deputy tells you this,—'In addition to my reply already given to this question, I may say that while the Department had no knowledge of any prospective interference with the Readers on the part of English publishers, or any anticipation of such trouble, yet, in view of questions of copyright which have come up in the past, it will not, as it need not, place itself in the position of guarantor that· no difficulty will arise.'' Now then, that is the answer they gave you?

A.—Yes,—but any person buying a set of plates to print from with the idea that the English firm would come down on him for it, would, to say the least, be doing a very unbusiness like action. The fact is, Mr. Staunton, I could not get them at all.

Q.—Is there anything more you can enlighten us on, Mr. Morang?

A.—Well, I do not want the Commission to get any idea that I made any kind of a deal with the Government.

Mr. STAUNTON: Perhaps you did not get the chance?

WITNESS: Probably I did not,—in any way, I made no agreement.

Q.—You only wanted to get the publication of these Readers?

A.—Yes,—of course I wanted to get the new ones; but I would have taken the old ones.

Q.—Have you a series that parallels these "Ontario Readers?"

A.—Yes.

Q.—Those are what you refer to when you say the new ones?

A.—Yes.

Mr. CROTHERS: Mr. Morang, are the statements you made in your letter to the Deputy Minister under date of January 21st, 1902, correct?

A.—Yes, in every respect.

Mr. STAUNTON: I want to ask you, Mr. Morang, about these books,— your Mr. Grantham has furnished us with a statement showing the cost of those books to you, and an estimate of the cost of the Ontario Readers to the various publishers. You have seen that statement, do you corroborate it?

A.—Yes, the estimate from our books is absolutely correct. What he thinks the Ontario Readers could be made for in their present form is correct.

Q.—You state in your letters that you would not put your imprint on those books?

A.—No, I would not.

Q.—Why not?

A.—It would be no advertisement to the house, it would be simply ruining your name.

Q.—Now the cost of these books to the pupils, and the cost of your books to the pupils seem to me to be very high, Mr. Morang.

A.—Do you mean that our price is high?

Mr. STAUNTON: No, it looks to me that these books cost the public a good deal of money when you come to think what the original cost to the publisher was. What percentage would a publisher add to his cost?

A.—Of course there is no definite rule as to that,—some publishers would have to add 100 per cent. and some 50 per cent.

Q.—Well, say you have a book,—I do not mean a fancy book; one that a man has to buy. What profit do you have, knowing that they are authorized and that there is a monopoly on them,—what profit would there be added to the cost?

A.—I think a man should take into consideration the cost of running his business, and then add on 10 per cent. clear profit.

Q.—Do you think a clear profit to the publisher of 10 per cent. would be fair?

A.—Yes, if a book cost 5c. he might be obliged to add another 5c., as it might cost him the 4c. to do the business and he would add another cent for profit.

Q.—Mr. Morang, supposing that the Government authorized one set of Readers in this Province, and the contract, on competition, coming to you for example, to supply the Government with all the Readers that would be used in this Province during the term of that contract which would extend over a period, say of from three to ten years, and that all the publisher had to do was to carry a sufficient stock of these books on hand to ship at any time, properly cased up, to any part of the Province, such a number of these books as the different school trustees and schools in the various parts of the Province would require, on requisition received for such books, the Government paying promptly for the books so sent out, could the publisher publish these books any cheaper than he does now?

A.—Certainly he could,—I mean, of course, if he had a monopoly. I should think he could afford to shave the price; anyway the public could save 35 per cent. right off.

Q.—How, by saving the handling charges?

A.—They would only have to pay one freight, and, perhaps, the price might be cut down finer.

Mr. CROTHERS: Supposing a man had a monopoly of this business, what would pay a fair profit on the contract for, say, ten years.

A.—I could hardly say.

Q.—What would be the advance on the prices that Mr. Grantham has given us?

A.—I do not know exactly what would be a fair advance to put on those prices, we are not making a big profit on the Readers we are making now.

Mr. STAUNTON: Well, for example, here I find on the profit portion of the 899,000 copies of Part I, First Reader, over 70,000 copies per year were sold all the time. If you had a monopoly for these Readers what, in your judgment, would be a fair offer?

A.—Well, we are only making one cent on the First Primer.

Q.—Yes, but what would be a fair profit on the turn over on these Readers?

A.—I should say, that the manufacturer should get his expenses and a clear 10 per cent. besides.

Mr. CROTHERS: What advance do you want on these prices under a ten year contract if all the elements of risk are eliminated?

A.—I would answer that question if I really could do so, I will think it over and tell you this afternoon.

Q.—What do you think then of the Government, for example, making such a contract to buy all the books from a publisher under this plan. Do you think it would be of benefit to the people?

A.—Yes, if they buy them from me.

Q.—Have you books authorized in different parts of the country?

A.—Yes. Our Readers in Nova Scotia.

Q.—It has been said here in justification for the price of these books in this country was owing to the fact that the United States books cost a great deal more. Do you know whether these books cost a great deal more in the United States?

A.—Well, competition over there is very keen, and they have heavy expenses. They often have what they call "contests" in the different States, and there might be forty or fifty agents trying to get the contract which runs into great expense.

Q.—What expense is there?

A.—Oh, they have some pretty oily men on the road. There is one of them sitting there (witness pointing to Mr. Wise), he may be able to tell you why they cost more.

Q.—As a matter of fact, are the books that are authorized in the United States, and which cost more than the books here; are they better from a literary and mechanical standpoint than the books you put up here?

A.—No, not a bit, take "Wrong" for instance, his book is published in the United States at $1.50; our price is $1.00.

Q.—You say that in the United States they are under greater expense than we are in this country in putting up these books?

A.—I think they are.

Q.—That is one reason why they are high?

A.—Yes.

Q.—Does that account for it,—that the cost for selling these books is so high that they have to put up the prices?

A.—Yes.

Q.—Then it is not fair to the people of Ontario to refer to the Americans at all?

A.—No.

Q.—Do you think they are more expensive?

A.—I think, on the whole, they are.

Q.—So that a comparison is not fair, I should think, where the conditions are different in the two countries?

A.—No, I do not think it would be.

Mr. COOPER: Do the publishers in the United States make different prices in the different States?

A.—I believe they do.

Q.—Why do they make prices different in one State from another?

A.—Well, they would probably get a monopoly in one State or another, and would have to make the prices lower, or the agent would not get the business.

Q.—Which price would you take?

A.—I would take the price he would make in a State where he has the contract.

Mr. COOPER: I will not ask you any more now, Mr. Morang.

The Commission then adjourned for lunch.

EVIDENCE OF MR. J. C. SAUL, TORONTO.

J. L. Staunton, Examiner.

Mr. STAUNTON: What are your initials, Mr. Saul?

A.—"J. C."

Q.—You are a Master of Arts, I believe?

A.—Yes.

Q.—You are engaged in the publishing business?

A.—Yes.

Q.—What is your position?

A.—I am Manager of the Education Department and Secretary of the Company.

Q.—Have you made an examination of the Ontario Readers for the purpose of ascertaining what selections are now in copyright?

A.—Yes.

Q.—Well, before I go on with that, I will ask you the question,— how long have you been in your present position?

A.—Four years.

Q.—How long have you been in the book-selling business?

A.—Four years, and a considerable time before that in editing various books.

Q.—What experience have you had in preparing books, Mr. Saul? Have you edited more than one?

A.—Yes, seven or eight altogether.

Q.—Have you had any experience in other parts of Canada in preparing Educational works?

A.—Yes, in Manitoba.

Q.—Do you know of any of the conditions prevailing in the United States?

A.—Yes.

Q.—Did you publish there?

A.—Yes.

Q.—Where the books are prepared?

A.—Yes.

Q.—So you consider yourself familiar with the trade engaged in the preparation of Educational works in Canada and the United States?

A.—Yes, I think I am pretty well conversant with them.

Q.—Well, be good enough to take up the copyrights with me, that is, in the preparation of the Ontario Readers?

A.—Well, in the Ontario Readers the matter of the compilation of the books was entrusted to the chairman of a committee of which Mr. John E. Bryant, now of the Bryant Press, was the principal member, and in the Junior books, Parts I and II, it is practically all original material, and, I presume, is copyrighted by the Government of the Province of Ontario. Nobody outside could possibly have any copyright,—in the two Junior books the material is practically all original,—by that I mean that there are not any selections taken from standard sets or other authors.

Q.—You have nothing to say about them?

A.—In the First Reader the lessons are manufactured for the book itself and are dependent upon words that happen to be used in the lesson,— there could be no possibility of there being any copyright in Part I.

Q.—Well, in Part Second book?

A.—In Part II, the material is really all out of copyright; I am not quite prepared to state in regard to some of it as to whether it was out of copyright in 1896, when the last contract was entered into.

Q.—Can you refer to a portion of it?

A.—I am not quite certain whether that poem, "Lady Moon," was at that time out of copyright. Then again, on page 43 of Part II—"What Birdie Says"—that was certainy in copyright; because the copyright has expired only on the 30th September last. That on page 29, "My Doll," by Charles Kingsley, was in copyright ten years ago. There is nothing in Part II at present in copyright.

Q.—Are these all in Part II that were in copyright at that time?

A.—Yes.

Q.—And there is nothing now in the book in copyright?

A.—No, that is as far as I know.

Q.—That is as far as you have been able to ascertain?

A.—Yes.

Q.—So that there was nothing, at all events, to prevent the First Reader, Part I, from being published by anyone?

A.—Nothing whatever.

Q.—Then, have you any knowledge of what it would cost to acquire the copyrights on these three articles?

A.—Two of them would cost $5 apiece at the very outside.

Q.—What would you say about the one by Charles Kingsley?

A.—It would not cost any more than $5.

Q.—Why do you accept the piece from Lord Tennyson's poems?

A.—I made the exception on the assumption that he would not allow his poems to be published by anybody,—besides one of the publishers was the Canadian agent for Lord Tennyson's poems, and it is altogether probable that they would obtain permission without paying anything for it,— for instance, Mr. Morang is the Canadian agent for Rudyard Kipling, and he is not charged anything for the use of his works.

Q.—Well, are there any more extracts?

A.—On page eighteen of the Second Book, "The Baby," by George Macdonald is still in copyright. I understand that the "Gage Company" hold the Canadian copyrights in that poem.

Q.—Who prints that book?

A.—The Copp, Clark Company.

Mr. STAUNTON: Well, resume, Mr. Saul.

Mr. SAUL: Then there are two lessons, one on page forty-three and the other on page sixty-eight, on "Tea" and "Coffee,"—these two lessons appear to have been taken from a Reader published in Great Britain by Blackwood. These two were copyrighted at that time and are still copyrighted.

Q.—How do you know they were taken from Blackwood?

A.—It is so stated in the index.

Mr. SAUL resuming: Then on page seventy-two there is another copied from an English Reader,—"The Lion," from "Blackies"—the chances are that that one also is copyrighted. Then again—"The Squirrel," by Norman Macleod, on page eighty-three, is also copyrighted,—I should say, however, that Morang & Company purchased the right to that lesson on "The Lion" from Blackie—it is one of the pieces that was secured by Mr. Morang in England. Then the piece "Grandpapa," by Mrs. Craik, on page one hundred, is a copyright piece. On page one hundred and two the story entitled "Two Sides to a Story," is taken from "Leisure Hour," and the probabilities are that was also copyright at the time. The lesson on page 110, "The Ostrich," was taken from "Blackie's" Third Reader, and was also copyrighted; but that copyright was secured by Morang & Company. On page 135, the chances are that "A True Hero, by Thomas Carlyle," was at that time copyrighted. As far as I know, that is all in this book.

Mr. STAUNTON: What do you say these would cost?

A.—There is not a single one of them that would cost any more than $5, and I doubt if most of them would cost anything at all.

Mr. STAUNTON: Well, take the next book, "The Third Reader."

Mr. SAUL: In checking this book over I did not check it for ten years ago, I checked it for the present. I may be mistaken in regard to one or two of them. In the first place, the lesson on page 24 was most probably prepared by the writer of the book,—there is no evidence as to where it came from, and if that is the case, the copyright is held by the Education Department. On page 55,—"The Hippopotamus," is taken from another English Reader, and is also copyrighted. A similar lesson on page 63, "The Black Douglas," also from that series, book IV. The lesson on page 71, "The Farmer and the Fox," is still in copyright. The lesson on page 96, "Ho! Breakers on The Weather Bow"—Swain—is in copyright yet. The two lessons from "Dickens," one on page 93, and the other on page 97, are out of copyright now. I cannot say as to whether they were in copyright ten years ago. On page 111, "A Narrow Escape," from an illustrated English Reader, No. IV, was probably copyrighted. On page 149, the poem "Zlobane"—is still copyrighted.

"The Monster of The Nile," on page 173, was at that time copyrighted,—and is yet—the copyright will expire next year.

The lesson on page 179, "The Thermometer," taken from "Illustrated Reader IV," was probably copyrighted,—similarly the lesson on page 194, on "Heat Conduction and Radiation." The lesson on "Canadian Trees"—in two parts—one on page 202 and the other on page 210, was specially prepared for this book, and I presume the copyright is held by the Education Department.

The lessons on the "Shapes of Leaves," on pages 229 and 235, and the lessons on "The Flower" and "The Fruit," on pages 252 and 257, are copyrighted, but I do not know who holds the copyright. The lessons on pages 132, 157, 233, 250 and 255, are out of copyright now, but were at that time in copyright,—they are from "Tennyson."

Mr. STAUNTON: Just go on to the next book, Mr. Saul,—the Fourth Reader.

Mr. SAUL—(taking up the Ontario Fourth Reader): The lesson on page 25, "The Little Midshipman," by Ingelow, Jean, is still copyright. On page 54, "Clouds, Rains and Rivers," by "Tyndall," is copyrighted.

On page 77 "Discovery of The Albert Nyanza," by Baker, is copyright. Also on pages 171 and 179—"The History of a Piece of Coal," is copyrighted.

Pages 189 and 195, lessons entitled "Lumbering," taken from "Picturesque Canada," are not copyrighted.

Page 199, lesson "Before Sedan," by Dobson, is copyrighted.

The lesson on page 200, entitled "Among The Thousand Islands," is copyrighted.

The lesson on page 214—"The Two Breaths," by Kingsley, is still in copyright,—it expires next year.

The lesson on page 230, entitled "To Florence Nightingale," by Edwin Arnold, is still in copyright.

And on page 231, the lesson entitled "Riding Together," by Morris, is still in copyright.

The lesson on page 272, entitled "After Death in Arabia," by Edwin Arnold, is still in copyright.

The lesson on page 282, "The Founders of Upper Canada," by Ryerson, is still in copyright.

The selection entitled "National Morality," by Bright, on page 295, I do not think that is copyrighted. It was a common newspaper article at the time and everybody was publishing it, and the chances are there was no copyright on it.

The lesson on page 303, entitled "Shakespeare," by Müller, is still in copyright.

The lesson on page 121 and 128—both selections from "Tennyson"—were at that time in copyright. Also the lesson on page 137 entitled "Dora."

Q.—There were then 53 lessons in all of the Readers at that time, and you say they would not cost more than $5 each or $250 to $300 for the whole lot?

A.—I do not think it would cost more than $250 for the whole thing.

Q.—You think, then, that you are pretty safe in your statement?

A.—Yes, anything I have said is in copyright; I may have missed one or two small selections, but I think it is all right.

Q.—The Morang Primers, they have been published in competition with the First and Second part of the First Reader, for some years, have they not?

A.—Yes.

Q.—How long?

A.—Well, the book has been in competition for four years, and was out for about one year before that.

Q.—Has any school in the Province a right to use it?

A.—Yes.

Q.—Have you had any sale for it?

A.—Yes.

Q.—How many of them have you sold?

A.—Last year we sold between 60,000 and 65,000.

Q.—Do you consider it is a greater favorite with the teachers?

A.—I can give you the name of the places where they are using it.

Q.—Well, give me some of them.

A.—It is used exclusively in the City of Hamilton, the City of St. Thomas, the Cities of Windsor, Guelph, Kingston and it is also used as one of the Readers in Brantford and in a very large number of towns in the Province.

Q.—How about Toronto?

A.—Toronto uses it also.

Q.—You have not got the whole market in Toronto?

A.—No, we have only one-half of the market; it is divided up between our company and the Canada Publishing Company.

Q.—How did they manage it?

A.—Well, our Readers are in use in the schools, while theirs are on the shelves to look at,—you will find that every time that the Morang Phonic Primer is the one that is used in the class.

Q.—The same class cannot use both Primers can they?

A.—As a matter of fact, the more Primers you have in a class room the better.

Mr. STAUNTON: When I went to school we had one book and we all learned out of the same book. They cannot use different books for the same lesson?

A.—No, but they may have lessons out of another book which may be introduced during the class.

Q.—Is this practice in general vogue?

A.—Yes.

Q.—Is this Primer of yours sold anywhere else?

A.—Yes, it is authorized on the supplementary list in Quebec.

Q.—Now Mr. Saul, as to the use of books generally, do you think it is in the interest of the public that one firm should have the publication of the books, or that it should be divided among many?

A.—I see no objection, if the Government is protected, why it should not be given to one firm.

Q.—Do you see any advantage in giving it to one firm,—that is, to the cost, getting the same quality of book, etc.?

A.—Yes, the larger the quantity of books you manufacture, the lower you can get your price.

Q.—If the books were published for the Government and delivered to the Government direct, would it be any advantage to the Government?

A.—Yes, we are doing that now in the Province of Manitoba.

10 T. B.

Q.—What are you doing in that Province?

A.—The Government of Manitoba buy "Our Home and Its Surroundings" Geography and Bi-lingual Reader.

Q.—How do they manage them?

A.—They purchase from us a certain number of books,—I think 20,000 Geographies to begin with, and 25,000 Arithmetics. We sell direct to them and we get our cash direct from the Government, and they distribute them to the schools.

Q.—Do you mean to say that the Government takes the consignment and keeps it in store?

A.—Yes, that is just what they do.

Q.—What was the first book that you disposed of?

A.—"Our Home And Its Surroundings."

Q.—What did you sell it at?

A.—I do not remember at present.

Q.—Can you tell me any of the prices?

A.—I cannot.

Q.—Is there a standard prescribed under contract for them as to excellence?

A.—No, not a written contract; but we submitted the book in its final form. Our position in the matter of book publishing has been quite different from that of other firms in the Province of Ontario. Every book that Morang & Company has published was a pure speculation. We have had to put money and time into these books, and run the risk of their being authorized. We have never been able to bank on a "sure thing." In the "Ontario Readers" that I well know, was done. It was simply handed over. The book was authorized before anything was printed,—and that is a most important factor.

Q.—These books you are selling, you paid all the cost of preparation?

A.—Every dollar of it.

Q.—As pure speculation?

A.—Yes. We depend on the excellence of our books to get in.

Q.—Do you think a better book could be got by permitting each publisher to prepare a sample and submit it for approval?

A.—Yes. They should always be open to competition by Publishing Houses.

Q.—Do you think that the Department would obtain better results by leaving it to the publisher to prepare a book?

A.—Yes I do.

Q.—Why?

A.—For this reason, that the various competing houses are going to give the very best that they possibly can,—one against the other.

Q.—You think a committee on book preparation might perform their work with a little less zeal than those who want to make money out of it?

A.—I think so.

Q.—Was that the plan adopted by the Manitoba Government?

A.—Yes, and I might say, I secured the contract for Nova Scotia with all the Publishers in Canada in open market.

Mr. COOPER: Mr. Saul, you are an Educationalist of some experience; what would think of a scheme whereby all the Provinces would combine and produce one National set of Readers.

A.—I think that as an ideal it would be very fine; but as an actual condition I do not think it is possible.

Mr. STAUNTON: Why not?

10a T. B.

A.—The various Provinces are so entirely different in this matter,—although I may say that the various Provinces are now coming round to the idea that the Readers of the Public Schools should be a purely literary set of "Readers." Now, if they would all agree on that, it would be a simple matter to get up a purely literary set of Readers; but if you want to select books like these here, you could never get the other Provinces to take them up.

Mr. Cooper: Outside of the Readers that Mr. Morang has had prepared for him under your direction, do you think there are any sets of Readers in the United States that would be literary models,—say "Stepping Stones to Literature"—would they be good models?

A.—I think "Stepping Stones to Literature" is fairly good; the "Sears" Readers are very good and the "Baldwin" and "(Brooks" Readers are very good. There are fifteen or twenty houses in the United States that publish very good Readers, but a large percentage is entirely contrary to our sentiments. The American writers, of course, predominate.

Mr. Cooper, continuing: You have had experience in the Province of Manitoba, Mr. Saul, do they follow much the same method as is followed in Toronto?

A.—Yes, they send a printed slip to each teacher in the province asking him how many books he will require and the teacher prepares a requisition which is sent in to the Department where it is filled and sent out.

Q.—Is that charged against the Government grant?

A.—I think not; the books are supplied in addition to the Government grant.

Q.—In whose charge are the books?

A.—Well, the pupils are allowed to take the books home; they are not retained in the class room—they take them home for the preparation of their ordinary work.

Q.—When a child is promoted to the Third Book, does he get a new "Third Reader" or an old one?

A.—He may get one that has been used before,—but the first three books are provided only.

Q.—The system then, is the same as in Toronto?

A.—Yes.

Q.—I do not know whether you have already stated or not, but is that system in Manitoba an ideal system?

A.—Yes, it seems to be working very well there; they are beginning to understand it and to extend it to higher grades.

Q.—You mean to say, in the Public and High Schools, they want to have free text books entirely?

A.—Not in the High Schools,—just in the Public Schools,—they are only supplying some of them free.

Q.—Well, take these books of yours that you are offering for sale and are selling; how do they compare in prices with the prices in the various states of the Union?

A.—They are lower, except in some places where there is a close contract.

Q.—What is the general rule in the United States as to closed or open competition?

A.—I think there are only eleven or twelve States in the Union where there is a State authorization; in the other parts of the Union there is State and Township authorization as the case may be. In some parts each High School is a "Law unto itself."

Q.—You gave us a list just now of books that you approve of in the United States for their literary and mechanical excellence; so far as those books are concerned, are they more expensive than those of yours?

A.—No, they are not.

Q.—Well, but to the purchaser?

A.—Yes, the price is higher for a corresponding book.

Q.—Can you give me any reasons why it should be so?

A.—In the first place, competition among publishers in the United States has taken the form,—until a short time ago—of excellence of manufacture: the publishers vied with one another in bringing out the best books and kept their prices uniform. There was a certain price that they put on a Primer, and competition took the form of striving to get the best books. Lately, however, it has become somewhat "cut-throat."

Q.—Are the expenses of the publishers in the United States greater than they are here?

A.—They are greater for the reason that they have a larger territory to cover. Most of the large publishing houses in the United States, in addition to their central agency have others in Chicago and San Francisco, and also keep State Agents, so that when there is a competition in a state they have to spend a great deal of money in securing authorization, so that their expenses would be somewhat greater than ours.

Q.—Can they manufacture books cheaper in the United States than they can here?

A.—No, they cannot. When you come to take it into consideration our paper will cost more in Canada,—that is, to get the same quality of paper. Take, for instance, the paper in these Readers (Morang's Modern Readers). We have a great many half-tones and consequently have to obtain a smooth surface paper. Now that paper in Canada would probably cost about from three-quarters to one cent more than it would in the United States. But the Press work is cheaper here than it is in the United States. Where the difference comes in is in the binding. It costs more here than in the United States.

Mr. Cooper: You say printing is cheaper here?

A.—Yes—Press work.

Q.—Is composition and making of plates cheaper also?

A.—As a matter of fact you cannot do very much of that here. It was simply impossible until the introduction of the "Monotypes"—Take Morang's Modern Reader, Second Book, there is not a Printing House in the City of Toronto that has a enough type to set up that book, so what are you going to do? You have to go where you can get the work done.

Q.—These plates the Government own, are they made in the United States?

A.—No.

Q.—Well, how were these books made up, if there was not sufficient type?

A.—Well, the way the Ontario Reader, Book Four, was made up, there was a certain amount of type used 34; 35 and 36 were set up; when that was set up it was completed and then that type was knocked down and used for another section of the book until the whole book was complete. When we set up Morang's books, the whole Reader was set up. Messrs. Brown and Searle Company simply told us over and over again that it would not pay them to bring type enough into the country to print a book of that kind for the reason that the type would lay idle on their hands, and we got them from the company that makes a specialty of making these plates.

Q.—Have you had any of your books printed and bound in the United States?

A.—We have had on certain occasions where we were absolutely forced to do it; but we saved nothing by it. We had to do so after the fire in Toronto.

By Mr. COOPER :

Q.—You say that binding here is more expensive than we will say Boston,—why?

A.—I do not know why it is ,—I do not know whether it is because they have to pay their girls more or what it is.

Mr. COOPER : I was in a publishing house the other day where their output was said to be 6,000,000 books, which is more than would be printed in Canada in a great many years. They have all the equipment for making covers and all the parts for the books. If that is true, we would get books made more cheaply in the United States than we could here, don't you think so?

A.—You could if you got your press work done.

Q.—What is the average price for press work per thousand,—say on the Fourth Reader?

A.—I cannot say, you would have to get that from Mr. Grantham.

Mr. STAUNTON : You say the press work is very much cheaper here?

A.—Yes.

Q.—The type setting, what is that worth?

A.—Well, we really have to do so little of that, and there is so little we can do, I really do not know what the comparison is.

Q.—Well, then, Mr. Saul, just take these books—The Baldwin set—do you know what these are sold at?

A.—No, I do not.

Q.—Can you take any of the books and compare them with yours?

A.—Yes. This Baldwin Reader, Second Book, corresponds with Morang's Modern Reader, Second Book—The price of the Baldwin Reader, I see, is 25c.

Q.—Can you produce the Baldwin Reader as cheap as Morang's?

A.—Yes,. it sells for 15c. more than ours.

Q.—This Baldwin,Third Reader corresponds with your Second Books?

A.—Yes, and ours retails for 25c., and the Baldwin for 40c.

Q.—Do you consider your books as good as theirs?

A.—Yes.

Q.—Compare that book with the Ontario Readers, comparisons have been made between Ontario Readers and Baldwin Readers,—Is there any justification in this?

A.—Yes, for the reason that Baldwin's is a more expensive book to manufacture than the Ontario Readers. There is no preparation to be made in these Readers, no illustrations to build up, and in the lower books the "cuts" are all small "line cuts."

Q.—They are just about as cheap a book as you can make, you think?

A.—Yes, I think they could not produce any cheaper book. They are just as cheap as can be made, in fact, it would be impossible for human ingenuity to devise a more inferior book; it is bad in every particular.

Q.—We have got down to the worst we could get, eh?

A.—Well, the plates are poor, and the paper is not extra, the very, ordinary,—in fact, very poor binding. What worse could you get.

Q.—Do you know anything about the 'Brooks' Readers?

A.—Yes, they run about 5c. cheaper than ours, and are a very good set of books.

Q.—Is there any difference?

A.—Well, the second year book has a little better color work.

Q.—Well, Mr. Saul, if it is true that the American firms have greater facilities, and can produce books cheaper than we can, they must be making more profit than we do.

A.—I think they are.

Q.—Well, is the binding any better?

A.—I do not think that it is.

Q.—Is the binding an improvement?

A.—Yes, it is an improvement.

Q.—Would it cost much more?

A.—No, I do not think so.

Q.—Well, is there any excuse for these wire bound books?

A.—No, except that where the bindery is equipped with wire binding machines they hate to throw them out and equip them with modern machinery.

Q.—Is there any difference in the price by adopting wire binding? We have been told it is very much cheaper.

A.—I do not believe there is much difference; but certainly a larger quantity can be turned out by the machines, and that might make a difference. But wire binding is not a good binding for school use.

Q.—But we have been told, Mr. Saul, that wire binding is very much cheaper than thread sewing,—are you speaking from experience or from your opinion of the work?

A.—Well, I made some enquiries and was told in regard to it by one of the houses, that there was not very much difference; the only advantage being, that you can bind very much faster by using wire machines, and you do not need so much help.

Q.—In fixing the price of these books, you have endeavoured to absorb the cost of producing the book by the author, and the plates too, have you not? In the Ontario Readers there is no such thing as that.

A.—No, they paid a lump sum to the Government, and did not have to pay for the plates. Of course, we have to pay for practically all of our books; and in connection with the set of books we are preparing we have to pay a royalty, and my time has to be counted in, and that means something.

Q.—What is the standard royalty?

A.—Ten per cent.

Q.—What do you mean,—on the retail price?

A.—Sometimes on the wholesale, but more frequently on the retail price.

Q.—That is a very good thing, is it not?

A.—Yes, sometimes the authors make more than the publisher. The royalties in the United States are not so high as they are here.

Q.—What are they over there?

A.—Oh, they run from say 5 to 7½ per cent.

Mr. CROTHERS: How do our school books,—from a mechanical standpoint—compare with those in use in the United States?

A.—They do not compare at all, Mr. Chairman, they are inferior in every respect. All you have to do is to put down a set of them beside the others, and you can see for yourself.

Q.—What do you think about a proposal to authorize one set of books in each Province, and make it a fixture for five or ten years?

A.—As a matter of fact, answering that question from a purely educational standpoint. I do not think it would be an advantage,—otherwise there is no particular reason that it should be done.

Mr. STAUNTON: To what do you attribute the superiority of the school books in the United States, Mr. Saul?

A.—I attribute it entirely to the system of open competition in vogue there.

Q.—You think, then, that the people of the United States attribute the superiority of their books to open competition?

A.—Yes.

Q.—Then there is no fair basis for comparing prices of books between the practice that obtains in the United States and Canada?

A.—No.

Q.—The very material elements of risk are wanting in our system, you think?

A.—Yes.

Q.—I suppose a manufacturer of binding, if he knew he was going to sell a large number, could make them very much cheaper?

A.—Yes.

Q.—Well, has a publisher not to take into consideration the "Exchange System" used in the United States?

A.—Yes, and that is one reason why the price of books is kept up.

Q.—Well, what about "Returned Books," have not all publishers a great number of books come back on their hands?

A.—No, we sometimes take back books to oblige people; but as a general rule, no, it is not the case. We do not put our books out on sale.

Well, that will do, Mr. Saul, thank you.

EVIDENCE OF MR. FRANK WISE—MACMILLAN & COMPANY, TORONTO.

G. L. STAUNTON, examiner:

Q.—What is your name?

A.—Frank Wise.

Q.—And your occupation?

A.—I am President of the Macmillan Company in Canada.

Q.—And you are connected with the English house.

A.—Yes.

Q.—The New York Company and yourselves are separate and individual companies, and distinct from the English house?

A.—Yes, but we have a connection with the parent house.

Q.—And you control in this country the Macmillan publications?

A.—Yes.

Q.—How long have you been in the publishing business, Mr. Wise?

A.—About eleven or twelve years.

Q.—Where have you been engaged?

A.—In New York.

Q.—How long have you been in Ontario?

A.—I started business on the first of January this year.

Q.—So that you have just come from New York?

A.—Yes.

Q.—You have been engaged in the publication of school books and Macmillan's publications and others?

A.—Yes, we are Macmillan's Agents in Canada.

Q.—Will you tell me about the Macmillan School Books. I am told that the books in the United States which correspond to our Ontario Readers, are much more expensive, and some people say they are no better, now, what do you say?

A.—If I am to compare them with the Ontario Readers, I would say there is no comparison at all.

Q.—Which got the worst of that remark, Mr. Wise?

A.—The Ontario Readers. I might say that ten years ago the American Book Company, which was an amalgamation of the then existing school book publishers which amounted to anything at all, published books about the same as the Ontario Readers are to-day in inferiority of literary and mechanical merit, and there seemed to be an inability to get them changed for the benefit of the public.

Q.—Did the American Book Company produce a better set of books?

A.—Not until they were compelled to do so.

Q.—How were they compelled to do so?

A.—By McCoy of New York.

Q.—You mean to tell me, then, that these other companies amalgamated with the American Book Company, and that McCoy came into the field and issued a series of Readers in competition with the American Book Company, and compelled them to improve their Readers from a literary and mechanical point of view; is that it?

A.—Yes, that is about the way it happened.

Q.—So that the people got better books, better literary matter, and at a much better price?

A.—Yes.

Q.—I understand that the books published by Macmillan and other publishers in the United States are more expensive than they are here. Is that a fact?

A.—I do not think that is so.

Q.—We had a few books here yesterday that showed that way.

A.—Well, the books, as far as I know them,—the First and Second Readers, contain a great deal more matter, and copyrighted articles, while frequently there is a more expensive paper and binding used.

Q.—Are you familiar with the expense of publishing Readers in this country?

A.—No, I am not.

Q.—Then you can not make a comparison?

A.—No.

Q.—Are you familiar with the expense of Readers in the United States?

A.—No, not enough to testify to, I was in the manufacturing line for a time.

Q.—Perhaps you can tell us about the composition and press work. Is it cheaper in the United States than it is in Canada?

A.—Yes, press work is cheaper in the United States than it is here.

Q.—Then you agree with what Mr. Saul said?

A.—Yes.

Q.—Are you satisfied that his evidence is correct?

A.—I cannot criticize it in any way; I think he has a very good idea of conditions there.

Q.—What do you say in criticism of the Ontario Readers. What do you think of them. Are they a credit to the Province of Ontario?

A.—Oh no. I heard all the evidence given yesterday, and I can not add anything to what was said then. They are simply the kind of books that were kicked out of the United States ten years ago. They did the work in your father's time and yours too.

Q.—Tell us how you managed to dislodge that ring in the United States?

A.—By letting loose a kind of moral wave wherever it was possible, and making public the scandalous side of the late regime where possible. Because they were controlled through political means,—that is, the poorest books always appeared where the strongest political control was held. In the City of Rochester, N.Y., where the people held a monster mass meeting, and turned out the then existing Board of Education and Superintendent of Education, they not only had old books that had been discarded everywhere else, but they insisted on the use in the rural schools of old editions of books.

Mr. STAUNTON: They had a reverence for the past?

A.—Yes. The reason for the disruption was that the "Regents" for the State of New York refused to grant certain privileges to the pupils of the rural High Schools because they were not in condition to compete with the other states, and that was just one instance where we managed to come in and get some of the business. This occurred all over the country, in states, townships, and cities.

Q.—How do these books of Morang's compare with the Ontario Readers?

A.—Well, the first thing that strikes one is the difference in the size of type and the difference in the amount of "leading". This Ontario Reader,—that is this tpye of it, would not be tolerated in the United States. It has bad type, is poorly leaded and its general appearance is bad. It would never be tolerated for a moment.

Q.—Compare these two books (hands witness one of Morang's Readers and an Ontario Reader).

A.—There is not so much difference as there is between the later books: but there is a very appreciable difference in favor of Morang. At the time these Ontario Readers were published—about twenty years ago—I should think they were a very decent lot of Readers; but for ten years they have been hopelessly out of date. But I presume in schools in the "Dismal Swamp," in Florida and other districts that put in out-of-date editions, then they would be masters of the situation.

Q.—Is that book of Morang's a first-class book?

A.—Yes. I would not be afraid to put a Macmillan imprint on that book.

Q.—Now, Mr. Wise, compare the Public School Phonic Primer, Part I., with the Ontario Reader, Part I. What do you find?

A.—Of course, for one thing, they have followed the example of the American publisher in putting in color work in this book (Morang's) but it is undoubtedly the best book of the two.

Q.—Have you a Primer published by your firm that is better than that?

A.—Yes.

Q.—Have you any other Primers?

A.—Yes, our book is a great deal better. Educational authorities have insisted on a large clear type—such as you find in the "Heath Primer".

Q.—Well, what about the "Brooks" First Reader?

A.—Yes, that is about the size of the type used in a modern Primer?

Q.—What about the price?

A.—Well, in a Primer of that size you cannot compare the price with the other books. I do not think the American books are more expensive than the Canadian. The American books are larger and contain more matter.

Mr. COOPER: Take Morang's Phonic Primer; how about the size of type in that book?

A.—I think it is a good size but I would put a little more lead in it.

Q.—What do you think of the First and Second Readers published by Morang?

A.—It looks to me very much like a book that I sold for the last five or six years—(witness turning to Mr. Morang) does it not, Mr. Morang? The greater part of this book is from the series of books which were instrumental in changing things in the United States.

Mr. STAUNTON: So he thought it best to bring this pilgrim here?

A.—Yes.

Q.—I have been under the impression that the American books cost more than the Canadian books. Is it true that they do, but the books are larger and more of them in every way; but comparing the same size and quantity of a book, they do not cost any more?

A.—No.

Q.—It is equally as cheap over there?

A.—Yes. It is the increased size of the book and the increased quality.

Q.—If they get a Morang Reader—which I understand you say is a modern book—the purchasers have not to pay any more money unless they get a better book.

A.—Yes, there is something in quality—because you get a better book.

Q.—Well, Mr. Wise, let me say that it has been pointed out again and again in Ontario that this "Ontario Reader" was not only an excellent book, but that the people of this country were getting their books much cheaper than the people in the United States. What have you to say to that?

A.—I think it was an impudent thing to say that they could get the same value as could be got from an American book at the same price.

Q.—What is the price of your Fourth Reader?

A.—Our Fourth Reader costs 45c. and contains 345 pages.

Q.—Is that book worth 40c. to publish—that Ontario Reader?

A.—Oh no. It is not worth more than 15 cents or 20 cents.

Q.—It would be a pretty smart man to make you pay 15 or 20 cents for it, would it not?

A.—Yes, it would, for I would not take it as a gift. It would not be used in the United States at all, where anybody knows anything of education.

Q.— Well, then, Mr. Wise, you have heard the evidence on the copyright. Under ordinary circumstances what does it cost to get the right to reproduce these articles here?

A.—I do not think I can answer that; it does not come under my knowledge. That question has never come up since I have been up here.

Q.—Well, if you cannot inform me on that point I will pass on to something you can. You have some of your books on the High School list, Mr. Wise?

A.—Yes.

Q.—What are they?

A.—Chiefly mathematical works.

Q.—Name some of them?

A.—Hall and Knight's Algebra—authorized in Nova Scotia, New Brunswick and Quebec. Hall and Knight's Higher Algebra—authorized in Manitoba, Alberta and Saskatchewan.

Q.—How is it that they have not been authorized here. They have not been refused authorization in Ontario, have they?

A.—Not as yet.

Q.—Will you show me some of those books?

A.—I have none of them here with me.

Q.—Well, are any of your books used in our schools?

A.—Yes, every Specialist and Mathematical Master uses as his desk book—for his own use—"Hall and Knight's Algebra", and wherever it is possible to make a selection of a book, the teacher always uses Hall and Knight, or a book as good.

Q.—What is it that commends that book to teachers?

A.—It is a practical mathematical book. Most Algebras treat the subject mechanically, but you cannot say "Hall & Knight" to any educated man in the English speaking world that he will not know what you are talking of. It is the recognized standard for teaching Algebra.

Q.—What is the price of the book?

A.—4 shillings and 6 pence or $1.08; but we make it $1.00.

Q.—Are they authorized in England?

A.—Yes, they are used all over England.

Q.—Is there such a thing as authorization in England?

A.—I think it applies only to sections. This book is one of our best sellers.

Q.—Is it used by the pupils in the provinces of Quebec, Nova Scotia and New Brunswick?

A.—Yes. It is the best book in existence.

Q.—What book takes its place in this Province?

A.—The High School Algebra.

Q.—What other books have you got in?

A.—Green's Short History of the English people, and a lot of classics—Latin and Greek and English classics. There is hardly a subject that we have not a great many books bearing on it.

Q.—Have you found it necessary to reduce your books from time to time?

A.—Oh, yes, when I same here I found that a very large number of pupils in Ontario, in order to kick out the High School Algebra, had to buy Hall & Knight's High School Algebra at a cost of $1.90 of which book they used about one-third or less. We made an edition covering the part they used at a cost to the pupils of 90 cents, so that in order to do this we were actually losing the sum of $1.00 on each copy.

Q.—Well, Mr. Wise, do you know anything of the merits of free books as against the system of books bought by the pupils?

A.—I think the honors are about easy on both sides. It is a question if you want to pauperize both parent and pupil by overcrowding them with books. The schools in the United States are up to the question of supplying books and pencils.

Q.—Is there any rule in the States compelling the pupils to supply "Second Books" themselves?

A.—No, and they are not allowed to administer corporal punishment.

Q.—Is that the effect of their particular system?

A.—No, I do not think so.

Q.—Well, Mr. Wise, can you enlighten us any further on this matter. You know what this Commission has to deal with?

A.—I would say that I think a long term contract is anything but a good arrangement. The city of Chicago for fifteen years kept in use an old Rand, McNally geography, and up to the time it was turned out, the pupils were taught geographical facts that were not proved. This is the worst example I have thought of. They were afraid to make a change for political reasons. If the term had been a definite one at the time the contract was made,—at the end of say six, eight, or ten years the old book would have to be removed and a new one take its place.

Q.—You believe, then, that the free book system is not absolutely faultless?

A.—Yes, it pauperizes, I think.

Well, that will do, Mr. Wise, thank you.

Toronto, October 25th, 1906.

EVIDENCE OF MR. A. W. THOMAS, TORONTO.

Mr. G. L. STAUNTON, Examiner:

Q.—What is your name?
A.—Arnold W. Thomas.
Q.—Are you a shareholder in the Copp, Clark Company?
A.—I am Secretary-Treasurer of the Company
Q.—You are a Director of the Company?
A.—I am, also a shareholder.
Q.—That Company is one of the publishers of the Ontario Readers, is it not?
A.—It is.
Q.—Who are the others?
A.—The W. J. Gage and the Canada Publishing Company.
Q.—I understand that the Canada Publishing Company is simply W. J. Gage, Warwick and Copp, Clark. is that right?
A.—I cannot really answer that question.
Q.—Are you a shareholder in the Canada Publishing Company?
A.—I really do not know, Mr. Chairman, that I should be called upon to answer as to my investments. The point is just this, Mr. Chairman, if the Commission wishes to investigate the properties of the various publishing companies I have no objection to supply a list of the stockholders of the company on the understanding that the other publishers do the same.

Mr. STAUNTON: What objection can there be? There is no reason why you should not answer that question. Do you hold any shares in the Copp, Clark Company?

A.—I do.
Q.—Are there any shareholders in the Canada Publishing Company who are not also shareholders in the Copp, Clark Company, Warwick Bros. and Rutter, and W. J. Gage?
A.—I cannot answer that question.
Q.—Do you say that you do not know whether there are any outsiders?
A.—I do not know the present construction or the present shareholders of that company.
Q.—Perhaps I can refresh your memory. Who are the Directors of the Canada Publishing Company?
A.—I am not a director myself and cannot tell you.
Q.—Who is the president of the company?

A.—Mr. Beatty.

Q.—Is he connected with any of these other companies?

A.—No.

Q.—Do you know the vice-president?

A.—I do not.

Q.—Do you know the Secretary?

A.—Yes, Mr. Builder.

Q.—Is he connected with any of the other companies?

A.—Now, this is a line of questions I was not prepared for at all, Mr. Chairman, and I can only tell you what I know. If you ask me if I think he is, I would say that "I think he is."

Q.—Would you bet on it?

A.—I do not bet, Mr. Staunton.

Q.—You think he is a Director, don't you?

A.—I cannot say.

Q.—Don't you know that the Canada Publishing Company is made up of these three firms?

A.—I cannot answer that question.

Q.—How long have you been connected with the company?

A.—Thirty-three years.

Q.—How long has the Canada Publishing Company been in existance?

A.—I don't know.

Q.—Have you been a shareholder?

A.—No.

Q.—Are you familiar as to how these books are published?

A.—In a general way.

Q.—Are they published by the Copp, Clark Co., Canada Publishing Company and the W. J. Gage Company?

A.—Yes.

Q.—Do they not publish them altogether,—each one of them publishing a part of each book?

A.—They are published as a syndicate. In a general way the publication is arranged that we shall each print as near as possible a certain number of a book and buy from the other concerns when we need to.

Q.—That is one of the agreements that equalizes the profits and losses of the respective publishers, is it not?

A.—Yes.

Q.—If you get a call from the trade for more than the number you are entitled to sell, you fill that order by buying from the others?

A.—Yes, it is a syndicate.

Q.—So that there is no competition among these firms?

A.—No.

Q.—Then there is no incentive to make any one of the firms publish a better book?

A.—The books are published strictly in accordance with the specifications.

Q.—There is no incentive to make one of the firms improve on the books by the requirements of the contract?

A.—No.

Q.—No matter how badly you print or turn out a book, if you can pass the Education Department, you will get your share of the trade?

A.—Yes, so long as the book is up to the specifications.

Q.—As long as it passes the Department, you will get your share of the trade?

A.—Yes.

Q.—Is there a written agreement to that effect?

A.—I do not think there is. I think it is simply a verbal arrangement.

Q.—Have you got any agreements made with any other publishers about these "Readers"?

A.—I have the agreements relating to copyrights.

Q.—Relating to the publication of the books, have you any agreements?

A.—Yes, I have.

Q.—What are they?

A.—I have an agreement with Macmillans.

Q.—I am not speaking about copyrights just now. Have you an agreement whereby your firm got into this business?

A.—Yes, we took the place of Thomas Nelson and Sons, Edinburgh, and made a contract.

Q.—What did you pay them for that privilege?

A.—That information I would rather give privately, Mr. Chairman. This is a matter of business arrangement between ourselves and the Nelsons and does not concern the case of text books at all, and I have no permission to make it public, and in that respect it would be a breach of confidence, and I would, therefore, request to be allowed to submit the agreements to the Commission to be used as they think best.

The Commissioners here drew together in private conference with their legal examiners, and after consulting for a short time the chairman gave the following ruling:—

"We have great faith in publicity, Mr. Thomas, and in the almighty power for good of a free press. We would be sorry unnecessarily to expose to the public any private affairs; but where persons or corporations enter into agreements with the Government it ceases to be a private affair, it is a public matter. Now, there was a good deal of criticism regarding the methods of secrecy adopted by the last Commission, and it resulted in rather concealing the truth and deceiving the public than otherwise, and now you suggest that these questions be answered to the Commission privately. I may say to you, that we think that anything this Commission is entitled to hear and see, the public is also entitled to hear and see. An investigation of this kind, to be of any use, must be open to the press, and everything must be given to the people. This is a question we think that affects the cost to you of the production of these books, and, therefore, a proper question for us to investigate. We, therefore, think that it is a question you ought to answer."

Mr. THOMAS: Well, Mr. Chairman, I bow to your ruling, of course. I just wanted to enter that protest so that it would be clear to our English friends that we had to disclose the bargain.

Mr. STAUNTON: What was the agreement you had with Nelson & Sons, of Edinburgh?

A.—The agreement in brief was that we took their place in the contract with the Education Department and paid them $30,000 for the rights for the first ten years, and for a continuance of the agreement we paid them a royalty on the trade prices varying from 2½ per cent. to 5 per cent. on the different books.

Mr. Staunton here reads copy of agreement as follows:—

This Indenture, made the Fourth day of December, A.D. 1884, between Thomas Nelson and William Nelson, both of the City of Edinburgh, Publishers, trading under the name, style and firm of Thomas Nelson & Sons, and hereinafter called Thomas Nelson & Sons, of the First Part, and

William Walter Copp, Henry James Clark and Charles Fuller, all of the City of Toronto, Publishers, trading under the name, style and firm of Copp, Clark & Co., hereinafter called Copp, Clark & Co., of the Second Part.

Witnesseth, that whereas a contract has lately been entered into, bearing date on or about the 26th day of November, A..D 1884, between the Government of Ontario, of the one part, and Mr. William James Gage and the Canada Publishing Company, Limited, and the said Thomas Nelson and William Nelson, of the other parts, for the printing and publication of certain Text Books or Readers for use in the schools of the Province, and the said Thomas Nelson & Sons have agreed to sell and assign, and the said Copp, Clark & Co. have agreed to purchase and acquire all the right, title and interest of the said Thomas Nelson & Sons in the said contract for the term of ten years from the first day of January, 1885, for the consideration hereinafter mentioned.

Therefore this indenture witnesseth that the said Thomas Nelson & Sons hereby sell, assign and transfer to the said Copp, Clark & Co. all the said contract for the term of ten years, and all their right, title and interest, and all profit and advantage to be derived therefrom for the said term, to have and to hold the same for their own sole use and benefit. And the said Copp, Clark & Co., in consideration of the premises, hereby covenant with the said Thomas Nelson & Sons, in manner following, that is to say :—To pay the said Thomas Nelson & Sons the sum of three thousand dollars per annum, during the said term of ten years in half-yearly payments, without any abatement or deduction, save as hereinafter mentioned ; the first of such payments to be made on the first day of October, 1885, by bank bill on London, at not more than ten days' notice. And also to pay to the Government of Ontario, whenever required, the half of the sum, not exceeding two thousand five hundred dollars, required by the said contract to be paid to the Government by the said Thomas Nelson & Sons for money expended in the preparation of the said school books or Readers, and the electrotypes therefore. And also to provide the two sureties, in the sum of two thousand five hundred dollars each, required by the said contract to be given to the Government of Ontario for the due fulfilment of the said contract. And also to do, fulfil, perform, keep, and observe, for and on behalf of the said Thomas Nelson & Sons, and in their place and stead, and at the costs, charges and expenses of the said Copp, Clark & Co., all the covenants provisoes, stipulations, conditions and agreements on the part of the said Thomas elson & Sons, in and by the said contract to be done, fulfilled, performed, kept or observed, whether positive or negative. And also to save harmless and keep indemnified the said Thomas Nelson & Sons, their heirs and each of their heirs, executors and administrators, and their and each of their estates and goods, of, from and against all actions, suits, claims, accounts and reckonings, by or on behalf of the Government of Ontario, and of, from and against all losses, damages, costs charges and expenses, for or by reason of the said contract, or of any matter or thing therein contained or arising thereout or therefrom, or from anything done or omitted in respect thereof.

Provided that if, at the end of any one year of the said term, the said Copp, Clark & Co. shall, by reason of actual and *bona fide* competition between the said Gage and the Canada Publishing Company, Limited and themselves, the said Copp, Clark & Co., in the sale of the said school books or Readers, the said Copp, Clark & Co. shall have actually and *bona fide* paid or allowed any commissions or discounts upon their sales for the said year, beyond the prices and discounts limited in the said contract with the Government of Ontario, and the further usual trade discount for cash, whatever the same may be from time to time, then the said Thomas Nelson & Sons, upon proof of the payment or allowance of any such commission or discount for the cause aforesaid having been made to them or their agent appointed for that purpose, hereby covenant and agree to allow to the said Copp, Clark & Co. an abatement or deduction from the payment due at the end of such year of one-half of the aggregate amount of said commissions or discounts for the year, such half however not to exceed in the whole the sum of five hundred dollars, the intention of these presents being that the annual payment by the said Copp, Clark & Co. to the said Thomas Nelson & Sons, shall never be less than the sum of two thousand five hundred dollars.

And this indenture further witnesseth, and it is hereby agreed that in case of the failure of the said Copp, Clark & Co. at any time during the said term, to carry out or fulfil the said contract with the Government according to its tenor and effect, or to make any of the half-yearly payments hereby agreed to be made at the times stipulated therefor; or if they shall make any assignment for the benefit of creditors, or shall become bankrupt or insolvent under any Act or law of bankruptcy or insolvency, or shall make, or attempt to make any assignment or transfer of the said contract, or of the benefit thereof, or of any interest therein, then, and in any such case, it shall be lawful for the said Thomas Nelson & Sons, their executors, administrators and assigns, and they shall have the right to resume the said contract, and to take and have the full benefit and advantage thereof for themselves, for the remainder of the term. Provided, that this clause shall not be acted upon in any case by reason of the non-payment of any semi-annual payment, unless and until the same shall remain overdue and unpaid for six calendar months after notice in writing to the said Copp, Clark & Co. left at their last or most usual place of business demanding payment thereof.

And the said Thomas Nelson & Sons hereby covenant with the said Copp, Clark & Co. to pay the other half of the sum not exceeding two thousand five hundred dollars, required by the said contract to be paid by the Government of Ontario for the preparation of the Readers, and the electrotypes therefor.

In witness whereof, the said parties have hereunto set their hands and seals, this fourth day of December, A.D. 1884.

Signed, sealed and delivered
in the presence of
(Sgd.) ARNOLD W. THOMAS.

(Sgd.) WILLIAM NELSON,
per Jos. Train Gray,
his Attorney.
THOMAS NELSON,
per Jos. Train Gray,
his Attorney.
W. W. COPP,
HENRY J. CLARK,
CHARLES FULLER.

Q.—2½ to 5 per cent. on your profit?
A.—No, on the trade prices of the books.
Q.—The prices from you to the trade?
A.—Yes.
Q.—Can you tell me what your turn-over, or business was for the first ten years?

A.—No, I cannot.

Q.—Can you tell me roughly, what it was per annum in the first ten years? What I want to see is how much percentage on your trade that $30,000 came to?

A.—I am afraid I cannot tell you that.

Q.—Can you tell me what it is now?

A.—No, I do not know,—you have returns which will show it.

Q.—Why was it necessary for you to pay Nelson & Sons the royalty on the renewal of the contract? Your first agreement was for ten years only, and they had no subsequent right in the Readers? .

A.—Well, we thought they had.

Q.—But they had no subsequent right?

A.—I am not arguing that and cannot say.

Q.—Well, you are an intelligent business man, and you know they had no rights after ten years?

A.—Well, we thought they had and our solicitors advised us that they had. That it still held on this contract which would entitle them to a renewal. .

Q.—You were so advised by your solicitors and you paid them a substantial sum for this royalty?

A.—Yes.

Q.—What does the royalty amount to?

A.—Well, it would be perhaps, say, $500 a year.

Q.—You do not know of any fact that you could put forward here to show that they had any legal right to a renewal of the contract?

A.—I think, perhaps, if their contract was referred to, it might clear up that point. The contract provides, Mr. Staunton, that we simply buy their rights for a term of ten years only.

Q.—Is there anything in your contract that compels you to pay them a royalty on a new contract?

A.—Nothing, except that one clause that we are limited to ten years.

Q.—So are they limited to ten years. Why should you pay them any money when you get a renewal from this Government? You did not bargain to do it?

A.—I do not remember the argument at the time; but I fancy they were the original contractors and certainly were entitled to their rights for renewal.

Q.—You have a contract for ten years now, have you not?

A.—Yes.

Q.—You have no rights under that for renewal?

A.—No.

Q.—You did not claim that you had any right in case the Government offered renewal, did you?

A.—Yes.

Q.—As a matter of fact, did not the publishers go to England and get hold of the copyright for the purpose of coercing the Government for a new contract?

A.—I cannot say as to that.

Q.—Did they not try to persuade the Government?

A.—No, I cannot say that either.

Q.—You had no claim then, after purchasing the Nelson interest, in all, to entitle you to a renewal of that contract by the Government?

A.—No.

11 T. B.

Q.—And you are not aware that Nelson had no claim under law, and yet you paid them a royalty?

A.—Yes.

Q.—And you are paying them to-day although the contract has expired?

A.—Yes.

Q.—It has been renewed a third time?

A.—Yes.

Q.—There is nothing in this agreement produced here compelling you to do that?

A.—No.

Q.—Who put up that money,—the $30,000?

A.—The Copp, Clark Company.

Q.—They had no contract with the Government in those days at all?

A.—No.

Q.—They wanted to get into this business?

A.—Yes.

Q.—And they alone contributed the $30,000?

A.—Yes.

Q.—They did not get a contribution from the other firms?

A.—Not a cent.

Q.—Are they paying the royalty now alone?

A.—Yes.

Q.—They will get that much less out of this business than your competitor did?

A.—Yes.

Q.—Were you personally connected with the negotiations with the Nelsons?

A.—In the original instance, no.

Q.—So that you cannot tell me how it was that they persuaded the Copp, Clark Company to pay a royalty on a renewal?

A.—It was a matter of controversy between the solicitors of both sides at that time, and the outcome of the controversy was that we had to pay royalty.

Mr. STAUNTON: Surely when you came to pay your money you knew what it was for. Were you told it would have a rather favourable effect on your application if you helped out Nelson & Sons?

A.—No.

Mr. STAUNTON: I cannot see why it was anything else.

WITNESS: I do not know anything more at all than what I have told you.

Q.—It never came to your ears how it was that they advised Copp, Clark to pay that price to Nelson & Sons?

A.—No.

Q.—They did not tell you why they had a right to it?

A.—No.

Q.—You cannot conceive that they have a right to it, can you?

A.—I think they have.

Mr. STAUNTON: Well, suppose you buy a man's lease for a house for ten years. You pay him what you think is sufficient, and when you make a new lease you will not come back and say, here is something for you—I do not owe it to you, but here it is for you. The Nelsons' original contract with the Government was for ten years, when the ten years expired they simply dropped out and they retained no original rights then under

11a T. B.

the contract. You bought the original contract for which you paid a certain sum of money,—they had no rights then,—they did not own the Government; they had no rights that you know of?

A.—I do not think it would have been honourable on our part to take the contract over their heads.

Q.—What you mean to tell me is that if you have a contract for ten years, and you sell it to me, it would not be honorable for me to get a new contract on the expiration of yours?

A.—I do not think so.

Q.—And that is the ground your firm took?

A.—Yes.

Q.—That was the only reason for paying that money that you know of?

A.—That is the only reason beyond the advice of our counsel at that time.

Mr. STAUNTON: When you made your original contract, you did not provide for renewal, did you?

A.—No.

Q.—Then you renewed that royalty on sentiments of honor apparently; but they thought they had better provide against you in case you might fall away on the second contract. Now I see here that,—"In the event of the existing contract being renewed with the Ontario Government, or continued on or after the first day of January, 1895, it is hereby agreed by and between the said parties hereto and contained in the said indenture of the 4th December, 1884, in respect to the said contract with the Ontario Government is to continue in force on and after the said first day of January, 1895, except as to the provisions therein contained, etc.," so that in 1895, the old agreement was still in force was it not?

A.—No.

Mr. STAUNTON: (Taking up copy of agreement.) Now, Mr. Thomas, just before you got your contract with the Government in 1894, you entered into this agreement of the 17th December, 1894, because this agreement recites as follows:—

Memorandum of agreement made in duplicate the seventeenth day of December A.D. 1894, Between The Copp, Clark Company (Limited), of the First Part, and the firm of Thomas Nelson and Sons, of the City of Edinburgh, Scotland, publishers, of the Second Part.

Whereas a certain contract dated on or about the 26th day of November, 1884, made between the Government of Ontario and the parties hereto of the second part, respecting the publication of Ontario School Readers, by indenture, dated 4th December, 1884, assigned by the parties of the second part to the parties of the first part, may soon expire, but may be renewed or continued, and in the latter event the parties hereto, in consideration of the benefits and advantages to them, respectively accruing by the continuation of the agreement now existing between them upon the terms herein mentioned, have agreed and do hereby agree in respect thereto as follows:—

In the event of the said existing contract with the Ontario Government being renewed or continued on or after the first day of January, 1895, it is hereby agreed by and between the said parties that the agreement now existing between the parties hereto and contained in the said indenture of the 4th December, 1884, in respect to the said contract with the Ontario Government is to continue in force on and after the said first day of January, 1895, except as to the provisions therein contained respecting the payment of an annual sum of $3,000 to the parties hereto of the second part, and respecting the reduction of the same to $2,500 under the circumstances in said indenture set forth and except as is hereby otherwise provided.

The parties hereto of the first part hereby agree to pay to the parties hereto of the second part, and the parties hereto of the second part hereby agree to accept in lieu of the annual payments provided for by said indenture of 4th Decmber, 1884, a royalty of ten per cent. on the retail prices of all copies of the series of Ontario School Readers at present in use, in stock on the first day of January, 1895, or completed and placed in stock thereafter, and published and sold by the parties of the first part during the renewal or continuance of the said contract with the Ontario Government on or after the first day of January, 1895.

It is hereby further agreed that an account of sales of said Readers is to be made for and forwarded to the parties hereto of the second part by the parties hereto of the first part on or about the 30th day of June and 31st day of December in each year, and the parties hereto of the first part hereby covenant and agree to pay to the parties hereto of the second part the amount due in respect of royalties under this agreement for each half year within one month from the expiration of each half year.

It is further understood and agreed that the parties of the first part will not renew the existing contract with the Ontario Government to the exclusion of the interests of the parties of the second part under this agreement.

In witness whereof the parties hereto of the first part have hereunto set their corporate seal attested by the signature of their President and Secretary-Treasurer, and the parties hereto of the second part have hereto set their hands and seals.

Witness,

(Signed) THOMAS LANGTON.

JOHN L. FORREST.

H. L. THOMPSON,
President.

ARNOLD W. THOMAS,
Sec'y.-Treas.

THOMAS NELSON & SONS,

FOR MR. THOMAS NELSON'S TRUST,
G. M. BROWN.

Q.—Now you are the signer of this contract, Mr. Thomas?

A.—Yes, I think so,—that contract lapsed on the 6th February, 1896, when a new one was made.

Q.—Who were your solicitors?

A.—Messrs. Thompson, Henderson & Bell.

Q.—I see that the agreement dated 6th February, 1896, states as follows:—

Memorandum of agreement made in duplicate this sixth day of February, 1896, between The Copp, Clark Company, (Limited), of Toronto, of the First Part, and Messrs. Thos. Nelson & Sons, of Edinburgh, Scotland, of the Second Part.

The Department of Education for Ontario having under consideration a new contract for the publication of the Ontario Public School Readers, for an interest in the publication of which Readers the parties of the first part have been paying to the parties of the second part a royalty of ten per cent. on the retail price of said Readers under agreement, dated seventeenth of December, 1894, it is hereby agreed.

1. That after the execution of the proposed new contract, and from the date on which the said contract shall take effect, the parties of the first part agree to pay to the parties of the second part, and the parties of the second part agree to accept in lieu of the payments to them, provided for in the agreement, dated seventeenth of December, 1894, aforesaid, a royalty on all copies of the Ontario Public School Readers, published and sold by the parties of the first part during the continuance of this agreement as follows : —

A royalty of two and one-half per cent. upon the trade price of the First Book (parts one and two), and the Second Book in the said series, and five per cent. upon the trade price of the Third and Fourth Book in the said series.

2. The royalty above mentioned is to be paid as long as the said Ontario Readers shall continue to be published by the present publishers, namely, the parties of the first part, Messrs. Gage & Co., and The Canada Publishing Company, and only by them or by parties to whom their interests may be transferred.

3. It is hereby further agreed that the parties of the first part shall make and forward to the parties of the second part an account of sales of the said readers on or about the thirtieth day of June and the thirty-first day of December of each year during the continuance of this agreement, and the parties of the first part hereby covenant and agree to pay to the parties of the second part the amount due in respect of royalties under this agreement for each half year within one month from the expiration of each half year.

4. In the event of the trade price of the said Readers being reduced below those specified in the contract now under consideration with the Education Department, it is understood that a reduced royalty is to be mutually arranged between parties of the first and second parts.

In witness whereof the parties hereto of the first part have hereunto set their corporate seal attested by the signature of their President and Secretary-Treasurer, and the parties hereto of the second part have hereto set their hands and seals.

H. L. THOMPSON,
President.
ARNOLD W. THOMAS,
Secy.-Treas.
Witness.
JAS. H. McDUNNOUGH.
THOMAS NELSON & SONS.

FOR MR. THOMAS NELSON'S TRUST,
G. M. BROWN.

Q.—Now, Mr. Thomas, had these people any powerful influence which would magnetise that contract and draw it your way?

A.—I do not know of any, Mr. Staunton.

Q.—Why, was it provided that you pay this royalty so long only as yourselves, the Canada Publishing Company, and Gage and Company had a monopoly of the business.

A.—The reason is that these were the three firms who had the original contract, and it was thought at the time that if other publishing firms published the Readers, the profits would be so largely reduced that we could not afford to pay it.

Q.—And if any other person got in you could drop this arrangement?

A.—I do not understand the question.

Q.—You must have been paying for the right?

A.—Yes, we paid for the right.

Q.—This is the only explanation you can give me on that point?

A.—Yes, that is the only explanation.

Q.—Have you any other agreement with the Nelsons or any of the other publishers concerning these Ontario School Readers?

A.—No, I have no other contracts that I am aware of or can find.

Q.—It is true, Mr. Thomas, is it not, that this is just a happy family. The publishers of the Ontario Readers are really one family, are you not?

A.—Oh no, not at all.

Q.—Is it not a fact that Warwick Bros. are interested in your company?

A.—Not a cent.

Q.—Are they interested in the "Canada Publishing Company"?

A.—I do not know.

A.—Do you know whether Mr. Gundy is interested?

A.—I do not know.

Q.—You don't know whether Mr. Warwick and Mr. Rutter are interested?

A.—I do not know for certain. I have never seen their list.

Q.—Well, have you ever seen them at a shareholders' meeting?

A.—Yes.

Q.—Mr. Warwick?

A.—Yes, Mr. George Warwick.

Q.—Have you seen Mr. Gundy there too?

A.—Yes.

Q.—And Mr. Thompson?

A.—Yes.

Q.—What firm is he connected with?

A.—He is the president of our company.

Q.—Did you see W. J. Gage there?

A.—Yes.

Q.—They all turn up there, do they not?

A.—Yes.

Q.—It is only fair to you to say that I see in this contract that Nelson and Sons paid half the cost of plates?

A.—Yes.

Q.—You only paid them $30,000 and half the cost of the plates?

A.—Yes, that is right.

Q.—They paid $1,200 into this?

A.—Yes.

Mr. STAUNTON: "They put in their thumbs and pulled out the plums," as it were?

A.—Yes.

Q.—When this contract ran out the Government did not want to renew that bargain, but wanted to have a free hand and go to the world at large for their "Readers," and get an improved Reader. Do you know anything about that?

A.—I cannot speak as to that.

Q.—Did you know that they wanted to break away from the syndicate?

A.—No.

Q.—So far as you know then, were the Government quite willing to renew with your firm among others?

A.—Yes.

Q.—If any professions were made that they did not want to renew, they were hollow professions?

A.—Yes.

Q.—You did not coerce the Government into renewing that contract?

A.—No, I can hardly agree with that; it was a matter of negotiation.

Q.—There was no undue influence on your part?

A.—No, but there was more than that; there was the fact that we had control of the copyrights.

Q.—What copyrights had you control of?

A.—We had the control of Macmillan & Co.'s Copyrights.

Q.—You heard a gentlemen here yesterday go over those copyrights, and he said there were very few of them that were of any value whatever. Now, see in the memo. he gave that there were really a great many on the list that he thought were outstanding copyrights.

Q.—Can you tell me how many pieces or extracts in these Readers that you control?

A.—No, I cannot tell you.

Q.—Do you control any?

A.—Yes.

Q.—Can you say that you control two or three?

A.—Yes. more than that.

Q.—Now, Mr. Thomas, I want you to justify yourself; I do not want you to put yourself in a false position?

A.—Well, in the year 1900, I asked the Macmillans to give me a list of the copyrights that were still in existence at that date because I had lost the previous list, and I have here a list of thirteen pieces that were in existence in 1900 and the property of the Macmillan Company.

Q.—Give me some of them?

A.—First Ontario Reader—Part II:
"My Doll," Kingsley.
"What Birdie Says," Tennyson.

Second Ontario Reader:
"Grandpapa," Mrs. Craik.
"My Fairest Child," Kingsley.

Third Ontario Reader:
"The Monster of the Nile," Baker.
"The Burial of Moses," Mrs. Alexander.
"The Road to the Trenches," H. Lushington.

Fourth Reader (Ontario):
"Tom Brown," Hughes.
"Loss of the Birkenhead," Doyle.
"Discovery of the Albert Nyanza," Baker.
"The Two Breaths," Kingsley.
"Song of the River," Kingsley.
"Extract from Speeches," Bright.

Q.—Had you these copyrights for Ontario before the contract was renewed?

A.—Yes, we had.

Q.—Did you know that your friends, the other publishers, were securing some of the others too?

A.—Yes.

Q.—It was planned among you to secure copyrights?

A.—Yes.

Q.—You knew at that time. did you not, that the Government when it made this contract with you for ten years, had composed those books at their

own expense and made the plates, using copyrighted articles and had never ʼ
been disturbed or troubled for ten years in their use?

A.—No, I did not know that.   It was during the first period of ten years
that we discovered that these selections were not secured.

Q.—You hunted up the copyrights instead of them hunting you up?

A.—I do not remember how it first started.

Q.—You do not know who was the "thinker" in the party?

A.—I cannot remember.

Q.—You never heard of anybody threatening you, did you?

Q.—Yes, we were in difficulties with the Macmillans.

Q.—Did they threaten you?

A.—Yes; they did not exactly threaten us, but were very much annoyed.

Q.—You had not done anything, you were merely the successors; the
Government was the guilty one if any?

A.—Clearly they were not guilty, but I should fancy that the publishers
were equally liable.

Q.—Was it expensive to secure these copyrights?

A.—Yes.

Q.—Can you tell me how much it cost?

A.—No, I cannot tell you.

Q.—Were all these secured from Macmillan?

A.—Yes, these thirteen were.

Q.—These are all you secured?

A.—Yes.

Q.—Do you know what the other people paid for theirs?

A.—I do not know.

Q.—I want to know what you paid; you did not pay Macmillan a sum
of money for these articles alone?

A.—There were others.

Q.—Well, I want to know what it cost you; have you been using them
for some time; now what did it cost you to publish books with these articles
in?

A.—The only figures I can give you are the Macmillan figures.

Q.—But you bought them all from Macmillan and he charged you so
much per copyright?

A.—No, we were charged an annual royalty on their copyright selections.

Q.—On these particular copyrights?

A.—On all that they had.

Q.—Now, what did it cost you?

A.—I am not quite clear yet.

Q.—Did you get control of certain extracts from British authors which
appear in the Ontario Readers?

A.—Yes.

Q.—What did it cost you to get the copyright for Ontario of these extracts?

A.—Well, I cannot tell you off hand; I can only tell you Macmillan's
figures.

Q.—Mr. Thomas, you first tell me that Macmillans were the people from
whom you got the right; now then, if you got the right for these thirteen
selections and paid a sum of money, and there was no other element in it,
you ought to be able to tell me?

A.—There were certain other elements in it; there were a great many
selections secured by the other firms and we paid our share in the cost of getting them.

Q.—As a matter of fact, did not the three publishers pay a certain sum each in one pool for all the selections got by the three of you?

A.—Yes, we divided it up.

Q.—Tell me how much money it cost the syndicate for the copyrights they obtained for the readers?

A.—No, I cannot tell you.

Q.—Well, you only paid one-third of it; how much did that amount to?

A.—I cannot tell you; I would have to go through all my cash books and pick out all the entries.

Q.—The Morang Publishing Company told us here that these selections are not very valuable and you could get some of them for $5 and sometimes for the honor of their appearing in the Ontario Readers?

A.—Well, about a guinea is a fair price.

Q.—You are Macmillan's agents, are you not?

A.—We were.

Q.—And on friendly terms?

A.—Yes.

Q.—You paid them for their goods?

A.—Yes.

Q.—And you want us to understand that they held you up?

A.—They certainly did.

Q.—You claim they did hold you up?

A.—I would not want to say that, but we paid them more than the selections were worth.

Q.—Do you mean to say that they took advantage of the fact that you were printing something somebody else had prepared to make you pay more money than you otherwise would have?

A.—Yes.

Q.—Can you tell me how much they increased the price on those particular selections?

A.—Would not the simplest way be to tell you what we paid them?

Mr. STAUNTON: No, it would not. There are all sorts of other elements which you have not described to me included in that cost. If you paid them for these selections alone I think it would be perfectly fair, but if your money payment was made in consideration of something else, it would not be fair?

A.—It was paid for the thirteen selections alone and if there were any others between 1896 and 1900.

Q.—Was that all for which your money was paid?

A.—Yes, we paid them £50 a year and we have paid it for fourteen years—£700 for those particular selections.

Q.—Did you not ask them to prevent anybody else getting them?

A.—Well, we paid for the right for Canada.

Q.—It was not the mere right to publish, but you wanted to have yourselves in a position that other publishing houses could not get into these Readers?

A.—That was not our sole object.

Q.—But that was the great object?

A.—It was one of the objects.

Q.—And you asked these English publishers to give you something more than you ordinarily asked for a guinea?

A.—No, we nearly always got the sole right.

Q.—You wanted them all and you wanted them to back you up if there was any litigation?

A.—No, they did not agree to that. I have a letter from the firm which explains the matter.

Mr. STAUNTON : Read it please.

MACMILLAN .& Co.,
BEDFORD STREET, COVENT GARDEN,
LONDON, May 18th, 1893.

DEAR SIR,—I enclose a formal letter giving you permission to make use of the copyright in the Ontario Readers, over which we have control, in consideration of an annual payment of fifty pounds (£50), to begin with the present year. We shall be glad to receive a cheque for this amount at your convenience, and in future we shall understand that the payment falls due in January of each year.

It is understood that we are to be at liberty to terminate this arrangement at any time by six months' written notice.

With reference to our conversation this morning as to books at special prices, I should like to put it on record that the general understanding is, that in the event of your taking up any book of ours at a special rate, we agree not to sell copies to any other Canadian bookseller at less than the ordinary trade terms, that is to say, ten per cent. off sale. We understand that this does not extend to the Maritime Provinces of New Brunswick and Nova Scotia.

I am, your faithfully,
(Signed) FREDERICK MACMILLAN.

H. L. THOMPSON, ESQ.,
c/o Messrs. John Walker & Co.,
Warwick Lane, Newgate Street, E.C.

(*Enclosure.*)

MACMILLAN & Co.,
BEDFORD STREET, COVENT GARDEN,
LONDON, May 18th, 1893.

DEAR SIRS,—We have carefully examined the series of Ontario Readers and find that they contain a considerable number of copyright pieces over which we have control. The publication of these pieces without our permission constitutes a very serious breach of copyright, but we are willing that the thing should be put upon a proper basis by a payment from you to us in respect of this copyright matter.

We propose that you should pay us the sum of fifty pounds (£50) in consideration of which we will agree to allow you to continue the publication, and further agree not to make a similar arrangement with the publishers of any other series of reading books, or of any other edition of this series in the Dominion of Canada. It is understood that this permission extends only to the three editions of the Ontario Readers which are published respectively by yourselves, Messrs. Gage & Co. and the Canada Publishing Co., and that you are not at liberty to extend the permission to anybody else.

You further undertake to assist us if necessary in taking legal proceedings against any person or persons by whom these copyrights are invaded.

We are, yours faithfully,

MACMILLAN & Co.

MESSRS. THE COPP, CLARK CO.,
Toronto, Canada.

Q.—You notice there, Mr. Thomas, that you undertake to assist them prosecuting any other person or persons who invade that copyright?
A.—Yes.

Q.—And you turned round and made an agreement with the Government that you would allow the whole world to publish these Readers.

A.—That was some years later.

Q.—Were you sincere in that?

A.—It seems, a little inconsistent.

Q.—It would appear from this letter then, that the representative of your firm took a set of the "Ontario Readers" over and pointed out to them that their rights had been invaded?

A.—I think I would have to refer you to Mr. Thompson for that.

Q.—Well, anyway, Mr. Thompson did go over and submit a set of Ontario Readers to them?

A.—I cannot answer that.

Q.—But he did go over and open negotiations with them, did he not?

A.—Yes.

Q.—But you do not know what passed between them?

A.—No.

Q.—As I understand you, the £50 a year was contributed by the three firms to Macmillan and Company?

A.—Yes.

Q.—And you were trustee for those rights for your co-members of the syndicate?

A.—I presume so.

Q.—You had the right to publish these articles in any other publication issued by you?

A.—No, I think it was confined to the "Readers" only.

Q.—Why did you refuse to let the Government see your list?

A.—That was a matter of legal advice; I do not know why.

Q.—Did you threaten the Government that if you did not get the Readers you would go for them?

A.—No.

Q.—It would have been an easy matter for the Government to exclude these copyrighted articles from any subsequent addition of the books and substitute others, would it not?

A.—It might have been done, but not easily done. There were probably over 100 selections altogether.

Q.—Well, they could easily have got 100 selections that were not copyrighted, don't you think so?

A.—I think so.

Q.—And by writing to the authors or publishers of those selections in England found out whether they claimed any copyright on them in Canada, could they not?

A.—They could.

Q.—So that the Government had it in its power to publish these books and exclude these selections and substitute others notwithstanding your action had it chosen to do so?

A.—Yes.

Mr. STAUNTON: You wanted to make an explanation and I cut you off, Mr. Thomas; go on now, please?

Mr. THOMAS: It was just along the lines of securing these British copyrights; I wanted to make our position clear before the Commission as so much adverse criticism has been made in the newspapers. When the publishers awoke to the fact that they were publishing books containing selections on which copyrights had not been secured by the Government, they found that they were in a very serious position indeed. The evidence yesterday by Mr.

Saul showed, in his opinion, there were fifty selections which were still in copyright, but taking his own figure at 50 pieces for a basis of this argument, the next point is what would have been the effect on us for publishing these selections.   In order to bring that to your notice I wish to direct attention to the suit brought by Mr. Morang, in which he claimed $25,000 damages. This suit failed, but if it had been brought against us by a British publisher, and we had not secured the copyright beforehand, it would not have failed. Now, if there were 50 cases, and we were sued for $25,000 in each case, that would not have been $250,000 as Mr. Saul stated, but $1,250,000, and if they did succeed, as no doubt they would, it would have meant financial ruin to the three publishers concerned.   I suppose you might say to me, why not proceed against the Government in this, but you know the uncertainty of the law, so the wisest thing to do was to make themselves safe by securing themselves against loss by getting copyrights; that was the reason these copyrights were secured.

Q.—You were alive to the effect on your business, and you knew that copyrights existed?

A.—Yes.

Q.—You knew at the time you entered into this contract, as old experienced publishers, the three of you, that it would be wise before you ventured to publish these articles to secure the copyright, did you not?

A.—The publishers thought they were secured.

Q.—Who told them they were secured?

A.—I cannot say now.

Q.—You hunted them up, did you?

A.—I cannot say?

Q.—Do you mean to tell me, if you infringed the copyrights it meant financial ruin, and that if you published 100 selections it might involve you in 100 law suits aggregating $1,000,000, and yet you did not think of enquiring whether or not the copyrights had been secured?

A.—I think they did.

Q.—You knew very well it was a trifling matter any way and that you could easily enough placate those people in England for taking extracts to put in a Government Reader?

A.—I do not know that.

Q.—Well, here we have a statement from a publisher in England, thinking it a compliment to put their works in the Government Readers. You are not sincere surely when you say that you believe a menace to your business really existed?

A.—I do think so, decidedly.

Q.—Why did you not come to the Government and say "Get up a new set of Readers as there is liable to be a suit against us for $1,000,000?

A.—Well, we did not do so.

Q.—Did the other people put up any more money?

A.—Oh, yes.

Mr. STAUNTON: Well, you are the easiest lot of publishers I ever knew of; I see here (referring to a memorandum) that a gentleman went to England and interviewed these publishers and he says (reads following memorandum):

Memorandum.

I reached London on February 5th. On making enquiry I found that Mr. Gage had called on most of the London publishers about six weeks previous. He represented that the Minister was about to injure his property in the Readers and that he wished to secure the copyright of a number of the pieces. He also urgd on some of them the advisability of proceeding against the Minister for infringement of the copyright. Mr. Isbister, trading under the name of Charles Burnett & Co., London, acceded to his wish in this respect and gave him a letter which was dictated by Mr. Gage, authorizing him to recover damages for infringement of copyright prospective and retrospective. Mr. Isbister declined to recall his letter as he had placed himself entirely in the hands of Mr. Gage. Mr. Gage had also obtained from Mr. Stanford permission to reprint Miss Buckley's articles, for which he paid the regular fee. I obtained from Mr Stanford a letter in which he disavowed having given Mr. Gage any instructions to proceed for infringement of copyright, and stated that he had again written to him on the subject.

Messrs. Macmillan & Co., of London, are the holders of the largest number of copyrights in question. I had two long interviews with the firm and they declined to grant any special copyright of those articles which they still held. They had transferred their copyrights some years before of all of Tennyson's Poems to Messrs. Copp, Clark & Co. They were satisfied that no action could lie against the Minister, because the Minister had never issued any book with his own imprint; he had never in that way infringed the copyright Act. Any action must lie against the three publishers. They assured me, however, that no action retrospective or prospective would be taken against the Minister or the publishers as long as the present series remained in the hands of the present publishers.

Messrs. Kegan, Paul & Co. had been visited by Mr. Gage and had sold to him at the rate of one guinea for each article, the poems of Dobson, Gosse and Locker. I purchased, however, from the right to reprint Tyndall's "Clouds" and Dobson's "Circe." I have forwarded their receipts for the accounts.

Messrs. Chatto & Windus had sold to Messrs. Gage the right to reprint Geo. Macdonald's "The Baby" and Swinburne's "Forsaken Garden."

Mr. Gage had applied to Smith, Elder & Co. for permission to reprint extracts from Mr. & Mrs. Browning's poems. He was refused. They have, however, consented to allow the Minister of Education to do so in terms of their letter of the 13th Feb., 1894.

Messrs. Ellis & Elbey have sold to Mr. Gage the right to reprint Rosetti's "Cloud Confines."

Prof. Max Müller wrote from Oxford that the right to reprint his article has been bought by Mr. Gage, but that the Minister had full permission to reprint anything else.

William Morris consents to the reprints of his poems.

W. H. Allen & Co. consent to the reprint of extracts from Mr. Proctor's book.

Mr. W. E. Gladstone also consents to the reprints of his articles. No reply could be obtained from Mr. Froude nor from Father Nevil, the literary representative of Cardinal Manning. The copyright is just about to expire as far as Cardinal Newman is concerned.

Second book. Sold to Mr. Gage. The articles Geo. Macdonald's "The Baby" and Norman McLeod's "The Squirrel;" articles on "Tea" and "Coffee" from Blackwood's Readers, the "Lion" from Blackie's Readers and the "Lazy Frog" from the Sunday School Union Readers are doubtful copyrights.

John S. Blackie; permission to reprint any of his poems.

Third Book. Tennyson's "Bugle Song," sold to Copp, Clark & Co.; Tennyson's "Song from the Princess," ditto. Tennyson's "Brook," ditto.

Tennyson's "My Queen," parts 1 and 2, ditto. Norman McLeod's "Trust in God," sold to Gage.

Fourth Book. Tennyson's "Lady Clare" sold to Copp, Clark; "Dora" ditto; "Wild Bells", ditto. Buckley's "Piece of Coal" parts 1 and 2 sold to Gage. Dobson's "Before Sedan", ditto; Edwin Arnold's "Florence Nightingale," ditto. Max Müller's "Shakespeare," ditto.

High School Reader, Rosetti's "Cloud Confines," sold to Gage. Ruskin's "Mystery of Life", ditto; Locker's "Old Cradle", ditto; Swinburne's "Forsaken Garden", ditto; Dobson's "Queen Elizabeth", ditto. Gosse's "Return of the Swallows", ditto; Tennyson's "Lord of Burleigh" sold to Copp, Clark. "Break, Break", ditto; and "Revenge", ditto.

Q.—You knew that the Government wanted to get control of these, did you not?

A.—I did not know of it.

Q.—There was a long correspondence between you and the Government, was there not?

A.—No.

Q.—Well, there was a correspondence between you and the Government in 1901?

A.—Yes.

Q.—And you refused to give them a list,—and the whole lot of you refused?

A.—Yes.

Q.—Did you have a conference before you refused?

A.—Yes.

Q.—You decided that you would all "stand pat"?

A.—We consulted our solicitors and refused.

Mr. COOPER: You assumed, on the advice of Messrs. Thompson, Henderson & Bell, in view of the fact that there was a suit brought against you by Mr. Morang, that it was but fair to withhold the list?

A.—I think so.

Mr. COOPER: I have never been able to understand what connection the suit that Mr. Morang brought against you had to do with the copyright question.

A.—I am afraid I cannot answer that.

Mr. STAUNTON: Did it strike you that when you had promised the Government under your hand and seal that you would allow any other publishers to publish anything that you control and allow them to come in to this business that it would have shown candor and frankness on your part to have given them immediately to the Government?

A.—I really cannot answer that.

Q.—Why did you rush off to your solicitors; you apparently wanted to get some legal breastwork to hide behind; you need not have paid them a fee to do that?

A.—I cannot answer that question.

Q.—Well, there is your own agreement with the Government that you would allow any one else to print them?

A.—If the Government had made it a part of the contract that we were to supply a list of the copyrights we would have done it.

Q.—Is there any other correspondence stating that fact?

A.—Yes.

Q.—Does that mean between man and man that you must tell them what you have got?

A.—I do not think so.

Mr. STAUNTON: Well, you seem to have made them think so. There has been a great deal of talk and criticism of your action and I thought you would have brought your mind to bear on it long ago. Some people say you simply "held the Government up", while other people say that both the Government and you took advantage of it; and I want you to say whether it was so or not. · If you can show us anything that would convince any ordinary man that such was not your intention, I wish you would do it?

A.—I can quite clearly state that there was no understanding with the Government whereby we acted together. It was a matter of stiff hard negotiation to get that contract through,—there was no collusion.

Q.—Why did the Government not want to give it to you?

A.—I cannot tell vou.

Q.—Well, here you were the only publishers printing them and apparently giving satisfaction at the cheapest price; now will you tell me why it was that they took a hostile position to you?

A.—They did not take a hostile position; what I said was, that there was a fight to get the best possible terms on the contract. The Government of course, as a matter of policy, wanted to make the best bargain they could for the trade.

Q.—So they divided the matter among the three of you and did not let anyone else into it?

A.—No.

Q.—It was a private deal between you and the Government?

A.—Yes.

Q.— There was no person else had an opportunity to come in to help the country out; that is, for the advantage of the country no person else was allowed to come in and compete with you under the renewed contract?

A.—No.

Q.—It was clearly a matter of benefit to the Government to have a number of people publishing these books, was it not?

A.—That is a matter of opinion.

Mr. STAUNTON: No, it is a matter of calculation; if they got ten of them to pay that much per year it would be an advantage, would it not?

A.—Yes.

Q.—How much did you pay?

A.—We paid $3,000.

Q.—That was really a tax put on the text books of the province?

A.—No, it was not that way; the Government said the prices must be so and so, and in addition to that we must pay $3,000.

Q.—You could have given the Government cheaper prices if they had not stuck on that $3,000?

A.—Yes.

Q.—It was a tax on you then?

A.—Yes, I suppose it was.

Q.—So that if they had got three publishers into the business they would have got $10,000, instead of the $3,000?

A.—Yes.

Q.—So it would be to the interest of the Government to get as many into it as possible?

A.—Yes.

Mr. CROTHERS: Then when you three publishers cease to publish the Ontario Readers you will have no further right in these copyrights?

A.—No.

Q.—They will then be open for the Government or anyone else to acquire them?

A.—Yes.

Q.—The agreement entered into with the Macmillan Company was confined to you three publishing houses, and at the same time you entered into an agreement with the Government that they might permit any others to come in and publish these books.

A.—Yes.

Q.—Well, how were these other publishers to get on with the MacMillans if the right to publish these selections was conveyed to your three publishing houses?

A.—They would have to negotiate that themselves with the British publishers; we could not do anything directly or indirectly.

Q.—Although the agreement between you three publishers and the Government seemed to give the right, it practically did not convey any such right, because you had the right to publish these selections and Macmillan might allow any other publisher to use them.

A.—Yes, that is right.

Q.—Does each one of these three publishing houses publish the whole of any one book?

A.—They each publish the whole of one book.

Mr. Staunton: Did you notice that you said to Mr. Crothers, the Chairman, that the agreement between you and Macmillan limited your right to publish these articles in the Ontario Readers.

A.—Well what I said is my understanding of it.

Q.—And only so long as you and the other two published them?

A.—Yes.

Q.—Now when you came to the Government was it not quite patent to them and to you that if the Government refused to let you publish the Readers, that Macmillan and Company could make a deal with the Government?

A.—I do not know about that.

Q.—Well, suppose the Government said we will not renew with you, then you would have no complaint if Macmillan wrote to the Government and said they would be delighted to have them use the articles in the Ontario Readers?

A.—Yes.

Q.—So that you really held no bludgeon at the head of the Government, did you?

A.—No. I do not like to answer any questions about "motives"; I will answer questions as to facts and that is all I would like to do. The publishers, of course, made the very best contract they could.

Mr. Staunton: Well, I think that will do, Mr. Thomas, thank you.

MEETING OF THE TEXT BOOK COMMISSION, THURSDAY, 25th OCTOBER, 1906, 2 O'CLOCK P.M., RESUMED.

Evidence of Mr. Edward M. Trowern.

T. W. Crothers, Examiner:

Q.—What is your occupation?

A.—Secretary of the Retail Merchants' Association. Toronto—for the Province of Ontario.

Q.—You desired to make a statement to the Commission dealing with the position of the Retail Merchants in the sale of books?

A.—Yes.

Q.—Just say what you desire to say?

A.—Gentlemen, as we have had a large number of letters from all parts of the Province with reference to the selling price of school books, we would like to say a few words to the Commission. Of course in Toronto where the public schools are supplied with books free to the children, there are not as many books sold as there are throughout the Province. The price at which the departmental stores sell the school books is detrimental to the store keeper who has to carry the stock and who needs to pay rent and taxes and help in order to accommodate the public. Ye thought while you were considering this whole question of books you might consider whether there would be a possibility of having the prices that are marked on the books and which are supposed to be the retail prices of the books maintained. We are not saying whether those particular prices on them should be the prices but we would like as far as possible to have the one price system adopted throughout the Province of Ontario. There is no reason in the world in our opinion why the book-sellers should be forced to handle these books for net cost so that a few dry goods stores can take these books and advertise them themselves and sell dry goods, to the disadvantage of the book-sellers.

Mr. COOPER: You are speaking now of the dry goods stores of Toronto only?

A.—There are a few in Hamilton and Ottawa that do the same, and throughout other parts of the Province. I can give you if you desire the names of the cities and towns where the prices are cut.

Q.—As long as you say it is general?

A.—Yes. But the dry goods stores take up books. We did not know whether this part of the enquiry would come under your observation or not. If you desire to get evidence on this issue as to what extent this difficulty exists we can get you the evidence.

Q.—What sort of evidence would it be?

A.—I suppose you would want to know whether these statements I am making are true and can be borne out in fact, whether the booksellers and stationers throughout the Province—whether this is a general grievance. I make the statement that it is the case. We have interviewed the book-sellers, and we have had meetings with them and the grievance is general.

Q.—How would you produce it, confirming what you have said?

A.—Well, we will either produce it in writing, or we can produce witnesses here to prove it.

The CHAIRMAN: Is this your objection then, that some retail merchant engaged in trade other than bookselling, are selling school books at lower prices than those marked on the books?

A.—Oh, yes.

Q.—And your association would like to have the price fixed so that they could not sell it below a certain price?

A.—Yes.

Q.—Now there is a maximum price fixed, and you want that to be fixed as the minimum price?

A.—We would prefer to have a fair profit, whatever profit you think is sufficient to handle the books. Put on the price and that would be the retail price.

Q.—A uniform price throughout the Province?

12 T. B.

A.—Yes, a uniform price throughout the Province, on the same principle as the Government sell marriage licenses.

Q.—They sell marriage licenses at $2, and any issuer of licenses that cuts the price his privileges are cut off. He does not get the right to sell. The same with postage stamps,—the Government fix the rates. The Globe or Mail would never tolerate such a thing for a minute. They would say, if you are going to use my papers to advertise something else, you cannot get the papers. If the principle is right, we want the right. We think it should be an adopted principle with school books.

Mr. STAUNTON: What would the Government do?

A.—It would largely depend on the way you decide to sell these books. The Government could fix the retail price and insist that they be sold retail at that price, allowing the retailers a discount off.

Q.—Would that not raise a great clamor against the Government?

A.—Well, if the Government contract to have publishers publish the book the publishers themselves can do that. That is a common thing; that is done with almost all staple lines of goods.

Q.—In order to make that one price, you would have to have a penalty against that?

A.—No, the penalty would be cutting off the supplies. The Ottawa Government do not fine you when you violate in selling postage stamps. They give you a condition, and they say you sell those postage stamps at that price, at two cents, and if you start selling them below that to the public, the penalty is you do not get any more to sell. They cut you right out. It is the same way with a large number of articles that are sold that way. Waterman Fountain pens have been sold that way, and Waterbury watches have been sold that way, the price is given to the retailer. We do not want to be unfair. We want to say to the publisher, or to the Government or whoever handles the books, it costs us so much to do business, and we want a profit. Now, if you say there is going to be a clamor against the Government, if the Government were to maintain the price there is going to be a good deal bigger clamor if you get all the booksellers and all the storekeepers all over the country handling them for nothing, and I assure you there is no more burning question in the Province of Ontario. There is nothing that makes a man feel cheaper or meaner than a storekeeper—probably a member of a church—when a little school boy or school girl comes in and asks for a school book, and he sells it for the price marked on it, and the school child or the parent finds by looking at the paper that the same book is sold in Toronto at twenty per cent. less, and these men are probably teachers in the Sunday School, and what do the children think? It is not a very nice thing. The principle is bad.

Q.—Supposing the Government did not publish the book, but they put them in the hands of publishers under contracts as now, only under as favorable a contract as they could obtain—then if these three or four or five publishers were to say they would not sell a book to you unless you sold at a certain price, do you not see they would just lay themselves open to the Dominion law of conspiracy?

A.—Not the publisher—

Q.—They leave themselves open to the law that they combined to keep up prices?

A.—Well, there has been no case yet in the courts. I have had a good deal of experience in that respect, and we are endeavoring to get the law changed, but there is no case before the courts yet. The publisher or

12a T. B.

manufacturer has never been, charged with an illegal act if he fixes the retail price to the seller.

Q.—Oh, yes, they have?

A.—If three or four of them come together. If I was publishing an arithmetic you understand, and that arithmetic was authorized by the Government and handed to me to publish, and no one else was publishing that book, and I put on the retail selling price of that book, and I said to you, you cannot buy that book from me or anybody else excepting you sell it for my price, you cannot quote any law in Canada where the publisher has been found guilty by doing that particular thing.

Q.—Although I am not familiar with the case, I think they did that with the Wampole people?

A.—No, not with that. I am familiar with that Wampole case, and that was an entirely different proposition. The Wampoles were selling their Cod Liver Oil at a dollar a bottle for ten years, but a few people such as I speak of cut the price, and the manufacturer said, I am not going to have the price of my goods cut, I want the price maintained, and the retail people said to Wampole, if you want your price maintained you had better adopt the contract that has been adopted in England, and we presented that contract and the first thing the manufacturer said was "how will the wholesale people look upon this," and then he said, "we will meet the wholesale and discuss it with him," and then we met with the wholesalers and discussed it with them this question, and then the manufacturer met with the wholesalers and retailers—there were three of us met, and the manufacturer said the contract is all right, we will adopt it. Now, in that case the three interests met together, and the penalty was imposed for that reason, not because Wampole fixed the price or adopted the contract, but because the three of us got together and decided that was a fair contract,—Judge Clute said we should not have come together. The law said we must not come together, and he is perfectly right.

Q.—There is the case of the coal dealers?

A.—That is a different case.

Q.—But your idea of escaping the penalty of the law is to deal with the retailer alone, and then you think there is no conspiracy, but if it just happened that I published an arithmetic, and you published an arithmetic, and the chairman published that arithmetic and Mr. Cooper published it, and each one went to the retailer, a Jury would infer that we had met together, and there we would be under the law?

A.—I quite agree with that case, but we do not agree that the law is right.

Q.—The Ontario Government cannot control the criminal law, and you would have to suggest some means, some plan that would not expose them, so that it could not be said even, they were trying to get within the law. The Government cannot put at defiance the criminal law?

A.—Our Retail Association quite understand that.

Q.—So far as I can see, and I have been over this Statute very carefully, and have had a good many cases under it, I think you would be open, and the jury would go against you immediately, particularly in a case of this kind. People all have school children, and they would say there is a combination?

A.—If you are going to have four or five publishers publishing the one book.

Q.—I do not know what the Commission will recommend,—I am just giving a supposititious case?

A.—If one publisher publishes—we would certainly be in favor of the Government publishing the books, and the Government are doing that very thing now. The Government are fixing prices. I can give you a dozen articles that they are fixing prices on.

Q.—Further, there is another thing, and I do not think you can show any decision to the contrary, that the mere fact that the publisher went to the retailer and agreed with him, and told him he would not let him have the book unless he sold at a certain price would be a conspiracy?

A.—No, we have been very careful on that point.

Q.—There is no decision against that proposition?

A.—Well, unfortunately we are the only country in the world that has such foolish legislation. England has not got it—France has not got it—Germany has not got it.

Q.—I quite agree with you, it is a great hardship, a great many times, but that is the condition. There is no good in presenting a proposition to the Commission asking them to violate the law. I think you should think it out and present a proposition which is within the law?

A.—Of course the position we are in now, we had a thousand retailers wait on the Dominion Government in regard to this law, and the Dominion Government are now considering changing it. Of course, it is right that I should come now before the Commission. If the Government at Ottawa change that law, which I hope they will do, they will give us selling rights. I think we should have the rights a laboring man has.

Q.—People say, and I have never heard it answered that the net result of the Dominion law is going to be to allow these great departmental stores to accomplish what the Act was intended to prevent, to control the prices?

A.—That is right, the law at the present time creates these large monopolies. I want to say, however, that the one price system is the system that the booksellers throughout the Province want adopted by the publishers, or by the Commission if it is possible to do it. Of course, Mr. Staunton is quite correct in instancing at the present time the difficulties, but if we can get that removed and you would be perfectly free to consider this afterwards.

Q.—That is your decision?

A.—Yes.

The CHAIRMAN: I have heard some of the retail men say they do not care much about the business of retailing books, because they have some left on their hands?

A.—That is the unfortunate part of it. They are only making three or four or five per cent., and a new edition comes out, and you leave them with the old edition that they should not have anything to do with, and if you do not carry them you are going to inconvenience the public. That is what the very system I am complaining of is doing. You are putting the public to inconvenience.

Q.—Do you think the trade is any good at all except to those who use it to advertise?

A.—It should be, but it is not any good to anybody.

Q.—There would not be any very great outcry then if we wiped it out altogether?

A.—In some small places where these big stores do not exist they get the price. It is marked on the books, and they get those prices.

Q.—Generally speaking, you do not think it is of much benefit at present?

A.—Not to large cities and towns.

Q.—It would not be much inconvenience in Toronto if it was done away with?

A.—No, the books are free you understand, but the High School books, of course, are you considering those? I would not like that statement to apply to the High School books.

Mr. Cooper: Your statement that it is not much good only applies to the public school book?

A.—Where free books were given, yes.

Q.—What discount do the retailers get from the wholesalers?

A.—Twenty-five per cent. I understand.

Q.—Have you any knowledge of the discount that the retailer gets in the United States?

A.—No, I do not. Mr. Carmen and Mr. Britnell are here. I am not up on the technical part of it.

Evidence of Mr. Albert Britnell.

Mr. Cooper Examiner:

Mr. Cooper: You have been in the book selling business a long time?

A.—Twenty-two years in this country.

Q.—And you have been selling school books here?

A.—Some, yes.

Q.—You know the discount in Ontario, twenty-five per cent.?

A.—Yes.

Q.—What is the usual discount in the United States by the publisher to the retailer?

A.—It varies; much the same there as here, twenty to thirty per cent.

Q.—That is your opinion?

A.—Yes.

Q.—Or is that your knowledge?

A.—That is what I find.

Q.—I am creditably informed that the maximum discount allowed by any American firm is sixteen and two-thirds per cent.?

A.—On the published prices?

Q.—On the school books?

A.—Well, we get them here for a lower price than they sell to the United States booksellers.

Q.—You get larger rates than that?

A.—If that is the maximum rate in the United States, we get more than that.

Q.—You do not know what they allow to the booksellers in the United States; you only know what they allow you?

A.—I have always understood it was between twenty and thirty per cent.

Q.—I know it is, unless you have some evidence to the contrary?

A.—I know only from experience as a Canadian bookseller. Even that may be a good profit if the same conditions do not prevail. In the large centres, for instance, here in Toronto, we sell at twenty per cent. discount, we sell at the same price as the departmental stores sell, and there is a profit of twenty-five per cent. to us, and as the chairman remarked, if we buy a thousand or two thousand of a good book at twenty per cent. discount, making five per cent. profit, and in the end we have to keep some copies—and the chances are the books may be changed—the profit is wiped out entirely. There is no profit in handling them to-day.

Q.—Where they get the prices?

A.—The same proportion, twenty per cent. Well, our discount is invariably twenty-five per cent., except we buy very large quantities, and then there is an extra five per cent.

Q.—Is not five per cent. a very good profit where sales are sure?

A.—I certainly do not think so. It does not pay for —

Q.—What would you say was a good fair profit?

A.—Ten or fifteen I would say—I would not be bothered with them.

Q.—It does not need to be twenty-five?

A.—I do not think so.

Q.—Twenty-five per cent. in a place where they are authorized?

A.—I think so. Of course in the smaller places they generally get the prices that the Government itself authorizes. There is no doubt about that, but here the booksellers are discriminated against by the public—the pupils and the parents where they can get these books cheaper. I think when a price is inscribed on a book it should be sold at that price. It could not be sold any higher because that is the evidence of the Government's price.

Mr. STAUNTON: You would put it down to a fair price, a living price?

A.—I would not allow it to be any lower. I would like more in the interests of the pupils and parents to say something about the overlapping of books—of authorized books. Take, for instance, the latin book,—you have two or three different books authorized. Now if an authorized book is good for one school it ought to be good for another. I certainly protest on behalf of the parents of the Province and the pupils of the Province. If a boy is going to school in the west they find a certain book authorized and they move away to another part of the city or country—High School books I refer to— they are compelled to discard the books they have been previously using and buy another one. That is a point which I think should be dealt with by the Commission and considered. I do not think there is any utility— any use in authorizing duplicate High School text books. If one book is good enough for one section it is good enough for the other, and, therefore, I do not see the use in the overlapping of books. It is an unnecessary expense.

Q.—Do you find many coming and selling second hand to you?

A.—Yes, quite a lot, and I hear parents constantly objecting. They buy a certain book for one school and move away and they find an entirely different book in use and they have to buy it over again.

EVIDENCE OF MR. EDWARD S. CASWELL.

Mr. STAUNTON, Examiner:

Q.—What is your position?

A.—I have charge of the book publishing there at the Methodist Book Room.

Q.—Do you publish school books?

A.—Some.

Q.—What books do you publish?

A.—We publish the Temperance and Physiology, Primary Latin Book and Clement's History of Canada and the Weaver History of Canada and the Algebra, Part One, which is I think, the only authorized one. We have also Part Two, I think those are all our Text Books.

Q.—Are your books in open competition, or are they exclusively authorized in the Province?

A.—I think the only one that does not have a competitor is Temperance and Physiology, Dr. Nattress.

Q.—Your books that are not exclusively authorized are all those except Temperance and Physiology?

A.—I think so. That is the only one that has a monopoly.

Q.—Which of the books do you pride yourself on most, which do you most credit?

A.—Well, it is a question. I hardly know. They are all pretty decent books.

Q.—What do you think is the best turned out book of the lot, if one is better than another?

A.—I fancy the new edition of Part One of the Algebra is perhaps the most creditable one. That is not yet authorized you know. Temperance and Physiology is fair—there is not very much to choose between them.

Q.—This book is stitched?

A.—It is machine sewn. We do not stitch any.

Q.—It is just held in the case by the mull?

A.—No tapes.

Q.—Why have you not adopted a tape or a hinge in your books?

A.—The chief reason I think is the expense. It would cost more to put the tape on.

Q.—What would it cost—have you ever figured it?

A.—Well, I will tell you now, we could bind it with using the tapes and with the cloth instead of the mull, and what they call cloth lining, the first and last section, at an additional cost of, I think, a cent a copy on the average sized book.

Q.—That should make the three improvements, add the tapes, put a cloth instead of a mull, and then put a cloth lining on the first section?

A.—Yes, a narrow piece of cloth that will come right over the bend of the section.

Q.—That was what I call a hinge?

A.—Yes, you could call it that.

Q.—It comes over each section?

A.—Yes, the first and last section.

Q.—As a matter of fact these books are not bound at all. They are just cased. I am told that a book should be properly laced into the cover? All the books we have before us, they are all simply cased in?

A.—I suppose that is merely a distinction of terms? The binding of ours is the binding that is ordinarily used in cloth board books in Canada and in other countries, I think.

Q.—We have not got any here in that way from the U. S. that I have seen?

A.—You mean perhaps school books. I cannot answer as to that. I have never examined American school books. That may be so with regard to them.

Q.—Then none of your books have the tapes. They are all put in just with the mull?

A.—None of our school books, no.

Q.—Have you a large sale for these books?

A.—No, not a very large sale for any of them. Of course if you put up against a Geography or History or Readers the sale is very insignificant.

Q.—This Temperance and Physiology, do you exclusively publish that as well?

A.—No, I cannot say that we do. I ought to correct what I said before, while we were given exclusive publication originally, W. J. Gage & Co. took advantage in the agreement, and another publisher, too, came after a certain time, and so to speak held us up on that.

Q.—The other publishers could not come in very well on the readers? Did you not know that?

A.—There is no copyright on the Physiology.

Q.—Do you mean to tell me they came to you and compelled you to let them have a part of the profits?

A.—Yes, it was either making a special price to them, making special consideration, or allowing them to make plates of their own, and bring the book out themselves.

Q.—Under that arrangement it cut into your business?

A.—It did.

Q.—Was the book paid for by you?

A.—Did you get the book compiled or did the Government have it?

A.—No, the Government had it compiled originally.

Q.—And furnished you with plates?

A.—Yes.

Q.—Then the Government had full control of all the copyrights of that book?

A.—Yes, I think the copyright was assigned to them.

Q.—You were given the contract similar to this you heard us discussing to-day, allowing the Government to make contracts with other publishers for bringing out this book?

A.—It gave us a monopoly only for a certain number of years.

Q.—At the end of that time Gage & Co. came and said unless you divide we will compete?

A.—That is the ultimatum we got.

Q.—You could not sell them?

A.—They could divide the market with us anyway.

Q.—What concession did you make?

A.—We made a special price with them and they supplied the paper.

Q.—At their own price?

A.—We gave them a price for printing, covering the royalty.

Q.—Did they print it for you?

A.—We would print it for them on their paper for a certain price.

Q.—You did the printing?

A.—Yes. They supplied their own paper and did their binding. We are not responsible for their book.

Q.—They are selling that book under their own name?

A.—Yes, they have the name on the imprint.

Q.—They have no contract with the Government?

A.—I do not think so, I am not sure. I do not know about that.

Q.—They simply go and publish the book and make whatever they can out of it?

A.—Yes.

Q.—And do you limit the output to a certain number?

A.—No, we do not.

Q.—They can sell all they like?

A.—They can sell 100,000 if they want to. We have no control of that.

Q.—Why did you not allow them to go and make a bargain with the Government?

A.—We got some profit out of printing the book for them, that we would lose otherwise. That was the only reason.

Q.—They were determined to have part of it? Did they let you into the Readers?

A.—Well, hardly.

Q.—Did they give you any consideration for this at all—just the threat they would go into the business?

A.—That was all we had out of it.

Q.—And the result is although they have no contract, they are sharing with you the profit whatever it is, in the business?

A.—I do not know what contract they have with the Government. They may have for all I know. I am relating only to what I know about our relation with them.

Q.—You make a return to the Government of how many you make? Do you make a return to the Government of the number of this Physiology and Temperance you publish?

A.—I think we make returns of sales.

Q.—Does that include Gage's output, too?

A.—I should suppose it would, though I could not answer that off hand. I do not make up the returns.

Q.—We have got 12 years, showing 185,940 of these sold?

A.—In 12 years.

Q.—The people seem to be getting less temperate because there was only 8,000 last year?

A.—Well, when the book came out first I suppose it was something of a curiosity, and there was a very large sale the first year or two, but latterly I think the book has not been used so much in the schools as it was formerly. I was given to understand that it would sell about 7,000 a year now. I think that return shows a little more than that.

Q.—When was it Gage came into it?

A.—I cannot tell you exactly. The agreement we have at the house; I have not got it here.

Q.—I asked you to bring any agreement that you had?

A.—Well, I overlooked that. I could get it for you.

Q.—Can you give me a reliable synopsis of it?

A.—Of the agreement?

Q.—Yes?

A.—No, I do not know that I can. I was not a party to the making of the agreement. It was made up by the manager of the wholesale department at that time, and while I could have brought the agreement—I could have got it and brought it if I had thought of it, coming into this. I would not consider that would come in here, you know.

Q.—Have you any agreement in respect to any of your other books extorted from you in this way?

A.—Yes, I think the first edition of the Primary Latin Book.

Q.—Who is that with?

A.—With Gage.

Q.—The same agreement?

A.—Yes, on the same principle, taking advantage of that clause.

Q.—In the contract?

A.—Yes.

Q.—Can you tell me when that was made?

A.—Yes, I think they were made at the same time but that would be some years ago, I should think five or six years ago at the least.

Q.—What price did you offer to sell that to Gage in sheets, these books?

A.—I suppose I should answer that question, should I?

Q.—We want to see what the cost of the books were, you know?

A.—Well, you see it is a little different proposition from the ordinary handling of a book. You know they come in as a publisher there and they supply the paper. It does not seem to me that should be.

Q.—Did you make him an offer to sell them in sheets before he made the present agreement with you?

A.—No, I think not.

Q.—He made the offer to you?

.A.—They came to us with the ultimatum that we were either to allow them—they would publish the book and set up their own plates or make terms with them. I was not a party to any of the conversation with them. It was all conducted by the manager of the department in which these books were handled, and I cannot give you very much information. I know they came in, and that is the most of my knowledge of it.

The CHAIRMAN: I think that is a proper question to be taken into account in ascertaining the price of these books, what you can afford to sell in that shape for.

Q.—It is done under compulsion, and he does not supply the paper, and I do not see how it would hurt you? It must be a rock bottom price?

A.—We had to give a very low price.

Q.—It is a question of press work?

A.—Yes. Well, the price is not the same now, I may say, as it was at the time the agreement was made.

Q.—Has his heart softened since?

A.—No, it has hardened; rather the hearts of our working men have hardened, they extort more wages. We had to raise their wages.

Q.—Can you give us the present price?

A.—I think it is $6\frac{1}{2}$ cents a copy.

Q.—That is for the Primary Latin book?

A.—No, that is Temperance & Physiology. I do not know the price of the Primary Latin book. I do not know what we are supplying for.

Q.—That is just the press work?

A.—Well, the press work and the royalty. The royalty is $2\frac{1}{2}$ cents.

Q.—How many of an edition would that apply to, how large?

A.—I think they order them in lots of 5,000.

The CHAIRMAN: They furnish the paper?

A.—Yes, and then they bind the book.

Mr. STAUNTON: Do you pay the royalty?

A.—Yes, we are under agreement with the author as to that. We cannot sell without paying him the royalty.

Q.—You give them the books at $6\frac{1}{2}$ cents, and they supply the paper?

A.—Yes.

Q.—Then these books that are authorized by the Government, you profess to publish them up to the standard prescribed under the contract?

A.—Yes.

Q.—There is no reason why you should make them above that?

A.—No.

Q.—Does that contract allow you to publish those books without tapes?

A.—Well, I will tell you, when the contract was first made on the Temperance & Physiology, and possibly the Algebra—I am not sure of the Algebra—we had all our books sewn by hand, and I think up to the time of the introduction of machine sewing, the tape or cord, the cord I think, was used—I do not think we ever used tape; but in machine sewn you cannot use either a tape or a cord, you understand.

Mr. COOPER: You can use a tape, not a cord?

A.—I am sure of that point.

Q.—Do you bind these yourself?

A.—We bind our own edition.

Q.—You have a binder?

A.—Oh, yes.

Q.—Your machine is not a machine where you put on the tape in a book bound in that way?

A.—Well, now, I do not know whether with the machine sewing we could put a tape on or not. I am not a practical enough man to tell that. I do not think we could.

Q.—The contract provided where they are sewn they shall also have the tapes?

A.—I think they did. I think the original contract calls for cord or tape.

Q.—Did the Inspector let them go through?

A.—They have been sent to the Department year by year, samples of all our new editions and no exception has ever been taken by the Department to this style in which they have been bound, so far as I am aware, I never have heard any.

Q.—You do not mean to say you have not been living up to that contract?

A.—We certainly have not in that respect; since using the machine we have not used the cord. Hand sewing has practically gone out. It is used only on job work or perhaps on leather work.

Mr. STAUNTON: Taking your High School Algebra—we have not had much on High School books—what do you sell that at, to the trade?

A.—Twenty-five per cent. off the retailer.

Q.—Seventy-five cents?

A.—Seventy-five cents, 25 off that.

Q.—Twenty-five off 75?

A.—Yes.

Q.—If you had a contract to supply that book exclusively to Educational Institutions of all kinds in which it is used that are under Government control, and you had a provision that the Government would pay you for all the books you manufacture, you to send these books out to any part of the Province where they were required, in such lots as those places required, at what price would you undertake to sell them to such a contractor as the Government?

A.—That is really a difficult question to answer. It would depend something upon the quantity of books I suppose.

Q.—You know what the number of books is, that are used—you know the demand for those books?

A.—We would give a good discount off.

Q.—I suppose you would arrive at your profit by adding it to your cost?

A.—Yes.

Q.—What percentage would you add to your cost, that would be perhaps the way to arrive at it?

A.—Well, I do not know, I should imagine one-third.

Q.—Remember you have got a customer who never fails to pay, you have got no bad debts, and no accounts to send out, you have got no left overs. You have got an ideal condition for the manufacturing of books?

A.—Yes, but then, of course, you can hardly disassociate one book from all the others in that way. You have to add to the original cost, the manufacturer's cost, a certain percentage for general expenses of the business you know. I should myself if I were making the book be well content at an advance of one-third on the manufacturer's cost.

Q.—What is the manufacturer's cost of that book?

A.—Our present cost on the last edition.

Q.—I am speaking of the High School Algebra?

A.—Would you include royalty?

Q.—Yes?

A.—Our cost of the last edition of that book, that is the old edition, we have got a later one—inclusive of royalty was 31¾ cents.

Q.—Exclusive of royalty?

A.—Inclusive.

Q.—What was the royalty?

A.—Eleven and a quarter cents, a royalty of 15% on the retail price.

Q.—It would cost you?

A.—Twenty and one-half cents.

Q.—Do I understand from you when you say it cost you that, it cost you that as a publisher or a manufacturer?

A.—That is the cost at which it is charged to the department that handles the book, by our printing department. That is a lower cost, of course, I should say, considerably, than it would be supplied to an outsider. That is what we consider our cost in the book.

Q.—Do you allow your printing department any profit?

A.—They certainly have some profit. They would have to have it, or they would be shown at a loss.

Q.—Do you not allow them some profit when they are selling to you as when they are selling to outsiders?

A.—No, not within the house.

Q.—You cannot keep a separate account?

A.—No, it is merely a matter if they are charging it up to the retail department or the wholesale department, they would give us a better price on the work than they would if they were supplying it to an outsider.

Q.—What would you supply those to Morang for, or any other reputable house?

A.—I could not give you the price. These prices are settled by the printing department. ·

Q.—That means any way the actual cost plus some profit to the printing department?

A.—Yes, some profit in the printing department, enough to cover their share of what is the expenses of the business and so on.

Q.—Then you want one-third more for handling them as publishers, one-third more of the 20½ cents?

A.—I would say we call our cost 31¾ cents. That would be one-third on that.

Q.—You want 10¼ cents on that for handling it?

A.—Yes.

Q.—That would make the price 42 cents?

A.—Yes.

Q.—What do you get for it now?

A.—Seventy-five cents is the retail.

Q.—You get for it?

A.—Well, if we are selling to the retail—

Q.—What is the net price to the retail?

A.—One-quarter off 75, that is 56¼ cents.

Q.—That is what you sell it at?

A.—Yes.

Mr. COOPER: Under the arrangement as stipulated by Mr. Staunton, you would be willing to sell at 42 cents?

A.—Oh, yes.

Q.—Or a difference in preference of this method of about 15 cents?

A.—Yes.

Mr. STAUNTON: Does anybody else publish that Algebra of yours?

A.—No, I think not.

Q.—I thought you did say that you were the sole publishers of these books, except that you allowed under the agreement you had made, Gage to publish two of them?

A.—Yes, that is right.

Q.—May I take it that those other books of yours would be sold to the Government at the same rate of profit, one-third on the cost?

A.—Yes, that would apply to all.

Q.—To all your publications?

A.—Yes.

Q.—Will you take the next one and tell me what that costs?

A.—The History of Canada by Clement. That costs us exclusive of royalty 28½ cents.

Q.—And it sells at how much to the public?

A.—At 50 cents.

Q.—So that you would sell it to the retailer at 37½ cents?

A.—To sell it to the retailer at ¼ off 50.

Q.—Thirty-seven and one-half cents?

A.—Yes.

Q.—They are all sold on the same arrangement?

A.—Yes.

Q.—You are going to charge the Government that much if you sell to them?

A.—We would like to get it.

Q.—At that rate it would amount to that?

A.—Of course, there is this, Mr. Staunton, that that price on the History is given on a comparatively small edition. If it is a large edition we are printing now, if we get an offer from the Government to purchase a larger edition we could, of course, afford to give it at a less price, and of course we would give it, I think, considerably below.

Mr. COOPER: The Copp, Clark Co. publishes this as well as the other?

A.—Yes.

Mr. STAUNTON: About 20,000 was the first, and now it is down to three?

A.—Our last edition I think was 2,000 copies.

Q.—Then you are figuring on an edition of 2,000 copies?

A.—Yes.

Q.—If you had the whole of it—The Copp, Clark apparently have 2,000 more copies?

A.—They have half of the market.

Q.—On a 4,000 tender could you do any better?

A.—We could, but I do not know how much though. We could do better.

Q.—Is it authorized to anybody else, this History?

A.—Clement's? Yes, it is, I think it is stated on the title page. The Departments of Education of the different Provinces agreed, in order to get up a national history to give a prize for the best history, and in the competition, Clement, the author of this book, was awarded the prize, and his book was published, and the publishing of it was given to Copp, Clark Co. and ourselves.

Q.—Have you two got it for the whole Dominon?

A.—Well, the Ontario Government cannot give us that.

Q.—Have you got it as a matter of fact?

A.—No, the book has been authorized but that is all, you know. We have exclusive right. I do not think there is any province where this is the only history used. You see in Ontario it has rivals.

Q.—Do you sell this book in any other Province?

A.—Yes.

Q.—For schools?

A.—Yes.

Q.—You must get out a much larger edition than this?

A.—No, that is our edition bona fide. While it had merit enough to win the prize, it apparently has not won the favor of the teacher or the parent or the scholar. The book has not a very large sale, and it is decreasing.

Q.—At the time it was published the critics were rather severe on it?

A. Yes, a good many of them criticised it as dry.

Q.—What other province do you sell it in besides Ontario?

A.—More or less in all of them. I think scattered orders from all. I think so.

Q.—It is not a popular book. It is not a book upon which we could ground anything as to circulation.

A.—No, it is a book with a decreasing sale. It is dying out.

Q.—Did you get this book by competition?

A.—The Clement History?

Q.—Yes.

A.—No, it was the gift of the Government.

Q.—To you two firms?

A.—Yes, a favor. We always look upon those things as going somewhat by favor.

Q.—Now take your next book?

A.—I have the Primary Latin book here. This is not one on which a fair basis can be made either. We have only half of the market, and now I think the policy of the Department is to put it into two separate books. I do not expect that edition will continue in much of a sale in Ontario.

Q.—What is the one you have in your hand?

A.—That is Miss Weaver's Canadian History.

Q.—Has that much of a sale?

A.—I think the sale of this is going to grow.

Q.—What is the cost of that?

A.—Exclusive of royalty it costs us 20¼ cents. I think there is a trifle more than that. When I was getting the cost together I could not get the exact cost of the colored map in front. It would be very little over 20¼ cents.

Q.—And the royalty?

A.—The royalty is usually 10 per cent. That includes the royalty, 65 cents. It is a 50 cent book.

Q.—The net cost is 15¼ cents.

A.—Exclusive of royalty. It might perhaps come to 16 cents.

Q.—What do you sell it to the trade at?

A.—At one quarter off 37½.

Q.—You would want about 36 cents from the Government on your sale?

A.—Yes, on that basis.

Mr. Cooper: Then on this book you are making about 100 per cent. profit?

A.—We are making a better profit on that than on others. You see in the others the Government started the books going and dictated the price.

Mr. Staunton: Now, why did you not apply to be authorized to publish, or have a contract rather to publish the books Gage was interested in when he came at you with this proposition, or did you do so?

A.—No, we did not.

Q.—You did not try to fight him with his own fire?

A.—No, we do not go in for that sort of business. We did not like it at the time, and it is a matter we would not have done with anybody else. They were the only firm that came to us in that way, and we did not retaliate on them.

Q.—You turned the other cheek?

A.—Yes, we kept our cheeks both to ourselves.

Q.—You did not do it?

A.—No.

Q.—You did not try to get their business?

A.—Not any of the other Public School books.

Q.—Did you ever try to get the Readers?

A.—We did.

Q.—When did you try to?

A.—When the old contract, the first contract was expiring.

Q.—What steps did you take?

A.—I think a personal application was all.

Q.—To the Government?

A.—To the Minister of Education.

Q.—What was the result?

A.—Well, the same result as with Mr. Morang. We failed to get it.

Q.—Did he give you these others as a sop?

A.—No, I do not think so. I do not think any of those came in in any relation to the Readers.

Q.—You do not mean to say you made any deal?

A.—No, you are speaking from his standpoint, that is the Government's standpoint?

Q.—He did not say I cannot give you the Readers so I will give you these?

A.—No.

Q.—Did they say why you could not get the Readers?

A.—The only reason given was that the firms who had the first contract had possession of certain copyrights and that made it necessary for the Government to make a new agreement with them.

Q.—Did you suggest to the Government that they might cut out these copyright selections?

A.—I do not know whether that suggestion was made or not.

Q.—It is a natural one?

A.—Yes. What we thought was that the Government should not have allowed themselves to be held up by a combination. There were two or three reasons for that if I may be allowed to make the statement. One was this, I had it in my mind at any rate, that since those Readers were first prepared Canadian literature had made advances and a new set of Readers more up-to-date and with selections from our own authors should have been prepared, and then we thought that the Government would have been safe in taking the onus, the responsibility, of getting a new set of Readers no matter what the cost, rather than place themselves in the humiliating position of being held up as they were. The Minister of Education at the time, Mr. Ross, professed very warm indignation at the position he found himself in, and he professed to be helpless in the matter. Those were the reasons that we thought. Then, of course, there was the further argument that those firms had had the Readers and they were considered a good property by the publishers, they had them for a term of years, and it was time that the outside house who had been looking on while they were picking the plums should have some share in it. We wanted to get into it, but not to get in as a part to any combine, but to get in as one of any other publishing houses who might be given these Readers. The books were given round, of course. from one house to another apparently at the caprice of the Government and the choice of the Government, and we always had the position of suppliants, glad to get what we could get, and we considered that as an old publishing house we should have had some consideration. When it came to matters of Readers, the monopoly should not be continued to any special houses who had no special right to it, that other houses should be allowed in. That was particularly speaking our claim for recognization.

Q.—And the answer was, it had to be given exclusively to these people?

A.—Yes, when I say exclusively, allowance has to be made for a clause in the agreement. We could have gone in I think if we had chosen to take the risk of an action.

Q.—But the risk was not minimized to you in any way?

A.—No, I do not think so.

Q.—You were simply in this position if you wanted to get what you considered the right of other publishing houses in this country to tender in open competition for the books published by the Government you had to do it with this sword hanging over you, that you might be sued?

A.—Yes.

Q.—You did not think that was what the Government should have done?

A.—No, we did not.

Q.—Now do you think as a publisher that ten years ago the time had arrived for improving the Readers in this country? At all events beyond that Ontario series?

A.—I certainly do and particularly thought, and perhaps it occupied my mind more than anything else in regard to selections, I thought they should be more Canadian.

Q.—Did you voice that to the Government?

A.—I think so. We had interviews with them.

Q.—And did you give them any samples of your books to show them what was going on in the publishing world?

A.—No, we did not.

Q.—I suppose the Department of Education would be at least familiar with up-to-date publications?

A.—They should be.

Q.—Were there not at that time many publications far in advance of those in your judgment?

A.—As Readers?

Q.—Yes?

A.—Well, I do not know that I could say that. These at that time were the only Readers. I do not think there was any other Canadian Reader.

Q.—You do not know anything about the American?

A.—No, I did not examine those at that time.

Q.—You heard it said to-day that ten years ago or twelve years ago they had contemporaries of these books in the U. S.?

A.—I was not here when that evidence was given. Of course, a new set of Readers prepared ten years ago would evidently be better than they would be ten years before that because an advance had been made in the art of printing.

Q.—I suppose as a matter of fact you would have been made in the art of printing.

Q.—I suppose, as a matter of fact, you would have been content to enter into a contract as onerous as this existing with the publishing houses on a new edition?

A.—Certainly we would.

Q.—So that the Government would have been recouped for all expenses in time?

A.—Certainly.

Q.—The country would get a new set of Readers and a better set of Readers and would not cost any more and ultimately it would be alright.

A.—The Government would have to meet I suppose some adverse criticism, parents who did not relish having to supply their children with new Readers, but that would only be temporary.

Q.—They could give reasonable notice when these books were coming in?

A.—They could.

Q.—They could make rules in the Educational Department so that it would not press hard on the pupils?

A.—Yes, the same as any other change in text books.

Q.—One of the necessities of education is to change the books at least within every 100 years?

A.—Yes.

. The CHAIRMAN: Of course the number of Readers sold in the province is very much larger than any other book?

A.—Yes, I think they were more than any book.

Q.—That was a trifle compared with the large transactions, and your garded by the other publishers as the best thing going in that line, more profit?

A.—Oh yes, it was regarded I think—I think the feeling of the trade generally, the publishers, was that the Readers were the prize of all the school books.

Q.—And that these three publishers had a snap in publishing them on the terms on which they had them?

A.—Yes, they had their plates, and simply had to continue printing as they had been.

Q.—About the end of the first ten years your house desired to come in?

A.—I suppose under the agreement they had to pay a certain amount, I think $3,000.

Q.—That was a trifle compared with the large transactions, and your house was anxious amongst other houses to get a share of the large profits that these other three fellows were getting?

A.—Yes.

Q.—And you were led to believe that owing to the position that these three houses held respecting the copyright transaction they were masters of the situation, and you could not get it.

A.—Yes, they had the whip hand so to speak.

The CHAIRMAN: It seems now that that was not the fact at all.

13 T. B.

EVIDENCE OF MR. GEORGE M. ROSE.

Mr. STAUNTON, Examiner:

Q.—Mr. Rose, your name is?
A.—George M. Rose.
Q.—What is your connection with the Hunter, Rose Company?
A.—President and Manager—Manager.
Q.—How long have you been manager?
A.—Three years.
Q.—How long have you been in the printing and publishing and book business?
A.—Four years.
Q.—And are you a practical bookmaker?
A.—No, I am not.
Q.—You are the business man, but I suppose you have a good knowledge?
A.—Yes, pretty fair.
Q.—You publish some of the authorized books of the province?
A.—Yes.
Q.—Have you got the books here?
A.—Yes, I have got them. (Produces books.)
Q.—Discuss the books in the order which you desire yourself. Which one will you take first?
A.—Take the Public School Euclid and Algebra.
Q.—That was authorized in September, 1894?
A.—Yes.
Q.—And you got an agreement with the Government for five years from the date of the agreement on the 31st January, 1894, and one year's notice in writing to be cancelled, expired 31st January, 1899. Are you still publishing it?
A.—We are still publishing it.
Q.—Under the old agreement?
A.—Under the old agreement.
Q.—That book retails at 25 cents, and had 156 pages in it. Does it comply with the contract as to binding?
A.—As far as I know it does.
Q.—I see it has no tapes and it is sewn. The contract usually provides that it shall have tapes?
A.—This book has no tapes; it is the ordinary case book.
Q.—What does that book cost you?
A.—Of course this is a small edition of this book that we print. Our sales last year were 1,500 books, and we printed 2,000.
Q.—It has kept about the same?
A.—Yes, it is a small seller.
Q.—It started 2,000 and last year it was 1,500?
A.—Yes.
Q.—What does that cost you?
A.—Eleven cents.
Q.—Is that inclusive of royalty?
A.—No, royalty two and a half cents.
Q.—Does that allow manufacturer's profit?
A.—It allows us the profit from one department to another; there is a printing and binders' profit in there.

13a T. B.

Q.—What do you sell that to the trade at?

A.—At 25 and ten off.

Q.—That is 18 cents is it not?

A.—About 18 cents.

Q.—If you were selling the whole edition to the Government and shipped them to different parts of the Province as required, without any risk of loss, bad debts, getting your money monthly, what price could you afford to sell that at?

A.—I would not like to sell that book any cheaper than we sell it to the jobbers. I do not think that is enough profit at that. I think that is selling them pretty close.

Q.—It is in competition in schools with other books?

A.—Yes.

Q.—Why does it not crowd the others out?

A.—I do not know.

Q.—It is cheap?

A.—It is cheap. It does not sell. The sale of the book is about dead now. It has not sold this year.

Q.—Was there any competition for the sale of this book?

A.—I do not think so. It was not connected with the firm at the time it was authorized and I could not tell.

Q.—You do not know anything about how you got the contract?

A.—No.

The CHAIRMAN: Is there any other public school book?

A.—No.

Mr. STAUNTON: What is the difference; I am told there is a substantial difference in the cost of binding a book with wire or stitching?

A.—Well, take for instance a larger book, you can figure it easier. Now, I should say on this Reader the difference between binding that by wire—

Q.—Which Reader?

A.—That is the High School Reader. Say a 500 page book would cost about half a cent to sew. Now, to wire stitch that, it would cost about seventy-five cents to stitch a thousand of those books.

Q.—To wire stitch it?

A.—Yes, on a thousand.

Q.—Seventy-five cents a thousand against $5 a thousand?

A.—Pretty near half a cent.

Q.—$5 versus 75 cents?

A.—Say a dollar.

Q.—One dollar for wire and five dollars for stitching?

A.—Yes, a thin book would cost only about 75 cents a thousand.

Q.—A book the size of the Ontario Reader, what would you say about wire stitching that?

A.—That is what I say—

Q.—That is not the Ontario Reader you are looking at. Take the Fourth Reader, what would be the difference in the cost of wire stitching and sewing that?

Q.—Sewing the Fourth Reader would cost about $3.15 a thousand books to sew, and about 75 cents to wire stitch.

Q.—$3.15 as against 75 cents?

A.—Yes.

Q.—It looked in the contract to a novice reading the contract as though that were the more expensive process. They allow them to leave out the tape?

A.—More expensive.

Q.—It said where they wire stitched them they could leave the tapes out?

A.—That makes it cheaper.

Q.—You would approve wire stitching a book?

A.—No, not in any case book.

Q.—You would in a pamphlet?

A.—Yes, I think in a saddle backed book something like this; that is plenty good enough for a copy book. In fact that is stitched that way.

Q.—But it is not allowable in your judgment?

A.—Not in any cloth case book.

Q.—What are the objections to it?

A.—Well, I think the chief objection is to the book opening. The book will not open. (Illustrates.) The case is more apt to break when in a wire stitched book.

Q.—Take the next book?

A.—The High School Arithmetic.

Q.—Is that book published?

A.—Yes, it has been a good seller. It has dropped now a little. We sold 4,200 copies last year. It is in competition now though.

Q.—It is in competition now with another book in the same field?

A.—Yes.

Q.—Say we eliminate the other book and give you the whole field, I presume it would be about double your present number?

A.—I suppose.

Q.—They get about half?

A.—Yes.

Q.—If you had the whole field what would you want above its cost to sell it to the Government under the conditions I have described?

A.—Above its cost?

Q.—Yes?

A.—Well, if I was doing business with the Government I would not want to do business for less than thirty-five per cent. at the very least, and as much more as I could.

Q.—About one-third?

A.—Yes.

Q.—You would want one-third?

A.—Fully one-third.

Q.—What is the cost of that book?

A.—That book costs us, paying the royalty, twenty-five and a half cents.

Q.—And sells at?

A.—We get forty and a half cents for that.

Q.—What is the royalty?

A.—Six cents.

Q.—You want about thirty-three cents?

A.—No, on small lines of school books where you are doing business in a general way and it is part of your own business, $33\frac{1}{2}$ per cent. is not enough.

Q.—Well, what is enough? You are giving the evidence. You want 35 per cent.?

A.—I would want from 35 to 50 per cent. on our small line of school books.

Q.—What do you consider a small line?

A.—Well, we have only got five books and they are High School books and the sales are small.

Q.—Up to 10,000 or 15,000—

Mr. Cooper: If he had ten or fifteen he could afford to sell them at a lower price I understand him to mean. This book has a limited sale.

WITNESS: Where we are only handling five or six High School books as part of our business. It is not the whole of your business you know; thirty-five to fifty per cent. profit.

Q.—If you had a large line about 33 1-3?

A.—I think about thirty-five per cent.

Q.—What would be the selling price for that book?

A.—Sixty cents.

. (High School Arithmetic.)

Q.—What is the next book you have?

A.—The High School Reader.

Q.—What does that sell at?

A.—Fifty cents.

Q.—And what would it cost you?

A.—Twenty-two cents.

Q.—Including royalty?

A.—There is no royalty on that.

Q.—You would sell that at?

A.—We sell that at 40½ cents to the trade now.

Q.—What would you sell that to the Government at under the same conditions?

A.—We could sell that book for 32 cents.

Q.—What is your next one?

A.—The High School Euclid. That book cost us 22 cents, a royalty of 7½ cents.

Q.—Is that included in the 22?

A.—Yes.

Q.—Sell that at the same price?

A.—We could sell that at the same price as the Reader.

Q.—What did you say the royalty was?

A.—7½ cents. That is fifteen per cent.

Q.—What is the next one?

A.—The French Grammar and Reader, the High School Grammar, that is a $1 book.

Q.—Cost you?

A.—Thirty-three cents, including ten cents royalty.

Q.—Have you got the exclusive field for that?

A.—No, we divide that with Copp, Clark Co.

Q.—Is that a wire stitched book?

A.—No, they all are sewn books.

The CHAIRMAN: What do you say you sell that to the trade at?

A.—Sixty-seven and a half cents.

Q.—You sell it now at 67½?

A.—Yes.

Mr. COOPER: And it costs you 33?

A.—Yes.

Q.—You are making one hundred per cent. on it?

A.—Yes.

Q.—Small sales?

A.—3,500.

Mr. STAUNTON: That is the last of your books?

A.—Yes.

Q.—Do you know that the Government on the 21st March, 1904, asked you to give a list of the copyright selections and extracts from authors used in your authorized text books?

A.—No.

Q.—I have it here; you were asked to and you did furnish it. Do you know whether it is correct?

A.—What was the date?

Q.—In 1904? That would come under your notice?

A.—Yes, I do not remember.

Q.—"Yours of the 19th inst., etc. We now beg to enclose you list which we trust will give you the necessary information?"

A.—Yes, I remember.

Q.—You did not scruple to give that to the Government?

A.—No, I wrote that.

Q.—It would not injure your business, would it?

A.—No, not at all.

Q.—You were quite willing to give it to them any time?

A.—Yes.

Q.—And it gives all the particulars. Can you tell me what those cost you?

A.—No, I could not.

Q.—Have you any doubt about Mr. Saul's and Mr. Morang's evidence that those can be secured from five shillings to a guinea?

A.—Yes, I think a great many of these could be secured for commission only.

Q.—Did you ever have any interference with your publications by any of these three publishers?

A.—Well, not to my personal knowledge, what I have gathered from the correspondence in the office.

Q.—What have you gathered from the correspondence in the office?

A.—I understand that Mr. Gage came to the office one time and wanted to make an arrangement to publish the High School Reader.

Q.—What did he want to do? What does the correspondence show? I have asked you to produce any correspondence of that kind?

A.—This is in 1901. It shows he made an offer to publish the book to the Minister of Education.

Q.—You had the contract?

A.—Yes.

Q.—And he wanted to get a piece of it?

A.—Yes.

Q.—And he made an offer to the Minister, and asked the Minister to let him have the contract?

A.—Yes, and then he afterwards—

Q.—And after having gone that far he came to you?

A.—Came to us and offered to withdraw this offer, provided we entered into a partnership arrangement with him in the book. We refused to enter into the proposal, and we laid the correspondence before the Minister, and told him we would oppose him in every way if he went further, and as far as I can see, Mr. Gage dropped the matter.

Q.—Have you got the letters there?

A.—Yes.

(Produces letter of November 21st, 1895.)

Q.—What other correspondence have you got?

A.—I have no other correspondence on that matter. It evidently dropped.

Q.—Did it just happen then that somebody came and threatened you for pirating certain authors?

A.—No, the arrangement was made with the Minister about the Readers. There was no trouble about it.

Q.—Did anybody ever trouble you for using selections?

A.—No.

Q.—Did you use them without permission?

A.—No, we had permission; the Department had permission for most of those selections.

Q.—Do you know that that book contains selections that permission was never gotten for?

A.—No, I do not know.

Q.—I do not know either, I thought you might. Have you any other correspondence now that comes within your subpœna, to produce anything that throws any light on it? What other letters have you got?

A.—These are copies of returns we made to the Government.

Q.—Does anybody else publish that High School Reader, but you?

A.—No.

Q.—It appears in this contract that Gage had the right to publish the High School Reader in 1896?

A.—I was not aware of it. That would be at the expiration of the first contract.

Q.—Yes. They never published it anyway if they did get the right?

A.—No, it was in 1891 they wanted the plates; that was years before.

The CHAIRMAN: Did you ever try to acquire the rights to publish these Readers with them?

A.—Not to my knowledge.

Mr. STAUNTON: Do you know that Gage tried to get you to enter into arrangement to publish your High School Arithmetic?

A.—I believe he did try to get in on that, but the authors would not have anything to do with him.

Q.—What do you know about it?

A.—That is all I know.

Q.—Did he threaten you on that?

A.—Yes, I think he tried to coerce there.

Q.—Here is a letter of March 3rd, to W. J. Gage & Co., by you: (Reads):—

TORONTO, March 3rd, 1897.

MESSRS. W. J. GAGE & Co.,
     City.

DEAR SIRS,—We have again looked into the matter of the High School Arithmetic, and have decided that we cannot improve the offer made you, namely, 20 cents for sheets.

Yours truly,
G. M. ROSE & SONS.
(Signed)   D. A. ROSE.

Q.—He wanted to buy the sheets from you in the same way as he wanted to buy them from Mr. Caswell?

A.—Yes.

Q.—And you put the price to him at twenty cents?

A.—Yes.

Q.—Can you tell me what he offered to give you for them?

A.—No, I do not know.

Q.—Then there is another one of March 3rd, 1897? (Reads):

TORONTO, March 3rd, 1897.

MESSRS. G. M. ROSE & SONS,
        City.

GENTLEMEN,—We regret to learn that you are not able to arrange with us on a satisfactory basis for sheets of High School Arithmetic, as we consider our proposition an eminently fair one. We must, therefore, withdraw from our proposal to apply for this book only, and now make application for the right to publish the High School Arithmetic, High School French Reader, High School French Grammar, and Public School Euclid and Algebra.

Yours faithfully.

That was giving another turn to the screw?
A.—Yes.
Q.—Did you wilt at that?
A.—I do not think so.
Q.—March 5th, 1897, they wrote to Mr. Ross. This is the second time they came after you?
(Reads letter):

TORONTO, March 5th, 1897.

HON G. W. ROSS, LL.D.,
        Minister of Education,
                City.

DEAR SIR,—The enclosed letter we have written in such form that you may show it, if you desire, to Messrs. G. M. Rose & Sons.

While we should prefer to go right in for all their books, yet in deference to your wishes for an amicable settlement we will close the matter with Messrs. Rose & Sons, for the Arithmetic only at 12 cents, if they can meet us on this point without further delay. We have no doubt at all that on presenting the case to them as you kindly proposed to do, that the matter can be closed up in a few minutes.

We have the honor to be,
        Sir,
        Your obedient servants,
        THE W. J. GAGE COMPANY, LIMITED.
                (Signed) W. P. GUNDY.

So they were sending Mr. Ross down to talk you up?
A.—I suppose.
Q.—Then this is the enclosed letter.
(Reads.)

TORONTO, March 5th, 1897.

Private.
HON. G. W. ROSS, LL.D.,
        Minister of Education,
                City.

DEAR SIR,—We regret to advise you that Messrs. G. M. Rose & Sons have declined to arrange with us for sheets of the High School Arithmetic, on anything like satisfactory terms.

We take the liberty of enclosing their letter, which states that the best offer they can make is 20 cents per book for sheets.

We enclose copy of our reply declining to pay this price, and stating that we must now apply to you for the right to publish not only the High

School Arithmetic, but the High School French Grammar, High School French Reader, and the Public School Euclid and Algebra.

Our letter was only sent them after we had exhausted every means of securing an amicable arrangement with them.

We offered to pay Messrs. Rose & Sons 12 cents per book for sheets, we supplying the paper.

The royalty is 6 cents: the cost of printing, at their own estimate, 1¾ cents, we, therefore, offered to pay them over three times their cost for printing. The offer which we have made them is not only a liberal one, but is practically on the same basis as the arrangement made with the Methodist Book Room, and the Copp, Clark Co., for sheets, viz., about 20% of the retail price. The royalty charged in all these cases being 10%.

The two Latin Books published by the Methodist Book Room, and Copp, Clark Co., retail at $1.00. We pay them 20 cents, and 20½ cents each respectively, for sheets.

Public School History retails at 30 cents. We pay 6 cents for sheets.

In view of these facts, you will, we are sure, agree with us that our offer to Messrs. Rose & Sons, is one that they should accept without hesitation.

We have lost so much time over this matter that we now prefer to make formal application for their other books (open to publication), above referred to, copyright of which is vested in the Department.

We informed Messrs. Rose & Sons, that we had arranged for some other books on a basis of price similar to that offered to them, but we did not tell them with whom we had arranged, nor for what books.

We have the honor to be,

Sir,

Your obedient servants,

THE W. J. GAGE Co.

(Signed) W. P. GUNDY,

Sec'y.-Treas.

Did the Minister have any more effect on you than anybody else?

A.—Evidently not. I think the matter was dropped.

Q.—Then there was a memo enclosed:

(Reads):

Memo.

Giving comparison of prices, showing what High School Arithmetic costs us at present from Rose & Co., and what it would cost if sheets were purchased at the price he proposes to give them to us. You will see that there is only a difference of some three cents.

Retail price of the book 60c. less dis. of 40% makes the book cost us .... 36c.

We have purchased at the above discount, viz., 40%, (the last lot was not quite so good, viz., 25, 5 and 2½%.

Price books would cost us, if we purchased sheets at his quotation.

Sheets .... .20

Paper, (supplied by us) .... .05

Binding book, per copy .... .08
                                                      ———
                                                      .33

Purchased in regular way costs 36 cents.

Q.—Now, the last one is this to the Hon. G. W. Ross, from Gage & Co.

(Reads):

TORONTO, March 26, 1897.

Hon. G. W. Ross, LL.D.,
    Minister of Education,
        City.

DEAR SIR,—Referring to our conversation of last evening with reference to a compromise with Rose, it seems to us that if we are to pay Mr. Rose 25 or 30% (that is 15 cents we furnishing the paper) more than has been paid to either the Methodist Book Room, or the Copp, Clark Co., for books which were controlled by them under precisely similar agreements to that relating to the High School Arithmetic we should have an arrangement with him which would cover at least one other of his books, viz., the High School French Grammar.

For the reasons given last night, there is no doubt whatever that under an arbitration he cannot secure more than the price we have offered for the High School Arithmetic sheets, viz., 12 cents. We would at the same time be able to secure the High School French Reader, French Grammar and other books.

With a view to a quiet settlement, however, that would be approved of by you and be acceptable to Rose, we are willing to forego any advantages that might come to us from an arbitration, paying Mr. Rose twenty-five per cent. more than we can secure under that method of settlement for the Arithmetic, and take one other only of his books instead of his list.

We have the honour to be,
        Sir,
    Your obedient servants,
            THE W. J. GAGE COMPANY, LIMITED.
            (Signed)   W. P. GUNDY.

A.—Yes.

Q.—Do you know of any other correspondence besides that?

A.—No, I have not found any correspondence there.

Q.—And they did not succeed in inducing you to part with what you had?

A.—No.

Q.—You told the Government they could make such contracts as they chose, you were going to stick to your rights?

A.—Yes, that is what we gave them to understand.

Q.—You defied Mr. Gage in all his works?

A.—We thought we were stronger than Mr. Gage with the Minister.

EVIDENCE OF S. CASWELL, RECALLED.

Mr. COOPER: Mr. Caswell has been given permission to use his selections and I would like to get his practice.

Mr. COOPER: You publish a great many Canadian books and you give permission to publish a great many extracts.

A.—Where we have had application for extracts we have given the permission without asking compensation for it. We consider if the extract is made from one of our authors and has incision in the school books that it is the best possible advertisement—we have other publishers advertising our works and for that reason we have never made any charge.

Q.—Just allow them to use it?

A.—Yes.

Q.—That is the common practice in this country?

A.—It may be—some of the other publishers maybe refuse permission or would ask something for it. It has never been our custom. We have welcomed it rather than charged for it.

Mr. STAUNTON: I see you had some correspondence with the Minister about the Gage trouble. Mr. Briggs wrote a letter.

(Reads) :

TORONTO, July 2nd, 1896.

HON. GEORGE W. ROSS, LL. D.,
    Minister of Education,
        Education Department, City.

DEAR SIR,—Complying with your request I herewith put into the form of a letter our statement with regard to the "Algebra, Part I." for the publication of which application has been made to your Department by the W. J. Gage Company.

The point to be settled is the amount to be paid by the W. J. Gage Co. to us as an allowance for the cost of making the book. The portion of the clause in the agreement dealing with this matter reads as follows.:—

"Provided always, however, that any other publisher shall have the right of publication at any time beginning one year after the transfer of the copyright of the book to the Education Department as provided for in this Indenture, by permission to be obtained from the Department of Education for Ontario, subject to a royalty of ten per cent. on the retail price, as at first issued or afterwards reduced, of each and every copy of said book as long as republished and subject to a proper allowance to cover cost of authorship and other necessary expenses in the preparation of the said books, to be settled as hereinafter provided, and to be paid to the publishers of the first part, or at the option of the Department of Education for Ontario a sum in gross may be paid in lieu of such royalty, and allowance and expenses, the amount of said allowance and expenses or sum in gross *to be settled by the Minister of Education and the publisher of the first part......*''

I may say that we are now engaged in making a new set of plates for this work, which we have almost completed. We have thus had to set the book up twice and make two sets of stereoplates, not to mention the cost of repairs on the old plates from time to time, which was not inconsiderable. The composition and stereotyping, therefore, have cost us between twelve and thirteen hundred dollars, and towards this we feel that we are entitled to an allowance of at least $700, to be paid as per agreement by the house applying for publication of the book.

In this, of course, we are dealing only with the plates, not taking into account expenses. which might be termed incidental, but which would sum up to a considerable amount more, and if these incidental expenses be taken as I think they should be, I would like to ask for a larger sum than the $700. say, at least, $800.

Will you kindly give this matter careful consideration, and advise us of your decision as the matter rests with you as to the amount which the W. J. Gage Company should pay us before publishing the book and giving to the author the same royalty as ours, and oblige,

            Yours truly,

            (Signed)   WM. BRIGGS.

TORONTO, July 2ud, 1896.

HON. GEORGE W. ROSS, LL. D.,
　　　Minister of Education,
　　　　　Education Department, City.
HON. GEORGE W. ROSS, LL.D.,
　　DEAR DR. ROSS,—I will be very glad indeed to call upon you personally when you consider the matter named in my letter to you of this date *re* The W. J. Gage Company's seeking the joint publication of "Algebra, Part I."
　　　　　　　　　　　　　　I am, yours truly,

A.—Yes.

Q.—Did you get that $800?

A.—I do not think so; I do not think Gage got in on that. I think that was dropped. I do not think he got in on that book at all.

EVIDENCE OF MR. FREDERICK CARMAN.

Mr. STAUNTON, Examiner.

　Mr. STAUNTON: You wished to make a statement?

A.—I am in the retail business with Vannevar & Company and it was just to corroborate Mr. Britnell's evidence. There was one question Mr. Cooper asked Mr. Britnell as regards to the discount to us and as regards to the American price. Our invoices coming from the States have the price to us and the price to the home dealers, and our price as a rule is five per cent. better than the home price. Of course where a publisher sets a price at $1.00 a dollar book that costs us seventy-five cents and we have to sell it at eighty cents,—that is, the price that is set by the larger stores, we have to fall into line.

Q.—What you mean is, what is on the book does not indicate the true price?

A.—No.

Q.—That does not apply to the province, that has reference to Toronto?

A.—What do you mean? Of course if we send them out to anyone in the province we would sell it at the retail price.

Q.—That applies to Toronto dealers?

A.—The large stores send the books out and for that reason I am speaking for the booksellers of the province.

Q.—You have no authority to speak for booksellers throughout the province?

A.—What I meant was, of course, booksellers generally in the city—

Q.—Speaking for yourself?

A.—Yes, we get our books laid down to us here at twenty-five per cent. and of course we have to sell on a five per cent. margin which I think is not enough.

　Mr. COOPER: That only applies to about ten per cent. and the other ninety per cent. get their full profits?

A.—No.

　Mr. STAUNTON: Do you know what the booksellers outside of Toronto are selling these books at, as a matter of fact?

A.—No, I cannot say that I do except the daily press. I see by the daily press that the prices are cut in the larger cities, such as Ottawa and Winnipeg.

Q.—You have seen them advertised at cut prices?

A.—I have seen the advertisement of the departmental stores in the daily press.

Q.—You could not have seen them in Hamilton?

A.—I have seen in the trade journals that the prices were cut in these larger places. I have no personal knowledge except what I see in the press. What I mean by with regard to the departmental stores I see they advertise at twenty per cent. off and where they send out I understand they add the charges—add the postage.

Mr. STAUNTON: You mean to say the department stores do sell outside Toronto and, therefore, they must affect the market outside of Toronto for the retailer?

A.—Exactly.

Q.—Your present knowledge is confined to the city of Toronto?

A.—Yes.

Q.—And you corroborate what Mr. Britnell says?

A.—Exactly.

Q.—Is that what you want to tell us now?

A.—Well, just simply as a bookseller, of course, I think it would be to the advantage of the public generally—to the pupils— that there should be one price for the simple reason if the Parkdale pupils have to pay the full price in Parkdale for a certain book, and they can come down town and get it at twenty per cent. off—while if there was one price—

Q.—You think the hardship should be uniform?

A.—Exactly, I think all should be treated alike.

Mr. COOPER: You are like Mr. Britnell, you would be satisfied with a straight ten or fifteen per cent. that you would be sure of?

A.—I would. Of course you can understand we have no way of getting even on our stock; we have a great deal of dead stock and we do not know just when we are going to get rid of it. It is almost impossible to do business on a five per cent. basis.

4.15 p. m.   Commission adjourned sine die.

FIFTH SITTING, MONDAY, NOVEMBER 5TH, 1906.

EVIDENCE OF CHARLES S. FLEMING, NORWOOD, U. S.

G. L. STAUNTON, Examiner:

Q.—Your name is?

A.—Charles S. Fleming.

Q.—You live in Norwood. do you not?

A.—Yes, I live in Norwood, near Boston. Mass.

Q.—You are connected with the Norwood Press, are you not?

A:—Yes.

Q.—It is a sort of combination of printing and publishing houses is it not?

A.—Yes, publishing, printing, and binding,

Q.—In the Norwood Press you can produce a book from the manuscript to the binding, can you?

A.—Yes.

Q.—Your particular department is?

A.—Binding.

Q.—What is the name of your firm?

A.—E. Fleming & Company.

Q.—Is it a large or small business that you do?
A.—We call it a large business.
Q.—One of the largest in the United States, is it not?
A.—Yes, sir.
Q.—You have been connected with this business for how long?
A.—About twenty years.
Q.—And from your experience are you able, in your judgment, to give the cost of such books as the Ontario Readers and the other school books which have been submitted to you?
A.—From my own experience, I can give you the cost of binding, and, in the other departments, I have it from the head of each department.
Q.—Have you made an estimate of the cost of a number of books?
A.—Yes.
Q.—Have you made an estimate on the cost of Part I of the Ontario Reader?
A.—Yes.
Q.—And also of Part II?
A.—Yes.
Q.—In making your estimate, I understand you have figured what you would reproduce the various books at, on such paper, type, and in such binding as you believe they should have?
A.—Yes, sir.
Q.—You have not undertaken to give estimates upon what the books would cost in the condition which you found them—such books as these for instance, that are in use in Ontario?
A.—No, sir.
Q.—Well, we will take the first part of the First Reader. Have you an estimate of what that would cost?
A.—Yes, sir, I have an estimate on 100,000 copies as follows:—

Title of Book—First Reader, Part I, 100,000 Copies.

Cost of typesetting and plates, 64 pages at $1.75 per page.........	$112 00
210 reams 30x40 paper, at .04½ per lb..................................	661 50
Printing, 2 32 pp. forms	376 00
Binding, at five cents. per copy	5,000 00

Remarks:—Weight of paper, 70 lbs. to ream, cost of book, per book, 6 1-10c., exclusive of plates.

Q.—That is exclusive of the plates, is it not?
A.—Yes, that includes paper, press work and binding.
Q.—What is the next book you estimate on?
A.—The First Reader, Part II, on 50,000 copies.
Q.—What do you estimate per book?
A.—6 9-10c.
Q.—Show me the binding and style of book that you would produce for that money?
A.—Here are two specimen books (submits two books, "Graded Speller") for examiner's inspection.
Q.—You would produce a book in that style of binding, paper and all?
A.—No, not that paper, just that style of binding.
Q.—Would you not use that paper?
A.—Not for an illustrated book like the Readers.

Q.—Have you a sample of the paper you would use here?

A.—Yes. (Witness submits sample of paper.)

Q.—Whose paper is this?

A.—That is paper made by the "Madenock Mills" and it is about 73 lbs. to the ream; it would average about 70 lbs. to the ream, with sheets 30x40.

Q.—This paper would cost about 4½c. a pound, I suppose?

A.—Yes.

Q.—What is its composition?

A.—It is made of chemical wood pulp, with a fair percentage of cotton rag.

Q.—Is that, in your judgment, a good paper for this class of work?

A.—Yes, I should say it was. It is a paper that is used for the best class of work in that line by the best publishers.

Q.—So you put in your estimate the very best quality of paper for that business?

A.—Yes. You can put in a more expensive paper, but you do not require it.

Q.—The binding you have shown us in the "Graded Speller" differs from the Ontario binding, does it not?

A.—Yes.

Q.—Why do you think this binding is preferable?

A.—It is stronger and has more wear to it.

Q.—Has it a cloth hinge?

A.—Yes.

Q.—Is the material in the cover as good as the other?

A.—It did not cost as much per yard, but I think it will wear as well.

Q.—Is the Second Part of the Reader wire stitched?

A.—Yes.

Q.—Do you know the difference in the price between thread sewing and wire stitching?

A.—Not of this kind of wire stitching. It is something we never do, and we could not bind a book that way; they would not allow us to bind a book that way.

Q.—Are any of the books wire stitched in the United States?

A.—I have never seen one stitched in this manner.

Q.—It might be wire stitched all through the book?

A.—Yes, but that is not in use now to any extent at all. It would be considered practically absurd.

Q.—Well, in your experience, there are no books wire stitched in use in the schools of the United States?

A.—No, not now. It is not used by the best class of publishers.

Q.—Well then, what is wire stitching used for?

A.—Mostly cheap pamphlets. etc.

Q.—Take then the Second Book—the Second Reader. Tell me what it would cost per book?

A.—9 1-5c. per copy, exclusive of the plates.

Q.—You are speaking exclusively of plates all the time now, are you not?

A.—Yes.

Q.—What style of binding?

A.—I should bind that in the style of this book here (shows examiner copy of, "Silver Burdett Reader—Third Book.")

Q.—You class that binding differently from the binding on the Second Reader?

A.—This Second Reader is sewed with thread through the whole book in the same manner that the Speller is sewed.   The main difference is, that the book is what we call "backed," the edges are turned over on each side.   A tight backed book.   It makes it a little stronger to bind it that way.

Q.—Is it a more durable book than the other?

A.—It is a more durable book.

Q.—Could you bind a book like the "Ontario Reader"?

A.—I could not.

Q.—What do you mean by that answer,—that you could not?

A.—Well, we think we bind them better.

Q.—Have you any books in the public schools bound after the manner of the Ontario Readers?

A.—I have never seen any.

Q.—Is it a superior or inferior class of binding?

A.—We think it is inferior.

Q.—What is the next book?

A.—The Third Reader.

Q.—What does that figure at?

A.—At about 11 3-10c. per copy.

Q.—The retail price of that book is how much?

A.—30c. per copy.

Q.—Is the binding the same as the Second Reader?

A.—I would make the binding the same as the Second Reader.

Q.—And the paper?

A.—The same paper would be all right, I should judge.

Q.—Have you got a Fourth Book estimate?

A.—The Fourth Book I should bind in a still different style.

Q.—Well, give me what it would cost first?

A.—The Fourth Reader, I find, figures at 13¾c. per copy.

Q.—And sells retail at 40c.?

A.—Yes.

Q.—Now, tell me how you would bind that?

A.—Well, I would bind it in a different style to the other two.   It is a thicker book, and is too thick to be sewed in this manner.   It would have to be sewn on a machine that sews with thread—"Syth Sewn"—taken from the name of the machine.   It would, instead of the cloth hinges, be ribbed entirely around the first and last 16 pages.

Q.—It is shown on a book of this kind—"Tarr and McMurray's Geography." It is bound something like this book, is it not? (Showing witness sample book.)

A.—Yes.   It is also reinforced at the top and bottom—a head bandage, as we call it in the trade.   It is practically bound with cloth all round the edges.

Q.—Have you the total figures?

A.—I have not.

Mr. Cooper: Do you think, Mr. Fleming, that the binding of the Fourth Reader would be sufficiently strong by sewing ordinary mull without this cloth around the first and last sections?

A.—That cloth is of great benefit in the strain.   You could leave off the "head band," but I would not like to leave off the cloth.

Q.—Most of our books in this country are bound without the cloth. You think that would be rather wrong on our part to leave that off?

A.—Yes, I should say put it on.   It is not absolutely necessary, but the best books that are being bound in the United States contain it now.

Mr. STAUNTON: Well, Mr. Fleming, what have you figured on the other books?

A.—I have the cost of the printing and binding.

Q.—Let us take the Public School Arithmetic, what is your price?

A.—I figure that it would cost 9 4-5 cents. per copy.

Q.—Is it bound in the same style by you?

A.—No, I would figure on a book with reinforcements on front and bank and "head band."

Q.—Similar to the one you have in your hand now?

A.—No, similar to "Tar and McMurray's" Geography.

Q.—The same paper?

A.—No, it would not require so good a paper, as there are no "cuts" in it.

Q.—What would the paper cost?

A.—4½ cents. per pound in the United States.

Q.—You have an estimate for this book, the same as you have for the Readers?

A.—Yes, I will read it to you (witness reads following statement of cost):—

Title of Book—Arithmetic—50,000 Copies.

Cost of type setting and plates, 216 pages at $2.50 per page... $540 00
367 10-20 reams 30x40 paper, at .04¼ per pound 1,093 31
Printing, 7 32 pp. forms 511 00
Binding, at 6½ cents. per copy 3,250 00

Remarks:—Weight of paper, 70 lbs. to ream.   Cost of book, 9 4-5 cents. per copy, exclusive of plates.

Q.—That book costs how much retail, 25 cents?

A.—Yes.

Q.—Now, the next one, Mr. Fleming?

A.—The next one is the Public School Grammar.   I figure on the style of that the same as the Arithmetic—cloth reinforcements, first and last sections and head band, sewed with thread, 11½ cents. per copy.

Q.—It costs retail, how much?

A.—Twenty-five cents.

Q.—The same papers as the Readers?

A.—No, the same paper as the Arithmetic.

Q.—Have you another one?

A.—No, that is all.

Q.—All these books that you have figured on, Mr. Fleming, your estimates are based upon what you, as a publisher, would sell these books at,—that is to say, you included all the profit of the various trades interested up to, and inclusive of the publisher?

A.—Yes.

Q.—All the profits then are included in your estimates, are they not?

A.—Yes, the profit on the press work, binding and cost of paper is included.   If I was manufacturing books to sell to the retailer, I would be willing to sell at that price.

Q.—Now then, we will come back to the plates.   You have made an estimate on all the plates on all of these books, have you not?   What can they be produced for?   Just go on with them all?

14 T. B.

A.—-First Reader, Part I—Ontario Reader, price per page for composition and plates, $1.75.

Q.—That is exclusive of paper, printing and binding?

A.—It is only for the manufacture of the plates themselves. On a book of this class there would be a charge on the First and Second Parts which could not be actually determined unless we were to follow this particular book. That would consist of any changes the author made after the type was set up—and also a charge for inserting "cuts." Of course, in the matter of author's changes, it would be impossible to estimate on what they would be. There would be a charge of 65 cents. per hour in making any changes the author wanted.

Q.—By the "author's" changes, you mean that after the proof is set up it is submitted to the author and he may arrange the plates differently and change the type, is that it?

A.—Yes, he might do either, but it is chiefly in the re-writing and changing of the wording.

Q.—Well, explain what you mean by "office changes"?

A.—For instance, the manufacturer receives all the type set up and a proof taken and sent to the author; he goes over the proof and possibly sees a mistake that the compositor made, and, in that case, the office would have to stand for it. Then again, he might see something he would like to have put in a different way, and sometimes, he might re-arrange a full page, necessitating the work to be done all over again, and that, of course, would be done by his order; so that to estimate what these changes by the author would be in a book that has been set up, a definite charge is made at so much per hour.

Q.—And you charge what price per hour?

A.—We charge 65 cents. per hour.

Q.—Now, supposing you supply a duplicate of these plates,—what would they be worth?

A.—We could supply a duplicate which could not be printed from, but could be used to make a new set of plates from at 45 cents. a page.

Q.—Then the plates you supply can be printed from and the duplicates can be used for making new plates?

A.—Yes.

Q.—How long will one of those plates last?

A.—With care, and in a good office, they ought to print 200,000 copies from them.

Q.—After that they would have to make a new set?

A.—Yes.

Q.—I am told that some publishers say that you can produce from 300,000 to 400,000. Is that possible?

A.—Yes, it has been done.

Q.—And produce a workman-like book always?

A.—Well, the last part of it did not look very fresh.

Q.—You think 200,000 copies is the fair life of a plate?

A.—Yes.

Q.—Do these Ontario Readers look as though the plates had been used for more than 200,000?

A.—These plates look to be in very good shape; I should say that they had not been used over that time.

Q.—I would like, Mr. Fleming, if you would tell me what you think of these Readers, generally. Take the binding for example, what is your opinion of the binding of these Ontario Readers?

14a T. B.

A.—I should say they might be bound better.

Q.—Should they be bound better?

A.—I should say so.

Q.—What is the matter with them? In what particular could they be improved?

A.—They might be sewed better and they might be reinforced with cloth on the cover.

Q.—Would you put out from your house books bound as these are for school books?

A.—Not unless I was obliged to by the person for whom I was doing the work. I would not do it for my own.

Q.—Is work like that justifiable? You say they retail to the public at 10 cents, 20, 30 and 40 cents?

A.—There is not so much discrepancy in the price of the First Reader as there is between it and Part II.

Q.—Is that a fair price for that book?

A.—I think somebody is making some money out of it.

Q.—What ought that book to sell at retail?

A.—I have the cost price only.

Q.—Well, what ought it to sell over the cost price to allow the dealer a profit?

A.—I do not think I can answer that question, not knowing local conditions.

Q.—Well, have you made any other estimates, Mr. Fleming?

A.—I have a partial estimate on the "History" and "Geography." Those are the only two. I will complete them for you.

Q.—That is all you can tell me then?

A.—I may say that I have figured on all those books on a different class of cloth, but I have figured on a better style of binding to my mind.

Q.—You have not figured on these books to reproduce them in the style of binding, paper, cloth. etc., that has been used in their production, but to produce them as you think they ought to be produced, with proper paper and proper binding, such as you would produce in the United States?

A.—Yes, that is how I figured it.

Q.—Now, I did not ask you for the cost of the plates in the other books. Is there any difference in the cost per page in the other books?

A.—Yes, there is; Part II of the First Reader, the price per page would be $1.65 with the same provisoes as to changes, cuts, etc. The understanding is that the "cuts" are to be furnished.

Q.—That is just the cost of the plates?

A.—Yes. The cost of making the plates with the cuts furnished.

Q.—In the Second Book what would be the cost of the plates?

A.—$1.35 per page.

Q.—What would be the total cost of that book?

A.—The total cost, exclusive of author's changes and inserting illustrations, would be for 184 pages, $248.40. The Third Book would cost for 280 pages $378, and the Fourth Book of 344 pages would cost $464.

Q.—What about the Arithmetic?

A.—The Public School Arithmetic of 216 pages at $2.50 per page would cost $540. There is a book that there would be no plates to be inserted. It would simply be a question of author's changes only.

Q.—What about the Grammar?

A.—The Grammar would cost for 192 pages at $2.50 per page, $480. I can give you the price for this History. The Public School History, 284 pages at $1.65, would cost $468.60. The Public School Geography I can give you the price per page. There are two kinds of type in that and it would be a question as to how much there would be and I have not measured it up, but I can give you a price of a page of which it would probably average about one-half of each kind of type. On the long primer type it would be $3.75 per page. On the smaller sized type $5.80 per page. On the tabular matter it would be double price. There are also boxes for storing plates, containing 48 plates at 75 cents each. Boxes for storing Geography plates, 32 plates, same price.

Mr. Cooper: Mr. Fleming, examine, please, this Fourth Reader, pages 240, 241, 334 and 335, and tell me if you think they are well printed?

A.—They look as if the plates were battered and that the plates are bad.

Q.—Do you think they have used a good quality of ink?

A.—I think it is more the condition the plates were in than the way the press work was done.

Q.—What would you say about the combination of color throughout the books?

A.—The color seems to be uneven in this book.

Q.—These Readers are printed by three firms, one-third being printed by each; do you think that satisfactory results can be obtained by this method of press work?

A.—No.

Q.—Why not?

A.—I do not see how they can keep the color uniform throughout the book.

Mr. Staunton: You have an estimate here, have you not, on all those various costs that I have asked you?

A.—Yes.

Mr. Staunton: Just hand them in to the Official Reporter, please, and I shall have them put in the evidence.

The following is the schedule of prices:—

Office of J. S. Cushing & Co.,

Norwood, Mass., Nov. 2nd, 1906.

Messrs. E. Fleming & Co.,

Dear Sirs,—We would submit the following estimates on the various Canadian books:—

Public School Arithmetic.

Size of page, 3 1-3 x 5 5-6.
Size of type, brevier and long primer.
Price per page for composition and one set of electros right through, $2.50.
Duplicate electros, 35 cents each.

Public School Grammar.

Size of page, 3 5-8 x 6 1-6.
Size of type, bourgeois and small pica.
Price per page for composition and one set of electros, $2.50.

Public School History of England.

Size of page, 3 1-2 x 6 1-6.
Size of type, bourgeois.
Price per page for composition and electros, $1.65.
Duplicate electros, 36 cents each.

Ontario Readers.

First Reader, Part I.

Size of page, 3 1-2 x 6 1-6.
Size of type, similar to sample book.
Price per page for composition and electros, $1.75.
Duplicate electros, 45 cents each.

First Reader, Part II.

Size of page, 3 1-2 x 6 1-6.
Size of type, similar to sample book.
Price per page for composition and electros, $1.65.
Duplicate electros, 40 cents each.

Second, Third and Fourth Readers.

Size of page, 3 1-2 x 6.
Size of type, 10, 11 and 12 point.
Price per page for composition and electros, $1.35.
Duplicate electros, 35 cents each.

Public School Geography.

Size of page, 6 2-3 x 9.
Size of type, long primer and brevier.
Price per page for long primer, larger size of type, $3.75.
Price per page for brevier, smaller size of type, $5.80.
Tabular matter, double price.
Duplicate electros, $1.20 each.

Time charge for author's changes and running in of cuts, 65 cents per hour. If original cuts are to be inserted in the plates, a time charge will be made at the rate of 80 cents per hour, which will average about 45 cents a piece.

If the original cuts are to be electrotyped, half tones will have to be put on solid bodies, for which a charge of 25 cents each will be made.

These prices are based on books like samples. If the copy is poorly prepared, or if the work is of a more difficult character, a new price will be given before starting on the work. The cuts and maps are to be supplied by the publishers.

Very truly yours,
J. S. Cushing & Co.,
Per O. J. Ban.

Note.—Boxes for storing plates. containing 48 plates each, 75c. a piece. Boxes for storing Geography plates, same price, but hold only 32 plates.

Mr. STAUNTON: Mr. Fleming, there has been some discussion here as to whether the press work is higher in the United States than it is here in Canada; can you give us an estimate?

A.—Yes; I will submit the following offer to print your books for your consideration:—

OFFICE OF BERWICK & SMITH Co.,
NORWOOD, Mass., Nov. 3, 1906.

To the Canadian School Book Commission:

GENTLEMEN,—We will print your books as follows:—

25,000 Geography, including maps, 10 forms text, 15 forms of maps	$1,404 00
Without maps, 10 forms of text	600 00
12,000 History, including maps, 9 forms text, 4 forms maps	270 24
Without maps, 9 forms text	192 24
100,000 First Reader, Part I, 2 forms	376 00
50,000 First Reader, Part II, 3 forms	324 00
50,000 Second Reader, 6 forms	600 00
50,000 Third Reader, 9 forms	900 00
20,000 Fourth Reader, 11 forms	338 80
50,000 Arithmetics, 7 forms	511 00

The above books are all printed on 30 x 40 paper, 32 pages to a form with the exception of the Geography, which is printed on 33 x 42, 16 pages to a form. To print the above books we should need the following amounts of paper:—

Geography	262½⅞ reams,	33 x 42,	for	text.
"	180 "	21 x 34,	"	maps.
History	113⁵⁄₇₀ "	30 x 40,	"	text.
"	6²⁄₂₀ "	15¾ x 30,	"	maps.
First Reader, Part I	210 "	30 x 40,	"	text.
" Part II	157½⅞ "	30 x 40,	"	"
Second Reader	315 "	30 x 40,	"	"
Third Reader	472½⅞ "	30 x 40,	"	"
Fourth Reader	231 "	30 x 40,	"	"
Arithmetic	367½⅞ "	30 x 40,	"	"
Grammar	189 "	30 x 40,	"	"

Yours sincerely,
BERWICK & SMITH COMPANY.

NOTE.—Cover sides for Geography, printing, $50.00.

Mr. STAUNTON (handing witness copy of Public School Geography): What do you say about this Geography?

A.—Well, the maps in all our Geographies are all "rounded" (witness here illustrates his meaning) with the rest of the book, so that when the book is sewed they are also sewed in, while your maps are just stuck in. The double maps are put in practically like yours, except that the "guard" is carried around the back of the book. We also print them on much different paper from that used in the book. The map paper would possibly cost about 3 cents per pound more.

Q.—Those maps in the Public School Geography are printed on the same paper as the rest of the book, are they?

A.—Apparently so.

Q.—Then you say the paper is too cheap?

A.—Yes, to get good results. I will show you the difference (witness shows examiner samples of maps to show difference in the color).

Q.—What do you think about the sewing?

A.—Well, there is the same trouble that you have with the other books; they are sewn with wire, instead of thread.

Q.—How many stitches of wire are there in that book?

A.—Three.

Q.—Is that strong enough to make it a durable book?

A.—Well, I should not think it was, because there is nothing to prevent them breaking in two.

Q.—How ought they to be sewn then?

A.—I should say with thread—what we call "Smyth" sewn—not through the book, but through the sections.

Q.—How should they be put in the covers?

A.—The books should have reinforcements on both sides; I do not know that a "Head Band" would be necessary, but in all cases they should have the reinforcement.

Mr. COOPER: (Handing witness a copy of "Fry's first steps in Geography). What do you think of the binding on that book?

A.—I think that is a good binding.

Q.—That has a cloth hinge, has it not?

A.—Yes, it is the same as we bind our Second Reader.

Q.—Here is a copy of the "Natural Advance Geography." What do you think of that one?

A.—That book is all right. It has a good binding.

Q.—Can you make a rough estimate as to the difference in cost as to binding a Geography in the way ours are bound, and the way those are bound?

A.—Of course, it depends upon the number of pages, maps, etc. I should say that these books ought to cost more than your books because they are very much more durable; at least that is my impression looking at the two books.

Q.—Do you think Geographies should be bound altogether in cloth, and not with board sides?

A.—Yes.

Mr. STAUNTON: The material is more, but the labor is less,—is that it?

A.—Yes.

Mr. COOPER: Do you think it would wear three times as long as the cover on our Public School Geography?

A.—Yes.

Q.—Have you ever bound any Geographies in that way—with board sides?

A.—No. There are a great many of them bound with a cloth back; but that is not absolutely necessary.

Mr. COOPER: ·Now come back to the readers again for a minute. How would you compare these books with the Readers that you have produced here? How much less should we get these books for then, the prices you have quoted? Would you say 25 per cent. less, or 50 per cent. less?

A.—The material used in the covers of these Readers cost more than I have figured on. The material used on my books cost more than on these. But I have figured on the two. With the regular thread sewing, which would make a book something like mine, I figure that I would want—particularly on the Second Reader—one cent more per copy for binding that book than I would for the other, but, at the same time, I do not think that it is as good a book.

Q.—How much longer would your binding wear?

A.—About twice as long.

Q.—You think, then, that you can bind a book cheaper, and that it will wear twice as long?

A.—Yes.

Mr. STAUNTON: Taking your cloth which you say is not as expensive in binding, you think it would wear twice as long as the "Ontario Reader?"

A.—Yes.

Mr. CROTHERS: What is the difference in cost of these books now as compared with that of ten years ago?

A.—I should say the cost should be somewhat less at the present time.

Q.—Does it cost more to produce the plates now than it did ten years ago?

A.—Not if they are hand made.

Q.—Is the price of paper as high now as it was then?

A.—I cannot answer that question.

Q.—Well, is not labor higher now than it was ten years ago?

A.—Yes.

Mr. COOPER: How long is it since the machine that makes the cases was made?

A.—Ten years.

Q.—How long have you been using the "Smyth Sewing Machines?"

A.—Twenty years.

Q.—Well, looking at the question from a little broader outlook, do you think the perfection to which the books have been brought in the United States is the result of a system whereby the publishers let their books out to people whose specialty 's making books, or would it be just as well if the publishers bound their own books. Does the practice enable very fine factories to be erected with the latest machinery?

A.—There are two ways of looking at that. The man that makes a specialty of press work should be able to do better work than the man who does all kinds of work, and so, in the same way should the other trades. A man might do plate making, press work and binding, but with so many interests to look after he cannot give his individual attention to anyone Department, as he could if he only had one thing to make.

Q.—Do you think your people in the Norwood Press can produce better books than the others can produce who work on a smaller scale?

A.—Yes, I think we can. Of course, there are a few in the United States, like Ginn & Company, and the American Book Company, who carry the thing along very well, but it takes a lot of money. There are very few persons who have money enough to put in a proper plant for the manufacture of books. But the publisher has his work done outside except in very few cases. It may be placed with three different firms, or it might be placed with persons who do all kinds of work, or it might be placed with persons who market the books. If a person has unlimited money he can put in a good plant.

Q.—If you were advising the Ontario Government on a policy for printing school books would you advise them to give the printing of the books to six firms, or to one firm:—that is, plate making, printing and binding?

A.—I should say that the best results would be obtained in giving parts to different firms, the plates to one firm and the binding to another.

Q.—Supposing we divided the printing, binding and plate making among six firms, that is, give so many books to each publisher—divide the whole business up into six parts, what then?

A.—Probably one man might give you better work than another. I do not think they would all give you the same kind of work.

Q.—Why?

A.—For the reason that one firm is better than another.

Q.—Supposing they have not enough money to put in this machinery; is that a reasonable answer?

A.—No. But I am speaking of good firms who have all the appliances for work.

Q.—Well, what would you suggest?

A.—I do not think you would get good work with the present equipment.

Q.—How could we best go about it to get good equipment?

A.—Well, get some of your books bound in the United States.

Q.—Supposing the Government asks for tenders from six different firms for the binding of say, "The Public School History," and they set forth specifications such as you suggest with reinforced cloth, etc. these people will do that, but will charge us an enormous price for it because they would have to put in special machinery, and would not have enough business to have the work properly done.

A.—Well, that might happen, and could not be overcome unless you opened the "bids" to everybody.

Well, thank you, Mr. Fleming, I will not examine you any further now.

OFFICIAL REPORT OF THE EVIDENCE TAKEN BEFORE THE TEXT BOOK COMMISSION AT ITS FIFTH SITTING ON TUESDAY, 6TH NOVEMBER, 1906.

Mr. JAMES A. MACDONALD, examiner:

GEORGE N. MORANG, recalled for further examination:

Q.—You were sworn before?

A.—Yes.

Q.—And you very kindly consented to come back and finish up your evidence where you left off. You made application to the Government for the purpose of publishing the Ontario Readers?

A.—Yes.

Q.—Can you give us the date when you made application first; in what year?

A.—We made the application on the 7th of March, 1901. That is the date of the letter to the Department.

(Letter produced in bound file by the witness, and read as follows:—

TORONTO, March 7th, 1901.

HON. RICHARD HARCOURT,
    Minister of Education,
        Toronto.

DEAR SIR,—We beg respectfully to make application for permission to print and publish the series of readers known as the Ontario Readers, according to the terms of the agreement entered into between the Government and certain other publishers.

We are prepared to conform to the terms therein set forth.

In connection with this, we would inform you that we are the exclusive owners in Canada of the copyrights of over forty pages of the matter which is contained in these readers.

Awaiting your favorable reply,

We have the honor to be,

Your obedient servants,

GEORGE N. MORANG & CO., LIMITED.

By GEORGE N. MORANG, President.

Q.—Was any answer given by the Government to that letter?

A.—Yes; one of the 8th, from the Minister of Education.

(Reads letter as follows:—)

TORONTO, March 8th, 1901.

MY DEAR SIR,—I have your letter of March 7th, in *re* readers, and will bring it to the attention of my colleagues as soon as possible. We cannot, I fear, take up these matters until the session is over. We should be able to finish in about three weeks.

Yours faithfully,

R. HARCOURT.

GEORGE N. MORANG, ESQ.,

90 Wellington Street West,

Toronto."

Q.—Did you have any personal interviews with any member of the Government concerning your application?

A.—Yes. I have had interviews for two or three years, off and on. I had had interviews with Mr. Ross before he was Premier.

Q.—And you did not publish eventually the Readers?

A.—No.

Q.—For what reason?

A.—The reason was that I could not get the plates.

Q.—You stated that in your former evidence?

A.—Yes.

Q.—Whom did you ask for the plates?

A.—I applied to the Government, the Minister of Education.

Q.—Who was the Minister of Education at that time?

A.—Mr. Harcourt.

Q.—And you could not get the plates?

A.—No.

Q.—What was the reason given for the refusal?

A.—There was not any reason except that he could not give them to me. That was the only thing. He said he could not do it.

Q.—Who gave that reason?

A.—Mr. Ross.

Q.—The Hon. Mr. Ross?

A.—Yes.

Q.—Did he go further and tell you why he could not?

A.—No, he never gave the reasons; he said "To tell you the truth, I can not do it." That is about all he said, but I imagined that there would be the copyright reason.

Q.—Was that shortly after you had made formal application?

A.—Oh no; that was away along after these letters that I sent in my protests about private and confidential letters, and all that.

Q.—You wrote protesting against letters coming to you marked "private and confidential?"

A.—Yes. August 1st, 1901, was my first protest.

(Reads letter as follows:—)

TORONTO, August 1st, 1901.

THE HONORABLE,

RICHARD HARCOURT,

Minister of Education,

Toronto.

DEAR SIR,—I am in receipt of your note of the 31st ult., marked "private and confidential," in which you ask me to "come and see you when convenient." This I should be pleased to do, but I have been treated with such marked discourtesy by members of the Government, that I cannot with any self respect expose myself to any further personal interviews without knowing the purpose and object of such interview. If you will kindly inform me as to this, you may rest assured that I will give immediate attention to any communication you may be pleased to make.

I have the honor to be,

Sir,

Your obedient servant

Q.—Then did you have any interview with Mr. Ross?

A.—I do not think I did; that month of August, I think, he was away.

Q.—Did you have any interview with Mr. Ross at all, concerning your application to publish the readers?

A.—Yes, I had that interview about the plates, when he was Premier, in which he told me he could not give them to me; the statements I made the last time I was here. Then here is another letter; August 7th, 1901, in which I protest against further communications being marked "private and confidential."

Q.—What letter or letters particularly did you receive marked "confidential;" have you any of those letters with you? There are none of them on the files here.

Mr. COOPER: Have you the Education Department file?

Mr. MACDONALD: Yes.

Q.—Have you any letter in your possession marked "confidential?"

A.—Yes; I have one dated the 31st of July, 1901, from Mr. Harcourt.

Q.—Have you that letter with you?

A.—Yes, I have got it attached to my reply.

Q.—I would like to see what that letter says; it is not on the file here?

A.—I have never made any of these letters public, these private and confidential letters, although they were concerning my business application; I have always held that I should not make them public.

Q.—You mean to say you have never published or caused to be published, those letters?

A.—I have not.

Q.—That is at the time of your effort to get into the publication of the books?

A.—No.

Q.—Have you got them here now?

A.—I have one dated 31st July, 1901.

Q.—Let me see that, please, or read it?

A.—Do I have to do that, Mr. Chairman?

The CHAIRMAN: Marked "private and confidential," is it?
A.—Yes.
Q.—How is it signed?
A.—R. Harcourt.
By Mr. MACDONALD:
Q.—Was it concerning your application?
A.—No. The way he did, he marked everything "private and confidential;" if I would write a letter about a matter connected with the Readers.
Q.—You would get a letter marked "private and confidential" in return?
A.—It was not until I actually protested on August 7th, that I got them to stop it.
Q.—I wish you would produce that letter; I cannot see any tangible ground for not producing it before this Commission; it is bearing directly upon your application to publish the readers?
A.—It does not amount to anything; there is nothing in it.
Q.—The Commission should be the judge of that?
A.—If the chairman rules that I should produce it, I will read it, that is all.
The CHAIRMAN: I feel reluctant to insist on a letter marked "private and confidential," being produced; still, I think such letters on business matters, matters of public interest, should not be so marked; and I, therefore, think that the public ought to have the benefit of any of these communications touching this public matter.
(The witness reads the letter as follows:—)

"Private and Confidential.

July 31st, 1901.
DEAR MR. MORANG,—I had a note from Mr. Barwick this morning. He is off for a holiday, having telephoned me. Come and see me when convenient.

Yours faithfully,
(Signed) R. HARCOURT."

WITNESS: His letters were marked "private and confidential," about the least thing, and I had to commence a correspondence regarding it. As I said, I would like to further produce my protests, by reading the letter of August 7th, 1901, to him.
(Reads letter as follows:—)

THE HONORABLE,
      RICHARD HARCOURT,
            Minister of Education,
                  Toronto.

DEAR SIR,—Your letter of the 2nd inst. marked "private and confidential," came duly to hand, but I was absent from the city, hence the delay in answering it.
As we are dealing with a question of general public concern, and one in which, for my part, there does not seem to be any necessity for privacy under present conditions, I trust you will allow me to suggest that any communications that pass between us should be on a business footing, and not "confidential or private."

As to the question of referring to anything contained in a letter marked "confidential," I may say, that if a letter addressed to me as "confidential" were indeed so, I should be the last one to make it public, either in whole or in part. But when I address a business letter, referring strictly to business, I cannot see why I should esteem an answer to such a letter as "confidential," particularly when the veracity of one of the parties concerned is called in question.

I appreciate the fact of you and Mr. Barwick, being college friends of long standing, but I cannot see why this should prevent you from taking notice of my application to print the Ontario Readers, dated March 7th. I engaged Mr. Barwick to look after my interests, and he has done so. The matter of friendship does not enter into the question. This fact I desire to emphasize as the Government seems to have overlooked it. I may also say that Mr. Barwick, from a business point of view, and independent of friendship, concurs in the course I have pursued.

Had I known that the call with which you favored me was a social one, I should have esteemed it highly, and would naturally have returned the compliment. But it was evidently a business call, and as I wrote you lately, I prefer to have any communications between the Government and myself in writing. Mr. Barwick, as well as myself, is convinced, from our experience of the past few weeks, that verbal expressions are not considered of any binding importance by the Government.

I certainly desire to reciprocate your wishes that our relations, business and otherwise, should be of the pleasantest kind possible, but I cannot agree with you that at the present time "there is no reason why they should not be so." I trust, however, that in time they may become more cordial.

I have the honor to be,
Your obedient servant.

Mr. MACDONALD: Have you any dealings with the three firms who were publishing the readers at all; did you negotiate or endeavor to negotiate with them in any way to secure some of the monopoly that they had?

A.—I did not negotiate with them, that is, really negotiate; but Mr. Ross, the Premier, intimated to me that I had better see them, and I just wrote him a letter that I would not see them. I indicated in the letter that if they wanted to meet me they could come and see me, I would not go near them.

Q.—For what purpose did the Hon. Mr. Ross suggest that you should see these firms?

Mr. COOPER: Was this while Mr. Ross was Minister of Education?

A.—This was while he was Premier.

Q.—He was not Minister of Education then?

A.—No, he was Premier.

Mr. MACDONALD: For what reason did he suggest that you should see them?

A.—The reasons are outlined in two letters he wrote me, that were marked "personal."

Q.—Letters from Hon. Mr. Ross?

A.—Yes.

Q.—In reference to publication of the Readers?

A.—In reference to the Reader question generally.

Q.—Where are those letters?

A.—I have never made those letters public, for just the reason I gave in former evidence.

Q.—You have been asked to produce all correspondence; have you got those letters with you?

A.—Yes. I know the subpœna called for bringing all correspondence, and I have brought these here.

Q.—Produce them, please, to the Commission?

A.—I would like to ask the chairman for a ruling as to that.

The CHAIRMAN: Were they in reference to this public matter, this public transaction?

A.—Yes.

The CHAIRMAN: I think we are entitled to see them.

WITNESS: On the 16th January, 1901, Mr. Ross wrote me a letter marked personal, in which he says:

Mr. COOPER: That is before your first written application for Readers?

A.—Yes, but after I had applied verbally a year or two back. I made a formal application on the 7th March, 1901; but Mr. Ross wrote me on the 16th January, 1901, as follows:

(Reads letter of the 16th January, 1901.)

"Personal.

TORONTO, 16th January, 1901.

MY DEAR MORANG,—I have seen a copy of your Phonic Primer. It is a splendid piece of work. I advised Mr. Barwick, who called upon me, to see the Minister of Education with a view to having it introduced as an alternative Primer for use in our schools. This, however, could not be done without the consent of the present contractors.

Yours truly,

(Signed) G. W. Ross.

GEORGE N. MORANG, ESQ.,
    Publisher, &c.,
        Toronto.''

Mr. MACDONALD: You thought that appealed to you as to securing the consent of the other contractors?

A.—I could not see the reason for it. I have read the agreement, and could not understand it.

Q.—Was there anything in the agreement that you saw to prevent the authorization of another book?

A.—I could not see anything, nor Mr. Barwick; he could not see anything.

Q.—You eventually did secure authorization for your Phonic Primer?

A.—Yes.

Q.—There was nothing in the agreement to prevent the Government authorizing any reader?

A.—Not that I could see, or my legal advisers could see.

Q.—Did you see the other publishers as a consequence of receiving that letter?

A.—No, I did not see them until I had received another letter from Mr. Ross.

Q.—Have you got that other letter with you?

A.—I made application, I may say, to print the Readers on the 7th March, 1901; and on the 8th March, 1901, I received the following letter:—

"Personal.

TORONTO, March 8th, 1901.

MY DEAR MORANG,—I think it would be to your advantage if you would open communication with Mr. Thompson of the Copp, Clark Co., in the matter of the Readers.

Yours truly,

(Signed) G. W. Ross.

GEORGE N. MORANG, ESQ.,

90 Wellington Street West,

Toronto."

Mr. COOPER: Your application was made to?

A.—The day before, I made it to the Minister of Education, Department of the Minister of Education.

Q.—Was the Minister of Education absent?

A.—No, he was in town. I registered the letter.

The CHAIRMAN: You received also a reply from Mr. Harcourt, on the 8th of March?

A.—Yes; I got a letter from each of them that day.

Mr. COOPER: You would judge from that, that the Minister of Education had been consulting the Premier on the matters?

A.—Yes, I would. It looked to me at the time as if Mr. Ross intended to take the matter up himself, by this, or steer it himself.

Mr. MACDONALD: Did you ask the Hon. Mr. Ross for any reason why you should see the other publishers?

A.—No, I did not see Mr. Ross,—did not go near him.

Q.—In answer to that letter; what did you do as a consequence of receiving that suggestion from the Hon. Mr. Ross?

A.—I don't know whether I answered it or, Mr. Barwick saw him. No, I never answered that letter of the 8th of March; never answered it.

Q.—Did you have any further interview with the Hon. Mr. Ross as a result of receiving that letter?

A.—No, I did not see Mr. Ross, regarding that at all.

Q.—Then you have told us of all the difficulties you had before in reference to this copyright: as a result of it all, you did not publish the Readers?

A.—No.

Q.—Although you had sent them your cheque for the amount required under the contract, $4,100?

A.—Yes.

Q.—That was returned to you?

A.—Yes.

Q.—Then you received permission to publish the Ontario Phonic Primer, or Modern Phonic Primer—I think it is called. What is the date of your application to the Government?

A.—I do not know the date of the application for that. Mr. Saul, I think, knows it; but the date of authorization I think you have there in the contract.

(A letter from the witness of September 3rd, 1902, to the Deputy Minister of Education, is read as follows:—)

"September 3rd, 1902.

JOHN MILLAR, ESQ.,
  Deputy Minister of Education,
    Education Office,
      Toronto.

SIR,—I notice that "A Public School Phonic Primer, Part One," appears upon the list of text books authorized for use in the Public Schools. I will be glad to know whether the agreement governing the authorization of this work contains a clause prohibiting the printing of copies of the book in the United States to be sold within the Province of Ontario. I refer to a clause similar to clause twelve of the agreement which governs the use of "The Modern Phonic Primer," published by Morang & Company.

I am, Sir,

Yours truly,
(Signed) GEORGE N. MORANG."

Mr. MACDONALD: Why did you make that enquiry from the Government as to the printing of the copies in the United States?

A.—Our modern Phonic Primer had been out, I should say, a year. and in getting it authorized we had to agree that it should be printed in Ontario. We assumed that as these people—the "School Book Ring," I called it that time, had had a monopoly of the Readers for eighteen years, that our Phonic Primer was to have a show; but I was very much surprised, on seeing the list of books on the 1st of September, to notice that a new Phonic Primer had been authorised to be published by the Canada Publishing Company.

Q.—You received then an answer from the Deputy Minister, dated September 4th, 1902, to your letter.

(Reads letter of September 4th, 1902, as follows:—)

September 4th, 1902.

DEAR SIR,—I have the honor to acknowledge the receipt of your letter of the 3rd instant, respecting the lately authorized book, "The Public School Phonic Primer, Part I." In the absence of the Minister of Education, I may simply state, there is no reason to suppose that any restriction in the agreement governing the use of "The Modern Phonic Primer," will be omitted in the case of the former.

Your obedient servant,
Deputy Minister.

GEORGE N. MORANG, ESQ.,
  Publisher, Etc.,
    Toronto.

By Mr. MACDONALD:

Q.—Had you any tangible ground for believing or knowing that the Canada Publishing Company were violating the agreement respecting the printing or publishing of books in the United States for use in Ontario?

A.—I knew that that book was printed in new York, and that Primer had been authorized contrary to the regulation in the contract.

The CHAIRMAN: Which one is that you are speaking of?

A.—The Phonic Primer of the Canada Publishing Company, the three combined firms. They published this Phonic Primer, had it authorized, shortly after I had mine authorized. My agreement called for me to make my Primer in Ontario.

Mr. MACDONALD: Your agreement was exactly the same as theirs?

A.—That is what I assumed.

Q.—I will read the clause; see if you can identify it as the same provision:—

"11. And that the said publisher shall not print or publish, nor cause nor authorize to be printed or published, nor be in any way accessory to the printing or publishing, of any edition or copy or copies of the said book in the United States, or anywhere else outside the limits of the Province of Ontario, to be sold within the said Province of Ontario."

That clause and that provision was contained in the agreement that the Government had with the Canada Publishing Company?

A.—That is what I assumed.

Q.—It was as a matter of fact?

A.—That is what I assumed.

Q.—You called the attention of the Government to the fact that that clause of the agreement was being violated?

A.—I did.

Q.—What knowledge had you about that?

A.—I went to New York and saw the vice-president of the American Colortype Company, who told me that he had printed an edition for them: and he brought me a sample of the sheets unbound.

Q.—Who was the vice-president?

A.—I forget his name; some German gentleman.

Q.—He told you?

A.—That he had just printed an edition for them. He went in to where he kept his samples and brought me out the different forms—the form folded up, printed on both sides.

Q.—What size of an edition?

A.—I think he told me he had printed some twenty thousand.

The CHAIRMAN: These were forms of what?

A.—Of the Phonic Primer.

Q.—It was in two parts?

A.—The Phonic Primer was printed on one sheet really, but it was thirty-two pages on each side. I am only speaking of the first part of the Phonic Primer, Part One.

Mr. COOPER: Did they publish two?

A.—Yes; they got out another one after I got out my second.

Q.—You are speaking of the Part One that I show you?

A.—Yes.

Mr. MACDONALD: The vice-president showed you a form?

A.— Yes, and I brought it back to Toronto with me.

Q.—I see that by letter of September 10th you notified the Minister of Education as follows:—

"September 10th, 1902.

THE HONORABLE, THE MINISTER OF EDUCATION,
            Toronto.

DEAR SIR,— I beg to inform you that I have evidence that the Ontario Phonic Primer published by the Canada Publishing Co., and now being sold for use in our public Schools was printed by the American Colortype Company at New York. The offices of this Company are at 277 Broadway. The introduction of this book is contrary to the agreement governing its use.

15 T. B.

which provides that the publisher shall not print or publish or cause or authorize to be printed or published nor be in any way accessory to the printing or publishing of any edition or copy or copies of the book in the United States or anywhere else without the limits of the Province of Ontario to be sold within the Province of Ontario.

In the publishing of our Modern Phonic Primer our house was of course governed by the similar clause and complied with it in every respect. The whole work was produced in Toronto. We cannot, submit to the Canada Publishing Co. being allowed to compète with us under such unfair discrimination, and we call on the Department to enforce the terms of the agreement governing the authorization of the Ontario Phonic Primer and the bond given that its terms would be complied with.

I have the honour to be sir,
Yours truly,
(Signed)　　George N. Morang."

Mr. Macdonald: That is the name of it? The Ontario Phonic Primer?
A.—Yes.
Q.—Published by the Canada Publishing Company?
A.—Yes.
Q.—In answer to that you received the following letter of the 13th of September, 1902, from the Deputy Minister:

"September 13th, 1902.
Dear Sir,—I am directed by the Minister of Education to acknowledge the receipt of your letter of 10th instant; and to state that the matter to which you refer is receiving the full attention of this Department.
Your obedient servant,
Deputy Minister.
George N. Morang, Esq.,
Publisher, etc., Toronto."

Mr. Cooper: What has been the result of this correspondence?
A.—I think I made an affidavit to the Government to the effect that this Primer was printed in the United States; and the only thing that I know of it is what I saw in "The Globe," that it had been what they call de-authorized on that account; but I never had any official communication that it was, nor can I find out, because they went right on selling it.
Mr. Macdonald: You wrote, then, to the Honorable the Minister of Education on the 16th of September, 1902, as follows:—

"September 16th, 1902.
The Honorable, The Minister of Education,
Toronto, Ontario.
Re "The Primer."
Dear Sir,—We understand that the Canada Publishing Co. has never yet signed the agreement governing the authorization of that Company's publication of the Ontario Phonic Primer, and we are induced to believe that the Canada Publishing Company will refuse to sign any such agreement.

Under these circumstances we will be glad to know what course is to be taken to prevent the introduction of the Ontario Phonic Primer into the public schools.

At the present time the Ontario Phonic Primer appears on the list of books authorized to be used in the public schools, and any Board of Trustees.

15a T. B.

and any one in trade, is justified in coming to the conclusion that the Ontario Phonic Primer is governed by the usual agreement.

We are publishing Morang's Modern Phonic Primer in strict compliance with the regulations of the Department and the terms of the prescribed agreement, and protest that we should receive protection against a book authorized under such circumstances, and produced by foreign workmen in direct competition with Canadian workmen.

We are, Sir, yours very truly,
GEORGE N. MORANG & Co., LIMITED.
(Signed) GEORGE N. MORANG, President.

WITNESS : In other words the book, Mr. Macdonald, was supposed to be authorized in September, and it really was not, according to my interpretation, but they were sending their men all over the Province, saying we had an authorized Primer and they had, too.

By Mr. MACDONALD :

Q.—There were men out canvassing for the book before it had really received official authorization?

A.—That is what I assume by the correspondence in the Department. and they had commenced early in July.

Q.—As a matter of fact they had commenced to canvass for the sale of the book?

A.—They commenced to canvass just as soon as my Phonic Primer was authorized; the ring got out their men all over the Province to stop its introduction into the schools, saying that they were going to publish one and that it would be authorized.

Q.—What authority had they for making that statement?

A.—I don't know; but they confused the school trustees all over the Province, much to our disadvantage.

Q.—Then on September 24th you wrote to the Minister of Education as follows :—

"I have the honor to call your attention to the fact that I have received no answers to the letters which I have addressed to the Department on the subject of the printing of the Ontario Phonic Primer in the United States.

"On the 21st of August last a carefully prepared statement from you appeared in the Toronto Globe, announcing that thereafter no text-book would be authorized for use in the schools of Ontario until after it had been published and in general circulation for at least six months. I was very much pleased to read this statement of policy to be pursued by the Department in the authorization of text-books, because it was the very thing for which I had been striving for some years.

"Shortly after the publication of this statement, however, I learned that the Department had in view the authorization of a Phonic Primer to be published by the Canada Publishing Company. I made every effort at this time to secure a copy of the book, but failed to do so. I was informed that this book was not printed in Canada, and I conveyed my information to the Government.

"The departmental regulations were issued this year a month later than they usually are, and when they did appear, I was amazed to find that the Department had not only authorized the Ontario Phonic Primer, which the Government knew was produced in the United States, but it had also authorized a Part II., which was not published at the time when the authorization was announced, nor has it been published since that time. I have tried to obtain a copy of Part II., but have not been successful."

WITNESS: Part II. was not out.

Mr. MACDONALD: Although it had been stated that thereafter no text book would be authorized for use in the schools of Ontario until after it had been published and in general circulation for at least six months?

A.—Six months.

Mr. COOPER: Was that a regulation, or merely an interview in The Globe?

Mr. MACDONALD: It was a regulation.

The Chairman: What do you mean by "Being in circulation six months?" You do not mean selling it to trustees and using it in the schools?

A.—Circulation amongst teachers, and really published.

Mr. COOPER: You could sell it to a school for supplementary reading?

A.—Yes; and the probable object for having a book out before authorization is that you get it around amongst teachers and get their opinion.

Mr. MACDONALD: But that regulation was evidently disregarded in the case of the book referred to?

A.—Yes.

(Mr. Macdonald continues the reading of the letter.)

"While I am aware that the Department of Education knew that the Ontario Phonic Primer was printed in the United States, yet, to put the fact beyond dispute, I yesterday forwarded to you a statutory declaration, verifying the information I had given the Government before the book was authorized. I have as yet said nothing about the action of the Department in authorizing, in the face of the declaration in the Globe of August 21st, a book, which has not yet been published, a month after the notice of authorization is given. The action which I have taken in the matter has been dictated by purely business motives and a desire to receive at least as fair treatment as the publishing houses, who, for years past, have held a practical monopoly of the school book trade of Ontario. I think you will not deny, that if our house had ventured to print any part of its Primer in the United States and this fact had been brought to the attention of your Department, by any one interested in the Canada Publishing Company, our house would speedily have had that justice meted out to it which is now delayed in the instance of the Canada Publishing Company."

Mr. MACDONALD: You thought you would receive harsher treatment than the other publishers?

A.—I never did receive any, what I call, decent treatment.

(Mr. Macdonald concludes the reading of the letter, as follows:—)

"I have always believed that the policy of the Department as to the production of school books by Canadian workmen was an earnest one. Believing so, I have at great expense established a business which enables our house to produce books manufactured by Canadian workmen, and at the same time to produce these books in strict compliance with the standard form of agreement governing the authorization of books for use in public and high schools. I may say that our house has, at great expense, produced in Toronto, the "Modern Phonic Primer," in all its parts, this being the first Phonic Primer with colored pictures produced by Canadian workmen. If I have been misled in all this, and if our house is in the production and sale of the Canadian produced school books, to meet the not over-honest competition of houses, who put upon the market books printed by United States workmen, then I would like to know it. It is only fair that I should be allowed to compete upon equal terms with my rivals who have, as I have said, for many years controlled the business of publishing school books for use in our Ontario schools.

I do not believe it was ever the intention of the Government that the regulations I am now referring to should be a farce, and, therefore, I demand from you, as Minister of Education that protection which I am entitled to as an employer of Canadian workmen, and as a Canadian contractor faithfully living up to the conditions imposed upon me by the Government.

I am led to believe that other trades are about to take this question up. I trust they will, and that they will agitate it as much as they possibly can. in which agitation they will have my most active support. I want no more than what is just and right; I want no favors, but I expect and require justice to be done to our house. If I cannot get protection I must endeavor in every public way I can to bring pressure to bear upon the Government to compel them to treat me justly.

The only course to protect our Canadian produced book is the immediate de-authorization of the foreign produced Primer.

           I have the honor to remain, Sir,

                      Yours truly,

           (Signed)   GEORGE N. MORANG.''

Mr MACDONALD: Have you any knowledge as to whether or not that Primer was de-authorized?

A.—Only what I saw in the newspaper.

Q.—At any rate, it was re-authorized; at any rate, if it was de-authorized, it was immediately re-authorized?

A.—All I know is from the paper. The Mail one day said it had been authorized, de-authorized, and re-authorized, and wanted to know what it meant. I did not get any communication from the Government.

Q.—Still, it was published as one of the authorized books?

A.—As a matter of fact, I do not believe it was ever de-authorized.

Q.—You got an answer from the Department to that letter, and you in reply say, on the 24th of September, in your letter of that date:—

                    "September 24th, 1902.

HON. RICHARD HARCOURT,

      Minister of Education, Toronto.

DEAR SIR:—I have the honour to acknowledge the receipt of your letter of to-day's date, in reply to mine of the 22nd, stating that the Canada Publishing Company have agreed that the Ontario Phonic Primer shall be printed in Ontario, that you are assured that no copies have been printed outside of Ontario since the authorization, and that it is especially stated that any books not printed or published as above required shall be sold, or offered for sale in Ontario.

I have to call your attention to the clause of the standard agreement governing the authorization of books for use in the public schools, and which provides that publishers will not print or publish, nor cause nor authorize to be printed or published, nor to be in any way accessory to the printing or publishing of any edition or copies of the book in the U. S. or anywhere else without the limits of Ontario to be sold within the Province. The proof is already in your hands that the Canada Publishing Company have printed in the U. S. an edition of 20,000 of the Ontario Phonic Primer, and have imported this edition into Ontario, and have sold and are now engaged in selling these books for use in the public schools. This edition bears the stamp of authorization by the Department.

It is impossible for me to understand what influence can induce you not to proceed against the Canada Publishing Company for their breach of this departmental regulation, which our Company was compelled to enter into substantial bonds to comply with.

Yours truly,
(Signed) GEORGE N. MORANG."

By Mr. MACDONALD:

Q.—You wanted the Government to avail itself of the right to cancel their contract by reason of the breach of that contract by the Canada Publishing Company?

A.—Yes; and I also thought that they had no business to authorize it at all after giving me an authorization of a Primer that had taken so much time and expense to get up.

Q.—You relied on one of the clauses of the agreement here, which states that:

"The publisher agrees that if the publisher shall carelessly or deliberately disregard the terms of this indenture, or fail to carry out the same in a matter of substance, the publisher so disregarding shall absolutely forfeit all their rights under this indenture."

You took the position that they had forfeited their rights under that agreement by reason of the breach of that term under the contract?

A.—Yes.

Mr. COOPER: Mr. Morang says he had another reason.

WITNESS: Yes. My other reason was that at the time my Primer was authorized I understood it was going to have a show and that we were going to realize something from its sale, because it had been the first Phonic Primer ever published here, and it cost me a lot. The color working was very expensive, on accont of so much experimenting. They were not accustomed to do that work here in Canada, and I had to go to a great deal of expense in that experimental stage; whereas in the United States they have got that down to the stage of a finished art.

By Mr. MACDONALD:

Q.—You could have produced the same thing in the United States at very much less expense?

A.—Yes.

Q.—Would you have done that if you had not been restricted by your agreement with the Government?

A.—Yes, I think I would have taken the color work only to the States, rather than have been delayed. The other work I would have done. As to the color or work at that time, I was really obliged to pay a man for learning something himself.

Q.—Yours was the introduction of that system of coloring?

A.—Yes; mine was really the introduction of the three-color work in school books in this country.

Q.—And you were at a great disadvantage with such unfair competition as permitting foreign work?

A.—Yes. They could do little better in New York at that time.

Mr. COOPER: Don't you think it was good policy on the part of the Government to let them do it in New York if it could be done so much better?

A.—Yes, if they would let me do the same thing.

Q.—You are not complaining about the work being done in New York; you only complain of the unfair competition?

A.—The Government led me to believe that the work must be done here; but when the other men went off to New York, where experimenting with color had been done and where the color work could be done better, it put me at a great disadvantage.

Q.—You would not have raised all this objection to the Canada Publishing Company having its books done in New York if you had been allowed to do the color work in New York?

A.—No, I would not have objected.

By Mr. MACDONALD:

Q.—All you wanted was to be placed on equal terms with the other publishers?

A.—That is all I wanted; to be able to produce the color work the same as they did.

Mr. COOPER: You said you expected to make some money out of this book: what right had you to think you were going to have a monopoly?

A.—I did not think I had any right to have a monopoly, but I thought it was only fair that I should have an opportunity to introduce the Phonic Primer without obstruction. The consequence of the Government authorizing a second Primer was that we had a fight on our hands for two years Our Primers were in the schools, and the Canada Publishing Company would come along and give theirs away in order to take ours out; and although the people wanted ours, there was so much confusion that they were afraid to take ours; and practically, even after the Primer was authorized, it was a losing game for us, a losing thing, because we had to go to so much expense in explaining to the people what we thought an unfair thing on the part of the Government, who had given us something with one hand and taken it away with the other. They were delighted with the construction of the Primer. Mr. Ross had told me privately that he had been wanting a Phonic Primer for years. Then I got one out, and the Canada Publishing Company immediately gets the tip and they get one out hurriedly; it is authorized before it is ever published; and their agents go all over Ontario, telling people that they were going to have one and not to take ours.

Q.—You have been protesting against a monopoly in regard to the public school Readers, the first, second, third, and fourth; and now you come to protest because you did not get a monopoly on your Phonic Primer?

A.—No, I do not protest. They already had another Primer; they did not take out the other Primer. The Canada Publishing Company had the old Ontario Primer, and my Primer was merely an alternative Primer, as a Phonic Primer. I did not have a monopoly for it, for the reason that many schools preferred the old Primer.

Q.—You were not asking for a monopoly, because the Canada Publishing Company really put three sets of Primers in the field?

A.—Three sets.

By Mr. MACDONALD:

Q.—On the 15th of May, 1902, you had authorization of Morang's Modern Phonic Primer?

A.—Yes.

Q.—On the 15th of May, 1902. Then in August, 1902, three months afterwards, the Phonic Primer published by the Canada Publishing Company was authorized?

A.—Yes.

Q.—That is, three months after the authorization of yours appears another primer paralleling yours?

A.—Yes, that is just what I stated.

Q.—Then there was not so long an interval elapsing between the appearance of the second Phonic Primer, published by the Canadian Publishing Company and the appearance of your own Phonic Primer, as there had been between that and the original Reader?

A.—No.

Q.—That was eighteen years?

A.—About eighteen years.

Q.—It went eighteen years without being paralleled by ·the publication of another Reader?

A.—Yes.

Q.—Until you got the privilege of printing your Primer?

A.—Yes.

Q.—That is a matter of fact?

A.—Yes, that is a matter of fact.

Q.—Then as soon as yours appears it is paralleled in three months?

A.—Yes, that is just the case.

Q.—They had a long period of tranquillity before that. Now you spoke of a regulation in regard to text books. Section 105 of the regulation pertaining to authorized text books is amended by adding the following:—

"Before application is made for the authorization of any text book th'e book must have been in circulation for at least six months, for examination by teachers, inspectors, and other educationists."

That was dated August 21st, 1902, the same date.

Mr. COOPER: That regulation was dated August 21st?

Mr. MACDONALD: Yes; and a notice of it appeared in the Globe of the same date.

Mr. COOPER: Was that before this Canada Publishing Company's Primer, Part I, was authorized?

A.—Was it?

Mr. MACDONALD: There is no date of authorization of that.

Mr. COOPER: Wait till we get that.

WITNESS: The list was prepared by the Government. What they did is, they delayed the list a month that year, would not let me see it, or anybody else; they delayed it a month, and when it came out the Canada Publishing Company's Primer was on it.

By Mr. MACDONALD:

Q.—Do you consider your Primer as good as the one published by the Canada Publishing Company?

Mr. COOPER: I do not think that is a fair question to ask Mr. Morang.

The CHAIRMAN: He is too modest to answer that.

WITNESS: You know what I would say to that.

By Mr. MACDONALD:

Q.—Were you able to discover any reason why three months after your book was authorized another one should parallel it after a period of eighteen years had elapsed?

A.—Yes, I will give you the reason.

Q.—Did you consider that the demands of the educationists of this province inspired the book?

A.—No, I did not. I assumed that the introduction of a carefully prepared Phonic Primer, one, was sufficient. The reason, I thought, for the other being authorized was merely that Mr. Ross was anxious to keep the Canada Publishing Company along the same lines as we were going on; that the Government was really—to be frank with you—working in favor of them; and I had every reason to believe, from start to finish, that they were. That was my reason.

Mr. COOPER: You have stated that you are aware that the Canada Publishing Company's Primer was published before authorization; do I understand you correctly?

A.—It came out on the authorized list of books before it was really authorized.

Mr. MACDONALD: But you said also that it was on the list before it was published?

A.—Yes. I could not get a copy.

Q.—Although there was a regulation in existence requiring that the book should be in circulation for six months?

Mr. COOPER: That was in August or September 1902. Do you know of any cases since September, 1902 where any books have been authorized that were not already published and in circulation for six months?

A.—There was Part Two of their Primer.

Q.—Part Two of their Primer is one example?

A.—Part Two of their Primer.

Q.—Any other?

A.—I think that they authorized some other books, but I cannot——

Q.—You cannot answer that question?

A.—I cannot answer. I think they authorized a history that had not been out, but I cannot swear to it.

Q.—Will Mr. Saul know that?

A.—I think so.

Q.—Do you know whether Rose's Geography was authorized before it was published?

A.—I heard it was, but, I could not swear that it was. I heard it was authorized before it was published.

The CHAIRMAN: Do you know whether any of these Phonic Primers were printed in the United States after you called the Government's attention to this twenty thousand?

A.—No, I think that they stopped that then; I think they stopped it.

EVIDENCE OF MR. H. M. GRANTHAM.

Mr. STAUNTON, Examiner:

Mr. STAUNTON: You have made a list of the manufacturing cost, consisting of the paper, press work and binding, of all the books published by Morang & Co., authorized in the Province of Ontario, which have not been already spoken of; am I correct in that?

A.—Practically so. Nearly all.

Q.—In a note on this list, you say, that this does not include the plate cost, royalties, editorial, and sundry other expenses; so that what you mean is that the manufacturing cost starts when the book has been written, revised, put in type, and turned into plate?

A.—Yes. The illustrations and so on all prepared and bought.

Q.—This shows that the Public School Arithmetic, retailing at twenty-five cents, costs?

A.—Eleven cents.

Q.—The Public School Algebra and Euclid, one hundred and sixty pages, retailing at twenty-five cents, costs?

A.—Nine cents.

Q.—Morang's Modern Geography, retailing at. seventy-five cents, costs twenty-five and three-quarter cents. Is there any necessity of going through all this?

WITNESS : There are fifty of them.

Mr. COOPER : Put it in.

(Following is the document referred to.)

The following list gives the manufacturing cost only, which consists' merely of the paper, press work and binding. The plate cost, royalties, editorial and sundry other expenses have not been considered.

These prices have been figurd on the basis of 10,000. lots. Should the editions be smaller, the cost would necessarily increase, probably anywhere from 1c. to 3c., or even more in some cases.

As we have had very little time to prepare this estimate, it has been impossible to figure these prices down to a fraction. They are, however, approximately right and should not be more than $\frac{1}{2}$c. or $\frac{3}{4}$c. a copy out in a few cases.

MORANG & CO., LIMITED.

Public School Arithmetic.

Contains 216 pages, 7 32's.

72 rms. 30x40—70, 5,000 at 4½	$226 80	
Printing 8 forms	120 00	
Binding at 6½c. per copy	650 00	
		$996 80

Cost per copy, 11c.

P. S. Algebra and Euclid.

Contains 160 pages, 5 32's.

52 rms. 30x40—75, 500 at 4½	$175 50	
Printing 5 forms	75 00	
Binding at 6½c	650 00	
		$900 50

Cost per copy, 9c.

Morang's Modern Geography.

Contains 432 pages, 13 32's and 1 16 and 24 5 color maps, 1 relief.

141 rms. 31x42½—85, 500 at 4½	$539 10	
Printing 14 forms	332 00	
Printing 1 form maps, 5 colors	125 00	
21 r. 85 lb. for maps	80 35	
Binding at 15c. a copy	1,500 00	
		$2,576 45

Cost per copy, 25¾c.

Public School Geography.

Contains 208 pages, 10 16's black, 16 single and 4 double maps.

137 rms. (including maps) 33x43—90, 500 at 4½	$554 85	
Printing 10 forms	200 00	
Printing maps 4 colors, back in black	170 00	
Binding at 12c. copy	1,200 00	
		$2,124 85

Cost per copy, 21¼c.

Our Home and its Surroundings.

Contains 160 pages, 5 32's, 3 colored maps.

52 rms. 31x42½—85, 500 at 4½	$198 90	
Printing 5 forms	110 00	
Printing 3 maps, 5 colors	50 00	
Paper for maps	7 00	
Binding at 7c.	700 00	
		$1,065 90

Cost per copy, 10½c.

Rose's Public School Geography.

Contains 408 pages, including maps, 14 single and 7 double maps, 4 color.

135 rms. 30½x41—80, 500 at 4¼	$486 00	
Printing 11 forms black	220 00	
Printing 1 form maps	90 00	
Binding at 13½c.	1,350 00	
		$2,146 00

Cost per copy, 21½c.

Public School Grammar.

Contains 192 pages, 6 32's.

62 rms. 30x40—70, 500 at 4½	$195 30	
Printing 6 forms	90 00	
Binding at 6½c. copy	650 00	
		$935 30

Cost per copy, 9 4-10c.

Morang's Modern English Grammar.

Contains 192 pages, 6 32's.

62 rms. 30½x41—75, 500 at 4½	$209 25	
Printing 6 forms	95 00	
Binding at 6¾c	675 00	
		$979 25

Cost per copy, 9 8-10c.

Public School History England and Canada.

Contains 284 pages, 9 32's and 2 4 color maps.

94 rms. 30x40—65, 500 at 4½	$274 95	
Printing 9 forms	130 00	
Printing maps and paper	30 00	
Binding at 7½c. a copy	750 00	
		$1,184 95

Cost per copy, 11 9-10c.

History Dominion Canada (Clement).

Contains 358 pages, 15 32's and 1 8 and 3 4 color maps and flag 5 colors.

118 rms. 30x40—70, 500 at 4½	$371 70	
Printing 12 forms	192 00	

Printing maps, etc. $95 00
Binding at 10⅜c. 1,075 00
                                                   ——————— $1,733 70

Cost per copy, 17 4.10c.

Story Canadian People.

Contains 476 pages, 15 32's and 1 colored and 1 relief map.
156 rms. 31x42½—85, 500 at 4½ $596 70
Printing 15 forms 340 00
Printing maps 25 00
Paper for maps 11 00
Binding at 11¼c. copy 1,125 00
                                                   ——————— $2,097 70

Cost per copy, 21c.

Weaver's Canadian History.

Contains 320 pages, 10 32's and 1 4 color map.
104 rms. 30x40—70, 500 at 4½ $327 60
Printing 10 forms 160 00
Printing map and paper 20 00
Binding at 8¼c. 825 00
                                                   ——————— $1,332 60

Cost per copy, 13 3-10c.

Public School Physiology and Temperance.

Contains 196 pages, 6 32's and 1 4.
63 rms. 30x40—70, 500 at 4½c $198 45
Printing 7 forms 105 00
Binding at 6¾c. copy 675 00
                                                   ——————— $978 45

Cost per copy, 9 8-10c.

Practical Speller.

Contains 208 pages, 6 32's and 1 16.
68 rms. 30x40—75, 500 at 4½ $229 50
Printing 7 forms 100 00
Binding at 6½c. 650 00
                                                   ——————— $979 50

Cost per copy, 9 8-10c.

Public School Book-Keeping.

Contains 88 pages, 5 16's and 1 8.
57 rms. 30x36—80, 500 at 4½ $205 20
Printing 6 forms .... · 90 00
Binding and printing cover at 6c. .... · 600 00
                                                   ——————— $895 20

Cost per copy, 9c.

Public School Agriculture (James).

Contains 212 pages, 6 32's, 1 16, 1 4.

    70 reams 31x42½—85, 500 at 4½ $267 75

    Printing 8 forms 130 00

    Binding at 7c. copy 700 00

                              ————   **$1,097 75**

    Cost per copy, 11c.

Public School Domestic Science.

Contains, 176 pages, 5 32's and 1 16.

    57 rms. 30x40—75, 500 at 4½ $192 37

    Printing 6 forms 90 00

    Binding at 6 3-8c. copy 637 50

                              ————   **$919 37**

    Cost per copy, 9 1-5c.

French-English Readers.

First Reader, Part I.

Containing 56 pages, 1 32, 1 16 and 1 8. (Print and bind 2 on.)

    Paper, 18½ rms. 30x40—70, 500 at 4 1-2 ...... $ 58 28

    Printing, about 35 00

    Binding at 2c. copy 200 00

                              ————   **$293 28**

    Cost per copy, 3c.

First Reader, Part II.

Containing 12 pages, 3 32's, 1 16.

    37 rms. 30x40—70, 500 at 4½ $116 55

    Printing 60 00

    Binding, 1 on, 4c. 400 00

                              ————   **$576 55**

    Cost per copy, 5¾c.

Second Reader.

Containing 128 pages, 4 32's.

    42 rms. 30x40—70, 500 at 4½ $132 30

    Printing 4 forms 65 00

    Binding at 5¾c 575 00

                              ————   **$772 30**

    Cost per Copy, 7¾c.

Third Reader.

Containing 192 pages, 6 32's.

    63 rms. 30x40—70, 500 at 4½ $198 45

    Printing 6 forms 96 00

    Binding at 6¼c. 625 00

                              ————   **$919 45**

    Cost per copy, 9 1-5c.

Ahn's First German Book.

Contains 76 pages, 2 32's and 1 16.
    26 rms. 30x41—95, 500 at 4½ $111 15
    Printing 2 32's and 1 16 .... 50 00
    Binding at 6c. per copy 600 00
                                                                           $761 15
    Cost per copy, 7 6-10c.

Ahn's Second German Book.

Containing 176 pages, 5 32's and 1 16.
    30½x41—95, 500 at 4½ $243 67
    Printing 105 00
    Binding at 11c. per copy 1,100 00
                                                                           $1,448 67
    Cost per copy, 14½c.
    Leather back, stamped in gold.

High School Reader.

Contains 512 pages, 16 32 page forms.
    166 rms. 30x40—65, 500 at 4½ $485 00
    Printing 16 32's 230 00
    Binding at 11½c. copy 1,150 00
                                                                          $1,965 00
    Cost per copy, 19 7-10c.

Principles, Practice of Reading.

Contains 256 pages, 8 32 page forms.
    85 rms. 30½x41—80, 500 at 4½ $298 80
    Printing 8 32's 125 00
    Binding at 7¼c. per copy 725 00
                                                                          $1,148 80
    Cost per copy, 11½c.

High School English Grammar.

Contains 416 pages, 13 32's.
    135 rms. 30x42—80, 500 at 4½ $486 00
    Printing 13 32's 195 00
    Binding at 10¾c. per copy 1,075 00
                                                                          $1,756 00
    Cost per copy, 17 6-10c.

Elementary English Composition.

Contains 242 pages, 7 32's, 16 and 1 4 and one insert.
    79 rms. 30x40—80, 500 at 4½ $284 40
    Printing 9 forms 165 00
    Insert, printing and paper 15 00
    Binding at 8c. per copy 800 00
                                                                          $1,264 40
    Cost per copy, 12 7-10c.

Composition from Models.

Contains 500 pages, 15 32's, 1 16 and 1 4.

161 rms. 33x44—99, 500 at 4½	$652 05
Printing 17 forms	265 00
Binding at 12c. per copy .,...........................	1,200 00

$2,117 05

Cost per copy, 21 1-5c.

High School Geography.   (Chase.)

Contains 478 pages, 15 32's and 8 colored maps, 4 colors.

156 rms. 30x42—80, 500 at 4½	$561 60
Printing 15 forms	300 00
Paper for maps, 5½ rms. 80 lb......:...............	22 00
Printing maps 4 colors	125 00
Binding at 11c. per copy	1,100 00

$2,108 60

Cost per copy, 21 1-10c.

High School History of England and Canada.

Contains 476 pages, 15 32's 8 2 color maps and 1 4 color.

156 rms. 30x40—75, 500 at 4½	$526 50
Printing 15 forms	225 00
3 rms. 30x40—100 maps at 4½	13 50
Printing 3 color maps and 1 5	35 00
Binding at 10½c.	1,050 00

$1,850 00

Cost per copy, 18 5-10c.

The British Nation.

Contains 616 pages, 30 32's and 1 8 and 5 5 color maps.

211 rms. 31x42½—80, 500 at 4½	$779 60
Printing 31 forms	510 00
Printing maps and paper	95 00
Binding at 13c. per copy	1,300 00

$2,684 60

Cost per copy, 26 9-10c.

High School Ancient History.

Contains 454 pages, 14 32's and 1 8 and 10 4 color maps.

148 rms. 31x41—85, 500 at 4½	$566 10
Printing 15 forms ·....................................	240 00
Printing color maps and paper	150 00
Binding at 12c. a copy	1,200 00

$2,156 10

Cost per copy, 21 6-10c.

Botsford's Ancient History.

Contains 512 pages, 16 32's and 19 colored maps.

167 rms. 31x42½—90, 500 at 5c	$676 35
Printing 16 forms	350 00

Printing maps $125 00
Paper for maps 55 00
Binding, 16c. per copy 1,600 00
                                                        ───────── $2,806 35
Cost per copy, 28 1-10c.

High School Arithmetic.

Contains 400 pages, 12 32's and 1 16.
    130 rms. 30x40—75, 500 at 4½ $438 75
    Printing 13 forms 185 00
    Binding at 10½c 1,050 00
                                                        ───────── $1,673 75
Cost per copy, 16¾c.

Arithmetic for High School (Delury).

Contains 284 pages, 9 32's.
    93 rms. 30x42—80, 500 at 4½ $334 80
    Printing 9 32's 130 00
    Binding at 8½c. copy 850 00
                                                        ───────── $1,314 80
Cost per copy, 13¼c.

High School Algebra.

Contains 352 pages, 11 32's.
    114 rms. 32x42—90, 500 at 4½ $461 70
    Printing 11 forms 165 00
    Binding at 10½c 1,050 00
                                                        ───────── $1,676 70
Cost per copy, 16¾c.

Elements of Algebra.

Contains 390 pages, 12 32's and 1 8.
    129 rms. 30x41—75, 500 at 4½ $435 38
    Printing 13 forms 190 00
    Binding at 9½c. per copy 950 00
                                                        ───────── $1,575 38
Cost per copy, 15¾c.

Elementary Plane Geometry.

Contains 148 pages, 4 32's and 1 16.
    47 rms. 30x40—80, 500 at 4½ $169 20
    Printing 5 forms 75 00
    Binding at 6½c. per copy 650 00
                                                        ───────── $894 20
Cost per copy, 9c.

H. S. Euclid, H. R. & Co.

Contains 238 pages, 7 32's and 1 16.

78 rms. 30x40—75, 500 at 4½	$263 25
Printing 8 forms	115 00
Binding at 7c. per copy	700 00
	$1,078 25

Cost per copy, 10 8-10c.

Geometry for Schools (Theoretical).

Contains 280 pages, 9 32's.

94 rms. 30x40—85, 500 at 4½	$359 55
Printing 9 forms	135 00
Binding at 7½c	750 00
	$1,244 55

Cost per copy, 12½c.

First Latin Book and Reader.

Contains 520 pages, 16 32's and 1 8.

170 rms. 30x40—70, 500 at 4½	$535 50
Printing 17 forms	250 00
Binding at 10¾c	1,075 00
	$1,860 50

Cost per copy, 18 6-10c.

New Primary Latin Book.

Contains 572 pages, 18 32's.

187 rms. 30x40—70, 500 at 4½	$589 00
Printing 18 forms	270 00
Binding at 11¾c	1,175 00
	$2,034 00

Cost per copy, 20½c.

Hagerty's Latin Grammar.

Contains 448 pages, 14 32's.

147 rms. 31x42½—85, 500 at 4½	$562 27
Printing 14 forms	270 00
Binding at 11¼c. copy	1,125 00
	$1,957 27

Cost per copy, 19 6-10c.

First Greek Book.

Contains 368 pages, 11 32's and 1 16 and 1 3 color map.

120 rms. 28x42—75 at 5c	$450 00
Printing 12 forms	215 00
Binding at 13¼c	1,325 00
	$1,990 00

Cost per copy, 20¼c.

16 т. в.

Beginner's Greek Book.

Contains 544 pages, 17 32's and 1 3 color map.

177 rms. 30x40—75, 500 at 4¾c	$630 56	
Printing 17 forms	280 00	
Binding, 13½c	1,350 00	
Printing map and paper	30 00	
		$2,290 56

Cost per copy, 22 9-10c.

High School French Grammar and Reader.

Contains 560 pages, 17 32's and 1 16.

183 rms. 30x40—70, 500 at 4½c	$576 45	
Printing 18 forms	270 00	
Binding, 11¼c. copy	1,125 00	
		$1,971 45

Cost per copy, 19¾c.

German Grammar Book.

Contains 590 pages, 18 32's and 1 16.

193 rms. 30x40—70, 500 at 4½	$607 95	
Printing 19 forms	295 00	
Binding at 11½c. copy	1,150 00	
		$2,052 95

Cost per copy, 20½c.

High School Physical Science. Part I.

Contains 224 pages, 7 32's.

73 rms. 30x40—70, 500 at 4½	222 95	
Printing 7 forms	115 00	
Binding at 7c. a copy	700 00	
		$1,037 95

Cost per copy, 10 4-10c.

High School Physical Science. Part II.

Contains 454 pages, 14 32's and 1 8.

149 rms. 30x40—70, 500 at 4½	$469 35	
Printing 15 forms	240 00	
Binding at 10¾c. copy	1,075 00	
		$1,784 35

Cost per copy, 17 9-10c.

High School Botany. Part II.

Contains 336 pages, 10 32's and 1 16.

109 rms. 30x40—80, 500 at 4½	$392 40	
Printing 11 forms	170 00	
Binding at 8c. copy	800 00	
		$1,362 40

Cost per copy, 13 6-10c.

16a T. B.

High School Chemistry.

Contains 224 pages, 7 32's.

75 rms. 30x40—75, 500 at 4½	$246 37
Printing 7 forms	115 00
Binding at 7c. copy	700 00
	$1,061 37

Cost per copy, 10 6-10c.

High School Book-Keeping.

Contains 304 pages, 9 32's and 1 16.

95 rms. 32x45—100, 500 at 4½	$427 50
Printing 10 forms	173 00
Binding at 10c. copy	1,000 00
	$1,600 50

Cost per copy, 16c.

Commercial Course in Book-Keeping.

Contains 112 pages, 7 16's.

73 rms. 30x40—90, 500 at 4½	$295 65
Printing 7 16's and 1 form red	125 00
Binding at 11c. copy	1,100 00
	$1,520 65

Cost per copy, 15 1-5c.

Cadet Drill Manual.

Contains 160 pages, 5 32's.

52 rms. 30x40—80, 500 at 5c	$208 00
Printing 5 forms	90 00
Binding at 6c. a copy	600 00
	$898 00

Cost per copy, 9c.

Mr. STAUNTON: That will do, Mr. Grantham, thank you.

EVIDENCE OF MR. JOHN C. SAUL.

Mr. COOPER, Examiner:

By Mr COOPER:

Q.—It has been drawn to our attention this morning that on August 21st, 1902, a regulation was passed by the Department that no book should be authorized until after it had been in circulation for six months?

A.—Yes; I was responsible for that to some extent.

Q.—Do you know of any school books that have been authorized since that date before they were published?

A.—Well, the first one that was authorized without the six months' notice was, of course, the re-authorization of the original Ontario Phonic Primer. That book, as the Ontario Phonic Primer, had a turn-over cover; and when it was de-authorized on account of being printed in the United States, and re-authorized again as the Public School Phonic Primer, it was as you see it now, with a cut flush edge. Then this Public School Phonic Primer, Part II, was placed upon the published list of authorized books for at least—if my memory serves me rightly—for at least four months before it saw the light of day. It was on the list of texts issued by the Government, but was not printed or put in circulation until some time after Christmas.

Q.—What time is that list usually issued each year?

A.—The list is supposed to issue in time for the opening of schools. The rural schools open on the third Tuesday in August. Of course, the list should be issued in time for their guidance. But I think in that particular year the list was delayed until some time in September.

Q.—Any other book?

A.—The third book that was authorized some time—I cannot tell the time to a certainty—but six months before it was published, was a Geography published by the Canadian Book Company, called Rose's Geography.

Q.—Published by the Canadian Book Company: "The World and its Continents." Who are the Canadian Book Company?

A.—I do not know; I have no information in regard to that at all; I understand that Mr. Dan. A. Rose is connected with it.

(To the Chairman): That was on the list of authorized books at least six months before it was published.

By Mr. STAUNTON:

Q.—Do you suppose it was on before it was written?

A.—It was submitted to the Department, according to what the Registrar of the Department told me, in dummy form. Certain chapters were written and certain alterations were made, and the book was authorized on that.

Q.—Went on its shape?

A.—Went on its shape.

The CHAIRMAN: Authorized on manuscript, you mean?

A.—Part of it was printed; I do not know how much, but not all of it. .

Mr. COOPER: You can tell us who the Canadian Book Company are?

A.—I cannot.

Q.—You have reason to believe that Mr. Dan. A. Rose was the man?

A.—Yes.

Q.—Is Mr. Dan. A. Rose connected with the Hunter-Rose Company?

A.—Not that I am aware of.

Q.—About the Manitoba situation; were you living in Manitoba at the time the free text book system was introduced into that Province?

A.—I left just when the Attorney-General, who was also the Minister of Education, was taking the matter up.

Q.—Are you aware how the system has worked there?

A.—Yes.

Q.—Will you outline that system, and tell us how the Government proceeds in the whole matter?

A.—The Government purchases from the publishers of the books a certain number, basing the number required on information that they procure from the inspectors and others. These books are kept in the Central Depository at Winnipeg, under the control of the chief clerk of the Department of Education. A circular is sent out to the various public schools of the Province some time prior to the school opening. The circular asks for information as to the number of copies required of each of the books that are provided free by the Government. The replies to that circular are immediately acted upon by the clerk, who is kept there during certain times of the year for the purpose of looking after the orders and the distribution of the books and having the books sent to the schools. Each book has in the front of it—and this is part of the arrangement with the publisher—a card book plate, stating that the book is the property of the particular school district, blanks being left to be filled in by the teacher before the books are given out. That is repeated each year, and the school is kept continuously supplied with the books required. That system, so far, is extended only to the junior classes; they have not as yet begun to supply any of the senior books. What I mean by the junior classes, is really the first four grades of the public schools in Manitoba. The last four are not supplied.

Mr. STAUNTON : Why do they have the book card?

A.—As a matter of fact, it is not separate and pasted on, but it is printed on the front of the paper and bound into the book. That is simply to identify the book as the property of the school district.

Q.—Is that for the benefit of the publishers?

A.—No. When the book is sent out, that is printed right on the paper itself.

Q.—Does it cost much to print that notice?

A.—We sold them the first edition of fifteen thousand copies of our Modern Arithmetic, Book One. When we were having the book bound we simply had this lining paper stamped or printed, and it was bound in.

Q.—The card is "This book belongs to school section blank"?

A.—Yes, and then certain directions given for handling the book.

Q.—They fill in the blanks themselves?

A.—Yes. The books are used in the school, and the pupils are allowed to take the books home, but the books must, of course, be turned in by the children at the end of the school term, or when they are through with the book.

Q.—Do they re-issue old books, re-bound books, to new pupils?

A.—Re-binding books is left entirely to the school district. New books are issued each year as required when books wear out.

Q.—Do the districts pay for the books?

A.—No. They are donated by the Government.

Q.—There is no reason why they should re-issue the books in the districts; the districts do not save anything by it?

A.—Nothing.

Mr. COOPER : You are sure it is not taken out of the school grant?

A.—It really began in Manitoba in connection with the Roblin Government's securing an additional grant in connection with the school lands shortly after going into office; and they felt when they got this money from the school lands that they ought to use it, as far as possible, in matters pertaining to education; and so they devote a certain amount of it, and will continue to do that, to the purchase of school books.

Q.—What discount is the Government of Manitoba able to secure from the publishers?

A.—I do not know anything about that. As a matter of fact all the books we sold to the Government were sold personally by Mr. Morang, and I do not remember what discounts were given. I knew at the time, but without looking it up I would not care to say.

Mr. STAUNTON : Are the books sold and taken to Manitoba and carried in stock by the Government?

A.—Yes, as a matter of fact, however, it may be of interest to the Commission to know that that system does not by any means interfere with a very large sale for the books outside of the books that are provided by the Government.

Mr. COOPER: How do you account for that?

A.—A great many parents prefer to have the children buy their own books, so that they may do what they like with them. Other parents object to their boys and girls bringing home books that have been used by pupils on previous occasions. I see no other reason for it than those two.

Mr. STAUNTON: And they destroy books and have to buy new ones for themselves?

A.—Yes.

Q.—Lose and destroy books?

A.—Yes.

(To the Chairman): There is only one book authorized in Manitoba on each subject. That applies both the Public and High School courses.

Mr. COOPER: As an educationalist, do you approve of that principle?

A.—There are advantages on both sides. I could make out a very good brief for both sides of the question without any trouble. The double and treble authorization was introduced into our schools by the late Government.

Q.—Do you think the Manitoba school system would be applicable to the Province of Ontario?

A.—I see no reason why it should not be applicable, but I do not say that the Government could afford to do it.

Mr. STAUNTON: Do you think that the one book in each subject is sufficient, without being allowed additional books to study from?

A.—Yes, decidedly, if plenty of allowance is made in the supplementary reading; I would be strongly in favor of having one single set of Readers authorized as the text.

Q.—Children are now-a-days provided in their homes with books suiting their age, for reading; nearly every civilized family supplies the children with books suitable to their ages?

A.—Yes; and then the library idea is growing largely in Ontario.

Q.—Give us some examples of the double and treble authorization that you speak of in this Province?

A.—In the first place, the Ontario Reader, Parts One and Two, were authorized as part of the Ontario Readers, and they formed for many years the single set used in the Province. Morang's Modern Phonic Primer was brought out in 1902, and placed on the authorized list. The reason for that, however, was very largely that the Ontario Reader is not on the phonic system, and there was a very vigorous demand all over the Province for a primer on what is known as the phonic system of teaching reading. But that Morang's Modern Phonic Primer was no sooner authorized than another phonic primer was authorized for the Canada Publishing Company. At the same time the Phonic Primer, Part Two, was authorized for the Canada Publishing Company, and two months later Morang's Modern Phonic Primer, Part Two, was authorized; so that in the public schools of Ontario there are three primers authorized for Part One, and three for Part Two.

Q.—Is there any necessity for it?

A.—Well, there is an advantage in it.

Q.—But is there any reason for it?

A.—No.

Q.—There is an advantage in a man having half a dozen pairs of boots, but some cannot afford it?

A.—One is enough.

Q.—There is no real necessity for it?

A.—No, none.

Q.—You said there are three books?

A.—Yes; do you want another example of three?

Q.—Yes?

A.—In the High School there are three Latin Grammars authorized: Latin Grammar, by Henderson and published by Copp, Clark & Co., Latin Grammar, by Robertson & Carruthers, published by Gage & Co., and by Hunter Rose, I think, and Hagerty's Latin Grammar, published by Morang.

Mr. Cooper: Which was authorized last?

A.—Morang's.

Mr. Staunton: Now, there is a dead language, a language in which the Grammar has been hard and fast for two thousand years; is there any reason why there should be more than one book?

A. From the standpoint of Morang & Co., there was a very strong reason for authorizing our Grammar, because it was a better book.

Q.—Educationists ought to know when they get a proper Grammar?

A.—Yes.

Q.—Is there any necessity for four of them, except ignorance in those who authorize them?

A.—None whatever.

Q.—Surely Latin Grammars have been authorized for the great schools of England and America which are correct?

A.—If there is to be more than one authorization in a book like a Latin Grammar the field should be thrown open to any book.

Q.—I am not talking for the good of the trade, I am talking for the good of the people and the saving of money; is there any necessity or any reason for authorizing more than one?

A.—Not if you get the right Grammar.

Mr. Cooper: You think if the Government had done what it should have done, when it authorized your Grammar, it should have de-authorized the other two; assuming that yours was the best book?

A.—Yes.

Mr. Staunton: They should have de-authorized two of them, anyway?

A.—Two out of the three.

Q.—When they made up their minds that the second one they authorized was better than the first, they should have de-authorized the first?

A.—Yes. Then in the High School, again, there are two books authorized in Ancient History: Myers' Ancient History, published by Copp, Clark & Co., and Botsford's Ancient History, published by Morang.

Q.—Which was authorized first?

A.—Myers'.

Q.—Why did they authorize Morang's?

A.—For this reason, I think; that we very strictly followed that clause in the Government regulations calling for six months' circulation. Myers' is a very old History, and, as a matter of fact, the edition of Myers published in the United States at the present time is a very good book and infinitely superior to the old one. We circulated Botsford's through the Province of Ontario, and had the teachers so enthusiastic over it that they were writing to the Minister of Education and to us, and we simply for-

warded those letters to the Minister.   There was such a demand for the
book raised in the Province that the Minister placed it on the authorized
list after he had taken measures to find out about it through its submission
to people in whom he had confidence.

Q.—The consequence was that a pupil who moved from one district
to another had to buy both of these books?

A.—We succeeded in displacing Myers in a great many institutions.
If you would compare those two books, you could see the reason in a moment.

Q.—Are you speaking from the mechanical point of view?

A.—I am speaking of both sides; both the literary matter and the
mechanical side. ("Ancient History for Beginners, Botsford," produced.)
That is bound by Fleming.   Owing to the fact that Professor Botsford
had not made all his corrections, and still wished to make further changes,
the Macmillan Company would not hand us the plates of the book; and we
bought the sheets from them and had them bound.

Q.—Has that got a hinge on it?

A.—It is reinforced around the first section and the last section of the
book, and has head bands on it.

Q.—That is a well bound book, is it?

A.—A well bound book.   That book retails at one dollar; the American
edition at $1.50.

Mr. COOPER: Do you think it would be better to bind that in two parts,
Roman in one and Grecian in the other?

A.—It would; but would cost more.

Q.—The High School teachers have protested against that book as not
wearing well?

A.—I do not see how they could do that, with it reinforced.   If the
tapes were added to that, it seems to me it would hold. It is a heavy book.
Of course in a book of that nature, you have to have a calendered paper,
and that paper contains clay, and, of course, it is heavy.

(To Mr. Staunton): One of the strong features of Botsford's book is
the very excellent maps in it.

Mr. STAUNTON: What is the price of Myers' High School Ancient
History?

A.—Seventy-five cents.

Q.—Do that and Botsford's sell at the same price?

A.—No; one is seventy-five cents. and the other is a dollar.   It is
easily seen that there is no comparison between the two books, either in
paper, maps, binding, or any other way.   Botsford's is filled with illustrations of all kinds.

(Commissioners and counsel compare the two books.)

Mr. COOPER: Are these books both copyright?

A.—Yes.   The original edition of Myers is published in the United
States by Ginn & Co.; the original edition of Botsford by the Macmillan Co.

Q.—So that they are both published under similar conditions?

A.—Yes.   For the purposes of comparison, I would suggest that you
take these three Histories.

Mr. STAUNTON: These three Histories are all authorized for use in the
Public Schools or High Schools?

A.—Weaver's Canadian History, Duncan's Story of the Canadian People,
and Clement's History of Canada, the three books are published at the same
price, fifty cents each.

Q.—Do you remember what the original cost of them was; was it given
at the meeting?

A.—I do not think it was.

Mr. COOPER: They are all the same price?

A.—The same price.

Q.—Do you think that the binding of your History might be improved?

A.—There is the last edition of that book, and you will see it is bound on tapes. As we have re-bound our books, we have been putting them on the tapes.

Q.—And it is your intention to use tapes in future?

A.—Yes.

Q.—What is the difference in the cost between Weaver and Duncan?

Mr. GRANTHAM: About six and a half cents.

Mr. STAUNTON: I want you to tell me about the American discounts, Mr. Saul?

A.—I notice some evidence was given the other day in regard to discounts by the American houses,—as a matter of fact, the American houses —Ginn & Co., D. C. Heath, the American Book Company, Macmillan— have a uniform discount of twenty per cent. for school books. It was said the other day that the discounts varied from 25 to 35 per cent. They do not.

Q.—You have ascertained that as a fact?

A.—Yes. The American School Book discount in the United States is twenty per cent. They have what is known as their export discount there, which is twenty-five per cent.

Q.—That is the dumping clause?

A.—Yes.

Mr. COOPER: Just on this point; is that a discount off the list price, or does that discount apply to dealers in States where there is State authorization?

A.—No, it does not; because where there is State authorization the wholesale price is fixed by contract, the price at which they sell it to the dealers.

Q.—Then it would not be fair to make a comparison between a discount given by New York publishers and the discount given by Ontario publishers, in the case of authorized books?

A.—Not except in States where there is open competition.

The CHAIRMAN: About Manitoba; do you sell any books to Manitoba except the Arithmetic?

A.—To the Government?

Q.—Yes?

A.—Yes, we sell "Our Home and its Surroundings," and we sell a bi-lingual French-English Reader, a Reader prepared especially for the French-English schools.

Q.—In each of these subjects there is only the book authorized that you supply them with?

A.—Yes.

Q.—What arrangement have they there with you as to authorizing a book before it is published?

A.—We have always submitted our books to the Advisory Board complete. They have absolute power in authorization. Once or twice we did submit a book in page form before it was bound; for instance, Morang's Complete Geography is authorized in Manitoba now. We have, altogether, in Manitoba, fourteen books on the authorized list that are sold in the Province. Three of those are sold to the Government; the rest are sold to the trade; and sole authorization in each case.

Q.—For how long a period is that authorization to last?

A.—Until such time as the Advisory Board think that a better book is in the field and desire to remove the books.

Q.—They may remove any one of these books of yours from the list at any time?

A.—At any time; except that when a change is made in Manitoba they give a year's notice, in order to allow the booksellers to clean out their stock, and after that they allow the book to be "worked out," as it is called; that is, no new books may be produced, but the old books may continue to be used.

Q.—Does that obtain in relation to the three books that you sell to the Government?

A.—Yes.

Q.—There is no particular time when they are to lapse?

A.—No.

Q.—There must be some limits to the Government sending out books to each section; you spoke of their sending out a circular and asking the number of books required for next year; there must be some limit?

A.—As far as I know, they have honored all the requisitions; we are supplying them with books constantly.

Q.—A section might make fuel of the books?

A.—I suppose there are proper restrictions in connection with it?

Mr. COOPER: Do you know what those restrictions are?

A.—No.

The CHAIRMAN: It would be interesting to know what you sold this Arithmetic for?

A.—The retail price is forty cents, but I do not recollect what it was sold to the Government for.

Commission takes recess.

EVIDENCE OF MR. GEORGE SMITH.

Mr. STAUNTON, Examiner:

WITNESS: I am going to place before you a few of our samples from George Philip & Son, Geographical Institute, Fleet Street, London, to show you their publications and their prices.

Q.—Are you their representative here?

A.—Yes.

Q.—Permanently settled here?

A.—Yes.

Q.—Where is your place?

A.—No. 21, Richmond Street West.

Q.—What are those books you have before you?

A.—They are different kinds of school books used in England in different parts of the country. My idea is not that they will apply to Canada particularly, but I thought there might be something suitable; and to show you the bindings and the get-up of them, and the prices.

(Submits a number of specimens.)

The discounts on these are thirty-three and one-third and ten per cent.

Q.—Those books are bound with tapes?

A.—Yes.

Q.—Is that used in the public schools in England?

A.—Yes, in some of them.

Mr. COOPER: Are there such things as authorized books in England?

A.—Each municipality gets its own.

Q.—The Government does not authorize any book for general use?

A.—No, the Government does not take any part in that whatever. The school boards have been abolished, and it is now the county councils. We get thirteen books as a dozen in England, or sometimes twenty-five as twenty-four. I am not showing these with the intention of supplying you direct with these books. Anything that the Commission might think favorably of, we would supply through Mr. Morang or anybody else.

Mr. STAUNTON: Through the trade?

A.—Through the trade. Of course we would sooner deal direct, but I know the sentiment in Canada.

Mr. COOPER: What do these copy books sell at?

A.—Twenty-four shillings a gross is the retail; sixteen shillings is the wholesale price, with ten per cent. off that. The specimen produced is a number bound together. I think you will find these books bound in a style that you like. They are all sewn with thread; there is no wire in them.

Q.—Is there anything else that you want to say?

A.—That is about all that I want to bring before you.

Q.—They are very nice books indeed; we will put them on fyle in the Department?

A.—I have only selected a few out of quite a number we have in the office. I may say that all these books are being adopted in Japan; they are taking quite a large quantity of these there. We have quite a number of other things, but these will give you an idea of the work we do. We have physical training books also.

That will do, Mr. Saul, thank you.

EVIDENCE OF MR. HENRY MOORE WILKINSON.

Mr. STAUNTON, Examiner:

Q.—What is your position?

A.—Chief Clerk and Accountant.

Q.—Do you know how early before the first ten-year contract ran out the Department of the Government was aware that the publishers of the school books claimed to have any exclusive right to the copyright in any of the selections in the Readers?

A.—I think it was three or four years before the expiration of the first agreement.

Q.—How did it come that it was brought to the notice of the Department?

A.—I could not say positively.

Q.—What is your recollection?

A.—I do not think the Department knew much about it until it drew near the time of the expiration of the first agreement.

Q.—You said they knew it three or four years before?

A.—Well, there was talk; but as for anything definite I do not know that you could lay your hands on it.

Q.—It was current rumor, anyway?

A.—Rumor that they were getting hold of the copyright.

Q.—So that the Department might, if it had chosen, have been prepared to meet them by having another set of Readers, or being prepared to exclude the copyrighted selections from any Readers which might be authorized after the expiry of the ten years?

A.—I think they had that option.

Q.—I see that Mr. Bain went to England; that is the Librarian of the City of Toronto, is it not?

A.—Yes.

Q.—And made a report to the Department in December, was it, 1894; do you know the date?

A.—No; I would have to verify it by the Department.

Q.—It says 1894 on the copy of the report that I have here; can you get any closer than that?

A.—No.

Q.—(Reads) "I reached London on February 5th." He had been sent over by the Government to ascertain the rights of the publishers in the copyrighted selections used in the Readers, had he not?

A.—I understood so. I understood it by Dr. Ross.

Q.—That report is made in February, 1894, because in the private letter in which it is enclosed that is the date given.

The report is read and put in, as follows:—

Memorandum.

I reached London on February 5th. On making enquiry I found that Mr. Gage had called on most of the London publishers about six weeks previous. He represented that the Minister was about to injure his property in the Readers and that he wished to secure the copyright of a number of the pieces. He also urged on some of them the advisability of proceeding against the Minister for infringement of the copyright. Mr. Isbister, trading under the name of Charles Burnett & Co., London, acceded to his wish in this respect, and gave him a letter which was dictated by Mr. Gage, authorizing him to recover damages for infringement of copyright prospective and retrospective. Mr. Isbister declined to recall his letter as he had placed himself entirely in the hands of Mr. Gage. Mr. Gage had also obtained from Mr. Stamford permission to reprint Miss Buckley's articles for which he paid the regular fee. I obtained from Mr. Stamford a letter in which he disavowed having given Mr. Gage any instructions to proceed for infringement of copyright, and stated that he had again written to him on the subject. Messrs. Macmillan & Co., of London, are the holders of the largest number of copyrights in question: I had two long interviews with the firm and they declined to grant any special copyright of those articles which they still hold. They had transferred their copyrights some years before of all of Tennyson's poems to Messrs. Copp, Clark & Co. They were satisfied that no action could lie against the Minister because the Minister had never issued any book with his own imprint; he had never in that way infringed the copyright Act. Any action must lie against the three publishers. They assured me, however, that no action retrospective or prospective would be taken against the Minister or the publishers as long as the present series remained in the hands of the present publishers. Messrs. Kegan Paul & Co. had been visited by Mr. Gage and had sold to him at the rate of one guinea for each article the poems of Dobson, Gosse and Locker. I purchased, however, from them the right to reprint Tyndall's "Clouds" and Dobson's "Circe." I have forwarded their receipts for the account.

Messrs. Chatto and Windus had sold to Messrs. Gage the right to reprint Geo. Macdonald's "The Baby" and Swinburne's "Forsaken Garden." Mr. Gage had applied to Smith, Elder & Co. for permission to reprint extracts from Mr. & Mrs. Browning's poems. He was refused. They have, however, consented to allow the Minister of Education to do so in terms of their letter of the 13th February, 1894. Messrs. Ellis & Elbey have sold to Mr. Gage the right to reprint Rosetti's "Cloud Confines."

Prof. Max Müller wrote from Oxford that the right to reprint his article had been bought by Mr. Gage, but that the Minister had full permission to reprint anything else.

William Morris consents to the reprints of his poems.

W. H. Allen & Co. consent to the reprint of extracts from Mr. Proctor's book.

Mr. W. E. Gladstone also consents to the reprints of his articles.

No reply could be obtained from Mr. Froude, nor from Father Nevil, the literary representative of Cardinal Manning. The copyright is just about to expire as far as Cardinal Newman is concerned.

Second Book. Sold to Mr. Gage, the articles Geo. Macdonald's "The Baby" and Norman MacLeod's "The Squirrel." Articles on "Tea" and "Coffee" from Blackwood's Readers, "The Lion" from Blackie's Readers, and "The Lazy Frog" from the Sunday School Union Readers are doubtful copyrights. John. S. Blackie, permission to reprint any of his poems.

Third Book. Tennyson's "Bugle Song," sold to Copp, Clark & Co. Tennyson's "Song from the Princess," ditto. Tennyson's "Brook," ditto. Tennyson's "May Queen," Parts I and II, ditto. Norman MacLeod's "Trust in God," sold to Gage.

Fourth Book. Tennyson's "Lady Clare," sold to Copp, Clark; "Dora," ditto. "Wild Bells," ditto. Buckley's "Piece of Coal," Parts I and II, sold to Gage. Dobson's "Before Sedan," ditto. Edward Arnold's "Florence Nightingale," ditto. Max Muller's "Shakespeare," ditto.

High School Reader. Rosetti's "Cloud Confines," sold to Gage. Ruskin's "Mystery of Life," ditto. Locker's "Old Cradle," ditto. Swinburne's "Forsaken Garden," ditto. Dobson's "Queen Elizabeth," ditto. Gosse's "Return of the Swallows," ditto. Tennyson's "Lord of Burleigh," sold to Copp Clark; "Break, Break," ditto, and "Revenge," ditto.

Q.—Mr. Bain says he purchased from Kegan Paul & Co. the right to reprint Tyndall's "Clouds" and Dobson's "Circe;" do you know how much was paid for them?

A.—I do not remember. It was a few pounds. It is on fyle.

Q.—At that time the Department was fully aware that these publishers had recently been in England acquiring copyrights so as to fortify themselves against the time to come when the new contract would be made?

A.—Yes, I think so.

Q.—And this contract was not made until 1896?

A.—No.

Q.—So that is there any reason why it can be said that the Department was forced into making this new contract with these publishers; had they chosen not to do so?

A.—No reason that I know of.

Q.—It has been said here by numerous witnesses that these books are not up to the standard prescribed by the contract?

A.—In mechanical execution?

Q.—Yes?

A.—Yes.

Q.—I see a memorandum here which I understand is by yourself, dated 13th November, 1901, which I now read to you:—

Memo for the Deputy Minister.

As the text book question is again being brought into the political arena it might be well to have the Minister look into the matter of mechanical execution of the books to see if his policy is in line with the ex-Minister's.

As far back as Hon. Mr. Crooks' time the Department from time to time made examination of the printer's and binder's work, but in the Hon. Mr. Ross' occupancy of the post of Minister of Education it was more carefully looked after. At first I had the work in hand and made visits several times a year to the publishers' printing and sales rooms, looking after the quality of the work. In order to give the examination work the prestige of the Queen's Printer's name, Mr. Thomas was afterwards associated with me in the work and for a time we made visits together and examined the stock from time to time at the warehouses or had specimen sheets, etc., submitted while printing was going on. The $_{w^ork}$ was so satisfactorily done that the examination gradually fell off to a yearly examination of books. Then it developed into the submission of specimen books annually of any new edition printed since the previous examination and a report upon these books. Since Mr. Thomas' death the work of examination has not been satisfactory because of the delay in the work of reporting on the sample books. For 1899 the report was very late in comparison with other years, while for 1900 no report has yet been made, although books were submitted last December and Mr. Grant has been told that to be of any use the publishers should be notified of any defects early in the year.

It is nearly time for another examination and report, and hence the submission of the matter for decision.

(Signed.)   **H. M. W.**

November 13th, 1901.

Mr. STAUNTON: Was there any regular and proper inspection of these books before they were accepted by the Department during the last four or five years?

A.—There has been no regular inspection for the last two or three years.

Q.—Is there any expert in the making of a book whose duty it was to make such a report?

A.—The late Mr. G. E. Thomas was a practical printer.

Q.—How long is it since he died?

A.—1899.

Q.—Has any practical printer taken his place?

A.—I do not know what Mr. Grant pretends to be. Mr. Grant is the assistant King's Printer.

Q.—Who is the Government printer?

A.—Lud K. Cameron, the official King's Printer.

Q.—You have seen the books that have gone through?

A.—Yes.

Q.—Have they been satisfactory, in your judgment, from a mechanical point of view?

A.—My work is on record.

Q.—I do not want to go over them, I want you to tell me what you think yourself?

A.—We have made many adverse reports during those years, as to the paper at times, as to the ink, as to the press work, as to the broken plates, and we stopped one edition because of the binding, long ago; it was being bound in 32-page sections instead of 16. We condemned the edition entirely, and it had to be gone over by hand. As to our report, I think you will find the expression is fairly satisfactory in most instances. We were on record in the beginning as being in favor of the thread sewing, but the wire sewing was on trial; it was thought at the time that we were too apprehensive, that it would be found effective; in fact, according to public opinion, the wire stitching was thought to be almost perfect, but we were afraid it would not be as lasting as the thread sewing, and so we put ourselves on record.

Q.—I have all the reports here, and insteal of reading them, I want you to summarize them. They are all here, and we will put them in.

Mr. COOPER: There was one particular one as to wire stitching?

A.—Yes; we preferred the thread stitching, and put ourselves on record at the time.

(The report of the witness and Mr. Thomas, dated October 31st, 1885, is read and put in.)

No. 9524. Draft of letter in reply to letter received, 14026.

EDUCATION DEPARTMENT,
TORONTO, November 7th, 1885.

GENTLEMEN,—Enclosed please find a copy of two letters received lately at this Department in reference to the binding of your Second Readers, and to which the Honorable, the Minister of Education calls your serious attention.

(Copy letter, 13,702, 13,354.)

(The letter when ready to be delivered to Mr. Thomas.)

W. J. GAGE & Co.,

Report on complaints in regard to Second Readers of W. J. Gage & Co., as contained in letters 13,354 and 13,702, with sample copy submitted.

Last April, Messrs. W. J. Gage & Co. bound a part of their edition of the Second Book, with the first three sections in 32 pp. each, the remaining sections in 16 pp., or 12 pp., but with a small section of 4 pp., merely pasted to the third section of 32 pp., near the centre of the book. This style of binding was objected to at once, and though Mr. Gage argued strongly, and at length in favor of it being strong enough, on our report the Department of Education caused a letter to be sent (May 1), to the three publishers of the Ontario Readers instructing them, from that time, to bind no more than 16 pp. to a section when the wire binding was used, and calling for the best work the Brehmer Machine can do. At the same time, the Department expressed its preference for the thread sewing as done by the Smythe Machine. It is the portion of the edition referred to in foregoing that is causing the complaints, and though without actual trial the degree of durability could not be tested, it is evident that their durability is less than was expected, and claimed by Mr. Gage.

The Department should press upon that firm the desirability and necessity for their own business reputation and credit sake, of replacing all these Second Readers, where complaint is made, with more satisfactorily bound books.

We report that though the publishers on obeying the instructions given in regard to 16 pp. to a section, there is a danger of all the wire bound books proving less satisfactory than desired as school books, and would like to see the desirability of discarding the wire, and coming to the thread sewing pressed upon the publishers, as we are confident that eventually the wire will have to be discarded as producing inferior work, as regards durability, to the thread sewing of the Smythe Machine.

(Signed) G. E. THOMAS,

Ass't. Q.P.

H. M. WILKINSON.

October 31st, 1885.

Mr. STAUNTON: Twenty years ago you made that expression of opinion?

A.—Twenty years ago I expressed that opinion.

Q.—Has your subsequent experience taught you that you should recall that opinion, or has it intensified your opinion?

A.—It has not caused us to recall it.

Q.—Do you think it was as bad as you thought it then?

A.—I do not know that it has proved as bad as we anticipated it to be; but at the same time we do not recall that opinion.

Q.—You from time to time condemned the books for one cause or another; sometimes binding, sometimes broken plates, sometimes type, sometimes paper; is that correct?

A.—Yes.

Q.—Did the Department accept books that were condemned by you?

A.—There was a clause in the agreement by which, unless the books were too bad the defective edition would be accepted, but they were to improve in the subsequent edition.

Q.—They were not to be naughty any more?

A.—About that.

Q.—Is that the way it has been done?

A.—If the defects were not considered too serious, so as to condemn the whole edition, they could dispose of that edition.

Q.—Where did you draw the line?

A.—In fact, it would be a report to the Minister, and he would be the one to draw the line.

Q.—Did you ever report that they were too serious?

A.—Not in those words. You will find our reports make very adverse criticism at times.

Q.—If you had been left to your own will, were there any books passed that you would not personally have passed?

A.—Well, I should have to look over the record.

Q.—What is your impression; do you think you would have refused?

A.—I think under that accepting clause, there was no edition bad enough to discard.

Q.—The fifth clause of the contract deals with that: "and that in case the Minister of Education points out to the said publisher any defect or defects in the sample copies furnished to the said Education Department as aforesaid, but not deemed by him of sufficient importance to cause him to hold his approval from such edition, then in such case the said publisher shall, in the next following edition or issue to that in which said defects shall have been pointed out, correct the same to the satisfaction of the said Education Department." But you did not understand that to apply to serious defects; that is only for trifling defects?

A.—It applies to defects of all kinds.

Q.—Do you not take it to mean trifling defects; because the clause goes on to say: "But in case serious defects are pointed out by the Minister of Education to the publisher in any edition published by the said publisher, and in case such edition is condemned by the Minister of Education as unfit for use in the schools, or for sale to the public, the condemned edition shall be withdrawn from sale for use in the Province of Ontario.''

Anyway, they could put anything through until the Minister came down on them and condemned it?

A.—Certainly.

Q.—As unfit for sale to the public?

A.—Yes.

Q.—And there never was any condemned, absolutely, was there?

A.—I think not.

Mr. Cooper: The original contract for the Readers was made in 1884; but this report of yours about the sewing was made in 1885?

A.—Yes.

Q.—A year and a half afterwards?

A.—About a year afterwards.

Mr. Staunton: Do you know whether any applications were made by any other publishers besides Mr. Morang, to be allowed to publish these books in competition with the three publishers?

A.—Warwick Brothers made application.

Q.—What became of their application?

A.—It would be on fyle.

Q.—Was that all that was done: received and fyled; was that the end of it?

A.—I could not say without looking up the records.

Q.—Were they ever authorized to publish them?

A.—No.

Q.—The Maclean Publishing Company applied also?

A.—I think so.

Q.—And they rapped at the door in vain, too?

A.—I would have to go by the record.

Q.—Were they ever allowed to publish them?

A.—I do not know whether they ever completed their application.

Q.—Did you ever make any report upon the duplication of books?

A.—Do you mean on the authorized list?

Q.—Yes.

A.—I may have,—there is a lot of my reports to the Department.

Q.—Did you ever form any opinion on it, whether it was overdone or not?

A.—It was certainly overdone in Dr. Ryerson's time.

Q.—But, in modern times?

A.—When Mr. Crooks came in he wished to improve it; at the same time, he gave an option. It is a matter of opinion. One Minister would prefer to have the option of two books, or so in a subject, and others prefer one. Dr. Ross's policy was to have one book as far as possible in a subject. I think that is the wisest course, so long as you get a book that will cover the course and be satisfactory to the great majority of the teachers who will handle the book.

Q.—You do not refer to all the teachers?

A.—A public school book satisfactory to the public school teachers who will use that book, and so with the High Schools, as far as possible. That is my own opinion.

Q.—I have a report here made by Mr. Jenkins; that is the report of Mr. Jenkins, is it not?

A.—Yes.

Q.—I will read that and put it in.

17 t. b.

Memo.

Re authorization of an additional text book in Geography.

At present two books on Geography are authorized for use in Public Schools, and these appear to be meeting the present requirements of teachers and pupils.

The multiplication of text books in any subject is quite defensible from a pedagogical point of view, but, in the interests of the parents, must have a limitation.

Moreover, the present Public School course of study is to be so thoroughly revised (and the revision will not probably take effect until after 1905), that any text book adapted to the present courses, or even to the course outlined in the "Draft" would in all probability require thorough revision within a year or two.

In my opinion, no additional text book on Geography should be authorized until the courses of study 'at present under consideration are finally settled, and not even then if the present authorized books meet the new requirements.

(Signed) W. H. JENKINS.

Mr. STAUNTON: They did authorize Mr. Rose's geography after that?

A.—I believe so.

Q.—Notwithstanding that report?

A.—Yes.

Mr. COOPER: I notice, Mr. Wilkinson—I have been reading a number of returns presented to the House, I have not been able to make head or tail of them; they seem to be broken very much. When a return was called for by the House, of correspondence in the Department, were all the letters in the Department put in that return?

A.—I could not say as to that. It would be the duty of the clerk of records to get out all the letters, and present them either to the Deputy Minister, or the Minister for supervision; and they would pass from him to the copyist. Personally I had nothing to do with those returns.

Q.—Who could give us that information out of the Department?

A.—The Clerk of Records will be the best one, Mr. Paull.

Q.—You had nothing whatever to do with the preparation of the returns?

A.—Not of such returns; not returns of correspondence. I have had to do with returns as to the authorization of text books, prices, discounts, and so on, but not as to the correspondence.

Q.—None of the correspondence is kept under your authority?

A.—No.

Q.—You know nothing whatever of the method of keeping it?

A.—Not in my charge.

Q.—You got up certain computations?

A.—Certain reports.

Q.—That related to the amount and number of text books used?

A.—Yes. I got up the last return to the House, the return got up this year, number 76.

Q.—Did you ever get up a return to show the number of books bought by the population of Ontario in any one year, and what the average cost per pupil was?

A.—I have made out several returns for a series of years.

17a T. B.

Q.—The Hon. Mr. Ross made a computation in some speeches that the cost per pupil was about sixteen and a half cents in the public schools of Ontario; did you get up the computation on which that was based?

A.—I think it was nineteen and a fraction.

Q.—Nineteen and a half; did you get up that return?

A.—I did.

Q.—Are you prepared to say now that you still find that correct?

A.—I am not, I regret to say. There is a clerical error in it.

Q.—I think that should be righted; I think we should have that on record; as that is an argument we shall have to answer?

A.—It is an unaccountable mistake.

Q.—What should be the correct figure?

A.—It should be between four and five cents more per book; instead of nineteen and a half, I would say about twenty-four and a half cents. Took too large an enrollment of the school children. I do not know whether I am primarily responsible for that, or the then chief clerk, but it was a very unfortunate mistake in the divisor that we used. After days of work, by accident a wrong divisor was taken, which made the average too small.

Q.—So far as you know, the other published records of that time are correct?

A.—I think so; to the best of my knowledge.

The CHAIRMAN: Was it part of your official duty to advise the Minister touching the mechanical execution of these text books?

A.—Merely to report, not to advise.

Q.—Was there any other officer in the Department whose duty it was, or who was competent to advise, or who was consulted respecting the mechanical execution of the book?

A.—Of course, the Deputy Minister was the next man responsible to the Minister.

Q.—I am not speaking of responsible, but competent as an expert?

A.—I never claimed to be an expert, but the assistant King's Printer was an expert, and I was associated with him as representing the Department. Anything I did is done as representing the Department, not claiming to be an expert, but just using common sense.

Q.—Were you consulted as to the use of wire stitching?

A.—Not at first.

Q.—You were not consulted then?

A.—I had nothing to do with it at first. The compilation Committee consulted with the Minister as to the style of binding and all details. I had nothing to do with it until the books were coming out.

Q.—When were you first employed to examine the mechanical execution of these books?

A.—I was appointed at first by Mr. Crooks, in connection with Dr. Hodgins.

Q.—And you have been connected afterwards with what has been done in that way?

A.—Since 1878 or 1879, looking after the mechanical execution of the text books.

Q.—Were you consulted about that when the contract was renewed in 1896?

A.—No.

Q.—Prior to that, I see by this report of the 7th November, 1885, you reported against wire binding?

"We report that though the publishers are obeying the instructions given in regard to sixteen pages to a section, there is a danger of all the wire bound books proving less satisfactory than desired as school books, and would like to see the desirability of discarding the wire and coming to the thread sewing pressed upon the publishers, as we are confident that eventually the wire will have to be discarded as producing inferior work, as regards durability, to the thread sewing of the Smythe machine."

That was your opinion in 1885?

A.—Yes.

Q.—Eleven years afterwards this contract was renewed, permitting this very thing that you were objecting to?

A.—Yes.

Q.—Do you know how that came about; did you change your mind, or do you know of any one in the Department after that who desired to continue the wire binding?

A.—The assistant King's Printer was the one that would have to do with that; he was consulted by the Minister of Education.

Q.—That was Mr. Thomas?

A.—Yes.

Q.—He signed this report with you?

A.—Yes.

Q.—Unless he changed his mind he could not advise to have wire binding?

A.—Of course, the experience of the ten years may have changed his opinion as to the want of durability in the wire binding.

Q.—It did not affect yours?

A.—The complaints coming in to the Department were very frequent as to the defectiveness of the wire binding.

Q.—Were there any coming in approving of it?

A.—You would not get reports of that kind.

Q.—Whatever was said about it was against it?

A.—Would be negative.

Q.—The objection now appears to be very general against it?

A.—Yes, it has had its trial.

Q.—Was not the first ten years enough for its trial? You were satisfied with the trial of one year?

A.—That was not one year.

Q.—You say, "We are confident that eventually the wire will have to be discarded as producing inferior work, as regards durability, to the thread sewing of the Smythe machine." Time has vindicated you in that respect. Notwithstanding that report, and notwithstanding all the reports which came in against wire binding, the contract permitting wire binding was renewed ten years?

A.—Yes.

Mr. STAUNTON: Nobody was paying any attention to it; it was just allowed to drift along?

A.—There was no action taken.

Q.—There was no real care or inspection made of these books the last ten years, as far as I can see?

A.—I think our reports will show otherwise than that.

Q.—You did, but nothing followed?

A.—It was not in the power of the inspectors to make any change; when we reported, our work was done.

The CHAIRMAN: Am I right on the conclusion that you were not consulted at all as to this mechanical execution just prior to the renewal of the contract?

A.—I was not consulted, but the assistant King's Printer was.

Mr. COOPER: Do you not think it should have been the duty of some person in the Department to help the Minister to keep the books up to the improving standard that was going on in the outside world?

A.—The inspection was to keep them fairly well up, as well as we could, up to the specifications of the agreement.

Q.—You did not take into account the standard—

A.—We had nothing to do with outside standards; our examination was in connection with the specifications. We would have been going beyond our duty if we reported otherwise.

Q.—Then the Minister cannot expect any help from this Department in preventing wrong contracts?

A.—He had his Deputy Minister to rely on. It might be considered impertinent for the staff to make suggestions.

Q.—Do you think down town in a business house a man would be considered impertinent to make a suggestion?

A.—We made our reports to the best of our belief from time to time; we honestly reported what we considered the defects, and we are on record.

The CHAIRMAN: Do you not think that although the Government might be bound for the first ten years it would have been well to make these improvements before any renewal of the contract was made?

A.—I do not know that I considered it my duty to offer any such opinion to the Minister at that time; in fact, I was not consulted in many instances in relation to the text books.

Q.—I notice several reports signed by you in writing, such as that of November 7th, 1885; did not you suggest in some of these that "although we may be bound to adhere to this contract for ten years, we had better not renew it, it is not satisfactory;" did you do anything of that kind?

A.—It is for the Minister to say. We would not offer him any suggestions.

Q.—You were rather serving the public than the Minister?

A.—Serving both.

Mr. COOPER: Most of the time you forgot about the public?

A.—I do not think our reports will show that. I think our reports are pretty hard on the publishers. You must remember that the style of binding was on trial. It is very easy to be wise after an event.

Q.—But that started in 1878?

A.—That was our opinion. You must remember that Mr. Gage advertised the superiority of the wire binding—"An iron bound book"—for years and years in the press, and there was a general public opinion that that was the best binding; and Mr. Gage is perhaps responsible more than anybody else as to the wire stitching. I think that when we made our representations as to the superiority of the thread binding that the publishers made representation to the Minister that we were unduly apprehensive, and it was decided that the wire binding should continue.

The CHAIRMAN: As representing and on behalf of the public, you would not expect the statement made by a publisher who was interested to be taken in preference to your opinion?

A.—It was not made to myself.

Q.—You gave that as a suggestion why the public was influenced by Mr. Gage; he was interested?

A.—And the head of the Department had the decision in the matter.

EVIDENCE OF MR. ARTHUR CHARLES PAULL.

Mr. COOPER, Examiner.

By Mr. COOPER:

Q.—You are the Clerk of Records of this Department. A certain number of returns were presented to the Legislature in the last ten years, containing a certain amount of correspondence?

A.—Yes, copies.

Q.—In reading those over I have found a great many breaks in them, and I had difficulty in understanding just what happened. When a return as asked for was all the correspondence put in there, or was a selection made?

A.—Some letters were left out. The Minister went through and made his own selections as to what he would put in. What was left out, of course, I could not say without checking the thing through.

Q.—Then it was in the discretion of the Minister what letters should be put in and what should be left out?

A.—Yes.

A.—And the returns do not necessarily contain all the correspondence?

A.—No.

The Commission adjourned at 3.30 p.m.

WEDNESDAY, NOVEMBER 7TH, 1906.

EVIDENCE OF MR. H. L. THOMPSON.

Mr. STAUNTON, Examiner.

By Mr. STAUNTON:

Q.—What is your position, Mr. Thompson?

A.—President of the Copp, Clark Company.

Q.—Do you take any active part in the management of the company?

A.—Yes.

Q.—What active part do you take, and for how long have you taken it?

A.—I have been president of the company for about fifteen years; since the death of Mr. Copp, in 1894. That would be only twelve years; and I have been connected with the company for forty years last March, that is, with the old company and the new one, and I have general oversight of matters. I have had to do with the educational part perhaps more than some of the other detail.

Q.—Then you were in the company's employment or as shareholder or director when the first contract was made with the Government for the Readers, were you not, in 1886?

A.—In 1886, yes; but not 1884.

Mr. COOPER: November, 1884, is the original contract.

Mr. STAUNTON: What was your position in November, 1884?

A.—I think I could call myself a confidential clerk.

Q.—Had you anything to do with the making of that contract?

A.—Nothing whatever.

Q.—You knew nothing whatever about it?

A.—Excepting what they told me as the matter proceeded.

Q.—You were in a more responsible position in 1896, when the new contract was made?

A.—In 1896 I was president of the company.

Q.—And as such you had a hand in the making of this new contract?

A.—Yes.

Q.—Prior to the making of that contract, did you personally do anything towards obtaining the copyright upon any of the selections that appeared in those Readers?

A.—Yes.

Q.—What selections did you interest yourself in obtaining the copyright of?

A.—A number of selections. The only list that we ever had was left with you by the Secretary-Treasurer, Mr. Thomas, when he was here under examination.

Q.—You obtained those yourself; you went to England?

A.—I went to England, yes, on my usual trip.

Q.—You did go there; what year?

A.—That was in 1893. I am speaking from memory there. The letter would show it.

Q.—Did any of the other publishers go with you?

A.—No.

Q.—Did you have any conference with them before you went?

A.—I had several conversations with them before I left.

Q.—I do not know about the distinction between the two. Had you a conference with them?

A.—As far as I know, you can call it a conference. We talked over it.

Q.—Who was present at the conference?

A.—That I cannot tell you. I talked the matter over with S. G. Beatty, the President of the Canada Publishing Company, and with Mr. Gage.

Q.—Were they interested in those selections that you were obtaining the copyright of?

A.—They were in the Readers that we were all publishing.

Q.—But were they interested in the selections you were obtaining copyright on?

A.—Only those that were in the Readers. They were publishing the Readers, so they were interested in the selections.

Q.—Why were they interested in obtaining copyright on them?

A.—We were all interested in securing the copyrights.

Q.—But I do not see why you were; you had been publishing them for eight or ten years?

A.—We had heard prior to this that a number of the selections that were in the Readers were not owned by the Government, who had given us the plates.

Q.—Had heard this in writing?

A.—No. I do not know how it first came out.

Q.—You had heard that the Government was not the owner of all the selections that were in the Readers; then, of course, you personally believed when you made the contract that the Government was the owner of all the selections in the Readers?

A.—If you had asked us at the time—

Q.—I ask you now; I want you to tell me frankly whether or not, before these rumors, which you speak about which were not in writing, came to your ears, you were under the *bona fide* impression that the Government was the owner of the selections in the Readers?

A.—The matter had not been discussed.

Q.—I did not ask you that. Were you or were you not under that impression?

A.—Certainly, if there was any impression at all, certainly that was it.

Q.—Then there may have been no impression at all. You do not publish a book without thinking whether you are going to have a law suit on your hands next week?

A.—I had nothing to do with the original arrangement.

Q.—Tell me, as definitely as you can, when and from whom you first heard that there was any doubt about the Government owning these copyrights?

A.—That is utterly impossible for me to say.

Q.—You cannot tell me anything that happened that put you on the alert until one of these conferences?

A.—No; I do not remember as to what brought the matter up at first. It may have been in the public press.

Q.—"It may have been." I like something definite, and I do not want to either trouble you or the Commission with anything indefinite. If you cannot tell me anything definite—

A.—Do not say anything.

Q.—Do not tell me that it may have been in the public press unless you can swear to it?

(No answer.)

Q.—Now, before you went to the first conference with these gentlemen, had you any information that you can now recall?

A.—No.

Q.—Then, so far as you know, your confreres in that conversation may have had all the information that was had by any of you at the time?

A.—As far as I know now.

Q.—You went to the meeting, and what happened, what did you hear there?

A.—There is no definite meeting in my mind.

Q.—You said you met these gentlemen two or three times?

A.—Yes.

Q.—Can you recall one time you met them?

A.—No.

Q.—You did meet them as a matter of fact?

A.—Yes.

Q.—You do not remember when you first met them?

A.—No.

Q.—What did you talk about?

Q.—You are asking me to answer something twelve or thirteen years ago now; I cannot tell.

Q.—You did not talk only about the weather?

A.—No.

Q.—You talked about this copyright?

A.—Yes.

Q.—What did you talk about in connection with the copyright?

A.—If I tell you what I am going to now, it is only just from memory.

Q.—That is the only thing you can call on unless you put it in writing; you did not put anything in writing?

A.—No.

Q.—What is your memory of it?

A.—My memory of it is that we discussed the dangerous position in which we were placed, that a number of these copyrights were apparently not belonging to us, and did not belong to the Government, and we were in the very unfortunate position of being assailed by anyone who might find that out.

Q.—That is what took place?

A.—As far as I can remember, that is what happened. '

Q.—You met there because you were fearful of an attack by the owners of the copyright?

A.—Not of necessity the owners of the copyright.

Q.—The controllers of the copyright?

A.—Or anybody who bought up any of these selections.

Q.—The owners or controllers, or a person interested or expecting to be interested?

A.—A person in that position, whose interest was against you:

Q.—So that you were fearful that having pirated these selections you might be attacked?

A.—Yes; we did not pirate them; we took what was given to us.

Q.—Having pirated them in law?

A.—Yes.

Q.—Having put yourself in the position of a pirate, you might be attacked?

A.—That is it; that is the reason.

Q.—And the only reason?

A.—That was my reason. I am speaking for myself.

Q.—That was the reason, and the only reason?

A.—There were other reasons that would grow out of that.

Q.—Let us see them grow?

A.—The first was that we did not know but that the owners of the copyrights might attack us. If I got control of those copyrights—I am speaking for myself—the only thing to do was the fair, straight thing, and tell the owners of the copyrights.

Q.—Never mind the owners. I want you to tell me the other grounds of your fear?

A.—The other point would be that at the end of the other term of ten years, the Government might give those to somebody else.

Q.—The Government might act like free men, and make another contract where they chose?

A.—The Government might take those Readers and give them to somebody else, and prevent our going on publishing them; taking away to that extent the rights that we had in the Readers.

Q.—Had you any rights?

A.—Well, we proposed to get some rights. We had no rights other than what were in the agreements.

Q.—And when your company—men of full stature in intelligence—made that contract, they knew that it was for ten years, and would terminate at the end of that time?

A.—Yes.

Q.—And you also knew that other people might be allowed to print these Readers?

A.—Yes.

Q. And you anticipated that perhaps somebody else, at the end of the term, would be allowed to compete for the Readers?

A.—Yes.

Q.—That would be perfectly legitimate and business like on the part of the Government?

A.—Yes. We did not propose to let them do that if we could help it.

Q.—After you had talked for a little while, the "dangerous position" disappeared, and the personal interest grew larger, in the reason of obtaining these copyrights?

A.—Put that again?

Q.—The real meaning and cause of this meeting was to fortify yourself against losing the renewal of the contract?

A.—It was to maintain our own position, and to hold—

Q.—Hold up anybody?

A.—No.

Q.—You wanted to leave the Government free?

A.—Free, if it did not hurt us.

Q.—Am I wrong in understanding that the real reason of this meeting was to see if you could not put the Government into such a corner that they would not be able to contract with anybody but yourself?

A.—That was not my intention at all.

Q.—So that they could not contract with anybody else?

A.—That was partly so.

Q.—That is what I mean by putting them in a corner?

A.—In the first place, we intended to secure ourselves, and if in doing so we could secure the rights for the longer term we proposed to do it.

Q.—That was in 1893. You did not, I suppose, communicate that to the Government?

A.—No.

Q.—You did not tell them that they had put you in a position where you might be injured, and ask them to protect you?

A.—I am sure I did not tell them.

Q.—You went about this matter secretly, as far as the Government was concerned?

A.—Did not tell them about it.

Q.—Did you go to England?

A.—Yes.

Q.—Anybody go with you?

A.—No.

Q.—Did you agree to obtain a certain lot of the copyrights, and the others to obtain another lot?

A.—No, there was nothing of that kind said.

Q.—No understanding between you?

Q.—Nothing as to what I was to get, because I did not know.

Q.—Was there no understanding between you?

A.—There was an understanding—

Q.—Was there an understanding as to what you should do and what they should do?

A.—There was an understanding before I went away; we had talked it over.

Q.—What was the understanding?

A.—There was an understanding that we were to secure the copyright, protect ourselves.

Q.—The three of you?

A.—We were all going to act together; we were going to secure all the copyrights we could.

Q.—Were you to pay for that out of a common purse?

A.—I do not think anything was said about that at the time. There was nothing said about that at the time.

Q.—In the result, did you charge it to the common purse?

A.—Yes. The largest charge that we made was paid part by each of the others.

Q. So that you pooled the copyrights in the end?

A.—Yes, I think you can say we pooled them.

Q.—You went to England?

A.—Yes.

Q.—I suppose you went to the publishers, saw them?

A.—Yes.

Q.—Did you do what Mr. Gage is said to have done, try to set them on to the Government?

Q.—Did you try to?

A.—No.

Q.—Did you urge upon any of the publishers the advisability of proceeding against the Minister for infringing the copyrights?

A.—No.

Q.—You did not try to set the heather on fire?

A.—No; I was looking after our own interest.

Q.—You did not point out to these publishers that they had the Government by the throat?

A.—No.

Q.—Did you indicate it to them?

A.—No.

Q.—I am told that you were the first gentleman from whom they found out that they had been hurt?

A.—I do not know whom you heard that from. That may be so.

Q.—It is so, is it not?

A.—No.

Q.—You took the books there yourself, and showed them; you said "In these selections your rights have been stepped 'on"; did you not do that?

A.—No. I showed them the whole of the books.

Q.—What did you take the books there for?

A.—To show them how we stood in the matter.

Q.—What books did you take?

A.—The set of Readers.

Q.—You went first to whom?

A.—I must ask you to let me state —

Q.—Tell me to whom you went?

A.—I do not know.

Q.—Can you tell me one publisher to whom you went?

A.—Yes; the Macmillan Company.

Q.—You went to Macmillan and you took these books to him; and had Macmillan, so far as you know, up to that time, any knowledge that his selections had been pirated, or any intention of commencing an action?

A.—I do not think he knew anything about it until I told him—till I asked him, rather.

Q.—Do you know of any other publisher who had any intention of taking any proceedings against the Government?

A.—No.

Q.—Not one?

A.—No.

Q.—Did you procure any of them to threaten the Government?

A.—No, certainly not, not to the best of my knowledge I never suggested that anyone should.

Q.—Did you get any authority from any of them to threaten the Government?

A.—No.

Q.—Did you threaten the Government either in your personal capacity, representing your firm,—or your firm?

A.—I do not remember doing so.

Q.—Then so far as you know you neither instigated any litigation or threatened any litigation or caused any person else to threaten any litigation against the Government or Department?

A.—No, but now, Mr. Staunton, there are papers in connection with this copyright matter in the hands of our solicitor, Mr. Nesbitt; and I saw him last night and he said he did not know what he had, and he wanted to see, and he wanted the matter to stand so that he might look them up.

Q.—I am asking you so far as you know; I want you to tell me what you know, if there is anything of that kind so far as you know?

A.—So far as I know, there was no threat made to the Government. I made no threats as far as I can remember. If Mr. Ross or any one else said "now do you not remember saying so-and-so," I might then remember it. I remember nothing of the kind now. It is twelve or fourteen years ago. Made no threat.

Q.—Then you obtained those that Mr. Thomas had already told us you obtained; and did the other members of the syndicate go with you to England at that time?

A.—No, I saw none of them.

Q.—Were you there together?

A.—Not as far as I know. I do not know when they were there.

Q.—Did you meet them after you returned?

A.—After I returned I reported what I had done to our own firm first and then to Mr. Gage and Mr. Beatty.

Q.—Have you any correspondence between you and the other firms as to this copyright?

A.—No, I have no correspondence whatever. Mr. Thomas handed in all there was.

Q.—Then you have nothing in writing that Mr. Thomas has not produced?

A.—Nothing in writing, no.

Q.—By what argument did you induce these people to give copyrights for Canada on the selections in the Readers?

A.—May I give you an answer in the story of the interview?

Q.—Yes.

A.—I went to Macmillan & Company and told them that we had been publishing a series of Readers for a number of years; that I had them with me, and I thought, although I did not know, I thought that a number of the selections were used without permission of the authors and owners. Mr. Macmillan, with whom I had the conference, said "What are they?" I showed him the books; he looked through them, and he said "Why, these are honeycombed with our selections." I said "That is what I was afraid of; I did not know but what you had given permission to the Government to use these." He said "No, never been asked permission, never gave any permission." I said "We have been using these now for a number of years; we shall have to make some arrangement with you, because we are under contract to publish these." He said "You will have to take them out." I said "We cannot do that very well, we are under contract and under bond to publish the books." I said "You should look to the Government." "No," he said, "We cannot look to the Government, we are looking to you, because your name is on the title page." I said "There is the position of affairs: we have published these books, and we do not know what selections are copyright and which are not." He said "You leave them with me, and I will look them through." I left them there for two days, and went back. Either the first or second time, he made use of this expression, he said "Do you know you have walked right into the lion's mouth" or "lion's den?" I said "We have done what we thought was right; we found ourselves using these without knowledge as to whether they are copyright or not. We fear they are not out of copyright"—in fact, I knew some were not, because I knew Tennyson's selections were not out of copyright, but I did not know about the others, I did not know but that they might have given permission to the Government when the set was arranged. He said something would have to be done. I said "What can we do?" He said "Take them out." I repeated what I said before as to our contract. He said "The only other way would be for you to pay us a sum of money." His first suggestion was that we should pay him seventy or seventy-five pounds per annum from the first year of publication. I felt a little uncomfortable when I heard that. I said, "That is a large sum;" and we talked it over, until at last he said "Well, we will arrange for fifty pounds a year, and you are to send me the money when you go back, and go on paying it, but no one else is to publish them."

Q.—Was that your suggestion or his?

A.—That was his suggestion. No other name had been mentioned by me, no other publisher. My name was on the title page. I said "No; I must tell you that these Readers are published by three houses who have been under contract with the Government: the Canada Publishing Company, the Gage Company, and ourselves; and really, what happens to one will happen to the others." "Oh," he says, "You want to make some money out of this; you are going to sell this to them?" I said "No, I will take them back, and whatever you charge I will see that we give them the same rights;" and it was from that, that the letter emanated that you have in your possesion; and that is all that has occurred, as far as I know, either before or since.

Q.—Did you ask them not to allow any other publishers except you to use them?

A.—No. That is in the letter, that they were not to allow anybody else to.

Q.—Did you not suggest it?

A.—If I did, it came from the suggestion that no one but ourselves should use it.

Q.—You remember the rest of the conversation pretty accurately; did you not suggest that no other publishers should be allowed to publish these books with those selections?

A.—Possibly I may have done so; I could not say yes or no to that. If I were doing it again I would.

Q.—Would you not venture it a little stronger than "Possibly?" Don't you think probably you did?

A.—I think probably I did. It was in a conversation.

Q.—That is what you went there for?

A.—I went there to secure ourselves.

Q.—Against the Government and any competition?

A.—Anybody else.

Q.—Was not the reason you went there to secure that copyright so that no other person could use it in those Readers?

A.—That was one of the reasons.

Q.—That was present in your mind when you went to that interview?

A.—Certainly.

Q.—And you asked him in consideration of your money to give you that right?

A.—Yes.

Q.—The exclusive right?

A.—The exclusive right, certainly.

Q.—And he acceded to that; you came away with that understanding?

A.—Yes.

Q.—That is what you were paying your money for?

A.—Yes.

Q.—So that there is no doubt about this position; that you gave them fifty pounds a year on the understanding that you, the Canada Publishing Company, and the Gage Company, alone should have the right to publish Readers with these selections in them in Ontario?

A.—Yes.

Mr. COOPER: That was in 1893?

A.—That was in 1893.

Mr. STAUNTON: Did you obtain personally any concessions from any other publishers?

A.—I think so, but I have no memorandum of those.

Q.—Was substantially the same bargain made with them as was made by Macmillan with you?

A.—The other arrangements were verbal and were made by me with some publishers; I have no memorandum, and I cannot speak definitely about it.

Q.—Did you pay anybody else any money?

A.—No.

Q.—Or your company?

A.—No, I paid no other money.

Q.—Do you remember what other publishers you saw?

A.—No, unfortunately I can give you no help in that matter. I had the whole memorandum of that in my little notebooks of my yearly trip to England, and they were destroyed.

Q.—Some of the people gave you the right for nothing?

A.—Yes.

Q.—And promised not to allow anybody else to use it?

A.—Yes, that was the general understanding.

Q.—Let me understand about the right you obtained; was that right perpetual?

A.—Well, whatever that letter says is an answer to your question.

Q.—They say here that they have a right to terminate on six months' notice. Has this sentence in the letter anything to do with the copyright: "I should like to put it on record that the general understanding is that in the event of your taking up any book of ours at a special rate, we agree not to sell copies to any other Canadian bookseller at less than the ordinary trade terms, that is to say, ten per cent. off sale."

A.—That was the arrangement we had with them about various books of theirs.

Q.—Had that anything to do with this copyright?

A.—No. I did not know it was there.

Q.—Had you been a customer of theirs a long while before this?

A.—Yes; as far back as I remember.

Q.—You said you feared—you told these gentlemen that you feared that those books might contain some selections that were copyright?

A.—Yes.

Q.—You knew that the Tennyson copyright was controlled by these people?

A.—Yes.

Q.—So that you were absolutely sure it had been so, unless the Government had got leave?

A.—Yes.

Q.—You knew that the moment you opened the book?

A.—I knew that before I went.

Q.—You knew that when you took the contract, or your Company did?

A.—I cannot speak for them.

Q.—Publishers know; that is part of their business to know that?

A.—They should have known.

Q.—They must have known?

A.—No, I would not say that . Mr. Copp and Mr. Clark attended to it.

Q.—Every publisher who knew his business would know it?

A.—You would think so. They ought to have known. They certainly should have looked into it, but I suppose they did not.

Q.—You are not supposing that they did not look into it?

A.—I am supposing they did not.

Q.—Did not you suppose that when these school books were being published by the Government these gentlemen concluded, and rightfully, that no person would ever interfere with it?

A.—I do not think they took it into consideration; I do not think it entered into their mind to discuss it. My impression is that when the plates came to us we did not know the selections that were in the books; when the plates were delivered to us by the Government we did not know what they contained.

Q.—You went on printing them for ten years?

A.—Yes.

Q.—Until 1893, at any rate?

A.—That was the first time that the matter was broached.

Q.—Did you ever discuss it with the senior members of the firm?

A.—Yes.

Q.—Had they been taking an active interest in the business?

A.—Yes.

Q.—Who were the officers?

A.—Mr. W. Copp was President and Mr. H. J. Clark was Vice-President.

Q.—Then you came back here at all events; you cannot tell me about the agreement that you made with the other publishers; you cannot remember anything about it?

A.—I have been trying since I knew I was to be asked; I have been trying to come by some means of answering that, but I have no memorandum; I have not anything to go by.

Q.—Then you came back and you reported to the other gentlemen interested in the publications?

A.—Yes.

Q.—And they reported what they had done?

A.—I never heard any report from them other than in a general way, I do not know what the others did.

Q.—Did you lay your plan of how you would operate after that when you got back?

A.—When we got our copyrights we proposed to protect them.

Q.—Did you come to the conclusion how you would proceed?

A.—I do not remember coming to any conclusion. Mr. Nesbitt can tell you as to that.

Q.—Did you?

A.—We discussed it continually. We had the copyrights then.

Q.—When you had the copyrights you waited?

A.—We waited, yes.

Q.—When did you first show your hand to the Government?

A.—I could not tell you that.

Q.—Surely you have some recollection of that?

A.—No, I have no record nor recollection of that?

Q.—Was there not a pretty warm discussion between you and the Government?

A.—The new contract came up in three or four years after that, and the records will speak as to what was done.

Q.—I want you to?

A.—I cannot give you any particulars as to what was done.

Q.—Did you go to the Government?

A.—I went to Mr. Ross several times.

Q.—I want you to tell me of any threats or any course of influence that after you obtained these copyrights you brought to bear upon the Department or the Government?

A.—I do not know of any.

Q.—As far as you are concerned you did not endeavor to use these copyrights to coerce or threaten the Government, personally?

A.—I think I can safely say no to that.

Q.—Then you left the Government perfectly free to act in the public interest as they thought best, personally?

A.—Personally I am almost certain to have told Mr. Ross that we had control of a number of the copyrights.

Q.—I understood you to say that you had no interviews with Mr. Ross about this copyright?.

A.—It must have been discussed.

Q.—We are only here to find facts, and there is no use in the world in telling me about anything that you do not sufficiently clearly recollect to swear to?

A.—I remember of no conversation with Mr. Ross about our holding copyrights.

Q.—Do not imagine there was one?

A.—No.

Q.—You cannot remember any?

A.—I remember of no conversation we had. ·

Q.—You did not write him any letters on the subject?

A.—I remember of none.

Q.—What I understand you to say is, you did not take any unfair advantage of the Government, or any advantage of the Government, to obtain these contracts; you simply went into the market like any honest publisher would for the contract?

A.—Oh, no. We knew we had these copyrights.

Q.—You knew you had a gun, but you did not draw the gun?

A.—We knew we had them, and Mr. Ross knew we had them.

Q.—I want you to tell me what you did; I would like you to clear your skirts if you can?

A.—You are asking me if any threats were made by me, is that it?

Q.—Yes?

A.—I say, no.

Q.—You did not, so far as you know, make any statement about these copyrights to the Government at all?

A.—I told Mr. Ross that we had them.

Q.—You should have told me that before?

A.—This would come out in the discussion of the new contract.

Q.—That is what I am referring to. After you got yourself fortified with these copyrights, I want to know if you then proceeded to use them against the Government?

A.—Yes. I can say yes; I think I can say yes.

Q.—What did you do?

A.—I told Mr. Ross that we had a number of them.

Q.—And what?

A.—I do not remember anything further. I don't remember.

Q.—Why did you tell him?

A.—So that he would see that our interests were looked after in the next contract.

Q.—Did you say that to him?

A.—I do not remember saying that.

Q.—You did not just say "Mr. Ross, by the way, I have got these copyrights;" you did not put it that way?

A.—I do not remember. You must not ask me, as you do, to imagine something.

Q.—I do not want you to imagine anything. Do you remember telling Mr. Ross?

A.—I do not remember any one occasion.

Q.—What did Mr. Ross say?

A.—I could not tell you what he said.

Q.—Did he say anything?

A.—I am not speaking of any special interview.

Q.—If you cannot recall any occasion on which you told him, I do not think you should say you did tell him?

A.—I can recall no one occasion on which I told him, but I am sure he knew.

Q.—So that if you had any conversation with Mr. Ross it was of a most informal nature?

A.—I had a good many with him.

Q.—Most informal?

A.—Yes.

Q.—Not such as would stick in your mind?

A.—No.

Q.—He did not require much persuading, apparently, to come down?

A.—To give the new contract?

Q.—To you?

A.—We took it with the others.

Q.—That is not the point. You have a fairly good recollection of anything important. He did not require much persuading?

A.—I do not know what persuading he required.

Q.—You were there?

A.—I do not remember any special occasion I was there.

Q.—I understood you to say that the discussions with Mr. Ross were so informal and so unimportant that they have faded entirely from your mind?

A.—Any definite one, yes.

Q.—So that you could not have said very much about this copyright?

18 T. B.

A.—I fancy it was talked about a good many times; but it ends up in a contract, and everything else is—

Q.—I want to get the preliminaries?

A.—I do not remember as to the preliminaries?

Q.— When did you tell him?

A.—I could not tell you that.

Q.—Surely you would remember when you came to talk to the Premier about a matter?

A.—I had a good many interviews with him. When I told him that, I do not remember at all.

Q.—Was it immediately after you came back?

A.—I have not the slightest recollection of when I told him.

Q.—Do you think you told him at all?

A.—I am sure he knew, and so I suppose I told him.

Q.—Why do you think you told him?

A.—Because he knew.

Q.—How do you know he knew?

A.—There was a contract made later on that showed it.

Q.—Then all your recollection is because of the contract?

A.—Yes, it ended up with the contract.

Q.—Have you told me all you recollect about all that you did personally in reference to these copyrights?

A.—Yes. You asked me not to imagine something.

Q.—No, all that you recollect?

A.—All that I can recollect.

Q.—You have told me all your negotiations with the English houses?

A.—Yes.

Q.—You have told me all the negotiations with the syndicate?

A.—Yes. What did you ask me about the syndicate?

Q.—I asked you to tell me about the interviews?

A.—I reported when I came back. I cannot recollect any definite one.

Q.—Can you recollect anything indefinite?

A.—We had constant interviews and talks over the copyright, because there was so much involved.

Q.—Arranging to open the campaign?

A.—I do not know that there was any campaign.

Q.—You were the only concerns that would publish the Readers?

A.—We were the only ones that could publish Readers with these selections in.

Q.—Could anybody hold you up with a threat of prosecuting for using these selections if you had the giving out of the contracts for these Readers?

A.—If there were any that we did not control, they could.

Q.—Could not you simply omit the selections?

A.—Yes; the selections might have been omitted.

Q.—Easily?

A. That would have been for the Government to say.

Q.—Did it not strike you that you could go to the Department and they would say "We do not propose, as trustees for the public, 'to allow you to dictate to us;" they could have done that quite easily?

A.—It depends on how many there were. I do not know what kind of a hole they would make in the symmetry of the book.

Q.—They would fill a hole in the cemetery of literature?

A.—That might be.

18a T. B.

Q.—You made the contract; did the Government object much to give you the contract?

A.—I do not think there was any great objections made. The contract was made; it speaks for itself.

Q.—No, it does not say anything as to whether there was an objection made. There was not much objection made, as far as you know, because you cannot recollect any ugly interviews at all?

A.—No.

Q.—Everything proceeded so smoothly that nothing has clung in your mind?

A.—That is the preliminary matters.

Q.—You signed a contract with the Government?

A.—Yes.

Q.—Your house is of first-class commercial standing, too, is it not?

A.—I must refer you to Bradstreet.

Q.—No; I mean commercial honor and standing?

A.—I think so.

Q.—And Mr. Thompson signed this as President, and I see in clause 4 of the contract these words:—

"And it is further understood and agreed that in the event of any other person or persons, corporation or corporations, making application to the said Minister of Education for a right to print or publish the said Readers as aforesaid, the said the Minister of Education shall have the power to grant such right as aforesaid from time to time to such person or persons, corporation or corporations, subject, however, to the same conditions as are set forth in the agreement hereinabove recited and also the conditions set forth."

You under your seal promised the Government that you would not obstruct them in giving the same rights of publication that you had to other people?

A.—Yes.

Q.—And you led the Government to think that you had power to grant those rights?

A.—Oh, no.

Q.—Why? There is your seal for it?

A.—The rights that we had, our own rights; we could not give other people's rights away.

Q.—You did not tell the Government that you had cut off the source of supply?

A.—I did not propose to tell them.

Q.—Did you propose to deceive them?

A.—No, I did not propose to deceive them, but they could find that out for themselves.

Q.—You told the Government under your seal that you would give that right?

A.—Our own rights.

Q.—Did you tell the Government that you had made a bargain that would render that clause utterly inoperative?

A.—No, because they knew it.

Q.—They knew it?

A.—They knew it.

Q.—Then you want us to understand that the Government entered into a contract with you and put in that clause as a blind for the other publishers?

A.—No.

Q.—You said the Government knew that they, the Government, could not give that right to or get that right for anybody else?

A.—I think they knew that well enough.

Q.—You knew?

A.—Yes.

Q.—So that this thing was just simply a waste paragraph, and everybody knew it?

A.—I could not say that everybody knew it.

Q.—When I say "everybody," I mean you and the Government?

A.—What did you mean by "that paragraph?"

Q.—Read it? (Hands contract to witness.)

A.—That is what we signed.

Q.—I see your seal there, and I am asking you if it was a piece of deceit on your part, or whether they knew it was utterly inoperative?

A.—I feel sure the Government knew; I think they knew it.

Q.—But you were a great publishing firm, entering into a contract with the Government of this Province; we would expect good faith. The Government knew they were utterly powerless in your hands?

A.—I think they had very good reason to think so.

Q.—For what reason?

A.—We had a number of the selections, and we agreed we would take no action—

Q.—Is there a contract to that effect?

A.—There is a contract to that effect.

Q.—Have you got a copy of it?

A.—I think so. (Produces a paper.) This is the same as you have.

Q.—Look at this?

A.—That is the same one as this.

Q.—That is the contract and the only contract about the copyright that I know of?

A.—There is another one. This is not the copyright one at all.

Mr. COOPER: There is an accompanying agreement to that that we have all seen here, whereby they enter into the agreement.

(Some discussion follows as to clause of contract.)

Mr. STAUNTON: Look at clause 3?

Mr. COOPER: Yes, that is the contract; you are right.

WITNESS: Here it is, clause 3.

Mr. STAUNTON: Yes, that is right.

WITNESS: I have here a copy of the agreement of the 24th of March, 1896, respecting the copyright.

Mr. STAUNTON: I read to you clause 4. Now you say that they knew at that time that you could prevent, and you fully intended to prevent anybody else, did you not?

A.—No, we were not going to, because we had given our rights away in these to the Government.

Q.—Did you intend to prevent anybody else?

A.—No, we did not propose to.

Q.—None of you?

A.—I am speaking for myself.

Q.—Did you not all agree; were you not all in the same boat?

A.—Yes.

Q.—And you all signed the same paper?

A.—We all signed the same paper, yes.

Q.—And you were all in the same mind about it, so far as you know?

A.—As far as I know, yes.

Q.—Did you consult any solicitor?

A.—Yes; Mr. Nesbitt.

Q.—After you made that contract with the Government?

A.—I do not remember after; but about that time.

Q.—Did you consult any solicitor as to restraining the Government from allowing any person else to use it?

A.—I do not remember doing that.

Q.—Did you write to England, and set Macmillan up to doing it?

A.—No, not to the best of my knowledge and belief we never wrote them at all.

Q.—You could have obtained the right from Macmillan to let anybody else do it?

A.—We did not propose to.

Q.—You could have?

A.—I could not say that. I do not know what they would have done.

Q.—You could have let Macmillan give the right if he had wanted to?

A.—If he had wanted to?

Q.—Yes?

A.—Yes, if he had wanted to.

Q.—You, at all events, are clear that the Government knew at that time that you had this agreement with Macmillan to prevent anybody else from using them?

A.—No, I am not clear that the Government knew that we had any contract with Macmillan.

Q.—Then, you deceived the Government?

A.—No, I would not say that we deceived the Government.

Q.—The Government would not have gone to all this trouble to get this contract unless they were standing in with you, or were deceived by you?

A.—We told them that we would put no obstacle in the way; and we did not, and did not propose to.

Q.—But you did not tell them that you had made a contract with Macmillan not to allow anybody else to print the Readers?

A.—I do not suppose for a moment that I told them that.

Q.—Do you not think it was the part of commercial honour to do so, when you were signing a contract with this clause in it: "That each of the said publishers, in consideration of the rights of publication granted to them as aforesaid, and in further consideration of the terms hereof, covenants and agrees with the said party of the fourth part not to attempt to restrain, prohibit, or obstruct in any way, directly or indirectly, so far as each of the said publishers has any control over such extracts or portions as aforesaid, the continued publication in the said Readers of any of the said extracts and portions as heretofore published therein by any other of the said publishers, or any other publisher who may hereafter become entitled to print and publish the said Readers under clauses 4 and 5 as hereinafter set forth."

A.—Yes, that is quite clear to me.

Q.—Was it not your duty, as you understood it, to have immediately written to Macmillan & Company, saying, "We have solemnly promised under our seal that nothing we shall do shall prevent the Government from permitting anybody else, and we therefore release you from that part of our arrangement?"

A.—No, I would not think of doing that.

Q.—You intended to hold the Government as tight as ever?

A.—Just as tight as we could.

Q.—And you think that was honorable?

A.—Yes, and I would do the same again.

Q.—You are not likely to have the chance. That is your view of it, and you are of opinion that the contract was just waste paper, as far as the Government was concerned they could not give it to anybody else?

A.—They would have to take their risks; we could not move a hand to prevent that.

Q.—And you concealed it from them?

A.—We were not telling them; we are not telling all our business to everybody.

Q.—Now, did you go to Thomson, Henderson & Bell, solicitors here, after this contract?

A.—I do not remember. I have not spoken to him about it. He has been our solicitor for a good many years.

Q.—Did not he refuse to tell the Government, on your instructions, what the copyright extracts were?

A.—I do not remember that.

Q.—We will see. If he did it, he got it from your personal instructions?

A.—Most likely.

Q.—I read to you from a letter from Thomson, Henderson & Bell, dated December 3rd, 1901, to the Deputy Minister of Education; "The Copp, Clark Company (Limited), has handed us your letter of the 30th ult." Do you remember what that letter was?

A.—No.

Q.—Here it is; a letter from the Deputy Minister, dated November 30th, 1901, which I read to you:

TORONTO, November 30th, 1901.

DEAR SIRS,—I am directed by the Minister of Education to state that there does not appear to be on file in this Department, any list of the copyrighted extracts in the Ontario Readers controlled by your firm, for the use of which any subsequent publisher, if permitted to publish, would be asked to pay to the present publisher $1,000.00, or a proper proportion of that sum, as compensation for the use of such extracts. Will you kindly furnish this Department, at your earliest convenience, with a statement of the extracts referred to above, controlled by your firm.

Your obedient servant,

Deputy Minister.

W. J. GAGE & Co.,
    Toronto, Ont.
CANADA PUBLISHING Co.,
    Toronto, Ont.
THE COPP, CLARK Co.,
    Toronto, Ont.

Q.—You got that letter?

A.—Yes.

Q.—Why did you not answer it?

A.—We did not propose to tell the Government, if we could help it, what selections we held.

Q.—Why?

A.—Tell them our business?

Q.—It was not your business, it was your contract?

A.—We never agreed to tell them what selections we had.

Q.—And you would not do it?

A.—We would not do it.

Q.—What did you sign this contract for?

Q.—We made the best bargain we could with the Government.

Q.—Did you sign this contract of the 24th of March with the inteution of not keeping to it?

A.—We kept to it. Does it say there that we are to give a list of selections?

Q.—Shylock said, "It is not so nominated in the bond." Is that the idea?

A.—That is the idea.

Q.—Now, Thomson, Henderson & Bell, on the 3rd of December, 1901, answered the Deputy Minister as follows:

TORONTO, December 3rd, 1901.

JOHN MILLAR, ESQ.,
        Deputy Minister of Education,
        Toronto.

SIR,—The Copp, Clark Company (Limited), has handed us your letter of 30th ultimo.

On perusal of the contract between the publishers and the Department, we do not find that the publishers have undertaken to supply any list of the copyrighted extracts, and as there is litigation now pending in the courts over the question-of some of these extracts we cannot advise the Copp, Clark Company (Limited), to supply such list at present.

We are, sir,
        Your obedient servants,
        (Signed) THOMSON, HENDERSON, & BELL.

That suggests a new idea: were the solicitors deceiving the Government?

A.—I could not answer that.

Q.—Did you tell them to say that?

A.—That, most likely was the result of an interview with them.

Q.—Did you say to the solicitors, "You hunt up some reason for not giving this to the Government;" or did you tell them the reason?

A.—I could not tell you what was said at that interview; I do not remember that interview except as these letters appear.

Q.—How much money did you pay for this right personally—your firm—what did it cost you?

A.—You are speaking of which right?

Q.—The right to these copyright extracts for these Readers?

A.—Fifty pounds a year.

Q.—How much did you pay personally for the right to these copyright extracts?

A.—The firm paid fifty pounds a year.

Q.—How much did it cost the firm?

A.—We paid that. We recouped ourselves. We charge the others up with a third each.

Q.—Do they charge you up with anything?

A.—I think they charge us with some small amount, but I do not remember as to that.

Q.—Did it amount to anything more than a pound or two?

A.—No. It was some small amount.

Q.—On the 16th of March, 1904, the clerk of the Legislative Assembly writes as follows to the Provincial Secretary:

LEGISLATIVE ASSEMBLY.

TORONTO, March 16th, 1904.

SIR,—I have the honor to forward you a copy of an order made by the house to-day as follows:—

Ordered, That there be laid before this house, a return, showing the copyrighted selections and extracts from authors, used in the authorized text-books of the Public Schools, indicating in each case, the pages, and the names of the persons or company controlling the copyrights.

And I have to request that you will cause a return to be made to the above order with all possible despatch.

I have the honor to be,
Sir,
Your obedient servant,
(Signed) CHARLES CLARKE,
Clerk, L.A.

The Honorable,
The Provincial Secretary.

Mr. STAUNTON: On the 19th of March, the Deputy Minister of Education writes as follows to the six publishers named:

TORONTO, March 19th, 1904.

DEAR SIR,—I am directed by the Minister of Education to ask you to be kind enough to furnish at your earliest convenience any information regarding your text book publications that will assist the Minister in complying with an order of the house, a copy of which is herewith enclosed.

Your obedient servant,
Deputy Minister.

MESSRS. THE COPP, CLARK CO.,
Toronto.
CANADA PUBLISHING CO.
W. J. GAGE CO.
G. N. MORANG.
METHODIST BOOK ROOM.
THE ROSE PUBLISHING CO.

Mr. STAUNTON: And on the 23rd of March, 1904, you wrote a letter to Mr. Millar, the Deputy Minister of Education, as follows:

TORONTO, March 23, 1904.

JOHN MILLAR, ESQ.,
Deputy Minister of Education,
Toronto.

SIR,—We have the honor to acknowledge receipt of your favor of the 19th inst., in reference to copyright selections in Public School Readers, and in reply have to say that arrangements were made with English Publishers by which, subject to certain payments amounting up to the present time to over £500 Sterling, we secured a general permission to use extracts controlled by such publishers.

Without their consent, however, we are not free to furnish the particulars asked for, and as some of such extracts have recently been made the subject of litigation, and may again come before the Courts, we think it doubtful whether we can obtain such consent.

We are, sir,
Your obedient servants,
THE COPP, CLARK CO., LIMITED.
(Signed) H. L. THOMPSON.

Q.—Did you try to obtain that consent?

A.—No.

Q.—Did not want to obtain it?

A.—No.

Q.—Are you a member of the Canada Publishing Company?

A.—I am a shareholder.

Q.—A director?

A.—And a director, yes.

Q.—Who are the other directors?

A. The other directors are Mr. Beatty, Mr. Gage, and Mr. Warwick.

Q.—What is your company's interest in it?

A.—I have stock in it.

Q.—To what extent

A.—I would rather not mention that.

Q.—I would not ask you only that you are bound to return it to the Government; it is on fyle in the Department?

A.—That is not so likely to get into the press as it is here; you can look it up.

Q.—Who owns the Canada Publishing Company? Gage and Company, and yourselves and Warwick?

A.—Oh, the shareholders own it.

Q.—But you do not want to tell me. I want you to tell me whom it is owned by?

A.—I could not tell you whom it is owned by.

Q.— I want to know whether those three publishing companies own that company or not?

A.—I could not answer that; I do not know who the shareholders are: I have never seen a list of them.

Q.—Tell me how much your company is interested in it?

A.—I would rather not mention the amount.

Q.—I will have to ask you if you will not tell me the other?

A.—The Copp, Clark Company have no interest in it.

Q.—How much of the stock of the Canada Publishing Company is held by members of the Copp, Clark Company?

A.—I cannot answer that without looking it up.

Q.—Take a fly at it, and see how near you can come to it?

A.—I think our interest would be about twenty thousand dollars.

Q.—What is the total capital of the company?

A.—That I could not tell you.

Q.—You do not know?

A.—No, not without looking it up.

Q.—Who is the president?

A.—Mr. Beatty.

Q.—You know that Boards of Directors are supposed to know something these days?

A.—Yes.

Q.—You had better learn. The day is past for not knowing. You do not know what the capitalization of that company is?

A.—I do not remember.

Q.—You cannot tell me?

A.—I should think between eighty and a hundred thousand dollars.

Q.—Have you not got a third of the issued capital?

A.—About that.

Q.—I thought so; and I am not on the board either. Can you tell me what Gage & Co. have got in that?

A.—I do not know.

Q.—And you cannot tell me how much their interest is?

A.—I do not know.

Q.—Have Warwick's got some interest?

A.—He is on the directoraté, so he must have an interest; but how much I do not know.

Q.—Did you know that other people were trying to break into this good thing—publishing the Readers—during the past five or six years?

A.—I knew that Morang & Co. had requested permission.

Q.—Did you do anything to head them off?

A.—I do not remember doing anything definite to head them off.

Q.—Did you not pay some solicitors something to do it?

A.—Possibly so.

Q.—Your contract said that you would not?

A.—Since that agreement?

Q.—Since that agreement?

A.—Oh no, certainly not.

Q.—Did you pay the Beatty-Nesbitt firm anything for any work done in April, 1901?

A.—Certainly, we may have; he was our solicitor, acting for us.

Q.—Did you not help pay them for their action in preventing the Government letting anybody else in?

A.—Yes, if there was any bill we paid it.

Q.—There was a bill?

A.—Yes, he was acting for us. I do not remember what it was. I am afraid I have misunderstood you; I thought you were speaking of 1891.

Q.—1901?

A.—I do not know of anything at that date.

Q.—Did you know of any arrangement made with Morang to put him to sleep?

A.—No; no. I am not in the drug business.

Q.—You do not know of anything of that kind?

A.—No.

Q.—No attempt to make him stop troubling you, worrying you in your business?

A.—Through our solicitors, do you mean?

Q.—Did you try and make a contract with him?

A.—Yes; we had a contract partially drawn out.

Q.— What for?

A.—For the publication of a primer.

Q.—He was to get the primer, and let you alone?

A.—There was nothing in it about that. As far as I know there was no talk about that.

Q.—Have you got anything concealed about your person that will prevent the Government making a contract?

A.—I can speak only for ourselves.

Q.—Yes?

A.—I do not know of any.

Q.—You do not know what weapon you may use if it comes to fighting. You have not got anything with you?

A.—No.

Q.—So far as you are concerned, they could publish the books, if they liked?

A.—After the contract has expired we have our own rights back again.

Q.—Whatever they are?

A.—Yes.

Q.—Have you got anything yourself that you can use to prevent the Government from publishing these Readers after you are out of it?

A.—If the contract were ended?

Q.—Yes.

A.—Yes.

Q.—What is it?

A.—Our hold on all the copyrights.

Q.—What copyrights?

A.—The copyrights in England that we secured, and any arrangement the English publishers might see fit to make with us.

Q.—Have you made any since the contract of 1896?

A.—No, nothing since then; at least, I remember of nothing just now.

Q.—So that all you have got with you to use as a persuader of this Government is whatever arrangement you made about these copyrights in 1893?

A.—I would not like to answer that off-hand. I do not know what we had.

Q.—You have not been ever since making arrangements?

A.—Not about the Readers.

Q.—Have you been contriving anything amongst the syndicate whereby you can re-secure this contract?

A.—I do not think so.

Q.—Have you?

A.—I do not think of anything. I could not tell until the occasion arose.

Q.—Oh yes, you could tell if you have been figuring how you were going to get the contract renewed?

A.—There has been no figuring out as to getting the contract renewed.

Q.—There is a letter here in which Mr. Ross said to Morang "You had better see Thompson?"

A.—Yes.

Q.—What did he say that for?

A.—I did not know that there was such a letter until I saw it in the paper last night. It had escaped my memory. I know now.

Q.—Had you not seen Mr. Ross re the letter?

A.—Not to ask him to write the letter or anything of the kind. I had seen Mr. Ross about the publication of a little Primer that we had, and I understood from him—I do not know how I knew about it—I understood that Morang had another Primer; and I went to Mr. Morang and told him that we would like to make some arrangement for publishing the two Primers.

Q.— Did you tell Mr. Ross, or ask Mr. Ross to write Morang that he had better see you?

A.—I do not remember telling him that.

Q.—What did he write the letter for?

A.—I could not tell you.

Q.—You cannot conceive any reason?

A.—I do not know of any reason why he should.

Q.—That letter was a complete surprise to you?

A.—It was when I saw it in the paper last night. I can recall now the circumstance.

Q.—I would like to know what the circumstances were that led up to the letter?

A.—I do not remember the circumstances that led up to the letter.

Q.—Do you all share equally in the profit from these Readers, the three firms?

A.—Yes.

Q.—And do you all share equally in all the publications that the three firms have?

A.— Oh no.

Q.—For school books?

A.— Oh no.

Q.—For school books?

A.— Oh no.

Q.—Did Mr. Gage ever try to persuade you that he should have a piece of any contract you had?

A.—He asked us once to take some part of one of our books.

Q.—I do not understand?

A.—He had a partial interest in one of our books at one time. It was a little public school history. That was some time ago.

Q.—How did he get that partial interest?

A.—Our right was for a certain length of time, and he applied for the right to publish the book, and then we arranged—

Q.—You came down?

A.—Yes.

Q.—Just the same proposition as he made to the Methodist Book Room?

A.—I do not know what that was.

Q.—Did not you see what Mr. Caswell said?

A.—Yes, but no two papers published the same account.

Q.—Could not you pick out of all the papers anything that looks like yours?

A.—A similar kind.

Q.—You published a book called "The Public School History of England and Canada?"

A.—Yes.

Q.—Authorized on the 24th of August, 1902; written by Mr. W. J. Robertson. What is the royalty you pay on that?

A.—We agreed with him for ten per cent. of the retail price. It was afterwards commuted; we bought his interest out for $2,500.

Q.—That was one of those you refused to tell the Government about?

A.—I think they asked for that return.

Q.—And you would not tell them?

A.—No; and I would rather not tell it now unless I am overruled.

Q.—It was $2,500, was it?

A.—Yes.

Q.—Cash?

A.—Yes.

Q.—When did you pay it?

A.—Soon after the book was published. Ten per cent. at first; it was commuted afterwards to $2,500.

Q.—That is all paid for long ago?

A.—Yes.

Q.—Public School Bookkeeping, August, 1900?

A.—Yes.

Q.—By Mr. J. S. Black; what did you pay for that?

A.—Ten per cent. on the retail price.

Q.—Is it ten now?

A.—Yes.

Q.—Never been changed?

A.—Never been changed, no.

Q.—Public School Domestic Science, Mrs. Hoodless?

A.—Ten per cent. on the retail price.

Q.—French and English Reader by various authors?

The royalty is paid to Nelson.

Q.—What did you pay Nelson?

A.—Will it be of service if instead of answering that I can hand you the whole list in?

Q.—Yes, that will do.

(A list of the Copp, Clark Co's list of royalties to authors is put in, as follows:)

Copp, Clark Company's List of Royalties to Authors.

Public School History, 3c. to W. J. Robertson, commuted for $2,500.

History of Canada, Clement, 5c. to W. H. P. Clement.

History of Canada, Weaver, 5c. to Miss E. P. Weaver.

Public School Bookkeeping, 2½c. to J. S. Black.

Public School Domestic Science, 5c. to Mrs. Hoodless.

French English Readers, 15 per cent. on trade price, that is retail price less 25 per cent. and 10 per cent. to Thos. Nelson and Sons.

Elementary English Composition, 8c. to F. H. Sykes.

Composition from Models, 7½c. to W. J. Alexander and 7½c. to M. F. Libby.

High School History, 4c. to W. J. Robertson, and 5c. to Macmillan & Company.

Myers Ancient History, 11¼c. to Ginn & Co.

First Latin Book, 5c. to John Henderson, and 5c. to John Fletcher.

High School French Grammar, 5c. to W. H. Fraser, and 5c. to John Squair.

High School German Grammar, 5c. to W. H. Vander Smissen and 5c. to W. H. Fraser.

Physical Science, Part I., 2½c. to F. W. Merchant, and 2½c. to C. Fessenden.

Physical Science, Part II., 7½c. to F. W. Merchant.

High School Chemistry, 2½c. to A. P. Knight, and 2½c. to W. S. Ellis.

High School Bookkeeping, 6c. to H. S. MacLean, commuted in January, 1904, including all his other books for $500.00.

Commercial Course, in Bookkeeping, 3 2-10c to J. H. Dickinson, and 8/10c. to David Young.

Cadet Drill Manual, 4c. to W. Bennett Munroe.

Mr. STAUNTON: That list shows how it is being paid for if the author has not already been bought out?

A.—Yes.

Q. That covers all the books?

A.—Yes.

Q.—You have got no other documents to be produced under this subpoena?

A.—I have two here that I judge should be given under the subpoena: a memorandum between Dr. Briggs and ourselves for the joint publication of a book; we each publish half; in the same way as each published a third of the Readers.

Q.—You produce what?

A.—I produce an agreement made December 30th, 1898, between Dr. Briggs, of the Methodist Book Room, and the Copp, Clark Co., for the production of Weaver's authorized history, whereby the parties agree that they shall produce the book jointly and share the profits equally between them. Also a second agreement between the same parties for the joint production of Clement's authorized book.

Q.—Do you share equally in that?

A.—We share equally in that.

Q.—Anything else?

A.—I have another here between Hunter-Rose and the Copp, Clark Company.

Q.—To the same effect?

A.—To the same effect.

Mr. COOPER: Relating to what?

A.—The French Grammar and Reader.

Q.—Are those all?

A.—Those are all.

Q.—You remember Warwick Brothers & Rutter applying to be allowed to print the Readers in 1901?

A.—I do not remember that.

Q.—Do you know that they did try to be authorized to publish them?

A.—It has quite escaped my memory, if I ever heard it.

Q.—Did any of the members of that firm get into the Canada Publishing Company about that time?

A.—I do not know how long they have been in.

Q.—It is more than two or three years?

A.—I am only guessing when I say four or five years; I do not know.

The CHAIRMAN: I suppose that ordinary precaution on the part of a publisher would lead him to settle the question of copyrights before publishing any selections?

A.—It would now, rather than ten or fifteen years ago.

Q.—Was it a common thing twenty years ago to publish selections without providing for the copyright?

A.—I do not think the question was considered in the way it is now at all.

Q.—When you had the conversation with these other gentlemen before going to England, having heard that the Government had not the copyright of these selections, you were all surprised?

A.—It was all supposition on our part as to whether the Government had them or had them not. •

Q.—I understood you to say that you had understood that the Government controlled these copyrights?

A.—No, I did not say we understood that.

Q.—You heard that they did not?

A.—Yes, we heard that they did not.

Q.—And that was discussed with these gentlemen before you went to England?

A.—Yes.

Q.—And was not it said then that they were led to believe that the Government did control them—that they were publishing the books on that supposition?

A.—I am speaking now for myself; we did not know whether the Government had them or not, but we felt very sure they had not.

Q.—But you heard that they did not control them?

A.—Yes.

Q.—Up to that time you supposed the Government did control them?

A.—We had not taken it into consideration.

Q.—You were all surprised to learn that?

A.—I do not think you can say that. They should have done so. It was a great piece of misfortune on their part, and ill advised work on the part of the Government, in not securing them.

Q.—Did you not impliedly say, when you said you heard that they did not control them, that up to that time you supposed that they did?

A.—I do not think the question was discussed.

Q.—Was not that the understanding of the publishers, that the Government controlled those copyrights?

A.—It would be supposed so.

Q.—If they then went to the Government and said, "We hear that you do not control those copyrights"—What are the facts as to that?

A.—We did not go to them.

Q.—You did not interview the Government with reference to it at all?

A.—No, we did not advise them.

Q.—And you went to England on the strength of this rumour?

A.—Yes.

Q.—Nothing more than rumour?

A.—No more than I have told you. We felt pretty sure they had not.

Q.—And when you went to England was it the understanding that you should secure the copyright of all these selections?

A.—Any that we could find.

Q.—I think Mr. Thomas said the other day that the only copyrights the Copp, Clark Company got were those controlled by the Macmillans?

A.—He would know of no others. There were others that I arranged verbally.

Q.—And that you secured?

A.—Yes, or their promise.

Q.—We have not a list of those?

A.—No, I have no list of those.

Q.—Cannot you tell by looking over the Readers the selections on which you secured copyright from Macmillan or somebody else?

A.—Only the Macmillan list. May I explain how that would come about?

Q.—Certainly?

A.—I went feeling that we were personally in danger, and I went to the various houses that I knew, and we were old customers of a great many of them ; and I said, "We are using this selection; is it copyright?" They would say Yes or No; and to some of those who said Yes I said, "We have published it, and we would like to go on publishing it." They replied, "That is all right; you are friends of ours."

Q.—Without paying anything?

A.—Yes.

Q.—And you have not anything now to show what those selections are?

A.—No. I had a list of them, but I have not now.

Q.—Was this fifty pounds a year only to be paid thereafter?

A.—To be paid annually thereafter.

Q.—How many sets of plates did the three publishers get from the Government?

A.—I do not know.

Q.—Do you know anything about how they are renewed from time to time?

A.—They are renewed from the original set.

Q.—Who has the original set?

A.—I suppose our own printers have our own part. We only print part of the books.

Q.—Each of the three publishers got a set of plates from the Government?

A.—Yes, but we only use our third of the book.

Q.—Each one of the three houses publishes one-third of each of the books?

A.—We make double sets of plates; one is always kept in the vault; and as there is a break in the press or as they wear out we make another one.

Q.—New plates are made when wanted from the set given by the Government?

A.—Yes.

Q.—The Government when they entered into the contract contemplated making large sums from you?

A.—Well, they did not know. Have I made it clear that we published, no books in connection with the Canada Publishing Company except the Readers; have I made that quite clear?

Q.—I think so.

A.—We published only the Readers. Otherwise we are interested in it just as shareholders.

Q.—I suppose from your examination it is the fact that you got those copyrights with the view of having the contract extended?

A.—That was partially so, certainly.

Q.—And when the time came for extending the contract, you used the fact that you had the copyright to induce the Government to extend the contracts?

A.—That is so.

Q.—You used that as a ground for getting it renewed?

A.—Yes. I think the Government sent an ambassador to England to look over the situation. What he found out I do not know. Dr. Bain went.

Q.—You were anxious to have it renewed for another ten years, and you used the fact that you had these copyrights, and the others could not use them, as a ground to induce the Government to give it to you for another ten years?

A.—Yes.

Q.—Your house bought out the Nelson Company at the beginning of the contract; bought out their interest?

A.—Yes.

Q.—For thirty thousand dollars?

A.—Not for thirty thousand dollars, but for three thousand dollars a year.

Mr. Cooper: What is the difference?

The Chairman: It would make a little difference as a matter of interest.

Witness: More than that. We were dealing then with John Train Gray as Nelson's representative, and the arrangement was that we were to pay $1,500 every six months, but no lump sum.

Q.—And that extended over the ten years.

A.—Extended over the ten years.

Q.—You simply bought out their interest in the original contract for ten years?

A.—That is it.

Q.—And paid him these sums of money?

A.—Yes.

Q.—Are you paying them anything on the second contract?

A.—Yes, we are paying them a royalty on the second contract.

Q.—I would like you to explain that. You bought out entirely their interest in the first contract?

A.—Yes.

Q.—What interest were you under to the Nelsons at the beginning of the second ten?

A.—We had legal advice to the effect that we were under obligations to pay them.

Q.—No legal obligation, surely; they simply had a contract with the Government for ten years; when you had paid three thousand dollars a year for ten years did that not end it?

A.—In a sense it did not, because they had some rights in the old Readers that we displaced.

Q.—But they had no rights after the expiration of ten years?

A.—Mr. Brown of the Nelson firm was the one who came out, and I speak a little more freely about that, because I had to do with that while I had not to do with the first one; and he said, "These are ours; the contract is ended."

Q.—What are "ours?"

A.—"The Readers are ours; anything in the Readers are ours;" and we were advised that that was right and it seemed to us if there was any reason at all why it should be done, morally we were bound to consider it.

Q.—Can you suggest any moral or legal reason why you should pay them five per cent. for the second ten; what was the consideration for that?

A.—There was no consideration beyond that we were to go on publishing the books.

Q.—There was a contract that they had made with two other firms and the Government for ten years; that was assigned to you for a certain sum of money; surely that ended at the end of the ten years and they had nothing to do with it afterwards: why did you pay a royalty after the expiration of the ten years?

A.—That was the bargain we made.

Q.—What was the reason of it; you gave them the five per cent. for nothing?

A.—For their rights in the Readers.

Q.—They dd not have any?

A.—We were advised that they had.

Mr. COOPER: Can you give us any proof of the fact that you were advised?

A.—I think Mr. Thompson took the matter in hand. We were given to understand that Nelson had a number of copyrights from the old Readers when the old Readers were used by the Government, and they took pieces here and there as they wanted them.

The CHAIRMAN: You had already secured a copyright on the selections used in the Readers so long as you published them?

A.—Only a few.

Q.—You and the others did secure them all?

19 T. B.

C—Precisely.

A.—I do not know what they secured. Dr. Bain went over and reported that he had found some that were not secured.

Mr. MACDONALD: It was careless on your part?

A.—Yes.

The CHAIRMAN: Is it true or is it not that the three firms together secured the copyrights of all the selections that were in the Readers so long as those firms had the right to publish them?

A.—I can only speak of what I secured, I really do not know what the others secured.

Q.—And you only secured the right to use those selections so long as you publishd the Readers?

A.—Whatever the letter says.

Q.—That is the fact, is it not; only while you publish them. Did you tell the Government that before the renewal?

A.—No.

Q.—"We have not anything to prevent anybody else publishing them after the ten years; we have only the right to use these selections as long as we publish the book?"

A.—No, we did not give them anything.

Q.—Did you then lead the Government to believe that they could not go on publishing these books afterwards, or get any one else to publish them, by reason of the rights you had in the copyrights?

A.—The Government would know that. I do not remember giving them to understand that.

Q.—Is it not very probable that you did, because unless you did that there was no reason in it at all?

A.—No.

The Commission takes recess.

EVIDENCE OF MR. WILLIAM J. GAGE.

Mr. STAUNTON, Examiner:

By Mr. STAUNTON:

Q.—Mr. Gage, you are, I believe, the head of the firm of W. J. Gage & Co.?

A.—I am.

Q.—Are you the sole proprietor of that business?

A.—No, sir.

Q.—Are there other shareholders outside of your own family?

A.—Yes.

Q.—And you were one of the original publishers of these books, were you not—of this present series of Readers?

A.—I have been one from the beginning.

Q.—You commenced publishing for the Government when?

A.—Do you refer to these books alone?

Q.—Yes; Readers?

A.—It will be about twenty-one years.

Q.—The first contract that you had for Readers was in 1886?

A.—No, sir.

Q.—Had you a contract prior to that?

A.—Yes.

Q.—When was that?

A.—About a year before that.

19a T. B.

Q.—Did that contract run out?

A.—No, sir.

Q.—What became of it?

A.—It was cancelled.

Q.—Were there any other publishers besides yourself for the Readers when that first contract was in existence?

A.—Yes.

Q.—Who were they?

A.—Nelson & Son, represented by Campbell & Son, and the Canada Publishing Company.

Q.—You three were publishing the present Readers prior to 1886?

A.—No, sir.

Q.—That is what I understood you to say?

A.—I said there were Readers.

Q.—Not these Readers?

A.—No, sir.

Mr. Cooper: Were they authorized Readers?

A.—Two series were.

Q.—Then when these present Readers came into existence you were one of those who received one of the first contracts?

A.—Yes.

Q.—There were Nelson & Sons and yourselves?

A.—Yes.

Q.—Nelson & Sons were succeeded by Copp, Clark & Co.?

A.—Copp, Clark & Co. purchased, I believe, from Nelsons.

Q.—You published the Readers for ten years before the renewal contract in 1896 was made?

A.—Yes.

Q.—You have been in the publishing business for some time?

A.—Yes.

Q.—You have been republishing British works?

A.—Yes.

Q.—I suppose you have a knowledge of copyright?

A.—To some extent.

Q.—Had you before you published these Readers?

A.—Yes.

Q.—And you are quite aware that there is such a thing known in the law of publication as piracy?

A.—Yes.

Q.—And were before you took up the Readers?

A.—Took up these Readers?

Q.—Yes?

A.—Yes.

Q.—Did you look over the Readers to see that there was nothing pirated in them before you made the contract?

A.—No.

Q.—Unwise and foolish, was it not?

A.—I do not know that it was.

Q.—Do you rush into a publication without enquiring as to the copyright, usually?

A.—Not usually.

Q.—Why did you in this case?

A.—We did not rush in.

Q.—I thought you made no enquiry as to the copyright?

Q.—Precisely.

Q.—You signed a long and serious contract for ten years' publication of books that you knew were made up of selections?

A.—Yes.

Q.—From authors, British and otherwise; and you made no enquiry as to copyright?

A.—No, sir.

Q.—Can you give me a reason why you did not?

A.—We supposed the Government had looked after these matters, if we supposed anything. Personally I took no concern about it.

Q.—You just simply published?

A.—Yes.

Q.—When did you commence to think it might be wise to look into it?

A.—Probably six or seven years afterwards. The matter was suggested in some way or other, that some of these pieces might not be copyrighted.

Q.—How was it suggested? Are you as much at sea as Mr. Thompson?

A.—I am not at sea at all; I am simply giving you the plain facts of the case.

Q.—I want to know when you first got any knowledge that the selections in these books were copyright?

A.—I have already answered the question.

Q.—No you have not, excuse me; you told me generally; I want you to localize the date?

A.—I found when I met some of the publishers in England that they had given no rights.

Q.—When were you put on the enquiry, and how?

A.—I cannot tell you how. I can tell you simply in a general way; we did not know that the Government had not copyright, and we first found out that they had not copyright in talking to the publishers in England.

Q.—You first found out from the publishers?

A.—Yes.

Q.—You did not talk this over with the other gentlemen in the syndicate before you went to England?

A.—Oh, yes.

Q.—The matter was discussed.

A.—Yes.

Q.—What led to that?

A.—Simply we made up our minds that we would see whether these copyrights were secure.

Q.—In plain English, you made up your minds you would see if you could not in some way get a renewal of the contract?

A.—If I—

Q.—Is that right?

A.—If you wish to put it—

Q.—By obtaining the copyrights you controlled the Government on the renewal of the contract?

A.—Yes, that is quite right. I want to be exceedingly frank; I want to give to this Commission all the information possible; there is nothing in the world I want to withhold. We are in business. Unfortunately, when these questions are asked, the question goes out with the answer, and we can-not help that, but it would be a pity if in my efforts to deal very frankly with this Commission something should go out which is not very complimentary. I want to help this Commission to get the fullest data.

Q.—Is it the fact or is it not, that you had no fear whatever that there was any risk in publishing these selections until you commenced to think about the renewal of the contract?

A.—Probably that was true.

Q.—And the whole object you had in getting these selections, this copyright, was that you might use it for your own purpose in obtaining a renewal of the contract?

A.—Partly.

Q.—Was there any other reason?

A.—Yes.

Q.—What was the other?

A.—To prevent another publisher coming in and possibly preventing us from publishing.

Q.—To prevent another publisher from getting part of the business; would that not be right?

A.—"And putting us out of the business" would be right.

Q.—Competing with you for the work with the Government?

A.—Yes.

Q.—To secure the business for yourselves was the object?

A.—That was part, with the other.

Q.—And you went to England personally, with that object in view, did you not?

A.—I had that in view, yes.

Q.—And when you got to England did you urge on any of the holders of these copyrights the advisability of proceeding against the Minister for infringement of the copyright?

A.—I do not remember of doing it there, but I remember there was something later in connection with one publisher.

Q.—I have a report from the Department to that effect: "He also urged on some of them the advisability of proceeding against the Minister for infringement of copyright?"

A.—I have no recollection of doing so.

Q.—Perhaps this will refresh your memory? "Mr. Isbister, trading under the name of Charles Burnett & Co., London, acceded to his wishes in this respect, and gave him a letter which was dictated by Mr. Gage."

A.—Probably in one case I had rather recommended it.

Q.—You did recommend them to go after the Minister?

A.—In that particular case I remember discussing the matter.

Q.—What did you do that for?

A.—I wanted the Minister to understand that there were certain rights on those Readers that he had not and that I had.

Q.—I do not think you had any rights. At this time you had no rights at all, and you were proceeding on the assumption that the Minister had acquired the rights. Then you went to England, and when you got there you urged upon these publishers the advisability of going after the Minister?

A.—Not until after we had secured the right.

Q.—They could not bring an action against the Minister if you owned the right?

A.—They could authorize me to do it, and they would practically have the bringing of it.

Q.—Then you wished the English publishers to sue the Minister for allowing you to publish these selections?

A.—No; I did not see the English publishers.

Q.—Was not Mr. Isbister a publisher?

A.—Yes.

Q.—You wanted him to allow you to sue the Minister for having given you the contract?

A.—No, sir.

Q.—What did you want him to do?

A.—To sue the publisher for infringement of copyright.

Q.—To whom did you dictate the letter referred to?

A.—I do not remember.

Q.—Did you dictate the letter?

A.—I do not remember such a letter.

Q.—Do you know a man named Edward Stanford?

A.—I do not know him, but I remember the firm; I think they are map publishers.

Q.—Do you remember getting them to do the same thing?

A.—I do not remember it now.

Q.—Did you write a letter to the Government under authority?

A.—Not that I know of.

Q.—Then did you get authority from Mr. Isbister?

A.—We did.

Q.—To do what?

A.—To proceed against the Minister for infringement of copyright.

Q.—In what had the Minister, in your opinion, erred?

A.—In issuing a series of Readers containing copyright matter.

Q.—Did you have the Readers with you?

A.—Do you mean in England?

Q.—Yes?

A.—I expect I did. I do not remember.

Q.—You referred then to the Readers that you had published yourself?

A.—Yes.

Q.—And you got a letter to the Government?

A.—Yes.

Q.—Threatening them with an action for having allowed you to publish that Reader?

A.—I do not know that there was a letter written to the Government in connection with the matter.

Q.—That was your purpose, anyway; to get litigation against the Government for allowing you to publish these Readers?

A.—No, sir.

Q.—Explain what you mean, then?

A.—We wanted to let the Minister know, in the most practical way, that there were copyright selections used there and that the publication of those selections was an infringement of the copyright.

Q.—Was it just a bluff you were putting up?

A.—No, sir.

Q.—Did you intend to bring an action against them?

A.—Did so.

Q.—When did you bring the action?

A.—In Mr. Isbister's name, we brought it shortly after.

Q.—Before you applied to renew the contract?

A.—Yes, three or four years before.

Q.—What was that action?

A.—For infringement of copyright.

Q.—In the publication of the Ontario Readers?

A.—Yes.

Q.—Did you join Mr. Gage as a party to that action?

A.—No; but we were virtually a party to it.

Q.—You were the plaintiff; Richard suing Richard, eh?

(No answer.)

Q.—What became of your action?

A.—I think it was withdrawn.

Q.—It was a bluff action?

A.—If you please.

Q.—Was it?

A.—If you like to call it so.

Q.—What do you call it?

A.—I do not call it anything at all.

Q.—Why did you not go on with it?

A.—I do not know now. I have no recollection.

Q.—How far did you get with it?

A.—The writ was issued in the matter.

Q.—You thought that sufficiently impressed the Minister?

A.—We desired to impress him.

Q.—That is all you brought it for?

A.—I do not remember the particular method, but we desired to let the Minister know there was a possibility of infringement of copyright.

Q.—That was how many years before the first contract ran out?

A.—I am not sure. Three or four years, speaking roughly.

Q.—You were frank with the Minister; you gave him timely notice that if you did not get a renewal of the contract there would be trouble?

A.—Yes, there would be trouble.

Q.—He knew that three or four years before he gave you the contract?

A.—Yes.

Q.—You did not wait until just before the expiry of the contract to spring that on him?

A.—No.

Q.—So that he might easily enough have had a new series of Readers prepared?

A.—I do not know. I suppose he could.

Q.—Three or four years is sufficient to get out a book of this kind?

A.—That was done, I think, in a year, or less than a year.

Q.—So that I suppose you pointed out to him wherein he was in the wrong in publishing these selections, told him what they were?

A.—I do not think I told him anything.

Q.—You told him in your action that he was guilty of piracy in publishing certain articles?

A.—Yes.

Q.—So that he knew what the articles were?

A.—Yes.

Q.—And could have eliminated them from the book if he had chosen?

A.—Yes, he could.

Q.—That was easy enough. When the Government could not do that so easily, what did you go to all that trouble for?

A.—Well, that is a matter for the Government to decide, whether they could do it or not, or whether they wished to do it.

Q.—What did you pay the English publishers for the copyright?

A.—I cannot tell you offhand. I had done this, I had got together all the memoranda, with the publishers in connection with it —

Q.—You cannot tell me what you paid for it?

A.—No, sir.

Q.—Cannot recall it?

A.—No, sir.

Q.—Did you pay anything?

A.—Yes.

Q.—Any sum of money more than a pound apiece?

A.—Yes.

Q.—Can you tell me more than one that cost you more than a pound?

A.—Yes. I would be very glad to give all these documents into the hands of the Commission, asking this condition, that the Commission would not allow other publishers to make use of them for business purposes. I want to give this Commission everything, only in a matter of this kind I can see how it has been the cause of litigation, and I can see how it might be hurtful from the business point of view. I take it that the Commission only want to get at the facts for themselves.

Q.—That is right. We want to find out where these copyrights' are and how they are held?

A.—For the benefit of the Commission, but not for that of rival publishers.

Q.—For the benefit of the Department of Education; we do not care for outside publishers, so far as I know. You refused to tell us what you had before getting this Commission, and so this is a method we have taken to find out where the Government is at?

(Witness produces certain letters.)

WITNESS: I have not read these letters for twelve or thirteen years. Mr. Burnside was my representative in England.

(The letters are handed to counsel, who look them over and select what they require to go in.)

WITNESS: Some of these are hardly bearing on the matter, but I pass the whole business up.

Mr. STAUNTON: Will you leave these letters here?

A.—Yes.

Q.—We just want to take a list of them with the prices?

A.—That will not be part of the record?

Q.—It would have to be?

A.—Mr. Nesbitt has been acting for twenty years, mixed up in this copyright business, and has many papers in connection with it; and he said "There is no question in the world, if you give them the information they require, for their own purposes, they will so far consider your business interests that they will not become part of the record."

Q.—It will have to be. We want to find out what you have copyright of, and what you paid for it?

A.—If you look over them to-day and examine me on them, as much as you desire, if you will give them back to me, and on consultaton with Mr. Nesbitt, who is acting in connection with this copyright question—and who will give to you a lot of additional information at our request but, if on the other hand, he says, "This Commission will not make use of this as part of the record," if he thinks it would be injurious, and in consultation with you, you agreed to that test, it would be a misfortune if it had already passed beyond that by my frankly turning over everything I have got.

Q.—I cannot make any bargain about it. I want to know what you have secured and what price you paid for them, and I want to know whether you have the exclusive right or not. That is all I am interested in this correspondence for; I am not interested in any other way. The Copp, Clark Company produced it, and I do not see how they are injured in any way. We are not here to injure your business; but you declined to give this information to the Government?

A.—At a time when there was litigation against us as publishers for issuing the school Readers.

Q.—How could it have hurt you in any way, when you had a right, to say so? When you have a right, how can it hurt you to say that you have the right? You are apparently under the impression that if you leave this here it may be used by other publishers. How can they? Any publisher can go to these houses and see if Gage & Co. got the copyright, and they see everything?

A.—Well, I may say that we were not satisfied in connection with what we could learn in regard to these copyrights. The best counsel in England advised Mr. Nesbitt on it, and there was some difficulty and uncertainty about it. There seems to have been some uncertainty when a Toronto publisher issued a writ against us to prevent us from publishing these Readers. He claimed to have the copyright.

Q.—Well, we will have to go through them?

A.—I want you to go through them; I want you to have all the information.

Q.—I cannot undertake anything. You may ask the Commission; they may give you some undertaking; I certainly cannot.

(Witness gathers up some of the letters.)

Mr. STAUNTON: I see, looking over this correspondence, that you paid from one to five guineas for the right to publish these extracts, to the various English publishers. "The sole right to print extracts of reasonable length."

(Reading from letter.)

"From any of the copyright works of Charles Dickens." Chapman & Hall gave you the right in consideration of five guineas; that is right, is it not?

A.—Yes.

The CHAIRMAN: What is the limit of that?

Mr. STAUNTON: (Reads.) "In the series of Ontario Government School Readers or in a separate book of extracts if you should find it desirable." Now, that is what you got from them on December 11th, 1893. Then Chatto & Windus gave you the right to publish Macdonald's poem "The Baby" in the Ontario Readers, for one pound, on December 11th, 1893, and undertook not to authorize the publication in any other Readers published in Canada or published by any other firm. Now, I think Mr. Macdonald had better go through these and make an extract.

(Some discussion follows, in the course of which it is arranged that copies shall be subsequently put in.)

Mr. STAUNTON: I see, in taking a hurried glance over these letters produced by you, that the copyright cost you about a pound to five pounds, according to the number that each publisher gave?

A.—I saw there was one eight guineas. I have not looked over them for ten or twelve years.

Q.—Do you know how much you paid altogether?

A.—No, sir. If that contains the record, I assume the total will give it to you.

Q.—Did you visit all the those publishers to get them?

A.—Some may have been secured by correspondence.

Q.—What did you tell them?

A.—We told them that the series of Readers had been published in Canada, and asked if permission had been given for the use of that particular copyright.

Q.—And when you found that there had not, you secured the copyright for yourself?

A.—Yes.

Q.—What did you do when you came back?

A.—Oh, I told the other publishers that we had secured certain selections.

Q.—And did they tell you that they had secured certain selections too?

A.—I remember the Copp, Clark Co. did.

Q.—This was some time before the contract ran out?

A.—Yes. The date of these letters will tell you.

Q.—It is 1893?

Mr. Cooper: The contract ran out in 1894.

Mr. Staunton: The contract ran out in 1896.

Mr. Cooper: 1894, according to my understanding; which was it, Mr. Gage?

A.—1896, I think.

Q.—It ran out in 1894 and was renewed in 1896?

A.—No.

Q.—When was the original contract?

The Chairman: Twenty-sixth of November, 1884.

Witness: But I think you will find the contract was dated a little ahead. It was to count from the 1st of January, 1885.

Mr. Cooper: The contract then ran out on the 31st of December, 1894.

Mr. Staunton: Did you have publication without a contract for a year?

A.—According to that it must be so.

(Some further conversation takes place on this point.)

Mr. Cooper: I want this correct. Mr. Gage's answer was that this took place three or four years before the contract ran out. Now, it was less than two years before the contract ran out.

Mr. Staunton: It was done in December, 1893, and you obtained the contract in January, 1896?

A.—That is right. I was basing my statement to the Commission on this renewal of contract that I had in my hand.

Q.—You told me that when you came back you met the other members of the publishers' syndicate?

A.—Yes.

Q.—You found what Copp, Clark got, and you stated what you got yourself?

A.—I do not remember stating what I got, but I have no doubt, I did. I assume that I did, although Mr. Thompson has no recollection—I do not remember having made any statement, but I take it for granted I did.

Q.—When did you first learn that the Government were going to make new contracts?

A.—I do not remember. I have no further information in my mind now than the renewal of the contract.

Q.—Why did you take all this trouble to obtain the rights to the copyright if you did not fear any trouble, or know anything was going to happen?

A.—We feared trouble.

Q.—What did you fear?

A.—We had learned not to put our trust in the Education Department, from very unfortunate experience we had passed through.

Q.—What was it?

A.—I want to be as concise as possible on this particular point.

Q.—Tell us the point. What is the point? You refer to something; I would like to know what it is?

A.—I said I feared that the Education Department might possibly refuse to give us the further privilege of publishing.

Q.—From what experience?

A.—We had published a series of Readers that had cost over thirty thousand dollars. We had spent fifty more. Two other firms did the same thing: one of them was made bankrupt, and the other very nearly, and we had found out that every book of ours except one was struck off the list, and it was quite possible that at the end of ten years we might be left out in the cold.

Q.—Why should they not leave you out in the cold at the end of your contract? Do you think because they do not renew a contract you have a right to reflect on them?

A.—I am going simply to state the facts.

Q.—If the Government give you a contract for ten years, and live up to it, do you say that at the end of that time you have got any claim on them?

A.—Yes.

Q.—What claim have you got on them?

A.—Because we were not fairly treated by the Government.

Q.—Speaking generally: if you get a contract for ten years, have you got any claim on them for another contract at the end of that time?

A.—It would depend on the conditions.

Q.—A contract exactly the same as you have got now?

A.—We thought we had.

Q.—What claim could you have on the Government, they having given you a ten-year contract to publish these books?

A.—Because we did not think it was a fair settlement of the question.

Q.—These books were new books, got out by the Government?

A.—Yes.

Q.—You had no expense in regard to these Ontario Readers at all?

A.—Yes, we had.

Q.—Did you get them up?

A.—No, sir.

Q.—Did the Government get them up?

A.—Yes.

Q.—And pay for them?

A.—Yes.

Q.—You were put to no expense for the preparation of these Ontario Readers?

A.—Yes.

Q.—How were you?

A.—By having to pay for the plates.

Q.—Did you prepare these Ontario Readers?

A.—No.

Q.—Did you pay anything towards preparing them?

A.—Yes; we paid part of the cost by paying some $7,500 between the three firms for the plates.

Q.—You paid that as part of your contract?

A.—As part of the contract and part of the cost.

Q.—They gave you the Readers on certain terms?

A.—Yes.

Q.—You chose to sign that contract?

A.—Yes.

Q.—Were you satisfied with it?

A.—No.

Q.—Did you sign it?

A.—Yes.

Q.—Why did you sign it if you did not like it?

A.—We were dealing with a Government.

Q.—There is no use in being mysterious about it: you made this contract with your eyes open?

A.—Yes.

Q.—And agreed to pay this money?

A.—Yes.

Q.—And the Government lived up to this contract?

A.—Yes.

Q.—And yet you reproach them?

A.—Yes.

Q.—You are not imagining a grievance now, are you, to justify you in getting these copyrights against them?

A.—No.

Q.—The Government paid you what they agreed to pay you?

A.—They did not pay us anything at all.

Q.—They agreed to pay you for the publication of these books?

A.—They did not pay us anything at all, nor did they agree to pay us anything.

Q.—I thought they did. You got the money that you contracted to supply the books for?

A.—No; we got no money from the Government.

Q.—You say that you made a contract with the Government, and you are justifying your action by saying you were improperly treated by the Government?

A.—Yes.

Q.—I do not care what the Government did to you outside of this contract; but you made this contract with them, and they lived up to it?

A.—Yes.

Q.—In every particular?

A.—Yes.

Q.—And you published the books?

A.—Yes.

Q.—They did not interfere with you?

A.—They did interfere with us.

Q.—Well, you published the books?

A.—Yes.

Q.—And you got your money for publishing them from those to whom you sold them?

A.—Yes.

The CHAIRMAN: That is where the misunderstanding came in just now.

Mr. STAUNTON: When the contract was to be renewed, you renewed it on better terms to the Government?

A.—Yes, if you put it that way.

Q.—The books were to be produced at a cheaper rate?

A.—Yes.

Q.—And you had the same number of people in the syndicate?

A.—Yes.

Q.—So that the profits had to be divided amongst the same number of people?

A.—Yes.

Q.—And you took a contract which was not as desirable as the old one?

A.—It was not.

Q.—You seemed to be awfully anxious to get this contract?

A.—We were.

Q.—It must have been a good thing, or you would not have been anxious to get it?

A.—A fairly good thing.

Q.—And you thought it was so good that you agreed to make a side agreement with the Government concerning the copyright, did you not?

A.—Yes, sir.

Q.—Did you object to the Government, after this contract of the 24th March, 1896, was made, did you object to the Government allowing any other publisher to publish these books?

A.—I have no recollection of doing so.

Q.—Did you get any solicitors to write, objecting?

A.—No, sir, not to my knowledge.

Q.—Did you make any effort to prevent anybody else from publishing the books?

A.—Not to my knowledge.

Q.—Are you a member of the Canada Publishing Company?

A.—I hold stock in it.

Q.—How much?

A.—I think it is about $28,000.

Q.—How much is their issue?

A.—I am not sure.

Q.—Are you a third holder; have you a third interest in it?

A.—I think I have.

Q.—Copp, Clark one-third, you one-third; who is the other?

A.—I know it is some of the members of the Copp, Clark firm have, and some of the members of the Warwick have.

Q.—Are you a director?

A.—I am.

Q.—President, or Vice-President?

A.—I am Vice-President.

Q.—Were you so on April 24th, 1901?

A.—I could not say.

Q.—Were you a director then?

A.—Yes, I would be a director then.

Q.—Who were the other directors then, do you recollect?

A.—No.

Q.—They have not changed?

A.—I do not know about that: I do not remember.

Q.—Did that company give the Beatty Blackstock firm instructions to protest against the publishing by any other publishers of a primer?

A.—I do not remember of their doing so.

Q.—(Reads), "April 24th, 1901. The Canada Publishing Company have called upon us, and instructed us to protect their interests in regard to certain agreements which they have with the Government regarding the publication of Readers."

I suppose those are the contracts of 24th of March, 1906, referred to in that letter?

A.—It would be this contract, I have no doubt.

Q.—(Reads.) "We have just learned that it is the intention of the Government."

(The examiner here reads from private communication.)

Q.—Would that have the effect of interfering with your rights?

A.—Under the renewal of that agreement it would.

Q.—How?

A.—My own interpretation was that in renewing that second agreement, the sum that we paid of nine thousand dollars for the right to renew, taken into consideration with the reduced rates at which the Readers were published, carried with it the thought that there would be only one series of Readers authorized in the schools.

Q.—Where does it say in the contract to that effect?

A.—I do not know that it does say so.

Q.—But you thought that the Government ought to live up to the contract in its spirit as well as in its letter?

A.—I presume so.

Q.—That is what you mean?

A.—That is the thought that is implied in which I said.

Q.—Was that your legal right, did you think?

A.—I do not know what the legal rights would be in the matter.

Q.—Why did you go to a lawyer about it?

A.—We always go to lawyers when we are in trouble or want to get out of trouble.

Q.—(Examiner reads further from private communication.) Does that recall anything to you?

A.—I have no knowledge of that letter.

Q.—Now you say that you thought that there was an understanding or that it was only right that the Government should live up to the spirit of that agreement?

A.—I would expect them to do so.

Q.—As an honorable Government that is what they ought to do?

A.—Yes, that is what Governments should do.

Q.—That is what anybody should do, surely; live up to the spirit, what is really meant?

A.—Yes.

Q.—Tell me why you objected, after you signed that agreement on the 24th of March, 1896, respecting the copyright, why you objected to anybody else publishing those Readers?

A.—I did not object.

Q.—Were you always willing they should?

A.—I am not willing, but I did not object.

Q.—Never made any objection at all?

A.—Not to my knowledge.

Q.—You considered that you had really pledged yourself to allow the Government to give a contract to anybody else?

A.—To put no difficulties in the way.

Q.—If you had the power to injure them or set anybody on them you considered you were in honor bound not to do it?

A.—Surely, if I agreed to that.

Q.—Did you not agree to that?

A.—I have not read the agreement, but if you say so—

Q.—No, I will not say anything about it?

A.—Well, I cannot refresh my memory.

Q.—I leave it to yourself, your own idea of what is right and wrong?

A.—If you say it is in the agreement; I have not read the agreement.

Q.—The agreement says this:

"And it is further understood and agreed that in the event of any other person or persons, corporation or corporations, making application to the said. Minister of Education for a right to print or publish the said Readers as aforesaid, the said the Minister of Education shall have the power to grant such right as aforesaid from time to time to such person or persons, corporation or corporations, subject, however, to the same conditions as are set forth in the agreement hereinabove recited, and also the conditions set forth."

Now is that not the plain meaning; that you led the Minister to understand that you authorized him to authorize anybody else to publish these selections in the Readers?

A.—That gives him that privilege.

Q.—And you apparently made him satisfied that he could give that privilege to anybody else without being interfered with?

A.—There is no doubt that he had it under the seal, and there was no assurance and no discussion about it.

Q.—The words are "shall have the power to grant." "It is understood that the said Minister of Education shall have the power to grant?"

A.—Yes.

Q.—You do not agree with Mr. Thompson's view of that?

A.—I do not know what his view was.

Q.—His view was that they suppressed this from the Government, did not let them know that they had made arrangements in England whereby the original owners of this copyright could come down on the Government if they allowed any person else to publish them?

A.—I never heard of such a thing being discussed with the Minister.

Q.—Then if the Government had given Morang or Warwick the right to publish these Readers you would think, so far as it was in your power, you ought to protect them?

A.—No, I ought not to protect them; but I would put no obstacle in the way; I would carry out the terms of the contract.

Q.—You had in the contract a clause that the Government should have the power to grant that. They could not have the power unless they had the authority of the English publisher?

A.—I do not know about that. We did not take and in that contract give any powers to the Government that we did not possess. We only assigned all rights that we had.

Q.—But you never showed the Government what you had?

A.—No, sir.

Q.—Is not the plain English of that clause that you were assuring the Government that you had the power to authorize the Government to let anybody else publish these Readers?

A.—No, it is nothing of the kind.

Q.—"And it is further understood"—leaving out some words—"that the said the Minister of Education shall have the power to grant such right as aforesaid from time to time to such person or persons, corporation or corporations, subject, however, to the same conditions?"

A.—Yes.

Q.—So that it was understood between you that the Government should have the power to grant those rights?

A.—So far as, speaking for myself personally—

Q.—It is absolute power; there is no string on it, no condition on it? (No answer.)

Q.—Is that right?

A.—I cannot answer yes or no to the question. If you let me answer it in my own way I will answer it.

Q.—So far as you could give the power?

A.—So far as we could give the power.

Q.—Why did you not let the Government see the list, in order that it might ascertain how far you could give this power?

A.—To what time are you referring now?

Q.—Any time?

A.—We were only asked last spring, so far as I remember.

Q.—You were asked in December, 1901?

A.—By whom?

Q.—By the Minister, and you flatly refused it yourself?

A.—Yes, we did, if you refer to the same period that I refer to.

Q.—I refer to the time in December, 1901, when the Minister asked you. On November 30th, 1901, Mr. Miller wrote you: "I am directed by the Minister of Education to state that there does not appear to be on file in this Department any list of the copyrighted extracts in the Ontario Readers controlled by your firm, for the use of which any subsequent publisher, if permitted to publish, would be asked to pay to the present publisher $1,000 or a proper proportion of that sum, as compensation for the use of such extracts. Will you kindly furnish this department, at your earliest convenience, with a statement of the extracts referred to above, controlled by your firm." Now you went and consulted your solicitors when you got that letter?

A.—I do not remember, but it is possible.

Q.—Your solicitor wrote a letter refusing to give that list?

A.—Yes.

Q.—Was that under your instructions?

A.—Well, I do not remember. I am quite willing to take the responsibility of it.

Q.—On the 3rd of December, 1901, Thomson, Henderson & Bell write to Mr. Miller thus: "The W. J. Gage Company, Limited, has handed us your letter of the 30th ultimo. On perusal of the contract between the publishers and the Department we do not find that the publishers have undertaken to supply any list of the copyrighted extracts."

A.—Yes.

Q.—Is that the reason you refused?

A.—That is one reason.

Q.—Why should you refuse for that reason?

A.—Because there was litigation, I think, pending.

Q.—That is a reason by itself?

A.—No, it was not a reason by itself, if my recollection is correct.

Q.—(Reads) "And as there is litigation now pending in the courts over the question of some of these extracts we cannot advise the W. J. Gage Company, Limited, to supply such list at present." Now, was there any one of those extracts that you had that there was any litigation about?

A.—There was litigation in connection with our publishing the Readers.

Q.—No; was there any litigation over any one of these extracts?

A.—I am not sure as to what are the special extracts.

Q.—I am instructed there was not, and I want you to say?

A.—I do not know.

Q.—Why did you not give the list?

A.—Simply because we did not want to put in the hands of a rival publisher material that would help his case.

Q.—You were not asked to put into the hands of a rival publisher anything; you were only asked for a list of the extracts that you had copyrights for, simply asked for that list?

A.—Yes.

Q.—And you would not give it to them?

A.—That is evident.

Q.—Although the Government told you that the purpose for which they wanted the information was for the purpose of making a contract with somebody else?

A.—I do not remember that they said so.

Q.—(Reads) "——list of the copyrighted extracts in the Ontario Readers controlled by your firm, for the use of which any subsequent publisher, if permitted to publish, would be asked to pay to the present publisher $1,000," etc.?

A.—The Minister does not say that he wished to make a contract with some other publisher.

Q.—But he speaks of making that use of the extracts?

A.—Yes.

Q.—Why did you not furnish the list?

A.—Because of litigation pending.

Q.—I am told there was no litigation over those extracts?

A.—I am not sure.

Q.—Will you say that there was?

A.—I do not know. If I go to my solicitor I put myself at his mercy and have to act on his judgment.

Q.—Were you the defendant in any action at that time?

A:—I think so. I cannot fix that certain date.

Q.—Did you ever furnish the Government with the list?

A.—No.

Q.—Had you any objection to furnish them with the list?

A.—I would furnish the Government of the day without a moment's hesitation with a list, as far as I am concerned.

Q.—Why did you not?

A.—When this litigation was on we felt it would be unsafe.

Q.—You have not been able to recall any one of these extracts that was attacked?

A.—No, I have not.

Q.—Could anybody attack them successfully?

A.—Well, we do not usually consider it wise, when a lawyer goes fishing, to give him all the evidence that—

Q.—But this was the Government?

A.—We cannot disassociate the two. There was litigation pending, by Mr. Thomson's letter. He said, "do not give these selections."

Q.—Do you remember yourself, or are you taking it from his letter?

A.—I know there was litigation.

20 T. B.

Q.—Is that a bona fide reason, or was it not as a matter of fact that you did not want any other publisher to be in a position to tender for this work; was not that the real reason?

A.—In this particular case the real reason was that we did not wish to give the information into the hands of the publisher who had issued a writ.

Q.—No; was not the real reason of withholding that list so as, as far as possible, to prevent any person going into the publication of these Readers?

A.—Not in this case at all.

Q.—Was not that the reason you did not want to give the Government your list?

A.—Not in this case at all.

Q.—Did not that actuate you?

A.—No; I am speaking for myself.

Q.—Speaking for yourself?

A.—Not in this case at all.

Q.—Were you asked more than once to give that list to the Government?

A.—I think last session we got a request.

Q.—Did you give it then?

A.—No.

Q.—Why?

A.—I do not know that there was any special reason. I do not remember how we replied to it.

Q.—I understand you to say that you were not actuated by any desire to prevent in 1901 any other publisher being granted the privilege of publishing these Readers in your refusal to furnish the Government with the list of the copyright selections you held?

A.—I answer just as I did before. There was no other reason than that I have already stated.

Q.—I am right, then, in my assumption that you had no other reason excepting to protect yourself against litigation?

A.—That is right.

The CHAIRMAN: I must have misunderstood you, then. I have taken down here that you did not wish to place in the hands of a rival publisher any assistance to enable him to get information?

A.—That would help him with his case. Not only had threats been made by the same publisher that he would drive us out of business——

Mr. STAUNTON: That is not the point. The Government made a request to you, and you have assured me that the whole object was——

WITNESS: I was answering the Chairman.

The CHAIRMAN: I understood Mr. Gage to say that he refused to give the list of the copyrighted selections because he did not desire to assist a rival publisher in publishing these Readers, to get in a position to publish these Readers. He says I misunderstood him in that respect.

Q.—How was that refusal, so far as this rival publisher is concerned, in accordance with the agreement you had entered into respecting these copyrights, that you would not in any way do anything to prevent any publisher from getting a share of the publication of those Readers? That is part of your agreement, there, if I remember rightly?

A.—Well, we simply were not going to furnish him with information to help his case.

Q.—Did not you undertake there not to prevent another person from coming in?

A.—We did not prevent him.

Q.—You simply refused to give him anything to help him?

20a T. B.

A.—We simply declared we would not furnish him with information to enable him to get in.

Q.—Not with information concerning the copyright?

A.—No, sir, surely.

Mr. STAUNTON: In 1904 what was your reason for refusing the Government that list?

A.—I do not remember really how it came. I would have to find out. I do not think we refused really. I do not remember how it came.

Q.—You did refuse, and here is your letter, dated March 24th, 1904, to the Deputy Minister of Education:—

(*Personal.*)

March 24, 1904.

JOHN MILLAR, ESQ.,
    Deputy Minister of Education,
        City.

DEAR MR. MILLAR,—Messrs. Copp, Clark Company have written you with reference to the copyright selections, and as their letter covers the ground very fully, we have thought it would be better not to make any formal reply, believing that if we replied (as we must) in a similar way, it might not be so satisfactory to the Minister, and might raise some question in the House as to collusion between the publishers, if both letters were presented.

Yours faithfully,

(Signed) W. J. GAGE.

Mr. STAUNTON: Mr. Thompson said perfectly frankly that they were not bound to produce this list, and they would not do it?

A.—Yes.

Q.—Not on account of any litigation, but they simply would not do it?

A.—He does not say that.

Q.—I think he did; however, we will be able to compare your evidence with his. Tell me what was your reason in 1904 for not giving the list?

A.—I fancy, as far as I am concerned——I have no recollection just at the present moment, but we anticipated that the same kind of information was desired in 1904 as in 1901.

Q.—For what reason; there was no litigation then?

A.—No.

Q.—There was no litigation; and you honestly had these rights?

A.—Yes.

Q.—And you refused to produce them?

A.—Yes.

Q.—Do you say now it was not for fear that some other publisher might not tender on the books?

A.—Not tender on them?

Q.—Yes, tender on them; ask the Government to allow them to publish them; was that not what you were afraid of?

A.—I have no doubt I did not wish to put any extra information in the hands of other publishers.

Q.—That is really the fact; that is what Mr. Thompson says; he says it was not in the bond, they would not do it, they were not going to help a bit?

A.—No, we did not want to help the Government one bit.

Q.—Then you refused to give the Government the information that they wanted about what extracts you controlled, and you did it for the purpose of hindering them in making a contract with anybody else?

A.—Not hindering them.

Q.—Is not that the truth?

A.—Not to hinder them.

Q.—What was it for; to help them?

A.—No.

Q.—What was it?

A.—Not to give this information into the hands of another publisher.

Q.—What other publisher was on the scene then?

A.—We knew they were sitting around, waiting.

Q.—For what?

A.—To publish.

Q.—The books?

A.—Yes.

Q.—You did not want to give the other publishers any information which might enable them to publish these Readers?

A.—You are asking at two different periods.

Q.—I am talking about 1904 now. You did not want to put the Government or the other publishers in a position where they could publish these Readers?

A.—Not to assist them.

Q.—Although you had promised under your seal that you would do so?

A.—I do not understand it so.

Q.—What do you understand it to mean?

A.—That we would allow the Government to do so, but not assist.

Q.—That is hindering them?

A.—I do not know about that.

Q.—If it did not hinder, why did you keep it back?

A.—I do not know whether it hindered them or not. The same information was available for them.

Q.—They could not get it until they brought you here?

A.—They could get it precisely in the same way that we got it ourselves.

Q.—The Government had to go to England for it, or get a Commission to get it out of you?

A.—They could get the knowledge from England by simply asking.

Q.—Now, we will see whether they could get it or not: "Without their consent, however, we are not free to furnish the particulars asked for, and as some of such extracts have recently been made the subject of litigation and may again come before the courts, we think it doubtful whether we can obtain such consent."

That is what the Copp, Clark Company wrote to Mr. Millar on the 23rd of March, 1904, and you wrote that that was all right; you saw that letter and agreed to it?

A.—Yes.

Q.—No doubt helped to compile it, did you not?

A.—No, sir.

Q.—Anyway, you agreed to it?

A.—The particulars of it.

Q.—And you wanted the Government to understand that you could not get the consent from England?

A.—I did not say so.

Q.—You said in your letter of the 24th of March, 1904, "If we replied,

A.—I do not know anything about the three firms.

as we must, in a similar way." That letter of Copp, Clark Company of the 23rd of March, 1904, was agreed to by the three firms?

Q.—Did not you three firms meet together and agree that you would not give up this information?

A.—I do not remember of our meeting, but I am quite sure that we would, and we ought to.

Q.—And did?

A.—I do not know whether we did or not.

Q.—But I ask you whether or not it would have been quite easy for the Government to have struck out of those Readers all these selections that were copyrighted?

A.—They could strike them out.

Q.—It was easy enough to ascertain what was copyrighted?

A.—Oh, yes.

Q.—Strike them out and substitute others for them?

A.—Yes.

Q.—Not the slightest trouble at all?

A.—Not at all. We found the Government could do most extraordinary things.

Q.—You found that it would?

A.—Would and could.

Q.—Were the Government compelled to give you this contract?

A.—I do not know.

C.—Did you hold them up?

A.—No, sir.

Q.—In no way at all?

A.—No, sir.

Q.—They were quite free not to give you the contract?

A.—Certainly they were free.

Q.—And they could have easily enough built a Reader up with extracts that were not under your control?

A.—Certainly.

Q.—And let the publication to the world at large?

A.—Certainly. They did more extraordinary things than that.

Q.—Tell me one of them?

A.—They authorized our Readers, and within twelve months they struck them off the list.

Q.—I am talking about modern times; after this contract was given?

A.—We think they did lots of extraordinary things.

Q.—Since then?

A.—I would not say just at that particular period. Within a year or two.

Q.—But during the currency of these two contracts, did they do anything extraordinary?

A.—I think I will confine my answer to the Reader question.

Q.—Did they do anything extraordinary?

A.—I do not recall to my mind any specific instance just now.

Q.—Did you know that Warwick & Co. wished to be allowed to publish the Readers at one time?

A.—I did not know until the letter was read this morning.

Q.—Were you in the Canada Publishing Company before Warwicks?

A.—Yes.

Q.—How did they get in?

A.—They must have bought some stock.

Q.—Did they not get in in order to prevent them from applying for the right to publish?

A.—No, sir; I do not think so.

Q.—You were a Director at that time?

A.—I do not suppose that opinions count for any evidence.

Q.—Oh, yes; I ask your opinion on that. Were they not let in to the Canada Publishing Company in order to induce them not to apply to publish the books?

A.—I can only give you my opinion, if you are willing to accept that.

Q.—I will take that?

A.—I would say No.

Q.—It was not for that reason?

A.—No; I knew that some of the stock had been offered for sale, and had been offered to myself and I would not buy, and it had been offered to other parties, and it was finally offered to Warwick; but I know that some others had the offer of that stock before Warwick bought.

Q.—You have been publishing the books with the other two firms in partnership all the time, have you not?

A.—Together, yes.

Q.—So all your interests were identical, you each got an equal share of the profits?

A.—That is not correct: no.

Q.—How were the profits divided?

A.—If we sold more we got that additional benefit.

Q.—Were you not limited in your sales?

A.—No, sir.

Q.—Were the other men limited in theirs?

A.—Not that I know of.

Q.—Did you not have to make an account to each other of what you said?

A.—Yes; but we did not sell the books for nothing.

Q.—You had an agreement which allowed you to sell up to a limited number; could you sell all you liked?

A.—We could sell all we liked, and did.

Q.—You had to account to the others?

A.—Yes.

Q.—You printed one section of the books?

A.—Yes.

Q.—The other publishers each printed another section, and those three sections were put into one book?

A.—If there were three sections in. Some books there were not.

Q.—Those that there were three sections in?

A.—Yes.

Q.—That book was bound at the joint expense?

A.—No.

Q.—Who bound it?

A.—We bound our own books?

The CHAIRMAN: Mr. Staunton is speaking of the Readers only.

WITNESS: So am I.

Mr. STAUNTON: How far were you partners in the production of these books?

A.—In the printing, if there were three sections, the Canada Publishing Company would print one section, Copp, Clark another, and we the third. We bound our own books. If we sold ten thousand more than the other publisher, we would have to make some credit to him on that amount.

Q.—You would divide the profits equally amongst you on the whole output?

A.—No; because we charged so much extra for selling because we sold so much extra.

Q.—The person who sold the books was allowed?

A.—That extra discount.

Q.—So, that if for selling the books there would be five per cent. allowed—I am not saying that was the amount?

A.—I would not like to allow so little.

Q.—There was a certain fixed amount allowed for selling charge, that went to whoever happened to sell the book?

A.—Yes.

Q.—But the rest of the profit was equally divided amongst you?

A.—Yes.

Q.—So that you acted as traveller for the firm, and were paid for whatever you sold?

A.—Yes.

Q.—And they acted as traveller for the firm, and were allowed a percentage on whatever they sold?

A.—I do not like the word "traveller."

The CHAIRMAN: Did you have any agents going around the country selling these Readers?

A.—Yes; fifteen or twenty.

Mr. STAUNTON: Do you not think it is a very expensive way of getting out these books?

A.—No, sir.

Q.—Do you think it is the cheapest way of obtaining books for the schools, the plan adopted by the Government?

A.—Well, I do not suppose that opinions count for much here.

Q.—That is a question of opinion. We will take that. Give me your opinion on that. Is it an expensive way of obtaining the books for the schools, that which has been adopted by the Government?

A.—Do you now refer to the Readers?

Q.—Yes; we will confine it to Readers for a moment. Is it?

A.—Well, it is a cheap way, I think, but at the same time I would like to use another word—I would not like to say "nasty," but it is not a very satisfactory way in order to get the best results.

Q.—What do you think is the best way to get the best results?

A.—We prefer to see competition amongst the publishers.

Q.—Go on and tell me a plan?

A.—I ought to just say, if you will allow me, that in the interests of the Commission, and in the interest of this whole question, there being a number of things of vital importance, that instead of answering offhand, I should have an opportunity of dealing with these matters later.

Q.—I asked you whether you thought the method adopted by the Government made it more expensive than was necessary to the pupils?

A.—Do you wish me to give an answer. Yes or No?

Q.—Yes.

A.—I think it is probably a very cheap way.

Q.—Then you cannot give us any information that would disabuse the Commission's mind of the impression that it is not a cheap way?

A.—I am not prepared to say. I have no means of knowing what the mind of the Commission is, and I do not think they have got the facts yet.

Q.—If you will tell me upon what matters you will give us information, perhaps we will adjourn to get it. Put it right down upon what point you wish to enlighten the Commission. You think this a very cheap way of getting the books?

A.—Yes.

Q.—If it is a very cheap way, you cannot help us?

A.—I think this Commission wants to get more than an idea of a very cheap way.

Q.—What do you think they want to get?

A.—I think they want to get all the information they can with reference to the present text book system, and what is the best way for getting a better. So far as the difficulties in the old system are concerned, they want to know them, and they want also to know, in the preparation of their recommendation, what would be a better way.

Q.—Are there any difficulties in your opinion in the old method?

A.—I am prepared to go into that question. I got the notice only last night that I was wanted here. I am prepared to come here and go into the whole question.

Q.—But you are not prepared to do it now?

A.—No.

Q.—You do not at present feel ready to discuss the question as to the cheapness or the proper plan to be adopted in obtaining a supply of school books for the future?

A.—I am not prepared.

Q.—At present to discuss the question?

A.—No.

Q.—Then I will not ask you.

The CHAIRMAN: I do not know whether I understood you or not, Mr. Gage: it seems very extraordinary that you, in the name of another person, instigated an action against the Minister of Education to have the publication of these Readers restrained?

A.—No, I did not say that. I do not think I said that. Possibly I may have said what involved that—that there was an infringement of copyright.

Q.—To have the publication of these books restrained which you had entered into a contract with the Government to publish for ten years?

A.—No.

Q.—There is no doubt, you were at the bottom of the action to bring a writ against the Minister?

A.—Yes.

Q.—What was that for?

A.—To make known the fact that there was an infringement of copyright.

Q.—Did you bring an action for damages, or to restrain the further use of these selections—or what was the writ asking for?

A.—This writ is probably thirteen years old, and I cannot tell you the terms.

Q.—Was it not for the purpose of restraining the further use of these selections by the Minister?

A.—That would involve that.

Q.—To restrain the Minister from using selections in a book which you had undertaken to publish for ten years?

A.—Yes.

Q.—Well, that is so extraordinary that I wanted to give you the opportunity of affirming or denying it?

A.—There is no denial necessary.

Mr. STAUNTON: A pure scare action, was it not?

A.—No.

Q.—You never went on with it?

The CHAIRMAN: You found fault with the Government for having de-authorized the series that preceded those provided for in the contract of 1884?

A.—Yes.

Q.—You and one other firm had each published a series of Readers, and the two had been authorized?

A.—Yes.

Q.—And had you entered into a contract with the Government for the publishing of that series that you had had authorized?

A.—Yes.

Q.—Did that contract provide that the Government was to have the right to cancel at any time?

A.—I do not think so.

Q.—I see the Minister of Education says so in a speech that he made in the House in introducing the contract of 1884. Speaking of that, he says, "Under the provisions of the agreement the Department had the right at any moment to cancel the authorization of the books." He is speaking of the series that just preceded that last one. Two had been authorized. You had got up a series and they were authorized, and one other firm had a series authorized. A third firm was asking authorization, but had not got it. You entered into a contract with the Minister for the publication of that series. The Minister says that that contract provided that the Government had the right at any moment to cancel it: was that so?

A.—I do not think there was any such—of course, that is twenty-four years ago.

Q.—If that were so, that the contract which you entered into provided that they might cancel it at any time, you had nothing to complain of when they did cancel it?

A.—We are presuming that they had the right. Now, I do not like to go on and argue from that, because I do not believe they had.

Q.—The Minister says they had?

A.—I am talking for myself, not for the Minister.

Q.—If the statement he made were true, you have nothing to complain of if he cancelled it; that is so?

A.—That is so.

Q.—You said something about spending large sums in agents going about the whole country; you have not agents going about the country for the sale of Readers that you publish under the contract?

A.—Yes, we have.

Q.—The retail people have to come to you?

A.—We want to get the orders.

Q.—The orders must come to you; where else could they go?

A.—To the Copp, Clark Co.

Q.—Had you three publishers rival agents through the country?

A.—Two of them had.

Q.—Just for these Readers alone?

A.—No.

Q.—As far as the Readers are concerned there was no object in going to any expense for the sale?

A.—Oh yes, there was.

Q.—I could understand the little profit that one of you three would gain by selling more than the other?

A.—That is what we sell the books for, is the margin; and they try very hard to get the orders, too.

Q.—Did not the agreement provide that you three were to publish these in equal shares, and be equally interested in that contract?

A.—No, s r.

Q.—You could not go on and publish as many as you chose and sell as many as you liked under the contract?

A.—Yes, we could.

Q.—That is your interpretation of it?

A.—Yes; under that contract with the Minister of Education.

Mr. STAUNTON: With yourselves?

The CHAIRMAN: Under the agreement with the Minister could any one of you go on and print and bind and sell just as many as you could?

A.—Yes.

Q.—And defeat the other two entirely?

A.—Yes. That is the intention, as the Minister, says, that we were supposed to be rivals and not a syndicate; and so we were rivals.

Q.—Did you divide equally the profit?

A.—I have already answered that: up to ten or fifteen per cent.

Q.—What you charged for handling?

Mr. STAUNTON: Do you mean to say there is a selling charge for these books that under these conditions would amount to ten or fifteen per cent.?

A.—As a separate item I do not know what the cost would be. We do not do our business that way.

Q.—I have always understood that in all commercial business every firm that runs their business properly have a selling charge as one of the items of expense; have they not?

A.—No, sir, I never knew that they had.

Q.—Do you mean to tell me that you do not know what it costs you to sell your wares?

A.—Yes, sir.

Q.—Do you not think that ten or fifteen per cent. on a book of which three firms have a monopoly is an enormous charge?

A.—Sixteen per cent.

Q.—But the selling charge for school books on which you three have a monopoly; is not ten or fifteen per cent. an enormous charge?

A.—I do not know that it is. We do not keep our school books separate.

Q.—Is it not an enormous charge?

A.—I do not know that it is.

Q.—Will you tell me what expense you could possibly be put to to sell these school books that you did not choose to incur?

A.—We have to have a place to put them in.

Q.—A warehouse to store them?

A.—Yes.

Q.—That does not come under the selling charge?

A.—Yes, it does.

Q.—What do you include in your selling charge?

A.—The management of the office; the rent; the help, taxes, light, and all incidental charges.

Q.—You tell me, then, that before you account to the members of the syndicate you add on an item for office management?

A.—No.

Q.—You said so?

A.—Excuse me.

Q.—You should wait until I am finished. You add on an item of the office management to your selling charge?

A.—Will you repeat your question?

Q.—Before you account to the other members of the syndicate you deduct or add on your expense that you keep from them an item partly composed of the office management?

A.—No, sir.

Q.—Expense of office management?

A.—No, sir.

Q.—You would not include office management in the selling charge?

A.—We would in the ordinary business.

Q.—In the sale of these books?.

A.—I would not include office management.

Q.—Will you tell me how you make up in your arrangement with the other members of the syndicate the selling charge?

A.—I think we credit those who sell a quantity of these books ten or fifteen per cent. extra. I can verify that.

Q.—So that if you sell fifty thousand books, and the other publishers sell ten thousand each, you get ten or fifteen per cent. on that fifty thousand of a profit?

A.—Yes.

Q.—Is that right?

A.—Yes. We are only talking figures that are merely guess work. I am not sure of the percentage. We will assume it is ten or fifteen per cent.

The CHAIRMAN: Is there an agreement amongst you three as to what you shall be allowed for selling?

A.—I think there is. There is.

Q.—I could understand if you were each selling about the same quantity it would not be material what that was; but suppose you sold ten thousand worth of books in a year more than each one of the other two, when you came to adjust your profits, how much would you be allowed extra?

A.—I think it is ten per cent. over and above the best discount given.

Mr. STAUNTON: How much in money would it be?

Mr. COOPER: That is clear enough.

Mr. STAUNTON: If it turned out in the course of the year you had sold ten thousand dollars more than they had of the Readers, how much more profit would you get?

A.—I cannot tell you.

Q.—Would you get a thousand dollars more?

A.—I do not think so.

Q.—You said you got ten per cent. for the selling of them?

A.—I know I said that. But I do not know that it would amount to a thousand dollars.

Q.—It would if you sold ten thousand dollars more than they did?

A.—Certainly.

Q.—Then you would get a thousand dollars more than they?

A.—If we sold ten thousand dollars more than they did.

The CHAIRMAN: Did the three firms together secure the copyright on all the selections in the Readers?

A.—In common, they did; for their own purposes.

Q.—Did it cover the whole of the selections in the Readers?

A.—I think it did.

Q.—There seems to have been a little time between the expiration of the first contract, and the making of the second. The first contract expired on the 1st of January, 1895; the second one, for the second period of ten years, was made, I think, in February, 1896; a year and a month or two afterwards?

A.—Yes.

Q.—Was there any agreement to cover that period?

A.—Not that I know of.

Q.—Just went right on without any new agreement?

A.—There was no interregnum.

Q.—There must have been an interregnum unless there was another agreement. The first one expired on the 1st of January, 1895; the next one commenced in February, 1896; you have no recollection of an agreement covering that intermediate period?

A.—There was none, I think.

Q.—You went right on under the first agreement until the second one was made?

A.—We have found it required considerable time to get an agreement through: sometimes six months.

Q.—I have told your solicitor that if you desire to make any further statement when he is present you will have the opportunity at our next session?

A.—Thank you, Mr. Chairman. Then may I say, possibly it would be to the advantage of the Commission.

Q.—Any statement you desire to make to the Commission we shall be glad to hear?

A.—It might be of some advantage to the Commission to have a copy of this evidence that has been given; it would not be very safe for us to give evidence on some of the newspaper reports, because we think it is something horrible, some of the evidence given.

Q.—The newspaper men, I think, have reported correctly the proceedings?

A.—But they cannot report all the evidence given.

Mr. COOPER: In the first agreement, 1884, you paid $7,500; that is $2,500 each; for a set of plates?

A.—Yes.

Q.—You say that was for plates and not for the right to publish?

A.—That included the right to publish.

Q.—For the plates and the right to publish?

A.—No doubt. I do not want to answer any questions any more fully than you desire; but the Minister claimed in his public speech that he was going to get from the publishers the cost of making these books, and he stated to us that this was the cost of preparing.

Q.—A portion of it; it would not be all. He paid about $17,000?

A.—Like some of the rest of us, we do not know what the cost is until we get the bills.

Q.—Here is a quotation from Mr. Ross's speech in the house in March, 1885, explaining this agreement: "The only subject now remaining for the consideration of the House is the cost of preparing the Readers. By the statement submitted it appears that the total cost is $17,686; against which we have $7,500 in cash, and about $7,000 in woodcuts and type, and a set of electrotypes worth at least $2,500; leaving the actual loss to the country at less than $2,000. It is well known to every person acquainted with the trade that the set of electrotypes furnished the publishers will require renewal a good many times in the course of ten years. The only possible way in which a new set can be obtained is by application to the Department. We are then in a position not only to receive $7,500 from these firms for the first set of electrotypes, but also to receive from them constantly a revenue for any renewals of the same; and I expect that during the ten years the entire cost to the country will be made up in this way."

Q.—Did you pay the Government anything for a set of plates after the first set?

A.—Yes.

Q.—You got further sets from them?

A.—I am not sure that we got a further set.

Q.—I mean during the life of the contract, the first ten years, did you pay them anything else?

A.—I do not think so.

Q.—Then, Mr. Ross's expectation here that the cost of the plates would be made up in ten years, did not come true?

A.—It evidently did not. Just within the ten years.

Q.—How did you keep your plates renewed during that ten years?

A.—We simply kept one set that we did not use.

Q.—Who do you mean by "We?"

A.—The three publishers kept one set which they did not use.

Q.—And from that you made any duplicates that might be necessary?

A.—Yes..

Q.—Much apparently to Mr. Ross's disappointment. In 1896, when you renewed the agreement, you paid $3,000 each, or $9,000 altogether?

A.—Yes.

Q.—Was that for a set of plates or entirely for the right to publish?

A.—I am not sure what special reason was given, but we had to pay that to get the right.

Q.—I am very anxious to know whether you got a set of plates at that time or whether it was entirely for the right to publish: you are not prepared to answer that just now?

A.—No.

Q.—You will get the information for us?

A.—Yes.

Q.—In the renewal for 1896, I understand the High School Reader was added?

A.—Yes.

Q.—The three firms never published the High School Reader?

A.—No.

Q.—Could you give us any explanation of that?

A.—The Minister did not give us a set of plates, although we thought we had paid in part for them; Mr. Ross would not let us have a set.

Q.—Somebody did block you a little?

A.—Yes, although we paid the Minister for them.

Q.—Did the Minister give you any reasons why he would not give you a set of plates of the High School Reader?

A.—I do not remember. I may say I have not had much conversation with the Minister during the last ten or fifteen years.

Q.—Can you tell me why Mr. Ross refused to give you the plates, or did he refuse?

A.—I cannot remember. We had some correspondence with him. He refused. We did not get them.

Q.—Will you look that up?

A.—Unfortunately, we all passed through a fire, and a lot of this correspondence was burned.

Mr. COOPER: Perhaps, Mr. Thompson could give us some information on those two points. I think it is a fair question. Just the two points that I have been asking Mr. Gage, as to why you did not publish the High School Reader under the new agreement, and whether the $3,000 paid in 1896, under the renewal agreement covered a new set of plates, or was merely a payment for the right to publish.

Mr. THOMPSON: There was no new set of plates, as far as I know.

Mr. COOPER: You are quite certain about that?

Mr. THOMPSON: No, there were no new plates.

Mr. COOPER: Then, Mr. Gage, what was the $3,000 for that you paid, if you did not get the set of plates?

A.—I do not think we did; but it was certainly for the privilege of having the contract renewed, and if the plates were included that would, no doubt, be part of it; and I would say the right to publish the High School Reader, if the plates were included, as they evidently must have been.

Q.—If you had not paid that $3,000 each, would the price of the text books have been lower?

A.—I do not think so.

Q.—Would it have tended to diminish the price of the text books?

A.—I do not think so.

Mr. STAUNTON: Three thousand dollars was not here or there on the production of these books.

Mr. COOPER: You think the payment of that $3,000 each, would not affect the price of the text books?

A.—It did not affect it, because the price was fixed by the Government.

Q.—If you had not had to pay it?

A.—Personally we would not have sold them any lower.

Mr. STAUNTON: Did you take any steps to prevent the publication of any other Primer than yours?

A.—Personally we did not.

Q.—Who are "we?"

A.—I am speaking for myself.

Q.—Did you engineer it, then?

A.—No sir.

Q.—Who did?

A.—I do not know.

Q.—Did you never hear of any effort being made to prevent the publication of another Primer?

A.—I heard to-day for the first time that there were legal steps taken.

Q.—Oh no; but any moral steps?

A.—Really, I am at a loss to know how you would have used moral steps with that Department.

Q.—You would not take an immoral step?

A.—No, we were not taking any steps at all.

Q.—Did you do anything to prevent the publication or to induce the Government not to allow the publication of another Primer than your own?

A.—We did not that I know of.

Q.—Did you know that Morang was taking steps to publish a Primer?

A.—All the world knew.

Q.—And did you not do anything to prevent that being published?

A.—Not that I know of.

Q.—If it was done, it was done by some other person than yourself and without your knowledge?

A.—I have no knowledge.

Q.—And never had any?

A.—I had no knowledge that I can call to mind of having done anything.

Q.—Did you know of any person else doing anything?

A.—No, sir.

Q.—Then so far as you are concerned you do not know of any steps having been taken to prevent the authorization of Morang's Primer?

A.—Personally I do not. I have no recollection.

Q.—"I do not remember;" is that what you mean?

A.—I have no recollection whatever.

Q.—Have you got any other information that you would like to give us?

A.—No, sir; I have not any that I am prepared to give now. I have already stated my position in that matter.

Q.—That you will prepare information?

A.—That I will be able to come here at the convenience of the Commission, if they desire it—

Q.—The Commission will be glad to hear you if you will tell us about what you will be able to give us information in the future. I would not like you to go away, and I am sure the Commission would not, with the idea that we had prevented you from telling us anything that you wished to tell us?

A.—You have not done so.

(Some conversation follows about methods of asking questions and of giving evidence.)

The CHAIRMAN: If you have answered any question Yes or No, that you want to answer more fully, we will give you the opportunity now?

A.—I am not finding fault.

Mr. STAUNTON: When I am examining you I like you to answer my questions; but I do not want you to be under the impression that I wish to prevent you from giving any fair answers or any fair explanation on any subject on which I have questioned you; and if you have any information or any explanation that you desire to make, I wish you would either do it now or let me know at any time before the business is over, and we will be glad to give you the opportunity.

The CHAIRMAN: That is fair enough.

WITNESS: It is very fair.

Mr. STAUNTON: You understand you can avail yourself of that offer at any time before the business of the Commission is over?

A.—If I am to give any information I would like a copy of the evidence; because I think that you are not going to be satisfied with just a statement of evidence that might be given to-day or last week. I picked up a paper yesterday and saw an extraordinary statement that no firms—I am quoting from a newspaper—that no firms published any Primers until this gentleman, who is giving evidence, published his.

Q.—That is not correct?

A.—You spoke of fourteen years of quiet during which there was tranquility. Now, the whole fringe of this question as far as publishing is concerned has not been touched. If that gentleman had known, who gave that evidence— he must have known—if the newspaper report is correct that there were at least two other series of Primers published within the time, and those were authorized in other Provinces of the Dominion; but the paper states that there was nothing done "until I brought out my Primer."

The CHAIRMAN: Mr. Morang stated here that his was the first Phonic Primer; is he correct in that statement?

A.—No.

Mr. STAUNTON: Now will you tell us what Phonic Primer there was published before his?

A.—I have got a parcel here some place. The report did not say "authorized Primers," and I have not said "authorized Primers" in my evidence.

Q.—Phonic Primers?

A.—Phonic Primers, yes.

(Produces book.)

Q.—You produce "New Canadian Readers, Twentieth Century Edition; the First Primer." Is that a Phonic Primer?

A.—Yes.

Q.—When was that first published in this Province?

A.—Let me see the title page; perhaps I can tell.

Q.—"For use in this Province?"

A.—This is all supplementary to the evidence; this is why I said it would be wise for us to have some official report. This was published in the year 1901.

Q.—For this Province?

A.—I said we had published not only for this Province but—

Q.—Let us stick to this Province?

A.—Yes, we published for this Province, if we could get authorized.

Q.—Was it ever authorized for the use of schools in this Province?

A.—No.

Q.—Then the first Phonic Primer in this Province was Morang's?

A.—Yes.

Q.—Then you got yours authorized immediately afterwards in this Province?

A.—No, we have not got it authorized yet.

Q.—Did the Canada Publishing Company get one authorized in the Province immediately afterwards?

A.—I do not know about that.

Q.—Did you apply to get yours authorized in the Province?

A.—Yes.

Q.—Was it refused?

A.—It was refused, I am sorry to say.

Q.—It was refused?

A.—Refused.

Q.—Is that all you want to say about that?

A.—We have other Primers here now. I am only now calling attention to the fact that before I could come here and give further explanation it would be necessary to have an official report, because it would not be safe to deal with a more condensed incomplete report.

The CHAIRMAN: This Commission was arranged some three or four months ago, and we have been taking evidence off and on for a couple of months; and you three publishing houses were especially notified of the sittings of the Commission. I suppose you knew that your transactions with the Government would be enquired into, yet only to-day you have seen fit to present yourself?

. A.—My only answer is this: we received the circular notice announcing it, and I do not know that we have by word, act, or in any other way shown any lack of courtesy; and so far as I am concerned personally I may say to the Chairman now that there is no man in the Government or out of the Government, or sitting in the Commission, who is more delighted to see a Commission sitting to enquire into this whole business, than myself; and if the Commission knew all in connection with school book educational work in this Province, I think they would confirm that statement. I have no doubt in the world they will.

Q.—What do you think about your remaining away until the work of the Commission is nearly over, and saying: "If you will give me a copy of what has taken place I will tell you something?"

A.—I do not put it that way. I say if we are to give full information on some of the matters that have been brought before you, some of the evidence, it will be very desirable in your interest—I am not worrying about the evidence given, but you want to get at the facts, and it will be impossible for me or some other witness to come here and volunteer evidence on a mere partial statement in a newspaper. That is only dealing with evidence already given.

Q.—If you have information that you think it would be to the advantage of the Commission to hear, cannot you give it regardless of what anybody else has said?

A.—Certainly; but I think in connection with that, if you are to get at the truth, if I am to answer a question of that kind and give you information, when misleading statements have gone to the public—

· Q.—We would have your statement as against that?

A.—I would not attempt to make an affidavit upon a mere statement like that.

The Commission adjourned at 5 p. m.

THURSDAY, NOVEMBER 8TH, 1906. 11 A. M.

EVIDENCE OF MR. DAN A. ROSE.

Mr. STAUNTON, Examiner:

Q.—Mr. Rose, are you a publisher?
A.—Yes.
Q.—What is your Company at present?
A.—I call it the Canadian Book Company.
Q.—It is a private business of your own, is it?
A.—Yes.
Q.—Have you any authorized books?
A.—One.
Q.—What is it?

21 T. B.

A.—A Public School Geography: "Rose's Public School Geography."

Q.—You have gone to the extravagance of binding that book with tape?

A.—Yes.

Q.—What did you do that for?

A.—It makes a more durable book.

Q.—What does the paper in that book cost you?

A.—Five and a quarter cents.

Q.—That is a very high price, is it not?

A.—It is a better quality of paper than is in the general run of school books.

Q.—Is it American or Canadian paper?

A.—Canadian. We are forced to use Canadian paper.

Q.—Is there any difference in the price of American and Canadian paper?

A.—American paper in the United States is fully twenty-five per cent. cheaper than in Canada. We pay a duty here.

Q.—I understand you to tell me that your paper cost you twenty-five per cent. more than the American paper costs the American?

A.—That is right.

Q.—How do they manage that?

A.—There is the tariff of twenty-five per cent. on imported paper.

Q.—But the Canadian paper is as cheap here as the American paper is there?

A.—No. Our paper here is fully twenty-five per cent. higher.

Q.—No matter whether you buy it in car load lots?

A.—No.

Q.—Do you buy the paper in that Geography by the car load lot?

A.—It would be about twelve tons of paper purchased for that book.

Q.—That is not half a car load?

A.—No.

Q.—You cannot buy that paper as cheaply in broken lots as by the car load?

A.—No.

Q.—If you bought by the car load it would cost you?

A.—Half a cent better.

Q.—It would cost you about five cents?

A.—Yes.

Q.—Did you ever try to publish the Readers?

A.—No.

Q.—Did you ever apply to publish them?

A.—No. We thought of it, but we were aware that copyrights existed.

Q.—You were aware that copyrights existed on the extracts?

A.—Yes.

Q.—Did you ever know that the publishers had made an agreement with the Government that they would aid in so far as they could,—or not hinder, to put it as favorably to them as possible—to not hinder the publication of these Readers by other publishers?

A.—Not until yesterday.

Q.—Do you mean to say that that public document was not accessible to you, that you did not know about it?

A.—Yes.

Q.—You never heard of it before?

A.—No.

Q.—If you had known about it, what would you have done?

21a T. B.

A.—I would have taken chances and published the Readers.

Q.—Why would you have taken chances and published the Readers?

A.—It strikes me that the signers of that agreement had conceded to the Department the right to allow anybody to publish the books.

Q.—You do not think they would have brought a real action against you?

A.—If they had, I would have fought it out.

Q.—You are an experienced publisher of many years, are you not?

A.—I have had charge of one of the largest printing and binding houses in the city.

Q.—For how many years?

A.—All my life, practically.

Q.—Did you ever publish the Readers?

A.—We have done press work on the Readers.

Q.—What do they pay for the press work on those Ontario Readers

A.—Anywhere from a dollar to a dollar twenty per thousand impressions.

Q.—What do you mean by a thousand impressions?

A.—The book is printed in 32 page forms; a thousand impressions of 32 pages.

Q.—They will give you a dollar for that?

A.—At one time it was as low as a dollar, but $1.20 is about the price.

Q.—You did not set the type for that?

A.—No, that is simply press work.

Q.—Have you ever read the specification for those books?

A.—I have read the general school book specification.

Q.—Looking at that third reader, is that specification lived up to in that reader, in your judgment?

A.—Certainly not.

Q.—Tell me why you think it is not?

A.—The book is inferior in every respect; binding, paper, press work, ink.

Q.—Would that book be passed as complying with the requirements of the contract by any person who was an expert in the business?

A.—No.

Q.—Could it honestly be passed by an expert?

A.—No.

Q.—If the requirements of the contract had been properly lived up to, is the specification in the contract a reasonably satisfactory one?

A.—The specifications would produce a really first-class book in every particular.

Q.—What class would you put the readers in that are now produced?

A.—Common printing and binding.

Q.—One man said they were somewhat like newspaper printing?

A.—They are a little bit better than a newspaper; but as a case of book-making they could not be much worse.

Q.—You are not extravagant in that statement?

A.—They are really inferior books.

Q.—Do you think that if the contract was complied with the result would be a satisfactory book according to modern ideas?

A.—It would produce a first class modern book.

Q.—What do you say about wire stitching?

A.—I do not believe in wire stitching; I think it is a mistake. The latest specifications withdraw the wire stitching on general book.

Q.—Not on the Readers?

A.—Not on the Readers.

Q.—What do you think of the profit in that book the way it is produced the third Reader, for example; what is your opinion about it if you could produce a book like that for the money that is got for the book?

A.—I would make fifty or sixty per cent. on the transaction.

Q.—You think that?

A.—That is a fact. I will give any man fifty per cent. and take the balance.

Q.—Supposing the book cost you ten cents to produce it; I am putting a suppositious case?

A.—If the book cost me ten cents I would get fifteen cents for it; on any of these books.

Q.—Then you say there is a fifty per cent. profit to the publisher in that book?

A.—Yes.

Q.—Does that give the printer and binder his profit too?

A.—Yes.

Q.—So that the publisher, who was really the middleman in the business. gets a fifty per cent. profit on the cost of that book?

A.—At least.

Q.—I see that Mr. Gage, on March 19th, 1888—long enough ago, I should have thought—said to Mr. Ross "I herewith submit a proposition which I am satisfied will more readily and satisfactorily carry into effect your wishes" etc. (Reads letter of March 19th.) Mr. Rose said to him, in reply to this: From a publisher's standpoint it appears to me that you are willing," etc. (Reads reply of Mr. Rose.) Nothing came of this, as I understand it. What do you say about that proposition to supply those books?

A.—I would say it was a bluff. Could not do it. He makes no reference there to the discount to the trade or anything of that kind. It was simply a bluff letter. If I had received the letter I would have regarded it as a bluff, it is an impossibility.

Q.—Does he mean that is what he would get?

A.—That is what he would get out of that book. He makes no provision for the retail trade.

Q.—Would you produce the books mentioned in the letter of W. J. Gage to the Minister of Education, dated 19th March, 1888, and set out in the Sessional papers of part one, 1890, at page 14, for those prices if you had to allow no discount off at all?

A.—Yes.

Q.—That is very much cheaper than they were being produced, as a matter of fact?

A.—Take the arithmetic; it was a twenty-five book; selling.

Q.—What is the ink worth in that third Reader?

A.—Fifteen or twenty cents a pound.

Q.—What priced ink should be used in a book of that description, the Third Reader?

A.—Fifty cents.

Q.—What is that paper in the Third Reader worth in your judgment?

A.—Oh, about four and a quarter cents a pound.

Q.—Is that enough money to pay for the paper in a school book?

A.—It is not the paper called for in the specification. The paper in the specification could not be bought, I think, under six cents in Canada.

Q.—What would it cost to bind these books, this book, the way it is now?

A.—Eight cents.

Q.—That includes the material in the binding?

A.—Yes.

Q.—What would it cost to bind this book according to the specification?

A.—Ten cents, that Third Reader.

Q.—Did you give evidence on one of the Commissions?

A.—Yes.

Q.—Which one was that?

A.—I gave evidence before two Commissions.

Q.—On the cost of school books?

A.—Yes.

Q.—What branch did you give the evidence on?

A.—Just general evidence.

Q.—Did you give evidence on the merits or demerits, as the case may be, of the Readers?

A.—I do not think so.

Q.—Were you asked anything about the Readers?

A.—I do not think so.

Q.—What were you asked about?

A.—Cost of paper, and questions of that kind. The cost of conducting a publishing business.

Q.—Did they not ever ask you what you thought of that book?

A.—They did not ask me, they asked paper experts about that.

Q.—Was there any evidence given as to whether or not these Readers were up to the specifications, that you remember?

A.—If my memory serves me, there was J. R. Barbour and W. D. Gillean gave evidence, but they only spoke generally of the paper; I do not think they gave a distinct reference to the—

Q.—To the books. Did anybody swear that the paper in those books was up to the requirements of the contract?

A.—I do not think so.

Q.—Was anybody asked that?

A.—It is so long ago I could not say.

Q.—Do you mean that evidence was confined to generalities?

A.—To a very great extent.

Q.—A sort of an academic discussion of the merits of the school books, was it?

A.—To a great extent, I think it was.

Q.—And you only gave evidence on the cost of paper?

A.—No; it was general evidence as to cost of press work and binding and things of that description; the cost of conducting a publishing business.

Q.—The cost of the production of that series of Readers or of the school books was not gone into minutely?

A.—Only in connection with the general publishing business.

Q.—From the evidence that you heard how were the Commission enabled to make up their mind as to whether the books were costing too much or not?

A.—Well, they had to satisfy themselves with the evidence they got.

Q.—Could you have made up your mind from the evidence you heard as to the cost of those books, leaving outside your own personal knowledge?

A.—To be frank, I left the Commission with the impression that they had very little evidence to go on; a good many generalities but nothing very definite.

Q.—You were in the Hunter, Rose Company when the High School Reader was prepared?

A.—Yes.

Q.—Who prepared that Reader?

A.—The Reader was prepared by the Department. The Department prepared the Reader, and we paid the cost of the authorship and made the plate.

Q.—Do you know what it cost?

A.—The author got a thousand dollars. The cost of the plates has passed out of my memory now.

Q.—Perhaps you can tell us the cost of the plates; as you were connected with the production of that book from the very beginning these alterations and changes would have been paid for by you?

A.—Yes.

Q.—Can you give me an idea of what those were?

A.—Oh well, if you take it roughly I suppose it would run three dollars and a half a page.

Q.—It cost $3.50 a page?

A.—Yes, to set the type, correct it, and produce the plate.

Q.—And there were a large number of copyrighted articles in that book?

A.—Yes, there was a number.

Q.—Did you have to pay anything for them?

A.—No.

Mr. COOPER: How did you get them?

A.—Just took them.

Mr. STAUNTON: Nobody ever bothered you about that at all?

A.—Nobody bothered.

Q.—Your firm gave a list of these selections to the Government?

A.—Some time ago there was a list supplied.

Q.—And you say they never cost you a brass farthing?

A.—No.

Q.—You say that all these authors in the list produced allowed you to publish without charge and without objection?

A.—Yes; the only one that made objection was the second one; Morang made an objection in regard to the extract from the Mill on the Floss.

Q.—You were under the impression that notwithstanding a book is written by an author who is alive, one may make an extract from that book without subjecting himself to liability?

A.—We were under that impression. We told Morang to go ahead with his writ; and the suit was never pressed.

Q.—You are under the impression that any person may publish a fair extract?

A.—Yes.

Q.—So there is really no foundation for the fear that the Ontario Government or its publishers might be successfully sued for having published extracts from British authors?

A.—I do not think that any reputable firm would take action; I think that instead of being offended they would be pleased. It is a good advertisement for any book to have an extract taken into a school book, excepting for the purpose of holding up to secure a contract.

Q.—Here we have seventy or eighty school books in this province, and they are filled with selections from standard authors whose works are copyrighted. Did you ever hear of an action being brought by any of them?

A.—Never.

Q.—So that even if there is a right to sue—which in your judgment I understand is questionable—to sue for publishing reasonable extracts from an author's work that is copyright, you think that no reputable firm would take action, but would rather be pleased?

A.—I took the trouble, when the question was up, to make a search and see if there is any record of any case in court being fought through on the question of extracts, *re* copyright.

Q.—Did you have your solicitors look up the question for you?

A.—Yes.

Q.—And there is no case where any person has ever been restrained from publishing extracts from an author?

A.—There is not.

Q.—You know that these copyright articles that Gage brought this fanciful action of his on, they were out for seven or eight years before there was any threat to the Government at all?

A.—Yes.

Q.—You have said to me that this High School Reader cost you a thousand dollars. The return to the Government puts it at eleven hundred dollars. Is that return incorrect?

A.—There is a typographical error, I see. Eleven hundred dollars is correct.

Q.—Could you ascertain for us what the cost of these plates were in the High School Reader?

A.—I think so.

Q.—Will you do it and let us have it?

A.—Yes.

Mr. Cooper: We think that $3.50 is a little high?

A.—In giving a price of that kind I am making an estimate that there is a certain amount of correction, as in a geography or grammar. On a Reader, where there is so much reprint copy, the chances are that I am high there. The typesetting in the Public School Geography alone cost over four dollars a page.

Mr. Staunton: Perhaps you can tell me what the plates of the Public School Geography cost?

A.—I am saying the mere mechanical work on that cost over four dollars a page. I could give the exact figures.

Q.—You mean?

A.—Labor.

Q.—Of producing the plates; is that right?

A.—Yes; setting the type and then casting it into a plate.

Q.—That cost over four dollars a page?

A.—Yes.

Mr. Cooper: Does that include the making of the illustrations?

A.—No.

Mr. Staunton: What would the illustrations cost you?

A.—The prices vary from three dollars to five dollars an illustration, the making of the plates.

Mr. Cooper: You say they cost you from $3 to $5; do you think they are worth that?

A.—They are not worth five.

Mr. Staunton: Could you get them any cheaper?

A.—I could not get them under the three dollars.

Mr. Cooper: I can buy them for less than three.

Mr. Staunton: When I ask you what these books cost per page, I mean with the illustrations and everything?

A.—The plates for that book, the Public School Geography, cost in the neighborhood of seven thousand dollars. There are twenty-four pages of maps. That is quite an item.

Mr. Cooper: Are those half-tone maps?

A.—Half-tone maps.

Q.—Printed in Canada?

A.—Printed in Canada. A plate like the map of Europe cost $125.

Q.—How many printings?

A.—Three.

Q.—Then there would be three cuts?

A.—Yes.

Q.—Do you think the press work in Rose's Geography is as good as it should be?

A.—No.

Q.—What is your defence for that book?

A.—The book was printed hurriedly, the first edition. The next will be better. I objected to the press work myself on that book. Some of the electrotypes were faulty. It will be altered in the next edition.

Q.—You say that the cuts in that book cost you from three to five dollars each. What is the ordinary rate per inch for first-class half-tones?

A.—Twenty cents.

Q.—Twenty cents per square inch.

Mr. STAUNTON: Does that include the photographing and everything?

Mr. COOPER: No, that is aside from the photograph. Twenty cents per square inch.

Q.—You do not know any person buying half-tone cuts at less than twenty cents per square inch?

A.—Yes.

Q.—Give us an example of some?

A.—I should imagine the Toronto Globe do.

Q.—For their illustrated section?

A.—Yes.

Q.—What do you think they pay per square inch?

A.—Likely about fifteen cents.

Q.—Would you be surprised to learn that they buy them for twelve cents a square inch?

A.—No.

Mr. STAUNTON: You cannot surprise him.

WITNESS: The general trade quotation on a half-tone is twenty cents.

Mr. COOPER: Do you consider that the half-tones in a publication like the *Canadian Magazine* are first-class half-tones?

A.—Yes.

Q.—Are you aware that the *Canadian Magazine* pays only fifteen cents for half-tones?

A.—No.

Q.—That is for your information?

A.—It depends a good deal on circumstances. You are citing the *Canadian Magazine* and the Toronto *Globe*, which are practically wholesale consumers of half-tones; but the consumer of small and less regular quantities, who comes in one day for half-a-dozen and another day for a few more, has to pay more.

Q.—Were you a member of the Hunter, Rose & Company when Mr. Gage made application to publish some of your text books?

A.—Yes.

Q.—On what ground did he apply to get the right to publish some of your books?

A.—The exclusive period had run out in our agreement with the Government.

Q.—How long did the exclusive period usually run?

A.—I imagine three years, as a rule.

Q.—Did you let him have the right to publish; did you make an agreement with him to allow him to publish some of your books with you?

A.—No. He tried to get us to enter into an agreement.

Q.—Why did you not?

A.—Because we thought perhaps we were being held up, and we would not stand for it.

Q.—Had not he the right to ask you to let him come in with you on those contracts?

A.—He had no right to threaten us.

Q.—What do you mean by "threaten"?

A.—He told me personally that if we did not take him in he would take all the books, and, with his opportunity to sell, he would probably practically have the whole control of the book and we would not have any sale at all.

Q.—In other words, you thought he was trying to crowd you out?

A.—Exactl .

Q.—Did he offer to compromise with you and take a portion of the profits and leave you alone?

A.—Yes.

Q.—He did?

A.—Yes.

Q.—And you objected to that?

A.—Yes.

Q.—Because you did not think it was fair?

A.—Yes.

Q.—Did any other publisher ever try to do the same thing with you?

A.—No.

Q.—Did you ever try to do the same thing with any other publisher?

A.—No.

Q.—Did you ever make an arrangement to publish a book with another firm?

A.—Yes.

Q.—What book?

A.—Made an arrangement for the public school copybooks with S. G. Beatty, and for a French Grammar with the Copp, Clark Co.

Q.—Why were you willing to make arrangements with Beatty and Copp, Clark and not W. J. Gage?

A.—We became joint publishers. These books were prepared jointly in both cases with Beatty and Copp, Clark; it was a joint undertaking from the beginning.

Q.—Therefore you were working under what you considered a fair agreement?

A.—Certainly. In the first place, we made an application to the Department for authorization, acting for ourselves and Mr. Beatty; and in the second place the Copp, Clark Company made application for authorization, acting for themselves and the Hunter, Rose Co.

Q.—What was the advantage to the publishers in making joint applications?

A.—Well, the Copp, Clark Co. were very large handlers of books, and handled more or less French books; and we had a French book; and to concentrate the trade on one book we came to an understanding.

Q.—It was a matter of economy?

A.—It was a matter of economy.

Q.—What do you think is a fair price, a fair price to add to the cost of a book to cover the distribution—the selling, advertising, canvassing, etc.?

A.—I am satisfied that there is no publishing.house in Toronto conducting their business under fifteen per cent. on their turnover. That is the actual cost for selling and running, and if they do it for that they are not extravagant.

Q.—Publishers have said here that they would want from thirty-three to fifty per cent.; do you think that excessive?

A.—I do not think that thirty-three and one-third per cent. is excessive by any means if they deduct their business charges from it. As a gross profit it is not excessive.

Q.—You said just now it cost them fifteen per cent.?

A.—Yes.

Q.—That the other eighteen and one-third per cent. would be their net profit?

A.—Would be their net profit.

Q.—Then you mean that if you want to make a fair profit out of a book you ought to add thirty-three and one-third per cent. to the actual cost of your printing and binding and preparation?

A.—Yes. You imagine that the mere preparation of a single text book covers the cost; but the publishers in many cases had to take big risks. For instance, a High School Arithmetic, the first edition of which was prepared by a man named Glashan. We printed fifteen or twenty thousand copies of that book. The Government authorized it. When the book was sent to the Department, the teachers complained that the book was too intricate. We had to prepare another book, and that fifteen or twenty thousand copies were simply thrown away. That is only one case of a number. It has occurred with the Copp, Clark Co., with the Canada Publishing Co., and it has occurred with them all; the Department has allowed them to go on with the book, and it got into the teachers' hands, and the book was unsatisfactory.

Mr. Staunton: Do you mean to say that they de-authorized it?

A.—Yes. They objected to the text.

Q.—After authorizing it they de-authorized it, and made no compensation?

A.—Made no compensation.

Q.—Did the publishers understand that beforehand?

A.—Yes.

Q.—It seems to me to be a great injustice?

A.—That is one of the risks.

Q.—Is that right; that the practice is for the Government to authorize a book, and then let you print it and put it out amongst the teachers to see how it will be received?

A.—And then they withdraw the authorization.

Q.—Is it a common practice?

A.—No; it is the exception, but these things have occurred. Of course, now under the regulations, Mr. Morang, in giving evidence here to-day, stated that this geography had not been published prior to authorization. We prepared the geography. There was a concession allowed us in the preparation of the geography; we were allowed to submit the text in print without the illustrations or maps; but that book was in circulation for a year prior to authorization, and the text was submitted to a committee of experts, who then recommended the Department to authorize it. It was published in that shape.

Mr. Cooper: Did you publish it in that shape in order to get around the regulation that a book should be published six months before it should be authorized?

A.—With their consent.

Q.—It does not make any difference whether it was with their consent. Did you or did you not publish the book in that shape in order to get around the regulation that a book should be published six months in advance of authorization; yes or no?

A.—Well, I would say yes.

Mr. Staunton: This is the book spoken of as a dummy the other day?

A.—That is the letter press of Rose's Public School Geography, without the illustrations.

Mr. Cooper: Then you actually got authorization before it appeared in the selling form?

A.—Yes.

The Chairman: What do you say would be a fair percentage of profit to the publishers of our Ontario Readers over and above the profit that would accrue to the trades for the mechanical execution of the book; over and above the profit of the press work, the profit of the binding, and all that sort of thing; just the publication alone; what would be fair?

A.—As a net profit, the publisher should make at least fifteen per cent.

Q.—He has nothing to do but send them out to the retailers when they order them?

A.—Of course, if you introduce that as a rule into business.

Q.—I am speaking of this particular time?

A.—It is hard to say where you draw the line.

Q.—From these Readers all this element of risk that you have referred to in connection with other books is eliminated. There is nobody else to publish them but these three; there is no cost of selling, no bad debts; they are bound to come to them for these Readers. What is a fair profit to the publisher under these particular conditions?

A.—Ten per cent. to fifteen; that is, a man who has got to live out of that.

Q.—I have some school books here published on the other side; I would like you to look at them and compare the mechanical execution of them with that of our Ontario Readers. In the first place, I show you Baldwin's Reader, fourth and fifth years combined. How would that compare in mechanical execution with our Ontario Readers?

A.—This is a hundred per cent. better made book.

Q.—I ask you next to look at Heath's Fifth Reader?

A.—It is precisely the same.

Q.—A hundred per cent. better than ours?

A.—Yes.

Q.—Here is Brooks' Sixth Year Reader, another American book?

A.—It is far ahead. There is no comparison between the books.

Q.—The Victoria Reader, fifth book; that goes to Manitoba; what about the mechanical execution?

A.—It is a far better book than ours; better paper, better press work, better binding.

Q.—You were giving certain percentages to Mr. Cooper, very much larger than ten per cent.; you were then referring to books published in different conditions from the Readers; for instance, Glashan's Arithmetic, which was not satisfactory, and the edition lost; you were referring to such cases when you were naming the higher percentages?

A.—Give a man the entire school book trade, and the percentage would naturally be lower.

Mr. STAUNTON: Give him the entire publication of the Readers for the Government, and he would only be obliged to fill the orders as they came in, and then come up here and get his money. What ought he to get on that?

A.—Ten per cent.

Q.—Ten per cent. would be a nice profit, would it not?

A.—Yes. I believe this: that for cheap production of books I believe to-day, if the Government were to prepare a set of plates and make them open to any publisher complying with the specifications, the Government naming the upset price to be sold at and discount to be allowed, I believe if those plates were thrown open to all printers you would get better school books, and you would get them cheaper.

Q.—Would you not have the retail price to add? It seems to me if the Government were to put it open to competition to produce the book, and then take the books—let the books be sent directly from the publisher to the schools—that would be the ideal way of supplying books to the schools?

A.—You might get in the same position that the Ross Government got into with their contract; you might be tricked. If you put it open to all comers you are going to get the books.

Q.—You mean, let the Government produce the plates?

A.—Yes.

Q.—Let the Government say, "Mr. Rose, you may publish that book to-day?"

A.—Yes.

Q.—You have got to publish it up to this standard?

A.—Yes.

Q.—You can get this price for it?

A.—Yes.

Q.—To-morrow, if another man comes in they will give him another set of plates?

A.—Yes.

Q.—But the books never pass to the schools unless they are up to the standard. So no contract at all; just simply say: "You publish the book, but it has got to be up to that specification?"

A.—Yes.

Q.—Can anybody publish a Bible?

A.—No. You cannot print a Bible in Canada; you have got to have a license from the British Government to print the Bible.

Q.—The Catholic Bible, the Douay Bible, is not printed under license?

A.—No.

Q.—You mean to say that the King James Bible is?

A.—Yes.

The Commission takes recess, 12.30 to 2 p.m.

EVIDENCE OF MR. WILSON F. BRAINARD.

Mr. STAUNTON Examiner:

Q.—Your residence is New York, is it?

A.—My place of business is New York City. I live in Glen Ridge, New Jersey—my house.

Q.—You are a University man?

A.—Yes, Amherst.

Q.—A graduate of Amherst University. After you left the University what business did you go into?

A.—Publishing.

Q.—What house?

A.—Hubbard Brothers, Philadelphia.

Q.—What were you engaged in when you were with them?

A.—In charge of the manufacturing department; and I curiously got in very suddenly; their manufacturing man left very suddenly one day, and I was put in until they got another; and they did not get another, and I continued at that work.

Q.—What was the volume of their business?

A.—Seven or eight hundred thousand dollars a year.

Q.—How long did you continue?

A.—I stayed on one or two years, and left them then.

Q.—Where did you go?

A.—I went to the United States Book Company, remained there between one and two years, and left them. That was a very large firm. There I had particular charge of the binding.

Q.—What is their turn over in a year?

A.—They did a business of something between three and four million dollars a year. They have since gone out of existence. The reason I left them was that they failed.

Q.—Under your management?

A.—No, it was under Mr. John W. Lovell's management.

Q.—And after you got through with that firm?

A.—I went to D. C. Heath & Co., the school book people in Boston. I had entire charge of their manufacturing department for seven years.

Q.—After that?

A.—I left them and went back to New York, and went to work for D. Appleton & Co.

Q.—What were you engaged in with them?

A.—Had entire charge of their manufacturing department. I stayed there about three years and left them.

Q.—Does that bring you nearly up to date?

A.—That brings me nearly up to date.

Q.—What are you engaged in now?

A.—I am engaged in book manufacturing by contract for publishers.

Q.—Have you a plant?

A.—None at all.

Q.—What do you do?

A.—I can explain to you. I had a pretty wide experience in the houses that I was with; school book end particularly, Mr. Heath's; they aid a very large business, and they grew very rapidly. My experience was a pretty wide one; I left each time that I thought I could earn more money, and when I left Appleton's the last time, I had discovered that there were very few men who actually made a specialty of understanding how books were manufactured. A great many men know it superficially, but very few people have taken the time and trouble to learn it thoroughly. I thought there was an opening for a business in New York, and there was no man there in exactly the same line of business; so I started business for myself, soliciting contracts from the book publishers as an expert to manufacture books. I got business the first day I went out, have had all I could do ever since, have got quite a large business to-day, and have built it up in three or four years: entirely by contract. I take the manuscript from them, and sometimes even tell them how much the book should sell for and what it is best adapted for, and whether it should be illustrated or not, and if so what kind of illustrations. Sometimes they have all laid out for me, and simply leave it to me to execute their plans. I then have drawings made, engravings made, type set, plates made, buy paper, have it printed, have it bound, and in some cases even ship the books all over the country. I transact the whole business for some of the smaller publishing houses; I take it from the manuscript and do all their shipping for them all over the United States. I simply have set up as an expert, and have been very successful, because I am very well known amongst the publishers there. In addition to that, just to prove the position—the New York Custom House have had me on their list of experts for five or six years. I appraise in cases of dispute very frequently for them without pay, simply as a little advertisement for me—in a case of l'spute about undervalued plates, books, sheets, or anything of that kind. I simply tell you that to show that I have a recognized position there as an expert.

Q.— We have brought you here to get your opinion upon the school books of this Province, and I would ask you first to take the school Readers. I would like you to take the Fourth Reader first. Before examining that book I would like you to read the specifications for its production, just what sort of a book it should be. I think it is contained in paragraph three of the contract of 1898.

(Witness examines contract and looks at books.)

Q.—What I am drawing your attention to that for is, I want you to tell me—if it is a fair question, you looking over it so hurriedly—whether that specification covers generally all that it should for the production of a first class book of its kind?

A.—It is not specific enough. I could make you a book corresponding to those specifications and make you a pretty poor book.

Q.—Will you criticise that specification in detail?

A.—"The book shall be bound in stiff covers, with the cloth turned in: the quality of the strawboard—" Strawboard is the cheapest thing that you can use in a book; we never use it in school books in the States; they would not allow it; it would not be accepted. It is used chiefly for binding holiday children's books, the cheapest kind of books. That should be binders' board," and there can be no mistake about that. "Heavy, extra finished, plain cloth." That does not mean much; you might use a cloth costing four cents a yard or eighteen cents a yard and still have it according to that. It is better in contracts drawn in the United States to-day; if cloth is specified they specify a particular make. The cloth is controlled by practically one firm in the States to-day, as most things are, and they make different grades of cloth: one at eighteen, one at sixteen, one at fourteen, one at twelve, and one at ten cents. They used to make them lower but they have cut out that, and we are no longer allowed to have very cheap cloth. This specification might mean cloth at from four to sixteen cents and still be complied with; but if you say "like sample submitted" and if you bind it in that only it is satisfactory then you would cover it. But merely to say "heavy, extra finished plain cloth" is entirely insufficient.

Q.—Without saying "by the sample submitted," how would you improve the wording of that?

A.—Without referring to a sample?

Q.—Yes; if it is a practical way of doing it?

A.—You would either have to refer to a specific cloth or to a sample.

Q.—You think it is wiser to refer to a sample?

A.—That is the way they do entirely in the State bids, and they are very strict about the cloth coming up to the samples. These samples are made with scrupulous care, in order that the final edition shall be exactly the same. I have had five reams of paper made to order at an expense of fifty or seventy-five dollars just in order to have it exactly as it would be in the State contract.

Q.—(Reading) "Heavy extra finished twilled cloth for the Second, Third, Fourth, and High School Readers?"

A.—That is open to the same criticism; the cloth might be of a cheap grade or a good grade.

Q.—"The covers of the book shall be embossed in black on first and last pages thereof?"

A.—That means exactly what you have there. Embossed in distinction to printing means this: embossing is going through a hot press which makes that sunken in, and through an inking machine which inks it.

Q.—Is that a good requirement?

A.—I think that is a very poor requirement for the users, the public: because it costs the publisher something which he had better put on somewhere else. It costs him as much to stamp the back of that book as the front of it. That costs a fraction of a cent, and you have to pay for it. If you leave it off all your books, you leave off that which is absolutely useless and is not on the majority of the modern books.

Q.—Leaving it off the back; but what about embossing the front?

A.—All the embossed books do not wear as well as the smooth books. When a child uses the book day after day with smutty fingers, the embossed cover catches the water and holds it, catches the dirt and holds it; and the cost of inking is greater than on a smooth surface.

Q.—Take the Ontario Reader, Part I., and the Fourth Reader; the First is smooth, the Fourth is embossed?

A.—All these items are a saving to the publisher; they are also an absolute saving to the consumer, because the consumer has to pay for the superficial thing.

Q.—(Reading) "The sections of the First Reader, Part I., shall be thread-sewed to extra strong evenly-made mull, extending to within one half inch from the top and bottom of the book and overlapping one inch on each side." What do you say as to that?

A.—That is perfectly correct. It is more elaborate than is necessary, because you cannot do it in any other way.

Q.—That is a proper requirement?

A.—That is a proper requirement.

Q.—Over the mull——"

A.—Excuse me; they do not call that in the States "mull;" they call it "super."

Q.—(Continues reading) "Over the mull a strong sheet of paper of approved quality and color shall be glued; and the First Reader, Part I., thus stitched with proper end papers, shall be strongly glued into covers approved of by the Minister of Education."

A.—That is perfectly correct.

Q.—Is that a sufficient requirement?

A.—You mean have you specified a sufficiently strong binding for the Fourth Reader?

Q.—Yes.

A.—Yes; as strong as it is customary to give for a book of that grade.

Q.—What do you say about requiring tapes or hinges?

A.—It has not been necessary to do that on a book as small as the Fourth Reader, which is not sufficiently heavy to pull out of the covers without very severe handling. The tapes are to make the book hold into the covers more strongly; and with a book of that weight it is not necessary. That has been very conclusively proven by the wear of the books.

Q.—Is not that so with some of the books that are there; are not books of that size bound in that way?

A.—Yes, you get it in books from Great Britain a great deal and all kinds of books whether they need it or not. It adds to the strength; it would make every book stronger, but it would cost more.

Q.—Here is the Progressive Course in Spelling, Hunt?

A.—Yes.

Q.—Is that book bound in the same way as required by this contract?

A.—Entirely different style.

Q.—What is that binding?

A.—That binding is described as stitched through the side to linen, which is then pasted on; and it is almost indestructible; but it is very awkward. They call it down there "the steel trap binding." You cannot hold your book open. That style of binding is used principally in spelling books and Primers, where the children give them very hard wear; and it has become quite universally used for those books within the last ten years, that exact style.

Q.—What is your opinion of it for the purposes of that kind of book?

A.—I think it is the best thing there is. I recommend it and do it. I have just manufactured a spelling book for the State of North Carolina, for the entire State; a new contract; a new spelling book which I manufacture for them; and I do it in that way.

Q.—Perhaps it is not quite fair to take that class of book. Give me an American Reader of that size, if you have one?

A.—I have Heath's Fourth Reader. This is sewed on one tape, and has in addition the waste leaf stitched to a piece of super, which makes it additionally strong. I have done it myself on very heavy books. Not on books of that grade as a rule—very rarely.

Q.—If you were drawing the specifications—if I understand you correctly—for such a book as I put before you, the Ontario book, you would not consider it necessary to improve upon that portion of the specification?

A.—The sewing?

Q.—Yes,

A.— No sir.

Q.—And fixing it to the case with the mull, as it is there?

A.—I am giving you what is the general custom of the large publishing houses in the States. It is not that it cannot be made better by binding but that is good enough.

Q.—And in your opinion is it good enough?

A.—It is. I have bound or overseen the binding of millions of books for the different houses; I have shipped half a million of books into one State in the fall; and have seen come back as damaged the smallest fraction of one per cent.; in those enormous state contracts.

Q.—"The sections of the First Reader, Part II., the Second, Third, Fourth, and High School Readers, shall be sixteen pages each, and each section shall be thread sewed to three tapes or strings." What do you say as to that requirement for these books?

A.—A very good specification; the best specification you have got there, that they shall be in sixteen pages each; because if they are in thirty-two pages each, it means that you will have a bulging back and it will be just half as strong. You have doubled the number of points to hold the thread when you specify sixteen pages; and sewing to three tapes is a very good thing, if you can afford it.

Q.—"The stitches and tapes or strings shall be covered with fine, strong, evenly-made mull, extending to within one-half inch from the top and bottom of the book and overlapping one inch in each side." Do you approve of that?

A.—No. One word there is absolutely the wrong one. Instead of "fine" it should be "coarse;" because fine mull will not not take glue. You see it is very coarse. If you put a fine mull in there it will not glue down at all. The fine is just the opposite of what you want.

Q.—"Over the mull a strong sheet of paper, or pressing, shall be glued, and the book thus stitched with proper end papers shall be strongly glued into its stiff covers?",

A.—Your term may be different here. If I were to describe it I should say: "over the mull a strong piece of paper or lining." What they mean by "pressing" I do not understand; it is not a term used in binding in the States. The rest of the specification is pecfectly correct; you could not im-

22 T. B.

prove on it; it describes the best process, practically the only one to make a good book.

Q.—Have you any criticism to make in the specification as far as I have gone?

A.—Not a word, except that the word "fine" does not describe the material.

Q.—Starting from that, is there anything that you would suggest?

A.—I would; just to make a little resume of it, I would specify binder's board instead of strawboard.

Q.—You have said that. Is there anything additional to what you have already stated, if you were drawing the specification?

Mr. COOPER: "Binder's Board" is their word for mill board. It was "millboard," and that was struck out and "strawboard" inserted.

WITNESS: There is not.

Mr. STAUNTON: You think that is all right. Then the specification proceeds: "If, however, the publisher prefer, he may substitute wire stitching for the thread sewing in above specifications as regards the First Reader, Part II., the Second, Third, Fourth, and High School Readers." What do you think of that?

A.—It is a very good thing for the publisher.

Q.—Why?

A.—If he had a large sale of the book he would make a large sum of money out of that.

(Note. The witness speaks here from a misconception, and corrects himself later.)

Mr. COOPER: It says, wire-stitched through the sections?

A.—That is impossible.

Q.—You will have to read the two paragraphs. Read the whole of it, and explain how it should be done. There are two kinds of wire stitching: one through the sections and the other through the entire book.

(Witness looks at contract again.)

A.—Yes, I see.

(Looks at "Elements of Algebra," a book that has been used.)

I have had little or no experience with a book bound in that way. It is a style that is not used in school books. I have never seen it used in a school book by any firm during the time that I have been connected with the business.

Q.—Would you recommend it?

A.—No; I do not recommend it for small books in that way, because the wires will rust and tear; a signature tears out of the wire that way more easily than it does from the thread. I am looking at a book wire-stitched through the signatures and then sewed.

Q.—You remarked that it would be a good thing for the publisher; why?

A.—I misunderstood the style. I thought it was to be wire-stitched through the side, like that spelling book I had in my hand a moment ago— like that Progressive Course in Spelling. That is sometimes done instead of thread stitching. The Progressive Course in Spelling method is more expensive than this.

Q.—In your opinion the wire-stitching is more expensive than the sewing?

A.—Yes. Take the Ontario Fourth Reader. This book, according to specifications, is to be folded in sixteens, then fed into the sewing machine, sixteen-page signatures at a time; and if you take this "Elements of Alge-

22a T. B.

bra'' you have to do the same thing with it; but to that process you have added the stitching of the signatures, which costs money. Any process costs money. It is an additional process.

Mr. COOPER: I do not quite catch that. The Algebra is sewed on a sewing machine?

A.—Where; did you not have a book there that was?

Q.—No. You said that. Excuse me, there is no thread in that book at all?

A.—He has wired it here?

Q.—Yes?

A.—I beg pardon.

Mr. STAUNTON: Describe it again and say why you think it is more advantageous, if you do think so?

A.—No, I do not think so now that I examine that more carefully. I looked at this, and listening to what you stated, without examining more carefully, I thought he had stitched every signature and then sewed them onto his tapes, that he had made a double process. That of course would cost additional, as I was describing it. I am inclined to think that the "Elements of Algebra" cost more to bind in that style than if sewed like the Heath Fourth Reader, because there are more processes. That has to be fed into a machine six times for every signature.

Mr. COOPER: They are alternate sections?

A.—Are they—

Q.—There are only three?

A.—Then it has to be fed by hand three times for every section; whereas in a sewing machine the signature is fed once.

Q.—Put in three staples at once?

A.—Yes, unless they are built specially.

Mr. STAUNTON: You do not approve of the wire stitching?

A.—I do not.

Q.—It is unknown in the modern trade in the United States, in regard to school books?

A.—Yes.

Q.—You have examined the specifications; I would like to direct your attention to the books themselves, the Readers. We are speaking entirely of the Readers now. Tell me whether in your opinion they comply with the specification even as it is. I am putting you in the position of being an expert who is going to pass or reject those books?

A.—I understand.

(The five Ontario Readers are placed before the witness, who examines them.)

Q.—You read about the paper, did you not?

A.—Yes. It does not mean much. Your specification of paper is open to the same criticism that part of the specification of binding is.

Q.—Tell me that, because I did not ask you that. "Of good quality and approved color and texture, weighing sixty-six pounds to the ream of 512 sheets?"

A.—Your word "good," does it mean three cents a pound or six?

Q.—Good for the price, it might be, and still be very poor?

A.—Yes.

Q.—The word is too general and not specific enough?

A.—Yes. You could use, and still live up to this contract, very poor paper or very good.

Q.—Would you substitute the use of a sample?

A.—That is the customary way. I would like to demonstrate that point. Here are two books, one "The Story of the Canadian People," and the other 'The Buccaneers History," Estill, an American book. There is over a cent a pound difference in the papers of those two books.

Q.—Are they both good?

A.—They are both good, and they both come up to specifications, I presume. That is not perceptible to you, and it would not be to any Board. I know the two papers; I know where they were made.

Q.—Which is the more expensive of those two papers?

A.—The one in "The Canadian People."

Q.—And you say both of these papers would pass under the specification?

A.—Yes, and there is a cent a pound between them. The paper in "The Canadian People" had got better stock in it. It has the quality of not dog-earing in a school book, which is a specification required in some state contracts—that the paper shall be long fibre so that it will not dog-ear or crackle. It is resilient. The Estill History paper is a very good paper and used in a million school books to-day, but it will not last as well. The reason of the use of that paper in that book is solely the lower price; they positively cannot afford to use the higher grade paper. So you can see the point I was trying to bring out.

Q.—I do; and I see the value of the suggestion. Now go on and pass or reject these Canadian Readers, giving your reason?

A.—I can see nothing in your five Readers which does not come up to that contract, except that this Fourth Reader which I have here, and which has been torn, does not seem to be on the tapes.

Mr. COOPER: There are no tapes on any of them?

A.—The specifications say?

Q.—That they may use wire instead?

A.—Then I take that back. So far as I can see, your five books come up to the specification.

Mr. STAUNTON: What do you say as to the press work?

A.—It is fair. It is not good. But the books are a little bit old fashioned, and are not modern books. I am looking at them purely from the point of view of the specifications there, not whether they are good.

Q.—Quite irrespective of what your opinion of the book is, if you are asked whether it had passed the specifications, it would pass?

A.—It would. They could even have furnished much poorer books and have passed the specifications, because the specifications are not carefully drawn.

Q.—Now tell me what you think of the books, speaking generally, apart from the specifications?

A.—Just to describe them very tersely, they are out-of-date.

Q.—In what way are they out-of-date; they have covers and leaves and they are printed and they have pictures in them?

A.—You can get better selections of type than they have here; in some, not all. Most of the modern Primers have a different arrangement of the type on a page, which is easier for the child, and a different selection of type, which also makes it easier for a child. Then the illustrations, personally, I like the old wood cuts, but they are old fashioned, and do not appeal to the children to-day as much as the line drawings and half tones. The main thing, of course this may be superfluous, but in building a Primer the main thing is to illustrate it. The idea that I have in my mind is that a great number of objects, such as there are in this picture, on page 18 of the Second Part of the First Reader, confuses the child. The modern idea of teaching children is to give them simple drawings as well as text, and that picture is involved. We do just the opposite thing in all illustrating of Primers. For that reason this book is very much out of date from a pedagogic point of view. Of course I have to take that into consideration when I take the illustrating of a Primer; I have to look at it from that point of view. The point as to the illustrations is applicable more or less right through the series; they are not up to the latest pedagogical point of view in illustrating a set of Readers.

Mr. Cooper : Is the type too small in that for a Fourth Reader?

A.—Not smaller than is used in most Fourth Readers to-day, but the tendency is to use larger type. The type in Heath's Reader is two sizes larger than in the Canadian Fourth. The Ontario Fourth Reader is ten-point modern, and Heath's is twelve-point old style. The type in the Heath Reader, the old style type, they believe is more easily read by a child, because it has not the little fine hair lines that the modern-face type has. It has not the hair lines nor the shade nor the little seriffs on the letters.

Q.—And you prefer old style type to modern?

A.—It is better for a child's eye, and better for any one's eye.

Q.—What would you specify for the type in each of these Readers?

A.—As to Readers, it is customary to use type beginning with eighteen-point for the first part of the book.

Q.—Eighteen-point modern or old style?

A.—I must say that eighteen-point modern has been used in most of the recent Primers, because there was no good old style made by the type founders of that size. Then farther over in the book, fourteen-point; and none smaller than twelve-point, in a Primer. This Ontario First Reader nearly agrees with that, but the type page is too crowded; there is too much matter. Look at pages 62 and 63 of the First Reader, Part I; I would never make a Reader like that. If the manuscript was given to me I should set that in type and return it to the author and request him to cut out a certain amount that was not permissible from the manufacturing point of view. That is, I look at it, in manufacturing the Primer, from the child's point of view.

Q.—The Second Reader is twelve-point modern.

Mr. Cooper : Do you think that is fairly good?

A.—That is very good for a Second Reader.

Mr. Staunton : Would you specify that?

A.—Yes.

Q.—And the Third?

A.—The Third drops to ten-point. It should be not smaller than eleven.

Q.—And the Fourth?

A.—The Fourth is ten-point, and some of it evidently nine. The Fourth Reader is ten and nine.

Q.—And it should have been?

A.—Nothing smaller than ten-point?

Q.—What would you specify?

A.—Nothing smaller than ten-point.

Q.—Ten or larger?

A.—Ten or larger. Quite frequently eleven is in that Heath Reader. It is even twelve in the Heath Fourth Reader.

Q.—If you were making specifications yourself?

A.—I should specify eleven and twelve.

Mr. Cooper : Did you criticize the paper?

A.—It is not a high class of paper, but it fulfils your specifications.

Mr. Staunton : You are criticizing it generally now?

Mr. Cooper : You are past the specifications.

WITNESS: It is a fair grade of paper, but not as good a grade as on the majority of Readers published in the States, and not as good as there is in "The Canadian People." That applies to all the four Readers.

Mr. STAUNTON: You told me that you would specify a sample; now what sample would you specify for the Readers?

A.—If I were asking to have bids submitted?

Q.—Yes?

A.—Well, you can specify paper that contains no free ground wood, and that it shall have a certain tensile strength, and shall have only a certain percentage of mineral. I have drawn State contracts in that minute way for Heath's when I was with them. That paper should have certain specifications; I could not tell you offhand what they are.

Q.—If you were picking out a paper yourself as a sample for that work, what kind of paper would you choose?

A.—I should choose a super-calendered paper of a good grade, and at the present day you cannot buy the grade that should go into them except around four and a half to five cents a pound. That of course would fluctuate with the market. If you were drawing very minute specifications you could specify tensile strength, and so on.

Q.—The result is that a man specifying the paper would have to examine the papers available, and his judgment should prevail. You do not know what papers would be available in this country for these books?

A.—No. That is the real practical way you have of getting at it, to get the available papers on the market which can be used under your laws, and select the one that is the best for the price that can be paid for it.

Mr. COOPER: You spoke of wood?

A.—No free ground wood should be used, because it makes a tender paper and one that discolors quickly.

Q.—You would not allow any?

A.—No, sir. My experience of seventeen years in State contracts is that it is absolutely specified that the paper shall contain no free ground wood. It must be soda and sulphite and some rag stock. I have seen a contract drawn giving minute specifications of paper to be used in a State contract, and no person except a chemist could tell whether it was lived up to or not; and if you are dealing with reliable people it is an unnecessary trouble. That is perfectly evident. If you specify this paper or the other, when the books are made and you lay them side by side a fairly good eye will tell the difference, especially when you tear them and look at them. It does not require an expert to tell when you are getting pretty nearly the same thing, but it is impossible for anybody except an expert to tell within a fraction of a cent a pound whether you are getting what you agreed to get or not.

Mr. STAUNTON: What ought the binding of these Readers to cost, bound as they are?

A.—Per copy?

Q.—Yes; take them in lots of fifty thousand?

Mr. COOPER: Do you want them all?

Mr. STAUNTON: There is an estimate I have made of what those books cost. I would like you to look at that and tell me what you think of it?

A.—The prices here are very reasonable. You could not duplicate them entirely in New York City.

Q.—You could not?

A.—Not some of them. Some of them you could.

Q.—Take them and tell me what percentage you would—

The CHAIRMAN: Perhaps you would take into account that there is only one man to publish the book for all these people.

WITNESS: He is taking fifty thousand lots. That is the maximum; you cannot reduce the price for a hundred thousand. Taking the paper, the paper is a little more than it is worth. We make better paper than that in the States for four and quarter cents. The printing of that First Reader is lower than they could do it there. The binding here at three cents a copy is lower than you could do it there. They will not do any cloth turned-in books at three cents a copy; cannot afford to do it, at the price of labor.

Mr. STAUNTON: How far is that price out, according to your estimate?

A.—It would cost fully a cent a copy more in New York City for the Primer.

The CHAIRMAN: That is Part I. Now, take Part II?

A.—In Part II, the percentage is not, I think, so different.

Q.—Approximately the same?

A.—Approximately the same. If there is any difference it would be fractional, and higher, not lower. Coming to your Ontario Reader, Second Book, it is still a little low, but to a trifling extent. The only variation would be on the printing. The binding you could do just as well there as here, perhaps a little less.

Mr. COOPER: Press work rules twenty-five to fifty cents a thousand cheaper here than in the United States?

A.—It does. I know that. As the books grow larger, the percentage grows less. The third book you could probably manufacture in New York, or any of the large manufacturing centres in the United States for less than ten and one-eighth cents a copy.

Mr. STAUNTON: A fraction, or a cent?

A.—That Third Reader could be made for one-half to three-quarters of a cent less in New York.

Q.—The Ontario Fourth Reader is quoted there at twelve and one-eighth cents?

A.—It could be made at fully a cent a copy less.

Q.—That would make it eleven and one-eighth cents, would it?

A.—Yes. Oh, I would guarantee to make it for eleven, and even less than that, I think, when I came to figure the paper, because you could buy that grade of paper in New York for less than four and a quarter cents.

The CHAIRMAN: You are counting in your estimates on stitching with thread?

A.—For the Second, Third, and Fourth Readers, with thread; and the small Readers just as they are bound.

Q.—On the whole, this estimate is pretty nearly right?

A.—Yes, and it favors the people who buy the books. Larger quantities of the lower grades are bought.

Mr. STAUNTON: You notice here that nothing is allowed for the plates. What ought the plates for these books to cost?

A.—The series?

Q.—Yes. Now, that is from the beginning. If I have to get a set of plates for these books and I have not got anything, photographs or anything else?

A.—This particular set?

Q.—Yes.

A.—Gotten up in this style, not in the modern style?

Q.—In that style?

A.—If you were very very lavish with your expenditure, and included in it the employ of the man who got the thing up, you could not spend ten thousand dollars on it.

Q.—On the lot?

A.—No, sir, if you were very lavish.

Q.—Tell me how you estimate?

A.—I arrive at it from having made perhaps fifteen or twenty different sets of Readers in the last ten years for different publishing houses. I can recall that on plain simple Readers, I spent for drawings, for engravings, five hundred dollars complete on some, two thousand dollars on others, three thousand dollars on others; and as high as four thousand dollars for drawings and engravings alone. The type-setting on the whole set, corrections and all, would not cost to exceed two thousand dollars. Twenty-five hundred dollars is a very liberal estimate for the type-setting and plates.

The CHAIRMAN: Type-setting and plates both?

A.—Yes, and that includes all the many illustrations which go into such a set.

Q.—You say $2,500?

A.—Yes. You asked me a question which I did not quite reply to. If you were going into it minutely to find out how much you could make another set for, you would figure how many drawings you wanted, and figure that they would cost you from five to fifteen dollars apiece for every drawing—two and a half, say, to fifteen dollars for a very large and elaborate one. Count this and multiply it up. They would cost you from one dollar to two and a half for the engraving of each one.

Mr. STAUNTON: How do you know which is two and a half, and which is more?

A.—By the size. Measure by the square inch. These are woodcuts.

Q.—And for half tones?

A.—Twenty cents a square inch for the very best grade of work done to-day. You first have to have the drawings or a photograph.

Q.—What will the drawing and photograph cost; is there any rule about that?

A.—No. That is entirely according to the quality you want. I can get drawings made for a dollar and a half apiece, or I can get them made for $150 apiece, depending on your artist. The average price paid by publishers to artists for first class work is from $2.50 to $15, according to the elaboration of the thing and the size of it. If you have a drawing with half a dozen figures in it, it is elaborate. If you have a drawing with a kitchen in it, it is simple. Then comes the cost of your half-tone or line plate. Anything that has a solid background has to be reproduced in a half-tone, photographed through a screen, and that work costs not to exceed twenty cents an inch; that is, for straight edge work; if it is vignetted, it is a little more expensive: wears out more easily, is more expensive to print.

Q.—When it is color made?

A.—Color work goes up much more rapidly. Your drawings would average to cost you at least twice as much as black drawings, and if at all elaborate say three times; two or three times as much. It cannot be very elaborate coloring that goes into a Primer, or it should not be; some of them are, but they should not be. Then the process of reproduction, getting your plates from which to print, is very much more expensive; costs from $25 to say $35 or $40 apiece for every picture. I have Heath's

Primer in my hand, open at a three-color-process plate, at page 34. The plate cost $25 to $30 to make. Here is a color picture in Second or Language Reader, Baker & Carpenter, on page 100, which is by an entirely different process. It is made from line blocks, and did not cost over twelve dollars. The result is not so natural. It is what they call flat printing: the other is process printing. On page 14 of Heath's Reader there are four little pictures. The probability is that the four little pictures were made at once, so some expense was saved.

(Witness looks at Primers.)

Q.—I want you to tell about the cost of these?

A.—The manufacturing cost?

Q.—Yes. The cost of the plates in Public School Phonic Primer, Part I. The other is Morang's Phonic Primer, Part I?

A.—Take the first?

A.—The large colored plate frontispiece undoubtedly cost them . thirty dollars, and those scattered through the book may have cost them twenty dollars apiece, but if so they were not worth it.

Mr. COOPER: They are not good cuts?

A.—No, they are poorly made and very poorly printed; so much so, that it is a detriment to the Primer. Charles Elliott Norton used to give me lectures on the subject of color work for children when making a set of Readers for Heath, and he said this style of color work for a child who is in that grade is worth nothing at all.

Q.—Why?

A.—It does not teach the child anything that is real.

Q.—What about this Morang's?

A.—This Morang's is better than the other.

Q.—It is a different style?

A.—It is an entirely different style. It is much better printed, but some of these would be better in black, I think. For instance, take the one at page seventeen. They demand color work nowadays, but I think the picture on page seventeen would be better in black. But it is much better than the color work in the Canada Publishing Company's Primer. The drawings are simpler and plainer, and the colors are more natural. But I think that about ninety-eight per cent. of the color work of the last five years in Primers would be better left out than left in. It is put in in the States mainly to sell books, not that it is in itself a good thing.

Mr. STAUNTON: It is to catch the barbarous adult, not the growing child?

A.—That is about it.

Mr. COOPER: Compare the Phonic Primer, Part II, of the Canada Publishing Company, and Morang's Modern Primer, Part II?

A.—The color work in the Phonic Primer, Part II, is very much better than in the one of the Canada Publishing Company, and very much better printed.

Mr. STAUNTON: Does it hold the mirror up to nature?

A.—You have not got quite a purple cow here, but it is somewhere near it. Here is Morang's Primer, Part II, page 85; there is a single page inserted which I think is better than all the other color work, because it is more natural. Here is this sort of thing: it is unnatural, and is not good from any possible point of view, artistic or teaching color work or anything else. (Referring to the frontispiece of the Canada Publishing Company's Phonic Primer, Part II.)

Q.—There is a second page in Morang's Primer, Part II, facing page 20?

A.—The colors are better, and it is a better drawing.

Q.—What is your opinion of it?

A.—I think that is a very fair color print, mainly because they have rot attempted to do great things, but have just made a simple picture.

Mr. Cooper: It is not so raw in color as the Canada Publishing Company's?

A.—Not at all. That is very much better printing. It is in the printing. The drawing in the Morang Primer is better drawing, and in addition to that it is better printing.

Mr. Staunton: How about the color work in Gage's Second Primer, will you examine that?

A.—The color work is better than the Canada Publishing Company's, but it is not as good as any one of the pictures in that Morang Primer. You have got a purple mill.

Q.—And a blue stream?

A.—Yes.

Q.—Now take the public school arithmetic, and tell me what you think of the cost in the list?

Mr. Cooper: We have an estimate here that the Public School Arithmetics can be produced for eleven cents a copy outside of the plates?

A.—That is pretty accurate.

Q.—Have you any criticism to make on the book?

A.—The only thing about that book is, the paper is a little too thin for an arithmetic. The arithmetic is a book that has to be thumbed a good deal, and the paper should always be a little bit heavier. The quality of that particular book is not as good as is ordinarily used in the States. In making an arithmetic paper I have it made especially to order, particularly strong ground, long fibre, run very slightly on a paper machine, so that the fibres will all get worked in well together, so that it does not dog-ear. That book is in too small type for any arithmetic work, and it is badly arranged.

Q.—What about the wire stitching?

A.—I think it does not add anything to its value.

Mr. Staunton: What do you mean by badly arranged type?

A.—It is very close together, very small, hard on children's eyes. These little examples on page 77 are jumbled right up close together. It is out of date book, you can see instantly from looking at it.

The Chairman: You are going to put all our books out of date?

A.—Well, I really do not think of it at all from that point of view.

Mr. Staunton: Go on; we want you to tell us what you think?

The Chairman: I want you to tell us the truth, even if it hurts us: do not spare us a bit.

Witness: Here is page 88; the type arrangement there is very bad. (Public School Arithmetic.)

Mr. Cooper: We have an estimate of the Public School Algebra and Euclid, that it can be produced at nine cents per copy?

A.—Yes; that means small editions. That is not out of the way.

Q.—You think that is a fair estimate?

Q.—Yes. A small edition is always printed of a book like that.

Mr. Staunton: What is your criticism of that book: tell us how that ought to be typed?

A.—That is better than the public school arithmetic just referred to; better in arrangement, better in size of type, and is not so very objectionable. It is a more modern book than the other.

Q.—Would you suggest any improvements in it?

A.—The type in parts of it is a little small.

Q.—What do you think of the cost of it?

A.—It is a fair cost. Among school books, of course, that book will have a comparatively small sale. The cost of getting up the plates is very great, and you do not get your money back except in small quantities over a large term of years. All that ought to enter into the cost of the book.

Q.—Is that Public School Algebra and Euclid as good a book as Geometry for schools, by Baker: mechanically?

A.—No, it is not.

Q.—What do you say of Baker's Geometry for schools?

A.—It is better typographically, and it is better paper. There is very little difference in the binding. It costs more to make than the Ontario book.

Q.—Is it well printed?

A.—That book is pretty well up-to-date typographically.

(Gage book, copyrighted 1904.)

Mr. COOPER: Morang's Modern Geography; we have an estimate of the cost of that, aside from the plates but including the printing of the maps and colors, and the paper of course included, and the cost is twenty-five and three-quarter cents. You can get the details in this list?

A.—It is very reasonable for that book, which has a great deal of work in it.

Q.—Is it strongly enough bound for a book that size?

A.—I was just looking at that. It would be better, where a book is as heavy as that, and has to stand constant use, to bind it on a tape; but a book of that size ordinarily is not bound on tape; but this is super calendered paper, on account of the illustrations, and the book has a good many maps in it, and it would be better if it were sewed on tapes.

Q.—Mr. Morang admits that himself. The next book is the Public School Geography. We have an estimate that that cost twenty-one and a quarter cents per copy outside of the plates?

A.—It undoubtedly did. There is very little of that done in the States now, because the machinery for making cloth covers brings the cost of the fully bound cloth book very nearly down to this. Hand labor is so expensive there that we prefer to bind the books in full cloth rather than boards; but I should say that was a reasonable price for the book.

Q.—You would say that if the Ontario Government wants to keep its books up-to-date it ought to bind all its Geographies in full cloth?

A.—Most of the Geographies in the States are.

Mr. STAUNTON: This has been given to us as a price according to the gentleman's experience who gave it to us. We want that guide for the Department. If I were the Minister or the person in charge I would want something I could rely on. You say that is a reasonable price; it may be too reasonable. I want you to say whether you could or could not get the work done for that?

A.—Well, I have been comparing them with New York.

Q.—When you say it is a reasonable price, you think the work can be done for that money?

A.—Yes. I mean that it could be done properly for that money. When I say the price is a little high, I mean that you could get that work done in New York City or in the States for a little less.

Q.—When you say it is a reasonable price, you mean you could do it for that?

A.—Yes, I should be very glad to take a contract back with me for the whole thing at these prices; and that is the most vital spot you can touch me on—when I am going to take it myself.

The CHAIRMAN: You think the Geography should be cloth covered?

A.—Yes.

Q.—Bound with three staples through each section?

A.—This style, years ago, when I was in the publishing business, was adopted because it was so much cheaper than the cloth binding. At that time they had no machinery for making cloth cases.

Q.—Would you be surprised to know that we have no machines in Canada for making cloth cases?

A.—I knew that; but now, as the price of labor in the department of covering a book has doubled in the States in the last twenty years and is restricted in the number of hours, and placing it over against the cost of making the case by machinery, the additional cost of cloth over that paper almost balances. I bid on a million and a half of spelling books for the State of North Carolina this summer, and a good many others bid at the same time. I offered to make them a cloth book just as cheaply as I would make the book with boards. They asked for boards or cloth. I said, "I will make the one just as cheaply as the other." Naturally, they took cloth; and I have the contract.

Q.—Now we come to "Our Home and its Surroundings," for which we have an estimated cost per copy of ten and a half cents; what do you think of that?

A.—The price is low.

Mr. STAUNTON: What would it cost?

A.—I could not tell you offhand, without figuring this up. The paper, press work and binding are low for what I should consider a small edition. If that edition was large it might be done; but in the main, the price is a low one. I would not say I could not duplicate it.

Mr. COOPER: Is it a well made book?

A.—It is very well printed and very good paper. That is the style in which the majority of school books are made. It is very well put together.

Q.—Rose's Public School Geography, estimated to cost twenty-one and a half cents?

A.—Yes, that is all it is worth. It is a more cheaply made book than the other Geography which you showed me there, Morang's. Morang's has a much more expensive paper and is much better printed.

Q.—Would you say that the printing in Rose's Geography is poor?

A.—It is. Partly the cause of that is poor paper.

Mr. STAUNTON: What do you say of the maps?

A.—It is impossible to get good printing on poor paper. The maps are very fair maps.

Q.—Is the paper in the maps as good as you usually put?

A.—It is the same as the rest of the book.

Mr. COOPER: Do you use usually the same paper for the maps as for the rest of the book?

A.—If you use very good paper for the rest of the book, but not unless you do.

Q.—The next is the Public School Grammar, for which we have an estimate that it is worth nine and four-tenths cents to produce?

A.—That is about right.

Mr. STAUNTON: What do you think of the book?

A.—Very much out-of-date. The typography is very poor.

Q.—Type too small?

A.—Too small, and very, very crowded.

Mr. COOPER: Unsuitable for public school use?

A.—The arrangement is not as good as can be done, and has been done in many other books.

Q.—Morang's Modern English Grammar; estimated cost, nine and eight-tenths cents?

A.—The paper in this is better than the last book I looked at. The typesetting is very much better. This is the modern book, the other is not.

Q.—The title of that book contains the word modern?

A.—Yes. The type of that book has been set in an up-to-date printing office, within, I should say, five or six years—six or seven years.

Mr. STAUNTON: Is not that pretty well crowded?

A.—Not so badly as the other, because the arrangement is better. They have got it packed closely in spots.

Q.—Would you improve it?

A.—Yes; I never saw a book yet that I could not.

Q.—But ought it to be improved, that is what I mean; is it a fair book; would it pass muster?

A.—Oh yes. I am on the publisher's side of the fence, anyway. They do not get enough for about nine-tenths of their books. When you figure that a man locks up so many thousand dollars and so much of his time, and then cannot make more than fifteen to twenty per cent. gross he might better go into some other business. It is looked upon as a very high grade sort of business, but is not one that brings money returns to the same amount of intelligent effort as many other kinds of business do. I would rather manufacture books at a profit than sell them as a publisher; that is, purely from the money end of it.

Mr. COOPER: In Ontario all books are authorized; and that is authorized, which is a certain guarantee as well?

A.—It is the same way in the States. The thing is to get it authorized.

Q.—Take the Public School History of England and Canada, published by the Copp, Clark Company: W. J. Robertson's. That is said to cost eleven and nine-tenths cents?

A.—It never should be used in the public school on account of the size of the type. It is an imposition to put a child to read that book. If I had a child, I would not let him do it; and I have two. They never read any books like that. It should be shut out of any school.

Q.—And you think both the publisher and the Minister of Education that authorized it ought to be indicted for an offence against children?

A.—I am not quite so strong in my statement as that, but I really think that is a very poor book for the public schools. That, of course, is perfectly self evident.

Q.—What about the paper?

A.—It is not a very good grade of paper.

Q.—What about the paper?

A.—It is not a very good grade of paper.

Q.—What about the ink?

A.—I should judge it is fair. The plates are worn, and have been used a long time. The cost of it is about right. It would cost that much to make it, but it should not be made.

Q.—History of the Dominion of Canada, by W. H. P. Clement; published by the Copp, Clark Company and the Methodist Book House; estimated to cost sixteen and four-tenths cents?

A.—The price is fair, but the book is open to that very severe criticism, the size of the type.

Q.—How about the cuts, the illustrations?

A.—Very old fashioned.

Mr. STAUNTON: So are the people that are in it?

A.—These were poor originally, and now do not look like human beings. That is a pretty poor book.

Mr. COOPER: Duncan's Story of the Canadian People: estimated to cost twenty-one cents?

A.—Well, that is the best book I have looked at for half an hour. Good type, good size, well leaded, clear to read; modern pictures; well printed; good paper.

Q.—Who is that published by?

A.—Morang.

Q.—Do you think that estimate is a little high, eleven and a quarter cents a copy?

A.—I was just looking at the book as a whole. It is a pretty large book; four hundred and forty-six pages. I think the binding on that Canadian People is a little high.

Q.—But you think it is a good book?

A.—It is a very well made book. It is a very well made book. It is a modern book, has good paper, good printing, good illustrations.

Q.—They are now binding them on tapes?

A.—That would improve that book, because it is very heavy.

Mr. STAUNTON: Ought to be bound on tape?

A.—It ought to be, if they can afford it. I have been accustomed to the publisher's standpoint. It is a question of how much is to be spent in making it.

Q.—But should it not be bound on tape, a book like that?

A.—I would lay down as a general principle to so bind any heavy book that is used, even in the High School; it should be sewed on tape. It is not necessary in college text books.

Mr. MACDONALD: What would you call a heavy book?

A.—That is a very heavy book.

Mr. COOPER: Here is Weaver's Canadian History. That is the third History we have given you. Costs thirteen and three-tenths cents; three hundred and twenty pages; one fair color map?

A.—It is too high.

Q.—Too high?

A.—Yes.

Q.—How much too high?

A.—At least two cents.

Q.—Should be produced for eleven and a half cents?

A.—I am figuring on big editions. You can easily add two cents a copy on small editions.

Q.—Say ten thousand?

A.—Well, call it a cent and a half difference, then.

Q.—Twelve cents?

A.—Yes. For ten thousand edition.

Mr. STAUNTON: What do you think of the get-up of the book?

A.—It is fair. It is very much better than Clement's; it is better than any of them, except the Canadian People.

Mr. COOPER: Is it better than the Public School History of England and Canada?

A.—Yes, very much better.

Mr. STAUNTON: It is good enough?

A.—You ought to get better. I do not know whether Weaver's covers the scope of the Canadian People.

Mr. COOPER: It is a competing book.

A.—Looking at it from the typographical and illustrative point of view—from a mechanical point of view—The Canadian People is worth at least fifty per cent. more than Weaver's Canadian History.

Q.—Public School Physiology and Temperance, by Nattress. The editions of that are much larger. The estimated cost is nine and eight-tenths cents?

A.—You can run it up half a cent or down half a cent?

Q.—Approximately?

A.—Yes, that is pretty nearly right.

Q.—What do you think of that as a book?

A.—The type is too small. The style of binding is somewhat out-of-date, but of course that does not militate against the value of the book very much. The illustrations are very fair, but they are not up to the best physiologies that are made to-day; but they are very fair.

Q.—The Practical Speller, published by Gage & Co., which it is estimated should cost nine and eight-tenths cents?

A.—Yes, it would undoubtedly cost as much to make it in that way here, but they never spend that much money in making a speller in the States.

Q.—They bind them differently?

A.—They bind them differently and make them cheaply. They have the spelling book proposition down there so fine that the State of North Carolina made a five year contract for their spellers at fifteen cents per copy. What does this sell for?

Q.—Twenty-five cents?

A.—It is not as large as this. The book was made for the States.

Q.—In North Carolina do the book sellers get a discount off that fifteen cents?

A.—They do.

Q.—How much discount do the retail book sellers get?

A.—I do not know in that State. It varies in different States. In some States they appoint State Depositories, who are allowed ten per cent. for handling the business. The State fixes the discount.

Q.—It would be at least ten per cent., you think?

A.—Oh, yes; never less. It was that way in the State of Texas several years ago.

Q.—Would twenty per cent. discount to retailers on that be too high?

A.—No, because the price is high.

Q.—That makes it worse?

A.—You say would twenty per cent. be too high?

Q.—Would it be too much to allow the retailer for handling it?

A.—It is the custom in the States, the regular discount on school books all over the country to the retailer is twenty per cent., one-fifth of the selling price.

Mr. STAUNTON: Where there is no authorization?

A.—Where there is no authorization.

Q.—What is the discount under authorization?

A.—In a State contract, where the retail price is cut down very close, it goes down in cases to my knowledge to ten per cent.

Q.—Take the case of Ontario, where we authorize all our books, what would be a reasonable discount to give the retailer a reasonable profit?

A.—I do not believe I could answer that, because I do not know the conditions of selling and collecting.

Mr. COOPER: Public School Bookkeeping, by J. S. Black, estimated to cost nine cents per copy?

A.—Yes, I think it would.

Mr. STAUNTON: What do you think of that book?

A.—Possibly a person might learn bookkeeping out of it, but I think it would be doubtful. It is not an up-to-date book. You ought to be able to get a better book on bookkeeping to-day.

Mr. COOPER: Typographically it is all right?

A.—It is fair. It is not up to the best of the books.

Q.—Public School Agriculture, by Charles C. James; retails at thirty cents and is estimated to cost eleven cents?

A.—Is this a Common School book?

Q.—Yes; it would correspond to about your middle grade in the Grammar School?

A.—I do not know what the object was in compressing it. It ought to have been a size larger type.

Q.—Type should be larger?

A.—That I have had well drilled into me by the publishers, and there is a constant tendency to larger type all the time; consequently I look at everything from that point of view, although there is a vast number of books in use to-day all over the United States which are not larger than this. This is leaded type; it is readable; it is a well printed book.

Q.—For the price?

A.—For the price it is a cheap book.

Q.—Public School Household Science, fifty cents; cost nine and one-fifth cents. Of course there is not a large sale for it?

A.—It did probably cost nine and one-fifth cents to make a small edition.

Q.—A fairly well made book?

A.—Yes, a fairly well made book. The paper in almost all of these books is not a very good grade; not as good as you usually see in the average school book in the United States.

Q.—Here is a series of French-English, Part I, Part II, Second and Third Readers; published by the Copp, Clark Company?

A.—The typesetting of all these books is modern; they are readable and properly done. The First Readers, Parts I and II, are very good indeed typographically. The illustrations are very fair. Very creditable little Primers for small ones, from a mechanical point of view.

Q.—Is the binding good enough?

A.—Oh, yes, plenty, for a little light book like that, it is good enough.

Q.—They are wire stitched?

A.—They are wire stitched through the signatures. That is a style of binding which I have never seen used in a school book before this afternoon right here.

Q.—You would sew them?

A.—Always.

Q.—Do you think that ink could be improved on?

A.—Not much. It is small type, and if you make it heavy it becomes blurred. If the type were larger you could. On the whole, mechanically, these four books are very good.

Q.—Take Ahu's First German book; that is estimated to cost seven and six-tenths per copy?

A.—Yes. Well, that is plenty low enough.

Q.—What would you say about that style of binding?

A.—I would rather have it in full cloth; it would wear better and would not cost any more.

Q.—High School Reader, The Hunter-Rose Company; estimated to cost nineteen and seven-tenths per copy?

A.—It is too high, and it is the worst looking sheet of paper of any book I have picked up; looks like newspaper; it is not good enough for a school Reader. Compare it with Heath's Fourth book. It is very poor paper and very poorly printed; bad margins. It could be made for several cents less. The margins are a matter for the eye; it does not injure the book, except that one might just as well have a proper margin on it.

Q.—On the whole you would say the High School Reader is a badly conceived book?

A.—Yes, in a general way it is a very poor book.

Q.—Principles and Practice of Oral Reading; it is said to cost eleven and one-half cents per copy?

A.—I think it would.

Q.—Pretty well printed book?

A.—Fairly well printed, but the paper is not good. The paper in almost all of these books is not as good as the paper they use in the United States; in fact, the Canadian mills here do not make as good paper as you can buy in the States.

Q.—Do you think the Ontario Government would be justified in allowing a publisher to use American paper?

A.—I certainly do. (Laughter.) Seriously, that is the fact. The mills here do not have the demand for that grade of paper that the mills there do. There are certain mills there that make nothing else but high grade school book papers, and made them from one year's end to the other; it is always the same; they make a special color, finish, and strength for school books. You have not any such mill here. The paper is all a little gray; it is not so good for the eyes as when it is a little creamy, a little bit on the cream shade.

Q.—You do not want any grayness in it?

A.—No; it all tells on a child's eyes, year after year.

Q.—Take the High School English Grammar; Canada Publishing Company; estimated to cost seventeen and six-tenths cents?

A.—Mechanically that book is a fair book—paper, press work, binding and typographically. I think the typography might be more prettily done, but it is well spaced and well set.

Q.—We have a great many complaints about that book, that the covers come off?

A.—Well, they should not. The experience I have had with about ten years at Heaths and Appletons; I used to make for them a million dollars worth I would actually spend for paper, printing and binding a year, and of the millions of books that I sent out all over the country, never sewing one of them on tape, even the heavy books, at that time—and this was five or six years ago—we did not use to get back, why, the smallest fraction of one per cent. of books badly bound or complaints from States or schools all over the country; practically no complaint at all.

23 т. в.

Q.—If they found a book badly bound they sent it back to the publisher?

A.—Sent it back right to the publisher. I have seen a whole edition of a thousand books sent back, but it was in a case of something radically wrong.

Q.—The wire cuts through the book?

A.—I have never seen wire binding of that kind.

Q.—"High School Geography?"

A.—It is very poorly illustrated for that kind of a book, very poorly.

Q.—Compare those two Ancient Histories?

A.—Myers' Ancient History, Greece and Rome; Botsford's Ancient History for Beginners. Botsford's is very much better than the other book; better paper, far better illustrations, better printing, better typographically and mechanically by far.

Q.—Here are two Arithmetics; High School Arithmetic, by Ballard, McKay and Thompson; and Arithmetic for High Schools, DeLury; both of these books are fair typographically?

A.—The DeLury is a little better typographically than the other one.

Q.—How about the paper?

A.—The paper of both is not good enough. The paper in the DeLury is better than in the Ballard.

Q.—It might be a little better still, you think?

A.—That is not a bad paper.

Q.—The DeLury is not a bad paper?

A.—It is not. It is better than many other books I have handled.

Q.—High School Algebra, by Robertson?

A.—That compares fairly well with most of the High School Algebras. It is an old book, but it is a fairly good book typographically.

Q.—The British Nation, by Professor Wrong?

A.—That ought to be on tapes.

Q.—The present edition is on tapes?

A.—This is a modern book, right up-to-date in illustrations and typography. You have got the latest thing you have here.

Q.—You think the type is large enough?

A.—Plenty. It is leaded, and very readable. That is as good a book as you can make to-day for a history.

Mr. MACDONALD: Who is the publisher?

A.—Morang.

Mr. COOPER: The First Latin Book and Reader, the Copp, Clark Company?

A.—This is a little bit old, but it is a very fair book typographically. There are better things on the market to-day.

.Q.—The Primary Latin Book and Reader, Methodist Book House; compare that with the First Latin Book of the Copp, Clark Company?

A.—Yes. They treat the subject very differently. There is very little to choose typographically between those two books.

Q.—Here is Hagarty's Latin Grammar, Morang; how does it compare with the other two Latin Grammars which you have already examined?

A.—This is a new book. It is very much better typographically, and the paper is better; the printing is better. That is a modern book. You have as good a thing as you can do here, and the others are both much poorer typographically and in paper and printing.

Q.—Could that book be bound on tapes?

A.—No. When you get up to that grade—

Q.—But still tapes would strengthen it?

A.—Yes; but it is no use throwing your money away.

23a T. B.

Q.—We do not agree with you, but we respect your opinion?

A.—I have had millions of books bound, and they do not use tapes because they do not find any trouble. We like to sell books frequently. The faster they wear out the more business.

Q.—High School Physical Science, Part I; the Copp, Clark Company?

A.—Typographically, it is fair, and the illustrations are fair; the paper is fair, and the printing.

Q.—High School Chemistry, paper and press work are—

Q.—Elements of Chemistry?

A.—It is a better book mechanically, typographically—paper and press work—than either of the Chemistries I have just looked at.

Mr. MACDONALD: You have now seen the books that we use in this Province in our Public and High Schools; do you not consider that there is or might be in all these authorized Public and High School publications such a uniform degree of similarity in the quality of paper and binding, style of printing and illustrations, as to enable you to suggest a reasonably accurate or standard estimate as to the cost per page for these publications on the basis of plates being supplied to the publishers?

A.—You mean, could I—

Q.—Set as a standard—not inflexibly, because we realize that is impossible—but could you set as a standard a cost per page which would be a guide to those who are responsible for the contract?

A.—Yes; but not a single standard.

Q.—We do not expect that. On a scale. I would be very much pleased if you could give it to us?

A.—The Grade of Readers, for example, so many pages, such a style, so much geographies, so much histories, so much?

Q.—That is the idea?

A.—Yes, that could be done.

Q.—Would you be in a position now to give us some idea, mentioning the books you have?

A.—No, I never made an estimate of that kind.

Q.—Do you not think that is the foundation after all, that there is a standard that could be worked out?

A.—Yes.

Q.—That idea occurred to me while listening to your criticism of these books, and from my experience in looking over these books it has occurred to me that there should be some standard price to regulate the Department?

A.—You can fix it, but your variation of grade there is very great. You have some very excellent books amongst those I have looked over, and some very poor ones.

Q.—Would you be able to suggest a standard price for the different books covering the various subjects; for instance, the Readers and the Arithmetic and the Geography and the History? My idea is to be able to secure if possible some reasonably accurate standard which would guide the Department in dealing with the publisher?

A.—I understand exactly what you are after, and it can be done. It is quite a piece of work to do that, and to do it carefully and accurately it requires pretty wide knowledge of books and conditions to-day. I am thinking of the United States. I could make such a scale as that. It would be quite a piece of work. I can see exactly.

Q.—In my humble opinion it would be of considerable assistance to the Department?

A.—It certainly would, if you had a basis from which to work up and down.

The CHAIRMAN: If the Department wanted such a scale you could make it for them?

A.—I could. I have never seen it done.

Mr. MACDONALD: It is an idea that occurred to me when watching your criticism of the books, and it seems to me a reasonable idea. With your vast experience in the handling of publications you ought to be in a position to say to somebody who comes to deal with you, asking for geographies, arithmetics, readers, that you have in your mind a standard price per page on the basis of the plates being supplied?

A.—Yes, I could make that.

Q.—Could you do that for us?

A.—Yes.

Q.—And give to this Commission a standard price—not inflexible, we admit—but some price that would guide the Department which has control of these books, in their dealings with the publishers?

A.—Yes.

Q.—Will you undertake to do that?

A.—I would hate dreadfully to do it, because it would be a tremendous job if it were done properly. You would have of course to draw an average. There are good books and bad books. For example, geographies: some books are profusely and well illustrated; the expense of printing such a geography would be considerably greater than a book poorly and sparsely illustrated. I would have to make an average for a geography; and then you, of course, having your starting price you say, "The average Geography should be so much: here is a poor book, that is below it; here is a good book, and the publisher thinks this is so much; this has undoubtedly cost more."

Q.—There is a middle standard of geography?

A.—Yes. If you had a fixed point you could work up or down according to your own judgment.

Q.—Do you think you would be able to give us that assistance, without incurring too much work on your own part, as a suggestion; not as a criticism, but as a suggestion to guide the Department?

A.—I would not answer that offhand: that would be a tremendous job to do that. I could sit here at this table and make it for you in twenty minutes or half an hour.

Q.—That is what I wanted; but if you are going to do it for the Department and set up a scale I would want the thing much more carefully worked out.

The CHAIRMAN: What do you think would be a fair advance to ask on the manufacturing prices on the part of the publisher?

A.—There is a fixed rule that governs all the publishers in the States.

Q.—I am speaking of where there is authorization?

A.—I am going on the business as a whole. Never less than a hundred per cent. on your actual cost of manufacture and your running expenses. These prices here are simply paper, printing and binding. To that should be added the cost of conducting your business, and doubled. Then figure that; figure your time and investment; as a business proposition it will not net you more than fifteen per cent., and it generally comes down to ten.

Q.—You are speaking of the United States conditions?

A.—Yes. And on High School Books, where the sale of the book is small, the cost of the plate is great, and the difference should be very much greater; two or three hundred per cent.; because if you only doubled on the cost of a small selling book which cost a large amount to get up, it would take you too long to get your investment back: the book would be old and out of date before you would get your investment.

Mr. Cooper: What do you think about spreading the books over, say, several publishers, or giving them to one publisher?

A.—I think that is pretty well answered. You can never give all the books to one publisher.

Q.—For instance, all the Readers, a set of Readers: would you give them to one?

A.—I think that; and it has in the main been followed when politics did not interfere, in the States; because the man has a homogeneous set, and from a pedagogic point of view it is perfectly uniform from the Primer up to the last Reader. If you undertake to mix the Primer of one publisher and the Higher books of another, they may not make a perfect set from a pedagogic point of view.

(Some discussion occurs.)

If you have got a first-class set of books you may make a publisher manufacture them properly; but I judge, without knowing the scope of this Commission at all, and not having known anything about it except having read a little bit in the papers, I suppose you are aiming to get at the bottom of the whole broad text book question and to set some standard.

Q.—You are raising more or less objection to all these books?

A.—Yes, all of them; they are a very heterogeneous mass. Some very bad, some very good, and some are fair; but for the same money on the average you could get better books.

Q.—Is there any general remark that you could make other than the one you have made?

A.—Comparing that entire lot of books with the books which are used in any American community of the same standing—they vary, you know, in the poor communities and the well to do ones— of the same standing, that lot of books is very considerably poorer from a mechanical standpoint than are used in the United States: for which there is absolutely no excuse.

Q.—Of course you cannot tell from looking at them whether it is the publisher's fault or the Department's fault?

A.—No. Take that set of Readers which he showed me at first: they may be as good as were asked for.

Q.—Those have been in use for twenty-one years?

A.—Considerable strides have been made in the teaching of children in twenty-one years.

Q.—Do you think that, estimating the English school population of Canada at three-quarters of a million, and dividing the work as we have done, that we can get good results?

A.—No, I do not; for the reason that there is not enough profit in the sale of books to the number of pupils mentioned to enable any firm to employ highly educated and experienced men to edit and market their books. In the United States the school population is so much larger and the sale so much greater. The way all the school book houses are run there, a teacher may become a superintendent, and his schools, are first class, and he arranges the work there and brings the standard for the teachers up high, and he writes a set of books or somebody goes after him, and the man who has the advanced ideas in education and is practical, that man will disappear in a year or so and reappear in one of the big publishing houses, and if he is adaptable he will make a success of it, he will bring you out some new books and new ideas which he has already put into effect before he tries to disseminate them through the publishing house. They cannot afford to do that here; they will not give a man like that a salary—four or five or six or seven thousand dollars a year. If he is successful he will get into a business from which he may make fifty thousand dollars besides his living, in ten years, and some have made half a million in ten years. Now, there is no such incentive here. A good man cannot afford to spend his time making school books for such a small sale as you have here. That is one argument for concentrating up here or else buying American books.

Q.—What do you mean by concentrating here?

A.—Not having the business so much split up.

Q.—What do you think of the plan of having the Government prepare the public school text books at its own expense?

A.—It has never worked out properly, because it is a business in itself.

Q.—I do not mean print, but prepare the manuscript and let them out to tender?

A.—They worked that in California.

Q.—Have they printed them there?

A.—No. A lot of manuscripts were prepared for the State, set up and printed. You get the effort there in California: they get the local effort. The publishing houses get the effort of the best men there are in the country.

Q.—I am sure, as far as I am concerned, I am delighted with what I have heard?

A.—I am very glad you are, although the conversation has been rather desultory.

Mr. COOPER: That is all right; we are taking it in a colloquial way.

The CHAIRMAN: We are very much obliged to you for coming.

The Commission adjourns.

December 19, 1906.

EVIDENCE OF MR. S. G. BEATTY.

Mr. GEORGE LYNCH-STAUNTON, Examiner:

Q.—What is your name?

A.—S. G. Beatty.

Q.—You are the President, I believe, of the Canada Publishing Company?

A.—Yes.

Q.—How long have you been connected with that Company?

A.—Twenty-two years.

Q.—Who are the other members of the Board?

A.—At the present time, the other members of the Board are W. J. Gage, H. L. Thompson, and George Warwick.

Q.—Is the stock at present held by the Directors, or is the Public generally interested in it?

A.—There are nine stock holders at the present time, namely:—W. J. Gage, George Warwick, H. L. Thompson, Warwick Brothers and Rutter, A. F. Rutter, Charles Warwick, A. W. Thomas and W. Copp.

Q.—Who incorporated the Company? Did you?

A.—No, I did not. The Company was organized six or seven years before I came in.

Q.—You have been how long, did you say?

A.—21 or 22 years.

Q.—It was organized then about 28 years ago?

A.—Yes.

Q.—By whom was it organized?

A.—By William Campbell.

Q.—Tell me how you became connected with it?

A.—I came in as Manager of the Company. The Company was in straightened circumstances at that time, and they came to me and asked me if I would take hold of the business and re-organize it, and, after investigating it, I came in and took hold of the Company on the understanding that I was to have a block of stock, under certain conditions, and the next year I purchased this stock. The balance of the stock was then held by Rice, Lewis & Son, A. B. Lee and John Lee.

Q.—Do you mean Rice, Lewis & Son of Toronto?

A.—Yes, their place of business is in King Street.

Q.—Then, when you got control of the Company, had it any school book business?

A.—Oh yes, the same business that the Company has carried on since; but there was a stationery business connected with it; but it was largely school book business.

Q.—Had they the "Ontario Readers" at that time?

A.—Yes, they had the new series,—the Royal Canadian Readers." ,

Q.—The Royal Canadian Readers were published by the Canada Publishing Company?

A.—Yes.

Q.—What became of them?

A.—Well, we have a large stock of them on hand still.

Q.—They are ostracized now?

A.—Yes, they are not used now. They were never used in the schools, they were never authorized. They unitized the series, but got up a new series before they were put in.

Q.—You had a series of authorized Readers at the time you joined the Company?

A.—No.

Q.—But your Company had a contract at the time the present series were recognized; you were one of the original contractors?

A.—Yes, we were the purchasers of a contract.

Q.—Did you pay anything to get your contract?

A.—Yes, we paid to Nelson & Son the same as the other three publishers, namely:— $7,500.

Q.—Did you pay anything besides that?

A.—No, nothing besides that amount.

Q.—Did you give a bonus to any one to get out of the way?

A.—No.

Q.—Your payment was the payment provided in the contract?

A.—Yes, we were recognized as having a vested right in having proposed these Readers,—that cost us over $30,000.

Q.—Did you spend $30,000 and Gage $30,000, and the other people $30,000.

A.—Oh yes, we paid over $30,000 and also spent a large amount in getting them introduced.

Mr. STAUNTON: Everybody seems to have spent $30,000,—I think about a million must have been spent in this business.

Q.—Your position then, Mr. Beatty, was this,—in the hope of change, re-organization and promises you got up a set of Readers and that set were not authorized?

A.—No.

Q.—Well, what publisher improved his chance?

A.—Mr. Gage got up a set of Readers.

Q.—Did he have a promise?

A.—No, there was a request made by the Department to the effect that a series of Readers would be authorized, and we went in on that understanding and prepared this series of Readers.

Q.—But you did not expect a trinity of Readers?

A.—No, we were in a position that we did not know what the other people were doing.

Q.—Well, how did you do it?

A.—We were promised authorization after the Readers came out, and on the strength of that we went on and had three or four of the Readers prepared.

Q.—Anyway that was the claim you had on the Government?

A.—That is the only claim we had on the Government.

Q.—You got a contract, however, from the Government for ten years?

A.—Yes.

Q.—Then, I believe, the three publishing houses had an understanding, that has been explained by previous witnesses, about how these books should be published after the ten years. At the end of that time, we have been told by several witnesses, that the publishing houses purchased the copyrights on all the selections which were in those Readers. Did you acquire any of those copyrights?

A.—No, we were interested, however, and paid a third of the cost of those copyrights.

Q.—Then the copyrights were acquired by Thompson and Gage alone?

A.—Yes.

Q.—So you have no copyrights directly or indirectly other than those we have been told of?

A.—Not of articles that are in those Readers.

Q.—So we have then, if Gage & Co., and the Copp, Clark Company have produced all in their possession, all the copyright selections in which you are interested?

A.—Yes.

Q.—There are no other copyright selections besides those that have been brought before this Commission?

A.—No, not connected with the Readers.

Q.—Did you take any active part in acquiring those copyrights, Mr. Beatty, or did you just pay?

A.—We, of course, discussed the matter.

Q.—Did you negotiate the purchase or agreement yourself?

A.—No, I did not.

Q.—Do you know of any copyrights excepting those of which we have been told by Gage and Company, and Copp, Clark?

A.—No.

Q.—There are some I understand that the English Publishers´ say were acquired by you and the three companies, that have not been accounted for.

A.—I am not aware of any.

Q.—Then in getting into the publishing business, under these contracts, you tendered for the publication of the Readers in the beginning and were all three accepted without any more difficulty, and it was just simply confined to the three houses?

A.—Oh, yes, the right to publish the books was given to the three houses simultaneously. All three houses were represented in the negotiations.

Mr. COOPER: Do you think that the Government intended at that time that there should be competition?

A.—No, not at that time.

Q.—The Government never intended that you should compete with the other firms?

A.—Of course, I cannot tell you what idea the Government might have had with reference to that. We were given the right to publish those books at a specified price and, of course, we might have reduced the price, and some of the other houses might have done so.

Q.—Did you expect competition when you entered into that contract?

A.—No, I did not expect it.

Q.—Then, if you did not expect competition you must have had some reason for it?

A.—I do not think the Government would imagine that there would be any competition. I do not think that any men capable of being placed in cabinet positions would cut one another's throat.

Q.—Did the Government expect you three firms would compete as to the quality of the binding, etc., and, in that way, you would keep up to the mark? Did you not expect that?

A.—We expected, of course, to bring these books up to the specifications and stipulations of the agreement, and expected to carry out our agreements.

Q.—Did you say you did not expect any competition?

A.—There may not have been competition as to quality, in fact, we had thought that we had better binding than the others ourselves.

Q.—You thought that?

A.—Yes.

REMARK: Then, if you have done any better, you should have produced some of it.

Q.—But, as a matter of fact, Mr. Beatty, there was no possibility of there being any considerable competition?

A.—No.

Mr. STAUNTON: Do you agree with Mr. Gage that open market is the best method to produce the best book?

A.—Yes, I agree with that.

Q.—I want to say to you now, that it was said in the House by Mr. Ross, that he expected that you publishers would pay him so much more money than would compensate him for all of the outlay in producing those plates. Did he ever realize that hope?

A.—We have never paid anything towards it.

Q.—How did he come to that conclusion? He said that the "plates" would wear out.

A.—There were three sets of "plates." One set was given to each publisher, and one set used to mould from so that when we wanted "plates" we always had them ready.

Q.—Any man, then, of ordinary ability should know that?

A.—He should.

Q.—How many thousands have you published in the last ten years? Have you published enough to wear out a set of plates?

A.—Oh, yes. Some plates would wear more than others, and sometimes we had to reproduce more, and they were reproduced from time to time as required.

Q.—And you have not knocked at the Minister's door for any more plates?

A.—No, we have not.

Q.—Then, he must have known that such a hope was illusionary, and that you would not have to go back for more plates.

A.—Yes, there was no occasion for it.

Mr. COOPER: At the time the negotiations were going forward, Mr. Beatty, to fix the price of those Readers for the first ten years, each one of the three firms represented that they had expended large sums in preparing the other three Readers,—about $35,000 each, I understood you to say, and that expenditure was an element in fixing the price of the books, was it not?

A.—I do not know that it was. The prices of the books were fixed the same as the Readers that had preceded them.

Q.—Did you personally negotiate?

A.—Yes.

Q.—You think then that was not taken into account as an element in fixing the price?

A.—No, I do not think it was.

Q.—It is said, Mr. Beatty, that there were offers at that time by other publishers to publish these Readers at a very much lower price. Mr. Ross said so at the time, and why then was the contract given to your people at a higher price?

A.—I did not know that any others had offers to make these books at a lower price; but we thought that we had a vested right to publish the books, and that would give us a right to come in and publish these books. I do not know of any other reason.

Q.—When you find it necessary to publish another edition of these Readers, how is that done among you publishers?

A.—We arrange between ourselves the number required by each,—we may take 10,000, Gage may take 15,000 and Copp, Clark may take 20,000 of the books.

Q.—Do you print all?

A.—Well, say the 45,000 would represent the edition to be printed. The plates are divided between us as follows:—say that there are nine forms in the books, we would have three, Copp, Clark three, and Gage three; and we would print the whole 45,000 of our three forms, and the others would do the same.

Q.—Each one would print his share?

A.—Yes, we would print our share of 45,000 and deliver to Gage his portion, and to Copp, Clark their portion, and we bind our own books.

Q.—You would only bind one-third of the books?

A.—Yes.

Q.—Would you get the other two-thirds from the others?

A.—Yes. One-third from Gage, and one-third from Copp, Clark.

Q.—Would you bind the whole book?

A.—Yes, our portion of the edition.

Q.—How about the sale of them?

A.—We sold as many as we got, and at a profit of ten per cent. on the number we sold.

Q.—That is the selling profit?

A.—Yes.

Q.—After adjusting matters between the three of you?

A.—Yes.

Q.—Do you have a net profit, or gross profit?

A.—We do not take it in that way. If we had $10,000 worth of books we would make ten per cent. on the deal.

Mr. STAUNTON: Do you consider that the book you produce is up to that contract?

A.—Yes. We have always thought so.

Q.—Up to the letter of it anyway?

A.—Yes. We have always realized that the contract might be cancelled at any time, and the whole edition thrown on our hands.

Q.—Did those books pass Government at any time?

A.—Yes, at all times.

Mr. COOPER: The Government inspection did not keep you awake at nights, did it?

A.—No.

Mr. STAUNTON: These drawing books and scribbling books, is there any authorization for them?

A.—There is authorization for the drawing books, but not for the scribbling books.

Q.—No person else could sell them but yourselves.

A.—There may be other drawing books and writing books.

Q.—Is there any reason on earth why these books should be authorized?

A.—Well, there are certain courses of drawing in the schools, and those courses are prescribed, and the books should come up to the standard. The quality of the drawings, and the grade of the books, etc.

Q.—Do you think that a teacher could not buy another sort of book equally as good as these books. Is there any necessity to buy these books?

A.—I presume a teacher of drawing teaches from a black board, one class at a time, and if there were individual drawing books he would have to give individual teaching.

Q.—Does that apply to writing books?

A.—Yes, for the same reason. If a teacher wishes to give a style of letter he explains the forms of this letter, etc., and that particular copy to the whole class at the same time. If he had a number of copies in writing by the pupils he would have to explain individually.

Q.—Have these books been authorized all the time?

A.—No, only since drawing has become a compulsory subject in the schools. The difficulty would be that you would have inferior teachers of writing throughout the country, and we have had a number of third class teachers throughout the Province, and these teachers would be allowed to select the books. Would it not be better to allow a committee of three experts to select these books instead of those who have no knowledge of the subject.

Q.—Usually there is no necessity of those books being authorized?

A.—The only necessity would be to have the best books authorized—there would be bad books and good books, and a teacher might use inferior books.

Q.—Would authorization increase the cost to the pupils?

A.—No.

Q.—You do not think that a monopoly would have that effect?

A.—No. I think our copy books are sold at as low a cost as they can be had.

Mr. STAUNTON: They have a method in Toronto where they buy drawing sheets instead of books. The teachers gives out one sheet at a time, and the pupil is not compelled to carry his book about with him, and when he is done drawing on that sheet it is put away. Is not that a good scheme?

A.—I have not considered that. I would have to look into that.

Q.—Will you explain the process of making drawing books and copy books?

A.—The plates are made by the engravers from copies that are produced by the author of the book. The originals are made by a photographic process and sometimes by wood engravings. I can hardly give you the process.

Q.—Is there any person who does know?

A.—Yes, Mr. Builder.

Mr. STAUNTON: Well, I will ask Mr. Builder, then.

Q.—Can you give me the cost?

A.—I cannot give the cost without looking it up.

Mr. STAUNTON: You said you have some other copyrights, what are they?

A.—We have a music course.

Q.—What is it?

A.—"The Canadian Music Course." Some of the articles that appear in it are English copyrights.

Q.—Did you secure them?

A.—Yes.

Q.—You say you own all the Canadian end of that book and have control of the English end of it also?

A.—Some of them.

Q.—Have you the particulars of these copyrights with you?

A.—No, I have not.

Q.—Have you any objection to giving them to me?

A.—No, I will let you have them.

Q.—Will you furnish a list?

A.—We have really no copyrights, except the rights we hold in connection with those songs, etc.

Q.—Have you no copyrights on articles that you have in the other books?

A.—No, except in that "Music Course." That Music Course is only approved for use in the schools. It is not authorized.

Mr. CROTHERS: The copyrights you have in connection with this "Music Course," are they only the rights to use them?

A.—Yes.

Q.—And if you cease to use them, they would be available for someone else?

A.—Yes.

Q.—Mr. Beatty, we have been told that Nelson & Sons were one of the original contractors and that Copp, Clark bought out Nelson & Sons and got the contract for ten years, and, that under the second contract for ten years five per cent. was paid to the Nelsons. I have never been able to ascertain what the consideration was. Can you explain why?

A.—No. I cannot.

Mr. STAUNTON: What do you think of wire binding, Mr. Beatty?

A.—I do not know much about binding really; we leave it with the foreman of the establishment.

Q.—But we mean as a school binding. Why did you get the Government to let you wire stitch those books?

A.—It was a quicker process than stitching the books by hand with thread stitching. Besides, it would be very difficult to get a sufficient number of girls to do the stitching.

Q.—What arguments did you use with the Government?

A.—I do not remember it. It was twenty years ago.

Q.—What would you use now?

A.—I do not know whether we would ask the question now.

Q.—Anyway, the object you had was that you could do it more cheaply?

A.—Our object was to get as good an arrangement as we could possibly get.

Mr. COOPER: Was your attention never called to the fact that this wire stitching was not as good as the other?

A.—Not to my knowledge. There might have been a communication from the Government, but I do not remember it. We have nad no representations of any kind made to us. Of course we did not seek the information as you have done.

Mr. COOPER: It strikes me that a publisher interested in his business would take the trouble to find out?

A.—We have been producing those books in that way for upwards of twenty years, and we never knew they were unsatisfactory.

Q.—You want us to believe that you did not care whether these books were satisfactory to the teachers or not, so long as you lived up to your contract?

A.—No, I do not want you to think that at all. Why, as a business proposition, should we borrow trouble at all?

Q.—Do you think it should be the business of a publisher to know whether his books are satisfactory or not?

A.—If he hears of anything that is wrong with the books, he should correct it and make his books as satisfactory as possible. We all attempt that.

Q.—You admit that you did not do it in the case of the Readers?

A.—We did not make any particular search in these matters.

Q.—Did you know that wire stitching had been abandoned in the United States ten year ago?

A.—No, I did not know that it had.

Q.—Well, can you produce any book publisher, or reputable firm using that stitching?

A.—I cannot say that I could.

Q.—Will you undertake to do it?

A.—No, I do not think I would care to.

Q.—Well, here is a binding that has been abandoned for ten years in the United States, and you say that you did not know it, and seem to think it is all right. I want to know why you think it is all right?

A.—We published the books under contract with the Government, and under that contract we had the right to bind with wire stitching, and that was the process we carried through at that time.

Q.—And you would have carried that on for the next fifty years on the same lines?

A.—I suppose so, unless the Government asked to have it changed.

Q.—What kind of inspection was made by the Government of these books?

A.—Well, the Inspector came in from time to time, but I do not know what kind of inspection he made. He had the privilege of going through the house and examining them if he saw fit.

Mr. COOPER: I suppose he was just careful to see that there were no improvements in them? (Laughter.)

Mr. COOPER: Are you aware that your readers are not bound in the way that the Readers in England and the American Readers are bound?

A.—Yes.

Q.—And you never tried to make any improvement in them?

A.—Of course there are better methods.

Q.—Do you think the method in which you have bound these Readers is good enough for the purpose for which they are designed?

A.—No, I do not think it is.

Q.—You do not think the binding is good enough?

A.—No, I do not.

Q.—How would you suggest improving it?

A.—I would suggest thread stitching.

Q.—Would you suggest anything else?

A.—No, I do not think that I could. I am not an expert in binding.

Q.—Have you a binder of your own?

A.—Yes. He would be able to give you an opinion on that line if you wish to call him.

Q.—Do you do your own stitching?

A.—Yes.

Q.—Have you any thread stitchers in your bindery?

A.—I really do not know; but I presume we have.

Mr. CROTHERS: You have had a great deal of experience, Mr. Beatty, not only as a publisher, but as a teacher, have you given any thought or attention to the system of Free Text Books?

A.—No, I cannot say that I have given the matter any thought, it has never interested me.

Mr. STAUNTON: Well, I think that will do, Mr. Beatty, we shall not ask you anything further.

EVIDENCE OF MR. CHAS. BUILDER.

By Mr. STAUNTON:

Q.—What is you name?

A.—Charles Builder.

Q.—And your position?

A.—Secretary Canada Publishing Company.

Q.—For how long?

A.—I have been with them ever since they were organized.

Q.—Can you give us an accurate list of the copyrighted articles controlled by that company?

A.—No, I do not know anything about the copyrights of the Readers at all. I know copyrights outside of the Readers.

Q.—Is Mr. Beatty correct in stating, that so far as the Readers are concerned, you have no copyrights?

A.—Yes.

Q.—So that we can eliminate copyright in so far as the Readers are concerned?

A.—Yes.

Q.—Then, you have copyrighted articles in the other books?

A.—Yes, we hold all of the copyrights for the other books. The whole of the copyrights belong to us.

Q.—What authorized books have you on which you have the Canadian copyright?

A.—As I understand the agreement between the Department and ourselves, that copyright is vested in the Department, and when the agreement is terminated that copyright comes back to us,—that is, as I understand the agreements.

Q.—That is not what I asked you. The question I am asking you is,—Can you give me a list of those copyrights?

A.—I can give you a list of our books.

Q.—What does your list contain?

A.—The names of the books, the authors, the amounts paid and the royalty.

Q.—Will you let us have it?

(Witness hands following list to Examiner):—

Books published by The Canada Publishing Company, Limited, and authorized for use in the Province of Ontario.

	Authors.	Amounts. paid.	Royalty.
		$	
Ontario Readers, Part I		2,500 00	
" " II.	Prepared by the Ontario		
" " 2nd Book..........	Gov		
" " 3rd Book...........			
" " 4th Book...........		3,000 00	
P. S. Phonic Primer, Pt. I	Prepared under the supervision of D. J. Goggin, M.A , D.C.L.........		
P. S. Phonic Primer, Pt. II	Mrs. M. R. Crawford....	....	6c. per dozen.
Public School Geography.............	Chas. Clarkson, B.A.....	140 00	
	Geo. R. Powell.........	500 00	
Public School Arithmetic.............	Wm. Scott, B.A........	....	5%.
	C. A. Barnes, B.A.......	....	5%.
Public School Grammar	H. I. Strang, B.A.......	....	10%.
" " Drawing, 1 to 5........	A. C. Casselman.........	600 00	
High School Geography	Geo. A. Chase, B.A	....	10%.
" " Grammar	Jno. Seath, M.A, LL.D..	250 00	10% paid to Jan. 1st, 1906, then commuted at $800.
		800 00	
High School Drawing, 1 to 3.........	A. C. Casselman	450 00	
Arithmetic for High Schools.........	A. T. DeLury, B.A......	100 00	10%
Principles and Practices of Oral Reading................................	Miss A. E. Marty, M.A..	....	10%
Elements of Algebra............... ..	J. A. McLellan, M.A, LL.D.	1,000 00	10%
Composition and Practical English ...	Wm. Willliams, B.A....	....	10%

Toronto, December, 1906.

Q.—Are all those books registered in Canada?

A.—Yes, every one.

Q.—And you own the copyright for the entire book in each case?

A.—Yes.

Q.—Subject to whatever claim the Department has under the contract with you?

A.—Yes.

Q.—Have you any other books on which you have control of the English copyright?

A.—No authorized books.

Q.—Then that list that you now put in includes all of the authorized publications for schools issued by your Company?

A.—That is right.

Q.—Mr. Cooper asked Mr. Beatty to give him the amount or cost of the manufacture of copybooks and drawing books. Can you give us that information?

A.—You mean in the preparation of the books?

Mr. STAUNTON: Yes.

A.—Well, I really cannot tell you off-hand. I would have to consult my books.

Q.—Now, Mr. Builder, take those books—the Public School Drawing Course—tell me what those books cost?

A.—Somewhere about two cents—but that does not include the first cost.

Q.—But I want you to tell me what that book costs you for "plates"?

A.—I cannot tell you that from memory.

Q.—Can you tell me what you figured out that these books cost you in order that you might put the selling price on that book? You know when you are tendering for that book what the market price is, and you do fix it by estimate.

A.—We do not make any estimate on it.

Q.—Do you mean to tell me, that you fix the price without estimating what it cost you?

A.—We do not fix the price, the Department fixes it.

Q.—Now, Mr. Builder you are an old experienced publisher, are you not, and you can surely tell me what the cost is?

A.—I cannot tell you off-hand.

Q.—Are you a practical publisher?

A.—Yes.

Q.—Can you tell me what the binding cost?

A.—I think the binding cost about $3 a thousand.

Q.—Well, now, will you tell me what the plates cost?

A.—I cannot tell you from memory.

Q.—Do you mean to tell me you do not know what the plates cost?

A.—Yes; I would not like to guess on it. I can find out for you.

Q.—I do not think you are entirely candid with me, Mr. Builder?

A.—Yes, I am, Mr. Staunton. I have a great many figures in my head, and I really cannot tell you off-hand.

Q.—Well, Mr. Builder, I will have to ask you to look it up and tell me this afternoon. Will you prepare a statement and give it to me, under oath, setting forth the first cost to you of these different publications?

A.—Yes. I will prepare it in tabulated form for you this afternoon.

Mr. STAUNTON: Very well, then, Mr. Builder, I will call you again.

MR. BEATTY RECALLED BY MR. STAUNTON.

Q.—Mr. Beatty, you have gone over carefully the cost of the various books prepared and produced here by Mr. Grantham; do you agree with him that these costs are correct?

A.—Yes, I agree with Mr. Grantham that these costs are correct.

As Mr. Beatty was leaving the stand, Mr. Wallace Nesbitt, K.C., Counsel for the Publishers, made the following request:—

Mr. Chairman and gentlemen of the Text Book Commission, I have a little statement here from Mr. W. J. Gage that I would like to read to you in behalf of the three publishers of school books.

Mr. Cooper: I strongly object to such a proceeding. I think we should have Mr. Gage here and let us hear what he has to say, for if Mr. Gage or any of the publishers have anything further to say, it should be said publicly before the Commission under oath and not by any statement or letter.

EVIDENCE SUBMITTED BY MR. NESBITT IN BEHALF OF THE THREE PUBLISHERS.

Mr. Nesbitt: Well, Mr. Chairman, I am not making any unreasonable request. A great many statements have been made here with reference to the alleged combine which have gone broadcast throughout the country, and I contend that I have a perfect right to come here and submit argument in behalf of my clients, and this statement merely contains what I would say in argument, and surely there should be no objection to it.

On Mr. Cooper still objecting to Mr. Nesbitt being permitted to read the statement, the Commissioners and their Counsel conferred together, after which the Chairman, Mr. T. W. Crothers, gave their decision as follows—

Mr. Crothers: Mr. Nesbitt, it has been the practice since this Commission began its sittings, that everybody should come here and give their evidence on oath, in order that our proceedings might be public and open, and I understand that these publishers were to be here this morning to be examined and cross-examined. Now I know there are precedents, but when I consented to act on this Commission, I determined not to follow precedent, and I would rather that these gentlemen should come here and make their statement under oath; but, however, as Mr. Staunton does not object, and still reserving the right to call either or all of these publishers, I will allow this statement to be put in.

Mr. Nesbitt: Thank you, Mr. Chairman, I will read the statement, which is as follows:—

To the Honourable, the Commissioners of the School Text Book Commission, Normal School Buildings, Toronto:

Dear Sirs,—When I last had the honour of appearing before the Commission, I was asked what suggestion I would make to secure the best results in text books.

I replied that there should be open competition among both authors and publishers.

I now repeat that if we are to secure the best results, both as to literary value and mechanical make-up, we must have competition among those who prepare the books, and those who publish.

The British and the United States system compel a text book to stand or fall on its merits and not by a Departmental edict; hence their excellence. In this competition authors and publishers have the strongest incentive to

24 T. B.

produce the best possible books in matter, pedagogical arrangement, paper, type, binding, etc.

The system adopted in Ontario has not encouraged authors and publishers to compete in the production of superior text books, with the result that many of the texts in use in our schools are inferior both educationally and mechanically.

Every school book publisher of experience has realized to his loss that notwithstanding the most vigilant care that he can exercise in the selection of authors and the sifting of material, that at least one-half of his books fail to meet successfully the supreme test—that of the school-room.

In many cases the practice of the Department in Ontario has been to select the author, not always with previous experience, to prepare a book, and a publisher to print it. To assert that this would produce satisfactory results is to ignore all past experience of publishers and to assume that more than *human wisdom is* bestowed upon the head of the Department.

Can it surprise anyone that the method of thus securing School Text Books has resulted in the authorization of so many inferior ones?

The work of the Text Book Commission has already directed attention to certain salient features:—

1. *Alleged existence of a Combine among certain publishers and inferior books.*

2. *A Hold-up of the Government through the buying of Copyrights.*

3. *School Book Ring.*

1. As to the alleged existence of a Combine, in order that the Commission may understand the status of the Reader publishers or so-called "Combine," may I be permitted to outline in a few words the story of the publication of the present series of Ontario Readers :—

About twenty-four years ago a Circular was issued by the Honourable Adam Crooks, the then Minister of Education, inviting publishers to submit Readers to the Department from which a series might be selected for use in the Public Schools.

Three firms, Campbell & Son (representing the Nelsons of Edinburgh), the Canada Publishing Co., and W. J. Gage & Co., submitted three new series of Reading Books.

Nelson's Readers and Gage & Co.'s Readers were authorized. The Canada Publishing Co. claimed that they were promised authorization.

After we had issued a very large edition of our Readers and had secured their adoption and use in the majority of the Schools of the Province, there was a sudden change of policy by the Government with the advent of the Honourable Mr. Ross as Minister of Education.

An order was issued by the Government de-authorizing the two newly authorized series—our own and the Nelson Books. It was further announced that the Department of Education would prepare a new series of their own. About a year later the present Ontario Readers were issued.

Our own firm had not only spent $30,000.00 in preparing a series, but we had published for use in the Schools a very large number of the books, amounting to about $30,000.00, which, by the changed policy of the Government, were left on our hands, and years afterwards many thousand dollars worth of the Nelson books were sold for a trifle at a Customs House sale for unclaimed goods.

The Government, realizing that the three publishers had a strong claim for damages and that we had suffered enormous loss, recognized this claim by giving the Nelson & Son firm, the Canada Publishing Co., and our own firm the exclusive right to publish the new series for a period of ten years, upon payment to the Government of $7,500.00 for plates of new books.

24a T. B'

At the end of ten years this contract was extended for a further period of ten years upon the three publishing firms paying a further sum of $9,-000.00—the latter also agreeing to improve the binding; reduce the prices of some of the books from fifteen to twenty-five per cent., as well as to increase the discounts to the trade.

The Reader publishers entered into a contract with the Government to publish the books according to a certain standard fixed by the Department as to quality of paper, presswork and binding; the Government also fixing the retail prices and discounts to the trade.

This brief outline shows how the present three Reader publishers through enormous outlay became the exclusive publishers of the present Ontario Readers.

Two matters will no doubt be perfectly clear to the Commissioners : —

(a) That whatever may be the requirements of the School Book trade to-day, the reasonableness of the action of those supplying books under the contract is demonstrated by the uncontradicted testimony of Mr. Brainard, the New York expert, summoned by the Commission to instruct it in the matter, who says, "I don't see anything in these books that does not come up to the specification," and further, "much poorer books might pass the specification."

This shows that the publishers need not have given as good books as they did under the Contract with the Government.

(b) It is equally clear that the arrangement made between the publishers did not come within any rule as to combines as the Government fixed the price which it thought reasonable for the production of the books in question beyond which the publishers could not go.

2. *A Hold-up of the Government through the buying of certain copyrights.*

It has been suggested that the Reader publishers secured certain copyrights with a view of strengthening their claim upon the Government for renewal of the Reader Contract.

In answer to this, speaking for my own firm, I may say unhesitatingly that while this was but one of the objects in view, it was the chief one. We felt that at the expiration of our agreement any vested rights we had in the School Readers were likely to be sacrificed by the Government. We had not forgotten our previous experience in this particular.

A large number of authorized text books, over forty in number, published by us when Mr. Ross took office, and a number of them greatly prized by the teaching profession, had, within a period of seven years, been taken off the authorized list, until we were left without a single book, outside of the one-third interest in the Readers on the Public School List, and only two on the High School List. Further, in some cases, new books which we had arranged for with the approval of the Department and had paid the author, on account, or the author desired us to publish, were transferred to other firms by order of the Education Department without our knowledge or consent.

Under these circumstances it seemed very proper, and indeed absolutely essential that we should try and retain any interests held in the Ontario Readers, practically the only books of any value left to our firm.

To protect these interests we purchased from the English publishers copyright selections in the Ontario Readers which they had control of.

After we had been stripped of all other school books, it is fair to assume that if we had not secured ourselves in this perfectly legitimate way in the solitary series left in which we held only one-third interest, we would have been driven out of the school book publishing so far as this great Province is concerned.

3. *School Book Ring.*

It is claimed there is a School Book Ring. We assume by this is meant a combination to control the publishing of school text books for the Province.

When the Hon. Mr. Ross took office, the Official Records show that we had forty books on the authorized list. When he left office we had but two exclusively published by our firm.

We had in addition to these a third interest in the Ontario Readers already referred to and a part interest in a series of Copy Books which were published jointly with another firm.

The official List of the Education Department when the Hon. Mr. Ross left office shows the number of books published by each Toronto firm as follows : —

Morang 13

Canada Publishing Co. ... 13   This is exclusive of Copy Books, which are published jointly with another firm, and does not include Ontario Readers.

Hunter, Rose   6

Briggs............................   6

Copp, Clark 25   Exclusive of Readers.

Gage & Co....................   2   This is exclusive of Copy Books, which are published jointly with another firm, and does not include Ontario Readers.

If, therefore, there was a Ring, the above shows that surely our firm was on the outside of it.

In conclusion, reverting to the publication of the Ontario Readers, I would say they were fairly good books when issued twenty years ago, but not as good as they should have been—not books that a publisher would be proud of. They were prepared under the supervision of the Government, and by men who had no experience in work of this kind, and were, therefore, mechanically at least, not up to the highest standard.

An examination, not only of the Reading Books, but of many other Text Books used in Ontario, when compared with those in other Provinces, will force the conclusion that this Province is very much behind other Provinces, both in the point of educational value and the mechanical make-up of the book.

In the other Provinces of Canada open competition has prevailed, the educational authorities have not attempted to make or supervise the making of the books, but have selected from the best that the publishers of the world could submit.

The improvement in our School Books should keep pace with the development in all the appliances in our schools. Matters now move so rapidly that each decade marks distinct progress.

If the Commission sees its way to report favorably on the suggestions made in this communication for a new series of betteryText Books in open competition among authors and publishers, we believe that the Government will not only secure in its books the best efforts of educational specialists in the various subjects, but also all the advantages that must follow open competition among publishers.

I have the honour to be, Sirs,

Yours faithfully,

(Signed)   W. J. GAGE.

Commission adjourned for luncheon.

On reassembling after luncheon, Mr. Charles Builder was recalled for further examination.

Mr. STAUNTON: Now, Mr. Builder, I see you have the statement, will you give it to me?

A.—Yes, sir, here it is (handing in statement to Examiner).

Q.—Does this give the exact prices?

A.—Yes, that is the original cost, including royalties, but not the cost of running the business.

Mr. Staunton reads statement:—

Canada Publishing Company, Limited.

—	Original Cost.	Cost of Production.	Estimated Sales Yearly
	$		
Ontario Readers, Part I	....	4.10	4,500
" " " II	....	5.75	2,000
" " 2nd Book	....	7.75	5,000
" " 3rd Book	....	10.50	6,000
" " 4th Book	....	12.00	3,500
Public School Geography	6,636 00	18.55	40,000
" " Arithmetic	499 00	10.60	30,000
" " Grammar	444 00	10.15	18,000
" " Drawing, 1-5	884 00	1.55	60,000
" " Phonic Primer	14,990 00	5.15	4,500
" " Phonic Primer II	2,016 00	8.25	1,500
High School Geography	3,890 00	28.00	6,000
" " Grammar	1,092 00	22.00	6,000
" " Drawing, 1-3	1,597 00	2.00	6,000
Delury's Arithmetic for High Schools	1,101 00	17.75	4,500
Principles and Practice of Oral Reading	765 00	16.30	5,000
Elements of Algebra (McLellan)	2,161 00	22.10	400
Williams' English Composition	308 00	16.00	250
Medial Slant Copy Books (Nos. 1 to 6)	590 00	1.35	75,000
No. 7	....	3.00	5,000

Q.—Is there no profit in these costs to you?

A.—None whatever.

Q.—Is that an exact statement?

A.—Yes, I think it is pretty accurate; it is as near as I can come to it.

Mr. COOPER: What is the retail price of drawing books?

A.—Five cents each.

Q.—They cost you two cents a piece?

A.—Between one and two cents.

Q.—How do you explain the small sale of "Elements of Algebra?"

A.—Well, that book has had a small sale for many years.

Q.—What is the retail price of the copy books?

A.—Seven cents each, and No. 7 sells at ten cents each.

Q.—You ought to be able to sell a book for less than seven cents when it costs you so little to produce it?

A.—Well, some of them we lose money on.

Q.—What discount do you get off?

A.—Twenty-five per cent., ten and five on the copy books.

Q.—How long have the Public School Drawing Books been in use, so far as your firm is concerned?

A.—I think since 1900.

Q.—How long have the High School Drawing Books been in use?

A.—Since 1894.

Q.—These "medium slant" drawing books, how long have they been in use?

A.—I think since 1902.

Mr. CROTHERS: These copy books, Mr. Builder, are there any others authorized for Public Schools?

A.—Not that I know of.

Q.—Have you a contract with the Government for these books?

A.—There is an agreement with the Government.

Q.—How long is that agreement for?

A.—I cannot say.

Q.—Now take that No. 7 book; how do you arrive at the price of that book?

A.—They cost us 36 cents a dozen.

Q.—Yes, but how do you get at it?

A.—It is the cost of press work, cover, paper, etc.

Q.—How many of these books do you put through at once?

A.—About 6,000.

Q.—Well then, you do not mean to tell me they would cost so much?

A.—I do.

Q.—That is about half as much as you estimate the cost for the Second Reader?

A.—Yes, but you pay a great deal more than you pay for the school books.

Q.—How much do you pay per pound for the paper?

A.—About six or seven cents a pound.

Q.—How many would a pound of paper produce?

A.—I cannot say.

Q.—What is the weight of a ream of that paper?

A.—I think somewhere about 45 pounds. It is 20 x 31. Gage & Co. and ourselves really publish these books between us. We print the same quantities together, and if we run out of books and want more of the same number we get them from the other firms.

Mr. CROTHERS: You did not tell me yet how you got at that price?

A.—I take six thousand and figure on them; so much paper at so much per pound, 24 reams of paper.

Q.—Yes, but how much money?

A.—About $75.

A.—What do you estimate for the binding?

A.—I do not remember; I did not go into detail.

Q.—Who figured up that cost?

A.—I did.

Q.—What purpose had you in figuring it up?

A.—I figured it up for the firm's information.

Mr. STAUNTON: This, then, is the whole manufacturer's cost plus his profit?

Q.—How did Mr. Thompson get into your company?

A.—He got in through the Copp, Clark Co.

Q.—What did he come in for?

A.—Mr. Beatty could tell you better than I can.

Q.—Well, tell me what you know anyway.

A.—All I can tell you is that he came into the company.

Q.—Well, tell me what you know.

A.—I do not know why he came in.

Q.—You are on your oath now, Mr. Builder?

A.—I know that, and that is the reason why I want to be careful. I have no idea why they came in. Mr. Beatty may have approached them for all I know.

Mr. COOPER: When did Mr. Thompson come in?

A.—In 1889 he came in first.

Q.—When did Mr. Warwick come in?

A.—In 1901.

Q.—When did Mr. Gage come in?

A.—In 1889.

Q.—They all came in together except Warwick?

A.—Yes.

Mr. STAUNTON: How did Warwick get in?

A.—It was through Mr. Beatty that he came in.

Q.—You do not know the reason?

A.—No, no more than they wanted to get an interest in the business.

Q.—Were you short of capital?

A.—No, they did not put in any of their capital. Mr. Warwick bought a part of Mr. Beatty's interest. Mr. Beatty had control of the stock of the company before that from the original stockholders.

Q.—Is this the "clearing house" for the other companies?

A.—No, not by any means. The Gage Company and the other companies print a great deal more than we do.

Q.—Was it the result of any arrangements about the publishing of the school books?

A.—No, not that I know anything about at all.

Q.—How about the Rice Lewis stock?

A.—Mr. Beatty got control of it.

Q.—Did he buy the stock?

A.—Yes.

Q.—So he practically owned the whole Company at one time?

A.—Yes.

Q.—And he let the other firms into it? '

A.—Yes.

Q.—Had it any bearing on your getting the contract for the Readers?

A.—No.

Mr. COOPER: Was not the agreement for the sale of the stock made about the same time as the contract came up?

A.—No.

Mr. STAUNTON: Warwick tried to get in to publish these Readers, did he not?

A.—I know nothing about that.

Q.—Well, instead of pressing his claim, did he not get stock in this Company?

A.—Not that I know of.

Mr. COOPER: I would like to ask you, Mr. Builder, if the Canada Publishing Company is the only Company which has its headquarters in your office?

A.—Yes.

Thank you, Mr. Builder, that will do.

EVIDENCE OF MR. ARTHUR F. RUTTER.

G. LYNCH-STAUNTON, Examiner:—

Q.—Your name in full, please?

A.—Arthur F. Rutter.

Q.—Mr. Rutter, you are a member of the firm of Warwick Bros. & Rutter?

A.—Yes,—Warwick Bros. & Rutter, Limited.

Q.—How long have you been a member of the Company?

A.—Of the present firm, about two and a half years, but of the original firm, since 1886.

Q.—What is your position in the Company?

A.—Vice-President.

Q.—Have you anything to do with the management of the business?

A.—Yes.

Q.—What?

A.—The manufacturing more particularly, and, of course, in the absence of the President, the duties of the Company.

Q.—Did your Company ever make application since its incorporation, to publish the Ontario Readers?

A.—No, not to my recollection.

Q.—I believe there is an application on file?

A.—I do not remember it if there was.

Q.—Tell us what you know about the 1884 deal?

A.—We were the publishers of the old series of "National Readers," and when the question of new Readers came up, I was not a member of the firm. The late William Warwick made application for the right to publish, and did make an offer at a greatly reduced price.

Q.—Do you know what that price was?

A.—I have just a recollection of it,—it was something like one-third less—that was the old series remember, not the present one.

Q.—The old Readers that you mention, did they differ in size and cost from these?

A.—Oh yes, they were a cheaper set of books than these.

Q.—The old Fourth Reader (National) was a cheaper book, was it not?

A.—Yes.

Q.—And you offered to publish it for a much less price?

A.—Yes.

Q.—You offered to publish it for 32 cents?

A.—Yes.

Q.—What is the price of that Fourth Reader you have in your hand?

A.—Forty cents.

Q.—It was a cheaper book than that?

A.—Yes.

Q.—And more expensive?

A.—I do not think so.

Q.—Without the plates, would it be a cheaper book?

A.—Yes. This was quite an improvement on the old series. That offer was made to preserve our right to publish it.

Q.—Would you have published these books at that time for one-third less?

A.—No sir, I do not think we could afford it.

Q.—Now, twenty years ago, could not that book have been published at one-third less?

A.—I am not sure of that.

Q.—Was binding more expensive then?

A.—No.

Q.—What was more expensive?

A.—The paper particularly.

Q.—Now, twenty years ago would that book have cost you, if I had handed you the plates, any more to publish than it would to-day?

A.—Yes. I think it would.

Q.—In what particular?

A.—Well, the reduction in cost is largely due to the machinery and material that it is made from. The stamping is done on a printing press instead of by an "embosser," as twenty years ago.

Q.—Well, can you publish it at one-third less to-day?

A.—No sir. That is from a general knowledge. I do not know what these books cost.

Q.—Then you cannot say whether it would cost more or less twenty years ago?

A.—No. Not having gone into it, I cannot say.

Q.—You do not know whether your firm ever did make a bid to publish these books at a cheaper rate?

A.—No. I do not think they did.

Q.—Did you ever apply to the Government to allow you to print the "Ontario Readers"?

A.—I think there was an application.

(The Examiner here showed the witness a copy of a speech made by the Hon. G. W. Ross in 1885, wherein he stated that Warwick would print them for one-third less.)

Q.—What have you to say to that?

A.—I think there was a mistake made there, as my recollection is, that it referred to the "National Readers"—not the present series of books.

(Mr. Staunton here read a letter from the report of the Minister of Education for 1886, offering to produce the Readers for a certain price, and asked witness how it contrasted with the prices that are on the books now.)

Mr. RUTTER: If Mr. William Warwick ever made such an offer it was a sincere one, as that gentleman never made an offer over his own signature that he was not prepared to carry out.

Q.—Mr. Ross states distinctly, that Warwick & Son did offer to produce those books at one-third less than they were costing the country, and you say that if he did it was a sincere offer?

A.—Yes, absolutely.

Q.—It would not have been a haphazard offer?

A.—No. He would have very carefully considered it before he made the offer.

Q.—You are confident it was sincere if it was made?

A.—Yes, absolutely. And I hope I am right in my recollection of it being made on the "Old Readers."

Q.—Well, you give us a reference as to what it was if you do find it?

A.—Yes I will. I think that all of those school book negotiations started by the late William Warwick were carried on by Mr. G. F. Warwick and our old late bookkeeper, Mr. Sylvester, and more particularly during the time that was going on I was confined very closely to the manufacturing department, and, while I had a knowledge of what was going on at the time, it is only a recollection now. I cannot give you the data. During this time you refer to, I know that there was sent out to every bookseller in the country a form asking them to sign and send in to the Government along the line of what Mr. William Warwick's offer was—which would show sincerity in the matter. There were several meetings took place—one gentleman coming here from St. Johns.

Q.—Were many of the circulars returned?

A.—To the best of my recollection about 700 were returned, and they ranged pretty well all over.

Q.—Who prepared this document that was sent out by Warwick & Sons?

A.—The firm of that date.

Q.—Now, then, the average profit on the sale of these Readers at the price fixed by the Department, and at the proposed aforesaid discounts, would not be less than one hundred per cent. on the cost of manufacture. Do you doubt the truth of that statement?

A.—I do not.

Q.—You say that it was notorious that there was one hundred per cent. profit there?

A.—Well, I would not like to say that it was notorious.

Q.—Do you know whether the publishers ever put in an answer to that statement?

A.—No, I do not.

Q.—You never heard of a public meeting being put in?

A.—Oh yes, there was a controversy in the papers forwards and back for upwards of a year.

Q.—Do you know how you got into that Company?

A.—Yes, by buying stock.

Q.—You do not say so! Did you get any of the stock?

A.—Oh yes, it is held by George Warwick, Charles Warwick and myself. It does not belong to the present firm.

Q.—What did they let you in for?

A.—Cash.

Q.—Well, what was back of it?

A.—I do not know any other reason than that.

Q.—Well, what would you think?

A.—There is absolutely no mystery about it. Mr. Beatty offered us stock. He made the offer to me personally because my partner was in Europe, and I cabled to him.

Q.—There was nothing behind it at all?

A.—Absolutely nothing. I may say, however, that Mr. Beatty having an affection of the throat, thought that he would have to live away from the country altogether, and he then offered to sell us his interest in the Canada Publishing Company and it was the subject of consideration talking at Mr. Beatty's house and at our office. He said that he feared he would never be able to live here again, and he wanted to dispose of it. The only thing that stood in the way was the cash—the purchase price. We had been extending the business to the limits of our capital and we did not feel as if we would like to ask the large amount of cash that he wanted for the business, and at that time Copp, Clark came in buying a part that he wanted to sell. Mr. Beatty said that he thought, as he had made an offer to us before, that he was bound to give us the first chance. I cabled Mr. George Warwick, who was then in Germany, and received the ordinary reply—"to do what I liked"—Mr. Beatty received a cheque for his stock, and we became stock-holders since that time. We do not carry school books or print them nor do we sell them. We fill an order for a retail dealer when he asks for them. Our travellers do not carry them because there is no profit to us in that. I want to give you the fullest and most complete answer as to how we got into the Company.

Q.—It all arose out of Mr. Beatty's ill health?

A.—Yes. He did not understand that it was necessary to sacrifice it.

Q.—I should judge Mr. Beatty intending to go away wished to dispose of his stock to people who would be experienced in the business, and who would continue it in the best interests of all concerned.

A.—Yes, that would be about it.

Mr. COOPER: Then we are to understand Mr. Rutter, that there was neither inducement or force used to get you into the Company?

A.—No Mr. Cooper, there was no inducement offered to me to come into the firm other than in a business way. I was not forced into it at all.

That will do, Mr. Rutter, we are obliged to you for appearing before the Commission.

The Commissioners and their Counsel conferred together and decided that they had obtained sufficient evidence upon which to base their report, and consequently, no more witnesses would be called.

APPENDIX.

COPIES OF LETTERS READ BEFORE THE COMMISSION AND REFERRED TO IN THE EVIDENCE.

TORONTO, April 20th, 1901.

HON. R. HARCOURT,
　　Minister of Education, Toronto.

DEAR SIR,—We desire permission to publish the Ontario Reader and are willing to conform to the regulation of the Department governing the same.

Are we correct in supposing that for the right to publish until July 1st, 1906, that it will cost us as follows:—

$1,250.00　for a set of plates.
　500.00　to be divided between the present publishers.
1,500.00　for rights to the Treasurer of Ontario, making a total of

---

$3,250.00

We understand that the Ontario Readers are the only series that will be authorized for use in the Public Schools until July 1st, 1906, and consequently are willing to incur the expense for that time.

It is our intention to have the books ready for sale in time to supply all orders by September 1st, 1901, and would, therefore, ask you to kindly favour us with your answer soon as convenient.

　　　　　We are, yours respectfully,
　　　　　　　WARWICK BROS. & RUTTER.

Memo for the Deputy Minister.

Messrs. Warwick Bros. and Rutter in applying for permission to print the Ontario Readers ask the price for the unexpired term of the present agreement with the three present publishers. The amounts they name for royalty to publishers and for the right are just one-half of the amounts in agreement for the ten years' term and are evidently correct. See their question about exclusive use of these books for the next five years and that the use of Phonic books does not clash with the same.

Another point to be guarded is in regard to the High School Reader for which the notes plates have not been transferred. I do not know the arrangement made regarding these between the Ex-Minister and the Rose Publishing Company and the other three Reader publishers.

For agreement please see Sessional Paper No. 73, 1896.

April 23, '01·   —————   H. M. WILKINSON.

Confidential.

TORONTO, July 3rd, 1901.

GENTLEMEN,—In reply to your four applications, asking for permission to print certain books, I wish to say that the Department will grant you the privilege as a matter of course, subject, however, to the conditions which must be carefully considered.

I would suggest that you would, at an early date, talk over some of these conditions with Mr. Millar, of my Department.

Faithfully yours,

MESSRS. WARWICK BROS. & RUTTER,
    Toronto, Ont.

—————

TORONTO, July 6th, 1901.

HON. R. HARCOURT,
    Minister of Education,
        Toronto.

DEAR SIR,—In reply to your favor of the 3rd inst., would say, that we will call on Mr. Millar, on Tuesday, respecting our application for publication of:

"High School Bookkeeping."
"Public School Bookkeeping."
"Public School History of England and Canada."
"High School History of England and Canada."

Regarding our application for right to publish Readers, may we ask that you instruct Mr. Millar to discuss at the same time, and oblige.

Yours truly,

WARWICK BROS. & RUTTER.

—————

TORONTO, July 11th, 1901.

GENTLEMEN,—I am directed by the Minister of Education to acknowledge the receipt of your letter of 6th instant, and to state that he is desirous of meeting your request regarding the publication of the other school books mentioned. After discussing the question further with the Minister, since our conversation of a few days ago, I am pleased to forward you the enclosed copy of agreement respecting the Readers, an extra copy having been on file in this Department. I am sending you this copy, in order that you may be in a position to get any legal advice you may deem necessary before taking further action. As soon as you feel free to enter upon an agreement for the publication of the Readers, a form will be prepared. As intimated, to you, some prior steps will have to be taken regarding some of the other books; but in order to save time, it may be better to have the question of the publication of the Readers alone settled at first.

Your obedient servant,

Deputy Minister.

MESSRS. WARWICK BROS. & RUTTER,
    Toronto.

Toronto, July 17th, 1901.

John Millar, Esq.,
    Deputy Minister of Education,
       Toronto.

Dear Sir,—We have your favor of July 11th, No. 5831. 04, 4667, respecting our application to publish the Ontario Readers and certain other books.

We have placed the printed Reader agreement in the hands of our solicitor, in order to ascertain if the right to publish, granted by your Department, will enable us to do so, without bringing us into legal conflict with the holders of copyright.

Should our solicitor advise us that we can proceed, we will avail ourselves of your permission to publish at once.

Respecting the other books for which we applied, kindly let us know as early as possible what steps it is necessary to take to be placed in a position to publish.

Thanking you for your promptness, we are,
                Respectfully yours,
                    Warwick Bros. & Rutter.

Toronto, July 19th, 1901.

Dear Sirs,—I am directed by the Minister of Education to state, in reply to your letter of 17th instant, that a copy of the indenture between The Copp, Clark Co. and this Department, respecting the Public School History of England and Canada, is herewith enclosed. I presume no difficulty will stand in the way of your purpose being reached regarding this agreement.

The agreements in the case of each of the other books mentioned will be examined, and information given you in due time. I am inclined to think that probably it will be necessary to wait until Mr. Thompson of the company mentioned returns.

                Your obedient servant,
                    Deputy Minister.

Messrs. Warwick Bros. & Rutter,
    Toronto.

Toronto, July 29th, 1901.

John Millar, Esq.,
    Deputy Minister of Education,
       Toronto.

Re Ontario Readers.

Dear Sir,—In reply to your favor of July 11th, No. 5831. 04, 4667, would say that, following your advice we have secured legal advice, as to the position we would occupy in regard to holders of copyrighted articles, and quote opinion received as follows:

I am of the opinion that it would be unsafe for your firm to proceed under the permission granted by the Educational Department with the publication and sale of the Readers referred to in said permission unless under the protection of an indemnity from the Educational Department.

I have arrived at this opinion because of the fact that there is apparently no data from which any conclusion can be arrived at which would enable you to determine that each and every selection contained in said Reader can be printed without the invasion of copyright. I think it reasonable that the Department should grant you this indemnity, because no doubt they have within themselves the full, complete and absolute knowledge that each selection is being rightfully printed, and that where the selection has been copyrighted that they have an assignment of the copyright, or the rightful authority to print and publish. In case there are one or more selections in the Reader the subject of copyright, which the Department has not the right to print and publish, your firm might be prevented by suit and injunction from proceeding at all, until after the time limit intended to be granted to you had expired.'

We have decided to follow the above advice, and request that we be given protection that will enable us on complying with regulations as to payment of money, and production of books up to standard, to proceed with their issue free from other expense.

Should you favor us with an immediate settlement of this question on a basis that is safe for us to proceed, we will at once have the matter closed, and go on with the work which we are anxious to do.

Trusting to be favored with an early reply,

We are,

Yours respectfully,

WARWICK BROS. & RUTTER.

TORONTO, July 31st, 1901.

GENTLEMEN,—I am directed by the Minister of Education to acknowledge the receipt of your letter of the 29th instant, and to state that your request for indemnity would appear to be one that has never been asked by any other publisher, and, of course, will require very careful consideration. In the meantime kindly furnish this Department with a list of the selections respecting which your publication of the same would be alleged as an infringement of copyright.

Your obedient servant,

Deputy Minister.

MESSRS. WARWICK BROS. & RUTTER,
    68 Front Street West,
        Toronto.

TORONTO, August 6th, 1901.

JOHN MILLAR, ESQ.,
    Deputy Minister of Education,
        Toronto.

DEAR SIR,—We have your favor of July 31st, No. 6897, G.M. 4, 4607, and in reply would say:

We desire indemnity against action that may be taken by original owners of any copyrighted articles contained in the Ontario Readers.

It seems plain from the agreement, that the present publishers have acquired rights from original owners, and have transferred same to Education Department, and before we can publish it is necessary for us to pay them a specified sum as reimbursement for their outlay. This we are quite willing to do, but we do not want to find ourselves liable to loss by any action from the parties who sold rights to present publishers, and it is against them we ask protection.

As to specifying articles, would say that we could hardly do this, and be sure we had them all. What we do ask is that we be placed in the same position as present publishers, with a free hand to publish the books after making the necessary payments, and producing the books to the satisfaction of the Department.

Your truly,
WARWICK BROS. & RUTTER.

TORONTO, October 30th, 1901.

DEAR SIRS,—I am directed by the Minister of Education to state, in reply to your letter of August 6th, that after giving full consideration to the questions mentioned in your communication, he wishes to inform you that he cannot undertake to promise you indemnity against any action that might be taken by the original owners of any copyrighted articles contained in the Ontario Readers. He is prepared to offer full facility to your firm, should it be contemplated to take advantage of the provisions of the agreement with the present publishers, in order that you may have, so far as this Department is concerned, freedom in publishing the Ontario Readers.

Your obedient servant,
Deputy Minister.

MESSRS. WARWICK BROS. & RUTTER,
    68 Front Street,
        Toronto.

List showing number of books published by various publishers from 1894 to 1905 inclusive.

PUBLIC SCHOOL.

Book.	Year.	Copp, Clark Co.	Gage & Co.	Can. Pub. Co.	Morang & Co.	Meth. BookCo.	Hunter Rose Co.	Total.
First Reader—	1894	30,000	50,000	28,000	....	....	....	95,000
Part I.	1895	45,000	45,000	20,000	....	....	....	110,000
	1896	15,000	49,930	....	....	....	....	64,930
	1897	32,677	....	25,000	....	....	....	57,677
	1898	32,031	38,000	....	....	....	....	70,031
	1899	23,946	40,000	20,000	....	....	....	86,946
	1900	23,623	35,000	25,000	....	....	....	83,623
	1901	29,905	20,000	3,000	....	....	....	54,905
	1902	31,342	30,430	15,000	....	....	....	76,772
	1903	25,389	20,887	10,000	....	....	....	56,276
	1904	19,194	21,000	13,000	....	....	....	53,194
	1905	16,606	11,097	3,000	....	....	....	30,703
								840,057
First Reader—	1894	15,000	20,000	15,000	....	....	....	50,000
Part II.	1895	45,000	45,000	20,000	....	....	....	110,000
	1896	5,000	35,018	....	....	....	....	40,018
	1897	15,421	....	15,000	....	....	....	30,421
	1898	18,469	40,000	....	....	....	....	58,469
	1899	21,936	30,000	20,000	....	....	....	71,936
	1900	16,713	10,000	15,000	....	....	....	41,713
	1901	22,303	20,000	5,000	....	....	....	47,503
	1902	24,305	22,173	10,000	....	....	....	56,478
	1903	22,496	16,044	10,000	....	....	....	48,540
	1904	11,947	15,000	10,000	....	....	....	36,947
	1905	12,359	9,927	....	....	....	....	22,286
								614,311
P.S. Phonic Primer	1902	....	....	10,000	....	....	....	10,000
Part I.	1903	....	....	15,000	....	....	....	15,000
	1904	....	10,000	10,000	....	....	....	20,000
	1905	....	9,945	10,000	....	....	....	19,945
								84,945
P.S. Phonic Primer	1903	....	....	20,000	....	....	....	20,000
Part II.	1904	....	10,000	10,000	....	....	....	20,000
								40,000
Mod. PhonicPrimer	1903	....	....	....	40,000	....	....	40,000
Part I.	1904	....	....	....	61,000	....	....	61,000
	1905	....	....	....	54,000	....	....	54,000
								155,000
Mod. PhonicPrimer	1904	....	....	....	41,000	....	....	41,000
Part II.	1905	....	....	....	47,000	....	....	47,000
								88,000
Second Reader....	1894	5,000	10,000	10,000	....	....	....	25,000
	1895	25,000	30,000	15,000	....	....	....	70,000
	1896	....	14,996	....	....	....	....	14,996
	1897	14,008	....	15,000	....	....	....	29,008
	1898	13,625	15,000	....	....	....	....	28,625

PUBLIC SCHOOL.—Continued.

Book.	Year.	Copp, Clark Co.	Gage & Co.	Can. Pub. Co.	Morang & Co.	Meth. Book Co.	Hunter, Rose Co.	Total.
Second Reader—	1899	21,901	30,000	10,000	....	....	....	81,901
Continued	1900	5,640	5,000	10,000	....	....	....	20,640
	1901	21,967	20,000	5,000	....	....	....	46,967
	1902	14,944	15,682	5,000	....	....	....	35,626
	1903	15,458	14,642	10,000	....	....	....	40,100
	1904	14,585	27,000	10,000	....	....	....	51,585
	1905	17,939	12,978	4,000	....	....	....	34,917
								459,365
Third Reader.....	1894	9,000	9,000	7,000	....	....	....	25,000
	1895	25,000	25,000	15,000	....	....	....	65,000
	1896	....	9,948	....	....	....	....	9,948
	1897	8,330	....	10,000	....	....	....	18,330
	1898	9,523	10,000	....	....	....	....	19,523
	1899	10,280	10,000	....	....	....	....	20,280
	1900	8,573	8,000	5,000	....	....	....	21,573
	1901	12,931	15,000	5,000	....	....	....	32,931
	1902	9,952	11,231	5,000	....	....	....	26,183
	1903	14,909	8,385	5,000	....	....	....	28,294
	1904	13,898	19,000	4,000	....	....	....	36,898
	1905	10,940	10,032	2,000	....	....	....	22,972
								326,932
Fourth Reader	1894	5,500	4,000	3,500	....	....	....	13,000
	1895	13,000	13,000	7,000	....	....	....	33,000
	1896	....	6,016	....	....	....	....	6,016
	1897	7,584	....	5,000	....	....	....	12,584
	1898	6,519	10,000	....	....	....	....	16,519
	1899	5,769	7,000	5,000	....	....	....	17,769
	1900	7,022	4,000	5,000	....	....	....	16,022
	1901	5,985	9,000	3,000	....	....	....	17,985
	1902	5,935	7,389	3,000	....	....	....	16,324
	1903	8,430	8,207	3,000	....	....	....	19,637
	1904	8,454	18,000	6,000	....	....	....	26,454
	1905	8,972	6,521	3,000	....	....	....	18,593
								213,903
Public School	1894	....	....	21,000	....	....	....	21,000
Arithmetic	1895	....	....	25,000	....	....	....	25,000
	1896	....	....	50,000	....	....	....	50,000
	1897	....	....	12,000	....	....	....	12,000
	1898	....	....	30,000	....	....	....	30,000
	1899	....	....	30,000	....	....	....	30,000
	1900	....	....	58,000	....	....	....	58,000
	1901	....	....	63,500	....	....	....	63,500
	1902	....	....	50,000	....	....	....	50,000
	1903	....	....	50,000	....	....	....	50,000
	1904	....	....	40,000	....	....	....	40,000
	1905	....	....	25,000	....	....	....	25,000
								454,500
High School	1900	....	....	....	....	....	4,000	4,000
Reader	1901	....	....	....	....	....	1,500	1,500
	1902	....	....	....	....	....	1,800	1,800
	1903	....	....	....	....	....	3,000	3,000
	1904	....	....	....	....	....	3,000	3,000
	1905	....	....	....	....	....	1,850	1,850
								15,150

25 T. B.

PUBLIC SCHOOL.—Continued.

Book	Year.	Copp, Clark Co.	Gage & Co.	Can. Pub. Co.	Morang & Co.	Meth. Book Co.	Hunter, Rose Co:	Total.
Principles of Oral Reading }	1904	....	....	8,500	....	....	....	8,500
Smith & McMurchy's Elem. Arith. }	1895	2,000	....	....	....	....	....	2,000
P. S. Algebra & Euclid	1894	....	....	....	....	....	2,000	2,000
	1895	....	....	....	....	....	2,000	2,000
	1896	....	....	....	....	....	2,700	2,700
	1897	....	....	....	....	....	3.200	3,200
	1898	....	....	....	....	....	....	....
	1899	....	....	....	....	....	2,000	2,000
	1900	....	....	....	....	....	....	....
	1901	....	....	...	....	....	1,000	1,000
	1902	....	....	....	....	....	1,500	1,500
	1903	....	....	....	....	....	1,500	1,500
	1904	....	....	... .	....	....	1,500	1,500
	1905	....	....	....	....	....	1,500	1,500
								18,900
Pub. A. Geog.	1894	....	....	19,000	....	....	....	19,000
	1895	....	....	10,000	....r.	....	....	10,000
	1896	....	....	....	....	....	....	....
	1897	....	....	29,000	....	....	....	29,000
	1898	....	....	24,000	....	....	....	24,000
	1899	....	....	15,000	....	....	....	15,000
	1900	....	....	13,000	...	....	....	13,000
	1901	....	....	35,000	....	....	....	35,000
	1902	....	....	40,000	....	....	....	40,000
	1903	....	....	25,000	....	....	....	25,000
	1904	....	....	25,000	....	....	....	25,000
	1905	....	....	25,000	....	....	....	25,000
								260,000
Morang's Modern Geog.	1903	....	....	....	3,123	....	....	3,123
	1904	....	....	....	2,000	....	....	2,000
	1905	....	....	..v.....	1,800	....	....	1,800
								6,923
Our Home, etc....	1903	....	....	....	24,698	....	....	24,698
	1904	....	....	....	1,650	....	....	1,650
	1905	....	....	....	3,200	....	....	3,200
								29,548
Rose's P. S. Geog.	1905	....	....	10,000	....	....	....	10,000
P. S. Grammar....	1894	....	....	20,000	....	....	....	20,000
	1895	....	....	20,000	....	....	....	20,000
	1896	....	....	20,000	....	....	....	20,000
	1897	....	....	20,000	....	....	....	20,000
	1898	....	... .	20,000	....	....	....	20,000
	1899	....	....	50,000	....	....	....	50,000
	1900	....	....	12,000	....	....	....	12,000
	1901	....	....	40,000	....	....	....	40,000
	1902	....	....	30,000	....	....	....	30,000
	1903	....	....	25,000	....	....	....	25,000
	1904	....	....	35,000	....	....	....	35,000
	1905	....	....	25,000	....	....	....	25,000
								317,000

PUBLIC SCHOOL.—Continued.

Book.	Year.	Copp Clark Co.	Gage & Co.	Can. Pub. Co.	Morang & Co.	Meth. Book Co.	Hunter Rose Co.	Total.
Morang's Modern Eng. Grammar.	1903	....	....	....	1,690	....	....	1,690
	1904	....	....	....	2,000	....	....	2,000
	1905	....	....	....	6,300	....	....	6,300
								9,990
History of Dom. of Canada.	1897	10,000	....	....	....	10,000	....	20,000
	1898	....	....	....	....	5,000	....	5,000
	1899	....	....	....	....	5,000	....	5,000
	1900	....	....	....	....	5,000	....	5,000
	1901	2,495	....	....	....	....	....	2,495
	1902	2,480	....	....	....	2,500	....	4,980
	1903	....	....	....	....	4,000	....	4,000
	1904	....	....	....	....	3,000	....	' 3,000
	1905	....	....	....	....	....	....	....
								49,491
Duncan's Story of Canadian People.	1905	....	....	....	5,000	....	....	5,000
Weaver's Canadian Histoy.	1905	2,500	....	....	....	....	....	2,500
P. S. Drawing Course.	1894	....	....	263,100	....	....	....	263,100
	1895	....	....	237,500	....	....	....	237,500
	1896	....	....	232,750	....	....	....	232,750
	1897	....	....	287,700	....	....	....	287,700
	1898	....	....	178,500	....	....	....	178,500
	1899	....	....	115,000	....	....	....	115,000
	1900	....	....	65,000	....	....	....	65,000
	1901	....	....	105,000	....	....	....	105,000
	1902	....	....	120,000	....	....	....	120,000
	1903	....	....	90,000	....	....	....	90,000
	1904	....	....	105,000	....	....	....	105,000
	1905	....	....	17,000	....	....	....	17,000
								1,816,650
Physiology and Temperance.	1894	....	....	....	....	65,000	....	65,000
	1895	....	....	....	....	18,400	....	18,400
	1896	....	....	....	....	14,040	....	14,040
	1897	....	....	....	....	15,000	....	15,000
	1898	....	....	....	....	15,000	....	15,000
	1899	....	....	....	....	8,500	....	8,500
	1900	....	....	....	....	10,000	....	10,000
	1901	....	....	....	....	....	....	....
	1902	....	....	....	....	10,000	....	10,000
	1903	....	....	....	....	15,000	....	15,000
	1904	....	....	....	....	7,000	....	7,000
	1905	....	....	....	....	8,000	....	8,000
								185,940
P. S. Copy Book ..	1894	....	....	....	....	....	117,000	117,000
	1895	....	....	....	....	....	92,000	92,000
	1896	....	....	181,600	....	....	84,000	264,600
	1897	....	....	40,000	....	....	....	40,000
	1898	....	....	72,000	....	....	....	72,000

PUBLIC SCHOOL.—Continued.

Book.	Year.	Copp. Clark Co.	Gage & Co.	Can. Pub. Co.	Morang & Co.	Meth. BookCo.	Hunter. Rose Co	Total.
P. S. Copy Book *Continued*	1899	....						
	1900	....	145,000	145,000	....	....	....	290,000
	1901	....	30,000	30,000	....	....	....	60,000
	1902 {	....	11,170	51,000	....	....	....	62,170
		....	80,824	32,500	....	....	....	113,324
	1903 {	....	90,737	22,500	....	....	....	113,237
		....	25,881	108,000	....	....	....	133,881
	1904	....	70,000	90,000	....	....	....	160,004
	1905	....	100,414	104,000	....	...:....	....	204,414
								1,724,426
Practical Speller...	1899	....	45,000	....	....	....	....	45,000
	1900	....	65,000	....	....	....	....	65,000
	1901	....	15,000	....	....	....	....	15,000
	1902	....	25,652	....	....	....	....	25,652
	1903	....	32,880	....	....	....	....	32,880
	1904	....	30,000	....	....	....	....	30,000
	1905	....	39,764	....	....	....	....	39,764
								253,296
P. S. Book-keeping	1903	2,462	....	....	....	....	....	2,462
	1904	....						....
	1905	1,500	....	....	....	....	....	1,500
								3,962
P. S. Agriculture..	1898	....	....	....	5,000	....	....	5,000
	1899	....	....	....	15,000	....	....	15,000
	1900	....	....	....	5,000	....	....	5,000
	1901	....	....	....	5,000	....	....	5,000
	1902	....	....	....	5,000	....	....	5,000
	1903							....
	1904	....	....	....	....	....	....	....
	1905	....	....	....	1,000	....	....	1,000
								36,000
P. S. Domestic	1898	993	....	....	....	....	....	993
French - English Readers— First Reader, Part I	1894	4,000	....	....	....	....	....	4,000
	1895	4,000	....	....	....	....	....	4,000
	1896	3,000	....	....	....	....	....	3,000
	1897	3,002	....	....	....	....	....	3,002
	1898	5,075	....	....	....	....	...—..	5,075
	1899	5,058	....	....	....	....	....	5,058
	1900	....	....	....	....	....	....	....
	1901	5,012	....	....	....	....	....	5,012
	1902	....	......:.	....	....	....	....	....
	1903	3,004	....	....	....	....	....	3,004
	1904	4,929	....	....	....	....	....	4,929
								37,080
French - English Readers	1894	4,000	....	....	....	....	....	4,000
	1895	....						....
	1896	4,000	....	....	....	....	....	4,000
	1897	4,968	....	....	....	....	....	4,968
	1898	2,525	....	....	....	....	....	2,525
	1899	2,875	....	....	....	....	....	2,875
	1900	....	....	....	....	....	....	....

PUBLIC SCHOOL.—Continued.

Book.	Year.	Copp, Clark Co.	Gage & Co.	Can. Pub. Co.	Morang & Co.	Meth. Book Co.	Hunter, Rose Co.	Total.
French - English Readers— *Continued*	1901	3,014	....	....	....	....	....	3,014
	1902	....	....	....	....	....	....	....
	1903	·3,005	....	....	....	....	....	3,005
	1904	5,012	....	....	....	....	....	5,012
	1905	....	....	....	....	....	....	....
								29,399
Second Reader	1896	1,000	....	....	....	....	....	1,000
	1897	1,350	....	....	....	....	....	1,350
	1898	1,669	....	....	....	....	....	1,669
	1899	2,018	....	....	....	....	....	2,018
	1900	1,012	....	....	....	....	....	1,012
	1901	1,008	....	....	....	....	....	1,008
	1902	....						
	1903	992						992
	1904	2,985						2,985
								12,034
French - English Readers— Third Reader	1896	1,000	....	....	....	....	....	1,000
	1897	....	....	....	....	....	....	....
	1898	1,023	....	....	....	....	....	1,023
	1899	1,016	....	....	....	....	....	1,016
	1900	1,008	....	....	....	....	....	1,008
	1901	....	....	....	....	....	....	....
	1902	....						
	1903	2,951	....	....	....	....	....	2,951
	1904	1,011	....	....	....	....	....	1,011
								8,009

STEIGER & Co., N.Y.

Book.	Year.	Number.	Total.
German-English Readers— Ahn's First Book	1894	150	150
	1895	150	150
	1896	150	150
			450
Ahn's Second Book	1894	100	100
	1895	100	100
	1896	100	100
			300
Ahn's Third Book	1894	75	75
	1895	75	75
	1896	75	75
			225
Ahn's Fourth Book	1894	50	50
	1895	50	50
	1896	50	50
			150
Ahn's First German Reader......	1894	150	150
	1895	150	150
	1896	150	150
			450

STATEMENT

Showing cash expenditure on construction

OF

The Temiskaming and Northern Ontario Railway

as of December 31st

1906

Presented to the Legislative Assembly

By Command

W. J. Hanna,
Provincial Secretary.

Provincial Secretary's Office,
Toronto, March 13th, 1907.

TORONTO, Ont., March, 12th, 1906.

HON. J. O. REAUME, M.D., M.P.P.,
Minister of Public Works, Ontario, Toronto:

SIR,—I have the honor, by direction, to submit to you for presentation to the Legislature, Statement showing cash expenditure on Construction as of December 31st, 1906.

I have the honor to be, Sir,
Your obedient servant,

A. J. McGEE,
Secretary-Treasurer.

DETAIL STATEMENT OF EXPENDITURE FOR YEAR 1906.

RECEIPTS AND EXPENDITURES ON CONSTRUCTION FOR YEAR ENDING DECEMBER 31ST, 1906.

Cash in hand December 31st, 1905		$ 32,605 71
Advanced by Provincial Treasurer	$1,639,619 87	
Discount, stamps and underwriting, London Loan, paid by Provincial Treasurer	232,666 66	
		1,872,286 53
Received from Miscellaneous Accounts rendered, and from operation......		395,729 75
		$2,300,621 99
By expenditure as per detail statement	$2,067,802 52	
Discount, stamps and underwriting, London Loan	232,666 66	
		$2,300,469 18
Cash in hand December 31st, 1906		152 81
		$2,300,621 99

JANUARY.

Voucher No.	Name.	Amount.
2818	C. B. Smith, Ma.E., salary Consult. Eng.....................................	$208 33
2819	H. W. Pearson, salary as Sec.-Treas.............................	150 00
2820	A. J. McGee, salary as Gen. Acct................................	125 00
2821	H. F. MacDonald, salary as Asst. to Acct................................	65 00
2822	John A. McDonald, salary as Clerk to Sec..............................	50 00
2823	Leland Pinkney, salary as Stenographer...............................	27 10
2824	W. G. Chase, salary as Elec. Engineer..............................	150 00
2825	S. R. A. Clement, salary as Draughtsman..............................	60 00
2826	Geo. Adair, timber, re repairing culvert..............................	75 00
2827	Margaret Dreany, lot 43 Park St., N. Bay.............................	1,550 00
2828	John Stockdale, lot 44 Park St., N Bay..............................	300 00
2829	Dept. Lands and Mines, half lot 11 con. 5 Evanturel....................	80 00
2830	C. B. Smith, expenses for January, 1906...............................	48 80
2831	J. L. Englehart, expenses for January, 1906.........................	48 50
2832	The Art Metropole, Ltd., engineer supplies, etc.............................	52 81
2833	H. W. Angus, plans and drawings, etc................................	105 00
2834	J. Blanchet, beef for boarding car................................	7 43
2835	J. R. Benoit, services re prospecting Cobalt	50
2836	Barber & Ellis, Ltd., envelopes for passes....................................	1 85
2837	Geo. Booth & Sons, lettering doors, etc..............................	19 75
2838	Pegg Bros., oil cloth car "Abbitibi"................................	10 40
2839	Brown Bros., Ltd., office supplies............................	3 55
2840	Bell Telephone Co. of Canada, service and exchange to August 1st...	48 85
2841	Can. Pac. Ry., steel rails and angle bars....................................	13,144 28
2842	John Clarke, cord wood............................	39 38
2483	Cobalt Bldg. & Supply Co., lumber for road approach	85
2844	A. W. Connor, check, design and draw, etc..........................	15 00
2845	Dodge Mfg. Co., 1 wood pulley............................	7 00
2846	A. Devine, "Traders Bank," transporting men and supplies	201 00
2847	R. J. Devine, hauling, etc............................	5 00
2848	D. Donovan, cartage	31 25
2849	Doheny & Grant, groc., prov., etc................................	320 63
2850	S. Eplett, hardware supplies............................	55
2851	Ferguson & McFadden, repairing tools, etc..............................	1 25
2852	K. Farah, board bills..................................	15 75
2853	Jas. Foster, Eng. supplies............................	35 00
2854	G. N. Goodall, board bills, etc............................	7 80
2855	Graham. Ferguson & Co., repairs, drills, etc..........................	7 10
2856	Gillies Bros., Ltd., board bills	141 25
2857	Demase Ganthier, repairing tools............................	9 90
2858	Gurney Foundry, Ltd., heat. equip., stats..............................	47 10
2859	Grand & Toy, Ltd., office supplies............................	7 05
2860	Herron's Livery, team hire............................	45 00
2861	Hawkesbury Lmr. Co., sharpening tools....................................	5 95

Voucher No.	Name.	Amount
	JANUARY.	
2862	F. H. Hopkins Co., Barrett jacks	102 00
2863	Mamilton Steel & Iron Co., tie plates	909 06
2864	Lester Joy, straw New Liskeard tank	3 75
2865	J. C. Johnston, testing cement	12 00
2866	H. I. Kerr, vegetables, etc	19 70
2867	D. O'Connor, board bill P. Laing	2 50
2868	London Bolt & Hinge Works, track bolts	1,509 51
2869	McDonald & Hay, galvanized iron pipe and parts	14 50
2870	A. McIntosh, beef supplies	52 11
2871	Jas. Morrison Brass Co., boiler tester and locomotive torches	130 04
2872	J. Marguerett, braces for signs	1 25
2873	Montreal Steel Works, Ltd., coil springs, etc	4 20
2874	Miller & Mahoney, lumber tel. line	7 35
2875	North Bay Lgt., Heat & Power Co., elec. lgt. and gas account	4 13
2876	Geo. Nicholson, expenses and wages of men	9 90
2877	National Life Assurance Co. of Canada, rent gen'l office, Jany., '06	125 00
2878	Nipissing Foundry & Machine Co., machine parts, etc	403 42
2879	Oliver Garvin, repairs and supplies	5 75
2880	A. G. Pittaway, photos of ties, Wallace suit	59 00
2881	D. Pike Co., Ltd., tents	44 20
2882	R. M. Ryan, team hire, etc	385 00
2883	Ry. & Marine World, subscription to December, 1906	8 75
2884	Robinson & Greenwood, 8 bags potatoes	10 00
2885	R. Herron, 13 cords wood	19 50
2886	E. H. Shepherd, board bills	17 50
2887	W. Switzer, board bills	1 15
2888	St. Ry. Journal, 1 year subscription	4 00
2889	W. H. Salter, supplies	8 63
2890	Jas. St. James, supplies	26 74
2891	Toronto Elec. Lgt. Co., elec. current	10 33
2892	Thomson, Stnry. Co., typewriter paper	4 00
2893	United Typ. Co., Ltd., typewriter & cabinet	145 00
2894	A. R. Williams Mc. Co., shop equipment	453 23
2895	N. Wickett, vegetables	13 00
2896	Warwick Bros. & Rutter, office supplies	11 45
2897	Thompson, Tilley & Johnston, legal services	634 24
2898	E. A. Sullivan, expense acct	8 80
2899	G. N. W. Tel. Co., telegrams, Jan., 1906	65
2900	Bank of Ottawa, E. Benoit, tie estimate, No. 3	2,708 55
2901	Wyse & Middlemist, tel. estimate, January, '06	5,231 70
2902	A. R. Macdonell, estimate No. 20, 2nd contract	54,714 90
2903	A. R. Macdonell, estimate No. 40, 1st contract	9,664 11
2904	G. A. McCarthy, C.E., expenses, Jan., 1906	29 35
2905	G. A. McCarthy, C.E., disbursements, Jan., 1906	124 53
2906	Nova Scotia Steel & Coal, anlge bars 80 lb. rails	20,029 89
2907	C. P. Sandberg, inspecting rails	91 50
2908	Wyse & Middlemist, enlarging gains, etc	247 11
2909	A. R. Macdonell, sundry accts	1,512 49
2910	T. & N. O. Ry., sundry accts	8,341 67
2911	W. G. Chace, expenses, Jan., 1906	41 60
2912	Geo. Taylor Hardware Co., hardware supplies	137 83
2913	Richardson & Co., hardware supplies	805 94
2914	A. J. Young, Ltd., supplies	1,502 62
2915	Purvis Bros., hardware supplies	369 19
2916	Rice Lewis & Son, Ltd., hand ratchet	102 22
2917	J. H. Marshall, lumber door sets	78 53
2918	G. A. McCarthy, engineer pay rolls, Jan., '06	9,662 27
2919	L. W. Read, eng. supplies	20 00
2920	C. P. R. Tel Co., telegrams	13 78
2921	J. H. Burd, expenses	48 80
2922	T. & N. O. Ry., amount paid by operation for account construction	10,565 50
2923	D. E. Thomson, fee as counsel, Jan., 1906	200 00
2924	E. F. Stephenson, work or crossing	10 00
2925	Dominion Concrete Co., bal. due on pipe	55 30
2926	H. W. Pearson, petty cash	20 00
2927	Mary A. McGregor, right of way, N. Bay	350 00

Voucher No.	Name.	JANUARY. Amount.
2928	Wm. Martin, right of way, N. Bay	1,000 00
2929	Letatia Lefevre, right of way, N. Bay	850 00
2930	Lotta Francis, right of way, N. Bay	300 00
2931	Thos. Dreany, right of way, N. Bay	1,250 00
2932	Matilda Bingham, right of way, N. Bay	1,500 00
2933	Amelia Parks, right of way, N. Bay	350 00
2934	Metcalf & McDonald, right of way, N. Bay	200 00
2935	Thos. Hines, right of way, N. Bay	1,550 00
2936	H. Biers, right of way, N. Bay	1,200 00
2937	Armstrong & Devlin, right of way, N. Bay	1,100 00
2938	J. H. Marshall, right of way, N. Bay	1,000 00
2939	Susan McLellan, right of way, N. Bay	1,000 00
2940	W. S. Parkes, right of way, N. Bay	1,000 00
2941	Rob. N. Fletcher, right of way, N. Bay	1,400 00
2942	Dominion Iron & Steel Co., steel rails	25,454 55
	Total	$188,290 73

FEBRUARY.

Voucher No.	Name.	Amount.
2943	C. B. Smith, Ma. E., salary as eng., Feb	208 33
2944	H. W. Pearson, salary as Sec. Treas., Feb	150 00
2945	A. J. McGee, salary as gen. acct	125 00
2946	H. F. MacDonald, salary as asst. to acct	65 00
2947	John A. MacDonald, salary as Clerk to Sec	50 00
2948	Leland Pinkney, salary as Stengrapher	40 00
2949	W. G. Chace, salary as elec. eng	150 00
2950	S. R. Clement, salary as draughsman	60 00
2951	E. N. May, salary as Clerk	37 50
2952	D. C. Leckie, bal. due acct., wages	15 00
2953	H. D. Graham, legal fees	1,127 72
2954	H. W. Pearson, petty cash	20 00
2955	C. C. Farr, re claim Temagami Townsite	1,000 00
2956	J. Ferguson, re claim Temagami Townsite	200 00
2957	J. L. Englehart, expenses for Feb., 1906	60 10
2958	Art Metropole, Ltd., engineer's supplies	100 29
2959	H. W. Angus, drawings, plans, etc	82 50
2960	Armstrong & Kingston, board bills	23 25
2961	Bell Tel. Co. of Can., telephone instruments	510 00
2962	Beardmore Belting Co., belting ne shop	271 50
2963	Oliver Berthiaume, crossing Cobalt stn	9 30
2964	Wm. Briggs, binding Street Ry. Journal	1 25
2965	J. Bertram & Sons Co., shop equipment	3,700 00
2966	Pinkley Bros., blankets	7 00
2967	Bell Tel Co. of Can., long dist. service	5 25
2968	Myles Bourke, supplies, etc	28 04
2969	Ed. Bryce, expenses and railway fare	12 10
2970	Brown Bros. Ltd., office supplies	15 35
2971	Canadian Inspection Co., inspection splice cars	45 81
2972	W. G. Chace, expenses for Feb., 1906	47 70
2973	Can. Foundry Co., Ltd., boiler pump	289 00
2974	Can. Pac. Ry. Co., fish plates	426 93
2975	Can. Westinghouse Co., elec. lgt. equipment	1,191 62
2976	Can. Pac. Ry. Tel., telegrams, Feb., 1906	11 58
2977	Chamber & McQuigge, board bills supplies, etc	309 18
2978	Can. Sewer Pipe Co., sewer pipe	172 38
2979	J. Charron, construction sid Cob. Frt shed	12 20
2980	J. Clarke, supplies	28 87
2981	Dept. Lands and Mines, dues on ties cut	718 80
2982	Dom. Bridge Co., Ltd., estimate bridge contract	6,484 00
2983	Davis & O'Connor, hardware supplies	142 31
2984	A. Devine, team hire, etc	35 00
2985	Dodge Mfg. Co. of Toronto, pulleys, etc	34 07
2986	Doheny & Grant, provisions	36 91
2987	J. R. Eaton, birch flooring	22 50

Voucher No.	Name.	Amount.
	FEBRUARY.	
2988	K. Farah, board bills	7 95
2989	J. Foster, engineer's supplies	8 00
2990	J. J. Gartshore. rail anchor and snatch block	52 50
2991	Grand & Toy, Ltd., office supplies	18 66
2992	Globe Printing Co., 1 year subscription	5 00
2993	Gillespie Co., photos for adv	16 00
2994	R. B. Herron, team hire, etc	142 66
2995	John Hughes. board bills	9 20
2996	A. G. Joy, 11 tel. poles	12 35
2997	J. C. Kennedy, board and lodging	3 90
2998	H. I. Kert, provisions	64 55
2999	Kruger & Gohr, board bill	27 90
3000	W. J. Keech, supplies boarding car	42 88
3001	A. R. Macdonell, estimates No. 1 and 2 contracts	35,980 09
3002	A. R. Macdonell, frt. charges, supplies, etc	507 75
3003	Miller & Mahoney, lumber, etc	33 07
3004	F. J. Martyn, matresses, etc	36 00
3005	H. Marceau & Son, Traders Bank, lumber	652 21
3006	W. Mussen & Co., velocipedies	121 66
3007	Mon. Steel Works, Ltd., Eureka spring frogs	3,291 00
3008	Robt. Morrison, board bills	3 00
3009	J. McBurney & Sons, lumber for North River bridge	207 36
3010	G. A. McCarthy, engineer's pay rolls, Feb......	10,866 33
3011	G. A. McCarthy, disbursements	67 78
3012	G. A. McCarthy, expenses, Feb., 1906	52 00
3013	A. McIntosh, supplies, etc	190 31
3014	Wm. Milne & Son, lumber	170 39
3015	Nipissing Foundry & Mach., supplies, repairs, etc......	921 51
3016	A. New, services rendered	2 50
3017	N. Bay Light, Heat & Power Co., elec and gas lgt. accts......	9 80
3018	Office Specialty Mfg. Co., desk and cabinet	63 60
3019	J. J. O'Neil, expenses	20 24
3020	Peck Rolling Mills, ry. spikes	1,214 26
3021	Poor's Ry. Manual Co., subsc. (1 copy)	10 00
3022	Purvis Bros., hardware supplies	240 58
3023	Richardson & Co., hardware supplies	223 12
3024	Rice Lewis & Son Ltd., shop equipment	212 42
3025	R. M. Ryan, board and lodging	25 30
3026	Sherwin-Williams Co., paint for stations	189 00
3027	E. H. Shepherd, board bills	12 00
3028	W. H. Salter, provisions	22 20
3029	J. St. James, provisions	92 33
3030	Scott & Jamieson, provisions	85 09
3031	J. H. Shivley, board bill	3 50
3032	M. Sinkovitsch, washing blankets	23 90
3033	Tem. & N. O. Ry., sundry accts	17,653 38
3034	T. & N. O. Ry., amt deducted Milne acct	502 03
3035	Tor. Elec. Light Co., elec. light & lamps	11 10
3036	Thompson Stnry Co., office supplies	2 25
3037	J. & J. Taylor, 5 safes for stations	885 00
3038	Tor. Weekly Ry. & S. Boat Guide, subsc. to April, 14	2 60
3039	Geo. Taylor Hardware Co., hardware supplies	23 13
3040	A. R. Williams Machry. Co., tank and shop equipment......	125 83
3041	Warwick Bros. & Rutter, forms, etc	117 10
3042	Chas. Wooley, reimbursement fire loss	40 50
3043	J. Welbourne, supplies	11 70
3044	Wyse & Middlemist, estimate per contract	2,242 00
3045	A. J. Young, Ltd., groceries and provisions	854 26
3046	Wyse & Middlemist, enlarging gains, etc......	879 76
3047	Geo. Gordon, lumber for stn. and sect. bldgs......	454 70
3048	D. E. Thomson, fee as Counsel......	200 00
3049	C. B. Smith, expenses February, 1906......	13 50
3050	Nat. Life Ass. Co., rent gen. office	125 00
	Total	$98,189 08

Voucher No.	Name. MARCH.	Amount.
3051	W. J. Dreany, right of way	$1,700 00
3052	A. Dreany, right of way	1,203 45
3053	T. J. Dreany, right of way	700 00
3054	J. Fulcher, right of way	902 42
3055	Sun-Hastings Sav. & Loan, right of way	597 58
3056	Letitia Lefevre, right of way	4 00
3057	Manitou Lumber Co., L., right of way	197 00
3058	W. Houser, right of way Township Armstrong	100 00
3059	T. Diamond, expenses Chicago, etc.	50 00
3060	H. W. Pearson, petty cash	20 00
3061	W. G. Chace, salary March, 1906	150 00
3062	S. R. Clement, salary March, 1906	60 00
3063	D. E. Thomson, fee as Counsel	300 00
3064	The Art Metropole, Ltd., eng. supplies	13 24
3065	H. W. Angus, specifications stations, etc.	13 24
3066	Myles Bourke, snow shoes	5 00
3067	J. H. Burd, expenses	24 35
3068	Brown Bros., office supplies	16 75
3069	Beardmore Belt Co., shop equip	72 25
3070	Burrows & Parmalle, parts for motor car	2 85
3071	Blanchet & Fitzpatrick, supplies	9 60
3072	Begg Bros., rubber boots	22 50
3073	Can. Inspection Co., inspecting bridge material	1 71
3074	W. G. Chace, expenses March	7 35
3075	C. P. R. Tel., telegrams	24 57
3076	Can. Westinghouse Co., air brake equip	29 25
3077	Can. Gen. Elec. Co., tel. wire, etc.	1,125 30
3078	Crossen Car Mfg. Co., frt. charges on air brake	12 10
3079	Can. Loco. Co., locos. 106 and 107	28,652 60
3080	William Costello, teaming	1,414 34
3081	Bernard Cairns, rubber stamps	2 00
3082	J. Clark, charges re Nelles, deceased	40 00
3083	Can. Pac. Ry. Co., steel rails and angle bars	8,688 71
3084	Peter Commando, western beef	35 00
3085	C. J. Campbell, board bills, etc.	11 35
3086	Firstbrooke Box Co., top pins and arm tel. line	382 50
3087	Margaret Gorman, rent. N. Bay office	330 00
3088	Grand Union Hotel, board bills	9 00
3089	Grand & Toy, Ltd., office supplies	136 93
3090	R. T. Gough, expenses	14 80
3091	J. F. Gillies, board bills	4 70
3092	Gillies Bros., Ltd., min. rights on right way	2 25
3093	Gutta Percha & Rubber Co., fire hose, etc.	268 65
3094	Ham. Stamp & Stencil Co., steel stamps	5 65
3095	R. B. Herron, board bills	11 05
3096	F. H. Hopkins Co., equip., etc.	746 32
3097	Ham. Steel & Iron Co., iron bars	9 44
3098	D. Moore, stage fares and board	4 70
3099	A. R. Macdonell, sundry accounts	119 15
3100	A. R. Macdonell, estimate 1st cont	1,735 02
3101	A. R. Macdonell, estimate 2nd cont	39,080 10
3102	The Mail Printing Co., adv. re tenders	27 00
3103	C. H. Mortimer Pub. Co., adv. re tenders	4 20
3104	J. H. Marshall, door brackets, etc.	39 00
3105	H. Marceau & Son, lumber	1,223 65
3106	J. McChesney, stage fares	16 00
3107	A. McIntosh, supplies boarding cars	140 55
3108	G. A. McCarthy, disbursements	325 54
3109	G. A. McCarthy, expenses on line	35 80
2110	G. A. McCarthy, pay rolls March, 1906	14,856 22
3111	North Bay Light, Heat & Power Co., elec. and gas light	4 13
3112	Will H. Newsome, office supplies	2 60
3113	Nipissing Foundry & Machine Co., repairing, etc.	46 47
3114	G. Nicholson, services	2 00
3115	J. J. O'Neil, expenses on line	12 60
3116	Office Spec. Mfg. Co., card cabinet	5 00

Voucher No.	Name.	MARCH.	Amount.
3117	Pembroke Lumber Co., lumber		1,575 99
3118	Purvis Bros., hardware supplies		382 20
3119	Peck Roll. Mills, Ltd., track spikes		2,392 31
3120	Rhodes, Curry & Co., Caboose No. 52		1,360 00
3121	Richardson & Co., hardware supplies		253 47
3122	Robert Reade, board bills		14 00
3223	Robinson & Greenwood, bread		99
3124	Scott & Jamieson, supplies to engrs		415 75
3125	G. Sands, axes and ropes		18 30
3126	J. Ross Robertson, adv. for tenders		18 00
3127	Toledo Foundry & Machine Co., part payment steam shovel		5,000 00
3128	Toronto Elec. Light Co., electric current		5 57
3129	S. E. Thicke, bread		2 70
3130	T. & N. O. Ry., propn. office salries, etc		1,052 35
3131	T. & N. O. Ry., sundry accounts		3,536 42
3132	T. & N. O. Ry., deducted Macdonell est		9,999 79
3133	T. & N. O. Ry., car rental deducted Wyse & Middlemist account...		33 80
3134	G. Taylor Hardware Co., hardware supplies		28 29
3135	Thomas Co., office supplies		37 00
3136	Tor. Bolt & Forging Co., track spikes		822 53
3137	C. A. Wismer, drugs eng. party		4 10
3138	A. J. Young, Ltd., groc. and prov.		5,802 72
3139	Wyse & Middlemist, final est. tel.		1,948 30
3140	Wyse & Middlemist, special cont. tel.		1,108 25
3141	Nat. Life Ass. Co., office rent March, 1906.		125 00
3142	J. M. McNamara, cost Fraser vs. N. O.		109 95
3143	J. M. McNamara, legal services		872 60
	Total		$142,941 67

		APRIL.	
3144	H. W. Pearson, petty cash		$ 20 00
3145	J. McKnight, right of way		25 00
3146	A. LaBracque, loss clothing, etc.		21 50
3147	J. M. McNamara, fees re town sites		312 80
3148	G. Carmichael, right of way		23 80
3149	W. G. Chace, salary as Elec. Eng.		150 00
3150	S. Clement, salary as Draughtsman		60 00
3151	Can. Bank Commerce, deposit for costs		500 00
3152	Thomson, Tilley & Johnston, advance for costs		1,000 00
3153	S. Clement, salary, May 1-12		23 23
3154	C. Horning, Pullman Toronto, North Bay		14 00
3155	H. W. Pearson, petty cash		20 00
3156	G. A. McCarthy, eng. pay rolls		18,777 41
3157	G. A. McCarthy, eng. disbursements		30 74
3158	G. A. McCarthy, eng. expenses		15 75
3159	J. J. O'Neil, expenses, April		19 01
3160	Toronto World, adv. mining lease.		171 30
3161	J. L. Englehart, expenses, April		30 25
3162	J. Tomlinson, expenses, April		75 00
3163	Art Metropole, Ltd., eng. supp.		11 35
3164	Wm. Abbott, track drills		48 00
3165	H. W. Angus, plans, etc		481 00
3166	J. E. Armstrong, expenses		38 45
3167	J. Arbathaum, expenses		3 00
3168	D. Barry, expenses		15 00
3169	The Brown Bros., Ltd., office supplies		12 90
3170	Begg Bros., blankets, etc		136 30
3171	Mrs. Baster, board bill		1 75
3172	Blanchet & Fitzpatrick, supplies		177 77
3173	W. G. Chace, railway fare		6 85
3174	Can. Loco. Co., 1 ten-wheel loco.		14,326 30
3175	L. O. Clake, surveying, etc		347 95
3176	Wm. Costello, team hire, etc		216 00
3177	R. J. Divine, team hire, etc		418 00

Voucher No.	APRIL. Name.	Amount.
3178	J. A. Cole, bldg. material	229 06
3179	A. J. Coombe, board bill	10 00
3180	Crossen Mfg. Co., heating equip	875 00
3181	Crossen Car Mfg. Co., 1st coach, 3 work cars	25,857 13
3182	J. Deegan, supplies	13 00
3183	Dom. Typewriter Co., office supplies	2 25
3184	Doheny & Donovan, board bills	116 20
3185	Dom. Wire Rope Mfg. Co., cable	85 45
3186	Treasury of Ont., team hire, lumber, etc., acct. Dept. L. & M	143 00
3187	J. R. Eaton, lumber	524 18
3188	Jas. Foster, repairing level, etc	9 50
3189	K. Farah, board bills	68 50
3190	G. N. W. Tel. Co., telegrams	1 78
3191	Grand & Toy, Ltd., office supplies	4 50
3192	Gutta Percha & Rubber Co., rubber boots	41 47
3193	R. Herron, team hire, etc	602 15
3194	Harris Ties & Timber Co., lumber	511 96
3195	Hart & Riddle, letter heads	12 00
3196	F. Hopkins & Co., equip	3,327 03
3197	Journal Printing Co., advertising	21 60
3198	H. Jack, telegraph poles	624 33
3199	H. I. Kert, vegetables	62 05
3200	J. C. Kennedy, board bills	5 60
3201	Lake & Lewis, photos	24 05
3202	Lindsay & McClusky, cement	1,062 72
3203	Mail Job Printing Co., printing	6 35
3204	Traders' Bank, H. Marceau. lumber	1,435 57
3205	Montreal Steel Works, Ltd., switches	2,503 40
3206	J. Martin, board bill	84 50
3207	J. Martyn, mattresses	320 95
3208	Milton Pressed Brick Co., bricks	212 00
3209	McKee & Campbell, board bills	53 50
3210	McLeod & Co., board bills	19 95
3211	A. McIntosh, supplies	199 32
3212	North Bay Light, Heat & Power Co., light	4 13
3213	Ottawa *Citizen* Co., advertising	33 30
3214	O'Boyle Bros., tank castings	512 00
3215	Purvis Bros., hardware supplies	717 50
3216	N. L. Piper Ry. Supp. Co., stn. seating	80 00
3217	Pembroke Lumber Co., lumber	1,307 06
3218	Rolf, Clarke Co., Ltd., checks	21 00
3219	Remington Typ. Co., ribbons	75
3220	Rice Lewis & Son, hose, etc	68 15
3221	Richardson & Con., hardware supp	245 67
3222	E. P. Rowe, oil barrels	2 00
3223	Scott & Jamieson, teaming	135 25
3224	Standard Inspection Bureau, inspection rolling stock	104 61
3225	Sault *Star*, advertising	1 80
3226	Swan Swanson, teaming	422 45
3227	W. H. Salter, prov	137 57
3228	T. Timlin, meals	8 75
3229	Toronto Electric Light Co., electric light, etc	4 82
3230	G. Taylor Hardware Co., hardware supplies	105 95
3231	T. & N. O. Ry., sundry accounts	4,095 76
3232	Wm. Wallingford, sharpening tools	13 35
3233	Zalahan & Abraham, board bills	50 50
3234	London Bolt and Hings Works, track bolts	31 00
3235	E. Johnston, teaming	73 32
3236	A. J. Young, Ltd., supplies	2,077 32
3237	G. A. McCarthy, orders *re* E. Johnston	668 68
3238	A. R. Macdonell, est. 2d cont. April	56,605 42
3239	A. R. Macdonell, sundry accounts	220 54
3240	Jas. McBurney, lumber	282 72
3241	H. Marleau, moving section house	200 00
3242	A. R. Williams Mach. Co., shop equip	1,420 00
3243	Office Specialty Mfg. Co., office furniture	147 45

Voucher No.	Name.	APRIL.	Amount.
3244	J. Inglis & Co., Ltd., boiler		185 00
3245	Darling Bros., Ltd., feed pump		232 00
3246	Bell Telephone Co., Ltd., long distance service		6 35
3247	Can. Loco. Co., Ltd., engine 105		14,200 30
3248	D. E. Thomson, salary		300 00
3249	Nat. Life Ass. Co., rent		125 00
3250	Can. Pac. Ry. Tel., telegrams		40 17
3255	A. R. Macdonell		18,637 36
3250A	Metropolitan Bank, interest		25
	Total		$180,325 71

MAY.

3251	J. M. McNamara, clearing permits tel. line		$140 00
3252	Toledo Fndry. & Mach. Co., bal. due acct. steam shovel		1,000 00
3253	W. G. Chace, salary, May		150 00
3254	J. H. Shaw, Ry. expenses, etc. *re* min. rights		44 75
3255	A. R. Macdonell, for April estimate, ent. April, '06		....
3256	Oscar Fulton, auctioneer on sale lots		225 00
3257	The *Journal* Print. Co., advertising tenders, etc.		76 30
3258	The *Mail* Print. Co., adv. tenders, etc.		37 80
3259	J. R. Robertson, adv. tenders, etc.		41 00
3250	*Globe* Print. Co., adv. tenders, etc.		131 70
3261	The *Gazette* Print. Co., adv. tenders, etc.		93 40
3262	Ottawa *Citizen* Co., adv. tenders, etc.		138 30
3263	*United Canada*, adv. tenders		14 00
3264	London *Free Press*, adv. tenders		63 00
3265	Kingston *News*, Ltd., adv. tenders, etc.		10 50
3266	*Spector* Print. Co., Ltd., adv. tenders		51 75
3267	The *Despatch*, adv. tenders		72 05
3268	Stephenson & Son, adv. tenders, etc.		15 12
3269	D. E. Bastedo, adv. tenders, etc.		4 48
3270	Petrolea *Advertiser*, adv. tenders, etc.		24 50
3271	*Time* Pub. House, adv. tenders, etc.		6 00
3272	Wesley & Crew, adv. tenders, etc		5 00
3273	Montreal *Star* Pub. Co., adv. tenders, etc.		109 20
3274	Pratt & McIvor, adv. tenders, etc.		24 50
3275	Sudbury *Min. News*, adv. tenders, etc.		5 70
3276	E. Stephenson, *Planet*, adv. tenders, etc.		5 60
3277	Brockville *Times*, adv. tenders, etc.		5 60
3278	*The Leader*, adv. tenders, etc.		5 50
3279	*The Times* Print. Co., adv. tenders, etc.		5 00
3280	*The Times* Print. Co., Peterborough, adv. tenders		18 90
3281	C. H. Mortimer Pub. Co., adv. tenders, etc.		10 00
3282	Can. Print. Co., adv. tenders, etc.		18 90
3283	*The Bruce Herold*, adv. tenders, etc.		6 72
3284	The Art Metropole, Ltd., eng. supp.		169 32
3285	H. W. Angus, details, etc., Englehart station		160 00
3286	Armstrong & Comisky, damage acct. ballasting		2 00
3287	Bell. Tel. Co., long distance service		8 75
3288	Bell Tel. Co., six months' service		14 25
3289	Phillippi Bousonnault, teaming		15 00
3290	E. Brice, expenses		15 45
3291	Begg Bros., towelling		1 50
3292	F. Burnes, board and lodging		37 25
3293	Brown Bros., Ltd., office supp.		7 00
3294	J. H. Burd, work on town site plans		20 00
3295	G. H. Carr, reimbursement fire loss		45 50
3296	J. A. Cole & Co., material stan. bldg.		84 83
3297	Chambers & McQuigge, labor and team hire		118 00
3208	Clinton I. Campbell, labor supp. Englehart		391 27
3299	W. M. Costello, moving camp		8 00
3300	Cobalt Hotel Co., board and lodging		18 50
3301	Cleveland & Sarnia Saw Mills Co., work on spur		3,721 20

Voucher No.	Name.	MAY. Amount.
3302	Can. & School Furniture Co., settees	94 50
3303	Can. Gen. Elec. Co., tel, wire, etc.	1,581 02
3304	Connor, Clarke & Monds, specifications, etc.	554 88
3305	H. C. Dunbar, lumber	18 00
3306	Dom. Typewriter Exchange, office supp.	1 50
3307	J. R. Eaton, lumber	1,721 27
3308	Davis & O'Connor, hardware supp.	20 52
3309	Dreany Bros., hardware supp.	20 33
3310	Jas. Foster, repairing level, etc.	8 50
3311	K. Karah, board bills	36 25
3312	Grand & Toy, Ltd., office supp.	9 05
3313	L. H. Hopkins & Co., ballast unloader parts	767 00
3314	Harris Tie & Lumber Co., lumber	231 40
3315	W. J. Keechl, meat supp.	55 56
3316	J. Kingston, board bills	26 00
3317	Mrs. G. Kirsch, board bills	8 00
3318	Langford Quarry Co., cutting stone for Temigami stan.	260 00
3319	A. Lindsay, cement and sacks	5 65
3320	A. R. Macdonell, sundry account	394 14
3321	Mail Job Print. Co., poster re sale town lots	5 00
3322	Mason Gordon Co., culvert cedar	327 84
3323	F. J. Martyn, mattresses, etc.	112 50
3324	U. Moore, stage fares	2 50
3325	A. McIntosh, supplies	269 27
3326	McKee & Campbell, board bills	14 00
3327	J. McChesney, supplies	18 25
3328	McLeod & Co., teaming and board bills	38 45
3329	G. A. McCarthy, expense acct.	26 25
3330	G. A. McCarthy, disbursements	34 83
3331	G. A. McCarthy, Eng. pay rolls, May	24,578 35
3332	A. R. Macdonell, est. May, 2nd contract	86,611 95
3333	W. F. McCann, ry. fare Tor. N. Bay	6 85
3334	N. Bay Light, Heat & Power Co., light N. B. offices	2 50
3335	G. Nicholson, measuring ballast pits	8 00
3336	D. O'Connor, lumber	67 10
3337	Ont. Lime Assn., lime and plaster	246 20
3338	Pembroke Lumber Co., lumber	1,461 00
3339	Purvis Bros., hardware supplies	300 93
3340	D. Pyke Co., Ltd., tents	104 80
3341	A. C. Rorabeck, drugs.	15 70
3342	W. A. Rutherford, office supp.	10 50
3343	Richardson & Co., hardware supp.	309 85
3344	Rice Lewis & Son, hardware supp.	201 72
3345	J. B. Smith & Son, lumber	327 17
3346	J. H. Sullivan, team hire	140 00
3347	J. Sears, board bills	16 25
3348	E. C. Shebherd, board bills	77 35
3349	Standard Inspection Bureau, inspection rails	369 59
3350	M. Sinkavitsch, laundry	29 00
3351	T. & N. O. Ry., acct J. Gartshore, rails	12,911 50
3352	T. & N. O. Ry., sundry accts.	13,639 59
3353	Tor. Elec. Light Co., elec. light gen. offices	3 49
3354	G. Taylor Hardware Co., hardware supplies	41 62
3355	United Typewriter Co., office supplies.	60 00
3356	Wyse & Middlemist, telegraph and telephone estimate, May. '06	2,824 29
3357	W. H. Walbourn, plate glass	12 00
3358	Young Wing, laundry.	14 10
3359	West & Trip, cartage	16 00
3360	Warwick Bros. & Rutter, office supplies.	19 75
3361	Warwick Bros. & Rutter, printing forms.	60 50
3362	Wood, Vallance & Co., hardware supplies.	553 42
3363	A. J. Young, Ltd., groc. and prov.	2,069 26
3364	W. J. Yates, Laurentian Water, one case.	1 35
3365	C. I. Campbell, clearing town site	630 00
3366	Wm. Shepherd, sharpening tools.	30 95

Voucher No.	Name.	Amount.

MAY.

3367	C. P. R. Tel., telegrams	19 44
3368	G. N. W. Tel., telegrams	51
3369	Mail Print. Co., adv	193 50
3370	Montreal Star Pub. Co., adv	11 20
3371	Spectator Print. Co., adv	49 00
3372	Journal Print. Co., adv	28 00
3373	Ottawa Citizen, adv	25 20
3374	Stephenson & Son, adv	18 60
3375	Herald Print. Co., subscription commissions	3 00
3376	Lindsay & McClusky, lime and cement	529 10
3377	J. J. Lacoste, supplies	1 55
3378	Robert Morrison, board bills	6 00
3379	Bell Tel. Co., long distance service	11 65
3380	Tor. World, adv	16 80
3381	New Pub. Co., adv	20 70
3382	Toronto Star, adv	9 00
3383	Mail Print. Co., adv	42 00
3384	H. McLean, est. moving section house	175 00
3385	Nat. Life Ass. C., rent office May	125 00
3386	C. B. Smith, expenses April and May, 1906	11 97
3387	J. L. Englehart, expenses May, 1906	62 00
3388	D. Murphy, expenses April and May, 1906	64 00
3389	D. E. Thomson, fee as Counsel, May, 1906	300 00
	Total	$163,556 40

JUNE.

3390	Queen City Oil Co., Ltd., part block F., North Bay	$200 00
3391	H. W. Pearson, petty cash	20 00
3392	H. W. Pearson, petty cash	20 00
3393	W. G. Chace, salary Elec. Eng. June	150 00
3395	J. E. Russell, bal. due on pile driver	50 00
3397	J. M. McNamara, Assurance fees Latchford plan	125 00
3399	T. Mansfield, ballast pit 2nd div	2,000 00
3401	G. A. McCarthy, advance acct	3,229 00
3403	Wm Milne & Son, ballast 1st div	250 00
3405	J. L. Englehart, expense acct. June	47 75
3407	C. B. Smith, expense acct. June	7 79
3409	Art Metropole, eng. supp	61 49
3411	J. E. Armstrong, expense acct	26 50
13	E. Benoit, Bank Ottawa, final estimate tie cont	3,006 91
3415	J. & S. Bessette & Son, Ltd., hardware supplies	70 00
3417	T. Birckett & Son, hardware supplies	333 37
3419	W. J. Bailey, Bank Ottawa, moving bldgs	500 00
3421	R. H. Burton, paint Latchford stan	20 90
3423	Bell Tel. Co., exchange serv	23 63
3425	Binkley Bros., blankets, etc	7 50
3427	C. I. Campbell, cleaning	31 50
3429	C. P. R. Tel., telegrams, June	27 42
3431	M. Courtright, transportation, etc	8 30
3433	J. Clarke, supp	37 85
3435	T. & N. O. Crossen Car Mfg. Co., roll stock	21,611 26
3437	Can. Inspection Co., inspecting br. matl	1 75
3439	Can. Gen. Elec. Co., insulators, etc	6 04
3441	Can. Print. Co., adv	5 60
3443	C. I. Campbell, labour, board bills	103 10
3445	Wm. Costello, teaming, etc	150 00
3447	H. Davis, gate hinges	4 17
3449	*The Despatch*, adv	5 00
3451	H. C. Dunbar, lumber	18 00
3453	Doheny & Donovan, board bills	72 45
3455	Doheny & Grant, board bills	18 00
3457	R. J. Devine, teaming supp	8 00
3459	J. R. Eaton, lumber	570 92

Voucher No.	Name.	JUNE. Amount.
3461	Wm. Errett, nail, felt, etc.	13 38
3463	K. Farah, board bills.	39 00
3465	J. E. Farrall & Co., time and material.	19 82
3467	A. G. Fernholm, services rendered.	15 00
3469	Globe Print. Co., adv.	16 80
3471	London *Free Press*, adv.	28 40
3473	G. N. W. Tel. Co., telegrams, June.	1 05
3475	Grand & Toy, Ltd., office supp.	12 25
3477	H. Gummer, adv.	24 50
3479	Grand Union Hotel, board bills	42 00
3481	T. Gunn, clearing.	100 00
3483	Harris Tie & Timber Co., lumber.	1,003 48
3485	F. H. Hopkins & Co., equip.	750 77
3487	R. Haggard, expenses, etc.	10 60
3489	Percy Harmer, clearing	25 00
3491	Imperial Varnish & Color Co., boiled oil	231 34
3493	T. Julien, lettering station	8 10
3495	H. I. Kirt, provisions	24 00
3497	Hugh Jack, tel. poles.	119 37
3499	Lindsay & McClusky, lime and cement.	694 67
3501	P. LeBlanc, teaming.	6 50
3503	H. Lefter, board bills.	18 11
3505	J. Loughrin, hiring Indians (fee).	17 50
3507	C. H. Mortimer Pub. Co., adv.	26 50
3509	Wm. Milne & Son, lumber.	628 26
3511	Montreal Steel Works, switch stands, etc.	2,031 70
3513	McKee & Campbell, board bills.	8 00
3515	McLellan & Co., lumber, etc.	30 78
3517	Patrick Murphy, hire canoes.	5 00
3519	J. D. McDonald, board bills.	84 00
3521	A. G. McGougan, transportation, etc.	16 15
3523	G. A. McCarthy, Engineer's pay rolls	27,046 47
3525	G. A. McCarthy, disbursements.	721 90
3527	G. A. McCarthy, expense account.	22 75
3529	A. R. Macdonell, est. 2nd contract, June.	43,028 72
3531	A. R. Macdonell, sundry accounts	5,890 10
3533	F. J. Martin, casket, etc.	130 00
3535	Nipissing Foundry & Machine Co., mach. pts. and casting.	136 44
3537	Union Bank (Miller & Mahoney), lumber.	519 22
3539	A. McIntosh, supplies.	75 80
3541	S. M. Newton, advertising.	37 65
3543	J. A. Nichol, scrap books.	3 00
3545	L. V. Neil, Laurentian water.	2 00
3547	S. W. Meadow, fixing speeder.	10 00
3549	J. J. O'Neil, expenses May and June.	35 93
3551	R. Parker, board bills.	46 00
3553	Pembroke Lumber Co., lumber, etc.	2,341 37
3555	Pembroke Lumber Co., lumber.	405 43
3557	D. Pyke & Co., Ltd., tents.	16 00
3559	Pembroke *Standard*, advertising	5 60
3561	Purvis Bros., hardware supplies.	115 74
3563	Rothschild Cobalt Co., box stoves.	7 00
3565	Ready & Joyce, board bills.	8 20
3567	Rice Lewis & Son, Ltd., hardware supplies.	208 95
3569	Richardson & Co., hardware supplies.	122 99
3571	Standard Inspection Co., insp. coach and rails.	203 85
3573	Standard Pub. Co., of Windsor, advertising	3 92
3575	Wm. Sheppard, sharpening tools.	2 70
3577	Sherwin-Williams Co., paint.	224 00
3579	W. H. Salter provisions.	110 80
3581	Swan Swanson, Bank of Ottawa, grading.	940 03
3583	Tor. Elec. Light Co., electric light.	3 36
3585	Temis. & Nor. Ont. Rly., cr. operation.	524 19
3587	T. & N. O. Rly., sundry accounts.	6.451 55
3587	T. & N. O. Ry., honorarium and salaries	969 70

3591	Geo. Taylor Hardware Co., hardware supplies	108 90
3593	G. Vanalastine, board bills	13 50
3595	Wyse & Middlemist, re Cons. tele line	897 31
3597	Wilson & Toye, time and material	26 42
3599	A. Young, Limited, groceries and provisions	1,830 21
3601	National Life Ass. Co., rent general office, June	125 00
3603	D. E. Thomson, fees as counsel, June	300 00

Total $132,554 62

JULY.

3394	H. W. Pearson, petty cash	$20 00
3396	Jno. Pool, Right-of-way	42 00
3398	J. M. McNamara, legal fees	433 33
3400	H. W. Pearson, petty cash	20 00
3402	J. L. Englehart, expenses	30 25
3404	J. J. O'Neil, expenses	22 50
3406	G. A. McCarthy, disbursements	111 89
3408	G. A. McCarthy, expenses	9 45
3410	G. A. McCarthy, pay rolls, July	30,176 63
3412	D. Murphy, expenses	41 75
3414	Art Metropole, engineering supplies	85 33
3416	The Algoma Steel Co., balance due on steel rails	52 45
3418	W. J. Bailey, work North Bay terminals	276 00
3420	W. J. Bailey, removing buildings	275 00
3422	W. Bailey, clearing	50 18
3424	E. Benoit (Bank of Ottawa), final estimate tie con	168 24
3426	J. S. Besette & Co., Ltd., driving wheels gear, etc.	5 95
3428	Thos. Birkett & Sons, stock and dies	43 15
3430	Brown Bros., Ltd., supplies	13 00
3432	Begg Bros., blankets	59 85
3434	Thos. Birkett & Sons, dis. not allowed	6 80
3436	Richard Bell, canoe	35 00
3438	Bell Telephone Co., long distance service	8 00
3440	Bell Telephone Co.. long distance and exc. ser	98 45
3442	J. Chabaneau, clearing	43 00
3444	Thos. Chester, clearing	42 75
3446	A. W. Connor, drawing, etc.	181 40
3448	C. P. R. Telegraph, telegrams	22 89
3450	Can. Genl. Electric Co., top pins, tele. line	16 59
3452	C. I. Campbell, cordwood	49 80
3454	Jas. A. Cole, lumber	40 45
3456	P. L. Davey, teaming	3 50
3458	Doheny & Donovan, teaming, meals, etc.	33 15
3460	Dom. Bridge Co., Ltd., timber	127 75
3462	S. D. Eplett, hardware supplies	45 15
3464	J. R. Eaton, frames, doors, etc.	161 88
3466	J. R. Eaton, frames, doors, etc.	45 11
3468	J. E. Farrell & Co., plumbing, etc.	1,000 00
3470	Thos. Filbury, clearing	26 75
3472	Forest City Paving Co., est. re roadhouse con	2,064 67
3474	Phillip A. Fetterley, railway fare	11 60
3476	Firstbrook Box Co., cross arms and top pins	23 10
3478	G. N. W. Telegraph Co., telegrams	1 70
3480	Grand Union Hotel, board bills	11 00
3482	Grand & Toy, Ltd., office supplies	4 25
3484	Gillies Bros., Ltd., teaming, meals	20 60
3486	Wm. Gohr, meals, etc.	2 35
3488	Thos. Gunn, clearing	190 50
3490	Hart & Riddell, office stationery	11 00
3492	Herald Ptg. Co., advertising	38 64
3494	J. C. Johnston, testing cement	73 05
3496	Gilbert Jones, clearing	18 81
3498	Mrs. Kerr, clearing	55 36
3500	Geo. F. Krick, lumber	501 93

Voucher No.	Name. JULY.	Amount.
3502	M. J. Kelly, expenses	10 85
3504	F. Kruger, meals	1 00
3506	Loco. & Mach. Co., 4 ten wheel locos	65,840 00
3508	M. C. Lodge, supplies	8 00
3510	R. P. Lang, railway fares, etc.	8 85
3512	Lindsay & McClusky, cement	441 80
3514	J. H. Marshall, lumber	162 67
3516	Miller & Mahoney, lumber	786 71
3518	H. F. MacDonald. elec. fan	13 75
3520	W. H. C. Mussen, ballast plow, etc.	630 22
3522	A. R. Macdonell, estimate July 2nd div.	85,517 79
3524	A. R. Macdonell, sundry accts.	1,568 24
3526	F. J. Martyn, mattresses, etc.	108 15
3528	Wm. Milne & Son, loading line, etc.	36 20
3530	H. J. McAuslan, expenses May and June	14 00
3532	McKee & Campbell, board bills	49 25
3534	McDonald & Hay, 1 oil stove	6 55
3536	W. McCracken, supplies	1 50
3538	A. McIntosh, supplies	659 28
3540	Wm. McLaren, eve troughs, etc.	162 83
3542	Nipissing Fndry. & Mach. Co., time and material	18 90
3544	Office Specialty Mfg. Co., office fixtures	52 10
3546	Office Specialty Mfg. Co., office fixtures	18 45
3548	R. Parker, clearing	176 75
3550	R. Parker, board bills	30 75
3552	Pecl. Rolling Mills lts., track spikes	1,232 00
3554	J. Peckover. clearing	52 25
3556	D. Pike Co., Ltd., awnings	15 00
3558	D. Pike Co., Ltd., car tarpaulins	18 00
3560	A. L. Perkins Co., supp.	22 75
3562	Pembroke Lumber Co., lumber	2,013 74
3564	Purvis Bros., hardware supp.	95 53
3566	Pratt & McIvor, adv.	28 00
3568	H. Reas, clearing	54 16
3570	Remillion Bros., axe handles	2 00
3572	Rice, Lewis & Son, Ltd., hardware supp.	21 42
3574	M. Rothchild & Son, axes	3 75
3576	Richardson & Co., hardware supp.	156 08
3578	Richardson & Co., hardware supp.	156 47
3580	Rise & Goldforb, board bills	51 00
3582	P. St. George, plaster boards	377 74
3584	Standard Inspection Bureau, insp. rolling stock	127 75
3586	Thos. Swords, clearing	58 90
3588	T. & N. O. Ry., sundry accts.	2,248 89
3590	T. & N. O. Ry., prop. office salaries	469 98
3592	Sault Star, adv.	5 10
3594	Swan Swanson, Bank of Ottawa, estimate, July	708 93
3596	Scown & Rogers, lumber	126 61
3598	Wm. Shepperd, sharpening tools	49 65
3600	T. & N. O. Ry., sundry accts.	1,713 57
3602	T, & N. O. Ry., amt. deducted A. R. Macdonell acct.	2,151 81
3604	T. Timlin, board bill	3 80
3606	Tor. Elec. Light Co., light accts.	2 38
3608	Geo. Taylor Hardware Co., supp.	192 10
3610	The Thomas Co., office supp.	8 15
3612	United Typewriter Co., office supp.	3 75
3614	Warwick Bros. & Rutter, office supp.	7 00
3616	Wyse & Middlemist, est. tel. cont.	1,815 00
3618	Wyse & Middlemist, re construction tel.	402 00
3620	Wyse & Middlemist, est. trestle and coat chute	2,017 66
3622	A. J. Young, Ltd., groc. and prov.	1,645 99
3624	A. J. Young, Ltd., groc. and prov.	968 94
3626	Nat. Life Ass. Co., rent	125 00
3628	D. E. Thomson, salary	300 00
	Total	$212,722 37

Voucher No.	Name. AUGUST.	Amount.
3605	J. M. McNamara, clearing tel. line	45 00
3607	T. Chester, right of way	81 60
3609	A. Chester, right of way	6 40
3611	F. W. Love, right of way	34 00
3613	C. C. Farr, right of way	15 30
3615	H. W. Pearson, petty cash	20 00
3617	The Art Metropole, sundry supplies	5 80
3619	J. E. Armstrong, expenses	31 50
3621	H. W. Anugs, plans, specifications, etc.	25 00
3623	Miles Burk, supplies	12 50
3625	E. Bryce, disbursements	7 15
3627	A. E. Brashear, board bills	9 75
3629	M. Backer, clearing	12 50
3631	R. Brtton, clearing	50 00
3633	Consolidated Plate Glass Co., glass	9 09
3635	J. A. Cole & Co., lumber	48 78
3637	R. Couthard, expenses	3 00
3639	Cobalt Meat & Prov. Co., supplies	22 87
3641	J. R. Eaton, lumber	3,279 69
3643	S. D. Eplett, snow shoes	5 00
3645	Englehart Supply Co., supplies	27 08
3647	Frost Wire Fenc Co., fencing	93 12
3649	Graham & Ferguson, lumber	41 16
3651	R. T. Gough, expenses	41 70
3653	Grand & Toy Ltd., supplies	7 00
3655	Grand Union Hotel Co., board bills	27 50
3657	B. Garner, clearing	75 00
3659	Harris Tie & Timber Co., lumber	665 37
3661	F. H. Hopkins & Co., parts ballast unloader	33 60
3663	F. H. Hopkins & Co., wrecking crane	14,170 00
3665	Hamilton Steel & Iron Co., iron bars	21 36
3667	R. Hagarty, expenses	6 10
3669	D. Harvey, ry. fare	8 85
3671	W. Harding, clearing	60 50
3673	J. Judge, expenses	9 00
3675	G. Krick, lumber	45 54
3677	Lindsay & McClusky, cement	447 60
3679	Locomotive & Mach. Co., stell angles	2,106 00
3681	F. H. Love, clearing	175 00
3683	Ludoueci-Celadon, roofing	1,037 69
3685	F. J. Martyn, window shades	27 70
3687	W. H. C. Mussen & Co., tel. wire	919 27
3689	H. Marceau & Son, lumber	931 75
3691	Mason & Gordon, lumber	797 35
3693	A. McGougan, expenses	82 85
3695	H. F. McAuslin, expenses	28 00
3697	Hotel Matabanick, board bills	5 50
3699	A. McIntosh, supplies	209 01
3701	A. R. Macdonell, sundry accts.	878 24
3703	G. A. McCarthy, eng. pay rolls	33,042 28
3705	G. A. McCarthy, expenses	23 15
3707	G. A. McCarthy, disbursements	59 73
3709	J. McGumery, clearing	97 25
3711	W. McLaren, services rendered	20 90
3713	McKee & Campbell, board bills	9 75
3715	Mrs. J. D. McFarlane, board bills	7 00
3717	J. J. O'Neil, expenses	23 25
3719	Office Specialty Mfg. Co., folders	75
3721	Prospect Hotel, board bills	15 00
3723	Wm. Palfreyman, board bills	7 50
3725	Purvis Bros.. hardware supplies	223 19
3727	Runping & Sons, lumber	52 48
3729	Rolph Clarke, Ltd., engraving treas. bills	140 00
3731	Rice Lewis & Son, Ltd., supplies	170 52
3733	Scott & Jamieson, supply board bills, etc	236 17
3735	Wm. Shepperd, welding shaft	1 00

Voucher No.	Name.	Amount.

AUGUST.

No.	Name	Amount
3737	J. H. Sullivan, handling material	26 00
3739	W. H. Salter, 1 pack strap	1 25
3741	S. Salmon & Co., lumber	19 84
3743	Tor. Weekly S. & R. Guide, subsc. 6 month	2 60
3745	Warwick Bros. & Rutter, envelopes	23 10
3747	W. Switzer, board bills	5 80
3749	T. & N. O. Ry., sundry accts	6,638 44
3751	J. W. Richardson, hardware supplies	197 16
3753	G. Taylor Hardware Co., hardware supplies	249 50
3755	A. J. Young, Ltd., groc. and prov	982 57
3757	Can. Westinghouse Co., air brake equipment	510 55
3759	Rhodes Curry & Co., conductor's van	1,535 42
3761	F. Hilliard, tile	255 00
3763	The Haileyburian, advertising	63 65
3765	The Journal Print. Co., adv	42 00
3767	J. R. Robertson, adv	42 00
3769	The Mail Print. Co., adv	63 00
3771	Nipissing Tribune Pub. Co., adv	16 80
3773	The Perth Expositor, adv	6 40
3775	Pratt & McIvor, adv	5 60
3777	S. Clement, expenses	7 55
3779	Forest City Paving Co., estimate round house	4,941 90
3781	Wyse & Middlemist, est. coal chute	2,942 46
3783	S. Swanson, Bank of Ottawa, N. B. Jct., grading	513 90
3785	A. R. Macdonell, 2nd cont., Aug. 1906.	78,064 23
3787	C. I. Campbell, clearing Englehart Townsite	189 00
3789	C. I. Campbell, Englehart tank cont.	146 88
3791	Wyse & Middlemist, estimate telegraph contract	1,080 00
3793	Wyse & Middlemist, estimate coal chute contract	761 40
3795	Woolings Bros., est. Englehart townsite, clearing	314 64
3797	H. Haw, carting	138 60
3799	Nat. Life Ass. Co., office rent Aug.	125 00
3801	D. E. Thomson, legal fees Aug	300 00
3803	J. L. Englehart, expenses Aug	46 75
	Total	$161,092 68

SEPTEMBER.

No.	Name	Amount
3630	H. W. Pearson, petty cash	10 00
3632	H. W. Pearson, petty cash	20 00
3634	J. L. Englehart, expenses	42 75
3636	G. A. McCarthy, eng. pay rolls	26,209 65
3638	G. A. McCarthy, disbursements	93 85
3640	G. A. McCarthy, expenses	12 35
3642	The Art Metropole, Ltd., eng. supplies	107 71
3644	E. Bryce, expenses, Sept.	5 40
3646	Begg Bros., blankets	97 65
3648	J. Burton, clearing	49 00
3650	Bell Tel. Co., long distance ser	14 95
3652	Bell Tel. Co., telephone service	85 00
3654	J. & S. Bessett Co., Lts., parts for velocipede	1 50
3656	C. J. Campbell, clearing	196 00
3658	Crossen Car Mfg. Co., frt. charges	6 84
3660	Can. Westinghouse Co., air brake equip	220 20
3662	S. B. Clement, expenses	8 15
3664	J. Clarke, meals supplies	20 70
3666	Can. Paint Co., Ltd., oil and paint	487 17
3668	Cobalt Meat & Prov. Co., supplies	33 36
3670	C. P. R. Ry. Tel., telegrams	38 75
3672	Can. Sewer Pipe Co., pipe	202 02
3674	Dom. Concrete Co., pipe	953 76
3676	S. D. Eplett, hardware supplies	13 29
3678	J. R. Eaton, lumber	6,626 64
3680	Empire Lumber Co., lumber	69 05
3682	W. Errett, hardware supplies	6 96

2 TEMIS.

Voucher No.	Name.	Amount.
	SEPTEMBER.	
3684	Forest City Paving Co., round house and machine shop contract, estimate Sept.	5,039 28
3686	Forest City Paving Co., mach. shop, round house contract, Sept....	2,970 00
3688	A. Fitzpatrick, clearing	20 00
3690	Jas. Foster, repairing field instrument	43 25
3692	G. N. W. Tel. Co., telegrams	1 61
3694	Grand & Toy, Ltd., office supplies	17 65
3696	Grand Union Hotel, board bills	17 00
3698	Wm. Gohr, board bills	95
3700	Grand Union Hotel, board bills	2 00
3702	P. Harner, clearing	25 00
3704	Chas. Harris, clearing	50 00
3706	R. B. Herron, labor, etc	347 73
3708	F. Hilliard, file	149 00
3710	Herold Print Co., adv	27 72
3712	L. G. Hovey, axe and handle	1 25
3714	W. Haw, Ctg	154 90
3716	Hart & Riddell, letter heads	11 00
3718	Journal Print Co., Ltd., adv	20 10
3720	J. Judge, expense, Aug. and Sept., 1906	17 00
3722	W. J. Kelly, expense, Aug. and Sept., 1906	8 85
3724	H. I. Kirt, vegetables	53 40
3726	J. Lundy, meals	5 25
3728	Lindsay & McClusky, cement	723 10
3730	W. H. Mussen & Co., hand car	45 00
3732	McGreggor & Ryan, meals	7 00
3734	A. McIntosh, beef, boarding car	66 52
3736	McNair & Murrison, supplies, etc	15 55
3738	H. Maclean, hauling gravel	126 00
3740	Miller & Mahoney, lumber	241 91
3742	H. J. McAuslin, expenses	25 50
3744	G. A. McCarthy, unclaimed wages	13 64
3746	A. R. Macdonell, est Sept. 2nd cont	114,673 48
3748	A. R. Macdonell, sundry expenses	5,217 87
3750	Montreal Star Pub. Co., adv	63 00
3752	Mail Print Co., adv	29 25
3754	W. Newberry, bldg. roadway	400 00
3756	New Pub. Co., adv	63 00
3758	Office Specialty Mfg. Co., office furniture	52 80
3760	Ont. Sewer Pipe Co., pipe	223 26
3762	Ont. Lime Ass., plaster, etc.	195 50
3764	Purvis Bros., hardware	317 91
3766	E. A. Peterson, rent camp	11 00
3768	D. Pyke Co., Ltd., tent and poles	123 20
3770	Pembroke Lumber Co., lumber	451 20
3772	J. W. Richardson, hardware supp	192 71
3774	Rice & Goldfarb, board and lodging	13 00
3776	Rice Lewis & Son, Ltd., hardware supp	419 69
3778	Sherwin-Williams Co., depot paint	168 00
3780	J. Sears, expenses	11 20
3782	S. Swanson, grading Nip. Jct., Regina St.	566 99
3784	Stephenson & Son, adv	36 40
3786	W. B. Sowden, board bills	151 30
3788	W. Salter, supp	45 35
3790	J. Stitt, board bills	7 50
3792	Standard Inspection Bureau, inspection	80 00
3794	E. G. Strathy, ry. fares	13 10
3796	Saturday Night, Ltd., agreement forms	5 00
3798	G. Taylor Hardware Co., Ltd., hardware supp	274 66
3800	T. & N. O. Ry., sundry accounts	4,982 95
3802	Temagami Trans. Co., board bills	3 00
3804	Tor. Elec. Light Co., elec. current	2 21
3806	A. M. Thorne & Co., Burlap	175 45
3808	J. T. Welbourn, glass, coal oil, etc	1 79
3810	Wyse & Middlemist, trestle and coal chute contract	2,497 64

Voucher No.	Name.	Amount.

SEPTEMBER.

Voucher No.	Name.	Amount.
3812	Wyse & Middlemist, Englehart coal chute	97 20
3814	Wyse & Middlemist, tel. cont.	900 00
3816	Wyse & Middlemist, telephone cont.	738 00
3818	Wooling Bros., cont. Englehart town site	181 08
3820	A. J. Gurney, Ltd., groc. and prov.	2,239 57
3822	Tor. *World* (Ont. Bank), adv.	63 00
3824	*Haileyburian*, subscription	5 75
3826	G. H. Newton (Despatch), adv.	59 00
3828	A. R. Macdonell, est. 43 and 44 1st cont.	99,719 89
3830	Nat. Life Ass. Co., rent September	125 00
3832	D. E. Thomson, legal fees, Sept.	300 00
3834	C. B. Smith, expenses.	8 35
3836	J. R. Hogarth, ry. fare, etc.	7 65
3838	J. M. McNamara, legal fees.	307 40
	Total	$282,001 16

OCTOBER.

Voucher No.	Name.	Amount.
3805	J. L. Englehart, expenses October	38 00
3807	G. A. McCarthy, pay rolls October	23,737 07
3809	G. A. McCarthy, disbursements October, 1906	27 21
3811	G. A. McCarthy, expenses	10 25
3813	The Art Metropole, Ltd., eng. expenses	18 00
3815	Acton Burrows, stan. sign.	18 91
3817	Baines & Peckover, bars, etc.	98 00
3819	W. Briggs, binding St. Ry. Journal.	1 75
3821	Bell Tel. Co., long distance serv.	6 45
3823	Brown Bros., Ltd., supp.	14 38
3825	J. & S. Bessett Co., Ltd., velocipede.	70 00
3827	Blair, Sinclair & Smith, plans, etc.	193 25
3829	T. Birkett & Sons, hardware supplies	256 70
3831	Commercial Acetylene Co., light equip.	890 00
3833	Can. Westinghouse Co., air brake equip.	455 55
3835	Cobalt Hotel Co., board bills.	20 50
3837	Crossen Car Mfg. Co., rolling stock	10,710 00
3839	Crossen Car Mfg. Co., rolling stock.	10,550 00
3841	Mrs. M. A. Delaney, board bills.	1 70
3843	Dom. Bridge Co., girders for bridge.	3,944 50
3845	D. E. Doncaster, board bills.	2 15
3847	Empire Lumber Co., bricks and laths	26 75
3849	J. E. Farrell & Co., stn. heating equip.	86 04
3851	J. Foster, repairing field instrument	25 00
3853	W. Gohr, board bills.	1 30
3855	Grand & Toy, Ltd., office supp.	3 35
3857	Grand Union Hotel, board bills.	14 50
3859	W. Haw, carting	30 65
3861	M. C. Hendry, expenses.	25 75
3863	Harris Tie & Timber Co., lumber.	803 94
3865	R. E. Hagarty, board bills.	33 00
3867	H. W. Johnston, glass.	2 45
3869	J. Kilby, team hire.	9 00
3871	W. J. Kelly, expenses.	8 40
3873	H. I. Kert, vegetables.	32 75
3875	Ludowici-Celadon. overcharge on freight	43 50
3877	London Free Press Co., adv.	64 80
3879	H. T. McAuslin, expenses.	5 75
3881	A. McGougan, expenses.	16 93
3883	C. P. Chamberlin, hardware.	3 58
3885	Lumsden Lime Steamers, transportation, etc.	21 83
3887	Lindsay & McClusky, lime, etc.	4 40
3889	C. H. Mortimer Pub. Co., adv.	6 80
3891	A. McIntosh, supp.	262 31
3893	McGill University, testing material.	14 50

Voucher No.	Name.	OCTOBER.	Amount.
3895	McKee & Campbell, board bills		24 75
3897	McNair & Murrison, meals		69 90
3899	R. M. McDougal & Co., Ltd., parts for pumps		68 00
3901	McCamus & McKelvie, lumber		5 35
3903	Montreal Steel Works, guard rails		1,266 50
3905	Wm. Milne & Son, bldg. material		817 40
3907	Miller & Mahoney, lumber		192 56
3909	L. D. Neil, Laurentian water		4 00
3911	Ont. Sewer Pipe Co., pipe		238 12
3913	O'Connor Steamboat & Hotel Co., board bills		32 25
3915	D. O'Connor, board bills		51 38
3917	Ottawa Steel Casting Co., Ltd., water tanks (4)		1,760 00
3919	Ottawa *Citizen*, adv		18 60
3921	Office Specialty Mfg. Co., desks for offices		164 50
3923	J. J. O'Neil, expenses		18 51
3925	Purvis Bros., hardware supp		105 98
3927	N. L. Piper Ry. Supp. Co., switch locks key		21 50
3929	A. L. Perkins, vegetables		32 48
3931	Rathbun Co., mill work for stations		1,657 00
3933	A. W. Richardson, hardware supp		239 42
3935	A. J. Rorabeck, drugs		4 45
3937	J. Robertson Ct., Ltd., supp. water stn		407 53
3939	Rice Lewis & Son, Ltd., bill hooks		26 25
3941	Rhodes, Curry & Co., Ltd., rolling stock		18,349 86
3943	J. B. Smith & Sons, timber for bridges		667 02
3945	Saturday Night, Ltd., printing		30 50
3947	Scott & Jamieson, meals, etc		33 98
3949	W. Salter, supp		13 26
3951	Spector Print Co., adv		19 60
3953	Tor. Bolt & Forging Co., bolts		28 88
3955	G. Taylor Hardware Co., hardware supp		92 10
3957	Tor. Elec. Light Co., elec. current		5 56
3959	Toledo Foundry & Mac. Co., parts for steam shovel		158 33
3961	T. & N. O. Ry., supp., etc		18 70
3963	T. & N. O. Ry., sundry accts		11,295 39
3965	Woolings & Woolongs, supp		13 97
3967	A. J. Young, Ltd., groc. and prov		948 87
3969	A. R. Macdonell, est. October 2nd div		74,241 29
3971	Forest City Paving Co., extra work rd. house		237 45
3973	Forest City Paving Co., rd. house and mach. shop		3,975 43
3975	Forest City Paving Co., rd. house and mac. eng		7,738 88
3977	J. E. Farrell Co., Ltd., cobalt and Temagami stn., plumbing		931 00
3979	Bank Ottawa, Swan Swanson, work done		2,170 16
3981	C. J. Campbell, Uno Park water tank		408 24
3983	C. J. Campbell, removing culvert		52 25
3985	C. J. Campbell, Englehart water tank		338 58
3987	Wyse & Middlemist, Englehart coal chute		828 32
3989	Wyse & Middlemist, tel. contract		1,440 00
3991	Wyse & Middlemist, N. B. coal chute		4,673 87
3993	Wyse & Middlemist, tel. contract		293 85
3995	Wyse & Middlemist, extrs. tel. 2nd div		64 20
3997	Standard Inspection Bureau, insp. roll. stock		80 00
3999	Pembroke Lumber Co., lumber		388 86
4001	J. B. Smith & Son, lumber		593 37
4003	Frost Wire Fence Co., wire stretcher		4 40
4005	T. & N. O. Ry., amt. deducted Milne & Co		1,029 00
4007	Nat. Life Ass. Co., rent gen. offices, Oct		125 00
4009	D. E. Thomson, legal fees, Oct		300 00
4011	S. Henerofsky, Right-of-way		32 85
4013	W. A. Houser, "		30 45
4015	Mrs. Mary Ferguson, "		69
4017	M. Backer, "		6 21
4019	Hugh Jack, "		10 05
4021	M. McLean, "		17 13
4023	W. Heaslip, "		17 37

Voucher No.	Name.	OCTOBER.	Amount.
4025	A. Sword,	Right-of-way	13 26
4027	T. S. Taylor, "		17 91
4029	J. Sharp, "		159 80

Total $191,733 97

NOVEMBER.

3840	The Art Metropole, supplies	$ 14 29
3842	H. W. Angus, plans, etc.	660 00
3844	Fred. Armstrong, estimate heating station	1,597 50
3846	Bell elephone Co., long distance	8 40
3848	Bell Telephone North Bay, exchange North Bay	37 00
3850	Brown Bros., Ltd., supplies, office	15 00
3852	Brooks, Sanford Hardware Co., tiling Temag. stn	311 90
3854	A. Bregbois, expenses	5 45
3856	Can. Pac. Ry. Telegraph, telegrams	41 41
3858	Can. Rail Joint Co., angle bars	193 32
3860	Can. Genl. Electric Co., insulators and cross arm	239 34
3862	Can. Loco. Co., switching engines	27,310 00
3864	Can. Westinghouse Co., air gauges	9 00
3866	S. B. Clement, expenses	6 50
3868	L. O. Clark, making levels, etc.	6 50
3870	C. J. Campbell, team hire, etc.	222 94
3872	Robt. Churchill, surveying station grounds	3 75
3874	J. Clark, hardware supplies	2 75
3876	*The Cobalt Nugget*, advertising	8 40
3878	Jas. A. Cole Co., building material	59 45
3880	L. Chambers, board bills	3 50
3882	Mrs. M. A. Delaney, meals, etc.	70
3884	DeLaplante Lumber Co., team hire, etc.	17 50
3886	J. F. Daly (Pacific Hotel), board bills	4 50
3888	Treasurer of Ontario (Dept. L. F. & M.), timber dues	61 15
3890	Forest City Paving Co., est. Englehart road house	2,734 46
3892	Ferguson & McFadden, meals	29 90
3894	Bank of Ottawa (T. Forsythe), water service, Haileybury	85 00
3896	R. T. Gough, expenses	17 60
3898	Grand Union Hotel, board bills	32 00
3900	W. Gohr, board bills 5	6 65
3902	Grand & Toy, Ltd., office supplies	20 20
3904	W. Haw, teaming	10 50
3906	R. B. Herron, supplies	270 13
3908	Wm. Hugh, supplies 5	2 46
3910	*Herald* Printing Co., advertising	20 16
3912	Hotel Vendome, board bills	5 00
3914	Hart & Riddell, letter heads	7 50
3916	Jas. Hope & Sons, carbon, pencils	1 50
3918	J. C. Johnston, testing cement	100 00
3920	Jno. Judge, expenses	19 25
3922	Frank Kruger, board bills	8 60
3924	J. Keable, reimbursement for clothing lost	40 80
3926	A. R. Macdonell, est. 2nd November	22,438 53
3928	Robt. Morrison, board bills	3 00
3930	W. Meadows, supplies	2 50
3932	Frank Monroe, empty cement bags	65 00
3934	Montreal Steel Works, Ltd., guard rails	1,173 00
3936	W. Milne & Son, lumber	642 73
3938	" " "	439 57
3940	Traders' Bank (H. Marceau), lumber	277 50
3942	Miller & Mahoney, lumber	12 32
3944	G. A. McCarthy, disbursements	158 24
3946	" " sundry accounts	8 60
3948	" " unclaimed wages account	3 67
3950	" " expenses	28 10
3952	H. J. MacAuslan, expenses	6 60

Voucher No.	Name. NOVEMBER.	Amount.
3954	W. C. McDougall, expenses	21 25
3956	John McChesney, teaming end of steel	38 50
3958	A. McDonald, supplies	85
3960	McNair & Murison, supplies, teaming, etc.	165 75
3962	McNair & Murison, meals	31 25
3964	A. McGougan, expenses	35 60
3966	A. A. McIntosh, supplies	324 83
3968	Nipissing *Tribune* Pub. Co., advertising	16 80
3970	Northern Elec. & Mfg. Co., telephone booths	225 00
3972	Nipissing Fndry. & Mach. Co., sundry accts	4 75
3974	J. J. O'Neil, expenses	56 35
3976	N. L. Piper Ry. Supply Co., train order signals	129 00
3978	N. L. Piper Ry. Supply Co., switch lamps, etc.	124 00
3980	R. Parker, board bills, etc.	44 00
3982	Roberts Car Wheel Co., wheels and axles	247 00
3984	R. Parker, services	30 70
3986	S. Robinson, vegetables	10 00
3988	Rice, Lewis & Son, hardware supplies	405 81
3990	Stephenson & Son, advertising	15 50
3992	Standard Inspection Bureau, insp. rolling stock	174 85
3994	Bank of Ottawa (Swan Swanson), extras N. B. Jct.	36 30
3996	Bank of Ottawa (Swan Swanson), work done Nov., '06 ......5...	2,578 61
3998	Scott & Jamieson, supplies	60 63
4000	W. B. Sowden, board bills	8 75
4002	Jno. Sears, expenses	13 70
4004	T. & N. O. Ry., sundry accts.	2,112 72
4006	" " refund	154 00
4008	" " sundry accounts	3,391 70
4010	" " engineer's pay rolls, November	22,563 74
4012	" " refund	115 96
4014	*Toronto Daily Star*, advertising	2 25
4016	Thomas Co., supplies	8 45
4018	Toronto Elec. Light Co., electric current	6 89
4020	T. Tomlinson & Son, castings	759 29
4022	Toronto Bolt & Forging Co., rod iron and spikes	1,114 57
4024	Geo. Taylor Hardware Co., hardware supplies	117 95
4026	Wyse & Middlemist, est. Englehart coal chute	2,451 50
4028	Wyse & Middlemist, est. North Bay trestle and coal chute	1,147 66
4030	Wyse & Middlemist, est. telephone construction	3,004 20
4032	Wilson Carbine Co., carbide	17 50
4034	J. T. Wilbourne, hardware supplies	1 25
4036	W. C. Woolings, supplies	88 73
4038	A. J. Young, Ltd., supplies	384 90
4040	J. W. Richardson, supplies	83 68
4042	Heavener Bros., board bills	8 00
4044	National Life Ass. Co., office rent, November	125 00
4046	D. E. Thomson, K.C., legal expense	300 00
4048	A. R. Macdonell, McDougall's chute	39,583 08
4050	A. R. Macdonell, penalty account	33,400 00
4052	T. & N. O. Ry., advance from operation	138,453 39
4054	D. C. Maymond, right of way, 2nd div	2 79
4056	H. Harmer, right of way	19 35
4058	Jas. Field, right of way	71 77
4060	Jas. Tomlinson, right of way 2nd div.	100 00
4062	Wm. Robinson, right of way 2nd div.	18 12
4064	Jno. Brisco, right of way 2nd div.	40 77
4066	Wm. Ferguson, right of way 2nd div.	20 40
4068	A. Heaslip, right of way 2nd div.	2 82
4070	Metropolitan Bank, interest	10 60
4075	Swan Swanson, grading 1st div.	500 00

$314,394 13

Total cash disbursements as of Dec. 31, '06............................$2,067,802 52

DECEMBER.

Expenditure 1906, Paid January 1907.

Voucher No.	Name.	Amount.
4031	Benjamin Mean, right of way	$ 25 45
4033	A. R. Macdonell	3,129 25
4035	G. A. McCarthy, pay rolls	18,057 06
4037	Thomson, Tilley & Johnson, legal expenses	783 00
4039	Macdonell, McMaster, Geary, legal expenses	1,208 95
4041	Long Lake Milling Co., lumber	495 40
4043	The Art Metropole, Ltd., office blue prints	7 44
4045	Fred. Armstrong Co., Ltd., est. plumbing	900 00
4047	Bell Tel. Co. of Can., long distance	4 15
4049	Blair, Sinclair & Smith, surveys	11 00
4051	Brown Bros., Ltd., office stationery	41 08
4053	Can. Pac. Ry. Tel. Co., telegrams	14 26
4055	S. B. Clement, expenses	25 95
4057	Can. Westinghouse Co., air brakes, etc	549 00
4059	Connor, Clarke & Monds, report	50 00
4061	Crossen Car Mfg. Co., 4 coaches	39,540 00
4063	Davis Acetylene Co., generators, etc., Temagami	370 85
4065	Treasurer of Ontario, Dept. Lands and mines, labour	10 50
4067	Treasurer of Ontario, Dept. Lands and Mines, board	6 00
4069	Dempster Bros., ties	100 30
4071	J. R. Eaton, lumber, sashes, etc	125 40
4073	Forest City Paving & Con. Co., labour	129 12
4075	McRae & McRae, Globe P. Co., subscriptions	5 00
4077	Grand & Toy, Ltd., office supplies	7 55
4079	Grand Union Hotel, board	4 50
4081	M. C. Hendry, travelling expenses	9 75
4083	W. Hugh, hardware supplies	1 75
4085	Hart & Riddell, letter heads	6 50
4087	W. J. Kelly, expenses	11 55
4089	J. McNamara, legal expenses	313 42
4091	A. McIntosh, meat	39 75
4093	G. A. McCarthy, disbursements	21 20
4095	G. A. McCarthy, expenses	23 65
4097	G. A. McCarthy, unclaimed wages	39 40
4099	A. R. Macdonell, Est. No. 31	57,849 58
4101	Jno. D. McDonald, board lodging	30 90
4103	H. J. McAuslan, expenses	11 10
4105	Wm. Pollock, ties	54 67
4107	Purvis Bros., supplies, shovels	27 10
4109	The Rathbun Co., conductors' vans	5,000 00
4111	A. C. Rorabeck, supplies	70
4113	Rice Lewis & Son, pipe cutters, lubricators, etc	124 93
4115	J. T. Sasche, inspection at "Y"	2 00
4117	W. H. Salter, washing blankets	16 80
4119	M. Sinkovitch, washing blankets	18 60
4121	Jos. Smith, ties	107 44
4123	W. D. Sowden, board	2 50
4125	Standard Inspection Bureau, insp. rolling stock	84 65
4127	Standard Inspection Bureau, insp. roof trusses, etc	20 66
4129	Geo. Taylor Hardware Co., hardware supplies	1 95
4131	Toronto Electric Light Co., Ltd., elec. light	14 65
4133	T. & N. O. Ry., advance	55,000 00
4135	T. & N. O. Ry., mattresses, etc	34 43
4137	T. & N. O. Ry., freight charges, etc	9,065 01
4139	T. & N. O. Ry., unclaimed wages	18 69
4141	T. & N. O. Ry., freight charges	95 26
4143	T. & N. O. Ry., wages of trainmen	759 14
4145	A. J. Young, Ltd., supplies	3 50
4147	Wyse & Middlemist, distributing tel. poles	230 45
4149	Wyse & Middlemist, Englehart coal chute	1,853 54
4151	Wyse & Middlemist, N. B. coal chute	675 00
4153	Woollings Bros., Englehart Townsite	57 78
4155	Woollings Bros., ties	303 67

Voucher No.	Name.	Amount.
	DECEMBER.	
4157	Warwick Bros. & Rutter, stationery, vouchers	14 00
4159	T. & N. O. Ry., prop. office salaries	2,239 70
4161	C. R. Boucher, expenses	16 76
4163	C. J. Campbell, Uno Park tank	45 36
4165	D. E. Thomson, legal fees	300 00
4167	National Life Ass. Co., rent general offices	125 00
4169	J. M. McNamara, legal expenses	75 00
4171	H. W. Pearson	250 00
4173	J. L. Englehart, remuneration as chairman, Nov. '06	208 33
4175	C. B. Smith, salary as consulting engineer, Nov. '06	83 33
4177	Edith Hayes, right of way	350 00
4179	Henry Leng, right of way	2,998 11
4181	Robert Scott, right of way	2,250 00
4183	McEwen & Morgan, right of way	282 11
4185	Can. Construction Co., refund deposit on contract	2,000 00

$208,770 58

REPORT

UPON

The Care of the

Feeble-Minded in Ontario

1907

PRINTED BY ORDER OF

THE LEGISLATIVE ASSEMBLY OF ONTARIO

TORONTO
Printed by L. K. CAMERON, Printer to the King's Most Excellent Majesty
1907

WARWICK BRO'S & RUTTER, Limited,] Printers,
TORONTO.

THE CARE OF THE FEEBLE-MINDED IN ONTARIO.

Sir,—I have the honor to present, in accordance with instructions, such information in regard to the care of the higher grades of the feeble-minded as I have been able to get from the best available sources, and also a Preliminary Special Report on the Census of the Feeble-minded in Ontario, as a part of "the securing and compiling of such information as would enable the Government and the House to fairly judge the necessity for and value of provision for the care of feeble-minded women from fifteen to forty-five. This would, it appears to me, require the co-operation of the Asylum authorities and the municipal authorities as well, all of which I should expect would gladly co-operate. The work of providing such a home would involve considerable initial expense, which should be incurred only on data as complete as we could get together."

"The value of a census is at once apparent." (Extract from a letter of instructions from the Hon. the Provincial Secretary.)

What "Feeble Minded" Means.

There is in different countries some slight variation of meaning in the term "Feeble-minded." Thus the French include all degrees of mental defect under the one term "L'Idiotie," and the Americans similarly use the term "Feeble-minded" to include all suffering from mental defect in any degree whatever from the lowest grade of idiocy to the highest grade of the feeble-minded. On the other hand, the practice of British authorities is to draw a careful distinction between idiots and imbeciles on the one hand, and those merely feeble-minded on the other. The following terms are convenient and accurate for use:

Ament—One whose mind from birth has been defective.

The Aments may be subdivided into:

1. Idiots.
2. Imbeciles.
3. Feeble-minded.

The word "Idiot" is derived from the Greek and denotes one who has no share in ordinary public affairs. The term "idiot" indicates those persons in whom certain brain cells are lacking. No amount of training can raise them into reasoning beings. Disease or defect of the brain, either congenital or acquired during the development of the brain, is the cause of idiocy.

An imbecile is an idiot of a higher grade. Thus imbeciles may be taught to perform more or less automatic actions. They can feed and dress themselves and even do simple work which does not require the power of initiative. Where the condition is not absolutely congenital, but brought about by disease of the brain subsequent to birth, the term "imbecile" is usually applied.

The highest grade of aments, the feeble-minded, differs considerably from the other two grades. The feeble-minded are capable of useful work. They are also capable of profiting by training and instruction. It would seem as if they possessed certain brain cells in a state of quiescence, capable of some development or of some degeneration. Thus, time spent in teaching them to read, write, and cipher is largely wasted. But they can do farm-work, household work, washing, cleaning, knitting, sewing, weaving, sometimes lace-making. They can make clothes under supervision and with some help. Cleaning and polishing operations they are often expert at. What they cannot do is to manage their own affairs, far less take any share in directing

[3]

others, as all normal persons do. They lack the power of restraint and in-
hibition. The feeble-minded are difficult to define, but not difficult to re-
cognize. They are below those of normal, though small, intellect, but above
actual imbeciles and idiots. They are able to act and may speak fairly well,
though usually more or less foolishly. They can partly, or even wholly,
earn their living under supervision, but they are not capable of protecting
and taking care of themselves out in the world at large. They lack prudence
and self-control. They have not proper will or judgment. Hence we find
them in maternity hospitals, refuges, gaols and poor houses. Thus I have
seen and carefully examined in the course of this inquiry a young woman
of 27 who can do a good day's work under direction. She does a large family
washing in a day under direction. She is strong and willing and kindly
in disposition, but she knows no better than to accept ten cents as her wage
for a day's washing, and certain well-to-do farmers in this Province were
not ashamed to pay her ten cents for her hard day's work. And her moral
sense is on a par with her financial sense, the result of which is that she is
the mother of four illegitimate children, the oldest of whom is in the Asylum
at Orillia, the next two are evidently feeble-minded, and the fourth, an in-
fant born the day before my first visit to the mother, is likely to be no better.
This woman will always remain a child as far as any financial and moral
control of herself and her affairs is concerned. In a home or institution
where she would be safe from evil persons she could be usefully and profitably
and happily employed and would be a burden on no one. As it is, she and
her four children have cost the Province and benevolent citizens no small
sum for maintenance already, and unless steps are speedily taken to prevent
it, the number will increase and the cost in proportion.

Historical.

Though the Abbess Euphrasia (A.D. 335-395), and St. Vincent de
Paul (A.D. 1576-1660) attempted to train idiots, it was really not till
1846 when Seguin published his great work "Traitement moral, Hygiene
et Education des idiots et des autres enfants Arrieres," that any
attempt was made to attack earnestly the problem of these mental defectives.
Dr. Edouard Seguin was one of the assistants of Itard, who in 1799 took
a "wild boy" found in the forests of Aveyron and attempted to teach and
train him. Though the efforts of Itard were not very successful, the efforts
of Dr. Seguin had better results, and in 1838 he established a School for
Idiots in the Hospital for Incurables at Paris. Dr. Seguin afterwards lived
in New York City and carried on his work there, assisting to establish the
first schools for Idiots in the United States.

Care of the Feeble-Minded in Great Britain—Special Classes.

· The recognition of and provision for the higher grades of aments, the
feeble-minded, was the next step. In England the guardians of workhouses
were the first to begin this movement. They saw the need of custodial care
for those workhouse girls who are evidently so mentally defective, and therefore morally weak, as to be in obvious danger themselves, and to be a danger
to the community when they take their discharge, as they are allowed to do,
at will. Homes for feeble-minded women and girls were opened by private
benevolence in London (1887 and 1890) and Birmingham, (by Miss Stacey)
in 1892. The Charity Organization Society and the British Medical Association took the matter up and a great interest was aroused in the subject.

Societies were established—the Lancashire and Cheshire Society for the Permanent Care of the Feeble-minded, the National Association for the Welfare of the Feeble-minded, the Society of the Crown of Our Lord, the National Union of Separate Schools, and the After-care Committees being the most important—the work of which increased the knowledge of the needs of the mentally defective classes, especially feeble-minded children, and impressed upon the public mind the dangers the feeble-minded were exposed to and unprotected from, and the danger and burden which the community and the nation were exposed to in the rapid increase of the feeble-minded and their tendency to swell the ranks of the unemployed, vagrant, degenerate and criminal classes. In April, 1892, the first "Special Classes" for mentally defective children in England were established in Leicester, and in July of the same year General Moberly, who will ever be remembered as the most prominently active friend on the London School Board that mentally defective children ever had, was instrumental in establishing these "Special Classes" in connection with the London School Board. There are now about 75 "Special Schools or "Special Classes" in London alone, with an attendance of about 5,000 children.

It is in connection with these Special Schools in London, in 1894, that we have the first evidence of public attention in Ontario being directed to this matter.

Royal Commission Appointed—Visit to America.

Meantime by the efforts of private individuals, School Boards, and the above mentioned Associations, as well as by the feeling of the general public that the problem of the feeble-minded in Great Britain is assuming gigantic proportions and becoming a public danger, the attention of the British Government was directed to these matters, and an act was passed in 1899 enabling School Boards to establish special schools or special classes for the feeble-minded, and finally, on the recommendation of the Home Secretary, a Royal Commission was appointed by His Majesty the King, in August, 1904, to consider the existing methods of dealing with idiots and epileptics, and with imbecile, feeble-minded, or defective persons, not certified under the lunacy laws, and in view of the hardship and danger resulting to such persons and the community from insufficient provision for their care, training and control, to report as to the amendments in the law and other measures which should be adopted in the matter, due regard being had to the expense involved in any such proposals, and to the best means of securing economy therein.

The members of the Royal Commission as at first constituted were:— The Marquis of Bath, Chairman; Mr. W. P. Byrne, C.B., of the Home Office; Mr. Charles Hobhouse, M.P.; Dr. Frederick Needham, Commissioner in Lunacy and Ex-President of Medico-Psychological Association; Mr. Henry D. Greene, K.C., M.P.; Mr. Charles Chadwyck-Healey, K.C.; Rev. Harold Nelson Burden, Mr. W. H. Dickinson, Chairman of the National Association for Promoting the Welfare of the Feeble-minded; Dr. Charles S. Loch, Secretary of the Charity Organization Society; Mrs. Hume Pinsent, of Birmingham, Chairman of the After-care Committee of the Birmingham School Board. There were afterwards added Dr. H. B. Donkin, one of H. M. Commissioners for Prisons, and Dr. J. C. Dunlop, Inspector under the Inebriates' Act in Scotland and Medical Adviser to the Prison Commissioners, Scotland. The Marquis of Bath having resigned, the King appointed the Earl of Radnor to his vacant place.

This Commission, in September, 1905, appointed five of its number, viz.: Mr. W. P. Byrne, Mr. Dickinson, Dr. Dunlop, Dr. Donkin and Mrs. Pinsent to visit America and inspect institutions for the feeble-minded and report on them.

On the arrival of the Commissioners in America the following letter was addressed to the Chairman, W. P. Byrne, C.B., by the Honorable the Provincial Secretary:—

DEPARTMENT OF THE PROVINCIAL SECRETARY OF ONTARIO,
TORONTO, Oct. 30th, 1905.

"W. P. BYRNE, C.B.,
    In care of Sir Percy Sanderson,
        British Consul General,
            New York:

DEAR SIR,—My attention has been called to the article published in the *British Medical Journal* to the effect that your Commission has been deputed to visit this Continent for the purpose of enquiring into the arrangements respecting such persons as might come within the terms of reference of your Commission. I have pleasure in extending to you a very cordial invitation to visit such of our institutions in Ontario as might best promote the objects you have in view. Our officials in charge of this work here would be delighted to meet your Commission and place themselves at your disposal.

Very truly yours,
(Sgd.) W. J. HANNA."

The reply received to this letter stated that the Commissioners greatly regretted that they were unable to accept the invitation of the Honorable the Provincial Secretary, as they had no instructions to visit Canada. (The explanation is given below).

In accordance with a letter of instructions received on Nov. 23rd, 1905, I left Toronto on that day at 5.20 p.m. and spent three days in New York in conference with the Commissioners.. Nothing could exceed the cordiality with which I was received and the kindness with which they gave me from the great store of valuable information possessed by the Commission and by each of its members. It should be mentioned that Dr. Dunlop, one of the Commissioners, had, on his own account, visited Toronto, as the Commissioners were travelling westward, and spent some hours in visiting the Infants' Home and The Haven in this city. Of his observations made in visiting these institutions he kindly gave me the benefit.

It is expected that the report of this Commission will be complete in three volumes, the first being mainly concerned with the English evidence taken from November 14th, 1904, to August 4th, 1905. The other volumes will contain an account of the visit of the Commissioners to America, the evidence for Scotland, and the evidence for Ireland. The complete report will probably not be ready for presentation to His Majesty and the Houses of Parliament until the end of 1907. It will then be the source of information on this subject.

I was informed by the Chairman of this Commission that on the appointment of this Royal Commission by His Majesty, letters were sent to all parts of the British Empire and elsewhere asking for information and assistance in regard to ascertaining methods and results of the care and control of the feeble-minded, and that the answer to this letter from Canada was in some three lines, of a purely formal character, and stated that nothing was done for the feeble-minded in Canada, and that little or not interest was taken in the subject. Consequently, when certain of the Commissioners were deputed to visit the United States, they were given no instructions to visit Canada. I have endeavored to trace this extraordinary communication from "Canada," but so far unsuccessfully.

As instructed, I laid before the Commissioners all the information at our disposal, including the 37th Annual Report of the Lunatic and Idiot Asylums of the Province of Ontario, and other information already laid before the Government, such as the number of feeble-minded women in certain Maternity Hospitals, Refuges, Homes, and charitable institutions, January to June, 1905; and further, the opinions of a number of Ontario Educationists in regard to the number of feeble-minded children in the schools of Ontario and what should be done for them.

Summary.

The things impressed upon my mind by study of this subject for years and more immediately by conference with the members of the Royal Commission are:

1st. The serious and important nature of the problem of the feeble-minded. Of all the witnesses examined by the Commission, every one has taken a serious view of the matter. A general opinion is expressed that the number of feeble-minded in Great Britain is probably as great as the number of the insane—not less than 100,000, and that the problem should be dealt with by Parliament.

2nd. The favorable position occupied in this matter by this Province as compared with the older parts of the Empire. As the Commissioners put it in conversation: "Ontario has an opportunity to take a fresh start in deal-"ing with this evil before it has grown too great to cope with it satisfac-"torily."

3rd. The number of mental defectives tends to increase, and there is not adequate provision to care for them. Existing institutions fail to reach milder cases of mental defect, i.e., the higher grades of the feeble-minded, though these higher grades on account of their numerous progeny and for other reasons, are more of a menace and a burden to the community than other feeble-minded persons.

4th. The function of "Special Schools" as a place of improvement and training for the feeble-minded, and also as a place of observation, a kind of "Sorting House." Home care is unsuitable for, at any rate, the majority of these cases, and special boarding-schools are urgently required in the interests of the individual, the family and the nation.

In Britain the feeble-minded children are, as far as possible, sent to the "Special Schools" established in Leicester, London, Birmingham and elsewhere, under the Act of 1899. So far, of these children in the "Special Schools" about ten per cent. become self-supporting or nearly so, thirty per cent. more might possibly be regarded, if they have very excellent home care, as having a chance to become fairly respectable citizens, but the remaining sixty per cent. cannot possibly be regarded as fit for anything but permanent custodial care in Homes with industrial colonies attached.

5th. The importance of having a census of the feeble-minded taken as a basis for action.

6th. The necessity of custodial homes for feeble-minded women and girls and the good results observed as a consequence of establishing such homes.

7th. It is possible to ascertain the cause of many, if not of all cases of mental defect, and if this knowledge were applied, the number of mental defectives would largely decrease instead of increasing.

There can be no doubt that feeble-mindedness goes hand in hand with moral weakness and physical weakness or at least a poor standard of physical health. Among other causes of feeble-mindedness are:

1st. Deficient nutrition in the early years of life. The brain is starved.

2nd. The employment of married women at the child-bearing period in factories, etc.

3rd. The marriage of relatives, e.g. cousins. The children are more often defective than the children of other marriages.

4th. Extreme age or extreme youth of the parents.

5th. A hereditary tendency to tuberculosis.

6th. Chronic alcoholism in one or both parents.

7th. Descent from a feeble-minded, criminal or insane ancestry.

These are not theories or conjectures. They are facts ascertained by the patient investigation and long experience of government officials, physicians, and others who have studied the problem of the feeble-minded, and been impressed with "the total inadequacy of the provision made for dealing "with the enormous class of mental incapables who, not being certified "lunatics, are unfit either to earn a livelihood or look after themselves or their affairs."—*The Lancet.*

Preliminary Report on the Census of the Feeble-minded in Ontario.

In preparing a census of the feeble-minded, I endeavored first of all to avail myself of the assistance of the large number of persons, both officials and private persons, who are known to be interested in this matter, especially Dr. R. W. Bruce Smith, Inspector of Hospitals and Public Charities; Dr. Beaton, Medical Superintendent of the Asylum for Idiots at Orillia; Mr. J. J. Kelso, Superintendent of Neglected and Dependent Children, members of the Local Council of Women and others.

To all these officials and others I beg to express my thanks for the very great assistance they have rendered. The municipal officials, the police authorities, the asylum authorities, as well as those in charge of hospitals, homes and charitable institutions generally, the officers and members of the National Council of Women, and of Benevolent Societies, as well as the educational authorities, have all expressed, by word and act, their sense of the importance of the Government's action, and their willingness to co-operate in any way.

The only Provincial institution for the care of the feeble-minded is the Asylum for Idiots in Orillia, which is one of the best known institutions in the Province, the site, a very beautiful one, extending over many acres and sloping down to the shores of Lake Couchiching. The site is well adapted to the work of the institution. A beautiful grove and extensive lawns add to its attractiveness and suitability as a permanent residence for those who by reason of their great and irremediable disabilities, can enjoy not many pleasures. This magnificent site was selected years ago by the present superintendent. Some of the higher grades of feeble-minded are confined here because there is nowhere else that they can be sent.

As to separate provision for the higher grades of the feeble-minded it would seem that the first public attempt in this direction in Ontario was made in 1894. In that year Mr. James L. Hughes, Inspector of Public Schools for Toronto, was in London, England, and took occasion to visit the "Special Schools" then just established. He saw some 400 children who were in attendance at these schools. On his return to Toronto he interested Dr. Fisher, the Chairman of the Toronto Public Schools, in the matter, and the Chairman and Inspector visited all the Toronto Public Schools during the autumn of 1894 with a view to ascertain how many mentally defective children were in attendance. They found about 20, and it was not thought that this was a large enough number to warrant the establishment of a "Special Class" for the feeble-minded.

In 1897, Dr. A. M. Rosebrugh, Secretary for Ontario of the National Conference of Charities and Corrections, wrote to the National Council of Women of Canada, then assembled in their fourth annual meeting at Halifax, asking the co-operation of the Council in making enquiries regarding the number of unmarried women in each Province under 40 years of age who are either idiotic, semi-imbecile, weak-minded, or who from any cause are incapable when at large of taking care of themselves. In answer to this request a committee was appointed to make enquiries and report at the fifth annual meeting held in Ottawa in 1898. The committee reported accordingly the result of their labours at length, including the following estimate of the number of such women in each Province as follows:—

Manitoba	5
Assiniboia	4
P. E. Island	2
Quebec	39
New Brunswick	150
Nova Scotia	135
Ontario	900

A similar committee has been appointed by the National Council of Women from year to year. In 1899 the following resolution was passed:—

RESOLVED. That in accordance with the suggestion of the Standing Committee upon "The care of feeble-minded Women," the National Council do petition the various Provincial Governments, asking them to conduct a careful investigation into the matter in the several Provinces. Be it further resolved that a deputation of members of the several Local Councils, with the several Provincial Vice-Presidents as Conveners, do wait upon their Provincial Governments to press the importance of the matter upon them."

In 1901, the committee again reported, emphasizing the necessity of enlightening the public about this evil, and at the suggestion of the National Conference of Charities and Corrections, and with the approval of the Ontario Government, Mrs. Evans of Hamilton, Convener of the Standing Committee, and Mrs. Willoughby Cummings, Secretary of the National Council, visited the institutions for the care of the feeble-minded at Rome, Syracuse, and Newark, New York State, and also at Orillia in Ontario, and a similar report was submitted at the annual meeting in 1902. On May 20th, 1903, a large deputation from the National Council, the Prisoners' Aid Association, the Associated Charities, and other organizations waited upon the Honorable G. W. Ross, Premier of Ontario, and the Honorable J. S. Stratton, Provincial Secretary, to present a largely signed petition from citizens of the Province of Ontario, requesting that provision should be made for the custodial care of feeble-minded women. The Premier and the Provincial Secretary both agreed as to the wisdom of the request, and promised to do what was possible to carry the same into effect.

The committee appeared again at the annual meeting in Winnipeg in 1904, reporting progress, and once more in 1905, at the annual meeting in Charlottetown, and in November, 1905, another large deputation including representatives from all parts of the Province, waited upon the Premier, the Honorable J. P. Whitney, and the Provincial Secretary, Honorable W. J. Hanna, to lay this matter before them. In June, 1906, the Honorable, the Provincial Secretary gave instructions to proceed at once with the taking of a census, and the first step was the issuing of the following letter. It was sent to officers of those associations who had already petitioned the Government, also to all municipal officials, police authorities, Governors of Gaols, Superintendents of all Asylums, Hospitals and Charitable Institutions, officers of the Children's Aid Societies, City Missionaries and Deaconesses, officers of Benevolent Societies, Educational Authorities, and private persons who were known to be interested, and others. In all about 3,000 letters were sent out, and a large number of replies have been received.

DEPARTMENT OF THE PROVINCIAL SECRETARY, ONTARIO.

Confidential.

Re Care of the Feeble-Minded

TORONTO, June 13th, 1896.

MY DEAR ————, —The Government of Ontario has received numerous petitions and requests for better provision for the care and control of the feeble-minded in this Province, who have not been certified to as insane or idiots, and yet are not able to protect themselves. Imbecility and heredity are known to be the most prolific of the causes of pauperism and crime. It has been determined to undertake a complete enumeration of such feeble-minded persons.

I am, therefore, instructed by the Hon. W. J. Hanna, Provincial Secretary, to ask your assistance in this matter, and respectfully request that you will forward to me at your earliest convenience the names and addresses of any such feeble-minded persons known to you and any further information in reference to this matter which you may deem of importance.

Any information you may be pleased to give me will be regarded as confidential.

I have the honor to remain,
Your obedient servant,
HELEN MACMURCHY.

Please address reply:
Dr. Helen MacMurchy,
133 Bloor St., East.
Toronto.

Results of the Census.

In all, the names and addresses of 1,385 feeble-minded persons have been thus obtained from responsible officials, either by letter or interview, frequently by my own examination of feeble-minded persons reported to me.

```
No. of women  ..............................................   676
No. of girls  ....................................................   183
No. of men ....................................................   418
No. of boys ....................................................   108
                                                                  ―――――
                                                                  1,385
```

This number is exclusive of school children as reported. See below. No doubt the fact that this enquiry was first set on foot in connection with the number of mentally defective women and girls in the Province may, to some extent, explain the proportion in the above figures. I have, however, reported all whose names were given to me by responsible officials and others well qualified to judge. In some cases the ages were given. Of 258 women where the age was given,

      66 were between 16 and 20 years
    101 were between 20 and 30 years
      44 were between 30 and 40 years
      29 were between 40 and 50 years
      10 were between 50 and 60 years
       8 were over 60 years.

Of 67 girls where the age was given—
      20 were under seven years
      47 were between 7 and 16 years.

Of 104 men where the age was given—
      24 were between 16 and 20 years
      37 were between 20 and 30 years
      19 were between 30 and 40 years
      15 were between 40 and 50 years
       6 were between 50 and 60 years
       3 were over 60 years.

Of 35 boys where the age was given—
      18 were under seven years
      17 were between 7 and 16 years.

The above figures do not include any allowance for such vague statements as "a large number," "many," &c., &c.

Urgent Cases—Home Care Inadequate.

It is manifest that these returns are not yet complete, and also require to be sifted and classified. [Since beginning to write this report sixty-one additional interviews and letters have been added, and some long lists have been received, none of which are included in the above figures.] There are, among the answers received, 43 special and urgent appeals for certain cases, in which it is felt that something should be done at once. The number of these urgent cases, so reported, is 121. These are all feeble-minded women and girls. In 48 cases the remark is made that these feeble-minded persons are well cared for, but in other cases even the best of home care is realised to be insufficient. E. G. File No. 112, Special Case, Girl of 19. A recent occurrence has impressed upon her father the fact that he cannot supervise her or give her the protection at home that is necessary. Able and willing to pay, he asks "Do you know of any institution, public or Church, where good but weak-minded girls could be trained, if possible?"

In a good many cases these mentally defective persons are in homes, and are sometimes very well cared for. A number of letters express great anxiety as to their fate when the home is broken up. Quite a number are kept as maids and workers under supervision in Government and charitable institutions. This also is often a good arrangement. They are placed as inmates in the Haven, Toronto, and similar institutions throughout the country, where the authorities feel that they dare not let them out, and yet it is a great detriment to the work of the institution and the other inmates to keep them. In the Industrial Refuge, Toronto, where 24 out of 36 inmates are at present more or less feeble-minded, they are well and permanently taken care of and usefully employed. This institution is filled to its utmost capacity. In the Home of the Good Shepherd at Toronto, a large number of mentally defective women and girls are permanently cared for, and are also successfully employed.

The Houses of Refuge.

It is quite different in the Houses of Refuge, where there are a large number of feeble-minded. My returns so far, which are by no means complete, give the names of 126 such persons in the Houses of Refuge or Poor Houses. In addition, 58 are now, or have recently been, in gaols, and 114 have been, during the last few years in the Mercer Reformatory, and from these places they come and go, each time coming back worse and more degraded, and there is at present no way to prevent the very great evils that constantly arise. Three examples among many are given below.

From a small town.

"There are two feeble-minded girls in the House of Refuge now with babies a few months old, according to rules they must stay a year and take care of the babies, then the girls are let go, perhaps to come back again before the year is out."

From the Governor of a gaol.

"I am decidedly opposed to the practice of sending feeble-minded persons to the gaol as has been done hitherto. I think it is barbarous and inhuman, and I am glad that the present Government have taken steps to partially remedy this state of things."

Visit to Rescue Home at ————, File No. 209.

"Have at present five girls, ages 30, 27, 22, 19 and 18, who are feeble-minded." One feeble-minded girl was admitted only four weeks before my visit with twin babies, both girls, (illegitimate, a few weeks old). The Superintendent has not room for these girls, and cannot well keep them, but feels that she cannot send them out, as they are not able to protect themselves. She "wishes there were any place where they would be cared for and kept from further harm."

Descendants of The Feeble-Minded.

In six cases special attention is drawn to consanguinity in the parents as a cause of feeble-mindedness in the children. In 158 cases the feeble-minded person mentioned is related closely to some other feeble-minded person also mentioned.

Of the numbers reported above it was stated that 8 of the men were married, and 71 of the women. Several of these who have written to the Department express themselves strongly on this serious matter. e.g., Case of H. R., File No. 425. "Parents insisted on taking her out of the institution where she was, in order to marry her to a man who was 'not very bright.' In two years returned to the same institution asking for admission with her child, also feeble-minded." The Superintendent of the Institution expressed himself as being of opinion that this marriage was a crime.

"Relatives should not be allowed to marry, as this seems a very great source of evil, and the issuing of Marriage Licenses should be left to the magistrates of the land. Idiots marrying is sure to bear its fruits." Township Clerk.

"Yours received this a.m. *re* feeble-minded. I am very much pleased to see that the Provincial Government are going to take steps in that direction, as it seems there is no place for these poor unfortunates except the County Gaols. We have one of such. We at first sent him to ————, but they let him go saying it was not a suitable place for him. He then wandered about the country, was arrested as a vagrant and sent to Gaol in Toronto, from there back here. We then had him arrested under the same charge, and he is now in ———— Gaol. His parents are living, neither very bright. This man has a wife, not much better than himself, and one child. I think a man who issues a license, and a Minister who marries people like these, should be prosecuted, as it peoples the world with a very undesirable class, and yet no fault of their own. Anything I can do to help on the work I will gladly do."

The marriage of such feeble-minded persons brings about such terrible consequences as are related in the next few cases.

Application from the County Attorney of ———— to admit to Orillia. A family, 17 in number, all descendants of one feeble-minded woman, all of whom are idiotic or feeble-minded and all illegitimate. Several were admitted to the Asylum at Orillia.

File No. 507. The B. family, three generations, consists of—
Grandparents—both over 70.

Parents—two daughters; elder married, has 4 children; younger married, has 5 children.

"This whole family are feeble-minded, and the Clergyman who married these two daughters should have been sent to prison." Opinion of the Police Magistrate.

The records at the Asylum at Orillia show the same thing. Number of inmates at present in the Asylum who are related to other inmates, at present in the Asylum.

Two of the same family, 18 times
Three of the same family, 9 times
Four of the same family, 2 times
Five of the same family, 2 times.

Total, 81 inmates are relatives of other inmates. We have a case here of a mother P.S. and her son J.S. Another A.R. and her son F.R., and one E.H. and her daughter V.H. Then we have one J.B. and her daughter W.B., and the history says that this mother gave birth to 8 illegitimate children. In nearly every case where there are two or more feeble-minded members of one family, the history of either one parent or the other is bad, showing that heredity has a great deal to do with feeble-mindedness. A. H. Beaton, Medical Superintendent.

The P. Family. Mr. J. J. Kelso, Superintendent of Neglected and Dependent Children for the Province of Ontario, to whom I am indebted for much valuable assistance, drew my attention to this case. It is a dreadful case. In April 1895, Mr. Kelso was asked to take charge of a neglected, dependent, illegitimate and feeble-minded child, E.P., then in the Industrial Home at ———— with her mother, S. P., who was an inmate of the same institution, and was also feeble-minded and illegitimate. On January 30th,

1897, Mr. Kelso discovered that a child, W. B., feeble-minded and illegitimate, whom he was asked to take charge of was the grandson of S.P. mentioned above. This boy is now in the Orillia Asylum. Finally, on May 3rd, 1906, Mr. Kelso found that a family of neglected children living in another place were also grandchildren of S.P. The history of this P. family was then investigated as fully as possible and may be briefly stated thus:

About thirty years ago there was in the Poor House at ————— a feeble-minded woman named S.P. She was able to do a good day's work, and she can do a good day's work still at the age of between 50 and 60. She was allowed to leave the Poor House and come back at her own will. Her history is mixed up with the history of at least three evil men. She was no more able to protect herself than a child. The consequence is that to-day, instead of one feeble-minded person, the Province has at least twelve such persons—this woman, her seven children, and her four grandchildren—every one, including the mother, illegitimate and all feeble-minded. Such a case as this needs no comment, but it may be pointed out that if S. P. had been cared for as a ward of the Province years ago, it would have saved the Province thousands of dollars.

Mentally Defective Children in Schools.

Sufficient time has not yet elapsed for the educational authorities to make anything like complete returns. But there are a number of teachers and others in Ontario who have been thinking of this problem for years, as the following letters will show.

"1· In my work of teaching here I have several times come in contact· with feeble-minded children, and I invariably found that they were clever mechanically, as clever as the other children and sometimes much more so. Do you not think that these children should be taken from the regular classes in the public schools where they are only a drag and where they feel their incapacity most keenly and be given special instruction along mechanical lines—wood carving, modelling, &c., so that they might develop and so enter into a larger life through what might be said to be the only possible door of entrance for them?"

"2. I greatly wish something could be done to provide suitable training for such unfortunates (children lacking mentally). They get little good in school—sit moping and brooding over what little they know, but learn very little."

"3. I have the names and ages of 15 such persons (feeble-minded) among my schools, all unable to learn, one 16 years of age and some quite young, 4, 6, 7, 8, most of these are not unruly. A few are very much so, and a source of much trouble and delay in the schools where I found them. There is in the common school no opportunity for care and training such as they need. The Province needs not merely places of confinement for these unfortunates but much more places where expert training, tender sympathy and loving patience can be given to every one."

"4· I have been teaching for the past 7 years. and during that time have had 4 or 5 children who have been as you describe (feeble-minded). I feel strongly that there should be some special place provided for such children."

I have received detailed reports from three School Inspectors that in their districts there are 119 children who, in the opinion of the teachers. are feeble-minded. The experience of other investigators shows that this statement is not likely to be far wrong. Taking this as a basis of calculation, it would show that there is a considerable number of feeble-minded children in our Ontario Public Schools to-day. And there is no doubt that if compulsory school attendance were really enforced, a larger number of such children would be found.

Public Opinion.

It is evidently the mind of the people of this Province that something should be done for the feeble-minded, and for the protection of the community from evils already referred to. Our present policy, resulting in such terrible consequences, for which we are responsible, as the history of the P. family shows, no one approves of. Besides the petitions presented to the Government for years, a large number of competent persons holding important official and other positions have so expressed themselves in writing to the Department. A few of these may be given.

From a Municipal Official.

"1. I sincerely hope the Government of Ontario will do something for the feeble-minded in this Province. It will reflect great credit upon them if they do."

From a Police Magistrate.

"2. We are heartily in sympathy with this movement, and will at any time be quite willing to furnish you with all the assistance in our power."

From a Municipal Officer.

"3. I consider this very matter of vital importance. No doubt our state will sooner or later have to care for such."

From a Municipal Officer.

"4. Our Municipal Council fully approve of the steps being taken by the Ontario Government in the direction intimated."

From a Municipal Officer.

"5. I am pleased to find that at last attention is to be given to the class of persons referred to, and any information or assistance I can give will be always at your disposal. It is a subject that has been neglected far too long."

From Private Citizens.

"6. In reply to your circular would like to say that I think there is a crying need for a Home or Institution of some sort for the care of the feeble-minded."

"7. I believe it would be in the interests of the public if all such persons were properly cared for."

"8. I have long thought that something was required for that class."

"9. I would be glad to do anything in my power to aid the work of caring for these unfortunate members of society. I have too often seen the awful results of allowing them to drift at large."

SUMMARY.

In summing up the results shown by this preliminary report it becomes clear that we have to deal with four classes of feeble-minded persons.

1. There are first of all habitual offenders, men and women who are never out of the gaol or the Mercer for more than a few months at a time. They now belong to the Criminal Class, and probably the reason that they belong to the Criminal Class is that they are feeble-minded. What can be done for them? The indeterminate sentence is the only solution. No one would be-

lieve, who had not personally visited the Mercer and carefully examined each inmate separately, what a very large proportion are distinctly and marked feeble-minded.

II. We then come to those who are not criminals—those girls who are constantly found in Maternity Hospitals, Infants' Homes, the Haven, the various Refuges, &c. These are all mothers. It should be required of all Superintendents of Maternity Homes and Hospitals, of all Poor Houses, Refuges, and other Charitable Public Institutions to report at once to this Department the admission of any feeble-minded woman in this position. Someone should be appointed to act for the Government and manage the affairs of the feeble-minded as the Official Guardian manages the affairs of infants, investigating each case and taking means to lessen the great, and at present, fast increasing burden of the mentally defective. If there were a Home where such persons could be taken care of and where they could work, their labour would render the Home nearly self-supporting and they themselves would be happy and safe, and the problem of the next generation would be solved to a large extent.

III. Then there are such cases as the young girl of 19 mentioned above. "Good but weak girls" should be classified by themselves in a separate department. In many cases their friends would pay for their maintenance. It is obvious that a Home for feeble-minded women is required by the Province in the best interests of the community and of these women themselves.

IV. Finally, Where were these feeble-minded persons thirty years ago? Where are the children who will fill their places thirty years hence? In our schools. Now is the time to take hold of these mentally defective children and make something of them, and for the 60 to 90 per cent. that will not be able to live in the world at large without becoming degenerate, unemployable, criminals, and alas, the parents of children still more mentally defective, degraded and dangerous than themselves, special schools and classes and permanent care afterwards are urgently required.

I have the honour to remain,

Your obedient servant,

September 30th, 1906.

HELEN MACMURCHY.

To the Hon. W. J. HANNA, M.PP., Provincial Secretary.

REPORT

OF THE

Special Investigation

ON

Horse Breeding in Ontario

1906.

(PUBLISHED BY THE ONTARIO DEPARTMENT OF AGRICULTURE, TORONTO)

PRINTED BY ORDER OF
THE LEGISLATIVE ASSEMBLY OF ONTARIO

TORONTO:
Printed by L. K. CAMERON, Printer to the King's Most Excellent Majesty.
1907.

WARWICK BRO'S & RUTTER, Limited, Printers,
TORONTO.

To the Honorable WILLIAM MORTIMER CLARK, K.C.,
Lieutenant-Governor of Ontario.

MAY IT PLEASE YOUR HONOR:

The undersigned begs to present herewith, for the consideration of Your Honor, the report on the Horse Industry of Ontario, 1906, which has been prepared by the Live Stock Branch of the Ontario Department of Agriculture.

Respectfully submitted,

NELSON MONTEITH,

Minister of Agriculture.

TORONTO, March, 1907.

CONTENTS.

[4]

Horse Breeding in Ontario.

INTRODUCTION.

The question of improving the quality of the horses bred in the Province has been considered at different times at annual and others meetings of live stock associations, as well as being a subject of concern to persons individually or officially interested .in the promotion of the horse industry. No unanimous and satisfactory scheme calculated to improve conditions could be decided upon, and when the matter was carefully inquired into, it was found that the reason, apparently, was a lack of accurate and detailed information as to the exact conditions throughout the Province which affect the quality of the horses produced. It was therefore decided by the Minister of Agriculture that before undertaking any comprehensive plan for the improvement of horse-breeding, it would be wise to procure more complete information upon which conclusions might be based. It was felt that detailed and accurate information along the following lines should be obtained before any comprehensive policy should be adopted looking to the general improvement of the horse industry in Ontario.

1. What conditions have affected or are affecting the quality and number of stallions and brood mares, in the various sections of the Province, and if the effect is for good, whether or not the same conditions could be applied in other sections; and if the conditions have not a good effect what could be done to remove them.

2. What class of horses can most profitably be raised in different sections of the Province, under the natural conditions found in those sections. '

3. The system of syndicating, and any other plan at present adopted in Ontario, other than private ownership.

4. The views of horsemen generally as to the advisability of a Stallion Inspection Act.

5. Suggestions from those interested in the horse business. as to what can be done to improve conditions of the horse business generally.

For the purpose of obtaining this information, the Legislature was asked to make an appropriation, which was done at the session of 1906. and the following plan of work was adopted : —

. The counties of the Province were divided into eight districts, and two Inspectors, one to represent light horses, and one to represent heavy horses, were appointed to investigate and report on the conditions in each district. The Inspectors were instructed to inspect each known stallion located in their district, and to obtain from the stallion owner and others with whom they came in contact, such information as might be possible regarding the mares. The information obtained in this way is practically accurate, regarding the stallions, and approximately correct regarding the mares. The Inspectors were instructed to make a report on the stallions covering the following points:

1. Owner.
2 Post office address.
3. Breed or breed most favored.
4. Pure-bred or grade.
5. If pure-bred, imported or Canadian-bred, and registration number and name of Record.
6. Average age.
7. Weight.
8. Sound or unsound.
9. If unsound, what disease.
10. Conformation.
11. Action.
12. Approximate value.
13. Number of mares-served.
14. Service fee.
15. Per cent. of foals.
16. If sound, score out of possible 100 points.
17. Remarks.

The following points are covered in the report on the mares:

1. Number in township.
2. Average number kept by each breeder.
3. Type.
4. Average weight.
5. Average quality.
6 Average age.
7. Average value.
8. Remarks.

Information regarding matters of a general nature covered by the investigation were obtained by meeting with those interested in the horse industry in each district, either individually or at the public meeting held in each county for this purpose. It was not the intention that at this meeting, or at any other time, the inspectors should endeavor to direct public opinion to obtain certain results or. decisions, nor was the work undertaken with the object of conducting an educational campaign. This latter point might be a natural result of the investigation, and form part. of a general plan to be adopted for improving conditions, but it was not a part of the work of the inspectors. What was required was a full and intelligent discussion of the different matters covered by the investigation, and to give every one interested an opportunity to express his opinion as to how the conditions relating to the breeding of horses could best be improved.

In order to facilitate the work of the Inspectors, the Secretary of the Farmers' Institute, in each institute district, was requested to organize the district, obtain the names of the stallion owners in his institute district, arrange the most convenient route for inspecting these stallions in their own stables, and also in order to avoid loss of time to drive with the inspectors throughout the district. The stallion owners were notified by circular letter as to the probable time of the visit of the Inspectors. The local officers also advertised and made the necessary arrangements for holding the public meeting in each county.

The result of the investigation in each institute district depended to a great extent upon the preliminary work being properly done, and the report will show that this work was well done in most cases by the local institute officers.

The list of Inspectors, the districts visited by them, and the counties comprising each district are given below:

DISTRICTS.

District No. 1.—Counties of Middlesex, Essex, Kent, Elgin, and Lambton. Wm. Smith, Columbus; J. D. Graham, Toronto.

District No. 2.—Counties of Halton, Wentworth, Brant, Oxford, Norfolk, Haldimand, Welland, and Lincoln. John Gardhouse, Highfield; Wm. Cain, V.S., Perth.

District No. 3.—Counties of Huron, Bruce and Grey. H. G. Reed, V.S., Georgetown; John Bright, Myrtle.

District No. 4.—Counties of Perth, Waterloo, Wellington, and Dufferin. Wm. Jones, Zenda; Peter Christie, M.P., Manchester; John A. Boig, Ravenshoe.

District No. 5.—Counties of Peel, Simcoe, York, and Ontario. Thos. McMillan, Seaforth; Wm. Mossip, St. Mary's.

District No. 6.—Counties of Hastings, Peterborough, Victoria, Durham, Northumberland and Prince Edward. J. G. Clarke, Ottawa; Jas. Irving, Winchester.

District No. 7.—Counties of Prescott, Russell, Carleton, Renfrew, and Lanark. W. F. Kydd, Simcoe; Geo. Gray, Newcastle.

District No. 8.—Counties of Glengarry, Dundas, Grenville, Leeds, Frontenac, and Lennox and Addington. H. S. Arkell, B.S.A., O.A.C., Guelph; Jas. Sinclair, V.S., Cannington; Arthur Thom, Elma.

NOTE.—Where more than two inspectors are given for one district, the work was divided so that but two inspectors were in the district at one time. The work of inspection in Stormont County was done by George Gray, Newcastle, and A. R. Walsh, V.S. Perth.

The following list shows the place and date at which it was arranged to hold the public meeting for each county.

PUBLIC MEETINGS.

County.	Town or city.	Date.	County.	Town or city.	Date.
Brant	Brantford	Oct. 20.	Lincoln	St. Catharines	Nov. 17.
Bruce	Paisley	" 26.	Middlesex	London	Oct. 19.
Carleton	Stittsville	" 30.	Northumberland	Brighton	Nov. 15.
Durham	Orono	Nov. 9.	Norfolk	Simcoe	" 3.
Dufferin	Shelburne	" 12.	Oxford	Woodstock	Oct. 27.
Dundas	Winchester	Oct. 18.	Ontario	Port Perry	Nov. 13.
Essex	Essex	" 26.	Perth	Mitchell	Oct. 16.
Elgin	St. Thomas	Nov. 9.	Peterborough	Madoc	" 17.
Frontenac	Harrowsmith	" 5.	Prince Edward	Picton	Nov. 20.
Grey	Markdale	" 8.	Peel	Caledon East	Oct. 12.
Grenville	Kemptville	Oct. 25.	Prescott	Vankleek Hill	" 13.
Glengarry	Alexandria	" 13.	Russell	Russell	" 22.
Hastings	Madoc	" 17.	Renfrew	Cobden	Nov. 6.
Huron	Clinton	" 11.	Simcoe	Barrie	Oct. 26.
Halton	Milton	" 11.	Victoria	Lindsay	" 31.
Haldimand	Fisherville	Nov. 8.	Wellington	Fergus	Nov. 7.
Kent	Chatham	" 2.	Waterloo	Berlin	Oct. 22.
Lanark	Carleton Place	" 12.	Wentworth	Dundas	" 16.
Lambton	Petrolea	" 19.	Welland	Welland	Nov. 14.
Leeds	Lansdowne	Oct. 31.	York	Richmond Hill	" 5.
Lennox and Addington	Napanee	Nov. 13.			

It was practically impossible to procure the name of every stallion owner in the Province, and in a very few of the townships it may be found that this may slightly affect the report on that particular township, but it will not affect the report of the county to any appreciable extent. In some few cases also, the owners would not allow their horses to be inspected, and wherever a stallion was not inspected, the report of the mares in the tabulated statement for the township in which such stallion is located will also be affected. It should also be borne in mind that stallions are credited to the townships in which they were located at the time of inspection, when they may possibly travel through the surrounding townships during the season; this may give a somewhat erroneous impression regarding the townships not credited, if this fact is not noted. It should also be specially noted that the number of mares credited to any township in the tabulated statement is the number of mares bred to stallions inspected in that township, and will not necessarily denote the number of breeding mares actually owned in the township. The information regarding the amount of service fees, and the number of mares bred to each stallion was supplied the Inspectors by the owner of the stallion. The Inspectors did not always have an opportunity of verifying this information, and referring specially to the service fees, it has been suggested that the advertised service fee was not always adhered to.

In this report standard-bred horses and pure-bred horses are classed together, the standard-bred horses being termed pure-bred as a matter of convenience in preparing the report. The same is also true of the term grade being applied to denote non-standard-bred horses of roadster type. Roadster stallions (Canadian-bred) include standard-bred horses bred in Canada and stallions of Roadster type bred in Canada, but registered in Records other than the American Trotting Register. Roadster grade stallions include grade stallions of Roadster type not registered in any record.

The report following is compiled from the statistics and general information supplied by the Inspectors, the report from each district being given separately. The report on each county in the above districts is given by townships, with a summarized table and general information regarding the whole county, given at the end of the county report. The remarks of the Inspectors regarding the work generally are given at the end of the report of the district which was under their charge. The report for each district after being finally prepared was submitted to and approved by the Inspectors for that district. A summarized report and statistics covering the Province, in accordance with the above districts, completes the report of the investigation.

DISTRICT NO. 1.

Counties.—Middlesex, Essex, Kent, Elgin and Lambton.
Inspectors.—Wm. Smith, Columbus, and J. D. Graham, Toronto.

MIDDLESEX.

The township of Biddulph was first gone over. Two Clydesdale stallions, two Shires, a Percheron, a Standard-bred, and a Roadster, were seen by the Inspectors. All of these were registered, and all the Clydesdales, Shires, and the Percheron were imported animals. The Clydesdales were of an excellent type, one weighing 2,100 lbs. and both had been used on a large number of mares. The Roadster was of good conformation and action, while the rest were described as, fair. All were sound. It is estimated that there are 1,000 breeding mares in the township, being mostly of Clydesdale and Roadster type, and averaging about 1,350 lbs. in weight. Their average quality is described as fair, and the average age 8 years. Service fees ran from $10 to $15, and in one instance was given as $25.

In McGillivray township, Clydesdales largely predominate; out of the nine stallions seen, five being of that breed, all imported but one. Their quality ranged from good to fair. One aged grade Clydesdale was seen, and one of the three Standard-breds and Roadsters was also a grade. Most of the stallions were sound, two coming under the head of "fairly sound." The average weight of the Clydesdales was about 1,750 lbs., and of the Standard-breds, about 1,050 lbs. Mares of Clydesdale type, averaging 1,200 lbs., are most generally found, and some 723 were bred, being of fair quality, their average age being 7 years. From $8 to $15, are charged as service fees.

In the township of West Williams, there were seen two Clydesdales, a Shire, a Roadster, and an Arabian (the latter a grade), standing for service. The four registered stallions were all sound, the two heaviest, a Clydesdale and a Shire, being reported at 2,000 lbs. Service fees ranged from $8 for the grade to $12 for one of the Clydesdales and the Roadster, the low fee for the grade evidently affecting adversely the average of the fees throughout the township. The Roadster was described as of very good conformation, that of the others ranging from fairly good to fair. The number of brood mares in the township is 500, being of Clydesdale and Roadster type, of fair average quality, and in weight 1,300 lbs. Average age was 6 years.

East Williams has fewer stallions than its sister township, only three being located by the inspectors, and of these, one was a grade. The Clydesdale, an imported horse, scored well, and had been used on a good number of mares. The Hackney was of good conformation and action, and had been used on a large number of mares, of which a very high percentage were in foal. All three stallions were sound. As regards mares, they are of good quality, in number about 600, of Clydesdale and Roadster type, and average in weight 1,250 lbs., and in years, 8. From $10 to $15 are the service fees, the higher fee being for the Hackney.

Two Clydesdales and a Percheron, all sound, and two of them of good conformation, comprised the sires seen in Adelaide township. The average value of the three was $1,200. All three were imported animals. As in the other townships of this county, the mares were mostly of Clydesdale and Roadster type, of good average quality, weighing about 1,200 lbs., in age averaging 8 years, and numbered some 600. $10 to $12 are paid for service fees.

Middlesex—Continued.

Out of the eight stallions in Lobo township (one of which was a grade), four were registered Clydesdales, three being imported. The German Coach stallion seen was of excellent conformation, and had good action, and had proved a successful foal getter. Of the two Roadsters, one was good, the other being undersized, and only fair in conformation. Service fees were from $9 to $15. The average quality of the mares in this township, which average 1,200 lbs. in weight, and are of the Clydesdale and Roadster type, is fair, and average age is 7 years.

Caradoc township makes a good showing in point of numbers of stallions. Out of the thirteen inspected, six were Clydesdales, four Roadsters, one a Percheron, one a Thoroughbred, and one an Arabian. Of these, four were grades or unregistered. A large proportion were out for their first season here, so that no record of their value as sires could be obtained. With one exception all were sound. The mares kept in this township are of the draught and general purpose type, weighing about 1,100 lbs., and are fair in quality, with an average age of 7 years. Service fees are from $8 to $15.

Metcalfe township is fairly well provided with sires, fairly equally divided between light and heavy breeds, the light somewhat preponderating. Three Roadsters, three Clydesdales, and one Coach stallion make up the list. The Clydesdales score highest in conformation and quality, and all are sound or fairly so. Here, again, the majority of the sires had put in their first season, and so no idea of their breeding abilities could be secured. Of those that had been standing for service more than one season, the percentage of foals was fairly good. The stud fees were from $10 to $15. The average weight of mares was no higher than 1,100 lbs.; quality fair, they being of a light or very slightly Clydesdale type. About 750 is the number of mares kept. Their average age is 8 years.

Mosa is a township with horses of a distinctly light type, hence the sires used are mostly of the lighter order. One Thoroughbred, two Roadsters, a grade Roadster, a German Coach, two Percherons, a Clydesdale, and a Clydesdale grade constitute the list. All but one are reported sound. Here, again, the service fee ranged from $10 to $15, the majority charging the lower fee. The mares in this township are described as partly general purpose, and partly Roadster in type. Their average quality is fair. Their average weight is about 1,100 lbs., and age, 8 years.

Ten to fifteen dollars is also the range of service fees in Ekfrid township, where there are only four stallions, two apiece of Roadsters and of Clydesdales, all sound and, as far as tested, fairly reliable sires. About 600 mares are kept, being of a Roadster type, with some inclined to a general purpose conformation. Their average age is 7 years, and weight, 1,100 lbs.

West Nissouri with its 1,000 mares of Roadster and Clydesdale type, averaging 1,200 lbs. in weight, leans towards the heavy type of sire, no less than 7 out of the 11 visited being Clydesdales, four imported, and three Canadian bred. There is also a Hackney kept for service for the first season, two Roadsters (one a grade) and a French sire. While most of the sires are young, one is 20 years old, and another 11. Most of them are reported sound. The fees are as low as $8, and up to $15. The average age of the mares is 7 years.

In North Dorchester township, while the type of mare is of the general purpose, Roadster and Hackney style, the tendency is to use mostly Clydesdale or Shire stallions, while two Hackneys have also put in their

Middlesex.—Continued.

'first season. In addition to these there is a Roadster. All are sound, and the conformation is fairly good, two scoring as very good. In age, the oldest is 11, and the youngest 3 years. Four are newcomers; the percentage of foals for the rest being good. Mares, which are of average quality, number 800. Their average weight is 1,100 lbs., and age 7 years.

The city of London is the headquarters for 12 stallions, being 7 Clydesdales, a Thoroughbred, and four Roadsters, one of these a grade. Six of the Clydesdales were newly imported, and the ages of the twelve ranged from 2 to "aged." All ranked as sound, and the service fee charged varied from $12 to $15, while for three Roadsters the fees are quoted at $20 to $50.

Westminster township excels the average of the surrounding townships, except that of London, in the total number of mares kept, 1,500, also in the average quality which is good. They scale about 1,200 lbs., and are of draught and roadster type, averaging in age 7 years. Of the sires kept, two are registered Clydesdales, and one a grade, and there is one apiece of the Shire, Percheron, and Roadster breed, the latter not being used for service. The oldest horse is 13 years, and all are sound. Service fees are placed at $8 to $15.

London township is the banner one of Middlesex county as regards the number of stallions and mares kept, there being 16 of the former and 2,500 of the latter, which the inspectors describe as mares of good quality, weighing 1,250 lbs., averaging in age about 7 years, and in type partly draught and partly roadster. The conformation of the sires does not seem to be in all cases as good as it might be, although a number scored well. The ages varied from 4 to 15 years. The list includes four Clydesdales, four Shires (two being grades), four Roadsters, two Hackneys and two Percherons. Eight to fifteen dollars are the service fees paid, and in the case of a Roadster stallion a fee of $20 is given.

STALLIONS.

Breeding.	Number.	Average weight. Pounds.	Average age.	Serviceably sound.	Average conformation.	Number of mares served.	Average service fee.
							$
Clydesdales, Imported	44	1,743	6	All	Good.....	3,443	12
Clydesdales, Canadian-bred	7	1,380	5	All	Fair......	432	10
Grades, Clydesdale	5	1,580	8	All	Fair......	343	9
Shires, Imported	8	1,812	7	All	Fair......	547	12
Grades, Shire	2	1,450	9	1....	Fair......	65	8
Percherons	8	1,744	6	All	Medium fair.....	921	11
Hackneys, Imported	5	1,350	6	All	Fairly good. ...	543	13
Standard-breds, Imported	14	1,053	8	All	Good.....	590	15
Roadsters, Canadian-bred	7	1,000	6	All	Good.....	358	14
Thoroughbreds, Imported	3	1,184	15	All	Medium good. ...	152	11
German Coach Horses	2	1,325	12	All	Good.....	251	13
English Coach Horses	1	1,300	9	All	Fair......	50	10
Grades.—Hackney, Roadster, Arabian and French Canadian (1 Hackney, 11 Roadsters, 2 Arabian, 1 French Canadian)	15	1,095	6	All	Fair......	704	10
Totals	121					8,399	

Middlesex.—Concluded.

MARES.

Townships.	Number of mares bred to stallions inspected in Township.	Type.	Average weight. Pounds.	Average quality.	Average age.
Biddulph...............	467	Clydesdale and Roadster	1,350	Fair. ..	8
McGillivray	723	Clydesdale......................	1,200	Fair. ..	7
West Williams...........	445	Clydesdale and Roadster	1,300	Fair. ..	6
East Williams	334	Clydesdale and Roadster	1,250	Good..	8
Adelaide	311	Clydesdale and Roadster	1,200	Good..	8
Lobo	644	Clydesdale and Roadster	1,200	Fair. ..	7
Caradoc	676	Draught and General Purpose......	1,100	Fair. ..	7
Metcalfe...............	605	Light and others half light Clydesdale	1,100	Fair. ..	8
Mosa ..... ,..........	668	General Purpose, Clydesdale and some Roadster	1,100	Fair. ..	8
Ekfrid	185	Roadsters and Grades inclined to General Purpose.	1,100	Fair. ..	7
West Nissouri...........	606	Roadster and Clydesdale..........	1,200	Fair. ..	7
North Dorchester	872	General Purpose, Roadster and Hackney	1,100	Fair. ..	7
London City...........	231	Draught and Roadster............	1,200	Good..	7
Westminster...........	443				
London	1,189	Draught and Roadster............	1,250	Good..	7
Total	8,399				

MARES BRED TO DIFFERENT CLASSES OF STALLIONS.

Stallions.	Total.		Serviceably sound.			Not serviceably sound.		
	Number of stallions.	Number of mares bred to.	Number of stallions.	Number of mares bred to.	Average fee.	Number of stallions.	Number of mares bred to.	Average fee.
Registered Stallions .	99	7,287	99	7,287	$ 12	......	......	$ ......
Grade Stallions	22	1,112	21	1,087	9	1	25	10
Totals........	121	8,399	120	8,374	....	1	25	....

The public meeting for the County of Middlesex was held in London on the 19th of October. Among those present were Col. McEwen, Dr. Fitzgerald, J. Courcey, Dr. Stevenson and Dr. Tennant. All agreed that there should be a license on stallions, and that the owner of a licensed horse should be entitled to a lien on the mare and foal for the amount of the service fee.

Essex.

In the township of Maidstone there are three registered Roadsters and three Clydesdales, one of the latter being a grade. All are sound, but as types of the breeds the Clydesdales have the advantage. One of the Roadsters is a pacer. Excepting the two sires that had been doing their first season, the percentage of foals reported is not high. From $9 to $15 is charged for service fees. Some 800 mares ranging from general purpose to Roadsters, with a few draughts, are kept, but the average quality is only fair; average weight 1,100 lbs.; and average age 9 years.

In Sandwich East township two Roadster stallions and one Percheron were inspected. The 600 mares to be found here are not of high quality, and average 9 years in age. Ten dollars is the service fee.

Sandwich West is on a par with her sister township as regards mares, which are described as poor, of bad type, weighing about 1,050 lbs. and numbering 700, while the average age is 10 years. Two Clydesdale stallions, both imported, are kept. One is an excellent individual; $12 and $16 are the stud fees charged.

Rochester township is distinctly in favor of raising heavy horses and boasts of eleven stallions, four being Clydesdales, three Shires (one a grade), two Percherons and two French Canadians. One Clydesdale and one Percheron are also grades. They are reported as ranging, with one exception, from medium to very good. Fees charged are $7, $8, $10, and $14. Mares range from light type to a few draughts; they number 1,100, and are fair in quality, average weight being 1,100 lbs., and age 8 years.

Six Roadsters, three being pure-bred and three grades, and two Clydesdales in their first season, comprise the sires in Mersea township all being sound, but some not rating high in conformation and quality. There are about 1,000 mares in this district, some draught, some general purpose, and others Roadster. Their average quality is medium, the average weight 1,100 lbs., and average age 8 years. From $10 to $15 is the service fee, while for one Roadster the fee is placed at $25.

The Percheron is the predominant breed in Gosfield South township and this type prevails largely among the mares, the balance being Roadsters. The quality of the mares is only fair, and the average weight 1,100 lbs. and average age 8 years. Of the eight stallions standing for service, 5 are pure-bred Percherons, one a German Coach, and two Roadsters. Of the eight, one is unsound, and the average rating is not high. Stud fees range from $10 to $12.

In Malden township only one stallion was inspected, a pure-bred Percheron, three years old, reported as being a good one. There are 600 mares in this township, of a general purpose type, weighing about 1,100 lbs., but only fair in quality. Their average age is 8 years.

In Gosfield North, too, only one stallion was seen, also a Percheron, 4 year old, that has not yet stood for service. The type of mares here is largely Percheron, scaling about 1,100 lbs., quality being fair. In number they are about 700, their average age is 7 years.

A Hackney, two Clydesdales, a Percheron, a Thoroughbred, and Roadster constitute the stallion stock of Colchester South township. With the exception of one, the standard is not very high, but all are sound, ages running from 6 to 15 years. Ten to fifteen dollars is the run of service fees, mostly at the lower figure. Mares number 700, and are principally light in type, scaling 1,050 lbs. with an average age of 8 years, while their average quality is not high.

Essex—Continued.

Colchester North has a somewhat similiar list of sires, viz., three Clydesdales, a Thoroughbred, a Percheron, and a Roadster, with ages from 4 to 16 years. The standard, too, is not as high as it should be, with one exception. Two of the horses were far advanced in years. The mares seen were fair in quality, averaging 1,150 lbs., and are inclined to the draught type, with some Roadsters and Percherons. In number they are about 800, and their average age is 8 years.

STALLIONS

Breeding.	Number.	Average weight. Pounds.	Average age.	Serviceably sound.	Average conformation.	Number of mares served.	Average service fee.
							$
Clydesdales, Imported	4	1,725	5½	All	Fairly good	340	13
Clydesdales, Canadian-bred	8	1,644	8	All	Good	722	11
Grades, Clydesdale	4	1,425	7½	All	Fair	301	9
Shires, Imported, and Gradés (1 pure-bred, 2 grades)	3	1,760	5½	All ...	Very fair	305	11
Percherons, Imported	8	1,650	8	All	Fair	586	12
Percherons, Canadian-bred	2	1,500	3½	All	Good	125	10
Grades, Percheron	2	1,400	6		Fair	100	10
Hackney, Imported	1	1,300	6	All	Excellent		
Standard-breds, Imported, and Roadsters, Canadian-bred, (6 imported, 1 Roadster,Canadian-bred)	7	1,084	10	All	Fair	371	14
Grades, Roadster	8	1,130	6	7 ..	Fair	333	10
Thoroughbreds	2	1,125	10	All	Fair	165	11
German Coach Horses and French Canadian (1 German Coach, 2 French Canadian)	3	1,475	13	All ...	Pretty good	279	10
Totals	52					3,627	

MARES.

Townships.	Number bred to stallions inspected in Township.	Type.	Average weight. Pounds.	Average quality.	Average age.
Maidstone	345	General purpose and a few draught and roadsters	1,100	Just fair	9
Sandwich East	286	Bad	1,050	Poor ...	9
Sandwich West	100	Bad	1,050	Poor ...	10
Rochester	1,042	Some draught and light kinds	1,100	Just fair	8
Mersea	505	Some draught, general purpose and roadsters	1,100	Medium	8
Gosfield South	488	A good many Percherons and some roadsters	1,100	Only fair	8
Malden		General purpose	1,100	Only fair	8
Gosfield North		Mostly Percheron	1,100	Fair	7
Colchester South	320	Mostly light kinds	1,050	Only fair	8
Colchester North	541	Inclined to draught, with some roadsters and Percherons	1,150	Fair	8
Total	3,627				

Essex.—Concluded.

MARES BRED TO DIFFERENT CLASSES OF STALLIONS.

Stallions.	Total.		Serviceably sound.			Not serviceably sound.		
	Number of stallions.	Number of mares bred to.	Number of stallions.	Number of mares bred to.	Average fee.	Number of stallions.	Number of mares bred to.	Average fee.
					$			$
Registered Stallions..	36	2,728	36	2,728	12	....	....	
Grade Stallions......	16	899	15	834	9	1	65	12
Totals........	52	3,627	51	3,562	......	1	65	....

The meeting held at Essex was not large, but it was enthusiastic over the future of the horse trade of this Province. The roads were bad, and a number of the breeders who came in by train had to remain all night The meeting was unanimously in favor of a Licensing Act and also registration. The only point upon which there was any difference was the amount of licensing fee, a fair majority wanting a moderate sum, and the balance going to the extreme.

KENT.

Some sections of, Kent County seem to favor heavy horse breeding more than others, but the main type is the lighter breeds. The city of Chatham is a great light horse centre, and of the sires owned by horsemen in this city, ten in number, four are Roadsters, one a Hackney, two Percherons, two Clydes, and one a Shire. The Roadsters are mostly a good class, and also the Hackney, while the two heavy breeds are fairly well represented. Two of the stallions are fifteen years old, and stud fees vary from $10 to $15, while for three Roadsters $20 is the fee stated.

The township of Raleigh inclines somewhat to the heavier breeds, there being two Clydesdales (one a grade), two Shires, a Percheron, and two Roadsters available here. The fee for a Roadster, $30, heads the list, the general run of fees being $10 and $13. All the horses are reported sound, and all have stood to a good number of mares. Of these latter there are in this township about 1,500, weighing about 1,100 lbs., and of fair average quality. They vary in type from Percheron to Roadster and general purpose. and are of an average age of nine years.

Tilbury East is mainly a heavy horse centre, there being five Clydesdales (two grades) and one Coach stallion. The average quality is not as high as it might be, and three of the horses are getting on in years, one being reported as unsound. Stud fees come at $9 to $15. Draught, general purpose, and Roadster are the three prevailing types among the mares in this section, which average in weight 1,200 lbs., and are fair in quality, age averaging seven years.

There are four Roadsters (two of them grades) and one Thoroughbred to a single Clydesdale stallion in Romney township, which indicates fairly well the type of mares kept, which are general purpose, Roadster, and some of heavier type of draught. Two of the stallions are aged, and with but two exceptions did not rank as high as they might. From $10 to $13 are the

Kent—Continued.

general fees charged for service, but for one Roadster the fee is $20. Mares are fair in quality, in weight averaging 1,150 lbs., and in age seven years.

With the exception of one Clydesdale all the stallions in the township of Zone are Roadsters, two of these and the Clydesdale scoring well as regards conformation and action. All are sound but one. Fees range from $10 to $20, Roadsters topping the list, as elsewhere. Mares of general purpose and Roadster type, of about 1,100 lbs. weight and medium quality, constitute the breeding stock of this township. Their average age is 8 years.

Howard township is well represented in the number and variety of sires kept for service, which include two Hackneys, a German Coach, a French horse, two Cleveland Bays, a French Canadian horse, three Roadsters, two Coach horses, and six Clydesdales. Seven of these stallions are grades. They are mostly a good lot and the majority are sound, but two are 14 and 19 years old respectively. Ten to fifteen dollars is the range of fees for service, with one given as $20. In all there are some 1,800 mares of fair quality in the township, of an average weight of 1,200 lbs., about a third being of the draught type, the rest general purpose and Roadsters. Their average age is eight years.

All the six stallions inspected in Camden township were young horses and sound, three of them having been out for their first season. The average quality is fairly high, and the service fees follow the general rule from $10 to $15. There are 1,200 mares in the township, of Clydesdale, general purpose, and Percheron type, whose quality is fair, and average weight about 1,150 lbs., average age being seven years.

Harwich township possesses what is rather a rarity in Ontario now, viz., Suffolk Punch sire. The heavy horse interests are served by two Clydesdales and two Shires, while there are in addition three Percherons, a Coach horse, and three Roadsters. Two of the stallions are grades. The majority are reported sound, but some are well up in years. The service fee is the usual range from $10 to $15. The percentage of mares bred out of the 3,000 in the township is about 35 per cent. They average 1,250 lbs. in weight, and are mostly general purpose, with some draughts and Roadsters. Their average quality is fair, and age seven years.

No stallions appear to be located in Chatham township. There are about 1,000 mares, chiefly of Percheron and light type, weighing on an average 1,100 lbs., and only fair in quality, average age being seven years.

Of the two stallions inspected in Dover township, one is a Percheron, the other a French Canadian, both pure-bred and of fair conformation. The fees are respectively, $15 and $11, and to them were bred rather more than a quarter of the 800 Percheron type of mare found in this township, their average weight being 1,100 lbs., quality only fair, and average age eight years.

Orford township has one Percheron stallion four years old, sound and well rated, and has a good percentage of foals to its credit. There is also a Clydesdale and Coach horse. Service fees are from $8 to $10. About 800 mares are kept by farmers, being mostly of general purpose stamp, with a very few of heavier build. They average about 1,150 lbs., and rate fairly well as to quality, age averaging about eight years.

Kent—Continued.

STALLIONS.

Breeding.	Number.	Average Weight. Pounds.	Average Age.	Serviceably sound.	Average confirmation.	Number of mares served.	Average service fee.
							$
Clydesdales, Imported............	6	1,825	7	All	Very fair..	404	13
Clydesdales, Canadian-bred.	7	1,657	10	6	Fair......	505	10
Grades, Clydesdale	6	1,600	6	All	Fairly good....	463	10
Shires, Imported.................	5	1,750	8	All	Fair	399	12
Shires, Canadian-bred............	1	1,600	7	All	Very fair .	85	10
Grades, Shire................	1	1,300	2	All	Medium ..	9	12
Percherons, Imported	5	1,493	9	All	Very fair .	558	14
Percherons, Canadian............	3	1,590	6	All	Very fair..	335	12
Suffolk, Punch...................	1	1,700	15	All	Fair	110	12
Hackneys, Imported	2	1,225	7½	All	Good.....	217	17
Hackneys, Canadian-bred	2	1,000	6	1	Good.....	14	10
Standard-breds, Imported	12	1,130	8½	10	Good.....	561	17
Roadsters, Canadian-bred	4	1,020	8	All	Good.....	60	10
Grades, Roadster................	4	1,000	8½	3	Only fair .	82	10
Thoroughbreds	1	1,050	13	All	Medium..	70	12
Grades, German Coach...........	4	1,300	10	All	Fair	228	9
Cleveland Bays and Grades (1 pure-bred, 3 grades).............	4	1,380	6	All	Very fair .	342	10
French Canadian and Grades (2 pure-breds, 1 grade............	3	1,325	15	All	Very fair .	314	11
Totals....................	71					4816	

MARES.

Townships.	Number of mares bred to Stallions inspected in Township.	Type.	Average weight. Pounds.	Average quality.	Average age.
City of Chatham	522	Light Roadster	1,050	Fair	9
Raleigh	525	Percheron, Roadster and General Purpose......................	1,100	Fair	9
East Tilbury	548	Draught, General Purpose and Roadster........................	1,200	Fair	7
Romney...............	310	Strongly General Purpose, Draught and Roadster	1,150	Fair	7
Zone	289	General Purpose and Roadster......	1,100	Medium	8
Orford	215	Mostly General Purpose, balance Roadster	1,100	Only fair	9
Howard	1,002	One-third Draught, balance General Purpose and Roadster	1,200	Fair	8
Camden	389	Clydesdales, General Purpose and Percheron	1,150	Fair....	7
Harwich..............	786	Mostly General Purpose, a few Draught and some Roadsters......	1,250	Fair....	7
Chatham		A good many Percherons and light kinds.......................	1,100	Only fair	7
Dover	230	Percherons........	1,100	Only fair	8
Total..............	4,816				

2—H.B.

Kent—Concluded.

MARES BRED TO DIFFERENT CLASSES OF STALLIONS.

Stallions.	Total.		Serviceably sound.			Not serviceably sound.		
	Number of stallions	Number of mares bred to.	Number of stallions.	Number of mares bred to.	Average fee.	Number of stallions.	Number of mares bred to.	Average fee.
Registered Stallions .	52	3,673	48	3,469	$ 10	4	204	$ 10
Grade Stallions......	19	1,143	18	1,118	10	1	25	10
Totals........	71	4,816	66	4,587	....	5	229	....

The public meeting for the county of Kent was held at Chatham on November 2nd. Representatives were present from nearly every part of the county. The meeting was unanimously in favor of an Inspection Act in regard to pedigree and individuality, and also expressed an opinion that syndicating of stallions was all right provided good individuals were purchased at proper prices. It was suggested that more attention be paid to subjects relating to the horse industry at Farmers' Institute meetings, and that Agricultural Societies should provide a separate class for each breed of horses.

ELGIN.

Southwold Township has nine stallions, made up as follows: Three Clydesdales, one Shire, a Percheron, two Roadsters (one a grade), a Thoroughbred and a coach horse. All are sound, and rate about the average, with two considerably above. Two were far advanced in years, and of the rest, five had travelled for the first time. Ten to sixteen dollars are the service fees, with one standing at $20. Draught, general purpose, and Roadster are the general types of the mares kept, which have an average weight of 1,200 lbs., an average age of 7 years, and being in quality fair.

Dunwich Township has some 1,200 mares of a heavier type, weighing 1,350 lbs. on the average, about 2 per cent. being lighter in build. Their quality is reported good, and age averages 5 years. The heavier type of mares is responsible for a corresponding increase in the proportion of sires of that stamp kept, which is 5 Clydes, a Percheron, a Hackney, and two Thoroughbreds (one a grade). Two of these horses are aged; the ages of the others range from 2 to 8 years. All pass muster as sound. Three of the horses are newcomers to this district. Fees charged vary from $10 to $17 with one at $20.

Ten stallions are on the routes in Yarmouth Township, where the prevailing type of mares is general purpose and Roadster, with a few draughts. The average weight of mares is 1,100 lbs., average age 8 years, and the number 1,200, their quality being only fair. The sires run pretty much to the lighter types, there being only one Clydesdale to seven Roadsters, a Thoroughbred, and a French Canadian. With two exceptions they are all sound, but some are up in years. $25 are the service fees in two cases for Roadsters, $12 to $15 being the usual fee charged.

Malahide is another township that favors the lighter breeds, the average weight of the mares being not more than 1,000 lbs., and they are of Hackney

2a H.B.

Elgin—Continued.

and Roadster type, and in quality fair. Their average age is 8 years. Roadster sires predominate, being five in number, but of these three are grades; Hackneys are four in all, one being a grade; Percherons number two, and Thoroughbreds one. No information could be obtained about one horse which with its owner was away from home. Most are sound, but two were very old. Fees are $10, $11, $13 to $15. The average quality is fair.

The Inspectors' report as to the mare stock in Bayham Township is not at all favorable, the 500 mares there being in quality bad, in type the same, and only averaging 950 lbs. in weight, their average age being 10 years. Roadster stallions number four out of six sires in use, and of these two are grades. There is also one Thoroughbred and a Percheron. Fees are as low as $5, $12 being the maximum sum.

In Aldboro' Township mares are of a somewhat heavier type, the greater number being general purpose, with others of a Clydesdale type. About 1,150 is the average weight, quality being medium. The number kept is about 1,200, the average age being 9 years. Two Clydesdales, two Roadsters, a Hackney and a French Canadian (two being grades) form the total of the sires kept. With one exception they are sound. One is well on in years. Conformation and action of four are good. As low as $7 is charged for fees, but the maximum is $15.

STALLIONS.

Breeding.	Number.	Average weight. Pounds.	Average age.	Serviceably sound.	Average conformation.	Number of mares served.	Average service fee.
							$
Clydesdales, Imported	10	1,740	6	All	Good	847	14
Clydesdales, Canadian-bred	3	1,550	7	All	Fair	354	10
Shires, Imported	1	1,900	5	All	Fair	110	15
Percherons	5	1,780	5	All	Fair	484	15
Hackneys, Imported..............	3	1,300	9½	All	Good	196	15
Hackneys, Canadian-bred	2	1,200	4½	All	Fairly good..	135	15
Grades, Hackney	1	......	......	......	......	......	...
Standard-breds, Imported	10	1,100	8½	All	Fairly good..	209	15
Roadsters, Canadian-bred	3	1,060	6	All	Medium.. Good.	160	11
Grades, Roadster	7	1,100	10	All	Fair.	154	10
Thoroughbreds, Imported.........	5	1,100	10	¼	Fair.	232	10
Grades, Thoroughbred	2	1,050	11	All	Fair.	40	10
German Coach Horses, and French Canadian and Grade French Canadian (1 German, 1 French, Canadian, 1 French Canadian Grade)......................	3	1,325	13	All	Medium. ..	229	10
Total	55					3,150	

Elgin—Concluded.

MARES.

Townships.	Number of mares bred to stallions inspected in Township.	Type.	Average weight. Pounds.	Average quality.	Average age.
Southwold.............	650	Draught, General Purpose and Roadster......................	1,200	Fair ...	7
Dunwich	741	Two per cent. light, rest Draught ..	1,350	Good. .	5
Yarmouth	324	General Purpose, Roadster and a } few draught .... }	1,100	{ Only { fair..	8
Malahide	751	Inclined to be light Hackney and Roadster	1,000	Fair. ..	8
Bayham................	288	Bad, very light	950	Bad ...	10
Aldboro	396	General Purpose and leaning to Clydesdale	1,150	Medium	9
Total...........	3,150				

MARES BRED TO DIFFERENT CLASSES OF STALLIONS.

Stallions.	Total.		Serviceably sound.			Not serviceably sound.		
	Number of stallions.	Number of mares bred to.	Number of stallions.	Number of mares bred to.	Average fee.	Number of stallions.	Number of mares bred to.	Average fee.
Registered Stallions..	44	2,845	43	2,775	$ 13	1	70	$ 10
Grade Stallions	11	305	11	305	9	....	....	....
Totals........	55	3,150	54	3,080	....	1	70	....

Public meetings in the County of Elgin were held at Aylmer on October 7th, and at St. Thomas on November 9th.

At the Aylmer meeting the majority of those present were in favor of stallions being licensed and registered, and it was also the opinion of the meeting that if an Inspection Act was enforced by the Government, there would be no difference whether a horse were syndicated or bought by a private individual. It was suggested that more time be devoted to questions relating to the breeding of horses at Farmers' Institute meetings, or that a special series of educational meetings should be held. It was stated that the sale of too many good mares, the use of too many poor stallions, the indiscriminate breeding of horses, and the importation of western horses, all contributed to the depreciation of the quality of our horses.

At the St. Thomas meeting it was resolved that the report prepared and presented by the St. Thomas and Elgin Horse Association be adopted. This report stated that resolutions had been passed favoring the syndicating of stallions, in favor of a Stallion Inspection Act, and in favor of the Government giving prizes for mares at horse shows and fairs in the County of Elgin.

LAMBTON.

In Brooke township, heavy breeds are to the light as 5 to 4. Three Clydesdales and two Shires, all pure-bred, and four Roadsters (one a grade), compose the list of sires. All are rated sound. Two are 13 years old. Their standard, as regards conformation, action and general worth is very fairly good. Ten dollars is the lowest, and fifteen the highest fee charged. The 1,200 mares kept are somewhat of the draught type, others are general purpose, and a few Roadsters. Average weight runs about 1,150 lbs., while quality is medium, and the average age 7 years.

The breeding stock of mares in Euphemia township, totals 700, are general purpose in style, and average 1,100 lbs. Their quality is only medium, and average age 9 years. Two Clydesdale sires, and one Hackney are kept for service; two of these have only been standing for service for one season. No unsoundness is reported, and the average rating is fairly good. For one Clydesdale, a grade, the service fee is $8, for the purebred, $12.

As the 1,800 mares kept in Warwick township are mostly draught, with some Roadsters, we find Clydesdale sires in the majority. The mares average 1,250 lbs., their quality is good, and average age is 6 years. No less than 8 out of the 13 stallions in service are Clydesdales, only o e being a grade. Roadsters come next in point of numbers with four, two of which are grades, and there is one Carriage stallion. Four of the total are newcomers. The average for conformation, and action is fairly good. Starting with $8 for a grade, the service fees run up to $12.

In Plympton township there are about 1,200 mares of very mixed type, averaging 1,100 lbs., and only fair in quality, with an average age of 8 years. Stallions number 18, 12 pure-breds, and 6 grades. Service fees are as low as $7, and as high as $12. Most of the stallions are sound, and barring some very aged horses, scored fairly well. Roadsters lead with eight. Clydesdales number six, and there is one each of Shires, French Canadians, German Coach, and Thoroughbreds.

Bosanquet township favors Clydesdales, 3 out of 4 of the sires being of that breed, and the other a German Coach. All are sound, but the average quality is not as high as it might be. There is considerable of a Clydesdale type in the 1,500 mares in this township, their average weight being 1,200 lbs., and quality fair, and average age 7 years. Service fees are $10 to $15.

In Sarnia township breeding proceeds largely on Roadster lines, there being four sires of this breed to one Clydesdale, one Percheron and a Hackney. Three of the Roadsters are grades; all the sires are sound. In conformation the average is fair, but the percentage of colts is small. Ten to fifteen dollars are the fees charged. The report on the mares describes them as of general purpose type, and not very good, averaging 1,100 lbs. in weight, and in quality not as good as they might be. Their average age is 9 years.

Considering that in Moore township there are about 1,100 mares of fair quality, weighing 1,200 lbs., and mostly of Clydesdale and Shire draught type, the balance being Roadster and Percheron, the proportion of 5 Clydesdale stallions to one Percheron, a German Coach Horse, and three Roadsters is not excessive. Of the stallions, three are grades, and all are fairly sound, while four are well up in years. Four rank well as to conformation and action, and others are about the average. Service fees are comparatively small, $7 to $12.

Lambton — Continued.

Two Roadsters, a Clydesdale, and a Percheron represent the breeds as sires in Sombra township, which contains 700 mares, general purpose and mixed in type and not very good in conformation or quality. They average 1.050 lbs., and average age is 9 years. The stallions are all sound, and are fair in conformation and action. They are all grades. Fees are low from $7 to $10.

Medium is the quality of the mares in Dawn township, which average 1,150 lbs. in weight, and are of a medium Clydesdale type, some having Roadster and Shire characteristics. Their average age is 8 years. There are only three stallions in the township, two Clydesdales (one a grade), and a Shire, the latter in his first season. They do not average very high in rating, and service fees average from $8 to $15, the former for the grade.

In Enniskillen township, sires of the heavy breeds are in the majority, there being five Clydesdales (two being grades), one Shire, two Roadsters, and a French Canadian. With four exceptions the quality is not extra good, but all are fairly sound. In ages, they range from 2 to 9 years, and service fees from $8 to $12. The percentage of foals is fairly good in most cases. Mares total 1,200, and are of Clydesdale and Roadster type. Their average weight is 1,200 lbs., quality fair and average age 7 years.

STALLIONS.

Breeding.	Number.	Average weight. Pounds.	Average age.	Serviceably sound.	Average conformation.	Number of mares served.	Average service fee.
							$
Clydesdales, Imported	16	1,760	8	All	Medium good	1,650	11
Clydesdales, Canadian-bred	11	1,740	10	All	Fair	1,287	10
Grades, Clydesdale	9	1,475	7	All	Fair	542	8
Shires, Imported	3	1,930	9	All	Good	393	12
Grades, Shire	2	1,625	8	All	Fair	155	10
Percherons, Imported and Grades. (2 Pure-bred, 1 Grade)	3	1,460	9	All	Medium good	272	9
Hackneys, Imported	2	1,250	5½	All	Good	189	12
Standard-breds, Imported	9	1,167	10	All	Good	675	12
Roadsters, Canadian-bred	5	1,150	7	All	Fairly good	245	10
Grades, Roadster	13	1,050	7	All	Very Fair	661	9
Thoroughbreds, Imported	1	1,300	20	All	Fair	75	10
German Coach Horses	3	1,350	13	All	Medium good	225	11
French Canadian, and Grades and Cleveland Bay (1 French Canadian, 1 Grade French Canadian, 1 Grade Cleveland Bay)	3	1,375	6	All	Fairly good	196	10
Totals	80					6,565	

Lambton.—Concluded.

MARES.

Townships.	Number of mares bred to stallions inspected in Township.	Type.	Average weight. Pounds.	Average quality.	Average age.
Brooke	976	Somewhat Draught, General Purpose and some Roadsters........	1,150	Medium..	7
Euphemia	226	General Purpose	1,100	Only middling...	9
Warwick	1,176	Mostly Draught with some Roadsters	1,250	Good	6
Plympton.............	1,420	Very mixed...................	1,100	Only fair	8
Bosanquet	472	A good deal of Clydesdale blood....	1,200	Fair	7
Sarnia...............	483	General Purpose and not too good..	1,100	Not too good ...	9
Moore...............	712	Mostly Draught, Clydesdale and Shire, and some Roadsters and Percheron....................	1,200	Fair	6
Sombra...............	156	General Purpose, not very good	1,050	Not good	9
Dawn	235	Medium, Clydesdale and some Roadster and Shire	1,150	Medium..	8
Enniskillen	709	Clydesdales and Roadsters	1,200	Fair	7
Total..............	6,565				

MARES BRED TO DIFFERENT CLASSES OF STALLIONS.

Stallions.	Total.		Serviceably sound.			Not serviceably sound.		
	Number of stallions.	Number of mares bred to.	Number of stallions.	Number of mares bred to.	Average fee.	Number of stallions.	Number of mares bred to.	Average fee.
Registered Stallions..	53	5,096	53	5,096	$ 11	....	....	$ ....
Grade Stallions......	27	1,469	27	1,469	9	....	....	....
Totals	80	6,565	80	6,565		....	....	...

The public meeting for the county of Lambton was held at Petrolea, on November 19th. There were present about thirty breeders and others interested in horse breeding.

After considerable discussion, those present put themselves on record as favorable to an Inspection and Licensing Act, and that after a reasonable time, there should be compulsory legislation. Some of the reasons given at the meeting for inferior quality among the horses were the sale of the best mares to outside buyers, the syndicating of inferior stallions, and the inability of the average farmer to detect unsoundness. The use of inferior sires, owing to cheaper fees charged, was also one prominent cause of deterioration of stock.

An informal meeting was held in the Council Chamber, Forest, November 13th. It was unanimously agreed that an Inspection and Registration Act would help the horse industry. The holding of spring shows for stallions, under the auspices of the Agricultural Society was highly recommended.

SPECIAL REPORT OF INSPECTORS.

In the first place we wish to say that it is not possible for us to give as full and comprehensive a report as we would have done had more time been placed at our disposal. We were not able to inspect every stallion in each district, and therefore did not come in contact with the breeders and users of such animals.

However, we are of the opinion that the Department could not have made a more popular move than to give consideration to the adoption of an Inspection and License Act. Resolutions in favor of these points have been unanimously adopted at all our meetings, and in fact by all individuals with whom we had the privilege of talking about these subjects.

As to the condition of the horse breeding industry, we might say that it certainly requires some directing. There are many causes for the present condition. The first and greatest has been indiscriminate and careless breeding. In the second place we hear complaints from the owners of stallions, of the great scarcity of good mares of all breeds or types to breed from. During our trip this was a very noticeable fact. Some attribute it to the high prices being offered by farmers and breeders of Manitoba and the other western provinces. This may be partially true at the present time; still we cannot but think that carelessness and lack of interest, or, in other words, lack of foresight on the part of the farmers and breeders, is to a great extent responsible for the present bad conditions of our brood mares.

As a Province we are peculiarly situated, having perhaps better facilities in this country than in any other for the breeding of high class, well bred horses of any type or breed. Our surroundings are such as to bring us in close proximity to the best markets of America. In fact, some years ago the great republic to the south of us were purchasers of a great number of high class horses which were bred in our Province at that time, namely, the draught horse, and the high class harness and saddle horse; and we venture to say if the people of this Province had been more careful to breed along the lines of the foundation laid in this country thirty or forty years ago, we would to-day be head and shoulders above any other country in being able to produce the best of the above mentioned classes.

The existing evils can partially be remedied by education, but the general opinion is that an Inspection Act will have the greatest tendency to improve the present conditions, from the fact that no stallion inferior in breeding and individuality would then be given a permit to go into commission. Therefore the breeders and users will not have to withstand the solicitations of wily horse owners inducing them to use undesirable animals. which, coupled with a desire for a cheap fee, has been one of the chief factors in bringing about the present low standard. It is impossible to buy a first-class horse for commercial use from the farmers of this Province.

Another cause which stands out prominently as a factor leading to the present conditions is the syndicating system. This fact has been impressed upon us for a number of years, and we found on our trip over five counties that in nearly every case animals sold by this system were of a very inferior quality, and cost from twenty to thirty per cent. more than a first-class animal of the same breed cost private individuals. This has also been the opinion of most of the people we met, and we believe that it is high time that this kind of unscrupulous plundering was stopped.

Another reason why an inspection placed in competent hands would be of great service, is that it would have a tendency to make importers and speculators more careful in making their selections, knowing that individuals

Report Inspectors District 1—Concluded.

or companies would not purchase unless the animal or animals had passed inspection.

LICENSING FEES.

In considering what fee should be charged in connection with licensing, it would be well to have as low a rate as possible, so that the horsemen might not consider it a hardship. In discussing this point at our meetings the concensus of opinion was that the fee should be large enough to make the Act workable. Some are of the opinion that five dollars should be the outside charge. We also think that this amount would be quite within the bounds of reason, and would be satisfactory to all concerned. This fee, of course, would cover the cost of issuing the license and inspection permit.

PUBLIC MEETINGS.

Public meetings were held at Chatham, Aylmer, St. Thomas, Forest, London, Essex and Petrolea. In each place the meetings were small in numbers, but made up for that in enthusiasm. Each meeting entered heartily into the discussion of the several points in question, namely, the licensing and inspection of stallions, together with a recommendation for registration. In every case we endeavored to encourage discussion on the part of those attending the meeting, our part being to receive the views placed before us. In each meeting we asked for a vote coupling together the license and inspection, taking up the registration separately. Each meeting gave an unanimous vote in favor of each of these votes. From the apparent feeling of those we came in contact with in the district visited by us, we are firmly of the opinion that public opinion is ready for regulations of this nature.

AS TO CONDITIONS FOUND IN EACH COUNTY.

Middlesex and East Lambton have probably the greatest number of good stallions in each and every class; they have also the best class of brood mares.

East and West Elgin come next, having a few as good as any we have seen in the above mentioned counties.

West Lambton being a comparatively new district, is somewhat behind, but breeders seem to evince a desire to improve their conditions.

East and West Kent seem to pay more attention to the producing of speed, irrespective of conformation and quality, yet in these ridings we met a few extra good types of the standard-bred trotting horse.

North Essex is away behind in all classes. We only saw one fairly good stallion in that riding.

South Essex has a mixed breed of a very poor quality.

As to the conditions predominating in each county, we find that they have all equal facilities for breeding any class of horse required for the market, of this or any country.

In our opinion the horse industry is one of the greatest, if not the greatest, branch of live stock, and we, together with all interested in the industry, are glad that the present important step has been taken, and trust, and in fact know, that you will receive the strong support of every right thinking man.

In conclusion, we think it would be well for the Department to place before the breeders of the Province the real requirements of our existing markets, what they are at present, and also the great expectations in connection with the development of our country.

(Signed) WM. SMITH,
J. D. GRAHAM.

DISTRICT NO. 2.

Counties.—Halton, Wentworth, Brant, Oxford, Norfolk, Haldimand, Welland and Lincoln.

Inspectors.—John Gardhouse, Highfield; Wm. Cain, V.S., Perth.

HALTON.

In the township of Esquesing the majority of the sires are of the lighter breeds, but two Clydesdales are kept for service. The different breeds represented are Roadsters, four (two being grades), Carriage, two (one a grade), and Clydesdales, two. In one instance the stallion was not seen owing to his owner being away from home. The average of soundness is low, only about one-half, while conformation also averages only fair. The service fees are correspondingly low, from $6 to $10, with one of $15. The Carriage stallions are among the best of those seen. Mares number but 262, of an average weight of 1,050 lbs. and average age 9 years; they are poor in type, and average quality is very poor. In commenting on this township the Inspectors say: "A large percentage of the stallions in this township should never be used for breeding purposes. Your committee are of the opinion that the horse industry would be very much improved in this township by the introduction of a few good stallions, as well as a large number of mares."

In Nassagaweya township there are four stallions, and only one pure-bred among them,—a Percheron. The rest are grades of Percheron, Roadster, and the French-Canadian type respectively. All are sound, and their conformation is generally good, the pure-bred being reported as of good type. $10 is the fee generally charged for service. There are 358 mares in the township, poor in type and average quality, average weight being 1,100 lbs. and age 9 years. Most of the mares in the township are bred. There are a few very good mares, but most are of no breeding, and not of good quality. One of the stallions would have made a good gelding.

Trafalgar township has long been noted as a breeding ground for light horses, of which some good specimens have been bred in the past. The leaning is still towards light horses, as is seen by the list of sires, among which are three Thoroughbreds, two Carriage horses (one a grade), two Hackneys. a German Coach, a Standard-bred, two Percherons (one a grade), two Clydesdales (one a grade). and a Shire grade. Eleven out of the list are sound and with the exception of four are of a good or fairly good type. Service fees are from $10 to $15, but in the case of a Thoroughbred the fee is given as $50. Mares number 784, and are of fair type and quality, averaging in weight 1,150 lbs. The Inspectors state: "Farmers in this township appear to be paying a little more attention to breeding, and also to the selection of sires, though, perhaps using more light sires than is in the best interests of the horse industry in a township like Trafalgar. A few young pure-bred mares have been purchased by farmers in this township for breeding purposes."

Nelson township runs a little more to heavy horses than Trafalgar. There are four Clydesdales and a Shire, all pure-bred, standing for service here as against two Standard-breds and a Roadster. Of the eight sires, six are sound or serviceably sound, and their type and conformation is mostly good. Two are 16 years old. There are a few very good registered mares in the township, but the type and quality of the majority, of the mares are poor. They average in weight, 1,100 lbs., and in age 7 years. More attention is paid to the breeding of heavy horses in Nelson township than in any of the other townships in Halton county.

*Halton—*Continued.

Inspectors' Remarks : "In the county of Halton your committee think that the heavy horse is the most suitable one for the average farmer to breed. We find that there are very few good mares to breed from, and no system followed by most of the breeders, some mares with one, two and even three heavy crosses in them being bred to poor light stallions, and poor light mares being bred to heavy horses. We also found that too often when a farmer has a mare that is used up and no good, he at once breeds her and tries to raise a colt. Suggestions were made that the Ontario Department of Agriculture distribute some literature that would impress on the farmers the advisability of breeding to type, and only breeding such mares as are suitable to raise colts that are sound, and that this would help the horse industry very much."

STALLIONS.

Breeding.	Number.	Average weight. Pounds.	Average age.	Serviceably sound.	Average conformation.	Number of mares served.	Average service fee.
							$
Clydesdales, Imported, Canadian-bred and Grades (4 Imported ; 3 Canadian-bred, 1 Grade)	8	1,635	5	3.....	Fairly good.	485	10
Shires, Imported and Grades (1 Pure-bred ; 1 Grade)	2	1,800	11	All....	Fairly good.	210	12
Percherons, Imported.............	2	1,800	5	All....	Good......	90	......
Grades, Percheron...............	2	1,575	5	All...	Good......	170	10 ·
Hackneys, Imported and Canadian-bred (1 Imported ; 1 Canadian-bred)	2	1,050	4	1.......	Good......	90	14
Standard-breds, Imported.........	2	1,100	9	All....	Good......	65	11
Roadsters, Canadian-bred.........	3	1,060	6	2......	Fairly good.	140	9
Grades, Roadster...... ·········	4	1,160	12	All....	Fairly good.	183	10
Thoroughbreds, Imported.........	3	1,170	14	All....	Good......	179	20
German Coach Horses and Grades and French Canadian Grades (1 Grade Coach ; 1 Grade French Canadian ; 1 German Coach Horse)........................	6	1,345	7	All....	Good......	347	10
Totals...............	34					1,959	

MARES.

Townships.	Number of mares bred to stallions inspected in Township.	Type.	Average weight. Pounds.	Average quality.	Average age.
Trafalgar...............	784	Some Clydesdale, Carriage and a few Roadsters......................	1,150	Fair.....	8
Esquesing..............	352	Light mostly......................	1,050	Very poor	9
Nassagaweya...........	358	General Purpose as a rule..........	1,100	Poor.....	9
Nelson.................	465	Heavy, with a few light	1,100	Poor.....	7
Total...............	1,959				

Halton.—Concluded.

MARES BRED TO DIFFERENT CLASSES OF STALLIONS.

Stallions.	Total.		Serviceably sound.			Not serviceably sound.		
	Number of stallions.	Number of mares bred to.	Number of stallions.	Number of mares bred to.	Average fee.	Number of stallions.	Number of mares bred to.	Average fee.
					$			$
Registered Stallions..	21	1,216	15	986	13	6	230	10
Grade Stallions......	13	743	12	708	10	1	35	10
Totals ....|	34	1,959	27	1,694	....	7	265	....

The public meeting for Halton was held at Milton on October the 11th. All the speakers recognized that there was room for great improvement in horse breeding in Halton county. The syndicating of stallions was very strongly condemned, and those present thought that there should be an inspection of all stallions before they were allowed to stand for service, some favoring a license fee, while others seemed to think that the stallion owner had enough expenses at present.

WENTWORTH.

In the townships of East and West Flamboro nine stallions are standing for service, and out of these there are two Thoroughbreds, both of excellent type, two grade Roadsters, two pure-bred Percherons, a grade Carriage horse, a Shire and a German Coach horse. Seven are serviceably sound, and the conformation and quality of most of them is up to the average. $8 to $10 are charged for service fees in most instances. Mares are poor in type and quality, averaging 6 years old, and 1,150 lbs. in weight. The Inspectors speak highly of the Thoroughbred sires, but think that some of the other sires should have been gelded. About twenty registered mares were found in the township.

There is not one sire heavier than a Percheron to be found in Beverly township. The list is made up of two Thoroughbreds, three Carriage stallions, a French-Canadian, a Roadster, a German Coach, and a Percheron. Only one case of unsoundness is reported, but quality and conformation is below what it should be. Fees for service range from $8 to $15. There are about 20 registered Clydesdale and Shire mares in this township, the balance being of a rather common type, averaging 1,150 lbs. in weight. Reporting on this township the Inspectors say: "We only found one imported horse here, and the stallions in general are not a very good class for the farmers to breed to. As there are a number of registered heavy mares it is important that there be good imported stallions of the same breeds to mate with them."

Out of the nine stallions in the City of Hamilton and surrounding township of Barton, one-third are not sound, while one is 21 years old, and another 11 years. Two are Thoroughbreds, three Standard-breds, one a Shire, one a Percheron, and the remaining one a grade. Their average for breeding purposes is low. The mares in this section are not of good type or quality,

Wentworth—Continued.

not over 1,100 lbs. on the average. One reason for this given by the Inspectors is that breeders are paying too much attention to race horses. The general run of service fees is $10 to $15, with one owner quoting $25.

A Percheron, a Roadster, and a Standard-bred comprise the sires in Saltfleet Township, the last named being of good type, and others fair. Two are reported sound, and their service fees run from $8 to $12. As regards the mares, these are of a poor light type not fitted for farming operations. "There seems to be very little breeding in Saltfleet Township" is the report of the Inspectors.

The Inspectors state: "We found a rather better class of horses in Binbrook Township, but there is still room for improvement. Farmers seem to have no fixed type. More heavy horses could be bred with advantage here. Mares are fair in type and quality, averaging 1,100 lbs. in weight." It is creditable that all the stallions standing for service are sound. Among them are a grade of Clydesdale blood, and another of French-Canadian. The breeding of the rest is: Standard-breds, three; English Coach, one; and Hackney, one. In conformation they average fairly good. The fees for the two grades are $7 and $8 respectively and for the pure-breds from $10 to $15.

Not one heavy stallion was inspected in Glanford Township, and farmers apparently are paying very little attention to horse breeding. The Inspectors report that some good heavy stallions and mares would be a good investment for farmers and breeders here. At present the mares are of no special breeding, and only average fair in quality, having an average weight of about 1,150 lbs. The rating of the stallions used is, on the whole, rather medium, but all are sound They include a Hackney, two Standard-breds, a grade German Coach, and a grade Carriage horse. Fees vary from $10 to $15.

Breeders in Ancaster Township are turning their attention more to breeding heavy horses and three Clydesdales were among the seven sires on service here. One is a Welsh pony, rated good, one a Percheron, one a Carriage horse, and two Roadsters (one being a grade). They are nearly all sound and score fairly well; service fees range from $10 to $15. There are twenty-one imported mares in the township, besides several registered Canadian-bred Clydesdale mares, and the general type and quality are fairly good.

Inspectors' Remarks: "In Wentworth farmers seem to have no fixed type. Far too many are breeding to light sires for the best interests of the horse industry. While we think that this county is one in which light horses can be raised with profit, yet too many farmers are making a mistake in breeding mares of a fair farm type to light road horses, some of which have very little breeding."

Wentworth—Continued.

STALLIONS.

Breeding.	Number.	Average Weight. Pounds.	Average Age.	Serviceably Sound.	Average Conformation.	Number of Mares Served.	Average Service Fee.
							$
Clydesdales, Imported, Canadian-bred and Grades (3 imported; 1 Canadian-bred; 1 grade)	5	1,640	6	All	Fair	322	10
Shires, Imported	2	1,800	4	All	Fairly good	105	12
Percherons	6	1,800	7	All	Mostly good	310	12
Hackneys, Imported and Canadian-bred (1 imported ; 1 Can.-bred)	2	1,375	5	All	Fairly good	195	12
Standard-breds, Imported and Roadsters, Canadian-bred (1 Standard-bred ; 7 Roadsters	8	1,190	9	7	Fairly good	234	12
Grades, Roadster	7	1,125	8	All	Fair	324	10
Thoroughbreds, Imported	3	1,060	9		Fairly good		
Thoroughbreds, Canadian-bred	3	1,100	5½	2	Fairly good	79	12
Grades, German Coach	3	1,370	8	2	Fairly good	270	10
English Coach Horse and Grades (1 pure-bred ; 6 grades)	7	1,350	13	6	Fair	366	9
Grades, French-Canadian and no particular breeding	3	1,225	10	All	Fairly good	278	11
Welsh Pony	1				Good	7	
Totals	50					2,490	

MARES.

Townships.	Number of Mares bred to Stallions inspected in Township.	Type.	Average Weight. Pounds.	Average Quality.	Average Age.
East and West Flamboro.	410	Mostly small, a few good registered Clydesdales	1,150	Poor	6
Beverly	538	A few registered Clydesdales and Shires, balance light	1,150	Fair	7
City of Hamilton and Barton	193	Light and rather poor	1,100	Poor	7
Saltfleet	120	Light and rather poor	1,000	Poor	8
Binbrook	534	More inclined to general purpose	1,100	Fair	8
Glanford	280	Light as a rule	1,050	Fair	8
Ancaster	415	Some Imported and Canadian-bred heavy mares, others general purpose and light	1,150	Fairly good	8
Total	2,490				

Wentworth—Concluded.

MARES BRED TO DIFFERENT CLASSES OF STALLIONS.

Stallions.	Total.		Serviceably Sound.			Not Serviceably Sound.		
	Number of Stallions.	Number of Mares Bred to.	Number of Stallions.	Number of Mares Bred to.	Average Fee.	Number of Stallions.	Number of Mares Bred to.	Average Fee.
					$			$
Registered Stallions.	30	1,271	28	1,262	13	2	9	8
Grade Stallions......	20	1,219	18	1,091	9	2	128	9
Totals	50	2,490	46	2,353	....	4	137	....

The public meeting for this county was held at Dundas on October 16th. Those present were in favor of the Government taking some steps to prevent poor, inferior, and unsound stallions from being used for breeding purposes, and if the time is ripe to have all stallions inspected. Some of the speakers stated that the stallions now used for breeding are not as good as those that used to travel some years ago.

BRANT.

While South Dumfries township favors the heavier sires to a considerable extent, having two Clydesdales, two Percherons, a general purpose grade, a French Canadian grade of a heavy type, and a grade Carriage horse, there is plenty of room for improvement in the ratings of the majority of them as regards soundness, conformation and quality. There are a number of very good mares in this township, some being newly imported Clydesdales. The general run of mares is of fairly good type, and very good quality, being young and of good average weight. From $8 to $15 is the run of service fees.

Brantford township has a fair representation of sires, consisting of five Clydesdales (of which no less than three are grades), two Hackneys, a Percheron, a general purpose horse, and a grade French horse. While some are of pretty fair type, the Inspectors state that some should not be used as sires. As regards soundness nearly all qualify as serviceably sound. Service fees vary from $7 and $8 for grades, to $15 for pure-breds. The general run of mares is rather poor as regards type and quality, 1,150 lbs. being the average weight, and 10 years the average age. A few Hackneys of a better type have lately been imported. Not many heavy mares are being bred.

Nothing but grade stallions, two Roadsters, a Carriage horse, and a general purpose horse were seen on the Indian Reserve, $10 is charged for service fee. The number of mares kept is 175, and out of these the Inspectors only saw two that looked like being useful brood mares. They report this section as being one in which many useful horses could be raised, and that something should be done to raise the standard of the horses, especially as to introducing heavy horses, as most of the land is heavy.

Brantford city and neighborhood, are well known as a centre of Standard-bred breeding, almost to the exclusion of other breeds. In the heavy

Brant.—Continued.

line, nothing better than two Clydesdale grades are found, only one of
which was seen by the Inspectors. They were also unable to see several of
the others. Besides eleven Roadsters and Standard-breds (five of which
are grades), and the two grade Clydesdales, there are, a Hackney, a
Hackney pony, a Shetland pony, and a German Coach horse. A few are
rated high, but several are below the average, and some are unsound. The
fees for services are in general from $9 to $15, with one quoted at $20, one
at $25, and one at $50, all three being for Roadsters. Mares are on the
whole a very inferior lot, but there are a few very good light ones. Their
average weight is 1,000 lbs., and age 10 years. The Inspectors think that
too many trotting bred stallions are being used for breeding purposes, and
that the horse interests would be served by the introduction of a few good
pure-bred heavy stallions.

The stallions located in Burford township are a very poor lot, being
all grades, one of Hackney blood, one Roadster, one Belgian, and the other
general purpose. Service fees are $8 to $10. Mares are also a very poor
class, not exceeding 1,000 lbs. in weight. The Inspectors comment as follows: "We understand that a few fair horses made stands in this township from adjoining townships."

Inspectors' Remarks: "The county of Brant is well supplied with
stallions so far as numbers are concerned, but there are not enough of the
right kind. Brant is well adapted for the raising of heavy horses, and we
think that if farmers and breeders would pay more attention to the breeding and raising of heavy horses, it would be a great advantage both to
themselves and to the horse industry of this county."

STALLIONS.

Breeding.	Number.	Average weight, Pounds.	Average age.	Serviceably sound.	Average con- formation.	Number of mares served.	Average ser- vice fee.
							$
Clydesdales, Imported	3	1,850	7	All	Fair....	345	14
Clydesdales, Canadian-bred	1	1,550	2	All	Good.....	....	.....
Grades, Clydesdale	5	1,600	9	4.......	Fair......	355	7
Percherons	3	1,870	5	All	Fairly good..	208	13
Hackneys, Imported	2	975	6	All	Fairly good..	190	12
Hackneys, Canadian-bred.........	2	1,250	4½	All	Fair......	210	15
Grades, Hackney	1	950	2	All	Fair......	8	10
Standard-breds, Imported.........	3	1,120	8	All	Good.....	180	18
Roadsters, Canadian-bred.........	3	1,090	6	2.......	Fairly good..	55	15
Grades, Roadster	8	1,000	7	6......	Fair.....	95	10
German Coach Horses and Grades (1 Pure-bred, 2 Grades).........	3	1,125	3½	1......	Fair......	138	10
Grades, French Canadian and Bel- gian (2 French Canadian, 1 Bel- gian)	3	1,525	10	2	Fair......	140	9
Shetland Pony	1	....	...	....	....	....	.....
Grades, (general purpose).........	4	1,300	10	3......	Only fair..	270	8
Totals...................	42					2,194	

Brant—Concluded.

MARES.

Townships.	Number of mares bred to stallions inspected in Township.	Type	Average weight.	Average quality.	Average age.
South Dumfries.........	425	A few very good imported Clydesdales........................:......	1,150	Very good	5
Brantford	824	Mostly light.................:......	1,150	Poor ..	10
Indian Reserve	49	Very light and poor `..............	950	Poor ..	9
City of Brantford and suburbs	746	Mostly light and inferior	1,000	Poor ..	10
Burford	150	Mostly light and inferior	1,000	Poor ..	10
Total...........	2,194				

MARES BRED TO DIFFERENT CLASSES ₁OF STALLIONS.

Stallions.	Total		Serviceably sound.			Not serviceably sound.		
	Number of stallions.	Number of mares bred to.	Number of stallions.	Number of mares bred to.	Average fee.	Number of stallions.	Number of mares bred to.	Average fee.
					$			$
Registered Stallions .	19	1,270	18	1,270	15	1	....	....
Grade Stallions	23	924	16	691	9	7	233	9
Totals........	42	2,194	34	1,961	....	8	233	....

The public meeting of Brant was held at Brantford, on October the 20th. There were not very many present, but every one there was given the opportunity to express his views. One speaker said that the only way to improve the standard of their horses was for the Ontario Department of Agriculture to get the Legislature to pass an Act making it compulsory that all stallions kept for service be inspected and registered. Another speaker said that while that would be a very stringent measure, he was unable to see how they were going to get rid of the mongrel class in any other way, and all were agreed that the mongrel horse was and has been most detrimental to the horse industry. As regards syndicating stallions, those present were generally agreed that the system could be successfully carried out, if there were not too many in the syndicate, and the horses were purchased at their proper value.

3 H.B

OXFORD.

There are a number of very good imported heavy stallions and mares in West Oxford township; also some good Hackneys. In spite of this many farmers are using some of the grade sires to be found here, for one of which, a grade Clydesdale, only $6, is asked for service fee. The usual range, however, is from $10 to $15, and one as high as $20. Among those on service are six pure-bred Clydesdales, one grade Clydesdale, two Hackneys, three grade Carriage horses, four Roadster grades, and a Coach grade. The majority are sound, but some are well up in years, one as old as 21 years. In this township are a number of very good Clydesdale fillies imported this year, and the average type and quality of the mares in the township, estimated at 680, is fairly good, average weight being 1,200 lbs.

The number of stallions in North Norwich township is not large, consisting of three, all grades, one respectively of Standard-bred, French, and Clydesdale blood. They are all sound. Eight and ten dollars are the service fees charged. Mares are only a fair lot, in number 250 and not of a distinctive type.

Stallions are more numerous in South Norwich township, among them being a good Clydesdale, Hackney and Percheron. Here, too, we find three grade sires, a Belgian, a general purpose, and a cross-bred Clydesdale and Shire. The service fees are as low as $8, and from $10 to $15 as the general run. The mares here are 420 in number, of a fair type and quality in general, while there are some 20 or 30 imported fillies to be found in the township, which are a very good lot, too good for some of the stallions used, so the Inspectors say.

Nineteen stallions travel in Dereham township, no less than eight being grades, and some of them of an inferior type, not to mention unsoundness. Among them are four pure-bred Clydesdales, one Shire, one Thoroughbred, four Roadsters, and a Percheron; while the grades are six Roadsters, one Belgian and a Clydesdale. The service fees range from eight to fifteen dollars, the lowest, of course, for grades. Mares are of various types, being only fair in quality, and evidently too many are being bred to poor sires.

There is an improvement of quality in the sires in North Oxford township, although only four in all, all being pure-breds, three Clydesdales and one a Standard-bred; all, too, are sound. From $10 to $15 are the service fees charged. Mares share in the improvement in quality which is fair, and there are a few very nice imported Clydesdale fillies and some Hackney fillies in the township.

"There are some useful animals in Blenheim township," say the Inspectors, "and most of the farmers seem to be breeding heavy horses and showing good judgment in the selection of sires." Out of the seven stallions found here, however, there are only three pure-breds (two Clydesdale and a Percheron) to four grades (two of Clydesdale, one of Roadster, and one of Carriage blood). Here fees run from $8 to $15. There are some very good mares to be found in the township, the average weight being 1,250 lbs., and average quality fair.

With the exception of a grade Roadster all the ten stallions found in Woodstock and the adjoining township of Blandford are registered. Quite a variety of sires are kept, ranging from two Clydesdales, three Standard-breds, a Thoroughbred, a Hackney, and an Arabian, to a Shetland pony. With a single exception they are sound, though not grading as high in quality and conformation as they might, a fact commented on by the Inspectors, who found some useful mares here, including a few imported Clydesdales. The general run of mares average 1,200 lbs., and are fair in type and quality.

3a H.B

Oxford—Continued.

The townships of East and West Zorra are well known as a section where heavy horses are well patronized, and, consequently we find nearly all the sires of the heavy breeds. Six Clydesdales (one a grade) a Shire, a Hackney and a Roadster comprise the total, and they all are rated fairly well, while the lowest service fee is $11, and the highest $20. Mares, too, among which are a number of excellent imported Clydesdale fillies, average very good and are of a good type, weighing about 1,300 lbs., and average age six years.

Of East Nissouri the Inspectors say: "In this township we did not see one real good stallion, but we learned that a few good imported heavy stallions from adjoining townships made stands in East Nissouri." The mares here are of a fairly good type, in weight about 1,150 lbs., and in quality very good. A number of them are registered Clydesdales, and a good many are of a very fair type with two or three crosses of heavy blood. Out of the six sires only one, a German Coach horse is pure-bred. There are three grade Clydesdales, and two Roadster grades.

Inspectors' Remarks: "In Oxford county there has been during the last few years quite a number of good imported Clydesdale stallions brought in, also a number of good imported young mares, which, if taken advantage of by the farmers, should, if properly mated, improve the present standard very much. As far as we are able to learn many of the farmers appear to be breeding a better class of mares and showing very good judgment in the selection of sires, but there are still quite a number that are using the poor, cheap horse."

STALLIONS.

Breeding.	Number.	Average weight. Pounds.	Average age.	Serviceably sound.	Average conformation.	Number of mares served.	Average service fee.
Clydesdales, Imported	20	1,700	6	All	Fairly good...	1,190	$15
Clydesdale, Canadian-bred	4	1,700	7	All	Fair......	265	10
Grades, Clydesdale	9	1,550	5	All	Fair......	324	9
Shires, Imported and Grades (2 imported, 1 grade)	3	1,785	8	All	Fairly good...	220	11
Percherons	3	1,400	6	All	Good.....	385	11
Hackneys, Imported	5	1,240	4	All	Very fairly good...	235	15
Standard-breds, Imported	6	1,130	13	All	Fair......	240	12
Roadsters, Canadian-bred	2	975	5	All	Fair......	1	15
Grades, Roadster	16	995	9	10	Fair......	516	9
Thoroughbreds, Imported	2	1,150	9	All	Good.....	162	15
German Coach Horses and Grades (1 Pure-bred, 1 Grade)	2	1,225	9	All	Fairly good...	130	11
Grades, English Coach Horse	4	1,250	12	3	Fair.....	233	11
Grades, French Canadian and General Purpose (1 French Canadian, 1 General Purpose)	2	1,225	8	All	Fair......	87	8
Grades, Belgian	2	1,575	5½	All....	Fair......	167	9
Ponies, Arab and Shetland (1 Arab, 1 Shetland)	2	725	9	All ...	Good.....	36	15
Totals	82					4,191	

Oxford—Concluded.

MARES.

Township.	Number of mares bred to stallions inspected in Township.	Type.	Average weight.	Average quality.	Average age.
West Oxford.............	736	Some good heavy mares, but many light ones.....................	1,200	Fairly good..	8
North Norwich	252	Fair	1,150	Fair	7
South Norwich.........	420	Some good heavy mares and others of lighter type................	1,150	Fair	8
Dereham...........·....	740	Fair	1,050	Only fair.	8
North Oxford...........	273	A few good Clydesdales, o t h e r s medium	1,150	Fair	9
Blenheim	520	Fair stamp of mares, including some good ones	1,250	Fair	8
Blandford and town of Woodstock	521	A few Clydesdales, others medium .	1,200	Fair	7
East and West Zora	505	Very good, including many imported Clydesdales..................	1,300	Very good	6
East Nissouri	224	Fairly heavy, with some good registered Clydesdales............	1,150	Very good	6
Total..............	4,191				

MARES BRED TO DIFFERENT CLASSES OF STALLIONS.

Stallions.	Total.		Serviceably sound.			Not serviceably sound.		
	Number of Stallions.	Number of mares bred to.	Number of Stallions.	Number of mares bred to.	Average fee.	Number of Stallions.	Number of mares bred to.	Average fee.
Registered Stallions .	47	2,734	47	2,734	13	....	....	....
Grade Stallions......	35	1,457	28	1,359	9	7	98	8
Totals	82	4,191	75	4,093	....	7	98	....

At the public meeting held at Woodstock, October 27th, attendance was not large, but most of the speakers seemed to think that stallions should be inspected. Some claimed that all stallions used for breeding purposes should be registered, while others asserted that it would not do to shut out stallions which had proved themelves good sires, although they could not be registered, claiming that really good individuals should be allowed a permit. It was thought that there should be an Act passed giving the stallion owners a lien on the mare as soon as she is bred. With regard to syndicating stallions, opinions were given that in some sections, if a syndicate was formed of four or five men and they selected a first-class stallion, better satisfaction would be given than the present system of syndicates which include too many men.

NORFOLK.

In Townsend township there are only two pure-bred sires out of thirteen, and with few exceptions they are not of a very good standard although there is only one case of unsoundness. The pure-breds are a Percheron and a Hackney. Grades are of Clydesdale, Hackney, Roadster, and general purpose stock. A Clydesdale grade is giving service for $5, the highest fee 's $15. for the Percheron. "Too many farmers are using grade sires. A few good heavy mares have been bought by breeders during the year."

Woodhouse Gore township is fortunate in being in close proximity to Simcoe, where a number of very good imported horses are owned. These are for sale. Some good fillies, too, have been imported and will make useful brood mares. Otherwise the quality of the average mare is fair. Weight 1,200 lbs., and type very fair. There is only one grade sire, a Hackney, out of nineteen kept. Of the eighteen pure-bred, nine are Clydesdales, two Shires, three Hackneys, three Percherons and one Standard-bred. Fees run from $10 to $15. All are sound and no less than eleven were imported last July.

In Windham township are a pure-bred Clydesdale, a registered Standard-bred and a Percheron grade, and strange to say, the grade earns a larger fee than the second named. $9 to $10 are the fees charged. All sires are sound. Mares are a very poor lot, with only a rare exception.

While the soil of Middleton township is light, and light breeds can be profitably raised, there is room for great improvement in the quality of the horses found here. There are very few good mares, the type and quality being described as poor. The average weight is 1,050 lbs. There are kept for service three pure-bred Roadsters, a Clydsdale, a Hackney, and a Roadster grade, and a general purpose grade. As high as $15, and as low as $8 is charged for fees. No unsoundness is reported.

The stallions in North Walsingham township are not of a very high order, there being too many inferior horses in service, and there is some unsoundness among them. Out of the thirteen, eight are grades of Clydesdale, Roadster, Hackney, and French stock. Among the pure-breds are four Clydesdales and a Suffolk Punch, one of the best. A Hackney grade and a Roadster grade have the lowest service fees, $5; other fees are $7, $8, $9, $10 and $12. There are practically no good mares in this township, and their average weight is about 1,100 lbs.

Charlotteville is another township that has a poor class of mares, and as many of the farmers are breeding to inferior grade stallions, prospects are not very bright for raising the standard of horse flesh here. There are only two pure-bred sires, Clydesdales. The rest are two grade Clydesdales, a grade Percheron, and a grade Roadster, and fees are from $6 to $12.

With two exceptions the average of the sires in Woodhouse township is not high, and also there are very few good mares in the section, the general run being poor. Among pure-bred sires kept, are a Hackney, a Thoroughbred, a German Coach horse, and a Percheron, while grades are of Clydesdale, German Coach, Hackney, and Standard-bred blood. Five to twenty-five dollars are the fees for service.

The only representatives of registered stock in Houghton township are a Hackney and a Suffolk Punch. Other sires are a Belgian, Clydesdale, and Roadster, all grades. Service fees run from $8 to $12. Mares are a very poor lot, and there is room for some good heavy stallions.

Inspectors' Remarks: "The County of Norfolk is very well supplied in some townships with a very good class of stallions, there having been a number of good imported horses brought out this year, a number of them

Norfolk—Continued.

being held by the importers for sale. If two or three good men would join together and select a good first-class stallion at a reasonable price, and a number of these were kept in the county it would help to improve the standard of the horses very much, as some of the townships have a very inferior lot of stallions."

STALLIONS.

Breeding.	Number.	Average weight, Pounds.	Average age.	Serviceably sound.	Average conformation.	Number of mares served.	Average service fee.
							$
Clydesdales, Imported	14	1,650	5	All	Fairly good	663	12
Clydesdales, Canadian-bred	3	1,700	4	All	Fair	230	10
Grades, Clydesdale	7	1,450	6	All	Fair	225	8
Shires, Imported	2	1,650	2	All	Good	1	15
Percherons	5	1,760	4	All	Fair	160	12
Grades, Percheron	2	1,375	3½	All	Only fair	33	10
Suffolk Punch	2	1,800	7²	All	Fairly good	157	10
Hackneys, Imported and Thorough- breds, Imported (4 Hackneys, 1 Thoroughbred)	5	1,150	9	All	Good	208	12
Hackneys, Canadian-bred	3	1,300	7	All	Good	380	14
Grades, Hackney	5	1,000	3	All	Fair	226	8
Roadsters Canadian-bred	6	1,130	9	All	Fair	397	10
Grades, Roadster	13	1,175	9	9	Fair	869	9
German Coach Horses	1	1,400	8	All	Fair	20	10
Grades, German Coach	1	1,250	4	All	Fair	65	8
Grades—French Canadian, Belgian and General Purpose (1 French Canadian, 1 Belgian, 3 general purpose)	5	1,265	7	All	Fair	369	8
Totals	74					4,003	

MARES.

Townships.	Number of Mares bred to Stallions inspected in Township.	Type.	Average weight.	Average quality.	Average age.
Townsend	700	Mostly light but a few good heavy mares	1,150	Rather poor	8
Woodhouse Gore	565	Several good imported heavy fillies, balance fairly good	1,200	Fair	7
Windham	122	Very poor		Poor	9
Middleton	610	Light and rather poor	1,050	Poor	8
North Walsingham	744	Very poor	1,100	Poor	9
Charlotteville	369	Very poor	1,100	Poor	9
Woodhouse	436	Not many good mares in this township	1,100	Poor	8
Houghton	457	Light and poor	1,050	Poor	9
Total	4,003				

Norfolk—Concluded.

MARES BRED TO DIFFERENT CLASSES OF STALLIONS.

Stallions.	Total.		Serviceably sound.			Not serviceably sound.		
	Number of Stallions.	Number of Mares bred to.	Number of Stallions.	Number of Mares bred to.	Average fee.	Number of Stallions.	Number of Mares bred to.	Average fee.
					$			$
Registered Stallions..	41	2,216	41	2,216	11	....	....	....
Grade Stallions......	33	1,787	29	1,522	8	4	265	9
Totals........	74	4,003	70	3,738	....	4	265	....

The system of inspection was very freely discussed at the public meeting held at Simcoe, November 3rd, the majority of those attending being strongly in favor of an Inspection Act, a number claiming that only pure-bred sires should be allowed to stand for service. Others, again, would favor allowing s allions that were good individuals and had proved themselves good producers to be used, although not eligible for registration. It was the general opinion that stallions unsound or of inferior type and quality should not be a..owed to stand for service. This meeting also favored an act giving the stallion owner a lien on the mare when bred.

The importation of bronchos into the county was very strongly condemned, and those present thought that some action should be taken to prevent any more being brought in, as they were considered a curse to the horse industry.

HALDIMAND.

Seneca township has a good type of mares, good in quality and averaging 1,300 lbs., being, apparently, superior to the sires in service there. The stallions are quite inferior on the whole, the list totalling two pure-bred Clydesdales, a grade Clydesdale and a grade Standard-bred. Fees quoted are $8 to $12.

Oneida township, too, has a good useful lot of mares of about the same weight, including a few registered ones. Here, there is a preponderance of grade sires, there being only one pure-bred Clydesdale to two Roadster grades and one Clydesdale grade. One of the grades earns the highest fee, $15; for the others, the fees are $9 and $10.

As regards Walpole township the Inspectors say: "There are a great many stallions in this township, but only a few really good ones. Farmers, though they have not very many registered horses, have a very good class of mares with some breeding in them, weighing about 1.300 lbs., which they appear anxious to breed to good stallions." Clydesdale sires are eleven in number (four being grades), Hackney three (two being grades), Standard-breds three (two grades), Cleveland Bay one, French Coach horse one, and French Draught one. The lowest fee is $5, and maximum $15.

Not a single pure-bred sire was inspected in Rainham township, and their quality is quite low. A number of good stallions from other townships, however, are being used by farmers who are anxious to secure first-

Haldimand—Continued.

class sires for their mares, which are a very good average lot, with practically no registered ones among them. Their average weight is 1,250 lbs. The sires for service in the township comprise grade Clydesdales, Roadsters, and a Coach horse.

The same condition as to sires prevails in Cayuga township, where four grades of Clydesdale, Thoroughbred, Coach, and Standard-bred breeding stand for service. They are far below the average, and service fees are $8 and $10. Mares are a useful lot, averaging 1,200 lbs., and of fair quality.

In Canboro township there are just three sires, a pure-bred Clydesdale, a Standard-bred and a grade—a general purpose. This is a township in which more and better horses should be raised, and a few good mares and one or two good stallions could do good work in improving the standard. Mares kept are fair in type and quality, weighing 1,200 lbs. on the average. Service fees are $8, $9 and $10. Stallions are rated as fair.

The Inspectors say: "While there are a few very fair horses in the township of Moulton, there is room for one or two good pure-bred sires, and we think that farmers would readily patronize them. Mares here are a very fairly god lot of 1,300 lbs. weight on the average." A pure-bred Clydesdale and a grade of that breeding, two Shire grades, a pure-bred Percheron, and two Roadsters (one a grade), form the stud list; fees are from $8 to $15.

Inspectors' Remarks: "It appeared to us, as far as we were able to learn, that the farmers in Haldimand County were using very good judgment in breeding. They seem to have a lot of very good mares, though very few are registered, and they are using the best stallions they have, and are breeding more to type."

STALLIONS.

Breeding.	Number.	Average weight Pounds.	Average age.	Serviceably sound.	Average conformation.	Number of mares served.	Average service fee.
							$
Clydesdales, Imported	5	1,775	13	4......	Very fairly good	399	10
Clydesdales, Canadian-bred	5	1,700	7	All	Fairly good.....	559	10
Grades, Clydesdale	12	1,625	6	10.....	Fair............	663	8
Percherons and Grade Shires (1 Percheron, 2 Grade Shires)......	3	1,700	6	All	Good..........	275	10
Hackneys, Imported, and Grades (1 Hackney, 2 Grades)..........	3	1,150	8	All	Fairly good.....	157	13
Standard-breds, Imported, and Roadsters, Canadian-bred (2 Imported, 2 Roadsters)............	4	1,150	12	3......	Fair..........	278	12
Grades, Roadster and Thoroughbred (9 Roadster, 1 Thoroughbred)	10	1,100	12	9......	Fair..........	372	10
French Coach and English Coach, Imported (1 French, 1 English)...	2	1,350	10	All	Fairly good.....	205	10
Grades, English Coach	2	1,250	6	All	Fair..........	88	9
French Draught and General Purpose (1 French Draught, 1 General Purpose)......................	2	1,550	5	All	Fairly good....	164	9
Totals	48					3,160	

Haldimand—Continued.

MARES.

Townships.	Number of mares bred to stallions inspected in Township.	Type.	Average weight, pounds.	Average quality.	Average age.
Seneca	430	Good, fairly heavy	1,300	Good..	8
Canboro'	263	A few heavy, mostly fairly light....	1,200	Fair...	8
Oneida	196	Good, useful type	1,300	Good..	7
Moulton	608	Fairly heavy	1,300	Good..	8
Walpole	1,297	Very good type	1,300	Good..	6
Rainham	227	Fairly good, tending to heavy	1,250	Very good.	8
Cayuga	139	Useful grade draught	1,200	Fair...	9
Total	3160				

MARES BRED TO DIFFERENT CLASSES OF STALLIONS.

Stallions.	Total.		Serviceably Sound.			Not serviceably sound.		
	Number of stallions.	Number of mares bred to.	Number of stallions.	Number of mares bred to.	Average fee.	Number of stallions.	Number of mares bred to.	Average fee.
Registered Stallions	19	1,679	17	1,452	$12	2	227	$10
Grade Stallions	29	1,481	26	1,318	9	3	163	9
Totals	48	3,160	43	2,770	....	5	390	....

'There was a very good turn out at the public meeting at Fisherville, on November 8th, and some very strong opinions were expressed on certain questions, the present system of syndicating being strongly criticised. It was claimed to be a dangerous one, and that more men had been robbed through it in Haldimand county than in any other district; that one man would be bribed in order to get another, and that it ought to be put down, unless some plan was devised whereby the members of the syndicate would be protected by a guarantee, as, in many cases, counterfeits were substituted.

It was generally held that there was room for great improvement in the horse industry, and that, if breeders would breed with a purpose, we would not have the country full of a class of horses for which there is no demand.

Holdimand—Concluded.

The question of inspecting stallions was also very freely discussed. The opinion of the meeting was taken, and twelve voted for it, while eight were against, the majority of those present not voting either way.

WELLAND.

Wainfleet is a township that would benefit by the introduction of some good sires in the place of the five grades that now stand for service for fees from $5 up to $10. The mares are a fair lot, but better than the stallions in quality.

As a rule there appears to be very little interest taken in breeding in Pelham township. The mares are only fair and are not over 1,150 lbs. in weight. A Thoroughbred, Clydesdale, Shire, Hackney and Standard-bred, all pure-bred, and a Roadster grade and Percheron grade make up the total of sires. serving for fees ranging from $6 to $15.

Humberstone is a township which also neglects the breeding of horses, those raised being a very poor lot not over 1,000 lbs. in weight. Three grades and two pure-breds represent the sires, the latter being a Shire and a Percheron, the former Standard-bred, Percheron, and Hackney breeding. Fourteen dollars is the maximum fee and the minimum eight dollars.

Bertie township has three pure-bred stallions, a Belgian, a Standard-bred and a Shire, and one Standard-bred grade for service at fees from $10 to $12. Mares are an inferior lot, poor in type and quality and not exceeding 1,100 lbs. "A better class of horses is needed here" say the Inspectors.

The same remarks as to stallions and mares apply to Willoughby township, where there is the same apathy as to horse breeding as seems to prevail so generally in this district. There were only two stallions inspected here. a Percheron and a general purpose grade, with fees of $12 and $7 respectively.

A lack of good stallions and mares is also visible in Stamford township. where a Suffolk Punch and a Standard-bred are the only representative sires. Eleven and ten dollars are the fees charged.

In Crowland township the conditions warrant the Inspectors to again remark that "As in the other townships, there is very little interest taken in horse breeding." Three grades (two Percherons and a Roadster) comprise the list of sires. all being sound. but not of a high standard of quality. Mares are a very poor lot all round.

Inspectors' Remarks: "In Welland very little interest has been taken in horse breeding, as far as we could learn. Some horsemen say that some years ago Americans bought up all the best mares and took them away to the United States, leaving only a very inferior lot of mares to breed from, which. in most instances, were bred to light racing horses, which have produced a very inferior lot of stock. This section is well adapted for raising heavy and light horses, and it certainly would be of great benefit to the breeders, as well as to the horse industry if a few good stallions and a number of good mares were brought into the district."

Welland—Continued.

STALLIONS.

Breeding.	Number.	Average weight Pounds.	Average age.	Serviceably sound.	Average conformation.	Number of mares served.	Average service fee
							$
Clydesdales, Canadian-bred and Shires, Imported and Canadian (1 Clyde, 1 Shire Imported, 2 Shires Canadian-bred)	4	1,710	4	All	Fair......	307	11
Percherons	2	1,650	4	All	Fair......	160	13
Grades, Percheron..............	3	1,530	7	All	Fair......	215	9
Suffolk Punch and Belgians (1 Suffolk Punch, 1 Belgian)..........	2	1,725	9	1......	Fair......	148	11
Hackneys and Grades (1 of each)..	2	1,150	5	All	Fair......	130	12
Standard-breds and Thoroughbreds Imported (3 Standard-breds, 1 Thoroughbred).................	4	1,135	13	All	Fair......	204	12
Grades, Roadster................	7	1,045	6	All	Fair......	177	9
Grades, Coach....................	2	1,150	4	All	Fair......	80	7
General Purpose................	2	1,200	7	All	Fair......	22	7
Totals....................	28					1,443	

MARES.

Townships.	Number of mares bred to stallions inspected in Township.	Type.	Average weight.	Average quality.	Average age.
Wainfleet...............	157	General purpose	1,150	Fair ...	10
Pelham	417	A few heavy, mostly light.	1,150	Just fair	9
Humberstone	230	Poor, light kind...............	1,000	Poor...	10
Bertie	262	Poor, light kind.................	1,100	Inferior	10
Willoughby	92	Poor, light kind.................	1,100	Poor...	9
Stamford	95	Poor, light kind.................	1,050	Poor...	9
Crowland	190	Poor, light kind.........	1,100	Poor...	10
Total	1,443				

Welland—Concluded.

MARES BRED TO DIFFERENT CLASSES OF STALLIONS.

Stallions.	Total.		Serviceably sound.			Not serviceably sound.		
	Number of stallions.	Number of mares bred to.	Number of stallions.	Number of mares bred to.	Average fee.	Number of stallions.	Number of mares bred to.	Average fee.
Registered Stallions..	13	909	12	859	$ 12	1	50	$ 11
Grade Stallions......	15	534	15	534	9	....	....	....
Totals	28	1,443	27	1,393	....	1	50	....

The Welland meeting on the evening of November 14th was not very well attended, and not much information was gleaned. The general opinion of those present appeared to be opposed to the present system of syndicating stallions. One speaker was in favor of inspection, and a few in favor of a Licensing Act. All present agreed that the horses in Monck and Welland were of a very poor type and quality, and that it would be in the best interests of the horse industry if some steps were taken by the Government to prevent some of the poorer sorts of stallions being used for breeding purposes.

LINCOLN.

One pure-bred Hackney and three unregistered sires are all the stallions of Grantham township. Twenty-five dollars is the highest and ten dollars the lowest fee. Mares are of fair average quality, but not good in type, and weigh 1,150 lbs. The Inspectors urge the introduction of one or two good sires into this township and also some good mares.

The quality of the horses in Niagara township has improved considably during the past few years, but is still far from satisfactory. There are a very few imported mares here, but the general average can only be stated as fair, and weight 1,150 lbs. There are nine stallions kept for service. including 4 Clydesdales, pure-bred, a registered Standard-bred three grades of that breeding and a Carriage grade. Stud fees are fairly good— $10 to $15. The quality of the sires averages fair.

Two grade Standard-breds and a Thoroughbred make up the sires in Louth township. This is a fruit section, and in consequence medium-sized horses are required for working in the orchards and under trees, hence, the mares are under-sized and poor, there being very few good mares found here.

Only one grade Carriage horse was inspected in Clinton township, and its fee is $12. Mares in this township also are a poor lot.

The same remarks apply to the mares in Grimsby township for the service of which there are a German Coach, a Standard-bred and a French Coach horse, a grade. All are sound and fair in conformation. Service fees are $12 to $15.

Mares are poor in type and quality in Gainsboro township, and there is room for improvement both as regards them and the stallions. At pre-

Lincoln—Continued.

sent there are four of the latter, a Percheron, a Standard-bred, a Road-ster grade and a Carriage horse. The lowest fee is $5 and highest $15.

Inspectors' Remarks: "In going over Lincoln county we did not see very many heavy horses, and, as this is a great fruit district, a number of medium sized horses are used by those engaged in the business, for working among the fruit trees. We think, that, perhaps, as many horses are being bred as can be raised with profit in a section like this."

STALLIONS.

Breeding.	Number.	Average weight. Pounds.	Average age.	Serviceably sound.	Average conformation.	Number of mares served	Average service fee.
Clydesdales, Imported	2	1,800	6½	All	Fair......	72	8 12
Clydesdales, Canadian-bred and Grades (2 Canadian-bred, 1 Grade)	3	1,710	4	All ..	F'rly good	245	12
Standard-breds and Thoroughbreds (1 Standard-bred Imported, 2 Canadian-bred, 1 Thoroughbred)	4	1,150	10	3......	F'rly good	205	12
Grades, Roadster	7	1,075	8	All	Fair......	207	9
German Coach and Grades of French and English Coach (1 German Coach, 1 French Coach and 3 English Coach)................	5	1,325	10	All	Fair......	289	11
Percheron and Carriage Grades (1 Percheron, 1 Grade)............	2	1,525	5	All	Good.....	217	12
Hackneys, Canadian-bred	1	1,200	5	All	Fair......	16	25
Totals..................	24					1,251	

MARES.

Townships.	Number of mares bred to stallions inspected in Township.	Type.	Average weight. Pounds.	Average quality.	Average age.
Grantham	146	Rather light	1,150	Fair	10
Niagara	410	Rather light	1,150	Fair.....!	9
Louth..................	42	Undersized	1,100	Poor ....!	9
Gainsboro	354	Small and poor....................	1,100	Rather p'r!	8
Clinton................	58	Poor and light	1,150	Poor	9
Grimsby	241	Poor and light	1,150	Poor ....!	9
Total	1,251				

Lincoln—Concluded.

MARES BRED TO DIFFERENT CLASSES OF STALLIONS.

Stallions.	Total.		Serviceably sound.			Not serviceably sound.		
	Number of stallions.	Number of mares bred to.	Number of stallions.	Number of mares bred to.	Average fee.	Number of stallions.	Number of mares bred to.	Average fee.
Registered Stallions..	11	756	10	716	$ 15	1	40	$ 12
Grade Stallions	13	495	13	495	11	....	....	....
Totals	24	1,251	23	1,211	....	1	40	....

There were a fair number present at the meeting, held at St. Catharines, November 17th. The majority of the speakers seemed to think that something ought to be done to try to improve the present condition of the horse industry, and a motion was carried in favor of an act being passed by the Government, giving the stallion owner a lien on the mare, and also on the colt until the service fee was paid. They also passed a motion in favor of an Inspection Act, and the majority appeared to be in favor of not allowing any stallion to stand for public service that was not registered in the recognized stud book of the breed to which it belonged, one speaker stating that all horses should be put out of business which would not register, pass a proper inspection and have a license. Another speaker thought that that would be a difficult measure to put into effect in a country like this, where most men like to be their own judges. Some thought that mares should be inspected as well as stallions.

SPECIAL REPORT OF INSPECTORS.

In submitting our report, we beg leave to say that we tried to keep our own counsel on all occasions, and to gather what information we could from the owners of stallions, and others who were interested in the horse business, without influencing them in any way by expressing our own opinions. In most sections, quite a large interest was taken in the investigation by most of the stallion owners, the large majority expressing themselves very freely as being in favor of the inspection and licensing of all stallions allowed to stand for service.

We were rather surprised on some occasions to find men who were in favor of this system, whose stallions would be among the first to fall, giving us the impression that they had not given the subject that serious consideration, that in our opinion it requires.

At most of the public meetings held we found those present quite ready to express their views; but with very few exceptions the opinions offered did not appear to your Inspectors to have received that due consideration and forethought that an important matter of this kind demands. In some sections we found those who were very much opposed to inspection and also licensing, claiming that while the class of sires that is being

Report Inspectors' District 2.—Concluded.

used is not what it should be, it would be much better for the Department of Agriculture to conduct an educational campaign by the distribution of literature on horse breeding throughout the Province, through the short course in judging at the Ontario Agricultural College, the Agricultural Societies and Spring Stallion Shows; and at Farmers' Institute meetings to have up-to-date and successful horse breeders as lecturers.

We found in some sections several stallions owned by syndicates, and on inquiring as to the success of said system learned in most cases that it had not proved to be very satisfactory; in many cases it was claimed that the stallions had been put in at very much more than their actual value; and in some cases it was claimed that the horses were not breeders, and should not have been sold for that purpose. While the system on the whole appears to have given very poor satisfaction, and should not be encouraged, we think it could be adopted with advantage in some sections, if three or four good farmers would join together, have a meeting, and decide just what kind of a stallion they should have in that section; then select two good judges to purchase said stallion at a right price; get the proper guarantee and then several first-class stallions might be used where there are none at present.

We found far too many inferior sires being used throughout the district. Unfortunately many farmers look at first cost only and use these sires. We also found a large number of inferior and unsound mares which in our opinion should never be used for breeding purposes. And in consequence it is important that more educational work be taken up along this line, in order to impress breeders with the idea of using a better class of females as well as sires.

In many sections we found a large number of breeders had no fixed type, some with very good heavy mares with two or three Clydesdale or Shire crosses in them, using a Percheron or some breed of light stallion, which can only have one result, and that is to injure the horse breeding industry of the Province.

We trust that the information received from this investigation may be of value to the Department in the effort to further the horse breeding industry, one of the most important branches of live stock development in the Province at the present time, and while at nearly every public meeting the majority appeared to be in favor of inspection and licensing, as already stated, we are of the opinion that the time is not yet ripe for such legislation.

We feel that the Department might by some well directed means endeavor to educate the people, so that in the near future they may be able to see the advisability of an Inspection Act at least, and probably a license act also, and trust that the labors of the Department may accomplish the desired end.

                 (Signed) JOHN GARDHOUSE,
                         WM. CAIN.

DISTRICT NO. 3.

Counties.—Huron, Bruce and Grey.

Inspectors.—H. G. Reed, V.S., Georgetown, and Jno. Bright, Myrtle.

HURON.

The township of Stephen in Huron county is a great centre for the heavy horse industry. In the list of sires are three imported Clydesdales, and two grades of that breeding, four imported Shires, a Percheron, an imported Hackney, two Standard-breds, and a Thoroughbred. With one exception there is no unsoundness, but some are up in years. The average conformation is fair, and the percentage of foals is pretty good. Fees run as low as $8 in two cases for unregistered stock, but the general run is from $10 to $15. The draught mares in this township are of a fairly good quality, although only a small percentage of them are registered, but the average mare would be likely to produce good draught horses when mated with good draught sires. The number of mares in the township is 1,360, about three-fourths being draught, and the balance general purpose and light.

The township of Hay is one in which the Inspectors found more Shires than Clydesdales, the proportion of the former to the latter being as six to four sires. The other sires are two Percheron and four Standred-bred. All are imported, and only one case of unsoundness was found. The general average, too, is good, and service fees vary from $10 to $20. As regards mares they number 1,585, about three-fourths being heavy draught the rest general purpose and light. Their average weights are draught, 1,400 lbs.; general purpose, 1,200 lbs.; and light, 1,000 lbs., about 5 per cent. of the draughts are registered, and the balance are good draught brood mares. Only a small percentage of the light mares are really good, their average type being poor.

Tuckersmith township runs to Clydesdales, there having been no Shires brought in lately. Two pure-bred Clydesdales and one grade, and one Standard-bred and two grades constitute the sires for service, and two of these are reported as unsound. The average quality and conformation is only fair. Service fees are $10 to $20, the latter for a Standard-bred. There are about 200 heavy draught mares in the township averaging 1,500 lbs.; 195 agricultural, about 1,300 lbs., and 265 of light type, all of fair quality.

Clydesdales also predominate in McKillop township, where there are six imported Clydesdale stallions, one Shire imported, and two Standard-breds. Here, again, there is one case of unsoundness, but the average conformation is fairly good. Service fees have the usual range of $10 to $15. Out of the 640 mares 200 are heavy, 300 of the agricultural class and 140 light, the average weights being 1,500, 1,300 and 1,000 respectively.

There seems to be a larger percentage of light mares in Grey township than in those previously considered, and here the sires stand three Clydesdales, a Shire, all registered, and three Standard-breds, which include a grade. The average conformation is fair, and two are rated as unsound. Eight to fifteen dollars is the range of fees. Heavy mares number 150,

Huron—Continued.

averaging 1,500 lbs.; agricultural are most numerous with 300, and light total 260.

In Turnbury and Morris townships the Inspectors found a large percentage of good heavy draught stallions, consisting of six imported Clydesdales and a grade, two imported Shires, and two Percherons, while the lighter breeds were represented by a Hackney and four Standard-breds, one being a grade. There is some unsoundness among both heavy and light sires, and while there are some excellent horses, including a sweepstakes winner at Toronto in 1906, the average rating is only fairly good. No service fees fall below $10, and the highest is $25 for a Standard-bred. Mares of agricultural type are most numerous, 400 in all; then come heavy mares, 395, and light, 270. The average weight are the same as given above.

Six imported Clydesdales, an imported Shire, and four Standard-breds, one a grade, make up the total of the stallions in the east part of Hullett township, and it is satisfactory to know that all are sound. Average conformation is fair, and the percentage of foals is satisfactory. Three of the sires are new arrivals, but for the others the fees are $10 to $15. In Hullett, as in the last two townships under review, the agricultural type leads among the mares, with the draught and light mares next respectively. In the west part of Hullett township heavy sires are most numerous, there being five pure-bred Clydesdales, a Shire, and three Standard-breds. In this section draught mares total 210; agricultural, 300, and those of light type, 205.

Contrary to the other townships passed in review, the township of Goderich leans more to the lighter breeds, as is seen by the fact that the light mares outnumber the draught and agricultural type, taken individually, and also by there being six Standard-bred sires and a Hackney to one Clydesdale and a Percheron. One sire is reported unsound and average quality and conformation is only fair. One grade out of the three standing for service has as low a fee as $7. The highest fee is $25.

In Colborne and Ashfield townships the Inspectors state that they found a good average lot of mares numbering, draught, 505; agricultural, 700, and light, 75, and averaging in weight as high as in the other townships; but there was a smaller percentage of really good draught stallions here than in the other parts of Huron county. There are three Clydesdales imported, one Canadian-bred, 3 grades of that breeding, four imported Shires and a grade, two Percherons, a Suffolk Punch, and a Standard-bred. There is a percentage of unsoundness, and conformation averages scarcely fair. The maximum service fee is $13 and minimum $8.

Inspectors' Remarks: "In Huron county we find the Clydesdale the popular draught horse, there being also a fair percentage of Shires and a few Percherons, one Belgian and a Suffolk Punch. The draught type of mares greatly predominates. Only a small percentage are registered, but the balance are a good average lot; there are very few really good light mares in this county.

"Our investigations have led us to conclude that very few really good mares are bred to any but Clydesdale or Shire sires.

"With regard to a Stallion Inspection Act, we find that the views of horsemen generally are that it does not go far enough. They are very much

4 H.B.

Huron—Continued.

oppo ed to a.lowing grade or unsound stallions to be used at all. A very strong fee!ing prevails against the cheap, mongrel, cross-bred and grade stallions. because they interfere so much with the business of the high-clas; and higher priced horses. We find breeders in general very much oppo⁻ed to syndicating stallions; very many poor animals are sold by this means."

STALLIONS.

Breeding.	Number.	Average weight. Pounds.	Average age.	Serviceably Sound.	Average conforma- tion.	Number of mares served.	Average service fee.
							8
Clydesdales, Imported	35	1,900	7	32.....	Fairly good.	3,011	13
Clydesdales, Canadian-bred	5	1,730	6	3.... .	Fair........	425	10
Grades, Clydesdale...............	7	1,600	5	6......	Fair........	431	11
Shires, Imported and Grades, (21 Imported Shires, 1 Grade).......	22	1,665	5	18.....	Fair........	2,340	11
Percherons......	9	1,880	6	8....	Fairly good.	840	12
Hackneys, Suffolk Punch and Grades (2 Hackneys; 1 Suffolk Punch, 1 Grade Hackney)......	4	1,390	3	All.....	Fair........	234	13
Standard-breds, Imported	19	1,110	12	17.....	Fair........	1,504	13
Roadsters. Canadian-bred.........	5	1,140	9	All....	Fair........	280	10
Grades. Roadster................	7	1.035	8	6.....	Fairly good.	363	10
Thoroughbreds, Canadian-bred	1	1,200	18	....	Fair........	30	8
Totals................	114	....		....	....	9,458	......

MARES.

Townships.	Number of mares bred to stallions inspected in Township.	*Type.				Average weight. Pounds.	Average quality.	Average age.
		Heavy Draught.	General Purpose.	Agricultural.	Light.			
Stephen	1,359	935	120	......	305	1,200	Fair...	8
Hay.....................	1,585	1,190	· 170	....	225	1,200	Fair...	8
Tuckersmith............	663	200	....	195	265	1,250	Fair...	8
McKillop...............	639	200	....	300	140	1,250	Fair...	8
Grey...:...............	714	150	....	300	260	1,250	Fair...	8
Turnberry and Morris...|	1,089	395	....	400	270	1,250	Fair...	8
Hullett.	1,382	520	....	600	355	1,250	Fair...	8
Goderich................	745	163	....	200	395	1,250	Fair...	8
Colborne and Ashfield...	1,282	505	....	700	75	1,250	Fair...	8
Total...............	9,458							

* The figures under this heading are only for the purpose of showing approximately the proportion of each class of mares in each township. The first column of the table gives the number of mares bred.

4a H.B

Huron—Concluded.

MARES BRED TO DIFFERENT CLASSES OF STALLIONS.

Stallions.	Total.		Serviceably sound.			Not serviceably sound.		
	Number of stallions.	Number of mares bred to.	Number of stallions.	Number of mares bred to.	Average fee.	Number of stallions.	Number of mares bred to.	Average fee.
					$			$
Registered Stallions..	98	8,604	86	7,492	12	12	1,112	11
Grade Stallions......	16	854	14	619	9	2	235	11
Totals........	114	9,458	100	8,111	....	14	1,347	....

The public meeting for the county of Huron was held at Clinton on October 18th. Owing to the inclemency of the weather the meeting was not so largely attended as would otherwise have been the case. However, each riding in the county was represented. After about two hours' discussion on the horse question, the meeting came to the unanimous decision that some steps should be taken to prevent a grade or unsound stallion standing for service. Those present also resolved that "In the opinion of this meeting a License Act would be preferable to an Inspection Act."

BRUCE.

The townships of Kinloss and Culross in Bruce County have a number of heavy sires, there being no less than 11 imported Clydesdales, 2 Canadian-bred ones, a Belgian and a French Draught, while the only representatives of the light breeds are 2 Standard-breds. There is not a single grade horse standing for service. With three exceptions they are all sound and one of these is not now used in the stud. The Inspectors state that the Clydesdales were the best average lot they saw in their investigations. The minimum fee is $11 and maximum $16. The mares are mostly agricultural in type numbering 1,000 of this class, 730 of the draught class and 153 light. They are of fair average quality.

In the township of Carrick the inspectors found only two draught horses, a Clydesdale and a Belgian, the rest being Standard-breds, one of them a grade, and two of the sires are unsound. Eight to sixteen dollars is the range of service fees. As a matter of fact over 20 stallions, from Huron County principally, covered a part of this township, and a number of the mares credited to that county should really be included in Carrick's and Brant's list. The number of mares as given to Carrick and Brant townships is draught 166, agricultural 200, and light 187. The mares of draught type are as numerous in these townships as in any of the other townships of Bruce.

Brant township has two imported Clydedales and a grade, all sound and standing for fees as follows: grade $8, pure-breds $15.

While Eastnor and Lindsay townships have a fair percentage of heavy sires, three Clydesdales, a Shire and a Percheron, two of these of Clydesdale

Bruce—Continued.

and Shire breeding are grades, and there is also a French Canadian grade and a Standard-bred grade. All are sound except one, but the average quality and conformation is only fair, and services are given for as low a price as $5 with a general run of $9 to $15. Mares are not numerous, and are chiefly of the agricultural type and in quality poor.

No draught stallions were seen in Amabel township, sires being Standard-breds and grades, one-half being unsound. Fees range from $8 to $10. The rating is not high. There are some draught mares in Amabel township and heavy stallions come in from Grey county, and consequently will be credited to townships in Grey where these stallions came from, the Inspectors being largely dependent for their information on the stallion owners themselves.

In Saugeen and Arran townships the Clydesdale is the predominant breed, there being five imported Clydesdales, five Canadian-bred, one grade, an imported Hackney, and two registered Standard-breds. There are four cases of unsoundness, all among the heavy ones and the average merit of these is only fair. Eight to seventeen dollars is the range of the fees. As in several of the other townships the agricultural type of mare is in the majority, but there are a good many draught and some light mares.

One Clydesdale, a Hackney, a Standard-bred and two grades of that breeding constitute the list of sires in Bruce township. Here, again, was found unsoundness in the proportion of two-fifths. Conformation is good in three-fifths and very bad in the remainder. Service fees are quoted as $7, $10 and $15. Mares average about 1,250 in weight.

Kincardine township contains no less than nineteen stallions, the majority being of the heavy type. Among them are five pure-bred Clydesdales, four grades of that breeding, five Percherons and five Standard-breds, of which three are grades. The grades, as usual are the cause of service fees being put as low as $5 and $8, but the owners of pure-bred sires get from $10 to $14. The average quality and conformation is only fair. Agricultural mares again lead in number with 600, draught come next with 433, followed closely by light mares 410. The average weight is 1,250.

The four stallions inspected in Huron township were two Clydesdales, an imported and a Canadian-bred one, respectively, an imported Shire and a Percheron. One-half are reported as sound. Service fees charged are $8, $10 and $12. Out of the 430 mares in this township, 300 belong to the agricultural and 130 to the draught type.

In Greenock township there are five pure-bred Clydesdale stallions, 3 imported and 2 Canadian-bred, an imported Shire, a Standard-bred, and 2 grades of French Canadian and German Coach blood respectively. The lowest service fee is $9 and the highest $15. No less than three out of the nine are not sound, and their standard of excellence is but fair. Mares average about the same weight as in the adjoining townships, viz,—1,250 lbs., and in point of numbers they stand agricultural 500; draught 255, and light 160. Their average quality is fair.

Inspectors' Remarks: "We find in Bruce county (and especially in the Centre Riding) a larger percentage of Percheron stallions than any other district that we have visited on this commission. These horses are in a

*Bruce—*Continued.

number of cases "syndicated" at high prices, above what we consider their value as regards merit."

STALLIONS.

Breeding.	Number.	Average weight. Pounds.	Average age.	Serviceably sound.	Average conformation.	Number of mares served.	Average service fee.
							$
Clydesdales, Imported	27	1,850	9	21.....	Fair.......	3,013	13
Clydesdales, Canadian-bred.......	14	1,775	7	10.....	Fair.......	1,066	10
Grades, Clydesdale	7	1,575	8	6.....	Only fair..	284	8
Shires, Imported and Grades (2 Shires ; 1 Grade Shire)..	3	1,975	6	1.....	Only fair..	320	10
Percherons......................	7	1,840	6	6.....	Fair.......	595	11
Belgians........................	2	1,850	7	1.....	Poor	192	12
Hackneys, Imported and Canadian-bred (1 Imported ; 1 Canadian-bred)	2	1,250	6	All.....	Good......	170	13
Standard-breds, Imported	9	1,165	11	7.....	Only fair..	568	10
Roadsters, Canadian-bred.........	2	950	3	All.....	Fair.......	35	10
Grades, Roadster.................	11	1,100	7	8.....	Fair.......	742	9
French Draught and Grades of German Coach and French-Canadian (1 French Draught ; 1 Grade German Coach ; 2 French-Canadian Grades)	4	1,525	6	All.....	Fair.......	385	11
Totals	88					7,370	

MARES.

Townships.	Number of mares bred to stallions inspected in township.	*Type.				Average weight. Pounds.	Average quality.	Average age.
		Draught.	Agricultural.	Light.	General Purpose.			
Kinloss and Culross.....	1,839	730	1,000	153	....	1,275	Fair....	8
Carrick and Brant.......	563	166	200	187	....	1,250	Fair....	8
Eastnor and Lindsay	348	85	200	60	....	1,210	Poor....	9
Amabel.................	185	....	....	100	85	1,125	Poor....	9
Saugeen and Arran......	1,226	356	600	265	....	1,250	Fair....	10
Bruce	395	50	70	245	....	1,125	Fair....	9
Kincardine	1,471	433	600	410	....	1,250	Fair....	9
Huron.................	430	130	300	....	....	1,400	Fair....	9
Greenock..............	913	255	500	160	....	1,250	Fair...	9
Total..............	7,370							

*The figures under this heading are only for the purpose of showing approximately the proportion of each class of mares in each township. The first column of the table gives the number of mares bred.

Bruce—Concluded.

MARES BRED TO DIFFERENT CLASSES OF STALLIONS.

Stallions.	Total.		Serviceably Sound.			Not Serviceably Sound.		
	Number of stallions.	Number of mares bred to.	Number of stallions.	Number of mares bred to.	Average fee.	Number of stallions.	Number of mares bred to.	Average fee.
Registered stallions..	66	5,971	50	4,563	$13	16	1,408	$10
Grade stallions......	22	1,399	18	1,162	10	4	237	8
Totals..........	88	7,370	68	5,725	....	20	1,645	....

The public meeting for the county of Bruce was held at Paisley on Friday, November 2nd. One hundred horsemen were present, representing all parts of the county, some having driven over 30 miles to be present.

After a lengthy discussion of the horse breeding industry in general it was unanimously resolved: "That this meeting strongly approves of some drastic legislation in favor of horse breeding, and is in favor of the compulsory inspection and licensing of all stallions standing for service; requirements for license to be freedom from hereditary unsoundness, and registration in a recognized record of the Dominion of Canada and a reasonably good formation."

Coupled with the above, the meeting also voted in favor of a Lien Act, giving the stallion owner a lien on the mare and foal until the insurance was paid.

GREY.

Sires of the heavy breeds have a monopoly in Bentinck and Normanby townships in the county of Grey. In Bentinck there are just two stallions an imported Clydesdale and a Percheron, both sound, and of fair merit. Fees are $13 and $12, respectively. Normanby has three more than Bentinck to its credit, viz., four Clydesdales (of which one is a grade), and a Percheron. There is one case of unsoundness, and the standard is fair. For the grade $9 is the fee charged, but two pure-breds have even lower fees $7 and $8, while the others stand at $12 and $13. Mares are mostly of the agricultural type, with some 135 of light, and 100 of heavy draught class.

Only three stallions are located in Glenelg township, an imported Clydesdale, a Percheron and a grade Roadster. Two out of the three are sound and conformation is fair. Eight, ten and eleven dollars are the fees charged. Of the 204 mares, 130 are agricultural in type, 50 draught and 24 light, with an average weight of 1,250 lbs. and of fair quality.

In Egremont, as in the other townships of the south riding of Grey, the Inspectors found a smaller percentage of draught mares than in the other districts through which they travelled. In this township the agricultural type is strong with 700 in number, the draught type comes next with 420, followed by the light with 320. The average weight of the whole is 1,250, and they are fair in quality. The percentage, on the other hand, of heavy draught stallions is very large as compared with the light breeds, being

Grey—Continued.

fourteen to four, viz.,—eleven pure-bred Clydesdales, one grade Clydesdale. a grade Shire and a Percheron. Light breeds are represented by one imported Hackney, and three grade Standard-breds. Three are unsound. and no high ratings as to conformation are given. Fees charged are all the way from $8 to $13.

With the exception of one Standard-bred, Clydesdales have a monopoly ot Sullivan township. Two out of the seven stallions found here are grades and six are sound. The average conformation is fairly good. Thirteen dollars is the maximum fee charged and $7 the minimum. Out of the 430 mares here only 10 are described as of light type, 80 of the draught type, and 340 agricultural.

The proportions of the mares in Derby township are very similar to those in Sullivan, viz.,—draught 50, agricultural 200 and light 25. Three pure-bred Clydesdale stallions, all sound and of fair conformation operate in this township, one of them putting in the first season. No fee is less than $10 and $15 is the highest charged.

There are a few more light mares in Keppel township, so we find two Standard-bred stallions (one a grade), to one Clydesdale. All are rated sound and of fair conformation, and earn fees of from $10 to $12. Draught mares are not numerous, only 40 being located, while light kinds number 60 and agricultural 160.

The number and average weight of mares in Sydenham township runs as follows: 100 draught, 1,500 lbs.; 600 agricultural, 1,300 lbs.; and 270 light mares, 1,000 lbs. The Inspectors explain the large percentage of light mares in this township by the fact that in Owen Sound there are a large number of light stallions.y As a matter of fact there are twelve light sires made up as follows: five registered Standard-breds and two grades of that breeding; two pure-bred Thoroughbreds, a pure-bred Hackney. and a grade, and a grade French Canadian. The heavy breeds are represented by three imported Clydesdales. Conformation is fair in all cases, but there is unsoundness in four of these animals. A Standard-bred grade is at the bottom of the list as regards fees, viz., $6, while a Thoroughbred heads it with $15.

In St. Vincent township, on the other hand, the heavy sires are the rule. almost to the exclusion of light stallions, there being only a solitary Standard-bred to five Clydesdales (one a grade), and three Percherons of which one is also a grade. Out of nine sires two are reported as not sound. For the two grades the service fees are $8 each, for the pure-breds from $10 to $15. Draught mares are given as 100, agricultural as 420 and light as 100. in this township. In average weight, quality, and age they are on a par with those in adjoining townships.

Heavy sires are also in the majority in Holland township where breeding interests are looked after by three Clydesdales, a Belgian, a Thoroughbred grade and a grade of Standard-bred stock. Nearly one-half are rated as wanting in soundness, and the average conformation is only fair. Service fees are about the same as elsewhere in this county, $8 for grade and $10 to $15, for the others. The agricultural type of mares predominates to the number of 350, light mares being next in number with 150 and draught with 120.

The proportion of light to heavy sires in Euphrasia township is as four to five consisting of two imported and one grade Hackney, a Standard-bred and three imported and one grade Clydesdale. No cases of unsoundness were reported here, but conformation is only fair. Service fees are the same as

Grey—Continued.

given for the previous township. Agricultural mares 500 in number; light 200, and draught 130, make up the total mares reported.

In Collingwood township light sires are not much in evidence, as is shown by the fact that there is only one grade Standard-bred to represent their interests, while there are five pure-bred Clydesdales. There are 200 agricultural and 100 draught mares kept in the township. The stallions have fair average conformation and all are sound, and they stand for $9 in one case and $10 in the rest.

Proton township is again a great district for the heavy breeds, of which there are the following representatives: ten Clydesdales, and a Shire, while other breeds are Thoroughbreds two, Standard-breds one and French Canadian one. All are pure-bred and all sound except one, and conformation is fair on the average. Stud fees are from $8 to $10. The mares found here are of about the usual fair quality and weight, the agricultural type leading in number with 500, draught come next with 250 and light last with 200.

Artemesia township contains a representation of several breeds varying from Clydesdale, Shire, Belgian, Hackney, French Coach, and Standard-bred, to a Shetland pony sire. While there are some good sires here there is still room for improvement, both as to conformation and soundness, no less than two-sevenths being reported as not qualifying for soundness. We find a pure-bred Clydesdale standing for $6, a grade for $8 and the balance for fees varying from $10 to $25, the latter for a Hackney. As regards purity of blood, the standing is eleven registered and three grades. Mares number 1,182, being composed of 600 of agricultural type, 382 of draught, and 200 of light mares.

STALLIONS.

Breeding.	Number.	Average weight. Pounds.	Average age.	Serviceably sound.	Average conformation.	Number of mares served.	Average service fee.
							$
Clydesdales, Imported............	33	1,850	7	28.....	Fair	3,532	11
Clydesdales, Canadian-bred.......	23	1,630	6	20.....	Fair	1,341	9
Grades, Clydesdale..............	7	1,470	4	All....	Fair	445	8
Shires, Imported.................	3	1,975	7	....	Fair	310	9
Percherons.....................	5	1,820	5	All....	Only fair..	405	11
Percherons, Canadian-bred........	1	1,600	5	All....	Good	85	12
Grades, Percheron and Shire (1 Percheron, 2 Shires).............	3	1,550	15	....	Poor......	187	8
Hackneys, Imported..............	5	1,310	9	All....	Fair	500	12
Grades, Hackney	2	1,250	6	All....	Fair	110	9
Standard-breds, Imported........	7	1,080	13	6......	Fair	570	12
Roadsters, Canadian-bred	3	1,100	11	2......	Fairly good	130	11
Grades, Roadster................	11	1,130	8	10. ...	Fair	510	9
Thoroughbreds, Canadian-bred....	4	1,050	7	3......	Fair	45	12
Grades, Thoroughbred............	1	1,300	7	All....	Good	100	12
French Coach, French Canadian, and Grades, (1 French Coach, 1 French Canadian, 1 Grade).....	3	1,330	6	All....	Fair	350	9
Belgians and Grades (2 Pure-breds 1 Grade)......................	3	1,875	6	1......	Only fair..	225	10
Shetland Pony..................	1	350	4	All....	Fair	12	10
Totals	115					8,857	

Grey—Continued.

MARES.

Townships.	Number of mares bred to stallions inspected in township.	Heavy draught.	Agricultural.	Light.	Average weight. Pounds.	Average quality.	Average age.
			*Type.				
Bentinck and Normanby	535	100	300	135	1,250	Fair ...	9
Glenelg..............	204	50	130	24	1,250	Fair ...	9
Egremont	1,498	420	700	320	1,250	Fair...	9
Sullivan	440	80	340	10	1,250	Fair ...	9
Derby................	278	50	200	25	1,250	Fair ...	9
Keppel..............	264	40	160	60	1,250	Fair ...	9
Sydenham...........	980	100	600	270	1,250	Fair ...	9
St. Vincent.........	640	100	420	100	1,250	Fair ...	9
Holland	620	120	350	150	1,250	Fair ...	9
Euphrasia	830	180	500	200	1,250	Fair ...	9
Collingwood	346	100	200	45	1,250	Fair...	9
Proton	1,040	250	500	200	1,250	Fair...	9
Artemesia	1,182	382	600	200	1,250	Fair...	9
Total..............	8,857						

* The figures under this heading are only for the purpose of showing approximately the proportion of each class of mares in each township. The first column of the table gives the number of mares bred.

MARES BRED TO DIFFERENT CLASSES OF STALLIONS.

Stallions.	Total.		Serviceably sound.			Not serviceably sound.		
	Number of stallions.	Number of mares bred to.	Number of stallions.	Number of mares bred to.	Average fee.	Number of stallions.	Number of mares bred to.	Average fee.
Registered Stallions..	89	7,295	74	5,892	8 11	15	1,403	8 11
Grade Stallions......	26	1,562	21	1,290	9	5	272	9
Totals	115	8,857	95	7,182	....	20	1,675	....

The public meeting for the county of Grey was held at Markdale on November 15th, about one hundred being present, representing nearly every township in the county. A discussion of a most lively kind took place lasting over three hours, when the following resolutions were carried:

"That this meeting is in favor of the compulsory inspection and licensing of all stallions standing for service."

"That all unregistered stallions be prohibited from serving mares."

"That all stallions suffering from hereditary unsoundness be prohibited from serving mares."

"That a Stallion *Lien Act* be passed."

Grey—Concluded.

A very lengthy and spirited discussion took place as to the amount that should be charged as a license fee, the suggestions varying from no charge to one hundred dollars. Finally, it was decided not to offer any suggestions as to the amount of the fee, but to leave that to the consideration of the Government.

The first resolution was carried almost unanimously; many, however, were opposed to the second and third, thinking it quite impossible to carry into effect such legislation. The minority were in favor of refusing a license to undesirable stallions and letting it go at that. There was also considerable opposition to a Stallion Lien Act.

SPECIAL REPORT OF INSPECTORS.

We, your Inspectors, beg leave to report that after investigating the horse industry in the counties of Huron, Bruce, and Grey, and inspecting the stallions in the above named counties, would strongly recommend the compulsory inspection and licensing of all stallions kept for service, the requirements for licensing to be freedom from hereditary unsoundness and registration in a recognized record of the Dominion of Canada; and we would also recommend a nominal license fee, sufficient to defray expenses in connection with said inspection. In reference to the Stallion Lien Act, we do not feel like recommending the Government to pass such legislation. While we have no doubt it might be some protection to the owners of stallions, yet we feel in many cases, it would be a hardship and an encumbrance to the owners of mares, and we believe there would be a good deal of opposition from farmers generally against such an Act. While we believe that much good has and can be done by the syndicating of good horses in many sections, yet we feel that there should be some protection to the farmers against being swindled by glib tongued salesmen, who sell inferior stallions, perhaps in the best of condition, to men who are not judges of horses. We would recommend that stallions about to be syndicated be compelled to pass inspection before being offered for sale. We believe the horse industry could be greatly benefited by holding a meeting of horse breeders in each riding, to be addressed by practical up-to-date horsemen, on the kind of horses required for the market to-day, and how to breed them.

(Signed) H. G. REED.
JOHN BRIGHT.

Counties.—Perth, Waterloo, Wellington and Dufferin.
Inspectors.—Wm. Jones, Zenda; Peter Christie, M.P., Manchester, (Perth, Waterloo, South a'nd Centre Wellington) and John A. Boag, Ravenshoe, (East and West Wellington, and Dufferin).

PERTH.

Perth is a county in which there are a number of breeders and importers of good horses, mostly Clydesdales. There are also several Hackneys, Percherons, Belgians and Standard-breds. In Downie townships, St. Paul's is the centre of a good horse district, and there were found five Clydesdales, a Standard-bred and a grade Shire. The effect of the presence of good sires is seen in the fact that even for the grade the service fee is not lower than $10, and it ranges from $12 to $15 in the other cases. There is one instance of unsoundness. The Inspectors report of the mares found here, 345 in number, that many of them are registered and are of a good class of Clydesdale type. The good stallions kept here have been of great value to the heavy horse business in Downie. Mares average 1,400 lbs. in weight.

Blanshard is another township well known as a good horse centre, especially for heavy horses. It is gratifying to find that of the nine stallions standing for service here not one is unsound, and the average conformation is good. The majority of stallion owners charge a fee of $15, some $10, and one $20. There are five imported Clydesdales, an imported Hackney, a Percheron, and two Standard-breds. Mares in Blanshard are mostly a very good lot, especially those of the heavy class, although it is said that farmers have sold off their best mares, especially near St. Mary's. The average weight of those of heavy type is 1,400 lbs., and of light type 1,100 lbs.

While there are not quite so many stallions in Hibbert township, they are all Clydesdales, imported, of a good serviceable age, good in conformation and all sound and stand for fees ranging from $10 to $15. Mares in this township ship are, so the Inspectors report, improving in quality and conformation, quite a number of good young mares having been bred this last season. The average weight of the mares is 1,400 lbs. and their average quality is fair.

Fullarton township has had the benefit of having brought into it an excellent class of stallions, some of which are also to be found in adjoining townships, where they are doing good service. Out of the 18 stallions here, ten are Clydesdales owned by one importer and there are two imported Clydesdales besides these. There is also an imported Hackney, an imported Shire, a Hackney grade, a Percheron, a Standard-bred, and a grade of the last named breeding. All are sound and mostly good in conformation and action and with three exceptions, in which the fee is $10, the standard fee is $15. In this township farmers are breeding the heavy mares to heavy sires and light mares to light sires, not as in some other districts breeding indiscriminately. Mares are in general of Clydesdale type, and average 1,400 lbs. in weight.

Heavy sires are in the majority in Logan township as well, where there are three imported Clydesdales, a Percheron, a grade Shire and a grade Roadster, standing for service fees from $8 to $15. All horses inspected are reported sound and of good conformation. Mares are of fair quality and average in weight the same as in the other townships of Perth.

Perth—Continued.

Two imported Clydesdales, a Canadian-bred one and a Clydesdale grade, a Thoroughbred and a Standard-bred were all the sires located in South Easthope. All were sound, of good conformation and the maximum fee is $15 and the minimum $10. The mares average 1,500 lbs. in weight and are of good Clydesdale type, with an average age of six years.

In North Easthope only two imported Clydesdales and an imported Hackney were found, and the latter was not seen, owing to its owner being away. For the Clydesdales the fees were $14 and $15. There are a good lot of mares in this section mostly of Clydesdale type and averaging 1,500 lbs. in weight.

Among the sires in Ellice township are three pure-bred Clydesdales, an imported Shire, a Belgian, a Standard-bred and a grade Coach. Conformation is not so good as in the other townships visited, but all are fairly serviceably sound. Mares number some 430 of which the greater proportion are of Clydesdale type and the balance of light type. Fees vary from $10 to $16.

Mornington is a township well provided with stallions, and as far as seen they were all reported sound and of fairly good average conformation. The general run of stud fees is $10 to $16, but one is given as $40. The list includes six imported and two Canadian-bred Clydesdales. There are 1,123 mares in this township of good average weight and quality.

With seven Clydesdale stallions (one a grade), a Belgian, a Hackney, a Percheron, 2 Coach horses, and three Standard-bred grades, Elma township has a fair range of sires of various types, but there is much lacking in regard to soundness and in conformation in some cases. The stud fees range from $10 to $15. Mares are in number 1,220, each breeder keeping two on the average. The average weight of the heavy mares of Clydesdale type is about 1,400 lbs. and the light Roadster mares 1,100 lbs. The average quality is fair all round.

STALLIONS.

Breeding.	Number.	Average weight. Pounds.	Average age.	Serviceably sound.	Average conformation.	Number of mares served.	Average service fee.
							$
Clydesdales, Imported............	42	1,860	7	All....	Good......	3,689	14
Clydesdales, Canadian-bred.......	7	1,590	6	All......	Good......	355	10
Grades, Clydesdale..............	5	1,650	9	4......	Good......	426	11
Shires, Imported.................	2	1,900	5	All....	Fairly good	227	14
Grades, Shire...................	2	1,700	13	1.......	Fairly good	188	9
Percherons	4	1,750	4	All....	Fairly good	295	14
Belgians.......................	3	1,930	4	All....	Fair.......	185	15
Hackneys and Grades (6 Hackneys, 1 grade).....................	7	1,235	7	All....	Good......	574	12
Standard-breds, Imported........	8	1,060	8	All....	Fairly good	434	17
Roadsters, Canadian-bred.........	2	1,150	9	All....	Good......	193	11
Grades, Roadster................	7	1,010	6	5......	Fair.......	108	10 •
Thoroughbreds, Imported........	3	1,050	6	All....	Fairly good	148	11
German Coach Horses and Grades (1 German Coach, 2 Grades)....	3	1,200	17	All....	Fairly good	85	10
Totals...................	95					6,907	

Perth—Concluded.

MARES.

Townships.	Number of mares bred to stallions inspected in township.	Type.	Average weight. Pounds.	Average quality.	Average age.
Downie	475	Clydesdale	1,400	Good	7
Blanchard	923	Clydesdale	1,400	Good	7
		Roadster	1,100	Fair	11
Hibbert	650	Clydesdale	1,400	Fair	8
Fullerton.............	738	Clydesdale.........................	1,400	Fair......	8
		Roadster	1,100	Not good.	10
Logan	559	Clydesdale.........................	1,400	Fair......	7
		Roadster	1,100	Fair......	10
South Easthope........	474	Clydesdale.........................	1,500	Good ...	6
North Easthope	262	Clydesdale.........................	1,500	Good....	6
Ellice	403	Clydesdale.........................	1,400	Fair......	8
		Light	1,100	Not good.	10
Mornington	1,203	Clydesdale.	1,400	Fair......	7
		Light	1,100	Fair......	10
Elma	1,220	Clydesdale.........................	1,400	Fair......	8
		Light	1,100	Fair......	10
Total............	6,907				

MARES BRED TO DIFFERENT CLASSES OF STALLIONS.

Stallions.	Total.		Serviceably sound.			Not serviceably sound.		
	Number of stallions.	Number of mares bred to.	Number of stallions.	Number of mares bred to.	Average fee.	Number of stallions.	Number of mares bred to.	Average fee.
Registered Stallions..	78	6,125	78	6,125	$ 13	......	......	8
Grade Stallions	17	782	13	641	10	4	141	11
Totals	95	6,907	91	6,766	....	4	141	... .

The public meeting held at Mitchell on October 16th was well attended and discussed fully the question of an Inspection Act, and a motion favoring the same was carried unanimously at the meeting.

Many of the stallion owners suggested that if stallions were under license and stallion owners had one-third of the insurance fee down at the time of service, it would put a stop to the breeding of a lot of mares that are not likely to get in foal.

WATERLOO.

The town of Berlin was first visited. Here, and in the adjoining territory there were found two pure-bred Hackneys, two Clydesdales (one of them a grade), two Percherons, and a Coach grade. With two exceptions the standard is not high and one horse is not sound. None of the horses stand at less than $10, while the highest price is $15. There are 400 mares here, mostly general purpose and light, the general average weight of which is 1,100 lbs., and quality only fair.

Waterloo—Continued.

In Woolwich township only a Clydesdale and Standard-bred, both good in conformation and sound, stand for service at $13 and $12 respectively. They both score well and are apparently successful sires. Of the 267 mares, part are of Clydesdale blood and part of Roadster, averaging in weight respectively 1,300 and 1,100 lbs. Quality is fair and their average age is 9 years.

Wellesley township is better off as regards numbers of stallions in its borders, some of which, of course, take in other districts not so well served locally. There are six Clydesdales (one a grade), a Thoroughbred grade, two Standard-bred grades, and a Coach grade in this township. Six of these are stated to be good individuals, both as regards conformation and action. Service fees range from $10 to $15. The type of mare found is general purpose, weighing about 1,200 lbs., but quality is inferior.

Waterloo township is another well furnished with sires, ten Thoroughbreds being found in one stable. It is also favored with some Standard-bred sires of the best quality, thirteen of which, together with some good Clydesdales and Hackneys were inspected in one stable, and it is worthy of note that out of 103 animals examined there, not one was found unsound. Besides these there are in the township a pure-bred Shire, four Clydesdales (one a grade), and a Standard-bred grade. Not all are sound, but their conformation is generally fairly good. As low as $5 and from $10 to $15 are the usual service fees. In some cases, however, they are from $25 to $50. The general run of the mares in this township are of the general purpose class.

The sires represented in Wilmot township are two Clydesdales, three Percherons, a Hackney, and three Standard-breds. Two of the sires could not be seen as they were away from home when the Inspectors paid their visit. Average conformation is fair, and there is some unsoundness. Stud fees vary from $8 to $20. The mares, as in most of the townships in Waterloo, are of general purpose class and are not very good in quality.

A pure-bred and grade Clydesdale, both sound, were the only stallions seen in North Dumfries township, and the stud fee is $10 in each case. There are a few good registered Clydesdale mares owned in this township, which are dependent on outside stallions for service. Most of the mares are of the general purpose type and deficient in quality.

STALLIONS.

Breeding.	Number.	Average weight. Pounds.	Average age.	Servically sound.	Average conformation.	Number of mares served.	Average service fee.
							$
Clydesdales and Shires, Imported (7 Clydesdales, 1 Shire)	8	1,800	6	7	Fairly good	845	13
Clydesdales, Canadian-bred	7	1,740	6	6	Fairly good	473	11
Grades, Clydesdale	4	1,400	4	All	Fair	155	8
Percherons	5	1,700	7	4	Fair	290	14
Hackneys, Imported	3	1,300	7	2	Fairly good	323	13
Standard-breds, Imported	16	1,050	6	All	Good	220	13
Roadsters, Canadian-bred and Grades (1 Roadster, 3 Roadster Grades, 2 Coach Grades)	6	1,150	6	All	Only fair	313	11
Thoroughbreds and Grades (10 Pure-bred, 1 grade)	11	1,040	8	All	Fairly good	205	14
Totals	60					2,824	

Waterloo—Concluded.

MARES.

Townships.	Number of mares bred to stallions inspected in township.	Type.	Average weight.	Average quality.	Average age.
Town of Berlin	460	General Purpose	1,200	Not good..	8
		Light	1,000	Fair.	7
Woolwich	267	Clydesdale	1,300	Fair.	9
		Roadster	1,100	Fair.	9
Wellesley	964	General Purpose	1,200	Not good..	8
Waterloo	613	General Purpose	1,200	Not good..	8
		Standard-bred	1,050	Good.	8
Wilmot	422	General Purpose	1,200	Not good..	8
North Dumfries........	98	General Purpose	1,200	Not good..	8
Total	2,824				

MARES BRED TO DIFFERENT CLASSES OF STALLIONS.

Stallions.	Total.		Serviceably sound.			Not serviceably sound.		
	Number of stallions.	Number of mares bred to.	Number of stallions.	Number of mares bred to.	Average fee.	Number of stallions.	Number of mares bred to.	Average fee.
Registered Stallions..	50	2,356	46	2,016	$ 13	4	340	$ 14
Grade Stallions	10	468	10	468	9	....	....	......
Totals ....,...	60	2,824	56	2,484	....	4	340	....

The public meeting for Waterloo county was held at Berlin on October 22nd, but was not very largely attended. The majority of those present were in favor of an Inspection Act.

WELLINGTON.

In the township of Guelph are four good Clydesdales, one of which is Canadian-bred, and there is a Thoroughbred sire for the light mares. No instance of unsoundness is stated, and the general conformation is good. The service fees run at about $10. There are many mares of Clydesdale breeding, more or less, and a few light ones averaging about 1,100 lbs. Quality is only fair.

Considering that there are a number of good Clydesdale stallions for service in Puslinch township the mares of heavy type in this township

Wellington—Continued.

are not as good as they might be, and one reason given is that farmers have sold their best mares. Of the 683 mares none are above medium in quality or fair in type. Of the fifteen stallions standing for service, eight are imported Clydesdales, two imported Hackneys, one a Thoroughbred, and four are Roadster grades. There is only one unsound, and some are considerably above the average stallion. Fees in general, run from $10 to $15, with one quoted at $25.

Of the stallions in Eramosa township, with few exceptions the Inspectors do not speak very highly, most of them being deficient in type and not likely to improve the class of horses found there, the mares, too, being of no special type. The sires include an imported Hackney, two Clydesdales (one a grade), two Thoroughbreds, and five Standard-breds, of which three are grades. $8, $10, $12 and $13 are some of the fees charged.

Seven stallions were inspected in Pilkington township belonging to the following breeds: Pure-bred Clydesdales, four; Standard-bred, Coach and Percheron, one each, and one Roadster grade, the latter standing at an $8 fee, the others from $10 to $15. All but one are sound, and the general average of conformation is fair, one Clydesdale being highly spoken of. The mares here are of fair average quality, those of Clydesdale breeding averaging 1,400 lbs., and light mares about 1,100.

Nichol township contains three pure-bred Clydesdale stallions, a grade Shire, and a grade Standard-bred, all qualifying as to soundness, but under the average as regards general conformation. One of the Clydesdales has only recently been brought in, and had not done any service at the time of the inspection. Ten dollars and twenty dollars are charged as fees, the latter for a heavy sire. The average of the heavy mares kept is rather higher than in other parts of the county, being 1,500 lbs., and averaging well as to quality.

While all the stallions in West Garafraxa township are pure-bred, there is some unsoundness among them, to the extent of two-sevenths. Clydesdales make up three, Standard-breds three, and there is one Percheron. There are no stud fees lower than $12, and the highest is $20. As this proportion of heavy sires would show, there are a number of fairly heavy mares in the township; also a good percentage of light ones, the respective weight averages being 1,400 to 1,100 lbs.

Of the stallions in East Garafraxa, the Inspectors state that their standard is not as good as it might be, and mares also are below the average of those in other sections of the county. It was the opinion of farmers met with here that something should be done to weed out inferior sires. The list of sires is made up of four imported and one Canadian-bred Clydesdales, and two grade Standard-breds. No less than three stallions are standing for as small a fee as $8, for the rest the fees are $10, $12 and $15. Unsoundness is again in evidence here.

In Erin township the general purpose mare is the rule, with an average weight of 1,200 lbs. The quality is poor. They total 736. The light breeds predominate among the stallions. There are three imported Clydesdales and one grade, a cross-bred Shire and Clydesdale, four pure-bred Standard-breds and a grade, and two imported Hackneys. There are two

Wellington—Continued.

cases of unsoundness, but the general average of the conformation is fairly good. Stud fees have a wide range from $6 to $20, with most of them from $10 to $12.

Mares in Luther township average 1,400 lbs. in weight for the heavy ones and 1,100 for the light. Their average quality is only fair however. The larger number of heavy mares is reflected in the proportion of heavy sires which are four Clydesdales to three Standard-breds, two of the latter being grades. All are sound and pretty fairly good in conformation and quality. The minimum stud fee is $7, the maximum $15.

Clydesdales again head the list in Arthur township, where six pure-breds of that breed and one grade, a grade Shire, a Thoroughbred, a Standard-bred, and two Roadsters make up the dozen stallions standing for service at varying fees from $6 to $15. No less than one-fourth are reported as not sound, but the average conformation is fairly good. The heavy mares found here are principally of Clydesdale blood, and average 1,400 lbs., light ones being 1,100 lbs.

There are no less than a baker's dozen of Clydesdales among the twenty stallions inspected in Minto township. The sires representing other breeds being Thoroughbreds, two; Hackneys, one; Coach grade, one; and Standard-breds, three, of which one is a grade. Four of the Clydesdales also are grades. Competition must be very keen here, for we find service fees quoted as $3 in one case and $5 in two others, but the better horses make $10 to $15. With one exception all are sound, but quality and conformation are only fair. The benefits of so many heavy sires is shown in the increase in the average weight of the heavy mares which is 1,500 lbs., and their quality is good.

There are seven Clydesdale stallions in Maryborough township, one being a grade; three pure-bred Percherons, an imported Hackney, a Thoroughbred, and a Roadster grade, and while there are a few good sires among them, the general average is not high. From $8 to $15 is earned in stud fees. Heavy mares only average 1,300 lbs.; light ones being about the same as usual, with average quality fair.

For the 618 mares in Wallace township there are four Clydesdales, a Belgian and a Standard-bred all registered and only one not sound. Conformation is only fair. Fees range from $10 to $16. The heavy mares of Clydesdale blood are of good average quality and fair weight.

Peel township, the last of the townships in Wellington to be visited, has a total of eleven stallions, made up as follows: Four Standard-breds, (two of them registered and two grades), three pure-bred Clydesdales, n imported Hackney, a Thoroughbred, and a Coach Horse. Nearly all are sound or serviceably so, and they have very fair average conformation and action. Some pure-bred sires stand at $8, while the average is $10 to $15. The average quality of both the heavy and light mares found here is described as not good, and the average weights are 1,300 and 1,100 respectively. In this township it was suggested that it would be an advantage if something could be done to secure the insurance of stallions at a lower rate than that now charged by companies engaged in this class of insurance.

5 H B

Wellington—Continued.

STALLIONS.

Breeding.	Number.	Average weight. Pounds.	Average age.	Serviceably sound.	Average conformation.	Number of mares served.	Average service fee.
							$
Clydesdales, imported............	47	1,735	7	44.....	Fairly good.	4,066	12
Clydesdales, Canadian-bred	15	1,590	4	14.....	Fairly good.	827	10
Grades, Clydesdale...............	8	1,450	5	7.....	Fair	508	7
Grades, Shire....................	3	1,665	8	1.....	Poor......	220	9
Percherons ..:...................	6	1,835	6	All....	Fair	505	14
Hackneys, imported	8	1,240	7	All....	Good	716	14
Standard-breds, imported	11	1,085	8	10.....	Fair	605	12
Roadsters, Canadian-bred	5	1,200	10	4.....	Good	394	15
Grades, Roadster	20	1,020	8	16.....	Fair	579	9
Thoroughbreds	6	1,060	11	4.....	Fair	305	10
Thoroughbreds, Canadian-bred	3	1,000	5	2.....	Only fair...	40	10
German Coach horses, Belgians and grades of Coach (2 German Coach, 1 Belgian, 1 grade)..............	4	1,465	8	2......	Only fair...	189	10
Totals	136					8,954	

MARES.

Township.	Number of mares bred to stallions inspected in township.	Type.	Average weight.	Average quality.	Average age.
Guelph.................	90	Clydesdale......................	1,400	Fair	7
		Light	1,100	Fair ..:..	10
Puslinch	683	Fair	1,200	Medium .	8
Eramosa...............	585	General purpose	1,200	Fair :....	8
		Light	1,000	Fair	10
Pilkington..............	434	Clydesdale.....................	1,400	Fair	7
		Light	1,100	Fair	10
Nichol	182	Clydesdale.....................	1,500	Good	6
		Light	1,100	Fair	10
West Garafraxa........	300	Clydesdale	1,400	Fair	8
		Light	1,100	Fair	10
East Garafraxa.........	576	Clydesdale.....................	1,400	Not good.	8
		Light	1,100	Not good.	10
Erin	736	General purpose	1,200	Poor.....	8
Luther	747	Clydesdale.....................	1,400	Fair	6
		Light	1,100	Not good.	10
Arthur	1,341	Clydesdale.....................	1,400	Fair	6
		Light	1,100	Fair	10
Minto	1,162	Clydesdale	1,500	Good	6
		Light	1,100	Fair	10
Maryboro	889	Clydesdale.....................	1,300	Fair	7
		Light	1,100	Fair	10
Wallace	618	Clydesdale.....................	1,400	Good	6
		Light	1,100	Fair	10
Peel...................	611	Clydesdale.....................	1,300	Not good.	7
		Light	1,100	Not good.	10
Total.............	8,954				

5a H. B.

Wellington—Concluded.

MARES BRED TO DIFFERENT CLASSES OF STALLIONS.

Stallions.	Total.		Serviceably sound.			Not serviceably sound.		
	Number of stallions.	Number of mares bred to.	Number of stallions.	Number of mares bred to.	Average fee.	Number of stallions.	Number of mares bred to.	Average fee.
Registered stallions..	104	7,632	94	7,112	$12	10	520	$12
Grade stallions......	32	1,322	25	997	9	7	325	7
Totals........	136	8,954	119	8,109	....	17	845	....

The meeting at Fergus for the county of Wellington was held on November 7th, when there was a very good attendance. The question of an Inspection Act was discussed by the meeting, and a motion favoring the same was carried by a two-thirds vote. The passing of a Lien Act was also discussed, and a motion in favor of it when put to the meeting was passed by a small majority.

DUFFERIN.

Melancthon township has the largest number of stallions to its credit, totalling seven Clydesdales, including two grades, two imported Hackneys, a grade Roadster, and a grade Coach horse. None of those seen were other than sound, but conformation does not average better than fair. The low service fee is again in evidence, such as $6 and $8, while the highest is $11. Not much can be said about the average quality of the mares, whether heavy or light, which average 1,300 and 1,100 lbs., respectively.

Mares in Mulmur township are mostly of the general purpose sort, are not very good in quality and average about 1,200 lbs. There are seven stallions standing for service in this section, consisting of a Canadian-bred Clydesdale and a grade, an imported Shire, a French Canadian grade, a Hackney grade, a Standard-bred grade and a Coach grade. Six-sevenths are sound, and conformation in general is fairly good, but low stud fees are the rule, the limit being $8 and $10.

Mono township has 450 mares, mostly of the general purpose type, and averaging in quality about the same as in Mulmur, and also in weight. Of the six sires in this township there are four imported horses, viz., one each of the Shire and Hackney breeds and two Clydesdales. There is also a pure-bred Coach horse and a grade Standard-bred and all are rated as sound and fair in average conformation, while service fees are from $10 to $15.

There are no more than four stallions in Amaranth township, all sound and fairly good in conformation and standing for fees running from $10 to $15 and in one instance, a Standard-bred, for $25. The list comprises an imported Clydesdale, two Standard-breds and a Percheron. As in the sister townships mares are general purpose in type and not good in quality.

Dufferin—Continued.

STALLIONS.

Breeding.	Number.	Average weight. Pounds.	Average age.	Serviceably sound.	Average conformation.	Number of mares served.	Average service fee.
							$
Clydesdales, Imported	6	1,880	7	All....	Fair........	660	12 .
Clydesdales, Canadian-bred.......	3	1,530	4	All....	Fair........	235	10
Grades, Clydesdale...............	3	1,450	5	All....	Fair........	118	7
Shires and Percherons (2 Shires, 1 Percheron)...................	3	1,925	5	All....	Fairly good.	260	10
Hackneys, Imported and grades (3 pure-breds, 1 grade).............	4	1,250	5	All....	Fair........	320	9
Standard-breds, Imported........	1	1,100	7	All....	Good.......	78	25
Roadsters, Canadian-bred.........	1	1,100	3	All....	Good.......	21	15
Grades, Roadster.................	3	1,110	9	All....	Fair........	135	9
Coach Horses, grades of same and of French (1 Coach Horse, 3 grades)	4	1,350	11	3......	Fair........	215	11
Totals...............	28					2,042	

MARES.

Townships.	Number of mares bred to stallions inspected in township.	Type.	Average weight.	Average quality.	Average age.
Melancthon.	830	Clydesdale.........................	1,300	Not good	6
		Light........................	1,100	Poor	10
Mulmur	493	General Purpose	1,200	Not good	8
Mono...................	450	General Purpose	1,200	Not good	8
Amaranth	269	General Purpose	1,200	Not good	8
Total.............	2,042				

MARES BRED TO DIFFERENT CLASSES OF STALLIONS.

Stallions.	Total.		Serviceably sound.			Not serviceably sound.		
	Number of stallions.	Number of mares bred to.	Number of stallions.	Number of mares bred to.	Average fee.	Number of stallions.	Number of mares bred to.	Average fee.
					$			$
Registered Stallions..	18	1,604	18	1,604	13	....	....	....
Grade Stallions......	10	438	9	403	8	1	35	10
Totals	28	2,042	27	2,007	....	1	35	....

Dufferin—Concluded.

The public meeting for the county of Dufferin at Shelburne, on November 12th, was well attended, about 40 being present, mostly farmers who did not own stallions. The question of an Inspection Act was discussed by them for some time before a vote was taken. The result was that only two voted against an Inspection Act, the rest voting in favor of it.

SPECIAL REPORT OF INSPECTORS.

We the undersigned committee appointed by the Ontario Department of Agriculture for the purpose of investigating the horse industry in the district known as No. 4, composed of the counties of Perth, Waterloo, Wellington, and Dufferin, beg to report as follows: "That we have inspected 306 stallions, Clydesdales 130, Standard-breds 40, Hackney 20, Thoroughbreds 22, Percherons 17, Shires 5, Belgians 4, Coach horses 4, and grades 64. Of the pure-bred stallions we found 15 unsound horses. We found the stallions of Clydesdale blood a good lot, the mares as a rule not nearly so good, owing to what the breeders say throughout the district, that until just recently the farmers have, as a rule, sold quite a number of their best mares, and in this way have lowered the standard of the heavy mares in the district. We find, however, that this policy has been to a great extent discontinued. We also find among the heavy class of horses in this district that the Percheron stallions, the Belgian stallions, and the Shire stallions are not nearly as good a lot as the Clydesdales; in fact, they were, with one or two exceptions, poor representatives of the respective breeds.

The Percheron and Belgian horses in this district have only been introduced recently. With few exceptions these horses have been brought in and sold to from six to fifteen individuals, in most cases farmers, under a system known as syndicating, and in every instance at prices away above their value. We found the universal opinion of those we came in contact with opposed to this system. The reason assigned was that it invariably places a poor horse in a community at a very high price, and further that it introduces a breed of horses in a section quite frequently that has a tendency to impair rather than improve present conditions. For instance, in this district the heavy class of mares are almost without exception Clydesdale-bred mares of from one to three crosses, and no greater mistake could be made than to breed such mares to either Percheron or Belgian stallions.

The light horses in this district are not so numerous and with few exceptions are not of nearly so high a standard. The Hackneys, as a rule, are a very good lot of the right kind. We also find some excellent Standard-breds, but the greater part of them are very inferior individuals. The grades are far too numerous, and, in most cases are of a very poor class, which would scarcely make good-looking workers.

Your committee are of the opinion, from what they learned and observed in passing through the district, that the heavy horse can be raised most profitably in this district. From the information we received we are convinced that there is no other plan of ownership of stallions that is giving as much satisfaction as private ownership.

We find that the views of horsemen generally favor a stallion Inspection Act with license attached that would permit of only pure-bred horses with registered pedigrees, free from all hereditary unsoundness and of reasonable

Report Inspectors' District 4.—Concluded.

merit standing for service. We also found that the farmers we came in contact with view this with favor, and we are of the opinion that this would be
the most effective way of materially improving the class of horses in this
district. We arrive at that conclusion for different reasons. In the first
place it would weed out largely the undesirable sires which in this district
amount of twenty-five per cent. of the whole. In the second place it would
to a considerable extent prevent the breeding of these poorest mares that
have been bred to these very poor stallions. We also believe that it would
prevent to a large extent the importation of horses of an inferior class of any
breed into this country. It would also put a stop to a system which has been
pursued, and is still in practice in this country, that of selling and taking back
and reselling again stallions that are known to be unsuccessful sires. But
while we are convinced that an Inspection Act with license attached would
without doubt very materially improve all classes of horses in this district,
we are of the opinion that legislation along that line should be deferred
until the people have had ample time to be better informed on the subject,
and with that object in view we would suggest that the Department of Agriculture should by some well directed course endeavor to enlighten the people thoroughly on this question by disseminating information bearing on
the subject, and by holding a series of meetings especially called for that
purpose, and that an Inspection Act be passed making it compulsory for all
stallions to be inspected, and that all stallions inspected be graded according
to merit and breeding, with provisions attached that all stallion owners be
compelled to give publicity to the certificates given. This conclusion is
arrived at taking for granted that the conditions and feelings of the people
are the same in other districts of this Province as in the districts visited by
ourselves.

(Signed)   PETER CHRISTIE.
WM. JONES
JOHN A. BOAG.

Counties.—Peel, Simcoe, York and Ontario.

Inspectors.—Thos. McMillan, Seaforth; and Wm. Mossip, St. Mary's.

PEEL.

While some of the townships in Peel county have a good proportion of heavy stallions, Brampton is a town that has long been known as a centre for carriage and saddle horses, especially the former, Hackney sires having been used here for some years, and also Thoroughbreds. The list includes four Hackneys, a Thoroughbred, a Clydesdale, and a Percheron. Some of the stallions are rather up in years, but all are sound, and the average conformation is certainly good. In one case the service fee is $12, while the fee for the other is $15. There are quite a number of pure-bred Clydesdales in this neighborhood, and their average quality and that of the light mares is very good. No breeding of old, unsound mares is reported.

The farmers in Chinguacousy township are taking an interest in horse breeding, but a good many light mares are being bred to heavy stallions in the neighborhood of Mono Road. The general type of the heavier mares is of the agricultural or general purpose class, ranging from 1,250 to 1,350 lbs. in weight. No less than eight pure-bred and two grade Clydesdale stallions stand for service here, one of the grades being a cross with a Shire. Besides these there are a Thoroughbred and three Roadsters, pure-bred and grades. The majority are sound and good in conformation. Stud fees are low, no less than five standing for fees of $8 each; for the rest the fees are $10 to $15.

Toronto township is well provided with sires, there being no less than eighteen here, among which are five Clydesdales (one a grade), two Shires, a Percheron, two Thoroughbreds (one aygrade), a Cleveland Bay grade, a Hackney and the balance Standard-breds and Roadsters. There was some unsoundness, but on the whole the conformation was good. The range of stud fees was from $10 to $20. The Inspectors report that most of the stallions are not given sufficient exercise. There are a good many imported Clydesdale mares in this township but no Shire mares. There are also some good carriage mares. The general average weight of mares is 1,350 lbs.

In Toronto Gore there were just two stallions inspected, a Canadian-bred Clydesdale and a Hackney grade, by a Hackney sire out of a Standard-bred mare. Both are sound and the fees are $8 and $10. Mares here average 1,500 lbs., and are good in quality and the heavy mares good in type. There is very little or no breeding of old mares.

The stallions in Albion township are not as a rule of very good type or conformation. The service fees average $10. The breeds represented are two Standard-breds, two grade and one pure-bred Clydesdale, and a French Canadian. Three of these horses do not travel, but stand for service at home. The mares found here are a good class, good in type and quality, and average 1,400 lbs.

Bolton township has seven imported Percherons. These horses are all a very good class, and if bred to suitable mares would do good service. It is doubtful, however, the Inspectors report, if crossing them on mares with Clydesdale blood would be advisable. Besides the Percherons, there are an imported Hackney, an imported and a Canadian-bred Clydesdale, and also

Peel—Continued.

a Canadian-bred Shire. All are sound and of good conformation; the average service fee is about $11. There are a number of mares of fair quality. and good type in this township scaling about 1,350 lbs.

There are seven stallions in Caledon township, made up as follows: an imported Hackney that was syndicated for $2,400, three Clydesdales, a Clydesdale-Shire cross, a grade Belgian, and a grade French Canadian. While mostly sound their average conformation is not high. They stand at fees varying from $8 to $15. Mares are only fair and their average weight is not over 1,300 lbs.

STALLIONS.

Breeding.	Number.	Average weight, pounds.	Average age.	Serviceably sound	Average conformation.	Number of mares served.	Average service fee.
							$
Clydesdales, Imported	12	1,745	6½	10.....	Fairly good...	868	11
Clydesdales, Canadian-bred	8	1,585	6	7......	Fairly good...	517	9
Grades, Clydesdale	6	1,430	5	All....	Fairly good...	188	8
Shires.	3	1,465	2	All....	Fairly good...	71	10
Percherons	9	1,670	4	All....	Good	72	13
Hackneys, Imported	7	1,280	10	All....	Good	485	15
Grades, Hackney and Belgian (1 Hackney, 1 Belgian)	2	1,250	5	All....	Good	16	9
Standard-breds, Imported	4	1,085	8	All....	Good	147	15
Roadsters, Canadian-bred	2	1,125	7	1......	Fairly good...	224	10
Grades, Roadster	5	1,080	8	All....	Fairly good...	170	9
Thoroughbreds	3	1,170	6	All....	Good	20	13
Grades, Thoroughbred and Cleveland Bay (1 of each)	2	1,185	12	All....	Good	110	11
Grades, French Canadian	2	1,275	15	All....	Fair	70	....
Totals	65					2,958	

MARES.

Townships.	Number bred to stallions inspected in township.	Type.	Average weight, pounds.	Average quality.	Average age.
Brampton Town	574	Good. Quite a number of pure-bred Clydesdales	1,400	Very good	6
Chinguacousy	545	General Purpose and Agricultural, and some light.	1,300	Good	7
Toronto	613	Fair.	1,350	Fair	7
Toronto Gore	16	Clydesdales; light	1,500	Good	6
Albion	364	Good	1,400	Good	8
Bolton	220	Good		Fair	8
Caledon	626	Fair.	1,300	Fair	8
Total	2,958				

Peel—Concluded.

MARES BRED TO DIFFERENT CLASSES OF STALLIONS.

Stallions.	Total.		Serviceably sound.			Not serviceably sound.		
	Number of stallions.	Number of mares bred to.	Number of stallions.	Number of mares bred to.	Average fee.	Number of stallions.	Number of mares bred to.	Average fee.
					$			$
Registered Stallions .	48	2,404	44	2,073	12	4	331	10
Grade Stallions	17	554	17	554	9	....	....	....
Totals	65	2,958	61	2,627	21	4	331	....

At the meeting held at Brampton for the county of Peel, the speakers were generally in favor of an Inspection Act for stallions, and one speaker went further and thought that it should include an inspection of the progeny, and, if these proved inferior, to cancel the sire's license. Much better results were obtained from the importation from Great Britain than from those from the United States, as regards the light classes. Another gentleman found that little confidence could be placed on the pedigrees of the light horses as furnished by owners. Nothing beneficial would follow inspection of the dams. If any system could be devised whereby stallions could be restricted to a certain number of mares it should be done. It was also thought by another speaker that the breeding of heavy horses was the most profitable for the farmer. He would encourage the crossing of Clydesdales and Shires. Another gentleman considered the breeding of speedy horses in Peel an ignominious failure, on the testimony of a light horse breeder. Another gentleman also spoke very strongly against syndicating, of which he had had bitter experience, some one always being given a good sum of money to put the deal through.

SIMCOE.

In Essa township honors are divided, there being three each of Clydesdales and Standard-breds, and only one grade, belonging to the latter. Two-thirds of them are sound, and the general average conformation is good. The fees charged run from $10 to $15. Mares average from 1,200 to 1,300 lbs., and the average kept is 1½ by each breeder.

Tecumseth township has three pure-bred Clydesdales, four grades of more or less Clydesdale breeding, a Percheron, a German Coach horse, and a Roadster grade. With one or two notable exceptions they are not of a very high order, although several qualify as regards conformation, but not all as to soundness. A minimum of $5 and a maximum of $15 is the range of the stud fees. The mares in this township are rather inclined to the light type, the heaviest averaging about 1,300 lbs. and the light about 1,175. They are of a fairly good type. The general opinion of the farmers seemed to be that syndicating stallions was a great mistake, for by this means the stallion costs nearly double what it should, and as in most cases there is no one whose special business it is to look after the stallion, in most cases it is

Simcoe—Continued.

not properly taken care of. Those spoken to thought that it would be a good thing to inspect stallions and also thought that they were not given enough exercise at this season of the year (October).

Clydesdales lead in point of numbers in Gwillimbury, with six pure-breds and two grades; Percherons, Roadsters, and Shires have one each to their credit. Two, at least, of the stallions are too old for service. There is not much unsoundness, but average conformation is only medium. $6, $8, $13, and $15 are fees charged. Mares are only medium heavy and fair in quality.

Adjala township has a Canadian-bred Clydesdale not registered and a grade Roadster, the latter well up in years. No unsoundness is mentioned and conformation is good. $10 is the fee in both cases. Mares average about the same as in the previous township, viz., 1,300 lbs.

Only one stallion, a Thoroughbred, was inspected in Innisfil township. Service fee is $10.

In Alliston town and surrounding district, quite a few old mares are being bred that are not fit for this purpose. Mares are of fair type, weighing 1,300 lbs. About one-half of the foals here die shortly after birth, and there is a good deal of *"navel and joint ailment."* "Something should be done to prevent horses without a pedigree from travelling for service," say those who were interviewed. There are two pure-bred Clydesdales and one Standard-bred in this township, all getting up in years, fairly good in conformation, but not all sound. $10 and $12 are the fees in this section.

Tossorontio township runs exclusively to Clydesdales of which two are imported, one Canadian-bred, and two grades. The stud fees are $5, $8, $10, and $13. In consequence of the absence of light sires, many small mares are being bred to heavy horses, making a rather violent cross. Mares average in weight 1,100 to 1,200 lbs.

In the township of Nottawasaga, which includes the town of Collingwood, and village of Creemore, there are a large number of sires, including many Standard-breds and a Hackney, besides a good complement of Clydesdales and two Percherons. Of Clydesdales there are eight pure-bred and one unregistered, and of Standard-breds seven. The greater number are sound and there are some good ones among them, the average conformation being good. Starting with $8 for a grade, the fees run up to $15. In this section the Inspectors saw more mares weighing 1,300 to 1,400 lbs., than in the districts previously visited.

In Stayner town and neighborhood Clydesdales again lead with four stallions, Standard-breds having two, and there is also a grade Hackney. Two of the horses are quite aged but all are sound and all fairly good as regards conformation. There is a unanimity as to fees, all charging $10.

The town of Barrie is a fairly good horse breeding centre, sires of light breeds being most in evidence. There are five Standard-breds and a Hackney grade to five Clydesdales (one a grade). Two of the Clydesdales and one of the Standard-breds are new arrivals. There is more or less unsoundness in evidence. Stud fees range from $9 to $15. Mares average about as in other townships of this county, viz.. 1,300 lbs.

There are seven Clydesdales (of which two are grades), a pure-bred Shire, an imported Hackney and a Roadster grade in Flos township. The average conformation of the lot is good, but there are two cases of unsoundness. Stud fees reach $16 and are as low as $8. There are some good mares in this township including some excellent Clydesdale imported ones, but the general average is not above 1,300 lbs.

Simcoe—Continued.

With one exception all the stallions in Tiny township are sound and of fairly good conformation. With reference to two grades, however, their value as sires is not great. There are two Clydesdale grades and one Roadster grade, whilst the pure-breds are repesented by two Standard-breds and a French Canadian, the latter standing for a fee of $12, while the others have fees up to $10 and as low as $7. Mares are poor in quality and of poor type, and a good many old used up mares are being bred. Two stallion owners gave their views on licensing stallions. One was strongly against inspection as he stated that he could raise better grades than pure-breds. The other was in favor of inspection, as that would give the owners of good pure-bred stallions a chance to earn something on their investment.

In Tay township one stallion was not seen on account of its owner being away. Of the six inspected, there are one imported Clydesdale, two grade Clydesdales, two cross-bred Clydesdales and Shires, and a French Canadian grade. The average standard is not as good as it might be although all those inspected were sound. The maximum fee is $10 and the minimum $5. Mares are in quality poor to fair, with an average weight of 1,200 to 1,250 lbs. Too many old mares are being bred, while any good ones are being sold to too great an extent. One breeder in this township, while in favor of government inspection and licensing stallions, thinks that this should be done gradually, as it would be a mistake to cut off unregistered sires immediately, the effect being to create a great dearth of sires from which to breed. He also thought the present custom of syndicating stallions should be discouraged. A man who sells a horse in this way generally gets three or four times as much as the horse was worth. He did not think that owners of good horses should be put to the additional expense of a license.

In Vespra township only two stallions were inspected, a pure-bred Clydesdale and a grade of mixed breeding. No unsoundness is reported, and while not of a high average, their conformation is fair. Fees are $12 and $8 respectively. The Inspectors add that the cutting off of poor stallions in a district like this should not be done hastily, as farmers here will not pay a fair fee for a good horse. The result would be to leave a section like this without any sires. Mares are poor in quality and type not averaging above 1,100 lbs., and too many culls are being bred.

The four sires in Medonte township are all more or less up in years, and have been good in their day and are all still sound. They consist of a pure-bred and a grade Clydesdale, an imported Shire, and a pure-bred Standard-bred. Three of the horses stand for a fee of $8, and the fourth for $12. As in the previously inspected townships of Simcoe county a good many old mares are bred, and the good ones sold. The quality on the average is poor, and mares are of no particular type. Their average weight is 1,200 lbs.

In Orillia township there are two pure-bred imported Clydesdales, four pure-bred Standard-breds, an imported Hackney and a Percheron, all sound as far as seen, one owner having refused to allow his horse to be inspected. In general, conformation was good. Two of the stallions were syndicated at high figures. Ten and twelve dollars are paid for stud fees. Here again the report mentions that many old mares are being bred, and as the average quality is poor even of the younger mares the results of breeding old, broken-down mares must be disastrous. Horse owners here agree that some steps should be taken to do away with scrub sires.

The Township of Oro is a good breeding centre; among the stallions were some of the best horses inspected. There is, however, some unsoundness. and, while some are extra good, others are only fair, and some unfit for use.

Simcoe—Continued.

There are four' pure-bred Clydesdales and a grade, a cross-bred Clydesdale and Shire, a Percheron and a grade, and a Hackney. A grade stands for a $9 fee, but the stud fees for the others range from $12 to $15. There are some good Clydesdale mares here, and the average quality and type among all mares is good. The average weight is 1,300 lbs. There is not much mortality among foals.

STALLIONS.

Breeding.	Number.	Average weight, pounds.	Average age.	Serviceably sound.	Average conformation.	Number of mares served.	Average service fee.
Clydesdales, Imported	33	1,660	7	30.....	Very fairly good.	3,084	$12
Clydesdales, Canadian-bred	16	1,390	5	All. ...	Good.......	841	11
Grades, Clydesdale	21	1,430	5	20.....	Fairly good.	1,036	8
Shires, Imported	3	1,680	11	2.....	Fair........	341	11
Percherons and Grades (6 pure-bred, 1 grade)	7	1,780	4	5......	Fair........	418	12
Hackneys. Imported..............	4	1,220	6	All. ...	Good.......	335	12
Grades, Hackney.................	2	1,200	5½	All. ...	Fair........	137	10
Standard-breds, Imported.........	14	1,165	10	12.....	Fairly good.	939	11
Roadsters, Canadian-bred	10	1,100	8	All. ...	Fairly good.	467	10
Grades, Roadster	.6	1,190	11	5......	Good.......	153	9
German Coach, Thoroughbred, French-Canadian and Grades (1 of each)	4	1,430	9	All. ...	Fair........	342	11
Totals...................	120					8,093	

MARES.

Townships.	Number of mares bred to stallions inspected in township.	Type.	Average weight, pounds.	Average quality.
Essa	420	General Purpose to Medium draught	1,200 to 1,300.	....
Tecumseth..............	619	Fairly good..................	1,175 to 1,300	Fair.
W. Gwillimbury.........	434	Fair........................	1,300	Fair.
Adjala	60	Fair........................	1,300	Fair.
Innisfil	25	Fair........................	....	Fair.
Alliston Town	279	Fair........................	1,300	Fair.
Tossorontio.............	190	Fair........................	1,100 to 1,200	Fair.
Nottawasaga and Collingwood Town	1,652	Fair........................	1,200 to 1,300	Fair.
Stayner Town.	608	Fair........................	1,300	Fair.
Barrie Town	419	Fair........................	1,300	Fair.
Flos	835	A few good Clydesdales, the rest fair	1,300	Fair.
Tiny....................	249	Poor	1,150	Poor.
Tay....................	607	Poor	1,200 to 1,250	Poor to fair.
Vespra.................	....	Fair	1,100	Poor.
Medonte	405	Only Medium	1,200	Rather poor
Orillia	511	Only fair	1,150 to 1,200	Poor.
Oro....................	780	Good	1,300	Good.
Total............	8,093			

Simcoe—Concluded.

MARES BRED TO DIFFERENT CLASSES OF STALLIONS.

Stallions.	Total.		Serviceably sound.			Not serviceably sound.		
	Number of stallions.	Number of mares bred to.	Number of stallions.	Number of mares bred to.	Average fee.	Number of stallions.	Number of mares bred to.	Average fee.
Registered Stallions..	89	6,615	81	5,991	$ 15	8	624	$ 11
Grade Stallions......	31	1,478	29	1,413	9	2	65	9
Totals........	120	8,093	110	7,404	....	10	689	....

The public meeting for the county of Simcoe was held at Barrie, on October 26th. Some of the speakers took the ground that syndicating horses should be encouraged, providing it is properly done and a good care-taker employed. Some of the views expressed by those present are as follows: Syndicating is a benefit if properly done otherwise it is an injury. Offspring should also be inspected, and future licensing based upon that. It is a question whether the people would stand the licensing and the consequent cutting off of poor sires. In syndicating, a syndicate should be formed first and then the animal afterwards purchased. If animals do not pass inspection they should not be allowed to stand for service at all. A small fee should be paid for license. It would be a great hardship to bring a license act into force if there was not enough serviceable animals on hand to do the work of service. Do not bring such an act into force at once. The heavy horse is the more profitable to breed but we have use for all classes of horses. The Government should do nothing to curtail the personal liberty of the individual. No horse should be licensed unless registered in some recognized Stud book. Unlicensed animals should not be allowed to stand for service. To make it illegal to allow the owners of scrub sires to charge a service fee would not be effective. Something should be done by the Government in preventing poor sires which are registered from entering the country. An inspection and license act should extend to imported stock at the time of landing. In the syndicating or selling of stallions the law should stipulate that notes taken in the sale of stallions should have written across the face of them *"Stallion sale notes not negotiable."* This would protect the purchaser in case the animal does not come up to any guarantee which may be given. If the notes do not bear this mark they should become void and the salesman liable to a fine or penalty.

At the conclusion of the meeting a vote of the audience numbering twenty-six was taken as to the advisability of the Government passing a Stallion Inspection and License Act and the voice of the meeting was unanimous in supporting such a measure. It was also considered that it would be a benefit to encourage Agricultural Societies to choose a good sire for the season, grant the owner a premium and restrict the horse to the service of a certain number of mares.

YORK.

The township of King, and Newmarket have a fairly long list of sixteen stallions to their credit, consisting of twelve Clydesdales, imported and Canadian-bred; two grade French Canadians, and a Standard-bred, and a Standard-bred grade. These are all of good serviceable age and mostly serviceably sound. Their average conformation is fairly good, and most of them serve successfully a good number of mares at fees from $7 to $13. There are not very many good mares in this section; their weight runs from about 1,100 to 1,250 lbs.

In the Gwillimbury townships there are a number of good sires, including five lately imported. One horse is pretty well up in years, but has been a good stud horse, and holds his age well. There is no unsoundness among any of them. As regards breeds, there are ten registered Clydesdales, a horse of mixed Clydesdale and Shire breeding, a Shire, a Hackney, a Percheron, a French grade and a Roadster grade. Five of the stallions are not rated high and the service fees are as low as $7 and from that amount up to $15. Some of the stallions are not kept in very good shape. There are a few good imported Clydesdale females which should be of benefit to the country, but the farmers as a rule have sold all their best females and kept the poorer ones for work and breeding. The average weight of the mares is not above 1,200 lbs.

In Sutton township a good many foals died of joint disease and rheumatism last season, due a good deal to lack of care on the part of the owners. There are eleven stallions in this district, and some of them certainly should not be used for breeding purposes. The majority are of the light type, Standard-breds and grades of this breeding; in addition there are three Clydesdales. Some idea of the class of sire may be gleaned from the fact that in one case the stud fee is $3, in another $5, and $7, $8, and $10. Mares average in weight 1,250 lbs., and are only fair in quality.

In Markham township both heavy and light stallions are almost without exception good individuals. There are thirteen Clydesdales, all pure-bred, two good Hackneys, a Percheron, and two very good Roadsters out of four (one a grade). Three of the stallions are getting up in years, but with one exception and one not seen, all are sound, and average well in conformation and fair in action. Stud fees are in the majority of cases from $12 to $15, but one Hackney stands for only $8. There are some good Hackney mares here, and the average quality of all the mares is above the general average. Too many old ones, however, are being bred. The average weight is 1,400 lbs.

The three sires in Scarboro township are an imported Clydesdale, an excellent Hackney, and a Standard-bred, the latter not being seen. Both the Clydesdale and the Hackney are doing good service. The fees are $15 and $20 respectively. Mares are of a fair type and their average quality is good.

In Whitchurch township, one importer has the field all to himself and two young imported Clydesdale stallions were inspected. The latter had just arrived when the inspection was made. The average quality of farm mares is good in this township, and they are of a good type, and are bred at a suitable age.

The stallion list in the township of York, is considerably augmented from time to time by the importation of Clydesdales, Shires, Hackneys, and Percherons. In all, there are six Thoroughbred stallions, twenty-two

York—Continued.

Clydesdales, five Shires, three Percherons, eight Hackneys and a Standard-bred. Where so many horses are imported for sale and newly arrived, they do not, as a rule, stand for service. and consequently no stud fees are available. For those in service fees run from $10 to $20. The mares in this township are mostly of pretty good type and quality, averaging about 1,400 lbs.

Vaughan township has a fairly good lot of sires, which include four Canadian-bred Clydesdales and a grade of that breeding, two Percherons (one syndicated at a high figure), and a grade each of Roadster and Carriage breeding. All are eligible as regards soundness and their conformation is pretty good on the average. While some of the grades stand at $8, the better horses make from $10 to $14. The mares here average the same as in York, and are much the same in type and quality which is good. There is no breeding of old mares, as a rule.

Etobicoke township, the last in York county to be visited, has just four sires within its limits, three of them Clydesdales, and one a grade Roadster. With one exception all are sound and fairly good as to conformation. Ten to thirteen dollars are the fees charged. Mares are good, and average well in type, with a weight of some 1,400 lbs. There are many young ones among them. In commenting on the stallions in this county the Inspectors remark on a defect found largely among Canadian-bred stallions of having rather small straight hoofs.

STALLIONS.

Breeding.	Number.	Average weight, pounds.	Average age.	Serviceably sound.	Average conformation.	Number of mares served.	Average service fee.
							$
Clydesdales, Imported	50	1,745	5	48.....	Good.......	2,551	12
Clydesdales, Canadian-bred	20	1,600	5	19.....	Fairly good.	1,162	10
Grades, Clydesdale	2	1,550	4½	All....	Fairly good.	176	8
Shires, (5 Imported; 1 Canadian-bred)	6	1,645	5	5....:.	Fair........	215	12
Percherons	7	1,745	5	6......	Fair........	273	13
Hackneys, Imported	12	1,040	4	All....	Good......	410	13
Standard-breds, Imported	5	1,090	12	All....	Fairly good.	374	11
Roadsters, Canadian-bred	5	1,080	7	All....	Good......	178	11
Grades, Roadster	8	1,160	9	All....	Fair........	270	10
Thoroughbreds	6	....	10	All....	Fairly good.	....	.....
Grades, Coach and French-Canadian (1 Coach; 3 French Canadians)	4	1,400	8	3......	Fairly good.	458	10
Unenumerated	9						
Totals	134					6,067	

York—Concluded.

MARES.

Townships.	Number of mares bred to stallions inspected in township.	Type.	Average weight, pounds.	Average quality.
King and Newmarket............	1,261	Fair	1,100 to 1,250	Fair
E. and N. Gwillimbury..........	964	Fair...................	1,200	Fair
Sutton........................	427	Fair...................	1,250	Fair
Markham......................	1,478	Good..................	1,400	Good
Scarboro	320	Fair...................	1,350	Good ·
Whitchurch	....	Good..................	1,400	Good
York..........................	492	Good..................	1,400	Good
Vaughan	639	Good	1,400	Good
Etobicoke	486	Good..................	1,400	Good
Total..................	6,067			

MARES BRED TO DIFFERENT CLASSES OF STALLIONS.

Stallions.	Total.		Serviceably sound			Not serviceably sound.		
	Number of stallions.	Number of mares bred to.	Number of stallions.	Number of mares bred to.	Average fee.	Number of stallions.	Number of mares bred to.	Average fee.
Registered Stallions.	111	5,163	106	4,793	$ 11	5	370	$ 10
Grade Stallions......	14	904	13	788	9	1	116	12
Unenumerated......	9	....	....	....	....	....	....	....
Totals........	134	6,067	119	5,581	....	6	486	....

The meeting for the County of York was held at Richmond Hill, November 5th.

· There were about thirty present, and it was not such a representative meeting of those interested in horse breeding as some previously held. It was urged by some speakers that the Government should do something to protect owners of good horses. Others took the ground that that would be a hard thing to get at, as the breeding of good horses depended on the class of mares in the county as well as on the stallions. One gentleman suggested that the Government might do something towards improving the standard of the mares by giving assistance to those bringing in good mares into the country. Regarding the inspection and licensing of stallions, he thought that nothing hasty should be done, as importers were doing their best in bringing in good sires, but he thought that an act should be passed to prevent grade sires being used.

All present agreed that the Government should take steps to prevent grade sires travelling and standing for service.

ONTARIO.

Uxbridge is a township where light sires are in majority. There are five Standard-breds and a French Canadian, to one Percheron and three Clydesdales. All are pure-bred as far as seen, and mostly sound, with good average conformation. There are no stud fees lower than $10, while the highest is $15 in three instances. Mares are good in type and fair in quality, averaging 1,250 to 1,300 lbs. in weight. No old mares are bred, and there is very little foal mortality in this section.

In Scott township there was only one sire inspected, a Thoroughbred, of fair type and sound, standing at $12. Mares in this township are much the same as in Uxbridge, but with an average of only one to each breeder.

Reach is a large township, and has a fair proportion of stallions, consisting of nine Clydesdales, a cross-bred Clydesdale and Shire, a Thoroughbred, and two Standard-breds (one of the latter a grade). All but one were serviceably sound, and they are in general a pretty good lot. Ten to thirteen dollars are charged for fees, but there is one grade standing for $6. The Thoroughbred is an old Queen's Plate winner, now well up in years. The average number of mares kept by farmers is 1½, and they are good in quality and of nice type, with an average weight of 1,300 lbs.

Brock township inclines mostly to heavy sires, there being six Clydesdales to two Standard-breds. In some cases the horses are not as well looked after as they should be, and three of them are getting on in years. They are nearly all (as far as inspected) serviceably sound, and of quite good average conformation. None are grades, but some of the service fees are quite as low as if they had been, viz., $8 and $9. The majority, however, run from $10 to $15.

In Thorah township, four Clydesdales, one Shire, and one Hackney were inspected. The minimum fee is $12, and the maximum $17. In this township there is an improvement in the average weight of mares, and also in their type and quality. Some horsemen here were of the opinion that little could be done to improve the standard of horses by licensing sires.

Four stallions, all Clydesdales have their routes in Mara township, one of these is a very old horse. The other three are sound and of good conformation, with fees of from $10 to $14. The average weight of the mares is 1,400 lbs., and they are of good average quality. Farmers here are well posted as to the injury that would be done by allowing scrub stallions to serve mares.

With the exception of one registered Standard-bred and two nondescripts, all the stallions inspected in East and West Whitby townships were Clydesdales, and they number 25, the list being largely made up of the horses in the stables of breeders and importers. The stallions throughout this township are almost without exception sound, and of a class to improve the standard of heavy horses in the Province. Eliminating the horses which stand for $8 each, the horses travelling in this district have service fees of from $10 to $15, and $25 in one instance for a Standard-bred. There are a good lot of mares, in weight 1,400 lbs., and of good Clydesdale character.

The number of stallions in Pickering township is 43, of which 26 are Clydesdales, 14 Hackneys and Hackney ponies, and three Standard-breds (two of these being grades). Many of these are for sale, and are not standing for regular service, but those that do, earn service fees of from $10 to $20. The general average is naturally good, and soundness is the rule. The mares in this township are a good lot, having an average weight of 1,400 lbs., and in type favoring the Clydesdale.

6 H.B.

Ontario—Continued.

STALLIONS.

Breeding.	Number.	Average weight, pounds.	Average age.	Serviceably sound.	Average conformation.	Number of mares served.	Average service fee.
							$
Clydesdales, Imported	55	1,655	5	54.....	Fairly good.	2,904	13
Clydesdales, Canadian-bred, and Grades (22 pure-breds, 1 grade)..	23	1,575	4	All....	Good.......	805	10
Shires and Percherons (1 Shire, 1 Percheron)....................	2	1,900	7	1......	Good.......	160	13
Hackneys.....................	15	1,225	7	All....	Good.......	80	14
Standard-breds, Imported........	7	1,140	9	All....	Good.......	368	15
Roadsters, Canadian-bred	3	1,075	5	All....	Good.......	130	11
Grades, Roadster ....'....	3	1,125	11	All....	Fair........	162	8
Thoroughbreds	2	1,050	12	All....	Fair........	129	12
Grades..........................	3	....	9	All....	....	237	9
Totals.....................	113					4,975	

MARES.

Townships.	Number of mares bred to stallions inspected in township	Type.	Average weight, pounds.	Average quality.
Uxbridge.......................	884	Good...................	1,250	Fair.
Scott..........................	65	Good...................	1,300	Fair.
Reach.........................	532	Good...................	1,250 to 1,300	Good.
Brock	835	Good...................	1,300	Good.
Thorah......	383	Good...................	1,400	Good.
Mara..........................	373	Good...................	1,400	Good.
Whitby and East Whitby	524	Good................	1,400	Good.
Pickering..............	1,379	Good...................	1,400	Good.
Total.....................	4,975			

MARES BRED TO DIFFERENT CLASSES OF STALLIONS.

Stallions.	Total.		Serviceably sound.			Not serviceably sound.		
	Number of stallions.	Number of mares bred to.	Number of stallions.	Number of mares bred to.	Average fee.	Number of stallions.	Number of mares bred to.	Average fee.
					$			$
Registered Stallions .	106	4,576	104	4,397	12	2	179	12
Grade Stallions......	7	399	7	399	8	....	....	....
Totals	113	4,975	111	4,796	....	2	179	....

6a H. B.

Ontario—Concluded.

At the Port Perry meeting held November 13th for the County of Ontario, sixty-five were present. The following are points taken by some of the speakers and approved of by those present:

An Inspection and License law might do good, but there might be considerable difficulty in carrying out the work of inspection and licensing. If a license law were passed it should also extend to an inspection of the progeny, and to imported horses at time of landing. Men should club together and in this way get good sires by forming a syndicate, if this is properly done. Horses not registered, and not serviceably sound should not be allowed to stand for service. A license fee should be only as high as will meet the cost of inspection. The Government should encourage Agricultural Societies to give premiums to good horses and get them into a neighborhood. Government should inspect and license first, and then encourage societies to give premiums afterwards. In Scotland, in lieu of premiums, 90 to 100 mares is the limit that district stallions are allowed to serve. There are just two classes of horses that are profitable, the heavy horse and the harness horse. The expert judges sent out should report to the Government the class of horses found in the different districts in the Province. There are many light horses travelling in this locality which have never left a good colt. This district is pre-eminently fitted for the breeding of heavy horses. A License law should be brought into operation at once. The following motion was moved by Jno. Vipond, seconded by Herb. Collacott, and carried unanimously: ·

"We the breeders and horsemen of the riding of South Ontario do hereby request that a license be placed on stallions in this riding, and also that none but a stallion of recognized breed be allowed to be used for service, and that he be recorded in our Stud Book, or in the book of the country in which he was bred. We also would request that an unsound stallion be not granted a license when his unsoundness is of an hereditary nature, such as side bones, spavin, ringbones, etc., and further, that there be a license fee of $25. Also that the Government should encourage horse breeders' associations and district societies."

SPECIAL REPORT OF INSPECTORS.

We beg to submit herewith our own impressions gained while engaged on the work of horse inspection, and our own opinion as to whether the horse industry of the Province would be best encouraged by means of a Government Inspection and License law.

At the outset, according to instructions we sought to keep our own counsel, and endeavored to draw out the opinions of the owners of stallions. uninfluenced by any ideas or suggestions made by us. Although the majority of the stallion owners seemed to favor inspection and license, yet with the exception of two or three individuals, none seemed to realize, that, in the event of such an act coming into force, their own animals would fall under the ban. Although the report shows that a large percentage of stallion owners favor the Inspection and License system, yet, in conversation your Inspectors were strongly impressed with the idea that the great majority of those had given the matter very little serious consideration, and therefore were not in a position to give an opinion as the result of careful and mature deliberation. As a consequence, when the public meetings were held, and some half dozen or so would express themselves as being favorable to inspec-

Report Inspectors' District 5.—Continued.

tion and license, the balance of the gathering as a matter of course fell in line, having no definite opinions of their own. Even those who carried the meetings did not impress your Inspectors with the idea that they had given the matter sufficient consideration to realize the difficulties which the Department may encounter in carrying out their suggestions.

In the prosecution of our labors, and as the result of serious consideration your Inspectors are so keenly alive to the following observations that we herewith present them to your judgment.

(1) Many inferior sires are being used in service throughout this district of the Province, and many, even some good sires are kept in miserable unhealthy and unthrifty condition.

(2) A number of sires have been sold to their present owners at exorbitant prices.

(3) That the crossing of Percheron sires (of which we saw quite a number) upon the class of heavy females of the Province, principally of Clydesdale and Shire breeding will result in serious injury to the horse breeding industry.

(4) In some sections of our district, if inferior sires were prohibited from standing for service, there would not, at present, be a sufficient number of suitable sires, and in those sections many farmers do not seem to realize the great advantage of breeding from good dams and to good sires, and in consequence, there is great need of educational work along this line, and the need of a better class of breeding females, both heavy and light.

(5) That the system of ownership by syndicate, although, in theory, it may appear to be ideal, yet in practice has proven such a signal failure, that great caution should be taken in giving the movement any further sympathy or encouragement.

(6) In some of the more advanced sections we found those who urged that instead of inspection and license a vigorous educational campaign be conducted, through the O. A. C. short course in judging, the Agricultural Societies, and the employment of well informed and successful horse-breeders as Institute lecturers, thus spreading the gospel of wisdom to those who desire information. These are mediums of instruction which we consider the Department would do well to endeavor to still further encourage and strengthen.

(7) While the information gleaned from this inquiry, will, as already intimated, be valuable to the Department in their further efforts in assisting this important branch of live stock development, yet we would be very cautious in advising the inspection, and more particularly the licensing of sires. What is to be gained thereby? Is it not a fact, that, in the mind of every successful breeder, no legislation is required in order to compel him to act in his own best interest in this matter. These men, although in some sections they may be comparatively few, yet practically speaking, are strewn all over the Province, and if their next door neighbors with this object lesson right before their eyes, are so blind they will not see, would it not be highly impolitic in this free democratic country for the Government to force upon an unwilling people, what their own best interests tell them they ought to do. Were it a matter of human life or health that was at stake, the case would be very different. Take for instance the handling and treatment of the farmers' milk supply. Milk and the products thereof, constitute a vital portion of the food of humanity. In the handling of that article of diet the health and vitality of our people are at stake, and the Government would be

Report Inspectors' District 5.—Concluded.

justified in interfering, entering upon the private farms and by law or regulation, forcing the removal of conditions which produce a dangerous contamination; yet thus far this is not done, and there is no parallel in the two cases. What would the matter of horse inspection alone accomplish? It would certainly compel stallion owners to stand and advertise their animals under their true colors. If this inquiry reveals any deception upon this score being practiced, (although under our present law a severe penalty is attached) then some further regulation may be enacted. In our five or six weeks labor, no such case has come under our notice. The matter has never been mooted. Every person in the locality seems to be quite conversant with the breeding of the animals they patronize. If the sire in question happens to be unsound in any particular, the owners of competing sires soon get to know, and publish the fact broadcast over the community.

(Signed)   THOMAS McMILLAN.
                WILLIAM MOSSIP.

DISTRICT NO. 6.

Counties—Hastings, Peterboro, Victoria, Durham, Northumberland and Prince Edward.

Inspectors—J. G. Clark, Ottawa, and Jas. Irving, Winchester.

Hastings.

In Sidney township the Inspectors report that the majority of the stallions are totally unfit for breeding a good class of horses; most of them are undersized and unsound and of poor quality, and colts of any kind are quite scarce. The horsemen here were found in favor of stallion inspection and the licensing of good horses for the protéction of breeders. Five of the stallions are Standard-bred, one being a good individual. There is also a good Hackney. The balance includes a fair Clydesdale and an aged Coach grade. Fees vary from $8 to $16. Mares are of only medium quality, many being unfit for breeding purposes; worn out and crippled mares being generally bred.

In the townships of Thurlow and Tyendinaga there are some very good stallions including Standard-breds, a French Coach, a grade English Coach horse and a Clydesdale. In numbers there are four Standard-breds and two grades of that breeding; a Clydesdale and a grade, a French Coacher, three French Canadians, unrecorded, an English Coach grade and a Shire grade. There is no absolute unsoundness and some of the horses have the reputation of being good stock getters. There is a wide range in fees from $7 to $20. As regards mares there is a tendency to breed too many light mares without regard to strength and substance. Mares are somewhat better than in Sidney township, but stallion owners claim that good ones are scarce and that the reputation of stallions is seriously injured by the mares with which they are mated being inferior and unsound, and the colts partaking of their unsoundness and inferiority. Among stallion owners the idea of stallion inspection seems to meet with universal approval. Some difference of opinion was met with in reference to a license fee. Many of those spoken to laid special emphasis on the necessity for the greatest care on the part of the Inspectors (if such were appointed) in inspecting the progeny of the stallions under consideration; as many had found that many registered stallions had not been successful as stock getters.

There are several grade sires in Hungerford township, and pure-bred stallions are considerably in the minority. The pure-breds are three Clydesdales and a Hackney; the grades are Clydesdales seven, Standard-breds three, Coach one, and Percheron one. With few exceptions the standard of merit is rather low and so are service fees, from $5 to $15, the majority not exceeding $10. Mares are chiefly cross-breds, light general purpose, with a few small Roadsters. A few heavy blocky mares were seen that would mate well with good Clydesdale or Shire stallions. Stallion owners are divided about the amount of a license fee; some favored a high one. The opinion seemed to be unanimous that the scrub stallion should be put out of business, but none of the owners apparently consider the possibility of their own horses coming within that class. Some favor an act of Parliament giving stallion owners a lien on the progeny until the service fee is paid. All the evidence goes to show that haphazard breeding and the patronizing of cheap horses are responsible for the slow progress being made in the improvement of horses here. The scope of a stallion act came in for a lot of discussion. Men who have had good results from cross-bred horses would not favor the

Hastings—Continued.

disqualifying of unregistered sires. Much evidence is forthcoming where cross-bred horses have given better results than some of those registered.

In the three townships of Elzevir, Madoc, and Marmora there are three pure-bred Clydesdales, an imported Hackney, a Clydesdale grade, two Standard-bred grades, and a French-Morgan horse. The inspectors state that some are very good horses, and that farmers are taking more interest as to the stallions used. Stud fees are from $7 to $12. All horsemen here think a stallion Inspection Act the most practical thing.

The quality of some of the imported stallions comes in for severe criticism, as their progeny compares unfavorably with those of Canadian-bred, and even cross-bred stallions. Here as elsewhere lack of judgment in the selection of suitable sires to mate with the type of mares on hand has led to failure. Opinions as to the amount of license fee differ, but all agree as to the expediency of a license law. There are some very good general purpose mares in these townships, but a large number are too small to give good results when mated to heavy sires.

There are only three pure-bred sires in Rawdon and Huntingdon townships, one an imported Clydesdale, one an English Coach horse, and the third a Standard-bred. Of grades there are three Clydesdales, three French, and a Standard-bred and a Percheron. Some of the grades are good-looking horses, but are not well enough bred to prove good sires. There is some unsoundness among them. They stand for fees from $6 up to $10, and one is quoted at $25. Mares vary in quality, there being some good, useful ones seen, but too few show signs of breeding among the heavy class. The Coach and Roadster average up better.

In the townships in the northern part of Hastings county there are three pure-bred Clydesdales, a pure-bred Shire, and a Percheron and French Canadian grade respectively, all sound except one, but only just fair in conformation. There are four syndicate horses among them purchased at pretty high figures. They serve for fees from $5 to $10.

STALLIONS.

Breeding.	Number.	Average weight, pounds.	Average age.	Serviceably sound.	Average conformation.	Number of mares served.	Average service fee.
							$
Clydesdales, Imported	7	1,700	7	6......	Fair........	506	10
Clydesdales, Canadian-bred	5	1,565	8½	4	Fairly good.	547	10
Grades, Clydesdale	12	1,420	5	All. ...	Fair........	905	7
Shires, Imported and Grades of Shire breeding	2	1,525	4	All. ...	Only fair ...	71	7
Grades, Percheron	3	1,375	10	2......	Fairly good.	165	7
Hackneys, Imported and Canadian-bred (2 Imported, 1 Canadian-bred)	3	1,325	6	2......	Fairly good.	250	14
Standard-breds, Imported	5	1,090	7	2......	Fairly good.	155	16
Roadsters, Canadian-bred	3	1,180	5	All. ...	Very good..	87	10
Grades, Roadster	10	1,090	5	6......	Fair........	244	8
Grades, German Coach	2	1,400	9	1......	Fair........	40	8
French and English Coach	2	1,250	9	All. ...	Good........	72	13
Grades, English Coach	2	1,250	10	All. ...	Fairly good.	96	10
Grades, French Canadian	8	1,200	6	All. ...	Fair........	454	7
Totals	64					3,592	

Hastings—Concluded.

MARES.

Townships.	Number of mares bred to stallions inspected in township.	Type.	Average weight, pounds.	Average quality.	Average age.
Sidney	416	Light, General Purpose and Drivers	1,000	Medium	12
Thurlow and Tyendinaga	796	Majority light, General Purpose with a few Standard-breds of fair quality..	1,075	Fair....	11
Hungerford............	835	Light General Purpose, some Standard-breds and Clydesdales	1,150	Medium	10
Elzevir, Madoc and Marmora	519	Mostly General Purpose, a few Clydesdales and some Hackney and Standard-breds	1,100	Fair....	10
Rawdon and Huntington	624	Light General Purpose.............	1.150	Medium	12
Dungannon, Monteagle and Wollaston	402				
Total...........	3,592				

MARES BRED TO DIFFERENT CLASSES OF STALLIONS.

Stallions.	Total.		Serviceably sound.			Not serviceably sound.		
	Number of stallions.	Number of mares bred to.	Number of stallions.	Number of mares bred to.	Average fee.	Number of stallions.	Number of mares bred to.	Average fee.
Registered Stallions..	26	1,677	20	1,429	$12	6	248	$14
Grade Stallions	38	1,915	32	1,709	8	6	206	7
Totals........	64	3,592	52	3,138	....	12	454	....

Very few of the horsemen spoken to hesitate to denounce the scrub stallion, and most of them speak of legislation against them as the only way of overcoming this nuisance. Some think that education through the Farmers' Institutes would bring more business to the owners of well bred horses. There is much difference of opinion among farmers as to the proper definition of the word "scrub" as applied to stallions, and this question was much discussed at the public meeting held at Madoc on October 17th. No recommendation was made by those present as the meeting was about evenly divided, half being in favor of legislation on the subject and the other half claiming that the Government should work along educational lines.

PETERBOROUGH.

As regards the townships of Belmont, Methuen, and Dummer in this county, the Inspectors report a decided improvement in the class of heavy horses inspected, and there is evidence of more intelligent interest being taken by farmers in horse breeding. The "scrub" is much complained of, however, and any legislation that will protect the owners of high class horses and encourage systematic breeding will be favorably received by most of the horsemen here. Stallion inspection and a license fee appear to be the only form of legislation considered likely to improve the present state of the horse industry. With but two exceptions, a Clydesdale and a Percheron, all the sires inspected were grades, viz., a Coach, Clydesdale, Percheron, and two Standard-breds. One is not sound, but on the whole they average up fairly well. The maximum for stud fees is $10, and minimum $5. Mares in these townships are a little better and heavier than in some of the other districts, but show no particular line of breeding with the exception of some grade Clydesdales. There are also a few registered mares of that breed. While there are a large number of light mares, there are not many high class drivers among them.

Peterborough town being adjacent to the townships of Otonabee and Asphodel, there are naturally a large number of stallions travelling in that section. Included in them are five pure-bred Clydesdales, and seven grades, eight pure-bred Shires, a German Coach horse, three pure-bred and two grade Standard-breds, a Percheron, a French Canadian, a pure-bred and a grade Hackney and a nondescript. There is a good deal of unsoundness among these horses, and some, at least, should not be travelling on this account, and also for poor conformation. There are some good sires amongst them, however, and some have good reports about them as stock getters. There is a pretty wide range of fees from $5 to $15, the former for grades. Mares here show some improvement along draft lines, not too many are old and worn out and not suited to give the best results in breeding. Very few give evidence of breed quality, and most of them are too light to mate with heavy stallions. Here, again, horsemen are nearly all a unit in asking that steps be taken to banish the "scrub" stallion, but opinions differ as to what action should be taken. Some would make registration a necessary qualification for all stallions, while a large number seem to favor inspection of all stallions as well as their progeny. The fact that some registered stallions have been failures in the stud, while some unregistered horses are recognized in the community as excellent stock getters, is put forward as an argument against pedigree qualification being made the standard. Many express the conviction that educating farmers as to the advantages of line breeding and the proper mating of their mares should be attempted before compulsory legislation is introduced.

The townships of North Monaghan, Smith, and Ennismore also benefit by the proximity of Peterborough, and no less than twenty-three stallions are found in this district. In this list are three pure-bred and six grade Clydesdales, three pure-bred and one grade Percheron, one Shire, four pure-bred and four grade Standard-breds and a grade Coach horse. Here, too, there is some unsoundness, but even among the grades there are some pretty goood horses. Six dollars is the lowest stud fee and $15, the highest. Mares are of fair average quality, but the age average is too high. The general purpose type of about 1,200 lbs. predominates, but there are a few Clydesdales and some good road mares. Stallion owners

Peterborough—Continued.

complain that the best mares are used on the road, and the culls kept for breeding. The greatest hindrance to improvements is the cheap stallion. Owners of high priced horses are anxious for legislation to protect them. The amount of the fee carries more weight with some farmers than the quality of the stallion or suitability of the mare. Education is much needed along the lines of intelligent breeding and mating of mares. The majority of those spoken to favor stallion inspection, and quite a number advocate a license fee on all stallions. Opinions vary as to the amount of the fee, some thinking that $25 would be sufficient, others $100. High prices offered for horses have induced farmers to part with their good mares. The introduction of the cayeuse into this district has also lowered the standard as many farmers have been foolish enough to breed them.

STALLIONS.

Breeding.	Number.	Average weight, pounds.	Average age.	Serviceably sound.	Average conformation.	Number of mares served.	Average service fee.
							$
Clydesdales, Imported	3	1,730	6	All....	Fairly good.	215	13
Clydesdales, Canadian-bred	6	1,700	4	All....	Fairly good.	432	11
Grades, Clydesdale	14	1,550	7	9....	Fair.	576	8
Shires, Imported	9	1,765	7	8.....	Fair.	166	9
Percherons	5	1,740	7	4.....	Fairly good.	360	11
Grades, Percherons	2	1,550	6	All....	Fairly good.	115	9
Hackneys and Grades	2	.....	5	All....	Fair.	100	12
Standard-breds, Imported	3	990	11	2.....	Good.	226	14
Roadsters, Canadian-bred	4	1,120	11	3.....	Pretty good.	141	12
Grades, Roadster	8	1,150	5	5.....	Fair.	143	8
German Coach and Grades (1 purebred ; 2 grades)	3	1,450	13	All....	Fairly good.	269	10
Grades, French Canadians and those of no particular breeding...	3	975	3	2.....	Poor.	21	7
Totals	62					2,764	

MARES.

Townships.	Number of mares bred to stallions inspected in township.	Type.	Average weight, pounds.	Average quality.	Average age.
Belmont, Methuen and Dummer	324	A few heavy, mostly light general purpose	1,200	Fair.	....
Otonahee and Asphodel	1,256	Mixed	1,200	Fair.	12
North Monaghan, Smith and Ennismore	1,184	Mixed	1,200	Fair.	12
Total	2,764				

Peterborough—Concluded. ·

MARES BRED TO DIFFERENT CLASSES OF STALLIONS.

Stallions.	Total.		Serviceably sound.			Not serviceably sound.		
	Number of stallions.	Number of mares bred to.	Number of stallions.	Number of mares bred to.	Average fee.	Number of stallions.	Number of mares bred to.	Average fee.
Registered Stallions..	32	1,740	28	1,572	$ 12	4	168	$ 14
Grade Stallions......	30	1,024	21	820	8	9	204	10
Totals..........	62	2,764	49	2,392	....	13	372	....

At the Peterborough meeting on October 24th, there was not a very large attendance owing to a severe thunderstorm that evening. A motion was carried favoring a standard of registration in the recognized stud book of the respective breeds in order to qualify stallions for service, and the majority were in favor of legislation to prevent "scrub" stallions doing business. Opinions varied as to the most profitable class of horse to breed, but the majority are breeding for the heavy horse market, and consider heavy horses most profitable. The syndicate system of ownership is not very popular. The opinion of many is that syndicate horses are purchased at prices much beyond their value. With very few exceptions, horsemen consider stallion inspection a good thing. This, and a license fee on all stallions seem to be the two principal methods suggested to improve the horse industry.

VICTORIA.

Two-thirds of the stallions standing for service in Emily township in this county are classified as sound, and, taken as a whole, they seem to be a fair lot. There are four registered Clydesdales and two grades, one of the latter being a cross on French stock, a cross occasionally found in this and adjoining counties; three Standard-breds and a grade, a Percheron, and a Thoroughbred. For most of these the fees range from $8 to $14. Ten being a common charge. Mares are medium, and of mixed type.

There is not much difference in the type of mares in Verulam township, except that occasionally heavier ones are met with, but the general quality is only medium and average weight about 1,150 lbs. In this township is found what is rather rare, seven Suffolk Punch stallions. They are all in the one stable, all typical of the breed and sound. Besides these there are three pure-bred and two grade Clydesdales, three grade Standard-breds and two French horses, one unregistered. There are a few unsound horses, and, apart from the Suffolk Punch and some Clydesdales, there are not many good ones in the district. Five, eight, ten, twelve and fifteen dollars are some of the fees charged. In this section a number of horsemen express themselves as opposed to compulsory legislation in any form in connection with horse breeding.

While there are in the townships of Fenelon and Somerville thirteen sires, some of these the Inspectors were unable to see, and therefor, there is

Victoria—Continued.

no report of such. Of those seen there were three pure-bred Clydesdales, two of them imported, and two Standard-breds, one of these not being registered, though eligible. They are a fairly good lot of horses, and their stud fees are from $10 to $15. Mares are of mixed types, as elsewhere, and average 1,250 lbs.

Mares in Ops township are fairly good, with a large percentage of draught type, averaging 1,300 lbs. There is a good percentage of Clydesdale stallions located in Lindsay, all seven being pure-bred. Besides these there are four Standard-breds, two Coach horses, and a French Draught. No less than four are unsound and are unfit for service. The balance are fairly good. $10 is the minimum service fee, and $15 the highest except for a Standard-bred for which the fee is $25. Horsemen interviewed, expressed opinions similar to those already given; while the majority favored stallion inspection, there are still quite a large number of breeders doubtful as to the wisdom of such legislation.

There is quite a noticeable improvement in the quality of both stallions and mares in Marposa township as compared with some of the districts previously visited. While mares are of mixed breeding and very few conform to any particular type, still they average fairly well in quality and weight. There is no unsoundness reported amongst the stallions inspected, which comprise six pure and four grade Clydesdales and two Standard-bred grades and a grade Thoroughbred. Service fees are only given in some cases and work out at $9 to $15. Some of these stallions only stand at their own stables. Inspection and license on stallions seem to be the most favored form of legislation.

The stallions in Eldon township are not so good as they might be, with perhaps, three exceptions. Heavy horses are most popular. A lack of good mares and the patronizing of unsuitable stallions hinder improvement. The majority of horsemen favor a stallion Inspection Act as a means to improve the horse industry. There are five Canadian-bred Clydesdales and a grade, a Standard-bred and a grade in this district, besides two that the Inspectors were unable to examine. One horse has passed his usefulness, but has been a good one.

The following suggestions made in writing to Inspectors by a horseman of this county are given here in full:

"There are two or three things a Government measure ought to deal with most stringently. One is unsoundness, whether acquired or otherwise. Unsound horses should not be allowed to do business, even should their breeding be all that is required. No license should be granted, and if their owners are known to collect fees, make it hot for them.

"The inspection made by a competent Inspector.

"I think too it is highly important that the Government define clearly the standard of character required. I am inclined to think it would not be wise to place that standard too high at first, but say in four or five years, by a gradual process of thinning out, reach a standard equal to or higher than our Associations require.

"My reasons are that a great number of men have purchased stallions for next year's service that will not begin to reach what is required by either the Clydesdale or Shire Associations. In these cases it would be a

Victoria—Continued.

great hardship if they were refused a license. Again, if the standard is placed high at first the licenses might be too few for the amount of service required. I do most strongly deprecate crowding a horse for all he is worth. Sixty or seventy mares ought to be the limit, and I would be an advocate for keeping the service down to this limit. Let a register of service be produced at the time of obtaining the license, and if service exceeds, withhold license. Again, let the Act say to those importing, 'You will not be able to obtain a license unless your horse comes up at least to the standard required by our associations; importation alone will not count.' This is a most important point and, if enforced, would I think, be the greatest boon to this business.

"In this section we have been confining ourselves principally (75 per cent.) to the Clydesdale and Shire, and I think perhaps we have some specimens of these as good as are to be found anywhere, but they are few. The reason is not far to look for. Although using imported stock this stock has not been of any higher character, and in very many cases, a good deal lower than the mares bred. As an instance, three years ago an imported horse was syndicated to the west to me, and I was approached to use my mares. They handed me his card, and I immediately found that he had but one cross on his dam's side, his being only the second cross. Now this horse cost about $2,500. That, with the fact that it was imported, brought to it some of the best mares. Can you look for improvement under such circumstances. We want to stop the introduction of such short pedigreed stock.

"Now in the case of Standard-breds I think that breeding (straight line) alone should count. There is no class of horses that needs such drastic measures applied as this class. Observation convinces me that but little improvement has been made, if any, in the appearance and gait of our Road and Carriage class for very many years, and if it is only through straight pure-breeding we get improvement in other breeds it cannot be otherwise in this class. Let us have a clear well defined law of registration along this line.

"Now as to license, I am of the opinion that it would be the wrong way of doing things to place a high license on the 'good horse'. Put it on the other horse. Those are the ones we want to get rid of, and I would grade up his license according to his character, making it as prohibitory as possible. If you place a high license on the good horse, of course he must increase his fee. Now, while I would willingly pay a good large fee for good service, my neighbor says 'Well, if I have to give that I simply cannot afford it,' and the consequence is he does not breed. Now that would be a great hardship and likewise a misfortune. My idea is to strive to keep the good service down as low as possible, and the poorer service up so near to it that the difference of fee would be so trifling as not to be considered or valued. If we can only get there we will be on the forward march.

"Again, I think it would be a good idea to publish a list of all the horses licensed to do service, in the local papers, this to be sent in by the Inspector and vouched for by him. This would act as a check on unlicensed service, assuming this service to be punishable.

"I would make it compulsory to have a certified copy of the character and inspection and name of the horse on the bills or whatever advertising medium he had. I think a commission ought to be appointed in every dis-

Victoria—Continued.

trict to inspect and issue licenses, the commission to sit in different places in the district; those days to be advertised in the local papers long enough ahead so that all could know and be prepared for it. The commission to consist of say four farmers well known as good stock men, and men with backbone enough to say what they think. The vote to be taken by ballot.

"Every sire receiving a license should be minutely described, etc., and the places of service given with owner's name, groom's name, amount of fee. As for the lien, I do not think it worth much."

STALLIONS.

Breeding.	Number.	Average weight, pounds.	Average age.	Serviceably sound.	Average conformation.	Number of mares served.	Average service fee.
							$
Clydesdales, Imported	8	1,700	6	All....	Fairly good.	554	15
Clydesdales, Canadian-bred	22	1,560	4	18.....	Fair........	971	10
Grades, Clydesdale	8	1,195	6	7......	Fair........	213	7
Percherons and French Draught	2	1,750	6	....	Poor.......	71	8
Suffolk Punch	7	1,455	3	All....	Fair......	67	....
Standard-breds, Imported	6	950	15	All....	Fair........	290	15
Roadsters, Canadian-bred	3	1,150	6	All....	Fair........	184	12
Grades, Roadster	8	1,100	7	7......	Fair........	267	8
Thoroughbreds and Grades	2	....	12	1......	Fair.......	....	
Cleveland Bay	2	1,500	7	All....	Good.......	140	10
French Canadians and Grades	2	1,200	7	All....	Fair........	111	10
Unenumerated	8						
Totals	78					2,868	

MARES.

Townships.	Number of mares bred to stallions inspected in township.	Type.	Average weight, pounds.	Average quality.	Average age.
Emily	573	Mixed	1,100	Medium	....
Verulam	708	Mixed	1,150	Medium	13
Fenelon and Somerville	309	Mixed	1,250	Medium	10
Ops	813	Mixed	1,300	Fair	10
Mariposa	197	Mixed	1,250	Fair	11
Eldon	268	Mixed	1,300	Fair	10
Total	2,868				

Victoria—Concluded.

MARES BRED TO DIFFERENT CLASSES OF STALLIONS.

Stallions.	Total.		Serviceably sound.			Not serviceably sound.		
	Number of stallions.	Number of mares bred to.	Number of stallions.	Number of mares bred to.	Average fee.	Number of stallions.	Number of mares bred to.	Average fee.
Registered Stallions .	52	2,312	45	1,975	$8 12	7	337	$8 9
Grade Stallions	18	556	16	421	. 8	2	135	8
Unenumerated......	8							
Totals	78	2,868	61	2,396	....	9	472	....

The meeting held in the Council Chamber, Lindsay, for the county of Victoria on October 31st, was not very largely attended, about twenty-five being present.

Several suggestions were made regarding licensing and line breeding. Some favored an inspection of the stallions, others opposed it. There was also a division of opinion as to syndicating stallions. Upon a vote being taken it was found that a majority of those in attendance were in favor of an Inspection Act.

DURHAM.

The Inspectors state that the breeders are paying a good deal of attention to selection of their stallions and improving the quality of their mares along draught lines, but the light horse breeding is suffering for want of a better class of mares and more careful mating.

The mares in the townships of Hope and South Monaghan are chiefly of Clydesdale blood, with a few of road and general purpose type. They average about 1,400 lbs. in weight, and are of fair quality. The sires in this neighborhood consist of three Standard-breds, two unrecorded, three Clydesdales, an imported Shire, a grade Coach, and a German Coach grade, Two-thirds of them qualify as regards soundness, but average conformation is only just fair. Stud fees are $7, $10 and $15.

The townships of Cavan and Manvers are well supplied with Clydesdale stallions of good average quality, also with Hackneys, Percherons, and Standard-breds. First class mares are much needed for improving the general average of the stock. The number of stallions here is considerably increased on account of the presence of a large number of imported horses in stables at Millbrook. Clyesdales number, pure-breds 25, grades 2; Hackneys 12; Percherons 4 and Standard-breds 4. There is too large a proportion of unsoundness, but there are some good horses both among the imported and Canadian-bred ones. Many of the sires being recently imported for sale do not stand for service. Service fees run from $7 to $15.

Durham—Continued.

Cartwright township has nine stallions within its limits comprising three registered and two grade Clydesdales, a registered Standard-bred and two grades and a French Canadian. They are all serviceably sound and of good average conformation. There is not a wide range of service fees which are $8 and $10. Mixed breeding is the rule among the mares here, but there are a few registered Clydsdales. The average weight is 1,200 lbs.

Bowmanville being in Darlington township, naturally swells the total stallions for this section, among which are some excellent horses. With three exceptions there is no unsoundness recorded against the nineteen stallions, of which six are registered and three unregistered Clydesdales, four Hackneys, four Standard-breds and a grade, and a Percheron. The maximum stud fee is $25 for a Hackney and minimum $10. Among the draught mares in this township are some very good animals, and the average quality is fair. Hackney mares are fair in quality, but other light types are poor. The general average is 1,250 lbs.

In Clarke township the breeds represented by stallions are Clydesdale, Percheron, Suffolk Punch, Hackney, and Standard-bred. Four stallions were not seen and their breeding is not given. Of Clydesdales there are five, Percherons one, Suffolk Punch one, Hackneys two, and Standard-breds two. All are pure-bred and sound and their average conformation is fairly good. From $8 to $15 is the variation in service fees. As to the mares they are of a mixed type averaging in weight 1,250 lbs., those of draugnt type being good in quality, but light type are only medium.

STALLIONS.

Breeding.	Number.	Average weight, pounds.	Average age.	Serviceably sound.	Average conformation.	Number of mares served.	Average service fee.
							$
Clydesdales, Imported	28	1,600	8	21	Fairly good.	1,926	12
Clydesdales, Canadian-bred	16	1,650	5	All	Fairly good.	901	10
Grades, Clydesdale	6	1,280	3	5	Pretty good.	214	9
Shires, Imported and Suffolk Punch.	2	1,600	7	All	Fair	218	12
Percherons	5	1,600	3	All	Fair	185	12
Hackneys, Imported	17	1,160	3	12	Good	378	15
Hackneys, Canadian-bred	1	1,200	4	All	Good	50	10
Standard-breds, Imported	6	1,030	10	5	Fairly good.	152	12
Roadsters, Canadian-bred	6	1,125	12	All	Fairly good.	361	10
Grades, Roadster	5	1,300	3	4	Only fair	40	10
Grades, German and English Coach, and French-Canadian	3	1,375	109	All	Pretty good.	129	8
Unenumerated	4						
Totals	99					4,554	

Durham—Concluded.

MARES.

Townships.	Number of mares bred to stallions inspected in township.	Type.	Average weight, pounds.	Average quality.	Average age.
Hope and S. Monaghan..	269	Mostly draught	1,400	Fair.....	10
Cavan and Manvers.....	2,015	Mostly draught	1,400	Fair.....	11
Cartwright	473	Mixed......	1,200	Medium .	10
Darlington	877	Mostly draught, some Hackneys and Standard-bred..................	1,250	Fair.....	10
Clarke......	920	Mixed...........	1,250	Draughts, good ; Roadsters, Medium	10
Total..............	4,554				

MARES BRED TO DIFFERENT CLASSES OF STALLIONS.

Stallions.	Total.		Serviceably sound.			Not serviceably sound.		
	Number of stallions.	Number of mares bred to.	Number of stallions.	Number of mares bred to.	Average fee.	Number of stallions.	Number of mares bred to.	Average fee.
Registered Stallions..	81	4,171	68	3,909	$10	13	262	$11
Grade Stallions......	14	383	12	350	9	2	33	8
Unenumerated......	4							
Totals.........	99	4,554	80	4,259	....	15	295	.....

At the public meeting held at Orono, November 9th, Mr. Thos. Cowan, Orono, moved, seconded by **Mr. H. C. Hoar**, Hampton, "That a tax of $100 be levied on all unregistered stallions kept for service, and that registered stallions be inspected and be required to measure up to a proper standard of quality, soundness, and conformation in order obtain a permit to be used as stock horses." Carried unanimously.

NORTHUMBERLAND.

Coming to Northumberland county the first townships visited were Hamilton and Haldimand. Some of the stallions found here are good, but too many are not of a quality to improve the horse standard. Patronage of inferior stallions and breeding from inferior mares appear to be the most serious hindrance to improved conditions. Here, too, the majority of horsemen are in favor of a Stallion Inspection Act. The stallions are twenty in number, being ten pure-bred Clydesdales, three grades of same blood crossed with French, two Shire grades, a Percheron, a Standard-bred, and two grades, and a grade Thoroughbred. Their average conformation is only fair. Service fees range from $8 to 15: As regards mares, those of Clydesdale type are good, but lighter stock is inferior.

7 H.B.

Northumberland—Continued.

The tendency of the sires in Cramabe township is towards the light breeds, there being six Standard-breds, two Hackneys, two Clydesdales, a Shire and two Percherons. It cannot be said that the average is good, although there are a few horses of nice quality, and the stud fees are not lower than $10 and as high as $15 and $25. The mares here do not scale over 1,200 lbs. on the average, and are rather an inferior class. "There is much room for improvement," say the Inspectors, and a hesitancy on the part of many farmers to breed their best mares seems to be one of the difficulties. Stallion inspection and more education along the lines of systematic breeding are among the suggested means of improvement.

There are rather more heavy sires in Percy and Seymour townships than in the last named, the proportion of heavy to light being about equal. There is considerable unsoundness, however, reported and average quality is not very high. Minimum stud fees are $5 in one case, and the general amount is from $8 to $16. Mares are, with few exceptions not of any particular type. The majority of the heavier class lack size and the lighter ones substance. Breeders in this section, as a rule, are ready to favor any legislation that will encourage improvement in stallions imported.

In too many cases much injury is being caused by inferior registered and imported stallions which do not compare as favorably as they should with the grade, either individually or by their progeny.

In Brighton and Murray townships more young mares have been bred lately, but there are still too many unsound and inferior ones being bred for improvement to be rapid. Their type is mixed, being on the average not above 1,100 lbs. and quality is medium. There are nine grade stallions in this section to three pure-breds, these latter being all Clydesdales. The grades are made up of the following breeding; Clydesdales four. Percheron one, Standard-breds three (one, it is claimed, being entitled to record), and French one. The highest service fee is $10 and lowest $5. Two, at least, are unsound.

STALLIONS.

Breeding.	Number.	Average weight, pounds.	Average age.	Serviceably sound.	Average conformation.	Number of mares served.	Average service fee.
							$
Clydesdales, Imported	6	1,680	7	4......	Fairly good.	590	12
Clydesdales, Canadian-bred	11	1,560	4	10......	Fair........	676	10
Grades, Clydesdale	9	1,475	7	8......	Fairly good.	546	8
Shires, Imported and Grades (1 pure-bred ; 3 Grades)	4	1,500	6	All....	Fairly good.	178	12
Percherons, Imported and Grades (2 pure-bred ; 2 Grades)	4	1,335	3	3	Fair........	198	11
Hackneys, Imported	3	1,365	8	All....	Fair........	105	14
Standard-breds, Imported	9	1,025	10	8......	Fairly good.	406	17
Grades (Roadster and Thorough-bred) (8 Roadsters; 1 Thorough-bred)	9	965	11	8......	Fair.......	250	8
Grades, French Canadian	3	1,350	12	All....	Fair........	170	10
Mixed Breeding	4	1,600	3	3......	Good.......	12	5
Totals	62					3,131	

7a H.B.

Northumberland—Concluded.

MARES.

Township.	Number of mares bred to stallions inspected in township.	Type.	Average weight, pounds.	Average quality.	Average age.
Hamilton and Haldimand	1,141	Mixed	1,300	Fair. ...	10
Cramabe	434	Mixed	1,200	Fair	11
Percy and Seymour	993	Mostly general purpose	1,200	Poor	10
Brighton and Murray	563	Mixed	1,100	Medium.	11
Total	3,131				

MARES BRED TO DIFFERENT CLASSES OF STALLIONS.

Stallions.	Total.		Serviceably sound.			Not serviceably sound.		
	Number of stallions.	Number of mares bred to.	Number of stallions.	Number of mares bred to.	Average fee.	Number of stallions.	Number of mares bred to.	Average fee.
Registered Stallions	32	1,907	28	1,547	$ 12	4	360	$ 12
Grade Stallions	30	1,224	26	1,122	9	4	102	5
Totals	62	3,131	54	2,669	....	8	462	....

The public meeting for the county of Northumberland was held at Brighton on November 15th, and after discussion a motion was carried favoring inspection of all recognized breeds: "That all stallions kept for service be required to pay a tax of $25; that the minimum fee charged for service should be $10 a mare; and that a Lien Act be passed to give the stallion owner a lien on the mare and foal until the service fee for sire of foal be paid."

PRINCE EDWARD.

In the townships of Hallowell and North and South Marysborough there are twenty-four stallions altogether, which include two imported Percherons and two grades, a pure-bred and three grade Clydesdales, a French grade, six Standard-breds and six grades, a German Coach horse, a Carriage horse and a Hackney. Some are too advanced in age to be of much use as sires, and again others are unsound. Altogether they cannot be described as a good average lot, although, as elsewhere, there are some good ones among them. Twenty-five dollars is quoted as the fee for a Standard-bred, but the general fee ranges from $15 to as low as $5. Mares are of a very mixed type, not over 1,100 lbs. in weight on the average, and their quality is poor. A few good ones are found here and there. Some of the stallion owners favor a stallion Inspection Act, but quite a number are indifferent, while others think that legislation is entirely unnecessary.

Prince Edward—Continued.

Mares are no improvement in Hillier township, being poor and very mixed in type. Stallions, too, are not a good lot, with very few exceptions. All are grades except an imported Clydesdale and a Percheron, and are as follows: one grade Clydesdale, two grade Standard-breds, a grade Shire, and two French grades. Their fees run from $8 to $15.

Of the five stallions in Ameliasburg township, four are grades and one a Canadian-bred registered Clydesdale. Three of the grades are of Standard-bred blood and one Percheron. They are a fair average lot. Five to ten dollars is the range of the fees. Mares are a little heavier here and somewhat better in quality.

Sophiasburg has also just five stallions, one a registered Standard-bred, one a grade of same breeding, a Clydesdale and Carriage grade, and two Percheron grades. Three are sound, but there is plenty of room for improvement all round. Service fees are $7 and $8. Mares average the same as in the township previous.

STALLIONS.

Breeding.	Number.	Average weight, pounds.	Average age.	Serviceably sound.	Average conformation.	Number of mares served.	Average service fees.
							$
Clydesdales, Imported and Canadian-bred (1 Imported, 2 Canadian-bred)	3	1,650	6	2......	Fairly good.	223	11
Grades, Clydesdale and Shire (5 Clydesdales, 1 Shire)	6	1,425	9	4......	Fair........	314	8
Percherons	3	1,800	12	2......	Fair........	235	13
Grades, Percheron	5	1,370	8	3......	Fair........	272	7
Hackneys, Imported	1	1,250	5	All.	Good......	80	15
Standard-breds, Imported	4	970	10	3......	Fair........	168	15
Roadsters, Canadian-bred	4	1,050	11	All. ...	Fairly good.	160	13
Grades, Roadster	11	1,090	6	7......	Fair........	271	.7
Grades, German and English Coach	2	1,325	8	1......	Fairly good.	137	10
Grades, French Canadian	3	1,100	5	All. ...	Only fair. ..	152	.7
Totals......	42					2,012	

MARES.

Townships.	Number of mares bred to stallions inspected in township.	Type.	Average weight, pounds.	Average quality.	Average age.
Hallowell, and South and North Marysburg	1,037	Mixed	1,100	Poor ...	12
Hillier	552	Mixed	1,200	Poor ...	11
Ameliasburg............	179	Mixed	1,200	Medium	12
Sophiasburg	244	Mixed	1,200	Medium	11
Total...........	2,012				

Prince Edward—Concluded.

MARES BRED TO DIFFERENT CLASSES OF STALLIONS.

Stallions.	Total.		Serviceably sound.			Not serviceably sound.		
	Number of stallions.	Number of mares bred to.	Number of stallions.	Number of mares bred to.	Average age.	Number of stallions.	Number of mares bred to.	Average age.
Registered Stallions..	15	866	12	717	12	3	149	13
Grade Stallions	27	1,146	18	790	8	9	356	8
Totals.	42	2,012	30	1,507	....	12	505	....

At the public meeting for the county of Prince Edward, held at Picton on November 30th, it was resolved: "That this meeting favor stallion inspection and a license fee on all stallions kept for stock purposes. That the stallion owners as a compensation for their license fee should be protected by a Lien Act, giving them a claim on all the mares bred to their horses until fee for said service is paid."

SPECIAL REPORT OF INSPECTORS.

As Inspectors having served in the investigation of horse industry of Ontario, we are convinced that a system of stallion inspection would be beneficial. The district through which we travelled has suffered from the practice of selling off too many of the best mares and using unsaleable, and in too many cases, unsound mares for breeding. Another thing which has had a bad effect on the industry is the importation of inferior, and in some cases, unsound stallions. In our opinion no stallion should be admitted from Britain or any other country that is unsound or does not measure up to the standard of breeding we require from our own breeders. Secondly, we would suggest that a standard should be fixed requiring all stallions for service to be free from hereditary unsoundness. Thirdly, that all stallions that qualify should be granted a certificate and be protected in the collection of service fee by a lien on colt. Fourthly, that at Winter Fairs and at Farmers' Institute meetings the subject of horse breeding and the selection of sires should be enlarged upon and given more attention than heretofore.

In the hands of the average farmer the draught and general purpose horses are most profitable, but there are also several men who have well bred, warm blooded mares that are producing high class carriage and road horses that sell for big prices. The system of syndicate ownership has not been generally satisfactory. Under that system there is nearly always too much paid for the stallions, and in many cases cull horses are foisted on the purchasers. The time is ripe for some action to be taken by the Department. Horse breeders and farmers generally expect it.

(Signed.)   J. G. CLARK.
             JAMES IRVING:

DISTRICT NO. 7.

Counties.—Prescott, Russell, Carlton, Renfrew and Lanark.

Inspectors.—W. F. Kidd, Simcoe; and Geo. Gray, Newcastle.

PRESCOTT.

In the townships of East and West Hawkesbury there are sixteen stallions, two pure-bred and three grade Clydesdales, one pure-bred and two grade Percherons, a pure-bred Shire, three pure-bred and two grade French Canadians, and a registered Standard-bred. All are serviceably sound and of good average conformation. The general average of service fees is very low, $5 being the figure for several; in two cases $10 are charged. One of the imported Clydesdales serving at the last named figure is marked as a very good horse. Mares are general purpose, and from that to very light, poor in quality, very few weighing over 1,150 lbs.

There are four grade stallions in Caledonia township, two being Clydesdales, one being Standard-bred and the remaining one of no breeding whatsoever. The two heavy ones are best as regards conformation, but the Standard-bred is fair in that respect. All are sound. In fact, only two really unsound horses were seen in this county. Fees are $5 in every instance. Mares are a very poor lot.

There are two pure-bred sires in South Plantagenet township, one each of the Clydesdale and the French Canadian breeds. The remaining seven are as follows: two Percheron grades, a Clydesdale grade, a Coach grade, two Standard-bred grades, and a cross-bred Pony and Coach. All qualify as to soundness, and the general average conformation is fair. The fee for the Pony-Coach stallion is $3, the lowest yet met with, and the highest fee is $7. Mares are light in type and poor in quality, showing no particular breeding.

With six grade stallions in North Plantagenet township, four are of Clydesdale breeding and two of French Canadian stock, one of the latter having some Clydesdale blood. Not one is unsound, and they are of fair conformation and action. Stud fees are $5 and $6. Mares are much the same as in the other townships of this county.

There is one pure-bred sire in Alfred township, an imported Shire. The six grades are Clydesdales, two; Percherons, three; and Standard-breds, one. The fee for the Shire is $10; for the others $5, $6, and $7. They are of fair conformation all round.

Two Percheron grades, a Clydesdale grade, a Standard-bred grade, and a Thoroughbred grade make up the list of stallions for Longueil township. Two here are unsound, and the general average conformation is not high. Fees are about the same as in the previous township, $5 and $6. Mares are poor and mostly light, with some general purpose.

Prescott—Continued.

STALLIONS.

Breeding.	Number.	Average weight, pounds.	Average age.	Serviceably sound.	Average conformation.	Number of mares served.	Average service fee.
Clydesdales, Imported and Canadian-bred (2 imported, 1 Canadian-bred)	3	1,700	7	All....	Good.......	241	$8
Grades, Clydesdale..............	13	1,455	5	12.....	Fairly good.	451	6
Shires, Imported, and Percherons (2 Shires, 1 Percheron).........	3	1,750	7	All....	Fairly good.	180	9
Grades, Percheron	9	1,445	5	All....	Fair......	501	6
Standard-breds and Grades (1 Pure-bred ; 5 Grades)	6	1,145	11	All....	Fair........	86	7
Grades, Thoroughbred and Coach (1 Thorough-bred, 2 Coach)	3	1,100	6	2......	Fair........	97	6
French Canadians...............	4	1,300	5	All....	Fair........	246	6
Grades, French Canadian.........	5	1,340	6	All....	Fair........	244	6
No Particular Breeding..........	1	1,300	8	All....	Fair........	16	5
Totals..................	47		·			2,062	

MARES.

Townships.	Number of mares bred to stallions inspected in township.	Type.	Average weight, pounds.	Average quality.
East and West Hawkesbury.................	894	General Purpose and Light	1,150	Poor ....
Caledonia	145	General Purpose and Light	1,150	Poor ....
South Plantagenet	438	Light, no particular breeding	1,150	Poor ....
North Plantagenet	182	Light, no particular breeding	1,150	Poor ....
Alfred................	217	Light, no particular breeding	1,150	Poor ....
Longueil ....·..........	186	Light, no particular breeding	1,150	Poor ....
Total............	2,062			

MARES BRED TO DIFFERENT CLASSES OF STALLIONS.

Stallions.	Total.		Serviceably sound.			Not serviceably sound.		
	Number of stallions.	Number of mares bred to.	Number of stallions.	Number of mares bred to.	Average fee.	Number of stallions.	Number of mares bred to.	Average fee.
Registered Stallions .	11	679	11	679	$8	.....	.....	$....
Grade Stallions	36	1,383	34	1,298	6	2	85	11
Totals.........	47	2,062	45	1,977	....	2	85	....

Prescott—Concluded.

There were 35 present at the meeting for the county of Prescott which was held at Vankleek Hill on October 13th. Those present were rather unwilling to express their ideas on the subject of stallions. Thirteen were in favor of giving certificates to registered, sound horses up to a certain standard of excellence. Nine were in favor of no stallion being permitted to travel unless licensed. A few were in favor of good grade stallions also being granted certificates. There was a strong feeling that something should be done. It was found that a great many stallions are being registered in some French Canadian book. As far as we can find out any light stallion can be registered for about $20.

RUSSELL.

Russell township is well stocked with stallions, and there are some excellent imported Clydesdales among them, while there are good ones among other breeds and all are sound. Twelve out of the nineteen are imported Clydesdales. The rest comprise a grade Clydesdale, a grade Shire, two grade Standard-breds, a grade Percheron and two French Canadian grades. There is one old horse; the rest are of a good breeding age. Service fees are $6 to $10.

So far as the Inspectors could ascertain, there are very few good mares in Clarence township, and those seen were of a very poor type. As regards the stallions there are two Clydesdales, two Hackneys, a Standard-bred, and a French Canadian, all pure-bred, a French Canadian grade, and a grade of nondescript breeding. Besides these, a French Canadian grade stood for service last year, but died in August last. All are of good average conformation, and all serviceably sound. One French Canadian grade stands for $3. and another grade for $4. With these exceptions fees run from $8 to $20.

There are three unsound sires among the thirteen standing for service in Cambridge township, and all are grades of the following breeds: Clydesdale, five; French Canadian, four; Standard-bred, one; Arabian, one; Belgian, one; no particular breeding, one. In conformation they stand fairly good on the average. Three of them have not travelled as yet. The maximum service fee is $8, and the minimum $4.

STALLIONS.

Breeding.	Number.	Average weight, pounds.	Average age.	Serviceably sound.	Average conformation.	Number of mares served.	Average service fee.
Clydesdales, Imported	12	1,700	4	All....	Fairly good.	910	$10
Clydesdales, Canadian-bred	2	1,600	11	All....	Good.......	223	9
Grades, Clydesdale	6	1,480	7	5......	Fairly good.	250	7
Grades, Percheron, Shire and Belgian (1 Percheron; 1 Shire; 1 Belgian)	3	1,750	5	All....	Good.......	238	7
Hackneys. Imported	2	1,085	3½	All....	Good.......	16	20
Standard-breds, Imported	1	1,075	17	All....	Good.......	40	12
Grades, Roadster and Arabian (3 Roadsters; 1 Arabian Grade)	4	1,050	4	All....	Fairly good.	59	5
French-Canadian and Grades (1 French-Canadian; 8 Grades)	9	1,210	7	8......	Fairly good.	574	6
No particular breeding	2	1,050	7	1......	Fair........	22	5
Totals	41					2,332	

Russell—Concluded.

MARES.

Townships.	Number of mares bred to stallions inspected in township.	Type.	Average weight, pounds.	Average quality.
Russell.................	1,374	Some Pure-bred Clydesdales ;......	1,450 to 1,500	Poor
		Light	1,150	
Clarence...............	494	Poor	....	Poor
Cambridge.............	464	Poor	....	Poor
Total.............	2,332			

MARES BRED TO DIFFERENT CLASSES OF STALLIONS.

Stallions.	Total.		Serviceably sound.			Not serviceably sound.		
	Number of stallions.	Number of mares bred to.	Number of stallions.	Number of mares bred to.	Average fee.	Number of stallions.	Number of mares bred to.	Average fee.
Registered Stallions..	18	1,304	18	1,304	$ 11	....	....	....
Grade Stallions......	23	1,028	20	999	8	3	29	6
Totals..........	41	2,332	38	2,303	....	3	29	....

The meeting for the county of Russell was held at Russell on October 22nd, but was not very well attended on account of the bad roads after heavy rain, which prevented many being present who would otherwise have been in attendance. There were twenty-four stallion owners and breeders present. Great interest was taken in the discussion. All considered the investigation of the horse industry a step in the right direction. Some spoke about the poor quality of many of the stallions, and considered them quite unfit to breed to mares. Seventeen expressed themselves as in favor of licensing all stallions, and that only sound pure-bred horses up to a certain standard of excellence should be granted the license.

The reasons given at the meeting why there were so few good mares in the county were that when horses were so cheap, anything good enough to sell was sold. Many, too, of the farmers have sons in the northwest, and these would take a pair of good mares from the old home or neighborhood, and the old mares were the only ones left to breed from.

CARLETON.

Taking the township of Gloucester, the Inspectors found in Ottawa and the adjoining sections ten sires which travelled in this township. There are three pure-bred Clydesdales, (two of them lately imported), three grades of that breed, an imported Hackney, a registered Standard-bred, and two pure-bred Belgians. Two of them are not entitled to be rated as sound, but average conformation is pretty good. They stand at fees varying from $7 to $10. There are a few fair agricultural mares, but on the whole they are under 1,100 lbs. and of poor quality.

There were only three stallions seen in Osgoode township, and, with one exception they are not of great value. They are an imported Shire, a Canadian-bred and a grade Clydesdale. Eight dollars and $10 are quoted as service fees. What has been said of the mares in Gloucester township will apply to this.

In Nepean township there are about 75 registered Clydesdales and Shires, mares and fillies. Many of the remaining mares are agricultural in type, weighing about 1,200 lbs. There are some light ones. Stallions found here belong to the following breeds; Clydesdales, two, pure-bred; Percherons, two, both grades; a Belgian pure-bred, and a pure-bred Standard-bred. They are a pretty good lot, all sound, and fees vary from $7 to $10.

There are seven stallions in North Gower township, consisting of two pure-bred and two grade Clydesdales, a pure-bred and grade Percheron, and a registered Standard-bred. Five are sound, and the majority are of good conformation. Six dollars, $7 and $10 are the fees charged.

In Goulbourne, as in the two previous townships, there are a few registered Clydesdale mares and fillies, but the bulk are agricultural and light. Out of the seven sires here two only, both Clydesdales, are registered. Three of that breeding are grades and so are two of Standard-bred blood. Six-sevenths are sound and average conformation is fairly good. The maximum fee here does not seem to exceed $10, the cheapest being $6.

Mares in Huntley township are an improvement on those in previous townships, and nearly every farm has good teams. The average weight will be about 1,400 lbs. and over. There are a few registered Clydesdales. Horse interests are looked after by seven pure-bred and three grade Clydesdales, a Percheron, a Hackney, four Standard-breds, (three being grades), and a grade Thoroughbred. No less than five are unsound, but rather more than half are rated good as regards conformation. Starting at $5, service fees in one instance reach $15. In one case it is said that the owner will take anything from $1 to $5.

In March township two stallions were inspected, one an imported Clydesdale, a good one, and a Standard-bred. Both have good conformation. The stud fees are $10 and $6 respectively. There are twenty registered mares and fillies in this townships, several agricultural, and a number of general purpose type.

In Fitzroy township mares are much the same in type and quality as in March township. There are about 15 registered Clydesdale mares and fillies here, but the majority are agricultural and general purpose. All the five stallions in this township are sound and of pretty good conformation. They are made up of two pure Canadian-bred Clydesdales and a grade; and one grade of Percheron and one of Standard-bred blood. Stud fees are $6, $7, $8 and $10.

Carleton—Continued.

The city of Ottawa has seven stallions, all pure-bred, and all, with the exception of a Canadian-bred Clydesdale, are registered Standard-breds. All except one inspected were serviceably sound, and all but one stood for a service of $10, one being quoted at $25.

STALLIONS.

Breeding.	Number.	Average weight, pounds.	Average age.	Serviceably sound.	Average conformation.	Number of mares served.	Average service fee.
							$
Clydesdales, Imported	8	1,850	6	7......	Good.......	570	10
Clydesdales, Canadian-bred........	13	1,700	6	7......	Fairly good.	904	9
Grades, Clydesdale	13	1,470	7	11.....	Fair........	656	6
Shires and Percherons (1 Shire, 2 Percherons)	3	1,800	4½	2......	Good.......	240	10
Grades, Percheron...............	4	1,575	9½	All	Good.......	210	8
Belgians	3	1,975	7	2......	Fair........	295	9
Hackneys, Imported	2	1,200	4	All	Good.... ..	75	10
Standard-breds, Imported........	4	1,225	4	3......	Fairly good.	225	12
Roadsters, Canadian-bred	7	1,200	9	6......	Fairly good.	374	7
Grades, Roadster and Thoroughbred (6 Roadsters, 1 Thoroughbred)..	7	1,210	6	6......	Fairly good.	· 263	9
Totals...................	64					3,812	

MARES.

Townships.	Number of mares bred to stallions inspected in township.	Type.	Average weight, pounds.	Average quality.
Nepean.................	468	Some registered Clydesdales and Shires, balance agricultural and light	1,200	Medium.
North Gower	320	Mostly draught ; a few registered heavy...............	1,200	Medium.
Gloucester..............	472	Mostly light ; a few agricultural	1,100	Poor.
Osgoode	257	Mostly light ; a few agricultural	1,100	Poor.
Goulbourne.............	149	Draught, agricultural and light	1,200	Medium.
Huntley...............	1,276	Draught	1,400·	Good.
March.................	170	Some Draught, General Purpose and Agricultural...........	1,250 to 1,300	Fair.
Fitzroy................	342	A few registered Clydesdales, Agricultural and General Purpose	1,250	Fair.
City of Ottawa..........	358	....	....	....
Total..........	3,812			

Carleton—Concluded.

MARES BRED TO DIFFERENT CLASSES OF STALLIONS.

STALLIONS.	Total.		Serviceably sound.			Not serviceably sound.		
	Number of stallions.	Number of mares bred to.	Number of stallions.	Number of mares bred to.	Average fee.	Number of stallions.	Number of mares bred to.	Average fee.
Registered Stallions..	40	2,683	29	1,860	$ 10	11	823	$ 8
Grade Stallions	24	1,129	21	1,036	8	3	93	8
Totals	64	3,812	50	2,896	....	14	916	....

About fifty men were present at the public meeting for the county of Carleton, which was held at Stittsville on October 30th. A deep interest was taken in the work. Many expressed their ideas, and, apparently, all thought it a good move for the Department to take up the horse question. The uppermost thought seemed to be how to stop the use of scrub stallions. Twenty-seven men were in favor of stallions being licensed; none wished the matter left as it is. A resolution was passed that the grant be withheld from Agricultural Societies who gave prizes to grade stallions.

RENFREW.

In McNab township the Inspectors were unable to see two out of the eight stallions owned here. Of the six seen, one-third were not serviceably sound. They are equally divided into four pure-bred and four grades. To the former list belong a Standard-bred, two Clydesdales and a Percheron. To the latter just the same numbers of the same breeds. One Standard-bred had only recently been brought in. For the others the stud fees are $6, $7 and $10. Mares are general purpose and light in type, very few weighing as much as 1,300 lbs.

There are four stallions in the town of Renfrew and in Horton township adjoining. These are a pure-bred Clydesdale and Belgian, respectively, and a grade Standard-bred and a nondescript. All are sound and pretty good in conformation; of those in service $8 to $10 are the fees. Not much can be said about the mares in this section.

In Admaston township only one stallion was inspected, a pure-bred Percheron, which stands for service at $5.

In Westmeath the quality of the mares improves, and there are a number of fair general purpose mares, as well as a few registered Clydesdales. There are the following sires in this township: two registered Standard-breds, a pure-bred Shire and two Percheron grades. One horse was sick and was not inspected. Three of the others were sound and two of them pretty good horses. Fees are about as usual in these townships, $6 to $8.

Of the seven stallions owned in the town of Pembroke and standing in Pembroke township, all but two are registered, and have fair average conformation. Clydesdales are represented by a grade, and there is a grade French Canadian. The pure-breds are one Percheron, two Standard-breds and a French Canadian. The fee of the grade French Canadian is given as $2; others at $7, $10 and $25.

Renfrew—Continued.

In Stafford, only one stallion was seen—a Percheron grade.

Stallion owners in Wilberforce township travel two pure-bred and one grade Clydesdale, a pure-bred Shire, a grade Percheron, a grade Coach, and a horse of no particular breeding. The pure-breds and the grade Percheron and Coach grade have good conformation. One grade is not sound. Only one owner charges $10 fees; the rest charge from $5 to $6.

Excepting a grade Clydesdale in Bromley township, which the Inspectors were unable to see, the four other sires are a Clydesdale, Shire, and Percheron, and a grade Clydesdale. They are of fair average conformation. Two cannot qualify for soundness. The service fee is highest for the Shire, viz., $10, the others stand for $5 and $8.

Two grade stallions, both of French Canadian breeding, one being a Percheron cross, serve in the township of Ross. Only one was seen by the Inspectors, and it was sound and of good conformation, standing for service at $8, while the fee of the other was $5. Very few mares were met with that could be called good. They are of a light type and of no particular breeding. The best mares are sold to the lumbermen. The Inspectors state that in this country they saw some really good stallions, and if these are well patronized, the result should be a considerable improvement in the future.

In the townships of Grattan, Hagarty, Ratcliffe and the districts adjoining, but stationed principally at Eganville and Killaloe, there are seventeen stallions, some of them quite good horses, and the majority of them serviceably sound. A number of them could not be seen by the Inspectors, but from reliable information furnished, those not seen work out a good average as regards conformation and also soundness. There is one syndicate horse. Clydesdales total three pure-breds and four grades; Shires, one pure-bred; Percherons, one pure-bred and two grades; Standard-breds, one pure-bred and two grades, and French Canadians three, two at least being grades. The maximum fee is $10, but the majority run from $8 down to $3, and in one case, anything between $1 and $3 is taken. The best mares seen were under 1,500 lbs., but they are very few in number; the majority are of a light general purpose type and of no particular breeding.

STALLIONS.

Breeding.	Number.	Average weight, pounds.	Average age.	Serviceably sound.	Average conformation.	Number of mares served.	Average service fee.
Clydesdales, Imported......... ...	6	1,730	7	5......	Fairly good.	255	$8
Clydesdales, Canadian-bred.......	3	1,540	5	2......	Fair........	300	6
Grades, Clydesdale...............	10	1,630	7	7......	Fair........	789	5
Shires, Imported.................	4	1,785	7	All....	Good......	377	8
Percherons.....................	5	1,730	11	4......	Good......	489	8
Grades, Percheron	7	1,450	5	6......	Fair........	260	4
Belgians......................	1	2,100	6	All....	Good.......	86	10
Hackneys and Standard-breds, Imported (1 Hackney, 1 Standard-bred).........................	2	1,200	8	All....	Fair........	76	12
Roadsters, Canadian-bred........	5	1,090	9	4......	Fair........	85	4
Grades, Roadster.................	4	1,050	7	3.. ...	Fair........	95	7
Grades, Coach	1	1,500	15	All....	Good......	80	6
French Canadians...............	2	1,250	8½	All....	Good......	94	8
Grades, French Canadian........	5	1,370	10	All....	Good.	328	4
Grades, No Particular Breeding....	2	1,375	9	All....	Fair........	141	5
Totals... :....................	57					3,455	

Renfrew—Concluded.

MARES

Townships.	Number of mares bred to stallions inspected in township.	Type.	Average weight, pounds.	Average quality.
McNab.................	656	Mixed ...., ...	1,100 to 1,200	Poor.
Horton &. Renfrew Town	152	Mixed..........................	1,100	Poor.
Admaston.............	93	Mixed..........................	1,100	Poor.
Westmeath	285	General Purpose, a few Regis-·tered Clydesdales	1,200	Medium.
Pembroke..............	307	Mixed..........................,	1,100	Poor.
Stafford.................	30	Mixed..........................	1,050	Poor.
Wilberforce	531	Mixed.....	1,050	Poor.
Bromley	255	Mixed	1,050	Poor.
Ross.................:...	179	Mixed	1,100	Poor.
Grattan, Hagarty, Rad-cliff and adjoining Townships...........	967	Mixed, a few very good ones...	1,100	Poor.
Total...............	3,455			

MARES BRED TO DIFFERENT CLASSES OF STALLIONS.

Stallions.	Total.		Serviceably sound.			Not Serviceably sound.		
	Number of stallions.	Number of mares bred to.	Number of stallions.	Number of mares bred to.	Average fee.	Number of stallions.	Number of mares bred to.	Average fee.
Registered Stallions.	28	1,762	24	1,642	$8 9	4	120	$6
Grade Stallions......	29	1,693	24	1,394	4	5	299	5
Totals	57	3,455	48	3,036	....	9	419	....

The meeting for the county of Renfrew was held at Cobden on November 6th, and was attended by about fifty men. Quite a number of those present dropped in from the village to see what was going on. About twenty men were horse raisers. All thought the draft horse the most profitable for farmers to raise. After considerable discussion and questions, seventeen (about all the horsemen present), voted in favor of stallions being licensed. Some thought that *first-class* grade stallions should be licensed because they were superior to many imported ones.

LANARK.

Ramsay township runs almost exclusively to Clydesdale sires, there being two pure-bred and two grades of that breed to one pure-bred Standard-bred. One of the heavy ones is unsound; and the light sire and one of the grade Clydesdales have the best conformation. It seems a pity that

Lanark—Continued.

a heavy horse of good conformation and sound only earns $3 in a service fee. The others earn $5 and $10.

Bathurst township also favors heavy horses, as is evident when the stallion list is made up of three pure-bred and one grade Clydesdale, a Shire and a Percheron. They are all sound and rather above the average in conformation, one Clydesdale especially being marked as extra good. The fee for the grade is $5, for the others $8 in each instance.

There are just four of the heavy, and four of the light sires in Drummond township, with representatives of the following breeds: Clydesdales, a pure-bred and a grade; a Shire, a Hackney, a Percheron, a Standard-bred and a grade of that breeding and a grade Coach horse. It is satisfactory to find them all sound and also fairly good in conformation. Stud fees are somewhat higher than in some of the adjoining townships. Beginning at $6 they go as high as $25.

In North Emsley only one sire was inspected, a registered Canadian-bred Clydesdale, sound, and of fair conformation, standing for $8.

This was also the case in Montague township—an imported Clydesdale, a good horse and sound, whose fee was $12.

Three Standard-bred stallions are owned in the town of Smith's Falls, one being recorded and two grades. Two are getting on in years, and have seen their best days. One is unsound. Their fees are $6, $8, and $10 respectively.

A pure-bred Clydesdale, and a grade each of Cleveland Bay and French Canadian blood, make up the trio of stallions in Beckwith township. Two-thirds of them are sound, but conformation is not very good. Five dollars and $8 are the fees charged.

Standard-breds are evidently the favorites in the town of Carleton Place, as there are three registered and two grade stallions of that breed there, the only other sire being a grade Hackney. Of the six, five are sound and of fair conformation. One horse has never stood for service, but the fees for the other five are from $5 to $15.

STALLIONS.

Breeding.	Number.	Average weight, pounds.	Average age.	Serviceably sound.	Average conformation.	Number of mares served.	Average service fee.
Clydesdales, Imported	5	1,690	6	All.	Fair to good	498	$9
Clydesdales, Canadian-bred	4	1,660	5	All.	Fair........	285	8
Grades, Clydesdale	4	1,475	8	3......	Fair to good	224	5
Shires, Canadian-bred	2	1,750	6½	All.	Good......	200	8
Percherons	2	1,850	7	All.	Fairly good.	300	10
Hackneys, Canadian-bred and Hackney Grades (1 Hackney, 1 Grade)	2	1,200	8	All.	Fairly good.	128	9
Standard-breds, Imported	3	1,130	10	2......	Good......	73	17
Roadsters, Canadian-bred	3	1,115	12	All.	Fair........	54	11
Grades, Roadster	5	1,120	10	4......	Pretty good.	210	9
Grades, Coach	2	1,350	6½	1......	Fair........	121	6
Grades, French Canadian	1	1,500	26	All.	Fair........		
Totals	33					2,093	

Lanark—Concluded.

MARES.

Townships.	Number of mares bred to stallions inspected in township.	Type.	Average quality.
Ramsay	322	Light to General Purpose	Poor.
Bathurst	700	Light to General Purpose	Poor.
Drummond	408	Light to General Purpose	Poor.
North Emsley	130	Light to General Purpose	Poor.
Montague	93	Light to General Purpose	Poor.
Town of Smith's Falls	175	Light to General Purpose	Poor.
Beckwith	81	Light to General Purpose	Poor.
Town of Carleton Place	184	Light to General Purpose	Poor.
Total	2,093		

MARES BRED TO DIFFERENT CLASSES OF STALLIONS.

Stallions.	Total.		Serviceably sound.			Not serviceably sound.		
	Number of stallions.	Number of mares bred to.	Number of stallions.	Number of mares bred to.	Average fee.	Number of stallions.	Number of mares bred to.	Average fee.
Registered Stallions	20	1,468	19	1,441	$12	1	27	$10
Grade Stallions	13	625	10	470	8	3	155	5
Totals	33	2,093	29	1,911		4	182	

The public meeting was held at Carleton Place, on November 12. It was a lively meeting, with plenty of discussion. When requested to give their views on stallion inspection, 21 voted for a license for stallions, but they must be sound, registered animals, up to a certain standard of excellence. A good deal was said about the poor quality of many imported stallions. Those present asked that the Government use its influence with some of the horse importers to get them to bring a carload of imported mares and fillies to Carleton Place for sale. They also asked the Government to give a liberal donation for prizes to be given at a 'spring show for stallions to be held at Carleton Place.

An additional meeting was held in the town of Perth. Fourteen men, all interested in horse-breeding attended, and all took part in the discussions and expressed themselves as pleased with the work undertaken by the Department. Some thought it might be advisable to license for one year really good grade stallions, but only those that were good stock getters. Many objected to grades being licensed. After full discussion all voted in favor of licensing all stallions that were sound and registered animals up to a certain standard of excellence.

SPECIAL REPORT OF INSPECTORS.

The meetings were fairly well attended, but in many cases the bad weather and distance kept those who were interested from attending. At every meeting there was a strong feeling that something should be done; most of the breeders of good horses favored licensing stallions. "None but sound registered animals up to a certain standard of excellence to be licensed," was the idea of the majority. We have seen horses in nearly all the Counties in Ontario and conversed with horsemen in those counties. Some districts have a better class of horses than others, but all over Ontario something requires to be done. In our conversation with horsemen met at Institutes during the last five years, many have favored licensing stallions. It is our opinion that now is the time to go on; the people expect that something more is to be done; the best thing to do is a matter of opinion and there will be great differences in ideas.

There are two points that must be kept in view, viz., enough stallions to serve mares, and how much regulation will the people tolerate. The idea of only having pure-bred stallions licensed is out of the question, because there are not nearly sufficient of them, and many imported ones are not deserving of a license. There must for several years be some grades permitted to travel, until there are enough pure-breds to take their place. After hearing many opinions, we think the following suggestion would find favor with a large majority of the horsemen: The cost of the license or permit, to be nominal, sufficient to cover the expense of inspection, etc. All horses to be free from hereditary unsoundness. Grant a first-class license to registered stallions of good conformation and good action; a second-class license to registered stallions of fair conformation and fair action, and a third-class license to the grade stallions, types of some breeds, producers of useful colts (if old enough to have colts).

We do not think it would be just to give the good and medium registered horse the same class of license. There would be no education in doing so. These three grades of permits, or licenses will certainly take in every horse that any horseman would be justified in using.

We are not in favor of second-class registered or grade horses, but the license would be for one year only, and the standard could be raised the second year, gradually getting rid of the most undesirable.

Anything less than the above appears to us, not likely to give favorable results. In some parts of Ontario the stallion fee is so much for the season. This is not fair to the owner of the mare—too one-sided a bargain. Let the owner of the mare pay half at time of service and the other half when the mare proves to be with foal. This method would prevent many barren or worn-out mares being bred, and would also prevent the stallion taking more mares than is reasonable for a fair percentage of foals.

We would suggest that prizes for stallions and mares be offered at the Winter Fair at Guelph. Farmers are there from all over Ontario, and we consider it would be a grand opportunity for the Government to educate those who are anxious to learn about horses. We would also suggest that spring stallion shows be encouraged by giving liberal prizes at one show in each county (not in the same place each year), horses receiving Government money prizes at said shows must travel part of the season where the prizes were awarded. None to compete unless they will travel in said county, if they receive a prize.

(Signed) W. F. KYDD.
GEORGE GRAY.

8 H.B.

DISTRICT NO. 8.

Counties.—Glengarry, Dundas, Grenville, Leeds, Frontenac, Lennox and Addington and *Stormont.

Inspectors.—Jas. Sinclair, V.S., Cannington; H. S. Arkell, B.S.A., O.A.C., Guelph, (Glengarry to Leeds); Arthur Thom, Elma, (Frontenac to Addington).

GLENGARRY.

In Charlottenburg township there are three stallions, a Clydesdale, a Hackney and a Standard-bred, all registered and sound and fairly good in conformation. Two stand for $10 and one for $15 service fees. Mares are light in type and are an exceedingly poor lot, averaging 1,100 lbs. This township is somewhat rough and the soil shallow. General purpose horses are in favor, and there are, practically, no heavy horses raised. There is very little system followed in breeding, and very few pure-bred mares in the township. Grade sires are not discriminated against. Light horses are mostly patronized. Carriage and general purpose horses, probably, suit the farmers here best.

Kenyon township is well provided with sires of both heavy and light kinds; the breeds represented being Clydesdales, pure-breds, three; grades, two; Shires, pure-bred, one; Percherons, grades, two; Hackney, pure-bred, one; Coach grades, five; Standard-bred, pure-bred, one; and French Canadians, grades, two. Out of the seventeen, four are unsound and the average quality and conformation is only fair, only a few qualifying as good. Mares are light in type, of poor quality and average 1,100 lbs. in weight. Service fees have a range from $5 to $10.

Not much can be said in favor of the sires standing in Lochiel township, but there is one very good horse. There is one grade, a Percheron, and six pure-breds, four Clydesdales, and two Standard-breds. Six-sevenths are sound. Their service fees vary from $5 to $15; mares are about the same as in the other townships.

Of the four stallions in Lancaster township there is only one really fair pattern of a horse. Three are sound or practically so. Two, an imported Clydesdale and a Standard-bred, are registered, while a Suffolk Punch and a Coach are grades. The grades' fees are $6 and $7, and the pure-breds, $10. Mares are small and poor, and there are very few registered Clydesdale mares.

---

* The County of Stormont was inspected by Geo. Gray, Newcastle, and A. R. Walsh, V.S., Perth.

8a H.B.

Glengarry—Continued.

STALLIONS.

Breeding.	Number.	Average weight, pounds.	Average age.	Serviceably sound.	Average conformation.	Number of mares served.	Average service fee.
							$
Clydesdales, Imported............	3	1,530	5	All....	Good.......	305	9
Clydesdales, Canadian-bred.......	6	1,585	6	5......	Fair........	555	9
Grades, Clydesdale...............	2	1,400	4	1......	Only fair....	87	5
Shires, Imported.................	1	1,800	8	All....	Very fair....	75	10
Grades, Percheron	3	1,400	6	1......	Fair........	253	5
Grades, Suffolk Punch............	1	1,400	4	All....	Fair........	92	6
Hackneys, Imported	2	1,400	6	All....	Good.......	215	10
Standard-breds, Imported and Roadsters, Canadian-bred (4 Imported, 1 Roadster)	5	1,210	11	All....	Fair........	194	11
Grades, Coach	6	1,325	8	4......	Fair........	400	6
Grades, French Canadian.........	2	1,325	7	1......	Poor........	180	6
Totals......................	31					2,356	

MARES.

Townships.	Number of mares bred to stallions inspected in township.	Type.	Average weight, pounds.	Average quality.	Average age.
Charlottenburg..........	210	Light............................	1,100	Poor	....
Kenyon	1,215	Light............................	1,100	Poor	....
Lochiel................	579	Light............................	1,100	Poor	....
Lancaster..............	352	Light......................	1,200	Poor	....
Total	2,356				

MARES BRED TO DIFFERENT CLASSES OF STALLIONS.

Stallions.	Total.		Serviceably sound.			Not serviceably sound.		
	Number of stallions.	Number of mares bred to	Number of stallions.	Number of mares bred to.	Average fee.	Number of stallions.	Number of mares bred to	Average fee.
					$			$
Registered Stallions..	17	1,344	16	1,219	9	1	125	8
Grade Stallions......	14	1,012	8	652	5	6	360	5
Totals	31	2,356	24	1,871	....	7	485	....

Glengarry—Concluded.

The public meeting for the county of Glengarry was held at Alexandria on October 13th, and was attended by about 25 people, principally farmers and breeders. The discussion was good and upon the following lines: the majority favored breeding to Clydesdales sires, which, they say, have been looked upon with disfavour here until the past year or two, but are fast coming into favor now. It was suggested that the Government aid in getting in pure-bred dams, not necessarily imported, and stop all grade stallions from leaving their own stables. The following resolution was carried. "That this meeting favor a license and inspection, also a small fee on·all stallions offered for public service." The people here seemed anxious to learn how to breed in the right direction.

Inspectors' Remarks: The greater portion of this county is well suited for raising good, heavy horses, and, in the greater portion of it, the farmers are beginning to wake up and look for a better class of sires. They require better dams also. Only one man was met with, who owned a pure-bred mare.

DUNDAS.

The class of horses and mares in Winchester township is an improvement on that of those in Glengarry county, the quality being better, and there is more good blood in the mares, which, however do not average over 1,100 lbs. The improvement is no doubt due to the fact that for some years a number of Clydesdales, Shires and Hackneys have been imported into the township for sale. There are eighteen stallions in this township, fourteen of them pure-bred and four grades. In regard to breeds they are as follows: Clydesdales, six pure-breds and one grade; one pure-bred Shire; one pure-bred Percheron; five pure-bred Hackneys, a Standard-bred; two grade French Canadians and a grade Coach horse. Nearly a third of them cannot qualify as being sound, and a number of them are not up to the average in conformation and quality. Starting with $5 for a grade, service fees run up to $10.

The quality of the mares in Mountain township is not as good as that of those in Winchester, nor are there so many bred. There are but three sires here, a pure-bred Percheron, and a grade of Clydesdale, and one of Coach breeding. One is unsound, and the average conformation and quality is not good. $6, $8 and $10 are the fees charged, the latter for the pure-bred sire.

Matilda township has only one registered sire, a French Coach horse, but eligibility to register is also claimed for a Clydesdale and a Standard-bred. In addition to these, there are two Clydesdales, a Roadster, and a Coach, all grades, and a grade of no particular breeding. They are all practically sound, but the average is not high in conformation and quality. Service fees for the French Coach horse are quoted as $20; for the rest $5, $6, and $8 are the amounts.

Two grades, a Clydesdale and a Hackney, stand in Williamsburgh township, both sound and of fair conformation. The stud fee is $7 in each case. Mares are of poor type and only fair quality, weighing about 1,050 lbs.

Dundas—Continued.

STALLIONS.

Breeding.	Number.	Average weight, pounds.	Average age.	Serviceably sound.	Average conformation.	Number of mares served.	Average service fee.
							$
Clydesdales, Imported.............	5	1,670	5	4......	Fairly good.	431	10
Clydesdales, Canadian-bred.......	2	1,600	5	All....	Very good..	184	9
Grades, Clydesdale...............	5	1,375	6	4......	Only fair ...	268	7
Shires, Imported and Percherons (1 Shire, 2 Percherons).........	3	1,700	3	2......	Very fair ...	236	10
Hackneys, Imported and Grades (5 Hackneys, 1 Grade)..........	6	1,155	5	All....	Fair........	707	8
Standard-breds Imported and Grades (2 Pure-bred, 1 Grade) ..	3	1,090	7	All.....	Fair.......	177	7
French Coach Horses and Grades (1 French Coach, 3 Grades).....	4	1,325	5	2......	Only fair ...	283	13
Grades, French Canadian.........	2	1,425	4½	1	Poor ......,	35	5
No Particular Breeding...........	1	1,175	7	All...	Poor	60	5
Totals......................	31					2,381	

MARES.

Townships.	Number of mares bred to stallions inspected in township.	Type.	Average weight, pounds.	Average quality.	Average age.
Winchester..............	1,586	Poor	1,100	Fair.....	10
Mountain...............	288	Not very good	1,050	Poor	10
Matilda	415	Poor	1,000	Poor	10
Williamsburg	92	Poor	1,050	Fair.....	10
Total..............	2,381		-		

MARES BRED TO DIFFERENT CLASSES OF STALLIONS.

Stallions.	Total.		Serviceably sound.			Not serviceably sound.		
	Number of stallions.	Number of mares bred to.	Number of stallions.	Number of mares bred to.	Average fee.	Number of stallions.	Number of mares bred to.	Average fee.
					$			$
Registered Stallions..	18	1,694	16	1,509	11	2	185	10
Grade Stallions	13	687	9	412	6	4	275	6
Totals	31	2,381	25	1,921	....	6	460	....

Dundas—Continued.

The public meeting for Dundas county, which was held at Winchester on October 18th, was not largely attended. Those present were all good horsemen, and each of the twenty men appeared anxious that something should be done for the improvement of the horse industry. After a general discussion a motion was passed as follows.: "That the Government pass an Act requiring all stallions to be inspected and certificates given after inspection.

Inspectors' Remarks: In this county is found a better class of horses generally than in Glengarry. There are better pure-bred sires, and a greater number of good mares. Farmers are breeding to Clydesdale sires for heavy horses and to Hackneys for light ones. If the farmers have good judgment and continue on in the good way Dundas will soon be ahead of the neighboring counties in the matter of horse-breeding. Its natural advantages are good, and the farmers require a horse with some breeding and substance to work the soil of this county. Hackneys are gaining in popularity, and will probably retain their hold in popular favor. A good many farmers in this county as well as in Glengarry are anxious to secure good pure-bred mares to breed from. This we think a good omen.

Views of two Stallion Owners.

Following are copies of letters received by the Inspectors from two prominent stallion owners in Dundas county who were unable to give their views personally to the Inspectors.

"I have noticed with great pleasure, that our Government is taking steps with a view to the improvement of the horse industry of this Province. and I believe that the result of the investigations being made by yourselves and your confreres, will prove of great value to those interested. I regret exceedingly, that it will be impossible for me to attend any of your meetings in this district, as a previous engagement in London, will prevent my personal attendance to express my own views and learn those of others.

"Will you permit me to place on record, a few matters which my somewhat extended experience in breeding and importing, leads me to think will tend to improve the quality of our stock and will bring adequate rewards to our breeders.

"First, I am strongly of the opinion that a simple and cheap system of registration of all stallions used for stock purposes, is necessary, and that all sires should be registered.

"Second, That every owner of a stallion used for stock purposes should be compelled to take out a license for each horse, under the penalty of not being able to collect stud fees, and, if deemed necessary, a fine for each later offence of using for stud purposes, a horse not registered.

"The above points, I deem to be of vital importance, among the many questions which affect the interests of both breeders and users of the horse."

"I regret that I will be unable to meet you when you visit my place on the 17th, but have instructed my man to give you all information you may require, and being very much interested in the bettering of the breed of horses, in our own Province, and especially in our own county, thought, as I will also be unable to attend the meeting which I see is to be held later on for the purpose of enabling those who have an interest in such betterment of expressing their views on the subject, that I would give them to you on paper.

Dundas—Concluded.

"In the first place—and to my mind the one of most importance—I believe that every stallion standing for public service should be licensed: that in each county, one, or more, veterinary surgeons should be appointed by the Government to inspect such stallions, examine their pedigrees, and report to the individual appointed by the Government to issue such licenses, which should be countersigned by the veterinary surgeon making the inspection.

"These should be produced for the examination of such owners as breed to such horse, and a certificate should be given them by the owner of the stallion, on receipt of service fee, that their mare has been bred to—or is in foal to, as the case may be—his stallion. This certificate should bear the name of the stallion, his particular breed, number in stud book, or name of his sire and dam, and should also state whatever description of the mare, that the owner of her could give.

"These certificates, while not necessary, would be of use in tracing the breeding of horses, would be of advantage in making a sale, and would be a guide to the owner of the mare in regard to her future breeding. They should be printed, with spaces left to be filled in by the stallion owner. A form could be attached to the Government license and copies could be obtained at any country printing office. This would insure their being uniform.

"Secondly, That no stallion should be accepted unless he is of pure breed, and registered in his Stud Book, is a fairly good individual, and sound, in so far as not possessing defects which are capable of transmission.

"A nominal fee, sufficient to cover cost of examination and issuance of license, should be charged.

"With regard to brood-mares, I look upon it as impossible to formulate any regulations that would prevent the breeding of such as are not desirable. A fairly good fee for stallion service would do more than anything else in preventing the breeding of poor, old broken down mares, that are physically unfit to produce sound, vigorous foals, as their owners would know, or would soon find out, that it is poor policy and a financial loss, to pay a good price to have them covered. The licensing of stallions would prevent this to a great extent, if carried out as I have outlined, as no one could afford to pay the price of such a stallion as described, and let it stand at too low a figure.

"In regard to any special breed, that is a matter the breeder will always use his own judgment on, and different conditions require different types of horses. To my mind, every pure type that has been evolved, is good—each for its particular use; otherwise they would not be bred to the high state of perfection they have attained.

"The Government could greatly benefit the farmers and breeders if they could induce the committees of the various Horse Shows now held throughout Ontario—or at least in certain sections—to have a class for green driving or saddle horses that are for sale. Price to be put on each entry by the owner, and this to be taken into account when making the awards. Each entry would be liable to be claimed by any *bona fide* purchaser, at the entered price. Once inaugurated, this would attract buyers from the States as well as other parts of Canada, and would provide means of showing horses to the public. Dealers should be excluded."

GRENVILLE.

Wolford township has n thing but grade stallions, and they are a poor lot, out of the seven, five being practically unsound and others not in very good shape. The breeding represented is, Roadsters, three; French, two; Clydesdale, one; and Coach, one. The cheapest fee is $5, and highest $10. Mares are a poor class of nondescript breeding, not over 1,000 lbs. in weight.

There are ten stallions in Oxford township and of these, three, an imported Shire, an imported Cleveland Bay, and a German Coach horse are pure-bred and fair horses. One of the grades is well up in years. Four grades and a registered sire are unsound. General average conformation is just fair, and fees are the same as in Wolford township. Mares, too, are no better than in that section.

The two stallions, an imported Shire and a grade Roadster, in South Gower are sound or practically so, but not of a high average as regards conformation and quality. They have a uniform service fee of $10. Mares are poor in quality and light in weight.

Not much can be said about the quality of the stallions in Augusta township or of their conformation. Five of the nine are sound, and four of the lot are pure-bred, including two imported Clydesdales. There are four of Clydesdale breeding, including two grades, and five are Standard-breds three being grades. Fees seem pretty uniform in Grenville county from $5 to $10.

There are eleven sires in Edwardsburgh township, but only one pure-bred and two grades are rated as good, two being very good in conformation. The rest are below the average, and three are unsound or practically so. As in the other townships stud fees range from $5 to $10. As regards breeding, there are one imported and two grade Clydesdales, two grade Hackneys, one registered and four grade Standard-breds, and a French grade.

STALLIONS.

Breeding.	Number.	Average weight, pounds.	Average age.	Serviceably sound.		Average conformation.	Number of mares served.	Average service fee.
								$
Clydesdales, Imported	3	1,550	6	1......	Fair........		204	9
Grades, Clydesdale..............	9	1,345	5	6......	Fair........		621	7
Shires, Imported................	2	1,800	4½	All....	Pretty fair..		204	10
Grades, Percheron and Hackney (1 Percheron, 2 Hackneys)	3	1,240	14	2......	Fair........		218	8
Standard-breds, Imported........	2	1,075	13	5......	Only Fair ...		125	10
Roadsters, Canadian-bred	1	1,100	15	All....	Fair........		76	8
Grades, Roadster................	12	1,020	5	5......	Only just fair		212	8
German Coach Horses, Cleveland Bays and Grades (1 German Coach, 1 Cleveland Bay, 1 grade)	3	1,375	9	2......	Fair........		210	9
Grades, French Canadian........	4	1,325	8	1......	Only fair ...		292	8
Totals	39						2,162	

Grenville—Concluded.

MARES.

Townships.	Number of mares bred to stallions inspected in township.	Type.	Average weight, pounds.	Average quality.	Average age.
Wolford	282	Light	1,000	Poor	10
Oxford	681	Light	1,000	Poor	10
South Gower	72	Light	1,000	Poor	10
Augusta	403	Poor	1,000	Poor	10
Edwardsburgh	724	Poor	1,000	Poor	10
Total	2,162				

MARES BRED TO DIFFERENT CLASSES OF STALLIONS.

Stallions.	Total.		Serviceably sound.			Not serviceably sound.		
	Number of stallions.	Number of mares bred to.	Number of stallions.	Number of mares bred to.	Average fee.	Number of stallions.	Number of mares bred to.	Average fee.
					$			$
Registered Stallions .	10	784	6	496	9	4	288	10
Grade Stallions	29	1,378	15	708	9	14	670	7
Totals	39	2,162	21	1,204	....	18	958	....

The public meeting for Grenville county was held at Kemptville on October 25th. The thirty or more persons present were practically all personally interested in horse breeding, and the discussions of the various questions were very good. The following resolution was moved and seconded, and received nearly the unanimous support of those present: "That all stallions standing for service should be registered as sound, and of good conformation after having passed a rigid inspection."

LEEDS.

Only one pure-bred stallion, an imported Clydesdale, was seen in Elizabethtown township. The rest were grades of Clydesdale, Shire, Percheron, and Roadster blood, one each of the first three and two of the last. None of them are good, and three only of the six are sound. Under the circumstances, the fees of $8 in one case and $10 in the others are fairly good.

The township of Rear of Yonge is a very poor section, and the horses are equally so. There is only one stallion here, a grade Percheron, sound, which stands for a fee of $8. In the township of Front of Yonge, there is, besides one not inspected, also a grade sire of Roadster breeding, and for which a very small fee is charged.

Leeds—Continued.

In Escott township farmers are trying to improve their horse stock somewhat. There was inspected here, only one stallion, a pure-bred Percheron, sound and of fair conformation. Its service fee is $12.

Bastard township contains a registered Standard-bred, a Roadster grade, and a French grade, only one of these three being sound, and none of them of much merit. Five dollars, nine, and ten, are the stud fees charged.

The five stallions whose routes are in North Crosby, are located in or near Westport, and comprise a Percheron and a grade and two Standard-breds and a grade. One of the Standard-breds is described as a very good horse, and two others have fair conformation. Only two-thirds of them, however, are sound. The maximum fee is $12 and minimum $8. Mares are, as is the rule in this and some of the adjoining counties, poor in quality and of a light type, about 1,000 lbs.

A pure-bred Clydesdale, of very good conformation, and a French grade, represent the sires seen in South Crosby. The first named is sound, the owner of the latter was away, and the horse was not seen outside of his stable. The pure-bred stands at $10. There are a great many poor, blemished mares in this section.

Out of the four stallions in Leeds township, two of which are Roadster grades, one an imported Coach, and the other a French grade, only two are sound. One of the Roadsters has the best conformation, the others are just fair. The fee for the Coach horse is $20; other fees are $8 and $10. Mares are a little improvement on those in the rear, as farmers here are giving more consideration to subjects' relating to horse-breeding. There is, however, plenty of room for further improvement.

There are six stallions in the township of Lansdowne, but only two of these were inspected, these being a pure-bred Clydesdale and a grade Percheron. The former is aged. One of them is unsound. The grade has the bigger stud fee $8. That of the other is $7.

STALLIONS.

Breeding.	Number.	Average weight, pounds.	Average age.	Serviceably sound.	Average conformation.	Number of mares served.	Average service fee.
							$
Clydesdales, Imported	2	1,500	13	1......	Fair........	157	8
Clydesdales, Canadian-bred	1	1,650	5	All	Very good..	85	10
Grades, Clydesdale and Shire (1 Clydesdale, 1 Shire)	2	1,350	5	....	Only fair ...	110	9
Percherons	2	1,675	5½	·1......	Fair........	178	12
Grades, Percheron	4	1,400	7	3......	Poor	152	9
Standard-breds, Imported	3	1,055	9	2......	Fair........	204	10
Grades, Roadster	7	1,045	7	5......	Rather good.	244	8
French Coach Horses	1	1,175	3	All	Fair........	....	20
Grades, French-Canadian	3	1,380	8	2......	Fair........	36	5
Unenumerated	5	....	......	....	....	....	......
Totals	30					1,166	

Leeds—Continue

MARES.

Townships.	Number of mares bred to stallions inspected in township.	Type.	Average weight, pounds.	Average quality.	Average age.
Elizabethtown	235	Light..............................	1,000	Poor...	10
Rear of Yonge..........	15	Light..............................	1,000	Poor...	10
Front of Yonge..........	12	Light..............................	1,000	Poor...	10
Front of Escott	103	Light..............................	1,000	Poor...	10
Bastard...............	227	Light......................	1,000	Poor...	10
North Crosby..........	281	Light..............................	1,000	Poor...	10
South Crosby..........	85	Light..............................	1,050	Poor...	10
Leeds	112	Light..............................	1,050	Poor...	10
Front of Lansdowne	96	Light and poor...................	1,050	Very inferior.	12
Total	1,166				

MARES BRED TO DIFFERENT CLASSES OF STALLIONS.

Stallions.	Total.		Serviceably sound.			Not serviceably sound.		
	Number of stallions.	Number of mares bred to.	Number of stallions.	Number of mares bred to.	Average fee.	Number of stallions.	Number of mares bred to.	Average fee.
Registered Stallions.	9	624	6	454	$12	3	170	$9
Grade Stallions	16	542	10	262	7	6	280	7
Unenumerated......	5	....	....	....	....	....	....	....
Totals	30	1,166	16	716	....	9	450	....

The public meeting at Lansdowne on October 31st, was well attended, considering the weather, and other adverse conditions; about 25 or 30 men, principally stallion owners being in attendance. The discussion was very good.

The following resolution was adopted: "That stallions in the county be inspected by a competent Inspector, and that all stallion owners whose horses do not pass inspection be given one year to dispose of them, and, after that date, all stallions that are advertised for service must be registered and pass inspection as to conformation, soundness and freedom from transmissable defects." This was carried by a vote of nine for, to four against. The others did not vote.

In addition to the motions favoring inspection and registration passed at the Lansdowne meeting, the opinions obtained from prominent horse breeders and others interested in horses residing near Brockville all tend to show the Governmental registration would be welcomed by them as tending to improve the quality of the horses in this county.

Leeds—Concluded.

Inspectors' Remarks: The mares are an exceedingly poor class, light, and very few good young mares are bred. Farmers do not think of breeding a mare until it is unfit for work, old, decrepit and unsound. This is an exceedingly poor county for mares, and we did not see one good sound pure-bred mare of any class used for breeding.

FRONTENAC.

Kingston township farmers evidently pin their faith almost entirely to the light breeds as there are a pure-bred and a grade Hackney, a Standard-bred and four Roadster grades, and one pure-bred Clydesdale standing for service here. No less than one-half are not sound, and are not likely to be successful sires. Conformation is rather poor on the whole. Service fees are $8 to $15. Mares average 1,000 lbs., are light in type and poor in average quality.

The two stallions, a Clydesdale and a Percheron, both pure-bred and sound, standing in Pittsburg township are two pretty fair horses. Service fee is $10. Mares are practically of the same type as in the previous township.

Two stallions were inspected in Storrington township, a pure-bred Percheron and a grade Shire.

Mares are very poor in Loughborough township, their average weight being given as 900 lbs., and quality poor. The three stallions found here, too, are not of good type, and two are unsound. All are pure-bred, being two Standard-breds, and a Clydesdale. Six dollars to $10 is the variation in fees.

Portland township has all grades for sires, two Roadsters, a Clydesdale, and a French Canadian. One half of them are sound, and they have fair conformation. Three stand for service at $8 and one for $15. Mares are very poor and light.

The only stallion inspected on Wolfe Island was a pure-bred French Coach horse of fair conformation, standing at $20, and also sound. The Inspectors were told that there were a great many common, nondescript stallions kept here, which serve all the mares they can at any price obtainable during the season. They are then put to work. The horses and mares are very inferior, and a great many unsound, and the people quite ignorant of breeding principles. This Island would be an ideal breeding ground if farmers gave more attention to breeding. Four stables were visited, but the owners and the horses were away from home.

Bedford township is poor and rocky, and the mares are very inferior. There is a pure-bred Canadian Clydesdale, serviceably sound. Its fee is $9.

A grade Shire and a grade Coach travel in Oso township; one being unsound. Six dollars and $4 are their respective fees. Mares, too, are poor, and the country rough and stony.

Olden township, also, has two grades, both of French blood, one of them unsound. Four dollars and $5 are the fees.

Kernebec, another of the rear townships, has one grade Clydesdale stallion on service.

Three of the six sires in Hinchinbrooke township were not inspected. The other three are a pure-bred Clydesdale, a grade of the same breed, and a French grade. Only one is sound, and none of them are very good.

Frontenac—Continued.

STALLIONS.

Breeding.	Number.	Average weight, pounds.	Average age.	Serviceably sound.	Average conformation.	Number of mares served.	Average service fee.
							$
Clydesdales, Imported and Canadian-bred (1 Imported, 4 Canadian-bred)	5	1,560	7	4......	Fair........	407	10
Grades, Clydesdale	3	1,380	5	1......	Poor	141	9
Grades, Shire	2	1,250	4	....	Poor	99	5
Percherons	2	1,650	3½	1......	Fair........	66	15
Hackneys, Imported and Grades (1 Hackney, 1 Grade)	2	1,150	10	All	Fair........	97	10
Standard-breds, Imported and Roadsters, Canadian-bred (2 Imported, 1 Canadian-bred)	3	1,110	9	1......	Fair........	152	11
Grades, Roadster	6	1,100	8	2......	Fair........	253	9
French Coach Horses and Grades (1 French Coach, 1 Grade)	2	1,250	4	All	Fair........	68	12
Grades, French-Canadian	4	1,150	11	1......	Fair........	229	6
Unenumerated	3	....	......	....	....	....	....
Totals	32					1,512	

MARES.

Townships.	Number of mares bred to stallions Inspected in township.	Type.	Average weight, pounds.	Average quality.	Average age.
Kingston	358	Light	1,000	Poor	10
Pittsburg	137	Light	1,000	Poor	10
Loughborough	181	Light	900	Poor	10
Storrington	81	Light	1,000	Poor	10
Portland	240	Light	900	Poor	10
Wolfe Island	46	Light	900	Very inferior	10
Bedford	112	Light	1,050	Poor	10
Oso	106	Light	1,000	Poor	11
Olden	60	Light	1,000	Poor	10
Kenebec	51	Light	900	Poor	12
Hinchinbrooke	140	Light	900	Poor	12
Total	1,512				

Frontenac—Concluded.

MARES BRED TO DIFFERENT CLASSES OF STALLIONS.

Stallions.	Total.		Serviceably sound.			Not serviceably sound.		
	Number of stallions.	Number of mares bred to.	Number of stallions.	Number of mares bred to.	Average fee.	Number of stallions.	Number of mares bred to.	Average fee.
Registered Stallions.	12	726	8	466	$ 9	4	260	$ 10
Grade Stallions	20	786	9	375	7	11	411	8
Total.........	32	1,512	17	841	....	15	671	....

The public meeting at Harrowsmith was held on November 5th, but not such a good meeting as previous ones, the discussion not being along such practical lines. Farmers in this section do not seem to appreciate breeding as they should.

The following resolution was moved: "That all stallions offered for service shall be inspected by a competent inspector, for soundness and conformation, and also be registered in a local register." An amendment was moved: "That all stallions offered for service be inspected by a competent Inspector for soundness and conformation, and must also be eligible for registration in their respective record books." The motion carried by 14 to 13.

Inspectors' Remarks: This meeting was by no means a representative one of the county. This particular locality is very much behind the times in horse breeding. Kingston horsemen are almost unanimous in asking for registration and inspection or license. All over the county the good men of the business favor a change from the present situation. Horses and mares are both of a very inferior quality in this county. Some of the syndicate stallions here are a disgrace.

LENNOX AND ADDINGTON.

While most of the townships have a rather inferior lot of mares, Camden East has the best average lot, the mares here being a little heavier than in the other townships. In such a wide district with but poor railroad facilities, it is probable that some of the stallions in the back townships were overlooked, but certainly nearly all were seen. The majority of the stallions in Camden are unsound and of poor conformation. Service fees are fairly good under the circumstances, viz., $8 to $15. Mares are of medium type, but of poor average quality. There are three registered stallions, and one grade Clydesdale, a pure-bred Shire, a grade Hackney and four Roadster grades.

Two grade Clydesdales and a grade Roadster make up the list of sires in Sheffield township, and of these one of the former is a pretty fair horse with good conformation. One is unsound. Service fees are $8 and $10. Mares are of a very poor quality and do not average more than 1,000 lbs. in weight.

Lennox and Addington—Continued.

No less than eight out of sixteen stallions travelling in Richmond township have to·be recorded as unsound, and there are only a few that come up to the requirements of a satisfactory sire. The breeds represented are two registered and five grade Clydesdales, a Percheron, two Standard-breds and three grades, a Thoroughbred, a grade Coach horse, and a grade of French breeding. Farmers can avail themselves of sires at fees ranging from $5 to $15, the latter being for a Standard-bred. Not only are mares of poor quality, but fully 25 per cent. of those bred are unsound.

Two-thirds of the stallions in North Fredericksburg township are sound, but that is about all that can be said of them in connection with their value as sires. There are three Percherons and three grade Clydesdales here, standing at fees as low as $2 for one grade and up to $15 for a pure-bred. Mares average slightly higher than in the previously mentioned townships of these counties, being about 1,200 lbs. in weight. Their quality, however, is no better.

Mares drop off again in weight in Adolphustown township. There are only three stallions here, one of which was away from its stable when the Inspectors called. One horse is unsound, and another one is very old. The sires are Roadster grades, and the only service fee given is $10.

There is no improvement in the quality or conformation of the sires in Ernestown township, nor as regard their soundness, for only one-third are sound. There are two pure-breds, a Hackney and an English Coach horse. The other four are composed of three grade Clydesdales and a grade Roadster. Mares are poor and light in type. As this is a good section of country, there is no reason why good horses could not be raised here, if farmers were inclined to do so.

In South Fredericksburg, three stallions were inspected, a registered Thoroughbred, and a Clydesdale grade, and a Roadster grade. There is the same report as to mares, being light in type and poor in quality, a state of things which need not be, as there is much good land here and the breeding of good horses would be profitable, especially heavy ones.

STALLIONS.

Breeding.	Number.	Average weight, pounds.	Average age.	Serviceably sound.	Average conformation.	Number of mares served.	Average service fee.
							$
Clydesdales, Imported and Canadian-bred (1 Imported, 4 Canadian-bred)	5	1,600	8	3......	Fair........	455	12
Grades, Clydesdale...............	15	1,350	6	7......	Not even fair	734	6
Shires, Imported and Percherons (1 Shire, 4 Percherons)........	5	1,800	7	2......	Just fair....	511	14
Hackneys, Imported and Grades (1 Hackney, 1 Grade)..........	2	1,175	5	1......	Good.......	117	10
Standard-breds, Imported.........	2	1,075	11	1......	Only fair ...	130	13
Grades, Roadster.................	13	1,055	7	8......	Fair........	361	8
Thoroughbreds	2	1,050	11	....	Fair........	12	10
English Coach Horses and Grades (1 English Coach, 1 Grade).....	2	1,350	14	1......	Fair........	141	8
Grades, no particular breeding....	1	800	24	....	Poor	....	....
Unenumerated.................	2	....	.....	....	....	....	....
Totals	49					2,461	

Lennox and Addington—Concluded.

MARES.

Townships.	Number of mares bred to stallions in township.	Type.	Average weight, pounds.	Average quality.	Average age.
Camden, East..........	570	Medium.........................	1,200	Poor	10
Sheffield	219	Light.......................	1,000	Poor	10
Richmond.............	812	Light.......................	1,050	Poor	10
North Fredericksburg ...	451	Medium.........................	1,200	Poor	10
Adolphustown	20	Light.............................	1,000	Poor	10
Ernestown..............	249	Light.........................	1,050	Poor	10
South Fredericksburg ...	140	Light.........................	1,050	Poor	10
Total..............	2,461				

MARES BRED TO DIFFERENT CLASSES OF STALLIONS.

Stallions.	Total.		Serviceably sound.			Not serviceably sound.		
	Number of stallions.	Number of mares bred to.	Number of stallions.	Number of mares bred to.	Average fee.	Number of stallions.	Number of mares bred to.	Average fee.
Registered Stallions .	16	1,184	8	598	$ 12	8	586	$ 12
Grade Stallions	31	1,277	15	642	7	16	635	8
Unenumerated......	2	....	....	....	....	....	....	....
Totals..........	49	2,461	23	1,240	....	24	1,221	....

The public meeting for Lennox and Addington was held on November 13th, at Napanee, and was attended by about twenty-five people. There was a fair discussion, and it was moved, "That in case the Government pass legislation prohibiting non-registered stallions standing for service, stallion owners receive compensation for those horses that do not fulfil the requirements."

It was moved in amendment: "That all stallions offered for service shall be pure-bred, registered in their respective books, of good conformation and sound." The amendment was carried.

Inspector's Remarks.—Lennox and Addington should be the breeding ground of good horses, inasmuch as there is plenty of good land and good water, but like all the eastern part of Ontario, there is a great lack of good mares. Farmers breed indiscriminately, crossing and re-crossing with no ultimate object in view, instead of trying to make each successive cross an improvement. Many of the farmers are unable to distinguish between true and bogus pedigrees, and can, therefore, be easily imposed upon by unscrupulous persons. Ignorance is widespread. Education is the watchword and remedy.

SPECIAL REPORT OF INSPECTORS.

The condition of the horse-breeding industry in District No. 8 was perhaps in a more backward state than the Inspectors were prepared to find it. We found a number of serviceable animals of what may be termed the general-purpose sort, but there was a marked absence in the district of market horses of each and every class. Of really good draught animals there were practically none, and the average of the Clydesdale, Shire, and Percheron grades was distinctly light in weight, and on the whole they were not of high quality. It was observed that a very large number of the horses of the district carried in their veins a noticeable percentage of trotting bred and French Canadian blood and were of corresponding conformation. The blood of the various breeds had, however, been so intermixed that no uniform type had been evolved, nor had any high standard of excellence been reached through the policy of breeding that had been followed. It may be remarked in passing that through the enterprise of certain importers and breeders in buying and using superior sires in a few townships in Dundas and Glengarry counties, there was a noticeable improvement over the average of the horses of the district. In the county of Glengarry both heavy and light horses are raised, but the former are more suitable and profitable. The difficulty in this county, as throughout the seven counties we traversed, is that breeders have not got heavy enough mares. This difficulty could be overcome by the importation of heavy mares, and in the opinion of some the Government might with advantage give pecuniary assistance for that purpose.

In no mistaken terms did a goodly number pronounce against the so-called general purpose horse that was permitted to travel the road for service to-day. There is no doubt that many of them should be barred out entirely or compelled to stay at the owner's stable. If this were done the better horses would almost invariably be used, and, as a consequence, a superior breed of horses would be raised and a better price be obtainable.

One point the people were all agreed upon, namely that there were a number of horses travelling the country that were a detriment rather than a help to the horse-breeding business.

In the popularity of the dairy industry in Eastern Ontario, in the lack of information among the farmers as to what constitutes real merit in horses, in the practice of indiscriminate breeding, and in the use of inferior breeding stock of both sexes, reasons may be found for the somewhat backward condition of the horse breeding business in the counties under consideration. The higher prices paid for horses within the last few years, together with the intelligent enterprise of a number of breeders in introducing a better class of stallions, have, however, awakened a very general interest in horse-breeding which should be the promise of a marked advancement in the near future. The movement undertaken by the Government to promote the horse interests in the Province has been, we think, a timely and popular one, and almost without exception the commissioners were cordially and courteously received by horsemen of the district. Under the advice of our instructions we attempted to gain the confidence of the stallion owners, and were repaid by generous treatment at their hands, and a ready response in an expression of opinion in answer to the questions asked. While large numbers did not attend the public meetings, these did not lack interest, and the attitude of these metings would, we think, be a fair gauge of the opinion of the horse-men of the whole district. This opinion is perhaps stated with sufficient clearness in the main body of the report, and need not be repeated here.

9 H.B.

Report Inspectors' District 8.—Concluded.

Your Inspectors beg to offer one or two suggestions by way of a summary relative to the information gathered while on this tour of inspection.

Supported by the opinion of many horsemen with whom we had conversation, we believe that the passing of a stallion License and Inspection Act would meet with very general approval, provided that it was reasonably moderate in its requirements. Horsemen are unanimous in their condemnation of the scrub sires that travel the country. We think, however, that an arbitrarily prohibitive act would be reactionary in its effect, and consequently would not produce the result desired. The greatest benefit must probably be brought about in an educative way. A system of Government inspection and registration of stallions should be practicable and desirable. A small registration fee might be charged to cover the cost of inspection, but we think the stallion owner should not be required to suffer the hardship of a high license fee. A certificate of registration, includng the finding of the Inspector as to soundness, utility, purity of breeding, etc., might be furnished each stallion owner, and he be required to publish such certificate in a conspicuous place on all bills, posters and advertising matter used by him. All stallions might be required to be registered and certain restrictions relative to eligibility for registration might be sufficiently prohibitive in its effect in retiring from active service undesirable animals. A catalogue of stallions in the different counties including an abridged statement of the inspector's report on each registered animal; and which could be obtained on application, would furnish useful information to the horsemen of the various districts. We think further that actual breeders should be protected against misrepresentation on the part of stallion owners in their being compelled to publish true statements of the breeding of their horses, together with the Government registration certificate on all advertising matter used by them. Breeders have been the victims of much fraud on the part of unscrupulous grooms, and should be protected against such misrepresentation. There might further be an advanced registry for superior stallions of approved merit and breeding, and the question of bonusing such stallions as would qualify might not be unwisely considered. We think, moreover, that the benefit of such an Act might be supplemented by the issuing of an up-to-date bulletin giving information not only as touching breeds and breeding, but as well upon markets, types, and classification of horses generally.

As regards syndicating, where a small syndicate of three, four or six persons, agree among themselves to buy a horse and go to a good reliable importer, we found this system to work all right. We asked for suggestions as to how to overcome the evil of syndicating stallions, but got no satisfactory answers. In our opinion the people are not educated, or rather are not good enough judges, to buy on their own judgment. Education is the most needful thing. This we think, can be partially done through the Farmers' Institutes, and through the employment of good men as judges at Agricultural Fairs.

The farmers as a rule, are not particular enough about breeding good mares. A great majority sell the good mares and breed the infirm and blemished ones, and also those unsound from diseases that are transmissable. This class of mares bred to a cheap, unsound, short-bred, nondescript stallion cannot help but produce poor offspring. If the breeders and farmers could only be taught to breed so that each succeeding cross would be one better than the previous, we would soon have a much better class of horses in Canada.

(Signed)   JAS. SINCLAIR.
H. S. ARKELL.

*STORMONT.

The general run of mares here were found to be of a light type and of very inferior quality. The majority of the sires are of the lighter kinds, but there is a fair sprinkling of heavy sires in every township except Osnabruck.

In Cornwall township there are seven stallions, all but one having their headquarters in the town of Cornwall. One is a registered Clydesdale, another a Percheron, and there are two Standard-breds, (one of which was not seen owing to the owner's absence), and three French grades, two of which are not used for service. For the other French grade, the fee is $5. while for the pure-breds it is $10. One of those used for service is unsound.

All the stallions in Osnabruck township are grades, and the breeding is as follows: Standard-breds, six; French Canadians, three. One of the former is unsound, and the average conformation is deficient. Fees are very low, being $4, $5, and $6.

There are six stallions in Roxborough township, but one of these appears among the horses in Glengarry. Of the remaining five one is a registered Clydesdale and one grade. There is one pure-bred Percheron and one grade, and there is also a French grade. Four are sound, but average conformation is only fairly good. The fees vary from $4 to $10.

Five grades of Standard-bred, Clydesdale, Percheron, and French Canadian breeding stand in Finch township, there being two of the first, and one each of the other three. Besides these there was another stallion which died recently. Another stallion has not done any service. There are two unsound horses and average conformation is only fairly good. $5 and $6 represent the service fees.

STALLIONS.

Breeding.	Number.	Average weight, pounds.	Average age.	Serviceably sound.	Average conformation.	Number of mares served.	Average service fee.
							$
Clydesdales, Imported	2	1,675	6½	All....	Fairly good.	156	10
Grades, Clydesdale..............	2	1,550	6	All....	Good.......	74	6
Percherons	2	1,775	5½	All....	Fairly good.	203	10
Grades, Percheron	2	1,350	7	1......	Only fair ...	107	5
Standard-breds, Imported, and Grades (1 Pure-bred, 9 Grades).	10	1,030	6	8......	Just fair....	239	7
Grades, French Canadian........	7	1,235	6	5......	Fair........	418	5
Unenumerated...................	1	....	......	....	....	....	....
Total.....................	26					1,197	

* This county was inspected by George Gray, Newcastle, and A. R. Walsh, V.S., Perth.

Stormont—Concluded.

MARES.

Townships.	Number of mares bred to stallions inspected in township.	Type.	Average quality.
Cornwall...................	281	Light............................	Inferior.
Osnabruck.................	314	Light............................	Inferior.
Roxborough.....	420	Light............................	Inferior.
Finch............	182	Light............................	Inferior.
Total.................	1,197		

MARES BRED TO DIFFERENT CLASSES OF STALLIONS.

Stallions.	Total.		Serviceably sound.			Not serviceably sound.		
	Number of stallions.	Number of mares bred to.	Number of stallions.	Number of mares bred to.	Average fee.	Number of stallions.	Number of mares bred to.	Average fee.
Registered Stallions..	5	384	5	384	$ 10	....	....	$ ....
Grade Stallions......	20♦	813	15	477	6	5	336	5
Unenumerated......	1	....	....	....	....	....	....	....
Totals	26	1,197	20	861	....	5	336	....

Summary for the Province showing by Counties the number of "serviceably sound" and also "not serviceably sound" registered and grade stallions and the number of mares bred to them.

Name of County.	Registered stallions serviceably sound.		Registered stallions not serviceably sound.		Grade stallions serviceably sound.		Grade stallions not serviceably sound.	
	Number of stallions.	Number of mares bred.	Number of stallions.	Number of mares bred.	Number of stallions.	Number of mares bred.	Number of stallions.	Number of mares bred.
Bruce	50	4,563	16	1,408	18	1,162	4	237
Brant	18	1,270	1		16	691	7	233
Carleton	29	1,860	11	823	21	1,038	3	93
Dufferin	18	1,604			9	403	1	35
Dundas	16	1,509	2	185	9	412	4	275
*Durham	68	3,909	13	262	12	350	2	33
Essex	36	2,728			15	834	1	65
Elgin	43	2,775	1	70	11	305		
Frontenac	8	466	4	260	9	375	11	411
Grenville	6	496	4	288	15	708	14	670
Glengarry	16	1,219	1	125	8	652	6	360
Grey	74	5,892	15	1,403	21	1,290	5	272
Haldimand	17	1,452	2	227	26	1,318	3	163
Halton	15	986	6	230	12	708	1	35
Huron	86	7,492	12	1,112	14	619	2	235
Hastings	20	1,429	6	248	32	1,709	6	206
Kent	48	3,409	4	204	18	1,118	1	25
Lambton	53	5,096			27	1,469		
Lincoln	10	716	1	40	13	495		
Lanark	19	1,441	1	27	10	470	3	155
*Leeds	6	454	3	170	10	262	6	280
*Lennox & Addington	8	598	8	586	15	642	16	635
Middlesex	99	7,287			21	1,087	1	25
Norfolk	41	2,216			29	1,522	4	265
Northumberland	28	1,547	4	360	26	1,122	4	102
Oxford	47	2,734			28	1,359	7	98
Ontario	104	4,397	2	179	7	399		
Perth	78	6,125			13	641	4	141
Prince Edward	12	717	3	149	18	790	9	356
Peterborough	28	1,572	4	168	21	820	9	204
Peel	44	2,073	4	331	17	554		
Prescott	11	679			34	1,298	2	85
Russell	18	1,304			20	999	3	29
Renfrew	24	1,642	4	120	24	1,394	5	299
Simcoe	81	5,991	8	624	29	1,413	2	65
*Stormont	5	384			15	477	5	336
*Victoria	45	1,975	7	337	16	421	2	135
Welland	12	859	1	50	15	534		
Waterloo	46	2,016	4	340	10	468		
Wentworth	28	1,262	2	9	18	1,091	2	128
Wellington	94	7,112	10	520	25	907	7	325
*York	106	4,793	5	370	13	788	1	116
Totals	1,615	108,109	169	11,225	740	35,202	163	7,127

* Unenumerated.—Durham, 4 ; Leeds, 5 ; Lennox and Addington, 2 ; Stormont, 1 ; Victoria, 8 ; York, 9.

Summary for the Province showing by Counties the per cent. of "serviceably sound" and also "not serviceably sound" registered and grade stallions and the per cent. of mares bred to them.

Name of County.	Registered stallions serviceably sound.		Registered stallions not serviceably sound.		Grade stallions serviceably sound.		Grade stallions not serviceably sound.	
	Per cent. of stallions.	Per cent. of mares bred.	Per cent. of stallions.	Per cent. of mares bred.	Per cent. of stallions.	Per cent. of mares bred.	Per cent. of stallions.	Per cent. of mares bred.
Bruce	57	62	18	19	20	16	5	3
Brant	43	58	2	....	38	31	17	11
Carleton	45	49	17	22	33	27	5	2
Dundas.............	52	63	6	8	29	17	13	12
*Durham.............	69	86	13	6	12	7	2	1
Dufferin.............	64	78	....	....	32	20	4	2
Essex	69	75	....	....	29	23	2	2
Elgin	78	88	2	2	20	10	.....	.....
Frontenac	25	31	13	17	28	25	34	27
Grenville............	16	23	10	13	38	33	36	31
Glengarry	52	52	3	5	26	28	19	15
Grey................	65	67	13	16	18	14	4	3
Haldimand	35	46	4	7	54	42	7	5
Halton	44	50	18	12	35	36	3	2
Huron...............	75	79	11	12	12	7	2	2
Hastings.............	32	40	9	7	50	47	9	6
Kent................	68	72	6	4	25	23	1	1
Lanark	58	70	3	1	30	22	9	7
Lambton	66	78	....	....	34	22	.....	.....
Lincoln..............	42	57	4	3	54	40	.....	.....
*Lennox & Addington.	16	24	16	24	31	26	33	26
*Leeds	20	39	10	15	33	23	20	23
Middlesex...........	82	87	....	....	17	13	1	.....
Norfolk..............	55	55	....	....	39	38	6	7
Northumberland......	45	50	6	11	42	36	7	3
Oxford..............	57	65	....	....	34	33	9	2
Ontario..............	92	88	2	4	6	8	.....	.....
Perth................	82	89	....	....	14	9	4	2
Prince Edward.......	29	36	7	7	43	39	21	18
Peterborough	45	57	6	6	34	30	15	7
Peel................	68	70	6	11	26	19	.....	.....
Prescott	24	33	....	....	72	63	4	4
Russell	44	56	....	....	49	43	7	1
Renfrew.............	42	48	7	3	42	40	9	9
Simcoe	67	74	7	8	24	17	2	1
*Stormont...........	19	32	....	....	58	40	19	28
*Victoria............	58	68	9	12	21	15	2	5
Welland.............	43	59	4	4	53	37	.....	.....
Waterloo............	76	72	7	12	17	16	.....	.....
Wentworth..........	56	51	4	....	36	44	4	5
Wellington	70	79	7	6	18	11	5	4
*York...............	79	79	4	6	10	13	1	2
	60	67	6	7	28	22	6	4

* *Unenumerated.*—Durham, 4 per cent. ; Lennox and Addington, 4 per cent. ; Leeds, 17 per cent. ; Stormont, 4 per cent. ; Victoria, 10 per cent. ; York, 6 per cent.

Summary for Province, showing by breeding the number of Imported, Canadian-bred, and Grade Stallions, the number of mares bred to them and the average service fees.

Breed. (Including Grades of same breed.)	Imported stallions. Serviceably sound. No. of stallions	mares bred to	Avg. service fee	Not serviceably sound. No. of stallions	mares bred to	Avg. service fee	Canadian-bred stallions. Serviceably sound. No. of stallions	mares bred to	Avg. service fee	Not serviceably sound. No. of stallions	mares bred to	Avg. service fee	Grade stallions. Serviceably sound. No. of stallions	mares bred to	Avg. service fee	Not serviceably sound. No. of stallions	mares bred to	Avg. service fee	Total. No. of stallions	No. of mares bred to
Shire	538	42,340	11	43	3,406	11	263	17,484	9	35	2,444	9	225	12,036	8	43	2,100	8	1,147	79,810
Clyde	75	5,866	12	16	1,454	12	8	481	10				20	1,354	9	9	562	8	128	9,717
Percheron	132	9,931	12	14	1,072	13	8	638	10	1	71	8	44	2,288	8	11	567	6	210	14,567
Belgian	9	736	11	4	378	11							5	307	8	2	115	8	20	1,536
Suffolk Punch	12	502	11	1	50	11							1	92	6				14	644
Hackney	123	7,671	13	7	180	15	16	1,247	14	2	24	11	25	1,065	10	1	69	8	174	10,256
*Standard-bred	203	10,238	14	23	1,245	12	114	5,315	11	11	540	9	256	8,863	9	63	2,126	8	670	28,327
Thoroughbred	50	1,621	12	7	262	11	8	185	13	3	9	15	9	361	10	1	35	6	78	2,473
German Coach.	17	1,353	11	1	90	10													18	1,443
English Coach.	10	676	10																10	676
French Coach.	6	377	16																6	377
French Draught	2	152	12	1															3	152
French breeding													60	3,369	8	15	710	7	75	4,079
French Can.							16	1,241	9				68	4,334	8	13	706	7	97	6,341
Miscellaneous	5	55	13										27	1,133	7	5	77	8	35	1,265
Totals	1,182	81,518		117	8,137		433	26,591		52	3,088		740	35,202		163	7,127		2,687	161,663

* Including those classified as Roadsters.

Note.—Unenumerated stallions—29.

INDEX.

Documents and Correspondence

REGARDING

Petawawa Camp

AND

Proceedings in the Legislature.

PRINTED BY ORDER OF

THE LEGISLATIVE ASSEMBLY OF ONTARIO

TORONTO:
Printed by L. K. CAMERON, Printer to the King's Most Excellent Majesty.
1907.

WARWICK BRO'S & RUTER, Limited, Printers
TORONTO

DESPATCH TO THE LIEUTENANT-GOVERNOR.

SIR,—His Excellency the Governor General has had under consideration in Council the urgent necessity of acquiring for the defence of Canada an area of ground conveniently situated to the capital upon which the artillery of the militia may safely practice with the long range guns with which they are armed, and where the infantry may be trained to use their rifles under modern service conditions.

The Minister of Militia and Defence states that he has caused· a number of localities in Ontario and Quebec to be examined and reported upon by competent officers, with a view to the selection of the most suitable area, and having considered the reports and all the circumstances of the case, he is of opinion that the area hereinafter described situate within the Province of Ontario is the most suitable one for the purpose.

The Minister is informed that there are certain outstanding timber licenses issued by the Government of Ontario conferring the right upon the licensees for the present to cut the trees growing upon the said lands.

Portions of the said lands are also in the possession of settlers who are entitled upon the performance of further settlement duties, or upon making further payments to the Government of Ontario, to obtain patents for the lands so occupied by them.

Except as to the aforesaid rights of the timber licensees and of the settlers in possession, the said lands are absolutely in his Majesty under the administration of the Government of Ontario

The Minister further states that it is not intended by the present recommendation to interfere with the existing rights of the said timber licensees or with the present interests of the settlers in possession ;.but he recommends that, subject to these rights and interests as they now exist, all the lands hereinafter described be, under the the authority of section 117, of the *British North America Act, 1867*, assumed by his Excellency the Governor General in the right of the Government of Canada for the defence of the country.

The·lands recommended to be so assumed are described as follows :—

All that parcel or tract of land situate and being within the Province of Ontario, bounded on the south by the south branch of the Petawawa river, on the north by the boundary line between concessions eight and nine of the township of Wylie, the Chalk river to the boundary line between the townships of Wylie and Buchanan, the line between concessions seven and eight of the township of Buchanan, the line between lots eighteen and nineteen, range A, and lots eighteen and nineteen, range B, of said township of Buchanan; on the east by the Ottawa river; and on the west by the western boundary of the townships of Mackay and Wylie, the whole being portions of the townships of Petawawa, Mackay, Wylie and Buchanan, in the County of Renfrew, in the Province of Ontario.

[3]

His Excellency the Governor General has been pleased to approve of these observations and suggestions of the Minister of Militia and Defence, and to direct that your Honour be notified of the assumption of the said lands for the purposes aforesaid.

I have the honour to be,

Sir,

Your obedient servant,

J. POPE,

His Honour   *Under-Secretary of State.*
    THE LIEUTENANT GOVERNOR OF ONTARIO,
        `Toronto, Ontario.`

COPY OF TELEGRAMS:

SIR FREDERICK BORDEN,   TORONTO, March 26th, 1907.
    Minister of Militia, Ottawa :

I do not understand the action taken by you regarding Petawawa as shown by your despatch to the Lieutenant-Governor of the 22nd of March. Having regard to the negotiations heretofore had between this Government and yourself, I would be glad to understand clearly the reasons and necessity for this action.

(Sgd.)   J. P. WHITNEY.

HON. J. P. WHITNEY,   OTTAWA, March 26th, 1907.
    Premier, Toronto.

Was under impression your Minister of Crown Lands was thoroughly familiar with action taken through Department of Justice. Impossible wire you particulars before to-morrow morning as office now closed.

(Sgd.)   F. W. BORDEN.

HON. J. P. WHITNEY,   OTTAWA, 27th March, 1907.
    Premier, Toronto.

Your telegram *re* Petawawa lands late Provincial Government having promised lease of Crown lands within Petawawa camp site for ninety-nine years at nominal rent and Honourable Mr. Cochrane having definitely since the interview I had with you refused to carry out promise without consent of timber licensees and timber license and having demanded compensation for surrender their licenses amounting to the exorbitant sum of $112 000 Department of Justice was consulted, on advice of the Minister of Justice that the lands could be taken for defence purposes under British North America Act steps were taken accordingly.

(Sgd.)   F. W. BORDEN.

MEMORANDUM BY THE DEPUTY MINISTER.

Memorandum for the Honourable the Prime Minister with respect to the Petawawa Camp Site.

Negotiations of an unofficial character were entered into in 1904 between Col. Biggar, acting for the Department of Militia and Defence, and Mr. Southworth, Director of Colonization, acting for the Department of Lands, Forests and Mines, with respect to certain lands, which the Department of Militia and Defence desired to acquire from the Government of Ontario for the purpose of a military camp, which lands were situated in the townships of Petawawa, Buchanan, Wylie and McKay, adjacent to the Petawawa river and near the Town of Pembroke in the Province of Ontario.

It would appear that Col. Biggar addressed a letter to the Honourable Mr. Davis, then Commissioner of Crown Lands, of date September 2, 1904, which letter is not with the papers.

On September 12, 1904, Honourable Mr. Davis wrote Col. Biggar stating that the Department would be glad to comply with his request for a lease of such lands within the areas mentioned as belonged the Crown for the period suggested, or such other tenure as might be mutually agreed upon for a nominal rental or charge, details to be worked out, that he would have an Order in Council passed covering the area and the terms and conditions agreed upon.

The official application for the land is of date October 3, 1904, and is for a lease for 99 years at a nominal rent, of the area required. No Order in Council was passed and no action was taken before Mr. Davis retired from the late Government.

The Honourable Mr. Mackay succeeded Mr. Davis, but no action with respect to the application was taken during his term of office.

The Ross Government retired from office and the present Government came in, Honourable Mr. Foy being Commissioner of Crown Lands.

Honourable Mr. Cochrane, the present Minister, succeeded Mr. Foy.

The undersigned was not a party to the early negotiations which took place between Colonel Biggar and Mr. Southworth, nor did he know of the correspondence which took place between the Minister, Mr. Davis, and the Department of Militia and Defence. The intention evidently was to turn the matter over to the undersigned after the principles had been agreed upon.

As soon as the undersigned became aware of what was proposed he immediately pointed out that the territory in question was under timber license, and that the rights of the licensees would have to be considered. The undersigned then prepared a statement showing in whose licenses the areas applied for stood, and communicated with the licensees informing them of the application asking if they would consent to the same and if not to state their objections. All the licensees replied, objecting to any disposition of their timber unless they were compensated for their loss.

The Minister of Lands, Forests and Mines, Honourable Mr. Cochrane, addressed a letter to the Minister of Militia and Defence explaining to him the whole position and offering to send a list of the licensees showing what lands were covered by their licenses, so that the Department of Militia and Defence might communicate with them. The Department of Militia and Defence asked for the lists which were duly transmitted.

Subsequently Sir Frederick Borden came to Toronto and, the undersigned believes, had an interview with the Prime Minister and the Honourable Mr. Cochrane. Subsequently, on January 21st, 1907, (L.2949/07) the Minister of Militia and Defence wrote asking, first, that this Department should issue direct to the Department of Militia and Defence patents for lands contained within the proposed camp site area, which the Department of Militia and Defence had purchased from settlers; secondly, that the Department of Militia and Defence should be given a lease or allowed to purchase the remaining lands which were vested in the Crown in the right of Ontario. The Minister of Militia and Defence requested that the lease should be given at a nominal rental for as long a period as the lands should be required for military purposes without reference to the holders of the timber licensees, "leaving the question of the acquisition of the rights of the timber licensees or otherwise compensating them for any encroachment by this Department to be adjusted by this Department and the licensees themselves." The Minister further asked in the event of sale that the Government of Ontario should sell the lands required at twenty-five cents an acre.

The total area required was approximately 73,000 acres; of this, the settlers' rights to 12,175 acres had been acquired by the Department of Militia and Defence by purchase from the settlers, 5,730 acres of which were unpatented. There were also 5,989 acres additional to be purchased from settlers, of which 2,870 acres are unpatented. The unpatented lands in the hands of the settlers would therefore approximate 8,600 acres, and the area remaining in the Crown would be approximately 55,000 acres.

The Department of Militia and Defence wrote again on February 6, 1907, (L. 5,299, /07), asking for a reply to its letter of January 21st.

On February 13, 1907, the Minister of Lands, Forest and Mines replied that patents would be issued to the Minister of Militia and Defence for such lots as that Department had purchased from settlers upon filing in this Department proper assignments from the settlers and paying in the balance of the purchase money due the Crown with interest thereon in accordance with the conditions under which the lands were sold, that the Government of Ontario would be prepared to issue a lease for the lands in the Crown required for military camp purposes by Order in Council at a nominal rental for such term of years as might be agreed upon, the lands to revert to the Crown in Ontario when no longer required for camp purposes, the proposals in both cases to be subject to the rights of the timber licensees being acquired by the Department of Militia and Defence and their consent to the issue of the lease being filed here, also that the Crown dues, which would accrue on the timber as cut would have to be paid by the Department of Militia and Defence. The Minister went on to say that he had had conversations with representatives of the Pembroke Lumber Company and had been supplied with an estimate of the kinds and quantities of timber on their part of the territory, that he knew the man who had made the estimate and considered him well qualified and regarded it as a conservative estimate though it was not as yet fully completed. The Minister enclosed for the information and consideration of the Department of Militia and Defence a copy of the estimate referred to, and intimated that if the Department of Militia and Defence acquired the rights of the licensees upon the estimate furnished, this Department would be prepared to accept payment of the dues upon the basis of such estimate at the rates fixed by the Crown Timber Regulations.

On February 21, 1907, the Deputy Minister of Militia and Defence wrote that with reference to the issue of patents for lots purchased from individual owners, the proposal of the Department of Lands, Forests and Mines was quite satisfactory and the assignments would be forwarded at an early date so that the matter might be speedily adjusted ; that with respect to the lands under license the Militia Department had no desire to interfere with the rights of the licensees, but would undertake to facilitate the cutting and removing of the timber if a lease were granted by the Department of Lands, Forests and Mines. The Deputy Minister of Militia and Defence again put the question :—Would the Provincial Government grant a lease of 55,000 acres to the Department of Militia and Defence for 99 years at a nominal rental, or would it sell to the Dominion Government the 55.000 acres at twenty-five cents per acre ?

On March 1, 1907, the undersigned by direction of the Minister acknowledged the receipt of this letter and said that with respect to the proposed lease of 55,000 acres the Department could not grant any rights which would interfere with the rights of the timber licensees, that if the Department of Militia and Defence could make arrangements with the licensees and file their consent a lease would be issued at a nominal consideration for the period mentioned, but without the consent of the timber licensees being procured it is not possible at the present time to give such a lease.

On March 5th, the Deputy Minister of Militia and Defence acknowledged the receipt of the undersigned's letter and informed him that the papers had been referred to the Minister of Justice.

A despatch has now been received at Government House and transferred to this Department informing His Honour the Lieutenant-Governor that His Excellency the Governor General has had under consideration the urgent necessity for the defence of Canada of acquiring certain lands convenient to the Capital for military purposes; that several localities had been examined ; that certain areas in the Province of Ontario had been found to be the most suitable ; that there are certain outstanding timber licenses issued by the Government of Ontario authorizing the licensees to cut the timber growing upon the said lands ; that portions of the said lands are in the hands of settlers, who are

entitled upon the performance of furthe se
further payments to the Government of O ar
so occupied by them, and except as to th ri
the settlers, the lands are absolutely in Hi Ia
the Government of Ontario; that it wa io
rights of the said licensees, or with the ri ts
that subject to these rights and interests n th
be assumed under section 17, of the Briti N
right of the Dominion of Canada for the er
a description of the lands, which are the s e
have taken place.

Upon receipt of this despatch, the I n
graphed the Minister of Militia and Def e
the action taken by the Government of C ad
Defence replied :—" Re Petawawa Lands. at
promised lease of Crown Lands within ta
years at nominal rent, and Honourable 1
the interview I had with you refused to ry
timber licensees, and timber licensees v
surrender of their licenses amounting t
Department of Justice was consulted O th
tice, that the lands could be taken for d n
America Act steps were taken accordingly

Section 117, of the British North An

" The several Provinces all
otherwise disposed of in this Ac.
lands or public property requir
country."

The timber licenses affecte
and have been ren for a
acquired by pur thin
Crown Timber
entitled to a re
of $3.00 per m
It will not sur
territory appr
standing, the I
$25,000 or $
begs leave to
ously jeopard
soldiers woul
for lighting

ment duties, or upon making
o obtain patents for the lands
s of the timber licensees and
ty under the administration of
itended to interfere with the
the settlers in possession, but
now exist all the lands are to
i America Act of 1867, in the
if the country. Then follows
hose about which negotiations

ble the Prime Minister tele.
the cause and particulars of
The Minister of Militia and
rovincial Government having
va camp site for ninety-nine
rane, having definitely since
promise without consent of
demanded compensation for
exorbitant sum of $112,000,
vice of the Minister of Jus-
rposes under British North

as follows:—
public property not
anada to
the de

consequences to the property .e licensees. The effect of the Order-in-Council, if the action is constit tical, is to t ay from the Province the surface rights and all rights in the timber and to deprive the licensees of their property, unless some provisio: i made for compensation both to the Province and the licensees.

AUBREY WHITE,
Deputy Minister.

Toronto, March 28th, 1907.

LETTER OF TRANSMISSION.

(Copy.)

GOVERNMENT HOUSE,

TORONTO, 2nd April, 1907.

SIR,—With reference to the despatch. f the Under-Secretary of State dated 22nd March, 1907, and ad lresed to m I have the honour to enclose herewith for your information the re rt to m on the subject matter of the said despatch, of the Honourable the irst Min ter and Acting Minister of Lands Forests and Mines, together wit te other : p rs indicated in the said report.

i hre the h r ir to be,

r

Your c lient servant,

i. WM. MORTIMER CLARK,
Lieutenant-Governor of Ontario

Honourable,
SECRETARY OF STATE
awa, Ontario.

REPORT F HE PRI MINISTER.

RTIMER CLARE SQ., K. C.
r of the P vnce of On t

nce to tl cspatch fr .. the Under-Secretary of State of our Ho ot, and d t the 22nd March, 1907, notifying assum io of cert lands for the Militia Camp at zned b ave to r : as follows:

epared to concede lands desired by the Dominion the word of sectio: 17 of the British North America *property required i fortifications or for the defence* does it apear fro ction 117 that lands of the Pro-thout compensatio the Province.

entitled upon the performance of further settlement duties, or upon making further payments to the Government of Ontario to obtain patents for the lands so occupied by them, and except as to the rights of the timber licensees and the settlers, the lands are absolutely in His Majesty under the administration of the Government of Ontario; that it was not intended to interfere with the rights of the said licensees, or with the rights of the settlers in possession, but that subject to these rights and interests as they now exist all the lands are to be assumed under section 17, of the British North America Act of 1867, in the right of the Dominion of Canada for the defence of the country. Then follows a description of the lands, which are the same as those about which negotiations have taken place.

Upon receipt of this despatch, the Honourable the Prime Minister tele-graphed the Minister of Militia and Defence for the cause and particulars of the action taken by the Government of Canada. The Minister of Militia and Defence replied :—" *Re* Petawawa Lands. Late Provincial Government having promised lease of Crown Lands within Petawawa camp site for ninety-nine years at nominal rent, and Honourable Mr. Cochrane, having definitely since the interview I had with you refused to carry out promise without consent of timber licensees, and timber licensees having demanded compensation for surrender of their licenses amounting to the exorbitant sum of $112,000, Department of Justice was consulted. On the advice of the Minister of Justice, that the lands could be taken for defence purposes under British North America Act steps were taken accordingly.

Section 117, of the British North America Act reads as follows :—

" The several Provinces shall retain all their respective public property not otherwise disposed of in this Act, subject to the right of Canada to assume any lands or public property required for fortifications or for the defence of the country."

The timber licenses affected have been granted by the Government of Ontario, and have been renewed for a great many years, although some of them have been acquired by purchase within recent periods from former owners. Under the Crown Timber Regulations, made under the Crown Timber Act, licensees are entitled to a renewal of their licenses upon payment of an annual ground rent of $3.00 per mile and Crown dues at such rates as may be fixed by Regulations. It will not surprise the undersigned if the stumpage value of the timber on the territory approximates $100,000, and in addition to the value of the timber standing, the Province has a direct pecuniary interest to the extent of probably $25,000 or $30,000 dues, payable on this timber as it is cut. The undersigned begs leave to state that, in his opinion, the safety of this timber would be seriously jeopardized by the presence of a large military camp in it, as bodies of soldiers would no doubt be moving about through the territory using matches for lighting pipes and fire for other purposes, without any thought or care of consequences to the property of the licensees. The effect of the Order-in-Council, if the action is constitutional, is to t   ay from the Province the surface rights and all rights in the timber and to deprive the licensees of their property, unless some provision is made for compensation both to the Province and the licensees.   .

AUBREY WHITE,
Deputy Minister.

Toronto, March 28th, 1907.

LETTER OF TRANSMISSION.

(Copy.)

GOVERNMENT HOUSE,

TORONTO, 2nd April, 1907.

SIR,—With reference to the despatch of the Under-Secretary of State dated 22nd March, 1907, and addressed to me, I have the honour to enclose herewith for your information the report to me, on the subject matter of the said despatch, of the Honourable the First Minister and Acting Minister of Lands Forests and Mines, together with the other papers indicated in the said report.

I have the honour to be,

Sir,

Your obedient servant,

(Sgd.) WM. MORTIMER CLARK,
Lieutenant-Governor of Ontario

To the Honourable,
  THE SECRETARY OF STATE,
    Ottawa, Ontario.

REPORT OF THE PRIME MINISTER.

To His Honour,
  WILLIAM MORTIMER CLARK, ESQ., K. C.
Lieutenant-Governor of the Province of Ontario.

SIR,—With reference to the despatch from the Under-Secretary of State of Canada, addressed to Your Honour, and dated the 22nd March, 1907, notifying Your Honour of the assumption of certain lands for the Militia Camp at Petawawa, the undersigned begs leave to report as follows:

(1) We are not prepared to concede that lands desired by the Dominion for a camp come within the words of section 117 of the British North America Act as "*lands or public property required for fortifications or for the defence of the country,*" neither does it appear from section 117 that lands of the Province can be assumed without compensation to the Province.

(2) From the despatch it appears that the Minister of Militia and Defence, after referring to the existing rights of timber licensees and the present interests of the settlers in possession, goes on to notify Your Honour of his recommendation that "subject to these rights and interests, as they now exist, all the lands hereinafter described be, under the authority of section 117 of the British North America Act, 1867, assumed by His Excellency the Governor General in the right of the Government of Canada for the defence of the country" and of the approval thereof by His Excellency the Governor General. The description and boundaries of the land so assumed appear in the despatch.

This action on the part of the Government of Canada has come to the knowledge of the Provincial Government, without either notice or warning and is a distinct surprise. Negotiations have been in progress between the two Governments for some time looking to the granting by the Department of Lands, Forests and Mines of a lease of the said lands to the Department of Militia and Defence for as long a time as the lands might be used for the purposes of a Militia Camp, and at a nominal rental, or for 99 years—the application of the Department of Militia and Defence asking for a lease for the latter term. For the information of Your Honour, as to the facts, I enclose report made to me by the Deputy Minister of Lands and Forests, together with telegrams to and from the Minister of Militia and Defence.

From statements made by the Minister of Militia and Defence, at the interview mentioned in the said report, the undersigned understood his views regarding the rights and property of the timber licensees to differ widely from the views held by the Minister of Lands, Forests and Mines. As stated by the Deputy Minister in his report "under the Crown timber regulations made under the Crown Timber Act, licensees are entitled to a renewal of the license upon payment of an annual ground rent of $3 per mile and Crown dues at such rates as may be fixed by regulation." It must not be forgotten either that the Provincial Government has, besides the ownership of the said lands, an interest in the said timber, under the terms of the licenses, equal to about one-quarter the value thereof. An estimate of the value of the timber,--not of course necessarily conclusive,-- was made by an expert, whose qualifications were well known to the Department, but this estimate has been characterized by the Minister of Militia and Defence as exorbitant. In any event, the value could have been easily ascertained and the Department of Lands, Forests and Mines would have been ready at any time to consider any method by which the value could have been satisfactorily arrived at.

Instead of co-operating with the Department to this end, viz. the determining the value of "the existing rights of the said timber licensees", the Department of Militia and Defence has peremptorily, without any notice being given to either the Provincial Government or the licensees, taken over the lands indicated and confiscated, as far as possible at any rate, the property both of the licensees and of the Province.

If this proceeding is constitutional, the rights of ownership of the Provincial Government have been taken away absolutely and without compensation, while the licensees must simply depend upon what may be called the bounty of the Department of Militia and Defence, the head of which has already, in a manner entirely *ex parte*, characterized the claims of the licensees as exorbitant. In other words, one of the parties to the dispute is to pronounce final judgment on the claim of the other party.

Further, if this proceeding is constitutional, the existing licenses cannot be renewed at the expiration of the present year (April 30th, 1907), at least, according to the view held by the Department of Militia and Defence, their renewal would have no legal effect, the property having been assumed by the Dominion Government and there being now no "existing rights of the timber licensees".

The undersigned hazards the opinion that this is a strange condition of affairs to obtain in a British country, and desires respectfully to inform Your Honour that, in the opinion of his colleagues and himself, the action of the Department of Militia and Defence in this matter was unnecessary, unwarranted and arbitrary in the extreme.

Respectfully submitted, .

J. P. WHITNEY,

First Minister and Acting Minister of Lands, Forests and Mines.

TORONTO, 2nd April, 1907.

LETTER OF ACKNOWLEDGMENT.

OTTAWA, 3rd April, 1907.

SIR,—I have the honour to acknowledge the receipt of Your Honour's despatch of the 2nd inst, transmitting the report of the Honourable the First Minister and Acting Minister of Lands, Forests and Mines, and enclosures, on the subject of the acquisition by the Government of Canada of certain lands for artillery practice.

I have the honour to be, Sir,

Your obedient servant,

J. POPE,

Under-Secretary of State.

His Honour,

    THE LIEUTENANT-GOVERNOR OF ONTARIO,

        Toronto, Ontario.

EXPLANATIONS BY THE PRIME MINISTER.

Extract from explanations by the Prime Minister to the Legislative Assembly on April 15th, 1907 :

Having read this correspondence I propose now, in order to show the animus which evidently pervaded the system of the Minister of Militia and Defence, to place before you the following report from the Hansard of an answer given by him to a question asked on the 3rd of April :

> "Mr. Boyce—by Mr. Taylor, asked :
>
> 1. Has the Government by Order in Council, assumed certain lands in the townships of Petawawa and McKay, in the Province of Ontario, for military camp purposes ?
>
> 2. If so, is it the intention of the Government to compensate the owners of the timber licenses covering the area of said lands, and the Ontario Government, for the timber thereon ?
>
> Hon. Sir Frederick Borden (Minister of Militia and Defence):
> 1. Yes.
>
> 2. The Government has not taken the interest of the lumber licensees, and they have, therefore, no claim to compensation. The Ontario Government is not by the British North America Act, entitled to compensation, and it is not intended to pay that Government any compensation."

That is equivalent, Mr. Speaker, to saying that the property belonging to the people of Ontario is to be taken in this wanton manner by the head of a Department of the Dominion Government, who had the assurance to say that he did not intend to pay any compensation after having offered a price for the land and after a lease of the land had been offered to him at a merely nominal figure time after time. But because he chooses to imagine that the claim made by the timber licensees was exorbitant, and without seeing if there could not be found a basis of proper valuation, he drops all question of negotiations with us, and without notice to the Government of Ontario takes advantage of a possible interpretation of the British North America Act, and at once takes away the land, the timber, the rights of licensees and the rights of the Province, which would accrue when the timber was cut. That is a bald statement of the actual, undisguised facts. All that the Department of Lands, Forests and Mines asked was that the licensees should be settled with. These licenses are issued each year. If the land is taken away, what right has the Province to issue licenses at the end of the year ? If this confiscation holds water the Province will have no right to issue a license, because the ownership of the Province will have been taken away. The timber licensees will have no rights either for the same reason. The Minister seems to think that because he says he takes over this, subject to the present existing interests of the licensees, that that means the licensees can go on and cut timber. But what is to become of the rights of the Province ? He says boldly he does not intend to give the Province any compensation because the British North America Act does not entitle the Province to it. As if the British North America Act contemplated taking away, for reasons of defence, the property of any individual without due consideration being given for it ! As I say in my report, there are two parties to this dispute as to the value of the timber, and by this action of the Minister the one party becomes the judge and says, ' I will give you, out of my bounty, what I think your property is worth.' That is the conclusion at which the Department of Militia and Defence has arrived.

Now, sir, I am not prepared to believe, and I do not wish to express an opinion hastily, that section 117 of the British North America Act authorizes or excuses any such taking over forcibly and without notice the property of this or any other Province. Let me read that section :—"The several Provinces shall retain all their respective public property not otherwise disposed of in this Act, subject to the right of Canada to assume any lands or public property required for fortifications or the defence of the country."

This land is so situated that it could never be used for purposes of defence. It is located hundreds of miles from the border of the only country that could ever become hostile, and it certainly could not be required for fortification purposes. Consequently this land does not, in my opinion, come under the operation of the section I have read. To the representations of this Government I have received no reply except a formal acknowledgment.

I regret this occurrence, first of all, because I am bound to say here, as leader of this Government, that all intercourse and communication between us and the Government of Canada have been of the most pleasant nature. This Government has nothing but good words with reference to their treatment when in the course of duty it has been necessary to communicate with the Government at Ottawa. I do not believe the principal members of the Dominion Government have anything to do with this attempt at the forcible taking away of our property. I do not believe the leader of that Government, or the principal members of that Government, knew anything about this action of the Department of Militia and Defence. I do not propose to take any hasty action. My first intention was to present a resolution to the House on the matter, but I refrained from that because of possible animadversions with reference to the motives which might have been charged as actuating this Government. But I say to the people of Ontario, and to the members of this House, that while this Government remain in power they will leave no stone unturned in the effort to stop this outrageous attempt on the part of a Minister at Ottawa to take over the property of the people of Ontario without compensation. If necessary we will go to the foot of the throne with our plaint, and we may well feel certain that when the time comes for final decision this